CPAR

OKLAHOMA BATTLEFIELDS & MILITARY FORTS

Oklahoma Almanac
Copyright ©2015—Oklahoma Department of Libraries
200 NE 18 Street, Oklahoma City, Oklahoma 73105–3298

Editor—**Connie G. Armstrong**

Cover and Book Design—**William R. Struby**

Further Assistance in Research and Data Gathering—**Steve Beleu,
Drenda Fisher, Kitty Pittman**, and **William R. Struby**.

Special Thanks—**Laura Martin** at the **Oklahoma Historical Society Research Division**, the
**John F. Kennedy Presidential Library, the Library of Congress, and the Oklahoma
Department of Tourism and Recreation.**

Prepared and issued by the Oklahoma Department of Libraries as authorized by 65 O.S.
2011§3–110. Three thousand (3,000) paperback copies have been printed. Printing costs
were approximately $23,257.^{00}. Copies deposited in the Publications Clearinghouse of the
Department of Libraries. (7/15)

International Standard Book Number 978–1–880438–15–2
Library of Congress Cataloging-in-Publication Data
Oklahoma Almanac / edited by Connie G. Armstrong
55th ed., 2015 revision. • Formerly *The Directory of Oklahoma*

1. Elections—Oklahoma—Statistics—Periodicals.
2. Oklahoma—Registers—Periodicals.
I. Oklahoma Dept. of Libraries.
II. Armstrong, Connie G.
JK7131.A36 2015
353.9766–dc23

Cover Image: Fort Reno, Oklahoma Territory 1891. ■ Fowler, T. M. (1842–1922).
Courtesy of the Library of Congress, Geography and Map Division

Oklahoma Almanac

2015–2016

Fifty-Fifth Edition

CONTENTS

Agencies, Boards, & Commissions 227

Federal Government 339

County Government 365

Oklahoma Municipal Government 527

Tribal Government   569

Election Information   581

Education   705

Oklahoma History   749

Commerce & Agriculture   929

Wildlife & Nature   953

General Index   1009

FOREWORD

It is often said that history is written in blood. Our books are filled with true tales of war and great battles that have changed the trajectory of human history. But history is also written on the land, and it is the proclivity of human beings to commemorate these patches of earth that have served as stages for the most violent of human interactions.

Perhaps this is our gift from past generations. By lending such land an almost sacred status, our ancestors have provided opportunities for re-enactments, ceremonies, and simple contemplation on a barren field or mountaintop. What was it like for these warriors? How different were they from us? How much do we still hold in common with these specters from the past?

The battlefields of Oklahoma have witnessed fighting for the most noble of reasons—the protection of homes, loved ones, and a way of life—and for the most ignoble of reasons—the perpetuation of slavery, dominance, and a fear of "the other."

Like the historic battlefields of our state, the forts established by the U.S. Government in Indian and Oklahoma Territories have their own stories to tell about dangerous times and a vanished way of life.

If our special *Almanac* section, "Oklahoma's Battlefields and Military Forts," inspires further exploration, your Oklahoma public library is ready to help with books, online resources, and recommendations on the subject. To know and understand the past is the key to a better future, and the future begins with all of us.

Susan McVey
Director, Oklahoma Department of Libraries
Oklahoma City • May 2015

OKLAHOMA

IN BRIEF

General Facts

Organized as a Territory May 2, 1890.

Admitted to the Union November 16, 1907, as the forty-sixth state.

State Name Oklahoma means "Red People" in the Choctaw language.

Population 3,878,051 (Resident Population, U.S. Census Bureau, 2014 estimate), 3,751,351 (2010); and 3,450,654 (2000). Oklahoma has the second largest American Indian population of any state, with California ranking first. Many of the more than 300,000 American Indians living in Oklahoma today are descendants of the original sixty-seven tribes inhabiting Indian Territory. According to the Census 2013 estimate, in Oklahoma 74.5 percent of the population is white; 9.0 percent American Indian and Alaska Native; 7.7 percent African American; and 2.0 percent Asian. Additionally, persons of Hispanic or Latino origin make up 9.6 percent of the population.

Major Cities (2014 U.S. Census Est.)			
Oklahoma City	620,602	Moore	59,196
Tulsa	399,682	Midwest City	57,039
Norman	118,040	Enid	51,386
Broken Arrow	104,762	Stillwater	48,406
Lawton	97,017	Muskogee	38,616
Edmond	88,605	Bartlesville	36,498

Source—U.S. Census Bureau at www.census.gov

Area There are 68,679 square miles of land and 1,224 square miles of water; a total of 69,903 square miles, divided into seventy-seven counties. Besides Minnesota, Oklahoma is larger than any other state east of it, and except for Washington and Hawaii, is smaller than any state to the north, west, and south.

Elevation The highest point in Oklahoma is in the extreme northwest on Black Mesa in Cimarron County (4,973 feet); the lowest point is located in the extreme southeast, east of Idabel in McCurtain County (287 feet).

Location Bordered by Texas, New Mexico, Colorado, Kansas, Missouri, and Arkansas. Closer to the equator than to the North Pole.

Latitude 33° 39′–37° North **Longitude** 94° 29′–103° West

Time Zones Oklahoma is on Central Standard Time from the first Sunday in November until the second Sunday in March. The rest of the year, Daylight Savings Time is in effect. The only exception is the city of Kenton in the far western tip of the Panhandle which is on Mountain Standard Time, one hour earlier all year. Time moves forward one hour in spring and back one hour in fall.

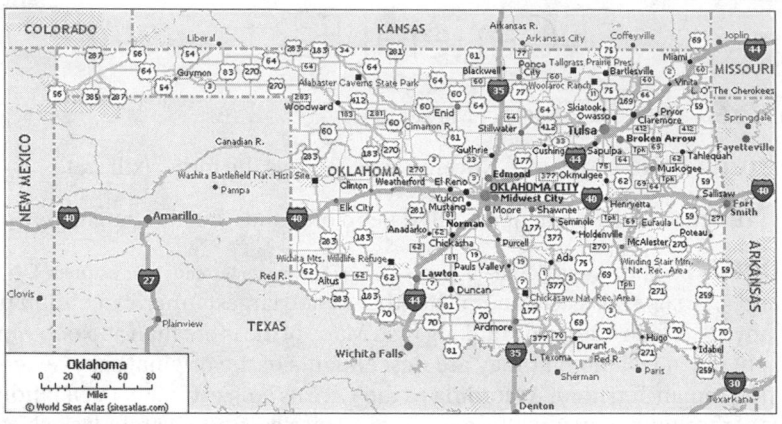

Driving Information
Oklahoma is crossed by three major interstate highways: I–35, I–40, and I–44. Additionally, US–412 extends from the state's eastern border with Arkansas near Siloam Springs, west through the Panhandle to the border with New Mexico. The speed limit on turnpikes is 75 mph, or 120 kph; on interstate highways, 70 mph, or 112 kph; and on other highways, 65 mph (104 kph), or 55 mph (88 kph).

Air Service
Will Rogers World Airport in Oklahoma City, and Tulsa International Airport are served by major and regional domestic airlines. The Lawton-Fort Sill Regional Airport is served by American Eagle. Also, Fort Smith, Arkansas; Wichita, Kansas; and Dallas, Texas, are served by major airlines.

Rail Service
Amtrak's Heartland Flyer offers daily service between Oklahoma City, Norman, Purcell, Pauls Valley, Ardmore, and Fort Worth, where travelers may connect to other Amtrak routes. Call 800/USA-RAIL or www.amtrak.com.

Bus Service
Greyhound and Jefferson bus lines operate within the state. Greyhound can be reached at 405/606–4382, or www.greyhound.com; Jefferson at 405/232–4214, or www.jeffersonlines.com.

Constitution and Government

Oklahoma's present constitution, dating from 1907, provides for amendment by initiative petition and legislative referendum. The legislature consists of a Senate of forty-eight members, elected for four-year terms; and a House of Representatives with 101 members, elected for two-year terms. The governor and lieutenant governor are elected for four-year terms. The governor can only be elected for two terms in succession. Electors are all citizens eighteen years or older, with the usual qualifications, i.e., resident of Oklahoma. There are restrictions on convicted felons running for office. The state is represented in the U.S. Congress by two senators elected to six-year terms, and five representatives elected for two-year terms.

Source—Secretary of State, State Election Board

Official Holidays in Oklahoma, 2015–2016
25 O.S. 1991, sec. 82.1 (as amended)

Holiday	Definition	2015	2016
New Year's Day	1st of January	Jan 1	Jan 1
Martin Luther King Jr. Day	3rd Monday in January	Jan 19	Jan 18
President's Day	3rd Monday in February	Feb 16	Feb 15
Memorial Day	Last Monday in May	May 25	May 30
Independence Day	4th of July	July 3	July 4
Labor Day	1st Monday in September	Sep 7	Sep 5
Veteran's Day	(Usually) 11th of November	Nov 11	Nov 11
Thanksgiving Holiday*	4th Thursday in Nov. & day after	Nov 26/27	Nov 24/25
Christmas Holiday**	25th of December	Dec 24/25	Dec 26/27

*HB 2480, April 23, 1996, designated the day after Thanksgiving an official holiday.

** HB 2607, November 1, 1998, designated the Monday before Christmas if Christmas is on a Tuesday, the Friday after Christmas if Christmas is on a Thursday as an official holiday; and such other days as may be designated by the President of the United States or the Governor of Oklahoma.

Additional Holidays (Optional Closing)
25 O.S. 1991, sec.82.2 (as amended)

Holiday	Date
Vietnam Veterans Day	3rd Thursday of March
Youth Day	3rd Sunday in March
Jefferson Day	13th of April
Oklahoma City Bombing Remembrance Day	19th of April
Oklahoma Day	22nd of April
Senior Citizens' Week	Beginning 1st Sunday in May
Senior Citizens' Day	Wednesday of Senior Citizens' Week
Mother's Day	2nd Sunday in May
Jim Thorpe Day	22nd of May
Purple Heart Week	Last week of May
Juneteenth National Freedom Day	3rd Saturday in June
Indian Day	1st Saturday after full moon in September
Grandparents' Week	Beginning 2nd Sunday in September
Cherokee Strip Day	16th of September
Oklahoma Historical Day	10th of October
Will Rogers Day	4th of November
Native American Day	3rd Monday in November
Pearl Harbor Remembrance Day	7th of December
Citizenship Recognition Day	On such day as may be fixed by the governor and each day in which the state election is held throughout the State of Oklahoma; and such other days as may be designated by the President of the United States or the Governor of the State of Oklahoma.

Economic Environment
Property Valuation

Locally Assessed	2013–14	2014–15	Increase/Decrease
Real Estate & Improvements	$20,614,938,633	$21,386,963,980	$772,025,347
Personal Subject to Tax	$5,954,320,039	$6,371,148,561	$416,828,522
Total Locally Assessed	$26,569,258,672	$27,758,112,541	$1,188,853,869
Homestead Exemptions Allowed	$927,755,318	$932,918,239	$5,162,921
Net Assessed Locally	$25,641,503,354	$26,825,194,302	$1,183,690,948
Public Service Assessments	$2,844,548,199	$2,999,603,600	$115,055,401
Net Assessed Valuation	$28,526,051,553	$29,824,797,902	$1,298,746,349
Locally Assessed	2011–12	2012–13	Increase/Decrease
Real Estate & Improvements	$19,374,046,614	$19,991,593,394	$617,546,780
Personal Subject to Tax	$4,961,899,643	$5,345,707,425	$383,807,782
Total Locally Assessed	$24,335,946,257	$25,337,300,819	$1,001,354,562
Homestead Exemptions Allowed	$778,562,754	$920,976,120	$142,413,366
Net Assessed Locally	$23,557,383,503	$24,416,324,699	$858,941,196
Public Service Assessments	$2,987,828,227	$3,005,837,463	$18,009,236
Net Assessed Valuation	$26,545,211,730	$27,422,162,162	$876,950,432

Source—State Board of Equalization

State Budget

Year Ending June 30, 2014

Total Revenue $17,819,000 • **Total Expenditures** $17,516,000.
Source—Office of Management and Enterprise Services
(*2014 Comprehensive Annual Financial Report*. Expressed in Millions of Dollars)

Year Ending December 31, 2014

Gross General Obligation Debt $152,280,000
Gross Contractual Obligation Debt $0
Gross Public Lease Purchase Obligation $2,815,000
Gross Lease Purchase Debt Privately Placed $14,551,000
Total Gross Tax-Supported Debt $2,028,995,000
Total Reductions to Gross Tax-Supported Debt   ($160,391,000)
Total Net Tax-Supported Debt $1,868,604,000.

Source—State Bond Advisor, *2014 Annual Report*, www.ok.gov/bondadvisor

Agriculture

According to the 2014 *Oklahoma Agricultural Statistics Report*, in 2013 Oklahoma had a total of 43,200 farms. The total land area in farms equaled 34,400,000 acres. The average size farm was 429 acres.

As of January 1, 2014, Oklahoma's farms and ranches held 4,300,000 cattle and calves, down 800,000 from 2011. The cow inventory consisted of 1,800,000 beef cows and 45,000 milk cows. The annual average milk production per cow increased to 17,125 lbs, an increase of 142 lbs. per cow. The total milk production in 2013 was 790 millions lbs. As of December 1, 2013, Oklahoma held 1,980,000 hogs, and 7,064,000 pigs. As of January 1, 2014, the state held 65,000 sheep; the 2013 lamb crop was 44,000 lambs. As of December 1, 2013, total chickens (excluding broilers) in Oklahoma totaled 4.23 million. Hens and pullets of laying age, at 3 million, were down 3 percent from 2012.

Cash receipts for all Oklahoma commodities sold in 2012 totaled 7.04 billion, up 1.7 percent from 2011. Receipts from livestock and related products, which accounted for 78 percent of the total cash receipts, totaled $5.51 billion, a 4.8 percent decrease from 2011. Receipts for cattle and calves sold were down 5.1 percent to $3.56 billion, as were hog receipts, at $914 million, down 3.4 percent. The third largest livestock item, based on cash receipts, was broilers at $710 million, down 2.7 percent from 2011. Dairy product receipts decreased 16 percent from 2011 sales, at $169 million.

Crop sales for 2012, at $1.53 billion, were up 35 percent from 2011. Sales of wheat totaled $758 million, up 93 percent from 2011. All hay sales, at $170 million, were more than double 2011 receipts. Cash receipts for corn, sorghum, cotton, soybeans, and sunflowers all declined from 2011. Cash receipts for canola, oats, and rye all increased from the previous year.

The average value per head of all cattle and calves on January 1, 2104, was $1,110, up $60 from a year earlier. The total inventory value of all cattle and calves was $4.77 billion. The average value per head of all sheep and lambs on January 1, 2014, was $238, up $15 from 2013. The total inventory value was $15.5 million. There were 150 thousand pounds of wool produced in 2013, level the amount with 2012. The average price received for wool was .60 cents per pound, .10 cents less than 2012. The average value per head of all hogs and pigs on December 1, 2013, was $125, up $20 dollars from 2012. The total inventory value of all hog and pigs was $249 million. The average price per pound for broilers, at 60.5 cents, was up 10.5 cents from the 2012 price. The calculated price per dozen eggs increased .11 cents from a year earlier to $1.58 per dozen.

The 2013 Oklahoma winter wheat market year average price was $6.90 per bushel, a decrease of .55 cents from 2012. The average sorghum price was $7.45 per hundredweight, a decrease of $4.55 from the previous year. Corn, at $5.20 per bushel, decreased $1.84 from 2012. Soybeans were $12.60 per bushel for 2013, down $1.80 for 2012. Cotton lint market year average price was up from 2012 to .77 cents per pound. Peanut prices decreased to 29.7 cents per pound. The average price for all hay was $147 per ton in 2013, 16.6 percent higher than 2012. Oat prices decreased, while rye prices increased and canola was down $2.60 to $22.60 per hundredweight. The market year average price of native pecans decreased by .5 cents, while prices for improved pecans increased by .50 cents. Cash rent paid for cropland in Oklahoma in 2014 was unchanged from 2013, at $33.50 per acre. Cash rent paid for pasture land was also static, at $12.00 per acre in 2014.

Topographically and geographically, Oklahoma's agriculture is diverse, ranging from the semi-arid high plains of the Panhandle with its heavy concentration of cattle feedlots and ranches, hog farms, and large-scale crop farms, to the flat, heavily irrigated southwest section devoted primarily to cotton, wheat, peanuts, and some cattle. Then there are the wheat and cattle farms of western and northern Oklahoma; the cross-timbered central sections where the emphasis is on dairying and diversified farming of crops such as peanuts and hay; the wetter eastern pastures and timbers; and the pine-rich southeastern section where timber, cattle, and poultry predominate.

Sources—*Oklahoma Agricultural Statistics 2014*; 2012 Census of Agriculture

Commerce

According to the Oklahoma Employment Security Commission's *Oklahoma Economic Indicators Report,* March 2015, Gross Domestic Product (GDP)—the output of goods and services produced by labor and property located in the United States—is the broadest measure of economic activity. It is also the measure that is most indicative of whether the economy is in recession. In the post-World War II period, there has been no recession in which GDP did not decrease in at least two quarters, (the exceptions being during the recessions of 1960–61 and 2001). There are four major components to GDP: personal consumption expenditures, investment, net exports, and government.

United States economic growth slowed as 2014 came to a close. Gross Domestic Product (GDP) increased at an annual rate of 2.2 percent in the fourth quarter of 2014. Consumer spending increased to 4.4 percent in the fourth quarter of 2014, the biggest gain in consumer spending in eight years. Durable goods expenditures rose to 6.2 percent, while nondurable goods spending increased to 4.1 percent during the fourth quarter of 2014. Spending on services grew at a 4.3 percent pace during the fourth quarter of 2014, which was the fastest pace since the second quarter of 2000. Business accumulated $80 billion worth of inventory in the fourth quarter of 2014. After-tax corporate profits declined $57.1 billion, the largest drop since the first quarter of 2001. Residential construction increased 3.8 percent during the fourth quarter of 2014. Exports also rose to 4.5 percent, and import growth rose to 10.4 percent during the fourth quarter of 2014. Foreign trade subtracted 1.03 percentage points from the fourth quarter GDP growth. A stronger dollar made U.S. exports more expensive and imports cheaper. Government spending in the last three months of 2014 was slightly weaker than previously estimated. Real federal government consumption expenditures and gross investment decreased 7.3 percent in the fourth quarter. National defense spending plunged 12.2 percent.

In the fourth quarter of 2013, Oklahoma's GDP was $165.7 billion in constant 2009 dollars, up from $164.5 billion in the third quarter. The state's fourth quarter real GDP increased by $1.19 billion, or 2.9 percent, ranking Oklahoma twenty-ninth among all other states and the District of Columbia.

For all of 2013, Oklahoma's real GDP was at a level of $164.3 billion in constant 2009 dollars, growing at a rate of 4.2 percent from 2012. That was the fourth-highest annual GDP growth rate among all other states and the District of Columbia. North Dakota was first with a 9.7 percent growth rate followed by Wyoming at 7.6 percent and West Virginia at 5.1 percent.

Fifteen Oklahoma industry sectors contributed to GDP growth in the fourth quarter of 2013, with six sectors subtracting from growth. The mining sector, which includes the oil and gas industry, was by far the largest contributor to Oklahoma's GDP growth in the fourth quarter, adding 2.39 percentage points to overall GDP growth, followed by non-durable goods manufacturing which contributed 0.94 percentage points. Agriculture, forestry, fishing, and hunting was the biggest drag to state GDP growth subtracting 1.95 percentage points.

Source—*Oklahoma Economic Report 2015*, Oklahoma Employment Security Commission

Petroleum and Natural Gas

Oklahoma's crude production in February 2015 was at 11,179,000 barrels, 79,000 barrels (or 6.0 percent) less than January 2015 level of 11,250,000 barrels. For 2014, Oklahoma's crude production was 127,730,000 barrels, 13,548,000 barrels or 11.9 percent more than the 114,182,000 barrels produced in 2013 and the highest annual crude production level since 1988.

The number of U.S. oil rigs (Baker-Hughes count) fell by eleven in March 2015 to 802, the lowest oil rig count in four years. The biggest declines came from North Dakota, which saw six rigs shut down, and Texas, which saw five rigs shut down. In March 2015, Oklahoma's active rotary rig count tumbled to its lowest level since July 2010. The number of active rigs in the state stood at 133. Of those 133 rigs, 124 were oil-directed and nine were natural gas-directed

The Baker Hughes rotary rig count for natural gas in Oklahoma gained a rig in March 2015. For the week ending March 27, 2015. Oklahoma's natural gas-directed drilling rig count was at a level of nine active rigs, the same rig count as the previous week but one more from the week ending March 6, 2015, and representing only six percent of total statewide drilling activity. Over the year, Oklahoma's natural gas-directed rotary rig count was down ten rigs from the nineteen rigs reported for the week ended March 28, 2014.

Source—*Oklahoma Economic Report 2015*, Oklahoma Employment Security Commission

Poverty

The national average of people in poverty in 2013 was 15.8 percent, a slight decrease from the 15.9 percent rate in 2012. The estimate for Oklahomans living below the poverty level in 2013 was 16.8 percent, a decrease from the estimated 17.2 percent in 2012. The number of Oklahoma children under the age of eighteen living below the poverty level in 2013 was 221,623. Poverty rates for 2013 from surrounding states include Arkansas, 19.7; Colorado, 13.0; Kansas, 14.0; Louisiana, 19.8; Mississippi, 24.0; Missouri, 15.9; New Mexico, 21.9; and Texas, 17.5.

Source—U.S. Census

Taxes

For the tax years 2013–2014, income tax on personal income ranged from .05 percent on the first $2,000 of taxable income to 5.25 percent for more than $15,000 if married filing jointly and head of household. (The rate is .05 percent on the first 1,000 to 5.25 percent over $8,700 if single or married filing separately.) The top tax rate on the 2013–2014

Oklahoma Individual Tax Form was 5.25 percent. The personal exemption is $1,000 per exemption. The corporate tax flat rate was 6 percent.

Only county governments with the local millage rates to meet local budgets levy real estate and tangible property taxes. County assessors must assess property at a single rate between 11 percent and 13.5 percent, and personal property between 10 percent and 15 percent. There is a general homestead exemption of $1,000 deducted from the gross assessed value of the homestead property.

Sales and use tax in Oklahoma is 4.5 percent. Many cities levy an additional sales tax. In addition, counties have the authority to levy a county sales tax not to exceed 2 percent. Counties can now levy a county use tax as well. Items not subject to sales tax are motor vehicles, mobile homes, travel trailers, gasoline, prescription drugs, water service, and others.

Source—Oklahoma Tax Commission, www.oktax.state.ok.us

Transportation

As of 2012, a total of 112,821 miles of public roads existed across Oklahoma. Of the 112,821 miles of public roads, the Oklahoma Department of Transportation is responsible for 12,267 miles. Oklahoma public and private roads consist of 933 miles of interstate roads; 8,420 miles are other principal and minor arterials; 25,311 miles are major and minor collectors; and 78,158 are local roads. Three major interstates make-up the highest traveled routes in the state. They are I–35, I–40, and I–44. The state also has ten toll roads, equaling 595.1 miles.

As of 2012 there were 22,912 road bridges in Oklahoma. Of the 22,912 road bridges, the Oklahoma Department of Transportation is responsible for 6,792. Moreover, of the 22,912 road bridges, 4,227 are structurally deficient or 18.4 percent, while 1,601 are functionally obsolete or 7.0 percent.

As of 2011, Oklahoma had 3,273 miles of freight railroad. Oklahoma had three "Class I" railroads. "Class I"railroads operate with revenues of at least $433.2 million annually.

As of 2015, there were 137 public-use airports in the state, including 110 that are owned by a public entity such as a city or town. There are forty-nine regional business airports in Oklahoma, forty-three of these airports have jet-capable runways that are at least 5,000 feet long.

Source—Department of Transportation, www.okladot.state.ok.us
Oklahoma Aeronautics Commission, www.ok.gov/OAC
U.S. Department of Transportation, *State Transportation Statistics Report 2014*

Workforce

As of December 2014, Oklahoma's civilian labor force was estimated at 1,782,238 with 1,712,315 employed and 69,923 unemployed. Oklahoma's unemployment rate fell to 3.9 percent in December, down from 5.0 percent in 2013.

In December 2014 Oklahoma's estimated leading employment areas were: Trade, Transportation, and Utilities, 303,900 jobs; Education and Health Services, 230,000; Government, 350,000; Professional and Business Services, 191,100; Leisure and Hospitality, 155,000; Manufacturing, 139,100; Financial, 79,700; Construction, 77,500; and Mining and Logging, 63,100.

The average wage per job in Oklahoma increased from the 2013 figure of $39,940 to $40,850 in 2014, while the estimated average median household income for 2013 was $45,690. The Bureau of Economic Analysis reported the national state per capita income for individuals in 2014 was $46,129. Oklahoma's reported per capita income for 2014 was $43,138. Other states in the region included Colorado, $48,730; Texas, $45,426; Kansas, $45,546; Missouri, $41,613; New Mexico, $37,605; and Arkansas, $37,751. Coming in first nationally was Connecticut at $62,467. Coming in last was Mississippi at $34,333.

Source—Oklahoma Department of Commerce, U.S. Bureau of Economic Analysis, U.S. Census, and the U.S. Department of Labor

Living Quarters of General Douglas H. Cooper, Fort Washita, 1856. An officer in the Confederate Army, Cooper was involved in two of the most important Civil War battles that took place in Indian Territory.

Natural Environment

Climate

Bright and sunny. The northwestern part of the state is cooler and drier than the southeast. The mean annual temperature ranges from 62 F along the Red River to about 58 F along the northern border. It then decreases westward to 56 F in Cimarron County. Temperatures of 90 F or greater occur, on average, about 60–65 days per year in the western panhandle and the northeast corner of the state. In the southwest, the average is about 115 days, and in the southeast about 85 days. Statewide-averaged precipitation ranges from about 17 inches in the far western panhandle to about 56 inches in the far southeast. Snowfalls usually do not remain on the ground more than a few days, ranging from two inches a year in the southeast to thirty inches in the western Panhandle. The growing season ranges from 175 days in the Panhandle to more than 200 days in the south central part of the state.

Source—Oklahoma Climatological Survey, www.ocs.ou.edu

Forests

A variety of soils, climate, and topography creates a rich diversity in Oklahoma's forest land. In the southeast, high rainfall and mountainous terrain support an expanse of pine and oak. In the northeast, Ozark hardwoods predominate. Through central Oklahoma, post oak and blackjack oak of the Cross Timbers mix with tallgrass prairies, pastures, and cropland. The streams and cypress swamps in the southeast coastal plain change to bottomland hardwoods, including cottonwood and willow, in the Panhandle.

In the southwest, oak shinnery and mesquite spreading onto rangeland offer a different "agroforest" environment. Eastern red cedar is spreading rapidly in some areas. Considered a pest as it spreads into rangeland and forest land, it is also becoming the basis for a new forest products industry. Through the northwest and Panhandle, limited rainfall isolates trees to water courses. In the far reaches of Cimarron County, pinyon pine, juniper, and even a remnant stand of ponderosa pine are reminiscent of the Rocky Mountains.

The economic impact of forestry statewide is estimated at more than $1.5 billion. In eastern Oklahoma, forestry accounts for 18 percent of manufacturing employment, and 12 percent of the value of shipments. When supporting industries are included, forestry accounts for 30 percent of the region's manufacturing employment. Timber is fifth in value of all agricultural commodities in Oklahoma.

Source—Oklahoma Department of Agriculture, Food and Forestry, www.oda.state.ok.us

Geography

Oklahoma, one of the Great Plains states, is slightly south of the geographic center of the contiguous 48 states. Most of the state is a great, rolling plain, sloping gently from northwest to southeast. Highest elevation is 4,973 feet above sea level at Black Mesa in the northwestern corner of the Panhandle; lowest, 287 feet, is near Idabel in the extreme southeast. Approximately one-fourth of the state's total area is forested, principally the region bordering Missouri and Arkansas. Although part of the Great Plains, Oklahoma has four mountain ranges: the Ouachita in the southeast, the Ozark Plateau in the northeast, the Arbuckle in the south central part of the state, and the Wichita in the southwest. Geographic center of the state is eight miles north of Oklahoma City.

Source—Office of State Geographer

Grasslands

Grass areas are abundant within Oklahoma's boundaries and are used for grazing. The grasses in the western sections are primarily short and mixed. Tall grasses are found in the northern and eastern sections of the state. Oklahoma's National Grasslands—Black Kettle District, Roger Mills County; and Rita Bianca District, Cimarron County—have been a part of the U.S. Forest Service since the 1950s. The Soil Conservation Service (now the Natural Resources Conservation Service) originally administered the program designed to demonstrate good, sound principles in grassland agriculture. In addition, the Nature Conservancy manages a Tallgrass Prairie Preserve in Osage County, consisting of 39,000 acres of rolling hills at the southern end of the Flint Hills

Source—*Atlas of Oklahoma* (Wikle, Ed.), Office of State Geographer

Minerals

Oklahoma's enormous mineral reserve can be divided into three types of mineral products: mineral fuels, metals, and non-metals. Mineral fuels are materials that can be burned, such as petroleum (crude oil and natural gas), and coal. These account for more than 90 percent of Oklahoma's annual mineral output. Metals are substances that can be melted and molded into any shape desired and are usually hard and heat resistant. There presently are no metals mined in Oklahoma. Zinc and lead are the principal metals previously mined in Oklahoma, but copper, manganese, iron, and uranium also were produced. A non-metal (industrial mineral) is any rock, mineral or other select naturally occurring or synthetic material of economic value often used in combination with other materials, such as sand and stone used in concrete. The principal industrial minerals produced in Oklahoma include crushed stone, portland cement, construction sand and gravel, industrial sand and gravel, iodine, and gypsum. Other Oklahoma non-metals include tripoli, feldspar, helium, common clay, granite, salt, volcanic ash, and lime.

Source—Oklahoma Geological Survey, www.ou.edu/special/ogs-pttc

Vegetation

The natural vegetation of Oklahoma can be divided into three large categories: grasslands, savannahs and woodlands, and forests. Grasslands of various kinds are found in all parts of the state, but they are the dominant natural vegetation in the drier and more elevated western regions.

The savannah and woodlands types of vegetation are found in all parts of the state, with the exception of the Ouachita Mountains and the Ozark Plateau. Large forest areas are located in eastern Oklahoma where rainfall is sufficient for good tree growth and the local topography is too rough for agricultural use other than grazing.

Source—*Atlas of Oklahoma* (Wikle, Ed.); Office of State Geographer

Recreation

Oklahoma has fifty state parks and resorts, and numerous wildlife refuges and recreation areas, offering a wealth of outdoor adventure, including fishing, camping, mountain biking, horseback riding, rappelling, scuba diving, and golf. Tourist attractions include elements from a rich cowboy heritage; American Indian history; and unspoiled, diverse natural beauty. The fabled "Main Street of America," Route 66, crosses Oklahoma for more than 392 miles.

The Tourism and Recreation Department produces brochures and Internet sites to help travelers learn about Oklahoma. Call 405/521–2413, write the Oklahoma Tourism and Recreation Department, 120 N Robinson, Sixth Floor, Oklahoma City 73102, or visit www.oktlatourism.gov.

Source—Tourism and Recreation Department

Water

In Oklahoma, there are approximately 500 named rivers and creeks, many of them short and intermittent during much of the year. Oklahoma's terrain is dominated by two major river basins: northern Oklahoma and much of the central part of the state is in the drainage basin of the Arkansas River; the remainder of the state is in the drainage basin of the Red River. Except for the rivers flowing from the Ozark Plateau or the Ouachita Mountains, the streams in Oklahoma flow in a general eastward direction. Water leaves the state through four watercourses (the Red, Arkansas and Little rivers, and Lee Creek), flowing into Arkansas. The Scenic Rivers of Oklahoma have such exceptional beauty and recreational value that six of them have been officially designated as scenic rivers, and are protected by the state legislature. One scenic river is in the Red River System—the upper part of Mountain Fork which flows into Broken Bow Lake in the Ouachita Mountains. The other five scenic rivers are in the Arkansas River System, in the Ozark Plateau, and include parts of the Illinois River and parts of Flint, Baron Fork, Lee, and Little Lee creeks.

Oklahoma has more man-made lakes than any other state, with more than one million surface acres of water and 2,000 more miles of shoreline than the Atlantic and Gulf coasts combined. All of the large lakes in Oklahoma are man-made. They were developed—most of the 60 major reservoirs constructed by the federal government— to control flooding and for conservation purposes, navigation, recreation, power, and municipal water supplies. The state has lakes ranging from 890 acres to 105,000 acres (Lake Eufaula). Other large lakes are: Texoma, Grand Lake O' the Cherokees, Fort Gibson, Oologah, Kerr, Pine Creek, Broken Bow, Keystone, and Tenkiller. The state's largest groundwater basin, the Ogallala Aquifer in western Oklahoma, contains 86.6 million acre-feet of supply—enough to cover the entire state two feet deep.

Source—*Atlas of Oklahoma* (Wikle, Ed.), Office of State Geographer, Oklahoma Water Resources Board, www.owrb.state.ok.us; Oklahoma Geological Survey, www.ogs.ou.edu

Wildlife

Once the hunting and trading ground of many Indian tribes, Oklahoma boasts five big game species, including white-tailed deer and wild turkeys in all seventy-seven counties. Mule deer inhabit the northwestern quarter of the state, and pronghorn antelope populations in the Panhandle have expanded to allow a special hunt for that species. Elk are present in the Wichita Mountains National Wildlife Refuge and have been introduced in the eastern part of the state. Among smaller upland game, the bobwhite quail still reigns supreme. Pheasant populations in the Panhandle remain stable and provide quality hunting opportunities. Scaled quail, squirrels, and rabbits are other fall favorites for hunters, along with migratory birds such as doves, ducks, and geese. Among native sport fish, the largemouth bass, small-mouth and spotted bass, channel, blue, and flathead catfish, white bass, crappie, and sunfish are popular. Hybrid stripers and saugeye have provided a fishing boom in some parts of the state, along with walleye and striped bass. Rainbow trout can be caught from eight designated trout fishing areas, and brown trout in the lower Illinois River and lower Mountain Fork trout areas.

Source—Department of Wildlife Conservation, www.wildlifedepartment.com

Dice games and gambling at Fort Reno.

OKLAHOMA BATTLEFIELDS & MILITARY FORTS

COLLISIONS

Civil War battles took place in Indian Territory? This fact comes as a surprise to some people. The Sooner State has one of the most unique and fascinating histories of all the fifty states. Ancient philosopher Herodotus wrote that history is both a story and an explanation. Oklahoma's narrative includes Native American resettlement, twin territories, cattle drives, land runs, oil and natural gas exploration, the Dust Bowl, civil rights activism, and aviation and space pioneers to name just a few. The forty-sixth state also experienced armed conflict as visions and cultures collided in American society. When European civilization migrated west across the Mississippi River, wars were fought between the United States military and Indians trying desperately to preserve their culture and lifestyle. Moreover, as the Civil War divided Americans and threatened the survival of the United States, it spilled over into Indian Territory with the same destabilizing effects on the Native American tribes.

The 2015–2016 *Oklahoma Almanac* showcases some of the Civil War battles that took place in Indian Territory. In addition, an essay featuring the Battle of the Washita details the plight of Native Americans under America's evolving Indian policies and westward expansion. Information regarding many of Oklahoma's early forts that played an integral role in Oklahoma and America's history is also highlighted in this edition. You will be introduced to fascinating individuals such as Stand Watie, a leader of the Cherokee Nation and a brigadier general of the Confederate States Army; Opotheyahola, a "Loyal Creek," who advocated neutrality while reaffirming his allegiance to the United States and President Abraham Lincoln; and the illustrious First Kansas Colored Volunteer Infantry, the first African Americans to see battle during the Civil War.

President John F. Kennedy stated, "Mankind must put an end to war before war puts an end to mankind." The people, who inhabited this area in generations past, experienced trials and tribulations along the way including the atrocities of war, and yet they and the nation survived.

I want to encourage you to learn more about the state's historical forts and battlefields. To do so, I suggest you visit the Oklahoma History Center website www.okhistory.org or the Oklahoma Department of Tourism and Recreation website www.TravelOK.com. Moreover, check out the sources page, and read a book or article regarding these notable landmarks. Many of these sites feature annual reenactments and activities. Take a weekend and travel to these locations and discover the people and events that helped shape the place we now call Oklahoma!

This edition of the *Oklahoma Almanac* could not have been completed without the assistance of several individuals. First, I would like to thank the wonderful staff at the Oklahoma Department of Libraries. Steve Beleu was especially helpful in finding statistics from the United States Bureau of Labor Statistics and the U.S. Census Bureau. Laura Martin at the Oklahoma Historical Society Research Division, assisted in the acquisition of many of the historical photographs pictured throughout the *Almanac*. I also need to thank the archivists at the John F. Kennedy Presidential Library in Boston, Massachusetts, who provided information and images of "Black Jack," the horse that served during several presidential funeral processions.

Connie G. Armstrong • Editor

BATTLEFIELDS

THE BATTLE OF ROUND MOUNTAIN

INCLUDING THE BATTLE OF CHUSTENAHLAH

If you are traveling in search of the first Civil War battle that occurred in Indian Territory, be prepared to look at different sites. There has long been debate among historians, Civil War enthusiasts, and area locals regarding the exact location of the Battle of Round Mountain. What is not in question, however, is the battle's participants and the ultimate outcome that would have a deep impact for Native American tribes living in Indian Territory.

The Battle of Round Mountain, also known as the Battle of Round Mountains or the Battle of Twin Mounds, took place on the evening of November 19, 1861, between Opothleyahola's forces and a Texas Cavalry detachment led by Lieutenant Colonel William Quayle. It would serve as the first of three military engagements between Opothleyahola, a Muscogee Creek Indian who led the Union Forces in Indian Territory, and Confederate troops, under the direction of Colonel Douglas H. Cooper assigned to command the Indian Department of the Confederate Army.

Cooper's mission was to locate Opothleyahola, and his approximate 3,500 followers, halt their advancement toward the Red Fork River, and compel Opothleyahola's recognition of the recent treaty signed between the Creek Nation and the Confederacy. Signed on July 10, 1861, the Treaty of Friendship and Alliance with the Creek Nation of Indians set forth a perpetual peace between the Confederacy and the Creek Nation; provided both an offensive and defensive alliance between the parties; and placed the Creek Nation under the protection and sovereignty of the Confederacy. It would be one of several treaties signed between the Confederacy and Indian tribes located in Indian Territory. Opotheyahola, however, did not support the treaty, and along with other "Loyal Creeks," advocated neutrality while reaffirming his allegiance to the United States and President Abraham Lincoln. President Lincoln informed Opotheyahola and other Loyal Creeks that the war between the United States and the Confederacy did not concern Native Americans, and the federal government did not offer them protection.

During the summer of 1861 Opothleyahola's followers continued to grow in numbers. Members of other Indian tribes such as the Delaware, Comanche, Kickapoo, Seminole, Wichita, and Shawnee, as well as freed slaves and runaway slaves, also joined him in opposing the Confederacy. Upon receiving instructions in early November 1861, Opothleyahola's supporters left their homes and dwellings and began to migrate to the area where the Cimarron and Arkansas Rivers join. Indians from both the Creek Nation and other tribes aligned with the Confederacy attempted to reach out to Opothleyahola in an attempt to reiterate that unity and peace among Indians should be preserved. Their efforts failed, however, and tension continued to rise between the two sides.

Cooper initially viewed Opothleyahola's opposition as a problem for the Creeks to resolve, but as time passed he became increasingly concerned that Opothleyahola and his forces planned to attack his Confederate camp. To increase his military strength, Cooper requested additional military personnel. Lieutenant Colonel William Quayle and his Texas Cavalry Regiment responded quickly to provide assistance. Cooper, along with a Texas Cavalry

Unit, and approximately 1,400 Indian troops representing the Choctaw and Chickasaw mounted riflemen, a Creek regiment, and Seminole warriors set out on November 15 to locate Opothleyahola's camp. They arrived at the campsite on November 18 only to discover the camp had been abandoned. Cooper reported that his group began to follow the trail left behind by the Loyal Creeks, located a few disgruntled members along the path, and had taken several of them prisoners. These prisoners provided Cooper with vital information regarding the location of a group of Opothleyahola's forces.

The loyalists informed Cooper that part of Opothleyahola's followers could be found near the Red Fork of the Arkansas River. Their destination was Walnut Creek where a Confederate fort was being constructed. Acting upon the intelligence, on November 19 Cooper's troops advanced across the Red Fork, where they discovered evidence the loyalists were in the area. Cooper immediately detached Quayle and his regiment to locate Opothleyahola's encampment. Quayle and his men identified and followed several Loyal Creek scouts approximately four

Battle of Round Mountain (Civil War), November 19, 1861 by Wayne Cooper

miles, when they unknowingly came in close proximity to the primary campsite that was concealed in a timbered area near a creek. As they tracked the scouts, Opothleyahola's men suddenly ambushed them, killing one soldier. Quayle's men engaged Opothleyahola's forces in a swift, bloody battle, before withdrawing. During the retreat the two groups continued to exchange gunfire. Several of Opothleyahola's men were killed, while one officer and four men in Quayle's regiment were killed, and one man was wounded. As night fell, it became increasingly difficult to ascertain friendly and enemy forces. Cooper ordered a cease fire until Opothleyahola's forces were within sixty yards. Confederate forces could then fire their weapons once the determination was made that they would be firing on the enemy. Once again gunfire

Creek Chief Opothleyahola

ensued between the opposing forces, until Opothleyahola's men began to retreat and escaped northward under the cloak of darkness.

In his official report, Cooper stated that the battle resulted in one Confederate officer and five soldiers killed, four wounded, and one missing. Opothleyahola's casualties were 110 killed or wounded. Cooper also reported that a large number of horses had been shot. Moreover, he made the decision not to immediately pursue Opothleyahola's forces, choosing to regroup and resupply his men.

After a short interval, Cooper and his forces once again located Opothleyahola's group at Chusto-Talasah (Bird Creek) and engaged them in a second battle on December 9, 1861. Beginning at approximately 11:00 am and lasting most of the day, the fierce, often chaotic battle took place over very rugged terrain, and at times included hand-to-hand combat. As the sun began to set, Opothleyahola's men began to disengage and once again retreat. As in the first engagement, Cooper reported that his soldiers had been victorious, with his forces suffering fifteen deaths, while the enemy dead numbered around 400. It is important to note that these Loyal Creek fighters, in defeat, had accomplished their objective to allow time for their women, children, and the older Indians to flee to safety. Opothleyahola's followers believed they had discouraged the Confederates, but the two battles had greatly depleted their food, number of horses, and other provisions. The Loyal Creek numbers continued to grow, however, as deserters of the First Cherokee Mounted Rifles, under command of Confederate Colonel John Drew, joined their ranks. Hoping to elude Cooper's forces, the Loyal Creeks decided to bypass the Cherokee Nation and set their sights on Kansas. Inclement weather and lack of supplies, however, resulted in their decision to seek refuge along Shoal Creek (Battle Creek), near present-day Skiatook.

Determined to continue his quest against Opothleyahola and his followers, Cooper mustered another group of Confederate units

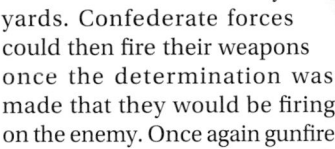

together and began pursuit of the enemy. On December 26, 1861, a Confederate unit under the leadership of Colonel James McIntosh, located a group of Opothleyahola's forces, numbering approximately 1,700, at Battle Creek. The Loyalists soon began to agitate the Confederate soldiers and their allies, enticing them to battle. Gunfire soon erupted, and following an intense four hour battle, McIntosh's forces crushed the Loyalists in what became known the Battle of Chustenahlah. The Confederate triumph over the Loyal Creeks in the Battle of Chustenahlah, resulted in the remaining members of Opothleyahola followers being scattered and driven out of Indian Territory whereby they became refugees in Kansas.

There has long been debate regarding the actual location where the Battle of Round Mountain took place. Some historians, including Angie Debo, place the battle near the present town of Yale in Payne County. Others argue the battle site is located near the mouth of the Cimarron River in southeastern Pawnee County. Regardless of the battle's actual location, a division took place in 1861 between the Creek Indians regarding the Civil War as some aligned with the Confederacy while others remained loyal to the Union. The division among the Creek Nation would create major reverberations. As noted historian Muriel H. Wright wrote, "... the Battle of Round Mountain began the bloodshed that led to this tragedy for the Union Creeks and their allies, and started the bitter division among the people of other tribes in the Indian Territory, during the Civil War."

Each year, the town of Yale conducts a Battle of Round Mountain re-enactment. For more information, call 918/399–9193.

BATTLE OF CABIN CREEK

Supply lines are vital to the outcome of war. Disrupt the enemy's ability to garner needed materials and their capability to maintain morale and fight effectively is greatly diminished. The two battles that occurred at Cabin Creek in the Indian Territory, southwest of present-day Vinita, resulted from the Confederate Army's attempt to impede Union supply lines. The Cabin Creek engagements, however, are historically significant. For the first time in American military history African American troops fought alongside white soldiers. The outcome of the Civil War was crucial to African Americans troops. They understood the ramifications involved if they took up arms against the Confederacy. Undeterred, many joined the military in defense of the Union. They fought for their own personal emancipation, and they did so valiantly. African Americans soldiers showcased their military prowess at Cabin Creek and on many other battlefields during the Civil War.

Union Army leaders realized in the summer of 1862 that more troops were essential to the outcome of the war. Congress quickly responded with legislation allowing African Americans to join the Federal forces. The First Kansas Colored Volunteer Infantry formed in August 1862, and by October it consisted of six companies with approximately 600 African American soldiers. Under the leadership of Colonel James M. Williams, the First Kansas Colored Regiment first saw battle in Butler, Missouri, in October 1862. In 1863 their mission involved escorting Union wagon supply trains headed south into the Indian Territory along the Texas Road.

On June 26, 1863, Colonel Williams received orders to meet and command a supply train from Fort Scott, Kansas, destined for Fort Gibson. Other units assigned to the wagon train included the Second Colorado Infantry Regiment; Third Wisconsin Volunteer Cavalry Regiment; Sixth Regiment Kansas Volunteer Cavalry; Ninth Regiment Kansas Volunteer Cavalry; Second Kansas Artillery; Fourteenth Kansas Cavalry; and First, Second, and Third Indian Home Guard. Guarding supply trains was a dangerous mission, because they often came under attack from Rebel forces. Williams had become aware of Confederate plans to attack the June supply train. According to captured Rebel troops, Confederate General William L. Cabell and approximately 2,000 troops had left Fort Smith and were on their way to attack the train. Moreover, Confederate Colonel Stand Watie, a Cherokee, with approximately 1,600 men also planned to attack the train at Cabin Creek.

Located approximately three miles north of present-day Pensacola, Oklahoma, the Texas Road crossed Cabin Creek. On July 1, 1863, the Union forces discovered Watie's troops were well entrenched on the south side of the Cabin Creek crossing. He also had a well-positioned picket on the north side of the creek. Watie's troops included the First Cherokee Mounted Rifles, First Creek Mounted Volunteers, a component of the Twenty-ninth Texas Cavalry, and a detachment from Martin's Partisan Rangers. As a result of heavy rains and high water, General Cabell and his enforcements were located on the Grand River, unable to cross and provide assistance to Watie.

The rain caused Cabin Creek to swell significantly as well. As Williams led his men toward the creek's ford, he ordered Major John Foreman, commander of the Third Indian Home Guard, to advance toward and attack the Confederate pickets. During the brief battle, the Union forces also launched a barrage from their heavy artillery weapons that drove the Confederates from their location. Realizing the water was too high to cross, Williams ordered the supply train back and placed troops into a defensive position north of the creek. They waited until the next day to engage Watie's forces.

On the morning of July 2, Williams ordered the supply train to remain behind under guard, and instructed some of the Union forces to march toward the creek. Major Foreman and the Third Indian Home Guard, along with five companies of the First Kansas Colored, took up the center position. Noting the creek level had rescinded from shoulder level to waist level, Williams gave the command to begin the heavy artillery barrage against Watie's forces. The heavy shelling lasted approximately forty minutes. At that point, Major Foreman proceeded to lead his troops down into the creek. The Union artillery shelling had been unsuccessful in dislodging the Confederates from their strongholds, however. As Foremen and his men crossed

the creek they were met with heavy gunfire from the Confederates. Foreman received serious gunshot wounds, and was forced to retreat. His men also began to pull back, when another artillery assault commenced against the enemy. Colonel Williams and the First Kansas Colored immediately began to push across the creek. This time the Union forces successfully crossed over, and dislodged the Confederates from their positions. Disorganized and demoralized, Watie's troops began to flee. Williams's forces pursued the enemy for about five miles, when they disengaged and returned to the supply train.

The Union supply train crossed Cabin Creek and continued unmolested to Fort Gibson. Watie's troops fled across the Arkansas River, while Cabell's forces journeyed to the Fort Smith area. The first battle at Cabin Creek resulted in one Union soldier dead and twenty wounded. The Confederate suffered approximately fifty killed and fifty wounded, and nine taken prisoner.

Surrender of General Stand Waite by Dennis Parker

The Union victory at the first battle at Cabin Creek resulted in a boost in morale for Union soldiers. They had soundly defeated Watie's forces, who in past fights, had proven to be a daunting opponent. More importantly, members of the First Kansas Colored Volunteer Infantry had proven their courage and merit in combat. They understood if they lost the battle they would surely meet their death, because the Confederates provided no housing or shelter for African American soldiers.

SECOND BATTLE OF CABIN CREEK

Following Watie's defeat at the Cabin Creek battle in 1863, he and members of the Cherokee Mounted Rifles regrouped along the Red River. In February 1864 Watie put forth a military strategy, whereby, the Confederates would initiate a major campaign in Kansas, forcing the withdrawal of Union troops from both Fort Gibson and Fort Smith. As he waited for approval for his plan, Watie (now a brigadier general) continued to harass and impede Union operations. His successful raids during the spring and summer of 1864 often targeted Union haying operations. Moreover, Watie planned and successfully carried out the surprise attack on the Union steamship the *J.R. Williams* on the Arkansas River. The steamship, destined for Fort Gibson, was loaded with supplies including food and other materials worth an estimated $120,000. Watie and his men ambushed the ship at Pleasant Bluff (northeast of present-day Tamaha, Oklahoma), looted the goods, set fire to the vessel, and then set it adrift to sink. The successful raid and sinking of the *J.R. Williams* improved the morale of Watie's men. It also resulted in the Union Army decision to utilize wagon trains over river travel to transport supplies.

By August 1864, the Confederate command gave approval to Watie's plan with some stipulation. The campaign should be carried out prior to October 1; be a joint exercise with Brigadier General Richard M. Gano of Texas; and it would take place in conjunction with General Sterling Price's raid in Missouri. That same month, Confederate leaders learned of another large Union supply wagon train being assembled at Fort Scott. The supply train would travel along the Texas Road in route to Fort Gibson with Fort Smith being its final destination. The report prompted Watie to alter his plans to include raids along the Grand River, north of the Arkansas River, to obstruct Union operations and communication. Their primary objective was to find and attack the Union supply train.

On September 12, the Union supply train, commanded by Major Henry Hopkins, left Fort Scott. The train consisted of 300 wagons, pulled by teams of six horses, and was accompanied by approximately 260 Union soldiers representing the Second Kansas Cavalry, the Sixth Kansas Cavalry, and the Fourteenth Kansas Cavalry as well as armed wagon drivers. The wagon train's value was over $1 million.

On September 14, Watie and Gano's forces embarked on their mission. Heading north across the Canadian River, Gano's troops numbered around 1,200 representing the Texas Cavalry and Captain Sylvanus Howell's Texas Artillery Battery. Watie's forces totaled 800 and featured members of the First and Second Cherokee regiments, the First and Second Creek regiments, and Seminole troops. Although both Gano and Watie each lead their own groups, Gano assumed command in its entirety, because he received his brigadier general's commission first, and many Texas soldiers refused to serve under a Native American commander.

On September 16, the Confederates engaged the enemy at a Union hay operation at Flat Rock Creek, near present-day Wagoner, Oklahoma. The small group of Union soldiers from the Second Kansas and First Kansas Colored Infantry quickly succumbed to the Confederate forces. Many white Union soldiers were taken prisoner, while those African Americans that were unable to escape were summarily executed. After their decisive victory at Flat Rock

General Stand Watie, the only Native American brigadier general in the Confederate Army • From *Mathew Brady Photographs of Civil War-Era Personalities and Scenes* series, documenting the period 1860–1865

Creek, Gano and Watie continued on toward the Texas Road, where they hoped to find the Union supply train.

Major Hopkins ordered the Union supply train to set camp at Horse Creek, about fifteen miles north of Cabin Creek, on the evening of September 17. At camp, Hopkins received notification that a large group of Confederates had been seen heading north. Hopkins was instructed to immediately head to Cabin Creek. Following their victory at the first battle of Cabin Creek, the Union Army had strengthened their position at the site. The site featured a new stockade built on the bluff above the creek, and fortifications had been made to the other buildings. Hopkins arrived at Cabin Creek on the morning of September 18, and by that afternoon, the wagon train was located in a defensive position behind the stockade. At approximately the same time the Union wagon train arrived at Cabin Creek, Gano's troops set camp at Wolf Creek, a few miles south of Cabin Creek.

On September 18 Gano and 500 troops left Wolf Creek to assess the area, and found the wagon train at Cabin Creek. Gano sent for the remainder of the Confederate troops who joined the others near the federal garrison at Cabin Creek around midnight. He deployed his troops, but did not give the order to advance. Meanwhile, Hopkins also sent out a detachment of men to survey the area, who located some of the Rebels. However, Hopkins was unable to ascertain the strength of Gano's forces.

Gano placed the artillery in the center, the Texas troops on the right, and Watie's Indian regiments on the left. Under a full moon, around 3:00 AM on September 19, Gano gave the order to advance. When the Confederates made it to within 300 yards of the enemy's position, rounds from their Union rifles began to reach the Rebels. Gano moved his men in such a way that placed the Union soldiers and the wagon train in a crossfire position. Panic among the teamsters and wagon masters ensued, and the majority fled in the direction of Fort Scott. Hopkins's men held back the advancing Rebel forces until 7:00 AM. By 2.00 PM, however, the Confederates had advanced their artillery to within 100 yards of the Union forces. Now disorganized, Hopkins's men began to retreat back across Cabin Creek where they scattered in all directions, leaving the wagon train in Gano's control. The Confederates headed south with as many units of the wagon train as they could hitch to remaining horses. Not wanting the Union to retrieve any of the supplies, they set fire to the remaining part of the supply train. Although Union forces were dispatched to recapture the train, Gano and the Confederates escaped.

The Confederate victory at the second battle of Cabin Creek provided a morale boost for Gano's forces. They had soundly defeated the Union soldiers, and seizure of the wagon train provided his troops with much needed provisions. Gano later reported that during the battle the Union had suffered twenty-three killed in action; an unknown number of wounded, and twenty-six taken prisoner. The Confederate casualties numbered six dead, and forty-five wounded. Although skirmishes between Union and Confederate forces would continue, the second battle of Cabin Creek would mark the end of major Civil War battles in the Indian Territory.

Today, the Oklahoma Historical Society maintains the battlefield site. A circle drive loop within the ten acres provides access to monuments and signage telling the story of the site. The site is open from dawn to dusk and is located at 442370 E. 367 Road in Big Cabin, Oklahoma. For more information, email cabincreek@okhistory.org.

THE BATTLE OF HONEY SPRINGS

The rain had been falling for several hours on July 17, 1863, when Major General James A. Blunt, commander of the Army of the Frontier for the Union forces, engaged Confederate forces under the leadership of Brigadier General Douglas H. Cooper. The engagement, known as the Battle of Honey Springs, or the Battle of Elk Creek, took place in McIntosh County, approximately four and one-half miles northeast of Checotah and would be the largest military battle to take place in Indian Territory. Moreover, it would serve as the turning point of the Civil War in Indian Territory, bringing it primarily under Union control.

During the first two years of the Civil War, the Confederacy had prevailed in the Indian Territory, having gone almost without confrontation by Union forces. The Union Army had focused primarily on campaigns west of the Mississippi River, thereby allowing the

Confederacy to control much of the Indian Territory. However, by the end of June 1863, the Union Army had experienced decisive victories in the east and south including Gettysburg in Pennsylvania and Vicksburg in Mississippi. In addition, Union forces had critical success in Arkansas. The Union Army could now focus troops and artillery to defeat the Confederate forces dominant in the Southwest. Honey Springs soon became a focal point for the Union Army.

Following the first Battle of Cabin Creek on July 1–2, 1863, Cooper garnered his forces at Honey Springs along the Texas Road and set up his headquarters there. The Texas Road served as the primary north-south overland route through Indian Territory. The thoroughfare was vital to the Confederates, and they established a substantial supply post near the Honey Springs settlement, located almost adjacent to the Texas Road. The Union Army controlled the Texas Road from Kansas to Fort Gibson, using it as a supply route. Moreover, by 1863 the Union

Major General James A. Blunt

Army had secured and occupied Fort Gibson. Confederates continued to pose a threat to Union control north of the Arkansas River, however; and they persistently harassed Union troop and supply movements. For example, Colonel Stand Watie, a Cherokee, led a group of Confederates in a raid on a Union supply train on its way to Fort Gibson on July 1, 1863.

The Union Army planned to deploy more troops before attacking Confederate forces in the Indian Territory. Blunt, having arrived at Fort Gibson on July 11, was unwilling to wait on additional support. Blunt received information that Cooper and his troops from Honey Springs planned to attack Fort Gibson. In a bold move, Blunt set out to locate Cooper and confront the enemy. He acted swiftly, because news arrived that Confederate Brigadier General William Cabell, along with 3,000 reinforcements, would march from Fort Smith to Honey Springs to assist Cooper in his campaign against Fort Gibson. Blunt's bravery should not be overlooked. At the time, he was suffering from a very high fever brought on by encephalitis.

In addition to his illness, Blunt faced the difficult task of crossing the swollen Arkansas River. At midnight on July 15, Blunt—with 250 cavalry, and four pieces of light artillery—traveled approximately thirteen miles up the northern bank of the Arkansas River, where his men drove out Confederate pickets, crossed the river, and led his men downstream toward the mouth of the Grand River. Blunt intended to take out any additional Confederate pickets, secure the area, and prevent enemy soldiers from returning to Honey Springs to warn Cooper of the advancing Union forces. By the morning of July 16, Blunt's men had secured the area around the mouth of the river, and by nightfall, the remainder of his troops and equipment had crossed the river on flat boats. Yet, his objective to maintain the element of surprise against the enemy proved futile. A few days earlier, Cooper learned of the Union Army's movements, and took countermeasures.

Determined to defend Honey Springs, on July 14, Cooper dispatched the First and Second Creek Regiments; the First and Second Cherokee Regiments; Texas Cavalry units, and Choctaw and Chickasaw forces along Elk Creek. The Confederates were strategically positioned and fortified at possible crossing points along the creek. Cooper enjoyed the advantage of troop

THE WAR IN ARKANSAS THE BATTLE OF HONEY SPRINGS, JULY 17—DEFEAT OF THE REBELS UNDER GENERAL COOPER BY THE U. S. TROOPS UNDER MAJOR-GENERAL JAMES G. BLUNT. From a Sketch by James R. O'Neil.

Lithograph depicting the Battle of Honey Springs

strength over Blunt, having approximately 6,000 men to Blunt's 3,000. However, Cooper's men were ill trained and not well equipped, while the Union forces had the benefit of having a full arsenal. Blunt's units included the Kansas First Colored Volunteers Infantry Regiment; the First and Second Indian Home Guard; Third Wisconsin Cavalry; Second Kansas Battery; Hopkins's Kansas Battery; and the Second Colorado Infantry.

At approximately 10:00 PM on July 16, Blunt's men began to advance down the Texas Road. Around midnight, an advance guard encountered Confederate scouts at Chimney Mountain, who after a brief skirmish, began to retreat. By dawn on the morning of July 17, the Union forces met another scouting party, located five miles from Elk Creek, and subsequently drove them back to the Confederate line. Cooper had concealed his main forces along a one and one-half mile stretch of the Elk Creek timberline. The Texas Road divided Cooper's troops in the middle. After assessing the enemy position and allowing his men time to rest and eat, Blunt divided his men into two columns and ordered them to advance on the enemy. Within minutes heavy fighting broke out, and continued for about two hours. During the battle, Confederate troops mistakenly believed the Union soldiers had been ordered to retreat. Cooper's men charged and came within twenty-five paces of the enemy, where they met a barrage of Union firepower from the First Kansas Colored Volunteer Infantry. The Union forces quickly breached the Confederate line and Cooper's men began to withdraw. Cooper instructed his men to secure the bridge at Elk Creek, but they were unsuccessful. Union forces crossed the bridge and other areas along the creek, and pursued the Confederates down the Texas Road to Honey Springs Depot, where the final stage of the battle occurred.

Confederate units repelled the Union soldiers long enough to evacuate their men and weaponry. However, as Cooper's forces left the depot, they torched the buildings and supplies. Blunt continued to pursue the Confederates for approximately three miles to the prairie south of Elk Creek. At approximately 4:00 PM, Blunt withdrew his pursuit, because his men and horses were near exhaustion, and his ammunition had almost been entirely depleted. Moreover, General Cabell with his 3,000 reinforcements had joined with Cooper's men.

During the night, the Confederates withdrew from the area and fled south of the Canadian River. A day later, Blunt's forces returned to Fort Gibson.

The Battle of Honey Springs resulted in seventeen Union soldiers dead and sixty wounded. The Confederate losses stood at 150 dead, 400 wounded, and 77 prisoners of war. The Battle of Honey Springs ended Confederate dominance in the Indian Territory, and began the Union offensive that resulted in the capture of Fort Smith. It also showcased the courage and capability of African American troops in battle.

The Honey Springs Battlefield is a National Historic Landmark and is also on the National Register of Historic Places. The site is under the direction of the Oklahoma Historical Society. It is located at 101601 S. 4232 Road in Checotah. The 1,100 acre site has six walking trails with a total of fifty-five interpretive signs. The battlefield is open Tuesday through Saturday from 9:00 AM to 5:00 PM. Admission is free. For more information, call 918/473-5572 or email honeysprings@okhistory.org.

THE BATTLE OF MIDDLE BOGGY

Take no prisoners!" These were the instructions Union Army Colonel William A. Phillips gave the Muscogee Creek troops before they embarked on their mission to eradicate Confederate forces from the Indian Territory. The Muscogee Creek soldiers made up part of the 1,500 men that would participate in the February 1864 military operation. In addition to driving out the Rebel forces, The Union Army's objective during the campaign was to sever the treaties signed between Indian tribes and the Confederacy, and to offer amnesty to Creek, Seminole, and Chickasaw Indians. Phillips's instruction to "take no prisoners" resulted in an intense and bloody engagement at Middle Boggy. The battle serves as a reminder regarding the brutality associated with war.

In his remarks to his men, Phillips also reiterated the Confederacy had been responsible for the "needless and wicked war." Moreover, he explained that as they marched south through Indian Territory destroying the enemy, they would help secure peace that had eluded the nation since the war began in 1861. For this campaign, Phillips decided to march west of the Texas Road, taking the old 1855 Dragoon Trail. It was believed the Dragoon Trail would provide the Union soldiers with enough food to sustain them. Moreover, the trail allowed them to sweep through the Creek, Seminole, and Chickasaw lands that Phillips planned to take back from the Confederacy.

Phillips and his troops left Fort Gibson and traveled along the Dragoon Trail for the first two

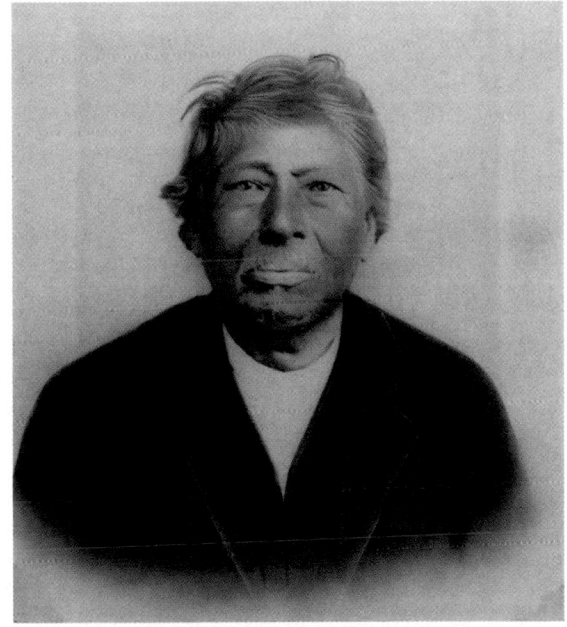

Lt. Colonel John Jumper, commander of a Seminole Confederate Battalion

days. On the third day they left the trail, and for the next few days his troops raided several Confederate Creek and Seminole camps. Phillips reported over 100 Rebel Indians killed during these raids. He rejoined the Dragoon Trail and headed southwest toward Middle Boggy River. At Middle Boggy the Union soldiers would once again engage the enemy.

Located approximately one mile north of present-day Atoka, and just north of Middle Boggy Creek, Middle Boggy became part of the defensive line established by the Confederate Army to help protect Texas and the Red River against Union encroachment. The line extended from Fort Washita, northeast of present-day Durant, through Middle Boggy and eastward into Arkansas. Confederate Lieutenant Colonel John Jumper and his Seminole Battalion led the defense of the Confederate western line including Middle Boggy. A small group of Confederates had set a picket near Middle Boggy in early February. On February 12, Union scouts discovered the encampment and both the Confederates and the Union soldiers reported the sighting to their leaders. Phillips responded quickly and made plans to attack the Rebel camp.

On the morning of February 13, Phillips ordered Major Charles Willets and 350 heavily armed Union troops that included an artillery section, to attack the Confederates at Middle Boggy. The Confederates, numbering approximately ninety, did not have adequate weaponry to match Willet's men. However, the Confederates at Middle Boggy withstood the assault for about thirty minutes before retreating. Following the skirmish, Confederates returned to the site to help the wounded and bury the dead. There at the battlefield, Jumper and his men made a gruesome discovery. There were no survivors. The Union soldiers had carried out Phillips's instructions to take no prisoners. Many of the forty-seven dead Confederate soldiers had received superficial wounds during the battle. Yet, when the Union soldiers came upon them, they scalped them and slit their throats. The Union soldiers did not suffer any casualties during the battle.

Phillips continued the expedition through Indian Territory until February 17, 1864. He and his men had traveled over 400 miles, and during their mission they wreaked havoc upon the Indian Territory and the enemy. Following a scorched earth policy, Phillips's men set fire to houses and crops, destroying lives as well as the landscape. Phillips's cruelty did not leash a final blow to the Confederate forces in Indian Territory, however. His tactics only reinforced the Rebel's steadfast resolve to fight on.

The Oklahoma Historical Society conducts a reenactment of the Battle of the Middle Boggy every three years.

THE BATTLE OF THE WASHITA

For as long as the waters run and the grass shall grow." These were the words promised to Native American tribes living on the Great Plains by the federal government following the adoption of the Concentration Policy in 1851. According to the policy, Indians would be removed to specific areas of land in the west. Indians also would be restricted to remain in these regions. The United States government informed the tribes that they could live uninhibited and would not be disturbed by white encroachment. In addition, the land would belong to the tribes indefinitely. However, by the 1850s Americans began a massive westward expansion across the Mississippi River. Many Indians refused to live on these restrictive land areas, leaving to follow the buffalo herds. They often clashed with settlers coming into the west. In an attempt to curtail the tension and violence between Native American tribes and westward migrants, the federal government implemented additional Indian policies. The U.S. Army, responsible for overseeing Indian tribes and maintaining peace, often used force to compel Indians to comply with federal Indian policies. The confrontation

General George Armstrong Custer

between the U.S. Army and these Indians sometimes resulted in catastrophic consequences. The Battle of the Washita, where Cheyenne Chief Black Kettle and a number of his followers were killed, serves as an example of those tragic times.

Following the 1851 Concentration Policy, many young male Indians became restless, blaming older tribesmen and chiefs for their plight. They left their assigned lands, and became nomadic again, choosing to hunt and follow the buffalo herds. Whites also began to encroach on Indian lands, and soon tension increased between the two groups. For example, following gold discoveries in the Pike's Peak region of Colorado, white miners began to intrude on land given to the Cheyenne, Arapaho, and seven other tribes in eastern Colorado. Warfare ensued between white settlers and members of the Cheyenne and Arapaho tribes. The fighting resulted in the U.S. government signing the Treaty of Fort Wise with these Indian tribes, resulting in the reduction of tribal lands to 1/13th its original size. A militaristic band of Cheyenne and Lakota warriors, known as "Dog Soldiers," refused to abide by the new treaty. They continued to hunt and roam in eastern Colorado and western Kansas.

Once again, tension resulted between the Dog Soldiers and white settlers. Fighting broke out between the Colorado militia, (led by Colonel John Chivington), and the Dog Soldiers. The conflict spilled over into civilian populations as Dog Soldiers attacked white settlements, killing men, women, and children. Hoping to avoid the conflict, Black Kettle and a group of 700 Cheyenne reported to Fort Lyon, Colorado, where they believed they had negotiated a peace treaty. Following the peace talks, Black Kettle and his followers made camp on Sand Creek. It was there that Colonel Chivington led an attack against the Cheyenne on November 29, 1864. Although Black Kettle survived the Sand Creek Massacre, Colorado militia slaughtered more than 100 innocent Cheyenne men, women, and children. Moreover, the carnage that took place at Sand Creek would breed further mistrust between Native Americans and federal officials.

Indian wars continued to plague the Great Plains. The federal government responded by introducing the 1867 Reservation Solution, whereby Native Americans would be relocated to two primary land areas: the Dakota Territory and Indian Territory. All land transactions with Indian tribes were required to go through the "treaty process," requiring approval of the U.S. Senate. Under the 1867 Medicine Lodge Treaty, the Cheyenne and Arapaho tribes would be placed in Indian Territory (present-day western Oklahoma). The federal government promised the tribes peace and protection from white intruders in return for amity and relocation to western Indian Territory. The U.S. Army would be responsible for

Depiction of the Battle of the Washita

enforcing the new reservation policy.

The 1867 Medicine Lodge Treaty and subsequent military campaigns in western Kansas failed to stem the tide of Indian raids on the southern Great Plains. In the latter part of 1867, Indians wreaked havoc on the Plains, burning homesteads, killing whites and taking their scalp. Moreover, the Indians often took white women and children captive. The U.S. Army recorded the following for 1867: 100 soldiers, including five officers, killed; fifty-eight whites murdered; numerous women and children kidnapped; and countless head of livestock stolen.

The U.S. government debated whether to continue to provide arms and ammunition to the Indian tribes, including the Cheyenne and Arapaho, who had been responsible for many raids in western Kansas. In August 1868, the federal government acquiesced to the demands of Indian agents and arms manufacturers that advocated providing weapons to the Cheyenne and Arapaho. However, within twenty-four hours of receiving the rifles and ammunition, young warriors left the hunting parties, made their way to Kansas, where they once again waged war against white settlers.

Settlers demanded the U.S. government pursue the hostile Indians, discipline them, and forcibly remove them to their assigned reservation. Army Major General Phillip Sheridan, given the task to resolve the Indian problem, realized the ineffectiveness of the army's summer military campaigns against the Indians. He immediately asked the army to reinstate Lieutenant Colonel George Armstrong Custer to active duty. Custer, a seasoned military veteran, served the Union Army during the Civil War but had been court martial and suspended. Sheridan and Custer developed a new military strategy known as the "Winter Campaign." The army would engage non-compliant Indians during the winter months, when they were less hostile and more likely to remain in camp. Custer wrote, "When the Indian pony is poor and thin; when he is weak from want of nourishing food; when the warrior is hibernating along the banks of Southern streams—then is the time to strike with vengeance." Black Kettle's camp fell prey to Sheridan's winter campaign strategy.

In early November 1868, Black Kettle, along with Arapaho Chief Big Mouth, asked permission from General William B. Hazen to locate their winter camp near Fort Cobb. Positioning their camps near Fort Cobb would offer the tribal chiefs and their followers a sense of security and protection. However, Hazen refused their inquiry citing he did not have the ability to grant their request. As a result, Black Kettle and his followers set camp along the Washita River near present-day Cheyenne, Oklahoma. The peace chief's camp included approximately 250 Cheyenne, more than 60 lodges, and 800 horses.

On November 12, 1868, the Seventh Cavalry, led by Custer and accompanied by a large supply train, marched from Fort Dodge, Kansas, to Camp Supply, Indian Territory. Camp Supply served as the army's headquarters for the winter campaigns. Sheridan soon joined Custer at the camp, where they studied maps of the Indian Territory. He then ordered Custer and his men to march deep into the Indian Territory, locate the winter camps, and inflict punishment on the Indians. Custer had been studying the Plains Indians in their habitat for more than a year. He understood his foe, and took with him forty sharpshooters.

On the morning of November 23, 1868, Custer and his troops set out in a severe blizzard, led by two Osage scouts. At one point, the scouts wanted to turn back, because the severe snowstorm impeded their sense of direction. Not to be deterred, Custer took over the lead using his maps and compass and headed toward the Antelope Hills. Once the Seventh Cavalry reached the Canadian River, Major Joel Elliott and a small group of soldiers were ordered to search upstream. Elliott reported that he had identified a trail that led south toward the Washita River. Custer left the wagon supply trains behind, and with a group of his men, decided to march on the Washita River. Custer and his Osage scouts soon found Black Kettle's peaceful Cheyenne village encamped along the river. On November 26 Custer arrived on a ridge above the Indian village. There, he and his men waited until dawn the next morning to attack.

Custer divided his men into four columns to ensure that Black Kettle and his followers could not escape. While the Indians slept, a rifle was fired as the bugler sounded the charge. Soon the federal troops had overrun the camp. Fighting continued until about three o'clock that

THE INDIAN CAMPAIGN—PRISONERS CAPTURED BY GENERAL CUSTER.—Sketched by Theodore R. Davis.—[See Page 826.]

Prisoners of the "Indian Campaign" captured by General Custer (from 1868 issue of *Harper's Weekly*)

afternoon, because Arapaho, Kiowa, and Cheyenne Indians camped further downstream heard the shots and came to assist Black Kettle's camp. At one point, Major Elliott took a group of soldiers and pursued Indians into the wooded area. Indians surrounded Elliot and his men, killing them. However, Custer's men killed Black Kettle and an indeterminate number of Cheyenne, and captured fifty-three women and children. In addition, soldiers burned fifty-one lodges and slaughtered roughly 800 horses. The Seventh Cavalry suffered twenty-two men killed including two officers, fifteen wounded and one missing. On the evening of November 27, the Seventh Cavalry with their prisoners in tow began their return march to Camp Supply.

The Sheridan-Custer winter campaigns continued into 1869, with troops representing the Seventh Cavalry and the Nineteenth Kansas Volunteer Cavalry roaming over much of present-day western Oklahoma searching for hostile Indians. In 1876 Custer and his men were killed at the Battle of Little Big Horn in Montana Territory. Indian wars continued on the Great Plains for several more

Battlefield marker.

years. The Battle of Wounded Knee in South Dakota in 1890 served as the final episode in the long history of Indian wars. Afterwards, Indians faced life under the Dawes Severalty Act, where they were often the victims of corruption and greed. Angie Debo's book entitled *And Still the Waters Run* detailed how Indian tribes in Oklahoma had been systematically deprived of their land and resources granted to them by treaties. She also argued the 1887 Dawes Severalty Act was used to swindle Indians out of their property. She also exposed the corruption, moral depravity, and criminal activity associated with the allotment system.

Today, the Washita Battlefield Historic site, created in 1996, is maintained by the National Park Service and is listed on the National Register of Historic Places. Visitors to the historic battlefield may also want to visit the Black Kettle Museum in Cheyenne, Oklahoma. For museum hours call 580/497-3929 or log on to www.garryowen.com/museum.htm.

OKLAHOMA'S MILITARY FORTS

FORT GIBSON

Along the banks of the Grand River where the Virdigris and Arkansas rivers join in Indian Territory, the United States Army established Fort Gibson in April 1824. At the time it served as the most westward military garrison for America. Named after Commissary General George Gibson, the fortification was manned by a small contingent of soldiers that numbered a little more than 100. The soldiers represented a portion of the Seventh Cavalry stationed at Fort Smith, and were under the leadership of Colonel Matthew Arbuckle. In addition to road construction, laying out the fort's grounds and erecting its first buildings that included barracks, the Fort Gibson soldiers' early mission was to monitor and quell the ongoing tension and conflict between the Osage and Cherokee Indians. Over the years, Fort Gibson would serve America in a variety of ways, including peacekeeper among the Indians and as a basis for operations for westward exploration.

Fort Gibson's importance to the nation as well as its prestige took place during the 1830s. The 1830 Indian Removal Act, signed by President Andrew Jackson, relocated the Five Civilized Tribes (Cherokee, Chickasaw, Choctaw, Creek, and Seminole) to Indian Territory. As these groups moved into Indian Territory, their first stop was Fort Gibson, where they received materials such as farm equipment, firearms, clothing, and food necessary for their survival. The soldiers also provided protection for the relocated tribes from white intruders and western Plains Indian tribes already living in present-day Oklahoma and the surrounding area. Providing protection for the relocated Indians, Fort Gibson served as the base of operations for several military expeditions to encounter Plains Indians and negotiate a peace between them and the Five Civilized Tribes. By 1837, peace treaties had been signed among a number of Plains Indian tribes, the relocated tribes, and the U.S. government. By the end of the decade, Fort Gibson had become a major hub for military personnel, transportation, and business. Its locations on the Grand River allowed for steamships to transport visitors, merchants, products that included luxury items, and supplies to the isolated frontier fort.

Although Fort Gibson had become one America's most important military garrisons, life at the fort was often arduous and many soldiers complained about the living conditions as well as the intense labor tasks they performed daily. Disease served as a primary concern. Disease had left many soldiers in a weakened condition, and resulted in the death of numerous others stationed at Fort Gibson during the 1830s. Moreover, soldiers often complained about conditions of the buildings. The initial buildings were not made of stone, and were crumbling, damp, and cold during the winter months. Disease and the living conditions resulted in many people lobbying government officials to abandon the fort and return back to Fort Smith, Arkansas. Colonel Arbuckle and other officers convinced U.S. officials that Fort Gibson was vital to American interests, and any thoughts to abandon the fort were temporarily dismissed.

The United States Army relocated Fort Gibson in 1845. The new stone buildings were

Officers quarters [top] and Soldier tents at Fort Gibson

constructed less than a mile from the original fort, on a higher elevation, where rising waters from the river would not pose a potential flood threat. Fort Gibson's prominence had declined by the 1840s, however, and by the 1850s renewed calls for the U.S. Army to abandon the fort emerged. This time, the Cherokee Nation became the primary proponent regarding the fort's closure.

Cherokee tribal leaders provided several reasons for abandoning the fort. They argued that the soldiers had not fulfilled their duty to keep alcoholic beverages away from the Indians. Moreover, the vices associated with military life, such as prostitution and gambling, were also a detriment to Native American life. The Cherokees also argued they were able to control their own population and could assume responsibility for the tribe. Despite other Civilized Tribes objecting to the fort's closure, the U.S. government relinquished its control of Fort Gibson in June 1857, and the buildings and grounds became the property of the Cherokee Nation.

During the Civil War, military personnel from both the Confederate and Union armies utilized Fort Gibson. During months of the Civil War, Confederate troops occupied Fort Gibson and used it as a base of operations. As the war progressed, and Union forces began to concentrate on the war's western front, the fort fell under Union control. The fort served as a point of protection for the Cherokees, who made the fort their seat of government during the war. In addition, the fort provided provisions, safety, and security to blacks and other refugees, who made their way to the fort.

Following the Civil War, the U.S. Army decided once again to abandon Fort Gibson. However, based upon the request of the Cherokee Nation, the army resumed a small presence at Fort Gibson. Their mission was to protect Cherokee lands, and curtail the outlaw and squatter activity that had been plaguing the area. Unfortunately, the fort became a magnet for vices that attracted outlaws and members of the lower socioeconomic classes. Many soldiers often lost their monthly pay to these individuals in games of chance or prostitution.

Soldiers continued to fulfill their duties in maintaining peace in the Indian Territory into the late 1880s. However, failure to provide routine maintenance left the fort in disrepair. The few soldiers that remained at the fort made their lodging outside the buildings. The military eventually abandoned Fort Gibson for the final time during the summer of 1890.

Today, Fort Gibson serves as a prominent tourist attraction, drawing visitors from all over the world. It is on the National Register of Historic Places and is generously supported by the Cherokee Nation. Visitors to the site can see a reconstruction of the early log fort as well as original buildings erected between the 1840s through the 1870s. The Commissary Visitor Center on Garrison Hill provides information regarding the fort's history. Fort Gibson hosts a number of special living history events and programs each year.

For more information contact, 918/478.4088 or email fortgibson@okhistory.org.

FORT RENO

ravelers on Route 66 heading west out of El Reno will find one of Oklahoma's most significant historical landmarks: Fort Reno. John Miles, an Indian agent located at the Darlington Indian Agency, staunchly advocated that a military camp be placed nearby to protect the Cheyenne and Arapaho Indians living in the area. The federal government heeded Miles's request and placed a military camp in the area in July 1874. A year later the camp became a permanent fixture in the Indian Territory, with the establishment of a fort on July 15, 1875. In January 1876 General Phillip Sheridan named it Fort Reno in honor of his friend and military veteran Jesse L. Reno, who had been killed during the Civil War. Fort Reno's mission changed over the years from Indian protector and overseer of Oklahoma's famous land runs to operating a prestigious remount station and serving as a prisoner-of-war camp. In the process, Fort Reno made a lasting impact on our nation's history.

Initially, soldiers at the camp were given the responsibility to safeguard the Cheyenne and Arapaho Indians that had been removed to central and western Oklahoma following the 1867 Medicine Lodge Treaty. Overseeing the Indians proved difficult at times for the soldiers stationed at Fort Reno. Many Indians were both resentful and suspicious of white authority figures. Their feelings were not unfounded. For example, in April 1875 a major battle between the camp soldiers and members of the Cheyenne Tribe occurred at Sand Hill, when the Indians believed the soldiers were indiscriminately firing into their teepees. The stray bullets resulted when troops fired at and killed Cheyenne Black Horse, a prisoner who had escaped. Following the battle, the military reported that both they and the Indians had suffered casualties that included the death of one soldier and nineteen Indians and many wounded. In 1878 another fierce engagement transpired between the troops at Fort Reno and approximately 300 members of the Cheyenne, who escaped the reservation and were attempting to return to Montana. As the soldiers pursued the Indians, they skirmished with them at present-day Freedom, Oklahoma, and again in western Kansas before relinquishing their mission to other northern military units.

Troops at Fort Reno also dealt with whites encroaching into the Indian Territory. David L. Payne, a leader of the Boomer Movement, had advocated the opening of the Unassigned Lands in

General Phillip Sheridan

central Oklahoma. Many individuals illegally came into the area and attempted to stake out land. Fort Reno dispatched "buffalo soldiers" (African Americans from the Ninth Cavalry), who sought out these squatters and removed them from the region. When the federal government finally opened the Unassigned Lands for settlement, Fort Reno helped supervise the land run openings in 1889, 1892, and 1893.

Texas cattlemen also created a hostile atmosphere for the Cheyenne Indians, resulting in Fort Reno troops coming to their assistance. Cowboys often drove their herds over reservation land, leaving many Cheyenne frustrated as the cattle tore up their pastures and gardens. These drovers often antagonized these Indians, and one encounter resulted in the death of a Cheyenne warrior attempting to protect his land. As a result, General Sheridan came to Fort Reno to investigate the situation, and he instructed the soldiers to remove all Texas cattle from the reservation. Fort Reno's role as guardian of the Cheyenne and Arapaho Indians diminished with the dawn of the twentieth-century. However, the fort would continue to play an important role for America.

From 1908 to 1947 Fort Reno served as one of the country's three Army Quartermaster Remount Stations. The fort was both expanded and upgraded to meet the equestrian requirements. Thousands of horses and pack mules were bred, groomed, and trained for military service at Fort Reno. From the garrison, they were shipped out on trains to all parts of the world, where they served a vital role in the Allied victories in both World War I and World War II. The military also utilized these animals in the Korean War. The most famous horse to be trained at Fort Reno was "Black Jack." He served as the ceremonial "horse with no rider," at the funerals of presidents Herbert Hoover, John F. Kennedy, Lyndon B. Johnson, and General Douglas MacArthur.

During World War II, Fort Reno became the home to German prisoners-of-war. The majority of the 1,300 Germans brought to the fort served under General Erwin Rommel in Africa. These prisoners worked for local farmers. They also assisted in the fort's expansion, building the

For nearly forty years, Fort Reno served as an Army Quartermaster Remount Station where horses and mules were bred and trained for military service. The most famous "trainee" was undoubtedly "Black Jack," who served as the time-honored "horse with no rider" at funeral ceremonies of four U.S. Presidents, including John F. Kennedy's, pictured here.

chapel in 1944. The Fort Reno Cemetery serves as the final resting place for both Italian and German prisoners-of-war. Except for one German who died at Fort Reno, the others buried at the post's cemetery were held at POW camps in Oklahoma and Texas. Also buried at the cemetery are Cheyenne Indians, pioneers, and military personnel. Following the war, the federal government transferred Fort Reno to the U.S. Department of Agriculture.

Over the years, some of America's most notable individuals visited Fort Reno including Will Rogers and famed aviatrix Amelia Earhart. Today, visitors to the historic site can explore the twenty-five buildings located on the campus, and the post cemetery. Fort Reno holds a number of events throughout the year, including the Tombstone Tales Re-enactment.

Fort Reno Visitors Center is located at 7107 W. Cheyenne Street, El Reno, OK 73036. For more information, call 405/262-3987 or email info@fortreno.org.

FORT SILL

Located in southwestern Oklahoma, near present-day Lawton, Major General Phillip Sheridan established Fort Sill on January 8, 1869, during a winter campaign against the Plains Indians. Originally designated as Camp Wichita, the fort was later renamed Fort Sill in honor of General Joshua Sill, a Civil War casualty and Sheridan's West Point classmate. Today, Fort Sill is the only active U.S. Army garrison established on the Southern Plains during the eighteenth century Indian Wars. It has played an integral part in every subsequent war and continues to have a vital role in our nation's defense.

Sheridan's expedition was not the first official military mission in the southwestern part of Indian Territory. In 1834 General Henry Leavenworth led the First Dragoon Expedition out of Fort Gibson to observe a Comanche village located near Medicine Bluffs. During this peaceful mission, artist George Catlin traveled with the group, and captured life of these southern plains Indians on canvas.

In 1867 the federal government implemented a new Indian policy that called for the relocation of Plains tribes to reservations. While many Plains Indians complied with the new policy, others resisted by refusing to move onto the reservations, or would leave to hunt and follow the decreasing buffalo herds. Oftentimes armed conflict ensued between settlers and Indians. The U.S. military, charged with the safety and security of peaceful Indians and whites, often engaged hostile Indians during the summer months. However, Sheridan implemented a new military strategy, whereby the army would pursue these rogue Indians during the winter months, when they were docile and less likely to engage in raiding activities.

It was during a massive winter campaign that Sheridan established Camp Wichita near the Medicine Bluffs. He acted on the recommendation of Colonel Benjamin H. Grierson, who had explored the area. Sheridan gave his approval for the military camp, because Indian tribes were drawn to the religious and cultural nuances associated with the bluffs. In fact, he held the first stake driven into the ground that created the parade ground. Some of the army's most notable units camped at Fort Wichita, including Brigadier General George Armstrong Custer and the Seventh Cavalry, the Nineteenth Kansas Volunteers, and the Tenth Cavalry that included a unit of African-American soldiers. These African-American soldiers would be named "buffalo soldiers" by local Native Americans. The buffalo soldiers were charged with keeping Indians on the reservations. They also kept unwanted intruders out of Indian Territory; maintained general law and order; built and maintained roads, telegraph lines, and forts; and assisted the cavalry in military actions. Another prominent individual that served as the camp's first Indian agent was Colonel Albert Gallatin Boone, grandson of famed frontiersman Daniel Boone.

During the early days of Fort Sill, soldiers and their family members lived in a stressful situation, as they were surrounded by many Indians who resented their presence. Yet, soldiers attempted to fulfill their duty to secure Texas from Indian raids, and maintain peace on local reservations. However, the vastness of the frontier impeded their success, as intruders and marauding Indians often evaded federal troops. As a result, the army established outposts around Fort Sill in order to provide a faster response to reported incidents. Eventually, peace was attained on the western prairie as defiant Indians eventually acquiesced to life on the reservation. Still, troops remained active as they dealt with cattle drives across Indian lands, outlaws, and people attempting to sell alcohol to Indians.

In 1894 Fort Sill became home to famed rebel Chiricahua Apache warrior Geronimo. Refusing to stay on the San Carlos Reservation in Arizona, Geronimo and his followers left the reservation and led a successful guerilla war into Mexico and against the United States. Following his surrender to General Nelson A. Miles, he and his fellow Apache warriors were branded prisoners-of-war by the federal government. They were sent to Florida and Alabama before being permanently relocated to Fort Sill. The Chiricahua Apaches believed Fort Sill would be their permanent home, and Fort Sill was enlarged to meet the needs of its growing population. During his stay at the fort, Geronimo continued to advocate the relocation of the Chiricahua Apache to their native land in Arizona. After twenty years of imprisonment, the majority of Apaches attained their freedom. Geronimo did not live to retain his independence. He is buried in the Apache cemetery at Fort Sill.

Fort Sill evolved throughout the twentieth century to meet both the military and the nation's

Apache leader Geronimo was held as a prisoner of war at Fort Sill.

defense requirements. Cavalry units gave way to field artillery units. Before World War I the fort had expanded to include the School of Fire; the Infantry School; and aircraft. Realizing the importance of aviation, Post Field was constructed in 1917 to handle the growing number of airplanes and pilots. By the end of World War I, approximately 50,000 military personnel were stationed at the base.

Following the war, Fort Sill continued to adapt to meet the nation's strategic military needs. It added a School for Aerial Observers, and when America found itself involved in another world war fighting Nazi aggression, the fort became the training grounds for the Forty-fifth

Infantry Division. Fort Sill continued to play an integral role in America's military missions including the Korean and Vietnam wars, and in the Middle Eastern conflicts including Iraq and Afghanistan.

Today Fort Sill is a major contributor to the state and local economies. According to the Fort Sill Public Information Office, in 2011 the fort paid $1 billion in payroll and contracts; $193 million in construction; $89 million in retail spending; $43 million in TRICARE; $1 million in legal claims; and another $536 million in other spending for a total of $1.9 billion. Moreover, 5.43 million gallons of gasoline pumped through filing stations at Fort Sill. The facility also provided 17,000 hours of free respite childcare. It also garnered over $3 million worth of volunteer contributions.

According to Fort Sill's official website, the population today at Fort Sill consists of 62,621 family members; 23,584 retirees; 8,831 military; 6,968 students; 3,115 civilian employees; 3,017 contractors; 836 NAF (numbered air force); 705 commercial employees; and 376 others.

CAMP SUPPLY

ocated in the northwestern portion of Indian Territory, in the valley where Wolf Creek and Beaver River meet, U.S. Army General Alfred Sully established Camp Supply as a temporary post in 1868. Its early mission: extend assistance to the army by providing provisions to soldiers and serve as a connection for the army's continuing supply chains. Camp Supply would play an integral part in America's strategic military mission, and would eventually be renamed Fort Supply.

During Camp Supply's early days, soldiers worked reinforcing the garrison by erecting stockades and storehouses as well as digging fresh wells. The site soon played an essential role in General Phillip Sheridan's winter campaign military strategy against resistant Indians. Camp Supply became Sheridan's headquarters and served as the base of operations for subsequent winter campaigns. The first campaign came in November 1868 when Lieutenant Colonel George Armstrong Custer led the Seventh Cavalry from Camp Supply and attacked Cheyenne Chief Black Kettle's camp located along the Washita River.

By 1870 the camp consisted of seven military units: five units from the Tenth U.S. Cavalry (an African American regiment), and two from the Third Infantry. The Tenth Cavalry and the Third Infantry were separated by approximately 600 yards. The camp had continued to grow with the addition of log buildings, a parade ground, and stables.

Camp Supply became a primary target for Indian raids, requiring the men to sleep with their weapons nearby. In fact, a series of incidents perpetrated by unfriendly Indians in 1870 led to a climactic battle at Camp Supply. In January 1870, warriors from the Southern Plains tribes, unhappy with their tribal leaders, worked to force the military out of the area. Indians accosted a group of Texas cowboys driving a herd of cattle destined for Camp Supply. Later that spring, Lieutenant Colonel Anderson Nelson, commander of Camp Supply, received warning that a group of Comanche and Kiowa Indians planned to attack the camp. Within days, a camp worker had been murdered, and horses belonging to the military had been stolen. Moreover, a band of Kiowa Indians attacked a supply train near the camp, killing one of the drivers.

In May and June 1870 soldiers provided assistance to a local mail station and supply train that had been attacked. Camp Supply itself became the focal point of attack during this time as well. Indians murdered another camp worker and assaulted the garrison's herd. Nelson took action to protect both the people and livestock at the camp. He gave specific instructions for the care and protection of the camp's horses, and he issued a command that Indians would not be allowed near the camp.

On the afternoon of June 11, 1870, a group of hostile Indians enticed soldiers into battle by attacking horses that had been placed outside Camp Supply. Soldiers, including Commander Nelson, dispatched to the areas along Wolf Creek and Beaver River to find those Indians responsible. Once they located the Indians, a fierce battle ensued, whereby the troops killed six warriors, and captured several of their horses. The Indians quickly retreated and the fighting ceased, but they remained in the area where they continued their aggressive actions against the camp.

Although soldiers were constantly on guard against Indian attacks, they continued to carry out their tasks that included guarding the route from Fort Dodge, Kansas, to the camp. The army used the path to transport supplies; later private citizens and wagon companies utilized the trail. Soldiers also kept the area safe from intruders encroaching on reservations, including merchants and individuals wanting to sell alcohol to the Indians.

David L. Payne

Camp Supply became a permanent garrison in 1878 and was renamed Fort Supply. Although Indian hostilities had diminished significantly by this time, soldiers at Fort Supply focused their attention on protecting Indians from intrusive whites. For example, demand for beef in eastern cities continued to increase throughout the late 1800s. Texas cattlemen, realizing the potential for substantial profit, were determined to meet the need. Cowboys drove Texas Longhorn cattle northward across Indian reservations to Dodge City and Abilene, Kansas, where they were sold and transported to Chicago. Soldiers often escorted these cattle drives through the Cheyenne-Arapaho Reservation as well as the Cherokee Outlet to help alleviate Indian resentment and make certain cowboys did not allow the cattle to feed on prime grazing lands.

Fort Supply also played a vital role in the land runs that opened up the Unassigned Lands to white settlement. For years, the Boomer Movement, led by David L. Payne, had advocated the opening of these lands. Hundreds of people came into these areas illegally, and soldiers from the fort were given the task to locate and remove them from the Cherokee Outlet. During the official openings of the Unassigned Lands, soldiers at Fort Supply answered the call and served as peacekeepers.

The U.S. Army closed Fort Supply in September 1894, and transferred it to the U.S. Department of the Interior. Today, Fort Supply is home to the William S. Key Correctional Center. It is on the National Register of Historic Places, and is under the direction of the Oklahoma Historical Society. Its mission is to preserve and maintain the historical buildings located on the site. The property is managed by the Plains Indians and Pioneers Museum in Woodward. Fort Supply, located thirteen miles north of Woodward on State Highway 183, is open to the public Tuesday through Saturday from 9:00 AM to 4:00 PM. Admission is free. For more information, call 580/256-6136.

FORT WASHITA

Following the Indian Removal Act of 1830, the Chickasaw Nation signed a treaty with the federal government in 1834, whereby they agreed to be relocated to the Indian Territory. However, Plains tribes occupied land nearby the new Chickasaw lands, and the tribe refused relocation, unless the federal government assured them protection. Non-Indian intruders into the area also posed a security risk for both the Chickasaw and Choctaw Indians. Federal agents had selected a possible site for a military garrison on the Old Texas Road along the Washita River. Before the final decision was made regarding the fort's location, General Zachary Taylor surveyed the site and gave his approval. In April 1842, soldiers from Company A of the Second Dragoon established the garrison, later named Fort Washita. At the time of its creation, Fort Washita served the United States as the nation's southwestern most military post. Its mission: protect the Chickasaw and Choctaw Indians from aggressive Plains tribes as well as non-Indians trespassing across the land.

Captain George Blake served as the post's first commander. Blake and his men began construction on the fort's first buildings. Located in a wooded, isolated area, soldiers had to utilize local resources, including lumber and stone, to erect the first barracks and other structures. Eventually, the fort would feature officer's quarters, a hospital, commissary, guardhouse, a sizable corral and stable, as well as blacksmith shops and farmhouses.

In the early days of Fort Washita, soldiers had to acquire their food locally (hunting and fishing) due to the scarcity of supplies. The fort would ultimately offer amenities including a bar, billiard table, bowling alley, school, library, and a newspaper. In their free time, troops stationed at the fort enjoyed hunting, fishing, and horse racing. Often times they would enjoy dances and parties at local Chickasaw homes.

Fort Washita experienced personnel and leadership changes over the years, but the fort and the region remained stable due to the military presence. Occasionally, troops were dispatched to deal with raiding Plains tribes, especially the Comanche Indians who proved to be the most menacing and formidable foe. It was during a skirmish with Comanche Indians that the garrison acquired a dog as the fort's mascot. A scouting patrol witnessed a struggle between the dog and an Indian. During the confrontation, the dog received several wounds. Soldiers retrieved the dog, took it back to the fort, and nursed it back to health. Placed on equal

Ruins of Fort Washita

Entrance to Fort Washita

rations with the soldiers, the dog became a highly regarded and protected addition to the fort. Penalty for any soldier menacing or attempting to harm the animal faced court martial.

From 1846 to 1848, military personnel also utilized the garrison as a rest stop on their march to the Mexican-American War. Although the average personnel at the fort averaged 150, during the Mexican-American War, the U.S. Army stationed approximately 2,000 troops at the fort. A year later, civilians travelling west to the California Gold Rush also stopped to rest at Fort Washita.

When the Civil War broke out in 1861, the U.S. Army abandoned Fort Washita on May 1, 1861. On May 3 Confederate forces from Texas occupied the garrison. The Confederacy utilized the fort as a primary supply depot, as a regional headquarters, and a hospital for Rebel troops in Indian Territory. Notable Confederate officers including General Douglas Cooper (who is buried on the grounds), General Albert Pike, General Ben McCulloch, and Brigadier General Stand Watie all called the fort home at some point during the war. Fort Washita never experienced a major attack during the Civil War.

Following the Civil War, the U.S. Army transferred Fort Washita to the U.S. Department of Interior, who transferred it to the Chickasaw Nation in 1870. A prominent Chickasaw family, the Colbert family, later acquired the property from the tribe in the early 1900s. It remained in private ownership, and over the years the buildings and grounds began to deteriorate. In 1962 the Oklahoma Historical Society obtained Fort Washita and continues to refurbish and maintain the site today. The fort is a National Historic Landmark and is on the National Register of Historic Places.

Fort Washita is located at 3348 State Road 199 in Durant, Oklahoma. Museum hours are Tuesday through Saturday from 9:00 AM to 4:30 PM, and Sunday from 1:00 PM to 4:30 PM. Admission is free. Visitors to Fort Washita can see reconstructed buildings, stone ruins, and get a glimpse of military life in the pre-Civil War west at the Fort Washita Visitor Center. The OHS conducts living history events at the site each year, including the Fur Trade Rendezvous. Moreover, according to legend and folklore several ghosts including one known as "Aunt Jane" haunt Fort Washita. Aunt Jane allegedly buried money, and was killed by thieves when she refused to disclose the money's location. The fort hosts Ghost Stories every Halloween for young and old alike. For more information, call 580/924–6502.

SOURCES

For the essays presented in this theme section, the editor relied heavily on both primary and secondary sources. Below is a list of secondary sources utilized for the essays. We would like to encourage you to read these books and articles to learn more about battles, battlefields, and military forts in Oklahoma.

Bahos, Charles—"On Opothleyahola's Trail: Locating the Battle of Round Mountains"—*Chronicles of Oklahoma* 63 (Spring 1985): 58–59

Cotrell, Steve—*Civil War in the Indian Territory* (Saint Greta: Pelican Publishing, 1995)

Debo, Angie—*And Still the Waters Run* (Princeton: Princeton University Press, 1935)

Debo, Angie—"The Site of the Battle of Round Mountain 1861"—*Chronicles of Oklahoma* 27 (Summer 1940): 187–206

Edwards, Whit—*The Prairie was on Fire: Eyewitness Accounts of the Civil War in the Indian Territory* (Oklahoma City: Oklahoma Historical Society, 2001).

Faulk, Odie B., Kenny A. Franks, and Paul F. Lambert editors—*Early Military Forts and Posts in Oklahoma* (Oklahoma City: Oklahoma Historical Society, 1978)

Goins, Charles Robert and Danney Goble—*Historical Atlas of Oklahoma* (Norman: University of Oklahoma Press, 2006)

Hancock, Marvin J.—"The Second Battle of Cabin Creek, 1864"—*Chronicles of Oklahoma* 39 (Winter 1961–1962): 414–426

Hoig, Stan—*Fort Reno and the Indian Territory Frontier: A Powerful Synthesis of Southern Plains History During the Late Nineteenth Century* (Fayetteville: University of Arkansas Press, 2005)

Hoig, Stan—*The Battle of the Washita: The Sheridan-Custer Indian Campaign of 1867–69* (Lincoln: Bison Books, 1979)

Janda, Lance—"Fort Sill"—*Encyclopedia of Oklahoma History and Culture*, www.okhistory.org

Jones, Ralph—"Honey Springs, Battle of"—*Encyclopedia of Oklahoma History and Culture*, www.okhistory.org

May, Jon D.—"Fort Washita"—*Encyclopedia of Oklahoma History and Culture*, www.okhistory.org

Rampp, Larry C.—"Negro Troop Activity in Indian Territory, 1863–1865"—*Chronicles of Oklahoma* 47 (Spring 1969): 531–559

Warde, Mary Jane—*When the Wolf Came: The Civil War and the Indian Territory* (Fayetteville: The University of Arkansas Press, 2013)

Warren, Steven L.—*The Second Battle of Cabin Creek: Brilliant Victory* (Mount Pleasant: The History Press, 2012)

Warren, Steven L.—"Middle Boggy, Battle of"—*Encyclopedia of Oklahoma History and Culture*, www.okhistory.org

Williams, Chad—"Round Mountain, Battle of"—*Encyclopedia of Oklahoma History and Culture*, www.okhistory.org

Wright, Muriel H.—"Colonel Cooper's Civil War Report on Battle of Round Mountain"—*Chronicles of Oklahoma* 39 (Winter 1961–1962): 352–397

WELCOME TO OKLAHOMA

People the world over know us as a place where the wind comes sweepin' down the plain—but that's just part of the story. We are a one-of-a-kind state with something for everyone. We have the most diverse terrain mile-for-mile than any other state, from gently rolling hills to expansive, fertile plains. Ancient mountains, ever-changing sand dunes, salt flats, pine forests, cypress swamps, and caves of alabaster all make for a vacation paradise. And, we claim more man-made lakes than any other state, with eleven official ecoregions recognized by the EPA.

You can rough it in our great outdoors, or take a drive along the Mother Road of the nation, historic Route 66. Traversing the Sooner State, the route reveals a wealth of unique and fascinating destinations.

Once known as Indian Territory, Oklahoma is still home to more American Indian tribes than any other state. Thirty-nine tribal headquarters and members of at least sixty-seven tribes make their home here. Indian heritage is woven throughout the modern culture. Visitors will find American Indian art, historic sites, interactive cultural experiences, museums, powwows, dances, and festivals.

That American Indian heritage is equaled by our Western heritage. Our cowboy roots were firmly planted by soldiers who constructed forts and outposts in the territory following the Civil War. Today, ranches dot the landscape, rodeos take place every month of the year, and you will find one horse for every twelve people, more per capita than any other state.

And if all of that were not enough, you can indulge your cultural side with visits to the ballet or philharmonic. Today's Oklahoma provides not only a diverse landscape and rich cultural heritage, but also major urban centers complete with entertainment of all kinds, fine dining, the arts, and world-class attractions.

To learn more about traveling in Oklahoma, visit www.TravelOK.com.

The Sooner State divides itself into six regional areas, each with its own unique appeal. An overview of each travel region is presented on the following pages.

Will Rogers Statue—Claremore.

All photographs in this section courtesy of the Oklahoma Tourism and Recreation Department

CHICKASAW COUNTRY

chickasawcountryma@gmail.com

The heart of south central Oklahoma is alive with excitement and attractions to suit every taste. With a landscape lush with mountains, valleys, lakes, and streams, Chickasaw Country is an ideal traveler's destination.

Start your exploration at the Bedré Chocolate Factory in Pauls Valley. The maker of the same chocolate bars you will find in the Neiman Marcus catalog, Bedre´ is known for its yummy chocolate-covered potato chips.

Just a few miles further, stroll through GW Exotic Animal Park, a non-profit sanctuary housing more than 1,000 exotic animals. Stop by at feeding time, and you will be surrounded by the thundering roar of lions, tigers, and other big cats as they "place their order" at mealtime.

For more animal adventure, continue south to Davis, home of Arbuckle Wilderness. This drive-through animal park contains herds of exotic beasts roaming freely through the driving area.

Head into Sulphur, where the waters from more than thirty mineral springs in the area are said to have magical healing powers. The Chickasaw National Recreation Area attracts visitors from around the world who come to enjoy breathtaking landscapes, outdoor recreation, great swimming holes, and the new Chickasaw Cultural Center.

Schedule a soothing massage at the nearby Sulphur Springs Inn. Housed in a 1905 bathhouse, the establishment also offers daily yoga, meditation, and nature walks. Spend the night at the inn to refresh yourself for the rest of your journey.

From Sulphur, head to Gene Autry, home of the Gene Autry Oklahoma Museum. The museum houses an impressive collection of memorabilia, with an emphasis on the famed Western movie star and singing legend.

Lake Murray—Ardmore

Continue south to Ardmore for some shopping and dining, then head to Lake Murray Resort Park, Oklahoma's first and largest state park. Fishing, boating, and all water sports are found at Lake Murray, as are camping, hayrides, horseback riding, hiking, biking, roller-blading, swimming, miniature golf, and paddleboats. Do not miss the Tucker Tower Nature Center, which sits on a point much like a lighthouse. Relax at the lodge or in a cozy cabin.

CHOCTAW COUNTRY

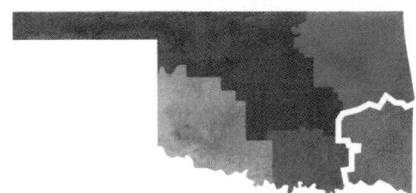

1002 HWY 2 North, Wilburton, OK 74578
580–317-9388
www.kiamichicountry.com

With seven mountain ranges, ten state parks and twenty-three lakes along with countless streams and rivers, southeast Oklahoma is an outdoor haven. The region is an angler's paradise, offering countless varieties of fish—including two rivers that feature year-round trout fishing. Add to that all types of water sports, camping, horse trails, hiking, sightseeing, hang-gliding and the best fall foliage in the Midwest, and you have found a getaway that beckons again and again.

Start your adventure at Robbers Cave State Park, just a few miles north of Wilburton. The park, located in the scenic hilly woodlands of the San Bois Mountains, is a favorite of rappellers, cave explorers, equestrians, hikers, and outdoor enthusiasts. Enjoy a peaceful night at a historic cabin, then wake up refreshed and head to Heavener Runestone State Park to view the famed Heavener Runestone, said to evidence some of Oklahoma's earliest Viking visitors.

Continue your driving tour by heading to Talihina, the entrance to the Talimena Scenic Drive. The drive takes you into the magnificent Ouachita National Forest for fifty-four miles of winding road known for vibrant spring and fall foliage.

Continue south to Beavers Bend Resort Park, and check into a cozy mountain cabin or lake-view lodge. After a restful night, enjoy the towering timbers, crystal clear waters and mountainous terrain of Oklahoma's "Little Smokies" throughout the park. Tee off for a game of golf, spend some time in the nature center, and stop by the Forest Heritage Center Museum.

After you leave the park, do not miss the Museum of the Red River in nearby Idabel. The museum features an outstanding collection of regional archaeological materials, Pre-Columbian Middle and South American artifacts, and more.

Beavers Bend State Park—Broken Bow

Head west to Millerton, home of Wheelock Academy, which served as a Choctaw day school and is currently being restored by the Choctaw Nation. Continue on to Hugo Lake State Park, where resort cabins provide comfortable accommodations and spectacular lake views.

FRONTIER COUNTRY

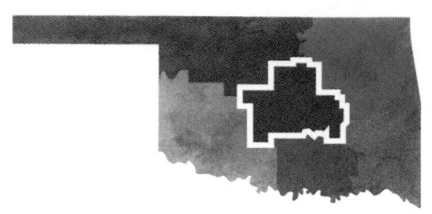

309 W Main Street, Norman, OK 73069
800–386–6552 • 405–232–6552
sherri@oktourism.com • www.oktourism.com

Frontier Country, in central Oklahoma, combines big city excitement with small town appeal. Experience the bustling state capital Oklahoma City, where family entertainment, shopping, art, sports, culture, and history combine for a total package. If you like a slower pace, visit some of the vibrant communities throughout Frontier Country where you can still find downtown main streets, courthouse squares, and mom and pop shops.

Start your tour in Norman, with a visit to The Sam Noble Oklahoma Museum of Natural History, located on the University of Oklahoma campus. Step back in time—way back— to see the Oklahoma "natives" that roamed this state millions of years ago—dinosaurs!

Stop by Campus Corner for shopping, then immerse yourself in culture at more OU landmarks: the newly-expanded Fred Jones Jr. Museum of Art and Jacobson House Native Arts Center, where the modern American Indian art movement began.

On day two, head to Oklahoma City, where you can pick and choose from a wide range of activities and attractions. Take in the Oklahoma City National Memorial, the Myriad Botanical Gardens, and the Oklahoma City Museum of Art. Take a walking tour, ride the trolley, or catch a water taxi for a cruise down the Bricktown Canal.

After those experiences, enjoy a short drive north on I–35 to Edmond, then go east on famed Route 66 to see Arcadia's restored 1898 Round Barn. Just a few miles away, drop by Tres Suenos Winery in Luther for a taste of the grape!

POPS on Route 66—Arcadia

On day three, continue north on I–35 to Guthrie and hop on the trolley for a tour of the Victorian splendor contained in the largest contiguous urban National Register Historic District in the United States. Grab a bite at a quaint bistro in downtown, browse the boutiques and antique stores, and book a night at one of Guthrie's numerous bed and breakfast inns.

You have barely scratched the surface of Frontier Country, so plan another trip with stops in Shawnee, Stillwater, Seminole, Bethany, El Reno, and more!

GREAT PLAINS COUNTRY

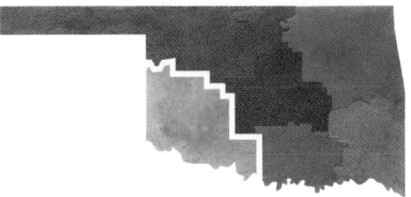

212 S Main Street, Suite 1,
Waurika, OK 73573
580–228-3400
www.greatplainscountry.com • gpc@greatplainscountry.com

Southwest Oklahoma is a prime location for a getaway. This rugged land, where Plains tribes once roamed and where boomtowns sprang up overnight, welcomes travelers with awe-inspiring landscapes and down-home good times.

Start your tour at Duncan's Chisholm Trail Heritage Center to experience the famed trail, then head to Lawton, home to Fort Sill, the largest army repository of military-related artifacts in the world. Visit The Old Post Guardhouse, the holding facility for Geronimo, the famed Apache warrior who is buried at the fort.

Next, head to the Wichita Mountains, site of the nation's first national wildlife refuge, where bison, longhorn cattle, elk, and other animals roam freely. While in the area, do not forget to explore Medicine Park, a 1920s mountain resort community regaining its heyday appeal.

Enjoy the spectacular prairie landscape as you drive to Quartz Mountain Arts and Conference Center, north of Altus. Located on sparkling Lake Altus-Lugert, this rustic resort is surrounded by a variety of recreational activities.

After a restful night, head north to Elk City, where the National Route 66 Museum encompasses all eight states through which the "Mother Road" travels.

Continue to Cheyenne to visit the Washita Battlefield National Historic Site, marking Lt. Col. George Custer's 1868 early-morning attack on Chief Black Kettle's sleeping village of Southern Cheyenne. After your tour of the site, settle in for the night at a local guest ranch or bed and breakfast inn.

Head back to I-40 for a short drive to Clinton and visit the Cheyenne Cultural Center for a look at tribal life on the Oklahoma plains. Continue just a few miles east on

I-40 to Weatherford for a visit to the General Thomas P. Stafford Space Museum, which chronicles the career of Weatherford's most famous son.

On your next visit to Great Plains Country, explore the American Indian culture of Anadarko, hit the links at Fort Cobb State Park, fish the waters of Foss Lake, and visit welcoming communities including Frederick, Cordell, Hobart, Mangum, and more.

Wichita Mountains—Indiahoma

GREEN COUNTRY

2825 E Skelly, #826, Tulsa, OK 74105
800–922–2118 • 918–744–0588
jstewart@greencountryok.com • www.greencountryok.com

From the tallgrass of Osage County to the pulsing energy of metropolitan Tulsa to the lush, cool greenery and beauty of the eastern lakes region, you will find fun and memorable times in northeast Oklahoma.

Start your trip in Jenks, the "Antique Capital of Oklahoma", for shopping and a stop at the Oklahoma Aquarium. Then head into Tulsa, where you will find something for everyone.

History buffs and art lovers will revel in visits to Philbrook Museum of Art and the Gilcrease Museum. At Philbrook, you will find a stunning collection of paintings and sculpture ranging from Renaissance legends to modern masters. At the Gilcrease, view the world's most comprehensive collection of American Indian and Western art.

Take the scenic route from Tulsa south to Stone Bluff Cellars Winery, where you can sample award-winning wines and add a bottle or two to your own wine cellar. Then continue onto Muskogee for a night at the Whitlock Wishouse Bed & Breakfast. The eclectic decor and spectacular cuisine are garnering national attention.

The next day, explore American Indian culture at The Five Civilized Tribes Museum, which preserves the heritage of the Cherokee, Creek, Chickasaw, Choctaw, and Seminole tribes. Then stop by Ataloa Lodge, one of Oklahoma's premier Native American museums.

Head back to Tulsa for a night at the Hotel Ambassador, where luxury goes hand-in-hand with sumptuous furnishings and world-class cuisine. The next morning, you will be ready to head to Bartlesville for more one-of-a-kind sites.

Visit the Woolaroc Ranch, Museum, and Wildlife Preserve, the 1925 country home of oilman Frank Phillips, then go back into town to tour the Frank Phillips Home, a twenty-six-room Greek Revival mansion. Next stop: Frank Lloyd Wright's only skyscraper, the Price Tower, home to the Price Tower Arts Center. Explore downtown Bartlesville's antique shops and boutiques, then call it a night at the elegant Inn At Price Tower.

Your tour of Green Country is far from complete, so plan another visit to explore welcoming destinations including Claremore, Grand Lake, Tahlequah, and more!

Philbrook Museum of Art—Tulsa

RED CARPET COUNTRY

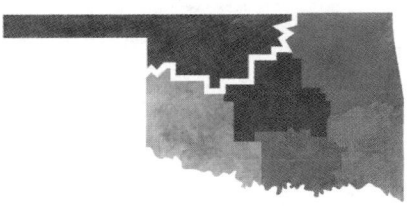

1040 8 Street, Shockley Hall #114, Alva, OK 73717
800–447–2698 • 580–327–4918
redcarpet@redcarpetcountry.com

Travelers embarking on a tour of Oklahoma's northwest corner will find a land marked by the footprints of dinosaurs, lined with red canyons, and blanketed in prairie grass and golden wheat.

Experience the luxury enjoyed by an early twentieth century oil baron at Ponca City's spectacular Marland Mansion and Marland's Grand Home. These houses of Governor E.W. Marland boast magnificent furnishings and lush surroundings.

Then tour the Poncan Theater, where the ornate interior recalls the luxury of this 1927 top-billing vaudeville house. And you will definitely want to stop for a photo at the Pioneer Woman Statue, one of America's most enduring images.

Next, journey west to the Salt Plains Federal Wildlife Refuge, where a vast sea of salt has become one of Oklahoma's most photographed locations. The region provides pristine salt plains, marshes, and a reservoir for more than 300 species of birds. Stay the night at nearby Great Salt Plains State Park.

Next stop: Oklahoma's very own sand dunes. Head to Little Sahara State Park for another unique landscape. Take a dune buggy tour of the towering sands, then enjoy a picnic at one of the park's shaded campgrounds.

On the way to Watonga, stop by the sparkling Glass Mountains and capture the glinting crystals on film—no easy task!

Then continue to Roman Nose State Park just north of Watonga. Set up camp in gypsum-streaked canyons or spend the night at the lodge or in a cozy cabin.

You have seen just a small portion of the unique sights of Red Carpet Country, so plan another visit to see Alabaster Caverns, Black Mesa (the state's highest point), the dinosaur tracks in Kenton, authentic cowboy life in Guymon and Woodward, and much more.

Great Salt Plains—Jet

Animal—**Buffalo**

Bird—**Scissor-Tailed Flycatcher**

Cartoon Character—**"Gusty"**

Fish—**White or Sand Bass**

STATE EMBLEMS

Amphibian
Bullfrog (Rana *catesbeiana*) [HCR1026, 1997]

Animal (Mammal)
American Buffalo (Bison *bison*) [SCR101, 1972]

Beverage
Milk [SCR2, 1985]

Bird
Scissor-Tailed Flycatcher (Muscivora *forficate*)
[25§98] [HJR21, 1951]

Butterfly
Black Swallowtail (Papilio *polyxenes*) [HB2082, 1996]

Cartoon Character
"Gusty" created by former Tulsa weatherman
Don Woods. [SB 464, 2005]

Children's Song
"Oklahoma, My Native Land" [HB3000, 1996]

Colors
Green and White [25§93]

Country and Western Song
"Faded Love" [Laws 1988, p.1902] [SCR65, 1988]

Day
Oklahoma Day, April 22 [25§82.3]

Dinosaur
Acrocanthosaurus atokensis [SB 1613, 2006]

Fish
White or Sand Bass (Morone *chrysops*) [25§98.2]

Flag
An Osage warrior's buckskin shield decorated
with pendent eagle feathers on a field of blue is

the basic design of the Oklahoma state flag.

In crossed positions over the shield are an Indian peace pipe and an olive branch. The latter is the white man's symbol of peace. The pipe has a red bowl and a pale yellow stem, with a red feather attached. The shield is a light tan, to which are attached white feathers, tipped with brown. Small crosses on the face of the shield are tan, but somewhat darker than that of the shield itself. The word "Oklahoma" in white is inscribed immediately below the shield. [25§91]

Flag Day
November 16 [25§91.3]

Flag Salute
"I salute the flag of the State of Oklahoma. Its symbols of peace unite all people." [25§91]

Floral Emblem
Mistletoe (Phoradendron *serotinum*)

The oldest of Oklahoma's symbols, adopted in 1893, 14 years before statehood. [25§92] [HJR49]

Flower
Oklahoma Rose [25 OS § 92]

Flying Mammal
Mexican free-tailed bat [SB1678]

Folk Dance
Square Dance [Laws 1988, p.1960] [SCR111, 1988] [HR1070]

Folk Song
"Oklahoma Hills" by Woody and Jack Guthrie [25§94.8]

Fossil
"Greatest king of the reptile eaters" (Saurophaganax *maximus*) [25§98.6]

Fruit
Strawberry [HB 1762, 2005]

Furbearer
Raccoon (Algonquian *arathkone*) [SCR25, 1stEx.Sess.1989]

Game Animal
White-Tail Deer [SCR24, 1stEx.Sess.1989]

Game Bird
Wild Turkey [SCR26, 1stEx.Sess.1989]

Furbearer—**Raccoon**

Flower—**Oklahoma Rose**

Game Animal—**White-Tail Deer**

Game Bird—**Wild Turkey**

Horse—**Oklahoma Colonial Spanish**

Insect—**Honeybee**

Monument—**Golden Driller**

Reptile—**Collared Lizard**

Governor's Flag [25§93.1]

Grass
Indiangrass (Sorghastrum *nutans*) [SCR72, 1972]

Horse
Oklahoma Colonial Spanish Horse [SCR34, 2014]

Insect
Honeybee (Apis *mellifera*) [SCR75, 1992]

Monument
Golden Driller, Tulsa [SCR23, 1979]

Motto
Labor Omnia Vincit (Labor Conquers All Things)
[1893, §5991; Art.6§35]

Musical Instrument
Fiddle [Laws 1984, p.1208]

Name
"Oklahoma"means Red People in the Choctaw
language [34Stat.267]

Nickname
Sooner State

Percussive Musical Instrument
Drum [25§98.3]

Pin
"OK" pin [Laws 1982, p.1258]

Poem
"Howdy Folks" by David Randolph Milsten (Tulsa)
[Laws 1973, p.568]

Reptile
Collared Lizard or Mountain Boomer
(Crotaphytus *collaris*) [HCR1009, 1969]

Rock
Rose Rock (Barite *rose*) [25§98.1]

Seal
Oklahoma has for its state seal a symbol that
was developed from the history of the state.

The central figures and wreath are from the Great Seal
of the Territory of Oklahoma. In each of the five arms

of the main star in the Great Seal of the state, is the official seal of one of the Five Civilized Indian nations that together comprised most of the area of present eastern Oklahoma. The upward arm depicts the seal of the Chickasaw Nation with an Indian warrior holding a bow and shield. In the upper left-hand arm is the seven-pointed star bearing a wreath of oak leaves which comprises the seal of the Cherokee Nation. The emblem of the Choctaw Nation is in the upper right-hand arm and is composed of a tomahawk, a bow, and three crossed arrows. In the lower left-hand arm is the seal of the Creek Nation, depicted by a sheaf of wheat and a plow. The lower right-hand arm shows houses and a factory on the shore of a lake. On the lake are an Indian hunter and a canoe, and this comprises the seal of the Seminole Nation. Forty-five small stars surround the central star and these represent the forty-five states that made up the Union at the time Oklahoma became the forty-sixth state on November 16, 1907. The original seal was designed for embossing purposes, and color was not a consideration. To this day, no official colors have been established for the Great Seal of the State of Oklahoma. Color design of the seal pictured is by Paul Lefebvre. [Art.6§18,35]

Rock—**Rose Rock**

Seal

Soil
Port Silt Loam (Cumulic *haplustolls*) [Laws 1987, p.1721]

Song/Anthem
"Oklahoma!" by Rodgers and Hammerstein [25§94.1]

Statehood Day
November 16 [25§88]

Tartan [HCR1025, 1999]

Theater
Lynn Riggs Players of Oklahoma [Laws 1961, p.726]

Tree
Redbud (Cercis *canadensis*) [2§16–69]

Waltz
"Oklahoma Wind" [SR42, 1982]

Western Band
"The Sounds of the Southwest" [HCR1053, 1997]

Wild Flower
Indian Blanket (Gaillardia *pulchella*) [25§92.1]

Tree—**Redbud**

Wild Flower—**Indian Blanket**

SOONER STATE GAZETTE

Some big issues that filled our news feeds and kept us talking the past two years ...

WELCOME BACK TO THE CITY

The urban renaissance in Oklahoma's two largest cities continues to advance thanks to public and private investments, a better understanding of the lifestyle millennials want and expect, and a realization that smart urban development is smart for the taxpaying public as well.

The investment in Oklahoma City and Tulsa's central business districts is buoyed by revitalization of adjacent older areas that sport big city hipster names— Film Row, Midtown, the Plaza District, Deep Deuce, Uptown, and SoSA (South of Saint Anthony's) in Oklahoma City; and Kendall-Whittier, the Blue Dome District, the Brady Arts District, and the Pearl District in Tulsa. As these neighborhoods add housing, restaurants, retail, and even hotel rooms, the momentum is supporting additional investment in already-successful districts: Brookside, Cherry Street, and Greenwood in Tulsa; Bricktown, The Paseo, and Stockyards City in OKC. Some completely new districts have emerged, like the Boathouse District and the proposed Wheeler District in OKC.

More city folk are riding their bicycles. Food trucks gather to create instant street fairs on Tulsa's Guthrie Green and at the capitol city's H&8th (Hudson and 8th street) events. Public transportation policy is moving to the top of city agendas, and there is a new appreciation for the sidewalk as the cities work to enhance, and in some instances re-create, an urban pedestrian environment that was anathema to America's 20th century car culture. Both towns are getting

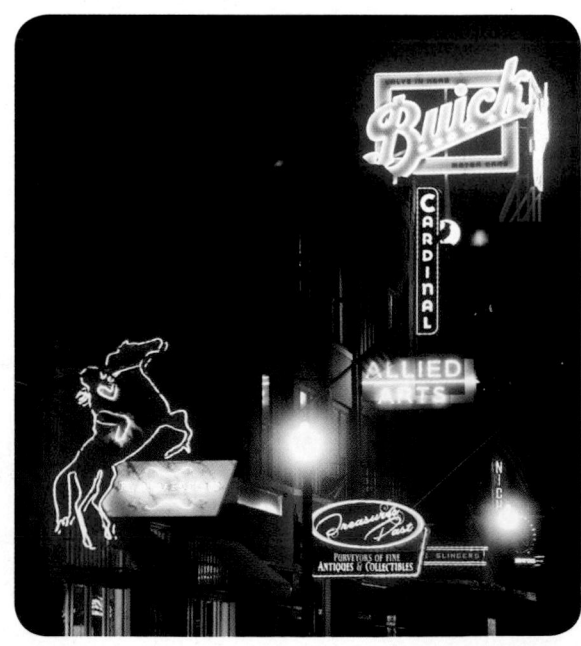

Neon lights announce new shopping and eating experiences on the revitalized Automobile Alley in downtown Oklahoma City.
(Photo by Doug Hoke, *The Oklahoman*)

Crowds flock to the businesses, galleries, and restaurants in Tulsa's Brady Arts District. (Photo courtesy of the *Tulsa World*)

big new urban parks: Core to Shore in OKC, and A Gathering Place on the banks of Tulsa's Arkansas River.

Urban development is the talk of both towns on the forum boards at *okctalk.com* and *tulsanow. net*. It's not unusual to see more than four hundred people join reporter Steve Lackmeyer for his OKC Central chats each Friday morning on *Newsok.com*.

The changes and developments are not without controversies. Oklahoma City continues to be shamed for demolishing more of its historic urban fabric to make way for new developments, and Tulsa is still trying to find a way to build dams to keep water in the Arkansas River to spur additional investments. And everybody's a critic when it comes to the architectural renderings that show up on the forum boards.

Other communities in Oklahoma are pursuing their own urban revival, sometimes with the help of the Oklahoma Department of Commerce's Main Street program. A new events center, restored convention center, and baseball park are spurring revitalization in downtown Enid. Broken Arrow is heaping love on its downtown and is marketing it as the Rose District. Shawnee looks toward loft living and mom and pop retail to keep downtown vital. State land near downtown Norman that houses Griffin Memorial Hospital is slated for a large multi-use development. And art is the catalyst for downtown revitalization in Ada, Alva, and Stillwater. Towns big and small are rediscovering their heart.

WELCOME TO THE
NEW EARTHQUAKE CAPITAL

A s if being a tornado capital isn't bad enough, Oklahoma is the current earthquake capital of America. In 2014, the state experienced three times the number of earthquakes as California, traditionally the most seismically active of the 48 contiguous states— and the Advanced National Seismic System global catalog reports Oklahoma even beat number one Alaska last year. More disturbing is the fact that quake activity is increasing. In 2014, Oklahoma had a total 585 quakes of magnitude 3.0 or higher. By May 14 of 2015, the state had already recorded 325 quakes of 3.0 or higher.

The consensus of national and state scientists is removing any doubt that the earthquake swarm in north central Oklahoma is man-made. The quakes are related to the deep-injection wells used by the oil and gas industry to dispose of toxic wastewater from hydraulic fracturing and other production methods. Scientists say injecting this water into existing, ancient fault formations is causing the earth to move. Joe Wertz of *State Impact Oklahoma* reports "scientists don't know if these earthquakes can be stopped now that they've started—even if these disposal wells are banned."

Oklahoma's Corporation Commission has instituted a system to help determine if disposal wells should be permitted in areas of increased earthquake activity, and has initiated a study of wells located within a six-mile radius of earthquake swarms. The commission's communication with well operators in the Arbuckle formation has led to changes in the depth or disposal volume of 200 wells.

This action is not enough for the Coalition to Stop Induced Seismicity, a group calling for a one-year moratorium on wastewater disposal wells in the 16 counties most affected, a move that would cost the state jobs and millions of dollars in taxes. And therein lies the crux: how does the state move to protect people and property without injuring the economic golden goose?

BOOM! BUST! BUDGET CRUNCH!

We've lived this story before, but every economic bust and state budget crisis has its own unique qualities.

The Big Picture Riding the wave of high energy prices in recent years, Oklahoma has become a major producer of oil and gas again, due primarily to advancements in horizontal drilling and hydraulic fracturing. As a consequence, Oklahoma has seen major economic and population expansion, and an enviable employment rate. Nevertheless, few state services saw any kind of relief from past budget cuts (funding reductions resulting from the national recession beginning in 2008 and from the legislature's move to lower the state's income tax rate). In 2014, voters opted to stay the course, meaning little or no change in investment in improving the state's low ranking in funding and outcomes under education,

Oklahoma's crumbling State Capitol building became a metaphor for the state's problem budget. In 2014, the legislature authorized a $120 million bond issue to begin repairs.
(Photo by Paul Hellstern, *The Oklahoman*)

healthcare, mental health, poverty, and correctional services. When oil and gas prices tumbled— due to market forces, including increased supply, OPEC's refusal to moderate Middle East oil production, and restrictions on exporting American oil outside the U.S.—and the bust hit, state officials estimated a $300 million shortfall for the state's 2015–2016 budget, only to see the shortage balloon to over $600 million. The bad news did not deter state leaders from signing off on the next step in the plan to cut the top income tax rate further for 2016, moving that rate down to 5%. When the 2015 legislative session ended, some state government agencies received increases, some received flat funding, and others saw continued reductions that have been adding up. Many agencies have seen their budgets cut by 24% to 30% since the 2008 recession.

Reviewing Tax Credits With the income tax rate falling, finding additional revenue is a tricky business in a state were politicians have signed pledges to not increase taxes, and where property taxes are anything but popular. Representative David Dank fought for years to reform the state's tax credit and reimbursement system. Many of the credits, according to Dank in *The Oklahoman*, "range from the questionable to the outrageous." Too often, Dank believed, the economic benefit simply didn't justify the credit. "Every dollar that's lost to an ineffective tax credit is a dollar that's not eligible to go to a core function of government services," he said. Dank saw no final action on this issue during his lifetime, but his death on April 10, 2015, spurred the legislature to pass two bills that would place business tax credits under greater scrutiny. The legislature later followed up with bills phasing out and eliminating most tax credits and reimbursements for wind energy.

How Big Will This Bust Be?   Oklahoma's economy may be more diverse than it was during that horrible energy bust in the 1980s, but energy is still king in the Sooner State. Roughly one-quarter of all jobs in the state are tied directly or indirectly to the oil and gas industry, according to economist Mickey Hepner in a *State Impact Oklahoma* report. The U.S. Labor Department reported that Oklahoma shed 12,900 jobs in March of 2015 alone as rigs went idle. The job loss was second only to Texas, the behemoth to the south, which lost more than 25,000 jobs. Because of the downturn, Oklahoma made the list in a Janaury *Forbes* column titled, "The States People Are Fleeing." State economists, though, are still optimistic our current bust will be nothing like the one in the 1980s. Plus, the job picture still looks good for Oklahoma college grads. Fracking pioneer Harold Hamm, CEO of Continental Resources, even predicts oil prices will top $85 a barrel by the end of 2015. Time will tell.

BAD NEWS RISING

If Oklahoma is not making the national news because of severe weather or earthquakes, we usually find our state mentioned on those "worst" lists. We're among the poorest states (CNBC), one of the unhealthiest states (America's Health Rankings report), and the state with the poorest access to the legal justice system for our residents (National Center for Access to Justice). We're also number one in spending cuts to education since 2008 (Center on Budget and Policy Priorities). Here are four additional stories that were "bad news" for the Sooner State:

Executing Executions   When Oklahoma "botched" the execution of Clayton D. Lockett, the state moved front and center into the discussion over capitol punishment, and whether or not lethal injection violated the U.S. Constitution's guarantee against cruel and unusual punishment. Lockett's execution began the evening of April 27, 2014, and things went wrong less than fifteen minutes in. After being declared unconscious "for ten minutes" following the injection of the first of three drugs, Lockett soon began to violently convulse, and even called out "oh, man," before the execution was halted. He died of a heart attack 40 minutes later.

The U.S. Supreme Court is expected to rule this summer on the constitutionality of lethal injection, in a case related to the botched execution. And while red state Nebraska ended the death penalty, Oklahoma is doubling-down, passing back-up legislation that would allow execution by nitrogen gas—a substance never used for executions in the United States. Oklahoma pioneered the use of execution by drug injection. Will it pioneer the use of nitrogen gas?

God, Guns, Gays, and Hoodies   You can always count on the annual legislative session to place the state in the national spotlight. Usually it involves controversy over proposed legislation. In 2015, one bill would have stopped the issuing of all marriage licenses by county court clerks, so that said clerks wouldn't have to issue licenses to same sex couples. One would have guaranteed parents the right to seek therapy for "same-sex attraction" for their minor child. Another bill would have allowed businesses to refuse service to certain customers due to the religious beliefs of the business owner. Another would have further penalized a criminal if they were wearing a "hoodie" (or masking their identity some other way) while committing a crime. And one would have prevented businesses from banning guns at events held at parks, recreational areas, and fairgrounds.

None of the bills made it into law, but they still caused damage to the state and its economic development efforts according to the Tulsa Regional Chamber of Commerce and the Greater Oklahoma City Chamber. Sky McNeil with the Tulsa Chamber said the bills give the state a "black eye," and that Oklahoma has to accept diversity to attract business. The OKC chamber warned that the gun bill would threaten dozens of high-profile events held in the city and state. The controversies on the LGBT side prompted Tulsa philanthropist Lynn Schusterman to write a

Organizer Marq Lewis chants as hundreds rally for justice outside the Tulsa County Sheriff's Department. (Photo courtesy of the *Tulsa World*)

letter to the state's two largest newspapers. "The people of Oklahoma deserve better," she wrote. "We deserve leadership that's willing and unafraid to take a public stand against bigotry and bullying."

Viral Video   A cell phone video of two University of Oklahoma fraternity men singing a racist chant flew across the social media world and national media outlets in March of 2015, embarrassing the university and outraging Oklahomans. OU President David Boren called for the immediate eviction of students from the Sigma Alpha Epislon chapter house, and the national SAE headquarters closed the chapter. When Boren threatened to expel two of the students, it triggered columns and blogs across the media challenging his action due to First Amendment protections of free speech.

"I shot him! I'm sorry!"   In April of 2015, a white volunteer reserve deputy with the Tulsa County Sheriff's Department shot an unarmed black man with his gun instead of his taser. The man would later die in the hospital, and this Oklahoma story would become another example in the national discussion about policing practices in communities of color. The police released a video of the incident, which included the deputy saying, "I shot him. I'm sorry." Following the incident, the deputy maintained he had meant to use his taser. Media coverage questioned the training and use of reserve deputies, citizens demonstrated for justice under the "black lives matter" banner, the Tulsa County sheriff announced he would not seek reelection, and residents pushed for a Grand Jury investigation.

OTHER NEWS THAT KEPT OKIES TALKING

Rainbow Weddings   When the U.S. Supreme Court refused on October 6, 2014, to review a U.S. 10th Circuit Court ruling finding Oklahoma's ban on same-sex marriage unconstitutional, marriage equality became a reality in the Sooner State. At press time, same-sex marriage was legal in 30 states, and the U.S. Supreme Court was expected to announce a major decision in June, 2015, that could make the practice legal in all 50 states.

Voter, Voter, Where Art Thou?   Voter turnout in 2014's gubernatorial and national mid-term election was historically low. The state saw a 9% drop in voters from the 2010 election.

Only 40.7% of registered voters, and 27% of eligible persons, voted. Nationally, 36.4% of the voting-eligible made it to the polls, making the 2014 election the lowest since 1942 according to the *Washington Post*.

Oh No You Don't!   In 2014, the Oklahoma legislature passed a law preventing municipalities from raising the local minimum wage. In 2015, the legislature passed a law preventing local municipalities from banning hydraulic fracturing within their city limits.

Museums In Limbo Get Their Day   The 2015 legislature authorized two bond issues that could finally bring two proposed museums to reality. Funds from one bond issue would combine with private funds to finally complete the American Indian Cultural Museum at the intersection of I-35 and I-40. The City of Oklahoma City would have to agree to run the museum before the bonds are let. Another bond issue would fund construction of the long-promised popular culture museum OKPOP, in Tulsa's Brady Arts District. The Oklahoma Historical Society will run OKPOP.

It's not Napa Valley, but ...   For a state that had prohibition baked into its constitution, the following news might surprise many Oklahomans: wine tourism is hot in the state right now. The Oklahoma Department of Tourism and Recreation is promoting the industry at www.travelok.com/wineries, and has joined forces with businesses to establish ten unique wine trails and a companion passport where tourists can note their impressions and favorite wines for each wine stop (oklahomawinetrails.com).

Drought Buster   May 2015 became the wettest month on record for communities across the state. After a four-year-long drought, many areas in Oklahoma—particularly western and southwestern parts of the state—saw relief from exceptionally dry conditions, and lakes across the state filled back up. But the 20+ inches of rain that many areas experienced came with another set of problems as flooding damaged property and even claimed lives. In addition, the state will be facing "tens of millions of dollars" in repairs to the state's roads and bridges according to a *KGOU* report.

Sharon Baldwin and Mary Bishop apply for a marriage license on Oct. 6, 2014 at the Tulsa County Courthouse. Their challenge to existing law, with other plaintiffs, led to the legalization of same-sex marriage in the state.
(Photo courtesy of the *Tulsa World*)

EXECUTIVE BRANCH

Governor Mary Fallin

Constitution, Article 6 § 1

Governor Mary Fallin was elected November 2, 2010, during a historic election in which she became the first-ever female governor of Oklahoma. She was inaugurated on the steps of the Oklahoma Capitol as the state's twenty-seventh governor on January 10, 2011. She won reelection in November 2014. After working in the private sector as a manager for a national hotel chain, Fallin made her first foray into public service in 1990 when she was elected to the Oklahoma House of Representatives. This began her long and distinguished career of public service dedicated to conservative, common sense solutions to the challenges facing Oklahoma families and small businesses.

During her time in the House, Fallin earned a reputation as a consensus builder who was willing to reach across the aisle. Serving in the Republican minority, she managed to pass more than a dozen bills that were signed into law by the state's Democratic governor, including Oklahoma's first "anti-stalker law," and measures aimed at improving the business climate in Oklahoma. She also worked to lower the health care costs of small businesses in Oklahoma and for her work in this area was honored as a Legislator of the Year by the American Legislative Exchange Council.

In 1994 Fallin would first make history by becoming the first woman and first Republican to be elected lieutenant governor of Oklahoma, an office she would hold for twelve years. In this capacity, Fallin focused her attention on issues affecting job creation and economic development. She served on ten boards or commissions involving business and quality-of-life issues in Oklahoma. In 1997 she chaired the Fallin Commission on Workers' Compensation, which released a comprehensive reform plan to lower costs of workers' compensation while creating a system that was fair to both businesses and workers. Fallin also used her position as president of the Oklahoma State Senate to allow the citizens of Oklahoma to vote on "Right to Work," which ended the practice of compelling workers to join and pay dues to a union. In 2001 Oklahoma became the first state in the country to pass such a law in more than twenty-five years.

Fallin was elected to the U.S. Congress in 2006 where she represented the Fifth District of Oklahoma. In Congress, Fallin served on the committees for small business, transportation and infrastructure, natural resources, and armed services. Fallin coauthored numerous pieces of legislation to lower taxes, reduce regulation on businesses and individuals, fight federal overreach, increase American energy production, create jobs and protect constitutional liberties.

Now serving as governor, Fallin has cited job growth and retention, education reform, government modernization, and protecting Oklahoma from the intrusions of Washington, D.C. as top priorities. Since taking office in 2011, Oklahoma has consistently ranked among the top states for job creation. Additionally, under Fallin's fiscally conservative, pro-growth agenda, the state's per capita income rose by 6.3 percent from 2011 to 2013, the second highest in the nation. The state's rainy day savings account has also gone from just $2.03 in 2011 to a high of over $570 million in 2013. Fallin has signed into law historic lawsuit reform and a complete overhaul of the state's workers' compensation system, eliminating frivolous lawsuits that hinder business growth and retention. Moreover, she has also signed bills to modernize and streamline government operations, responsibly cut the income tax, increase compensation for public employees, and address the state's fiscally unstable pension system.

At Fallin's direction, the state has appropriated more than $154 million in the past two years for K–12 education, allowing more money into the classroom and a boost to student performance. In 2012, she launched Complete College America, an initiative to increase the number of college graduates and career certificate holders in Oklahoma to help the state attract and retain jobs. In addition to her statewide education initiatives, Fallin has lead a nationwide dialogue among state legislators and governors through her past-chairmanship of the National Governor's Association to better align education and workforce needs of the 21st century called America Works: Education and Training for Tomorrow's Jobs. In addition, she has also worked with local and state officials to implement a road and bridge plan that aims to eliminate all of the deficient bridges on the state's highway system. Fallin has also introduced the state's first-ever comprehensive energy plan that focuses on developing and finding new markets for Oklahoma's natural resources. Fallin is a graduate of Oklahoma State University. She is married to Wade Christensen, Oklahoma's first "First Gentleman." The couple has six children between them

Key Personnel

Denise Northrup—Chief of Staff

Alex Weintz—Director of Communications

Michelle Waddell—Executive Assistant to the Governor

A.J. Mallory—Executive Assistant to the Chief of Staff

Steve Mullins—General Counsel

Katie Altshuler—Director of Policy

Michael McNutt—Press Secretary

Cindy Harper—Director of Operations

Monica Houston—Director of Scheduling

Cody Inman—Director of Constituent Services

Chris Bruehl—Director of Appointments

Chris Benge—Native American Liaison

Office

Oklahoma City—State Capitol, Room 212, Oklahoma City 73105-3207
    405/521-2342, FAX 405/521-3353

(Agency Code 305, IA)

Office Hours—8:30 AM–5 PM Monday-Friday

www.gov.ok.gov

Qualifications—Citizen of the United States, at least thirty-one years of age, qualified elector at least ten years preceding election. State Constitution, Article 6, Section 3.

Salary—$147,000 annually

Personnel—unclassified

Oklahoma Elected Officials

Governor—Mary Fallin

State Capitol, Room 212
Oklahoma City 73105 3207
405/521-2342, FAX 405/521-3353
www.gov.ok.gov

Lieutenant Governor—Todd Lamb

State Capitol, Room 211
Oklahoma City 73105-3207
405/521-2161, FAX 405/522-8694
www.ltgov.ok.gov

Attorney General—Scott Pruitt

313 NE 21 Street
Oklahoma City 73105-3207
405/521-3921, FAX 405/521-6246
Tulsa—907 Detroit, Suite 750,
Tulsa 74120-4200
918/581-2885, FAX 918/938-6348
www.oag.ok.gov

State Auditor and Inspector—Gary Jones

State Capitol, Room 100
Oklahoma City 73105-3207
405/521-3495, FAX 405/521-3426
www.sai.ok.gov

State Treasurer—Ken Miller

State Capitol, Room 217
Oklahoma City 73105-3207
405/521-3191, FAX 405/521-4994
www.treasurer.ok.gov

Insurance Commissioner—John Doak

3625 NW 56 Street, Suite 100
Oklahoma City 73112-4511
PO Box 53408 73152-3408
405/521-2828, 800/522-0071
FAX 405/521-6633
Tulsa—7645 E 63 Street, Suite 102
Tulsa 74133-1249
918/295-3700, FAX 918/994-7916
www.oid.ok.gov

Commissioner of Labor—Mark Costello

3017 N Stiles
Oklahoma City 73105-2808
405/521-6100, 888/269-5353,
FAX 405/521-6018
www.labor.ok.gov

Superintendent of Public Instruction—Joy Hofmeister

Oliver Hodge Building
2500 N Lincoln Boulevard, Rm. 121
Oklahoma City 73105-4599
405/521-3301, FAX 405/521-6205
www.sde.ok.gov

Corporation Commissioners—Bob Anthony, Todd Hiett, and Dana L. Murphy

2101 N Lincoln Boulevard,
Oklahoma City 73105-4905
PO Box 52000 73152-2000
405/521-2211, FAX 405/521-6045
Tulsa—440 S Houston, Suite 114
Tulsa 74127-8917
918/581-2296
www.occeweb.com

Office of the Lieutenant Governor
Constitution, Article 6 § 1

Todd Lamb, Republican, was born on October 19, 1971, in Enid, Oklahoma. Oklahoma elected Lamb as lieutenant governor on November 2, 2010. After a term in which he successfully advocated for workers' compensation reform, higher pay for Oklahoma's troopers, and growing Oklahoma's oil and gas industry, Lamb was reelected in 2014, winning in each of Oklahoma's seventy-seven counties.

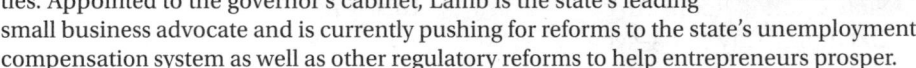

Lamb continues to focus on being the voice of Oklahomans in the capitol. Every year he visits each of Oklahoma's seventy-seven counties. Appointed to the governor's cabinet, Lamb is the state's leading small business advocate and is currently pushing for reforms to the state's unemployment compensation system as well as other regulatory reforms to help entrepreneurs prosper.

Lamb played football at Louisiana Tech University, then returned to Oklahoma earning a bachelor's degree from Oklahoma State University, and his law degree from Oklahoma City University School of Law.

At the start of his career, Lamb worked for then gubernatorial candidate Frank Keating, and then served in the Keating administration until 1998, when Lamb became special agent with the United States Secret Service. During his U.S. Secret Service tenure, he investigated and made numerous arrests in the areas of counterfeiting, bank fraud, threats against the president, and identify theft. His duties included domestic and international protection assignments during the Clinton and George W. Bush administrations. In early 2001, he was appointed to the national Joint Terrorism Task Force, and after the terrorists' attacks, he was assigned to portions of the 9-11 investigation.

In 2004 Lamb was elected to serve in the Oklahoma State Senate. Lamb was reelected in 2008, and in 2009 he became the first Republican majority floor leader in state history. Lamb has worked in the private sector as a landman in Oklahoma's energy industry, and was general counsel for an energy and wireless company in Edmond, Oklahoma. He has been consistently recognized as a leader. He was elected chair of the National Lieutenant Governors Association. He is currently serving as chair of the Republican Lieutenant Governors Association. For four years Lamb has been vice chair of the Aerospace States Association.

Lamb and his wife, Monica, have been married nineteen years and have two children, Griffin and Lauren. They are active members of Quail Springs Baptist Church, where Lamb serves as a church deacon.

Key Personnel—Keith Beall, Chief of Staff; Bailey Lynn, Director of Scheduling; Zach Sumner, Director of Constituent Services.

Office—Room 211, State Capitol, Oklahoma City 73105-3207 (Agency Code 440, IA)

Office Hours—8:30 AM–5 PM, Mon.-Fri.

405/521-2161, FAX 405/522-8694

www.ltgov.ok.gov

Salary—$114,713 annually

Personnel—8 non-merit, unclassified;
    1 temporary

Qualifications for Office—The individual must be a citizen of United States, at least thirty-one years of age and a qualified elector of the state for ten years prior to election to office. State Constitution, Article 6, Section 3.

Office of the Attorney General
Constitution, Article 6 § 1

E. Scott Pruitt, Republican, was elected as Oklahoma's seventeenth attorney general on November 2, 2010. He is the second Republican in the history of the state to hold the office, which oversees eighty attorneys. Pruitt has quickly risen as a national leader in the cause of restoring limited government and the proper balance of power between the states and the federal government. As a first priority in office, Pruitt established Oklahoma's first Federalism Unit in the Office of Solicitor General to more effectively combat unwarranted regulation and systematic overreach by federal agencies, boards, and offices.

Pruitt served two terms as chair of the Republican Attorneys General Association (RAGA), and one term as chair of the Midwest Region of the National Association of Attorneys General (NAAG). Under his leadership, attorneys general have come together to advance policies and legal strategies that protect the interests of their states from an overly intrusive federal government, with a particular focus on domestic energy security and production. Pruitt has led the charge with repeated notices and subsequent lawsuits against the United States Environmental Protection Agency for their leadership's activist agenda and refusal to follow the law.

Establishing and respecting the rule of law is a hallmark of Pruitt's administration. He made national headlines when Oklahoma became the first state in the nation to challenge the Affordable Care Act.

Before he was elected attorney general, Pruitt represented Broken Arrow, Coweta, and Tulsa in the Oklahoma State Senate for eight years, serving four of those years as assistant Republican floor leader. He used his legislative experience to transform the Attorney General's Workers' Compensation and Insurance Fraud Unit, and the Medicaid Fraud Control Unit.

Pruitt grew up in Lexington, Kentucky. He received a bachelor's degree in communications and political science from Georgetown College, and earned his Juris Doctor degree from the University of Tulsa College of Law. While in private practice, Pruitt specialized in constitutional and employment law. Pruitt and his wife of twenty-five years, Marlyn, are raising two children, McKenna and Cade in Tulsa. The Pruitts are members of First Baptist, Broken Arrow, where Pruitt serves as deacon.

Key Personnel—Tom Bates, First Assistant Attorney General; Melissa McLawhorn Houston, Chief of Staff; Diane Clay, Director of Communications; Patrick Wyrick, Solicitor General; Aaron Cooper, Director of Public Affairs

Oklahoma City—313 NE 21 Street,
Oklahoma City, 73105-3207
405/521-3921, FAX 405/521-6246

Tulsa: 907 Detroit, Suite 750,
Tulsa, 74120-4200
918/581-2885, FAX 918/938-6348

(Agency Code 049, IA)

Office Hours—7:45 AM-5:30 PM, Mon.-Fri.

www.ok.gov/oag

Qualifications—The individual must be a U.S. citizen, at least thirty-one years old and qualified elector in state for ten years prior to election to office. State Constitution, Article 6, Section 3.

Salary—$132,825 annually

Personnel—161 unclassified employees

Office of State Auditor and Inspector
Constitution, Article 6 § 1

Gary Jones, Republican, has spent much of his adult life seeking to expand the accountability of elected officials and to improve the delivery of government services.

As a certified public accountant and certified fraud examiner, Jones understands the important contributions the state auditor can make in identifying inefficiencies in government entities and in offering recommendations and solutions to provide a better product for taxpayers.

Jones's strong personal belief in the importance of public service led him to run for Comanche County Commissioner in 1994.

Jones graduated from Lawton Eisenhower High School in 1972, and earned a bachelor's degree in business administration and accounting from Cameron University in 1978.

Along with Mary Jane, his wife of thirty-eight years, Jones values Oklahoma's rugged, rural heritage. They live on their farm southwest of Cache, where they raised two children, and built their cow-calf operation for over thirty years. Mary Jane retired in 2011 after a thirty-six year career teaching kindergarten.

Daughter Kelly is married with three children and is a math teacher at Cache High School. Son Chris manages the family farm and is employed at the Comanche County Juvenile Detention Center. When it comes to getting the most out of life, Jones holds close the three traditional virtues of God, country, and family. These values have defined his life as they have molded his character.

Key Personnel—Sheila Adkins, CISA, CPM, CIA, Information Services; Melissa Capps, CFE, CGFM, Performance Audit Division; Trey Davis, Continuing Education; Lisa Hodges, Deputy State Auditor for State Agency and Information Services; Mark Hudson, CPA, Gaming and Horse Racing, Minerals Management Division; Cindy Byrd, CPA, Deputy State Auditor for Local Government; Brenda Holt, CPA, Special Investigative Unit.

Office—Room 100, State Capitol, Oklahoma City, 73105-3207 (Agency Code 300, IA) 405/521-3495, FAX 405/521-3426, Fraud Hotline—1/855-372-8366

Office Hours—8 AM–5 PM Mon.-Fri.

www.sai.ok.gov

Qualifications For Office—The individual must be a U.S. citizen, at least thirty-one years of age and qualified elector of the state for ten years prior to election and at least three years experience as an expert accountant. State Constitution, Article 6, Sections 3 and 19.

Salary—$114,713 annually

Personnel—120 non-merit, unclassified

Office of the State Treasurer
Constitution, Article 6 § 1

Ken Miller, Republican, is the eighteenth state treasurer of Oklahoma. Miller was first elected to a four-year term in 2010 and was unopposed for re-election in 2014. As the state's top elected financial officer, Miller protects and manages more than $22 billion of taxpayer money deposited each year, safeguards the financial health of the state, promotes responsible fiscal policy, and operates the state's unclaimed property program. Miller chairs the Oklahoma College Savings Plan Board of Trustees, the State Pension Oversight Commission, and the Tobacco Settlement Endowment Trust Fund Board of Investors. He is a member of the State Board of Equalization, which certifies funds available for the state budget.

Miller earned his PhD from the University of Oklahoma, a MBA from Pepperdine University and a bachelor's degree in economics and finance from Lipscomb University. In addition to his duties as state treasurer, Miller is a tenured economics professor at Oklahoma Christian University, where he teaches at the graduate and undergraduate levels and has been honored with the "Who's Who Among American Teachers" award and the Merrick Foundation Award for Excellence in Teaching Free Enterprise.

Miller served six years in the Oklahoma House of Representatives, where he had 225 bills signed into law and led efforts to modernize state government and enhance transparency and accountability. Miller served his last three years in the House as chair of the Appropriations and Budget Committee, where he guided Oklahoma through the largest spending cuts in state history while maintaining the delivery of core government services. He took his reputation as a reformer and common-sense fiscal conservative to the treasury where he continued to reduce waste and inefficiency by eliminating leased office space and consolidating the agency into one location in the State Capitol Building, cutting the agency's operating budget and staff while increasing service delivery and output. Miller's fiscal policy experience in both the executive and legislative branches, combined with his credentials in economics and finance, led him to become an influential voice on major initiatives in areas of taxation, budget, and incentives.

Prior to his election to the Oklahoma Legislature, Miller served in the administration of Governor Frank Keating as chair of the Legislative Compensation Board where he established a 10-year freeze on legislative salaries that remains in effect today.

Key Personnel—Susan Nicewander, Chief Deputy Treasurer; Regina Birchum, Deputy Treasurer for Policy and Chief of Staff; Tim Allen, Deputy Treasurer for Communications and Program Administration; Jeff Ringer, Director of Constituent Engagement; Craig Sanger, Compliance Officer/Internal Auditor; Lisa Murray, Chief Investment Officer; Sherian Kerlin, Portfolio Accounting and Reporting Director; Kathy Janes, Unclaimed Property Director.

Office—Room 217, State Capitol, Oklahoma City 73105-3207 (Agency Code 740, IA) 405/521-3191, FAX 405/521-4994

Office Hours—8 AM–5 PM (Administration), 10 AM–3:30 PM (Cashier window)

www.treasurer.ok.gov

Qualifications for Office—The individual must be a U.S. citizen, at least thirty-one years old and qualified elector in the state for ten years prior to election. State Constitution, Article 6, Section 3.

Salary—$114,713 annually

Personnel—43 unclassified

Insurance Commissioner
Constitution, Article 6 § 1

John Doak, Republican, was sworn in as the twelfth insurance commissioner of Oklahoma on January 10, 2011. He was sworn into office for a second term on January 12, 2015, after receiving 77 percent of the vote.

Doak graduated from the University of Oklahoma with a Bachelor of Arts degree in political science. Shortly after graduation, he opened a successful insurance business in Tulsa. As his career thrived, Doak worked in numerous roles within the insurance industry. He served as an executive for several risk and insurance service companies including Marsh, Aon, HNI, and Ascension.

Under Doak's leadership, each year the Oklahoma Insurance Department has operated under budget. In the last four years, the department has returned a total of $22.5 million in unspent funds to the state treasury, and has generated more than $1 billion in revenue for the state. As an active member of the National Association of Insurance Commissioners, Doak is the vice chair of the Property and Casualty Insurance Committee, the chair of the American Indian and Alaska Native Liaison Committee, and a member of the International Insurance Relations Committee. He also shapes important national insurance policy issues as a member of the Government Relations Leadership Council.

Doak is committed to protecting all Oklahomans by his pledge to visit all seventy-seven counties annually. During his visits, which he has done each year since taking office, he promotes public awareness of important insurance issues through education and community outreach.

Doak and his wife Debby live in Tulsa with their children, Zack and Kasey. They are members of the South Tulsa Baptist Church.

Key Personnel—James Mills, Chief of Staff; Tyler Laughlin, Chief of Operations; Mike Rhoads, Deputy Commissioner of Health Insurance; Joel Sander, Deputy Commissioner of Finance; Susan Dobbins, General Counsel; Buddy Combs, Director of Public Policy and Assistant General Counsel; Julie Meaders, Deputy General Counsel; Kelly Dexter, Director of Communications; and Frank Stone, Chief Actuary.

Oklahoma City—3625 NW 56 Street, Suite 100, Oklahoma City 73112-4511 405/521-2828, 800/522-0071, FAX 405/521-6633

Tulsa—7645 E 63 Street, Suite 102, Tulsa 74133-1249 918/295-3700, FAX 918/994-7916

Office Hours—8 AM-5 PM, Mon.-Fri.

www.oid.ok.gov

Qualifications for Office—The Oklahoma State Code specifies that the commissioner shall be at least twenty-five years of age and a resident of the State of Oklahoma for at least five years, and have had at least five years experience in the insurance industry in administration, sales, servicing or regulation. The commissioner shall not be financially interested directly or indirectly, in any insurer, agency or insurance transaction except as a policy holder or claimant under a policy. 36 O.S. Section 302

Personnel—122 non-merit, unclassified

Salary—$126,713 annually

Commissioner of Labor
Constitution, Article 6 § 1

Mark Costello, Republican, holds the distinction of defeating an incumbent Democrat with over 64 percent of the popular vote. He is a businessman with thirty-two years experience in meeting the bottom line. Costello has taken a sabbatical from his businesses in order to fulfill his role as a public servant. He founded AMCAT, a telephone software company, in 1991, employing over one hundred employees and generating hundreds of millions of dollars of payroll until it was successfully sold in 2007. In 1998 he founded USA Digital Communications, Inc., a telecommunications company that is a licensed common carrier in over forty states. Costello's business experience and perspective uniquely qualifies him to advance conservative principles and encourage the generation of jobs and opportunities for Oklahomans.

Costello is an active labor commissioner who deploys existing resources to better aid Oklahoma job producers. He supports legislative efforts to reduce government bureaucracy, cut taxes, and works hard to promote private-sector job creation. In that vein, Costello holds that it is necessary to adopt an administrative system of workers' compensation in order to reduce the burden on existing businesses and justly compensate injured workers.

Costello is a fourth generation Oklahoman born in Bartlesville. He graduated from College High in Bartlesville and following his older siblings, entered the University of Kansas from which he graduated in 1980. He married Cathy (Cerkey) in 1982, and together they are raising their five children in Edmond, Oklahoma. Costello holds a lifetime membership in the National Rifle Association.

Key Personnel—Jim Marshall, Chief of Staff; Don Schooler, General Counsel; Stacy Bonner, Finance Director; Liz McNeill, Communications; Danielle Wade, Special Assistant to the Commissioner; Diana Jones, Director of OSHA Consultation Program/PEOSH/Abestos; James Bick II, Director of Licensing Division; and Angela Cobble, Director of Safety Standards Division.

Office—3017 N Stiles, Oklahoma City, OK 73105-2808
405/521-6100, 888/269-5353, FAX 405/521-6018

www.labor.ok.gov

E-mail—labor.info@labor.ok.gov

Qualifications For Office—There are no constitutional or statutory requirements.

Salary—$105,053 annually

Personnel—47 classified, 19 unclassified

Superintendent of Public Instruction
Constitution, Article 6 § 1

Joy Hofmeister, Republican, was sworn in as Oklahoma's fourteenth state superintendent of public instruction on January 12, 2015. Since taking office, Hofmeister has traveled throughout Oklahoma to advocate for school children, launched common sense steps to improve performance of the education system, and has begun transforming the Oklahoma State Department of Education into an inclusive and transparent service-oriented organization. In her first fourteen weeks as state superintendent, she visited more than twenty school districts in every part of the state. She is an advocate for solutions to Oklahoma's teacher shortage and the elimination of unnecessary mandates and assessments.

Hofmeister is a former public school teacher and small business owner. She served on the Oklahoma State Board of Education from January 2012 through April 2013 as an appointee of Governor Mary Fallin.

In the private sector, Hofmeister spent fifteen years operating Kumon Math & Reading Centers of South Tulsa, which works through parent partnerships to ensure higher academic achievement for children. During that time, she personally worked with more than 4,000 students to improve their educational outcomes.

Hofmeister graduated with a bachelor's degree in education from Texas Christian University, and holds teaching certificates in English and elementary education. In May 2015, she earned her master's degree in education administration with a specialty in education policy and law from the University of Oklahoma.

As a mother of four graduates of Oklahoma's public school system, Hofmeister served as an officer for the Jenks Public Schools Foundation Board of Directors, the Select Committee for the Study of School Finance, and other committees within the Jenks Public School District. She and her husband maintain residence in Tulsa.

Key Personnel—Dr. Cindy Koss, Deputy State Superintendent of Academic Affairs and
   Planning; Dr. Robyn Miller, Deputy State Superintendent of Educator Effectiveness;
   Matt Holder, Chief Operations Officer; Lance Nelson, Chief of Staff; Heather
   Griswold, Deputy Chief of Staff; Carolyn Thompson, Director of Government
   Relations; and Phil Bacharach, Director of Communications.

Office—Room 121, Oliver Hodge Memorial Education Building
   2500 N Lincoln, Oklahoma City 73105-4599
   405/521-3301, FAX 405/521-6205

Office Hours—8 AM-4:30 PM, Mon.-Fri.

www.ok.gov/sde

Qualifications For Office—The individual must be a U.S. citizen, not less than thirty-one
   years old and qualified elector of state for ten years prior to election. State Constitution,
   Article 6, Sec. 3.

Salary—$124,373 annually

Personnel—284 unclassified

Corporation Commission
Constitution, Article 9 § 15

Oklahoma City—2101 N Lincoln Boulevard, Jim Thorpe Building, Oklahoma City 73105-4905
  PO Box 52000, Oklahoma City 73152-2000
  405/521-2211, FAX 405/521-6045

Tulsa—440 S Houston Ave., Suite 114, Tulsa 74127-8917 ▪ 918/581-2296

www.occeweb.com

Bob Anthony, Republican, is currently the longest serving utility commissioner in the United States and has served six times as chairman of the Oklahoma Corporation Commission. He is a member of the board of directors for the National Association of Regulatory Utility Commissioners and past chairman of the National Regulatory Research Institute. The United States Secretary of Energy has twice appointed Anthony to the National Petroleum Council. He is past president of the Mid-America Regulatory Conference, a member and past president of the Economic Club of Oklahoma, and a delegate to the worldwide General Conference of the United Methodist Church.

Anthony holds a BS from the Wharton School of Finance at the University of Pennsylvania; a Master of Science from the London School of Economics; a Master of Arts from Yale University; and a Master of Public Administration from Harvard University. He rose to the rank of captain in the U.S. Army Reserve. In 1972 he served as staff economist for the United States House of Representatives Interior and Insular Affairs Committee (now called the Natural Resources Committee). From 1979 to 1980 Anthony served on the Oklahoma City Council as Ward 2 Councilman and as vice mayor. In 1980, at age thirty-two, Anthony became president of C.R. Anthony Company retail stores, then the largest privately-owned firm headquartered in Oklahoma. During his seven-year term as president, annual sales for the retail chain increased from $256 to $411 million with payroll, employment, and dollar profits reaching all-time record levels. In 1988 he was chairman of the Trust Committee of Oklahoma's largest bank trust department.

In 1995 the Federal Bureau of Investigation honored Anthony with its highest award given to a citizen who "at great personal sacrifice, has unselfishly served his community and the nation." Among other recognitions, the American Association of Retired Persons of Oklahoma presented Anthony with an award "in appreciation of his tireless efforts on behalf of Oklahoma consumers."

Anthony has served as a statewide elected official longer than any current Oklahoma office holder, winning his fifth consecutive six-year term on the Oklahoma Corporation Commission in 2012, winning all seventy-seven counties. He initially ran for the Corporation Commission in 1988, becoming the first Republican elected to that body in sixty years and receiving more votes than any Republican since statehood. In 1994 Anthony became the first Republican incumbent in Oklahoma history to win statewide reelection to a state office. In 2000 he was reelected, receiving more votes at that time than any candidate for state office in Oklahoma history.

All four of Anthony's grandparents came to Oklahoma before statehood. His father was born in Cleveland, Oklahoma, and his mother grew up in Enid, Oklahoma. He and his wife, Nancy, were married in 1975. They are the parents of four daughters, and have three grandchildren.

Todd Hiett, Republican, was elected to serve as Oklahoma's newest corporation commissioner. Hiett, a graduate of Oklahoma State University, was elected to the Oklahoma House of Representatives in 1994, at the age of twenty-seven. Hiett quickly ascended into leadership and was selected by his colleagues to serve as House minority leader in November 2002. Two years later, he led the state House Republicans to their first majority in eight decades and their largest victory in nearly a half-century. Marking a historic shift in power at the capitol, Hiett was chosen the first Republican Speaker of the House in more than eight decades.

During his first year as Speaker, Hiett oversaw a smooth transition as House Republicans ascended to power with a bold agenda. Hiett pushed through the largest tax cut in state history, the most significant right-to-life legislation in thirty years, an innovative highway-funding bill, and significant education reforms, collectively known as the ACE Initiative, which raised the bar for curriculum standards and graduation requirements in Oklahoma.

After a successful twelve years in the Oklahoma Legislature, Speaker Hiett has worked for the past eight years with various entities in manufacturing, navigation, and energy industries. In this role, he has enjoyed the opportunity to work with many pro-growth companies such as Webco Industries and Callidus Technologies to strengthen and expand their ability to provide jobs.

Hiett and his wife, Bridget, have three children, Jimmy, John, and Hillary. The Hiett family lives on a ranch, two miles south of Kellyville, that they continue to operate. Bridget teaches fourth grade at Kellyville Elementary; son Jimmy graduated from Oklahoma State University; son John is attending Oklahoma State University; and daughter Hillary is a junior at Kellyville High School. The Hietts attend First Baptist Church of Kellyville.

Dana L. Murphy, Republican, was born in Woodward, Oklahoma, and is a fifth generation Oklahoman deeply committed to her home state. After attending Central State University in Edmond, Oklahoma, where she received the Best All-Around Freshman Athlete Award, she attended Oklahoma State University. She graduated in the top 10 percent in her class at OSU, and received a bachelor's degree in geology. After practicing as a geologist for ten years, she obtained her law degree cum laude, while working and attending night school at Oklahoma City University.

On November 4, 2008, Murphy was first elected to the statewide office of Oklahoma Corporation Commissioner for a partial two-year term. On July 27, 2010, she was re-elected to a full six-year term. Murphy served as chair of the commission, following election by her fellow commissioners, from January 3, 2011, through July 31, 2012.

Murphy's prior experience includes working for almost six years as an administrative law judge at the commission, where she was named Co-Employee of the Year in 1997, and received the Commissioners' Public Servant Award in 2001. She has more than twenty-two years experience in the petroleum industry including owning and operating her own private law firm focused on oil and gas title, regulatory practice and transactional work, and working as a geologist.

Prior to joining the commission, Murphy was a member of the board of directors for Farmers Royalty Company. She is a member of the National Association of Regulatory Utility Commissioners (NARUC), where she serves on the Electricity Committee. Murphy is the Oklahoma member and president of the Regional State Committee of Southwest Power

Pool, Inc., the Oklahoma Water Resources Research Institute Advisory Board, the Financial Research Institute Advisory Board, and the Salvation Army's Central Oklahoma Area Command Advisory Board. She is also a member of the Oklahoma Bar Association, American Association of Petroleum Geologists, Oklahoma City Geological Society, and the Oklahoma Women's Coalition. She is as a member of Energy Advocates, and in March 2007 was recognized as an outstanding woman in energy. In 2010 she was recognized for dedicated service by the National Association of Royalty Owners, and in 2011 received the Friends of Agriculture Cooperatives Award. Murphy is also a recipient of the University of Central Oklahoma Distinguished Alumni Award for 2012. She previously served as a trustee and a care chaplain for the Church of the Servant United Methodist Church in Oklahoma City. In January 2014, Murphy became the chair of the Financial Research Institute Advisory Board. In January 2015, she became the president of the Southwest Power Pool Inc., Regional State Committee. Murphy, a part-time personal fitness trainer, lives in Edmond, but continues to be actively involved in her family's farm and ranch in Ellis County, Oklahoma.

In 1915, while waiting for the construction of a new post (near Fort Sam Houston, San Antonio, Texas), the U.S. Air Force's 1st Aero Squadron was ordered to Fort Sill, Oklahoma, to conduct observation and fire control experiments with the field artillery. Some of the squadron's first flights occurred at Fort Sill, though their airplanes and engines were plagued by persistent manufacturing problems.

Governor Fallin's Cabinet

(74 O.S. 2001 § 10.3)

Secretary of State and Native American Affairs—Chris Benge

State Capitol, Room 101
2300 N Lincoln Boulevard
Oklahoma City 73105-4897
405/521-3912, FAX 405/521-2031

Secretary of Agriculture—Jim Reese

2800 N Lincoln Boulevard
Oklahoma City 73105-4298
PO Box 528804, 73152-8804
405/522-5719, FAX 405/522-0909

Secretary of Commerce and Tourism— Deby Snodgrass

900 N Stiles, Oklahoma City 73126-0980
405/815-5306, FAX 405/815-5290

Secretary of Education and Workforce Development— Natalie Shirley

State Capitol, Room 105
2300 N Lincoln Boulevard
Oklahoma City 73105-3207
405/521-4634, FAX 405/521-3353

Secretary of Energy and Environment—Michael Teague

100 N Broadway, Suite 2350
Oklahoma City 73102-9211
405/285-9213, FAX 405/285-9212

Secretary of Finance, Administration, and Information Technology— Preston Doerflinger

State Capitol, Room 122,
2300 N Lincoln Boulevard
Oklahoma City 73105-3207
405/521-2141, FAX 405/521-3902

Secretary of Health and Human Services—Terry Cline

1000 NE 10 Street
Oklahoma City 73117-1207
405/271-5600

Secretary of the Military— Major Gen. Robbie L. Asher

3501 Military Circle
Oklahoma City 73111-4398
405/228-5201, FAX 405/228-5524

Secretary of Safety and Security— Michael C. Thompson

3600 N Martin Luther King
Oklahoma City 73111-4223
PO Box 11415, Oklahoma City, 73136-0415
405/425-2424, FAX 405/419-2050

Secretary of Science and Technology— Dr. Stephen W.S. McKeever

145 Physical Sciences
Oklahoma State University
Stillwater 74078-1016
405/744-4625, FAX 405/744-6811

Secretary of Transportation— Gary Ridley

3500 Martin Luther King Boulevard
Oklahoma City 73111-4221
405/425-7412, FAX 405/427-8246

Secretary of Veterans Affairs— Major Gen. Myles Deering

2311 N Central
Oklahoma City 73105-3200
405/521-3684, FAX 405/521-6533

Secretary of State and Native American Affairs
Chris Benge

State Capitol, Room 101, 2300 N Lincoln Boulevard, Oklahoma City
73105-4897 ▪ 405/521-3912, FAX 405/521-2031 ▪ www.sos.ok.gov

Chris Benge was appointed as Oklahoma's thirty-third secretary of state by Governor Mary Fallin on November 8, 2013. In addition to his duties as secretary of state, Benge serves on the governor's cabinet.

Benge was elected to the Oklahoma House of Representatives in 1998 and left office in November 2010 due to legislative term limits. He served six years in leadership positions, including three years as chair of the Appropriations and Budget Committee, a position that is responsible for negotiating and writing the state budget. He spent his last three years in office as Speaker of the House.

After his legislative service, Benge worked in Tulsa Mayor Dewey Bartlett's administration as the director of Intergovernmental and Enterprise Development. His focus was on public policy and special project development, such as river development, transportation, infrastructure needs, and energy leadership. He also concentrated on strengthening working partnerships between Tulsa County and the surrounding communities in the region.

Most recently, Benge served as senior vice president of government affairs with the Tulsa Regional Chamber, leading the organization's advocacy efforts at the state and federal level through the OneVoice process, as well as working with city and county officials on local policy issues.

His legislative service was highlighted by focusing on ways to encourage economic development and job growth for the citizens of Oklahoma. He was committed to funding transportation infrastructure, addressing physician training by stabilizing the OSU Medical Center, and promoting education initiatives. He also focused on pension reform, government efficiency, and responsible use of excess oil and gas tax collections.

As a way to increase the focus on growing the state's economy, Benge brought focus to the Oklahoma Quality Jobs Program and the Closing Fund, which have brought numerous high caliber jobs to the state. He also pushed for incentives that assisted local industry growth in aerospace and energy. He received recognition for his efforts to help the state create a favorable business climate from the Oklahoma State Chamber with the organization's Defender of Free Enterprise Award for 2009.

Benge also brought particular attention to the use of domestic energy in the state by working to establish a set of energy goals for Oklahoma that included increased use of natural gas for transportation. These efforts led to his testifying before a congressional committee on the benefits of using more natural gas for transportation purposes.

On February 9, 2015, Governor Fallin appointed Benge to fill the position of the Native American Liaison. In addition to his duties as secretary of state, he will work directly with the Tribal Nations of the State of Oklahoma. He will work to further the relationship between the state and tribal leadership, and build on the momentum the state and tribal nations have developed over the last few years.

A lifetime Tulsa area resident, Chris and his wife Allison, along with their two children, reside in the community of Berryhill. He earned a bachelor's degree in business administration from Oklahoma State University.

The secretary of state is responsible for the following executive entities:

Access to Justice Commission, Oklahoma
Archives and Records Commission
County Government Personnel Education
and Training, Commission on
Election Board, State
Ethics Commission, Oklahoma
Judicial Compensation, Board of
Judicial Complaints, Council on
Judicial Nominating Commission
Library Board, State
and Department of Libraries
Licensed Architects, Landscape Architects
and Interior Designers of Oklahoma,
Board of Governors of
National Conference of Commissioners on
Uniform State Law

Native American Cultural and Educational
Authority
Native American Liaison, Oklahoma
Professional Engineers & Land Surveyors,
State Board of Registration for
Professional Responsibility Tribunal
Real Estate Appraiser Board
Real Estate Commission, Oklahoma
Real Estate Contract Form Committee,
Oklahoma
Secretary of State
Workers' Compensation, Advisory Council
on
Workers' Compensation Commission

Secretary of Agriculture
Jim Reese

2800 N Lincoln Boulevard, Oklahoma City 73105–4298 ▪
405/522–5719, FAX 405/522–0909

Jim Reese was appointed secretary of agriculture by Governor Mary
Fallin and has been serving in that capacity since January 10, 2011. Reese
was raised on a wheat and dairy farm in north central Oklahoma, where
he continues to farm today. He attended Deer Creek-Lamont High
School, Northern Oklahoma College, and Oklahoma State University
and received a bachelor's degree in engineering technology. In 1986
he was elected to the House of Representatives where he served for
fifteen years. While serving in the Oklahoma Legislature he was selected by the George W.
Bush administration to serve as state executive director of the Farm Service Agency for eight
years. He was then chosen by House Speaker Chris Benge to serve as policy advisor to the
Speaker of the House. Secretary Reese is a long time agricultural and rural advocate. He and
his wife Margaret have four children.

The secretary of agriculture is responsible for the following executive entities:

Agriculture, State Board of
Agriculture, Food and Forestry,
Department of
Apiary Committee
Boll Weevil Eradication Organization
Commodity Commissions, Peanut, Oilseed,
Sheep and Wool, Sorghum, and Wheat
Conservation Commission, Oklahoma

Horse Racing Commission, Oklahoma
Industry Advisory Committee
South Central Interstate Forest Fire
Protection Compact and Advisory
Committee
Southern Dairy Compact
Standards, Bureau of
Veterinary Medical Examiners, State
Board of

Secretary of Commerce and Tourism
Deby Snodgrass

900 N Stiles, Oklahoma City 73126–0980 ▪ 405/815–5306,
800/879–6552, FAX 405/815–5290

Snodgrass currently serves as the Oklahoma Secretary of Commerce and Tourism. In addition to her duties as executive director of the Oklahoma Department of Commerce. Snodgrass previously served as secretary of tourism and executive director of the Oklahoma Department of Tourism and Recreation. During her four year tenure at the tourism department, the economic impact of the tourism industry in Oklahoma grew from $6.2 billion to $7.5 billion, despite substantial cuts in the agency's appropriated budget. In 2012, Snodgrass was awarded the Oklahoma Council of Public Affairs Sheer Vision Award for her efforts to "right size" state government. In 2014, she received the Byliner Award for Public Service from the Association of Women in Communication.

As secretary of commerce and tourism, Snodgrass is responsible for thirty-two state agencies, boards, and commissions, in addition to her duties as executive director. She serves on the Oklahoma Industrial Finance Authority, Oklahoma Science and Technology Research and Development Board, Oklahoma Development Finance Authority, Executive Bond Oversight Commission, Governor's Council for Workforce and Economic Development, and the Oklahoma Ordnance Works Authority. Additionally, she has been appointed by Governor Mary Fallin to the Oklahoma Standards Setting Steering Committee and the Oklahoma Compensation and Unclassified Positions Review Board. Snodgrass also serves as an ex-officio board member of Allied Arts, State Chamber of Oklahoma Board of Directors, and the Native American Cultural and Educational Authority.

Prior to her public service, Snodgrass served as senior director of Public Affairs for Chesapeake Energy (NYSE CHK). In that role, she developed and executed strategic political and public policy initiatives, managed both state and federal political action committees, and monitored federal, state, and local issues. Previous to her tenure at CHK, she was a founding partner of the public policy and research firm, Cole, Hargrave, Snodgrass and Associates.

Snodgrass's commitment to community service is also well-documented. In 2013, she served as chair of the State Charitable Campaign for United Way of Central Oklahoma. In 2012, she served as the fund coordinator for the Oklahoma National Guard Camp Gruber Chapel. She was also the founding member of the Board of Directors for Friends of the Mansion, Inc., inaugural chair of Septemberfest, and a former co-chair of "Opening Night," Oklahoma City's annual New Year's Eve celebration. She served eight years on Oklahoma's Capitol Preservation Commission, and is a former board member of the Arts Council of Oklahoma City.

The secretary of commerce is responsible for the following executive entities:

1921 Tulsa Race Riot Memorial of
　Reconciliation Design Committee
African American Centennial Plaza Design
　Committee
Alarm and Locksmith Industry Committee
Arts Council, Oklahoma
Commerce, Oklahoma Department of
Employment Security Commission,
　Oklahoma and State Advisory Council
　and Board Review

Geographic Information Council, State
Greenwood Area Redevelopment Authority
Historic Preservation Review Committee,
　Oklahoma
Historical Records Advisory Board
Historical Society, Oklahoma
Housing Finance Agency, Oklahoma
Industrial Finance Authority, Oklahoma
J.M. Davis Memorial Commission
Jazz Hall of Fame Board, Oklahoma

Labor Commissioner, and Department of Labor
Midwestern Oklahoma Development Authority
Northeast Oklahoma Public Facilities Authority
Office of Minority and Disadvantaged Business Enterprises
Ordinance Works Authority, Oklahoma
Quartz Mountain Arts and Conference Center and Nature Park, Board of Trustees, and Quartz Mountain Arts and Conference Center and Nature Park
Register of Natural Heritage Areas, State
Rural Action Partnership Program
Rural Area Development Task Force
Rural Development, Center for
Sam Noble Museum of Natural History, Oklahoma
Scenic Rivers Commission
Tourism and Recreation Commission, Oklahoma, and Department of Tourism and Recreation
Tourism Promotion Advisory Committee, Oklahoma
Will Rogers Memorial Commission

Secretary of Education and Workforce Development
Natalie Shirley

State Capitol, Room 105, 2300 N Lincoln, Oklahoma City 73105-3207
▪ 405/521-4634, FAX 405/521-3353

Shirley concurrently serves as president of Oklahoma State University-Oklahoma City, and as Oklahoma Secretary of Education and Workforce Development. She was hired in May 2011 as the first female president in the OSU system. In January 2015, Shirley was appointed by Governor Mary Fallin to serve in her cabinet as secretary of education and workforce development. In this position, she is working with the governor to implement the Oklahoma Works program, which is designed to increase educational attainment for Oklahomans in order to produce a more educated workforce to support and cultivate the state's economy.

From 2007 to 2011, Shirley also served in Governor Brad Henry's cabinet as Oklahoma Secretary of Commerce and Tourism. In this position, she was the liaison between the governor, five major state agencies, and more than thirty small agencies, authorities, and institutions. During this time, she also served as executive director of the Oklahoma Department of Commerce, the state's leading economic development agency.

Formerly, Shirley was president of ICI Mutual in Washington, D.C., after serving in various leadership offices in the company. ICI Mutual is the captive insurance company of the mutual fund industry.

In addition to her dual roles as OSU-OKC president and secretary of education and workforce development, Shirley also serves on the United Way board, as well as several business boards, including the Greater Oklahoma City Chamber of Commerce, Oklahoma City Convention & Visitors Bureau, BancFirst, AAA Oklahoma/South Dakota, and the Oklahoma State Fair Board. She also serves on the Jasmine Moran Children's Museum Board of Trustees.

As an Oklahoma native, Shirley graduated from Oklahoma State University and earned a law degree from the University of Oklahoma. Shirley and her husband, Russ Harrison, live in Oklahoma City. They have six children and are members of the Saint Luke's United Methodist Church.

The secretary of education and workforce development is responsible for the following executive entities:

Accrediting Agency, State

Anatomical Board, State

Career and Technology Education, State Board of

Career and Technology Education Department

College and University Boards of Regents or Trustees

Dyslexia Teacher Training Pilot Program Advisory Committee

Education Commission of the States

Education Quality and Accountability, Office of, and Commission for Education Quality and Accountability

Education, State Board of, Superintendent of Public Instruction, and State Department of Education

Educational Television Authority, Oklahoma (OETA)

Governor's Council for Workforce and Economic Development

Municipal Clerks and Treasurers Division of the Oklahoma Career and Technology Education Advisory Committee

Partnership for School Readiness Board, Oklahoma

Physician Manpower Training Commission

Private Vocational Schools Board

School and County Funds Management Commission

School of Science and Mathematics, and Oklahoma Board of Trustees of

Student Loan Authority

Student Tracking and Reporting Coordinating Committee (STAR)

Teacher and Leader Effectiveness Commission

Textbook Committee, State

Virtual Charter School Board, Statewide

Secretary of Energy and Environment
Michael Teague

100 N Broadway, Suite 2350, Oklahoma City 73102-9211 ▪ 405/285-9213, FAX 405/285-9212 ▪ www.ok.gov/energy

Michael Teague is serving as Oklahoma's first secretary of energy and environment.

Prior to his appointment, Teague served in the U.S. Army for nearly thirty years before retiring with the rank of colonel.

Teague served in many capacities during his time in the army including commander for the Tulsa District of the U.S. Army Corps of Engineers where he was responsible for a civil works program encompassing all of Oklahoma, a large portion of southern Kansas and the panhandle of northern Texas. He oversaw over 700 employees in engineering, construction, and operations, as well as an annual budget of $700 million.

Throughout his career, Teague has dealt with power generation and distribution, water desalinization, and environmental impact studies. He has facilitated and negotiated numerous solutions regarding federal and state agencies, tribes, and local stakeholders, and has acted as a liaison between the Tulsa District and the United States Congress.

Teague also served in operational assignments in Germany, Honduras, Saudi Arabia, Egypt, and numerous stateside duty stations. He deployed several times to the Middle East and central Asia including commanding the 52nd Engineer Battalion in Mosul, Iraq, in support of the 101st Airborne Division as part of Operation Iraqi Freedom in 2003.

Teague received a bachelor's degree in civil engineering from Norwich University. He also received master's degrees in operations analysis from the Naval Postgraduate School, and in national security and strategic studies from the Naval War College.

The secretary of energy and environment is responsible for the following executive entities:

Arkansas River Basin Compact Commission, Arkansas-Oklahoma
Arkansas River Basin Compact Commission, Kansas-Oklahoma
Canadian River Commission
Carbon Sequestration Advisory Committee
Central Interstate Low-Level Radioactive Waste Compact and Commission
Climatological Survey
Corporation Commission
Energy Resources Board, Oklahoma
Energy Initiative and Energy Initiative Board, Oklahoma
Environmental Quality Board and Air Quality Advisory Council, Hazardous Materials Emergency Response Commission, Hazardous Waste Management Advisory Council, Radiation Management Advisory Council, Solid Waste Management Advisory Council, Water Quality Management Advisory Council, and Department of Environmental Quality
Grand River Dam Authority (GRDA) and GRDA Board of Directors
Geological Survey

Interstate Oil Compact Commission
Liquefied Petroleum Gas (LPG) Board, Oklahoma
LPG Research, Marketing, and Safety Commission, Oklahoma
Mining Commission, Interstate,
Mining Commission, Oklahoma, and Department of Mines
Miner Training Institute, Oklahoma
Municipal Power Authority Board, Oklahoma
Oil and Gas Compact Commission, Interstate
Red RiverCompact and Commission, Arkansas-Louisiana-Oklahoma-Texas
Southern States Energy Compact and Southern States Energy Board
Storage Tank Advisory Council
Sustaining Oklahoma's Energy Resources Committee
Water for 2060 Advisory Council
Water Resources Board, Oklahoma
Well Drillers and Pump Installers Advisory Council
Wildlife Conservation Commission and Wildlife Conservation Department

Secretary of Finance, Administration, and Information Technology
Preston Doerflinger

Room 122, State Capitol, 2300 N Lincoln Boulevard, Oklahoma City 73105-3207 ▪ 405/521-2141, FAX 405/521-3902

Doerflinger was appointed by Governor Mary Fallin on January 19, 2011. He also serves as director of the Office of Management and Enterprise Services (OMES), the state's central finance and operations agency.

Prior to his state appointment, Doerflinger founded and served as chief executive officer of PLD Management, a business consulting and investment firm, in addition to founding several health care and supply companies. In 2009, he was elected city auditor of Tulsa. He received a bachelor's degree in organizational leadership from Southern Nazarene University.

Since joining the Fallin administration, Doerflinger has become known as the governor's chief problem solver and a leader of her efforts to modernize state government. He is also the governor's lead budget negotiator with the legislature.

As director of OMES, Doerflinger is the state's chief non-elected finance, administrative, and operations officer. Doerflinger's cabinet duties were expanded in summer 2013 under the new cabinet position of secretary of finance, administration, and information technology that reflects the widened responsibilities assigned to OMES through major consolidation initiatives in 2011 and 2012.

Between March and November of 2012, Doerflinger served as interim director of the Department of Human Services, the largest state agency. At DHS, Doerflinger was instrumental in implementing the beginning stages of the Pinnacle Plan, the largest child welfare reform in recent state history.

The secretary of finance, administration, and information technology is responsible for the following executive entities:

Abstractors Board, Oklahoma
Accountancy Board, Oklahoma
Alternative Fuels Technician Examiners and Board, Oklahoma
Auditor and Inspector, State
Banking Board, State, and State Banking Department
Bipartisan Legislative Apportionment Commission
Bond Advisor, State
Bond Oversight, Council of
Building Bonds Commission
Capital Investment Board, Oklahoma
Capitol-Medical Center Improvement and Zoning Commission
Capitol Preservation Commission, State
Cash Management Oversight Committee
Compensation and Unclassified Positions Review Board, Oklahoma
Construction Industries Board
Consumer Credit Commission and Department of Consumer Credit
Contingency Review Board
Development Finance Authority, Oklahoma
Electronic and Information Technology Accessibility Advisory Council
Employee Assistance Program, State, and Advisory Council
Employee Insurance & Benefits Board, Oklahoma
Equalization, State Board of
Firefighters Pension and Retirement System and Board
Home Inspector Examiners, Committee of
Incentive Approval Committee
Incentive Awards for State Employees, Committee for
Insurance Commissioner and State Insurance Department
Interstate Cooperation, Oklahoma Commission on
Land office, Commissioners of the

Law Enforcement Retirement System and Board, Oklahoma
Legislative Compensation, Board on
Life and Health Insurance Guaranty Association and Board of Directors, Oklahoma
Long-Range Capital Planning Commission
Lottery Commission and Board of Trustees, Oklahoma
Management and Enterprise Services, Office of
Manufactured Home Advisory Committee
Market Assistance Association and Board of Directors
Merit Protection Commission
Motor Vehicle Commission, Oklahoma
Multiple Injury Trust Fund
Oversight Committee for State Employee Charitable Contributions
Pension Commission, Oklahoma State
Police Pension and Retirement System and Board, Oklahoma
Program Development and Credit Review Committee
Public Employees Relations Board
Public Employees Retirement System and Board, Oklahoma
Securities Commission, Oklahoma, and Department of Securities
State Credit Union Board, Oklahoma
State Governmental Technology Applications Review Board
Streamlined Sales and Use Tax Agreement Committee
Tax Commission, Oklahoma
Teachers' Retirement System, Board of Trustees of the, and Teachers' Retirement System
Treasurer, State
Used Motor Vehicle and Parts Commission, Oklahoma

Secretary of Health and Human Services
Terry L. Cline, PhD

1000 NE 10 Street, Oklahoma City 73117-1207 ▪ 405/271-5600

Cline was appointed secretary of health and human services by Governor Mary Fallin on January 31, 2011. Cline also serves as Oklahoma's Commissioner of Health, a position he has held since June 30, 2009. Cline previously completed a post as Health Attache at the U.S. Embassy in Baghdad, Iraq, where he advised the U.S. Ambassador, the Iraqi Minister of Health, and the U.S. Department of Health and Human Services on health-related challenges in Iraq. He served in this capacity under the administrations of President George W. Bush and President Barack Obama. Cline also served as administrator for the federal Substance Abuse and Mental Health Services Administration from 2006–2008, a position for which he was appointed by President George W. Bush and confirmed by the U.S. Senate. In 2004 he was appointed by Governor Brad Henry as Oklahoma's secretary of health. He also served as the commissioner of the Oklahoma Department of Mental Health and Substance Abuse Services. His professional history also includes staff psychologist at McLean Hospital in Belmont, Massachusetts; clinical instructor in the Harvard Medical School Department of Psychiatry; and chair of the governing board for a Harvard teaching hospital in Cambridge, Massachusetts. Cline earned a bachelor's degree in psychology from the University of Oklahoma in 1980. He received a master's degree and doctorate degree in clinical psychology from Oklahoma State University.

The secretary of health and human services is responsible for the following executive entities or their successors:

Advancement of Wellness Advisory Council
Agent Orange Outreach Committee
Alcohol and Drug Counselors, Oklahoma Board of Licensed
Alcohol, Drug Abuse and Community Mental Health Planning and Coordination Boards
Alzheimer's Research Advisory Council
Athletic Commission, Oklahoma State
Athletic Trainers Advisory Committee
Behavioral Health Licensure, Board of
Blind Vendors, Committee of
Catastrophic Health Emergency Planning Task Force, Oklahoma
Cerebral Palsy Commission and J.D. McCarty Center for Children with Developmental Disabilities
Child Abuse Examination Board of
Child Abuse Prevention Training and Coordination Council
Child Abuse Prevention, Office of
Child Death Review Board
Children and Youth, Oklahoma Commission on
Chiropractic Examiners, Board of

Citizens Advisory Panels for Administration, Aging Issues, Children and Family Issues, and Disability Issues
Community Hospitals Authority
Community Social Services Center Authority
Cosmetology and Barbering, State Board of
Consumer Advocacy, Office of
Consumer Protection Licensing Advisory Council
Dentistry, Board of
Dietetic Registration, Advisory Committee
Developmental Disabilities Council
Disability Concerns, Governor's Advisory Committee to the Office of, and Office of Disability Concerns
Early Childhood Intervention, Interagency Coordination Council for
Employment of People with Disabilities, Governor's Advisory Committee on
Faith-based and Community Initiatives
Food Service Advisory Council
Funeral Board, Oklahoma
Governor's Council on Physical Fitness and Sports

Group Homes for Persons with Developmental or Physical Disabilities Advisory Board
Health Care Authority, Oklahoma
Health Care Information Advisory Committee
Health, State Board of, and Department of Health
Home Care and Hospice Advisory Council
Hospital Advisory Committee, Oklahoma
Hospital Advisory Council, Oklahoma
Human Services, Department of
Infant and Children's Health Advisory Council
Juvenile Affairs Board of, and Office of Juvenile Affairs
Juvenile Justice, State Advisory Group on
Licensed Social Workers, State Board of
Long-Term Care Administrators, Oklahoma State Board of Examiners for
Long-Term Care Facility Advisory Board
Medical Care for Public Assistance Recipients, Advisory Committee for
Medical Licensure and Supervision, Board of
Mental Health Advisory Committee on Deafness and Hearing Impairment
Mental Health and Substance Abuse, Board of, and Department of Mental Health and Substance Abuse
Mental Health, Interstate Compact on
Nursing, Board of, and Formulary Advisory Council
Occupational Therapy Advisory Committee, Oklahoma
Oklahoma State University Medical Authority
Optometry, Board of Examiners in

Osteopathic Examiners, State Board of
Partnership for Children's Behavioral Health
Perfusionists, State Board of Examiners of
Pharmacy, Board of
Physician's Assistant Advisory Committee
Placement of Children, Interstate Compact
Podiatric Medical Examiners, Board of
Post Adjudication Review Advisory Board
Prevention of Adolescent Pregnancy and Sexually Transmitted Diseases, Interagency Coordinating Council for Coordination of Efforts for
Psychologists, State Board of Examiners of
Public Guardian, Office of
Registered Electrologists, Advisory Committee of
Rehabilitation Services Commission, Oklahoma Rehabilitation Services, Department of
Residents and Family State Council
Respiratory Care Advisory Committee
Sanitarian and Environmental Specialist Registration Advisory Council
Santa Claus Commission
Self-Directed Services Program Committee
Speech Pathology and Audiology, Board of Examiners for
Statewide Independent Living Council
Suicide Prevention Council, Oklahoma
Tobacco Settlement Endowment Trust Fund Board of Directors
Trauma and Emergency Response Advisory Council
Traumatic Spinal Cord and Traumatic Brain Injury, Advisory Council on
University Hospitals Authority
Vulnerable Adult Intervention Task Force

Secretary of the Military
Major General Robbie Asher

3501 Military Circle, Oklahoma City 73111-4398 ▪ 405/228-5201, FAX 405/228-5524

Major General Robbie L. Asher serves as the secretary of the military as well as the adjutant general of Oklahoma. As such, he is responsible for commanding units of the Oklahoma Army and Air National Guard. He also serves as the military advisor to the governor. Asher was commissioned in 1976 through the Texas Army National Guard.

Asher joined the United States Army in June 1974, and was assigned to the 101st Airborne Division, where he served until June 1976. The day after his release from active duty, Asher began his career with the Oklahoma National Guard, when he enlisted in the 2nd Battalion, 158th Field Artillery, 45th Field Artillery Brigade. He was commissioned in 1981 through the Reserve Officer Training Corps program at the University of Oklahoma.

Asher's key assignments have included: chief, Officer Personnel Actions Branch/Detachment; executive officer, Headquarters, State Area Command; commander, 1st Battalion 279th Infantry, 45th Infantry Brigade; deputy commander, 45th Infantry Brigade; and director, Joint Staff, Oklahoma Joint Force Headquarters, Oklahoma National Guard. While serving as the deputy commander for the 45th Infantry Brigade, Asher deployed to Afghanistan in support of Operation Enduring Freedom.

On February 7, 2015, Governor Mary Fallin appointed Asher as the twentieth adjutant general for Oklahoma since statehood, and to the cabinet position of secretary of the military.

The secretary of the military is responsible for the following executive entities or their successors:

Adjutant General, State   Military Department

Secretary of Safety and Security
Michael C. Thompson

3600 Martin Luther King Boulevard, Oklahoma City 73111–4223;
PO Box 11415, Oklahoma City 73136–0415 ▪ 405/425-2424,
FAX 405/419-2050

Michael C. Thompson was appointed secretary of safety and security by Governor Mary Fallin on December 20, 2010. He also serves as commissioner of the Department of Public Safety. As commissioner, Thompson is directly responsible for the Department of Public Safety, which includes the Oklahoma Highway Patrol (OHP). Thompson rose to the rank of major with the OHP before being appointed commissioner by Governor Fallin. Thompson is also a brigadier general in the Oklahoma National Guard, and a decorated combat veteran of two deployments to Iraq in support of Operation Iraqi Freedom. He received a bachelor's degree in criminal justice from Langston University; a master's degree from Oklahoma State University; and a master's degree in strategic studies from the U.S. Army War College. He is a graduate of the 208th Session of the FBI National Academy in Quantico, Virginia.

The secretary of safety and security is responsible for the following executive entities:

Adult Offender Supervision, Oklahoma
State Council for Interstate
Alcohol and Drug Influence Board of Tests
Alcoholic Beverage Laws Enforcement
Attorney General, Oklahoma
Bureau of Investigation Commission,
Oklahoma State, (OSBI), and Oklahoma
State Bureau of Investigation
Bureau of Narcotics and Dangerous Drugs
Control Commission, Oklahoma State,
and Oklahoma State Bureau of Narcotics
and Dangerous Drugs

Chief Medical Examiner, Office of, and
Board of Medicolegal Investigations
Corrections, Department of, and Board of
Corrections
Crime Victims Compensation Board
District Attorney's Council
Domestic Violence Fatality Review Board
Driver's License Compact
Driver's License Medical Advisory
Committee
Emergency Management, Oklahoma
Department of
Homeland Security Director, Office of

Indigent Defense System Board, Appellate
Law Enforcement Education and Training,
  Council on (CLEET), and CLEET
  Advisory Council
Motorcycle Safety and Education,
  Committee for
National Crime Prevention and Privacy
  Compact Council

Nonresident Violator Compact Board
Pardon and Parole Board
Polygraph Examiners Board
Public Safety, Department of
State Fire Marshal Commission, and State
  Fire Marshal, Office of
Statewide Nine-One-One Advisory Board

Secretary of Science and Technology
Dr. Stephen W.S. McKeever

145 Physical Sciences, Oklahoma State University, Stillwater 74078–
1016 ▪ 405/744–4625, FAX 405/744–6811

McKeever is the Oklahoma Secretary for Science and Technology,
and Regents Professor of Physics at Oklahoma State University. He
is the former vice president for Research and Technology Transfer at
Oklahoma State University (2003–2013). As secretary of science and
technology, he serves on the governor's cabinet and is chair of the
Governor's Science and Technology Council and Unmanned Aerial
Systems Advisory Council. He also sits on numerous boards, including
Oklahoma EPSCoR, and the Oklahoma Biosciences Association, and has served on several
national scientific committees. He is also currently the director of the National Energy Solu-
tions Institute at OSU.

He obtained his PhD from the University of Bangor, UK, and after postdoctoral work at the
universities of Birmingham and Sussex in the United Kingdom, he joined the OSU physics
faculty in 1983, attaining the rank of associate professor in 1986 and full professor in 1990.
He was named a Noble Research Fellow in Optical Materials in 1987, served as head of the
Department of Physics from 1995–1999, and as associate dean for research in the College of
Arts & Sciences from 2000–2003. McKeever was named the MOST (More Oklahoma Science
and Technology) Chair of Experimental Physics in 1999.

McKeever's research and technology transfer experience led him to interests and substantial
experience in how best to transition technology from the state's research institutions into
commercial enterprises for the benefit of the local and state economies, and the creation
of innovative and scalable models for technology commercialization and job growth. His
personal research interest involving radiation sensor development has led to new patents
and licenses, and new company formation.

He has authored or co-authored over 200 scientific publications and six books, and has six
United States and nine international patents in the area of radiation detection and measure-
ments, specializing in development and applications of luminescence in radiation dosim-
etry. He is a Fellow of the American Physical Society, a Fellow of the Institute of Physics, a
Fellow of the National Academy of Inventors, and a member of the Health Physics Society.
He has also served as co-editor-in-chief and is presently consulting editor of the journal
Radiation Measurements.

The secretary of science and technology is responsible for the following executive entities:

Center for the Advancement of Science and
  Technology, Oklahoma (OCAST)

Experimental Program to Stimulate
  Competitive Research Advisory
  Committee (EPSCOR)

Science and Technology Council
Science and Technology Research and
   Development Board, Oklahoma

Space Industry Development Authority,
   Oklahoma

Secretary of Transportation
Gary Ridley

3500 Martin Luther King Boulevard, Oklahoma City, 73111–4221 ▪ 405/425–7412, FAX 405/427–8246

Longtime transportation executive Gary Ridley was appointed secretary of transportation by Governor Brad Henry in May 2009 and reappointed by Governor Mary Fallin in November 2010. Ridley has a wealth of knowledge regarding transportion having served as the director of both the Oklahoma Department of Transportation (ODOT), and the Oklahoma Turnpike Authority. Ridley's journey up through the ranks provided him with first-hand insights into the whole spectrum of department operations. His ODOT service began in 1965, when he joined the department as an equipment operator. He has served as maintenance superintendent in Kingfisher; traffic superintendent in Perry as well as field maintenance engineer; and Division Five maintenance engineer and division engineer in Clinton. In 2001 he was named assistant director of operations, and later ODOT director. A native of Chicago, Ridley is a registered professional engineer. He and his wife Eula live in Yukon. They have two children, Daphne and Joe.

The secretary of transportation is responsible for the following executive entities:

Aeronautics Commission
Highway Construction Materials Technician
   Certification Board
Port Authorities
Tourism Signage Advisory Task Force,
   Oklahoma
Transportation Commission, and
   Transportation Department

Transportation County Advisory Board,
   Department of
Transportation Tribal Advisory Board,
   Department of
Turnpike Authority, Oklahoma
Waterways Advisory Board

Secretary of Veterans Affairs
Major General Myles Deering

2311 N Central, Oklahoma City 73105–3200 ▪ 405/521–3684, FAX 405/521–6533

Major General Myles L. Deering serves as the secretary of veterans affairs. He formerly served as secretary of the military and adjutant general under Governor Brad Henry and Governor Mary Fallin. Deering was commissioned in 1976 through the Texas Army National Guard. After his transfer into the Oklahoma Army National Guard, he rose through the ranks to command the 700th Support Battalion and served as director for the Human Resources Directorate as well as the director for the Plans, Operations, and Training Directorate. He served as joint staff director before he assumed command of the 45th Infantry Brigade in December 2004. He commanded the 45th Infantry Brigade during deployments to Hurricane Katrina in 2005 and Operation Iraqi Freedom in 2008. Governor Henry appointed Deering as secretary of the military in February 2009, and Governor Mary Fallin reappointed on December 13, 2010. Fallin appointed Deering as secretary of veterans affairs in February 2015.

The secretary of veterans affairs is responsible for the following executive entities:

Strategic Military Planning Commission, Oklahoma
Veterans Affairs, Department of
Veterans Commission

On April 2, 1913, in an event recalled by the Fort Sill Apache as "the Parting," 180 Apache prisoners of war were relocated from Fort Sill to Mescalero, New Mexico.

LEGISLATIVE BRANCH

The Legislative Service Bureau, Jan Eric Cartwright Memorial Library, and the staffs of the Senate President Pro Tempore and the Speaker of the House provided information in this chapter.

The Oklahoma Legislature

Oklahoma's bicameral legislature is composed of forty-eight members of the Senate and 101 members of the House of Representatives. As of the election in November 2010, there are thirty-two Republicans and sixteen Democrats in the Senate. The House has seventy Republicans and thirty-one Democrats.

The legislature meets annually at noon on the first Monday in February. Its sessions must be finished by 5 PM on the last Friday in May every year. In odd-numbered years, the regular session will also include one day in January—the first Tuesday following the first Monday in January, with recess no later than 5 PM on the same day. Normally, the legislature is in session Monday through Thursday. However, during the last several weeks of a session, either or both houses of the legislature may decide to convene Fridays, depending upon work remaining. Extraordinary sessions may be called by the governor or the legislature.

Each house of the legislature organizes independently to function during the legislative session. By law, the lieutenant governor is president of the Senate. Members of both houses take office fifteen days after the General Election. Senators serve staggered four-year terms. Senators in even-numbered districts were elected in 2010. Those in odd-numbered districts were elected in 2012. Members of the House of Representatives serve two-year terms, and are elected every even-numbered year.

Legislators are paid $38,400 annually and certain necessary expenses. The President Pro Tempore and the Speaker of the House are paid an additional $17,932 annually. The majority floor leader, minority floor leader, appropriations chair in each house, assistant speaker (House), and the assistant majority leader of the Senate are paid an additional $12,364 per year. Salaries are set by the Board of Legislative Compensation.

Each house considers four types of legislation: bills that can become law if passed by both houses and signed by the governor; joint resolutions that have the force and effect of law when passed by both houses, but may not become part of the statutes; concurrent resolutions that expresses the will of both houses; and simple resolutions that express the will of the house of origin. Legislation that originates in the Senate is numbered consecutively beginning with "1" and legislation that originates in the House is numbered consecutively beginning with "1001."

Any member of either house may introduce legislation. Once prepared by the legislative staff, the legislation is introduced (first reading) by being read in the house of origin. The following day the bill is assigned to a committee (second reading) for study in the house of origin. After study by the assigned committee, the bill is printed with any changes made by the committee and considered by the full membership of the house of origin (third reading). The bill is then printed to include any changes made by the house of origin and transmitted to the other house to repeat the same process. When it is again returned to the house of origin, any amendments made by the opposite house are considered, and if agreed to by the house of origin it is printed in its final form and considered for final passage (fourth reading) and transmitted to the governor for consideration. If the house of origin is unable to agree with changes made by the opposite house, a conference committee is appointed with members from both houses to work out differences. The conference committee report goes first to the house of origin and then to the opposite house.

Legislatures are identified by consecutive numbers. For example, the 2013 session was the First Session, 54th Legislature; and the 2014 session, the Second Session, 54th Legislature. The 2015 session is the First Session of the 55th Legislature.

The legislature occupies the third, fourth, and fifth floors of the capitol. The Senate is on the east side of the rotunda and the House of Representatives is on the west side. Joint sessions are held in the House Chambers. Chambers for both houses are on the fourth floor, with visitors' galleries on the fifth.

Members of the legislature may be addressed at the State Capitol, Oklahoma City, 73105. Telephone number for the Senate is: 405/524-0126, website is www.oksenate.gov; for the House of Representatives: 405/521-2711, website is www.okhouse.gov.

Paula George, Senate Staff

Legislative Leadership Offices Contact Information

Senate President Pro Tempore

Senator Brian Bingman
State Capitol Building
2300 N Lincoln Boulevard, Oklahoma City, OK 73105
Telephone: 405/521-5565
E-mail: bingman@oksenate.gov

Speaker of the House of Representatives

Representative Jeffrey Hickman
State Capitol Building
2300 N Lincoln Boulevard, Oklahoma City, OK 73105
Telephone: 405/557-7339
E-mail: jwhickman@okhouse.gov

Legislative Service Bureau

The Legislative Service Bureau is responsible for fiscal services and any area of production of proposed legislation as directed by the Speaker of the House of Representatives and President Pro Tempore of the Senate. The Legislative Service Bureau also serves as a clearinghouse for the legislature for all budgetary forms, research reports and information. The office is located in Room B-30, State Capitol. Telephone 405/521-4144.

Find Your State Legislators and District Maps

www.oklegislature.gov

Oklahoma State Senate

Senate Leadership

President	Lt. Gov. Todd Lamb		Vice Caucus Chair	AJ Griffin
President Pro Tempore	Brian Bingman		Rural Caucus Chair	Ron Justice
Majority Floor Leader	Mike Schulz		Minority Leader	Randy Bass
Assistant Floor Leader	Eddie Fields		Asst. Minority Leader	Kay Floyd
Assistant Floor Leader	Greg Treat		Asst. Minority Leader	Susan Paddack
Majority Whip	Nathan Dahm		Asst. Minority Leader	John Sparks
Majority Whip	Kim David		Asst. Minority Leader	Charles Wyrick
Majority Whip	Frank Simpson		Asst. Minority Leader	Earl Garrison
Majority Whip	Rob Standridge		Min. Whip	Anastasia Pittman
Caucus Chair	Bryce Marlatt			

State Senators by District

This list of senators by district is given as a cross-reference. In the section following, senators' names are arranged in alphabetical order.

Dist.	Name	Dist.	Name	Dist.	Name
1	Charles Wyrick (D)	17	Ron Sharp (R)	33	Nathan Dahm (R)
2	Marty Quinn (R)	18	Kim David (R)	34	Rick Brinkley (R)
3	Wayne Shaw (R)	19	Patrick Anderson (R)	35	Gary Stanislawski (R)
4	Mark Allen (R)	20	A.J. Griffin (R)	36	Bill Brown (R)
5	Joseph Silk (R)	21	Jim Halligan (R)	37	Dan Newberry (R)
6	Josh Brecheen (R)	22	Stephanie Bice (R)	38	Mike Schulz (R)
7	Larry Boggs (R)	23	Ron Justice (R)	39	Brian Crain (R)
8	Roger Thompson (R)	24	Anthony Sykes (R)	40	Ervin Yen (R)
9	Earl Garrison (D)	25	Mike Mazzei (R)	41	Clark Jolley (R)
10	Eddie Fields (R)	26	Darcy Jech (R)	42	Jack Fry (R)
11	Kevin Matthews (D)	27	Bryce Marlatt (R)	43	Corey Brooks (R)
12	Brian Bingman (R)	28	Jason Smalley (R)	44	Ralph Shortey (R)
13	Susan Paddack (D)	29	John Ford (R)	45	Kyle Loveless (R)
14	Frank Simpson (R)	30	David Holt (R)	46	Kay Floyd (D)
15	Rob Standridge (R)	31	Don Barrington (R)	47	Greg Treat (R)
16	John Sparks (D)	32	Randy Bass (D)	48	Anastasia Pittman (D)

Senators Contact Reference List

Due to renovations in the State Capitol, call 405/524-0126 for senators' current room numbers.

Senator	Phone	E-mail
Allen, Mark (4)	405/521-5576	allen@oksenate.gov
Anderson, Patrick (19)	405/521-5630	anderson@oksenate.gov
Barrington, Don (31)	405/521-5563	barrington@oksenate.gov
Bass, Randy (32)	405/521-5567	bass@oksenate.gov
Bice, Stephanie (22)	405/521-5592	bice@oksenate.gov
Bingman, Brian (12)	405/521-5528	bingman@oksenate.gov
Boggs, Larry (7)	405/521-5604	boggs@okenate.gov
Brecheen, Josh (6)	405/521-5586	brecheen@oksenate.gov
Brinkley, Rick (34)	405/521-5566	brinkley@oksenate.gov
Brooks, Corey (43)	405/521-5522	brooks@oksenate.gov
Brown, Bill (36)	405/521-5602	brownb@oksenate.gov
Crain, Brian A. (39)	405/521-5620	crain@oksenate.gov
Dahm, Nathan (33)	405/521-5551	dahm@oksenate.gov
David, Kim (18)	405/521-5590	david@oksenate.gov
Fields, Eddie (10)	405/521-5581	efields@oksenate.gov
Floyd, Kay (46)	405/521-5610	floyd@oksenate.gov
Ford, John W. (29)	405/521-5634	fordj@oksenate.gov
Fry, Jack (42)	405/521-5584	fry@oksenate.gov
Garrison, Earl (9)	405/521-5533	whitep@oksenate.gov
Griffin, A.J. (20)	405/521-5628	griffin@oksenate.gov
Halligan, Jim (21)	405/521-5572	halligan@oksenate.gov
Holt, David (30)	405/521-5636	holt@oksenate.gov
Jech, Darcy (26)	405/521-5545	jech@oksenate.gov
Jolley, Clark (41)	405/521-5622	jolley@oksenate.gov
Justice, Ron (23)	405/521-5537	justice@oksenate.gov
Loveless, Kyle (45)	405/521-5618	loveless@oksenate.gov
Marlatt, Bryce (27)	405/521-5626	marlatt@oksenate.gov
Matthews, Kevin (11)	405/521-5598	matthews@oksenate.gov
Mazzei, Mike (25)	405/521-5675	mazzei@oksenate.gov
Newberry, Dan (37)	405/521-5600	newberry@oksenate.gov
Paddack, Susan (13)	405/521-5541	paddack@oksenate.gov
Pittman, Anastasia (48)	405/521-5531	pittman@oksenate.gov
Quinn, Marty (2)	405/521-5555	quinn@oksenate.gov
Schulz, Mike (38)	405/521-5612	schulz@oksenate.gov
Sharp, Ron (17)	405/521-5539	sharp@oksenate.gov
Shaw, Wayne (3)	405/521-5574	shaw@oksenate.gov
Shortey, Ralph (44)	405/521-5557	shortey@oksenate.gov
Silk, Joseph (5)	405/521-5614	silk@oksenate.gov
Simpson, Frank (14)	405/521-5607	simpson@oksenate.gov
Smalley, Jason	405/521-5547	smalley@oksenate.gov
Sparks, John (16)	405/521-5553	sparks@oksenate.gov
Standridge, Rob (15)	405/521-5535	standridge@oksenate.gov
Stanislawski, Gary (35)	405/521-5624	stanislawski@oksenate.gov
Sykes, Anthony (24)	405/521-5569	lewis@oksenate.gov
Thompson, Roger (8)	405/521-5588	thompson@oksenate.gov
Treat, Greg (47)	405/521-5632	treat@oksenate.gov
Yen, Ervin (40)	405/521-5543	yen@oksenate.gov
Wyrick, Charles (1)	405/521-5561	wyrick@oksenate.gov

President Pro Tempore of the Senate

Brian Bingman

Occupation—Oil and Gas ▪ **Education**—University of Oklahoma, BBA ▪ **Party**—Republican ▪ **District**—12 ▪ **Legislative Experience**—Oklahoma House of Representatives, 2004–2006; Senate Member, 2007–present; Assistant Floor Leader, 2009; Senate Pro Tempore, 2010–present ▪ **Committee Membership**—As President Pro Tempore of the Senate, Bingmam serves as an Ex-Officio Voting Member of all Senate Committees

Bingman was born in Tulsa, Oklahoma. He received a bachelor's degree in petroleum land management from the University of Oklahoma. He is currently employed by Uplands Resources in Tulsa as vice-president of land operations. Bingman served as mayor of Sapulpa from 1994 to 2004, and served in the Oklahoma House of Representatives, District 30, from 2004 to 2006. He was elected to the Oklahoma Senate in November 2006 from Senate District 12, which represents Creek and Tulsa counties. On January 4, 2010, Bingman was elected President Pro Tempore of the Oklahoma Senate. Before becoming Pro Tem of the Senate, he served as an assistant majority floor leader, chairman of the Energy and Environment Committee and vice chairman of the Appropriations Subcommittee on General Government. He and his wife, Paula, have three children; Annie, Blake, and Rebecca. He is an active member of the First Presbyterian Church of Sapulpa. Bingman was a past chairman of the Energy Council, and the Oklahoma Independent Producers Association. He is also a member of the Sapulpa Chamber of Commerce. His hobbies include playing golf, working on and around his house, and most of all spending time with his family and his four grandchildren; Blake, Merrit, Ellie, and Madilyn.

To contact Bingman—2300 N Lincoln Blvd., Oklahoma City, OK 73105 ▪ 405/521-5528 ▪ bingman@oksenate.gov

Membership

Mark Allen

Occupation—Legislature ▪ **Party**—Republican ▪ **District**—4 ▪ **Legislative Experience**—Senate Member, 2011 ▪ **Committee Membership**—Agriculture and Rural Development, Chair; Appropriations; Appropriations Subcommittee on Natural Resources; Energy; Tourism and Wildlife; Rules, Vice Chair.

Allen won election to the Oklahoma Senate from District 4, which is comprised of Sequoyah County and the northern half of LeFlore County, on November 2, 2010. He was reelected November 4, 2014.

Allen was born and raised in Enid, Oklahoma, and moved to Wilburton, in 1962. In 1963 Allen's father started Allen Rathole. He worked side by side with his father in the business until he and a partner bought the business from his father in 1989. Allen and his wife, Nikki, continue to own and operate Allen Rathole today.

Allen is a graduate of Wilburton High School and served in the U.S. Navy Seabees as a heavy equipment operator from 1968 to 1970. Except for the time spent serving his country, he has always lived in southeastern Oklahoma. He knows rural values and works to ensure that we preserve our close-knit communities and agricultural heritage. Allen is a firm believer in God and country and the U.S. Constitution America was built on, and praises the men and women who defend it.

A staunch conservative, Allen is concerned about safeguarding traditional values, keeping our families and communities strong and ensuring that our natural resources benefit Oklahomans and create jobs in this state. A Lifetime National Rifle Association member, Allen stands strong for Second Amendment rights. His other affiliations include Pajaro Gun Club Board of Directors, National Sporting Clays Association, Ducks Unlimited sponsor, life member of the American Quarter Horse Association, Spiro Chamber of Commerce, U.S. Chamber of Commerce, Better Business Bureau, National Federation of Independent Business, and Oklahoma Independent Petroleum Association. Allen and his wife have been married 18 years. They are members of the Victory Worship Center in Spiro, Oklahoma.

To contact Allen—2300 N Lincoln Blvd., Oklahoma City, OK 73105 ▪ 405/521-5576 ▪ allen@oksenate.gov

Patrick Anderson

Occupation—Attorney/Banker/Farmer ▪ **Education**— Oklahoma State University, BS; University of Oklahoma, JD ▪ **Party**—Republican ▪ **District**—19 ▪ **Legislative Experience**— Senate Member, 2005–present ▪ **Committee Membership**— Appropriations; Appropriations Subcommittee on Natural Resources and Regulatory Services; Pensions; Tourism and Wildlife; and Veterans and Military Affairs, Vice Chair

Anderson was born and raised in Enid, Oklahoma. He holds a bachelor's degree from Oklahoma State University and a Juris Doctor degree from the University of Oklahoma. Anderson won election to the Oklahoma Senate from District 19 in 2004. He represents District 19 that includes Alfalfa, Garfield, Grant, and Kay counties. He is employed as a vice president at Central National Bank & Trust Company of Enid. He also farms in Garfield County. Anderson and his wife, Kelly, live in Enid, with their two daughters.

To contact Anderson—2016 Comanche Trail, Enid, OK 73703 ▪ 405/521-5630 ▪ anderson@oksenate.gov

Don Barrington

Occupation—Fire Chief/Retired ▪ **Education**—AS ▪ **Party**— Republican ▪ **District**—31 ▪ **Legislative Experience**—Senate Member, 2005–present ▪ **Committee Membership**—Agriculture and Rural Development; Appropriations; Appropriations Subcommittee on Public Safety and Judiciary; Public Safety and Homeland Security, Chair; and Transportation

Barrington was born on September 7, 1947, in Pryor, Oklahoma. He graduated from Rexford High School in Rexford, Kansas, in 1965. He served in the United States Army from 1966 to 1969. He spent an eighteen-month tour in Vietnam, where he received an Army Commendation Medal. Barrington began his professional career as a rookie with the Lawton Fire Department in 1969. During his thirty-two year tenure, he spent twenty-six years on shift at the fire station. He advanced through testing to the levels of driver, lieutenant, and captain, and was then promoted to deputy chief. He received an associate degree in engineering technology from Oklahoma State University–Oklahoma City in 1993. He was appointed as Lawton Fire Chief in 1996, and served in that position until his retirement in 2002. Barrington won election to the Oklahoma Senate from District 31 in 2004. He married the former Jennifer Morgan. They have two children, Alicia and Jaron. Barrington continues active participation in the Lawton Salvation Army Advisory Board, Gideon's International Lawton Chapter, Oklahoma Firefighters Association, Oklahoma State Firefighters Association, and the Oklahoma Retired Firefighters Association. He also serves as co-chair of the Steering Committee for Law Enforcement and Public Safety through the Great Plains Technology Center.

To contact Barrington—2300 N Lincoln Blvd., Oklahoma City, OK 73105
▪ 405/521-5563 ▪ barrington@oksenate.gov

Randy Bass

Occupation—Cattle Rancher and Wheat Farmer ▪ **Education**—Lawton High School; Cameron University ▪ **Party**—Democrat ▪ **District**—32 ▪ **Legislative Experience**—Senate Member, 2005–present; Minority Leader, 2015 ▪ **Committee Membership**—Appropriations; Appropriations Subcommittee on General Government and Transportation; Insurance; Pensions; Tourism and Wildlife; and Transportation

Bass was born on March 13, 1954, in Lawton, Oklahoma. In 1972 the Minnesota Twins drafted Bass, and he spent several years playing major league baseball for the Kansas City Royals, Montreal Expos, San Diego Padres, and the Texas Rangers. From 1983 to 1988 he played first base and power hitter for the Hanshin Tigers, a Japanese baseball team. Considered a baseball legend in Japan, Bass set the all-time season batting average of .389 in 1986. He is the only player to win back-to-back Triple Crowns, and hit 200 home runs faster than anyone in baseball history. Governor George Nigh appointed Bass ambassador to Japan in 1986. Bass has two children from a former marriage, Zach and Staci. He and his wife, Kelley, have one daughter, Remi. He has four grandchildren. Bass recently served as councilman for the City of Lawton from 2001 to 2004. He won election to the Oklahoma Senate from District 32 in November 2004. He continues active participation in the Lawton Ambucs, Major League Baseball Association, and the Oklahoma Municipal League. His hobbies include golf and spending time with his family.

To contact Bass—2300 N Lincoln Blvd., Oklahoma City, OK 73105 ▪ 405/521-5567
▪ bass@oksenate.gov

Stephanie Bice

Occupation—Vice President of Business Development, Smirk New Media ▪ **Education**—Oklahoma State University ▪ **Party**—Republican ▪ **District**—22 ▪ **Legislative Experience**—Senate Member, 2015 ▪ **Committee Membership**—Appropriations; Appropriations Subcommittee on Select Agencies; Business and Commerce, Vice Chair; General Government; and Transportation

Bice won election to the Oklahoma Senate in November 2014. She represents District 22 that comprises northern Oklahoma County and eastern Canadian County, including parts of Edmond, Deer Creek, Piedmont, and Yukon. Bice is a fourth generation Oklahoman, and graduated from Putnam City High School in Oklahoma City. She earned a bachelor's degree in marketing with a minor in international business from Oklahoma State University.

Bice is a vice president of business development at Smirk New Media, a digital marketing agency, located in downtown Oklahoma City. Prior to her employment at Smirk, Bice worked for eight years for her family's technology company in a variety of capacities, including financial oversight, business strategy, and marketing.

Bice has served on the Oklahoma City Chapter of American Marketing Association Executive Board, as well as School Advisory Board member and chair of the Pastoral Board for St. Eugene Catholic Church and School.

Bice is keenly aware of the challenges small business owners face as they strive to grow their companies, and is committed to ensuring no undue burdens are placed on Oklahoma small business owners. Bice, and her husband, Geoffrey, were married in 1996, and are members of St. Eugene Catholic Church in Oklahoma City. They have two daughters.

To contact Bice write to 2300 N Lincoln Blvd., Room 531, Oklahoma City, OK 73105 ▪ 405/521–5592 ▪ bice@oksenate.gov

Larry Boggs

Occupation—Conservationist, Cattle Rancher ▪ **Party**—Republican ▪ **District**—7 ▪ **Legislative Experience**—Senate Member, 2013 ▪ **Committee Membership**—Agriculture and Rural Development; Appropriations; Appropriations Subcommittee on General Government and Transportation; Tourism and Wildlife, Vice Chair; and Veterans and Military Affairs

Born in southeastern Oklahoma to hard working Christian parents, Boggs worked as a general contractor during his early career. He and his wife, Karla, operate Rockland at Eagles Rest, and founded Eagles Rest Sanctuary, a corporation centered on protecting and providing for the nesting American bald eagle on land once owned by Karla's family. He and his wife also run a cattle operation and raise horses. Boggs was elected to the Oklahoma Senate on November 6, 2012 from District 7.

To contact Boggs write to 2300 N Lincoln Blvd., Oklahoma City, OK 73105 ▪ 405/521–5604 ▪ boggs@oksenate.gov

Josh Brecheen

Occupation—Motivational Speaker ▪ **Education**—Oklahoma State University ▪ **Party**—Republican ▪ **District**—6 ▪ **Legislative Experience**—Senate Member, 2011; ▪ **Committee Membership**—Appropriations; Appropriations Subcommittee on Public Safety and Judiciary; Education; Public Safety; and Tourism and Wildlife, Chair

Brecheen was elected to the Oklahoma Senate in November 2010. He represents District 6, consisting of Atoka, Coal, Bryan, Johnston, and Marshall counties. Brecheen earned a dual degree in agricultural communications and animal science from Oklahoma State University. Prior to his election to the Oklahoma Legislature, he served almost six years as a field representative for United States Senator Tom Coburn, M.D. As a field representative, Brecheen was one of Senator Coburn's "boots on the ground," working directly with constituents on issues, and evaluating government programs for waste, fraud, and abuse. Brecheen owns a motivational speaking business, Brecheen Keynotes and Seminars. Since the inception of the business, he has provided inspirational presentations to over 600,000 people in more than 600 school systems, conferences, and universities in many states. A committed Christian, Brecheen is married to Kacie Ann Brecheen and has two small step children, Micah and Makayla. Additionally, the couple's third child, Colt Justice was born on October 20, 2010. The family resides in Coal County.

To contact Brecheen—2300 N Lincoln Blvd., Oklahoma City, OK 73105 ▪ 405/521-5586 ▪ brecheen@oksenate.gov

Rick Brinkley

Occupation—Legislator ▪ **Education**—Langston University; Oral Roberts University; and Oklahoma State University ▪ **Party**—Republican ▪ **District**—34 ▪ **Legislative Experience**— Senate Member, 2011-present; Majority Whip, 2013-2014 ▪ **Committee Membership**—Appropriations; Appropriations Subcommittee on General Government and Transportation; Energy; and Rules

Brinkley was elected to the Oklahoma State Senate in November 2010 and brings a broad range of business and consumer experience to the legislature. He has served as a leader of the Better Business Bureau serving Eastern Oklahoma from 1999 to 2015, and in 2008 was honored with the BBB's National Meritorious Service Award in recognition of his "Call to Excellence." In addition, he served as a member of the board of directors of the National Council of Better Business Bureaus for six years as well as on its executive and strategic planning committees. Brinkley's priorities in the senate are to allow the economy to grow itself through making Oklahoma "job friendly" and to protect the core conservative values of District 34. He believes there are very few problems facing our state that cannot be solved through successful job growth. Professionally, for over ten years, Brinkley served as pastor of the Community Church in Collinsville. Brinkley also worked as a television producer, investigative producer, writer, and on-air personality. His work in television culminated with a National Emmy Award nomination. In addition, he serves as a leader in communications and personal impact for corporations, non-profits, and educators. Brinkley was the first person on either side of his family to attend college and is a graduate of both Langston University and Oral Roberts University's School of Theology and Missions, and has completed some doctoral work at Oklahoma State University's College of Education. He is an active member of First Christian Church in Owasso and serves on the associate board of Oasis Adult Day Care Facility, and the board of directors of the Petroleum Club of Tulsa. He is the former president of the Kiwanis Club. Brinkley is a supportive "Peepaw" for his grandson's soccer team, '98 Sheffield Eagles FC. However, his greatest achievements are his son John and his grandson Christian.

To contact Brinkley—2300 N Lincoln Blvd., Oklahoma City, OK 73105 ▪ 405/521-5566 ▪ brinkley@oksenate.gov

Corey Brooks

Occupation—Rancher ▪ **Education**—Oklahoma Baptist University, BA; US Naval War College, MA ▪ **Party**—Republican ▪ **District**—43 ▪ **Legislative Experience**—Senate Member, 2013 ▪ **Committee Membership**—Appropriations; Appropriations Subcommittee on Public Safety and Judiciary; General Government; Judiciary; and Public Safety, Vice Chair

A Washington, Oklahoma, native, Brooks won election to the Oklahoma Senate on November 6, 2012, from District 43 He received a bachelor's degree (summa cum laude, with honors) in political science and foreign missions from Oklahoma Baptist University. He also earned a master's degree in national security and strategic studies (with distinction) from the U.S. Naval War College. Following his undergraduate education, Brooks began his career in the White House of President George W. Bush, serving in the Executive Office of the President. Bush appointed him to serve as a special assistant to the secretary of defense in the Pentagon. Brooks served in this role for over six years with duties including political advisement, Congressional and interdepartmental liaison, special projects and policy development covering areas such as defense strategy, the US global military footprint, Base Realignment and Closure (BRAC), energy independence and security, privatization, and budget development. At the close of the Bush administration, Brooks transitioned to the active component of the United States Navy. As a naval officer, Lieutenant Brooks worked on the secretary of the navy's staff as a military assistant and flag aide, followed by a tour as the secretary's deputy branch chief for Special Operations/Irregular Warfare Support. He also spent time at sea on the USS Blue Ridge out of Yokosuka, Japan; worked as a team lead in the Office of Naval Intelligence; and attended various Navy schools and exercises across the globe. Brooks culminated his active duty service with a year-long combat tour in Afghanistan, serving as the officer-in-charge of the forward-deployed Afghan Threat Finance Cell (ATFC) with responsibility for operations in the remote provinces of Khost and Paktiya. Brooks led a joint team charged with identifying and disrupting terrorist and insurgent networks by way of their funding/financing operations, both on the battlefield and around the globe. Throughout his career, Brooks has also worked for the Heritage Foundation; the Oklahoma County District Attorney's Office; as a deputy sheriff in McClain County, Oklahoma; and was appointed by Governor Frank Keating to serve on the State Advisory Group for Juvenile Justice and Delinquency Prevention. Brooks is very active in his local church and community. He attends the First Baptist Church of Washington, Oklahoma. He has served as a deacon, lay youth minister, committee chair, and Sunday school teacher. He is a member of the American Legion and VFW, a former OK Boys' State chief of staff, a pilot, scuba diver and sky diver.

To contact Brooks—2300 N Lincoln Blvd., Oklahoma City, OK 73105 ▪ 405/521–5522 ▪ brooks@oksenate.gov

Bill Brown

Occupation—Insurance ▪ **Education**—Northeastern State University ▪ **Party**—Republican ▪ **District**—36 ▪ **Legislative Experience**—Senate Member, 2007-present ▪ **Committee Membership**—Appropriations; Appropriations Subcommittee on Public Safety and Judiciary; Insurance, Chair; Pensions; and Tourism and Wildlife

Brown was born and raised in Henryetta, Oklahoma. He attended Northeastern State University, where he received a bachelor's degree in education. He taught school for four years, before going into the insurance business. Brown served as president of the Broken Arrow Rotary Club, and was president of Gatesway Foundation, an organization that helps the mentally and physically disabled. He is married to Linda Brown, a longtime teacher at Park Lane Elementary School. They have four children and nine grandchildren.

To contact Brown—2300 N Lincoln Blvd., Oklahoma City, OK 73105 ▪ 405/521–5602 ▪ brownb@oksenate.gov

Brian A. Crain

Occupation—Attorney ▪ **Education**—University of Oklahoma, BBA; University of Tulsa, JD; and University of Oklahoma, MPA ▪ **Party**—Republican ▪ **District**—39 ▪ **Legislative Experience**—Senate Member, 2005-present ▪ **Committee Membership**—Appropriations; Appropriations Subcommittee on Health and Human Services; Energy; Health and Human Services; and Judiciary, Vice Chair

Crain was born at Andrews Air Force Base, Maryland, and moved to Oklahoma City, at the age of three. He graduated from Putnam City West Senior High School in 1979, and received a bachelor's degree in management from the University of Oklahoma in 1983. Crain worked for a national distributor for electrical and electronic wiring for twelve years, living throughout the southern and mid-Atlantic states before moving to Tulsa in 1987. Crain remained in Tulsa, and graduated from the University of Tulsa Law School in 1991. In 2014 he graduated from the University of Oklahoma with a master's degree in public administration.

Crain became an assistant district attorney in 1996, and in 1999, he left to pursue a law practice focusing primarily on title and real property law. He now belongs to Hanson and Holmes PLC. He is currently pursuing a master of public administration degree at the University of Oklahoma. Crain and his wife, Lori, have two daughters, Sarah and Catherine. He continues active participation in Leadership Tulsa, Masonic Lodge, Tulsa County Bar Association, Tulsa Lawyers Helping Children, Tulsa Hispanic Chamber of Commerce,

Tulsa Title and Probate Lawyers, and is a lifetime member of the Tulsa Hispanic Chamber of Commerce. Crain first won election to the Oklahoma Senate from District 39 in 2004.

To contact Crain—2300 N Lincoln Blvd., Room 417-B, Oklahoma City, OK 74105 ▪ 405/521-5620 ▪ crain@oksenate.gov

Nathan Dahm

Occupation—Business Owner ▪ **Party**—Republican ▪ **District**—33 ▪ **Legislative Experience**—Senate Member, 2013; Majority Whip, 2015 ▪ **Committee Membership**—Appropriations; Appropriations Subcommittee on Select Agencies; Business and Commerce; Finance; General Government, Chair; and Rules

Dahm spent his childhood years in Broken Arrow, Oklahoma, while his parents attended Bible school. In 1994 he moved with his family to Romania, serving as missionaries to the former communist nation. Upon graduating from high school, Dahm returned to Romania to work as a missionary. While there, he actively served in each department of his local church and designed and served as general manager of the 65-acre Bible school campus that was built a few miles outside Romania's capital city of Bucharest. In 2003 Dahm became the dean of students for the school's charter class. He served in that position for four years, when he returned to Broken Arrow. Upon his return to Oklahoma, Dahm became active in politics, serving on the executive committee of the Tulsa County Republican Party; as a precinct chair and vice chair; and as president of the Tulsa Area Republican Assembly. He has been employed as an engineering technician for a local municipality and as producer for a local production company. He currently manages the daily operations of his family-owned cleaning company, as well as being self-employed with a smartphone/tablet application development company. Dahm won election to the Oklahoma Senate from District 33 on November 6, 2012.

To contact Dahm—2300 N Lincoln Blvd., Oklahoma City, OK 73105 ▪ 405/521-5551 ▪ dahm@oksenate.gov

Kim David

Occupation—Owner, Sweetgum Properties, Inc. ▪ **Education**—Oklahoma State University, BS ▪ **Party**—Republican ▪ **District**—18 ▪ **Legislative Experience**—Senate Member, 2011-present; Majority Whip, 2013-present ▪ **Committee Membership**—Appropriations; Appropriations Subcommittee on Health and Human Services, Chair; Finance; Health and Human Services; Public Safety; and Rules

Senator Kim David is proud to represent Senate District 18, serving portions of Cherokee, Mayes, Muskogee, Tulsa and Wagoner counties. She has the distinction of serving as majority whip and is the first Republican woman to hold that post. David currently serves as chair of the Appropriations Subcommittee on Health and Human Services. She is also a member of the full Appropriations Committee, and also serves on the Finance, Health and Human Services, Public Safety and Rules committees. In addition to her Senate committees, David serves as chair of the Grand River Dam Authority Legislative Task Force and vice chair of the Governor's Impaired Driving Prevention Advisory Council.

A native of Oklahoma, David is an experienced businesswoman and entrepreneur, as well as a wife, and mother of a United States Air Force officer and a Marine.

David was born in Tulsa, Oklahoma, and grew up in Owasso where she graduated high school in 1979. In 1984 Kim graduated from Oklahoma State University with a degree in geology and a minor in geography. She worked in petroleum marketing for ten years before making the decision to stay home and raise her two children. When her children were school-age, she received her alternative teaching certification so she could work at their school. In 1999, Kim formed her own properties company which she still owns and operates.

To contact David—2300 N Lincoln Blvd., Oklahoma City, OK 73105 ▪ 405/521–5590 ▪ david@oksenate.gov

Eddie Fields

Occupation—Agri-Business ▪ **Education**—Oklahoma State University, BS ▪ **Party**—Republican ▪ **District**—10 ▪ **Legislative Experience**—Senate Member, 2011–present; Assistant Majority Floor Leader, 2015 ▪ **Committee Membership**—Agriculture and Rural Development, Chair; Appropriations; Appropriations Subcommittee on Natural Resources; Energy; Rules, Vice Chair; and Tourism and Wildlife

After serving two years in the Oklahoma House of Representatives in House District 36, representing Osage and Tulsa counties, Fields was encouraged to run for the Oklahoma Senate by friends, family, and mentors. He won election to the Oklahoma Senate on November 2, 2010 by voters of District 10. Fields served the citizens of Osage and Pawnee counties and portions of Kay, Payne, and Tulsa counties. After redistricting two years ago, District 10 now serves Osage and Kay counties.

Fields currently serves the Oklahoma Senate as assistant majority floor leader; chair of the Agriculture and Rural Development Committee; and vice chair of the Rules Committee. He also serves as a member of the Appropriations Committee; Energy Committee; and Tourism and Wildlife Committee. He was recently selected to serve as 2nd vice president of the national Board of State Agriculture and Rural Leaders (SARL)

Fields was born January 21, 1967, in Monterey, California, to Dennis and Jan Fields, where his father was stationed with the National Guard at Fort Ord. He graduated from Wynona High School in Wynona, Oklahoma, in 1985 and earned a Bachelor of Science degree in agri-business from Oklahoma State University in 1990. Fields married Christina (Guthrie) Fields on May 12, 1990, in Vici, Oklahoma. They have made their home in northeastern Oklahoma for over twenty-five years, and have three daughters—Tailor, Jacie, and Tristan. Christina is a fourth grade teacher at Cleveland Public Schools, and has served Oklahoma's public school system for twenty years. They are members of the First Baptist Church of Wynona.

To contact Fields—2300 N Lincoln Blvd., Oklahoma City, OK 73105 ▪ 405/521–5581 ▪ efields@oksenate.gov

Kay Floyd

Occupation—Administrative Law Judge ▪ **Education**—
Oklahoma State University, BS; University of Oklahoma School
of Law, JD ▪ **Party**—Democrat ▪ **District**—46 ▪ **Legislative
Experience**—Senate Member, 2015; Assistant Minority
Leader, 2015 ▪ **Committee Membership**—Appropriations;
Appropriations Subcommittee on Education; General
Government; Health and Human Services; Judiciary; and Rules

Floyd graduated from Oklahoma State University in 1980 with a Bachelor of Science degree
in psychology, a minor degree in political science, and a minor degree in philosophy. After
graduating from OSU, she attended law school at the University of Oklahoma where she
received her Juris Doctor degree in May 1983 at the age of twenty-four.

After two years in private practice, Floyd became an assistant attorney general for the State
of Oklahoma working in both the civil and criminal divisions. During the development
of Oklahoma's equine industry in 1987, Floyd became deputy executive director for the
Oklahoma Horse Racing Commission. In 1989 Floyd was appointed as an administrative
law judge for the State of Oklahoma and served in that capacity for twenty-two years.
Her appointment made her one of the youngest women in Oklahoma history to receive
a judicial appointment. During that time she also served as a special municipal court
judge for the City of Oklahoma City.

Along with her judicial duties, Floyd has been an adjunct professor at Oklahoma State
University, and an attorney for the senior citizens division of Legal Aid of Western
Oklahoma. Floyd has worked as a volunteer on the Citizens Action Committee for the
Oklahoma City Animal Shelter and is also a member of the Oklahoma Bar Association's
Women in Law committee, Legislative Monitoring committee, and Government and
Administrative Law Practice committee.

Floyd is a founding member and vice president of the Justice Alma Wilson SeeWorth
Academy Board of Directors, which was established in 1998 and which currently serves
485 at-risk youth in the Oklahoma City community. She has served on the OKC AIDS Walk
Board of Directors and is currently a member of the Lyric Theatre Board of Directors in
Oklahoma City.

Floyd won election to the Oklahoma House of Representatives in 2012 where she focused
on improving our education system and working for Oklahoma's women and children.
She authored bills to provide suicide prevention assistance in Oklahoma's schools, curb
domestic violence and study its correlation with poverty, and worked to provide measures
to analyze the frivolous costs of the Legislature considering and approving unconstitutional
legislation. Floyd won election to the Oklahoma Senate in 2014 from District 46. As senator,
she plans to continue her work and service to the people of Oklahoma.

To contact Floyd—2300 N Lincoln Blvd., Room 522 A, Oklahoma City, OK 73105
▪ 405/521–5610 ▪ floyd@oksenate.gov

John W. Ford

Occupation—ConocoPhillips/Retired ■ **Education**—University of Tulsa, BS ■ **Party**—Republican ■ **District**—29 ■ **Legislative Experience**—Senate Member, 2005–present; Caucus Chair, 2009; Assistant Majority Floor Leader, 2011–present ■ **Committee Membership**—Appropriations; Appropriations Subcommittee on Education; Education, Chair; Finance; and Public Safety

Ford was elected to the Oklahoma Senate from District 29 in November, 2004, and re-elected without opposition in 2008 and 2012. Prior to his election to the senate, Ford had a thirty-four-year career with Phillips Petroleum Company. Ford has a business degree from the University of Tulsa. He has lived, worked, and worshiped in the area for over forty years. He is involved in various community organizations and city and chamber committees. He is a founding member and past president of both the Bartlesville Area Friends of the Parks and the Daybreak Rotary Club. His priority issues are education, tort reform, workers' compensation, and Highway 60 from Ponca City to Vinita. Ford has distinguished himself as a strong advocate for Oklahoma's children and for excellence in education. The Oklahoma Institute for Child Advocacy has listed him as having earned an "A" voting record on children's issues. He also annually visits local classrooms as part of the "Legislators Back to School Program," which is a bipartisan national program to give children the opportunity to get to know their elected officials. In addition, the Oklahoma Youth Services Association recognized Ford by presenting him the "2008 Youth Advocate Award." He has been honored with the "Legislator of the Year" award by the Oklahoma Association for Home Care. He also earned one of the highest scores possible in the "Legislative Report on Aging Issues" published by the Oklahoma Aging Partnership (OAP). He currently serves as assistant majority floor leader. Ford and his wife, Mary, reside in Bartlesville, Oklahoma, and attend the Good Shepherd Presbyterian Church. They have two married children and four grandchildren.

To contact Ford—2300 N Lincoln Blvd., Oklahoma City, OK 73105 ■ 405/521–5634 ■ fordj@oksenate.gov

Jack Fry

Occupation—State Senator ■ **Party**—Republican ■ **District**—42 ■ **Legislative Experience**—Senate Member, 2015 ■ **Committee Membership**—Appropriations; Appropriations Subcommittee on General Government and Transportation; General Government, Vice Chair; Transportation; and Veterans and Military Affairs

Fry served in the United States Air Force Reserves from 1970 to 2004. He started a small business in 1978 as the owner of Fry Electric and still owns and operates Custom Homes by Jack Fry. He also worked for Oklahoma Gas and Electric from September 1971 through April 1984. He worked for the Midwest City Fire Department from April 1984 through July 2009 where, as a firefighter, he was a captain and assistant chief-training officer. Fry served as the mayor of Midwest City from May 2010 through November 11, 2014. He won election to the Oklahoma Senate from District 42 in November 2014. Fry is currently the vice chair of the General Government Committee. He also serves on the Transportation Committee, Veterans and Military Affairs, General Government and Transportation Appropriations subcommittees.

Public service to his community is very important to Fry, and he has served on numerous committees and boards. Fry and his wife, Gail, have been married forty-three years. Their son Shane and wife, Brittney, have four children. Their daughter, Jamie, died in 1991 at age fifteen in an automobile accident. The Fry's are active members at Country Estates Baptist Church.

To contact Fry—2300 N Lincoln Blvd., Oklahoma City, OK 73105 ▪ 405/521-5584 ▪ fry@oksenate.gov

Earl Garrison

Occupation—Retired Educator/Rancher ▪ **Education**—University of Oklahoma, EdD ▪ **Party**—Democrat ▪ **District**—9 ▪ **Legislative Experience**—Senate Member, 2005-present; Minority Whip, 2011-2014; Assistant Minority Floor Leader, 2015 ▪ **Committee Membership**—Appropriations; Appropriations Subcommittee on Health and Human Services; Education; Rules; Tourism and Wildlife; and Veterans and Military Affairs

Garrison was born on May 24, 1941, in Muskogee, Oklahoma. He holds a doctorate degree in education from the University of Oklahoma. He has been employed as a teacher and coach in the Mid-Del School System, a professor and coach at Rose State College, regional accreditation officer with the State Department of Education, and as superintendent of the Fort Gibson School System and the Indian Capital Career Tech. Garrison won election to the Oklahoma Senate from District 9 in 2004. He is a 32nd Degree Mason and a Shriner. He attends the First Baptist Church in Muskogee.

To contact Garrison—3806 Club View Drive, Muskogee, OK 74403 ▪ 918/781-0612 ▪ whitep@oksenate.gov

A.J. Griffin

Occupation—Not-for-Profit Agency Executive ▪ **Education**—Oklahoma State University, BS; University of Central Oklahoma, MS ▪ **Party**—Republican ▪ **District**—20 ▪ **Legislative Experience**—Senate Member, 2013; Majority Caucus Vice Chair, 2013-present ▪ **Committee Membership**—Appropriations; Appropriations Subcommittee on Health and Human Services, Vice Chair; Energy, Vice Chair; Health and Human Services; Judiciary; and Rules

Griffin graduated from Adair High School. She holds a bachelor's degree in hotel and restaurant administration from Oklahoma State University, and a master's degree in human environmental science from the University of Central Oklahoma. While attending OSU, she had the honor of participating in the Cowboy Marching Band as a drum major. Griffin began her professional career in the restaurant industry. She then spent several years as a family and consumer sciences teacher and hospitality careers instructor. Griffin has spent the last eight years managing not-for-profit businesses dedicated to improving the lives of children and families. Griffin has served as a board member for the Oklahoma Association of Youth Services, Oklahoma Substance Abuse Service Alliance, Oklahoma Child Abuse Training and Coordination Council, the Logan County United Way, the Guthrie Rotary Club, and the Guthrie Chamber of Commerce. She won election to the Oklahoma Senate from District 20 on November 6, 2012. She and her husband, Trey, serve as deacons for First Christian Church in Guthrie. They have two children, Alexandra and Reagan.

To contact Griffin write—2300 N Lincoln Blvd., Oklahoma City, OK 73105
■ 405/521-5628 ■ griffin@oksenate.gov

Jim Halligan

Occupation—University Educator ■ **Education**—Iowa State University, BS, MS, PhD ■ **Party**—Republican ■ **District**—21 ■ **Legislative Experience**—Senate Member, 2009 ■ **Committee Membership**—Appropriations; Appropriations Subcommittee on Education, Chair; Business and Commerce; Education; and Finance

Halligan received undergraduate and graduate degrees as well as a doctorate degree in chemical engineering from Iowa State University. His teaching, research, and administrative positions have taken him to Arkansas, Texas Tech, and New Mexico State University, where he served as president for ten years before coming to Oklahoma State University (OSU). Halligan joined OSU as its sixteenth president on August 1, 1994. As chief executive officer of the Oklahoma State University system and president of OSU, he was responsible for OSU campuses in Oklahoma City, Okmulgee, Stillwater, and Tulsa as well as the school's health sciences center and medical school. At OSU Halligan emphasized student success, increasing retention and graduation rates, encouraging the development of national scholars, and investing more than $200 million in facilities. Those financial investments include a Center for Services to Students, a student leadership complex, multi-media classrooms, and suite-style student housing. He also stressed the university's role in research and economic development. Among $380 million in new facilities brought online during the Halligan years, are the Advanced Technology Research Center, designed to host joint industry-university research, and the Food and Agricultural Products Research and Technology Center, which offers pilot plant space to Oklahoma entrepreneurs. Halligan won election to the Oklahoma Senate from District 21 in November 2008.

To contact Halligan—2300 N Lincoln Blvd., Oklahoma City, OK 73105 ■ 405/521-5572
■ halligan@oksenate.gov

David Holt

Occupation—Attorney ■ **Education**—The George Washington University, BA; Oklahoma City University, JD ■ **Party**—Republican ■ **District**—30 ■ **Legislative Experience**—Senate Member, 2011–present; Majority Caucus Vice Chair, 2011; Majority Whip, 2013 ■ **Committee Membership**—

Appropriations; Appropriations Subcommittee on Select Agencies, Chair; General Government; Judiciary; and Public Safety

Holt was elected in 2010 and re-elected in 2014. He has successfully shepherded almost forty pieces of conservative legislation into law, and has received awards from Freedom of Information Oklahoma, the Oklahoma Commission on the Status of Women, Prevent Child Abuse Oklahoma, and the National MS Society. Holt's dynamic record of service has garnered national attention, as in 2014 when he was named to the national board of GOPAC, and Chuck Todd of NBC News named him a "Rising Star." Born and raised in Oklahoma City, Holt's roots are deep.

The son of a teacher and a social worker, Holt is a fourth-generation Oklahoman and an alumnus of Putnam City Schools, which he attended from kindergarten until his graduation as a National Merit Scholar. He brings a wide range of prior experiences to his position in the Oklahoma Senate. At the time of his 2010 election, Holt had already served a United States president, a U.S. Speaker of the House, a lieutenant governor, and members of Congress. He also stood at the center of the Oklahoma City renaissance during five years as chief of staff to its mayor.

A tireless volunteer, Holt has been a member of many community organizations, including current service as president of the Ralph Ellison Foundation Board, and on the boards of the Oklahoma City National Memorial & Museum, Allied Arts, and the Oklahoma City Arts Council. Holt is also a graduate of Leadership Oklahoma City Class XXVI and has previously been named "40 Under 40" by *OKC Business News* and an "Achiever Under 40" by the *Journal Record*.

Holt is director of investor relations at Hall Capital, is a licensed attorney, and has served as an adjunct professor at Oklahoma City University. He is also the author of the 2012 book *Big League City: Oklahoma City's Rise to the NBA*. Holt and his wife, Rachel, an Oklahoma County prosecutor, married in 2003. They have two children, George and Margaret. The Holts are members of St. Augustine of Canterbury Episcopal Church. He is a member of the Osage Nation. The Holts also maintain a home at the Holt Ranch west of McAlester, Oklahoma.

To contact Holt—2300 N Lincoln Blvd., Oklahoma City, OK 73105 ▪ 405/521-5636 ▪ holt@oksenate.gov

Darcy Jech

Occupation—Business Owner, Farming ▪ **Education**—Southeastern Oklahoma State University, BS ▪ **Party**—Democrat ▪ **District**—26 ▪ **Legislative Experience**—Senate Member, 2015 ▪ **Committee Membership**—Appropriations; Appropriations Subcommittee on Public Safety and Judiciary; Finance; Insurance; and Pensions, Vice Chair

Jech won election to the Oklahoma Senate from District 26 in November 2014. Born and raised east of Kingfisher, Oklahoma, Jech attended first through eighth grade at Big 4 School, and graduated from Kingfisher High School. Jech attended Seminole State College, and graduated from Southeastern Oklahoma State University degree with a Bachelor of Science degree. He is the owner and operator of an independent insurance agency in Kingfisher. He also is a partner with his brother in a cow-calf operation on the family farm east of Kingfisher.

Jech's wife, Vicky, is a career educator. They have two grown children, Sarah and Ryan, who are graduates of Oklahoma State University. They have one granddaughter, Macy.

To contact Jech—2300 N Lincoln Blvd., Oklahoma City, OK 73105 ▪ 405/521–5545 ▪ jech@oksenate.gov

Clark Jolley

Occupation—Attorney ▪ **Education**—Oklahoma Baptist University, BA, BME; University of Oklahoma, JD ▪ **Party**—Republican ▪ **District**—41 ▪ **Legislative Experience**—Senate Member, 2005-present; Whip, 2007–2008; Assistant Majority Floor Leader, 2009–2011; Redistricting Co-Chair, 2011 ▪ **Committee Membership**—Appropriations, Chair; Education; Energy; Finance; and Rules

Jolley was born in Oklahoma City, and grew up in Del City, Oklahoma. He earned a Bachelor of Music Education and a Bachelor of Arts in political science from Oklahoma Baptist University in 1992, and a Juris Doctor degree from the University of Oklahoma in 1995. Jolley began a private law practice in 1995, and served as administrative law judge for the Oklahoma Department of Labor from 1996 to 1998. In 1999 Jolley married Verlyne Simmons. Together they expanded his law practice into a partnership, Jolley and Jolley. The couple have two children, Lauren and Alex. Jolley won election to the Oklahoma Senate from District 41 in 2004, and was quickly selected by his colleagues to serve in the leadership as a whip and then as assistant majority floor leader. In 2011 he was chair of Appropriations for the senate. Jolley is an adjunct professor in the School of Business at Oklahoma Christian University, and also has served on the worship staff at Henderson Hills Baptist Church in Edmond since 1990.

To contact Jolley—2300 N Lincoln Blvd., Oklahoma City, OK 73105 ▪ 405/521–5622 ▪ jolley@oksenate.gov

Ron Justice

Occupation—OSU County Extension Agent/Retired ▪ **Education**—Oklahoma State University, BS, MS ▪ **Party**—Republican ▪ **District**—23 ▪ **Legislative Experience**—Senate Member, 2005-present; Rural Caucus Chair, 2011-present ▪ **Committee Membership**—Agriculture and Rural Development; Appropriations; Appropriations Subcommittee on Natural Resources, Chair; Energy; Rules, Chair; Tourism and Wildlife

Elected to the Oklahoma Senate in 2004 from District 23, Justice has proven himself a leader in his own caucus and a champion for rural Oklahoma. Justice received both his bachelor's and his master's degree from Oklahoma State University. He is a member of the Chickasha Lions Club, Grady County Cattle Producers, Mineral Owners Association and the Alfalfa Hay Association. He has gained even more knowledge and experience from his time with the Chickasha Chamber of Commerce, the other civic organizations in District 23, and Epsilon Sigma Phi. Justice is a retired Oklahoma State University County Extension Agent. He and his wife, Darlene, live in Chickasha and have three children;

Greg, Yvonne, and Yvette. They are the proud grandparents of nine grandchildren, and are members of the Sharon Baptist Church in Chickasha.

To contact Justice—2300 N Lincoln Blvd., Oklahoma City, OK 73105 ▪ 405/521-5537 ▪ justice@oksenate.gov

Kyle Loveless

Occupation—Business Owner/Consultant ▪ **Education**— University of Oklahoma; Georgetown University, BA ▪ **Party**— Republican ▪ **District**—45 ▪ **Legislative Experience**—Senate Member, 2013 ▪ **Committee Membership**—Appropriations; Appropriations Subcommittee on General Government, Chair; Energy; Health and Human Services; and Transportation

Loveless was born in Oklahoma City, Oklahoma in 1974. He graduated from Westmoore High School in 1992. While attending the University of Oklahoma, Loveless accepted an internship in Washington, D.C. working for Congressman Ernest Istook. At the end of the internship, he accepted a job and worked his way up from staff assistant to legislative assistant advising Istook on legislative matters concerning Oklahomans. He was involved in several pieces of legislation affecting many areas of the country, especially Oklahoma. Through his efforts, Congressman Istook was able to secure the necessary resources to help the revitalization and restoration of the North Canadian (now Oklahoma) River. These monies provided Oklahoma City with the resources necessary to complete the final piece of the MAPS projects. While working for Congressman Istook during the day, he attended night classes completing his bachelor's degree in American studies at Georgetown University in 2000. Loveless married Summer Sullins in 1999. The couple returned home to south Oklahoma City in the summer of 2000, and he immediately became civically involved, ultimately returning to work for Congressman Ernest Istook, successfully managing the re-election of Oklahoma City's most conservative congressman through two consecutive election cycles. In 2005, Loveless opened Phoenix Consulting, a corporate and political consulting firm in south Oklahoma City. He and his wife have one daughter, Isabella Josephine.

To contact Loveless—2300 N Lincoln Blvd., Oklahoma City, OK 73105 ▪ 405/521-5618 ▪ loveless@oksenate.gov

Bryce Marlatt

Occupation—Oil and Gas/Real Estate ▪ **Education**— Northwestern Oklahoma State University ▪ **Party**— Republican ▪ **District**—27 ▪ **Legislative Experience**—Senate Member, 2009–present; Caucus Chair, 2011–present ▪ **Committee Membership**—Appropriations; Appropriations Subcommittee on General Government and Transportation, Chair; Energy, Vice Chair; General Government; Rules; and Transportation

Marlatt was born March 29, 1977. He attended Northwestern Oklahoma State University, where he received a bachelor's degree in agriculture and business. He was elected to the Oklahoma Senate from District 27 in November 2008. Marlatt's affiliations include the

National Rifle Association, Oklahoma Farm Bureau, and the Woodward Rifle and Pistol Club. He and his wife, Tatum, have three children together; Kade, Kole, and Kloey. He enjoys hunting and fishing as well as family time. He attends Living Word Fellowship Church.

To contact Marlatt—2300 N Lincoln Blvd., Oklahoma City, OK 73105 ▪ 405/521-5626 ▪ marlatt@oksenate.gov

Kevin Matthews

Occupation—Tulsa Fire Department, Retired ▪ **Education**—Central State University ▪ **Party**—Democrat ▪ **District**—11 ▪ **Legislative Experience**—Oklahoma House of Representatives, 2013-2015; Senate Member, 2015

Matthews, a long-time resident of the Tulsa area, won a special election to the Oklahoma Senate in April 2015 from District 11. He filled the seat vacated by Senator Jabar Shumate. He began his legislative career, when he was elected to the Oklahoma House of Representatives in November 2012. Matthews graduated from Booker T. Washington High School, and attended Central State University, where he pledged Phi Beta Sigma. He earned a degree in fire protection technology, and has served twenty-five years with the Tulsa Fire Department. He retired in January 2010 as the administrative fire chief, chief of personnel. During his career, Matthews completed the Middle Management Curriculum at the National Fire Academy and the Executive Development Institute at Dillard University. He also attended the 2012 Center for Advanced Leadership Studies and the Andrew Young School of Policy Studies in Atlanta, Georgia.

Matthews is the proud, single parent of two grown sons, Kevin Matthews II, who is a graduate of Hampton University and "Teach for America" participant in Dallas, Texas, and Sterling Matthews, who is a certified medical assistant and "Spoken Word" artist who teaches the craft to local high school students.

To contact Matthews—2300 N Lincoln Blvd., Oklahoma City, OK 73105 ▪ 405/521-5598 ▪ matthews@oksenate.gov

Mike Mazzei

Occupation—Financial Planner ▪ **Education**—George Mason University, BA ▪ **Party**—Republican ▪ **District**—25 ▪ **Legislative Experience**—Senate Member, 2005-present; Co-Assistant Floor Leader, 2007; Assistant Majority Floor Leader, 2009 ▪ **Committee Membership**—Appropriations; Appropriations Subcommittee on Natural Resources and Regulatory Services; Finance, Chair; Insurance; and Pensions

Mazzei attended George Mason University in Fairfax, Virginia, graduating with a bachelor's degree in government and politics. He also is a graduate of the College of Financial Planning, and is a certified financial planner practitioner. Mazzei is the president of Tulsa Wealth Advisors, which operates a branch of Raymond James Financial Services in Tulsa, Oklahoma. Mazzei won election to the Oklahoma Senate from District 25 in 2004. He is a member of the Asbury United Methodist Church, Financial Planners Association, and serves on the board of the Salvation Army. Mazzei, and his wife Noel, have five children; Maria; triplets Caleb, Carissa, and Mykaela; and Jackson.

To contact Mazzei—2300 N Lincoln Blvd., Oklahoma City, OK 73105 ▪ 405/521-5675 ▪ mazzei@oksenate.gov

Dan Newberry

Occupation—Mortgage Banker ▪ **Education**—Oral Roberts University, BS ▪ **Party**—Republican ▪ **District**—37 ▪ **Legislative Experience**—Senate Member, 2009; Majority Whip, 2011-present ▪ **Committee Membership**—Appropriations; Appropriations Subcommittee on Select Agencies; Business and Commerce, Chair; Pensions; and Transportation

Newberry was born on November 22, 1975. He is a third generation Tulsan and is an active member of Victory Christian Center. He earned a diploma of "charismatic ministry" as well as a bachelor's degree in liberal arts with a focus on leadership and organizational management from Oral Roberts University. He has been a business professional in the mortgage banking industry for sixteen years and is now the vice president of real estate development at Tulsa Teachers' Credit Union. Newberry is a member of the Glenpool, Jenks, and Sand Springs chambers of commerce, the Rotary Club, and the OU Capitol Society.

Newberry won election to the Oklahoma Senate from District 37 in November 2008. He authored a constitutional amendment during his first session fighting the Patient Protection Affordable Care Act, otherwise known as Obamacare. He has received multiple awards from Americans United for Life and Oklahomans for Life for authoring legislation which protects the sanctity of human life at all stages. As a strong supporter of the military, he established the Gold Star Medal of Honor, which is given to the spouse or family members of an American soldier killed in action since 9/11.

Newberry is the founder of the Paul Revere Reading Society, created to motivate elementary students to read. The Oklahoma Farm Bureau named him a member of the prestigious "100 Percent Club" and the Oklahoma State Chamber honored him with the Guardian of Free Enterprise Award for championing the economic development and growth of business in our state. He and his wife, Laura, have four children, Claire, Paige, Eva, and Alex.

To contact Newberry—2300 N Lincoln Blvd., Oklahoma City, OK 74105 ▪ 405/521-5600 ▪ newberry@oksenate.gov

Susan Paddack

Occupation—Nonprofit Consultant ▪ **Education**—University of Colorado, BS; East Central University, ME ▪ **Party**—Democrat ▪ **District**—13 ▪ **Legislative Experience**—Senate Member, 2005-present; Majority Whip, 2007; Minority Whip, 2009; Minority Caucus Vice Chair, 2011-2014; Assistant Minority Leader, 2015 ▪ **Committee Membership**—Appropriations; Appropriations Subcommittee on General Government and Transportation; Appropriations Subcommittee on Public Safety and Judiciary; Education; Finance; Pension; and Transportation

Paddack received a bachelor's degree in education from the University of Colorado, and a master's degree in secondary education from East Central University. She has been employed as a secondary science teacher in Colorado, Oklahoma, and Texas. Paddack was employed as the director of Local Education Foundation Outreach for the Oklahoma Foundation for Excellence. She won election to the Oklahoma Senate from District 13 in 2004, and serves as the Democratic Whip. Paddack's civic involvement is extensive. She served as president of the American Medical Association's Alliance. Her other civic involvement included serving on the boards of the Ada Arts and Humanities Council, Ada Board of Adjustments, Communities Foundation of Oklahoma, Kiwanis Club of Ada, Oklahoma Institute for Child Advocacy, Center for Nonprofit Management, and the Pontotoc County Medical Alliance. She currently serves on the board of the Oklahoma Academy, Jasmine Moran Children's Museum, the Oklahoma Arts Institute, and the Oklahoma Foundation for Excellence. She serves professionally on the Achieving Classroom Excellence Task Force, Education Commission of the States, Governor's Catastrophic Health Emergency Planning Task Force, Governor's Elimination of Health Disparities Task Force, Healthcare Workforce Resource Center Board, Oklahoma Educational Technology Trust, Southern Regional Education Board, and the State Coverage Initiative to Reform Healthcare in Oklahoma.

To contact Paddack—500 SE County Road, Ada, OK 74820 ▪ 405/521–5541 ▪ paddack@oksenate.gov

Anastasia Pittman

Occupation—Educator, Journalism, Public Relations ▪ **Education**—University of Oklahoma, BA; Langston University, MEd ▪ **Party**—Democrat ▪ **District**—48 ▪ **Legislative Experience**—Oklahoma House of Representatives, 2007–2014; Senate Member, 2015; Minority Whip, 2015 ▪ **Committee Membership**—Appropriations; Appropriations Subcommittee on Health and Human Services; Appropriations Subcommittee on Select Agencies; Business and Commerce; General Government; Health and Human Services; Transportation; and Veterans and Military Affairs

Pittman was born on July 19, 1970, in Miami, Florida, and has resided in Oklahoma City for over thirty-five years. She earned a bachelor's degree in journalism and public relations from the University of Oklahoma, and a master's degree in urban education and behavioral science from Langston University. Pittman is an educator, consultant, public relations specialist, radio broadcaster, registered tutor with the Oklahoma City Public Schools System, former case manager, and former mentor for the United States Department of Justice, Western District. She won election to the Oklahoma House of Representatives from District 99 in November 2006, and the Oklahoma State Senate from District 48 in November 2014.

Pittman is the second Seminole citizen to serve in the legislature, and currently serves as co-chair of the Oklahoma Native American Caucus. She chairs the Oklahoma Legislative Black Caucus and serves as Senate minority whip. She is also Housing vice chair for the National Black Caucus of State Legislators, and chair of Education and vice chair of Health for the National Caucus of Native American Legislators. Pittman is the state director for the National Foundation of Women Legislators.

Pittman has international honors from Turkey, Malaysia, and Israel. She is a member of Northeast Church of Christ, Leadership Oklahoma Class XXII, Downtown Rotary Club, Alpha Kappa Alpha Sorority, Inc., Top Ladies of Distinction, Inc., American Council of Young Political Leaders Alumni, Rose State College Foundation Board of Trustees and Board of Governors, advisory board member of the Oklahoma City University Meinders School of Business, Close Up, Red Earth, Junior League of Oklahoma, the Commission on the Status of Women, NOBEL Women, Women in Legislators' Lobby, Urban League Young Professionals, and is a life member of the National Association for the Advancement of Colored People (NAACP). Moreover, Pittman has received numerous honors including 2013 Woman of the Year nominee, Outstanding Community Service Recognition for Magic Star Foundation from former United States President Bill Clinton, Asian Legislative Excellence Award, and the Media Advocacy Award from the Oklahoma Coalition Against Domestic Violence and Sexual Assault. She received the state, district, and national TRIO awards, and the Oklahoma Achiever under 40 Award. Pittman is a Henry Toll Fellows Graduate, and is the host of the Anastasia Pittman Show, co-host on Caliedascope Radio Network, and featured guest on the Touch 1140 AM, and Heart & Soul 92.1 FM.

Pittman is married and has one daughter, one foster son, and three step children. She is the great granddaughter of Abner Burnett, Tulsa Race Riot survivor, and granddaughter of the late Jazz Hall of Fame member C.E. Pittman.

To contact Pittman—2300 N Lincoln Blvd., Oklahoma City, OK 73105
▪ 405/521-5531 ▪ pittman@oksenate.gov

Marty Quinn

Occupation—Insurance Agent ▪ **Education**—Dierks, Arkansas High School, Henderson State University ▪ **Party**—Republican ▪ **District**—2 ▪ **Legislative Experience**—Senate Member, 2015 ▪ **Committee Membership**—Appropriations; Appropriations Subcommittee on Natural Resources and Regulatory Services, Vice Chair; Finance, Vice Chair; Education; and Insurance

Quinn was elected without opposition to the Oklahoma Senate from District 2 in 2014. He presently serves as Appropriations and Budget Subcommittee on Natural Resources vice chair, and is a member of the Education, Finance, and Insurance committees. Quinn and his wife, Kelly, have two grown children, Lynsay and Tyler. They are members of the Blue Starr Church of Christ in Claremore, Oklahoma.

Quinn has participated in many civic and legislative organizations, such as Noon Rotary Club, Hope Harbor Children's Home (past board member), Claremore Public Schools Foundation, and as a member of the National Conference of Insurance Legislators.

To contact Quinn—2300 N Lincoln Blvd., Oklahoma City, OK 73105 ▪ 405/521-5555
▪ quinn@oksenate.gov

Mike Schulz

Occupation—Farmer ▪ **Education**—Oklahoma State University, BS ▪ **Party**—Republican ▪ **District**—38 ▪ **Legislative Experience**—Senate Member, 2006–present; Majority Whip, 2009; Majority Floor Leader, 2011–present ▪ **Committee Membership**—As Majority Floor Leader, Schulz serves as ex-officio member of all committees

Schulz was born on March 5, 1964, in Cheyenne, Oklahoma. He received a bachelor's degree in agriculture from Oklahoma State University. He first won election to the Oklahoma Senate from District 38 in a special election held in April 2006, following the death of Senator Kerr. He was re-elected in November 2006. Schulz is an active member of the Oklahoma Farm Bureau, where he served as chairman of the Young Farmer and Rancher Committee in 1996 and also worked for the organization for many years as a field representative. He is a graduate of Oklahoma Agriculture Leadership Class V. Schulz continues to be an active member in the Altus Kiwanis Club as well as the First United Methodist Church. He married the former Reenie Reid, and the couple have two children, Benjamin and Abby.

To contact Schulz—2300 N Lincoln Blvd., Oklahoma City, OK 73105 ▪ 405/521–5612 ▪ schulz@oksenate.gov

Ron Sharp

Occupation—Education ▪ **Education**—Southeastern State College, BS; MS, Central State University; and Kensington University, EdD ▪ **Party**—Republican ▪ **District**—17 ▪ **Legislative Experience**—Senate Member, 2013▪ **Committee Membership**—Appropriations; Appropriations Subcommittee on Education; Business and Commerce; Education, Vice Chair; and Tourism and Wildlife

Sharp graduated from Shawnee High School. He earned his bachelor's degree from Southeastern State College, his master's degree from Central State University, and his doctorate in education, with an emphasis in political science, from Kensington University. He won election to the Oklahoma Senate from District 17 on November 6, 2012. Sharp was named 2011 Oklahoma State Teacher of the Year by the Veterans of Foreign Wars and Shawnee High School Teacher of the Year in 1994, 1996, and 1997. He is a member of the United States Selective Service Board, the National Council for the Social Studies, and the Oklahoma Bar Association's Foundation for the U.S. Constitution. He has been named to Who's Who Among America's Teachers for eighteen straight years. Sharp received the "United States Congressional Award of Special Recognition for Outstanding Service" recognizing coaching and teaching accomplishments in 1998. During his career, Sharp also served as head coach of the Shawnee High boys and girls tennis teams, helping win five state boys' championships and one state girls' championship. He was recognized as one of the "Best 50 Tennis Coaches in the World" by the US Professional Tennis Registry, has been a member of the Oklahoma Coaches Association for twenty-nine years and was co-founder and first President of the Oklahoma Tennis Coaches' Association. He is active in his home church, Liberty Baptist, and is strongly pro-life, believing that society must defend the right to life from the womb to the grave. He is a long-time member of the National Rifle Association and the Sons of the American Revolution.

To contact Sharp—2300 N Lincoln Blvd., Oklahoma City, OK 73105 ▪ 405/521-5539 ▪ sharp@oksenate.gov

Wayne Shaw

Occupation—Pastor ▪ **Education**—Lamar University, BS; Lincoln University, MDiv; Fuller Theological Seminary, DMin ▪ **Party**—Republican ▪ **District**—3 ▪ **Legislative Experience**— Senate Member, 2013 ▪ **Committee Membership**— Appropriations; Appropriations Subcommittee on Select Agencies, Vice Chair; Education; Public Safety; and Tourism and Wildlife

Shaw was born and raised on a farm. He attended a one-room country school until he was in the eighth grade. He received a bachelor's degree in secondary education with math and history teaching fields from Lamar University; a master's degree in divinity from Lincoln University, and a doctorate degree in ministry from Fuller Theological Seminary. Shaw taught in the public high school at Yellville, Arkansas. He and his wife, Anna, married in 1968. The couple served as missionaries to Liberia, West Africa, where he taught in Liberia Christian High School and Liberia Christian College. Over the past few years, he has served as an adjunct professor for Oklahoma Wesleyan University in Bartlesville. Shaw has served as a pastor most of his life. He served as the senior pastor at First Christian Church in Grove for fifteen years before being elected to the Oklahoma Senate from District 3 on November 6, 2012. He has been working with Dr. Joe Wilson in the Oklahoma Prison Chapel Program, which has successfully built five chapels in Oklahoma prisons. Shaw has visited many of the state's prisons and spoken in several, because he believes this program will provide prisoners an opportunity for change.

Shaw has officiated football for the past twenty-nine years. He served as volunteer chaplain for the Grove Police Department. Before his election to the senate, he served on the board for Court Appointed Special Advocates (CASA), advocates for neglected and abused children; Abundant Blessing Center, a pregnancy center; and Grove Community Action Network, all in Grove. Shaw and his wife have three children; Doug, Teresa, and Timothy. They also have five grandchildren. Over their forty-seven year marriage, the couple felt led to foster numerous children in their home which enriched their lives and broadened the ministry which they love so much.

To contact Shaw—2300 N Lincoln Blvd., Oklahoma City, OK 73105 ▪ 405/521-5574 ▪ shaw@oksenate.gov

Ralph Shortey

Occupation—Legislator ▪ **Party**—Republican ▪ **District**—44 ▪ **Legislative Experience**—Senate Member, 2011–present ▪ **Committee Membership**—Appropriations; Appropriations Subcommittee on Public Safety and Judiciary; Energy; General Government; and Transportation

A member of the Rosebud Sioux Indian Tribe, Shortey was born in Casper, Wyoming. He spent part of his childhood on the Rosebud Sioux Indian Reservation in Grass Mountain, South Dakota, before moving to Oklahoma City where he attended Moore Public Schools. Shortey graduated from Westmoore High School in 2000, and following graduation he attended Heartland Baptist Bible College in Oklahoma City in preparation for mission work in Uganda. In 2002 he married his high school sweetheart, Jennifer, and continues to make his home in south Oklahoma City with their two children, Kaitlyn and Elena. With a growing family, Shortey decided against pursuing mission work and instead entered the oil and gas industry, working as a production consultant. In 2010 Shortey, a long-time political volunteer, won election to the Oklahoma Senate from District 44 on November 2, 2010. He is currently pursuing a degree in finance and economics. Shortey's legislative priorities include personal liberty, fighting illegal immigration, and strengthening public safety in Oklahoma.

To contact Shortey—2300 N Lincoln Blvd., Oklahoma City, OK 73105 ▪ 405/521-5557 ▪ shortey@oksenate.gov.

Joseph Silk

Occupation—Vacation Property Manager ▪ **Party**—Republican ▪ **District**—5 ▪ **Legislative Experience**—Senate Member, 2015 ▪ **Committee Membership**—Agriculture and Rural Development; Appropriations; Appropriations Subcommittee on Education; Business and Commerce; and Transportation, Vice Chair

Silk won election to the Oklahoma Senate from Disrict 5 in November 2014.

To contact Silk—2300 N Lincoln Blvd., Oklahoma City, OK 73105 ▪ 405/521-5614 ▪ silk@oksenate.gov

Frank Simpson

Occupation—Part-time Pastor ▪ **Education**—Cedar Valley College ▪ **Party**—Republican ▪ **District**—14 ▪ **Legislative Experience**—Senate Member, 2011; Majority Whip, 2015 ▪ **Committee Membership**—Agriculture and Rural Development; Appropriations; Appropriations Subcommittee on Health and Human Services; Finance; Rules; and Veterans and Military Affairs, Chair

Having been encouraged to seek public office by his friends and family, Simpson was elected to the Oklahoma Senate from District 14 on November 2, 2010. Simpson's professional career began at the age of eighteen, when he enlisted in the United States Navy. During his twenty-six year navy career, he earned several awards and honors. Among those were the Navy Commendation Medal for service with the Multinational Force in Beirut, Lebanon, and the Navy Achievement Medal for professional performance. Simpson earned a warrant commission and retired in 1988 with the rank of CWO-4. After retiring from the navy, he worked in the private sector for almost twenty years. Simpson served as a facilities manager for several large retail companies. He has also served as a part-time pastor in the United Methodist Church since 2000. He currently pastors the First United

Methodist Church in Mannsville. Simpson and his wife Linda have been married since 1964. They have four daughters, fifteen grandchildren, and a growing number of great grandchildren. The couple lives on their "Little Piece of Heaven" in Springer.

To contact Simpson—2300 N Lincoln Blvd., Oklahoma City, OK 73105 ▪ 405/521-5607 ▪ simpson@oksenate.gov

Jason Smalley

Occupation—Business Owner ▪ **Education**—University of Oklahoma, BS ▪ **Party**—Republican ▪ **District**—28 ▪ **Legislative Experience**—House Member, 2012 to 2014; Senate Member, 2015 ▪ **Committee Membership**—Appropriations; Appropriations Subcommittee on Education, Vice Chair; Education; Pensions, Chair; Transportation; and Veterans and Military Affairs

Smalley was raised by his grandparents, Ed and Aleta, in Stroud, Oklahoma. He graduated from Stroud High School, where he earned a music scholarship to the University of Central Oklahoma. While attending college, Smalley enlisted in the United States Marine Corps. He was deployed to both Iraq and Afghanistan, where he served multiple tours.

Following an honorable discharge from the Marine Corps in 2006, Smalley earned a bachelor's degree in social science from the University of Oklahoma. After graduation, he worked as a technology consultant. He currently runs a restaurant in Stroud, and is a third generation restaurant and business owner.

Smalley won election to the Oklahoma House of Representatives in 2012, where she served on the Appropriations and Budget Revenue and Tax, Common Education, and Government Modernization Committee, and as chair of the Appropriations and Budget Transportation Committee.

Smalley won election to the Oklahoma Senate from District 28 in November 2014. He presently serves on the Appropriations, Education, Transportation, and Veterans and Military Affairs committees, as well as the Appropriations Subcommittee on Education as vice chair.

Smalley is active in the Lions Club, American Legion, and local school as a coach. He is a member of the First Baptist Church of Stroud, where he met his wife and high school sweetheart, C'Anne. They have been married for twelve years, and have a four-year old son, Gideon.

To contact Smalley—2300 N Lincoln Blvd., Oklahoma City, OK 73105 ▪ 405/521-5547 ▪ smalley@oksenate.gov

John Sparks

Occupation—Small Businessman/Rancher/Attorney ▪ **Education**—Harvard College, AB; University of Oklahoma, JD ▪ **Party**—Democrat ▪ **District**—16 ▪ **Legislative Experience**—Senate Member, 2007-present; Assistant Minority Leader, 2011-present ▪ **Committee Membership**—Appropriations; Appropriations Subcommittee on Education; Education; Energy; Finance; Insurance, Vice Chair; Judiciary; and Rules

Sparks was raised in Sulphur near his family's ranch, which was founded before statehood. He remains actively involved in family ranching. He attended Harvard College, where he was an All Ivy League defensive tackle and also served as an intern for then Senator David Boren. After receiving his degree, he returned home, earning a law degree from the University of Oklahoma. Upon graduation from law school, his strong attraction to public service took him to Washington, DC, where he served as a legislative aide to Oklahoma Congressman Bill Brewster. Sparks spent over a year serving the people of Oklahoma, working on issues such as the environment, defense, agriculture, international trade and Native American affairs. Committed to improving Oklahoma, he again returned home to begin his legal career. Most of his legal career, including time with the law firms of Crowe & Dunlevy and Foliart, Huff, Ottaway & Bottom, has been spent in the health care sector. He is now a founding partner of the Odom, Sparks & Jones law firm. Sparks community actvities include: serving as past president of the Cleveland County Bar Association and the Cleveland County Workforce Investment Board. He is a past member of the boards of Health for Friends and the Thunderbird Clubhouse, which supports adults recovering from mental illness in Cleveland and McClain counties. He is also a dedicated member and volunteer with the United Way of Norman. Sparks continues to be an active member of the Sooner Rotary Club, as well as a member of the Norman Chamber of Commerce. Following a long family tradition, he is a member of the Oklahoma Farm Bureau and Oklahoma Cattleman's Association. He won election to the Oklahoma Senate from District 16 in November 2006, and was reelected in 2010 and without opposition in 2014. He and his wife, Elizabeth, are raising their two sons in Norman where they have lived since college. They are active members of McFarlin Memorial United Methodist Church and have served the church in numerous capacities, including the Administrative Board.

To contact Sparks—2300 N Lincoln Blvd., Oklahoma City, OK 73105 ▪ 405/521-5553 ▪ sparks@oksenate.gov

Rob Standridge

Occupation—Pharmacist ▪ **Education**—University of Oklahoma, BS ▪ **Party**—Republican ▪ **District**—15 ▪ **Legislative Experience**—Senate Member, 2011; Majority Whip, 2015 ▪ **Committee Membership**—Appropriations; Appropriations Subcommittee on Health and Human Services; Energy; Health and Human Services, Chair; Judiciary; and Rules

Standridge, a native of Midwest City, earned a bachelor's degree in pharmacy from the University of Oklahoma in 1993. In 1995 he and his wife, Lisa, also a pharmacist, purchased their first pharmacy in Blanchard, Oklahoma. One year later, he developed one of the first online pharmacies. Legend Care Pharmacy specializes in the care and treatment of juveniles and the mentally disabled across the state. A few years later, Standridge taught himself how to write computer programs and created a software program call *Compound Assist*. Since his original program, he has written several software programs including a complete pharmacy management system that is used throughout the country. His most recent business venture has been a start-up technology and equipment company for pharmacies. Health Engineering Systems (HES) has a number of products for pharmacies, including a line of mixing equipment that is sold throughout North and South America. HES is located in Norman, and houses a working pharmacy and compounding lab, as well as a training facility for pharmacists on the use of its equipment and software.

Standridge is an ACA Fellow and a member of numerous pharmacy organizations. He also founded Business Leaders for Oklahoma. In addition, he belongs to several aviation organizations, several business leaders organizations, and is a member of Toastmasters. He is a Rotarian and a Sooner Centurion. He and his wife have been married since 1992 and have two daughters, Holley and Harper. They make their home in Norman.

To contact Standridge—2300 N Lincoln Blvd., Oklahoma City, OK 73105
▪ 405/521-5535 ▪ standridge@oksenate.gov

Gary Stanislawski

Occupation—Financial Planner ▪ **Education**—Oregon State University, BS; Oral Roberts University, MA ▪ **Party**—Republican ▪ **District**—35 ▪ **Legislative Experience**—Senate Member, 2009; Majority Whip, 2011 ▪ **Committee Membership**—Appropriations; Appropriations Subcommittee on Education; Education; Insurance; and Transportation, Chair

Stanislawski was awarded a four year ROTC scholarship and attended Oregon State University, where he earned a bachelor's degree in business administration. Upon graduation, he entered the air force and subsequently earned his wings as a pilot in 1984. He flew for eight years flying such planes as the B-52 and the B-1 Bomber. He has approximately 2,000 hours flying time. Stanislawski also earned a master's degree from Oral Roberts University. He serves as the president of Regent Financial Services, and he is a member of the Financial Planning Association. Stanislawski works with individuals and businesses in investment, retirement, and estate planning services. He won election to the Oklahoma Senate from District 35 in November 2008. He and his wife, Dayna, have been married since 1981, and they are active members of the Victory Christian Center in Tulsa. They have two children, Shawn and Kristie.

To contact Stanislawski—2300 N Lincoln Blvd., Oklahoma City, OK 73105
▪ 405/521-5624 ▪ stanislawski@oksenate.gov

Anthony Sykes

Occupation—Attorney ▪ **Education**—University of Oklahoma, BA, JD ▪ **Party**—Republican ▪ **District**—24 ▪ **Legislative Experience**—Senate Member, 2007-present; Majority Whip, 2009; Assistant Floor Leader, 2011 ▪ **Committee Membership**—Agriculture and Rural Development; Appropriations; Appropriations Subcommittee on Public Safety and Judiciary; Judiciary, Chair; and Veterans and Military Affairs

Sykes received a bachelor's degree and a Juris Doctor degree from the University of Oklahoma. He won election to the Oklahoma Senate from District 24 in November 2006.

To contact Sykes—2300 N Lincoln Blvd., Oklahoma City, OK 73105 ▪ 405/521-5569
▪ lewis@oksenate.gov

Roger Thompson

Occupation—President, News Leader Company, Inc. ■ **Education**—Southwestern Bible College & Seminary, MA, PhD ■ **Party**—Republican ■ **District**—8 ■ **Legislative Experience**—Senate Member, 2015 ■ **Committee Membership**—Appropriations; Appropriations Subcommittee on General Government and Transportation, Vice Chair; Business and Commerce; Education; and Judiciary

Thompson won election to the Oklahoma Senate from District 8 in November 2014. District 8 is comprised of Okmulgee and McIntosh counties, and parts of Okfuskee and Muskogee counties. In 1883 Thompson graduated from Preston Road School of Preaching, and later attended Southwestern Bible College and Seminary, where he earned a master's degree in theology in 1999 and a doctorate in theology in 2001.

Thompson is president of the News Leader Company, Inc., which owns and publishes the Okemah News Leader and the Tri-county Herald newspapers. He co-owns, along with his wife Pamela Thompson, Pamela's Flowers and the Okemah Office Supply. He is an active realtor with Carl Alls Real Estate. He also is currently the president of Okemah Community Improvement Association (CIA).

Thompson was a non-lawyer member of the Professional Responsibility Commission of the Oklahoma Bar Association from 1992–1994. He also served on the Okfuskee County Election Board, and the Okfuskee County Excise Board. He is past president of the Okemah Chamber of Commerce and Agriculture, Okemah Lions Club, and Rock Creek Youth Camp in Norman, Oklahoma. Thompson has served as president of the board and CEO of Good News International Foundation, where he was recognized for partnering with the secretary of religion and science in Ukraine, while operating a publishing and benevolent outreach in Ukraine after the fall of the Soviet Union. During this same time, he served as an advisory member of Global Christian University.

Thompson and his wife, Pamela, were married in 1976 and are the parents of two children. They are members of New Beginnings Church.

To contact Thompson—2300 N Lincoln Blvd., Oklahoma City, OK 73105 ■ 405/521-5588 ■ thompson@oksenate.gov

Greg Treat

Occupation—Legislator ■ **Education**—University of Oklahoma, BA ■ **Party**—Republican ■ **District**—47 ■ **Legislative Experience**—Senate Member, 2011–present; Majority Whip, 2013–2014, Assistant Majority Floor Leader, 2015 ■ **Committee Membership**—Appropriations, Vice Chair; Appropriations Subcommittee on Public Safety and Judiciary, Chair; Energy; Health and Human Services; Judiciary; and Rules

Treat was elected to the Oklahoma Senate on January 11, 2011, in a special election to replace Lieutenant Governor Todd Lamb from District 47. After graduating from Catoosa High School, Treat attended the University of Oklahoma, where he earned a bachelor's degree in history and political science. He graduated from OU with honors earning him membership in the prestigious Phi Beta Kappa honor society. Following graduation, he was named legislative advisor to former State Representative Fred Morgan. Treat researched and advised House members on important policy decisions. He left to become legislative director for then Lieutenant Governor Mary Fallin, where he helped guide and implement her legislative agenda. In 2004 Treat began work as regional director for Dr. Tom Coburn's successful United States Senate campaign. Senator Coburn hired Treat as a field representative and state government liaison. In 2010 Senator Coburn and other Republican members of Oklahoma's congressional delegation asked Treat to serve as executive director of the Victory Program. As executive director, he helped raise more than $500,000, helped register 28,000 new voters, and lead the effort as Republicans won every statewide elected office for the first time in Oklahoma history. Treat and his wife, Maressa, reside in northwest Oklahoma City with their two young sons, Mason and Cooper. They are both active members of Highpointe Church. Treat enjoys spending time with his family, playing sports, hunting, fishing, and reading.

To contact Treat—72300 N Lincoln Blvd., Oklahoma City, OK 73105 ▪ 405/521–5632 ▪ treat@oksenate.gov

Charles Wyrick

Occupation—State Legislator ▪ **Party**—Democrat ▪ **District**—1 ▪ **Legislative Experience**—Senate Member, 2005–present; Whip, 2007; Minority Whip, 2009; Assistant Minority Leader, 2011–present; Minority Caucus Vice Chair, 2015 ▪ **Committee Membership**—Agriculture and Rural Development; Appropriations; Appropriations Subcommittee on Natural Resources; Business and Commerce; Energy; Finance; Public Safety; and Tourism and Wildlife

Wyrick graduated as co-valedictorian from Fairland High School and attended classes at Northeastern Oklahoma A&M College. Wyrick started his family dairy in 1980 and is currently raising dairy and beef cows. In 1990 he started a heavy equipment contracting business specializing in soil conservation work. That operation grew into commercial work, but has since scaled back to a seasonal operation. He served on the board of directors of the Ottawa County Conservation District from 1999 through 2004; From 1996 to 2003 Wyrick served on the board of directors for several state, regional, and national dairying promotion organizations with annual budgets ranging from $9 to $165 million dollars and partnering with corporate organizations such as McDonalds, Disney, and NASCAR. From 1998 to 2006, he served as representative of the Southeast Council of Dairy Farmers of America, which is the nation's largest milk marketing cooperative. Wyrick won election to the Oklahoma Senate from District 1 in 2004. He is currently serving as Assistant Minority Floor Leader. Wyrick and his wife, Pamela, have been married for thirty-five years. They have two sons, Michael and his wife, Wendy, who have a six-year-old daughter, Josilynn, a four-year-old son, Talon and a one year old daughter, Malynn; and Randy and his wife, Crystal, who have been married eight years and have a three-year-old daughter, Remington Jo.

To contact Wyrick—58500 E 155 Road, Fairland, OK 74343 ▪ 405/521–5561 ▪ wyrick@oksenate.gov

Ervin Yen

Occupation—Physician, Anesthesiologist ▪ **Education**—
University of Oklahoma, BS, MD ▪ **Party**—Republican ▪
District—40 ▪ **Legislative Experience**—Senate Member,
2015 ▪ **Committee Membership**—Appropriations;
Appropriations and Subcommittee on Health and Human
Services; Business and Commerce; Finance; and Health and
Human Services, Vice Chair

Yen was born in Taipei, Taiwan, in 1954. After the Communists took over China and several relatives were imprisoned, Yen's parents, fearing an invasion of Taiwan, made the difficult decision to leave their families behind and pursue a better life in America. At the age of four, Yen and his family immigrated to America. In 1960, the family moved into what is now Oklahoma Senate District 40, and Yen has made his home there ever since. When Yen was nine, he and his family became naturalized United States citizens.

Yen graduated from Putnam City High School in 1973, earned a bachelor's degree in zoology from the University of Oklahoma, and then put himself through OU Medical School. After completing his residency, he began practicing as an anesthesiologist in 1984. He has worked as a cardiac anesthesiologist at Saint Anthony Hospital and Integris Baptist Medical Center for more than twenty years.

Yen and his wife, Pam, have been happily married for over twenty-eight years. They have five children and are active members of Christ the King Catholic Church. Yen is a past president of the Oklahoma Society of Anesthesiologists and past chief of the anesthesiology section at Saint Anthony Hospital. He has served as a member of the University of Oklahoma's President's Associates program for thirty-one years. Yen won election to the Oklahoma Senate from District 40 in November 2014.

To contact Yen—2300 N Lincoln Blvd., Oklahoma City, OK 73105 ▪ 405/521-5543
▪ yen@oksenate.gov

Senate Committees

Chairs and Vice Chairs of committees are listed first.

Senate President Pro Tempore Brian Bingman is ex-officio voting member of all senate committees.

Agriculture and Rural Development—Eddie Fields, Mark Allen, Don Barrington, Larry Boggs, Earl Garrison, Ron Justice, Joseph Silk, Frank Simpson, Anthony Sykes, and Charles Wyrick.

Appropriations—Clark Jolley, Greg Treat, Mark Allen, Patrick Anderson, Don Barrington, Randy Bass, Stephanie Bice, Larry Boggs, Josh Breechen, Rick Brinkley, Corey Brooks, Bill Brown, Brian Crain, Nathan Dahm, Kim David, Eddie Fields, Kay Floyd, John Ford, Jack Fry, Earl Garrison, A.J. Griffin, Jim Halligan, David Holt, Darcy Jech, Ron Justice, Kyle Loveless, Bryce Marlatt, Mike Mazzei, Dan Newberry, Susan Paddack, Anastasia Pittman, Marty Quinn, Ron Sharp, Wayne Shaw, Ralph Shortey, Joseph Silk, Frank Simpson, Jason Smalley, John Sparks, Rob Standridge, Gary Stanislawski, Anthony Sykes, Roger Thompson, Charles Wyrick, and Ervin Yen.

Appropriations Subcommittees—

All subcommittee members are members of the standing Appropriations Committee. The chair of the Appropriations Committee is an ex officio and voting member of each subcommittee.

Education—Jim Halligan, Jason Smalley, Kay Floyd, John Ford, Ron Sharp, Joseph Silk, John Sparks, and Gary Stanislawski.

General Government and Transportation—Kyle Loveless, Roger Thompson, Mark Allen, Randy Bass, Rick Brinkley, Larry Boggs, Jack Fry, Bryce Marlatt, and Susan Paddack.

Health and Human Services—Kim David, A.J. Griffin, Brian Crain, Earl Garrison, Anastasia Pittman, Frank Simpson, Rob Standridge, and Ervin Yen.

Natural Resources and Regulatory Services—Ron Justice, Mary Quinn, Patrick Anderson, Randy Bass, Eddie Fields, Darcy Jech, Mike Mazzei, and Charles Wyrick.

Public Safety and Judiciary—Greg Treat, Ralph Shortey, Don Barrington, Josh Breechen, Corey Brooks, Bill Brown, Kay Floyd, Susan Paddack, and Anthony Sykes.

Select Agencies—David Holt, Wayne Shaw, Stephanie Bice, Nathan Dahm, Kay Floyd, Dan Newberry, and Anastasia Pittman.

Business and Commerce—Dan Newberry, Stephanie Bice, Nathan Dahm, Jim Halligan, Anastasia Pittman, Ron Sharp, Joseph Silk, Roger Thompson, Charles Wyrick, and Ervin Yen.

Education—John Ford, Ron Sharp, Josh Breechen, Earl Garrison, Jim Halligan, Clark Jolley, Susan Paddack, Marty Quinn, Wayne Shaw, Jason Smalley, John Sparks, Gary Stanislawski, and Roger Thompson.

Energy—Bryce Marlatt, A.J. Griffin, Mark Allen, Randy Bass, Rick Brinkley, Brian Crain, Eddie Fields, Clark Jolley, Ron Justice, Kyle Loveless, Ralph Shortey, Rob Standridge, John Sparks, Greg Treat, and Charles Wyrick.

Finance—Mike Mazzei, Marty Quinn, Nathan Dahm, Kim David, John Ford, Jim Halligan, Darcy Jech, Clark Jolley, Susan Paddack, Frank Simpson, John Sparks, Charles Wyrick, and Ervin Yen.

General Government—Nathan Dahm, Jack Fry, Stephanie Bice, Corey Brooks, Kay Floyd, David Holt, Bryce Marlatt, Anastasia Pittman, and Ralph Shortey.

Insurance—Bill Brown, John Sparks, Randy Bass, Darcy Jech, Mike Mazzei, Marty Quinn, and Gary Stanislawski.

Health and Human Services—Rob Standridge, Ervin Yen, Brian Crain, Kim David, Kay Floyd, A.J. Griffin, Kyle Loveless, Anastasia Pittman, and Greg Treat.

Judiciary—Anthony Sykes, Brian Crain, Corey Brooks, Kay Floyd, A.J. Griffin, David Holt, John Sparks, Rob Standridge, Roger Thompson, and Greg Treat.

Pensions—Jason Smalley, Darcy Jech, Patrick Anderson, Randy Bass, Bill Brown, Mike Mazzei, Dan Newberry, and Susan Paddack.

Public Safety—Don Barrington, Kim David, Roger Ballenger, Larry Boggs, Josh Brecheen, David Holt, Al McAffrey, Wayne Shaw, and Ralph Shortey.

Rules—Ron Justice, Eddie Fields, Rick Brinkley, Nathan Dahm, Kim David, Kay Floyd, Earl Garrison, A.J. Griffin, Clark Jolley, Bryce Marlatt, Frank Simpson, John Sparks, Rob Standridge, and Greg Treat.

Tourism and Wildlife—Josh Breechen, Larry Boggs, Patrick Anderson, Randy Bass, Bill Brown, Eddie Fields, Earl Garrison, Ron Justice, Ron Sharp, Wayne Shaw, and Charles Wyrick.

Transportation—Gary Stanislawski, Joseph Silk, Mark Allen, Don Barrington, Randy Bass, Stephanie Bice, Jack Fry, Kyle Loveless, Bryce Marlatt, Dan Newberry, Susan Paddack, Anastasia Pittman, Ralph Shortey, and Jason Smalley.

Veterans and Military Affairs—Frank Simpson, Patrick Anderson, Larry Boggs, Jack Fry, Earl Garrison, Anastasia Pittman, Jason Smalley, and Anthony Sykes.

Oklahoma State House of Representatives

House of Representatives Leadership

Speaker	Jeffrey Hickman
Speaker Pro Tempore	Lee Denney
Majority Floor Leader	Charles Ortega
Majority Floor Leader	Jason Nelson
Majority Floor Leader	Lisa Billy
Majority Whip	Gary Banz
Assistant Majority Whip	Lisa J. Billy
Majority Caucus Chair	David Brumbaugh
Majority Caucus Vice Chair	Elise Hall
Majority Caucus Secretary	Katie Henke
Minority Leader	Scott Inman
Minority Floor Leader	Ben Sherrer
Assistant Minority Floor Leader	Eric Proctor
Minority Whip	Chuck Hoskin
Minority Caucus Chair	Jerry McPeak
Minority Caucus Vice Chair	Steve Kouplan
Minority Caucus Secretary	David Perryman

State Representatives by District

This list of representatives by district is given as a cross-reference. In the following section, representative's names are arranged in alphabetical order.

Dist.	Name	Dist.	Name	Dist.	Name
1	Johnny Tadlock (D)	35	Dennis Casey (R)	69	Chuck Strohm (R)
2	John Bennett (R)	36	Sean Roberts (R)	70	Ken Walker (R)
3	James Lockhart (D)	37	Steve Vaughan (R)	71	Katie Henke (R)
4	Mike Brown (D)	38	John Pfeiffer (R)	72	Seneca Scott (D)
5	Doug Cox (R)	39	Marian Cooksey (R)	73	Vacant*
6	Chuck Hoskin (D)	40	Chad Caldwell (R)	74	David Derby (R)
7	Ben Loring (D)	41	John Enns (R)	75	Dan Kirby (R)
8	Ben Sherrer (D)	42	Lisa Billy (R)	76	David Brumbaugh (R)
9	Mark Lepak (R)	43	John Paul Jordan (R)	77	Eric Proctor (D)
10	Travis Dunlap (R)	44	Emily Virgin (D)	78	Jeannie McDaniel (D)
11	Earl Sears (R)	45	Claudia Griffith (D)	79	Weldon Watson (R)
12	Wade Rousselot (D)	46	Scott Martin (R)	80	Mike Ritze (R)
13	Jerry McPeak (D)	47	Leslie Osborn (R)	81	Randy Grau (R)
14	George Faught (R)	48	Pat Ownbey (R)	82	Kevin Calvey (R)
15	Ed Cannaday (D)	49	Tommy Hardin (R)	83	Randy McDaniel (R)
16	Jerry Shoemake (D)	50	Dennis Johnson (R)	84	Sally Kern (R)
17	Brian Renegar (D)	51	Scott R. Biggs (R)	85	Vacant**
18	Donnie Condit (D)	52	Charles Ortega (R)	86	William Fourkiller (D)
19	R.C. Pruett (D)	53	Mark McBride (R)	87	Jason Nelson (R)
20	Bobby Cleveland (R)	54	Paul Wesselhoft (R)	88	Jason Dunnington (D)
21	Dustin Roberts (R)	55	Todd Russ (R)	89	Shane Stone (D)
22	Charles A. McCall (R)	56	David L. Perryman (D)	90	Jon Echols (R)
23	Terry O'Donnell (R)	57	Harold Wright (R)	91	Chris Kannady (R)
24	Steve Kouplen (D)	58	Jeffrey Hickman (R)	92	Richard Morrissette (D)
25	Todd Thomsen (R)	59	Mike Sanders (R)	93	Mike Christian (R)
26	Justin F. Wood (R)	60	Dan Fisher (R)	94	Scott Inman (D)
27	Josh Cockroft (R)	61	Casey Murdock (R)	95	Charlie Joyner (R)
28	Tom Newell (R)	62	John Montgomery (R)	96	Lewis H. Moore (R)
29	James Leewright (R)	63	Jeff Coody (R)	97	Mike Shelton (D)
30	Mark McCullough (R)	64	Ann Coody (R)	98	Michael Rogers (R)
31	Jason Murphey (R)	65	Scooter Park (R)	99	George Young (D)
32	Kevin Wallace (R)	66	Jadine Nollan (R)	100	Elise Hall (R)
33	Lee Denney (R)	67	Pam Peterson (R)	101	Gary Banz (R)
34	Cory T. Williams (D)	68	Glen Mulready (R)		

*Representative Kevin Matthews from District 73 vacated his House seat to be a candidate in a special election for the Oklahoma Senate District 11 seat.   **Representative David Dank from District 85 died on April 10, 2015.

Representatives Contact Reference List

Due to renovations in the State Capitol, call 405/521-2711 for representatives' current room numbers.

Representative	Phone	E-mail
Banz, Gary W. (101)	405/557-7395	garybanz@okhouse.gov
Bennett, John (2)	405/557-7315	john.bennett@okhouse.gov
Biggs, Scott R. (51)	405/557-7405	scott.biggs@okhouse.gov
Billy, Lisa J. (42)	405/557-7365	lisajbilly@okhouse.gov
Brown, Mike (4)	405/557-7408	mikebrown@okhouse.gov
Brumbaugh, David (76)	405/557-7347	david.brumbaugh@okhouse.gov
Caldwell, Chad (40)	405/557-7317	chad.caldwell@okhouse.gov
Calvey, Kevin (82)	405/557-7357	kevin.calvey@okhouse.gov
Cannaday, Ed (15)	405/557-7375	ed.cannaday@okhouse.gov
Casey, Dennis (35)	405/557-7344	dennis.casey@okhouse.gov
Christian, Mike (93)	405/557-7371	mike.christian@okhouse.gov
Cleveland, Bobby (20)	405/557-7308	bob.cleveland@okhouse.gov
Cockroft, Josh (27)	405/557-7349	josh.cockroft@okhouse.gov
Condit, Donnie (18)	405/557-7376	donnie.condit@okhouse.gov
Coody, Ann (64)	405/557-7398	anncoody@okhouse.gov
Coody, Jeff	405/557-7307	jeff.coody@okhouse.gov
Cooksey, Marian (39)	405/557-7342	mariancooksey@okhouse.gov
Cox, Doug (5)	405/557-7415	dougcox@okhouse.gov
Denney, Lee (33)	405/557-7304	leedenney@okhouse.gov
Derby, David (74)	405/557-7377	david.derby@okhouse.gov
Dunlap, Travis (10)	405/557-7402	travis.dunlap@okhouse.gov
Dunnington, Jason (88)	405/557-7396	jason.dunnington@okhouse.gov
Echols, Jon (90)	405/557-7354	jon.echols@okhouse.gov
Enns, John (41)	405/557-7321	john.enns@okhouse.gov
Faught, George (14)	405/557-7310	george.faught@okhouse.gov
Fisher, Dan (60)	405/557-7311	dan.fisher@okhouse.gov
Fourkiller, William (86)	405/557-7394	will.fourkiller@okhouse.gov
Grau, Randy (81)	405/557-7360	randy.grau@okhouse.gov
Griffith, Claudia (45)	405/557-7386	claudia.griffith@okhouse.gov
Hall, Elise (100)	405/557-7403	elise.hall@okhouse.gov
Hardin, Tommy (49)	405/557-7383	tommy.hardin@okhouse.gov
Henke, Katie (71)	405/557-7361	katie.henke@okhouse.gov
Hickman, Jeff (58)	405/557-7339	jwhickman@okhouse.gov
Hoskin, Chuck (6)	405/557-7319	chuck.hoskin@okhouse.gov
Inman, Scott (94)	405/557-7370	scott.inman@okhouse.gov
Johnson, Dennis (50)	405/557-7327	dennis.johnson@okhouse.gov
Jordan, John Paul (43)	405/557-7352	jp.jordan@okhouse.gov
Joyner, Charlie (95)	405/557-7314	charlie.joyner@okhouse.gov
Kannady, Chris (91)	405/557-7337	chris.kannady@okhouse.gov
Kern, Sally (84)	405/557-7348	sallykern@okhouse.gov
Kirby, Dan (75)	405/557-7356	dan.kirby@okhouse.gov
Kouplen, Steve (24)	405/557-7306	steve.kouplen@okhouse.gov
Leewright, James (29)	405/557-7353	james.leewright@okhouse.gov
Lepak, Mark (9)	405/557-7380	mark.lepak@okhouse.gov
Lockhart, James (3)	405/557-7413	james.lockhart@okhouse.gov
Loring, Ben (7)	405/557-7399	ben.loring@okhouse.gov
Martin, Scott (46)	405/557-7329	scott.martin@okhouse.gov
McBride, Mark (53)	405/557-7346	mark.mcbride@okhouse.gov
McCall, Charles A. (22)	405/557-7412	charles.mccall@okhouse.gov

Representative	Phone	E-mail
McCullough, Mark (30)	405/557-7414	mark.mccullough@okhouse.gov
McDaniel, Jeannie (78)	405/557-7334	jeanniemcdaniel@okhouse.gov
McDaniel, Randy (83)	405/557-7409	randy.mcdaniel@okhouse.gov
McPeak, Jerry (13)	405/557-7302	jerrymcpeak@okhouse.gov
Montgomery, John (62)	405/557-7374	john.montgomery@okhouse.gov
Moore, Lewis H. (96)	405/557-7400	lewis.moore@okhouse.gov
Morrissette, Richard (92)	405/557-7404	richardmorrissette@okhouse.gov
Mulready, Glen (68)	405/557-7340	glen.mulready@okhouse.gov
Murdock, Casey (61)	405/557-7384	casey.murdock@okhouse.gov
Murphey, Jason (31)	405/557-7350	jason.murphey@okhouse.gov
Nelson, Jason (87)	405/557-7335	jason.nelson@okhouse.gov
Newell, Tom (28)	405/557-7372	tom.newell@okhouse.gov
Nollan, Jadine (66)	405/557-7390	jadine.nollan@okhouse.gov
O'Donnell, Terry (23)	405/557-7379	terry.odonnell@okhouse.gov
Ortega, Charles (52)	405/557-7369	charles.ortega@okhouse.gov
Osborn, Leslie (47)	405/557-7333	leslie.osborn@okhouse.gov
Ownbey, Pat (48)	405/557-7326	pat.ownbey@okhouse.gov
Park, Scooter (65)	405/557-7305	scooter.park@okhouse.gov
Perryman, David L. (56)	405/557-7401	david.perryman@okhouse.gov
Peterson, Pam (67)	405/557-7341	pampeterson@okhouse.gov
Pfeiffer, John (38)	405/557-7332	john.pfeiffer@okhouse.gov
Proctor, Eric (77)	405/557-7410	eric.proctor@okhouse.gov
Pruett, R.C. (19)	405/557-7382	rcpruett@okhouse.gov
Renegar, Brian (17)	405/557-7381	brian.renegar@okhouse.gov
Ritze, Mike (80)	405/557-7338	mike.ritze@okhouse.gov
Roberts, Dustin (21)	405/557-7366	dustin.roberts@okhouse.gov
Roberts, Sean (36)	405/557-7322	sean.roberts@okhouse.gov
Rogers, Michael (98)	405/557-7362	michael.rogers@okhouse.gov
Rousselot, Wade (12)	405/557-7388	waderousselot@okhouse.gov
Russ, Todd (55)	405/557-7312	todd.russ@okhouse.gov
Sanders, Mike (59)	405/557-7407	mike.sanders@okhouse.gov
Scott, Seneca (72)	405/557-7391	seneca.scott@okhouse.gov
Sears, Earl (11)	405/557-7358	earl.sears@okhouse.gov
Shelton, Mike (97)	405/557-7367	mikeshelton@okhouse.gov
Sherrer, Benjamin (8)	405/557-7364	bensherrer@okhouse.gov
Shoemake, Jerry (16)	405/557-7373	jerryshoemake@okhouse.gov
Stone, Shane (89)	405/557-7397	shane.stone@okhouse.gov
Strohm, Chuck (69)	405/557-7331	chuck.strohm@okhouse.gov
Tadlock, Johnny (1)	405/557-7363	johnny.tadlock@okhouse.gov
Thomsen, Todd (25)	405/557-7336	todd.thomsen@okhouse.gov
Vaughn, Steve (37)	405/557-7355	steve.vaughn@okhouse.gov
Virgin, Emily (44)	405/557-7323	emily.virgin@okhouse.gov
Walker, Ken (70)	405/557-7359	ken.walker@okhouse.gov
Wallace, Kevin (32)	405/557-7368	kevin.wallace@okhouse.gov
Watson, Weldon (79)	405/557-7330	weldon.watson@okhouse.gov
Wesselhoft, Paul (54)	405/557-7343	paulwesselhoft@okhouse.gov
Williams, Cory T. (34)	405/557-7411	cory.williams@okhouse.gov
Wood, Justin F. (26)	405/557-7345	justin.wood@okhouse.gov
Wright, Harold (57)	405/557-7325	harold.wright@okhouse.gov
Young, George (99)	405/557-7393	george.young@okhouse.gov

Speaker of the House of Representatives

Jeffrey W. Hickman

Occupation—Farming/Ranching ▪ **Education**—University of Oklahoma, BA ▪ **Party**—Republican ▪ **District**—58 ▪ **Legislative Experience**—House Member, 2005-present; Deputy Majority Whip, 2007; Speaker Pro Tempore, 2011; Speaker of the House, 2014-present ▪ **Committee Membership**—The Speaker of the House is the ex-officio member of all House special and standing committees.

Hickman was born on November 28, 1973, in Alva, Oklahoma. He received a bachelor's degree in journalism from the University of Oklahoma. He won election to the Oklahoma House of Representatives from District 58 in 2004. Hickman has been involved in his family's farming operation in Alfalfa and Woods counties all of his life, and is the fifth generation to own and farm land in District 58. Prior to his election, he worked in the private sector as vice president of Omni Media Group in Woodward, Oklahoma,. From 1997 to 2003 he served at the University of Oklahoma as assistant to the athletic director, special projects coordinator, and university press secretary. Hickman and his wife, Jana, have three children; Taylor, Ashley, and Austin. He serves on the boards of 101 Classic Bowl Foundation, Oklahoma Summer Arts Institute, and Children's Hospital Foundation. He is a member of the Woodward Rotary Club and Cherokee Lions Club.

To contact Hickman—2300 N Lincoln Blvd., Oklahoma City, OK, 73105
▪ 405/557-7339 ▪ jwhickman@okhouse.gov

Membership

Gary W. Banz

Occupation—Education/Retired ▪ **Education**—Southern Nazarene University, BS; University of Central Oklahoma, MEd ▪ **Party**—Republican ▪ **District**—101 ▪ **Legislative Experience**—House Member, 2005-present; Assistant Majority Floor Leader, 2011; Majority Whip, 2015 ▪ **Committee Membership**—Appropriations and Budget Subcommittee on General Government; Elections and Ethics; Rules; and Tourism and International Relations

Banz was born on December 7, 1945, in Sylvia, Kansas. He received a bachelor's degree from Southern Nazarene University and a master's degree in education from the University of Central Oklahoma. He served in the United States Army from 1968 to 1970 and the U.S. Army Reserve from 1982 to 1990. During his military career, Banz received the Army Commendation Medal and the Army Achievement Medal. He is a retired educator, having taught in the Ada, Midwest City, and Putnam City schools. Banz won election to the Oklahoma House of Representatives from District 101 in 2004. He continues active participation in the Choctaw and Midwest City chambers of commerce, Choctaw Church of the Nazarene, Kiwanis Club of Midwest City, Midwest City Rotary, and Oklahoma

Coaches Association. Banz married the former Linda Burchett. They have three children; Michelle, Mindy, and Mark; and six grandchildren. Banz was a co-founder of Oklahoma Honor Flights in 2009.

To contact Banz—2300 N Lincoln Blvd., Oklahoma City, OK, 73105 ▪ 405/557-7395 ▪ garybanz@okhouse.gov

John Bennett

Occupation—US Marine ▪ **Party**—Republican ▪ **District**—2 ▪ **Legislative Experience**—2011 ▪ **Committee Membership**— Appropriations and Budget; Appropriations and Budget Subcommittee on Public Safety, Chair; Government Oversight and Accountability; and Transportation

Bennett won election to the Oklahoma House of Representatives from District 2 on November 2, 2010.

To contact Bennett—2300 N Lincoln Blvd., Oklahoma City, OK 73105 ▪ 405/557-7315 ▪ john.bennett@okhouse.gov

Scott R. Biggs

Occupation—Legislator ▪ **Education**—Oklahoma State University, BS; University of Oklahoma, JD ▪ **Party**— Republican ▪ **District**—51 ▪ **Legislative Experience**—House Member, 2013 ▪ **Committee Membership**—Agriculture and Rural Development, Vice Chair; Appropriations and Budget Subcommittee on Natural Resources and Regulatory Services; Criminal Justice and Corrections; and Public Safety

Biggs attended Oklahoma State University, where he received a bachelor's degree in agricultural economics. He later received a Juris Doctor degree from the University of Oklahoma. While in law school, Biggs served as a legal intern for the Grady County District Attorney's office, and later served as a prosecutor until January 2012 when he opened his own law practice. Biggs won election to the Oklahoma House of Representatives from District 51 on November 6, 2012. He married Rosslyn Spencer, a veterinarian, in 2002. The couple maintain an equine operation on their farm outside of Chickasha, marketing their stock across the nation. They also manage family farms in the Verden area where they raise wheat and alfalfa. They have two daughters, Maguire, born in 2010, and Spencer born in 2014. They attend Holy Name of Jesus Catholic Church in Chickasha.

To contact Biggs—2300 N Lincoln Blvd., Oklahoma City, OK 73105 ▪ 405/557-7405 ▪ scott.biggs@okhouse.gov

Lisa J. Billy

Occupation—Legislator ▪ **Education**—Northeastern State University, BA; University of Oklahoma, MEd ▪ **Party**— Republican ▪ **District**—42 ▪ **Legislative Experience**— Chickasaw Tribal Legislator, 1996–2001; House Member, 2004–present; Deputy Majority Whip, 2007; Majority Caucus

Vice Chair, 2007; Majority Floor Leader, 2009; Assistant Majority Floor Leader, 2011; Assistant Majority Whip, 2013; Majority Floor Leader, 2015 ▪ **Committee Membership**—Appropriations and Budget; Appropriations and Budget Subcommittee on Public Safety, Vice Chair; and Criminal Justice and Corrections

Billy was born in Purcell, Oklahoma. She received a bachelor's degree in business and fine arts from Northeastern State University and a master's degree in education from the University of Oklahoma. She and her husband, Phillip, led Cub Scout Pack 247, serving four years. Billy also served nine years on the National Board for Girl Scouts of the USA. She attends Lighthouse Worship Center in Purcell. Billy is a member of the National Rifle Association. She is married to Phillip Billy. They have three children; Masheli, Nahinli, and Anoli. Together they enjoy high school band events, Choctaw/Chickasaw dancing, horses, and little league sports.

To contact Billy—PO Box 1412, Purcell, OK 73080 ▪ 405/557-7365 ▪ lisajbilly@okhouse.gov

Mike Brown

Occupation—Business Owner ▪ **Education**—Fort Gibson High School ▪ **Party**—Democrat ▪ **District**—4 ▪ **Legislative Experience**—House Member, 2005–present; Assistant Minority Floor Leader, 2007; Minority Floor Leader, 2009; Minority Appropriations and Budget Advisor, 2013 ▪ **Committee Membership**—Appropriations and Budget; Energy and Natural Resources; and Wildlife

Brown was born on April 7, 1957, in Albuquerque, New Mexico. A graduate of Fort Gibson High School, Brown is a self-employed businessman. He founded and is the owner of Northeastern Oklahoma Sign Company. He won election to the Oklahoma House of Representatives from District 4 in 2004. Brown married the former Tammy Taylor. They have two children, Brandi and Dustin. He continues active participation in the Oklahoma Signage Task Force and the Tahlequah Chamber of Commerce. His hobbies include fiddle making and playing, and horseback riding.

To contact Brown—PO Box 1460, Tahlequah, OK 74465 ▪ 405/557-7408 ▪ mikebrown@okhouse.gov

David Brumbaugh

Occupation—Business Owner/Electric Power Industry ▪ **Education**—Belmont Abbey College, BA; Pacific Western University, MBA; Oklahoma State University ▪ **Party**—Republican ▪ **District**—76 ▪ **Legislative Experience**—House Member, 2011–present; Majority Caucus Chair, 2015 ▪ **Committee Membership**—Appropriations and Budget Subcommittee on General Government; Energy and Natural Resources; Transportation; and Utilities, Vice Chair

Brumbaugh was born on December 2, 1960, in Abington, Pennsylvania. He holds a bachelor's degree in political science, a minor in theology, and master's degree in business administration. Brumbaugh also has executive education in energy policy. He is the president and owner of DRB Industries LLC, a leading company in the electric power industry. He was named to Who's Who of Outstanding U.S. Business Executives. Brumbaugh is also a published author and noted speaker. He is a decorated U.S. Army veteran having served with the 101st Airborne Division and an American Legion Member. From 2008 to 2010 Brumbaugh served as a Tulsa City-County Library Commissioner, and from 2006–2010 as vice chairman of Mingo Valley Christian School Board. He also served on government relations committees with the Broken Arrow Chamber of Commerce. Brumbaugh won election to the Oklahoma House of Representatives from District 76 in 2010. He was ordained as a deacon in 2000, and has served as chairman of the deacon board at Tulsa Bible Church. Brumbaugh serves on the executive board of the Tulsa County Republican Party, as precinct chairman and as a delegate to the county and state Republican conventions. He is a member of the NRA, National Right to Life, Oklahoma Sheriffs Association, and Prison Invasion Ministry. He married the former Shelley Edwards and they have two children, Abigail and Hannah.

To contact Brumbaugh—PO Box 364, Broken Arrow, OK 74013 ▪ 405/557-7347
▪ david.brumbaugh@okhouse.gov

Chad Caldwell

Occupation—State Legislator ▪ **Party**—Republican ▪ **District**—40 ▪ **Legislative Experience**—House Member, 2015 ▪ **Committee Membership**—Appropriations and Budget Subcommittee on Health, Vice Chair; Common Education; Rules; and Utilities

Caldwell won election to the Oklahoma House of Representatives from District 40 in November 2014. He has served as executive director of Hospice Circle of Love. He has also been employed with the University of Oklahoma Athletic Department, Garth Brooks Teammates for Kids Foundation, and Frantz Insurance Agency. Caldwell is an elder at Westminster Presbyterian Church, and serves on several non-profit boards including, president of the Oklahoma Hospice & Palliative Care Association; president-elect of the Enid Rotary Club; and chair of the Enid Chamber's Federal Government Relations Committee. He is also an "Honorary Wing Commander" for Vance Air Force Base. Caldwell and his wife, Hallie, have three children, Holden, Clara, and Caroline.

To contact Brown—2300 N Lincoln Blvd., Oklahoma City OK 73105 ▪ 405/557-7317
▪ chad.caldwell@okhouse.gov

Kevin Calvey

Occupation—State Legislator ▪ **Education**—University of Dallas, BA; Georgetown University, JD ▪ **Party**—Republican ▪ **District**—82 ▪ **Legislative Experience**—House Member, 1998–2006; 2015 ▪ **Committee Membership**—Appropriations and Budget Subcommittee on Judiciary; Energy and Natural Resources; Environmental Law, Chair; and Judiciary and Civil Procedure

Calvey was born on July 13, 1966, in Milwaukee, Wisconsin. He earned a bachelor's degree in 1988 from the University of Dallas, and a Juris Doctor degree from Georgetown University in 1993. He served in the Oklahoma House of Representatives from 1999 to 2006. He won election to the Oklahoma House of Representatives from District 82 in November 2014.

To contact Calvey—2300 N Lincoln Blvd., Oklahoma City, OK 73105 ▪ 405/557-7357 ▪ kevin.calvey@okhouse.gov

Ed Cannaday

Occupation—State Legislator ▪ **Party**—Democrat ▪ **District**—15 ▪ **Legislative Experience**—House Member, 2007–present ▪ **Committee Membership**—Administrative Rules; Appropriations and Budget Subcommittee on Education; Common Education; and Utilities

Cannaday was born in Radisson, Wisconsin, on October 31, 1940. He served in the United States Army, 25th Infantry Division from 1959 to 1962, achieving the rank of Sergeant E-5. In 1964 he received an associate degree from Cameron College. He studied education, social studies, and political science at the University of Tulsa, earning both a bachelor's and master's degree. He has accumulated fifty post graduate hours in psychology and administration. After teaching four years in Kenosha, Wisconsin, Cannaday returned to Oklahoma to help establish the Pontotoc County Alternative Education Program. He later owned and operated the Cannaday Dairy Farm in the Porum, Oklahoma, area from 1976 to 1989. He returned to education as a government and history teacher at Stigler High School, where he also served as principal from 1998 to 2002. He also served as a teaching principal at Webbers Falls from 2002 to 2006. Cannaday won election to the Oklahoma House of Representatives from District 15 in November 2006.

To contact Cannaday—2300 N Lincoln Blvd., Oklahoma City, OK 73105 ▪ 405/557-7375 ▪ ed.cannaday@okhouse.gov

Dennis Casey

Occupation—Educator/Rancher ▪ **Education**—Oilton Public School; Northeastern State University, BS, MS ▪ **Party**—Republican ▪ **District**—35 ▪ **Legislative Experience**—House Member, 2011–present; Assistant Majority Floor Whip, 2011–present ▪ **Committee Membership**—Agriculture and Rural Development; Appropriations and Budget, Vice Chair; and Higher Education and Career Tech

Casey was born on August 6, 1960, in Wellington, Kansas. He received both his bachelor's and Master in Education degree from Northeastern State University. He spent twenty-nine years as a teacher, coach, principal, and superintendent in Oklahoma. Casey won election to the Oklahoma House of Representatives from District 35 in 2010. He and his wife, Kelly, live north of Morrison on a ranch in Pawnee County. They have three children; Heath, Kelcey, and Kamie. They also have three grandchildren. His hobbies are family, fishing, hunting, and raising cattle. They are members of Stillwater Bible Church.

To Contact Casey—2300 N Lincoln Blvd., Oklahoma City, OK 73105 ▪ 405/557-7344
▪ dennis.casey@okhouse.gov

Mike Christian

Occupation—Retired State Trooper ▪ **Education**—University of Arkansas; University of Oklahoma ▪ **Party**—Republican ▪ **District**—93 ▪ **Legislative Experience**—House Member, 2009 ▪ **Committee Membership**—Appropriations and Budget Subcommittee on Public Safety; County and Municpal Government; Public Safety, Chair; and Utilities

Christian was born on January 12, 1970 in Durant Oklahoma. He served as a state trooper for the Oklahoma Highway Patrol for nine years, until his career was cut short by a line-of-duty injury that forced his retirement. He is the recipient of the Purple Heart, and has received numerous awards for his efforts to curb drunk driving and drug trafficking. Christian won election to the Oklahoma House of Representatives from District 93 in November 2008. He is a member of the Choctaw Nation, University of Oklahoma "O" Club, Retired Troopers Association, and the Retired Peace Officers Association. He and his wife, Veda, have one son, Michael Jr.

To contact Christian—2300 N Lincoln Blvd., Oklahoma City, OK 74105 ▪ 405/557-7371
▪ mike.christian@okhouse.gov

Bobby Cleveland

Occupation—Business Owner ▪ **Party**—Republican ▪ **District**—20 ▪ **Legislative Experience**—House Member, 2011–present ▪ **Committee Membership**—Appropriations and Budget Subcommittee on Public Safety; Criminal Justice and Corrections; Long-term Care and Senior Services; and Public Safety, Vice Chair

Cleveland grew up in south Oklahoma City. He started his own small business when he was just out of school. After some early struggles, he began working with a company in Northwest Arkansas that was just gaining steam: Walmart. Over the next thirty years, Cleveland built his business, manufacturing different products for Walmart. His companies have sold everything from Bible covers to refurbished golf balls (Experienced Golf Ball®). An inventor, Cleveland holds two patents and at least ten trademarks. He and his wife, Barbara, live in Slaughterville. Married for forty-nine years, they have two boys, Rob and Rod, and eight grandchildren. The couple are members of Bethel Baptist Church in Norman. Cleveland won election from District 20 to the Oklahoma House of Representatives on November 6, 2012.

To contact Cleveland—2300 N Lincoln Blvd., Oklahoma City, OK 74105
▪ 405/557-7308 ▪ bobby.cleveland@okhouse.gov

Josh Cockroft

Occupation—Legislator ▪ **Party**—Republican ▪ **District**—27 ▪
Legislative Experience—House Member, 2011–present;
Assistant Majority Whip, 2013 ▪ **Committee Membership**—
Appropriations and Budget Subcommittee on Natural Resources
and Regulatory Services; County and Municipal Government;
State Government Operations; and Tourism and International
Relations, Chair

Cockroft, a Republican from Tecumseh, won election to the House of Representatives
from District 27 on November 2, 2010. At the time, he was the second youngest (twenty-
one years old), state representative in state history. He is currently serving in his third
term as representative from District 27, which covers southern Pottawatomie County and
Northern Cleveland County. Cockroft comes from an extensive background in ministry,
and is a devout man of faith. His desire is to bring accountability and accessibility to state
government through honesty and integrity.

To contact Cockroft—2300 N Lincoln Blvd., Oklahoma City, OK 73105 ▪ 405/557-7349
▪ josh.cockroft@okhouse.gov

Donnie Condit

Occupation—Retired Educator ▪ **Education**—East Central
University, BS, MS ▪ **Party**—Democrat ▪ **District**—18 ▪
Legislative Experience—House Member, 2011–present;
Minority Caucus Secretary, 2011 ▪ **Committee Membership**—
Appropriations and Budget Subcommittee on Public Safety;
Common Education; Elections and Ethics, Vice Chair; and Rules

Condit was born in Fort Stockton, Texas. His parents only spent a
couple of months in the Fort Stockton area before they moved back home to south central
Oklahoma. Condit grew up in the Lindsay area, and graduated from Lindsay High School
in 1975. Condit received a bachelor's degree in education in 1980 and a master's degree
in education in 1982, both from East Central University. He is a retired educator, having
served as a teacher, K-12 counselor, and administrator in the McAlester Public School
District. He has been married to his wife, Karen, for more than thirty years. They have
three children; Ami Bax, M.D., and husband Benjamin, Christopher, and Brittany. They
are proud grandparents of Emma, Jack, Joey, and Jude.

To contact Condit—2300 N Lincoln Blvd., Oklahoma City, OK 73105 ▪ 405/557-7376
▪ donnie.condit@okhouse.gov

Ann Coody

Occupation—Education/Retired ▪ **Education**—Hardin-
Simmons University, BA; University of Oklahoma, MEd ▪
Party—Republican ▪ **District**—64 ▪ **Legislative Experience**—
House Member, 2005–present; Majority Caucus Secretary, 2007–
2008 ▪ **Committee Membership**—Appropriations and Budget;

Appropriations and Budget Subcommittee on Education; Common Education, Chair; and Veterans and Military Affairs

Coody was born in Shreveport, Louisiana. She received a bachelor's degree in speech and drama from Hardin-Simmons University in Abilene, Texas, and a master's degree in education from the University of Oklahoma. For thirty-nine years, she served as a teacher, counselor, assistant principal, and principal for the Lawton Public Schools. Coody won election to the Oklahoma House of Representatives from District 64 in 2004. She is an active member of First Baptist Church of Grandfield, Oklahoma, Comanche County Retired Educators, and the Oklahoma Retired Educators Association. She is married to Dale Coody, an evangelistic singer and rancher. Their family includes Nina, intermediate school principal; Jeff, an insurance agent and former U.S. Navy pilot, and his wife, Julie; and granddaughters, Addie and Olivia; and grandson Payne. Coody's hobbies include reading and singing.

To contact Coody—2300 N Lincoln Blvd., Oklahoma City, OK 73105 ▪ 405/557-7398 ▪ anncoody@okhouse.gov

Jeff Coody

Occupation—Business Owner ▪ **Education**—Hardin Simmons University, BA ▪ **Party**—Republican ▪ **District**—63 ▪ **Legislative Experience**—House Member, 2015 ▪ **Committee Membership**—Agriculture and Rural Development; Appropriations and Budget Subcommittee on Health; Environmental Law; and Insurance, Vice Chair

A lifelong resident of southwest Oklahoma, Coody grew up on a farm in Comanche County. In high school he was active in sports, 4–H, and the Future Farmers of America. Coody earned a bachelor's degree in business administration from Hardin Simmons University, where he was named "Outstanding Student in Finance" in 1982, and served as president of the Student Foundation. Coody served in the United States Navy from 1993 to 1999, when he received an honorable discharge. During his tenure in the navy, he flew the P3 Orion, and served as an instructor in the T-34C, readying navy and Marine pilots for Operation Desert Storm. Following his service in the navy, he worked as a corporate pilot, and started his own business as an independent insurance agent in 2002. Coody and his wife, Julie, have three children, Addie, Olivia, and Payne. He won election to the Oklahoma House of Representatives from District 63 in November 2014.

To contact Coody—2300 N Lincoln Blvd., Oklahoma City, OK 73105 ▪ 405/557-7307 ▪ jeff.coody@okhouse.gov

Marian Cooksey

Occupation—Realtor ▪ **Education**—University of Central Oklahoma ▪ **Party**—Republican ▪ **District**—39 ▪ **Legislative Experience**—House Member, 2005-present; Assistant Majority Whip, 2007; Deputy Majority Whip, 2009; Majority Caucus Secretary, 2009; Assistant Majority Whip, 2011 ▪ **Committee Membership**—Appropriations and Budget Subcommittee on Natural Resources and Regulatory Services; Crinimal Justice and

Corrections; Economic Development, Commerce, and Real Estate, Vice Chair; and Energy and Natural Resources

Cooksey was born on November 6, 1943, in Ada, Oklahoma. She attended the University of Central Oklahoma. She has been employed in the Oklahoma Lieutenant Governor's Office, the oil and gas industry, and real estate. Cooksey won election to the Oklahoma House of Representatives from District 39 in 2004. She continues active participation in the Edmond First Baptist Church, Edmond Chamber of Commerce, and Edmond Meals on Wheels. She has one child, Ronnie Anne. Cooksey's hobbies include decorating, reading, and travel.

To contact Cooksey—1105 Columbia Court, Edmond, OK 73003 ▪ 405/330-3976 ▪ mariancooksey@okhouse.gov

Doug Cox

Occupation—Physician ▪ **Education**—Oklahoma State University, BS; Oklahoma University College of Medicine, MD ▪ **Party**—Republican ▪ **District**—5 ▪ **Legislative Experience**— House Member, 2005-present ▪ **Committee Membership**— Alcohol, Tobacco, and Controlled Substances; Appropriations and Budget; Appropriations and Budget Subcommittee on Health, Chair; and Public Health

Cox was born on August 9, 1952, in Tulsa, Oklahoma. He received a bachelor's degree from Oklahoma State University and a Doctorate of Medicine from the University of Oklahoma. A physician at Grove General Hospital, Cox won election to the House of Representatives from District 5 in 2004. He continues active participation in the American College of Emergency Physicians, Oklahoma Academy of Family Practice, and the Oklahoma State Medical Association. He married the former Drenda Butterfield. They have three children; Matt, Scott, and Cassie. Cox's hobbies include flying and water sports.

To contact Cox—33471 S 595 Road, Grove, OK 74344 ▪ 405/557-7415 ▪ dougcox@okhouse.gov

Lee Denney

Occupation—Veterinarian ▪ **Education**—Oklahoma State University, BS, DVM ▪ **Party**—Republican ▪ **District**—33 ▪ **Legislative Experience**—House Member, 2005-present; Assistant Majority Floor Leader, 2007, 2013; Speaker Pro Tempore, 2015 ▪ **Committee Membership**—As Speaker Pro Tempore, Denney is ex-officio voting member on all House committees.

Denney was born on September 19, 1953, in Cushing, Oklahoma. She received a bachelor's degree in agricultural economics and a Doctor of Veterinary Medicine degree from Oklahoma State University. She was employed as a veterinarian for twenty-five years at Veterinary Medical Associates. Denney won election to the Oklahoma House of Representatives from District 33 in 2004. She continues active participation in the American Veterinary Medical Association, Cushing Arts and Humanities Council, Cushing Lion's Club, Daughter's of the American Revolution, First United Methodist Church of

Cushing, Habitat for Humanity, Oklahoma Veterinary Medical Association, and the P.E.O. She has two children, Will Denney and Kate Kupiec. Denney's hobbies include reading and volunteer work.

To contact Denney—2300 N Lincoln Blvd., Oklahoma City, OK 73105 ▪ 405/557-7304 ▪ leedenney@okhouse.gov

David Derby

Occupation—Forensic Scientist ▪ **Education**—Hillsdale Free Will Baptist Bible College, AS; University of Central Oklahoma, BS; University of Oklahoma College of Pharmacy ▪ **Party**— Republican ▪ **District**—74 ▪ **Legislative Experience**—House Member, 2007-present ▪ **Committee Membership**—Alcohol, Tobacco, and Controlled Substances, Chair; Appropriations and Budget Subcommittee on Human Services; Public Health; and Public Safety

Derby was born on May 30, 1976, in Saint Louis, Missouri. He attended the University of Central Oklahoma, where he earned a bachelor's degree in forensic chemistry. In 2012 he earned a doctorate of pharmacy degree from the University of Oklahoma College of Pharmacy. He has worked for the Missouri State Highway Patrol as a forensic chemist, and was an expert witness for district attorneys in fourteen counties. In 2002 the Tulsa Police Department hired Derby for their forensic laboratory, where he specialized in controlled substances. He was the only forensic chemist in the Tulsa area that tested and testified on "clandestine labs," which manufacture Methamphetamine. While working for the Tulsa Police Department, he became aware of the recidivism that plagues Oklahoma. He won election to the Oklahoma House of Representatives from District 74 in November 2006. As a representative, he has introduced legislation each year that focuses on drugs and controlled substances. He has introduced legislation to set up "defacto" drug courts in every Oklahoma county. The purpose of these "defacto" courts is to intervene in the addicts' life before they become a ward of the state.

Derby and his wife, Kim, have two sons, Quinton and Evan. They attend the Rejoice Church in Owasso, where they work with the youth and are involved in choir, drama, and Sunday school class. He is a member of the National Rifle Association.

To contact Derby—PO Box 2150, Owasso, OK 74055 ▪ 405/557-7377 ▪ david.derby@okhouse.gov

Travis Dunlap

Occupation—Business Owner ▪ **Education**—University of Oklahoma ▪ **Party**—Republican ▪ **District**—10 ▪ **Legislative Experience**—Member, 2015 ▪ **Committee Membership**— Appropriations and Budget Subcommittee on Human Services; Economic Development, Commerce, and Real Estate; Environmental Law, Vice Chair; and Tourism and International Relations

Dunlap was born on September 22, 1985, in Bartlesville, Oklahoma. He earned a bachelor's and master's degree in music from the University of Oklahoma in 2008 and 2010.

He spent two years in Southeast Asia with the Southern Baptist International Mission Board Journeyman Program. He operates a small music business in Bartlesville. Dunlap won election to the Oklahoma House of Representatives from District 10 in November 2014. He continues active participation in the Bartlesville Daybreak Rotary, Bartlesville Symphony Orchestra, and the Bartlesville Southern Baptist Church.

To contact Dunlap—2300 N Lincoln Blvd., Oklahoma OK 73105 ▪ 405/557-7402 ▪ travis.dunlap@okhouse.gov

Jason Dunnington

Occupation—Professor/Business Owner ▪ **Education**— Southern Nazarene University, BS; Nazarene Theological Seminary, MA; University of Oklahoma, PhD ▪ **Party**— Democrat ▪ **District**—88 ▪ **Legislative Experience**—House Member, 2015 ▪ **Committee Membership**—Appropriations and Budget Subcommittee on Education; Appropriations and Budget Subcommittee on Public Safety; Environmental Law; State Government Operations

Dunnington was raised in Oklahoma City, but transferred to and graduated from rural Cashion High School. He received an academic scholarship to Southern Nazarene University where he earned a bachelor's degree in psychology and later earned his master's degree in theology from Nazarene Theological Seminary. After pastoring at a local church in Oklahoma City, Dunnington went on to receive his PhD at the University of Oklahoma in Sociology. In addition to teaching, he worked in the oil and gas industry for six years until joining the faculty at Oklahoma City University. Dunnington is currently a Sociology professor at Oklahoma City University, where he enjoys challenging his students to examine and analyze the complex and diverse world we live in. He won election to the Oklahoma House of Representatives from District 88 on August 26,, 2014. Dunnington is a proud father of a son and daughter and is an active member in his community.

To contact Dunnington—2300 N Lincoln Blvd., Oklahoma City, OK 73105 ▪ 405/557-7396 ▪ jason.dunnington@okhouse.gov

Jon Echols

Occupation—Attorney/Business ▪ **Education**—University of Oklahoma, BA; Oklahoma City University, JD ▪ **Party**— Republican ▪ **District**—90 ▪ **Legislative Experience**—House Member, 2013; Assistant Majority Whip, 2013 ▪ **Committee Membership**—Appropriations and Budget Subcommittee on Judiciary; Energy and Natural Resources; Judiciary and Civil Procedure, Vice Chair; and Public Health

Echols received a bachelor's degree in political science from the University of Oklahoma, and a Juris Doctor degree from Oklahoma City University. After spending four years coaching football at Community Christian's junior high and high school, Echols started a group of private businesses with two partners. Those businesses center around taking care of Oklahoma's elderly. They include Sooner Medical Staffing, a medical staffing company that specializes in elder care, Cornerstone Sourcing, a medical permanent placement company, and Absolute Senior Care, a licensed and certified service that assists seniors in their home. He and his wife, Kristen, have three children—David, Ethan, and Kaylee. The family attends First Southern Baptist Church in Del City, where he serves as a deacon. Echols won election to the Oklahoma House of Representatives from District 90 on November 6, 2012.

To contact Echols—2300 N Lincoln Blvd., Oklahoma City, OK 73105 ▪ 405/557-7354 ▪ jon.echols@okhouse.gov

John Enns

Occupation—Farmer/Rancher ▪ **Education**—Tabor College, BA ▪ **Party**—Republican ▪ **District**—41 ▪ **Legislative Experience**—House Member, 2007-present ▪ **Committee Membership**—Agriculture and Rural Development, Chair; Alcohol, Tobacco, and Controlled Substances; Appropriations and Budget Subcommittee on Natural Resources and Regulatory Services; and Veterans and Military Affairs

Enns was born on January 30, 1967, in Enid, Oklahoma. He received a bachelor's degree in natural sciences: biology and chemistry from Tabor College in 1989. He taught microbiology at Northern Oklahoma College for three years. Enns won election to the Oklahoma House of Representatives from District 41 in November 2006. He attends church at Cornerstone Evangelical Free Church in Enid. He is an active member of the Civil Air Patrol and the National Rifle Association. He married the former Charla Peck.

To contact Enns—1741 Pawhuska, Enid, OK 73703 ▪ 405/557-7321 ▪ john.enns@okhouse.gov

George Faught

Occupation—Business Owner ▪ **Education**—Bryan Institute ▪ **Party**—Republican ▪ **District**—14 ▪ **Legislative Experience**—House Member, 2006-2012; 2015 ▪ **Committee Membership**—Administrative Rules, Chair; Appropriations and Budget Subcommittee on General Government; Transportation; and Veterans and Military Affairs

Faught was born on July 14, 1962, in Brownfield, Texas. His family relocated to Muskogee, Oklahoma, when he was six months old. He graduated from Muskogee High School in 1980, and from Bryan Institute in 1987. Faught owns Clean Pro, a carpet cleaning company specializing in fire and water damage restoration. In 2006 Faught became the first Republican in state history elected to House District 14. He served as assistant majority floor leader from 2009-2012. In 2011 he received the Eagle Award from the Oklahoma Eagle Forum, presented by Eagle Forum founder and conservative icon, Phyllis Schlafly. Other honors include being named "Representative of the Year" by the Oklahoma Department of Rehabilitation Services (2011); "Legislator of the Year" by the Oklahoma Psychological Association (2011); and "Patriot of the 2nd Amendment" in 2011 and 2012 by the Oklahoma 2nd Amendment Association (OK2A). In 2012 Faught was one of six seeking the Republican nomination for United States Congress and made it into a run-off where he lost to the eventual winner of the seat. In 2014 he was re-elected to represent Oklahoma House District 14. He is a member of the Muskogee and Fort Gibson chambers of commerce, Gideon's International, National Rifle Association and Oklahoma 2nd Amendment Association. Faught is an active member of Tulsa Bible Church where he serves as deacon, usher, and Discovery Class teacher. He and his wife, Becky, have three grown children: Tyler (married to Rachelle), Jamison (married to Kristen) and Savannah (attending College of the Ozarks). They are expecting their first grandchild in July 2015. His hobbies include traveling, cooking, gardening, and beekeeping.

To contact Faught—2300 N Lincoln Blvd., Oklahoma City, OK 73105 ▪ 405/557-7310 ▪ george.faught@okhouse.gov

Dan Fisher

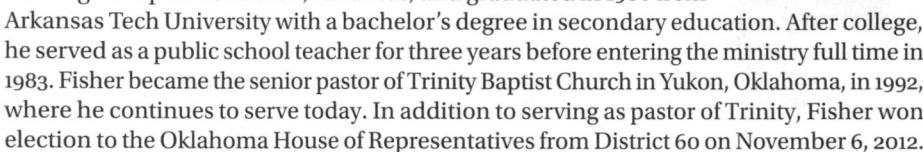

Occupation—Pastor ▪ **Education**—Arkansas Tech University, BS ▪ **Party**—Republican ▪ **District**—60 ▪ **Legislative Experience**—House Member, 2013 ▪ **Committee Membership**—Administrative Rules; Appropriations and Budget Subcommittee on General Government; Common Education; and State and Federal Relations, Vice Chair

Fisher grew up in Van Buren, Arkansas, and graduated in 1980 from Arkansas Tech University with a bachelor's degree in secondary education. After college, he served as a public school teacher for three years before entering the ministry full time in 1983. Fisher became the senior pastor of Trinity Baptist Church in Yukon, Oklahoma, in 1992, where he continues to serve today. In addition to serving as pastor of Trinity, Fisher won election to the Oklahoma House of Representatives from District 60 on November 6, 2012.

Fisher is a published author and recently released his book entitled *Bringing Back the Black Robed Regiment*, which documents the history of the "Patriot Pastors" who led out in the fight for liberty in the war for independence. He is a national conference speaker and a leader in the modern Black Robed Regiment. Fisher travels the country presenting his "Brining Back the Black Robed Regiment" presentation. He serves on the boards of a number of organizations including Reclaiming America, vision America, BOTT Radio Network, and the OKC Tea Party. Fisher and his wife, Pam, have two children, Jacob and Rebekah, who are both married. Jacob is in his final year of medical school at Oklahoma State University, and Rebekah recently graduated from nursing school and serves as a nurse in Weatherford, Oklahoma. Fisher and his wife live on thirty acres west of Yukon, in a log house they built themselves. They raise a few horses in their spare time.

To contact Fisher—2300 N Lincoln Blvd., Oklahoma City, OK 73105 ▪ 405/557-7311 ▪ dan.fisher@okhouse.gov

William Fourkiller

Occupation—Registered Nurse/Elementary Teacher ▪ **Education**—Northeastern State University, BS; University of Oklahoma Health Science Center Tulsa, BS ▪ **Party**—Democrat ▪ **District**—86 ▪ **Legislative Experience**—2011-present ▪ **Committee Membership**—Alcohol, Tobacco, and Controlled Substances, Vice Chair; Appropriations and Budget Subcommittee on Health; Business, Labor, and Retirement Laws; and Public Health

Fourkiller was born on February 26, 1972, in Tahlequah, Oklahoma. He received a bachelor's degree from Northeastern State University, and a bachelor's degree from the University of Oklahoma Health Sciences Center in Tulsa. Fourkiller was employed as an elementary teacher for twelve years in Adair County, teaching in three different schools: Maryetta Elementary, Zion Elementary, and Stilwell Public Schools. Fourkiller returned to nursing school in May 2007, and graduated in August 2008. He worked at W.W. Hastings Hospital in the operating room full time until December 2010. He won election to the Oklahoma House of Representatives from District 86 on November 2, 2010. Fourkiller is a member of Colcord, Stilwell, and Westville chambers of commerce, the National Rifle Association, and Oklahoma Nurses Association. He and his wife, Kerrie, have one son, Toss Mabrey. Fourkiller is a citizen of the Cherokee Nation. His hobbies include spending time with his family, exercising, watching his son participate in sports and other school activities, and officiating Oklahoma high school football. He is an active member of Antioch Baptist Church.

To contact Fourkiller—2300 N Lincoln Blvd., Oklahoma City, OK 73105
▪ 405/557-7394 ▪ will.fourkiller@okhouse.gov

Randy Grau

Occupation—Attorney ▪ **Education**—Pepperdine University; University of Oklahoma College of Law ▪ **Party**—Republican ▪ **District**—81 ▪ **Legislative Experience**—House Member, 2011–present; Assistant Majority Floor Leader, 2013 ▪ **Committee Membership**—Alcohol, Tobacco, and Controlled Substances; Appropriations and Budget Subcommittee on Judiciary; Criminal Justice and Corrections; and Judiciary and Civil Procedure, Chair

Grau won election to the Oklahoma House of Representatives from District 81 on November 2, 2010. He grew up in the district he now serves. He is an award-winning attorney, who frequently speaks regarding ethics and professionalism. Grau served as deputy county commissioner for Oklahoma County, District 3, from 2007 to 2010. As deputy county commissioner he assisted in the administration of a county with over 700,000 residents. The Oklahoma Bar Association selected Grau in 2007 to represent Oklahoma as its representative to the Czech Republic to encourage citizen participation in government. In 2009 Grau climbed Mount Kilimanjaro in Tanzania to raise money for African school children. He is married to Dr. Renee Hamel Grau, and they are active members of Quail Springs Church of Christ. The couple have two children. Grau volunteers monthly with Oklahoma Lawyers for Children, and Epworth Villa Retirement Community.

To contact Grau—2300 N Lincoln Blvd., Oklahoma City, OK 73105 ▪ 405/557-7360 ▪ randy.grau@okhouse.gov

Claudia Griffith

Occupation—Nurse/Public Health ▪ **Education**—University of Oklahoma ▪ **Party**—Democrat ▪ **District**—45 ▪ **Legislative Experience**—House Member, 2015 ▪ **Committee Membership**—Alcohol, Tobacco, and Controlled Substances; Appropriations and Budget Subcommittee on Health; and Public Health

A native of Norman, Oklahoma, Griffith earned a master's degree in public health from the University of Oklahoma. A registered nurse, Griffith served as Norman Regional Hospital's first full time patient education coordinator. She has worked at Cleveland County Health Department, and was a program consultant at Oklahoma University Health Promotions, working with Native American tribes all over the United States on health issues. She served as a former executive director of Health for Friends, a healthcare non-profit organization which provided prenatal, chronic disease, pharmacy, and dental services to the under served. She has been active in the Norman community including the Norman Chamber of Commerce, Leadership Norman, Imagine Norman and the Boy Scouts of America. She was one of the first Oklahomans to volunteer as a responder in the aftermath of the Oklahoma City bombing in 1995. Claudia and her husband, Jim, have been married forty-two years and together they have built a successful dentist practice in Norman. She won election to the Oklahoma House of Representatives from District 45 in November 2014.

To contact Griffith—2300 N Lincoln Blvd., Oklahoma City, OK 73105 ▪ 405/557-7386 ▪ claudia.griffith@okhouse.gov

Elise Hall

Occupation—Marketing ▪ **Education**—University of Central Oklahoma, BBA ▪ **Party**—Republican ▪ **District**—100 ▪ **Legislative Experience**—House Member, 2011-present; Majority Caucus Secretary, 2013-2014; Majority Caucus Vice Chair, 2015 ▪ **Committee Membership**—Appropriations and Budget Subcommittee on Revenue and Taxation; Economic Development, Commerce, and Real Estate; Government Oversight and Accountability; and Public Health, Vice Chair

Hall was born on March 26, 1989. As a teenager, she founded Anna Elise Photography and Design, and learned how to run a successful business, mastering budgeting, expense reports, and income statements. She later became the director of marketing and advertising for WesternLawns in Oklahoma City. Hall received a bachelor's degree in marketing from the University of Central Oklahoma. She worked with TeenPact Leadership Schools, teaching students in thirteen states about how government works and how they can make a difference. Hall won election to the Oklahoma House of Representatives from District 100 on November 2, 2010. She serves in many ways at her local church, Bethany First Church of the Nazarene. When the legislature is not in session, she provides freelance design, marketing, and advertising services to Oklahoma City.

To contact Hall—2300 N Lincoln Blvd., Oklahoma City, OK 73105 ▪ 405/557-7403 ▪ elise.hall@okhouse.gov.

Tommy Hardin

Occupation—Air Traffic Controller, Retired ■ **Party**—Republican ■ **District**—49 ■ **Legislative Experience**—House Member, 2011–present ■ **Committee Membership**—Appropriations and Budget Subcommittee on Public Safety; Energy and Natural Resources; Rules, Chair; and Wildlife

Hardin was born on January 6, 1962, and is a retired air traffic controller. He won election to the Oklahoma House of Representatives from District 49 on November 2, 2010.

To contact Hardin—2300 N Lincoln Blvd., Oklahoma City, OK 73105 ■ 405/557-7383 ■ tommy.hardin@okhouse.gov

Katie Henke

Occupation—Educator ■ **Education**—University of Alabama, BS ■ **Party**—Republican ■ **District**—71 ■ **Legislative Experience**—House Member, 2013; Majority Caucus Secretary, 2015 ■ **Committee Membership**—Appropriations and Budget Subcommittee on Education, Vice Chair; Common Education; Higher Education and Career Tech; and Transportation

After graduating from Cascia Hall Preparatory School in 1999, Henke went on to study education at the University of Alabama, graduating with a bachelor's degree in early childhood development. During her career, she has taught special needs children at Tulsa's Little Light House, as well as pre-kindergarten classes at Montessori and Riverfield schools. In her spare time, Henke enjoys volunteering. In addition to various local charities, she has spent time with the Tulsa County Republican Party serving on their executive and platform committees. She is a member of the Tulsa Republican Club, the Republican Women's Club of Tulsa, the Oklahoma Federation of Republican Women, the National Federation of Republican Women, and the Oklahoma First Ladies (OFRW). Henke and her husband Frazier have been married since June 2009. Henke won election to the Oklahoma House of Representatives from District 71 on November 6, 2012.

To contact Henke—2300 N Lincoln Blvd., Oklahoma City, OK 73105 ■ 405/557-7361 ■ katie.henke@okhouse.gov

Chuck Hoskin

Occupation—Educator ■ **Education**—Northeastern Oklahoma A&M College, AA; Northeastern State University, BA, MEd ■ **Party**—Democrat ■ **District**—6 ■ **Legislative Experience**—House Member, 2007–present; Minority Caucus Chair, 2009; Minority Floor Leader, 2011; Minority Whip, 2013–present ■ **Committee Membership**—Appropriations and Budget; Appropriations and Budget Subcommittee on General Government; and Veterans and Military Affairs

Hoskin was born on January 29, 1952, in Claremore, Oklahoma, and has been a life long resident of District 6. He graduated from Vinita High School in 1970, and enlisted in the

United States Navy. Hoskin was stationed aboard the *USS Independence*, and upon his honorable discharge became a journeyman ironworker. He received an associate of arts degree from Northeastern Oklahoma A&M College, and a bachelor's degree in social sciences from Northeastern State University. He served as an American History and government teacher in the Vinita Public School system. He later received his master's degree in education from NSU. He worked as an administrator for Locust Grove Public Schools. Hoskin has been an elected member and deputy speaker of the Cherokee Nation Tribal Council, representing Craig and Nowata counties. He won election to the Oklahoma House of Representatives from District 6 in November 2006. He is married to the former Stephanie Reichert, and they have three children; Amy, Charles Jr., and Amelia.

To contact Hoskin—PO Box 941, Vinita, OK 74301 ■ 918/256-3229
■ chuck.hoskin@okhouse.gov

Scott Inman

Occupation—Attorney ■ **Education**—University of Oklahoma, BA, JD ■ **Party**—Democrat ■ **District**—94 ■ **Legislative Experience**—House Member, 2007–present; Minority Leader, 2010–present ■ **Committee Membership**—Appropriations and Budget; Appropriations and Budget Subcommittee on Judiciary; and Energy and Natural Resources

Inman was born on October 2, 1978, in Midwest City, Oklahoma. Raised in Del City, Oklahoma, Inman graduated first in his class from Del City High School in 1997. He then graduated summa cum laude in 2001 from the University of Oklahoma with a bachelor's degree in political science with a Spanish minor. In 2004, he received a Juris Doctor degree from the University of Oklahoma School of Law. He practiced law in downtown Oklahoma City until he won election to the Oklahoma House of Representatives from District 94 in November 2006. Upon his election, Inman became the first graduate of Del City High School to ever represent the community at the state capitol. In 2009 Inman was elected by his caucus to serve as House democratic leader. At age thirty-two, he became the youngest person in state history to lead a caucus in either the house or senate. He was reelected to his second term as democratic leader in 2011. Inman has been recognized for his legislative accomplishments by the Oklahoma Public Employees Association. In 2010 he received the OPEA Legislator of the Year Award. In 2012 OPEA again honored him with a Special Recognition Award for his work that session. He was also honored with the 2012 Outstanding Speaker Award by Embry-Riddle Aeronautical University. Inman continues active participation in the community as president of the Del City Rotary; an executive board member of the Oklahoma Parkinson Foundation; an executive board member of the Oklahoma Bar Association's High School Mock Trial Program; a board member of the DelQuest Student Leadership Program; and a member of the 2010 Tinker Air Force Base COMSTAR Program. Inman married the former Dessa Baker. They have two children, Ella Grace and Sophia Claire.

To contact Inman—2300 N Lincoln Blvd., Oklahoma City, OK 73105 ■ 405/557-7370
■ scott.inman@okhouse.gov

Dennis Johnson

Occupation—Business Owner ▪ **Education**—Weber State University, BS ▪ **Party**—Republican ▪ **District**—50 ▪ **Legislative Experience**—House Member, 2007-present; Assistant Majority Floor Leader, 2009-2012; Majority Leader, 2013 ▪ **Committee Membership**—Appropriations and Budget; Appropriations and Budget Subcommittee on General Government, Chair; Energy and Natural Resources; and Public Safety

Johnson was born in July 1953 in Long Beach, California. He received a bachelor's degree in marketing from Weber State University in Ogden, Utah. Following his college graduation, he moved to Duncan, Oklahoma, and co-founded A-1 Appliance. He served on the Duncan City Council from 1996 to 1999, and as mayor of Duncan from 1999 to 2003. Johnson won election to the Oklahoma House of Representatives from District 50 in November 2006. He and his wife, Susan, have three children; Bryan, Caroline, and Laura.

To contact Johnson—2300 N Lincoln Blvd., Oklahoma City, OK 73105 ▪ 405/557-7327 ▪ dennis.johnson@okhouse.gov

John Paul Jordan

Occupation—Attorney ▪ **Education**—University of Central Oklahoma, BA; University of Oklahoma College of Law, JD ▪ **Party**—Republican ▪ **District**—43 ▪ **Legislative Experience**—House Member, 2015 ▪ **Committee Membership**—Appropriations and Budget Subcommittee on Human Services; Children, Youth, and Family Services; Common Education; and Government Oversight and Accountability, Vice Chair

Jordan is a lifelong resident of Canadian County, Oklahoma. He earned a bachelors degree in education at the University of Central Oklahoma. He taught United States history and government at Roosevelt Middle School in Oklahoma City. He earned a Juris Doctor degree from the University of Oklahoma College of Law, and in 2010 founded the Jordan Law Firm. He is currently active with the Oklahoma County and Canadian County bar associations, and is licensed to practice law in all the federal courts in Oklahoma. He also serves as an adjunct professor at Redlands Community College. Jordan won election to the Oklahoma House of Representatives from District 43 in November 2014. Jordan and his wife, Christi, have been married since 2007, and live in Yukon, where they are active members of Trinity Baptist Church.

To contact Jordan—2300 N Lincoln Blvd., Oklahoma City, OK 73105 ▪ 405/557-7352 ▪ jp.jordan@okhouse.gov

Charlie Joyner

Occupation—Fire Chief, Retired/Businessman, Retired ▪ **Education**—Midwest City High School; Oklahoma State University/OKC; National Fire Academy ▪ **Party**—Republican ▪ **District**—95 ▪ **Legislative Experience**—Midwest City Council; Midwest City Vice Mayor; House Member, 2007-present ▪ **Committee Membership**—Appropriations and Budget Subcommittee on Transportation; Business, Labor, and Retirement Laws; Elections and Ethics; and Transportation, Chair

Joyner was born on July 22, 1940, in Rose Hill, North Carolina. He attended Midwest City High School, Oklahoma State University/OKC, and the National Fire Academy. He served on the Midwest City Fire Department for twenty-two years, retiring as fire chief. He served as the operations manager for Tony Caesar's Flower and Greenhouses, his wife's family-owned business, until the business was sold in 1999. He has served on the Midwest City Chamber Community Economic Development Committee, as chair of the Midwest City Comprehensive Planning Committee, and on the Midwest City Credit Union Board of Directors and the Midwest City Tree Board. Joyner won election to the Oklahoma House of Representatives from District 95 in November 2006. He served as president of the Midwest City Rotary Club from 2006-2007; as past president of Metro Area Fire Chiefs Association; and past president of the Oklahoma Fire Chiefs Association. He is a member of the Midwest City Chamber of Commerce, Midwest City Rotary Club, Mid-Del Tinker 100 Club, the Oklahoma Retired Fire Chiefs Association, and the Oklahoma Retired Firefighters Association. He and his wife, Gwen, have four children and seven grandchildren. His hobbies include family, sports, auctions, and politics.

To contact Joyner—3500 Bella Vista Drive, Midwest City, OK 73110 ▪ 405/557-7314 ▪ charlie.joyner@okhouse.gov

Chris Kannady

Occupation—Attorney ▪ **Education**—University of Oklahoma, BA, MA, JD; George Washington University, MA ▪ **Party**—Republican ▪ **District**—91 ▪ **Legislative Experience**—House Member, 2015 ▪ **Committee Membership**—Appropriations and Budget Subcommittee on Judiciary, Vice Chair; Higher Education and Career Tech; Judiciary and Civil Procedure; and Rules

Kannady won election to the Oklahoma House of Representatives from District 91 in November 2014. He earned a bachelor's degree, a business administration degree, and a law degree from the University of Oklahoma. He served as a judge advocate in the United States Marine Corps, and served multiple tours in both Iraq and Afghanistan. He continued his education, while stationed at the Pentagon, at George Washington University earning a master's degree in national security and foreign relations. Kannady and his wife, Renee, have two children.

To contact Kannady—2300 N Lincoln Blvd., Oklahoma City, OK 73105 ▪ 405/557-7337 ▪ chris.kannady@okhouse.gov

Sally Kern

Occupation—Education ▪ **Education**—University of Texas at Arlington, BA; East Texas State University ▪ **Party**—Republican ▪ **District**—84 ▪ **Legislative Experience**—House Member, 2005–present ▪ **Committee Membership**—Appropriations and Budget Subcommittee on Education; Children, Youth, and Family Services, Chair; Common Education; and State and Federal Relations

Kern was born on November 27, 1946, in Jonesboro, Arkansas. She received a bachelor's degree in sociology from the University of Texas at Arlington in 1971. She also obtained teacher certification in social studies with emphasis on government from East Texas State University in 1986. Kern won election to the Oklahoma House of Representatives from District 84 in 2004. She continues active participation in the American Legislative Exchange Council, Eagle Forum, Frontier Country Republican Women, Heart and Hand Ministries, Northwest Chamber of Commerce, Olivet Baptist Church, and Tri-City Republican Women's Club. She is married to Steve Kern, pastor of Olivet Baptist Church. They have two sons, Jesse and Nathan, and one daughter-in-law, Amie. She also has two grandsons, Luke and Grant. Kern's hobbies include golf, playing games, spending time with family and friends, and reading.

To contact Kern—2713 Sterling Avenue, Oklahoma City, OK 73127 ▪ 405/557-7348 ▪ sallykern@okhouse.gov

Dan Kirby

Occupation—State Legislator/Real Estate Associate ▪ **Education**—Apostolic Bible Institute ▪ **Party**—Republican ▪ **District**—75 ▪ **Legislative Experience**—House Member 2009–present ▪ **Committee Membership**—Appropriations and Budget Subcommittee on Public Safety; County and Municipal Government; Economic Development, Commerce, and Real Estate, Chair; and Insurance

Kirby attended Apostolic Bible Institute. He won election to the Oklahoma House of Representatives from District 75 in November 2008. Kirby is very active in the community, and serves on several boards and committees within his district.

To contact Kirby—2300 N Lincoln Blvd., Oklahoma City, OK 73105 ▪ 405/557-7356 ▪ dan.kirby@okhouse.gov

Steve Kouplen

Occupation—Rancher ▪ **Education**—Oklahoma State University, BA, MA ▪ **Party**—Democrat ▪ **District**—24 ▪ **Legislative Experience**—House Member 2009–present; Assistant Minority Floor Leader, 2011–2014; Minority Caucus Vice Chair, 2015 ▪ **Committee Membership**—Agriculture and Rural Development; Appropriations and Budget Subcommittee on Natural Resources and Regulatory Services; Energy and Natural Resources; and Insurance

Kouplen is a lifelong resident of District 24. He attended Oklahoma State University, where he received a bachelor's degree and a master's degree in agricultural education. He is self-employed as a rancher. He has served as past president of the Oklahoma Farm Bureau. He is currently a member of the American Farmers and Ranchers, American Hereford Association, Beggs School District, Beggs Masonic Lodge, East Central Electric Cooperative, National Rifle Association, Oklahoma Beef Industry, Oklahoma Cattlemen's Association, Okmulgee County Fair, and Okmulgee County Rural Water District #6. Kouplen won election to the Oklahoma House of Representatives from District 24 in November 2008.

To contact Kouplen—2300 N Lincoln Blvd., Oklahoma City, OK 73105 ▪ 405/557-7306 ▪ steve.kouplen@okhouse.gov

James Leewright

Occupation—Business Owner ▪ **Party**—Republican ▪ **District**—29 ▪ **Legislative Experience**—House Member 2015 ▪ **Committee Membership**—Appropriations and Budget Subcommittee on Transportation; Banking and Financial Services, Vice Chair; Government Oversight and Accountability; and Higher Education and Career Tech

Leewright won election to the Oklahoma House of Representatives from District 29 in November 2014. He has worked for a Fortune 500 company for ten years, and is now a small business owner of Dynamic Restoration in Creek County. He was named "Entrepreneur of the Year" for Creek County in 2007, and was named one of "Oklahoma's Top 40 Under 40" professionals in the state by Oklahoma Magazine. He has served as a "Big Brother" for Big Brothers, Big Sisters, and has served on the board of directors and executive board for the Sapulpa Chamber of Commerce. He has been captain for the Red Cross Heroes Campaign, and is past president of Sapulpa Ambassadors. Leewright and his wife, Cari, have four children: Blake, Jack, Kendall, and Carington. They attend the First Baptist Church of Bristow.

To contact Leewright—2300 N Lincoln Blvd., Oklahoma City, OK 73105 ▪ 405/557-7353 ▪ james.leewright@okhouse.gov

Mark Lepak

Occupation—Telecommunications ▪ **Education**—University of Oklahoma, BS ▪ **Party**—Republican ▪ **District**—9 ▪ **Legislative Experience**—House Member, 2015 ▪ **Committee Membership**—Appropriations and Budget Subcommittee on Natural Resources and Regulatory Services; State and Federal Relations; State Government Operations, Vice Chair; and Tourism and International Relations

Lepak won election to the Oklahoma House of Representatives from District 9 in November 2014. He earned a bachelor's degree in engineering physics from the University of Oklahoma, and has been employed for over thirty-five years in the telecommunications field with AT&T. At the time he announced his candidacy for the Oklahoma House of

Representatives, he served as a council member on the Claremore City Council. Lepak and his wife, Linda, have five children.

To contact Lepak—2300 N Lincoln Blvd., Oklahoma City, OK 73105 ▪ 405/557-7380 ▪ mark.lepak@okhouse.gov

James Lockhart

Occupation—Rancher/Farmer/Biologist ▪ **Education**—
Carl Albert State College, AS; University of Phoenix, BS ▪
Party—Democrat ▪ **District**—3 ▪ **Legislative Experience**—
House Member, 2011–present ▪ **Committee Membership**—
Appropriations and Budget Subcommittee on Transportation;
Transportation; Utilities; and Wildlife

Lockhart resides in Heavener, where he was raised. He received an associate degree in biology and zoology from Carl Albert State College, and a bachelor's degree in business management from the University of Phoenix. He holds an Oklahoma Teaching Certificate, and is certified to teach business and economics. His family operates a cow and calf operation. He and his wife, Carrie, have two children, Hope and Jakob. Lockhart has worked on several scientific research projects including alternative energy. He won election to the Oklahoma House of Representatives from District 3 on November 2, 2010. He is a member of the First Baptist Church of Heavener, LeFlore County Cattlemen's Association, Masonic Lodge, and Poteau Chamber of Commerce. He is a card holder in the Professional Rodeo Cowboys Association. He also served as a team leader at the World Trade Center Recovery Effort in 2001 and 2002.

To contact Lockhart—2300 N Lincoln Blvd., Oklahoma City, OK 73105 ▪ 405/557-7413 ▪ james.lockhart@okhouse.gov

Ben Loring

Occupation—Attorney ▪ **Education**—University of
Oklahoma, BS, JD ▪ **Party**—Democrat ▪ **District**—7 ▪
Legislative Experience—House Member, 2015 ▪ **Committee
Membership**—Appropriations and Budget Subcommittee on the
Judiciary; Appropriations and Budget Subcommittee on Public
Safety; Public Safety; Relations; and Tourism and International
Relations

Loring was born on February 23, 1953, in Lake Charles, Louisiana. He grew up in Bartlesville, Oklahoma. Loring earned a bachelor's degree in political science and a Juris Doctor degree both from the University of Oklahoma. He practiced law in Miami, Oklahoma, where he served as the district attorney from 1991 to 1999. He then entered private practice with Eddie Wyant. When Wyant became district attorney in 2004, Loring served as his first assistant.

Loring won election to the Oklahoma House of Representatives from District 7 in November 2014. He has served on the Oklahoma Commission on Children and Youth for fifteen years, serving three years as chair. He and his wife, Barbara, have two sons, David and Ian. Both sons served in the United States Army. Barbara is a special education teacher in the Miami Public Schools. The Lorings purchased a small farm next to their home in Miami. Loring continues to serve as a Boy Scout leader, and enjoys camping, canoeing, hiking, rappelling, and other outdoor adventures with his scouts.

To contact Loring—201 16 Place SW, Miami, OK 74354
- 405/557-7399■ ben.loring@okhouse.gov

Scott Martin

Occupation—Banking ▪ **Education**—University of Oklahoma, BS ▪ **Party**—Republican ▪ **District**—46 ▪ **Legislative Experience**—House Member, 2007-present; Assistant Majority Whip, 2007 ▪ **Committee Membership**—Appropriations and Budget; Appropriations and Budget Subcommittee on Eduation, Chair; Joint Committee on Appropriations and Budget; Banking and Financial Services; and State Government Operations

Martin was born on December 28, 1971, in Tulsa, Oklahoma. He received a bachelor's degree in political science from the University of Oklahoma in 1995. Martin won election to the Oklahoma House of Representatives from District 46 in November 2006. From 1995 to 1999, Martin worked for the City of Noble as projects director and public works director. From 1999 to 2006, he worked for the City of Norman as the assistant to the city manager. He is currently employed as an assistant vice president for a local community bank. He continues active participation in the Boy Scouts of America, National Rifle Association, Noble and Norman chambers of commerce, Norman Business Association, OU Alumni Association, and United Way. Scott is an Eagle Scout, served as student body president at OU from 1994 to 1995, and is a member of the Kappa Sigma Fraternity. He is married to the former Angela Berglan. They have two sons, Luke and Blake, and a daughter Gentry. They attend Bethel Baptist Church in Norman, where he serves as a deacon and teaches Sunday school.

To contact Martin—2916 Stonebridge Court, Norman, OK 73071 ▪ 405/701-8811
- scott.martin@okhouse.gov

Mark McBride

Occupation—Business Owner ▪ **Education**—Northwestern Oklahoma State University ▪ **Party**—Republican ▪ **District**—53 ▪ **Legislative Experience**—House Member, 2013 ▪ **Committee Membership**—Appropriations and Budget Subcommittee on Public Safety; Business, Labor, and Retirement Laws; Energy and Natural Resources, Vice Chair; Resources, Vice Chair; and Utilities

McBride is a fifth generation Oklahoman. The McBride family has called Moore home since the 1940s. He graduated from Moore High School in 1979, where he was active in Future Farmers of America, serving his junior and senior years as vice president. McBride attended Northwestern Oklahoma State University before going into farming and ranching opera-tions that he managed for several years. He also worked in the western Oklahoma oil fields for a brief time. McBride and his wife, Alana, are active members of First Baptist Church in Moore. He has been involved in several areas of mission ministry and humanitarian aid. He has consulted with mission projects in Central America, Eastern Europe, and Africa. Since 2003, McBride has personally led mission teams several times a year into remote village areas of Nicaragua and Ethiopia where they help with agricultural and veterinar-ian projects. He is the owner of two successful Moore businesses: McBride Construction and Roofing, and McBride Homes. Among his civic and community activities, he is a member of the Moore and South Oklahoma City chambers of commerce, as well as the Central Oklahoma Homebuilders Association, the National Homebuilders Association, Cleveland County Rebuilding Together, the National Federation of Independent Business, and the National Rifle Association. McBride won election to the Oklahoma House of Representatives from District 53 on November 6, 2012.

To contact McBride—2300 N Lincoln Blvd., Oklahoma City, OK 73105 ▪ 405/557-7346 ▪ mark.mcbride@okhouse.gov

Charles A. McCall

Occupation—President and CEO of AmeriState Bank ▪ **Education**—University of Oklahoma, BS; University of Colorado ▪ **Party**—Republican ▪ **District**—22 ▪ **Legislative Experience**—House Member, 2013 ▪ **Committee Membership**—Appropriations and Budget; Appropriations and Budget Subcommittee on Revenue and Taxation, Vice Chair; Banking and Financial Services; and Commerce and Real Estate

A fourth-generation southern Oklahoma native, McCall graduated from Atoka High School in 1988. He received a bachelor's degree in finance from the University of Oklahoma in December 1992, and completed his state license as a nursing home administrator in 1993. McCall then went on to complete the Graduate School of Banking at the University of Colorado in 2000. Although McCall began working at the family bank as a young boy, shredding paper for $2 per bag, he later worked as a part-time bank teller his junior and senior year in high school. After returning to the bank from the University of Oklahoma, he worked through every department, learning the family business and earning the respect of his co-workers and peers in the community. After eight years of full-time service, he was named President of AmeriState Bank in 2001, and then was also named CEO of AmeriState Bank in 2008. McCall is a member of Cornerstone Church in Atoka, where he serves as a church elder and teacher. He has served in many community organizations and has held the position of president of the Atoka Chamber of Commerce and the Atoka Lions Club; vice-chairman of the Planning and Zoning Commission; trustee of the Atoka County Health Care Authority; and trustee of the Atoka Perpetual Cemetery Trust. He was elected mayor of Atoka in 2005. As mayor, he successfully accomplished the completion of a new water treatment plant, a new waste water treatment plant, and a multi-million dollar sports complex. His leadership over the past seven years has resulted in over $48 million dollars of new investment; over 500 jobs created or saved; and a new school cafetorium and new elementary school facility. McCall was selected as a state finalist for "Mayor of the Year" by the Oklahoma Municipal League in 2010. He and his wife, Stephanie, have two sons, Chase and Carson. McCall won election to the Oklahoma House of Representatives from District 22 on November 6, 2012.

To contact McCall—2300 N Lincoln Blvd., Oklahoma City, OK 73105 ▪ 405/557-7412 ▪ charles.mccall@okhouse.gov

Mark McCullough

Occupation—State Legislator ■ **Education**—Oklahoma State University, BA, MEd ■ **Party**—Republican ■ **District**—30 ■ **Legislative Experience**—House Member, 2007-present ■ **Committee Membership**—Appropriations and Budget; Appropriations and Budget Subcommittee on Judiciary, Chair; Criminal Justice and Corrections; and Judiciary and Civil Procedure

McCullough was born on August 7, 1967, in Sapulpa Oklahoma. He received a bachelor's degree in agriculture and a master's degree in technology education from Oklahoma State University. He also received a Juris Doctor degree from the University of Tulsa. He served in the United States Peace Corps as a high school teacher in Botswana, Africa. He served as assistant attorney general for the Illinois Attorney General's Office, and in the Special Victims Unit of the Indianapolis Prosecutor's Office. He has also worked in medical sales. McCullough won election to the Oklahoma House of Representatives from District 30 in November 2006. He and his wife, Charlotte, have two sons, Clayton and Everett. His hobbies include fishing, hunting, and spending time with his family.

To contact McCullough—4825 Dogwood Place, Sapulpa, OK 74066 ■ 405-557-7414 ■ mark.mccullough@okhouse.gov

Jeannie McDaniel

Occupation—State Legislator ■ **Education**—Tulsa Community College, AA; University of Oklahoma, BLS ■ **Party**—Democrat ■ **District**—78 ■ **Legislative Experience**—House Member, 2005-present; Assistant Minority Floor Leader, 2009-present ■ **Committee Membership**—Appropriations and Budget; Common Education; Long-term Care and Senior Services; and Public Health

Born on December 10, 1948, McDaniel received an associate degree from Tulsa Community College in 2002 and a bachelor's degree in liberal studies from the University of Oklahoma in 2004. She has been employed as executive director of the Metropolitan Tulsa Citizens Crime Commission, as coordinator of neighborhoods for the Tulsa Mayor's Office, and with the City of Tulsa. McDaniel won election to the Oklahoma House of Representatives from District 78 in 2004. She continues active participation in Habitat for Humanity, League of Women Voters, YMCA Tulsa Advisory Board, Tulsa First United Methodist Church, and Will Rogers Rotary Club. She married Joe L. McDaniel. They have five grown children and seven grandchildren. McDaniel's hobbies include jogging and volunteer work.

To contact McDaniel—1416 S Marion Avenue, Tulsa, OK 74112 ■ 918/834-3259 ■ jeanniemcdaniel@okhouse.gov

Randy McDaniel

Occupation—Financial Advisor/Stockbroker ▪ **Education**—University of Oklahoma, BA; Georgetown University, Institute of Business and Government Affairs; Cambridge University MPhil ▪ **Party**—Republican ▪ **District**—83 ▪ **Legislative Experience**—House Member, 2007-present; Deputy Majority Whip, 2009-2010; Assistant Majority Whip, 2011-2012; Assistant Floor Leader, 2013-2014 ▪ **Committee Membership**—Appropriations and Budget; Business, Labor, and Retirement Laws, Chair; Economic Development, Commerce, and Real Estate; and Insurance

McDaniel is a fourth-generation Oklahoman. He received a bachelor's degree in economics from the University of Oklahoma, where he was selected the Outstanding Senior Man, and served as the student body president. He also graduated from the Institute of Business and Government Affairs at Georgetown University, and received a master's degree in land economy from Cambridge University in England. McDaniel has worked in the financial services for more than twenty years, and is a vice president of investments at Wells Fargo Advisors. He served in the Oklahoma Army National Guard as a field artillery officer and an engineer officer from 1988-1999. McDaniel won election to the Oklahoma House of Representatives from District 83 in 2006. He and his wife, Julie, have two children, Grace and John. McDaniel has served on numerous community boards. He continues active participation in the Crossings Community Church, Rotary Club 29, Southern Legislative Conference, and American Legislative Exchange Council. His hobbies include golf and other outdoor sports.

To contact McDaniel—to 2300 N Lincoln Blvd., Oklahoma City, OK 73105 ▪ 405/557-7409 ▪ randy.mcdaniel@okhouse.gov

Jerry McPeak

Occupation—Cattleman/Education ▪ **Education**—Oklahoma State University, BS; Northeastern State University, MS ▪ **Party**—Democrat ▪ **District**—13 ▪ **Legislative Experience**—House Member, 2005-present; Assistant Minority Floor Leader, 2007; Deputy Minority Floor Leader, 2009; Minority Caucus Chair, 2011-present ▪ **Committee Membership**—Appropriations and Budget; Energy and Natural Resources; and Transportation

McPeak was born on October 21, 1946, in Checotah, Oklahoma. He received a bachelor's degree from Oklahoma State University, and a master's degree from Northeastern State University. McPeak has been employed in the cattle industry in a variety of areas including a livestock feed business and a packing house and feed yard. He also has been employed at Connors State College as dean of men, a livestock judging coach, and psychology instructor. McPeak won election to the Oklahoma House of Representatives from District 13 in 2005. He continues active participation in Connors State College Agriculture Alumni, Farm House Fraternity, Higher Education Alumni Council of Oklahoma, Little League Coaches Association, Muskogee County NAACP, National Collegiate Livestock Judging Coaches, Oklahoma Farm Bureau, the Oklahoma Farmers and Ranchers Association, and Future Farmers of America. McPeak and his wife, Veda, have operated "Be A Champ" for three decades. They have four children; Jeff, Jason, Jinger, and Jori. His hobbies include serving as a volunteer 4–H leader, motivational speaking, and youth work, including coaching for little league baseball, basketball, and softball. McPeak is a citizen of the Muscogee (Creek) Nation.

To contact McPeak—PO Box 932, Warner, OK 74469 ▪ 405/557-7302
▪ jerrymcpeak@okhouse.gov

John Montgomery

Occupation—State Legislator ▪ **Education**—University of Oklahoma, BA ▪ **Party**—Republican ▪ **District**—62 ▪ **Legislative Experience**—House Member, 2015 ▪ **Committee Membership**—Administrative Rules, Vice Chair; Appropriations and Budget Subcommittee on Health; Environmental Law; and International Relations and Tourism

Montgomery was born on August 13, 1991, in Lawton, Oklahoma. He graduated Eisenhower High School, and began his college studies at Cameron University. He earned a bachelor's degree in international studies at the University of Oklahoma. Montgomery worked at Northwestern Mutual and the governor's office, prior to running for the state legislature. He won election to the Oklahoma House of Legislator from District 62 in November 2014. His hobbies include violin and competitive swimming.

To contact Montgomery—2300 N Lincoln Blvd., Oklahoma City, OK 73105
▪ 405/557-7374 ▪ john.montgomery@okhouse.gov

Lewis Moore

Occupation—Insurance ▪ **Education**—New Mexico Military Institute, AS; University of Arkansas, BA ▪ **Party**—Republican ▪ **District**—96 ▪ **Legislative Experience**—House Member, 2009 ▪ **Committee Membership**—Appropriations and Budget Subcommittee on Health; Environmental Law; and Insurance

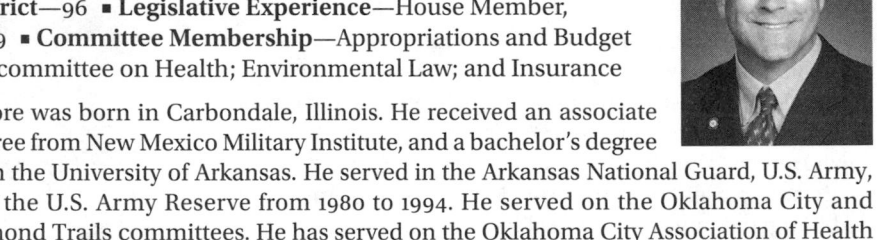

Moore was born in Carbondale, Illinois. He received an associate degree from New Mexico Military Institute, and a bachelor's degree from the University of Arkansas. He served in the Arkansas National Guard, U.S. Army, and the U.S. Army Reserve from 1980 to 1994. He served on the Oklahoma City and Edmond Trails committees. He has served on the Oklahoma City Association of Health Underwriters, and on the Philmont Staff Association Membership Committee. He is a member of the National Rifle Association, the Boy Scouts of America, and the Choctaw, Edmond, and Harrah chambers of commerce. He and his wife, Patti, have three children; Micah, Nathan, and Jackson. Moore's hobbies include scouting, coaching his kids' teams, bicycling, and backpacking.

To contact Moore—PO Box 250, Arcadia, OK 73007 ▪ 405/396-9023
▪ lewis.moore@okhouse.gov

Richard Morrissette

Occupation—Attorney ▪ **Education**—University of New Hampshire, BA; University of Tulsa, JD ▪ **Party**—Democrat ▪ **District**—92 ▪ **Legislative Experience**—House Member, 2005-present ▪ **Committee Membership**—Appropriations and Budget; Economic Development, Commerce, and Real Estate; Judiciary and Civil Procedure; and State Government Operations

Morrissette was born on April 28, 1956, in Rochester, New Hampshire. He received bachelor degrees in both economics and political science from the University of New Hampshire and a Juris Doctor degree from the University of Tulsa. Morrissette has been employed as an Oklahoma Senate staff member and in the Western Oklahoma Public Defender's Office. Currently a practicing attorney, Morrissette won election to the Oklahoma House of Representatives from District 92 in 2004. He continues active participation in the Capital Hill Lions Club, Oklahoma Bar Association, Oklahoma City YMCA, South Oklahoma City Chamber of Commerce, South Oklahoma City Rotary Club, and the South Oklahoma City Democratic Women's Club. Morrissette has a daughter, Danielle. His hobbies include collecting baseball cards, watching movies, swimming, and reading.

To contact Morrissette—6609 S Harvey Avenue, Oklahoma City, OK 73139 ▪ 405/557-7404 ▪ richardmorrissette@okhouse.gov

Glen Mulready

Occupation—Insurance Broker/Consultant ▪ **Education**— Bridgewater State College ▪ **Party**—Republican ▪ **District**—68 ▪ **Legislative Experience**—House Member, 2011; Assistant Majority Whip, 2013 ▪ **Committee Membership**— Administrative Rules, Government Oversight, and Repealer; Appropriations and Budget Subcommittee on Public Health and Social Services; and Insurance Chair

Mulready was born on November 21, 1960, and is an insurance broker and consultant. He attended Bridgewater State College. Mulready won election to the Oklahoma House of Representatives from District 68 on November 2, 2010.

To contact Mulready—2300 N Lincoln Blvd., Oklahoma City, OK 73105 ▪ 405/557-7340 ▪ glen.mulready@okhouse.gov.

Casey Murdock

Occupation—Farming/Ranching ▪ **Education**—Oklahoma Panhandle State University, BS ▪ **Party**—Republican ▪ **District**—61 ▪ **Legislative Experience**—House Member, 2015 ▪ **Committee Membership**—Appropriations and Budget Subcommittee on Transportation; Transportation, Vice Chair; Utilities, and Wildlife

Murdock grew up on a farm in Felt, Oklahoma, and graduated from Felt High School. He earned a bachelor's degree in agricultural business from Oklahoma Panhandle State University in 1992. Since college graduation, he has farmed and ranched near his hometown. He has also worked at the New Mexico State University Clayton Livestock Research Center. He has served on the Felt School Board for the past eight years, and is currently the board president. Murdock and his wife, Aimee, have three children, Cash, Oliver, and Cosette. Murdock won election to the Oklahoma House of Representatives from District 61 in November 2014.

To contact Murdock—2300 N Lincoln Blvd., Oklahoma City, OK 73105 ▪ 405/557-7384 ▪ casey.murdock@okhouse.gov

Jason Murphey

Occupation—Small Business Owner ▪ **Education**—Charter Oak State College, BA ▪ **Party**—Republican ▪ **District**—31 ▪ **Legislative Experience**—House Member, 2007–present ▪ **Committee Membership**—Appropriations and Budget Subcommittee on General Government; County and Municipal; State Government Operations, Chair; and State and Federal Relations

Murphey is a third generation, lifelong resident of Logan County. At the age of 19, he started his own business, G&C Security, where he provided security services to the Oklahoma City area. In 2001 Murphey was elected to the Guthrie City Council, where he won approval for placing government proceedings on television and the Internet, and lead the successful effort to defeat property and sales tax increase proposals. Murphey won election to the Oklahoma House of Representatives from District 31 in 2006. In 2008, he was named chairman of the Government Modernization Committee, becoming the first House District 31 representative to chair a standing House committee. In this capacity, Murphey has authored numerous legislative proposals designed to enhance transparency, cut state spending, and apply best technology practices to state governance processes. He holds the designation of Distinguished Toastmaster (DTM) from Toastmasters International. He received a bachelor's degree with national honors from Charter Oak State College. He and his wife, Raleah, have two children, Jarod and Jarel. They attend the Church of God Outreach.

To contact Murphey—1521 Olison Turn Trail, Guthrie, OK 73044 ▪ 405/557-7350 ▪ jason.murphey@okhouse.gov

Jason Nelson

Occupation—Public Relations Consultant ▪ **Education**— Oklahoma State University; University of Central Oklahoma ▪ **Party**—Republican ▪ **District**—87 ▪ **Legislative Experience**— House Member, 2009; Majority Floor Leader, 2015 ▪ **Committee Membership**—Appropriations and Budget; Common Education; and Rule, Vice Chair

Nelson, age forty-three, is a native Oklahoman. Nelson attended Oklahoma State University and the University of Central Oklahoma. He has extensive experience in government and politics. From 1994 to 2002, Nelson served in a variety of roles on Governor Frank Keating's staff. Nelson won election to the Oklahoma House of Representatives from District 87 in November 2008. In 2010 Nelson led the successful bipartisan effort to pass the Lindsey Nicole Henry Scholarships for Students with Disabilities Program Act. In 2011 he led a four member Department of Human Services working group in a comprehensive review of the state's child welfare system. During the 2012 legislative session, the DHS working group proposed sweeping reforms that became law, including passage of State Question 765, that was passed by Oklahoma voters. Nelson and his wife, Lori, have two children, Benjamin and Grace. They attend Metropolitan Baptist Church in Oklahoma City.

To contact Nelson—2300 N Lincoln Blvd., Oklahoma City, OK 73105 ▪ 405/557-7335 ▪ jason.nelson@okhouse.gov

Tom Newell

Occupation—Pastor ▪ **Education**—Mid-America Christian University, BA; Liberty University, MBA ▪ **Party**—Republican ▪ **District**—28 ▪ **Legislative Experience**—House Member, 2011 ▪ **Committee Membership**—Appropriations and Budget Subcommittee on Revenue and Taxation; Business, Labor, and Retirement Laws; and Children, Youth, and Family Services

Newell was born on December 4, 1968, in Bristow, Oklahoma. He grew up on a small ranch, and as a youth, was a state champion bull rider and state champion extemporaneous speaker in the Future Farmers of America. He received a bachelor's degree from Mid-American Christian University in Bible and pastoral ministry in Oklahoma City, and has pastored churches in Oklahoma, Missouri, and Pennsylvania. He also received a master's degree in business administration from Liberty University in Lynchburg, Virginia. He is married to the former Holly Wilson, and they have three sons; Ethan, Andrew, and Levi. In 2005 they started a church in Seminole, Oklahoma. He has also taught business and economics classes at Seminole State College, and he is a past member of the board of directors for the Seminole Chamber of Commerce. Newell is a member of the American Quarter Horse Association. He is past president of the Oklahoma Assembly of the Church of God, and past vice chair of the Business and Leadership Resource Committee of the General Assembly of the Church of God in North America.

To contact Newell—2300 N Lincoln Blvd., Oklahoma City, OK 73105 ▪ 405/557-7372 ▪ tom.newell@okhouse.gov

Jadine Nollan

Occupation—Executive Director ▪ **Education**—Oklahoma State University, BS ▪ **Party**—Republican ▪ **District**—66 ▪ **Legislative Experience**—House Member, 2011 ▪ **Committee Membership**—Alcohol, Tobacco, and Controlled Substances; Appropriations and Budget Subcommittee on Education; Common Education; and Long-term Care and Senior Services, Chair

Nollan was born on September 29, 1958. She earned a bachelor's degree from Oklahoma State University in 1981. Nollan has served as the executive director of the Sand Springs Community Service, Inc., from 2007 to 2010. She founded and pastored C3 Ministries, Word of Life Fellowship from 2006 to 2010, and was a Sand Springs School Board member from 1999 to 2010. She has been a member of the Cooperative Counsel Oklahoma School Administration, Oklahoma Secondary School Board Association, Sand Springs Board of Education, Sand Springs Rotary, Sand Springs Chamber of Commerce, Tulsa Chamber of Commerce, and Word of Life Church. Nollan won election to the Oklahoma House of Representatives from District 66 on November 2, 2010.

To contact Nollan—to 2300 N Lincoln Blvd., Oklahoma City, OK 73105
- 405/557-7390 ▪ jadine.nollan@okhouse.gov

Terry O'Donnell

Occupation—Attorney ▪ **Education**—Baylor University, BA; University of Tulsa College of Law, JD ▪ **Party**—Republican ▪ **District**—23 ▪ **Legislative Experience**—House Member, 2013 ▪ **Committee Membership**—Appropriations and Budget Subcommittee on Judiciary; Criminal Justice and Corrections, Vice Chair; Judiciary and Civil Procedure; and Transportation

O'Donnell was born in 1963, and was raised in Tulsa. He graduated from Memorial High School in 1982, where he lettered in football and baseball, and was a member of the Memorial 1980 State Championship Football Team. He received a bachelor's in political science from Baylor University. In 1989 he received a Juris Doctor degree from the University of Tulsa College of Law. Since law school, O'Donnell has built his practice and a full-service law firm. As an attorney, he has been awarded Martindale-Hubbel's highest AV® rating for competence and ethics, as well as being named to Tulsa's Top Lawyers. O'Donnell is actively involved in the life of his family. Terry has coached his daughters in basketball, soccer, and softball for more than seven years. He also serves on the Advisory Board of Metro Christian Academy. O'Donnell won election to the Oklahoma House of Representatives from District 23 on November 6, 2012.

To contact O'Donnell—to 2300 N Lincoln Blvd., Oklahoma City, OK 73105
- 405/557-7379 ▪ terry.odonnell@okhouse.gov

Charles Ortega

Occupation—Business Owner ▪ **Education**—General ▪ **Party**—Republican ▪ **District**—52 ▪ **Legislative Experience**—House Member, 2009-present; Assistant Majority Floor Leader, 2013-2014; Majority Floor Leader, 2015 ▪ **Committee Membership**—Appropriations and Budget; Business, Labor, and Retirement Laws; Energy and Natural Resources; and Tourism and International Relations

Ortega was born on September 23, 1955, in Fort Worth, Texas. He attended public schools in Altus, Oklahoma, and San Antonio, Texas. Ortega has been a business owner in Altus, for twenty years. He is an active member of Altus First Baptist Church, where he works with the Spanish Mission and the men's ministry. He is also a member of the Altus Hispanic Association. Ortega won election to the Oklahoma House of Representatives from District 52 in November 2008. He has been married to his wife, Margaret, for thirty-four years. They have two sons, and one daughter; two daughters-in-law; four grandchildren; and one more grandchild on the way. His hobbies include flying and going on mission trips.

To contact Ortega—1509 N Main PMB 292, Altus OK 73521 ▪ 405/557-7369
▪ charles.ortega@okhouse.gov

Leslie Osborn

Occupation—Small Business Owner ▪ **Education**—Oklahoma
State University, BS ▪ **Party**—Republican ▪ **District**—47 ▪
Legislative Experience—House Member, 2009-present; Deputy
Majority Whip, 2009-2012; Assistant Majority Floor Leader, 2011-
2012 ▪ **Committee Membership**—Appropriations and Budget;
Appropriations and Budget Subcommittee on Natural Resources
and Regulatory Services; Banking and Financial Services; and
Judiciary and Civil Procedure

Osborn was born on October 17, 1963, in Salina, Kansas. She received a bachelor's degree
from Oklahoma State University in 1986. She owned her business, Osborn Pick-Up
Accessories, for twenty-two years. Osborn won election to the Oklahoma House of
Representatives in November 2008. She is a member of the Mustang and Tuttle cham-
bers of commerce, the National Rifle Association, the Oklahoma Farm Bureau, and the
Oklahoma Council of Public Affairs. She is also a board member for the Canadian Valley
Technology Center Foundation Board. Osborn resides in Mustang and has two children,
Will and Katie.

To contact Osborn—2300 N Lincoln Blvd., Oklahoma City, OK 73105 ▪ 405/557-7333
▪ leslie.osborn@okhouse.gov

Pat Ownbey

Occupation—Broadcasting ▪ **Education**—University of
Oklahoma, BS ▪ **Party**—Republican ▪ **District**—48 ▪
Legislative Experience—House Member, 2009-present ▪
Committee Membership—Appropriations and Budget;
Appropriations and Budget Subcommittee on Human Services,
Chair; and Children, Youth, and Family Services

Ownbey received a bachelor's degree in communications from the
University of Oklahoma. His love of broadcasting kept him involved in that profession for
more than thirty years, both in radio and television. He is president and general manager
of On the Air Property Management. He is the former owner and general manager of KICM
Radio, and the former vice president and general manger of KKAJ-KVSO Radio. He has
previously served as the president of both the Ardmore Kiwanis Club and the United Way
of Southern Oklahoma. He also has served as vice president of the Southern Oklahoma
Blood Institute. His community involvement has also involved board membership in the
Ardmore Crime Stoppers, Ardmore YMCA, Greater Ardmore Scholarship Foundation,
and Take Two Academy. He won election to the Oklahoma House of Representatives from
District 48 in November 2008. Ownbey, and his wife Kathy, have two children, Scott, and
his wife Megan; and Susan, and her husband Will Perkins. The have one granddaughter,
Anna Katherine, and one grandson, Maddox. He is an active member of the First Baptist
Church of Ardmore, where he has taught Financial Peace University, and traveled on
mission trips to Zimbabwe.

To contact Ownbey—2303 Cloverleaf Place, Ardmore, OK 73401 ▪ 405/557-7326
▪ pat.ownbey@okhouse.gov

Scooter Park

Occupation—Farming/Ranching ▪ **Party**—Republican ▪
District—65 ▪ **Legislative Experience**—House Member, 2015 ▪
Committee Membership—Agriculture and Rural Development;
Appropriations and Budget Subcommittee on General
Government; County and Municipal Government, Vice Chair;
and Wildlife

Park is a fourth generation cattleman and farmer. He has been a long-
time volunteer at the Devol Fire Department, and has volunteered to fly surveillance for
the Cotton County Sheriff's Department. CLEET certified, Park has also served as a reserve
deputy for Tillman County. He is a former president of the Cotton County Farm Bureau,
member of the National Federation of Independent Business, National Rifle Association,
Oklahoma Cattleman's Association, and American Farmers & Ranchers. He won election
to the Oklahoma House of Representatives from District 65 in November 2014. He and
his wife, Lisa, have four children, Jeron, Marissa, Meredith, and Allison. They are active
members of the First Baptist Church of Grandfield.

To contact Park—2300 N Lincoln Blvd., Oklahoma City, OK 73105 ▪ 405/557-7305
▪ scooter.park@okhouse.gov

David L. Perryman

Occupation—Attorney ▪ **Education**—Eastern Oklahoma
State College, AA; Oklahoma State University, BS; University
of Oklahoma College of Law, JD ▪ **Party**—Democrat ▪
District—56 ▪ **Legislative Experience**—House Member, 2013;
Minority Caucus Secretary, 2015 ▪ **Committee Membership**—
Appropriations and Budget Subcommittee on General
Government; Appropriations and Budget Subcommittee on
Judiciary; Business, Labor, and Retirement Laws; and Elections
and Ethics

Perryman was raised in Haskell County and graduated from Kinta High School in 1975.
He was active in Future Farmers of America, and earned the State Farmer Degree. At
Eastern Oklahoma State University, Perryman served as student government president.
He received a bachelor's degree from Oklahoma State University, and a Juris Doctor degree
from the University of Oklahoma College of Law. David and his wife, Jo, have lived in Grady
County since 1980 where Perryman practices law. They have four adult children and eight
grandchildren. Perryman and his wife attend the Southern Oaks Church of Christ, where
he serves as an elder. Perryman won election to the Oklahoma House of Representatives
from District 56 in November 2012.

To contact Perryman—2300 N Lincoln Blvd., Oklahoma City, OK 73105
▪ 405/557-7401 ▪ david.perryman@okhouse.gov

Pam Peterson

Occupation—Television Spokesperson/Associate Producer ▪ **Education**—Oral Roberts University, BA ▪ **Party**—Republican ▪ **District**—67 ▪ **Legislative Experience**—House Member, 2003–present; Majority Whip, 2005; Majority Floor Leader, 2013 ▪ **Committee Membership**—Appropriations and Budget; Children, Youth, and Family Services, Vice Chair; Criminal Justice and Corrections, Chair; and Public Safety

Peterson was born on June 28, 1955, in New York City, and came to Oklahoma in the 1970s. She received a bachelor's degree in communications from Oral Roberts University in 1977. She has been employed as a television spokesperson as well as an associate television producer. She served as Tulsa County Republican chairman, as the Republican Party's First Congressional District vice chairman, and as a national delegate to the Republican Convention. Peterson won election to the Oklahoma House of Representatives from District 67 in January 2004. She was appointed commissioner for the Oklahoma Commission on the Status of Women, and served as chair of the Task Force to Stop Sexual Violence (2006). Her activities include: Oklahoma Commission on the Status of Women, 2007 to 2011; Human Services Committee chair, 2008 to 2012; and Oklahoma House Human Services working group renewing policy, procedures, and administration, vice chair, 2011–2012. Peterson was named Public Official of the Year in 2011 by the Oklahoma Chapter of the National Association of Social Workers, received the Guardian Award 2012 from the Oklahoma Commission on the Status of Women, Legislator of the Year 2012 from the Oklahoma Bureau of Narcotics and Dangerous Drugs, and the Kate Bernard Award in 2013.

To contact Peterson—6528 E 101 Street, PMB 422, Tulsa, OK 74133 ▪ 918/289-3003 ▪ pampeterson@okhouse.gov

John Pfeiffer

Occupation—Farmer/Rancher ▪ **Education**—Oklahoma State University ▪ **Party**—Republican ▪ **District**—38 ▪ **Legislative Experience**—House Member, 2015 ▪ **Committee Membership**—Agriculture and Rural Development; Appropriations and Budget Subcommittee on Natural Resources and Regulatory Services, Vice Chair; State Government Operations; and Veterans and Military Affairs

Pfeiffer is a fifth generation, Logan County farmer and rancher. He graduated from Mulhall-Orlando High School, and attended Oklahoma State University. While he was in high school, Pfeiffer was a Future Farmers of America "Star Farmer," and president of the 4-H and FFA chapters. In 2009 he joined the United States Marine Corps, and served in Afghanistan. A decorated Marine, Pfeiffer was awarded the United States Navy and Marine Corps Achievement Medal, Marine Corps Good Conduct Medal, and the National Defense Service Medal. He won election to the Oklahoma House of Representatives from District 38 in November 2014. Pfeiffer lives in Orlando, Oklahoma, and is a member of the Orlando United Methodist Church.

To contact Pfeiffer—2300 N Lincoln Blvd., Oklahoma City, OK 73105 ▪ 405/557-7332 ▪ john.pfeiffer@okhouse.gov

Eric Proctor

Occupation—State Legislator ▪ **Education**—Tulsa Community College, AA; Northeastern Oklahoma State University, BA; University of Oklahoma, MPA ▪ **Party**—Democrat ▪ **District**—77 ▪ **Legislative Experience**—House Member, 2007–present; Minority Caucus Secretary, 2007–present; Deputy Minority Floor Leader, 2011–2014; Assistant Minority Leader, 2015 ▪ **Committee Membership**—Banking and Financial Services; Energy and Natural Resources; State and Federal Relations; and Transportation

A fifth generation Oklahoman, Proctor was born on August 6, 1982. He earned an associates degree from Tulsa Community College; a bachelor's degree from Northeastern Oklahoma State University; and a master's degree in public administration from the University of Oklahoma. He has served as a youth minister and as a high school economics, history, and government teacher. His associations include the Big Brothers and Big Sisters of Tulsa, Oklahoma Honor Flights, National Rifle Association, Promise Keepers, and Sons of the American Legion. Proctor won election to the Oklahoma House of Representatives from District 77 in November 2006. He and his wife, Tara, have two daughters, Molly and Caroline.

To contact Proctor—2300 N Lincoln Blvd., Oklahoma City, OK 73105 ▪ 405/557–7410 ▪ eric.proctor@okhouse.gov

R.C. Pruett

Occupation—Business Owner ▪ **Education**—East Texas State University ▪ **Party**—Democrat ▪ **District**—19 ▪ **Legislative Experience**—House Member, 2005–present ▪ **Committee Membership**—Public Safety; Rules; Tourism and International Relations, Vice Chair; and Utilities

Pruett was born on September 19, 1944, in Houston, Texas, and attended East Texas State University. He has been self-employed for thirty-five years, and currently owns and operates supermarkets. Pruett won election to the Oklahoma House of Representatives from District 19 in 2004. He continues active participation in the Antlers Chamber of Commerce, Lion's Club, and the Oklahoma Grocery Association. Pruett married the former Barbara Gentry. They have three children; Shannon, Ray, and Stacie. His hobbies include golf and hunting.

To contact Pruett—PO Box 969, Antlers, OK 74523 ▪ 580/298–5577 ▪ rcpruett@okhouse.gov

Brian Renegar

Occupation—Veterinarian ▪ **Education**—Northeastern State University, BS; Oklahoma State University, DVM ▪ **Party**—Democrat ▪ **District**—17 ▪ **Legislative Experience**—House Member, 2007–present; Assistant Minority Floor Leader, 2013 ▪ **Committee Membership**—Agriculture and Rural Development; Economic Development, Commerce, and Real Estate; and Public Safety

Renegar was born on September 16, 1950, in Oklahoma City, Oklahoma. He received a bachelor's degree in biology, chemistry, and psychology from Northeastern State University in 1972. He also received a Doctor of Veterinary Medicine degree from Oklahoma State University in 1976. Renegar has been in mixed animal practice for the past thirty-nine years. He won election to the Oklahoma House of Representatives from District 17 in November 2006. In 2005 Governor Brad Henry appointed Renegar to the State Board of Veterinary Medical Examiners, where he was elected vice president in 2006. He continues active participation in the Frink Baptist Church, McAlester Rotary Club, National Rifle Association, Oklahoma Farm Bureau, Oklahoma Veterinary Medical Association, Pittsburg County Cattlemen's Association, and South McAlester Mason Lodge #96. He married the former Theresa Pallan, and they have four children; Amanda, Cory, Glen, and Luke. They also have eight grandchildren.

To contact Renegar—1550 S Main, McAlester, OK 74501 ▪ 918/426–0113 ▪ brian.renegar@okhouse.gov

Mike Ritze

Occupation—Physician/Surgeon ▪ **Education**—Northeast Missouri State University, BS; Kirksville College of Osteopathic Medicine, DO; Oklahoma State University Center for Health Sciences, MS ▪ **Party**—Republican ▪ **District**—80 ▪ **Legislative Experience**—House Member, 2009 ▪ **Committee Membership**—Appropriations and Budget Subcommitee on Human Services; Long-term Care and Senior Services; Public Health, Chair; and Public Safety

Ritze was born in Trenton, Missouri. He received a bachelor's degree in zoology from Northeast Missouri University, and a doctor of osteopathic medicine from Kirksville College of Osteopathic Medicine. He also holds a master's degree in forensic science administration (summa cum laude) from Oklahoma State University Center for Health Sciences. Ritze has been a practicing physician and surgeon, and has delivered over 2,000 babies. He received an honorable discharge from the U.S. Army Captain Medical Corps. He has served in a variety of professional positions including adjunct professor at Oklahoma State University College of Medicine, Northeastern Oklahoma State University, and Council Law Enforcement Education Training. His past service includes: medical staff secretary and treasurer for the Broken Arrow Medical Center; president of the Tulsa County Osteopathic Medical Society; senior medical examiner for the Federal Aviation Administration; State of Oklahoma Medical Examiner and Child Abuse Examiner; and City of Broken Arrow police physician. He is a private helicopter pilot. Ritze won election to the Oklahoma House of Representatives from District 80 in November 2008. He and his wife, Connie, have been married for thirty-seven years and have four children. Ritze is an ordained Southern Baptist deacon and Sunday school teacher at Arrow Heights Baptist Church. He and his wife have served as medical missionaries to Mexico and Honduras.

To contact Ritze—2300 N Lincoln Blvd., Oklahoma City, OK 73105 ▪ 405/557-7338 ▪ mike.ritze@okhouse.gov

Dustin Roberts

Occupation—Small Business Owner ▪ **Education**—Durant High School ▪ **Party**—Republican ▪ **District**—21 ▪ **Legislative Experience**—House Member, 2011–present ▪ **Committee Membership**—Appropriations and Budget Subcommittee on Transportation; Economic Development, Commerce, and Real Estate; Tourism and International Relations; and Veterans and Military Affairs, Chair

Roberts was born in McAlester and raised in Durant. He graduated from Durant High School in 2003, and enlisted in the United States Navy. In his five-year career in service, Roberts was the recipient of two U.S. Navy and Marine Corps Achievement medals for his efforts in the Horn of Africa situation and again in Operation Iraqi Freedom. In 2004, Roberts was awarded the Blue Jacket of the Year and honored with an invitation to the Presidential Inaugural Ball and Inaugural Address. He was promoted, through the Command Advancement Program, to 3rd Class Petty Officer by the Command Master Chief and Commanding Officer of VFA-143. Later, Roberts was awarded Junior Sailor of the Year for the leadership role he took on his second deployment. Roberts and his wife, Lindsay, are entrepreneurs and active members of their community. He is a member of the Choctaw Nation of Oklahoma, while his wife is a member of the Chickasaw Nation of Oklahoma. Together, they volunteer with organizations such as Relay for Life and March of Dimes, and are avid supporters of the local 4-H, FFA, and athletics programs. In their spare time, Dustin and Lindsay love to go camping, kayaking, and boating on Lake Texoma, and spending time with their families. Roberts won election to the House of Representatives from District 21 on November 2, 2010.

To contact Roberts—to 2300 N Lincoln Blvd., Oklahoma City, OK 73105 ▪ 405/557-7366 ▪ dustin.roberts@okhouse.gov

Sean Roberts

Occupation—Physical Therapist/Business Owner ▪ **Education**—University of Oklahoma ▪ **Party**—Republican ▪ **District**—36 ▪ **Legislative Experience**—House Member, 2011–present; Assistant Majority Whip, 2013 ▪ **Committee Membership**—Appropriations and Budget Subcommittee on Health; Energy and Natural Resources; and Public Health

Roberts was born on October 18, 1973. He attended the University of Oklahoma, where he earned a master's degree. He has worked as a physical therapist, and he and his wife, Amber, own Snider's Soda Shoppe in Hominy, Oklahoma. He is a member of the Hominy Chamber of Commerce, the Oklahoma Farm Bureau, and is a lifetime member of the National Rifle Association. Roberts won election to the House of

Representatives from District 36 on November 2, 2010. He and his wife have three sons, Kevin, Jeremy, and Andrew.

To contact Roberts—to 2300 N Lincoln Blvd., Oklahoma City, OK 73105
▪ 405/557-7322 ▪ sean.roberts@okhouse.gov

Michael Rogers

Occupation—Education ▪ **Education**—Oral Roberts University ▪ **Party**—Republican ▪ **District**—98 ▪ **Legislative Experience**—House Member, 2015 ▪ **Committee Membership**—Appropriations and Budget Subcommittee on Education; Elections and Ethics; and Insurance

Rogers came to Oklahoma on a baseball scholarship and attended Oral Roberts University, where he earned a bachelor's degree in marketing. He was drafted by the Cleveland Indians, and played with the major league baseball organization for three years before injury forced his retirement. Following his baseball career, Rogers served as the athletic director, and later principal, at Summit Christian Academy in Broken Arrow, Oklahoma, where he worked to transform the athletic program from a recreation program to one of the best small school programs in the state. Rogers's wife, Krystal, is an elementary school teacher. He won election to the Oklahoma House of Representatives from District 98 in November 2014.

To contact Rogers—to 2300 N Lincoln Blvd., Oklahoma City, OK 73105
▪ 405/557-7362 ▪ michael.rogers@okhouse.gov

Wade Rousselot

Occupation—Rancher ▪ **Education**—Oklahoma State University, BS ▪ **Party**—Democrat ▪ **District**—12 ▪ **Legislative Experience**—House Member, 2005-present; Assistant Minority Floor Leader, 2007-present ▪ **Committee Membership**—Agriculture and Rural Development; Appropriations and Budget; Appropriations and Budget Subcommittee on Human Services, Vice Chair; and Appropriations and Budget Subcommittee on Revenue and Taxation

Rousselot was born on April 13, 1959, in Joplin, Missouri. He attended Oklahoma State University, where he received a bachelor's degree in animal science. A self-employed rancher, Rousselot won election to the Oklahoma House of Representatives from District 12 in 2004. He continues active participation in the Oklahoma Cattlemen's Association, Oklahoma Farm Bureau, Wagoner County Cattlemen's Association, Wagoner Farm Bureau, Wagoner Lions Club, and Wagoner Sheriff's Association. Rousselot married the former Margie Wicks. They have a daughter, Lelia. Rousselot lists his favorite pastime as spending time with family.

To contact Rousselot—5298 E 110 Street N, Wagoner, OK 74467 ▪ 405/557-7388
▪ waderousselot@okhouse.gov

Todd Russ

Occupation—Rancher/Small Business Owner ▪ **Education**—Southwestern Oklahoma State University, BS; University of Colorado; Berean University ▪ **Party**—Republican ▪ **District**—55 ▪ **Legislative Experience**—House Member, 2011–present; Assistant Majority Whip, 2013 ▪ **Committee Membership**—Administrative Rules; Appropriations and Budget; Banking and Financial Services, Chair; and Insurance

Russ was born on January 8, 1961. He received a bachelor's degree in international finance from Southwestern Oklahoma State University. He attended the University of Colorado Graduate School of Banking and the Berean University School of the Bible. His professional career includes serving as president, CEO, director, and shareholder of Washita State Bank in Burns Flat, Oklahoma; executive vice president, director, and interim president and CEO of Frontier State Bank in Oklahoma City; vice president of commercial loans at the First National Bank and Trust Company in Chickasha, Oklahoma; and as the owner and founder of Commercial Growers, in Cordell, Oklahoma. He has served on the following boards: Washita State Bank, Frontier State Bank, Cordell Chamber of Commerce, Cordell Municipal Airport, Oklahoma Bankers Association, and Washita County 2000 Economic Development. Russ won election to the Oklahoma House of Representatives from District 55 on November 2, 2010. He and his wife, Khristy, have been happily married for thirty-one years. They have three children; Ryan, Lacey, and Lauren.

To contact Russ—to 2300 N Lincoln Blvd., Oklahoma City, OK 73105 ▪ 405/557-7312 ▪ todd.russ@okhouse.gov

Mike Sanders

Occupation—Funeral Business ▪ **Education**—Oklahoma Christian University, BA ▪ **Party**—Republican ▪ **District**—59 ▪ **Legislative Experience**—House Member, 2009–present; Assistant Majority Whip, 2011–present ▪ **Committee Membership**—Agriculture and Rural Development; Appropriations and Budget; Appropriations and Budget Subcommittee on Transportation, Chair; and Energy and Natural Resources

A native of western Oklahoma, Sanders has dedicated his life to public service, and began working on political campaigns at the age of nine. He graduated from Kingfisher High School in 1993, earned a bachelor's degree in history and pre-law from Oklahoma Christian University in 1997, and has worked on his Master's in Government at Georgetown University in Washington, D.C. After making a strong impression on the Bush Campaign, he was given a position at the White House as Director of Interns where he managed more than 1,000 interns. For his service to the White House and Nation on September 11, 2001, Sanders was awarded the Distinguished Honor Service Award by President George W. Bush. He continued his public service as Deputy Chief of Staff for Rural Development as well as the Senior Advisor to the Chief of the Natural Resources Conservation Service for the United States Department of Agriculture (USDA). He served on the Council for Small Business for Governor Frank Keating and Lt. Governor Mary Fallin from 1999–2003. He was elected to the Oklahoma House in 2008, was unopposed in the 2010 election, was elected with 95% of the vote in 2012, and was unopposed in 2014. For his service to children and families, he was honored with the 2013 Outstanding Elected Official Award by the State Interagency Child Abuse Prevention Task Force. He is a member of the Kingfisher County Farm Bureau, the Knights of Columbus #3113, Kingfisher Elks Lodge, Kingfisher Rotary Club, and the National Rifle Association. He is also a lifetime member of the American Council of Young Political Leaders and has served in many leadership positions with the Kingfisher County Republican Party, serving as Chairman from 1999-2001. He currently works for his family's business, Sanders Funeral Service. He is married to Nellie Tayloe Sanders, and they live in Kingfisher with their sons, Davis Lee Sanders and Walker Tayloe Sanders.

To contact Sanders—2300 N Lincoln Blvd., Oklahoma City, OK 73105 ▪ 405/557-7407 ▪ mike.sanders@okhouse.gov

Seneca Scott

Occupation—Energy Management/Service Clearing Company ▪ **Education**—University of Oklahoma, BA ▪ **Party**—Democrat ▪ **District**—72 ▪ **Legislative Experience**—House Member, 2009-present ▪ **Committee Membership**—Appropriations and Budget Subcommittee on Natural Resources and Regulatory Services; Energy and Natural Resources; Government Oversight and Accountability; and State and Federal Relations

Scott is a fifth-generation Oklahoman. He received a bachelor's degree in history and Native American studies from the University of Oklahoma. He won election to the Oklahoma House of Representatives from District 72 in November 2008. His extensive community involvement includes serving on the board of directors for the Oklahoma Sustainability Network, the Springdale Economic Development Council, the Kendall-Whittier Neighborhood Task Force, and the Turley Community Association. Scott has two children, Clay and Harper. He resides in north Tulsa, near the beautiful Mohawk Park area.

To contact Scott—3102 E 2 Street, Tulsa, OK 74104 ▪ 405/557-7391 ▪ seneca.scott@okhouse.gov

Earl Sears

Occupation—Educator/Principal, Retired ▪ **Education**—Northeastern State University, BA, MA ▪ **Party**—Republican ▪ **District**—11 ▪ **Legislative Experience**—House Member, 2007-present ▪ **Committee Membership**—Appropriations and Budget, Chair

Sears was born on September 2, 1952, in Bartlesville, Oklahoma. He received a bachelor's and master's degree from Northeastern State University. After receiving his master's degree in counseling, Sears obtained his administrative certificate and served as principal of Central Middle School in Bartlesville for twenty-four years. A dedicated community member, Sears has served on numerous boards including the Bartlesville Area Rotary, Bartlesville City Council, Symphony Board,

Youth and Family Services, Bartlesville United Way, Bartlesville Community Foundation, Cherokee Area Boy Scouts, and countless others. Sears is also a proud member of the Bartlesville Sportsman Club. For the last thirty years, he has faithfully fought for community improvement initiatives including city capital improvements, political campaigns, and school bond proposals. He won election to the Oklahoma House of Representatives from District 11 in November 2006. He married the former Jane Anne Grove, and they have two children, Hollye and Ryan.

To contact Sears—1721 Cherokee Place, Bartlesville, OK 74003 ▪ 405/557-7358 ▪ earl.sears@okhouse.gov

Mike Shelton

Occupation—Community Relations ▪ **Education**—Langston University, BS ▪ **Party**—Democrat ▪ **District**—97 ▪ **Legislative Experience**—House Member, 2005-present; Assistant Minority Floor Leader, 2011-present ▪ **Committee Membership**—Administrative Rules, Appropriations and Budget Subcommittee on Health; Banking and Financial Services; and Insurance

Shelton was born on February 28, 1973, in Tulsa, Oklahoma. He received a bachelor's degree in economics with emphasis in agricultural business from Langston University. Shelton has been employed as community relations director for Langston University as well as Oklahoma County. He also worked as district executive director for the Boy Scouts of America. Shelton won election to the Oklahoma House of Representatives from District 97 in 2004. He continues active participation in the Alpha Phi Alpha Fraternity, Prince Hall Masons & Shriners, Ryan White Board, and the Urban League Young Professionals. Shelton married the former Clarissa Franklin, and they have two children. His hobbies include fishing and movies.

To contact Shelton—2300 N Lincoln Blvd., Oklahoma City, OK 73105 ▪ 405/557-7367 ▪ mikeshelton@okhouse.gov

Benjamin Sherrer

Occupation—Attorney ▪ **Education**—Oklahoma State University, BS; Oklahoma City University, JD ▪ **Party**—Democrat ▪ **District**—8 ▪ **Legislative Experience**—House Member, 2005-present; Assistant Minority Floor Leader, 2005; Deputy Minority Floor Leader, 2007; Minority Whip, 2009-2012; Minority Floor Leader, 2013-present ▪ **Committee Membership**—Appropriations and Budget; Children, Youth, and Family Services; Criminal Justice and Corrections; and Judiciary and Civil Procedure

Sherrer was born on June 18, 1968, in Anchorage, Alaska, when his father was serving in the U.S. Army. He received two bachelor's degrees from Oklahoma State University and a Juris Doctor degree from Oklahoma City University. Sherrer has been employed as a bailiff and a staff auditor for the State of Oklahoma, before and while attending law school. A practicing attorney, Sherrer won election to the Oklahoma House of Representatives from District 8 in 2004. He continues active participation in the Pryor Rotary, and is a graduate of Leadership Oklahoma, the Department of Corrections Leadership Academy, and Oklahoma Partners in Policy Making. Sherrer married the former Margo DeRose. They have three children; Bennett, Samuel, and Delanie. His hobbies include attending his children's activities, running, cycling, and OSU athletics.

To contact Sherrer—123 N Hayden, Chouteau, OK 74337 ▪ 405/557-7364 ▪ bensherrer@okhouse.gov

Jerry Shoemake

Occupation—Farming/Ranching ▪ **Education**—Morris High School ▪ **Party**—Democrat ▪ **District**—16 ▪ **Legislative Experience**—House Member, 2005–present ▪ **Committee Membership**—Agriculture and Rural Development; Appropriations and Budget Subcommittee on Natural Resources and Regulatory Services; Rules; and Veterans and Military Affairs, Vice Chair

Shoemake was born on April 1, 1943, in Morris, Oklahoma. He graduated from Morris High School, and has been self-employed in the farming and ranching industries. Shoemake won election to the Oklahoma House of Representatives from District 16 in 2004. He continues active participation in the American Quarter Horse Association, Morris Lion's Club, Oklahoma Fairs and Festivals Association, Oklahoma Cattlemen's Association, Oklahoma Quarter Horse Association, Okmulgee County Cattlemen's Association, and Okmulgee County Fair Board. Shoemake married the former Lynda Mills. His hobbies include team roping.

To contact Shoemake—15160 N 310 Road, Morris, OK 74445 ▪ 918/733-2522 ▪ jerryshoemake@okhouse.gov

Shane Stone

Occupation—Business/Construction ▪ **Education**—Oklahoma City Community College; University of Oklahoma ▪ **Party**—Democrat ▪ **District**—89 ▪ **Legislative Experience**—House Member, 2015 ▪ **Committee Membership**—Appropriations and Budget Subcommittee Revenue and Taxation; Business, Labor, and Retirement Laws; Common Education; and Insurance

Stone, a fourth generation Oklahoman, won election to the Oklahoma House of Representatives from District 89 in November 2014. He attended Oklahoma City Community College as well as the University of Oklahoma. At the time of his election, Stone worked as the building superintendent at Dub Stone Construction Company, a family business that has built homes in south Oklahoma City for over fifty years. He is a member of the South Oklahoma City Chamber of Commerce and attends St. James the Greater Catholic Church.

To contact Stone—2300 N Lincoln Blvd., Oklahoma City, OK 73105 ▪ 405/557-7397 ▪ shane.stone@okhouse.gov

Chuck Strohm

Occupation—Electronics/Software Engineering ▪ **Education**—Oral Roberts University, BS ▪ **Party**—Republican ▪ **District**—69 ▪ **Legislative Experience**—House Member, 2015 ▪ **Committee Membership**—Appropriations and Budget Subcommittee on Revenue and Taxation; Business, Labor, and Retirement Laws, Vice Chair; Common Education; and Long-term Care and Senior Services

Strohm graduated from Oral Roberts University in 1988, earning a bachelor's degree in engineering. He is a small business owner and the sole inventor on two wireless patents. Strohm has spent more than twenty-five years as an electronics and software engineer in the Tulsa area. His engineering background includes aircraft simulation, oil and gas, wireless systems, and classified work in support of missile defense. He is the only practicing engineer in the Oklahoma House of Representatives.

Strohm served on the Jenks Planning Commission as vice chair, Jenks Bond Oversight Committee as chair, and is a graduate of Leadership Jenks. He currently serves on the Tulsa County Republican Party Executive Committee, having served as the Precinct 700 chair, and authored the Tulsa County Republican Party Precinct Organization Handbook. Strohm and his wife, Angela, have four children—Tamara, Brittany, Andre, and Reagan. Tarmara is a neurology resident at the Cleveland Clinic in Ohio; Brittany is a third-year medical student at the University of Oklahoma; Andre and Reagan attend Victory Christian School. The Strohm family attends both Church on the Move in Glenpool, where he serves as an usher, and Grace Church on Wednesday evenings.

To contact Strohm—2300 N Lincoln Blvd., Oklahoma City, OK 73105 ▪ 405/557-7331 ▪ chuck.strohm@okhouse.gov

Johnny Tadlock

Occupation—State Legislator ▪ **Education**—Haworth High School ▪ **Party**—Democrat ▪ **District**—1 ▪ **Legislative Experience**—House Member, 2015 ▪ **Committee Membership**—County and Municipal Government; Criminal Justice and Corrections; Government Oversight and Accountability; and Tourism and International Relations

Tadlock won election to the Oklahoma House of Representatives from District 1 in November 2014. He graduated from Haworth High School. He and his wife, Jamie, live in Idabel.

To contact Tadlock—2300 N Lincoln Blvd., Oklahoma City, OK 73105 ▪ 405/557-7363 ▪ johnny.tadlock@okhouse.gov

Todd Thomsen

Occupation—East Central Oklahoma Area Representative for the Fellowship of Christian Athletes ▪ **Education**—University of Oklahoma, MIS ▪ **Party**—Republican ▪ **District**—25 ▪ **Legislative Experience**—House Member, 2007-present; Assistant Majority Floor Leader, 2009; Chaplains, 2011; Majority Whip, 2013-2014 ▪ **Committee Membership**—Appropriations and Budget Subcommittee on Education; Common Education; Energy and Natural Resources; and Utilities, Chair

Thomsen was born on June 24, 1967, in Oklahoma City, Oklahoma. He received an MIS degree from the University of Oklahoma. He is employed as a East Central Oklahoma Representative for the Fellowship of Christian Athletes, which involves public speaking and interacting with students and school faculty. He won election to the Oklahoma House of Representatives from District 25 in November 2006. He and his wife, Melanie, have lived in Ada for more than twenty years, and they have four children; Aneli, Tovan, Mene'e, and Tyde. They are members of the First Baptist Church of Ada.

To contact Thomsen—PO Box 2347, Ada, OK 74821 ▪ 405/557-7336 ▪ todd.thomsen@okhouse.gov

Steve Vaughan

Occupation—Financial Planner, Retired ▪ **Education**—Northeastern Oklahoma A&M, AAS; School of the Ozarks, BS ▪ **Party**—Republican ▪ **District**—37 ▪ **Legislative Experience**—House Member, 2011-present; Assistant Majority Whip, 2013 ▪ **Committee Membership**—Agriculture and Rural Development; Appropriations and Budget Subcommittee on Natural Resources and Regulatory Services; and Environmental Law

Born in Cassville, Missouri, in October 1958, Vaughan attended nearby Northeastern Oklahoma A&M on a football scholarship and received an associate degree. He received a bachelor's degree from the School of the Ozarks in 1979. That same year, he married his wife, Diane, and the couple have five children—Stephen, Chris, Ashley, Matt, and Amber. The couple have five grandchildren. Vaughan retired after thirty years as a financial planner and insurance representative in the Ponca City area for three decades. He established Buffalo Waller Ranch. He built his own home and most of the ranch outbuildings. For over thirty years, he has been a scout leader for Boy Scouts of America, and a youth football and basketball coach. He is a longtime member of the National Rifle Association, and is a leader at First Lutheran Church, Ponca City. Vaughan won election to the Oklahoma House of Representatives from District 37 on November 2, 2010.

To contact Vaughan—to 2101 N 14 Street, Suite 138, Ponca City, OK 74601 ▪ 580/761-4654 ▪ steve.vaughan@okhouse.gov

Emily Virgin

Occupation—Law Clerk ▪ **Education**—University of Oklahoma ▪ **Party**—Democrat ▪ **District**—44 ▪ **Legislative Experience**—House Member, 2011-present; Assistant Minority Floor Leader, 2013 ▪ **Committee Membership**—Appropriations and Budget Subcommittee on Education; Higher Education and Career Tech; and Judiciary and Civil Procedure

Virgin was born on October 1, 1986, and attended the University of Oklahoma. She has been employed as a law clerk. Virgin won election to the Oklahoma House of Representatives from District 44 on November 2, 2010.

To contact Virgin—to 2300 N Lincoln Blvd., Oklahoma City, OK 73105 ▪ 405/557-7323 ▪ emily.virgin@okhouse.gov

Ken Walker

Occupation—State Legislator ▪ **Education**—Baltimore International Culinary College, AA; Rhema Bible Training Center; Oral Roberts University ▪ **Party**—Republican ▪ **District**—70 ▪ **Legislative Experience**—House Member, 2013 ▪ **Committee Membership**—Administrative Rules; Appropriations and Budget Subcommittee on Transportation, Vice Chair; Public Safety; and State and Federal Relations

Walker graduated Arundel Sr. High School in Gambrills, Maryland, and afterword, pursued his dream of going to culinary school after serving in the military. Walker joined the U.S. Army at the age of seventeen, and was an airborne paratrooper, and was stationed with the 3rd Special Forces Group in Ft. Bragg, North Carolina, for almost three years as an interrogator, intelligence analyst, and French and Spanish linguist. He is a Desert Storm veteran. He walked across the country from Maryland to California between April 1996 and 1997. Walker graduated valedictorian from Baltimore International Culinary College with an associates degree in professional cooking. Walker is also a 2004 graduate of Rhema Bible Training Center, and he studied leadership, management, and public policy at Oral Roberts University. He moved to the Tulsa area in 2002 with his family. He is a former restaurant critic for the *Tulsa Beacon* newspaper, and he started *Shepherd's Guide Christian Yellow Pages* for metro Tulsa in 2003. Walker won election to the Oklahoma House of Representatives from District 70 on November 6, 2012.

To contact Walker—2300 N Lincoln Blvd., Oklahoma City, OK 73105 ▪ 405/557-7359 ▪ ken.walker@okhouse.gov

Kevin Wallace

Occupation—Business Owner ▪ **Party**—Republican ▪ **District**—32 ▪ **Legislative Experience**—House Member, 2015 ▪ **Committee Membership**—Agriculture and Rural Development; Appropriations and Budget Subcommittee on Natural Resources and Regulatory Services; and Business, Labor, and Retirement Laws

Wallace graduated from Wellston High School, and worked his way through college earning a bachelor's degree in business administration. He has founded several successful businesses, including American Cellular Service and Dynatek Development Services, which he sold in 2000. He also founded SWT Construction, a civil construction company. He owns an equipment rental company, and a small investment firm. Wallace is co-owner of The Wilderness Refuge, a hunting reserve, as well as Wallahachie LLC, a whitetail deer and cattle breeding operation. Wallace is a committed father of two daughters, Ashlynn and Hailey. He is an active member of First Baptist Church of Wellston.

To contact Wallace—2300 N Lincoln Blvd., Oklahoma City, OK 73105 ▪ 405/557-7368 ▪ kevin.wallace@okhouse.gov

Weldon Watson

Occupation—Energy Industry, Retired ▪ **Education**—University of Oklahoma, BA ▪ **Party**—Republican ▪ **District**—79 ▪ **Legislative Experience**—House Member, 2007-present; Deputy Majority Whip, 2009; Majority Caucus Chair, 2011-present ▪ **Committee Membership**—Appropriations and Budget on Judiciary; Energy and Natural Resources, Chair; Rules; and Utilities

Watson was born on December 8, 1947, in Oklahoma City, Oklahoma. He received a bachelor's degree in journalism from the University of Oklahoma in 1970. He spent eight years as a reporter finishing his career in that profession working for WKY-TV in Oklahoma City, where he covered the Oklahoma House of Representatives. He also worked twenty-eight years in the energy business, retiring from ONEOK as a corporate officer on March 1, 2006. He won election to the Oklahoma House of Representatives from District 79 in November 2006. His recent memberships include American Gas Association, Association of Investment Management and Research, Leadership Tulsa, National Investor Relations Institute, Public Relations Society of America, Society of Professional Journalists, Southern Gas Association, Summit Club of Tulsa, Tulsa Chamber Government Affairs Committee, Tulsa Citizens Crime Commission Board, Union Public Schools Planning Committee, University of Oklahoma Gaylord College of Journalism and Mass Communications Board of Visitors, and Woodlake Assembly of God Board of Deacons. He married the former Cheryle Satterlee, and they have two sons, Matthew and Stephen.

To contact Watson—2300 N Lincoln Blvd., Oklahoma City, OK 73105 ▪ 918/281-9370 ▪ weldon.watson@okhouse.gov

Paul Wesselhoft

Occupation—Minister ▪ **Education**—University of Central Oklahoma, BA; Southern Nazarene University, MA; Gordon-Conwell Theological Seminary, MDiv ▪ **Party**—Republican ▪ **District**—54 ▪ **Legislative Experience**—House Member, 2005-present; Assistant Majority Whip, 2011; Assistant Majority Floor Leader, 2013 ▪ **Committee Membership**—Appropriations and Budget; Elections and Ethics, Chair; Energy and Natural Resources; and Public Safety

Wesselhoft was born on August 16, 1947, in Oklahoma City, Oklahoma. He received a bachelor's degree in drama from the University of Central Oklahoma, a master's degree in religion from Southern Nazarene University, and a master of divinity degree in theology from Gordon-Conwell Theological Seminary. A highly decorated military veteran, Wesselhoft served in front line combat during the liberation of Kuwait in the Persian Gulf War. He is a retired United States Army Airborne Ranger chaplain. An ordained Baptist minister, Wesselhoft pastored the Community Chapel in Vicenza, Italy. He also worked as the state coordinator of Oklahoma Abstinence Sex Education for Teens for the Oklahoma State Health Department. Wesselhoft won election to the Oklahoma House of Representatives from District 54 in 2004. He continues active participation in the Heritage Foundation, a conservative think-tank. Wesselhoft married the former Judy Albright. They have two children, Justin and Holly.

To contact Wesselhoft—1105 NE 29 Street, Moore, OK 73160 ▪ 405/794-9464
▪ paulwesselhoft@okhouse.gov

Cory T. Williams

Occupation—Attorney ▪ **Education**—Oklahoma State University, BS, MS; Oklahoma City University School of Law, JD ▪ **Party**—Democrat ▪ **District**—34 ▪ **Legislative Experience**—House Member, 2009; Minority Caucus Secretary, 2009; Assistant Minority Whip, 2011–present ▪ **Committee Membership**—Appropriations and Budget Subcommittee on General Government; Criminal Justice and Corrections; Environmental Law; and Higher Education and Career Tech

Born and raised in Stillwater, Williams graduated from Stillwater High School in 1996. He received a bachelor's degree in political science with an emphasis on applied politics in 2001, and a master's degree in international trade and development from the OSU School of International Studies in 2003. While in graduate school, he was awarded the Boeing Company Fellowship for his overseas work with American Airlines. He completed his law degree from Oklahoma City University School of Law in 2006. He won election to the Oklahoma House of Representatives from District 34 in November 2008. An active leader in the Stillwater community, Williams has taken an interest in both the health care and education of local residents. He serves on the board of directors for the Stillwater Community Health Center, a non-profit health clinic for the indigent and under-served residents of Stillwater. He is also a trustee for the Stillwater Public Education Foundation, which provides private fund raising for special projects at his local alma mater. He is a member of the American Bar Association as well as the Oklahoma and Payne counties' bar associations. He married the former Shannon Jacobson, a dentist.

To contact Williams—2300 N Lincoln Blvd., Oklahoma City, OK 73105 ▪ 405/557-7411
▪ cory.williams@okhouse.gov

Justin F. Wood

Occupation—State Legislator ▪ **Education**—Shawnee High School; University of Central Oklahoma ▪ **Party**—Republican ▪ **District**—26 ▪ **Legislative Experience**—House Member, 2013 ▪ **Committee Membership**—Alcohol, Tobacco, and Controlled Substances; Appropriations and Budget Subcommittee on Human Services; Energy and Natural Resources; and Higher Education and Career Tech, Vice Chair

Wood was born on December 23, 1989, in Shawnee. Wood has been employed by Oklahoma Baptist University. He won election to the Oklahoma House of Representatives from District 26 on November 6, 2012. He married his high school sweetheart, the former Olivia Goss. They have two children.

To contact Wood—2300 N Lincoln Blvd., Oklahoma City, OK 73105 ▪ 405/557-7345 ▪ justin.wood@okhouse.gov

Harold Wright

Occupation—Radio Broadcasting/CEO ▪ **Education**—Southwestern Oklahoma State University, BA ▪ **Party**—Republican ▪ **District**—57 ▪ **Legislative Experience**—House Member, 2009–present; Assistant Majority Floor Leader, 2009; Majority Caucus Vice Chair, 2011–present ▪ **Committee Membership**—Agriculture and Rural Development; Appropriations and Budget; Higher Education and Career Tech, Chair; and Rules

Wright attended Texas Tech University, Oklahoma State University, and received a bachelor's degree in speech from Southwestern Oklahoma State University in 1971. His interest in radio broadcasting began in college, while working at university and community radio stations. He worked in programming and sales at KWEY Radio in Weatherford. He served as sales manager at WMBR Radio in Jacksonville, Florida, before moving back to Oklahoma in 1975 to become part owner and general manager of KRPT Radio in Anadarko. Wright fulfilled a dream when he purchased his hometown radio station and moved back to Weatherford in 1991. Since then he has added stations in nearby Clinton, Cordell, and Elk City. He now operates five stations in western Oklahoma. He actively manages Wright Radio and helps promote community affairs. He served as mayor of Anadarko from 1985–1987, and was past president of Rotary and the chamber of commerce. He was also president of the Oklahoma Association of Broadcasters (OAB) in 1986. He was elected to the OAB Hall of Fame in 2009. Wright won election to the Oklahoma House of Representatives from District 57 in November 2008. He and his wife, Carol, have two children, Angela and Heston. They have two grandchildren, Abby and Rudy. He is a member of the First United Methodist Church in Weatherford, and is a certified lay speaker.

To contact Wright—2300 N Lincoln Blvd., Oklahoma City, OK 73105 ▪ 405/557-7325 ▪ harold.wright@okhouse.gov

George Young

Occupation—Retired Minister/Pastor/CEO ▪ **Education**—
Lambuth University, BS; Oklahoma Christian University,
MA; Phillips Theological Seminary, MDiv; D.Min ▪ **Party**—
Democrat ▪ **District**—99 ▪ **Legislative Experience**—House
Member, 2015 ▪ **Committee Membership**—Appropriations and
Budget Subcommittee on Human Services; Children, Youth, and
Family Services; and Long-term Care and Senior Services

Young earned a bachelor's degree in business administration from Lambuth University,
a master's degree from Oklahoma Christian University, and a master's degree in divinity and a doctorate degree in ministry from Phillips Theological Seminary, where he
was recognized as a "Distinguished Alumnus." He is a former board certified chaplain
with the Association of Professional Chaplains. He is also a certified case manager and
a former commissioner for the Oklahoma Department of Human Services. Young has
completed the Master Trainer Program through Standford University Patient Education
Research Center in chronic disease and self-management. He also completed a Merrill
Fellowship with Harvard Divinity School in Cambridge, Massachusetts, in 1996. He was
awarded and completed the "Sabbatical Grant for Pastoral Leaders" from the Louisville
Institute of Louisville Seminary (Lily Foundation). He is an alumnus of the Lott Carey
Pastors of Excellence Program, where he completed a three-year missionary program in
three foreign countries.

Young is a board member of The Red Cross of Central Oklahoma, United Way for Greater
OKC, Oklahoma Health Foundation, University of Central Oklahoma President's Advisory
Council, Leadership Oklahoma City, and Youth Services of Oklahoma County. He is a
former trustee for Phillips Theological Seminary, where he also serves as an adjunct profes-
sor. He has also received community service awards from Urban League of Greater OKC,
Oklahoma Health Foundation, Midwest City Martin Luther King Breakfast, Oklahoma
Conference of Churches, and the Interfaith Alliance. He is an alumnus of Leadership
Oklahoma Class XVIII, where he was selected by his class to receive the Golden Bull
Award, which is awarded to a class member who exemplifies the mission of the class.

A former senior pastor at Holy Temple Baptist Church in Oklahoma City, Young led
Holy Temple in the construction of an independent living senior housing project known
as "Temple Gardens." He is currently an adjunct professor at Mid-American Christian
University, and works with the Oklahoma County Drug and DUI Court. He won election
to the Oklahoma House of Representatives from District 99 in November 2014. Young is
married to the Reverend Dr. Thelma Chambers-Young. The couple have two children and
three wonderful grandsons.

To contact Young—2300 N Lincoln Blvd., Oklahoma City, OK 73105 ▪ 405/557-7393
▪ george.young@okhouse.gov

House Committees

Committee chair is listed first—the second name is vice chair.

The Speaker of the House and Speaker Pro Tempore are ex-officio voting members of all committees.

Administrative Rules—George Faught, John Montgomery, Ed Cannaday, Dan Fisher, Glen Mulready, Todd Russ, Mike Shelton, and Ken Walker.

Agriculture and Rural Development—John Enns, Scott Biggs, Dennis Casey, Jeff Coody, Steve Kouplen, Scooter Park, John Pfeiffer, Brian Renegar, Wade Rousselot, Mike Sanders, Jerry Shoemake, Steve Vaughn, Kevin Wallace, and Harold Wright.

Alcohol, Tobacco, and Controlled Substances—David Derby, Will Fourkiller, Doug Cox, John Enns, Randy Grau, Claudia Griffith, Jadine Nollan, and Justin Wood.

Appropriations and Budget—Earl Sears, Dennis Casey, John Bennett, Lisa J. Billy, Mike Brown, Ann Coody, Doug Cox, Chuck Hoskin, Dennis Johnson, Scott Martin, Charles McCall, Mark McCullough, Jeannie McDaniel, Randy McDaniel, Jerry McPeak, Richard Morrissette, Jason Nelson, Charles Ortega, Leslie Osborn, Pat Ownbey, Pam Peterson, Wade Rousselot, Todd Russ, Mike Sanders, Ben Sherrer, Paul Wesselhoft, and Harold Wright.

Appropriations and Budget Subcommittees

Education—Scott Martin, Katie Henke, Ed Cannaday, Ann Coody, Jason Dunnington, Sally Kern, Jadine Nollan, Michael Rogers, Todd Thomsen, and Emily Virgin.

General Government—Dennis Johnson, Gary Banz, David Brumbaugh, George Faught, Dan Fisher, Chuck Hoskin, Jason Murphey, Scooter Park, David Perryman, and Cory Williams.

Health—Doug Cox, Chad Caldwell, Jeff Coody, Will Fourkiller, Claudia Griffith, John Montgomery, Lewis Moore, Glen Mulready, Sean Roberts, Mike Shelton.

Human Services—Pat Ownbey, Wade Rousselot, David Derby, Travis Dunlap, John Paul Jordan, Mike Ritze, Justin Wood, and George Young.

Judiciary—Mark McCullough, Chris Kannady, Kevin Calvey, Jon Echols, Randy Grau, Scott Inman, Ben Loring, Terry O'Deonnell, David Perryman, and Weldon Watson.

Natural Resources and Regulatory Services—Leslie Osborn, John Pfeiffer, Scott Biggs, Josh Cockroft, Marian Cooksey, John Enns, Steve Kouplen, Mark Lepak, Seneca Scott, Jerry Shoemake, Steve Vaughn, and Kevin Wallace.

Public Safety—John Bennett, Lisa J. Billy, Mike Christian, Bobby Cleveland, Donnie Condit, Jason Dunnington, Tommy Hardin, Dan Kirby, Ben Loring, and Mark McBride.

Revenue and Taxation—Charles McCall, Elise Hall, Tom Newell, Wade Rousselot, Shane Stone, and Chuck Strohm.

Transportation—Mike Sanders, Ken Walker, Charlie Joyner, James Leewright, James Lockhart, Kevin Matthews, Casey Murdock, and Dustin Roberts.

Banking and Financial Services—Todd Russ, James Leewright, Scott Martin, Charles McCall, Leslie Osborn, Eric Proctor, and Mike Shelton.

Business, Labor, and Retirement Laws—Randy McDaniel, Chuck Strohm, Will Fourkiller, Charlie Joyner, Mark McBride, Tom Newell, Charles Ortega, David Perryman, Shane Stone, and Kevin Wallace.

Children, Youth, and Family Services—Sally Kern, Pam Peterson, John Paul Jordan, Jason Nelson, Tom Newell, Pat Ownbey, Ben Sherrer, and George Young.

Common Education—Ann Coody, Michael Rogers, Chad Caldwell, Ed Cannaday, Dennis

Casey, Donnie Condit, Dan Fisher, Katie Henke, John Paul Jordan, Sally Kern, Jeannie McDaniel, Jason Nelson, Jadine Nollan, Shane Stone, Chuck Strohm, and Todd Thomsen.

County and Municipal Government—Sean Roberts, Scooter Park, Mike Christian, Josh Cockroft, Dan Kirby, Kevin Matthews, Jason Murphey, and Johnny Tadlock.

Criminal Justice and Corrections—Pam Peterson, Terry O'Donnell, Lisa J. Billy, Scott Biggs, Bobby Cleveland, Marian Cooksey, Randy Grau, Mark McCullough, Ben Sherrer, Johnny Tadlock, and Cory Williams.

Economic Development, Commerce, and Real Estate—Dan Kirby, Marian Cooksey, Travis Dunlap, Elise Hall, Kevin Matthews, Charles McCall, Randy McDaniel, Richard Morrissette, Brian Renegar, and Dustin Roberts.

Elections and Ethics—Paul Wesselhoft, Donnie Condit, Gary Banz, Charlie Joyner, David Perryman, and Michael Rogers.

Energy and Natural Resources—Weldon Watson, Mark McBride, Mike Brown, David Brumbaugh, Kevin Calvey, Marian Cooksey, Jon Echols, Tommy Hardin, Scott Inman, Dennis Johnson, Steve Kouplen, Jerry McPeak, Charles Ortega, Eric Proctor, Sean Roberts, Mike Sanders, Seneca Scott, Todd Thomsen, Paul Wesselhoft, and Justin Wood.

Environmental Law—Kevin Calvey, Travis Dunlap, Jeff Coody, Jason Dunnington, John Montgomery, Lewis Moore, Steve Vaughn, and Cory Williams.

Government Oversight and Accountability—Tom Newell, John Paul Jordan, John Bennett, Elise Hall, James Leewright, Seneca Scott, and Johnny Tadlock.

Higher Education and Career Tech—Harold Wright, Justin Wood, Dennis Casey, Katie Henke, Chris Kannady, James Leewright, Emily Virgin, and Cory Williams.

Insurance—Glen Mulready, Jeff Coody, Dan Kirby, Steve Kouplen, Randy McDaniel, Lewis Moore, Michael Rogers, Todd Russ, Mike Shelton, and Shane Stone.

Judiciary and Civil Procedure—Randy Grau, Jon Echols, Kevin Calvey, Chris Kannady, Mark McCullough, Richard Morrissette, Terry O'Donnell, Leslie Osborn, Ben Sherrer, and Emily Virgin.

Long-term Care and Senior Services—Jandine Nollan, Jeannie McDaniel, Bobby Cleveland, Mike Ritze, Chuck Strohm, and George Young.

Public Health—Mike Ritze, Elise Hall, Doug Cox, David Derby, Jon Echols, Will Fourkiller, Claudia Griffith, Jeannie McDaniel, Glen Mulready, and Sean Roberts.

Public Safety—Mike Christian, Bobby Cleveland, Scott Biggs, David Derby, Dennis Johnson, Ben Loring, Kevin Matthews, Pat Ownbey, Pam Peterson, R.C. Pruett, Brian Renegar, Mike Ritze, Ken Walker, and Paul Wesselhoft.

Rules—Tommy Hardin, Jason Nelson, Gary Banz, Chad Caldwell, Donnie Condit, Chris Kannady, R.C. Pruett, Jerry Shoemake, Weldon Watson, and Harold Wright.

State and Federal Relations—Lewis Moore, Dan Fisher, Sally Kern, Mark Lepak, Jason Murphey, Eric Proctor, Seneca Scott, and Ken Walker.

State Government Operations—Jason Murphey, Mark Lepak, Josh Cockroft, Jason Dunnington, Scott Martin, Richard Morrissette, and John Pfeiffer.

Tourism and International Relations—Josh Cockroft, R.C. Pruett, Gary Banz, Travis Dunlap, Mark Lepak, Ben Loring, John Montgomery, Charles Ortega, Dustin Roberts, and Johnny Tadlock.

Transportation—Charlie Joyner, Casey Murdock, John Bennett, David Brumbaugh,

George Faught, Katie Henke, James Lockhart, Jerry McPeak, Terry O'Donnell, and Eric Proctor.

Utilities—Todd Thomsen, David Brumbaugh, Chad Caldwell, Ed Cannaday, Mike Christian, James Lockhart, Mark McBride, Casey Murdock, R.C. Pruett, and Weldon Watson.

Veterans and Military Affairs—Dustin Roberts, Jerry Shoemake, Ann Coody, John Enns, George Faught, Chuck Hoskin, and John Pfeiffer.

Wildlife—Steve Vaughan, Kevin Wallace, Mike Brown, Tommy Hardin, James Lockhart, Casey Murdock, and Scooter Park.

Fort Reno, circa 1910—building was originally a hospital, later used for boarding civilian employees.

JUDICIAL BRANCH

Oklahoma Court System

The Oklahoma Court System is made up of the Supreme Court, the Court of Criminal Appeals, the Court of Civil Appeals, and seventy-seven District Courts.

Courts of Last Resort	Civil—Supreme Court
	Criminal—Court of Criminal Appeals
Intermediate Appellate Court	Court of Civil Appeals
Courts of General Jurisdiction	District Courts
Courts of Limited Jurisdiction	Court on the Judiciary
	Court of Tax Review
	Workers' Compensation Court
	Municipal Criminal Courts of Record
	Municipal Courts Not of Record
Court-Related Entities	Judicial Nominating Commission
	Dispute Resolution Advisory Board

Unlike most states, Oklahoma has two courts of last resort. The Oklahoma Supreme Court determines all issues of a civil nature, and the Oklahoma Court of Criminal Appeals decides all criminal matters. Members of these courts, and of the Court of Civil Appeals, are appointed by the governor from a list of three names submitted by the Oklahoma Judicial Nominating Commission. The Oklahoma Supreme Court has nine justices; the Court of Criminal Appeals, five judges; and the Court of Civil Appeals, twelve judges.

The Court of Civil Appeals is responsible for the majority of appellate decisions. These opinions may be released for publication by either the Oklahoma Supreme Court or the Court of Civil Appeals. When the opinions are released by the Oklahoma Supreme Court, they have precedential value. The Court of Civil Appeals is made up of four divisions, each composed of three judges. Two divisions of the Court of Civil Appeals are located in Oklahoma City, and two are in Tulsa.

Deciding cases is only one of the Oklahoma Supreme Court's functions. The court is also responsible for administering the state's entire judicial system. The court establishes rules of operation for all other courts in the state. The court formulates rules for practice of law, which govern the conduct of all attorneys, and it administers discipline in appropriate cases.

Administrative services for the court system are provided by the Administrative Office of the Courts. For more information please contact the Administrative Office of the Courts at 405/556-9300.

Supreme Court Judicial Districts

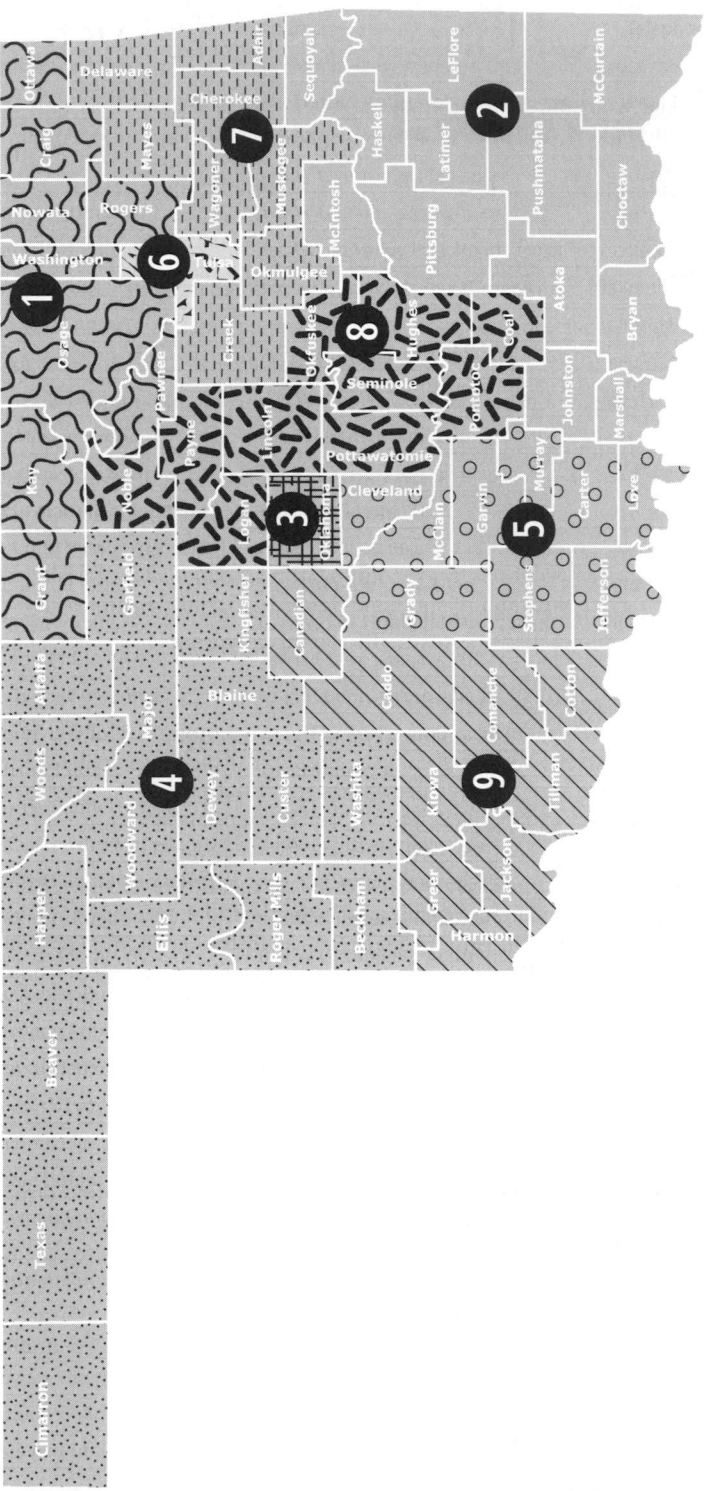

Supreme Court

Constitution, Article 7 § 1

History and Function—The Oklahoma Supreme Court determines all issues of a civil nature in the State of Oklahoma. Members of this court are appointed by the governor from a list of three names submitted by the Oklahoma Judicial Nominating Commission.

Name	City	District
John F. Reif, Chief Justice	Tulsa	1
Douglas L. Combs, Vice Chief Justice	Shawnee	8
Tom Colbert	Tulsa	6
James Edmondson	Muskogee	7
Noma D. Gurich	Oklahoma City	3
Yvonne Kauger	Colony	4
Steven W. Taylor	McAlester	2
Joseph M. Watt	Altus	9
James R. Winchester	Chickasha	5

Administration—Michael D. Evans, Administrative Director of the Courts; Debra Charles, General Counsel. Administrative Office of the Courts is located in the Oklahoma Judicial Center, 2100 N Lincoln Blvd., Suite 300, Oklahoma City 73105 ▪ 405/556-9300 ▪ www.oscn.net ▪ Agency Code 677, IA

Clerk of the Appellate Courts (Constitution, Article 7 § 5; 20 O.S. 2001, § 78), Michael S. Richie. Clerk Office is located in the Oklahoma Judicial Center, 2100 N Lincoln Blvd., Oklahoma City, OK 73105 ▪ 405/556-9400

Staff Attorneys

Name	Justice	Name	Justice
David Dixon	Tom Colbert	W. Kyle Shifflett	Yvonne Kauger
Kate DoDoo	Tom Colbert	Sharon Schooley	John Reif
Sheldon Jones	Douglas L. Combs	Hilda Harlton	John Reif
John Holden	Douglas L. Combs	Kyle Rogers	Steven W. Taylor
Vacant	James Edmondson	Barbara Kinney	Steven W. Taylor
Michael Elliott	James Edmondson	Paul White	James Winchester
John W. Turner	Noma Gurich	Jill van Egmond	James Winchester
Jana Knott	Noma Gurich	Vicki Angus	Joseph M. Watt
Julie Rorie	Yvonne Kauger	Marissa Lane	Joseph M. Watt

Referees—Greg Albert, Louise Helms, Daniel Karim, Barbara Swimley

Justices of the Supreme Court

Chief Justice John F. Reif, District 1. Reif is currently serving as Chief Justice of the

Oklahoma Supreme Court for 2015 and 2016. Reif was appointed to the court in October 2007 by Governor Brad Henry. He was chosen to serve on the Oklahoma Court on the Judiciary, Appellate Division, March 1, 2011, through March 1, 2013. Prior to his service on the Oklahoma Supreme Court, Reif was appointed by Governor George Nigh to the Oklahoma Court of Civil Appeals in May 1984, where he served twenty-three years, exercising jurisdiction over civil appeals as assigned by the Oklahoma Supreme Court. Reif started judicial service in February 1981 as a special district judge for the Fourteenth Judicial District in Tulsa County, where his primary duties included arraignments and preliminary hearings. Reif began his legal career in 1977 with the Tulsa County District Attorney's Office, where he worked in the civil division; providing general legal services to the county. Before practicing law, he provided planning and grant assistance to law enforcement agencies in the Tulsa area through the Indian Nations Council of Governments from 1974 to 1977. Reif also served as a police officer for the City of Owasso from 1973 to 1975. While on the bench, teaching has been Reif's way of giving back to the community. He has made over 120 presentations for Oklahoma Bar Association sponsored CLEs and community education programs. In 1995 Reif was the recipient of the Distinguished Service Award from Oral Roberts University for his teaching at ORU. In December 2010 the Oklahoma Bar Association awarded Reif the Earl Sneed Award in recognition of his continuing legal and community education presentations and programs over the past thirty years. From 1994 through 2001, Reif completed extensive judicial training provided by The National Judicial College, and joined the faculty of the National Tribal Judicial Center at the NJC in 2003. He presents classes in essential skills for both appellate and tribal court judges at The National Judicial College. Reif also is an active participant in The Sovereignty Symposium, annually presenting the ethics portion of the program. Reif was born June 19, 1951, in Skiatook, Oklahoma. He attended high school at Cascia Hall, in Tulsa, Oklahoma, under a work study scholarship and graduated as valedictorian of his Class of 1969. He attended the University of Tulsa, receiving a bachelor's degree in criminal justice in 1973, and his Juris Doctor from the College of Law in 1977. Reif was married for thirty-five years to Aylo (Brewer) Reif until her death in 2008. Reif can be reached at Suite N–230, Oklahoma Judicial Center, 2100 N Lincoln, Oklahoma City, OK 73105, or 405/556–9360.

Vice Chief Justice Douglas L. Combs, District 8, was born on October 17, 1951,

in Shawnee, Oklahoma. He is a member of the Muscogee Nation. Combs was appointed by Governor Brad Henry to the Oklahoma Supreme Court on January 1, 2011. He served as district judge in the twenty-third judicial district from 2003 through 2010, and served as special judge from 1995 to 2003. Prior to taking the bench, Combs was in private practice and served as an assistant state attorney general and as a deputy clerk for the Oklahoma Supreme Court. Combs graduated from Shawnee High School in 1969. He attended St. Gregory's Junior College, now St. Gregory's University, and the University of Oklahoma to earn a bachelor's degree in political science in 1973. He earned his juris doctorate from the Oklahoma City University School of Law in 1976, and was admitted to the bar the same year. Combs has served as chief judge of the twenty-third judicial district and as the presiding judge of the North Central Administrative Judicial District. He served as a board member of the Oklahoma Judicial Conference from 2006 to 2010, and held the office of president of the Oklahoma Judicial Conference in 2009. Combs is married to Janet Lea Combs, and they have two children: Christopher T. Combs and Eric L. Combs, both members of the Oklahoma Bar Association. He is a resident of Shawnee, Oklahoma. Combs can be reached at Suite 1, Oklahoma Judicial Center, 2100 N Lincoln, Oklahoma City, Oklahoma 73105, or 405/556-9361.

Justice Tom Colbert, District 6. Colbert, the first African-American to serve on the Oklahoma Supreme Court, was born in Oklahoma City. He graduated from Sapulpa High School, earned an associate's degree from Eastern Oklahoma State College in 1970, and a bachelor of science degree from Kentucky State University in 1973. While at Kentucky State, Colbert was named an All-American in track and field. Colbert served in the United States Army and received an honorable discharge in 1975. He earned a master of education degree from Eastern Kentucky University in 1976 and taught in the public schools in Chicago, Illinois. Colbert received his juris doctorate from the University of Oklahoma in 1982. He was an assistant dean at Marquette University Law School from 1982–1984, and  an assistant district attorney in Oklahoma County from 1984–1986, before entering private law practice at Miles-LaGrange and Colbert from 1986 to 1989. Colbert continued his practice under the name Colbert and Associates from 1989 to 2000. He also served as an attorney for the Oklahoma Department of Human Services from 1988 to 1989 and again in 1999. In March 2000, Colbert became the first African-American appointed to the Oklahoma Court of Civil Appeals. He was appointed by Governor Brad Henry. He served as chief judge of that court in 2004. On October 7, 2004, Governor Brad Henry appointed Colbert to the Oklahoma Supreme Court. In January 2011, Colbert was sworn in as the court's first African-American vice chief justice. On January 1, 2013, he became the first African-American to be sworn in as the court's chief justice. Colbert is a member of the American Bar Association, the National Bar Association, the Oklahoma Bar Association, and the Tulsa County Bar Association. He is a frequent speaker at schools. Colbert can be reached at Suite 1, Oklahoma Judicial Center, 2100 N Lincoln, Oklahoma City, Oklahoma 73105, or 405/556-9365.

Justice James E. Edmondson, District 7. Born in Kansas City, Missouri, Edmondson received a bachelor's degree from Northeastern State University in 1967. He served in the United States Navy from 1967 to 1969. Following his military service, Edmondson enrolled at Georgetown University Law School and received his law degree in 1973. His legal career includes serving as Muskogee County's assistant district attorney from 1976 to 1978, assistant United States attorney from 1978 to 1980, and acting U.S. attorney for Oklahoma's Eastern District from 1980 to 1981. Edmondson entered private law practice and was a partner in the Edmondson Law Office from 1981 through 1983. He served as district judge for District 15  in 1983 and continued in that capacity for twenty years. Governor Brad Henry appointed Edmondson as justice to the Oklahoma Supreme Court on December 2, 2003. He served as chief justice in 2009 and 2010. He and his wife, Suzanne, have two grown children, Jimmy and Sarah, and a grandson, Jack. Edmondson can be reached at Suite 1, Oklahoma Judicial Center, 2100 N Lincoln, Oklahoma City, OK 73105, or 405/556-9316.

Justice Noma D. Gurich, District 3. Born on September 26, 1952, in South Bend, Indiana, Gurich graduated from Penn High School in Mishawaka, Indiana.

She graduated magna cum laude from Indiana State University in 1975 with a degree in political science. Gurich received her juris doctorate degree from the University of Oklahoma College of Law in 1978. She was an editor of the *American Indian Law Review*, and received the Professional Responsibility Award. Gurich has lived in Oklahoma City for more than thirty years. Before she began her judicial career, Gurich was engaged in private law practice in Oklahoma City for ten years. In 1988 she was appointed by Governor Henry Bellmon to serve as a judge on the Oklahoma Workers' Compensation Court. She served as presiding judge of that court for four years. She was reappointed for a second term by Governor David Walters in 1994. After being appointed by Governor Frank Keating to the district court bench in July 1998, she won a countywide election for district judge that same year. She was re-elected without opposition in 2002, 2006, and 2010. Gurich served as the presiding administrative judge for the Seventh Judicial District, Oklahoma County, from January of 2003 to December 31, 2004. She presided over more than 190 jury trials during her career as district judge. While serving as a district judge, Gurich served as the presiding judge of both the 11th and 12th Multicounty Grand Juries (2007–2008 and 2009–2010) by order of the chief justice of the Oklahoma Supreme Court. Gurich was appointed by Governor Brad Henry as the third woman justice of the Oklahoma Supreme Court, and she took office on February 15, 2011. Gurich served as president of the William J. Holloway, Jr. American Inn of Court from 2007 to April of 2008. She continues as a master member of the Inn. She received the 2003 Mona Salyer Lambird Spotlight Award from the OBA Women in Law Committee. Gurich was a three time *Journal Record* Honoree for Woman of the Year in 2005, 2008, and 2011, and a member of the Circle of Excellence. She was named Judge of the Year by ABOTA in 2011. Indiana State University selected her as a 2012 Distinguished Alumni. In 2013, the Association of Women in Communications honored Gurich with a Byliner Award. In March 2014, Gurich received a Valuable Volunteer Award by the Foundation for Oklahoma City Public Schools. She is the Key Club advisor for the Southeast High School Key Club, and a volunteer with El Sistema Oklahoma, an after school music program for elementary school children attending Oklahoma City Public Schools. Gurich is past president and member of the Kiwanis Club of Oklahoma City, and was only the second woman president of the ninety-year-old club when she served from 2006 to 2007. She is the Kiwanis Advisor for the Southeast High School Key Club. She was honored in 2013 as a valuable volunteer by the Oklahoma City Public Schools Foundation. She serves annually on the Application Screening Committee for the Oklahoma School of Science and Mathematics. She is an active member of St. Luke's United Methodist Church, where she is a volunteer Mobile Meals driver and television camera operator. Gurich is married to John E. Miley, who is the general counsel of the Oklahoma Employment Security Commission. Gurich can be reached at Suite 1, Oklahoma Judicial Center, 2100 N Lincoln, Oklahoma City, Oklahoma 73105 or 405/556–9362.

Justice Yvonne Kauger, District 4. A fourth generation Oklahoman, Kauger was born in Cordell, Oklahoma, on August 3, 1937, and raised in Colony. A graduate of Southwestern Oklahoma State University and the Oklahoma City University School of Law, Kauger served as presiding judge for the Court on the Judiciary, and on the Law School and Bench and Bar Committees of the Oklahoma Bar Association. Governor George Nigh appointed her as justice to the Oklahoma Supreme Court on March 11, 1984. She served as the court's chief justice from January

1997 to December 1998, and she is the only woman to serve as the court's chief justice and vice chief justice. Kauger founded the Gallery of the Plains Indian in Colony, co-founded Red Earth, and has served as coordinator for the Sovereignty Symposium since its inception in 1987. The symposium is a seminar on Indian law sponsored by the Oklahoma Supreme Court. Kauger has received numerous honors and awards throughout her distinguished career including being named valedictorian of her graduating class at Colony High School, and graduating first in her class from the OCU School of Law. In 1984 she was adopted by the Cheyenne and Arapaho tribes of Oklahoma. She was named National Delta Zeta in 1988, and received the Oklahoma City Pioneer Award in 1989. Kauger served as the featured speaker at the Twentieth William O. Douglas Lecture Series at Gonzaga University in 1990. She received an honorary doctorate degree from OCU in 1991, and has been named as an honorary alumnus by both OCU and Southwestern Oklahoma State University. In June 1999 the American Judicature Society awarded Kauger the Herbert Harley Award in recognition of her outstanding efforts to improve the administration of justice. That same year, the Oklahoma Bar Association honored her with the Judicial Excellence Award. In March 2001 Justice Kauger was inducted into the Oklahoma Women's Hall of Fame. In 2004 she was named one of the ten most notable women in Oklahoma City by the Oklahoma City Orchestra League. In July 2004 she donated Main Street in Colony, Oklahoma, which her great grandfather built, to Southwestern Oklahoma State University to be used to promote the arts in western Oklahoma. In 2005 Kauger received the Governor's Art Award. In addition, she is a member of the District State-Federal Judicial Council and the Washita County Hall of Fame. She chaired the Oklahoma Judicial Center Building Committee, and the Building Art Committee. After the move into the new Center in 2011, the committee received the Governor's Art Award. In 2012 she received the Lifetime Achievement Award from the Paseo Arts Association. Kauger can be reached at Oklahoma Judicial Center, 2100 N Lincoln, Oklahoma City, OK 73105, or 405/556–9364.

Justice Steven W. Taylor, District 2. Born on June 7, 1949, in Henryetta, Oklahoma, Taylor attended McAlester Public Schools. He received a bachelor's degree in political science from Oklahoma State University in 1971 and a Juris Doctor degree from the University of Oklahoma College of Law in 1974. He is the only person to have received the highest alumni awards at both OSU and OU. Taylor joined the United States Marine Corps and served on active duty from 1974 to 1978. He was trained as an infantry platoon commander and later served as a prosecutor and chief defense counsel. In 1977 he became the youngest judge in the U.S. armed forces. He achieved the rank of major. Following his military career, Taylor practiced law in McAlester from 1978 to 1984. Taylor's public service career began in 1980, when he was elected to the McAlester City Council. In 1982 he was elected mayor of McAlester, making him the youngest in the city's history. In 1983 he received recognition as one of three "Outstanding Young Oklahomans." Recognizing Taylor's leadership in economic development, the City of McAlester named a multi-million dollar industrial park for him, where many industries now employ several hundred Oklahomans. The city further honored Taylor in 1997 by naming him "Citizen of the Year." He is the co-author of *University of Oklahoma College of Law: A Centennial History*, a book published in 2009 detailing the history of the OU Law School. Governor George Nigh appointed Taylor associate district judge in 1984. Taylor became the first associate district judge elected president of the Oklahoma Judicial Conference. In 1994 he was elected district judge and chief judge of the eighteenth Judicial District that included McIntosh and Pittsburg counties. In 1997 and 2003 he was elected presiding judge of the East Central Judicial Administrative District that encompasses ten counties. During the twenty years Taylor served as a trial judge, he presided over more than 500 jury trials including the Oklahoma City bombing trial. He has received numerous awards including the Oklahoma Bar Association 2003 "Award of Judicial Excellence." On September 23, 2004, Governor Brad Henry appointed Taylor as justice of the Oklahoma Supreme Court. In 2007 *Oklahoma* magazine named him as one of the "100 Who Shaped Us," a list of Oklahomans who influenced the first one hundred years of the state. In 2009 he was inducted into the Oklahoma Hall of Fame. Taylor can be reached at Suite 1, Oklahoma Judicial Center, 2100 N Lincoln, Oklahoma City, OK 73105, or 405/556-9368.

Justice Joseph M. Watt, District 9. Watt was born on March 8, 1947, in Austin, Texas. He graduated from Austin High School in 1965, received a bachelor's degree in history/government from Texas Tech University in 1969, and a Doctor of Jurisprudence from the University of Texas Law School in 1972. Admitted to practice law in both Texas and Oklahoma, Watt moved to Altus, Oklahoma, in 1973, where he worked in private law practice from 1973 to 1985. He also served as Altus city prosecutor from 1973 to 1985, and as city attorney from 1980 to 1985. Watt was appointed special district judge for Jackson County in 1985, and was elected associate district judge in 1986. He served in that capacity until January 1991, when he was asked to serve as general counsel in Governor David Walters's administration.

Watt was appointed as justice to the Oklahoma Supreme Court on May 18, 1992. Watt's judicial service also includes Oklahoma Supreme Court chief justice for two terms from 2003 to 2006; and vice chief justice from 2001 to 2002; Oklahoma Judicial Conference vice president, 1993 to 1994; Oklahoma Judicial Conference president elect, 1995; Oklahoma Judicial Conference president, 1996; Court on the Judiciary Appellate Division, 1997-2002; and Supreme Court Liaison to the Oklahoma Bar Association, 1997-2002. His honors include the Delta Theta Phi Law Fraternity Outstanding Law Student in the Nation in 1972; University of Texas Circle of Omnicron Delta Kappa National Honorary Leadership Society, 1972; Paul Harris Fellow; Graduate of the Inaugural Oklahoma State Bureau of Investigation Citizens Academy, 2004; Honorary Alumnus, Oklahoma City University School of Law, 2005; and Honorary Highway Patrol Trooper, 2006. He has served as secretary and as president of the Altus Rotary Club. Watt is a member of the Oklahoma and Texas bar associations. He and his wife, Cathy, have four grown children and three grandchildren. Watt can be reached at Suite 1, Oklahoma Judicial Center, 2100 N Lincoln, Oklahoma City, OK 73105, or 405/556-9359.

Justice James R. Winchester, District 5. Winchester was appointed as a member of

the Oklahoma Supreme Court by Governor Frank Keating in 2000. He served as chief justice of the court January 2007 to December 2008. A native of Clinton, Oklahoma, he received his Bachelor of Arts degree from the University of Oklahoma and his juris doctorate from Oklahoma City University. After graduating from law school, Winchester practiced law in western Oklahoma before being named associate district judge for Caddo County in January 1983. In December 1983, at age 30, he became one of the youngest district judges in the state when he was appointed by Governor George Nigh as district judge for the Sixth Judicial District of Oklahoma. He was named an Outstanding State Trial Court Judge and is a past president of the Oklahoma Judicial Conference. During his fifteen years on the bench, he presided over both civil and criminal cases, including death-penalty trials and multi-million dollar oil and gas disputes. He oversaw hundreds of jury trials ranging from dog bites to first degree murder. For two years, Winchester served as a U.S. administrative law judge in Oklahoma City and New Orleans. Winchester is a graduate of Leadership Oklahoma and the recent recipient of the Boy Scouts of America Silver Beaver Award. He recently completed the Program on Negotiation at Harvard Law School. He resides in Chickasha, Oklahoma, with his wife, Susan Winchester, and their son Davis. Winchester can be reached at Suite 1, Oklahoma Judicial Center, 2100 N Lincoln, Oklahoma City, OK 73105, or 405/556-9367; www.oscn.net.

In 1910, President Theodore Roosevelt's War Department dispatched Army Capt. Dan T. Moore to Fort Sill, Oklahoma, to organize America's first School of Fire for Field Artillery to train officers and noncommissioned officers. ❦ In 1942 [pictured above], the men of Battery C, 26th Battalion, Field Artillery Replacement Training Center practised traversing difficult terrain in the Wichita Mountains. With guns and auxiliary equipment slung on the backs of army mules, the cannoneers/muleteers were trained to go where mechanized and horse-drawn artillery could not, advancing through dense forests, fording rivers, and scaling mountains.

Criminal Appeals Judicial Districts

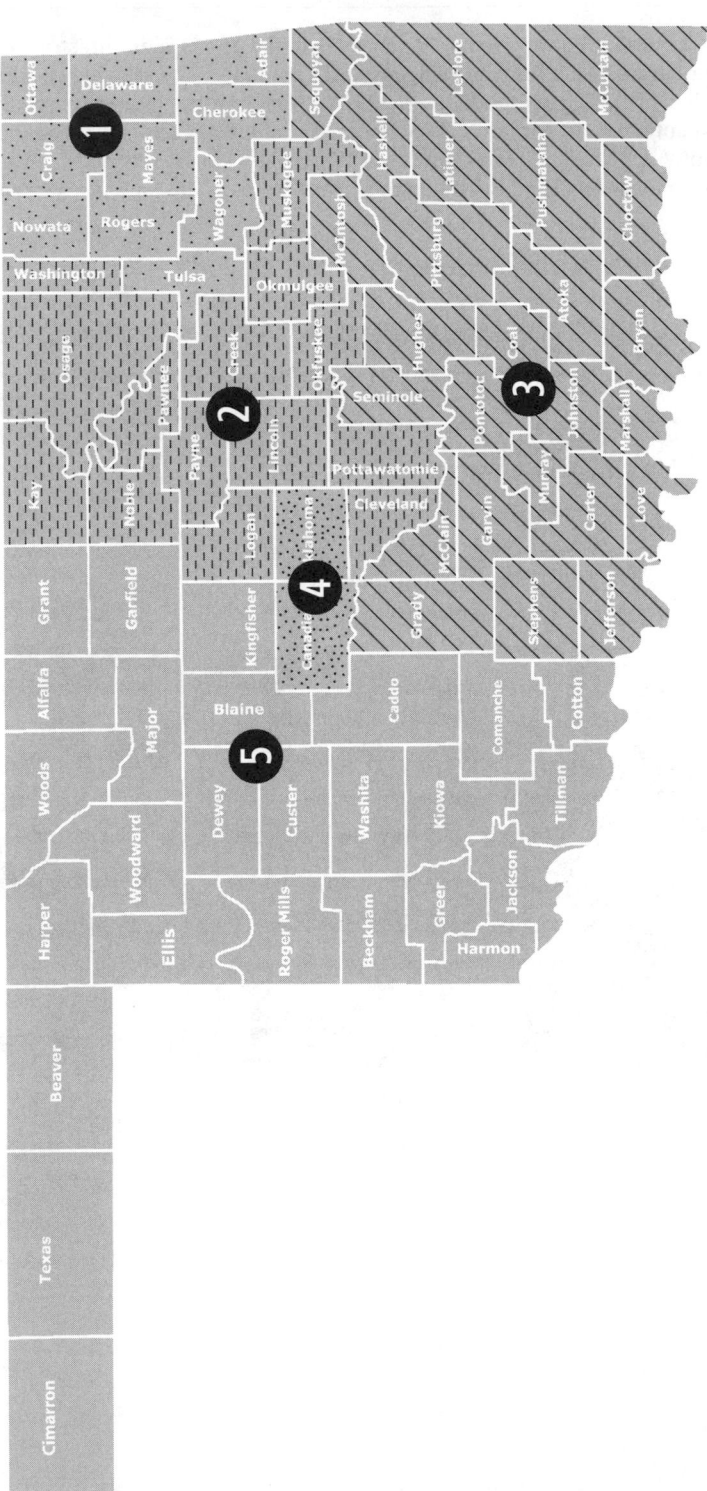

Court of Criminal Appeals

Constitution, Article 7 § 1

History and Function—The Oklahoma Court of Criminal Appeals is the highest court in Oklahoma with appellate jurisdiction in criminal cases. It is the state court of last resort in criminal matters. The court derives its origin and jurisdiction from the state constitution, which was formulated by the constitutional convention and submitted to and adopted by the people of Oklahoma at the first election on September 17, 1907. Members of this court are appointed by the governor from a list of three names submitted by the Oklahoma Judicial Nominating Commission.

Name	City	District
Clancy Smith, Presiding Judge	Tulsa	1
Gary L. Lumpkin, Vice Presiding Judge	Madill	3
Robert L. Hudson	Guthrie	2
Arlene Johnson	Oklahoma City	4
David Lewis	Lawton	5

Administration Office—Oklahoma Judicial Center, Suite 2, Third Floor, Oklahoma City, OK 73105 ▪ 405/556-9600 ▪ www.okcca.net ▪ Agency Code 199, IA

Staff Attorneys

Lendell S. Blosser
David C. Bugg
Jake Burks
Brant Elmore
Byran Dupler
Pete Gelvin
Patty Grotta
Suzanne Heggy

Gaylene Henley
Lou Ann Kohlman
Maria Kolar
Melanie Stucky
M. Caroline Mitchell
Allen Smith
Russ Wheeler

Judges of the
Court of Criminal Appeals

Presiding Judge Clancy Smith, District 1. Smith was appointed to the Oklahoma Court of Criminal Appeals on September 1, 2010, to fill the unexpired term of Judge Charles S. Chapel. She was named presiding judge on January 1, 2015. Smith is a native of Hugo, Oklahoma, and graduated from Hugo High School. She attended Oklahoma State University, receiving a bachelor's degree in English in 1964. She taught high school English in Tulsa, Oklahoma, and Jacksonville, Florida. She received her juris doctorate from the University of Tulsa College of Law in 1980. After graduating law school, she worked in private practice of law from 1980 to 1994. She then served as a special judge in Tulsa County from 1994 to 1998 in the family division. Smith received the Outstanding Family Law Judge Award from the family law section of the Oklahoma Bar Association in 1996. From 1998 to 2005, she served in the criminal division of Tulsa County, conducting preliminary hearings, arraignments, plea hearings, and bond hearings. In 2005 Governor Brad Henry appointed Smith as district judge for the Fourteenth Judicial District. From 2005 to 2010, Smith served the criminal division in Tulsa County and has presided over more than 110 felony jury trials. Smith is a member of the Tulsa County Bar Association, the Oklahoma Bar Association, and the American Bar Association. She served as president of the Johnson-Sontag Chapter of the America Inns of Court for three years and received the James Sontag Award in 2010. In 2013 she received the OBA Award of Judicial Excellence. She has two children and four grandchildren. Smith can be reached at Suite 2, Oklahoma Judicial Center, 2100 N Lincoln, Oklahoma City, OK 73105, or 405/556–9643.

Vice Presiding Judge Gary L. Lumpkin, District 3. Originally a native of Sentinel, Oklahoma, Lumpkin graduated from Weatherford High School in 1964. He received a bachelor's degree in business administration from Southwestern State College in 1968, and a Juris Doctor degree from the University of Oklahoma School of Law in 1974. Lumpkin served in the United States Marine Corps from 1968 to 1971, serving eighteen months in Vietnam. He retired in 1998, after thirty years of service, with the rank of colonel in the Marine Corps Reserves. He completed his military service as one of only two Marine Reserve judges assigned to the Navy-Marine Corps Court of Criminal Appeals. Lumpkin worked as a staff attorney for the Oklahoma Department of Consumer Affairs.  He was appointed assistant district attorney for Marshall County in 1976, and subsequently first assistant district attorney for the Twentieth District. Lumpkin served as associate district judge for Marshall County from 1982 to 1985, and as district judge, Twentieth Judicial District, Division II from 1985 to 1989. Governor Henry Bellmon appointed him to the Oklahoma Court of Criminal Appeals, and he began his service on the court in January 1989. Lumpkin was named Outstanding Young Man of America by the U.S. Jaycees in 1979, and Outstanding Assistant District Attorney of the Third Congressional District by the Oklahoma District Attorneys Association in 1981. He also received the 1999 William J. Holloway Jr. Professionalism Award from the William J. Holloway Jr. American Inn of Court. Southwestern Oklahoma State University selected him as their 2007 Distinguished Alumnus and inducted him into the University Hall of Fame. Lumpkin is a member of the Marine Corps Reserve Association;

Oklahoma, Oklahoma County, and Marshall County bar associations; Benefactor Fellow of the Oklahoma Bar Foundation; Oklahoma Judicial Conference; Veterans of Foreign Wars Post 4611; and the William J. Holloway Jr. American Inns of Court CV. From 2001 to 2007, he was a member of the National Center for State Courts Board of Directors in Williamsburg, Virginia. He is a current member of the advisory board for the Trinity Legal Clinic. Lumpkin and his wife, Barbara, are from Madill and have one child. They are members of Waterloo Road Baptist Church. Lumpkin can be reached at Room N 308, Oklahoma Judicial Center, 2100 N Lincoln, Oklahoma City, OK 73105, or 405/556–9642.

Judge Robert L. Hudson, District 2,
was born in Guthrie, Oklahoma, and graduated

from Guthrie High School in 1975. He graduated from Oklahoma State University in 1980 with a double major in agricultural economics and accounting. He earned his Juris Doctor degree from the University Of Oklahoma School Of Law in 1983. After graduating from law school, Hudson was in the private practice of law in Guthrie, Oklahoma, from 1983 to 1996. In April 1996 he was appointed by then Governor Frank Keating as district attorney for Payne and Logan counties, a post he was re-elected to four consecutive terms. In 2011 Hudson accepted the position of first assistant attorney general in the Attorney General's Office. In November 2012, he became special judge in the 9th Judicial District, where he served the citizens of Logan and Payne counties for over two years before being appointed to the Oklahoma Court of Criminal Appeals by Governor Mary Fallin in April 2015. Among Hudson's achievements, honors, and awards, in 1980 he was named Oklahoma State University College of Agriculture's Most Outstanding Graduate and one of OSU's Top Five Graduating Senior Men. While in law school, he was a member of the 1983 Regional Winning National Mock Trial Team. In 2000 and 2011, he was named the state's Outstanding District Attorney by the Oklahoma District Attorneys Association, and served two terms as president of the Oklahoma District Attorneys Association (2000 and 2008). Hudson is a member of Leadership Oklahoma Class XVII. He served as a commissioner for the Oklahoma State Bureau of Investigation for nearly ten years. Hudson has been married for thirty-three years. His wife, Mary Hughes Hudson, of Bartlesville, is a school teacher. They have five adult children and numerous grandchildren. Hudson also owns and operates a wheat and cow-calf operation in the Guthrie area. He is a deacon in the First Southern Baptist Church in Guthrie.

Judge Arlene Johnson, District 4.
Johnson received a Bachelor of Arts degree in English from the University of Oklahoma and Juris Doctor degree from the OU School of Law. After admission to the Oklahoma Bar on July 29, 1971, she practiced law with the Oklahoma City law firm of Bulla and Horning, and subsequently served as judicial law clerk to the Court of Criminal Appeals. Johnson worked as Oklahoma County assistant district attorney and as assistant Oklahoma Attorney General. She served as assistant United States attorney for the Western District of Oklahoma for twenty-one years. She received the U.S. Attorney General's John Marshall Award for Outstanding Legal Achievement (1998), and the FBI's Commendation for Exceptional Service in the Public Interest (1998). Johnson is admitted

to practice before the United States Supreme Court, Tenth Circuit Court of Appeals, and the United States District Court for the Western District. Governor Brad Henry appointed Johnson to the Court of Criminal Appeals, District 4, on February 18, 2005. She is a former member of the Tenth Circuit Uniform Criminal Jury Instruction Committee, the Admissions and Grievance Committee for the Western District of Oklahoma, and is a former member of the United States Magistrate Merit Selection Panel for the Western District of Oklahoma. Johnson has also served as an adjunct professor at the University of Oklahoma College of Law. Johnson may be reached at Suite 2, Oklahoma Judicial Center, 2100 N Lincoln, Oklahoma City, OK 73105, or 405/556-9640.

Judge David Lewis, District 5. Lewis was born in Ardmore, Oklahoma. Governor Brad Henry appointed him to the position on August 4, 2005. He served as  presiding judge for 2013-2014. Lewis earned a bachelor's degree with high honors from the University of Oklahoma in 1980. He also earned his law degree from the University of Oklahoma College of Law in 1983. He served four years as a Comanche County prosecutor, after serving four years in private practice. Lewis served as Comanche County special district judge from 1991 to 1999. He was a district judge for Comanche, Stephens, Jefferson, and Cotton counties from 1999 to 2005. He has served as president of the Oklahoma Judicial Conference and is a fellow of the Oklahoma Bar Association. Lewis was selected as a member of the Class of 2008 Henry Toll Fellowship Program of the Council of State Governments, and also served as chairman of Reach Out and Read Oklahoma. Lewis has two children—a son, David Jr., and a daughter, Danielle. Lewis can be reached at Suite 2, Oklahoma Judicial Center, 2100 N Lincoln, Oklahoma City, OK 73105, or 405/556-9611.

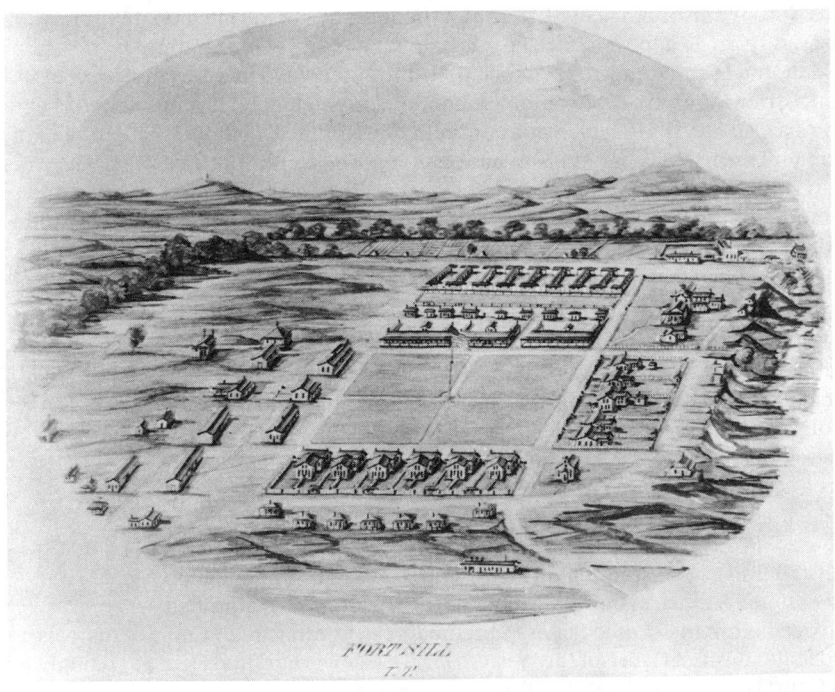

Drawing of Fort Sill in Indian Territory, from Historic American Buildings Survey.

Court of Civil Appeals

20 O.S. § 30.1

History and Function—The Oklahoma Court of Civil Appeals is the intermediate Court of Appeals for all civil cases filed in Oklahoma. Created by the Oklahoma Legislature in 1968, six new positions were added to the original six judges of the Oklahoma Court of Civil Appeals in 1982. With terms of six years each, judges are elected on a non-partisan retention ballot from each of the six congressional districts as they existed before the 2002 election. If a majority of those who cast ballots vote in favor of retention, the judge will serve another term. If a vacancy occurs on the Court of Civil Appeals prior to the expiration of a term, the governor appoints a successor, from three names submitted by the Judicial Nominating Commission. The clerk of the Oklahoma Supreme Court serves as clerk of the Court of Civil Appeals. The Court of Civil Appeals consists of twelve judges, six that sit in Oklahoma Ctity, and six that sit in Tulsa. Those judges from Congressional Districts 1, 2, and 3 comprise Divisions 2 and 4 in Tulsa. Those judges from Congressional Districts 4, 5, and 6, comprise Divisions 1 and 3 in Oklahoma City. These divisions are three-judge panels, the membership of which changes each year. Divisions 2 and 4 in Tulsa will each be comprised of a combination of three of the following judges: Deborah Barnes, Jerry L. Goodman, John F. Fischer, Keith Rapp, Tom Thornbrugh, and Jane P. Wiseman. Divisions 1 and 3 in Oklahoma City are comprised of a combination of three of the following judges: Robert D. Bell, Kenneth L. Buettner, Brian Jack Goree, William C. Hetherington Jr., Larry Joplin, and E. Bay Mitchell. The chief judge and vice-chief judge are selected and rotate each year between Oklahoma City and Tulsa.

Divisions 1 & 3—Oklahoma City			
Robert D. Bell	OKC	W. C. Hetherington Jr.	Norman
Kenneth L. Buettner	Edmond	Brian Jack Goree	Tulsa
Larry Joplin	OKC	E. Bay Mitchell	Enid
Divisions 2 & 4—Tulsa			
Deborah Barnes	Tulsa	W. Keith Rapp	Tulsa
John Fischer	Tulsa	Tom Thornbrugh	Tulsa
Jane P. Wiseman	Tulsa	Jerry L. Goodman	Tulsa

Administration Offices

Oklahoma City—2100 N Lincoln Boulevard, Suite 3, Oklahoma City, OK 73105 ▪ 405/556-9300

Tulsa—440 South Houston, Suite 601, Tulsa, OK 74127 ▪ 918/581-2711 ▪ www.oscn.net

Clerk of the Appellate Courts—Michael S. Richie, Oklahoma Judicial Center, 2100 N Lincoln Blvd., Oklahoma City, OK 73105 ▪ 405/556-9400

Civil **Appeals** Judicial Districts

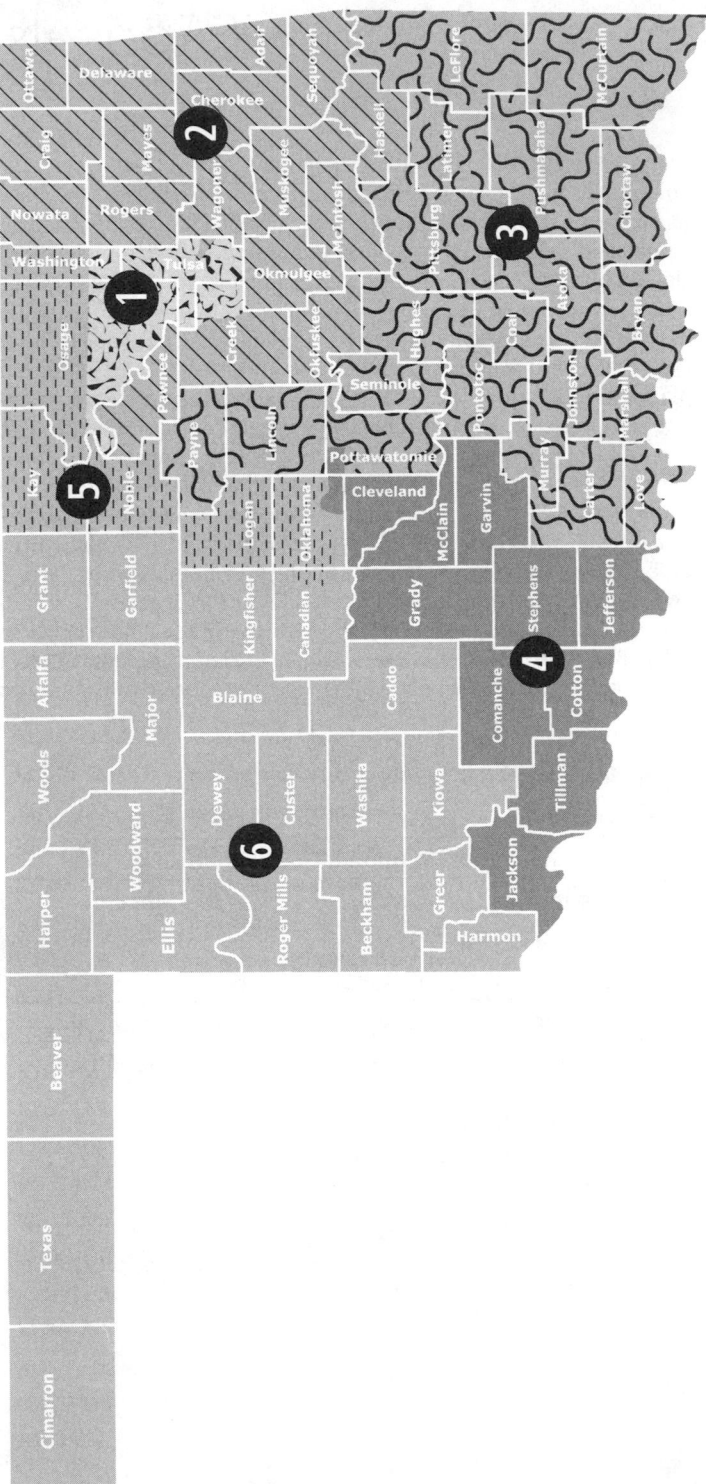

Judges of the Court of Civil Appeals

Oklahoma City

Judge Robert D. Bell, District 5, Office 2. Born on May 11, 1967, in Norman, Oklahoma, Bell graduated from the Norman Public School system. He received a bachelor's degree in 1989 from the University of Oklahoma and a Juris Doctor degree from the University of Tulsa College of Law in 1992. In law school, Bell received the award for distinguished service to the House of Delegates for recognition of being elected to office all three years of school. Following law school, Bell worked in private law practice in Norman for thirteen years. During the same time, he served as municipal judge for the cities of Blanchard, Broken Arrow, Noble, Moore, and Purcell. He has served as an adjunct professor at the University of Oklahoma College of Law since 1998. In June 2005 he was  appointed to the Oklahoma Court of Civil Appeals. He was retained in a statewide vote in 2006 and 2012. He was elected chief judge for 2011. The *Journal Record* named Bell as one of Oklahoma's Achievers Under 40 (Class III) in 2006. Bell has been given commendations for judicial service by both Governor Brad Henry and Governor Mary Fallin. He is a member of the District of Columbia and Oklahoma bar associations. Bell and his wife, Carolyn, have two children, Bradleigh and Addy.

Judge Kenneth L. Buettner, District 5, Office 1. Born on June 17, 1950, in Oklahoma  City, Oklahoma, Buettner received a bachelor's degree from Texas Christian University in 1972, and a Juris Doctor degree from Southern Methodist University in 1975. He has completed additional graduate work at the University of Denver and the University of Central Oklahoma. Buettner served in the United States Air Force from 1976 to 1980 in the Judge Advocate General's Corps. Professionally, he served as president of the Oklahoma Judicial Conference in 2005, and has served on its executive board from 2002 to 2006. Buettner's civic participation includes Leadership Edmond Class IX; Leadership Oklahoma Class XVI; Edmond Public School Foundation trustee from 1995 to 2001; Oklahoma Foundation for Excellence trustee, 2001 to present; St. John's Endowment Fund trustee, 1995 to 2003; St. John the Baptist Catholic Church Finance Board from 1990 to 1996, and 2006–2012; and the Board of Christian Education, 1998 to 2003. He is a member of the Oklahoma and Oklahoma County bar associations as well as the Colorado Bar and State Bar of Texas. He is an Oklahoma Bar Foundation Sustaining Fellow, and a master of the Luther Bohanon American Inn of Court.

Judge Brian Jack Goree, District 6, Office 2. Born March 18, 1964, Goree was raised in Tulsa and earned a bachelor's degree in chemistry from the University of Oklahoma in 1986. He received his law degree from the University of Tulsa in 1989, and is a registered patent attorney. Goree worked in private practice in Tulsa for twenty-three years, primarily focusing on legal research and writing. He has been an active volunteer with Tulsa Lawyers for Children, a past chairman of the Appellate Practice Section of the Oklahoma Bar Association, and is dedicated to encouraging and advising law school students.

Governor Mary Fallin appointed Goree to the Oklahoma Court of Civil Appeals in 2012. He and his wife, Jill, live in Oklahoma City.

Judge William C. Hetherington Jr., District 4, Office 1. Born in February 1947, in

Oklahoma City, Oklahoma, Hetherington has been a sixty-five year resident of Norman, Oklahoma. He is a graduate of Norman High School, the University of Oklahoma, and received the Juris Doctor degree from the Oklahoma City University School of Law in 1979. He served on the OCU School of Law Alumni Board of Trustees through the end of his term in 2004. Hetherington's judicial career began in 1982 as a special district judge. He retired from the bench and worked in private practice law from 1986 through 1991. He was appointed district judge in Cleveland County in 1992, He was re-elected to five four-year consecutive terms, unopposed. Hetherington has served the judicial branch as a district judge since that time. During his tenure as district judge, he served as chief judge for Judicial District 21, Cleveland County, for seven terms, and was elected by his peers as presiding judge of the South Central Administrative Judicial District, serving in that capacity in 2001 and 2002. He also served on the Oklahoma State Judicial Conference Executive Board for six years, and as president of the Conference in 2000. Hetherington shared both civil and criminal felony case load dockets with District Judge Tom Lucas and District Judge Lori Walkley, while serving in Cleveland County. He has extensive experience in handling mass tort litigation, having been assigned judge in the State of Oklahoma Attorney General Tobacco case, several oil field class-action cases, and class-action tort cases involving the Oklahoma Walmart employees and the "Hepatitis C" cases out of central Oklahoma. He was assigned judge and responsible for judicial administration of the Cleveland County Community Corrections Intervention system. He designed and implemented the Cleveland County Mental Health Court, and was co-assigned judge with Judge Jequita Napoli. In 2000 Hetherington was nominated by the Judicial Nominating Commission as one of three nominees to then Governor Frank Keating for appointment consideration to the Oklahoma Supreme Court. Governor Brad Henry appointed Hetherington to the Oklahoma Court of Civil Appeals on November 19, 2009. He regularly serves as a visiting lecturer at the University of Oklahoma School of Law, and is a master member and past president of the Luther Bohanon American Inn of Court.

Judge Larry E. Joplin, District 4, Office 2. Born on August 9, 1946, in Oklahoma City,

Oklahoma, Joplin received a bachelor's degree and a Juris Doctor degree from the University of Oklahoma. While in law school, Joplin was selected for the Oklahoma Law Review, and Moot Court, with his team placing third nationally his junior year. Joplin served as an attorney with Pierce and Couch from 1971 to 1973, and Bohannon and Barth from 1973 to 1976. He was a partner in his own law firm, Wheatley and Joplin, from 1978 to 1982, and a partner with Crowe and Dunlevy from 1982 to 1993. Joplin also served as a special prosecutor for the Oklahoma County District Attorney's office from 1976 to 1978, as director of the State of Oklahoma Office, Washington, D.C. in 1993, and as general counsel for  the State Insurance Department from 1993 to 1994. Joplin was appointed as judge to the Oklahoma Court of Civil Appeals in November 1994. He married the former Susan Colley. They have three children—Karen, David, and Matthew. Joplin's hobbies include travel and reading.

Judge E. Bay Mitchell, III, Enid, District 6, Office 1. Mitchell was born on November

6, 1953. He grew up in Enid, Oklahoma, and graduated from Enid High School in 1972. He attended the University of Oklahoma, where he received a bachelor's degree in 1976 and a Juris Doctor degree in 1979. Mitchell worked in private law practice for fourteen years in Oklahoma City and in Enid. In 1993 he became staff attorney to the Honorable Carl B. Jones of the Oklahoma Court of Civil Appeals. Governor Frank Keating appointed Mitchell to the Oklahoma Court of Civil Appeals in 2002, and the voters retained him in 2004, 2006, and 2012. He served as chief judge of the Court of Civil Appeals in 2009. Mitchell is a member of the Oklahoma Bar Association, and from 2008 to 2010 was on the board of directors of the Oklahoma County Bar Association, where he has also served as chairman of the C.L.E. Committee, and the Bench and Bar Committee. He is also a member of the OBA Appellate Practice Section, a Sustaining Fellow of the Oklahoma Bar Foundation, and a member of the Oklahoma Supreme Court Committee for Uniform Jury Instructions. He is a master emeritus  of the Ginsburg Chapter of the American Inns of Court. He is a former member of the OBA Administration of Justice Committee, Oklahoma Association of Defense Counsel, Defense Research Institute, and a volunteer at Legal Aid of Western Oklahoma. He has been admitted to practice in all Oklahoma state courts, the U.S. District Courts for the Western and Northern Districts of Oklahoma, the U.S. Court of Appeals for the Tenth Circuit, and the U.S. Supreme Court. Mitchell and his wife, Debra, have three grown children—Elliot, Madeline, and Adam.

Tulsa

Judge Deborah Barnes, District 2, Office 1. Born in 1954 in Tulsa, Oklahoma, Barnes  is a native of Sand Springs. She received a bachelor's degree in journalism from the University of Oklahoma in 1976, and in 1983, a Juris Doctor degree, with distinction, from the Oklahoma City University School of Law where she graduated first in her class. While in law school, she served as articles editor of the Law Review, and received the Faculty Award for Most Likely to Succeed. Barnes was an attorney with Crowe and Dunlevy and subsequently a staff attorney for the late Supreme Court Justice Ralph Hodges. In 1989 she resumed private practice at Stack and Barnes in Oklahoma City until 1991, when Barnes moved to Tulsa to join Transok. Barnes was named vice president, human resources and administration for Transok in 1996, and later became vice president, secretary, and associate general counsel for ONEOK, Inc., from 1997–2001. In 2002 she joined the firm of Crutchmer, Browers, and Barnes. In 2008 Governor Brad Henry appointed her to the Oklahoma Court of Civil Appeals. Barnes is a member of the American, Oklahoma, and Tulsa bar associations and past chairperson of the Oklahoma Board of Board Examiners. She is an Oklahoma Fellow of the American Bar Foundation; served as chair of the OBA Mineral Law Section; chair of the Tulsa County Court Operations Committee; and was a barrister of the American Inns of Court, Council Oak Chapter of Tulsa. She is the recipient of the Mona Salyer Lambird Spotlight Award, and a three-time finalist for the Journal Record Woman of the Year. She is a member of Leadership Oklahoma Class XII, and First United Methodist Church of Tulsa. Barnes has been married to Ronald M. Barnes, an attorney, since 1974 and they have one son, Grayson.

Judge John F. Fischer, District 3, Office 2. Born in Stillwater, Oklahoma, Fischer received Bachelor of Arts and Master of Arts degrees in English Literature from the University of Oklahoma. He received his Juris Doctor degree from the University of Oklahoma in 1975, and was admitted to practice law in Oklahoma in 1976. He has been admitted to practice before the United States Supreme Court since 1979. From 1976 to 1980 Fischer served as an assistant attorney general for the State of Oklahoma. He was in private law practice from 1980 to 2006, during which time he was selected by his peers as one of the "Best Lawyers in America" in commercial litigation. While in law school, Fischer received the Liberty National Bank Research Scholarship. He is a Master of the Bench and past president of the William J. Holloway American Inn of Court CV, and author of various articles on antitrust law and health care issues. He has been involved in various arts and community activities, and served as a member and chair of several state and county bar committees. He is a member of the American and Oklahoma bar associations, the Oklahoma Judicial Conference, a Oklahoma Bar  Foundation Fellow, a American Bar Foundation Fellow, and a former Oklahoma representative to the United States Court of Appeals for the Tenth Circuit Advisory Committee. In 2011 he received the Appellate Judge of the Year award from the Oklahoma Association for Justice. He was appointed to the Oklahoma Court of Civil Appeals in May 2006. Fischer and his wife, Pam, have been married since 1972. They have two daughters, Jennifer and Andrea.

Judge Jerry L. Goodman, District 1, Office 1. Born in Mangum, Oklahoma, Goodman received a bachelor's degree from the University of Tulsa, and a Juris Doctor degree from Georgetown University Law Center. He was appointed to the Oklahoma Court of Civil Appeals on July 26, 1994. He is a member of the Oklahoma and Tulsa County bar associations, and the Oklahoma Judicial Conference. He has previously served as vice president of the Tulsa County Bar Association, and president of the Oklahoma Judicial Conference. He served to the rank of lieutenant in the United States Naval Reserve. Goodman and his wife, Donna, have four children—Courtney, Polly, Mallory, and Benjamin.

Judge Keith Rapp, District 2, Office 2. Born in Wheelersburg, Ohio, Rapp received a bachelor's degree from Southwest Missouri University, a Juris Doctor degree from the University of Tulsa, and a Master of Laws degree from the University of Virginia. He was named Outstanding First-Year Law Student, awarded a Scholarship Key, named three times to the Dean's List, and was a member of the Tulsa Law Review. Rapp is a former aerospace engineer specializing in guidance and navigation systems. He worked on the Mercury, Apollo, Lunar Lander, and Skylab projects. He has publications in these areas including original research in mathematics. He served as an instructor of Sino Soviet Relations and Atomic and  Biological Warfare in the Naval Reserves Officers' School, and as a business law instructor at Tulsa Junior College. Rapp retired as a commander in the United States Naval Reserve. He also served as Tulsa Junior College regent. He served as counsel and director of banks and as director of two national insurance companies. Rapp worked as public defender in Tulsa; a city prosecutor in Broken Arrow; a municipal judge in Bixby; an alternative municipal judge for the City of Tulsa; and as district court judge. He was appointed as judge to the Oklahoma Court of Civil Appeals in 1984. Rapp is a member of the Oklahoma and Tulsa County bar associations, as well as, the bars of the U.S. Court of Appeals and U.S. Supreme Court. He is a member of Tulsa Arts Council Advisory Board. He married the former Mary Lynn Clanton. He has three children—Elizabeth, Kathy, and Joseph—and his dog Belle.

Judge Tom Thornbrugh, District 3, Office 1. Governor Mary Fallin appointed Thornbrugh to the Oklahoma Court of Civil Appeals on September 2, 2011. He earned a bachelor's degree in speech and political science from Emporia State University in Emporia, Kansas. He  later received a law degree from the University of Tulsa, where he was a member of the Dean's Honor Roll and *Res Nova* law review. Thornbrugh spent more than twenty years in private law practice in Tulsa. He also served as prosecuting attorney for the city of Bixby and as a municipal court judge for the city of Tulsa. In addition, he served as a legislative advisor for United States Senator Dewey Bartlett. Thornbrugh served as district court judge for the Fourteenth Judicial District from 1997 to 2011, and served as that court's presiding judge at the time of his appointment to the Court of Civil Appeals. Thornbrugh is a member of the Oklahoma Judicial Conference, where he serves on the conference executive board; former president of the Assembly of Presiding Judges; and currently serves on the conference's legislative committee. He is also an adjunct professor at the University of Tulsa. Thornbrugh is married to Dr. Jean Thornbrugh, who is a member of the faculty at St. Gregory's University in Shawnee, Oklahoma. They have five adult children.

Judge Jane P. Wiseman, District 1, Office 2. Wiseman received a Bachelor of Arts degree from Cornell University, a Master of Arts degree in American History from the University of North Carolina at Chapel Hill and a Juris Doctor degree from the University of Tulsa College of Law. She began clerking for Rosenstein, Fist, and Ringold in her second term in law school, and continued as a legal intern and later as an associate until her first child was born when she practiced as a sole practitioner until she was appointed as special judge for Tulsa County. Governor George Nigh appointed her district judge, when she was assigned to the Family Relations Division and then to the Civil Division. As a trial judge, Wiseman tried close to  1,000 jury trials. In March 2005 Governor Brad Henry appointed her to the Court of Civil Appeals in Tulsa where she currently serves. Wiseman has served as president of the Oklahoma Judicial Conference and currently serves on its executive board and legislative committee. She has taught trial court case management as a member of the National Judicial College faculty in Reno, Nevada. She has also served on the Oklahoma Bar Association's Professionalism Committee, Evidence Committee, and the OBA Special Task Force on Tort Reform. Wiseman is active with the Tulsa County Bar Association, serving on its awards and nominations and bench and bar committees, and is a frequent continuing legal education presenter. She is married to Jim Hodges and has two sons, Jamie and John, and two sons-by-marriage, Clayton and Kevin.

10th Circuit Court of Appeals

Colorado, Kansas, New Mexico, Oklahoma, Utah, Wyoming

This court sits primarily at Denver, Colorado; however, it is customary to hold at least one session annually in other cities in the circuit. Sessions may last as long as one week and are usually held every other month. ▪ www.ca10.uscourts.gov

Mary Beck Briscoe (Chief Circuit Judge)
645 Massachusetts, Suite 400
Lawrence, KS 66044-2235
785/843-4067

Stephanie K. Seymour (Senior Judge)
4-562 U.S. Courthouse
Tulsa, OK 74103-3877
918/699-4745

Bobby R. Baldock (Senior Judge)
PO Box 2388, Roswell, NM 88202-2388
505/625-2388

David M. Ebel (Senior Judge)
Byron White U.S. Courthouse
1823 Stout Street, Denver, CO 80257-1823
303/844-3800

Paul. J. Kelly Jr.
PO Box 10113, Santa Fe, NM 87504-6113
505/988-6541

Scott Matheson Jr.
125 S State Street, Suite 5402
Salt Lake City, UT 84138-1153
801/524-5145

Carolyn B. McHugh
4201 Federal Building
Salt Lake City, UT 84138-1102
801/524-6950

Carlos F. Lucero
Byron White U.S. Courthouse,
Rm. 422, 1823 Stout Street
Denver, CO 80257-1823
303/844-2200

Michael R. Murphy (Senior Judge)
5438 Federal Building
125 S State Street
Salt Lake City, UT 84138-1181
801/524-5955

John C. Porfilio (Senior Judge)
Byron White U.S. Courthouse
1823 Stout Street, Denver, CO 80257-1823
303/844-2067

Monroe C. McKay (Senior Judge)
Suite 6012, Federal Building
125 S State Street
Salt Lake City, UT 84138-1181
801/524-5252

Harris Hartz
201 Third Street NW, Suite 1870
Albuquerque, NM 87102-4391
505/843-6196

Terrence O'Brien (Senior Judge)
2120 Capitol Avenue
Cheyenne, WY 82001-3633
307/433-2400

Timothy M. Tymkovich
Byron White U.S. Courthouse
1823 Stout Street, Denver, CO 80257-1823
303/335-3300

Jerome Holmes
215 Dean A. McGee Ave. Rm. 315
Oklahoma City, OK 73102-3423
405/609-5480

Neil Gorsuch
Byron White U.S. Courthouse
1823 Stout Street, Denver, CO 80257-1823
303/335-2800

Robert Bacharach
Federal Building
PO Box 1767
Oklahoma City, OK 73101-1767
405/609-5420

Gregory A. Phillips
2120 Capitol Avenue
Cheyenne, WY, 82001
307/433-2121

Nancy L. Moritz
444 SE Quincy
Topeka, KS 66683
785/338-5400

Circuit Executive—Dave Tighe
Byron White U.S. Courthouse
1823 Stout Street, Denver, CO 80257-1823
303/844-2067

Clerk—Elisabeth A. Shumaker
Byron White U.S. Courthouse
1823 Stout Street, Denver, CO 80257-1823
303/844-3157

Courts of General Jurisdiction

District Courts
Article VII: Section 7, 20:92.1

Judicial District	Administrative	Judicial District	Administrative
1	Northwestern	14	Tulsa-Pawnee
2	Northwestern	15	East Central
3	Southwestern	16	Southeastern
4	Northwestern	17	Southeastern
5	Southwestern	18	East Central
6	Southwestern	19	Southeastern
7	Oklahoma	20	South Central
8	North Central	21	South Central
9	North Central	22	South Central
10	Northeastern	23	North Central
11	Northeastern	24	East Central
12	Northeastern	25	Southeastern
13	Northeastern	26	Canadian

Judges of the District Courts
East Central Judicial Administrative District
Jim D. Bland, Presiding Judge

15th Judicial District
(Adair, Cherokee, Muskogee, Sequoyah, Wagoner Counties)

Division I—Wagoner and Cherokee Counties

District Judge .... Darrell Shepherd
    Associate District Judges—
        Cherokee County.. Mark L. Dobbins
        Wagoner County...Dennis Shook
        Special Judges, Cherokee County..............................Saundra Crosslin ▪ Larry Langley
        Special Judge, Wagoner County ....Douglas Kirkley

Division II—Muskogee County

District Judges.. Mike Norman ▪ Thomas H. Alford
    Associate District Judge..Norman D. Thygesen
    Special Judges .... Robin Watt Adair ▪ Weldon Stout

Division III—Adair and Sequoyah Counties

District Judge .... Jeff Payton
    Associate District Judges—
        Adair County... L. Elizabeth Brown
        Sequoyah County ....Kyle Waters
    Special Judge, Sequoyah County .... Vacant

18th **Judicial District** (McIntosh and Pittsburg Counties)

District Judge .... Jim D. Bland
    Associate District Judges—
        McIntosh County..Jim Pratt
        Pittsburg County.. Tim Mills
    Special Judge, Pittsburg County .... Matthew Sheets

24th **Judicial District** (Creek, Okfuskee, and Okmulgee Counties)

Division I—Creek County

District Judges.. Douglas W. Golden ▪ Joe Sam Vassar
    Associate District Judge...Mark Ihrig
    Special Judges .... Richard Woolery ▪ Lester Henderson

Division II—Okfuskee County

District Judge .... Lawrence W. Parish
    Associate District Judge.. David N. Martin

Division III—Okmulgee County

District Judges..Ken Adair ▪ H. Michael Claver
    Associate District Judge.. Cynthia Pickering
    Special Judge..Pandee Ramirez

North Central Judicial Administrative District

Cynthia F. Ashwood, Presiding Judge

8th **Judicial District** (Kay and Noble Counties)

District Judge .... Phillip A. Ross
    Associate District Judges—
        Kay County..David Bandy
        Noble County .... Nikki Leach
    Special Judges, Kay County.. Jennifer Brock ▪ Lee Turner

9th **Judicial District** (Logan and Payne Counties)

District Judge ....Phillip C. Corley
    Associate District Judges—
        Logan County... Louis A. Duel Jr.
        Payne County ....Stephen Kistler
    Special Judge, Logan County .... Rob Hudson
    Special Judges, Payne County.................................R.L. Hert, Jr. ▪ Kathering E. Thomas

District Courts

23rd **Judicial District** (Lincoln and Pottawatomie Counties)

District Judges.. John Canavan Jr. ▪ Cynthia F. Ashwood
   Associate District Judges—
      Lincoln County .... Sheila Kirk
      Pottawatomie County..John D. Gardner
      Special Judges, Pottawatomie County........................ David Cawthon ▪ Dawson Engle

Northeastern Judicial Administrative District

Terry McBride, Presiding Judge

10th **Judicial District** (Osage County)

District Judge ....John Kane
   Associate District Judge...Bruce David Gambill
   Special Judge .... Stuart Tate

11th **Judicial District** (Nowata and Washington Counties)

District Judge ....Curtis L. DeLapp
   Associate District Judges—
      Nowata County ....Carl G. Gibson
      Washington County...Russell Vaclaw
      Special Judges, Washington County........................ John M. Gerkin ▪ Kyra K. Williams

12th **Judicial District** (Craig, Mayes, and Rogers Counties)

District Judges.................................... Terry McBride ▪ Sheila Condren ▪ J. Dwayne Steidley
   Associate District Judges—
      Craig County .... Harry Bud Wyatt
      Mayes County ....Shawn Taylor
      Rogers County..Steve Pazzo
      Special Judge, Mayes County.. Rebecca Gore
      Special Judges, Rogers County............ David N. Smith ▪ Terrell Crosson ▪ Lara Russell

13th **Judicial District** (Delaware and Ottawa Counties)

District Judge .... Robert G. Haney
   Associate District Judges—
      Delaware County .... Barry V. Denney
      Ottawa County ....Robert E. Reavis II
      Special Judge, Delaware County...Alicia Littlefield
      Special Judge, Ottawa County...William E. Culver

Northwestern Judicial Administrative District

Paul Woodward, Presiding Judge

1st **Judicial District** (Beaver, Cimarron, Harper, and Texas Counties)

District Judge .... Jon K. Parsley
    Associate District Judges—
        Beaver County..Ryan D. Reddick
        Cimarron County.. Ronald L. Kincannon
        Harper County .... Aric Alley
        Texas County... A. Clark Jett

2nd **Judicial District** (Beckham, Custer, Ellis, Roger Mills, and Washita Counties)

District Judge ....Doug Haught
    Associate District Judges—
        Beckham County .... Michele Kirby-Roper
        Custer County .... Jill Weedon
        Ellis County.. Laurie E. Hayes Thompson
        Roger Mills County ....Pat Ver Steeg
        Washita County..Christopher Kelly
    Special Judge, Custer County.. Donna Dirickson

4th **Judicial District** (Alfalfa, Blaine, Dewey,
Garfield, Grant, Kingfisher, Major, Woods, and Woodward Counties)

Division I—Alfalfa, Dewey, Major, Woods, and Woodward Counties

District Judge ....Justin P. Eilers
    Associate District Judges—
        Alfalfa County ....Loren E. Angle
        Dewey County...Rick Bozarth
        Major County ....Tim Haworth
        Woods County...Mickey J. Hadwiger
        Woodward County.. Don Work

Division II—Blaine, Garfield, Grant, and Kingfisher Counties

District Judges.. Paul Woodward ■ Dennis Hladik
    Associate District Judges—
        Blaine County .... Mark A. Moore
        Garfield County .... Tom Newby
        Grant County ....Jack Hammontree
        Kingfisher County...Robert Davis
    Special Judges, Garfield County .... Norman L. Grey ■ Brian Lovell

Oklahoma Judicial Administrative District

Ray C. Elliott, Presiding Judge

7th **Judicial District** (Oklahoma County)

District Judges—
  Don Andrews
  Bernard M. Jones
  Glenn Jones
  Donald Deason
  Bryan C. Dixon

Ray C. Elliott
Thomas Prince
Bill Graves
Timothy R. Henderson
Roger H. Stuart
Patricia G. Parrish

Lisa Davis
Cindy Truong
Barbara G. Swinton
Alicia H. Timmons

Associate District Judges—Richard Kirby

Special Judges—
  James B. Croy
  D. Fred Doak
  Don Easter
  Barry Hafer
  Russell D. Hall
  Lisa K. Hammond

Howard Haralson
John Jacabson
Larry A. Jones
Roma M. McElwee
Lynn McGuire
Marth Oakes
Richard Ogden

Gregory J. Ryan
Larry Shaw
Geary L. Walke
Allen J. Welch Jr.
Cassandra Williams

Canadian Judicial Administrative District

Ray C. Elliott, Presiding Judge

26th **Judicial District** (Canadian County)

District Judge .... Gary E. Miller
  Associate District Judge...Bob Hughey
  Special Judges .... Barbara Hatfield ▪ Gary D. McCurdy ▪ Jack McCurdy

South Central Judicial Administrative District

Wallace Coppedge, Presiding Judge

20th **Judicial District** (Carter, Johnston, Love, Marshall, and Murray Counties)

Division I—Carter County

District Judge ....Dennis Morris
  Associate District Judge... Stephenn Baldwin
  Special Judge...Carson Brooks

Division II—Johnston, Love, Marshall, and Murray Counties

District Judge ....Wallace Coppedge
  Associate District Judges—
      Johnston County...Charles Migliorino
      Love County ....T. Todd Hicks
      Marshall County ....Gregory L. Johnson
      Murray County... Aaron Duck

21st Judicial District (Cleveland, Garvin, and McClain Counties)

Division I—Cleveland County

District Judges...Tracy Schumacher ▪ Thad Balkman
Jeff Virgin ▪ Lori Walkley
Associate District Judge... Stephen W. Bonner
Special Judges ....Janet A. Foss ▪ Michael Tupper ▪ Jequita H. Napoli ▪ Steven Stice

Division II—Garvin and McClain Counties

District Judge ....Vacant
Associate District Judges—
Garvin County..Steven C. Kendall
McClain County..Charles Gray
Special Judge, Garvin County .... Trisha A. Misak
Special Judge, McClain County ....Lee Shilling

22nd Judicial District (Hughes, Pontotoc, and Seminole Counties)

Division I—Pontotoc County

District Judge .... Steve Kessinger
Associate District Judge..Lori Jackson
Special Judge... Greg Pollard

Division II—Seminole County

District Judges.. George W. Butner
Associate District Judge.. Timothy Olsen
Special Judge...Gayla M. Arnold

Division III—Hughes County

District Judge .... George W. Butner
Associate District Judge.. Gordon Allen

Southeastern Judicial Administrative District

Mark Campbell, Presiding Judge

16th Judicial District (Haskell, Latimer, and LeFlore Counties)

District Judge .... Jon Sullivan
Associate District Judges—
Haskell County.. Brian Henderson
Latimer County...Bill D. Welch
LeFlore County ....Marion D. Fry
Special Judge, LeFlore County..................................... Jeffrey Singer ▪ Jennifer McBee

17th Judicial District (Choctaw, McCurtain, and Pushmataha Counties)

District Judge ....Kenneth Farley
Associate District Judges—
Choctaw County .... James R. Wolfe
McCurtain County..Kenneth Farley

Pushmataha County...Jana Wallace
Special Judges, McCurtain County............................... John W. Dewitt ▪ Gary L. Brock

19th **Judicial District** (Bryan County)

District Judge .... Mark Campbell
Associate District Judge...Rocky L. Powers
Special Judge... Trace C. Sherrill

25th **Judicial District** (Atoka and Coal Counties)

District Judges...Paula Inga
Associate District Judges—
    Atoka County .... Preston Harbuck
    Coal County ....Clay D. Mowdy

Southwestern Judicial Administrative District

Mark Smith., Presiding Judge

3rd **Judicial District** (Greer, Harmon, Jackson, Kiowa, and Tillman Counties)

District Judge ....Richard Darby
Associate District Judges—
    Greer County... Eric Yarborough
    Harmon County.. W. Mike Warren
    Jackson County .... Clark E. Huey
    Kiowa County... Norman L. Russell
    Tillman County ....Bradford L. Benson
Special Judge, Jackson County...Brad Leverett

5th **Judicial District** (Comanche, Cotton, Jefferson, and Stephens Counties)

Division I—Comanche and Cotton Counties

District Judges...Keith Bryon Aycock ▪ Gerald F. Neuwirth
                                                   Mark Randall Smith ▪ Emmit Taylor
Associate District Judges—
    Comanche County..Lisa Shaw
    Cotton County ....Michael C. Flanagan
Special Judges, Comanche County .... Kenny D. Harris ▪ Susan Zwaan

Division II—Jefferson and Stephens Counties

District Judges...Ken Graham
Associate District Judges—
    Jefferson County..Dennis Gay
    Stephens County..Brent G. Russell
Special Judge, Stephens County .... Jerry Herberger

6th **Judicial District** (Caddo and Grady Counties)

District Judge ....Richard G. Van Dyck

Associate District Judges—
Caddo County .... S. Wyatt Hill
Grady County .... John E. Herndon
Special Judge, Grady County .... Timothy A. Brauer
Special Judge, Caddo County .... David A. Stephens

Tulsa-Pawnee Judicial Administrative District

Carlos Chapelle, Presiding Judge

14th Judicial District (Tulsa and Pawnee Counties)

District Judges—
Daman H. Cantrell
James M. Caputo
Carlos Chapelle
Doug Drummond

Mary Fitzgerald
Doris Fransein
Kurt Glassco
Sharon Holmes
William D. LaFortune

Linda G. Morrissey
Bill Musseman
Rebecca Nightingale
Jefferson D. Sellers
Caroline Wall

Associate District Judges—
Tulsa County .... Dana Kuehn
Pawnee County .... Patrick Pickerill

Special Judges—
Martha Rupp Carter
Terry Bitting
Tammy Bruce
Stephen Clark
Teresa Dreiling
Kyle B. Haskins

Bill Hiddle
James W. Keeley
Deborrah Ludi-Leitch
Tony Miller
Dawn Moody
Millie Otey
Kirsten Pace

Wilma Palmer
Clifford J. Smith
Sarah Day Smith
Rodney Sparkman
David Youll

Members of the "A" battery of the 349th Field artillery regiment of Fort Sill, 1941, sitting on the barrel and carriage of a heavy artillery piece.

Court on the Judiciary

Article VII, Section 1; Article VII, Section A:2

Appellate Division

Name	Designated By
Douglas Combs	Oklahoma Supreme Court
Jefferson Sellers	Secretary of State
Bryan C. Dixon	Secretary of State
Noma Gurich	Oklahoma Supreme Court
Clancy Smith	Court of Criminal Appeals
Betty O. Williams	Oklahoma Bar Association
Richard Van Dyck	Secretary of State
Mark Smith	Secretary of State
Douglas Golden	Secretary of State

Trial Division

Name	Designated By
W.B. Heckenkemper	Oklahoma Bar Assoc.
John Kane	Secretary of State
Mark Campbell	Secretary of State
Barbara Swinton	Secretary of State
Paul Woodward	Secretary of State
Lori Walkley	Secretary of State
Jeff Payton	Secretary of State
Richard Darby	Secretary of State

Administrative Office—2100 N Lincoln Blvd., Suite 300, Oklahoma City, OK 73105 • 405/556-9300 • Michael Richie, Clerk of the Supreme Court, Clerk of the Court on the Judiciary.

Judges of the Court of Tax Review

(Statutory re-creation of the Court of Tax Review can be found in 68 O.S. Supp 1998, Sec. 3024)

History and Function—The Court of Tax Review is vested with jurisdiction to hear complaints relating to ad valorem taxation. Actions may be brought by—railroad and public service corporations as to the valuation of property by the State Board of Equalization; a district attorney, upon direction of the Board of County Commissioners as to the intra-county or inter-county equalization; a county assessor as to the orders of the Oklahoma Tax Commission relating to non-compliance of the county assessor with the regulations governing the four-year revaluation cycle; a taxpayer as to the illegalities in ad valorem tax levies; a taxpayer as to illegalities in the budget for the taxing entities within the county; or through requests of the Oklahoma Tax Commission for reimbursement of costs resulting from the supervision of the county in the validation of property due to noncompliance with the regulations governing the four-year revaluation cycle.

Administrative Office—2100 N Lincoln Blvd., Suite 300, Oklahoma City, OK 73105 • 405/556-9300.

Judges of the Workers' Compensation Court of Existing Claims

Constitution, Article 7 § 1; 85a O.S. § 400 (State Industrial Court)

L. Brad Taylor, Presiding Judge—Oklahoma City and Tulsa

Margaret A. Bomhoff	Oklahoma City	David P. Reid	Tulsa
Owen T. Evans	Tulsa	Carla Snipes	Oklahoma City
Michael W. McGivern	Tulsa		

History and Function—In 1951 the Oklahoma Legislature created the State Industrial Court and added to the Judicial Department by Constitutional amendment in 1967. The court was changed in composition and renamed by statue in 1978. The court is a court of record that adjudicates workers' compensation cases. Court awards and decisions are final and conclusive unless appealed to the Oklahoma Supreme Court or the Court En Banc. Due to legislative changes, on February 1, 2014, the Workers' Compensation Court became the Oklahoma Workers' Compensation Court of Existing Claims. The Oklahoma's Compensation Court of Existing Claims sits in Oklahoma City and Tulsa. It consists of six judges appointed by the governor.

Administration—Michael J. Harkey, Administrator; Timmye Porter, Judicial Assistant; and Katrina Stephenson, Court Clerk.

Personnel—31 non-merit, 8 exempt employees.

Offices—

Oklahoma City—1915 N Stiles, Suite 127, Oklahoma City, OK 73105 ▪ 405/522-8600
Tulsa—440 S Houston, Rm. 210, Tulsa, OK 74127 ▪ 918/581-2714

www.cec.ok.gov

Assembly of Presiding Judges

(By order of the Supreme Court)

Jud. Admin.	Dist.	Presiding Judge	Courthouse
Southwestern	3, 5 & 6	Mark Smith	Comanche County
Northwestern	1, 2 & 4	Paul Woodward	Garfield County
Northeastern	10, 11, 12 & 13	Terry McBride	Craig County
Southeastern	16, 17, 19 & 25	Mark Campbell	Bryan County
Okla. & Canadian	7 & 26	Ray C. Elliott	Oklahoma County
South Central	20, 21 & 22	Wallace Coppedge	Marshall County
Tulsa-Pawnee	14	Carlos Chapelle	Tulsa County
East Central	15, 18 & 24	Jim D. Bland	Pittsburg County
North Central	8, 9 & 23	Cynthia F. Ashwood	Lincoln County

History and Function—By order of the Oklahoma Supreme Court, on and after January 9, 1969, all district and associate district judges selected for service in courts, sitting within a statutorily designated judicial administrative district (as prescribed by 20 O.S. Supp. 1968 [S] 22), assemble to select a district judge as presiding judge of their respective administrative district. Subject only to the rules, orders, and directives of the Oklahoma Supreme Court or the chief justice, the presiding judge shall have general administrative authority and supervision over all courts within the district and over all judicial personnel and court officials serving in the district; this authority shall include, but not be limited to, temporary intra-district assignment of any judge or court official to service or duty with a court other than that for which he was selected or to which he was originally assigned. The Administrative Office of the Courts assists the Assembly of Presiding Judges in administrative matters.

Administration—Administrative Office of the Courts, 2100 N Lincoln Blvd., Suite 300, Oklahoma City, OK 73105 • 405/556-9300.

Judicial Nominating Commission
Article VII, Section B:3

John H. Tucker	Tulsa	Steve Turnbo	Tulsa
Deborah Reheard	Eufala	Ed Crocker	Norman
Michael Mordy	Ardmore	Lee Evans	Ponca City
Peggy Stockwell	Norman	Jenny Dunning	Nichols Hills
Larry D. Ottaway	Oklahoma City	Jim Hamby	Ada
Stephen D. Beam	Weatherford	Kimberly Fobbs	Broken Arrow

History and Function—Established as part of the Judicial Department, the commission consists of thirteen members: six members appointed by the governor, one from each of the six congressional districts as they existed before the 2002 election; six members elected from and by the membership of the Oklahoma Bar Association; and one member at large who shall not have been admitted to the practice of law in any state, to be selected by no fewer than eight members of the commission. The commission has jurisdiction to determine whether the qualifications of nominees for judicial office have been met and to determine the existence of vacancies on the commission.

Administration—2100 N Lincoln Blvd., Suite 300, Oklahoma City, OK 73105 • 405/556-9300. FAX (405)521-6815

Dispute Resolution Advisory Board
Article 12, Section 1803.1

Christina Winkel Roach	Oklahoma City	Michael T. Oakley	Oklahoma City
Jane Wheeler	Oklahoma City	Ted Roberts	Norman
Stan Foster	Oklahoma City	Terry Winn	Edmond
Michael D. Evans	Oklahoma City	Ray Vaughn	Oklahoma City
Bobbie Burbridge Lane	Oklahoma City	Phil Cotton	Norman
Mike Cotrill	Tulsa	Shirley Cox	Oklahoma City
Timothy Harris	Tulsa	Lori Walkley	Norman
Bonnie Cliff	Norman	Margaret Love	Tulsa

History and Function—The Oklahoma Dispute Resolution System began in November 1986 and focuses on mediation services. The statutory purpose is to provide Oklahomans a fast, economical way to solve conflicts. The Early Settlement service has offices throughout the state to handle conflicts between neighbors, family members, landlords and tenants, customers and merchants, employers and employees, roommates, farmers/lenders, or victims/offenders. All mediators are trained and must be certified by the court administrator. Mediators do not order decisions, but function as neutral facilitators, encouraging communication and creative problem solving. Proceedings are voluntary, confidential, and may not be used in any court litigation.

Administration—Sue D. Tate, ADRS System Director; Michael E. Evans, ex officio • Administrative Office of the Courts, 2100 N Lincoln Blvd., Suite 300, Oklahoma City, OK 73105 • 405/556-9300.

Council on Judicial Complaints
Article 20, Section 1652

History and Function—Created by the 1974 Oklahoma Legislature as the investigatory body for the Court on the Judiciary, the council is empowered to investigate all complaints made against a member of the judiciary. The council may dismiss a complaint, refer it to the chief justice for discipline, or recommend that the matter be made the subject of proceedings before the Court on the Judiciary. The council consists of three members. They serve staggered five-year terms and may serve no more than two terms on the council.

Council Members—Glen Huff, Chair; Cathy M. Christensen, member; and Jerry Franklin, member.

Administration—Eric Mitts, Director; Laurie Robinson, Principal Assistant; Terry West, General Counsel • 1901 N Lincoln Boulevard, Oklahoma City, OK 73105 • 405/522-4800, FAX 405/522-4752.

District Attorneys

For more information about district attorneys and their assistants, contact the **District Attorneys Council**, 421 NW 13 Street, Suite 290, Oklahoma City, OK 73103 ▪ 405/264–5000 ▪ Hours: 8 AM to 5 PM, Monday through Friday ▪ Suzanne McClain Atwood, Executive Coordinator; Trent H. Baggett, Assistant Executive Coordinator ▪ 1200 non-merit, unclassified employees.

Dist.	Name	Address	City	Zip	Telephone	Fax
1	Mike Boring (R)	319 N Main	Guymon	73942	580/338-3388	580/338-0528
2	Angela Marsee (R)	PO Box 36	Arapaho	73620	580/323-3232	580/323-9377
3	John M. Wampler (D)	101 N Main	Altus	73521	580/482-5334	580/482-5346
4	Mike Fields (R)	114 W Broadway	Enid	73701	580/233-1311	580/233-7065
5	Fred Smith (D)	315 SW 5 Street, Rm. 502	Lawton	73501	580/585-4444	580/585-4435
6	Jason Hicks (R)	101 S 11 Street	Duncan	73533	580/255-8726	580/255-1889
7	David Prater (D)	320 Robert S. Kerr, #505	Okla. City	73102	405/713-1600	405/235-1567
8	Brian Hermanson (R)	201 S Main	Newkirk	74647	580/362-2571	580/362-2335
9	Laura Thomas (R)	606 S Husband, Rm. 213	Stillwater	74074	405/372-4883	405/372-4590
10	Rex Duncan (R)	628½ Kihekah, 3rd Floor	Pawhuska	74056	918/287-1510	918/287-3137
11	Kevin Buchanan (R)	420 S Johnstone, Rm. 222	Bartlesville	74003	918/337-2860	918/337-2896
12	Matthew Ballard (R)	200 S Lynn Riggs Blvd.	Claremore	74017	918/923-4960	918/923-4545
13	Kenny Wright (D)	PO Box 528	Jay	74346	918/253-4217	918/254-4183
14	Steve Kunzweiler (R)	500 S Denver, Suite 900	Tulsa	74103	918/596-4805	918/596-4830
15	Orvil Loge (D)	220 State Street	Muskogee	74401	918/682-3374	918/687-3347
16	Jeff Smith (D)	100 S Broadway, Ste. 300	Poteau	74953	918/647-2245	918/647-3209
17	Mark Matloff (D)	108 N Central	Idabel	74745	580/286-7611	580/286-7613
18	Farley Ward (D)	109 E Carl Albert Pkwy.	McAlester	74501	918/423-1324	918/423-8575
19	Emily Redman (D)	117 N 3 Street,	Durant	74701	580/924-4032	580/924-3596
20	Craig Ladd (D)	20 "B" Street SW, Ste. 202	Ardmore	73401	580/223-9674	580/221-5504
21	Greg Mashburn (R)	201 S Jones, Suite 300	Norman	73069	405/321-8268	405/360-7840
22	Chris Ross (D)	PO Box 146	Ada	74820	580/332-0341	580/332-7393
23	Richard Smothermon (D)	331 N Broadway	Shawnee	74801	405/275-6800	405/275-3575
24	Max Cook (R)	222 E Dewey, Suite 302	Sapulpa	74066	918/224-3921	918/227-6346
25	Rob Barris (D)	314 W 7 Street	Okmulgee	74447	918/756-0794	918/756-4712
26	Chris Boring (R)	1600 Main Street, Suite 5	Woodward	73801	580/256-8616	580/256-3959
27	Brian Kuester (R)	213 W Delaware	Tahlequah	74464	918/456-6173	918/456-1885

AGENCIES, BOARDS, & COMMISSIONS

Profiles of Agencies, Boards, and Commissions

For information about boards or board members, contact the administrator. In the case of subordinate entities, unless a separate address and phone number are given, contact the main agency for information. For governor's task forces, for example, contact the governor's office; for legislative committees, contact the Legislative Service Bureau (405/521-4144). If the entity is not listed, consult the index, as it may be listed alphabetically beneath a parent entity. Personnel figures are provided by the agency. Interagency Mail availability is indicated by (IA).

2-1-1 Oklahoma Coordinating Council (56 O.S. § 3021)
Formerly named the 2-1-1 Advisory Collaborative, Oklahoma

www.211oklahoma.org

Abstractors Board, Oklahoma (1 O.S. § 22) Re-created until July 1, 2019
Agency Code 022 (IA)   www.abstract.ok.gov
2401 NW 23 Street, Suite 60B, Oklahoma City 73107   405/522-5019, FAX 405/522-5503

Mission Statement The Oklahoma Abstractors Board regulates the abstracting industry and issues abstractor licenses, certificates of authority, and permits to construct abstract plants.

Administration Glynda Reppond, Executive Director

Personnel 2 unclassified

History and Function The board consists of nine members, six of whom are in the abstracting industry, one real estate representative, one banking representative, and one attorney. All members are appointed by the governor and serve staggered four year terms. The board is responsible for promulgating rules, setting forth guidelines for agency operations, and governing the professional practices of the licensees. The entity is self-supporting through fees.

Accountancy Board, Oklahoma (59 O.S. § 15.2; 74 O.S. § 3905)
Agency Code 020 (IA)   www.ok.gov/oab
201 NW 63 Street, Suite 210, Oklahoma City 73116   405/521-2397, FAX 405/521-3118

Mission Statement To safeguard the public welfare by prescribing and assessing the qualifications of and regulating the professional conduct of individuals and firms authorized to engage in the practice of public accounting in Oklahoma.

Administration Randall A. Ross, Executive Director

Personnel 19 unclassified, non-merit

History and Function The first accountancy law was enacted by the Oklahoma Legislature in 1917 and the board was recreated by the legislature in 2004 in accordance with the Oklahoma Sunset Law to administer the provisions of the Oklahoma Accountancy Act for the protection of the public. The board is composed of five certified public accountants and one public accountant (or meets the criteria to become a public accountant), who serve for five-year terms and one lay member who serves coterminous with the governor. All members are appointed by the governor and confirmed by the Senate, and are responsible for promulgating rules of general application, setting forth guidelines for agency operations and governing the professional practices of the registrants. The agency is self-supporting through fees. Re-created until July 2020.

Accrediting Agency, State (72 O.S. § 241, 72 O.S. § 241, 74 O.S. § 3908)

4045 NW 64 Street, Suite 205, Oklahoma City 73116 (IA)
405/879-9600, FAX 405/879-3400

PO Box 53067, Oklahoma City 73152
www.ok.gov/saa

Administration   Gina M. Wekke, Director

History and Function   The agency was established in 1949 and is responsible for the approval and the monitoring of education and training programs for veterans, their dependents, active duty military, and reservists in Oklahoma. Re-created to continue until July 1, 2017.

Aeronautics Commission, Oklahoma (3 O.S. § 84)

Agency Code 060 (IA)
120 N Robinson, Suite 1244W, Oklahoma City 73102
E-mail—oac@oac.ok.gov

www.aeronautics.ok.gov
405/604-6900, FAX 405/604-6919

Administration   Victor N. Bird, Director
    Elaine Spell, Operations Officer
    Dan Stroud, Director of Communications
    Dale Williams, Planning Division Manager
    Jane Mitchell, Grants Administrator/Executive Assistant to the Director
    Vivek Khanna, Engineering Division Manager
    Treasure Tytenicz, Liaison AVEO & Government Affairs

History and Function   The commission was created in 1963 by the Oklahoma Legislature to encourage, foster, and assist in the development of aeronautics in Oklahoma and to encourage the establishment and maintenance of public airports. This includes the preservation and improvement of the state's 110 public airports, which make up the state airport system; and the promotion of the aerospace industry, a top employer in Oklahoma, providing approximately 144,000 direct and indirect jobs.

Center for Aerospace and Defense Supplier Quality (3 O.S. § 85.3)

Agriculture, Food, and Forestry; Department of

(2 O.S. § 1–2 est. Dept.; 2 O.S. § 1–3 name change)   **Board** (Constitution, Article 6 § 31)

Agency Code 040 (IA)
PO Box 528804, Oklahoma City 73152-8804

www.ag.ok.gov
405/521-3864, FAX 405/521-4912

Mission Statement   To look at agriculture with a vision as to what it will be in the next one hundred years. The agency must increase the value of agriculture produce and enhance the value of life in the rural communities. The agency also must develop the state's food and fiber resources in a manner that will always protect consumer health and safety, natural resources, property, and the environment.

History and Function   The agency began at statehood in 1907 and was primarily a regulator. It has since branched into services such as animal and plant disease control, crop and livestock market reporting, agricultural product marketing, laboratory services, water quality, animal damage control, and forestry. The department is supervised by a five-member board, with the commissioner as its president. The board's duties involve regulating all areas of agriculture. The commissioner is by law assigned to the Board of Equalization, the Board of Regents for A&M Colleges, and the School Land Commission.

Administration   Jim Reese, Secretary of Agriculture
    Blayne Arthur, Deputy Commissioner and Public Information, 405/522-6105
    Jane Swank, Executive Assistant, 405/522-5488
    Agriculture Environmental Management Services, Jeremy Seiger, Director, 405/522-5492
    Animal Industry Services, Dr. Rod Hall, DVM, Director, 405/522-6131
    Food Safety, Stan Stromberg, Director, 405/522-6127
    Forestry Services, George Geissler, Director, 405/522-6148

Laboratory Services, Paul Kerr, Director, 405/522-5431
Legal Services, Teena Gunter, Director, 405/522-5996
Market Development Services, Jamey Allen, Director, 405/522-5509
Consumer Protection Services, Sancho Dickinson, Director, 405/522-5972
Statistics Services, Wilbert Hundl Jr., 405/522-6190
Wildlife Services, Kevin Grant, 405/522-4039

Personnel 336 classified, 56 unclassified, 26 temporary

Apiary Advisory Committee (2 O.S. § 3–101)

Eastern Red Cedar Registry Board (2 O.S. § 18–403)

State Bureau of Standards (2 O.S. § 14-1)
PO Box 528804, Oklahoma City 73152-8804   405/521-3864, EXT 370, FAX 405/521-4912
Administration Paul Kerr, Director
History and Function This board is authorized to determine the standards of weights, measures, and tests of all kinds. Bureau functions within the Department of Agriculture, Food, & Forestry.

Agriculture Mediation Board (2 O.S. § 2–30)
www.ok.gov/mediation   800/248-5465

Alcohol and Drug Counselors, Oklahoma Board of Licensed
(59 O.S. § 1873) Re-created until July 1, 2020
Agency Code 448 (IA)   www.okdrugcounselors.org
405/521-0779

Alcohol and Drug Influence, Board of Tests for (47 O.S. § 759)
Agency Code 772 (IA)   www.ok.gov/bot
Building 9, 3600 Martin Luther King Avenue   PO Box 36307, Oklahoma City 73136-2307
405/425-2460, FAX 405/425-2490

Administration   Kenneth E. Blick, Ph.D., Chairman of the Board; Kevin Behrens, State Director of Tests for Alcohol and Drug Influence

History and Function   Created by the Oklahoma Legislature, the board began functioning January 1, 1969. Recreated by the legislature in 1982 with a name change and expanded responsibilities, it is the state agency charged with the authority and responsibility for approving laboratories for analysis of alcohol and other intoxicating substances in blood, breath, and saliva, under the Oklahoma Chemical Tests Act for traffic law enforcement purposes; issuing permits to persons qualified to conduct such tests; approving methods, techniques, devices, equipment, and records for such tests and for collection and handling of specimens. In 2005 the Oklahoma Legislature transferred responsibility for oversight of the ignition interlock devices to the Board by amendment 47 O.S. § 754.1(D). Copies of the rules set by this board (Administrative Code 40) may be obtained from the Secretary of State's office. Re-created until July 1, 2015.

Alcoholic Beverage Laws Enforcement Commission (ABLE Commission) (Constitution, Article 28 §1; 37 O.S. § 506.1)
Agency Code 030 (IA)   www.able.ok.gov
3812 N Santa Fe Avenue, Suite 200, Oklahoma City 73118
405/521-3484, Toll Free 866/894-3517, FAX 405/521-6578

Mission Statement   To protect the public's welfare and interest in the enforcement of the laws pertaining to alcoholic beverages, charity games, and youth access to tobacco in Oklahoma.

Administration   A. Keith Burt, Director; Jim Hughes, Assistant Director

Personnel 30 classified, 4 unclassified, merit

History and Function   Created by the Twenty-eighth Amendment to the Oklahoma Constitution, the commission consists of seven members appointed by the governor and subject to the advice and consent of the Oklahoma Senate, who in turn appoint the director. The purpose of the commission is viewed as an exercise of the police power of the State of Oklahoma for the protection, welfare, health, peace, temperance, and safety of the people of the state through the enforcement of the laws pertaining to alcoholic beverages, charity games, and youth access to tobacco. The agency enforces the Oklahoma Beverage Control Act, Charity Games Act, and Youth Access to Tobacco Act.

Anatomical Board of the State of Oklahoma (63 O.S. § 91; 74 O.S. § 3907)

Agency Code 044 (IA)
PO Box 26901, BSEB 100, Oklahoma City 73126
405/271-2424, EXT 48531, FAX 405/271-8397   E-mail—kayla-mcneill@ouhsc.edu

Mission Statement   To ensure, for the State of Oklahoma, the respectful and consensual disposition and use of human bodies and parts donated for education, research, and the advancement of medical, dental, forensics or mortuary science. The Anatomical Board oversees all entities that provide or use donated bodies and body parts for education and research.

Administration   Daniel O'Donoghue, Ph.D., Chairman; Kayla McNeill, Executive Director.

History and Function   Created by the 1935 Oklahoma Legislature, the board is composed of deans, or their designees, of each accredited medical school and osteopathic medical school within the state; heads of the Department of Anatomy, or their designees, two persons appointed jointly by the presidents of institutions of higher education with programs other than medical which require, on a regular basis, human and anatomical material, provided they have been approved by the State Regents for Higher Education, and one at-large member appointed by the governor to represent the interests of the citizens of this state. Board functions are to provide for the collection, preservation, storage, distribution, delivery, recovery from users, cremation, and final disposition of all dead human bodies used for health science education and research in the state. Re-created until July 1, 2016.

Archeological Survey, Oklahoma (74 O.S. § 241)

The University of Oklahoma, 111 E Chesapeake, Building 134, Norman 73019-5111
405/325-7211, FAX 405/325-7604   www.ou.edu/cas/archsur
E-mail—rbrooks@ou.edu

Administration   Robert L. Brooks, State Archeologist/Director

Mission Statement   To research Oklahoma's archeological record; to work with state and federal agencies, and the citizens of Oklahoma to preserve significant archeological sites; and to disseminate information about Oklahoma's cultural heritage through publications and public presentations.

History and Function   Established in 1970, the survey studies prehistoric and early historic sites; conserves, maintains, and exhibits archeological materials; enforces laws protecting archeological sites; maintains archeology programs; does anthropological and archeological research under the direction of the Board of Regents of the University of Oklahoma.

Archeological Survey Advisory Board

Architects, Landscape Architects, and Registered Interior Designers of Oklahoma, Board of Governors of the Licensed
(59 O.S. § 46.4; 74 O.S. § 3905)

Agency Code 045 (IA)   www.ok.gov/architects
PO Box 53430, Oklahoma City 73152   405/949-2383, FAX 405/949-1690

Mission Statement   To protect the life, safety, and welfare of the people of Oklahoma, by administering the State Architectural and Registered Interior Designers Act which provides that all persons and firms practicing or offering to practice architecture, landscape architecture, or using the title registered interior designer in this state submit evidence that he, she or the entity is qualified to practice and is licensed and registered.

Administration   Jean Williams, Executive Director

Personnel   3 unclassified, non-merit

History and Function   Established by the Oklahoma Legislature in 1925, the board is responsible for the examination and licensing of architects and landscape architects after determining their eligibility. The board also examines and determines the eligibility for registered interior designers and registers them and their entities. It also regulates the practice of architecture and landscape architecture with power to suspend, revoke, deny, refuse to renew, or reinstate licenses and/or registrations. The board is self-sustaining through collection of fees. Re-created until July 1, 2020.

Arts Council, Oklahoma (53 O.S. § 163)

Agency Code 055 (IA)
PO Box 52001-2001, Oklahoma City 73152-2001
405/521-2931, FAX 405/521-6418, TDD 405/521-2931

www.arts.ok.gov
Jim Thorpe Building, Suite 640
E-mail—okarts@arts.ok.gov

Mission Statement   To lead in the development, support, and enrichment of a thriving arts environment, which is essential to quality of life, education, and economic vitality.

Administration   Amber Sharples, Executive Director; Amy Weaver, Deputy Director; George Taylor, Director of Finance; Joel Gavin, Director of Marketing and Communications

Personnel   14 unclassified, non-merit

History and Function   Created by the Oklahoma Legislature in 1965 to encourage and stimulate all forms of artistic endeavors, the Oklahoma Arts Council receives appropriations from the state legislature and the National Endowment for the Arts to provide matching grants to Oklahoma non-profit arts organizations.

Athletic Commission, Oklahoma State

(HB 3070, 2008; 3A O.S. § 604.1; 74 O.S. § 3906) Recreated until July 1, 2015

www.ok.gov/osac

405/271-9444

Attorney General (Constitution, Article 6 § 1)

Agency Code 049 (IA)
313 NE 21 Street, Oklahoma City, OK 73105
Tulsa Office: 907 Detroit, Suite 750, Tulsa, 74120-4200

www.ok.gov/oag
405/521-3921, FAX 405/521-6246
918/581-2885, FAX 918/581-2917

Administration   Scott Pruitt, Attorney General; Tom Bates, First Assistant Attorney General; Melissa McLawhorn Houston, Chief of Staff; Diane Clay, Director of Communications; Patrick Wyrick, Solicitor General; Aaron Cooper, Director of Public Affairs

Office of Civil Rights Enforcement (SB 763, 2011) (IA)

Workers' Compensation Fraud Investigation Unit (85A O.S. § 6) (IA)

Banking Department, Oklahoma State (Constitution, Article 14 §1; 6 O.S. § 201)

Agency Code 065 (IA)
2900 N Lincoln, Oklahoma City 73105
Tulsa Office: Triad Center 1, 7666 E 61 Street, Suite 305, Tulsa 74133

www.ok.gov/banking
405/521-2782, FAX 405/522-2993
918/295-3649, FAX 918/893-6405

Mission Statement   To preserve and promote sound, constructive competition among financial services and to help ensure the security of deposits through the promulgation of rules and regulations governing the banking industry in Oklahoma and by promoting diversity in financial products and services.

Administration   Mick Thompson, Bank Commissioner; O. Dudley Gilbert, Deputy Commissioner; Sherbie Kiffin, Assistant Deputy Commissioner; Harold A. Reel, Assistant Deputy Commissioner; Paul Qualls, Regional Examiner; Jeff Bagby, Regional Examiner; Rhonda Bruno, Director of Administration; Regina Rainey, Chief of Staff; Angela Morris, Administrative Assistant

Personnel   40 unclassified, 1 temporary, non-merit

History and Function   Through its boards, the department supervises all state chartered banks, trust companies, savings and loan associations, credit unions, and licensed sellers of checks and money transmitters; makes periodic examinations of the institutions under its supervision; conducts public hearings on charter applications and processes all documents submitted by state chartered financial institutions seeking corporate powers and changes in their articles of incorporation.

State Banking Board (6 O.S. § 202) (IA)

Banking Board, State (6 O.S. § 202)

State Banking Department (IA)
2900 N Lincoln Boulevard, Oklahoma City 73105   405/521–2782, FAX 405/522–2993
Tulsa Office: 7666 E 61 Street, Suite 305, Tulsa 74113

Administration   Mick Thompson, Commissioner; O. Dudley Gilbert, Deputy Commissioner; Angela Morris, Administrative Assistant

Mission Statement   To preserve and promote sound, constructive competition among financial services, and to help ensure the security of deposits through the promulgation of regulations governing the banking industry in Oklahoma and by promoting diversity in financial products.

History and Function   Established by the Oklahoma Legislature in 1965, the Banking Board is authorized to adopt and promulgate reasonable and uniform rules and regulations to govern the conduct, operation, and management of all banks or trust companies created, organized or existing under or by virtue of the laws of this state, and otherwise to govern the administration of the Oklahoma Banking Code.

Bar Association, Oklahoma

(Integrated bar under the jurisdiction of the Supreme Court. 5 O.S. § 12–14, 16, and Appendix.)

1901 N Lincoln Boulevard, Oklahoma City 73105   www.okbar.org
PO Box 53036, Oklahoma City 73152–3036   405/416–7000, 800/522–8065, FAX 405/416–7001

Administration   John Morris Williams, Executive Director; Craig D. Combs, Director of Administration; Gina Hendryx, General Counsel; Carol A. Manning, Director of Public Information; Susan Damron Krug, Director of Educational Programs; Jim Calloway, Management Assistance Program Director; Jane McConnell, Law Related Education Coordinator; Robbin Watson, Information Technology Director; Beverly Petry, Administrator of MCLE Commission; Travis Pickens, Ethics Counsel

Mission Statement   To advance the administration of justice according to law and the rules of the Oklahoma Supreme Court.

History and Function   The Oklahoma Bar Association was created in 1939 by the Oklahoma Supreme Court to assist the court in the regulation of the practice of law. (In Re Integration of State Bar of Oklahoma, 185 OK 505, 95 P.2d 113).

Oklahoma Bar Foundation Founded 1949, Private non-profit institution   405/416–7070

Bar Examiners, Board of 5:12–14, 16   405/416–7075

Continuing Legal Education Title 5, Chapter 1, Appendix 1–B, Rule 3   405/416–7029

Law Related Education Program Created by the Bar Association   405/416–7005

Mandatory Continuing Legal Education Commission Title 5, Chapter 1, Appendix 1–B   405/416–7009

Professional Responsibility Commission (Title 5, Chapter 1, Appendix 1–A, Rule 2.1)   405/416–7007

Professional Responsibility Tribunal Title 5, Chapter 1, Appendix 1–A, Rule 4.1   405/416–7007

Behavioral Health Licensure, State Board of (59 O.S. § 5011)

www.ok.gov/behavioralhealth   405/522–3696

Biological Survey, Oklahoma (70 O.S. § 3314)

(Placed under the direction and supervision of the Board of Regents of the University of Oklahoma.)

University of Oklahoma, 111 East Chesapeake Street, Norman 73019–0575   www.biosurvey.ou.edu
405/325–4035, FAX 405/325–7702   E-mail—jkelley@ou.edu

Administration   Jeffrey F. Kelley, Director; Bruce Hoagland, Coordinator, Oklahoma Natural Heritage Inventory; Wayne Elisens, Curator, Bebb Herbarium; Steve K. Sherrod, Executive Director, Sutton Avian Research Center; Kurt Kuklinski, Director of Fishery

History and Function   The Oklahoma Biological Survey, established in 1927, is both a research unit of the University of Oklahoma and a state office. The mission of the survey is to scientifically investigate the diversity of plants and animals in Oklahoma and associated regions and to contribute to conservation and education concerning these important resources. The survey includes: (1) the General Biological Survey program; (2) the Oklahoma Natural Heritage Inventory; (3) the Bebb Herbarium, jointly operated with the Department of Botany and Microbiology; (4) the Oklahoma Fishery Research Laboratory, jointly operated with the Oklahoma Department of Wildlife Conservation; (5) the Sutton Avian Research Center, a bird conservation center located in Bartlesville, and (6) the Oklahoma Natural Areas Registry. Personnel in the survey include faculty, staff, graduate students, and undergraduates who engage in a wide range of research, teaching, and service activities.

Boll Weevil Eradication Organization, Oklahoma (2 O.S. § 3–50.5)

Agency Code 039
Department of Agriculture, Food, and Forestry   www.obweo.org
800 S Main Street, Hobart 73651   PO Box 100, Hobart 73651
580/726–4280, FAX 580/726–8401

Administration   Mr. John Henderson, Executive Director

Mission Statement   To eradicate the boll weevil from Oklahoma.

Personnel   6 unclassified, 1 temporary, non-merit

Bond Advisor, Oklahoma State (62 O.S. § 695.7)

9220 N Kelley Avenue, Oklahoma City 73131 (IA)   www.ok.gov/bondadvisor
405/602–3100, FAX 405/848–3314   E-mail—jjoseph@oksba.org

Administration   James C. Joseph, State Bond Advisor; Vacant, Senior Bond Analyst; Rachael Blanchard, Administrative Assistant

Mission Statement   To administer the Private Activity Bond Allocation Act, and to provide advice and assistance to the Long-Range Capital Planning Commission and serve as staff to the Council of Bond Oversight.

History and Function   Created by statute in 1987. The function of the office is to improve the debt issuance and management practices of all municipal bond issuers in Oklahoma and to promote improved capital planning.

Bond Commissioner (62 O.S. § 11)

The Attorney General is ex officio Bond Commissioner of the State.
Office of the Attorney General, 313 NE 21 Street, Oklahoma City 73105
405/521–3921, FAX 405/521–6246

Administration   Scott Pruitt, Attorney General, ex officio Bond Commissioner

Bond Oversight, Council of (62 O.S. § 695.11A)

The five-member Council of Bond Oversight is responsible for the review and approval of all financing requests by state agencies, authorities, departments, and trusts. The council meets monthly to review financing requests and may set specific conditions that must be satisfied prior to issuance. The council consists of the Office of Management and Enterprise Services director, two members appointed by the governor, one member appointed by the Speaker of Oklahoma House of Representatives, and one member appointed by the President Pro Tempore of the Oklahoma Senate.

Boxing Commission, Oklahoma Professional (3A O.S. § 604.1)

State Department of Health   405/271-9444 EXT 57992
E-mail—boxing@health.ok.gov   FAX 405/271-1695

Building Bonds Commission, Oklahoma (62 O.S. § 57.302)

Secretary of State (IA)   State Capitol Room 101, 2300 N Lincoln Blvd. Oklahoma City 73105-4897
405/521-6434, FAX 405/521-2031

Administration   Tookie Hayes, staff

History and Function   Established in 1949 by the Oklahoma Legislature, this is the agency by which the state incurs indebtedness for the purpose of constructing, equipping, remodeling, and repairing any and all buildings of the state, including those of its educational, recreational, penal, and charitable establishments, pursuant to Section 31, Article 10 of the Constitution of Oklahoma and subsequent legislative acts.

Business License Information Office (74 O.S. § 5058.4)

Department of Commerce (IA)   900 N Stiles, Oklahoma City, 73104
Business Solutions Division, 900 N Stiles Avenue, Oklahoma City 73104-3234

Administration   Rana Steeds, 405/815-5143

History and Function   Provides information to existing businesses and individuals starting a business about compliance with state licensing and registration requirements. Information is also available in the form of a business start up workbook, and finance referral. A group of coordinators, designated by the directors from the twenty-five state agencies knowledgeable about business license, permit, or filing requirements for their respective state agencies, provides current information to the office of business license information.

Capital Investment Board, Oklahoma (74 O.S. § 5085.2)

(State-beneficiary public trust)
13905 Quail Point Drive, Suite A, Oklahoma City 73134 (IA)   405/848-9456, FAX 405/842-6389

Administration   Devon L. Sauzek, President

Mission Statement   The Oklahoma Capital Investment Board (OCIB) is established to mobilize sources of equity and near-equity capital for Oklahoma businesses.

History and Function   OCIB was established under a 1987 legislative act and began functioning in 1992. OCIB currently operates the Venture Investment Program which supports the funding of venture capital partnerships that meet the investment and strategic objectives of OCIB. OCIB guarantees investments in carefully selected venture capital partnerships, which agree to focus a portion of their time, talent, and capital on potential investment opportunities in high growth, high return Oklahoma businesses.

Capitol Improvement Authority, Oklahoma (73 O.S. § 152)

Will Rogers Office Building, 2401 Lincoln, Suite 206 (IA)
PO Box 53218, Oklahoma City 73152-3218   405/522-8519, FAX 405/521-6403

Mission Statement   To provide buildings and facilities for state government offices.

Administration   Travis Monroe, OCIA Administrator

History and Function   Created by legislative act in 1959 to issue revenue bonds to provide buildings and facilities for state government offices, the authority cannot issue bonds without legislative authorization. The authority consists of the governor who serves as chairman, the state treasurer, the lieutenant governor who serves as vice chairman, the director of the Office of Management and Enterprise Services, the director of the Department of Human Services, the vice chairman of the Tax Commission, the director of the Oklahoma Department of Tourism and Recreation, and the director of the Department of Transportation.

Capitol-Medical Center Improvement and Zoning Commission

(73 O.S. § 83.1, 73 O.S. § 3908)

Will Rogers Office Building, 2401 Lincoln, Suite 212 (IA)
PO Box 53448, Oklahoma City 73152-3448   405/521-3678, FAX 405/521-6403

Administration   Denise Martin, Administrative Officer

Mission Statement   To efficiently promote the general welfare of Oklahoma and private property owners by providing effective direction for the orderly development of the Capitol-Medical Center Improvement and Zoning District.

History and Function   The commission was established under a 1970 legislative act and has as its principal purpose the orderly development of certain designated areas of land surrounding the state capitol and the Oklahoma Health Center. It has authority to grant or deny zoning permits for any changes or new construction within the district in accordance with a comprehensive master plan. Re-created until July 1, 2014.

Citizen's Advisory Committee (73 O.S. § 83.12)

Historical Preservation and Landmark Board of Review (120 O.S. § 10–11–2) (Created by Commission)

Oklahoma Administrative Code 120: Chapter 10

Capitol Preservation Commission, State (74 O.S. § 4102)

Will Rogers Office Building, 2401 Lincoln, Suite 206 (IA)
PO Box 53218, Oklahoma City 73152-3218   405/522-0440, FAX 405/521-6403

History and Function   The commission was created in 1982 to plan and supervise the preservation and restoration of the interior and exterior of the Oklahoma State Capitol Building. Similar responsibilities were added in 1983 with respect to the governor's mansion. The commission also controls the display of art objects in public areas of the state capitol and the first floor of the governor's mansion. The commission consists of fifteen members. Re-created until July 1, 2015.

Career and Technology Education, Oklahoma Department of

(70 O.S. § 14–104)   **Board** (70 O.S. § 14–101)

Agency Code 800 (IA)   www.okcareertech.org
1500 W Seventh Avenue, Stillwater 74074   405/377-2000, FAX 405/743-6809

Mission Statement   To prepare Oklahomans to succeed in the workplace, in education, and in life.

Administration   Dr. Marcie Mack, Interim State Director

Personnel   250 unclassified

Advisory Committee to the Municipal Clerks and Treasurers Division (11 O.S. § 52–103)

Cash Management and Investment Oversight Commission

(62 O.S. §71.1)

Legislative Service Bureau
State Capitol, Room 309-1, Oklahoma City 73105   405/521-5662

Cerebral Palsy Commission (63 O.S. § 485.3, 485.9)

Agency Code 670   www.jdmc.org
J.D. McCarty Center for Children with Developmental Disabilities
2002 E Robinson, Norman 73071   405/307-2800, 800/777-1272

Mission Statement   To provide a comprehensive program of rehabilitative care to Oklahoma's children (0 to 21) with developmental disabilities; to utilize measurable quality standards and to ensure excellence in health care through a comprehensive, multi-disciplinary approach to service delivery which will enable children with developmental disabilities to maximize their potential and enhance their quality of life; to provide an intensive and comprehensive habilitative environment through direct services, referrals, and consultations that will lead to increased productivity and a quality standard of living throughout adulthood; to increase the physical and emotional well-being of patients and their families through an empowering process of education, training, transitional planning, and community support; to advocate for the needs of children with developmental disabilities by increasing awareness and supplementing habilitative services in all communities as well as pro-actively seeking solutions to expressed concerns; and to facilitate ongoing educational training for staff to ensure continuous quality improvements.

Administration   Vicki Kuestersteffen, Director; Erik Paulson, Business Manager; Becky Melsek, Director of Nursing; Debbie L. Barrett, Human Resources Director; Greg Gaston, Director of Marketing

Personnel   235

History and Function   The McCarty Center was founded in 1946 by the 40 et 8 of Oklahoma, an honor society within the American Legion. A member of the 40 et 8 had a grandson who had cerebral palsy. The grandfather could not find any entity in the state that could help his grandson to learn to walk or talk. The 40 et 8 took it upon themselves to create a place where children with cerebral palsy could get the physical, occupational, and speech and language therapy they needed to reach their highest level of independence and functionality. Today, the McCarty Center has treated more than one hundred different diagnoses in the developmental disability category. In 1948 the McCarty Center became a state agency.

Chief Medical Examiner (63 O.S. § 934)

901 N Stonewall, Oklahoma City 73117 (IA)   www.ok.gov/ocme
405/239-7141, FAX 405/239-2430   E-mail—medicalexaminer@ocme.ok.gov

Mission Statement   To protect the public health and safety of Oklahomans through the scientific investigation of deaths as defined by state statutes. This process involves scene investigation and medicolegal autopsy (including radiology, toxicology, histology, and microbiology) complementing the activities of law enforcement agencies, district attorneys, and public health officials.

Children and Youth, Commission on (10 O.S. § 601.1)

Agency Code 127 (IA)   www.okkids.org
1111 N Lee Avenue, Suite 500, Oklahoma City 73103   405/606-4900, FAX 405/524-0417

Mission Statement   The mission of the Oklahoma Commission on Children and Youth is to improve services to children by facilitating joint planning and coordination among public and private agencies; independent monitoring of the children and youth service system for compliance with established responsibilities; and entering into agreements to test models and demonstration programs for effective services.

Administration   Lisa Smith, Director; Jack Chapman, Assistant Director

Personnel   25.5 classified, 7 unclassified, merit

History and Function   The Commission on Children and Youth was created by the Oklahoma Legislature on May 28, 1982, to develop and improve services to children and youth in Oklahoma.

Child Abuse Examination, Board of (10 O.S. § 601.30; 10 O.S. § 1150.2)
1111 N Lee Avenue, Suite 500, Oklahoma City 73103; 405/271-2429
Administration   John Stuemky, M.D., Chief Child Abuse Examiner

Child Death Review Board (10 O.S. § 1150.2) Re-created until July 1, 2020
405/606-4933, FAX 405/524-0417
Administration   Lisa Rhoades, Administrator

Children of Incarcerated Parents
405/606-4918; FAX 405/524-0417
Administration   Treasa Hansdowne, Coordinator

Juvenile System Oversight, Office of (10 O.S. § 601.6)
405/606-4900; FAX 405/528-0455
Administration   Lisa Smith, Director; Jack Chapman, Assistant Director

Office of Planning and Coordination for Services to Children and Youth (10 O.S. § 601.3)
405/606-4931; FAX 405/524-0417
Administration   Anthony Kibble, MSW, Coordinator

Post Adjudication Review Advisory Board (10 O.S. § 1116.6)
405/606-4922; FAX 405/524-0417
Administration   Sara Vincent, Coordinator

Chiropractic Examiners, Board of (59 O.S. § 161.1; 59 O.S.161.4)

Agency Code 145 (IA)   www.chiropracticboard.ok.gov
421 NW 13 Street, Suite 180, Oklahoma City 73103   405/522-3400, FAX 866/245-2748

Mission Statement   To enhance public health and safety by regulating the practice of chiropractic in Oklahoma to insure that only properly qualified chiropractors practice in the state and that the profession as a whole is conducted in the public's best interest. Re-created until July 1, 2016.

Administration   Beth Carter, Executive Director; Joseph English, Investigator

Personnel   3 unclassified, non-merit

History and Function   The board serves as the administrative agency for the conduct and licensing of chiropractic physicians; has authority to enforce statutory laws relating to the profession and is self-sustaining through collection of licensing fees.

Civil War Sesquicentennial Commission, Oklahoma American

(53 O.S. § 400) Created until July 1, 2015

www.okcivilwar.org

Advisory Council, Oklahoma American Civil War Sesquicentennial Commission
(53 O.S. § 402) Created until July 1, 2015

Climatological Survey, Oklahoma (74 O.S. § 245) Re-created until July 1, 2020.

(Under direction and supervision of Board of Regents of University of Oklahoma.)
University of Oklahoma, 120 David L. Boren Boulevard, Suite 2900, Norman 73072-7305
405/325-2541, FAX 405/325-2550   www.climate.ok.gov

Mission Statement   To acquire, archive, process, and disseminate, in the most cost-effective way possible, all climate and weather information of value to policy and decision makers in the state.

Administration   Kevin Kloesel, Ph.D., Director; Renee A. McPherson, Ph.D., State Climatologist

History and Function   The Oklahoma Climatological Survey (OCS) is a state agency mandated to acquire, archive, process, and disseminate, in the most cost-effective way possible, all climate and weather information of value to policy and decision makers in the state. OCS was first established by the University of Oklahoma in 1980 to serve as a supporting structure for the state climatologist. The state legislature in 1982 formalized the OCS's existence with enabling legislation. Re-created until July 1, 2014.

Since 1991 the OCS has been the operational home of the Oklahoma Mesonet (www.mesonet.org), the state's weather network, designed and implemented by the University of Oklahoma (OU) and Oklahoma State University (OSU). The addition of the Mesonet expanded OCS's role from retrospective climate studies to supporting real-time weather-impacted decisions. OCS initiated outreach programs for Oklahoma's K–12 teachers and public safety agencies in 1992 and 1996, respectively, and provides additional decision-support tools in support of rural electric cooperatives and agriculture.

OCS provides tailored information to address particular needs for Oklahoma's citizens and state and local decision makers. OCS scientists utilize all available weather and climate information, both historical and real-time, to assist citizens and state decision makers with understanding current weather conditions and historical circumstances of weather events and climate variability. By integrating weather and climate information from multiple data sources, OCS relieves other state agencies of the necessity to have expertise on staff to assemble and evaluate the multiple information sources. OCS climatologists provide similar expert assessments for citizens of Oklahoma.

OCS is located at OU in Norman, and is under the governance of the OU Board of Regents. OCS is home to the state climatologist. The director of OCS is appointed by the OU Board of Regents, based upon recommendations by a search committee conducted within the OU College of Atmospheric and Geographic Sciences and School of Meteorology. The director also serves as co-chair of the Mesonet Steering Committee.

Climate Services
climate.mesonet.org   Mark Shafer, Director of Climate Services, 405/325-3044

K–12 Educational Outreach
earthstorm.mesonet.org   Andrea Melvin, Program Manager, 405/325-2652

Mesonet, The Oklahoma (Partnership with OSU, Division of Agricultural & Natural Resources)
www.mesonet.org   Chris Fiebrich, Associate Director for Mesonet; 405/325-6877

OK-First Public Safety Outreach
okfirst.mesonet.org   James Hocker, Program Manager, 405/325-3230

College Savings Plan, Board of Trustees (70 O.S. § 3970.4)

877/654-7284   www.ok4saving.org

Commerce, Oklahoma Department of (74 O.S. § 5003.1)

Agency Code 160 (IA)   www.okcommerce.gov
900 N Stiles Avenue, Oklahoma City 73104-3234
405/815-6552, National Toll Free 1-800-TRY-OKLA; FAX 405/815-5199

Mission Statement   To create and deliver high-impact solutions that contribute to job creation and lead to prosperous lives and communities for all Oklahomans.

Administration   Larry V. Parman, Executive Director, 405/815-5306; Jamie Maddy, Chief of Staff, 405/815-5153; Don Hackler, General Counsel, 405/815-5359; Vaughn Clark, Director, Community Development, 405/815-5370; Charles Kimbrough, Director, Business Development, 405/815-5361; Deidre Myers, Deputy Secretary, Workforce Development, 405/815-5383

Personnel   123 unclassified

History and Function   Established in 1986, the Department of Commerce is the state's lead economic development agency. Its responsibilities include assisting and developing local communities through the investment of federal and state resources; stimulating growth of existing businesses; attracting new domestic and international businesses; and promoting the development and availability of a skilled workforce. The department has offices in Oklahoma City, Tulsa, and has representation in three foreign countries.

Community and Faith Engagement, Office of

2400 N Lincoln, Oklahoma City 73105   PO Box 25352, Oklahoma City 73125
405/522-0606, FAX 405/522-4360

Mission Statement   Helping Oklahoma's poor and needy by promoting collaboration between government agencies and faith-based/community organizations to provide social services.

Administration   Karen Jacobs, Director

Community Hospitals Authority (63 O.S. § 3240.3)

CompSource Oklahoma

On January 1, 2015, CompSource became CompSource Mutual Insurance Company (85 O.S. § 396.3). Organized under state law, the company operates as a private entity independent of the state. It is required to provide worker's compensation insurance to any employer in the state.

Conservation Commission, Oklahoma (27A O.S. § 3-2-101)

Agency Code 645 (IA)   www.conservation.ok.gov
2800 N Lincoln Boulevard, Suite 160, Oklahoma City 73105-4201   405/521-2384, FAX 405/521-6686

Mission Statement   To conserve, protect, and restore Oklahoma's natural resources, working in collaboration with the conservation districts and other partners on behalf of the citizens of Oklahoma.

Administration   Mike Thralls, Executive Director 405/521-2384; Robert W. Toole, Assistant
    Director 405/521-4818; Kim Tweed, Executive Secretary; Stacy Hansen, Communications
    Coordinator
    Abandon Mine Land Division, Mike Sharpe, Acting Director
    Conservation Programs Division, Robert W. Toole, Director
    District Services and Human Resources, Lisa Knauf Owen, Director
    Financial Management/Human Resources Division, Steve Coffman, Director
    Office of Geographic Information and Technical Services, Mike Sharp, Director
    Water Quality Division, Shanon Phillips, Director

Personnel   3 classified, 42 unclassified, merit

History and Function   Authorized under the Conservation District Act in 1937 when Oklahoma landowners faced the serious problem of erosion from wind and water, the early-day work for the Conservation Commission was to eradicate these problems. Today the Conservation Commission, the federal USDA Natural Resources Conservation Service, and a network of eighty-seven local conservation districts cooperatively carry out the conservation program in Oklahoma. In addition to providing direct technical assistance to local land users for soil and water conservation, the commission and conservation districts are responsible for upstream flood control protection, a state-funded conservation cost-share program, reclamation of abandoned mine land and nonpoint source water quality monitoring, planning, and management, in addition to a variety of educational and informational activities.

Conservation Districts—Oklahoma's eighty-seven conservation districts are legal subdivisions of state government organized by local residents. The entire state is divided into conservation districts, often but not always along county lines. Each conservation district office offers a variety of natural resource information including soil surveys. Conservation districts provide services to large segments of the public, including farmers, ranchers, community planners, public health officials, developers, educators, students, and rural and urban citizens. A directory of conservation district offices, addresses, and telephone numbers is available on the Conservation Commission's web site at www.conservation.ok.gov.

Small Watershed Upstream Flood Control Program—The Conservation Commission assists the state's eighty-seven local conservation districts in the construction of new and rehabilitation of aging Small Watershed Upstream Flood Control Program structures (most often dams) as well as operation and maintenance of those structures. Oklahoma has more than 2,100 upstream flood control dams, the most of any state in the nation.

Conservation Cost-Share Program—The Oklahoma Legislature established the Oklahoma Conservation Cost-Share Program in 1998. The Oklahoma Conservation Commission administers the program at the state level and local conservation districts administer local programs. The program provides funds, as appropriated by the legislature, to conservation districts to be used to install conservation practices on the land to reduce soil erosion and improve water quality.

Conservation Education—The Conservation Education program involves a number of activities including teacher training, technical assistance to conservation districts, outdoor classroom development, and cooperative projects with other state and federal agencies and higher education entities. The agency co-sponsors education curriculum for Project WET (Water Education for Teachers).

Environmental Education Coordinating Committee—The Oklahoma Environmental Quality Act of 1993 designated the OCC to coordinate environmental education with all other state agencies in a statewide effort involving government, environmental advocates, business community, private citizens, and students to educate the citizenry of Oklahoma about the importance of the environment and our natural resources. In response, the Conservation Commission established the State Environmental Education Coordinating Committee with the goal of more efficiently serving the public by increased networking among agencies and reduced duplication of effort.

Wetlands—Federal funding from the U.S. Environmental Protection Agency assisted the Conservation Commission in preparing the Oklahoma Comprehensive Wetlands Conservation Plan. The commission continues to coordinate the implementation of the state comprehensive wetlands management plan.

Nonpoint Source Water Quality—The Oklahoma Environmental Quality Act (Laws 1992, c. 398) statutorily designated the Conservation Commission as the state's nonpoint source technical lead agency in carrying out Section 319 Nonpoint Source Management Programs of the Federal Clean Water Act Amendments of 1987. The Water Quality Division is responsible for the assessment, prioritization, and management program of nonpoint source pollution of the state's waters required under Section 319 of the Federal Clean Water Act. The Water Quality Division developed a strategy to monitor small feeder streams on a rotational basis to determine the impact of nonpoint source pollution on the state's water resources. This rotational monitoring program, which rotates into two new basins every two years, supports the state's ambient monitoring program. The division coordinates the development and management of a performance-based Priority Watershed Cost-Share Program, in which federal and state funds are made available to landowners to install conservation practices to reduce the state's nonpoint source pollution. The division director chairs the NonPoint Source Working Group, which is made up of federal, state and local agencies, environmental and producer groups, and Indian tribes. The NonPoint Source Working Group identifies priorities where funds and technical assistance will be directed. The Water Quality Division also includes the Conservation Commission's Wetlands Program, which coordinates implementation of the Oklahoma Comprehensive Wetlands Conservation Plan. The plan promotes private and public cooperation in managing wetlands through a voluntary system using education, technical assistance, and incentives to bring the private and public sectors into wetlands management.

Abandoned Mine Land Reclamation Program—The Oklahoma Conservation Commission is the state agency designated to administer the federally-funded Abandoned Mine Land (AML) Reclamation Program. The purpose of this program is to reclaim abandoned mined land in Oklahoma. The AML Program, through the Office of Management and Enterprise Services, contracts with private contractors to perform the reclamation work. All AML lands are prioritized based on potential threat to the public health and safety. Oklahoma's abandoned mine land sites are reviewed by the State Reclamation Committee, which includes state and federal agencies and private nonprofit associations.

Pollution Complaints Tracking—The Oklahoma Environmental Quality Act of 1993 also directed the Conservation Commission to establish and maintain a geographic information database for all citizen pollution complaints. This system became operational July 1, 1993.

Carbon Sequestration Certification Program—This program encourages Oklahomans to voluntarily protect water quality; prevent soil erosion and improve soil quality; and improve air quality by adopting conservation practices that sequester or avoid emissions of greenhouse gases. By developing a program, that combines research, natural resource protection, and state-backed verification of carbon offsets, Oklahoma has a model, voluntary program that strives to maximize the quality of offsets from agriculture, forestry, and ecologic sequestration.

Construction Industries Board (59 O.S. § 1000.2)
Re-created until July 1, 2017

2401 NW 23 Street, Suite 2F, Oklahoma City 73107–2428   www.ok.gov/cib
405/521-6550, FAX 405/521-6525

Mission Statement   To protect life and property by licensing and inspection of the related trades for the health, safety, and welfare of the public.

Administration   Janis Hubbard, Administrator; JaNeal Beougher, Office Manager; Linda Ruckman, Board Secretary/Executive Assistant

Personnel 34 unclassified

History and Function   Created in 2001 for the licensing and oversight of the construction industries trades, which include the Plumbing License Law of 1955, the Oklahoma Inspectors Act, the Electrical Licensing Act, the Mechanical Licensing Act, the Home Inspectors Licensing Act, and the Roofing Contractor Registration Act.

Entities included under the direction of the Construction Industries Board include:
Electrical Examiners, Committee of (59 O.S. § 1683)
Electrical Hearing Board (59 O.S. § 1689)
Electrical Installation Code Variance & Appeals Board (59 O.S. § 1697)
Home Inspector Examiners, Committee of (59 O.S. § 858–624)
Inspector Examiners Committee (59 O.S. § 1034)
Mechanical Hearing Board (59 O.S. § 1850.14)
Mechanical Examiners, Committee of (59 O.S. § 1850.4)
Mechanical Installation Code Variance & Appeals Board (59 O.S. § 1850.16)
Plumbing Examiners, Committee of (74 O.S. § 3903; 59 O.S. §1004) Re-created until July 1, 2016
Plumbing Hearing Board (59 O.S. § 1010)
Plumbing Installation Code Variance & Appeals Board (59 O.S. § 1021.1)
Roofing Examiners, Committee of (59 O.S. § 1151.26)
Roofing Hearing Board (59 O.S. § 1151.28)
Roofing Installation Code Variance and Appeals Board, Oklahoma State (59 O.S. § 1159.79)

Consumer Credit, Commission on (14A O.S. § 6–501)

Agency Code 635 (IA)   www.okdocc.state.ok.us
3613 NW 56 Street, Suite 240, Oklahoma City 73112   405/521-3653, 800/448-4904, FAX 405/521-6740

Mission Statement   We protect and educate consumer buyers, lessees, and borrowers against unfair practices, and are fair and impartial in the regulation of consumer credit transactions in Oklahoma.

Administration   Scott Lesher, Administrator

Personnel   20 classified, 5 unclassified

History and Function   The Oklahoma Department of Consumer Credit was created by the Oklahoma Legislature in 1969. The department is responsible for the regulation of consumer credit sales and consumer loans in the state of Oklahoma. The department also is responsible for the licensing and regulation of mortgage brokers, mortgage lenders, mortgage loan originators, pawnshops, deferred deposit lenders, rental purchase lessors, health spa contracts, credit serve organizations, precious metal and gem dealers, and consumer litigation funders.

Consumer Credit Advisory Committee (14A O.S. § 6–501

Cooperative Extension Service at Oklahoma State University

(19 O.S. § 130.2) Formerly Center for Local Government Technology and Cooperative Extension Service

www.oces.okstate.edu   405/744-5339

Corporation Commission, Oklahoma

(Constitution, Article 9 § 15; 17 O.S. § 1 et seq.)

Agency Code 185 (IA)
Jim Thorpe Building, 2101 N Lincoln Boulevard   www.occeweb.com
PO Box 52000, Oklahoma City 73152-2000   405/521-2211, FAX 405/522-1623, TDD 405/521-3513

Consumer Services:
   Pollution Complaint/Royalty Owner Information Hot line 800/522-0034
   Public Utility Complaints 800/522-8154

Commissioners   Bob Anthony—405/521-2261, Patrice Douglas—405/521-2264, and Dana Murphy—405/521-2267.

Administration   Lori Wrotenbery, Director, 405/521-2307;
   Administrative Proceedings Division, Michael Decker, 405/521-2241
   Consumer Services Division, Kim Dobbins, Interim Director, 405/522-0478
   Information Technology Division, Michelle Smith, Director, 405/521-4520
   Finance Department, Cleve Pierce, Director, 405/521-3526
   General Counsel Office, Michele Craig, Interim General Counsel, 405/521-2078
   Human Resources, Christine Jolly, Director, 405/521-2217
   Oil & Gas Conservation Division, Ron Duncan, Interim Director, 405/521-2302
   Petroleum Storage Tank Division, Robyn Strickland, Director, 405/521-4861
   Public Utility Division, Brandy Wreath, Director, 405/521-2322
   Transportation Division, Sam Macaluso, Director, 405/521-4131

Mission Statement   To regulate and enforce the laws and supervise the activities associated with the exploration and production of oil and gas; the storage and dispensing of petroleum based fuels; the establishment of rates and services of public utilities; and the operation of intrastate transportation to best serve the economic needs of the public. In the interests of the public, the commission will oversee the conservation of natural resources; avoid waste; abate pollution of the environment; and balance the rights and needs of the people with those of the regulated entities which provide essential and desirable services for the benefit of Oklahoma and its citizens.

Personnel   308 classified, 147 unclassified, 10 temporary, merit

History and Function   The Corporation Commission was established at statehood. The First Legislature empowered and directed the commission to regulate and supervise the activities of "all public businesses," whose services were considered by the legislature to be essential to the public welfare. The legal principle for state regulation of rates and services of public businesses had been established after the Civil War, and that principle was sustained by the U.S. Supreme Court in 1877. Regulation to assure fair rates and prevent discrimination in rates and services began as a legislative matter, but as the nation grew and the need for regulation increased, legislative bodies began establishing specific agencies to administer regulation. The Corporation Commission serves as both a tribunal and agency of investigation, accomplishing regulation through a combination of legislative, executive, administrative, and judicial powers. Commission orders carry the same weight of authority as laws enacted by the legislature.

The Oklahoma Constitution authorized the Corporation Commission to regulate transportation and transmission companies, mainly railroads and telephone and telegraph companies. The First Legislature (1908) added authority for "all public businesses." The Second Legislature (1909) put regulation of oil pipeline companies under commission jurisdiction. The commission began regulating the prices of telephone calls in November 1908 and telegrams in April 1912. Regulation of water, heat, light, and power rates began in December 1913. The commission began regulating oil and gas in 1914 when it restricted drilling and production of oil from the Cushing and Healdton fields to prevent waste when production exceeded pipeline transport capacity.

The commission acted under its authority to regulate pipelines as common carriers. In 1915 the legislature passed the Oil and Gas Conservation Act and directed the commission to enforce it; declared cotton gins to be public utilities under commission regulation; and extended commission authority over utility companies to include practices and rates.

The businesses regulated by the commission and types of regulation administered have changed through the years as technology has advanced and services considered essential to the public welfare have changed. The commission presently regulates public utilities, except those under municipal or federal jurisdiction; oil and gas drilling, production, and environmental protection; motor fuel quality and containment; gas and hazardous liquid pipeline safety procedures; and some aspects of motor carrier transport and railroad operations. The commission also administers and enforces federal programs for underground injection control (in connection with oil and gas enhanced recovery programs and disposal of certain oil and gas drilling waste fluids) and remediation of soil and ground water pollution caused by leaking underground storage tanks. The commission also manages the state Petroleum Storage Tank Release Indemnity Fund, which reimburses a portion of the cost of remediating environmental pollution caused by leaking storage tanks.

Carbon Sequestration Advisory Committee (27A O.S. § 3–4–102)

Storage Tank Advisory Council (17 O.S. § 340)

Corrections, State Department of (57 O.S. § 505)   Board (57 O.S. § 503)

Agency Code 131 (IA)
3400 N Martin Luther King Avenue 73111–4298   www.doc.state.ok.us
PO Box 11400, Oklahoma City 73136–0400   405/425–2500, FAX 405/425–2578

Mission Statement   To protect the public, the employees, and the offender.

Administration   Vacant, Director, 405/425–2505, FAX 405/425–2578; Kimberley Owen, Executive Assistant, 405/425–2506, FAX 405/425–2578; Marilyn Davidson, Executive Assistant, 405/425–7267; FAX 405/425–2578; Edward L. Evans, Associate Director, Field Operations, 405/425–2550, FAX 405/425–2578; Tina Hicks, Associate Director, Administrative Services, 405/425–2722, FAX 405/425–7216; Terri Watkins, Director of Communications, 405/425–2565, FAX 405/425–2578; Joyce Jackson, Executive Communications Administrator, 405/425–2520, FAX 405/425–2502; and David Cincotta, General Counsel, 405/425–2515, FAX 405/425–2683

Personnel   3,531 classified, 343 unclassified, 37 temporary, merit

History and Function   In May 1967 the Oklahoma Corrections Act was signed into law by Governor Dewey F. Bartlett. Governed by a bipartisan, seven-member board of gubernatorial appointees serving six-year staggered terms, the Board of Corrections establishes and reviews policies for the department's operation, appoints a director, and reviews appointments of management personnel. The department protects the public, the employees, and the offenders, and is responsible for the operation of seventeen institutions ranging from maximum to minimum security, seven probation and parole districts, six community corrections centers, and fifteen work centers.

Board of Directors for Canteen Services (57 O.S. § 537) (Parent Canteen Board Director)
   Administration   Robert Patton, Director of Board Administration; Tom James, Chief Financial Officer, Finance and Accounting, 405/425–2646, FAX 405/425–2021

Inmate Reentry Policy Council (57 O.S. § 521.1)

Inspector General
    Administration   Johnny Blevins, Inspector General, 405/425-2571, FAX 405/425-7216

Investigations Division (57 O.S. § 508.4)

Oklahoma Correctional Industries (57 O.S. § 549.1)   www.ocisales.com
    3402 N Martin Luther King Avenue, Oklahoma City 73111   405/425-7525, FAX 405/425-7502
    Administration   J.D. Colbert, Administrator
    Oklahoma Correctional Industries is a program within the Oklahoma Department of Corrections. Its mission is to provide work opportunities that emphasize the development of work ethics and provide skills training to a maximum number of offenders in the Oklahoma correctional system. To successfully accomplish this goal, OCI strives to maintain cost effective operations that provide qualified customers with necessary products and services. It is the goal of OCI to provide products and services that are comparable in quality and workmanship to private sector goods, competitively priced, and delivered in a timely manner.

Sex Offender Level Assignment Committee (57 O.S. § 582.5) Formerly Sex Offender Risk Assessment Review Committee.

Cosmetology and Barbering, State Board of (59 O.S. § 199)

Agency Code 190 (IA)   www.cosmo.ok.gov
2401 NW 23 Street, Suite 84, Oklahoma City, 73107   405/521-2441, fax 405-5212440

Mission Statement   To safeguard and protect the health and general welfare of the people of the state of Oklahoma by performing a variety of services from developing curriculum for schools to administering examinations for prospective practitioners of the cosmetology and barbering profession.

Administration   Sherry G. Lewelling, Executive Director; Jennifer McRee, Principal Assistant

History and Purpose   The State Board of Cosmetology was created by the Oklahoma Legislature in 1935, primarily as a self-sustaining licensing agency. Recreated in 2014 as the Oklahoma State Board of Cosmetology and Barbering, the entity licenses and regulates the profession of cosmetology, barbering, esthetics, manicuring, instructors and establishments where these services are performed. It also regulates health and safety issues in schools approved by the Board. Anyone who provides these types of services including but not limited to, haircutting, hairdressing, nail care, skin care and the application of make-up must be licensed by the Board.

County Government Personnel Education and Training, Commission on (19 O.S. § 130.1) Re-created until July 1, 2015

318 Agriculture Hall, Oklahoma State University, Stillwater 74078-6026   agecon.okstate.edu/ctp
405/744-6160

Administration   Notie H. Lansford; Gayle Hiner, Publications Officer at Oklahoma Cooperative Extension Service, 405/744-3659

Credit Union Board, Oklahoma State (6 O.S. § 2001.1)

State Banking Department
2900 N Lincoln Blvd., Oklahoma City 73105   405/521-2782, FAX 405/522-2993
Tulsa Office: 7666 E 61 Street, Suite 305, Tulsa 74133   918/295-3649, FAX 918/893-6405

Mission Statement   To promote and preserve sound constructive competition among financial services and to help ensure the security of deposits through the promulgation of rules and regulations governing the credit union industry in Oklahoma and by promoting diversity in financial products and services.

Administration   Mick Thompson, Bank Commissioner; O. Dudley Gilbert, Deputy Commissioner; Deborah Moore, Executive Secretary

History and Function   Established by the Oklahoma Legislature in 1974, the board is authorized to exercise the powers given to the state banking commissioner under previous legislation and is authorized to promulgate rules and regulations to carry out the department's responsibilities.

Crime Victims Compensation Board (21 O.S. § 142.4)

Agency Code 220 (IA)
421 NW 13 Street, Suite 290, Oklahoma City 73103   405/264–5006

Administration   Suzanne Breedlove, Director of Victim Services; Suzanne McClain Atwood, Executive Coordinator, District Attorneys Council.

Davis, J.M. Memorial Commission (53 O.S. § 201A)

Agency Code 204   www.jmdavis.state.ok.us   www.thegunmuseum.com
330 North J.M. Davis Boulevard, PO Box 966, Claremore 74018–0966   918/341–5707, FAX 918/341–5771

Mission Statement   To house, preserve, and display the unique items collected by J.M. Davis, and to provide an educational experience, entertainment, and pleasure to viewers of the collection.

Administration   Wayne McCombs, Executive Director

Personnel   4 permanent, 3 temporary

History and Function   The duty of the J.M. Davis Memorial Commission is to house, preserve, and display the arms collections and historical artifacts. The J.M. Davis Arms and Historical Museum houses more than 50,000 guns and related items, including 1,200 steins from all over the world, John Rogers's Statuary, Gallery of Outlaw Guns, western memorabilia, Native American artifacts, antique music boxes, antique musical instruments, swords and knives, World War I posters, a very extensive research library, and a gift shop.

Dentistry, Oklahoma Board of (Constitution, Article 5 § 39; 59 O.S. § 328.7)

Agency Code 215 (IA)   www.ok.gov/dentistry
2920 N Lincoln Boulevard, Suite B, Oklahoma City 73105   405/522–4844 FAX 405/522–4614

Mission Statement   To enhance public health and safety by regulating the practice of dentistry in the state in accordance with the State Dental Act and ensuring that the dental profession as a whole is conducted safely and in the public's best interest.

Administration   Susan Rogers, Esq., Executive Director

Personnel   5 classified, 5 unclassified

History and Function   The Oklahoma Board of Dentistry was created in the Oklahoma Constitution in 1935. The board is responsible for the regulation and oversight of the licensing and practice of dentistry in Oklahoma. In conjunction with the practice of dentistry, the board also regulates the practice of dental hygiene, certifies dental assistants, and issues permits to dental laboratories. The board is not appropriated state funds, but is self-sustaining on licensing fees and regulatory fines.

Developmental Disabilities Council, Oklahoma

(Executive Order 93–20, as retained by Executive Order 2011–10)

2401 NW 23 Street, Suite 74, Oklahoma City 73107   www.okddc.ok.gov
405/521–4984, 800/836–4470, FAX 405/521–4910   E-mail—ann.trudgeon@okdhs.org

Administration   Mark Liotta, Chair; Ann Trudgeon, Director

Mission Statement   The mission of the Oklahoma Developmental Disabilities Council is to lead and advocate for systems change in the field of developmental disabilities, leverage collaborations and partnerships toward improved services and supports for Oklahomans with developmental disabilities, and promote positive perceptions and attitudes toward people with developmental disabilities.

Diabetes Center, Comprehensive (70 O.S. § 3318)

Oklahoma City: haroldhamm.org   Tulsa: tulsa.ou.edu/diabetes

Mission Statement   Authorized establishment of a diabetes center on the campus of the University of Oklahoma Health Sciences Center in Oklahoma City (Harold Hamm Diabetes Center), and a diabetes clinic at the OU Schusterman Center in Tulsa.

Disability Concerns, Office of (74 O.S. § 9.21)

Agency Code 326 (IA)   www.ok.gov/odc
2401 NW 23 Street, Suite 90, Oklahoma City 73107-2423
405/521-3756, 800/522-8224, FAX 405/522-6695

Mission Statement   To serve all Oklahomans with disabilities, meeting their concerns and needs.

Administration   R. Douglas MacMilan, Director; Dalene Barton, Office Manager; William Ginn, Client Assistance Program Director; Peppi Boudreau, Disability Program Specialist; Valencia Stiggers, Disability Program Specialist; Cathy Miller, Disability Program Specialist

Personnel   5 classified, 2 unclassified, merit

History and Function   The Office of Handicapped (Disability) Concerns was formed in 1980 as referenced in Title 74, Sections 9.21-9.35 of the Oklahoma Statutes. The purpose of the agency is to help state government develop policies and services that meet the needs of Oklahomans with disabilities. The agency is served by two advisory committees with separate functions. These committees are the Governor's Committee on Employment of People with Disabilities and the Governor's Advisory Committee to the Office of Disability Concerns. For a list of members, call 405/521-3756 or 800/522-8224.

Client Assistance Program
405/521-3756, FAX 405/522-6695, Toll Free 800/522-8224
Administration   William Ginn, Director
History and Function   Section 112 of the Rehabilitation Act of 1973, as amended. This program provides clients, client-applicants, and former clients with assistance in obtaining services under the Rehabilitation Act. As of 1973, as amended, CAP serves clients, client-applicants and former clients of Rehabilitative and Visual Services (RVS), federally funded centers and programs.

District Attorneys Council (19 O.S. § 215.28)

Agency Code 220 (IA)   www.ok.gov/dac
421 NW 13 Street, Suite 290, Oklahoma City 73103   405/264-5000, FAX 405/264-5099

Mission Statement   To strengthen the criminal justice system in Oklahoma by providing a professional organization for the education, training, and coordination of technical efforts of all state prosecutors.

Administration   Suzanne McClain Atwood, Executive Coordinator; Trent H. Baggett, Assistant Executive Coordinator, 405/264-5000, FAX 405/264-5099; Suzanne Breedlove, Victims Services Division, 405/264-5006, FAX 405/264-5097; DeLynn Fudge, Director, Federal Programs/ Grants Division, 405/264-5008, FAX 405/264-5095; Bud Webster, Director, Finance Division, 405/264-5004, FAX 405/264-5099; Robert Eubank, Director, IT Division, 405/264-5002, FAX 405/264-5099

Personnel   44 unclassified, non-merit

Drought Commission, Emergency (27A O.S. § 2251) Formed if needed.

Education, State Board of (Constitution, Article 13 § 5, 70 O.S. § 3-101)

Agency Code 265 (IA)
Oliver Hodge Building, 2500 N Lincoln Boulevard, Room 118, Oklahoma City 73105

405/521-3308, FAX 405/521-6205   E-mail—Janet.Barresi@sde.ok.gov

Administration   Janet Barresi, State Superintendent of Public Instruction and Chairperson of the State Board; Kalee Isenhour, Chief Executive Secretary

Education, State Department of (70 O.S. §1–105, 1–115)

Agency Code 265 (IA)   www.ok.gov/sde
Oliver Hodge Building, 2500 N Lincoln Boulevard, Oklahoma City 73105-4599
405/521-3301, FAX 405/521-6205

Mission Statement   To improve student success through services to schools, parents, and students; to provide leadership for education reform; and for the regulation/deregulation of state and federal laws to provide accountability while removing barriers to student success.

Administration   Janet Barresi, State Superintendent of Public Instruction; Joel Robinson, Chief of Staff, 405/521-4516; Liz Young, Executive Assistant to the Superintendent, 405/521-4885
Marsha Thompson, Assistant State Superintendent of Instruction, 405/522-3521
Kerri White, Assistant State Superintendent of Educator Effectiveness, 405/522-8618
Lisa Chandler, Assistant State Superintendent of Accountability and Assessments, 405/522-6250
Romona Coats, Assistant State Superintendent of Federal Programs, 405/522-0217
Rene Axtell, Assistant State Superintendent of Special Education, 405/521-4873
Colleen Flory, Assistant State Superintendent of Policy Implementation, 405/522-0717
Richard Caram, Assistant State Superintendent for School Turnaround, 405/522-0855
Phil Bacharach, Executive Director of Communications, 405/521-4894
Kim Richey, Legal, General Counsel, 405/521-4889
John Kraman, Executive Director of Student Information, 405/521-4892
Mathangi Shankar, Director of Financial Services, 405/522-0162
Lynn Jones, Executive Director of Accreditation, 405/521-3333

Personnel   284 unclassified

History and Function   Responsible for all phases of state public school education, the department is under the direction of the State Board of Education, consisting of seven members. The superintendent of public instruction is elected to a four-year term by the people, or appointed by the governor to fill an unexpired term, and serves as a voting member and chair of the board. The other six members are appointed by the governor, and confirmed by the Oklahoma Senate and serve staggered six-year terms. In addition to an Administrative Services section, the department has other divisions: Accreditation Services, Professional Services, School Improvement, Special Education Services, and Federal Fiscal and Financial Services. Within the divisions are various sectional functions such as child nutrition programs, teacher certification, school finance, school transportation, school accreditation, reading, student testing, gifted/talented, adult-community education, literacy, Indian education, and multicultural programs.

Military Children, Oklahoma State Council for Educational Opportunity for (70 O.S. § 510.2)

Teacher and Leader Effectiveness Commission
(70 O.S. § 6–101.17) Until July 1, 2016. Formerly Oklahoma Race to the Top Commission

Virtual Charter School Board, Statewide (70 O.S, § 3–145.1)
www.ok.gov/sde/statewide-virtual-charter-school-board

Educational Quality and Accountability, Office of
(70 O.S. § 3–117)

Agency Code 275 (IA)
840 Research Parkway, Suite 455, Oklahoma City 73104   405/522-5399, FAX 405/525-0373
www.SchoolReportCard.org   405/225-9470, FAX 405/225-9474
www.octp.org   405/525-2612, FAX 405/525-0373

Administration   Dr. Sherry Labyer, Executive Director

History and Function   Originally established as the Office of Accountability under the Education Oversight Board by HB 1017, the Education Reform Act of 1990, the Office of Educational Quality and Accountability became operational under its new name in July of 2013. It is governed by the Commission for Educational Quality and Accountability which is composed of seven members, all appointed by the Governor. The original charge to the office was to establish and administer the Oklahoma Educational Indicators Program, serving as a clearinghouse for statistical information from common education, career and technical education, higher education, and several other state agencies. The Educational Indicators Program provides comparative statistics for each of the 520 school districts and the nearly 1,800 schools in the state. Publications include a state report, a district report, and school report cards. An additional charge to the office was to establish and administer the Oklahoma School Performance Review Program, which comprehensively analyzes the performance of Oklahoma's public school districts in all areas of operation. he reviews are collaboratively conducted by OEQA staff and outside review teams on a district-by-district basis with the findings published in a detailed report presented to the local board of education at the conclusion of the review process. Effective July 1, 2014, the Oklahoma Commission for Teacher Preparation's programs and personnel became a part of the Office of Educational Quality and Accountability. The responsibility for ensuring quality teacher preparation will still continue under the guidelines established by the Oklahoma Legislature in House Bill 1549. This landmark educational reform legislation establishes that the office will approve and accredit new teacher education programs, review and assess existing teacher education programs, assess teacher candidates for licensure and certification and encourage studies and research designed to improve teacher education. The commission is committed to developing and sustaining a well-prepared professional teacher workforce ensuring that all Oklahoma students have the opportunity to be academically successful.

Educational Quality and Accountability Commission (70 O.S. § 3–116.2)

Educational Television Authority, Oklahoma (70 O.S. § 23–105)

Re-created until July 1, 2020

Agency Code 266 (IA)   www.oeta.tv
7403 N Kelley Avenue   PO Box 14190, Oklahoma City 73113
405/848-8501, 800/879-6382, FAX 405/841-9216, FAX News 405/841-9226,
TDD 405/841-9294 (Oklahoma City area); TDD 800/292-1397 (other Oklahoma areas).

Mission Statement   OETA's mission is to provide essential educational television content and multimedia services that inform, inspire, and connect Oklahomans to ideas and information that enrich our quality of life.

The intent of OETA is to assure that new educational technologies, both over the air and on-line, benefit all citizens of the state. This opens new opportunities for more educational content, improved local services, increased civic engagement, and more coverage of state government and innovative bandwidth management. With the right investment in equipment and personnel, the state of Oklahoma will be able to provide instant, statewide, essential two-way communication for emergencies/public safety, training and citizen involvement via OETA's broadcast spectrum and ancillary bandwidth.

Administration   Dan Schiedel, Executive Director; Ashley Barcum, Director of Communications; Holly Emig, Director of Programming; Richard Ladd, Director of Engineering; Janette Thornbrue, Operations Manager; Mark Norman, Deputy Director, Technology; and Toni Matthews, Deputy Director, Finance and Administration

Personnel   56 unclassified, non-merit

History and Function   A statutory corporation created by law in 1953, OETA makes instructional and public television services available to all citizens of Oklahoma on a coordinated statewide basis. Four transmitters, located at Channel 13 in Oklahoma City, Channel 11 in Tulsa, Channel 3 in Eufaula, and Channel 12 in Cheyenne, with fourteen translators located statewide, extend OETA's services throughout Oklahoma. OETA has offices and production studios in both Oklahoma City and Tulsa.

Documentary Program Unit (Laws 1998, c. 280§23)

Election Board, State (26 O.S. § 2–101)

Agency Code 270 (IA)
State Capitol, Room B–6
405/521–2391, FAX 405/521–6457, TDD 405/521–3028

www.elections.ok.gov
PO Box 53156, Oklahoma City 73152
E-mail—info@elections.ok.gov

Mission Statement   To achieve and maintain uniformity in the application, operation, and interpretation of the state and federal election laws with a maximum degree of correctness, impartiality, and efficiency.

Administration   Paul Ziriax, Secretary; Fran Roach, Assistant Secretary; Jay Smith, Information Services; Suzanne Cox, Support Services; Pam Slater, Ballot Generation Services

Personnel   14 classified, 5 unclassified

History and Function   Established under the Oklahoma Constitution in 1907, the board functions under the laws enacted by the Oklahoma Legislature as the administrative agency for the conduct of state elections, and the conduct of county election boards. Specific functions are: accepts filings for all state, judicial, district attorney, U.S. Senate and congressional offices; prints and distributes state and federal ballots to each county along with other election supplies; promulgates rules and regulations for the conduct and administration of elections. Board members are appointed to four year terms by the governor, with the advice and consent of the Oklahoma Senate, from a list of ten nominees recommended by the Democratic State Committee, and a list of ten nominees recommended by the Republican State Committee. The secretary of the Senate serves as secretary of the board.

Emergency Management, Oklahoma Department of (63 O.S. § 683.4)

Agency Code 309 (IA)
PO Box 53365, Oklahoma City 73152   (Duty officer on 24-hour call) 405/521–2481, FAX 405/521–4053
E-mail—albert.ashwood@oem.ok.gov

www.ok.gov/oem

Mission Statement   To minimize the effects of attack, technological and natural disasters upon the people of Oklahoma by preparing and exercising preparedness plans, assisting local government sub-divisions with training for and mitigation of disasters, and by coordinating actual disaster response/recovery operations.

Administration   Albert Ashwood, Director; Michelann Ooten, Deputy Director; Keli Cain, Public Information Officer

Personnel   12 classified, 16 unclassified, merit

History and Function   Created by the Oklahoma Legislature in 1951, later laws combined the responsibilities of the Department of Emergency Resources Management with the Department of Civil Defense. The department now implements programs designed to minimize the effects of national and natural disaster upon the people of Oklahoma.

Employment Security Commission, Oklahoma (40 O.S. § 4–102)

Agency Code 290 (IA)
Will Rogers Memorial Office Building, 2401 N Lincoln Boulevard, Oklahoma City 73105
405/557–7100, Local Offices Toll Free 888/980–9675, TDD 405/557–7531
E-mail—webmaster@oesc.state.ok.us

www.oesc.ok.gov

Mission Statement   To enhance Oklahoma's economy by providing unemployment compensation to support unemployed workers and their communities, matching jobs and workers to increase the efficiency of local labor markets, referring workers to training opportunities to enhance and align their skills to meet local labor market needs, and gathering, analyzing, and disseminating information about the labor force to improve local economic decisions.

Administration   Richard McPherson, Executive Director; Teresa Keller, Deputy Director;

Personnel   692 classified, 88 temporary

History and Function   Created by the Oklahoma Legislature in 1941, the Oklahoma Employment Security Commission (OESC) governs the operation of local workforce centers. These centers provide testing, career counseling, and placement services; solicit job orders from employers; refer job seekers; provide an online job bank; and provide special services for veterans and disabled veterans including job development, counseling, and placement. OESC also collects unemployment insurance taxes from employers to fund unemployment benefits to jobless workers. Unemployment insurance claims are filed online and through call centers. The OESC, in cooperation with the Bureau of Labor Statistics (BLS), manages research programs that provide current labor market information to employers, job seekers, employment and guidance counselors, and students to assist them in making informed decisions. The agency is part of a national network of employment service agencies receiving funding (OESC is funded solely with monies issued by the U.S. Department of Labor) from the federal government and is governed by a five-member commission appointed by the governor with consent of the Oklahoma Senate.

Board of Review (40 O.S. § 4–202)
Employment Security Commission
3815 N Santa Fe, #10, Oklahoma City 73118

Employment Service, Local Offices
City (Office Number)—Counties Served

Ada (62)—Garvin, Pontotoc
   580/332-1533, FAX 580/421-9265
   1628 E Beverly Street, Suite 115
   (PO Box 850, 74820)

Altus (33)—Greer, Harmon, Jackson, Kiowa
   580/482-3262, FAX 580/482-3284
   1115 N Spurgeon Street, 73521
   (PO Box 551, 73522)

Ardmore (10) Carter, Love, Murray
   580/223-32910, FAX 580/226-2730
   2421 Autumn Run, Suite B, 73401
   (PO Box 1457, 73402)

Bartlesville (74)—Nowata, Osage, Washington
   918/331-3400, FAX 918/331-0044
   6101 SE Nowata Road, Suite C100 74006
   (PO Box 4039, 74006-4039)

Chickasha (26) Grady, McClain, Caddo
   405/224-3310, FAX 405/222-1215
   301 S 2 Street, 73108
   (PO Box 398, 73023)

Claremore (66)—Rogers
   918/341-6633, FAX 918/341-7723
   1810 N Sioux, 74018   (PO Box 908, 74017)

Clinton (20)—
   Beckham, Custer, Roger Mills, Washita
   580/323-1341, FAX 580/323-9176
   1120 Frisco Avenue (PO Box 605, 73601)

Duncan (69)—Jefferson, Stephens
   580/255-8950
   FAX 580/255-8959
   1927 W Elk Avenue, 73533
   (PO Box 750070, 73575)

Durant (07)—
   Atoka, Bryan, Coal, Johnston, Marshall
   580/924-1828, FAX 580/920-2464
   4310 W Highway 70, 74701
   (PO Box 1000, 74702)

Enid (24)—Alfalfa, Blaine, Garfield,
   Grant, Kingfisher, Major
   580/234-6043, FAX 580/234-8405
   900 W Cherokee, 73701 (PO Box 1269, 73702)

Guymon (70)—Beaver, Cimarron, Texas
   580/338-8521, FAX 580/468-1814
   225 E Highway 5
   (PO Box 929, 73942)

Holdenville (32)—Hughes, Okfuskee
   405/379-5452, FAX 405/379-6355
   115 N Rogers Drive (PO Box 937, 74848)

Hugo (2)—McCurtain
   580/286-2303, FAX 580/326-0958
   107 S 3 Street, 74743

Idabel (45)—Choctaw, McCurtain, Pushmataha
   580/286-6667, FAX 580/286-7867
   2202 SE Washington
   (PO Box 1197, 74545)

Lawton (16)—Comanche, Cotton, Tillman
   580/357-3500, FAX 580/357-9629
   1711 SW 11 Street
   (PO Box 989, 73502)

McAlester (61)—
   Haskell, Latimer, Pittsburg
   918/423-6830, FAX 918/429-1175
   1414 E Wade Watts Avenue, 74501
   (PO Box 1108, 74502)

Miami (58)—Craig, Ottawa
918/542-5561
FAX 918/542-7505
121 N Main, 74354
(PO Box 670, 74355)

Muskogee (51)—
McIntosh, Muskogee, Wagoner
918/682-3364, FAX 918/682-4311
717 S 32 Street, 74401 (PO Box 1688, 74402)

Norman (5514)—Cleveland
405/701-2000
FAX 405/701-2042
1141 E Main, 73071

Oklahoma City (5503)
South Canadian, Cleveland, Oklahoma
405/639-3640, FAX 405/639-3682
416 Hudiburg Circle, 73108

Oklahoma City (5509) East—
Canadian, Logan, Oklahoma
405/713-1890, FAX 405/713-1898
7401 NE 23 Street, 73141

Oklahoma City (5520) Reno—
Canadian, Logan, Oklahoma
405/470-3200, FAX 405/470-3223
12777 N Rockwell, 73142

Okmulgee (56)—Okmulgee
918/756-5791, FAX 918/756-0937
1801 E 4 Street, 74447
(PO Box 2218, 74447)

Ponca City (36)—Kay, Noble, Osage
580/765-3372, FAX 580/765-6145
1201 W Grand Ave., 74601
(PO Box 309, 74602)

Poteau (40)—LeFlore
918/647-3124, FAX 918/647-8939
106 Rogers Avenue
(PO Box 9, 74953)

Pryor (49)—Delaware, Mayes
918/825-2582, FAX 918/825-6494
219 NE 1 (PO Box 427, 74362)

Sallisaw (5)—Sequoyah
918/775-5541, FAX 918/775-6385
401 W Houser, 74955

Sand Springs (6)—Tulsa, Creek, Pawnee
918/245-9544
FAX 918/245-9566
401 E Broadway, Suite B1, 74063

Sapulpa (19)—Creek
918/224-9430, FAX 918/227-2859
1700 S Main Street, 73533
(PO Box, 1403, 74066)

Seminole (67)—Seminole
405/382-4670, FAX 405/382-0104
229 N 2 Street, 74868
(PO Box 910, 74818)

Shawnee (63)—Lincoln, Pottawatomie
405/275-7800
FAX 405/878-9742
2 John C. Bruton Blvd., 74804

Stilwell (7)—Adair
918/696-6608
FAX 918/696-5983
219 W Oak, 74960

Stillwater (60)—Payne
405/624-1450, FAX 405/372-0295
3006 E 6 Street, 74074
(PO Box 1987, 74076)

Tulsa—Eastgate (7207)—
Osage, Pawnee, Tulsa
918/796-1200, FAX 918/796-1313
14002 E 21 Street, Suite 1030, 74134

Tulsa Skyline (7209)—
Osage, Pawnee, Tulsa
918/384-2300, FAX 918/384-2310
6128 E 38 Street, Suite 405, 74135

Tahlequah (1116)—
Cherokee, Adair, Sequoyah
918/456-8846, FAX 918/456-3256
1755 S Muskogee, 74464
(PO Box 689, 74465)

Woodward (77)—
Dewey, Ellis, Harper, Woods, Woodward
580/256-3308, FAX 580/254-3093
1117 11 Street
(PO Box 608, 73801)

Energy and Environment, Secretary of (27A O.S. § 1–2–101)

3800 Classen Boulevard, Oklahoma City 73118
405/530-8995, FAX 405/530-8999

www.environment.ok.gov

Mission Statement   To protect and enhance Oklahoma's environment and natural resources through preservation, conservation, restoration, education, and enforcement in order to maintain and improve the environmental quality and natural beauty of our state and better the standard of living for all Oklahomans.

Administration   Colonel Michael Teague, Secretary of Energy and Environment;
Tyler Powell, Director

History and Function   The Office of the Secretary of Environment (OSE) was created, in response to Laws 1999, c.413 § 3 by the Oklahoma Legislature, to coordinate pollution control activities of the state, disburse Clean Water Act monies to Oklahoma agencies with environmental jurisdiction, and other duties as deemed appropriate by the governor. OSE serves as liaison between Oklahoma's environmental agencies, the U.S. Environmental Protection Agency, and the Office of the Governor.

Energy Initiative Board, Oklahoma (17 O.S. § 802.3)

Energy Resources Board, Oklahoma
(52 O.S. § 288.3) Re-created until July 1, 2017

Agency Code 359 (IA)   www.oerb.com
500 NE 4 Street, Suite 100, Oklahoma City 73104   405/942–5323, 800/664–1301, FAX 405/942–3435

Mission Statement   To educate Oklahomans about the importance of petroleum (oil and natural gas) in their lives through traditional and non-traditional school curriculum, advertising, and public relations; to environmentally restore abandoned well sites to productive land use; to promote environmentally sound production methods and technologies; and to research and provide educational activities concerning the petroleum exploration and production industry.

Administration   Mindy Stitt, Executive Director

History and Function   Created by the Oklahoma Legislature in 1993, the OERB is a privatized state agency funded through a voluntary one-tenth of one percent assessment on oil and natural gas, also known as the "Oklahoma Oil Check-Off." The assessment, paid for by oil and natural gas companies and royalty owners, is refundable annually between January 1 and March 31 for any contributor who does not wish to participate in the program.

OERB provides hands-on energy-related curricula for grades K–12. The OERB created "Little Bits" and "Fossils to Fuel" and "Fossils to Fuel 2" for elementary students, "Petro Active" for middle school students, and "Core Energy" for high school students. Other student education programs include "Petroleum Professionals in the Classroom" (Petro Pros), in which industry volunteers give energy presentations in classrooms across the state, and a petroleum scholar program for students pursuing careers in the oil and natural gas industry. The agency produces television and newspaper advertisements, and maintains a public relations campaign to help Oklahomans better understand the petroleum industry. The OERB has restored more than 13,000 abandoned and orphaned oil and natural gas exploration and production sites to productive use since 1994.

Energy Resources, Committee for Sustaining Oklahoma's (52 O.S. § 288.5A)

Engineers and Land Surveyors,
State Board of Licensure for Professional (59 O.S. § 475.1; 74 O.S. § 3905)

Agency Code 570 (IA)   www.pels.ok.gov
220 NE 28 Street, Room 120, Oklahoma City 73105
405/521–2874, FAX 405/523–2135   E-mail—Khart@pels.ok.gov

Mission Statement   Charged with the responsibility for safeguarding life, health, and property as affected by the practice of professional engineering and land surveying. To facilitate the prosecution of persons found in violation of established rules. Re-created until July 1, 2020.

Administration   Kathy Hart, Executive Director; Bill Dickerson, Principal Assistant

Personnel   4 classified, 5 unclassified, merit

Environmental Quality, Department of (27A O.S. § 2–3–101)

Board (27A O. § 2–2–101)

Agency Code 292 (IA)
707 N Robinson, Oklahoma City
405/702–7100, FAX 405/702–7101

www.deq.state.ok.us
PO Box 1677, Oklahoma City 73101–1677

Administration   Scott Thompson, Executive Director
Jimmy Givens, Deputy Executive Director
Air Quality Division, Eddie Terrill, 405/702–4100
Environmental Complaints/Local Services, Gary Collins, 405/702–6100
External Affairs Division, Lloyd Kirk, 405/702–710
General Counsel, Martha Penisten, 405/702–7184
State Environmental Laboratory Services, Chris Armstrong, 405/702–1000
Administrative Services, 405/702–0100
Land Protection Division, Kelly Dixon, 405/702–5100
Water Quality Division, Shellie Chard-McClary, 405/702–8100

Mission Statement   The mission of the Oklahoma Department of Environmental Quality is to enhance the quality of life in Oklahoma and protect the health of its citizens by protecting, preserving, and restoring the water, land, and air of the state. Thus, fostering a clean, attractive, healthy, prosperous, and sustainable environment.

Personnel   457 classified, 36 unclassified, 43 temporary, merit

Environmental Quality Board (27A O.S. § 2–2–101)   **Administration**   Scott Thompson 405/702–7100

Oklahoma Hazardous Materials Emergency Response Commission (27A O.S. 4–2–102)
This commission is jointly administered by the Department of Environmental Quality and the Department of Civil Emergency Management.

Air Quality Advisory Council (27A O.S. § 2–2–201(H))   **Administration**   Eddie Terrill 405/702–4100

Hazardous Waste Management Advisory Council (27A O.S. § 2–2–201(D))   **Administration**   Kelly Dixon 405/702–5100

Radiation Management Advisory Council (27A O.S. § 2–2–201(F))   **Administration**   Kelly Dixon 405/702–5100

Small Business Compliance Advisory Panel (42 U.S.C. 7661f(e) 27A O.S. § 2–5–115(c))   **Administration**   Lloyd Kirk 405/702–7100

Solid Waste Management Advisory Council (27A O.S. § 2–2–201(E))   **Administration**   Kelly Dixon 405/702–5100

Water Quality Management Advisory Council (27A O.S. § 2–2–201(C))   **Administration**   Shellie Chard-McClary 405/702–8100

Equalization, State Board of (Constitution, Article 10 § 21, 68 O.S. § 2864)

State Auditor and Inspector
2300 N Lincoln Boulevard, Room 100, Oklahoma City 73105
E-mail—ngrantham@sai.ok.gov

Agency Code 295 (IA)
405/521–3495, FAX 405/522–4306

Administration   Gary Jones CPA, State Auditor and Inspector, Secretary;
Nancy Grantham, Administrative Assistant

History and Function   The board consists of six elected officials and the president of the State Board of Agriculture, now an appointive office. The governor serves as chairman, with the state auditor and inspector serving as secretary. The board's functions are to adjust and equalize the valuation of real and personal property of the seventy-seven counties; assess all railroad, air carrier, and public service corporation properties; perform such other duties as may be prescribed by the Oklahoma Legislature; and provide an estimate of revenue that will be available for appropriation by the legislature.

Ethics Commission (Constitution, Article 29 § 1)

Agency Code 296 (IA)   www.ethics.ok.gov
2300 N Lincoln Boulevard, Room B-5, Oklahoma City 73105-4812   405/521-3451, FAX 405/521-4905

Mission Statement   To promulgate rules of ethical conduct for campaigns for state office and for campaigns for initiative and referenda; to promulgate rules of ethical conduct for state officers and employees; to investigate, settle or prosecute in the district court violations of its rules and to make binding interpretations of its rules.

Administration   Lee Slater, Executive Director; Ashley Kemp, Deputy Director

Personnel   6 unclassified, non-merit

History and Function   Created in 1990, by a vote of the people under Article 29 of the Oklahoma Constitution, the Ethics Commission promulgates rules of ethical conduct for campaigns for elective state office and for campaigns for initiative and referenda, including civil penalties for violation of these rules; promulgates rules of ethical conduct for state officers and employees, including civil penalties for violation of these rules; investigates and, when deemed appropriate, settles investigations or prosecutes in the district court of the county where the violation occurred and responds to questions of specific individuals seeking interpretation of the commission's rules governing ethics conduct for campaigns, state officers, or state employees.

Film and Music Office, Oklahoma

120 N Robinson, Suite 600, Oklahoma City 73102   www.ok.gov/oklahomafilm
405/230-8440, 800/766-3456   FAX 405/230-8641

Mission Statement   Created in 1979, the Oklahoma Film and Music Office attracts film, television, video, and music industries to Oklahoma for the promotion and growth of these industries within the state. The office strives to share all that Oklahoma has to offer by welcoming filmmakers to the state. The office can save filmmakers time and money when arranging a production. Within Oklahoma exists a very strong and enthusiastic network of contacts capable and ready to meet daily production needs.

Administration   Tava Maloy Sofsky, Director

Fire Marshal Commission, State (59 O.S. § 1820.6)

Agency Code 310 (IA)   www.ok.gov/fire
2401 NW 23 Street, Suite 4, Oklahoma City 73107   405/522-5005, FAX 405/522-5028
Arson Hot line—800/522-8666

Mission Statement   The Office of the Oklahoma State Fire Marshal is a state law enforcement agency charged with the task of preservation of life and property through enforcement of criminal statutes and mandated fire prevention/life safety codes. The agency will be guided by the following principles: a commitment to provide leadership in the fire service through effective communication with the Oklahoma Legislature, public officials, and citizens; a commitment to provide continual public relations and education; a commitment to interact positively with law enforcement, government agencies, and other interested professional entities; and a commitment to the improvement and the financial stability of the Office of the Oklahoma State Fire Marshal in order to provide more efficient service to the citizens of Oklahoma.

Administration   Robert Doke, State Fire Marshal; Luke Tallant, Assistant Fire Marshal

Personnel   24 classified, 4 unclassified, merit

History and Function   The State Fire Marshal's Office was originally established in 1910, but then abolished in 1957. Recognizing the need for a state fire marshal, the Oklahoma fire service voiced concerns and the office was re-established in 1965. Prior to this, fires were investigated by agents with the Oklahoma State Bureau of Investigation (OSBI) and code enforcement/plan review regulations were conducted only in cities having an established code enforcement office. In 1965 the Oklahoma Legislature established the Office of the Oklahoma State Fire Marshal and a five-member commission was appointed to oversee the agency's operations, including the hiring of the state fire marshal. The agency began its operations with the state fire marshal and only three agents. They were given statewide jurisdiction and responsibility for conducting fire investigations and building inspections. In 1970 the plans review unit of the code enforcement division of the agency was formed. Today, the agency has three divisions: Administration and Public Education, Fire Investigations, and Code Enforcement. It has approximately thirty employees with an annual appropriated budget of approximately $2.2 million. All agents are sworn peace officers. Field agents are located throughout the state and office from their homes.

Firefighter Training, Oklahoma Council on (74 O.S. § 325.1)

2716 NE 50 Street, Oklahoma City 73111   E-mail—contact@coft-oklahoma.org
405/601-8862, FAX 405/601-7996

Administration—Jon Hansen, Executive Director

Firefighters Pension and Retirement System, Oklahoma
(11 O.S. § 49–100.2 **Board** (11 O.S. § 49–100.3)

Agency Code 315 (IA)   4545 N Lincoln Boulevard, Suite 265, Oklahoma City 73105–3414
405/522–4600, 800/525–7461, FAX 405/522–4643   www.ok.gov/fprs

Mission Statement To be responsive in administering retirement benefits to firefighters of Oklahoma; to manage the firefighters' retirement funds prudently; and to embrace the highest ethical standards with regard to these endeavors.

Administration Robert E. Jones Jr., Director

Personnel 10 unclassified, 1 temporary, non-merit

History and Function Governor Charles N. Haskell signed into law the first fireman's pension benefit statute May 14, 1908. The new law contained a 1 percent tax on insurance premiums to fund the pension benefits for both paid and volunteer firefighters. Oklahoma cities and towns administered the program until the Oklahoma Legislature created the current Oklahoma Firefighters Pension and Retirement System in 1980. The Oklahoma Firefighters Pension and Retirement System was created to better fund the total system and administer the system equally. The agency is vested with the power and duties specified by statutes and such other powers as may be necessary to enable it and its officers and employees to carry out fully and effectively the intent of the law to provide pension benefits to all participating firefighters in Oklahoma.

Food Service Advisory Council, Oklahoma (63 O.S. § 1–106.3)

State Department of Health (IA)   www.health.ok.gov
1000 NE 10 Street, Oklahoma City 73117–1299   Board of Health 405/271–4200
405/271–5243, FAX 405/271–3458

Mission Statement The purpose of the advisory council shall be to advise the State Board of Health, the State Commissioner of Health, and the department regarding food service establishments. The council will recommend actions to improve sanitation, consumer protection, and have the duty and authority to review and approve in an advisory capacity the rules and standards for food service establishments operating in this state. The council evaluates, reviews, and makes recommendations regarding department inspection activities, and approves quality indicators, and data submission requirements for food service establishments. The department monitors compliance with licensure requirements and publishes an annual report of food service establishment performances.

Administration Bill Ricks, Chair, Independent Food Service Operator with W. H. Braums Inc.

Forensic Center, Oklahoma

Agency Code 452 (IA)

PO Box 69, Vinita 74301   24800 E 4420 Road, Vinita 74301
918/256–7841, FAX 918/256–4491

Administration   Lori Jordan, MBA, Executive Director; Satwant Tandon, MD, Clinical Director; Samina Christopher, PhD, Director of Forensic Psychology; Steve Willy, LSW, MSW, Director of Patient Services; Glenda Satterwhite, RN, Director of Nursing; Darrell Praytor, Director of Information Technology; Julie Jacobs, Human Resources Manager; Miriam Harris, Director of Operating Services.

History and Function   Formerly Eastern State Hospital, the Oklahoma Forensic Center (OFC), an inpatient forensic facility within the Oklahoma Department of Mental Health and Substance Abuse Services (ODMHSAS), conducts outpatient evaluations of adjudicative competency, as well as competency restoration treatment services to all persons deemed incompetent to stand trial (due to mental illness) by district courts in Oklahoma counties. OFC also provides mental health treatment and evaluation for all persons deemed "not guilty by reason of insanity," by district courts in Oklahoma counties. OFC provides training to ODMHSAS forensic evaluators and professionals from other state agencies across Oklahoma and authors the Oklahoma Forensic Mental Health Services Manual.

Forensic Review Board (22 O.S. § 1161)

Members   Verna Foust, Chair; Rand Baker, member; Edward C. Cunningham, Member; Richard Hartman, MD, Member; David Tiller, MD, Member; Cliff Thomas, PhD, Member; Mike Segler, JD, Member.

History and Function   The Forensic Review Board is composed of seven (7) members appointed by the governor with the advice and consent of the Oklahoma Senate. The Board meets quarterly to review and determine which individuals adjudicated "not guilty by reason of insanity" and confined with the Department of Mental Health and Substance Abuse Services are eligible for therapeutic visits, conditional release or discharge, and whether the Board wishes to make such a recommendation to the court of the county where the individual was found "not guilty by reason of insanity."

Foresters, State Board of Registration for Registered

(59 O.S. § 1201) Advisory Board to the State Department of Agriculture, Food, & Forestry

Agency Code 040 (IA)
2800 N Lincoln Boulevard, Oklahoma City 73105–4298   405/522–6147, FAX 405/522–4583

Mission Statement   To protect the public from irresponsible disregard for the conservation of the state's forests by licensing individuals qualified to be foresters by reason of education or experience in the practice of forestry.

Administration   Kurtis L. Atkinson, Secretary; Ed Miller, Chair

History and Function   Appointed by the State Board of Agriculture, board members must have ten years experience in forestry or related industries. Their principal duty is to register and license foresters for the benefit and protection of the public.

Funeral Board, Oklahoma (59 O.S. § 396; 74 O.S. § 3905)

Agency Code 285 (IA)   www.ok.gov/funeral
3700 N Classen, Suite 175, Oklahoma City 73118   405/522–1790, FAX 405/522–1797
E-mail—info@okfuneral.com

Mission Statement   The mission of the Oklahoma Funeral Board is to act in the public interest, and for the public protection and advancement of the profession within the police powers vested in the board by the Oklahoma Legislature, entirely without appropriated funds. The board shall serve as a resource on funeral service to the general public and members of the funeral profession.

Administration   Chris Ferguson, Agency Director; Jenna Barry, Deputy Director

History and Function   Originally established in 1905 by the Legislative Assembly of the Territory of Oklahoma. The board is made up of seven members appointed by the governor. The agency provides regulatory oversight for funeral establishments, commercial embalming establishments, crematories, funeral directors, embalmers, apprentices, burial associations, and burial agents. It is self-sustaining by fee collection. Recreated until July 1, 2020.

Geographic Information, State Office of (82 O.S. § 1501–205.3)

Oklahoma Conservation Commission (IA)
4545 N Lincoln Boulevard, Suite 11A, Oklahoma City 73105   405/521-2384, FAX 405/522-6686

Administration   Mike Sharp, State Geographic Information Coordinator, mike.sharp@conservation.ok.gov

Mission   To provide geographic information services to governments, academia, industry, and the public. The office supports the State Geographic Information Council, coordinates and promotes geographic information awareness, activities, data and training, and develops standards, policies, and operating procedures. In addition, it maintains a centralized statewide clearinghouse of accurate and timely data, facilitates data development, sharing, and access as well as fosters the values and benefits of geographic information system technology to ensure good stewardship of the state's resources.

History and Function   Created by HB 2457 in 2004, and administratively housed in the Oklahoma Conservation Commission.

Geographic Information Council, State

(82 O.S. § 1501–205.1; 82 O.S. § 1501–205-3)

Oklahoma Conservation Commission (IA)
2800 N Lincoln Boulevard, Suite 169, Oklahoma City 73105   405/521-2384, FAX 405/521-6686

Administration   The commission serves as chair of the council. The nineteen member council consists of state agencies, universities, and representatives from local, county, and regional governments. The council generally meets on a monthly basis to share information about developing technology and applications in the geographic information field. Contact— mike.sharp@conservation.ok.gov

Duties and Function   Overseeing the Office of Geographic Information concerning the development, adoption, and recommendation of standards and procedures that may be applied to geographic information and geographic information systems to promote consistency of data elements and the promotion of collaboration and sharing of geographic data and data development.

Geographic Names, Oklahoma Board on (70 O.S. § 3310)

Oklahoma Geological Survey   405/325-3031, FAX 405/325-7069
Sarkeys Energy Center, 100 E Boyd Street, Room N-131, Norman 73019-0628

Administration   G. Randy Keller, Director, Oklahoma Geological Survey; Ken Luza, Chairman, Board on Geographic Names

History and Function   Created in Laws 1965, c.396 § 310, the responsibility to "Act as Oklahoma Board on Geographic Names" was designated to the Oklahoma Geological Survey. The board has the responsibility to cooperate with local, state, and federal agencies to establish, change, and determine the appropriate names of geographic features in Oklahoma. Decisions of the board are forwarded as recommendations to the United States Board on Geographic Names. The Oklahoma Board is a member of the Council of Geographic Name Authorities, a national association of state name authorities that promotes standardization of procedures, cooperation among all agencies, and the sharing of geographic-name information.

Geological Survey, Oklahoma

(Constitution, Article 5 § 38, 70 O.S. § 3310, 74 O.S. § 231)

Agency Code 325   www.ogs.ou.edu

Sarkeys Energy Center, 100 E Boyd, Room N-131, Norman 73019-0628
405/325-3031, FAX 405/325-7069

Administration   Dr. G. Randy Keller, Director; E-mail—grkeller@ou.edu

History and Function   In 1908, in accordance with the Oklahoma Constitution, the First Legislature created the Oklahoma Geological Survey. It is now supervised by the University of Oklahoma Board of Regents and charged with the responsibility of collecting and disseminating information about the geology, mineral, energy, and water resources of the state.

The Oklahoma Geological Survey (OGS) studies the state's geology including hydrocarbon and mineral resources, and makes this information available through publications and workshops. The OGS also examines non-fuel minerals, coal and coal bed methane resources, earthquakes in Oklahoma and throughout the world, natural hazards, and other geological issues concerning the state.

The survey conducts a number of mapping programs in Oklahoma, maintains a web site, and presents programs for teachers, scouting groups, rock hound clubs, and other educational and civic organizations. These research and public service programs are conducted from main offices on the Norman campus of the University of Oklahoma. In addition, the OGS maintains a geophysical observatory near Tulsa, and a map and publication sales office at the Oklahoma Petroleum Information Center (OPIC) in Norman (2020 Industrial Boulevard). The OPIC maintains an extensive collection of petroleum information. The data includes cores, samples, well logs, scout tickets, completion reports, and related data on petroleum activity in Oklahoma. Some petroleum data are available for other states.

Grand River Dam Authority (82 O.S. § 861)

Agency Code 980
226 W Dwain Willis Avenue   www.grda.com
PO Box 409, Vinita 74301-0409   918/256-5545, FAX 918/256-5289

Administration   Dan Sullivan, Chief Executive Officer/Director of Investments; Tim Brown, Chief Operating Officer; Ellen Edwards, General Counsel; Charles Barney, Assistant General Manager/Thermal & Hydro Generation; Carolyn Dougherty, Chief Financial Officer/Treasurer; Mike Herron, Assistant General Manger/Engineering, System Operations, and Reliability; Dale Willis, Assistant General Manager/Transmission; Dr. Darrell Townsend, Assistant General Manager/Ecosystems & Lake Management; Allison Carter, Superintendent of Human Resources; Brian Edwards, Assistant General Manager/Chief of Law Enforcement and Lake Operations; Justin Alberty, Corporate Communications Director

Personnel   390 classified, 60 unclassified, 11 temporary

History and Function   The Grand River Dam Authority was created by the Fifteenth Oklahoma Legislature in 1935 to serve as a conservation and reclamation district for the waters of the Grand River. The Grand River Dam Authority Act (SB 395) established GRDA as a state agency and authorized it to build dams on the Grand River for the purposes of hydroelectric production, recreation, and flood control. Development of natural resources for Oklahoma were also responsibilities included in the act. The powers and functions of GRDA are exercised by a seven-member board of directors.

Dams   The Pensacola Dam hydroelectric project was completed in 1940. At 5,680 feet in length, it is one of the longest multiple-arch dams in the world. Pensacola Dam creates Grand Lake O' the Cherokees (Grand Lake) with 46,500 surface acres, a 1,300-mile shoreline, and a 66-mile channel. Six Francis-type hydroelectric turbines at Pensacola Dam's powerhouse have a total capacity of 112,000 kW. Pensacola Dam impounds 1,672,000 acre-feet of water and has a floodwater storage capacity of 540,000 acre-feet.

In 1964, GRDA completed construction on the Markham Ferry project. Also known as the Robert S. Kerr Dam, the project created Lake Hudson. This 12,000-surface-acre lake has a 200-mile shoreline and contains thirty channel miles of the Grand River in a fairly constant lake level, maintained the year round. Four Kaplan-type hydroelectric turbines at the Kerr Dam powerhouse have a total capacity of 114,000 kW, and an average water year can provide 211,000,000 kWh.

The Salina Pumped Storage Project was planned to be developed in four stages, 130,000 kW each. Two stages have been completed, the first in 1968 and the second in 1971. These two stages combine for a total capacity of 260,000 kW. The project is used for storing energy in the form of water pumped from Lake Hudson to the west.

W.R. Holway Reservoir was formed by an earthen dam, which stretches 2,300 feet across the Chimney Rock Hollow southeast of Salina. The Salina Pumped Storage Project also supplies energy during peak loads and supplies emergency power to the system.

In 1976, the Oklahoma Legislature authorized bonds to be issued to construct a 490,000 kW coal-fired power generating unit (GRDA 1). Construction was begun in 1978 and completed in 1981 when the legislature authorized bonds to be issued to construct a second coal-fired generating station (GRDA 2) near Chouteau, adjacent to GRDA 1. GRDA 2 is jointly owned by the authority (62%) and KAMO Power, Inc., an electric cooperative (38%). The unit is rated at 520,000 kW. Construction began on GRDA 2 in 1981 and was completed in March 1986. The two facilities comprise the Coal-Fired Generating Complex (CFC).

In 2008 GRDA purchased 36 percent interest in the Redbud Gas Plant near Luther, Oklahoma. This further diversified the organization's generation portfolio, adding natural gas to a beneficial mixture that already included hydroelectric and coal fire generation.

In addition to these projects, GRDA operates and maintains an integrated electric transmission system including approximately 2,090 miles of line and related switching stations and transformer substations.

Hazard Mitigation Team, State (63 O.S. § 683.6)

Oklahoma Department of Emergency Management (IA)
Tunnel, Will Rogers-Sequoyah Buildings
Duty officer on 24-hour call

PO Box 53365, Oklahoma City 73152
405/521-2481, FAX 405/521-4053

Health, State Department of

(63 O.S. § 1–105)   **Board** (Constitution, Article 5 § 39, 63 O.S. § 1–103)

Agency Code 340 (IA)
1000 NE 10 Street, Oklahoma City 73117-1299
405/271-5600, 800/522-0203, FAX 405/271-3431
AIDS/HIV Hot line 800/535-AIDS
Home Health Care Hot line 800/234-7258
Nurse Aide Registry 800/695-2157

www.health.ok.gov
Board of Health 405/271-8097

Birth Certificates 405/271-4040
Newborn Hearing Screening 800/766-2223
Women, Infants, and Children (WIC) 888/OKLAWIC

Mission Statement   To protect and promote health, to prevent disease and injury, and to cultivate conditions by which Oklahomans can be healthy.

Administration   Terry L. Cline, PhD, Commissioner; Julie Cox-Kain, Senior Deputy Commissioner; Janice Hiner, Senior Advisor; Mark Newman, Director of State & Federal Policy; Steve Ronck, Deputy Commissioner Community & Family Health Services; Henry Hartsell, Deputy Commissioner Protective Health Services; Toni Frioux, Deputy Commissioner, Prevention & Preparedness Services; VaLauna Grissom, Secretary to the Board of Health; Vacant, Director, Office of Communications

Personnel   1522 classified, 522 unclassified, 138 temporary, merit

History and Function   For more than one hundred years—first as the Territorial Board of Health, then following statehood, as the Oklahoma State Department of Health—the people of Oklahoma have entrusted the Oklahoma State Department of Health to be this state's prudent steward of public health.

Public health service in Oklahoma was signed into law Christmas Day, 1890, by Governor George Washington Steele, who immediately appointed a superintendent of health. After statehood in 1907, the Oklahoma Legislature created the State Board of Health under a commissioner appointed by the governor. In 1917 the legislature placed control of all public water supplies and sewer systems under the Board of Health.

Today, the Board of Health has nine members appointed by the governor with Senate confirmation. The board appoints the commissioner of health, chief administrative officer, who coordinates activities of the agency with the federal government and other agencies, and directs activities of county health departments.

Each county health department has a board of health with authority to establish a health department. Through this system of local health services delivery, the Oklahoma State Department of Health protects and improves the health status of Oklahoma communities through strategies that focus on preventing disease and promoting health. Sixty-eight counties now operate health departments.

Advisory Bodies to State Board and State Department of Health
   Advancement of Wellness Advisory Council (63 O.S. § 1-103a.1)
   Catastrophic Health Emergency Planning Task Force, Oklahoma (63 O.S. § 6105)
   Consumer Protection Licensing Advisory Council (63 O.S. § 1-103a.1)
   Food Service Advisory Committee (63 O.S. § 1-106)
   Health Care Information Advisory Committee (63 O.S. § 1-122)
   Home Care and Hospice Advisory Council (63 O.S. § 1-103a.1)
   Hospital Advisory Council (63 O.S. § 1-707)
   Infant and Children's Health Advisory Council (63 O.S. § 1-103a.1)
   Long-Term Care Facility Advisory Board (63 O.S. § 1-1923)
   Sanitarian & Environmental Specialist Registration Advisory Council (59 O.S. § 1150.5)
   Trauma and Emergency Response Advisory Council (63 O.S. § 1-103a.1)

Health Care Authority, Oklahoma (63 O.S. § 5006)

Agency Code 807 (IA)   www.okhca.org
4545 N Lincoln, Oklahoma City 73105   405/522-7300, FAX 405/522-7100

Mission Statement   To purchase state and federally funded health care in the most efficient and comprehensive manner possible, and to study and recommend strategies for optimizing the accessibility and quality of health care.

Administration   Joel Nico Gomez, CEO

Personnel   487.75 unclassified, 20 grant, 7 temporary

Health Information Infrastructure Advisory Board (63 O.S. § 1-131)

Hospital Advisory Committee (63 O.S. § 3241.2)

Medicaid Drug Utilization Review Board (63 O.S. § 5030.1)

Nursing Facility Funding Advisory Committee, Oklahoma (63 O.S. § 1-1925.2)

Public Assistance Recipients, Advisory Committee on Medical Care for (63 O.S. § 5009.2)

Health Care Authority Board, Oklahoma (63 O.S. § 5007)

4545 N Lincoln, Oklahoma City 73105   405/522-7417, FAX 405/530-7162

Administration   Lindsey Bateman, Board Secretary

Health Care Workforce Resources Board (74 O.S. § 3200.2)

www.okhealthcareworkforce.com

Health Insurance High Risk Pool

(36 O.S. § 6535) Repealed effective January 1, 2017.

Insurance Commission   www.bcbsok.com/ohrp
405/741-8434, 877/885-3717

Administration   Frazier Farley, Plan Administrator

Function   Every insurer or reinsurer providing health insurance or reinsurance, as a condition of doing business in the state, must participate in the Health Insurance High Risk Pool, a nonprofit legal entity. The pool operates under the supervision and approval of a 9-member board of directors, appointed by the insurance commissioner.

Healthy and Fit School Advisory Committee (70 O.S. § 24–100A)

Calls for the establishment of Healthy and Fit School Advisory Committee in each public school.

Highway Construction Materials Technician Certification Board
(69 O.S. § 1953)

Department of Transportation Training Center   www.oktechcert.org
1025 SE 59 Street, Oklahoma City 73129   405/632–8022

Historic Preservation Review Committee, Oklahoma (53 O.S. § 353)

Agency Code 350 (IA)
800 Nazih Zuhdi Drive, Oklahoma City 73105-7917   405/521–6249

Mission Statement   To provide advice to the Historic Preservation Officer

Administration   Bob L. Blackburn, State Historic Preservation Officer; Melvena Heisch, Deputy State Historic Preservation Officer

History and Function   Established in 1969 as a part of the State of Oklahoma's participation in the newly created federal preservation programs, the committee membership is composed of citizen members as well as professionals in the areas of history, architecture, architectural history, historic archeology, and prehistoric archeology. The committee provides comments to the state historic preservation officer about proposed nominations to the National Register of Historic Places and other preservation issues as appropriate. Additionally, the committee comments on nominations to the State Register of Historic Places.

Historical Society, Oklahoma (53 O.S. § 1.2)   Board (53 O.S. §1.6)

Agency Code 350 (IA)   www.okhistory.org
800 Nazih Zuhdi Drive, Oklahoma City 73105-7917   405/521–2491, FAX 405/521–2492

Mission Statement   The mission of the Oklahoma Historical Society is to collect, preserve, and share the history and culture of Oklahoma and its people.

Administration
   Bob L. Blackburn, PhD, Executive Director & State Historic Preservation Officer 405/522–5202
   Tim Zwink, PhD, Deputy Executive Director, 405/522–8989
   Kathy Dickson, Museum & Sites Director, 405/522–5231
   Melvena Heisch, Deputy State Historic Preservation Officer, 405/521–6249
   Terry Howard, Comptroller, 405/522–5299
   Sherri Henderson, Human Resources Director, 405/522–5204
   Nicole Harvey, Executive Secretary, 405/522–5202
   Dan Provo, Director, Oklahoma Museum of History, 405/522–5380
   Chad Williams, Research Division Director, 405/522–5207
   Larry O'Dell, Development Director, 405/522–6676

Personnel   129 classified, 13 unclassified, 48 seasonal

History and Function   The Oklahoma Historical Society, both a state agency and a private membership organization, is dedicated to the preservation and perpetuation of Oklahoma's history. Founded in May 1893 by the Oklahoma Territorial Press Association, it was declared an agency of the territorial government in 1895. The Oklahoma Historical Society Board of Directors consists of twenty-five members, twelve of whom are appointed by the governor and thirteen elected by the society membership for three-year terms. Members of the board are appointed and elected by congressional district to help ensure statewide representation.

The central offices; the State Museum; extensive collections of books, manuscripts, newspapers, photographs, genealogical, and other historical research materials, maintained in the Research Division, are housed in the Oklahoma History Center. The *Chronicles of Oklahoma* and *Mistletoe Leaves* are both published by the society.

African American Centennial Plaza Design Committee (74 O.S. § 8403)

Tribal Relations (53 O.S. § 1.4A)

Homeland Security, Oklahoma Office of (74 O.S. § 51.1)

PO Box 11415, Oklahoma City 73136–0415   www.homelandsecurity.ok.gov
405/425–7296, FAX 405/425–7295   E-mail—okohs@dps.state.ok.us

Mission Statement   To develop and coordinate the implementation of a comprehensive statewide strategy to secure the state of Oklahoma from the results of terrorism, from natural disasters, cyberterrorism, from weapons of mass destruction, and perform other duties assigned to it by the governor.

Administration   Kim Edd Carter, Director

History and Function   Recognizing the need for coordinated preparedness and security efforts after 9/11, the Oklahoma Legislature passed Senate Joint Resolution 42 in February 2002 and the Office of Interim Oklahoma Homeland Security Director was created. A staff was assembled and the Oklahoma Office of Homeland Security (OKOHS) began focusing on homeland security efforts within the state. In January 2004 Governor Brad Henry appointed Kerry Pettingill as the Oklahoma Homeland Security director. That same month, the governor sent a letter to the US Department of Homeland Security designating OKOHS as the State Administering Agency (SAA) for homeland security grant programs in Oklahoma. The Oklahoma Legislature passed and the governor signed the Oklahoma Homeland Security Act (HB 2280) in May 2004 and OKOHS was established in Oklahoma statute.

The Oklahoma Homeland Security Act of 2004 outlined OKOHS's strategic objectives which include: 1) prevent a terrorist attack in Oklahoma; 2) reduce Oklahoma's vulnerability to terrorist attacks; and 3) minimize the damage from and respond to a terrorist attack should one occur. The duties of the office include developing and implementing a comprehensive statewide homeland security strategy; planning and implementing a statewide response system; administering the homeland security advisory system; coordinating, applying for and distributing federal homeland security grant funds; and implementing homeland security plans. In February 2011, Governor Mary Fallin appointed Kim Edd Carter as director of OKOHS.

Information Fusion Center Governance Board, Oklahoma (Executive Order 2007–41; Executive Order 2011–39)

Homeland Security, Regional Planning and Coordination Advisory Councils for (74 O.S. § 51.3)

Oklahoma School Security Institute (74 O.S. § 51.2d)

Horse Racing Commission, Oklahoma (3A O.S. § 201)

Agency Code 353 (IA)
2401 NW 23 Street, Suite 78, Oklahoma City 73107   www.ohrc.org
405/943–6472, FAX 405/943–6474   E-mail—ohrc@socket.net

Mission Statement   The Oklahoma Horse Racing Commission encourages agriculture, the breeding of horses, the growth, sustenance, and development of live racing, and generates public revenue through the forceful control, regulation, implementation, and enforcement of commissioned-licensed racing and gaming.

Administration   Constantin A. Rieger, Executive Director; Mary Ann Roberts, Staff Attorney; Bonnie Morris, Assistant to the Administrator; Mike Dixon, Director of Law Enforcement; Robin Helt, Fiscal Administrative Officer; Lisa Hanson, Licensing Supervisor; Phyllis Dean, Oklahoma-Bred Claims; Tara Teel, Oklahoma-Bred Registrar

History and Function   State Question 553 (Initiative Petition 315) adopted at an election held September 21, 1982, authorized the pari-mutuel system of wagering on horse races in Oklahoma. The Oklahoma Horse Racing Act, Title 3A, Chapter 2 of the Oklahoma Statutes, was enacted with an emergency provision and became effective March 22, 1983. The function of the agency is to regulate state-sanctioned horse racing. State Question 712 adopted by an election held on November 2, 2004, authorized the State-Tribal Gaming Act. The act allows commission-licensed racing facilities who meet statutory criteria to have authorized gaming within the enclosure of the racetrack.

Personnel   42 FTE unclassified, non-merit

Oklahoma Breeding Program (3A O.S. § 208.3–208.3a)

State-Tribal Gaming Act (3A O.S. § 261–282)

Hospitals Authority, University (63 O.S. § 3207)

Agency Code 825   Children's Hospital of Oklahoma, Nicholson Tower, Room 6N6900
PO Box 26307, Oklahoma City 73126   405/271–4962, FAX 405/271–1301

Mission Statement   The purposes of the University Hospitals Authority are to provide for an effective and efficient administration, to ensure a dependable source of funding, and to effectuate the mission of the authority. The mission of the authority is to provide state oversight to the Joint Operating Agreement (JOA) with HCA Health Services of Oklahoma, and to contract with the venture from state appropriated dollars for the services of indigent care for the people of Oklahoma. The mission of the JOA is to assure the continuation of the university as a patient care, education, and research organization for Oklahoma. The principal purpose of the University Hospitals Trust is to effectuate the purposes of the authority as established in the University Hospitals Authority Act.

The authority and trust are officially scheduled to meet the third Thursday of the month and meet at least quarterly at 8:30 AM and 8:45 AM, respectively. The authority is composed of six members as follows: one member shall be appointed by the governor, with the advice and consent of the Oklahoma Senate; one member shall be appointed by the President Pro Tempore of the Senate; one member shall be appointed by the Speaker of the House of Representatives; one member shall be the director of the Oklahoma Health Care Authority or his/her designee; one member shall be the provost of the University of Oklahoma Health Sciences Center; and the executive director of the University Hospitals Authority who shall be an ex officio, non-voting member. The trustees of the trust are the acting members of the authority as provided in the University Hospitals Authority Act.

Administration   Dean H. Gandy, Executive Director; John Johnson, Deputy Director; Tadra Jones, Secretary to Board and Trust

Personnel   11 unclassified, non-merit

Housing Finance Agency, Oklahoma (60 O.S. § 176)

(State-beneficiary public trust)
Agency Code 922 (IA)   www.ohfa.org
100 NW 63 Street, Suite 200, Oklahoma City 73116   PO Box 26720, Oklahoma City 73126
405/848–1144, 800/256–1489, TDD 405/848–7471

Administration   Dennis Shockley, Executive Director; John Marshall, Housing Development Team Leader; Deborah Jenkins, Rental Assistance Team Leader; Eldon Overstreet, Finance Team Leader; and Holley Mangham, Communications Director

Mission Statement   "Creating Housing Solutions for Oklahomans." Oklahoma Housing Finance Agency (OHFA) helps people own a home, rent a place to live, or rehabilitate an existing home. Some families become homeowners at below-market interest rates through the agency's single-family loan program. Those in need of rental assistance can afford to live in safe neighborhoods with help from the rental assistance program. Private developers can receive federal housing tax credits that allow them to build apartment complexes or single-family homes at affordable rates, passing the savings on to residents. Cities, towns, and non-profit organizations can help their communities with the aid of HOME dollars to rehabilitate existing homes or construct new homes to meet the housing needs in rural Oklahoma. OHFA also administers a homeless program, HOPWA Program, and Contract Administration. OHFA is governed by a five-member board of trustees appointed by the governor. Trustees serve five-year terms.

Human Services, Department of (Constitution, Article 25 § 2; 56 O.S. § 162.1)

Agency Code 830 (IA)   www.okdhs.org
Sequoyah Building, 2400 N Lincoln Boulevard, PO Box 25352, Oklahoma City 73125
405/521-3646, FAX 405/521-6458

Mission Statement   To help individuals and families in need help themselves lead safer, healthier, more independent and productive lives.

Administration   Ed Lake, Director of Human Services, 405/521-3646
    Chief of Staff, Lee Anne Bruce Boone, 405/521-3646
    Adult and Family Services, Jim Struby, Director, 405/521-3076
    Aging Services, Lance A. Robertson, Director, 405/521-2281
    Business Quality, Office of; Mark A. Robison, Director, 405/522-5704
    Child Care Services, Lesli Blazer, Director, 405/521-3561
    Child Support Services, Gary Dart, Director, 405/522-2273
    Child Welfare Services, Deborah Smith, Director, 405/521-3777
    Citizens Advisory Panels, Connie Holland, Executive Assistant, 405/521-3646
    Civil Rights, Office for; Bill Drapala, Administrator, 405/521-3529
    Client Advocacy, office of, Kathryn Brewer, Advocate General, 405/525-4850
    Communications, Office of; Sheree Powell, Director, 405/521-3027
    Community Living & Support Services, Mark L. Jones, Chief Coordinating Officer, 405/521-6395
    Developmental Disabilities Council, Ann Trudgeon, 405/521-4984
    Developmental Disabilities Services, JoAnne Goin, Director, 405/521-6267
    Finance and Administration, David Ligon, Director, 405/521-3577
    Human Resource Management, Diane Haser-Bennett, Director, 405/521-3613
    Information & Referral, Office of; Cynthia Kinkade, Coordinator, 405/521-3646
    Inspector General, Office of;, Tony Bryan, Inspector General, 405/522-5880
    Intergovernmental Relations & Policy, Office of; Samantha Galloway, Coordinator, 405/521-6392
    Legal Services, Ron Blaze, General Counsel, 405/522-3535
    Office of Community and Faith Engagement, Karen Jacobs, Coordinator, 405/522-2528
    Planning, Research & Statistics, Office of, Connie Schlittler, Director, 405/521-3552
    Support Services, Kelly Kappelman, Director, 405/521-3095

History and Function   Oklahoma voters created what is now the Department of Human Services in the Great Depression year of 1936. By a two-to-one margin, voters approved a state constitutional amendment "to provide ... for the relief and care of needy aged ... and other needy persons." Voters also approved a 1 percent sales tax for use by the Welfare Department. The amount was increased to 2 percent by the 1937 Oklahoma Legislature. In the 1950s, the agency's responsibilities were expanded, and, in 1980, its name was changed by the legislature. Today, DHS has offices in each of the seventy-seven counties.

Administration, Citizens Advisory Panel for (56 O.S. § 162.1b) Created until July 1, 2016.

Aging Issues, Citizens Advisory Panel for
    (56 O.S. § 162.1b) Created until July 1, 2016; Effective Date November 7, 2012, by SQ 765 passage.

Children and Family Issues, Citizens Advisory Panel for (56 O.S. § 162.1b) Created until July 1, 2016

Developmental or Physical Disabilities Advisory Board, Group Homes for Persons with
    (10 O.S. § 1430.4; 74 O.S. § 3905) Recreated until July 1, 2020

Disability Issues, Citizens Advisory Panel for (56 O.S. § 162.1b) Created until July 1, 2016.

Disability Services Rate Review Committee, Advantage Waver and Developmental (10 O.S. § 1430.42)

Guardian, Office of Public (30 O.S. 6-101)

Pharmacy Connection Council, Oklahoma (56 O.S. § 1010.23)

Self-Directed Services Program Committee
(56 O.S. § 198.16; HB 2777, 2010) Created until four years after implementation of programs.

Volunteer Service Credit Bank Program (56 O.S. § 703)

Incentive Approval Committee (68 O.S. § 3603)

Oklahoma Department of Commerce (IA)
Quality Jobs Program, 900 N Stiles, Oklahoma City 73104–3234
405/815–6552, 800/879–6552, FAX 405/605–2869

Administration   Richard Schwalbach 405/815–5269

Independent Living Council, Oklahoma Statewide (29 U.S.C. 796d)

3535 NW 58 Street, Suite 480, Oklahoma City 73112   www.oksilc.org
405/951–3581, FAX 405/951–3504   E-mail—smadden@oksilc.org

Administration   Sidna Madden, Executive Director

Mission Statement   To provide leadership in guiding the state's planning process for independent living services so that needed services are available statewide.

Indigent Defense System, Oklahoma (22 O.S. § 1355)   Board (22 O.S. § 1355.1)

Agency Code 047   www.oids.state.ok.us
PO Box 926, Norman 73070   405/801–2601, FAX 405/801–2649

Mission Statement   To provide indigents with legal representation comparable to that obtainable by those who can afford counsel and to do so in the most cost-effective manner possible. The Oklahoma Indigent Defense System is responsible for implementing the Indigent Defense Act by providing trial, appellate, and post-conviction criminal defense services to persons judicially determined to be entitled to legal counsel at state expense.

Administration   Joe P. Robertson, Executive Director; W. Craig Sutter, Deputy Executive Director; Angie Cole, Chief Administrative Officer

Personnel   135 unclassified, 10 temporary, non-merit

Industry Advisory Committee (2 O.S. § 5–60)

Robert M. Kerr Food & Agricultural Products Center
Oklahoma State University, Room 148, Food and Agricultural Products Center, Stillwater 74078–6055

History and Function   Created to assist and advise the Robert M. Kerr Food & Agricultural Products Center in prioritizing projects, setting fees, creating and designing joint ventures for the development and advancement of the production, processing, handling, and marketing of agricultural commodities, so that the center may meet the needs of the state's value-added processing entities. Composed of sixteen members, the committee receives staff assistance from the center.

Insurance Department (Constitution, Article 6 § 22; 36 O.S. § 301)

Agency Code 125 (IA)   www.oid.ok.gov
3625 NW 56 Street, Suite 100, Oklahoma City 73112   405/521–2828, 800/522–0071, FAX 405/521–6652
Tulsa Office—7645 E 63 Street, Suite 102, Tulsa 74133   918/295–3700, FAX 918/994–7916

Mission Statement   To protect and enhance the financial security of Oklahoma and Oklahomans.

Administration   John Doak, Insurance Commissioner; James Mills, Chief of Staff; Tyler Laughlin, Chief of Operations; Mike Rhoads, Deputy Commissioner of Health Insurance; Paul Wilkening, Deputy Commissioner of Administration; Joel Sander, Deputy Commissioner of Finance; Susan Dobbins, General Counsel; Buddy Combs, Director of Public Policy and Assistant General Counsel; Kelly Collins, Director of Communications; and Frank Stone, Chief Actuary.

Personnel   125 unclassified, non-merit

History and Function   The office of the insurance commissioner regulates the many facets of the insurance industry. The department was created by the Oklahoma Constitution that called for election of a state insurance commissioner through a statewide vote of the people. The department is the regulatory agency for the insurance industry, bail bondsmen, real estate appraisers, adjusters, agents, and companies.

Insurance Commission (Constitution, Article 6 § 23, 36 O.S. § 302)

Advisory Board (36 O.S. § 6221)

Bail Bondsmen (59 O.S. § 1301)

Fraud Unit, Anti- (36 O.S. § 361)

Health Care for the Uninsured Board (36 O.S. § 4602)

Health Insurance High Risk Pool Board (36 O.S. § 6535)

Health Reinsurance Program Board, Oklahoma Small Employer (36 O.S. § 6522)

Real Estate Appraiser Board (59 O.S. Article VII § 858–700)

Investigation, Oklahoma State Bureau of (OSBI)
(74 O.S. § 150.1)   **Commission** (74 O.S. §150.3)

Agency Code 308 (IA)   www.osbi.ok.gov
6600 N Harvey, Oklahoma City 73116   405/848-6724 (24 Hours), 800/522-8017, FAX 405/843-3804

Mission Statement   The mission of every OSBI member is to ensure the safety and security of the citizens of Oklahoma.

Administration   Stan Florence, Director; Charles Curtis, Deputy Director; Bob Harshaw, Division Director, Investigative Services; Andrea Swiech, Division Director, Criminalistics Services; Dave Page, Division Director, Information Services; Darrel Wilkins, Division Director, Administrative Services; Jimmy Bunn, Chief Legal Counsel

Personnel   245 classified, 34 unclassified, 29 temporary

History and Function   The OSBI was created by statute in 1925. On July 1, 1976, the agency, by law, was removed from the Governor's Office and placed under the newly created OSBI Commission, whose members are appointed by the governor and confirmed by the Oklahoma Senate. The OSBI is the general investigative agency of Oklahoma and provides services in support of law enforcement throughout the state. Its statutory duties are to: (1) Maintain a nationally accredited scientific laboratory to assist all law enforcement agencies in the discovery and detection of criminal activity; (2) Maintain fingerprint and other identification files including criminal history records, juvenile identification files, and DNA files; (3) Establish, coordinate, and maintain the automated fingerprinting identification system (AFIS) and the deoxyribonucleic acid (DNA) laboratory; (4) Operate teletype, mobile and fixed radio or other communication systems; (5) Conduct schools and training programs for the agents, peace officers, and technicians of the state charged with the enforcement of law and order and the investigation and detection of crime; (6) Assist the director of the Oklahoma Statue Bureau of Narcotics and Dangerous Drugs Control, the chief medical examiner, and all law enforcement officers and district attorneys when such assistance is requested, in accordance with the policy determined by the OSBI Commission established in section 150.3 of this title; (7) Investigate and detect criminal activity when directed to do so by the governor; (8) Investigate, detect, institute, and maintain actions involving vehicle theft pursuant to sections 152.2 through 152.9 of this title; (9) Investigate any criminal threat made to the physical safety of elected or appointed officials of this state or any political subdivision of the state and forward the results of that investigation to the Department of Public Safety, and provide security to foreign elected or appointed officials while they are in this state on official business; (10) Investigate and detect violations of the Oklahoma Computer Crimes Acts; and (11) Investigate and enforce all laws relating to any crime listed as an exception to the definition of "nonviolent offense" as set forth in section 571 of Title 57 of the Oklahoma Statutes that occur on the turnpikes.

Child Abuse Response Team (74 O.S. § 150.38)

Criminal Justice Resource Center (22 O.S. § 1517)

Criminal Justice Statistics, Office of (74 O.S. § 150.17a)

Information Fusion Center, Oklahoma (Executive Order 2007–41; Executive Order 2011–39)

Internet Crimes Against Children (74 O.S. § 151.1)

Jazz Hall of Fame Board of Directors, Oklahoma (74 O.S. § 1910)

111 E 1 Street, Upper Level, Tulsa 74103
E-mail—info@okjazz.org

www.okjazz.org
918/281–8600, FAX 918/948–7737

Judicial Compensation, Board of (20 O.S. § 3.2)

Mission Statement   The board recommends and establishes compensation for members of the state judiciary, unless such compensation is rejected or amended by law passed by the legislature, or vetoed by the governor. The board is composed of seven members; two appointed by the President Pro Tempore of the Senate; two members appointed by the Speaker of the House; two appointed by the Governor; and one appointed by the Chief Justice of the Supreme Court.

Judicial Complaints, Council on (20 O.S. § 1652)

Agency Code 678 (IA)
405/522–4800, FAX 405/522–4752

1901 N Lincoln Boulevard, Oklahoma City 73105
E-mail—eric.mitts@cojc.ok.gov

Mission Statement   To efficiently and impartially investigate complaints regarding the conduct of persons holding judicial positions and to determine if such complaints should be the subjects of an action before the Court on the Judiciary, the Oklahoma Supreme Court, or should be dismissed.

Administration   Eric Mitts, Director; Terry West, General Counsel; Members: Glen Huff, Chair; Jerry Franklin, Vice Chair; Cathy Christensen, Member

Judicial Nominating Commission (Constitution, Article 7B § 3)

2100 N Lincoln Blvd. Suite 3, Oklahoma City 73105   405/556–9300

History and Function   Established as part of the Judicial Department, the commission consists of fifteen members. Six members are appointed by the governor, one from each congressional district as they existed in 1967, six members elected from and by the membership of the Oklahoma Bar Association; one member-at-large who shall not have been admitted to the practice of law in any state, to be selected by no fewer than eight members of the commission; one member by the Speaker of the House; and one member by the President Pro Tempore of the Oklahoma Senate. The commission has the jurisdiction to determine whether the qualifications of nominees to hold judicial office have been met and to determine the existence of vacancies on the commission.

Juvenile Affairs, Office of (10A O.S. § 2–7–202)   Board (10A O.S. § 2–7–101)

Agency Code 400 (IA)
3812 N Santa Fe, Suite 400, Oklahoma City 73118
405/530–2800, FAX 405/530–2893

www.ok.gov/oja
PO Box 268812, Oklahoma City 73126–8812

Administration   T. Keith Wilson, Executive Director; Kelli Huffman, Secretary, Board of Juvenile Affairs 405/530–2806

Personnel   633 classified, 58 unclassified, 11 temporary

History and Function   In 1994, the Oklahoma Legislature passed the Juvenile Reform Act creating the Office of Juvenile Affairs (OJA) as the state juvenile justice agency, and the Board of Juvenile Affairs. This legislation also created the Youthful Offender Act to provide swift justice for serious and habitual juvenile offenders 15 through 17 years of age.

The **Board of Juvenile Affairs** is comprised of seven members, all of whom are appointed by the governor and shall include persons having experience in social work, juvenile justice, criminal justice, criminal-justice-related behavioral sciences, indigent defense, and education. Additionally, one member must be appointed from each of the five congressional districts and two are appointed from the state-at-large.

The board typically meets in regular session once per month on the third Friday. Meetings are usually held at the Office of Juvenile Affairs office in Oklahoma City.

Juvenile Justice, Department of (10A O.S. § 2–7–202)

Juvenile Justice and Delinquency Prevention, State Advisory Group on (42 U.S.C. 5633, 28 C.F.R. 31.302)
3812 N Santa Fe, Suite 400, Oklahoma City 73118   PO Box 268812, Oklahoma City 73126–8812
405/530–2853, FAX 405/530–2913
Mission Statement   To identify the root causes of juvenile crime, to seek solicitations utilizing intervention and prevention strategies; to advise the governor and legislature concerning delinquency prevention and juvenile justice matters and to effectively administer federal funds received through the Juvenile Justice and Delinquency Act (JJDP), Formula Grant Program, Title V, and Challenge Grants.
Administration   Anna Kelly, Federal Grant Administrator, 405/530–2804, FAX 405/530–2913
History and Function   The Office of Juvenile Affairs is the state agency responsible for the oversight of this office. The OJA will insure federal funds made available are properly dispersed to qualified applicants.

Juvenile Supervision, State Council for Interstate (10A O.S. § 2–9–116)

Santa Claus Commission (10 O.S. § 361)   Agency Code 621
3812 N Santa Fe, Oklahoma City 73118   405/530–2800, FAX 405/530–2890
History and Function   Created in 1937 for the purpose of purchasing Christmas presents for eligible youth in state custody who are in state-supported facilities. The SCC solicits private donations. Since 1996, the commission is supervised by the Office of Juvenile Affairs.

Juvenile Justice Reform Committee, Oklahoma

(HJR 1065, 2010; SB 674, 2011; Executive Order 2013–18) Established until January 1, 2014

Labor, Department of (Constitution, Article 6 § 20; 40 O.S. § 1)

Agency Code 405 (IA)   www.labor.ok.gov
OKC Office: 3017 N Stiles, Oklahoma City 73105   405/521–6100, FAX 405/521–6018
Toll-free 888/269–5353   E-mail—laborinfo@labor.ok.gov

Mission Statement   To help ensure fairness, equity, and safety in Oklahoma workplaces through ethical behavior, conscientious guidance, and loyal service to Oklahoma's employers and employees.

Administration   Mark Costello, Commissioner of Labor; Jim Marshall, Chief of Staff; Don Schooler, General Counsel; Stacy Bonner, Deputy Commissioner/Finance Director; Liz McNeill, Communications; Danielle Wade, Special Assistant to the Commissioner; Diana Jones, Director of OSHA Consultation Program/PEOSH/Abestos; James Buck II, Director of Licensing Division; Angela Cobble, Director of Safety Standards Division

Personnel   47 classified, 19 unclassified

History and Function   The commissioner of labor is a constitutional office defined by Article VI Section 20. The department is responsible for administration and enforcement of minimum wage; child labor laws; workers' compensation insurance compliance; regulation of private employment agencies; investigation and mediation of unpaid wages; inspection of welded steam lines, boiler and pressure vessels, elevators (other than Oklahoma City and Tulsa), amusement and water rides, and water heaters in public facilities; certification of welders and weld-testing laboratories; regulation and certification of asbestos workers; and enforcement of occupational safety and health for public employees.

Alarm and Locksmith Industry Committee (59 O.S. § 1800.4)

Alternative Fuels Technician Certification 40 O.S. § 142.1)

Compressed Natural Gas (52 O.S. § 348)

Elevator Inspection Bureau (59 O.S. § 3023)

Land Office, Commissioners of the (Constitution, Article 6, § 32; 64 O.S. § 1)

Agency Code 410 (IA)   www.clo.ok.gov
120 N Robinson, Suite 1000 W, Oklahoma City 73102   405/521-4000, 888/355-2637, FAX 405/521-4444

Administration   Harry W. Birdwell, Secretary; Keith Kuhlman, Assistant Secretary; Terri Watkins, Director of Communications; Diana Nichols, Internal Auditor; Karen Johnson, Chief Financial Officer; Trey Ramsey, Director of Information Systems; Lisa Blodgett, General Counsel; Dave Shipman, Director, Minerals Management Division; James Spurgeon, Director, Real Estate Management Division; Steve Diffee, Director, Royalty Compliance Division; and Debra Sprehe, Executive Secretary and Human Resources

Commissioners   Mary Fallin, Governor; Todd Lamb, Lieutenant Governor; Gary Jones, State Auditor and Inspector; Janet Barresi, Superintendent of Public Instruction; and Jim Reese, President, State Board of Agriculture

History and Function   The Commissioners of the Land Office, a constitutional agency, was created to manage and control lands and funds granted to the state under the provisions of the Enabling Act. The act, passed by the U.S. Congress in June 1906, gave to the state certain lands and funds for the support of schools and charged the commission with the sale, rental, disposal, and management of the lands as well as the trust funds and proceeds derived.

Personnel   39 classified, 18 unclassified, 4 temporary

Langston University–Oklahoma City and Langston University–Tulsa, Board of Trustees for (70 O.S. § 3431)

Law Enforcement Education and Training, Council on (CLEET) (70 O.S. § 3311)

Agency Code 415 (IA)   www.cleet.state.ok.us
2401 Egypt Road, Ada, Oklahoma, 74820-0669   405/239-5100, FAX 405/239-5180

Mission Statement   To provide the citizens of Oklahoma with peace officers who are trained to be professional, ethical, conscientious, sensitive to needs of the public, knowledgeable, and competent in identified learning objectives; and to protect the public by regulating private security in Oklahoma through education and licensing requirements, and to ensure licensees practice within the provisions of law.

Administration   Steve Emmons, Director 405/239-5152; Chuck Gerhart, Assistant Director, 405/239-5153

Personnel   42 unclassified, non-merit

History and Function   Created by the Oklahoma Legislature in 1961, the Council on Law Enforcement Education and Training is the governing body for the training and education of peace officers who must receive a minimum of 576 hours of basic academy instruction. In 1987 CLEET assumed the responsibility to license security guards and private investigators, pursuant to the Oklahoma Security Guard and Private Investigators Act.

Advisory Council (70 O.S. § 3311 B1)

Bomb Dog Advisory Council (70 O.S. § 3311 M2)

Curriculum Review Board (70 O.S. § 3311 B16)

Drug Dog Advisory Council (70 O.S. § 3311 L2)

Polygraph Board (59 O.S. § 1455)

Private Security Advisory Committee (59 O.S. § 1750.3)

Law Enforcement Retirement System, Oklahoma

(47 O.S. § 2–301)   **Board** (47 O.S. § 2–303)

Agency Code 416 (IA)   www.olers.state.ok.us
421 NW 13 Street, Suite 100, Oklahoma City, 73103   405/522–4931, 877/213–0856, FAX 405/522–5004

Mission Statement   To ensure that all members who contribute to the system will find upon retirement adequate funds to meet the benefits guaranteed them by directing investment of the funds of the system, attempting to maximize gains, minimize losses, and protect the trust.

Administration   Ginger Poplin, Executive Director

Personnel   7 unclassified, non-merit

Legislative Apportionment, Bipartisan Commission on

(Constitution, Article 5 § 11A) Formerly Apportionment Commission

History and Function   This commission becomes active only if the Oklahoma Legislature fails to accomplish apportionment during the first regular session of the legislature following each Federal Decennial Census. Consists of the attorney general, superintendent of public instruction, and the state treasurer.

Legislative Compensation, Board on (Constitution, Article 5 § 21; 74 O.S. § 291.2)

2300 N Lincoln Boulevard, Room 122, Oklahoma City 73105 (IA)   405/521–2141, FAX 405/521–3902

History and Function   Created in 1968 by the adoption of a constitutional amendment, the board's duties are to review, every two years, the compensation paid to legislators, with the power to change such compensation, which becomes effective on the fifteenth day following the succeeding general election. Currently, Oklahoma legislators are paid $38,400 annually and the President Pro Tempore of the Senate and Speaker of the House of Representatives receive an additional $17,932. The floor leaders of the majority and minority parties receive an additional $12,364, as does the Appropriations Committee chair in each house. The speaker pro tempore of the House of Representatives and the person holding the position of assistant majority leader of the Senate each receive an additional $12,364 per year for extra duties. Legislators are reimbursed for expenses.

Legislative Service Bureau (74 O.S. § 450.1)

Agency Code 423 (IA)   www.lsb.state.ok.us
State Capitol, Room 309-1, Oklahoma City 73105   405/521–5662

Mission Statement   To serve the Oklahoma Legislature by providing services as directed by the Speaker of the House of Representatives and the President Pro Tempore of the Senate.

Administration   Dale Wythe, Director

Personnel   9 unclassified

History and Function   Legislative Council created in 1939, fully implemented in 1949 with full-time director. Abolished in 1980, when the Legislative Fiscal and Joint Bill Processing Office was formed. The Legislative Fiscal Office was abolished in 1985, when the Legislative Service Bureau was created. Each of these entities were created to serve the legislature jointly.

Libraries, Oklahoma Department of (65 O.S. § 3–101)   Board (65 O.S. § 2–101)

Agency Code 430 (IA)   www.odl.state.ok.us
Allen Wright Memorial Library Building, 200 NE 18 Street, Oklahoma City 73105

405/521–2502, 800/522–8116, FAX 405/525–7804   E-mail—webteam@oltn.odl.state.ok.us

Mission Statement   The mission of the Oklahoma Department of Libraries is to serve the people of Oklahoma by providing excellent information services and by preserving unique government information resources.

Administration   Susan McVey, Director, 405/522–3172
Vicki Sullivan, Deputy Director, 405/522–3172
Cindy Mooney, Executive Assistant, 405/522–3172
Archives and Records Management, Jan Davis, 405/522–3191
Business Manager, Kristi Hawkins, 405/521–2508
Federal Operations, Judy Tirey, 405/522–3317
Library Development, Vicki Mohr, 405/522–3217
Library Resources, Kitty Pittman, 405/522–3192
Oklahoma Almanac, Connie G. Armstrong, 405/522–3383
Public Information, William R. Young, 405/522–3562
State Government Information, Judith Matthews, 405/522–3189
U.S. Government Information, Steve Beleu, 405/522–3327

Personnel   46 classified, 3 unclassified

History and Function   The Department of Libraries is the official state library of Oklahoma. It is responsible for providing information and records management services to state officials and employees, for assisting public library development in the state, and for coordinating information technology projects statewide. It serves the general public through its specialized collections, and has published the *Oklahoma Almanac* since 1981. Its history as the legal reference library for the executive, legislative, and judicial branches began with the establishment of the Territorial Library in the 1890s, which in 1907 became the State Library.

The board members serve six-year staggered terms and are appointed by the governor with approval of the Oklahoma Senate. The director of the department, who is appointed by and serves at the pleasure of the board, is an ex-officio, non-voting member of the board and serves as secretary.

The law reference collection provides reference services from its Jan Eric Cartwright Memorial Library branch in the capitol. The department also preserves the state's archives and provides records management assistance to state agencies, boards, commissions, and institutions.

Archives and Records Commission (67 O.S. § 305, 74 O.S. § 3908)
200 NE 18 Street, Oklahoma City 73105   405/522–3191, 800/522–8116, FAX 405/525–7804
www.odl.state.ok.us/oar
Mission Statement   To assist state agencies in establishing and administering records management programs that apply efficient and economical methods for the creation, utilization, maintenance, preservation, retention, and disposal of state government records.
History and Function   The primary basis of the Archives and Records Commission lays in the creation of a Records Commission in 1939, passage of act establishing the commission in 1947, and the Records Management Act that became effective in 1961. Re-created until July 1, 2017.
Administration   Susan McVey, State Archivist and Records Administrator
Contact   Jan Davis, State Coordinator

Historical Records Advisory Board (36 CFR, Sect. 1206.30)
200 NE 18 Street, Oklahoma City 73105   405/522–3191, 800/522–8116, FAX 405/525–7804
www.odl.state.ok.us/oar/administration/ohrab.htm
Mission Statement   To provide leadership in encouraging and assisting in the development of programs to preserve and enhance access to historical records pertaining to Oklahoma and to serve as Oklahoma's liaison with the programs of the National Historical Publications and Records Commission.
History and Function   Members are appointed by the director of the Oklahoma Department of Libraries. The board serves as Oklahoma's liaison with the programs of the National Historical Publications and Records Commission.
Contact   Jan Davis, State Coordinator

Jan Eric Cartwright Memorial Library (Law)
State Capitol, Room B-8, Oklahoma City 73105
405/522-3212, 800/522-8116, FAX 405/521-2753
Contact   Christine Chen, Senior Reference Librarian

Oklahoma Center for the Book
200 NE 18 Street, Oklahoma City 73105   405/522-3383, 800/522-8116, FAX 405/525-7804
Mission Statement   The center is located in the Department of Libraries and affiliated with
the Library of Congress Center for the Book in Washington, D.C. Its mission is to promote
Oklahoma authors, celebrate the state's literary heritage, and encourage reading for pleasure by
all Oklahomans.
Contact   Connie G. Armstrong, Executive Director

Oklahoma Literacy Resource Office
200 NE 18 Street, Oklahoma City 73105   405/521-2502, 800/522-8116, FAX 405/525-7804
Mission Statement   The mission of the Oklahoma Literacy Resource Office is to provide assistance and support to Oklahoma's library and community based literacy programs. The office
provides technical assistance, funding opportunities, training, and awareness. Additional services
include serving as the state contact for volunteer literacy initiatives, and forming partnerships
with public, private, and non-profit agencies to assist with family literacy and welfare-to-work
programs.
Contact   Leslie Gelders, Literacy Coordinator

State Records Center
426 E Hill Street, Oklahoma City 73105   405/524-4416, 800/522-8116, FAX 405/524-7567
Contact   Jan Davis
Hours: Monday, 8 AM to 5 PM (closed 12 noon to 1 PM); Wednesday, 8 AM to 11 AM; closed Tuesday,
Thursday, and Friday. For information and assistance call 405/522-3579.

Life and Health Insurance Guaranty Association, Oklahoma
(36 O.S. § 2023)   Board (36 O.S. § 2026)

201 Robert S Kerr Avenue, Suite 600, Oklahoma City 73102   405/272-9221, FAX 405/236-3121

Mission Statement   To protect Oklahoma insureds against failure in the performance of
contractual obligations, under life and health insurance policies and annuity contracts, because of
impairment or insolvency of the member insurer. Created in 1981.

Administration   James W. Rhodes, Administrator and General Counsel;
Shari J. Mounce, Assistant Secretary

Linked Deposit Review Board, Oklahoma
(Small Business Board) (62 O.S. § 88.3)

Office of the State Treasurer (IA)   www.treasurer.ok.gov
State Capitol, Room 217, Oklahoma City 73105   405/522-6860, FAX 405/522-0056

Administration   Ken Miller, State Treasurer, Chair

History and Function   The Oklahoma Small Business Linked Deposit Program was established
October 1, 1988. The purpose of the board is to insure eligibility and compliance with the linked deposit
program by lenders and applicants. The board reviews applications and makes recommendations
for approval or rejection of a linked deposit loan package.

Liquefied Petroleum Gas Board, Oklahoma (52 O.S. § 420.3)

Agency Code 445 (IA)   3815 Santa Fe, Suite 117, Oklahoma City 73118
405/521-2458, FAX 405/521-6037   E-mail—lpgasinfo@lpgas.state.ok.us

Mission Statement   To protect the health and welfare of the citizens of Oklahoma by promulgation of standards for the storage, handling, and installation of liquefied petroleum gases as adopted

by the National Fire Protection Association (NFPA) in 1969 and published in its Pamphlet No. 58 and No. 54 including subsequent changes and/or additions to these standards adopted by NFPA.

Administration   W. A. Glass, Administrator

Personnel   8 classified, 2 unclassified, temporary

History and Function   Created by the Oklahoma Legislature in 1953 to regulate the industry within the state, the board issues dealer and manager permits after applicants qualify by written examination. It also executes and enforces all laws relating to the handling, using, storing, selling, distributing, transporting, and manufacturing of butane, propane, and other liquefied petroleum gases and installation of liquefied petroleum gas systems. Administrative costs of the board are borne by collection of licenses and other fees that are deposited in L.P. Gas Administration Revolving Fund.

Liquefied Petroleum Gas Research, Marketing and Safety Commission (52 O.S. § 420.22)

Agency Code 444 (IA)   E-mail—lpgascomm@rhess.com
6412 N Santa Fe Avenue, Suite C, Oklahoma City 73116

Administration   Richard Hess, 405/879-9828, FAX 405/879-0304

History and Function   The LP Gas Research, Marketing and Safety Commission was created in 1994 to enhance safety training and education for both propane marketers and the state's propane consumers. The LP Gas Commission created the nation's first Regulator Rebate Program, and has now replaced more than 35,000 faulty or out-of-date propane regulators in the state. The commission has also distributed more than 400,000 safety pamphlets to Oklahoma consumers, and offers a Propane Consumer Guide to new propane customers at no charge. Each year, the commission assists with approximately thirty safety programs for propane marketers, and offers specific training for persons planning to take the Class I owners exam or the Class X managers exam. The LP Gas Research, Marketing and Safety Commission has primary responsibility for propane marketing activities in Oklahoma, and works with the national Propane Education and Research Council on research programs and the development of new propane technology.

Long-Term Care Administrators, Oklahoma State Board of Examiners for (63 O.S. § 330.51)

Formerly Oklahoma State Board of Examiners for Nursing Home Administrators

Agency Code 509 (IA)   www.ok.gov/osbeltca
2401 NW 23 Street, Suite 62, Oklahoma City 73107   405/522-1616, FAX 405/522-1625

Mission Statement   OSBELTCA ensures that Oklahoma's long term care administrators are suitable and qualified to serve and continue to serve in this profession.

Administration   Gaylord Z. Thomas, Executive Director

Personnel   3 unclassified, non-merit

History and Function   Established by the 1968 Oklahoma Legislature with revisions being made by the 1973 legislature, principal duties of the board are licensing of long term care administrators and approval of continuing education programs. Re-created until July 1, 2018.

Lottery Commission (3A: O.S. 2004, § 701–735)

3817 N Santa Fe, Oklahoma City, 73118   www.lottery.ok.gov
405/522-7700   E-mail—info@lottery.ok.gov

Administration   Rollo Redburn, Director

History and Function   The Lottery Commission was created following approval of the voters on November 2, 2004. The commission supervises and administers the operation of the lottery.

The commission is governed by a board of trustees composed of seven members appointed by the governor with the advice and consent of the Oklahoma Senate.

Management and Enterprise Services, Office of

(62 O.S. § 41.3; 62 O.S. 34.3) Formerly Office of State Finance

Agency Code 090 (IA)   www.omes.ok.gov
2300 N Lincoln Boulevard, Room 122, Oklahoma City 73105   405/521–2141, FAX 405/521–3902

Administration   Preston Doerflinger, Director of OMES, Secretary of Finance, Administration, and Information Technology; Susan Perry, Executive Assistant
Budget and Policy, 405/521–2141
Capital Assets Management, 405/522–3620
Central Accounting and Reporting, 405/521–2141
Central Purchasing, 405/522–0955
Human Capital Management, 405/521–2177
Information Services, 405/521–2444
Legal, 405/717–8911
Performance and Efficiency, 405/521–2141
Public Affairs, 405/521–3097

Total Personnel   285 classified, 1,020 unclassified, 64 temporary

History and Function   The Office of Management and Enterprise Services was formed through a series of agency consolidations in 2011 that created a central, unified government operations agency that provides financial, property, purchasing, human resources, and information technology services to all state agencies. OMES also assists the governor's office on budgetary policy matters.

Market Assistance Program Association, Voluntary (36 O.S. § 6420)

9417 N Kelly Avenue, Oklahoma City 73114
PO Box 13488, Oklahoma City 73113   405/842–9883, FAX 405/840–4450

Administration   Denise Johnson, Executive Director; Cindy Munden, Program Administrator

History and Function   Title 36, Section 6412—The Oklahoma Market Assistance Program Association (OK-MAP) was created in 1986 to assist in the placement of homeowners' insurance coverage for residents of this state. The OK-MAP is not a carrier capable of assuming insurance risks. While it is believed that the association will be able to solve or at least reduce problems of availability, it has no power to guarantee successful conclusion of all assistance efforts and it is assumed that some risks may not be entitled to coverage.

Medical Authority, Oklahoma State University (63 O.S. § 3275)

www.osumc.net   918/599–1000

Medical Licensure and Supervision, State Board of

(59 O.S. § 481; 74 O.S. § 3904) Re-created until July 1, 2019.

Agency Code 450 (IA)   www.okmedicalboard.org
101 NE 51 Street, Oklahoma City 73105   PO Box 18256, Oklahoma City 73154–0256
405/962–1400, 800/381–4519, FAX 405/962–1499

Mission Statement   To promote the health, safety, and well-being of the citizens (patients) of Oklahoma by requiring a high level of qualifications, standards, and continuing education for licensure of medical doctors, physician assistants, physical therapists, occupational therapists, radiology assistants, anesthesiology assistants, respiratory therapists, athletic trainers, dietitians, electrologists, orthotists, prosthetists, and pedorthists. To protect the on-going health, safety, and well-being of the citizens (patients) of Oklahoma by investigating complaints, conducting public hearings, effectuating, and monitoring disciplinary actions against any of the aforementioned licensed professionals, while providing the licensee with proper due process and all rights afforded under the law. To provide any member of society upon request, a copy of the specific public records and information on any of the aforementioned licensed professionals.

Administration   Lyle R. Kelsey, C.A.E., Executive Director; Reji T. Varghese, Executive Deputy Director; Gerald Zumwalt, M.D., Secretary; Eric E. Frische, MD, Medical Director

Personnel   13 classified, 6 unclassified, 2 temporary

History and Function   The agency was mandated in 1923 to license qualified individuals to practice medicine. Since then, other health care professions have been added to the agency's jurisdiction and the board has been further charged by the Oklahoma Legislature to enforce laws related to medical practice by disciplinary action.

Advisory Committees
   Athletic Trainer Advisory Committee (59 O.S. § 529)
   Advisory Committee on Dietetic Registration (59 O.S. § 1723)
   Advisory Committee on Registered Electrologists (59 O.S. § 536.5
   Allied Peer Assistance Committee (59 O.S. § 518.1))
   Anesthesiologist Assistants Committee (59 O.S. § 3201–3208)
   Occupational Therapy Advisory Committee (59 O.S. § 888.12)
   Advisory Committee on Orthotics and Prosthetics (59 O.S. § 3005)
   Advisory Committee on Pedorthics
   Re-created until July 1, 2019 (HB 1069, 2007, HB 1318, 2007, HB 1688, 2013, 59 O.S. § 3005, 74 O.S. § 3908, 59 O.S. § 2305)
   Physical Therapy Committee (59 O.S. § 887.4)
   Physician Assistant Committee (59 O.S. § 519.3)
   Radiologist Assistant Advisory Committee (59 O.S. § 541.2)
   Respiratory Care Advisory Committee (59 O.S. § 2028)
   Therapeutic Recreation Committee (59 O.S. § 540.4)

Medical Trust, Oklahoma State University (63 O.S. § 3290)

www.osumc.net   918/587–2561

Medicolegal Investigations, Board of (63 O.S. § 931)

Agency Code 342 (IA)   www.ok.gov/ocme
901 N Stonewall, Oklahoma City 73117   405/239-7141, FAX 405/239–2430
Tulsa 918/295–3400, FAX 918/585–1549   E-mail—medicalexaminer@ocme.ok.gov

Mission Statement   To protect public health and safety by investigating cases of sudden, violent, or unexpected and suspicious deaths that occur to its residents or to people passing through Oklahoma, and by identifying possible public health hazards.

Administration   Eric Pfeifer, MD, Chief Medical Examiner
   Byron Curtis, PhD, Chief Forensic Toxicologist
   Amy Elliott, Chief Administrative Officer
   Kari Learned, Senior Executive Secretary
   Timothy Dwyer, Investigative Supervisor
   Tulsa Office: Joshua Lanter, MD, Deputy Chief Medical Examiner; Callie Farrar, Office Manager

Personnel   74 unclassified

History and Function   The agency was created in 1961 as the Board of Unexplained Deaths and the Office of the State Medical Examiner. The Oklahoma Legislature in 1972 changed the name to Board of Medicolegal Investigations that appoints the Chief Medical Examiner and supervises and controls the Office of the Chief Medical Examiner.

Office of the Chief Medical Examiner (63 O.S. § 933)
   Oklahoma City—405/239-7141, FAX 405/239-2430   Tulsa—918/295-3400, FAX 918/585-1549

Mental Health and Substance Abuse Services, Department of

(43A O.S. § 2–101)   **Board** (43A O.S. § 2–101, 2–103)

Agency Code 452 (IA)   www.odmhsas.org
1200 NE 13 Street, Oklahoma City 73117   PO Box 53277, Oklahoma City 73152–3277
405/522–3908, FAX 405/522–3650

Mission Statement   To promote healthy communities and provide the highest quality care to enhance the well-being of all Oklahomans.

Administration   Terri White, Commissioner; 405/522–3908; Durand Crosby, Chief Operating
   Officer, 405/522–3908; Carrie Slatton-Hodges, Deputy Commissioner/Treatment and Recovery
   Services, 405/522–3908; Steven Buck, Deputy Commissioner/Communications and Prevention
   Services, 405/522–3908
   Consumer Advocate General, 405/521–4256
   General Counsel, 405/522–3871
   Human Resources, 405/522–3902
   Inspector General, 405/522–3871
   Provider Certification, 405/522–3800
   Public Information/Public Affairs, 405/522–3907
   General Information, 405/522–3908

History and Function   The Oklahoma Department of Mental Health and Substance Abuse Services (ODMHSAS) was established through the Mental Health Law of 1953, although services to Oklahomans with mental illness date back to early statehood. The department is responsible for mental health and substance abuse prevention and treatment services statewide. This includes acute care and inpatient services, residential treatment, community-based treatment and outpatient services, crisis stabilization, programs for assertive community treatment, services for children and families, and a statewide community prevention network along with education and awareness activities. In addition, the department is responsible for the establishment of rules regulating all substance abuse treatment programs and related services in Oklahoma, as well as rules that regulate residential care and community mental health treatment programs. The department also oversees and manages the behavioral health component of Oklahoma's medicaid program. The ODMHSAS governing board is an eleven-member body appointed by the governor and confirmed by the Oklahoma Senate.

Drug Court, Juvenile (10 O.S. § 7303–5.5)

Suicide Prevention Council, Oklahoma (43A O.S. § 12–104) Created until January 1, 2020

Merit Protection Commission (74 O.S. § 840–1)

Agency Code 298 (IA)   www.mpc.ok.gov
3545 NW 58 Street, Suite 360, Oklahoma City 73112   405/525–9144, FAX 405/528–6245

Mission Statement   To design, implement, and enforce a dispute resolution system for state employees and applicants for state employment. Our mission is accomplished primarily through the training, counseling, consultation, and advice given by the commission in conjunction with voluntary mediation program and mandatory negotiation. The rights and responsibilities of state employees are protected through the commission's investigative powers, dispute resolution systems, and administrative hearing process.

Administration   Carol Shelley, Interim Director

Personnel   5 positions, 2 unclassified, 1 vacant

History and Function   Created in July 1982, the commission has essentially three functions: (1) to investigate allegations of violations of the Oklahoma Personnel Act and employment discrimination in state service; (2) to serve as an administrative appeal agency for state employees having disputes with their agency; and (3) to enforce the provisions of the Oklahoma Personnel Act. In addition to its original functions, this agency is now responsible for providing specific training on grievance resolutions in state employment and training for its administrative law judges. Agency functions also include a component designed to assist agencies in voluntarily complying with the Oklahoma Personnel Act.

Military Department (44 O.S. § 21)

Agency Code 025 (IA)   www.ok.ngb.army.mil
3501 Military Circle, Oklahoma City 73111–4305   405/228–5000, FAX 405/228–5524

Mission Statement   To preserve the state and the nation through the organization and training of the Oklahoma National Guard, to be ready for federal duty when called upon by the president of the United States, pursuant to congressional authority, and to be ready for state duty when called upon by the governor of Oklahoma.

Administration   Major General Myles Deering, Adjutant General
   405/228–5201, FAX 405/228–5524

Personnel   96 classified, 234 unclassified, 38 temporary

History and Function   Initiated by the U.S. Congress in 1890 when it authorized one regiment of organized militia for Oklahoma Territory, the Territorial Legislature passed a law, in 1895, providing for the organization and development of the Volunteer Militia, the Oklahoma National Guard. The Oklahoma Military Department was established in 1951 and serves as the administrative agency for all matters concerning the Oklahoma National Guard and other military organizations. The governor, as commander-in-chief of the National Guard, appoints the adjutant general, the executive and administrative officer. The Army National Guard operates with an authorized strength of 6,983 personnel in 95 units statewide. Its main components are the Forty-fifth Infantry Brigade, Combat Team, Ninetieth Troop Command, and the Forty-fifth Fires Brigade. The Air National Guard has an authorized strength of 2,344 personnel operating from air bases in Oklahoma City and Tulsa.

The National Guard has three missions: (1) to provide trained units and individuals available for active duty during war or national emergency; (2) to provide units organized, equipped, and trained to function efficiently in the protection of life and property and preservation of peace, order, and public safety under competent orders of federal or state authorities; and (3) to participate in local, state, and national programs which add value to America.

Architect Selection Board (44 O.S. § 227)

National Guard Relief Program Review Board, Oklahoma (44 O.S. § 237)

Military Planning Commission, Oklahoma Strategic

(74 O.S. § 5401; 74 O.S. § 3905) Re-created until December 31, 2020

Mission Statement   The purpose of this commission is to analyze state policies affecting military facilities currently in use by the U.S. Department of Defense and the Oklahoma Army and Air National Guard located within the state, and such infrastructure as may support or be affected by these facilities or any activity therein. Responsibility for the administrative direction, coordination, and support of the Commission is with the Office of the Governor.

Mines, Department of (Constitution, Article 6 § 25; 45 O.S. § 3)

Agency Code 125 (IA)   www.mines.ok.gov
2915 N Classen Blvd., Suite 213, Oklahoma City 73106–5486   405/427–3859, FAX 405/427–9646

Mission Statement   To protect the environment of the state, to protect the health and safety of the miners, and to protect the life, health, and property of affected citizens through enforcement of the state mining and reclamation laws.

Administration   Mary Ann Pritchard, Director; Doug Schooley, Deputy Director; Rhonda Dossett, Coal Program Director (918/485–3999); Mark Secrest, Chief Counsel; Suzen Rodesney, Chief Financial Officer; Bret Sholar, Minerals Division Administrator

Personnel   32 unclassified

History and Function   The Department of Mines enforces and implements various provisions of state and federally-mandated programs in health, safety, mining, and land reclamation practices associated with surface and subsurface mining. The department has programs to 1) safeguard human health and safety; 2) issue permits and inspect all mining operations for land reclamation; 3) minimize environmental impact to land, air, and water quality; and 4) regulate blasting of a mine site. The department also conducts miner courses in first aid, mine safety, and accident prevention through the Oklahoma Miner Training Institute.

Oklahoma Miner Training Institute (45 O.S. § 1e)
    EOSC—Baker Hall, 1301 W Main, Wilburton 74578–4999   918/465–1799, FAX 918/465–4490
    Mission Statement   To provide training for mining health and safety.
    Administration   Aaron Farris, Executive Director

Mining Commission, Oklahoma (45 O.S. § 1)

2915 N Classen Blvd., Suite 213, Oklahoma City 73106–5486   405/427–3859, FAX 405/427–9646

Mission Statement   The Oklahoma Mining Commission determines broad plans and programs for the Department of Mines designed to facilitate the regulation, safety, and promotion of the Oklahoma mining industry.

Administration   George Fraley, Chair; Mary Ann Pritchard, Director, Department of Mines

History and Function   The membership of the commission consists of one person with experience in each of the following fields: engineering or geology, labor or worker's safety, agriculture or soil conservation, transportation, economic development or banking, public utilities, natural resources, and two persons selected at large. The commission is the policy-determining agency for the Department of Mines and also selects the director under the commission.

Motor Vehicle Commission, Oklahoma (47 O.S. § 563)

Agency Code 475   www.omvc.ok.gov
4334 Northwest Expressway, Suite 183, Oklahoma City 73116   405/607–8227, FAX 405/607–8909

Mission Statement   To prevent frauds, impositions, and other abuses upon Oklahoma citizens; to preserve the franchise system of motor vehicle distribution; to prevent undue control of independent new motor vehicle dealers by the manufacturers or distributors; and to prevent false and misleading advertising and unfair trade practices by dealers, manufacturers, distributors, and salespersons of new motor vehicles.

Administration   Roy K. Dockum, Executive Director; Marilyn Maxwell, Deputy Director; Jennifer Bates, Licensing Coordinator

Personnel   4 unclassified, non-merit

History and Function   Established by the Oklahoma Legislature in 1953 as the licensing agency for motor vehicle manufacturers, distributors, representatives, dealers, and salesmen, the commission is empowered to provide supervision for the industry and to enforce the legislative act relating to the distribution and sale of new vehicles.

Municipal Power Authority, Oklahoma (11 O.S. § 24–103)

2701 W I–35, Edmond 73013   www.ompa.com
PO Box 1960, Edmond 73083–1960   405/340–5047, FAX 405/359–1071

Mission Statement   To provide competitively priced electric service at the lowest cost possible, offering additional services that allow members to enjoy the full benefits of municipal ownership and giving consideration to the needs of member cities served.

Administration   David Osburn, General Manager; Drake N. Rice, Director of Member Services; Randy Elliott, General Counsel; John Vanzant, Director of Corporate Services and CFO

History and Function   Authorization for formation of the OMPA was granted by the Oklahoma Legislature under the auspices of the Oklahoma Municipal Power Authority Act passed in June 1981. A joint action agency created for the purpose of providing an adequate, reliable, and affordable supply of electrical power and energy to Oklahoma's municipally owned electric systems. OMPA is a consumer-owned public entity. OMPA serves thirty-nine cities in Oklahoma. Four-member cities—Kingfisher, Laverne, Mangum, and Pawhuska—have municipal diesel generating plants, which are contracted to OMPA for operation and dispatched through the OMPA Operations Center in Edmond. Ponca City also has two steam generating units that are leased to OMPA. Through OMPA, member cities also are joint owners of generating plants in four states: Arkansas, Louisiana, Texas, and Oklahoma. In addition, the authority owns 100 percent of the Kaw Hydroelectric Plant located on Kaw Reservoir, just east of Ponca City, and two combustion turbines at the Ponca City Power Plant.

Narcotics and Dangerous Drugs Control, Oklahoma Bureau of

(63 O.S. § 2–102)

Agency Code 477 (IA)   www.ok.gov/obndd
419 NE 38 Terrace, Oklahoma City 73105
405/521–2885, 800/522–8031, FAX 405/524–7619 or 405/530–3192

Mission Statement   Committed to honor, integrity, and excellence, the Oklahoma Bureau of Narcotics will serve the citizens of Oklahoma in the quest for a drug-free state.

Administration   R. Darrell Weaver, Director

Personnel   75 classified, 66 unclassified, 2 OMES positions, 1 grant position

History and Function   The Oklahoma Bureau of Narcotics and Dangerous Drugs Control (OBNDDC) is the state agency responsible for drug enforcement in Oklahoma. Primary responsibilities are to enforce the Uniform Controlled Dangerous Substance Act as outlined in the Oklahoma Statues, Title 63; to train state and local law enforcement officers; provide leadership, logistical, technical, and tactical support to local, state, and federal agencies for drug enforcement; and to compile drug-related statistics; OBNDDC is also tasked with investigating and reducing human trafficking and money laundering in Oklahoma. Additionally, OBNDDC coordinates the Oklahoma Drug Endangered Children program to respond to children living in a drug environment.

The strength of OBNDDC lies in the unique skills and abilities of dedicated agents and support staff. They conduct a wide variety of specialized programs to combat the local availability of various domestic and foreign produced drugs, human trafficking and money laundering. Rural and metro enforcement, intelligence, diversion, regulatory, wire intercept, legal, analytical, and educational activities are directed from OBNDDC headquarters in Oklahoma City; five (5) district offices located in Ardmore, Lawton, McAlester, Tulsa, and Woodward; and fifteen (15) regional offices in Ada, Altus, Chickasha, Clinton, Duncan, Durant, El Reno, Enid, Guymon, Idabel, Muskogee, Okmulgee, Poteau, Stillwater, and Vinita. OBNDDC partners with various local, state, and federal agencies on major long-term projects. OBNDDC provides leadership, training, resources, and infrastructure for the federally funded District Attorneys drug task forces and local law enforcement entities throughout the state. From direct case support to overseeing major statewide program initiatives, OBNDDC works directly with a multitude of federal, state, and local agencies to identify and remove primary sources of drug supply, human trafficking and money laundering networks, as well as aggressive demand reduction efforts. OBNDDC maintains an aggressive and proactive approach toward reducing the local availability of drugs and addressing the ever-changing climate of narcotics distribution and abuse, human trafficking and money laundering. This, combined with future strategies, defines the character of OBNDDC and drives this agency toward the ultimate quest of creating a "drug-free," human trafficking-free," and "money-laundering free" Oklahoma.

Native American Cultural and Educational Authority (74 O.S. § 1226)

Agency Code 361 (IA)   www.theamericanindiancenter.org
900 N Broadway, Suite 200, Oklahoma City 73102–5843   405/239–5500, FAX 405/602–5013

Administration J. Blake Wade, Executive Director, Native American Cultural and Educational Authority, 405/239-5500

History and Function The Native American Cultural and Education Authority, a state agency created in 1994 by the Oklahoma Legislature, has a singular mission: to develop a world-class cultural and educational institution that will bring an awareness and understanding for all people of the Oklahoma American Indian cultures and heritage. The cultural center will serve as a living center for cultural expressions of the diverse American Indian cultures of Oklahoma. The 173 thousand square foot center is to be located on a 210-acre landscaped park that will positively impact the cultural and economic environment for the state.

Natural History, Sam Noble Oklahoma Museum of (70 O.S. § 3309.1)

Directed and supervised by the Board of Regents of the University of Oklahoma
University of Oklahoma, 2401 Chautauqua, Norman 73072-7029   www.snomnh.ou.edu
405/325-4712, FAX 405/325-7699   E-mail—snomnh@ou.edu

Administration Michael A. Mares PhD, Director

History and Function An organized research unit of the University of Oklahoma, the Sam Noble Oklahoma Museum of Natural History was founded in 1899, and was designated the state museum of natural history by act of the Oklahoma Legislature in 1987 (Okla. Statutes, Title 70, Section 3309.1). The mission of the museum is to conduct research, participate in higher education, disseminate information to the people of Oklahoma, and collect and preserve the tangible record of Oklahoma's natural and cultural history, which the museum holds in trust for the people of Oklahoma. The museum is accredited by the American Association of Museums and regularly undergoes national accreditation reviews.

Nursing, Oklahoma Board of (59 O.S. § 567.4)

Agency Code 510 (IA)   www.ok.gov/nursing
2915 N Classen Boulevard, Suite 524, Oklahoma City 73106   405/962-1800, FAX 405/962-1821

Mission To safeguard the safety of citizens in the state of Oklahoma by regulating the practice of Registered Nurses, Certified Nurse Practitioners, Certified Nurse-Midwives, Clinical Nurse Specialists, Certified Registered Nurse Anesthetists, Licensed Practical Nurses, and Advanced Unlicensed Assistants.

Administration Kim Glazier, M.Ed., RN, Executive Director; Jackye Ward, MS, RN, Deputy Director of Regulatory Services

Personnel 27 unclassified, non-merit

History and Function Enacted by the Oklahoma Legislature in 1909, the Oklahoma Nursing Practice Act was revised through the years, with the most recent revisions effective November 2014. Purpose of the act is to safeguard the public health and welfare by requiring persons in professional or practical nursing to be licensed. The Board is responsible for regulating the practice of nursing and establishing minimum standards for education programs. At the end of Fiscal year 2014 (as of June 30, 2014), there were 48,989 Registered Nurses, 17,909 Licensed Practical Nurses, and 2,597 Advanced Practice Registered Nurses holding licenses in the state. In addition, there are 630 Advanced Unlicensed Assistants in the state. There are thirty-four approved schools preparing Registered Nurses at fifty-seven different sites; thirty-two approved schools preparing Licensed Practical Nurses at fifty different sites; and fourteen approved schools for Advanced Unlicensed Assistants. The Board is self-sustaining through collection of licensing and renewal fees.

Formulary Advisory Council (59 O.S. § 567.4a)
Consists of twelve members, created to make recommendations for an exclusionary formulary that will list drugs or categories of drugs that will not be prescribed by advanced practice nurses.

Certified Registered Nurse Anesthetist (CRNA) Formulary Advisory Council (59 O.S. § 567.4b)
Composed of five members who shall be active in clinical practice at least 50 percent of their time

within their defined area of specialty. CRNA is authorized to order, select, obtain, and administer drugs pursuant to provisions of the Oklahoma Nursing Practice Act (SB 275, 1997).

Oilseed Commission, Oklahoma (2 O.S. § 18–272) Re-created until June 1, 2017.

www.okoilseed.org

Optometry, Board of Examiners In (59 O.S. § 582)

Agency Code 520
2008 S Post Road, Suite 200, Midwest City 73130

www.optometry.ok.gov
405/733–7836

Mission Statement   To protect the public by regulating the practice of optometry in Oklahoma through education and licensing requirements and to ensure that optometrists practice optometry within the provisions of the law.

Administration   Russell Laverty, OD, Executive Director

Personnel   3 unclassified, 1 temporary, non-merit

History and Function   The board was created by an act of the 1911 Oklahoma Legislature and was known then as the Board of Optometry. The board is the regulatory agency for the profession of optometrists, and is self-sustaining through collection of fees. Re-created until July 1, 2016.

Osteopathic Examiners, State Board of

(59 O.S. § 624; 74 O.S. § 3906; 74 O.S. § 3909) Re-created until July 1, 2014

Agency Code 525 (IA)
4848 N Lincoln Boulevard, Suite 100, Oklahoma City 73105

www.osboe.ok.gov
405/528–8625, FAX 405/557–0653

Mission Statement   To protect the public by regulating the practice of osteopathic medicine in Oklahoma through education and licensing requirements as well as ensure that each licensee practices osteopathic medicine within the provisions of the Osteopathic Medicine Act.

Administration   Deborah J. Bruce, Executive Director

Personnel   2 classified, 3 unclassified

History and Function   Established by the Oklahoma Legislature in 1921, the board's principle duty is licensing of applicants for the practice of osteopathic medicine and adoption of rules and regulations governing enforcement of laws relating to the profession.

P–20 Data Coordinating Committee (70 O.S. § 3–163) Created until July 1, 2015

Mission Statement   The Council advises the State Department of Education, the State Regents for Higher Education, the Department of Career and Technology Education, the Office of Accountability, the Oklahoma Employment Security Commission, the Legislature, and the Governor on coordination of the creation of a unified, longitudinal student data system to provide interoperability and efficient and effective storage, use and sharing of data among agencies, other policy makers, and the general public.

Pardon and Parole Board (Constitution, Article 6 §10; 57 O.S. § 332.2)

Agency Code 306 (IA)
120 N Robinson, Suite 900W, Oklahoma City 73102–7436

www.ok.gov/ppb
405/602–5863, FAX 405/602–6437

Mission Statement   To provide the Parole Board with the best possible information, through a case-by-case investigative process, for their use in making decisions whether or not to recommend the supervised release of adult felons.

Administration   Jari Askins, Interim Executive Director

Personnel   31 classified, 2 unclassified, 5 temporary

History and Function   The Oklahoma Pardon and Parole Board is a constitutional, part-time body composed of five members. Members of the board are appointed, three by the governor, one by the chief justice of the Oklahoma Supreme Court, and one by the presiding judge of the Oklahoma Court of Criminal Appeals. Board members hold office co-terminous with the governor and can be reappointed. If vacancies occur, the appointing authority selects a replacement member before the term expires. Board members are removable only for cause in the manner provided by law for elected officers not liable for impeachment. The board meets each month at one of the state penal institutions. The positions of chairperson are elected by majority vote of the board. The board is vested with the following statutory and constitutional powers; 1) granting or denying paroles; 2) revoking, modifying, or rehearing paroles; and 3) making recommendations for paroles, revocations, pardons, and commutations to the governor.

Pension Commission, Oklahoma State (74 O.S. § 941)

2300 N Lincoln, Rm. 100, Oklahoma City 73105   www.ok-pension.state.ok.us
405/521-3495, FAX 405/521-3426   E-mail—rchicoine@sai.ok.gov

Administration   Ruth Ann Chicoine

History and Function   As directed by statute, the commission consists of seven members as follows: (1) The state auditor and inspector, or designee; (2) The director of the Office of Management and Enterprise Services, or designee; (3) The state treasurer, or designee; (4) one member who shall be a member of the Oklahoma Senate appointed by the President Pro Tempore of the Senate who shall serve at the pleasure of the appointing authority; and, (5) one member who shall be a member of the House of Representatives appointed by the Speaker of the House of Representatives who shall serve at the pleasure of the appointing authority; (6) one person to be appointed by the governor who shall have at least ten years of demonstrated experience in the banking industry; and (7) one person to be appointed by the governor who shall have at least ten years of experience in professional pension planning, including demonstrated experience with defined benefit retirement plan design.

The Oklahoma State Pension Commission was formed to provide guidance to public officials, legislators, and administrators in developing public retirement objectives and principles, identifying problems and areas of abuse, projecting costs of existing systems and modifications to those systems, and recommending pension reform programs. As directed by statute, the commission publishes a report of the most recent actuarial valuation including total assets, total liabilities, under-funded liability or over-funded status, contributions, and any other information deemed relevant by the commission, and also makes recommendations on administrative and legislative changes, which are necessary to improve the performance of the retirement system.

Perfusionists, State Board of Examiners of (59 O.S. § 2053)

Agency Code 343 (IA)   www.okperfusionists.org
101 NE 51 Street, Oklahoma City 73105   PO Box 18256, Oklahoma City 73154-0256
405/962-1400, FAX 405/962-1499   E-mail—lkelsey@okmedicalboard.org

Mission Statement   To regulate the practice of perfusion, issue licensure where appropriate, and assure the public that the practice of perfusion will be conducted with reasonable skill and safety.

Administration   Lyle R. Kelsey, CAE, Executive Director;
Reji T. Varghese, Deputy Executive Director

History and Function   On behalf of the people of the state, the Oklahoma Legislature created the Oklahoma Board of Examiners of Perfusionists to regulate the practice of perfusion, issue licensure where appropriate, and in general, assure the public that the practice of perfusion will be conducted with reasonable skill and safety. To enforce the act, the board reviews applications for licensure and complaints relative to the conduct of licensed perfusionists. In addition, the board makes rules and policies in conformity with the stated purpose of the board and the mission mandated by law. Re-created until July 1, 2015.

Pharmacy, Board of (Constitution, Article 5 § 39; 59 O.S. § 353.3)

Agency Code 560 (IA)   www.pharmacy.ok.gov
2920 N Lincoln Boulevard, Suite A, Oklahoma City 73105   405/521-3815, FAX 405/521-3758
E-mail—pharmacy@pharmacy.ok.gov

Mission Statement   To protect the citizens of Oklahoma by regulating and enforcing the laws regarding pharmacy practice and the manufacture, sales, distribution, and storage of drugs, medicines, chemicals, and poisons.

Administration   Dr. John A. Foust, Pharm. D., DPh, Executive Director

Personnel   2 classified, 8 unclassified

History and Function   Authorized by the Oklahoma Constitution under Article V, Section 39 and implemented by acts of the Oklahoma Legislature, the board is the regulatory agency for the practice of pharmacy and for the sale, storage, and handling of prescription drugs, medicines, chemicals, and poisons. One of the chief board functions is to conduct examinations for the granting of licenses to pharmacists. The board is responsible for licensing and inspection of premises where prescription drugs are dispensed, sold, or stored.

Physician Manpower Training Commission (70 O.S. § 697.2, 697.3)

Agency Code 619 (IA)   www.pmtc.ok.gov
5500 N Western Avenue, Suite 201, Oklahoma City 73118   405/843-5667, FAX 405/843-5792
E-mail—PMTC@pmtc.ok.gov

Mission Statement   To enhance medical care in rural and under served areas of Oklahoma by administering residency, internship, and scholarship incentive programs that encourage medical and nursing personnel to practice in rural and under served areas. Further, PMTC is to upgrade the availability of health care services by increasing the number of practicing physicians, nurses, and physician assistants in rural and under served areas of Oklahoma.

Administration   James R. Bishop, Executive Director; Charlotte Jiles, Deputy Executive Director; Terrie Hardin, Executive Secretary; Michelle Cecil, Nursing Scholarship Coordinator

Personnel   4 classified, 3 unclassified

History and Function   Created by the Oklahoma Legislature in 1975 to increase the number of practicing physicians in rural and under served areas of Oklahoma, the commission is charged to administer the Oklahoma Medical Loan Repayment Program, Oklahoma Rural Medical Education Program, Physician Placement Program, Physician/Community Match Program, Internship and Residency Programs, Nursing Student Assistance Program, and the Physician Assistant Program.

Podiatric Medical Examiners, Oklahoma State Board of

(59 O.S. § 137, 74 O.S. § 3906) Re-created until July 1, 2015

Agency Code 140 (IA)   www.okpodiatrists.org
101 NE 51 Street, Oklahoma City, 73105   PO Box 18256, Oklahoma City 73154-0256
405/962-1400, FAX 405/962-1499   E-mail—lkelsey@okmedicalboard.org

Mission Statement   On behalf of the people of Oklahoma, the state legislature created the Oklahoma Board of Podiatric Medical Examiners to regulate the practice of podiatry, issue licensure where appropriate, and in general, assure the public that the practice of podiatry will be conducted with reasonable skill and safety. To enforce the act, the board administers the State Licensing Examination, reviews applications for licensure, and reviews complaints relative to the conduct of licensed podiatrists. In addition, the board makes rules and policies in conformity with the stated purpose of the board and the mission mandated by law. The board is charged with assuring the public the podiatrist will practice ethically, with competency, and will be of good moral character.

Administration   Lyle R. Kelsey, Executive Director; Reji T. Varghese, Deputy Executive Director

History and Function   The board was established in 1935 to regulate the profession of chiropody (podiatry) which relates to the treatment of ailments, diseased conditions, deformities or injuries to the foot. The board conducts examinations to qualify applicants for licenses to practice; issues renewals annually, and is authorized to revoke licenses for causes defined by law. It is self-sustaining through collection of fees.

Police Pension and Retirement System, Oklahoma

(11 O.S. § 50–102.1)   **Board** (11 O.S. § 50–103.1)

Agency Code 557 (IA)   www.opprs.ok.gov
1001 NW 63 Street, Suite 305, Oklahoma City 73116   405/840-3555, 800/347-6552, FAX 405/840-8465
E-mail—opprs@opprs.ok.gov

Mission Statement   To provide secure retirement benefits for members and their beneficiaries.

Administration   Steven K. Snyder, Executive Director

Personnel   12 unclassified, non-merit

Polygraph Examiners Board

(59 O.S. § 1455, 74 O.S. § 3906) Re-created until July 1, 2015

Council on Law Enforcement Education and Training (CLEET)
2401 Egypt Road, Ada 74820   405/239-5164, FAX 405/239-5182

Mission Statement   To establish standards for polygraph examiners.

Administration   Dennis McGrath, Chair

History and Function   Authorized by the Oklahoma Legislature in 1971 as a regulatory body for those performing in the field of lie detection through use of instrumentation equipment (polygraph), the board is authorized to give examinations for polygraph examiners' licenses and also has the power to suspend or revoke such licenses after proper hearings, or to levy fines.

Ponca City, Board of Trustees of University Center at (70 O.S. § 3213.1)

www.ucponcacity.com

Port Authorities (82 O.S. § 1102)

Muskogee City-County Port Authority, PO Box 2819, Muskogee 74402, 918/682-7886, FAX 918/683-4811, www.muskogeeport.com

City of Tulsa-Rogers County Port Authority, 5350 Cimarron Road, Catoosa 74015; 918/266-2291, 888/572-7678, FAX 918/266-7678, www.tulsaport.com

History and Function   Authorized under laws enacted in 1959, port authorities may be established by incorporated cities and towns and by counties and may be combined to form joint port authorities. The authorities have broad powers for the development, operation, and expansion of ports. Governing bodies of cities, towns, and counties are the appointing authorities for members of the board of directors of the port authorities.

Private Vocational Schools, Oklahoma Board of (70 O.S. § 21–101)

Agency Code 563 (IA)
3700 N Classen Boulevard, Suite 250, Oklahoma City 73118-2864   405/528-3370, FAX 405/528-3366
E-mail—nhouse@obpvs.ok.gov

Administration   Nora House, Director

Personnel   3 unclassified, non-merit

Mission Statement To protect the people of Oklahoma by licensing, monitoring, and regulating private vocational schools and school representatives. Training conducted in Oklahoma or via correspondence or online to Oklahoma residents is regulated.

History and Function Established by the Oklahoma Legislature in 1970, the board was authorized to set minimum standards for private vocational schools which include standards for courses of instruction and training qualifications of instructors, financial stability, advertising practices, and reasonable rules and regulations for operation of private vocational schools.

Psychologists, State Board of Examiners of

(59 O.S. § 1354) Re-created until July 1, 2019

Agency Code 575 (IA)
421 NW 13 Street, Suite 180, Oklahoma City 73103

www.osbep.ok.gov
405/522–1333

Mission Statement To protect the public by regulating the practice of psychology in Oklahoma to ensure that only properly qualified psychologists practice psychology in the state and that the psychology profession as a whole is conducted in the public's best interest.

Administration Teanne Rose, Executive Officer, E-mail—teanne.rose@psychology.ok.gov

Personnel 3 unclassified, non-merit

History and Function Established under the Psychologists Licensing Act of 1965, the board is the official licensing agency for the practice of psychology and in the investigation of complaints and enforcement of the laws and rules of the profession.

Public Employees Relations Board

(11 O.S. § 51–104; 74 O.S. § 3903) Re-created until July 1, 2016

Agency Code 580 (IA)
2401 N Lincoln Blvd., Room 206, Oklahoma City 73105
E-mail—perb@omes.ok.gov

www.ok.gov/DCS/PERB
405/522–6723, FAX 405/521–6403

Administration Debbie Tiehen, Administrator

History and Function Established in 1972, the Public Employees Relation Board (PERB) administers the provisions of the Fire and Police Arbitration Act (FPAA), 11 O.S. § 51–101 et seq., which governs collective bargaining for police officers and firefighters. PERB prohibits certain practices by municipal employers and employee organizations, provides procedures for filing, investigation, and adjudication of election petitions and unfair labor practice charges.

Public Employees Retirement System, Oklahoma

(74 O.S. § 903) **Board** of Trustees (74 O.S. § 905)

Agency Code 515 (IA)
5801 N Broadway Extension, Suite 400, Oklahoma City 73118–7484
PO Box 53007, Oklahoma City 73152–3007
FAX/Administration 405/848–5967

www.opers.ok.gov
405/858–6737, 800/733–9008
FAX/SoonerSave 405/848–5946
FAX/Member Services 405/858–6714

Mission Statement To provide and promote comprehensive, accountable, and financially sound retirement services to Oklahoma's public servants in a professional, efficient, and courteous manner.

Administration Tom Spencer JD, Executive Director
   Chief Investment Officer, Brad Tllberg, CFA
   Chief Financial Officer/ Director of Finance, Susan Reed, CPA
   Communications & Customer Contact Director, Patrick Lane
   Defined Benefits Administrator, Rebecca Catlett
   Defined Contributions (SoonerSave) Administrator, Ray Pool, CPA
   Human Resources Manager, Diana Byrd, CEBS, SPHR
   Information Technology Director, Garry McCoy

General Counsel, Joseph A. Fox, JD
Investment Accounting/Financial Reporting, Brian Wolf, CPA, Asst. CFO
Legislative & Policy Director, Kristi Ice, JD
Member Services Director, Linda Webb

Personnel   13 classified, 42 unclassified, merit

History and Function   The Oklahoma Public Employees Retirement System, created by the Oklahoma Legislature, was established in 1964. The board is the supervisory authority for the operation of the system; as well as the Uniform Retirement System for Justices and Judges, the Deferred Compensation Plan, and the Oklahoma State Employees Deferred Savings Incentive Plan.

Audit Committee   **Investment Committee**

Budget and Policy Committee

Quartz Mountain Arts and Conference Center and Nature Park, Board of Trustees for (70 O.S. § 4451)

www.quartzmountainresort.com

Mission Statement   Created to act as the administrative agency for the Quartz Mountain Arts and Conference Center and Nature Park ("Center").

Real Estate Appraiser Board (59 O.S. § 858–705)

Insurance Department (IA)   www.reab.oid.ok.gov
3625 NW 56 Street, Suite 100, Oklahoma City 73112   405/521–6636, FAX 405/522–6909
E-mail—christine.mcentire@oid.ok.gov

Administration   Christine McEntire, Director

History and Function   In response to federal legislation passed in 1989, the State of Oklahoma established the Oklahoma Real Estate Appraiser Board. The insurance commissioner is the ex officio chair of the board, and the other members are appointed by the governor to five-year terms. The board oversees the state's system of licensing and certifying real estate appraisers. This is accomplished in conjunction with uniform guidelines established by various independent boards of the Appraisal Foundation of Washington, D.C., and under the oversight of the Appraisal Subcommittee of the Federal Financial Institutions Examinations Council (FFIEC). In January 2011, the board became responsible for regulation of appraisal management companies, also under the oversight of the Appraisal Subcommittee.

Real Estate Commission, Oklahoma

(59 O.S. § 858–201; 74 O.S. § 3904) Re-created until July 1, 2017

Agency Code 588 (IA)   www.orec.ok.gov
1915 N Stiles, Suite 200, Oklahoma City 73105   405/521–3387, 866/521–3389

Mission Statement   To safeguard the public interest by requiring high standards of knowledge and ethical practices of licensees; to discipline licensees who engage in dishonest, fraudulent, or criminal activities in the conduct of real estate transactions; and to facilitate the prosecution of any person who is found in violation of the Oklahoma Real Estate License Code.

Administration   Charla J. Slabotsky, Executive Director

Personnel   10 classified, 4 unclassified, merit

History and Function   The commission is the regulatory agency for the Real Estate License Act which became effective through legislative enactment January 1950. The commission has authority to conduct certain examinations for applicants for sales associate and broker licenses and to either grant or deny licenses. It also has authority to conduct hearings on complaints within the industry and make rulings on such complaints.

Real Estate Contract Form Committee, Oklahoma (59 O.S. § 858–208)

Regents for Higher Education, Oklahoma State

(Constitution, Article 13A § 2; 70 O.S. § 3202)

Agency Code 605 (IA)   www.okhighered.org
655 Research Parkway, Suite 200, Oklahoma City 73104-6266   405/225-9100, FAX 405/225-9230
PO Box 108850, Oklahoma City 73101-8850   Student Information Hot line 800/858-1840

Administration   Dr. Glen D. Johnson, Chancellor, 405/225-9100; Amanda Paliotta, Vice Chancellor for Budget and Finance, Information Technology, Telecommunications and OneNet, 405/225-9130; Blake Sonobe, Vice Chancellor for Academic Affairs, 405/225-9170; Dr. Kermit McMurry, Vice Chancellor for Student Affairs, 405/225-9173; Bob Anthony, General Counsel, 405/225-9129; Richard Edington, Executive Director of the Oklahoma College Assistance Program, 405/234-4300; Kylie Smith, Vice Chancellor for Administration, 405/225-9122; Tony Hutchison, Vice Chancellor for Strategic Planning and Analysis and Workforce and Economic Development, 405/225-9175; Vonley Royal, Executive Director of OneNet and Higher Education Chief Information Officer.

Personnel   225 unclassified, non-merit

History and Function   The Oklahoma State Regents for Higher Education is the statewide coordinating board of control for the state's twenty-five colleges and universities, and ten constituent agencies. The State Regents for Higher Education prescribe academic standards of higher education, determine functions and courses of study at state colleges and universities, grant degrees, recommend to the Oklahoma Legislature budget allocations for each college and university, and recommend proposed fees within limits set by the legislature. The state regents also manage twenty-three scholarship and special programs. In addition, in cooperation with the Office of Management and Enterprise Services, the state regents operate OneNet, the state's information and telecommunications network for education and government. The regents also oversee the Oklahoma College Assistance Program.

Experimental Program to Stimulate Competitive Research Advisory Committee, Oklahoma (EPSCOR) (70 O.S. § 3230.1)   Office of Accountability, Robert Buswell, Administrator

Dyslexia Teacher Training Pilot Program Advisory Committee (70 O.S. § 7001)

Rehabilitation Services, Oklahoma Department of (74 O.S. § 166.1)

Commission (74 O.S. § 166.2)

Agency Code 805 (IA)   www.okdrs.gov
3535 NW 58 Street, Suite 500, Oklahoma City 73112-4824
405/951-3400, 800/845-8476, FAX 405/951-3529, TTY/TDD 405/951-3400

Mission Statement   To provide opportunities for individuals with disabilities to achieve productivity, independence, and an enriched quality of life.

Administration   Joe Cordova, Executive Director, 405/951-3400; Public Information Administrator, Jody Harlan, 405/951-3473; Chief Fiscal Officer, Kevin Statham, 405/951-3422; Chief of Staff, Cheryl Gray, 405/951-3418; Disability Determination Division, Noel Tyler, Administrator, 405/419-2200; Vocational Rehabilitation Division, Mark Kinnison, Administrator, 405/951-3491; Visual Services Administrator, Doug Boone, 405/951-3485
Library for the Blind & Physically Handicapped, Kevin Treese, Programs Manager,
    800/523-0288, 405/521-3514, www.library.state.ok.us
Oklahoma School for the Blind (Parkview School) James C. Adams, Superintendent,
    918/781-8200, 877/229-7136, www.osb.k12.ok.us
Oklahoma School for the Deaf, KaAnn Varner, Superintendent,
    580/622-4900, 888/685-3323, www.osd.k12.ok.us

History and Function   The Oklahoma Department of Rehabilitation Services (DRS) provides assistance to Oklahomans with disabilities through vocational rehabilitation, employment, independent living, and residential and outreach education programs. The agency also determines medical eligibility for disability benefits. The commission meets monthly (except in July), at the DRS State Office, Disability Determination Division, Oklahoma School for the Blind, or Oklahoma School for the Deaf.

Personnel   798 classified, 194 unclassified, 19 temporary

Statewide Independent Living Council
3535 NW 58 Street, Suite 480, Oklahoma City 73112–4824   www.oksilc.org
405/951–3581, TTY/TDD 405/325–4927   FAX 405/951–3504
Administration   Sidna Madden, Director

Oklahoma Rehabilitation Council (29 U.S.C. 725)
3535 NW 58 Street, Suite 500, Oklahoma City 73112–4824   www.ok.gov/orc
Administration   Theresa Hamrick   405/951–3579, Voice/TTY/TDD 800/569–7974

Rural Development, Center for (70 O.S. § 4803)

124 W Shawnee, Suite C, Tahlequah, OK 74464   918/458–9687
E-mail—murphyrf@nsuok.edu

Mission Statement   Housed at Northeastern State University in Tahlequah, the Center provides economic development services for the State of Oklahoma. The office provides geographic, demographic, economic, and growth information about Oklahoma communities and the state itself.

Safety, Department of Public (47 O.S. § 2–101)

Agency Code 585 (IA)   www.dps.state.ok.us
3600 N Martin Luther King Avenue, Oklahoma City 73111–4223
PO Box 11415, Oklahoma City 73136   405/425–2424, FAX 405/425–2324

Mission Statement   Working to provide a safe and secure environment for the public through courteous, quality, and professional services.

Administration   Michael C. Thompson, Commissioner of Public Safety, 405/425–2001;
Gerald Davidson, Assistant Commissioner, 405/425–2002
Administrative Rules Liaison, Kim Dammen, 405/425–2140
Driver Compliance, Doug Young, 405/425–2156
Driver License Examining, Jeff Hankins, 405/425–7732
General Counsel, Stephen Krise, 405/425–2148
Highway Patrol Chief, Ricky Adams, 405/425–2004
Law Enforcement Telecommunications Systems Division, Gene Thaxton, 405/425–2224
Oklahoma Highway Safety Office, Garry Thomas, 405/523–1570
Public Affairs Office, Captain George Brown, 405/425–7709
Records Management, Virgil Bonham, 405/425–2047
Wrecker Services, Virgil Bonham, 405/425–2047

History and Function   The Oklahoma Department of Public Safety is a multi-service safety and law enforcement organization, created by state statute to administer to the protection and needs of Oklahoma citizens including both their personal well-being and their vehicular safety.

Personnel   1,404 classified, 39 unclassified, 48 temporary, merit

Driver's License Medical Advisory Committee (47 O.S. § 6–118)
The Driver's License Medical Advisory Committee is composed of seven members appointed by the commissioner of health (2 appointments), the commissioner of public safety (2), the governor (1), the President Pro Tempore of the Oklahoma State Senate (1), and the Speaker of the House of Representatives (1).
Administration   R. LeRoy Carpenter, M.D., Executive Secretary, 405/425–2071

Injury Review Board (47 O.S. § 2–310.1)

Motorcycle Safety and Education, Advisory Committee for (47 O.S. § 40–122) www.ok.gov/okiemoto

Scenic Rivers Commission, Oklahoma

(82 O.S. § 1461 & 74 O.S. § 3904) Re-created until July 1, 2017

Agency Code 630
www.twitter.com/OKScenicRivers
15971 HWY 10, Tahlequah, PO Box 292, Tahlequah 74465–0292

www.oklahomascenicrivers.net
www.facebook.com/OKSRC
918/456–3251, FAX 918/456–8466

Administration   Ed Fite, Administrator, ed.fite@osrc.ok.gov; Cheryl Allen, Administrative Manager, admin.manager@osrc.ok.gov; Cassandra Carter, Education Outreach, education.outreach@osrc.ok.gov; and Bill James, Captain, Ranger Department, river.ranger@osrc.ok.gov

Board of Commissioners   Gerald Hilsher, Chair, Tulsa; Dr. Riley B. Needham, Vice-Chair, Bartlesville; John Larson, Secretary/Treasurer; Jeff Bashaw, Member, Jay; Monte Bradford, Member, Westville; Randy Corp, Member, Edmond; Michael Fuhr, Member, Tulsa; Archie "Trey" Peyton III, Member, Tahlequah; David Pickle, Member, Tahlequah; Steve Randall, Member, Kansas; David Spears, Member, Tahlequah; and George Rick Stubblefield, Member, Proctor

History and Function   The Oklahoma Scenic Rivers Act (OSRA) was enacted in 1970. The purpose of the OSRA is to protect and preserve scenic rivers in their natural and free-flowing state with attention provided to enhancing scenic beauty, water conservation, fish, wildlife, and outdoor recreational values of present and future benefit to citizens of Oklahoma. There are six (6) designated scenic rivers areas: 1) Flint Creek and Illinois River above the confluence of the Barren Fork Creek in Cherokee, Adair, and Delaware counties; 2) Barren Fork Creek in Adair and Cherokee counties from present alignment of US Highway 59 west to the Illinois River; 3) Upper Mountain Fork River above the 600-foot elevation of Broken Bow Reservoir in McCurtain and LeFlore counties; 4) Big Lee Creek above the 420-foot elevation in Sequoyah County; and 5) Little Lee Creek in Adair and Sequoyah counties. In 1977 the present commission was created to oversee and implement provisions of the Oklahoma Scenic Rivers Act for the Illinois and Flint Creek located in Adair, Cherokee, and Delaware counties, and that portion of the Barren Fork Creek located within Cherokee County.

School and County Funds Management, Oklahoma Commission on (60 O.S. § 177.2)

State Department of Education   405/521–3460, FAX 405/522–3559
Oliver Hodge Building, Room 4–27, 2500 N Lincoln Boulevard, Oklahoma City 73105–4599 (IA)

School Health Coordinators Pilot Program Steering Committee

(70 O.S. § 24–100C)

Mission Statement   Committee created to help the State Department of Education and the State Department of Health facilitate the development of a physical fitness assessment software program customized for public schools that has the capability to track the components of student health-related physical fitness.

School of Science and Mathematics, Oklahoma

(70 O.S. § 1210.401(A))   **Board** of Trustees (70 O.S. § 1210.401(B))

Agency Code 629 (IA)
1141 N Lincoln Boulevard, Oklahoma City 73104–2847

www.ossm.edu
405/521–6436, FAX 405/521–6442

Mission Statement   To foster the educational development of Oklahoma high school students who are academically talented in science and mathematics and who show promise of exceptional development through participation in a residential educational setting emphasizing instruction in the field of science and mathematics; and to assist in the improvement of science and mathematics education for the state by developing, evaluating, and disseminating instructional programs and resources to all schools and students of the state.

Administration   Frank Y.H. Wang, PhD, President

Personnel   3 classified, 60 unclassified

School Readiness Board, Oklahoma Partnership for

(10 O.S. § 640.1; 74 O.S. § 3904) Re-created until July 1, 2017

www.smartstartok.org

Science and Technology, Oklahoma Center for the Advancement of (OCAST) (74 O.S. § 5060.2)   Board of Directors (74 O.S. § 5060.6)

Agency Code 628 (IA)
755 Research Parkway, Suite 110, Oklahoma City 73104-3612
405/319-8400, FAX 405/319-8426, Toll Free 866/265-2215

www.ocast.ok.gov
E-mail—info@ocast.ok.gov

Mission Statement   To foster innovation in existing and developing businesses by 1) supporting basic and applied research; 2) facilitating technology transfer between research laboratories and businesses; 3) providing seed capital for innovative firms in the development of new products or services; and 4) helping Oklahoma's small and medium-sized manufacturing firms become more competitive through increased productivity and modernization.

Administration   C. Michael Carolina, Executive Director; Dan Luton, Director of Programs; Chad Mullen, Director of Government Relations & Special Projects; Diane Lewis, Director of Administration and Finance

Personnel   19 unclassified, merit

History and Function   Created in 1987 to be Oklahoma's technology-based economic development agency, OCAST oversees the programs necessary for the development, transfer, and commercialization of technology. Those programs are: Inventors Assistance Service, Oklahoma Manufacturing Alliance, Oklahoma Applied Research Support, Oklahoma Health Research, Oklahoma Nanotechnology Applications Project, Oklahoma Seed Capital Fund, Oklahoma Technology Commercialization Center, Plant Science Research Program, R&D Intern Partnerships, Small Business Research Assistance, and Technology Business Finance Program.

Advisory Bodies
Oklahoma Applied Research Committee, Ed Shreve, PhD, Chair
Oklahoma Health Research Committee, Mary Beth Humphrey, MD, PhD, Chair
Oklahoma Nanotechnology Applications Project Committee, Dale Teeters, Chair
Oklahoma Plant Sciences Research Advisory Committee, Rodd Moesel, Chair
Seed Capital Investment Committee, Sherri Wise, Chair
Small Business Research Assistance Committee, Rafal Fanjo, Chair

Nanotechnology Initiative, Oklahoma (SCR 23, 2003) www.omhof.com

Science and Technology Research and Development Board, Oklahoma (74 O.S. § 5060.2)

Secretary of State, Office of

Agency Code 625 (IA)
State Capitol, Room 101, 2300 N Lincoln Blvd., Oklahoma City 73105-4897
405/521-3912, FAX 405/521-3771
Office of Administrative Rules and Public Services—220 Will Rogers Building, 2401 N Lincoln Boulevard, Oklahoma City 73105
405/521-4911, FAX 405/522-3555

www.sos.ok.gov

Mission Statement   To provide the registry and safekeeping of vital state instruments through prompt, accurate service and complete satisfaction for our public, business, and government agency clients.

Administration   Chris Benge, Secretary of State; Chris Morriss, Assistant Secretary of State and Chief International Protocol Officer; Tookie Hayes, Executive Assistant to the Secretary of State; Peggy Coe, Director/Managing Editor of the Oklahoma Administrative Code/Register; Tod Wall, Director of Information Systems
Accounting, 405/522-4568, FAX 405/521-2031
Administrative Rules, 405/521-4911, FAX 405/522-3555
Agriculture Liens, 405/521-2474, FAX 405/522-3555
Apostilles, 405/521-4211, FAX 405/521-3771
Business Filings, 405/522-2520, FAX 405/521-3771
Business Records, 405/521-4211
Certification Department, 405/521-4211, FAX 405/521-3771
Charitable Organizations, 405/522-2520, FAX 405/521-3771
Executive/Legislative, 405/522-4564, FAX 405/521-3771
Information Systems, 405/522-2495, FAX 405/521-3771
International Protocol Office, 405/522-2076, FAX 405/521-2031
Notary, 405/521-2516, FAX 405/522-3555
Public Meeting Notices, 405/521-4911, FAX 405/522-3555
Trademarks, 405/522-2520, FAX 405/521-3771

History and Function   The Secretary of State's Office is the official repository and filing agency for all official acts of the governor, legislation and state questions, business entity filings, state agency rules and regulations, agricultural lien filings, notary public applications, and athlete agent registrations. The secretary of state serves as the Oklahoma Chief International Protocol Office.

Personnel   29 classified, 4 unclassified, 4 temporary

Protocol Office, Oklahoma Chief International (74 O.S. § 5017.7)
The secretary of state serves as the central point of contact for foreign governmental officials and the Houston and Oklahoma City Consular Corps. The secretary of state is the first point of contact for foreign government officials and delegations and it the chief international protocol officer. The office has the responsibility for Oklahoma's international relations. The secretary of state represents the state at official functions with members of the international diplomatic community; and serves as a resource to local and state government officials and agencies for information regarding procedure and protocol for international diplomats, government officials, and visitors.
Administration   Chris Morriss, Assistant Secretary of State, International Protocol Officer, 405/522-2076, FAX 405/521-2031

Securities Commission, Oklahoma (71 O.S. § 1–101–1–701)

Agency Code 630 (IA)   www.securities.ok.gov
Oklahoma Department of Securities   405/280-7700, FAX 405/280-7742
120 N Robinson, Suite 860, First National Center, Oklahoma City 73102

Mission Statement   The mission of the Oklahoma Securities Commission is investor protection through the administration and enforcement of the Oklahoma Uniform Securities Act of 2004, an act prohibiting fraud in securities transactions and requiring the registration of broker-dealers, agents, investment advisors and investment advisor representatives, as well as the registration of securities. The Commission also administers the Oklahoma Business Opportunity Sales Act, the Oklahoma Subdivided Land Sales Code, and the Oklahoma Take-over Disclosure Act of 1985.

Administration   Irving L. Faught, Administrator; Melanie Hall, Deputy Administrator; Kenneth Mailard, Chief of Registrations and Exemptions; Carol Gruis, Chief of Securities Professional Registrations; W. Charles Kaiser, Chief Information Officer; Faye Morton, General Counsel

Personnel   23 unclassified, merit

History and Function   The commission as well as the Department of Securities were created by the Oklahoma Legislature in 1959. Their functions include the regulation of securities agents, broker-dealers, investment advisor representatives and investment advisors. These persons and firms are registered and examined under provisions of the Oklahoma Uniform Securities Act of 2004. The department also handles the registration of stocks, bonds, and many other types of securities as provided under the very broad definition of securities in the act. The objectives of the department are protecting the investing public from securities fraud, eliminating unfair sales practices in the market place, and maintaining the market's integrity in Oklahoma.

Sheep and Wool Utilization Research and Market Development

Commission (2 O.S. § 18–181, 74 O.S. 3908) Re-created until July 1, 2017

Agency Code 631
PO Box 502, Tonkawa, OK 74653   405/755–1558

Mission Statement   To promote greater use of Oklahoma's sheep and wool products.

Administration   Rebecca Bolene, Executive Director

History and Function   Authorized by the Oklahoma Legislature in 1973, the commission became operative through a referendum election conducted by sheep and wool producers. The legislation also called for the election, by the producers, of seven members of the commission, four from districts, one at-large, and two from producers of major purebred sheep in Oklahoma. The commission's purpose is to conduct utilization, research, and market development of sheep and wool produced in Oklahoma. The commission is financed through fees assessed on each head of sheep and each pound of wool produced. The name was changed from the Sheep and Wool Commission in 2001. (Laws 2001, c. 146 § 60). Re-created until July 1, 2013.

Shorthand Reporters, State Board of Examiners of Certified

(20 O.S. §1501; 74 O.S. §3903)

2100 N Lincoln, Suite 3, Oklahoma City 73105   405/556–9300

Administration   Michael D. Evans, Court Administrator; Tammy Reaves, Administrator of Court Services Programs; Kinsey Hicks, Certified Shorthand Reporter Liaison

History and Function   Created by the Oklahoma Legislature in 1970, the board is composed of five court reporters appointed by the chief justice of the Oklahoma Supreme Court. Functions of the board include licensing of shorthand reporters as either certified or licensed shorthand reporters and conducting proceedings to recommend suspension, revocation, or reinstatement of licenses of certified or licensed reporters. Re-created until July 1, 2015.

Social Workers, Oklahoma State Board of Licensed

(59 O.S. § 1253) Recreated until July 1, 2020

Agency Code 622 (IA)   www.ok.gov/socialworkers
4545 N Lincoln Blvd., Suite 162, Oklahoma City 73105   405/521–3712, FAX 405/521–3713

Agency Mission   To safeguard the welfare of the public of the State of Oklahoma by establishing, promoting, and enforcing high standards of practice for licensed social workers.

Agency Vision   To have strong public awareness of social work practices within the state. To maintain high standards that reflect best practice in the profession of social work. To ensure that qualified professionals are available to the citizens of Oklahoma.

Agency Values   To be responsive to the needs of the potential licensees. The OSBLSW strives to process an application for licensure within a reasonable length of time. To be committed to protecting the public from the aberrant practices of any licensed social work professional. To be sensitive to the complaints concerning a professional licensed by the agency. Complaints in any form and from any source will be reviewed, acknowledged, and adjudicated with due process to a conclusion within a reasonable period of time. To perform the responsibilities of this board with integrity and professionalism.

Administration   James Marks, Executive Director, james.marks@oswb.ok.gov

Sorghum Commission, Oklahoma

(2 O.S. § 18–242) Re-created until July 1, 2018

4201 N Interstate 27, Lubbock, TX 79403   806/749-3478, FAX 806/749-9002

Mission Statement   To increase Oklahoma grain sorghum profitability through research, education, and promotion. Oklahoma's commission has contracted for administrative services through the national office in Lubbock, Texas. Created until July 1, 2018.

Space Industry Development Authority, Oklahoma

(74 O.S. § 5203)   **Board** (74 O.S. § 5207)

Agency Code 346   www.okspaceport.state.ok.us
121 First Street, Burns Flat, Oklahoma, 73624   PO Box 689, Burns Flat, Oklahoma, 73624
580/562-3500, FAX 580/562-3499

Mission Statement   To be aggressive, deliberate, and forceful in the planning and development of spaceport facilities, launch systems, and projects, and to successfully promote and stimulate the creation of space commerce, education, and space-related industries in Oklahoma.

Administration   Bill Khourie, Executive Director, Bill.khourie@okspaceport.state.ok.us

Personnel   4 unclassified, non-merit

Special Advocate, Court Appointed

Office of Attorney General   405/521-3921 FAX 405/521-6246   www.oklahomacasa.org

Speech-Language Pathology and Audiology, Board of Examiners for (59 O.S. § 1607)

Agency Code 632 (IA)   www.obespa.ok.gov
Speech Pathology and Audiology
3700 N Classen Blvd., Suite 248, Oklahoma City 73118 or PO Box 53592, Oklahoma City 73152
405/524-4955, FAX 405/524-4985   E-mail—amy.hall@obespa.ok.gov

Mission Statement   To protect the health and general welfare of the people of Oklahoma by ensuring that no person practices speech pathology or audiology unless he/she is licensed under the Speech Pathology and Audiology Licensing Act.

Administration   Amy Hall, Executive Secretary

Personnel   2 unclassified, non-merit

History and Function   The board was recreated by the Oklahoma Legislature in 1982 to conduct examinations for the licensing of speech pathologists and audiologists.

Statewide Nine-One-One Advisory Board (63 O.S. § 2847)

www.ok.gov/911

Student Loan Authority, Oklahoma (70 O.S. § 695.3)

(State-Beneficiary Public Trust)
Agency Code 618 (IA)   www.osla.org
525 Central Park Drive, Suite 600, Oklahoma City 73105   Box 18145, Oklahoma City 73154-0145
405/556-9200, 800/456-6752, FAX 405/556-9255, 800/261-7529

Administration   James T. Farha, President; Larry Hollingsworth, Vice President, Loan Management; W. A. Rogers, Vice President Operations and Controller; Ken Ontko, Vice President, Information Systems; Kay Brezny, Vice President, Human Resources and Special Projects

History and Function   Created by the Oklahoma Legislature on August 2, 1972, as an express trust for the benefit of the state by a trust indenture executed pursuant to the Public Trust Act. Acceptance of the beneficial interest in the trust was authorized by the legislature in the Oklahoma Student Loan Act. As a federal contractor, the authority services federal student loans for students or their parents for post-secondary education. The authority is authorized to incur indebtedness through the issuance of revenue bonds or notes. Student or parent borrowers are required to repay their loans with interest that provides for the authority's operating costs. The authority receives no state appropriated funds.

Tax Commission, Oklahoma (68 O.S. § 102)

Agency Code 695 (IA)   www.tax.ok.gov
M.C. Connors Building, 2501 N Lincoln Boulevard, Oklahoma City 73194-0001
405/521-3160, 800/522-8165   Tulsa Office 918/581-2979

Mission Statement   To serve the people of Oklahoma by promoting tax compliance through quality service and fair administration.

Tax Commissioners   Thomas E. Kemp Jr., Steve Burrage, and Dawn Cash

Administration   Tony Mastin, Executive Director, 405/521-3214; Mary Frantz, Deputy Executive
Director, 405/522-6233
Account Maintenance Division—Jerry Statton, 405/521-2944, FAX 405/522-2072
Ad Valorem Division—Joe Hapgood, 405/319-8200, FAX 405/521-0166
Central Processing—Fredda Puckett, 405/521-3177, FAX 405/522-4373
Communications Div. & Public Information—Paula Ross, 405/521-3637, FAX 405/522-1711
Compliance Division, Jim Fourcade, 405/522-4101, FAX 405/522-1783
Management Services—Melissa Reames, 405/522-4809, FAX 405/522-0196; Carol McCullar,
Chief Financial Officer; 405/521-6168, FAX 405/522-0196
Counsel to the Commissioners—Andrew Messer, 405/521-3213
Economist—Reece Womack, 405/521-4309, FAX 405/522-5162
General Counsel—Doug Allen, General Counsel, 405/319-8550, FAX 405/601-7144
Human Resources—Kanda Woods, 405/521-3167, FAX 405/522-1043
Motor Vehicle—Russ Nordstrom, 405/521-2510, FAX 405/522-3740
Tax Policy And Research Division—Rick Miller, 405/521-3123, FAX 405/522-0063
Taxpayer Assistance Division—Joanne Kurjan, 405/522-1626, FAX 405/522-1942

Personnel   517 classified, 218 unclassified

History and Function   The first Tax Commission was composed of three members appointed by the governor with the consent of the Oklahoma Senate. The gubernatorial appointment contingent on Senate confirmation has remained in effect since 1931, but the terms, numbers, and removal of commissioners have undergone a few changes.

The commission is responsible for the administration and enforcement of state tax laws, the collection of a majority of all state-levied taxes, fees, and licenses; and the subsequent apportionment and allocation of revenues earmarked to various state agencies and local units of government. In its quasi-judicial capacity, the commission has the authority to subpoena witnesses and records, to administer oaths and to render decisions appealable directly to the Oklahoma Supreme Court.

The Oklahoma Legislature, in 1947, fixed the terms of the commissioners at six years each, staggered so that one new appointment would come up every two years. The first appointments under this reorganization were to expire on the second Monday of the years 1949, 1951, and 1953. Thereafter, each term would run six years. The 1947 statute also removed the power of the governor to dismiss a commissioner except for cause and in the manner provided by law.

Tobacco Tax Advisory Committee, Cigarette and (68 O.S. § 302-6)

Teachers' Retirement System of Oklahoma (70 O.S. § 17–102)

Trustees (70 O.S. § 17–106)

Agency Code 715 (IA)   www.ok.gov/trs
5th Floor, Oliver Hodge Building, 2500 N Lincoln Boulevard, Oklahoma City 73105
PO Box 53524, Oklahoma City 73152-3524
405/521-2387, FAX 405/522-2521, Toll Free 877/738-6365

Mission Statement   To oversee the administration of the Teachers' Retirement System and to ensure that adequate funds are maintained to meet its financial obligations to its entire membership. In directing the investments of the system's funds, the board seeks to maximize gains, minimize losses, and protect the trust.

Administration   Tom Spencer, Interim Executive Director, 405/521-4745; Julie Ezell, General Counsel; Dixie Moody, Director of Client Services; Riley Shaull, Comptroller; Kim D. Bold, Director of Human Resources; Melissa Kempkes, Investment Analyst

Personnel   39 unclassified, merit

History and Function   Following voter approval of a constitutional amendment, the system was established by legislative act and became effective July 1, 1943. Active members contribute 7 percent of their gross salary per school year. Employer contributions are a combination of 5.0 percent of the state's sales and income taxes and contributions from local school districts. The board of trustees has responsibility for the general operations of the Teachers' Retirement System. The board is composed of thirteen members: six appointed by the governor, and four appointed by the legislature, and three ex-officio members. Eight of the thirteen members are plan participants and five members are from the business community.

Textbook Committee, Oklahoma State

(Constitution, Article 8 § 6; 70 O.S. § 16–101)

State Department of Education, Instructional Materials Section (IA)
Oliver Hodge Building, 2500 N Lincoln Boulevard, Oklahoma City 73105-4599
405/521-3456, FAX 405/521-2971   E-mail—timmie.spangler@ade.ok.gov

Administration   Timmie Spangler, Director, Instructional Materials

History and Function   The Oklahoma Constitution was amended in 1946 to provide for a system of free textbooks for common schools and for the appointment of a committee by the governor to supervise the selection of multiple lists of textbooks from which local school district committees make a final selection of textbooks.

Tobacco Settlement Endowment Trust Fund, Board of Directors of the (Constitution, Article 10 § 40)

Agency Code 092   www.tset.ok.gov
3800 N Classen Boulevard, Suite 200, Oklahoma City 73118
866/530-8738, 405/521-3888, FAX 405/525-6104

Mission Statement   To improve the health and quality of life of all Oklahomans through accountable programs and services that address the hazards of tobacco use and other health issues.

Administration   Tracey Strader, Executive Director

History and Function   The Oklahoma Tobacco Settlement Endowment Trust was established in November 2000 by a vote of the people of Oklahoma, directing the earnings from the trust to fund programs that are designed to improve the health and well-being of all Oklahomans, especially children and senior adults.

Tobacco Settlement Endowment Trust Fund, Board of Investors of the (Constitution, Article 10 § 40)

Tourism and Recreation Department, Oklahoma (74 O.S. § 2201)
Commission (74 O.S. § 2201)

Agency Code 566 (IA)   www.oklatourism.gov   www.travelok.com
120 N Robinson, 6ᵗʰ Floor; PO Box 52002, Oklahoma City, 73152-2002
405/230-8300, FAX 405/230-8600, Literature Requests—800/652-6552, Reservations—800/654-8240

Mission Statement   To advance the exceptional quality of life in Oklahoma by preserving, maintaining, and promoting our natural assets and cultural richness.

Administration   Deby Snodgrass, Executive Director, 405/230-8301
   Administrative Services, Zettie Farrow, 405/230-8331
   Discover Oklahoma, Barbara Merckx, 405/230-8431
   Human Resources, Denise Edwards, 405/230-8354
   Oklahoma Film & Music, Jill Simpson, 405/230-8441
   Oklahoma Today magazine, Colleen McIntyre, 405/230-8454
   State Parks Division, Kris Marek, 405/230-8476
   Tourism Promotion Division, Dick Dutton, 405/230-8414

Personnel   204 classified, 238 unclassified, 271 temporary (seasonal)

History and Function   Administered by an executive director, under the guidance of a nine-member commission, the department began in 1931 when the Oklahoma Legislature appropriated $90,000 for the land on which Lake Murray is located. In the late 1930s, Congress directed the U.S. Corps of Engineers to begin construction on several large reservoirs, primarily for flood control and water supply. In 1951 Lake Murray State Park also became the site for the first of seven state-owned lodges. Through the years, park, lodge, and tourism programs rested in the Planning and Resources Board, the Department of Commerce and Industry, and the Industrial Development and Park Department. In 1972 the legislature created the Oklahoma Tourism and Recreation Department, now made up of five divisions.

Oklahoma Tourism Promotion Advisory Committee (68 O.S. § 50015)   405/230-8402

Oklahoma Today Magazine (74 O.S. § 2237)   405/230-8454

Transportation, Department of (69 O.S. § 4002)

Agency Code 345 (IA)   www.okladot.state.ok.us
R.A. Ward Transportation Building, 200 NE 21 Street, Oklahoma City 73105
405/522-8000, FAX 405/521-2524

Mission Statement   To provide a safe, economical, and effective transportation network for the people, commerce, and communities of Oklahoma.

Administration   Mike Patterson, Executive Director; Tim Gatz, Deputy Director; Casey Shell, Chief Engineer; Tim Tegeler, Director of Engineering; Paul Green, Director of Operations

Personnel   2,259 classified, 66 unclassified, 2 temporary

History and Function   Created by the Oklahoma Legislature in 1976 as an overall coordinating agency for the state's highways, railways, and waterways, this agency superseded the original Oklahoma State Department of Highways, implemented by legislation in 1911. The Oklahoma Aeronautics Commission and Rail Planning were also placed under ODOT jurisdiction. The Waterways Branch was transferred from the Commerce Department to ODOT in 1993. The Oklahoma Aeronautics Commission became a separate agency as of July 1, 2002. The department is primarily funded by motor vehicle fuel taxes, legislative appropriations, and a return of federal matching dollars from the Federal Highway Trust Fund. ODOT's annual budget, totaling more than $2 billion in federal and state funds, is applied to highway construction and maintenance activities, railways, waterways, public rural transit programs and administration statewide. While the primary business is construction and maintenance of the state's highways, the agency also promotes intermodal transportation. An eight-member Transportation Commission appointed by the governor and confirmed by the Oklahoma Senate sets departmental policy and oversees general operations. The members represent eight geographic districts corresponding with ODOT's eight field divisions. The commission meets on the first Monday of each month in the R.A. Ward Transportation Building in Oklahoma City.

Field Divisions Division 1, Muskogee, 918/687-5407; Division 2, Antlers, 580/298-3371; Division 3, Ada, 580/332-1526; Division 4, Perry, 580/336-7340; Division 5, Clinton, 580/323-1431; Division 6, Buffalo, 580/735-2561; Division 7, Duncan, 580/255-7586; Division 8, Tulsa, 918/838-9933.

Highway Construction Materials Technician Certification Board (69 O.S. § 1953)

Oklahoma Tourism Signage Advisory Task Force (74 O.S. § 1891)

Tribal Advisory Board (69 O.S. § 302.2)

Tuition Aid Grant Program, Oklahoma (OTAG)

Oklahoma State Regents for Higher Education   www.otag.org
655 Research Parkway, Suite 200, Oklahoma City 73104
405/225-9456, 800/858-1840, FAX 405/225-9392   E-mail—studentinfo@osrhe.edu

Administration Irala K. Magee, Director of Scholarship and Grant Administration

Turnpike Authority, Oklahoma (69 O.S. § 1703)

Agency Code 978 (IA)   www.pikepass.com
3500 Martin Luther King Avenue, Oklahoma City 73111   PO Box 11357, Oklahoma City 73136-0357
405/425-3600, FAX 405/427-8246

Mission Statement Partnering with others, we provide our customers with a choice of a safe, convenient, efficient, user-funded transportation network focusing on fiscal responsibility and promoting economic development.

Administration Tim Stewart, Director, 405/425-3650; Jim Hazeldine, Assistant Director, Operations and Capital Planning, 405/425-7201; Phil Motley, Assistant Director, Finance and Administration, 405/425-7078; David Murdock, Assistant Director, Maintenance, Engineering, and Construction, 405/425-7396

Personnel 491 classified, 52 unclassified, merit

History and Function Inaugurated during the administration of Governor Roy J. Turner in 1947, the authority constructed the Turner Turnpike between Oklahoma City and Tulsa. This toll road reached its fifty-fifth year of service May 16, 2008. Created to facilitate traffic throughout the state, this system of toll roads, approved by the legislature, has been financed through the sale of revenue bonds. The authority now operates ten turnpikes totaling 612 miles. The membership of the authority consists of the governor, an ex officio member, and six members appointed by the governor with confirmation by the Oklahoma Senate. There are six districts within the Turnpike System and one member is appointed from each district.

Used Motor Vehicle and Parts Commission, Oklahoma (47 O.S. § 582)

Agency Code 755
2401 NW 23 Street, Suite 57, Oklahoma City 73107   405/521-3600, FAX 405/521-3604

Mission Statement To license and regulate used motor vehicle dealers, wholesale motor vehicle dealers, automotive dismantlers, rebuilders, manufactured home dealers, manufacturers, and installers; to create an atmosphere of fair competition among equally regulated dealers; and to protect the interests of the consuming public.

Administration John W. Maile, Executive Director

Personnel 10 unclassified, non-merit

Manufactured Home Advisory Committee (47 O.S. § 582.1)

Veterans Affairs, Oklahoma Department of (72 O.S. § 63.1)

Agency Code 650 (IA)   www.odva.ok.gov
War Veterans Commission of Oklahoma, 2311 N Central, Box 53067, Oklahoma City 73152
405/521-3684, FAX 405/521-6533

Mission Statement   To ensure all Oklahoma veterans and their families receive all possible benefits and to provide excellent health services and long-term skilled care in a residential environment to all qualified wartime veterans residing in the state.

Administration   Major General Myles Deering, Executive Director; Danny Stewart, Deputy
  Director; Shantha Varahan, Chief Financial Officer
  Claims and Benefits, Jim Pass, Manager
  Lawton: Joe Pinkowski, Claims Service Officer, 580/354-3033
  Muskogee: Rick Shaughnessy and Lorainne McReynolds, Claims Service Officer, 918/680-3630
  Tulsa: Larry Jordan and Connie Wilson, Claims Service Officer, 918/835-5033, 918/764-7266
  Oklahoma City: David Dupuis, Claims Service Officer, 405/270-0501, EXT 5477
  Ardmore Veterans Center: Regeana McCreacken, Administrator, 580/223-2266
  Claremore Veterans Center: Tim Potteiger, Administrator, 918/342-5432
  Clinton Veterans Center: Katherine Kreizenbeck, Administrator, 580/331-2200
  Lawton Veterans Center: Terry Wilkerson, Acting Administrator, 580/351-6511
  Norman Veterans Center: Kim Praytor, Administrator, 405/360-5600
  Sulphur Veterans Center: Stacie Paige, Administrator, 580/622-2144
  Talihina Veterans Center: Roy Griffith, Administrator, 918/567-2251

History and Function   Created by the Oklahoma Legislature in 1947 as the successor to the Soldiers Relief Commission, the department is responsible for the administration of the general duties of the commission, which includes assistance to veterans and their dependents in obtaining benefits.

Personnel   1,929 classified, 65 unclassified

Claims Offices
  Muskogee: 125 S Main, Room 1B38, Muskogee 74401, 888/655-2838
  Lawton: 501 SE Flower Mound Road, PO Box 849, Lawton 73502, 580/354-3033
  Tulsa: c/o VA Outpatient Clinic, 9322 E 41 Street, Tulsa 74145; 918/764-7266 or 918/764-7267
  Medical Center, Muskogee, Honor Heights Dr., Muskogee 74401; 918/680-3633 or 918/680-3630
  Medical Center, Oklahoma City, 921 NE 13 St., Oklahoma City 73104; 405/270-0501, EXT 5477, 5478

Veterans Commission (72 O.S. § 63.1)
  2311 N Central, Oklahoma City 73105   405/521-3684

Veterinary Medical Examiners, Board of (59 O.S. § 698.3)

Agency Code 790 (IA)   www.okvetboard.com
2920 N Lincoln Boulevard, Suite C, Oklahoma City 73105   405/522-8831, FAX 405/522-8034

Mission Statement   To regulate the practice of veterinary medicine by the licensure of veterinarians and veterinary technicians, as well as the investigation of complaints to ensure that licensed veterinarians and euthanasia technicians are practicing within the provisions of the law.

Administration   Cathy Kirkpatrick, Executive Director

Personnel   6 unclassified, non-merit

History and Function   The board was established by the Oklahoma Legislature in 1913 and is the chief regulatory agency for the practice of veterinary medicine, including the licensing and enforcement of state laws and rules and regulations of the board. This also includes the veterinary technicians. Re-created until July 1, 2020.

Animal Commission Advisory Committee (59 O.S. § 529)

Examination Committee (59 O.S. § 698.30a)

Visual and Performing Arts, Oklahoma School for the (70 O.S. § 1210.451)

www.okarts.us

Mission Statement   OKArts will provide excellence in Arts education and will deliver comprehensive academic programs for gifted and talented visual and performing Arts students from across the State of Oklahoma. This extraordinary high school will fulfill a two-fold mission: It will provide each student with outstanding, professional preparation via a conservatory Arts education; it will also equip the students with college preparatory academics.

Visual and Performing Arts Board of Trustees, Oklahoma School for the (70 O.S. § 1210.451)

Viticulture and Enology Center

(37 O.S. § 563.1) Created within Redlands Community College, El Reno, Oklahoma.

Redlands Community College, 1300 S Country Club Road, El Reno, OK 73036

Mission Statement   To develop viticulture-related and enology-related education programs; develop technologies, strategies, or practices that aid in the production of grapes and wine in Oklahoma; and increase the positive economic impact of the Oklahoma wine industry on this state.

Administration   Annie Pearson, 405/422–1486; E-mail—pearsona@redlandscc.edu

Water Resources Board, Oklahoma (82 O.S. § 1085.1)

Agency Code 835 (IA)
3800 Classen Boulevard, Oklahoma City 73118

www.owrb.ok.gov
405/530–8800, FAX 405/530–8900

Tulsa—440 S Houston, Room 2, 74127, 918/581–2924
McAlester—321 S 3 Street, Suite 5, 74501, 918/426–5435
Woodward—2411 Williams Avenue, Suite 116, 73801, 580/256–1014

Mission   The mission of the OWRB is to enhance the quality of life for Oklahomans by managing, protecting, and improving the state's water resources to ensure clean, safe, and reliable water supplies, a strong economy, and a healthy environment.

Administration   JD Strong, Executive Director; Jerry Barnett, General Counsel; Joe Freeman, Chief, Financial Assistance; Derek Smithee, Chief, Water Quality Programs; Julie Cunningham, Chief, Planning And Management; Amanda Storck, Chief Administrative Services

Personnel   65 classified, 35 unclassified, 5 temporary

History and Function   Created in 1957, the nine-member board is composed of nine members appointed by the governor for terms of seven years each, with the advice and consent of the Oklahoma Senate. Beginning July 1, 2014, the membership of the board shall transition from congressional district and at-large representation to regional representation based on nine regions of the state, as provided in Title 82, Oklahoma Statues, section 1085.1 At all times, at least one member of the board shall be well versed in each of the following types of water use: recreational, industrial, irrigational, municipal, rural residential, agricultural, soil conservation work, and oil and gas production. Not more than two members may be selected representing any one of the major types of water use. The board administers water use permits, the water well drillers licensing program, dam safety, floodplain management programs, the Clean Lakes program, promulgates state water quality standards, and monitors the state's surface and ground waters.

Water for 2060 Advisory Council (82 O.S. § 1088.14) Created until December 31, 2015

Waterways Advisory Board (69 O.S. § 4018)

Agency Code 345 (IA)
ODOT Waterways Branch
4002 N Mingo Valley Expressway, Tulsa, OK 74116–5002

Oklahoma Department of Transportation
E-mail—waterways@odot.org
918/838–9933, FAX—918/834–5233

The board consists of seven members to advise the Oklahoma Department of Transportation (ODOT), and ODOT Waterways Branch on matters relating to the promotion and viability of Oklahoma's commercially-navigable waterway, the McClellan-Kerr Arkansas River Navigation System (MKARNS). Members are appointed by the director of the Oklahoma Department of Transportation and shall consist of the two executive directors of Oklahoma's two active public ports, commonly known as the Tulsa Port of Catoosa and the Port of Muskogee; two members from private port operations with existing waterfront facilities which regularly employ the use of barge transportation, one handling bulk commodities and one handling liquids; one economist with not less than five continuous years of experience in inland navigation feasibility studies, operation, maintenance, and rehabilitation issues who possesses demonstrated knowledge of the maritime and towing industry; and two members appointed at large from business and/or industry associated with inland navigation. The board shall serve in an advisory capacity to ODOT, the governor's office and the Oklahoma Legislature in accomplishing its mission, assist in the directions of the ODOT Waterways Branch, and recommend specific public and private actions that would enable this state to utilize its waterways to promote future growth. The Waterways Branch works with local, state, and federal agencies to promote a better understanding of the state's navigable waterway and works to ensure adequate funding is appropriated to the Corps of Engineers for the operation and maintenance of the system. The Corps of Engineers has the role of operating and maintaining the MKARNS and to maintain a 9-foot channel depth. Congress has approved the deepening of the channel to twelve feet, but funds have not been appropriated for the project. The U.S. Coast Guard is responsible for the safety, security, and regulations on the MKARNS, including setting the markers and tendering buoys on the navigation channel. The 445-mile long MKARNS is an international water route to the Mississippi River and seaports of the world. Forty-two countries have traded commerce with the Arkansas River Basin region via the MKARNS. Completed in 1970 at a cost of $1.3 billion, the system has eighteen locks and dams (five in Oklahoma) and an elevation differential of 420 feet from mile 600 on the Mississippi River to the head of navigation at the Tulsa Port of Catoosa. Port and dock facilities on the MKARNS in Oklahoma total eighty plus industries, nearly $5 billion in private investments, 7,500 jobs, and $350 million in annual payroll. The 2,500-acre Tulsa Port of Catoosa is one of the largest, most inland, ice-free ports in the nation, with over sixty industries and more than 3,600 employees. Oklahoma's 2012 waterborne commerce totaled over 5.75 million tons worth over $2.2 billion. The tonnage is equivalent to the carrying capacity of 3,831 barges, 57,471 railcars, or 229,885 semi-trucks. 2012 tonnage on the entire McClellan-Kerr Arkansas River System totaled 11.7 million tons, with a value of $3.75 billion. Commodities with the most tonnage were chemical fertilizer, iron and steel, wheat and other grains, sand, gravel and rock, coal and coke, and soybeans. More than 2,000 semi-trucks per day travel into and out of Oklahoma's port and terminal facilities to load and off-load commodities to and from barges.

Wildlife Conservation, Department of (Constitution, Article 26 § 1;29:3–101)

Commission (Constitution, Article 26 §1;29:3–101)

Agency Code 320 (IA)
1801 N Lincoln Boulevard, Oklahoma City
405/521–3851, FAX 405/521–6535

www.wildlifedepartment.com
PO Box 53465, Oklahoma City 73152

Mission Statement   The mission of the Oklahoma Department of Wildlife Conservation is to manage Oklahoma's wildlife resources and habitat to provide scientific, educational, aesthetic, economic, and recreational benefits for present and future generations of hunters, anglers, and others who appreciate wildlife.

Administration   Richard Hatcher, Director, 405/522–6279; Wade Free, Assistant Director, 405/521–4660; Melinda Sturgess-Streich, Assistant Director, 405/521–6685; Alan Peoples, Wildlife, Chief, 405/521–2739; Nels Rodefeld, Information/Education, Chief, 405/521–3855; Barry Bolton, Fisheries, Chief, 405/521–3721; Robert Fleenor, Chief Law Enforcement, 405/521–3719; Nels Rodefeld, *Outdoor Oklahoma* magazine, Editor, 405–521–3855

Personnel   325 unclassified, 59 temporary, non-merit

Will Rogers Memorial Commission (53 O.S. § 47.1)

Agency Code 880
1720 W Will Rogers Boulevard
918/341–0719, 800/324–9455, FAX 918/343–8119

www.willrogers.com
PO Box 157, Claremore 74018–0157

Mission Statement   To collect, preserve, and share the life, wisdom, and humor of Will Rogers for all generations.

Administration   Tad Jones, Director

Personnel   2 classified, 5 unclassified, 16 temporary, merit

History and Function   Created by the Oklahoma Legislature in 1937, the Will Rogers Memorial Commission honors the famed Oklahoma cowboy humorist. The main museum building at Claremore was constructed in 1938 on land given to the state by Mrs. Rogers, who also contributed many museum exhibits depicting her husband's career. Will Rogers's birthplace on Lake Oologah is also under the direction of the commission and the Memorial administration offices. Both are open from 8 AM to 5 PM daily.

Worker's Compensation Commission, Oklahoma (SB 1062)

1915 N Stiles, Oklahoma City, OK 73105   405/522–8600, 800/522–8610

Administration   Robert Gilliland, Chair; Dr. Leroy Young, Vice-Chair; Mark Liotta, Commissioner; Troy Wilson, Special Commissioner; and Kim Bailey, Interim Director

History and Function   Created by the Oklahoma Legislature in 2013 (SB 1062), the commission moved the workers' compensation system from a judicially based system to an administrative system. The commission consists of three commissioners appointed by the governor with the advice and consent of the Oklahoma Senate. Workers who are injured on or after February 1, 2014, may have their cases heard by an administrative law judge appointed by the commission. The commissioners also serve as an appellate body, and they perform other regulatory duties as they pertain to workers compensation issues.

State Government Institutions

Department of Corrections

Institutions

Charles E. "Bill" Johnson Correctional Center (57 O.S. § 509) ▪ 1856 E Flynn Street, Alva, 73717–3005 ▪ Telephone 580/327–8000, FAX 580/327–8018 ▪ West Institutions, ▪ Janice Melton, Warden; Jason Bryant, Deputy Warden

Clara Waters Community Corrections Center (57 O.S. § 509) ▪ 9901 N I-35 Service Road, Oklahoma City, 73131 ▪ Telephone 405/254–3200, FAX 405/254–3290 ▪ Oklahoma County Community Corrections/ Residential Services ▪ Brian Thornburgh, District Supervisor; Kristin Tims, Assistant District Supervisor

Eddie Warrior Correctional Center (57 O.S. § 509) ▪ 400 North Oak, Post Office Box 315, Taft, 74463–0315 ▪ Telephone 918/683–8365, FAX 918/682–4782 ▪ East Institutions, ▪ Sharon L. McCoy, Warden; Gregory Breslin, Deputy Warde

Enid Community Corrections Center (57 O.S. § 509) ▪ 2020 E Maine Avenue, Enid, 73702–6445 ▪ Telephone 580/977–3800, FAX 580/977–3834 ▪ Community Corrections, Northwest ▪ Mike Carr, District Supervisor; Chris Frech, Assistant District Supervisor; Vacant, Assistant District Supervisor; John Lipsey, Assistant District Supervisor

Howard McLeod Correctional Center (57 O.S. § 509) ▪ 1970 E Whippoorwill Lane, Atoka, 74525 ▪ Telephone 580/889–2264, FAX 580/889–2264 ▪ East Institutions, ▪ Bruce Howard, Warden; Debbie Aldridge, Deputy Warden

Jackie Brannon Correctional Center (57 O.S. § 509) ▪ 900 N West Street, Post Office Box 1999, McAlester, 74502–1999 ▪ Telephone 918/421–3339, FAX 918/426–0004 ▪ East Institutions, ▪ Emma Watts, Warden; David Wortham, Deputy Warden

James Crabtree Correctional Center (57 O.S. § 509) ▪ 216 N Murray Street, Helena, 73741–9606 ▪ Telephone 580/852–3221, FAX 580/852–3104 ▪ West Institutions, ▪ Janet Dowling, Warden; Vacant, Deputy Warden

Jess Dunn Correctional Center (57 O.S. § 509) ▪ 601 S 124 Street West, Post Office Box 316, Taft, 74463–0316 ▪ Telephone 918/682–7841, FAX 918/682–4372 ▪ East Institutions, ▪ Mike Mullin, Warden; Mike Murry, Deputy Director

Jim E. Hamilton Correctional Center (57 O.S. § 509) ▪ 53468 Mineral Springs Road, Hodgen, 74939–3064 Telephone 918/653–7831, FAX 918/653–7813 ▪ East Institutions, ▪ Michael Wade, Warden; Mike Murry, Deputy Warden

John Lilley Correctional Center (57 O.S. § 509) ▪ Route 1 Box 407971, 105150 N 3670 Road, Boley, 74829–0308 ▪ Telephone 918/667–3381, FAX 918/667–3959 ▪ West Institutions, ▪ Kameron Harvanek, Warden; Rita Cooksey, Deputy Warden

Joseph Harp Correctional Center (57 O.S. § 509) ▪ 16161 Moffat Road, Post Office Box 548, Lexington, 73051–0548 ▪ Telephone 405/527–5593, FAX 405/527–4841 ▪ East Institutions, ▪ Mike Addison, Warden; Jay Hodges, Deputy Warden; Michael Shelite, Deputy Warden

Kate Barnard Community Corrections Center (57 O.S. 509) ▪ 3300 Martin Luther King Avenue, Oklahoma City, 73111 ▪ Telephone 405/425–2900, FAX 405/425–2911 ▪ Female Offender Community Corrections/Residential Services, ▪ Sharon Harrison, District Supervisor; Lydia McBride, Assistant District Supervisor

Lexington Assessment and Reception Center (57 O.S. § 509) ▪ 15151 Highway 39, Post Office Box 260, Lexington, 73051–0260 ▪ Telephone 405/527–5676, FAX 405/527–9892 ▪ West Institutions, ▪ Jim Farris, Warden; Jenny Dillon, Deputy Warden; Jimmy Shipley, Deputy Warden

Lawton Community Corrections Center (57 O.S. § 509) ▪ 605 SW Coombs Road, Lawton, 73501–8294 Telephone 580/248–6703, FAX 580/355–1081 ▪ Community Corrections, Southwest District. Jeff Woody, District Supervisor; Angela Hearell, Assistant District Supervisor

Mabel Bassett Correctional Center (57 O.S. § 509) ▪ 29501 Kickapoo Road, McLoud, 74851–8339 ▪ Telephone 405/964–3020, FAX 405/964–3014 ▪ East Institutions, ▪ Rickey Moham, Warden; Carla H. King, Deputy Warden; Debbie Morton, Deputy Warden

Mack H. Alford Correctional Center (57 O.S. § 509) ▪ 1151 N Highway 69, Post Office Box 220, Stringtown, 74569–0220 ▪ Telephone 580/346–7301, FAX 580/346–7214 ▪ East Institutions, ▪ Jerry Chrisman, Warden; Tommy Sharp, Deputy Warden; Art Lightle, Deputy Warden

Northeast Oklahoma Correctional Center (57 O.S. § 509) ▪ 442586 E 250 Road, Vinita, 74301–4126 Telephone 918/256–3392, FAX 918/256–2108 ▪ East Institutions, ▪ Rodney R. Redman, Warden; John Somers, Deputy Warden

Oklahoma City Community Corrections Center (57 O.S. § 509) ▪ 315 West I–44 Service Road, Oklahoma City, 73118–7634 ▪ Telephone 405/848–3895, FAX 405/848–6635 ▪ Oklahoma County Community Corrections/Residential Services ▪ Brian Thornburgh, District Supervisor; Carmen Jackson, Assistant District Supervisor

Oklahoma State Penitentiary (57 O.S. § 509) ▪ Corner of West and Stonewall streets, Post Office Box 97, McAlester, 74502–0097 ▪ Telephone 918/423–4700, FAX 918/423–3862 ▪ East Institutions, ▪ Anita Trammell, Warden; Linda Morgan, Deputy Warden; Maurice Warrior, Deputy Warden

Oklahoma State Reformatory (57 O.S. § 509) ▪ 1700 East First Street, Post Office Box 514, Granite, 73547–0514 ▪ Telephone 580/480–3700, FAX 580/480–3997 ▪ West Institutions, ▪ Tracy McCollum, Warden; Ted Durfey, Deputy Warden; Bruce Bornheim, Deputy Warden

R.B. Dick Conner Correctional Center (57 O.S. § 509) ▪ 129 Conner Road, Post Office Box 220, Hominy, 74035–0220 ▪ Telephone 918/594–1300, FAX 918/594–1324 ▪ East Institutions, ▪ Terry Martin, Warden; Carl Bear, Deputy Warden; Vacant, Deputy Warden

Union City Community Corrections Center (57 O.S. § 509) ▪ Post Office Box 129, Union City, 73090–0129 ▪ Telephone 405/483–5900, FAX 405/483–5431 ▪ Community Corrections, Northwest District ▪ Mike Carr, District Supervisor; Chris Frech, Assistant District Supervisor; Vacant, Assistant District Supervisor; John Lipsey, Assistant District Supervisor

William S. Key Correctional Center (57 O.S. § 509) ▪ One William Key Boulevard, Post Office Box 61, Fort Supply, 73841–0061 ▪ Telephone 580/766–2224, FAX 580/766–2908 ▪ West Institutions, William Monday, Warden; Lonnie Lawson, Deputy Warden

Probation and Parole Offices

Jeffrey M. McCoy Central District Probation and Parole Services ▪ 1131 W Sheridan Avenue, Oklahoma City, 73106 ▪ Telephone 405/778–7100, FAX 405/778–7245 ▪ James Reed, District Supervisor; Courtney Jones, Assistant District Supervisor; Camille Porter, Assistant District Supervisor

Jeffery M. McCoy Central District Oklahoma County Intake Office ▪ 217 N Harvey, Suite 301, Oklahoma City, 73102–3802 ▪ Telephone 405/319–3560, FAX 405/319–3570, James Reed, District Supervisor; Camille Porter, Assistant District Supervisor; Courtney Jones, Assistant District Supervisor

Northeast District Community Corrections ▪ 3031 N 32 Street, Muskogee, 74401 ▪ Telephone 918/681–6600, FAX 918/680–3041 ▪ Teresa McCoin, District Supervisor; Marvin Holmes, Assistant District Supervisor

Northwest District Community Corrections ▪ 2613 N Van Buren, Enid, 73703–1713 ▪ Telephone 580/977–3400, FAX 580/977–3420 ▪ Mike Carr, District Supervisor; Chris Frech, Assistant District Supervisor; John Lipsey, Assistant District Supervisor; Vacant, Assistant District Supervisor

Oklahoma County Community Corrections ▪ 3031 N 32 Street, Muskogee, 74401 ▪ Telephone 918/681–6600, FAX 918/680–3041 ▪ Brian Thornburgh, District Supervisor; Kristin Tims, Assistant District Supervisor; Carmen Jackson, Assistant District Supervisor; Peggy Carter, Assistant District Supervisor

Southeast District Community Corrections/Residential Services ▪ 9901 North I–35 Service Road, Oklahoma City, 73131–5228 ▪ Anthony Rowell, District Supervisor; Joe Hankins, Assistant Supervisor; Dwayne Howell, Assistant Supervisor

Southwest District Community Corrections ▪ 602 SW Highland Avenue, Lawton, 73501–8252 Telephone 580/248–9146, FAX 580/248–7617 ▪ Jeff Woody, District Supervisor; Joshua Young, Assistant District Supervisor; Dwayne Janis, Assistant District Supervisor; Angela Hearrell, Assistant District Supervisor

Tulsa County District Community Corrections ▪ 440 S Houston, Suite 701, Tulsa 74127–8911 ▪ Telephone 918/581–2931, FAX 918/581–2694 ▪ Kathryn King, District Supervisor; Tom Nelson, Assistant District Supervisor; Cameron Rose, Assistant District Supervisor

Work Centers

Altus Community Work Center ▪ 308 W Broadway, Altus, 73521–3806 ▪ Telephone 580/482–0790, FAX 580/477–4073

Ardmore Community Work Center ▪ Ardmore Industrial Park, 316 Grumman, Ardmore, 73401 ▪ PO Box 100, Gene Autry, 73436–0100 ▪ Telephone 580/389–5469, FAX 580/389–5472

Beaver Community Work Center ▪ 215 1/2 Avenue E, PO Box 1210, Beaver 73932–1210 ▪ Telephone 580/625–3840, FAX 580/625–3862

Carter County Community Work Center ▪ 5268 Santa Fe Road, Wilson 73463 ▪ Telephone 580/668–3700, FAX 580/668–3706

Earl A. Davis Work Center ▪ 3297 N 369 Road, Holdenville, 74848–9435 ▪ Telephone 405/379–7296, FAX 405/379–7298

Elk City Community Work Center ▪ 1309 Airport Industrial Road, Elk City, 73648–1924 ▪ Telephone 580/243–4316, FAX 580/243–2721

Frederick Community Work Center ▪ 18205 County Road, NS 215 Street, Frederick, 73542–9614 ▪ Telephone 580/335–2142, FAX 580/335–3090

Hobart Community Work Center ▪ 311 S Washington Street, Hobart, 73651–4023 ▪ Telephone 580/726–3341, FAX 580/726–3342

Hollis Community Work Center ▪ 105 W Jones Street, PO Box 171, Hollis, 73550–3003 ▪ Telephone 580/688–3331, FAX 580/688–3699

Idabel Community Work Center ▪ 2001 Industrial Parkway, Suite B, Idabel, 74745–4000 ▪ Telephone 580/286–7286, FAX 580/286–5382

Madill Community Work Center ▪ 210 S 11 Street, Madill, 73446 ▪ Telephone 580/795–7348, FAX 580/795–7346

Mangum Community Work Center ▪ 215 E Lincoln, Mangum, 73554–4265 ▪ Telephone 580/782–3315, FAX 580/782–3316

Sayre Community Work Center ▪ 1107 N Broadway, Sayre, 73662–1813 ▪ Telephone 580/928–5211, FAX 580/928–9516

Walters Community Work Center ▪ RR 3, Box 9, Walters, 73572–9312 ▪ Telephone 580/875–2885, FAX 580/875–2029

Waurika Community Work Center ▪ 109 W Anderson, Waurika, 73573–3095 ▪ Telephone 580/228–3521, FAX 580/228–2565

Department of Human Services

Northern Oklahoma Resource Center of Enid (10 O.S. § 1406) ▪ 2600 E Willow, Enid, 73701 ▪ Telephone 580/213–2700, 800/457–1893, FAX 580/548–2600 ▪ Sally E. Randall, Director. (Formerly the Enid State School)

Robert M. Greer Center (10 O.S. § 1414.1) ▪ 2501 NE Delaware, Enid, 73701–9410 ▪ Telephone 580/213–2700 Extension 2599, 800/457–1893, FAX 580/213–2799 ▪ Hugh M. Sage PhD, Director

Southern Oklahoma Resource Center of Pauls Valley (10 O.S. § 406) ▪ 3210 S Chickasaw Street, Pauls Valley, 73075 ▪ Telephone 405/238–6401, FAX 405/238–8261 ▪ Jeff Livingston, Director. (Formerly the Pauls Valley State School)

Office of Juvenile Affairs

Central Oklahoma Juvenile Center (HB 1978, 1995) ▪ 700 S 9 Street, Tecumseh, 74873 ▪ Telephone 405/598–2135, FAX 405/598–8713 ▪ Mike Moriarity, Superintendent

Southwestern Oklahoma Juvenile Center ▪ 300 S Broadway, Manitou, 73555 ▪ Telephone 580/397–3511, FAX 580/397–3491 ▪ Marc Norvell, Superintendent

Department of Mental Health and Substance Abuse Services

Carl Albert Community Mental Health Center
(43A:3–102) ▪ 1101 East Monroe, PO Box 579, McAlester, 74502 ▪ Telephone 918/426-7800, 800/448-0740, FAX 918/426-5526

Central Oklahoma Community Mental Health Center (43A:3–103) ▪ 909 East Alameda, PO Box 400, Norman 73070 ▪ Telephone 405/360-5100, FAX 405/573-3958

Children's Recovery Center of Oklahoma
(43A:3–101) ▪ 320 12 Avenue NE, Norman, 73071 ▪ Telephone 888/506-3775, FAX 405/573-3804

Griffin Memorial Hospital (43A:3–101) ▪ 900 E Main, PO Box 151, Norman, 73070 ▪ Telephone 405/321-4880, FAX 405/321-4514

Jim Taliaferro Community Mental Health Center (43A:3–102) ▪ 602 Southwest 38 Street, Lawton, 73505 ▪ Telephone 580/248-5780, FAX 580/248-3610

Northwest Center for Behavioral Health
(43A:3–107A) (formerly known as Western State Psychiatric Center) ▪ 1222 10 Street, Suite 211, Woodward 73801 ▪ Telephone 580/571-3233, FAX 580/254-2985

Oklahoma County Crisis Intervention Center
▪ 2625 General Pershing Blvd., Oklahoma City 73107 ▪ Telephone 405/942-2300, FAX 405/942-2303

Oklahoma County Recovery Unit ▪ 1200 NE 13 Street, PO Box 53722, Oklahoma City 73152 ▪ Telephone 405/522-8100, FAX 405/522-3195

Oklahoma Forensic Center ▪ PO Box 69, Vinita 73152 ▪ Telephone 918/256-7841, FAX 918/526-4491

Rose Rock Recovery Center
(43A:3–107) Formerly, Vinita Alcohol and Drug Treatment Center ▪ 24919 S 4420 Road, Vinita, 74301 ▪ Telephone 918/256-9210, FAX 918/256-6377

Department of Rehabilitation Services

Oklahoma School for the Blind
(Constitution, Article 21 § 1, 10 O.S. § 1418, 70 O.S. § 1721) ▪ 3300 Gibson Street, Muskogee, 74403 ▪ Telephone 918/781-8200, 877/229-7136 ▪ www.osb.k12.ok.us ▪ Jim Adams, Superintendent

Oklahoma School for the Deaf
(Constitution, Article 21 § 1, 10 O.S. § 1418, 70 O.S. § 1731) ▪ 1100 E Oklahoma, Sulphur, 73086 ▪ Telephone 580/622-4900, 888/685-3323 ▪ www.osd.k12.ok.us ▪ KaAnn Varner, Superintendent

Department of Veterans Affairs

Oklahoma Veterans Center, Ardmore Division (72 O.S. § 221) ▪ 1015 S Commerce, PO Box 489, Ardmore, 73402 ▪ Telephone 580/223-2266, FAX 580/221-5606 ▪ Regeana McCracken, Administrator

Oklahoma Veterans Center, Claremore Division (72 O.S. § 221.2) ▪ 3001 West Blue Starr Drive, PO Box 988, Claremore, 74018 ▪ Telephone 918/342-5432, FAX 918/342-0835 ▪ Tim Potteiger, Administrator

Oklahoma Veterans Center, Clinton Division (72 O.S. § 226) ▪ 1701 S 4 Street, PO Box 1209, Clinton 73601 ▪ Telephone 580/331-2200, FAX 580/323-4834 ▪ Katherine Kreizenbeck, Administrator

Oklahoma Veterans Center, Lawton/Fort Sill Division (72 O.S. § 221.2a) ▪ 501 SE Flower Mound Road, PO Box 849, Lawton, 73502 ▪ Telephone 580/351-6511, FAX 580/351-6526 ▪ Terry Wilkerson, Administrator

Oklahoma Veterans Center, Norman Division (72 O.S. § 221.1) ▪ 1776 E Robinson, PO Box 1668, Norman, 73070 ▪ Telephone 405/360-5600, FAX 405/364-8432 ▪ Kim Praytor, Administrator

Oklahoma Veterans Center, Sulphur Division (72 O.S. § 221) ▪ 304 E Fairlane, Sulphur, 73086 ▪ Telephone 580/622-2144, FAX 580/622-5881 ▪ Stacie Paige, Administrator

Oklahoma Veterans Center, Talihina Division (72 O.S. § 229) ▪ 10014 Southeast 1138 Avenue, PO Box 1168, Talihina, 74571 ▪ Telephone 918/567-2251, FAX 918/567-2950 ▪ R. Roy Griffith, Administrator

Interstate Compacts, Regional Entities, and State-beneficiary Public Trusts

Adult Offender Supervision, Interstate Compact for (22 O.S. § 1091–1095)

Department of Corrections
3700 Classen Drive, Suite 110, Oklahoma City 73118   405/525-4510, FAX 405/525-4524

Administration   Milton Gilliam, Commissioner

History and Function   The Interstate Compact for Adult Offender Supervision was established to control the transfer of offenders (Probation/Parole) across the state lines in a manner that promotes effective supervision strategies consistent with public safety, offender accountability, and victim's rights. This unit is part of the Department of Corrections, Community Corrections Division and is responsible for ensuring Oklahoma's compliance with the Compact.

Arkansas-Oklahoma Arkansas River Compact Commission

(82 O.S. § 1421)

Oklahoma Water Resources Board
3800 Classen Boulevard, Oklahoma City 73118   405/530-8800, FAX 405/530-8900

Administration   R. Tyler Powell, Scott Thompson, and JD Strong, Oklahoma Commissioners; Julie Cunningham, Oklahoma Member, Engineering Committee; Derek Smithee, Oklahoma Member, Environment and Natural Resources Committee; Jerry Barnett, Oklahoma Member, Legal Committee.

History and Function   The major purposes of the compact are to promote interstate comity between the states of Arkansas and Oklahoma, to provide an equitable apportionment of the waters of the Arkansas River between the two states, and to address water quality issues. The compact was approved in 1971 by both states and revisions approved by both states in 1972.

Canadian River Commission (82 O.S. § 526.1)

Oklahoma Water Resources Board
3800 Classen Boulevard, Oklahoma City 73118   405/530-8800, FAX 405/530-8900

Administration   Les Kamas, Oklahoma Commissioner; JD Strong, Assistant to Oklahoma Commissioner; Julie Cunningham, Oklahoma Member, Engineering Committee; Jerry Barnett, Oklahoma Member, Legal Committee.

History and Function   Composed of representatives from the states of Oklahoma, New Mexico, and Texas, the commission's principal duties are to promote interstate comity in relation to the waters of the Canadian River; to provide for the construction of additional works to conserve the waters of the Canadian River, all in cooperation with the federal government under the terms of the Canadian River Compact.

Centennial Botanical Garden Authority, Oklahoma

(62 O.S. § 4001; Executive Order 2011–45) Created as a public trust.

www.ocbg.org or www.tulsabotanic.org   918/289-0330

Children, Interstate Compact on the Placement of (10 O.S. § 577)

Department of Human Services
2400 N Lincoln Boulevard, Oklahoma City 73105-4601   405/522-0672, FAX 405/522-4488

Administration   Ed Lake, Director of Human Services, Compact Administrator; Misty Pollard, Programs Field Representative

Children, Interstate Commission for the Placement of (SB 906, 2008; 10 O.S. § 577)

Corrections Compact, Interstate Institutions (57 O.S. § 601–602)

Lexington Assessment and Reception Center
Department of Corrections, PO Box 260, Lexington 73051   405/527-5676, FAX 405/527-3699

Mission Statement   To protect the public, the employees, and the offender.

Administration   Staci Bliss, Compact Coordinator

Parole and Interstate Services
3700 Classen Blvd., Suite 110, Oklahoma City, 73118   405/523-3075, FAX 405-525-4524
Administration   Milt Gillam, Administrator
History and Function   Interstate transfer to enhance safety for offenders, employees, and the public. To enhance offender/family relationships.

County Energy District Authority

(19 O.S. § 460.2) Created as public trusts with a county option.

Mission Statement   Allows county governments to establish PACE (Property-Assessed Clean Energy) programs to incentivize permanently fixed renewal energy or energy efficiency improvements to private properties through PACE loans.

Crime Prevention and Privacy Compact Council, National

(74 O.S. § 150.9B; Article VI)

Dairy Compact, Southern (2 O.S. § 7–10) Commission (Article III)

Detainers, Interstate Agreement on (22 O.S. § 1347)

Office of the Governor
State Capitol Building, Room 212, Oklahoma City 73105   405/522-8861, FAX 405/521-3353

Administration   Audrey Rockwell, Detainer Administrator

Driver's License Compact (47 O.S. § 781)

Department of Public Safety   3600 N Martin Luther King Avenue, Oklahoma City 73111
PO Box 11415, Oklahoma City 73136   405/425-7034, FAX 405/425-2061

Administration   Michael C. Thompson, Commissioner and Oklahoma Compact Administrator; Gerald Davidson, Assistant Commissioner; Doug Young, Director, Administrator, Driver Compliance Division

History and Function   Oklahoma enacted legislation in 1967 whereby the state became a member of the Driver's License Compact; an agreement whereby the various states recognize the laws of other member states relative to the operation of motor vehicles. In effect, the compact provides that Oklahoma, for the purpose of suspension, revocation or limitation of the license to operate a motor vehicle, shall take appropriate action against a driver if he/she is convicted of violating certain laws of other states.

East Central Oklahoma Building Authority (60 O.S. § 176)

(State-beneficiary public trust)   300 W Main Street, Ada 74820

East Central Oklahoma Gas Authority (60 O.S. § 176)

(State-beneficiary public trust)   www.eastcentralokgas.com
PO Box 776, Gore 74435   918/489-5592

Administration   Horace Lindley, Administrator; Ryan Callison, Chairperson

Education Commission of the States, The (70 O.S. § 506.1 [Article III] [A])

Janet Barresi, Superintendent of Public Instruction (IA)
2500 N Lincoln Boulevard, Room 121, Oklahoma City 73105
405/521-4885, FAX 405/521-6205   E-mail—Janet.Barresi@sde.ok.gov

History and Function   The Interstate Compact for Education has as its purpose the further-ance of education through the close cooperation and understanding among executive, legislative, professional, educational, and lay leadership on a nationwide basis, and at the state and local levels; and to provide a forum for the discussion, development, and recommendation of public policy alternatives in the field of education.

Educational Personnel, Interstate Agreement on Qualification of (70 O.S. § 508.1)

(Nat'l. Assn. of State Directors of Teacher Education & Certification Interstate Contract)

State Department of Education   www.ok.gov/sde
2500 N Lincoln Boulevard, Room 212, Oklahoma City 73105   405/521-3337, FAX 405/522-1520
E-mail—Jeff.Smith@sde.ok.gov

Administration   Jeff Smith, Executive Director, Teacher Certification, OKSDE

Teacher Education and Certification Interstate Contract, National Association of State Directors of
   www.nasdtec.net

Emergency Management Compact (63 O.S. § 684.1)

PO Box 53365, Oklahoma City 73152   www.ok.gov/oem

Administration   Oklahoma Department of Emergency Management
   Albert Ashwood, Director; Michelann Ooten, Deputy Director, 405/521-2481, FAX 405/521-4053

History and Function   Purpose is to provide for mutual assistance among the states entering into this compact in managing any emergency or disaster that is duly declared by the governor of the affected state, whether arising from natural disaster, technological hazard, man-made disaster, civil emergency aspects of resources shortages, community disorders, insurgency, or enemy attack. Also provides for mutual cooperation in emergency-related exercises, testing, or other training activities.

Energy Compact of the Southern States (74 O.S. § 1051)

Southern States Energy Board   www.sseb.org
6325 Amherst Court, Norcross, Georgia 30092   770/242-7712, FAX 770/242-9956
E-mail—sseb@sseb.org

Mission Statement   Through innovations in energy and environmental programs, policies, and technologies, the Southern States Energy Board enhances economic development and the quality of life in the South.

Administration   Kenneth J. Nemeth, Executive Director and Secretary to the Board

History and Function   The Southern States Energy Board is a non-profit interstate compact organization created in 1960 and established under Public Law 87–563 and 92–400. As an institution that has led to economic growth in the South, the Southern States Energy Board endeavors to reach the goal of sustainable development by implementing strategies that support its mission. SSEB develops, promotes, and recommends policies and programs that protect and enhance the environment without compromising the needs of future generations. Sixteen southern states and two territories comprise the membership of SSEB. Each jurisdiction is represented by the governor and a legislator from the House and Senate. A governor serves as chairman and legislators serve as vice chairman and treasurer. Ex-officio, non-voting board members include a federal representative appointed by the president, the Southern Legislative Conference Energy and Environment Committee chairman and SSEB's executive director, who serves as secretary.

Energy Council, The (Laws 1982, C. 282, § 3)

(For list of Oklahoma legislative members, call Oklahoma Senate 405/524–0126)

5400 LBJ Freeway, Suite 985, Dallas, TX 75240   972/243-7788, FAX 972/243-7722
E-mail—energy@theenergycouncil.org

Administration   Lori Cameron, Executive Director

Finance Authority, Oklahoma Development (ODFA)

(74 O.S. § 5062.2, 5062.6)

(State-beneficiary public trust)   Agency Code 900 (IA)
9220 N Kelley Avenue, Oklahoma City 73131   405/848-9761, FAX 405/848-3314

Mission Statement   To assist in the creation and retention of employment throughout Oklahoma by providing a financing conduit or by providing loans to communities, businesses, and institutions without jeopardizing the credit rating of the state and at a minimum cost and minimal risk exposure to the taxpayers.

Administration   Michael D. Davis, President; Jeremy Stoner, Senior Vice President; Sunny Dobbins, Vice President; Sarah Hardy, Vice President, Operations; Lorie Collier, Assistant Vice President

Program Development and Credit Review Committee (74 O.S. § 5062.6A)

Finance Authority, Oklahoma Industrial

(Constitution, Article 10 § 33A; 74 O.S. § 854)

(State-beneficiary public trust)   Agency Code 370 (IA)
9220 N Kelley Avenue, Oklahoma City 73131   405/842-1145, FAX 405/848-3314

Mission Statement   To increase employment in Oklahoma and to help diversify the state's economy by issuing bonds and serving as a capital source for businesses.

Administration   Michael D. Davis, President; Jeremy Stoner, Senior Vice President; Sunny Dobbins, Vice President; Sarah Hardy, Vice President of Operations; Lorie Collier, Assistant Vice President

Personnel   5 unclassified, non-merit

Health Care Commission, Interstate Advisory (63 O.S. § 7300)

Health Information Exchange Trust, Oklahoma (OHIET)

(63 O.S. § 1–132) Created as a public trust.

www.ohiet.org

Juveniles, Interstate Compact for (10 O.S. § 7309)

Office of Juvenile Affairs, Juvenile Services, 3812 N Santa Fe, Suite 400 Oklahoma City 73118
PO Box 268812, Oklahoma City 73126–8812   405/530–2894, FAX 405/530–2885

Administration   Robert Hendryx, Deputy Compact Administrator

History and Function   The Interstate Compact for Juveniles was drafted by the Council of State Governments with the assistance of many other organizations to meet the needs of juvenile probationers and parolees who abscond or travel across state lines for placement purposes and to assist in returning runaway youth to their home states. The Interstate Compact for Juveniles was adopted in 2001 by Oklahoma and has been ratified by forty-nine states.

Juvenile Supervision, State Council for Interstate (10 O.S. § 7309–1.10)

Juveniles, Interstate Commission for (10 O.S. § 7309–1.7)

Kansas-Oklahoma Arkansas River Commission (82 O.S. § 1401)

Oklahoma Water Resources Board
3800 Classen Boulevard, Oklahoma City 73118   405/530–8800, FAX 405/530–8900

Administration   Bryce Benson, Ross Kirtley, and JD Strong, Oklahoma Commissioners; Julie Cunningham, Secretary, Oklahoma Member, Budget Committee; Lou Klaver, Oklahoma Member, Legal Committee

History and Function   The Kansas-Oklahoma Arkansas River Compact was approved by the states in 1965 and 1966 and by the U.S. Congress in 1966. The major purposes of the compact are to promote interstate comity between the states of Kansas and Oklahoma, and to provide and apportion equitably between the states the waters of the Arkansas River Basin.

Kiamichi Economic Development District of Oklahoma (KEDDO) (60 O.S. § 176)

(County-beneficiary public trust)   www.keddo.org
1002 HWY 2 North, Wilburton 74578   918/465–2367, FAX 918/465–3873, 800/722–8180

Mission Statement   KEDDO's purpose is to achieve total community development which will result in a balanced blend of industrial, recreational, social, cultural, and educational forces to bring about a broadened socio-economic base of the seven county region. The objective of KEDDO is to enhance the living conditions and standards in the area for all communities.

Administration   Danny Baldwin, Executive Director

History and Function   In 1967 a group of local civic and business leaders met and petitioned the Economic Development Administration (EDA) for funding of a local organization to accomplish overall economic planning and development for the seven county region of Choctaw, Haskell, Latimer, LeFlore, McCurtain, Pittsburg, and Pushmataha counties. KEDDO is a legal trust authority set up to assist people of southeastern Oklahoma plan and promote growth and development for the seven county area. The organization is directed by a board of trustees of persons from each of the counties. The financing for KEDDO is a cooperative effort between federal, state, and local governments.

Lone Chimney Water Association (60 O.S. § 176)

346400 East 5200 Road, Glencoe 74032   918/762–3581, FAX 918/762–3874

Mission Statement   To serve potable water to its customers. Formed in 1985.

Administration   Paul Kinder, Manager

Mental Health, Interstate Compact on (43A O.S. § 6–201)

1200 NE 13 Street, PO Box 53277, Oklahoma City 73152   405/522–3908

Oklahoma Compact Administrator—Designee of Commissioner of Mental Health and Substance Abuse Services (ex officio).

Mid-South Industrial Authority (60 O.S. § 176)

(State-beneficiary public trust)

For information, contact the McAlester Chamber of Commerce, 918/423-2550.

Midwestern Oklahoma Development Authority (60 O.S. § 176)

(State-beneficiary public trust)
500 N Holcomb Drive, Burns Flat 73624   PO Box 549, Burns Flat 73624
580/562-3111, FAX 580/562-3113   www.moda4counties.org

Mission Statement   To promote economic development in Beckham, Custer, Kiowa, and Washita counties.

Administration   Kathy Carlisle, Executive Director; Don Greteman, Chair, Board of Trustees

History and Function   A not-for-profit organization, established as a public trust with the state as beneficiary. In operation for approximately forty-three years, the staff performs daily maintenance on rental units. The revenue generated is invested in development and economic issues.

Military Children, Interstate Compact on Education Opportunity for (70 O.S. § 510.1)

Mining Compact Commission, Interstate (45 O.S. § 851)

Secretary of Energy
100 N Broadway, Suite 1880, Oklahoma City 73102   405/285-9211, FAX 405/285-9212

Administration   Secretary of Energy and Energy, Vacant; Jay Albert, Deputy Secretary

History and Function   When Oklahoma enacted the necessary legislation in 1970 and joined the compact as the fourth state, the compact was activated. The governor, or his designee, serve on the commission governing the compact operations whose functions are to advance the protection and restoration of the land and other resources affected by mining.

Mutual Aid Compact, Oklahoma Intrastate (63 O.S. § 695.2)

Nonresident Violator Compact (47 O.S. § 790)

Department of Public Safety, Driver Compliance Division   www.dps.state.ok.us
PO Box 11415, Oklahoma City 73136   405/425-2148, FAX 405/425-2061

Administration   Douglas R. Young, Director, Driver Compliance; Larry Williamson Sr., Driver Compliance Hearing Officer; Mike Bailey Sr., Driver Compliance Hearing Officer

North Central Oklahoma Municipal Power Pool Authority

(60 O.S. § 176) (State-beneficiary public trust)

Northeast Oklahoma Public Facilities Authority (60 O.S. § 176)

(State-beneficiary public trust)
103 N College Avenue, Tahlequah 74464   918/456-5621, FAX 918/458-0765

Administration   Jim Reagan, General Manager

Pest Control Compact (2 O.S. § 3–35)

www.pestcompact.org

Offender Supervision, Oklahoma State Council for Interstate Adult
(22 O.S. § 1094)

Created in accordance with Article IV of the Interstate Compact for Interstate Adult Offender Supervision.

Oil Compact Commission, Interstate (52 O.S. § 204(Article VI), 205)

Agency Code 307
Secretary of Energy and Environment   100 N Broadway, Suite 1880, Oklahoma City 73102
405/235-285-9211, FAX 405/285-9213

Administration   Colonel Michael Teague, Secretary of Energy and Environment

Ordnance Works Authority, Oklahoma (60 O.S. § 164, 178)
(dba MidAmerica Industrial Park)

(State-beneficiary public trust)   www.maip.com
PO Box 945, Pryor 74362   918/825-3500, 888/627-3500, FAX 918/825-4022

Administration   David R. Stewart, CAO

History and Function   Created as a state beneficiary public trust December 30, 1960, the trust
owns and operates the MidAmerica Industrial Park to promote industrial development in the state.
One trustee is appointed by the President Pro Tempore of the Oklahoma Senate, one by the Speaker
of the House of Representatives and three by the governor.

Racing with Pari-mutuel Wagering, Interstate Compact Committee on Licensure of Participants in Live Horse (3A O.S. § 240)

Radioactive Waste Compact Commission, Central Interstate Low-level (27A O.S. § 2–8–102(Article IV))

Department of Environmental Quality
707 N Robinson, PO Box 1677, Oklahoma City 73101-1677   405/702-5100, FAX 405/702-5101

Administration   Jon Roberts, Commissioner

Rail Compact, Interstate Midwest Regional Passenger
(66 O.S. § 326) Commission (66 O.S. § 327)

Red River Compact Commission (82 O.S. §1432)

Oklahoma Water Resources Board
3800 Classen Boulevard, Oklahoma City 73118   405/530-8800, FAX 405/530-8900

Administration   Charles Dobbs, JD Strong, Oklahoma Commissioners; Julie Cunningham,
    Oklahoma Member, Engineering Committee; Derek Smithee, Oklahoma Member, Environment
    and Natural Resources Committee; Jerry Barnett, Oklahoma Member, Legal Committee

History and Function   The Red River Compact Commission has been approved and ratified
by the legislatures of the affected states, Arkansas, Louisiana, Oklahoma, and Texas, and serves to
administer each state's apportionment of the waters of the Red River and its tributaries.

Southern Oklahoma Development Association (SODA) (60 O.S. § 176)

2704 N 1 Street, Durant 74701   www.soda-ok.org
PO Box 709, Durant 74702   580/920–1388, 800/211–2116, FAX 580/920–1391

Mission Statement   A voluntary association of Oklahoma local governmental jurisdictions that performs functions for the benefit of and exists for the primary benefit of Oklahoma local governmental jurisdictions.

Administration   Tommy Shepard, Executive Director; Jon McCormick, Chief Financial Officer; Brenda McCarty, Accounting Administrator; Mark Ellis, Area Agency on Aging; Dottie DeMeulenaere, Planning and Development; Cecil Mackey, Rural Fire Defense

History and Function   The Southern Oklahoma Development Association (SODA) was first organized November 19, 1957, and consisted of Carter, Garvin, and Murray counties. The agency's primary objective was to promote and support construction of Arbuckle Dam and Reservoir. When Congress passed the Interlocal Cooperation Act, the present ten county configuration was recognized. These ten counties are: Atoka, Bryan, Carter, Coal, Johnston, Garvin, Love, Marshall, Murray, and Pontotoc. The Economic Development Administration of the U.S. Department of Commerce recognized SODA as an Economic Development District February 21, 1967, allowing SODA to become the first such district in the nation to be founded by EDA.

South Western Oklahoma Development Authority (SWODA)

(60 O.S. § 176)

PO Box 569, 420 Sooner Drive, Burns Flat 73624   www.swoda.org
800/627–4882, FAX 580/562–4880

Mission Statement   The authority's mission is to strengthen governments by providing services and technical assistance; promote orderly growth and development through job creation and the preservation of the environmental integrity; and improve the quality of life by maximizing economic and social opportunities for the region and its population.

Administration   Debora Glasgow, Executive Director

Uniform State Laws, Commissioners to National Conference on

(74 O.S. § 471)

History and Function   Established as an advisory committee to the Oklahoma Legislature and to the governor. Composed of four members of the Oklahoma Bar appointed by the governor with the advice of the president of the Oklahoma Bar; two members, at least one of whom is a member of the Oklahoma House, to be appointed by the Speaker of the House; and two members, at least one of whom is a member of the Oklahoma Senate, to be appointed by the President Pro Tempore of the Senate. Members are appointed for four-year terms. The commissioners attend the annual meetings of the National Conference (see below).

Uniform State Laws, National Conference of Commissioners on   www.uniformlaws.org
111 N Wabash Ave., Suite 1010, Chicago, IL 60602   312/450–6600, FAX 312/450–6601

Wildland Fire Protection Compact, South Central Interstate

(2 O.S. § 16–35) Formerly South Central Interstate Forest Fire Protection Compact

Advisory Committee (2 O.S. § 16–35, 2 O.S. § 16–38)

Department of Agriculture, Food, and Forestry (IA)
PO Box 528804, Oklahoma City 73152   405/522–2295, FAX 405/522–4583
E-mail—george.geissler@ag.ok.gov

Administration   Mary Fallin, Governor, Compact Administrator; George Geissler, Assistant Compact Administrator and Representative of the State of Oklahoma.

History and Function   As part of the Agricultural Code, the compact's purpose is to promote effective prevention and control of forest fires in the south central region of the United States, mainly in Oklahoma, Arkansas, Louisiana, Mississippi, and Texas. The Advisory Committee has been authorized to meet with other compact state administrators to formulate a regional forest fire protection plan for the member states.

Sam Houston Cabin, Fort Gibson, from *Historic American Buildings Survey*, 1934, Fred Q. Casler, photographer. From 1829 to 1833, Sam Houston was a practicing lawyer in Indian Territory, settling in Cherokee country to assist Indians with legal advice regarding their agents, the government, and persons who had illegally entered their land. His practice has been described as "international law, frontier style" due to the mix of overlapping authority and lawlessness in the Territory.

Public Libraries In Oklahoma

Oklahoma's public libraries loaned more than 25 million items and hosted more than 4.2 million public Internet sessions in 2014. For updates visit www.odl.state.ok.us/go/pl.asp.

City	Library	Address	Telephone
Ada	Hugh Warren Memorial	124 S Rennie, 74820-5189	580/436-8124
Allen	Allen Public	214 E Broadway, 74825-0343	580/857-2933
Altus	Altus Public	421 N Hudson, 73521-3605	580/477-2890
Altus	Southern Prairie System	421 N Hudson, 73521-3605	580/477-2890
Alva	Alva Public	504 7 Street, 73717-2247	580/327-1833
Anadarko	Anadarko Community	215 W Broadway, 73005-2807	405/247-7351
Antlers	Antlers Public	104 SE 2 Street, 74523-3856	580/298-5649
Apache	Apache Public	111 W Evans, 73006-0593	580/588-3661
Ardmore	Ardmore Public	320 "E" St. NW, 73401-4398	580/223-8290
Ardmore	Chickasaw Regional System	601 Railway Express, 73401-2999	580/223-3164
Arkoma	Arkoma Public	1101 Main, 74901-0446	918/875-3971
Atoka	Atoka County	215 East A Street, 74525-2041	580/889-3555
Barnsdall	Ethel Briggs Memorial	410 S 5 Street, 74002	918/847-2118
Bartlesville	Bartlesville Public	600 S Johnstone, 74003-4630	918/338-4161
Battiest	Battiest Reading Center	PO Box 199, 74722	580/241-5686
Beaver	Beaver County Pioneer	201 Douglas, 73932-0579	580/625-3076
Bethany	Bethany Public	3510 N Mueller, 73008-3971	405/789-8363
Binger	Binger Public	217 W Main, 73009	405/656-2543
Bixby	Bixby Public	20 E Breckenridge, 74008-4427	918/549-7514
Blackwell	Blackwell Public	123 W Padon, 74631-2805	580/363-1809
Blanchard	Blanchard Public	205 NE 10 Street, 73010-0614	405/485-2275
Boise City	Soutar Memorial	102 S Ellis, 73933-1088	580/544-2715
Boley	Boley Public	17 N Cedar, 74829	918/667-3337
Boswell	Boswell Reading Center	610 Valliant, 74727-0811	580/566-2866
Bristow	Montfort & Allie B Jones Memorial Library	111 W 7 Street, 74010-2401	918/367-6562
Broken Arrow	Broken Arrow Public	300 W Broadway, 74011	918/549-7500
Broken Arrow	South Broken Arrow	3600 S Chestnut, 74011-1444	918/549-7662
Broken Bow	Broken Bow Public	404 N Broadway, 74728-2942	580/584-2815
Buffalo	Buffalo Public	11 E Turner, 73834-0265	580/735-2995
Canton	Canton Public	PO Box 694, 73724	580/886-2266
Carmen	Carmen Public	110 N 6 Street 73726-0098	580/987-2301
Carnegie	Carnegie Public	6 E Main, 73015	580/654-1980
Catoosa	Catoosa Public	105 E Oak, 74015-0662	918/266-1684

City	Library	Address	Telephone
Chandler	Chandler Public	1021 Manvel, 74834–3853	405/258–3204
Checotah	Jim Lucas Public	626 W Gentry, 74426–2218	918/473–6715
Chelsea	Chelsea Public	618 Pine, 74016–1820	918/789–3364
Cherokee	Cherokee City/County	123 S Grand, 73728–3020	580/596–2366
Cheyenne	Minnie R. Slief Memorial	201 S Cearlock, 73628	580/497–3777
Chickasha	Chickasha Public	527 Iowa, 73018–3445	405/222–6075
Choctaw	Choctaw Public	2525 N Muzzy, 73020	405/390–8418
Chouteau	Chouteau Public	111 N McCracken, 74337	918/476–4445
Claremore	Will Rogers	1515 N Florence, 74017–7032	918/341–1564
Clayton	Cartwright Memorial	113 Lawson, 74536	918/569–4776
Cleveland	J.C. Byers Memorial	215 E Wichita Avenue, 74020	918/358–2676
Clinton	Clinton Public	721 Frisco, 73601–3320	580/323–2165
Clinton	Western Plains System	501 S 28 Street, 73601–1027	580/323–0974
Coalgate	Coal County Public	115 W Ohio, 74538–0049	580/927–3103
Collinsville	Collinsville Public	1223 Main, 74021–3114	918/549–7528
Cordell	Cordell Public	208 S College, 73632–0340	580/832–3530
Coweta	Coweta Public	120 E Sycamore, 74429	918/486–6532
Crescent	Crescent Community	205 N Grand, 73028	405/969–3779
Cushing	Cushing Public	215 N Steele, 74023	918/225–4188
Davis	Davis Public	209 E Benton, 73030–2306	580/369–2468
Del City	Del City Public	4509 SE 15 Street, 73115–3098	405/672–1377
Dewey	H.F. Tyler Memorial	821 N Shawnee, 74029–1629	918/534–2106
Drumright	Drumright Public	104 E Broadway, 74030–3610	918/352–2228
Duncan	Duncan Public	2211 N Hwy 81, 73533–4686	580/255–0636
Durant	Donald W. Reynolds Community Center and Library	1515 W Main, 74701–4315	580/924–3486
Edmond	Edmond Public	10 S Blvd, 73034–3798	405/341–9282
Elgin	Elgin Community	HWY 17, 73538	580/492–5650
Elk City	Elk City Carnegie	221 W Broadway, 73644–4741	580/225–0136
El Reno	El Reno Carnegie	215 E Wade, 73036–2753	405/262–2409
Enid	Enid & Garfield County	120 W Maine, 73701	580/234–6313
Erick	Erick Community	200 S Sheb Wooley, 73645	580/526–3425
Eufaula	Eufaula Memorial	301 S First Street, 74432–3201	918/689–2291
Fairfax	Fairfax Public	158 E Elm, 74637–2017	918/642–5535
Fairview	Fairview City	115 S 6 Street, 73737–0419	580/227–2190
Fort Gibson	Q.B. Boydstun	201 E South Avenue, 74434	918/478–3587
Frederick	Frederick Public	200 E Grand, 73542–5627	580/335–3601
Gage	Gage Public	515 N Maine, 73843	580/923–7727

City	Library	Address	Telephone
Gate	Gateway/Panhandle	Main Street, 73844-0027	N/A
Geary	Geary Public	106 W Main, 73040-0216	405/884-2372
Glenpool	Glenpool Public	730 E 141 Street, 74033-3604	918/549-7535
Grandfield	Grandfield Public	101 W 2 Street, 73546-9789	580/479-5598
Grove	Grove Public	1140 NEO Loop, 74344	918/786-2945
Guthrie	Guthrie Public	201 N Division, 73044-3201	405/282-0050
Guymon	Guymon Public	1718 N Oklahoma, 73942-5110	580/338-7330
Harrah	Harrah Public	1930 N Church, 73045	405/454-2001
Hartshorne	Hartshorne Public	720 Pennsylvania Avenue, 74547	918/297-2113
Haskell	Rieger Memorial	116 N Broadway, 74436-0429	918/482-3614
Healdton	Healdton Community	554 S 4 Street, 73438-2109	580/229-0590
Heavener	Heavener Public	203 East C Avenue, 74937-0246	918/653-2870
Hennessey	Hennessey Public	525 S Main, 73742-1701	405/853-2073
Henryetta	Henryetta Public	518 W Main, 74437-4244	918/652-7377
Hinton	Norman Smith Memorial	115 E Main, 73047-0034	405/542-6167
Hobart	Hobart Public	200 S Main, 73651-3628	580/726-2535
Holdenville	Grace Pickens Public	209 E 9 Street, 74848-3499	405/379-3245
Hollis	Hollis Public	201 W Broadway, 73550-0073	580/688-2744
Hominy	Hominy Public	121 W Main, 74035-1031	918/885-4486
Hooker	Olive Warner Memorial	111 S Broadway, 73945-0576	580/652-2835
Hugo	Choctaw County	703 E Jackson, 74743	580/326-5591
Hulbert	Hulbert Community	210 N Broadway, 74441	918/772-3383
Hydro	Hydro Public	530 N Broadway, 73048-0041	405/663-2009
Idabel	Idabel Public	103 E Main, 74745	580/286-6406
Inola	Inola Public	15 N Broadway, 74036-1237	918/543-8862
Jay	Delaware County	429 S 9 Street, 74346-0387	918/253-8521
Jenks	Jenks Public	523 West B, 74037-3713	918/549-7570
Jones	Jones Public	111 E Main, 73049-0425	405/399-5471
Kansas	Kansas Public	200 W Tulsa Avenue, 74347	918/868-5257
Kaw City	J.A. Walker Memorial	900 Morgan Square, 74641-0026	580/269-2525
Kellyville	Kellyville Public	230 E Buffalo, 74039-1260	918/247-3740
Kingfisher	Kingfisher Memorial	505 W Will Rogers, 73750-4334	405/375-3384
Kiowa	Kiowa Reading Center	7th and Harrison, 74553	918/423-6279
Konawa	Kennedy of Konawa	701 W South St, 74849-0003	580/925-3662
Langley	Langley Public	Third and Osage, 74350-0655	918/782-4461
Laverne	Laverne Delphian Municipal	214 W Jane Jayroe, 73848	580/921-7323
Lawton	Lawton Public	110 SW 4 Street, 73501-4076	580/581-3450
Lawton	Kathleen Wyatt Nicholson	1304 NW Kingswood, 73505	580/581-3457

City	Library	Address	Telephone
Lindsay	Lindsay Community	112 W Choctaw, 73052-5417	405/756-3449
Locust Grove	Locust Grove Public	715 Harold Andrews, 74352-0697	918/479-6585
Luther	Elizabeth Threatt Luther	310 NE 3 Street, 73054	405/277-9967
Madill	Madill City/County	500 W Overton, 73446-2221	580/795-2749
Mangum	Margaret Carder	201 W Lincoln, 73554-4601	580/782-3185
Mannford	Mannford Public	101 Green Valley Park Road, 74044	918/865-2665
Marietta	Love County	500 S Highway 77, 73448-9418	580/276-3783
Marlow	Garland Smith	702 W Main, 73055-2459	580/658-5354
Marshall	Angie Debo	PO Box 130, 73056	580/935-6736
Maysville	Maysville Public	508 Williams St., 73057	405/867-4748
McAlester	McAlester Public	401 N 2 Street, 74501-4625	918/426-0930
McAlester	Southeastern System	401 N 2 Street, 74501-4625	918/426-0456
McCurtain	McCurtain Reading Center	407 W Oak, 74994	918/945-7385
McCloud	McLoud Public	133 N Main, 74851	405/964-2960
Medford	Medford Public	123 S Main, 73759-1530	580/395-2342
Meeker	Meeker Public	616 W Carl Hubbell Blvd., 74855	405/279-1139
Miami	Miami Public	200 N Main, 74354-5918	918/541-2292
Midwest City	Midwest City Public	8143 E Reno, 73110-3999	405/732-4828
Moore	Moore Public	225 S Howard, 73160-5240	405/793-5100
Mooreland	Altrusa Public	107 S Main, 73852	580/994-5924
Morris	Morris Public	321 S Hughes, 74445	918/733-2222
Mounds	Julia Crowder McLellan	15 W 14 Street, 74047	918/827-3949
Mt. View	Addie Davis Memorial	301 N 4 Street, 73062-0567	580/347-2397
Muldrow	Muldrow Public	711 W Shawntell Blvd., 74948-0449	918/427-6703
Muskogee	Eastern Library System	814 W Okmulgee, 74401-6839	918/683-2846
Muskogee	Muskogee Public	801 W Okmulgee, 74401-6800	918/682-6657
Mustang	Mustang Public	1201 Mustang Road, 73064	405/376-2226
Newcastle	Newcastle Public	705 NW 10 Street, 73065-0780	405/387-5076
Newkirk	Newkirk Public	116 N Maple Ave, 74647	580/362-3934
Nicoma Park	Nicoma Park Public	2240 Overholser Dr., 73066	405-769-9452
Noble	Noble Public	204 N 5 Street, 73068	405/872-5713
Norman	Norman Public Library Central	225 N Webster, 73069	405/701-2600
Norman	Norman Public Library West	300 Norman Center CT, 73072	405/701-2644
Norman	Pioneer System	300 Norman Center CT, 73072	405/801-4500
Nowata	Nowata City/County	224 S Pine, 74048	918/273-3363
Oilton	Oilton Public	105 W Main, 74052	918/862-3294
Okeene	Okeene Public	215 N Main, 73763	580/822-3306

City	Library	Address	Telephone
Okemah	Okemah Public	301 S 2 Street, 74859	918/623-1915
Okla. City	Almonte	2914 SW 59 Street, 73119	405/606-3575
Okla. City	Belle Isle	5501 N Villa, 73112-7164	405/843-9601
Okla. City	Capitol Hill	334 SW 26 Street, 73109-6711	405/634-6308
Okla. City	Metropolitan System	300 Park Avenue, 73102	405/606-3726
Okla. City	Patience Latting Northwest	5600 NW 122 Street, 73142	405/606-3580
Okla. City	Ralph Ellison	2000 NE 23 Street, 73111-3402	405/424-1437
Okla. City	Ronald J. Norick	300 Park Avenue, 73102	405/231-8650
Okla. City	Southern Oaks	6900 S Walker, 73139-7299	405/631-4468
Okla. City	Southwest Oklahoma City	2201 SW 134 Street, 73170	405/979-2200
Okla. City	Wright	2101 Exchange Avenue, 73108	405/235-5035
Okmulgee	Okmulgee Public	218 S Okmulgee, 74447-4436	918/756-1448
Owasso	Owasso Public	103 W Broadway, 74055-2908	918/549-7624
Pauls Valley	Nora Sparks Warren	210 N Willow, 73075-3287	405/238-5188
Pawhuska	Pawhuska Public	1801 Lynn Avenue, 74056	918/287-3989
Pawnee	Pawnee Public	653 Illinois, 74058	918/762-2138
Perkins	Thomas-Wilhite Memorial	101 E Thomas, 74059-0519	405/547-5185
Perry	Perry Carnegie	302 N 7 Street, 73077-6406	580/336-4721
Pickens	Pickens Reading Center	100 Main Street, 74752	580/241-5686
Piedmont	Piedmont Municipal	1129 7 Street NW, 73078	405/373-9045
Ponca City	Ponca City	515 E Grand, 74601-5499	580/767-0345
Pond Creek	Pond Creek City	105 S 2 Street, 73766	580/532-6319
Poteau	Patrick Lynn Public Library	206 S McKenna Street, 74953	918/647-3833
Prague	Haynie Public	1619 W Main 74864	405/567-4013
Pryor	Thomas J Harrison Public	505 E Graham, 74361-4804	918/825-0777
Purcell	Purcell Public	919 N 9 Street, 73080-2098	405/527-5546
Quinton	Quinton Reading Center	PO Box 180, 74561	918/469-2218
Red Oak	Red Oak Reading Center	PO Box 470, 74563,	918/754-2832
Ringling	Gleason Memorial	101 E Main, 73456	580/662-2925
Rush Springs	Glover Spencer Memorial	100 S 6 Street, 73082-0576	580/476-2108
Salina	Salina Public	420 E Ferry Street, 74365	918/434-8001
Sallisaw	Stanley Tubbs Memorial	101 E Cherokee, 74955-4621	918/775-4481
Sand Springs	Charles Page	551 E 4 Street, 74063	918/549-7521
Sand Springs	Pratt Public	3219 S 113 W Avenue, 74063	918/549-7638
Sapulpa	Bartlett-Carnegie Public	27 W Dewey, 74066-3909	918/224-5624
Sayre	Sayre Public	113 E Poplar, 73662-0399	580/928-2641
Seiling	Seiling Public	209 N Main, 73663-0070	580/922-4259
Seminole	Seminole Public	424 N Main St, 74868-3481	405/382-4221

City	Library	Address	Telephone
Sentinel	Sentinel Public	210 E Main, 73664-0178	580/393-2244
Shattuck	Shattuck Public	101 S Main, 73858-0129	580/938-5104
Shawnee	Shawnee Public	101 N Philadelphia, 74801	405/275-6353
Shidler	Shidler Public	N 4 & Cosden, 74652	918/793-4171
Skiatook	Skiatook Public	316 E Rogers, 74070	918/549-7676
Snyder	Snyder Public	805 E Street, 73566	580/569-4572
Spiro	Spiro Public	208 S Main, 74959-2506	918/962-3461
Stigler	Stigler Public	410 NE 6 Street, 74462-2208	918/967-4801
Stillwater	Stillwater Public	1107 S Duck, 74074-4449	405/372-3633
Stilwell	Stilwell Public	5 N 6 Street, 74960-2829	918/696-7512
Strang	Strang Community	PO Box 12, 74367	918/593-2350
Stratford	Chandler-Watts	340 N Oak, 74872-0696	580/759-2684
Stroud	Stroud Public	301 W 7 Street, 74079-0599	918/968-2567
Sulphur	Mary E. Parker Memorial	500 W Broadway, 73086-4606	580/622-5807
Tahlequah	Tahlequah Public	120 S College, 74464-3842	918/456-2581
Talala	Talala Public	104 W Watova, 74080	918/275-4540
Talihina	Talihina Public	900 2 Street, 74571	918/567-2002
Tecumseh	Tecumseh Public	114 N Broadway, 74873-3226	405/598-5955
Texhoma	Texhoma City Public	PO Box 647, 73949	580/423-7150
Thomas	Hazel Cross	115 W Broadway, 73669-0410	580/661-3532
Tipton	Tipton Municipal	PO Box 340, 73570-0340	580/667-5268
Tishomingo	Johnston County	116 W Main, 73460-1732	580/371-3006
Tonkawa	Tonkawa Public	216 N 7 Street, 74653-3537	580/628-3366
Tryon	Tryon Public	25 S Main, 74875-0065	918/374-2220
Tulsa	Brookside Public	1207 E 45 Place, 74105-4508	918/549-7507
Tulsa	Central Library	400 Civic Center, 74103	918/549-7323
Tulsa	Genealogy Center	8316 E 93 Street, 74114	918/746-5222
Tulsa	Hardesty Regional	8316 E 93 Street, 74133	918/549-7550
Tulsa	Helmerich	5131 E 91 Street, 74137-3506	918/549-7550
Tulsa	Herman & Kate Kaiser	5202 S Hudson Ste B, 74135	918/549-7542
Tulsa	Kendall-Whittier	21 S Lewis, 74104	918/549-7584
Tulsa	Martin Regional	2601 S Garnett, 74129-5113	918/549-7590
Tulsa	Maxwell Park	1313 N Canton, 74115-5305	918/549-7610
Tulsa	Nathan Hale	6038 E 23 Street, 74114-3835	918/549-7617
Tulsa	Rudisill Regional	1520 N Hartford, 74106-4312	918/549-7645
Tulsa	Schusterman-Benson	3333 E 32 Place, 74135-4449	918/549-7670
Tulsa	Suburban Acres	4606 N Garrison Avenue, 74126	918/549-7655
Tulsa	Tulsa City/County	400 Civic Center, 74103-3857	918/549-7323

City	Library	Address	Telephone
Tulsa	Zarrow Regional	2224 W 51 Street, 74107–7748	918/549–7683
Valliant	Mattie Terry Public	311 N Johnson, 74764	580/933–4883
Village	Village Public	10307 N Penn, 73120	405/755–0710
Vinita	Vinita Public	215 W Illinois Ave, 74301	918/256–2115
Wagoner	Wagoner City Public	302 N Main, 74467–3834	918/485–2126
Walters	Walters Public	202 N Broadway, 73572–2042	580/875–2006
Warr Acres	Warr Acres	5901 NW 63 Street, 73132–2401	405/721–2616
Warner	Warner Public	207 8 Street, 74469–0120	918/463–2363
Watonga	Watonga Public	301 N Prouty, 73772–3644	580/623–7748
Waurika	Waurika Public	203 S Meridian, 73573–3063	580/228–3274
Waynoka	Waynoka Public	1659 Cecil, 73860–1233	580/824–6181
Weatherford	Weatherford Public	219 E Franklin, 73096–5134	580/772–3591
Westville	John F. Henderson	116 N Williams, 74965–0580	918/723–5002
Wetumka	Wetumka Public	202 N Main, 74883–3099	405/452–3785
Wewoka	Wewoka Public	118 W 5 Street, 74884–3102	405/257–3225
Wilburton	Latimer County Public	301 W Ada, 74578–1026	918/465–3751
Wilson	Wilson Public	1087 US Hwy 70–A, 73463	580/668–2486
Wister	Wister Public	211 Plum Street, 74966	918/655–7654
Woodward	Woodward Public	1500 W Main, 73801–3053	580/254–8544
Wynnewood	Wynnewood Public	108 N Dean McGee, 73098–7810	405/665–2512
Yale	Yale Public	213 N Main, 74085–2509	918/387–2135
Yeager	Yeager Public	2815 7 Street, 74848	405/379–2049
Yukon	Mabel C. Fry Memorial	1200 Lakeshore Drive, 73099–3263	405/354–8232

Daily and Weekly Newspapers

Visit Oklahoma's online newspapers at www.okpress.com/business-members

City	Newspaper	Telephone	FAX	E-mail
Ada	Ada News	580/332-4433	580/332-8741	adanewseditor@cableone.net
Allen	Allen Advocate	580/857-2687	580/857-2573	allennews@aol.com
Altus	Altus Times	580/482-1221	580/482-5709	firstinitiallastname@cibitasmedia.com
Alva	Alva Review-Courier	580/327-2200	580/327-2454	marione@alvareviewcourier.net
Anadarko	Anadarko Daily News	405/247-3331	405/247-5571	news@anadarko-news.com
Antlers	Antlers American	580/298-3314	580/298-3316	ed.antlers.amer@sbcglobal.net
Apache	Apache News	580/588-3862		apachenews@pldi.net
Ardmore	Ardmoreite	580/223-2200	580/226-0050	marsha.miller@ardmoreite.com
Arnett	Ellis County Capital	580/885-7788		
Atoka	Atoka County Times	580/889-3319	580/889-2300	rlinscott@atokaspeedynet.net
Barnsdall	Bigheart Times	918/847-2916	918/847-2654	info@bighearttimes.com
Bartlesville	Bartlesville Examiner-Enterprise	918/335-8200	918/335-3111	firstinitiallastname@examiner-enterprise.com
Beaver	Beaver Herald-Democrat	580/625-3241	580/625-4269	
Blackwell	Blackwell Journal-Tribune	580/363-3370	580/363-4415	news@blackwelljournaltribune.net
Blanchard	Blanchard News	405/485-2311	405/485-2310	blanchardnews@pldi.net
Boise City	Boise City News	580/544-2222	580/544-3281	bcnews@ptsi.net
Bristow	Bristow News & Record-Citizen	918/367-2282	918/367-2724	bristowenews@sbcglobal.net
Broken Arrow	Broken Arrow Ledger	918/259-7500	918/259-7583	news@baledger.com
Broken Bow	Broken Bow News	580/286-3321	580/286-2208	
Buffalo	Harper County Leader	580/921-3391		hcjbuffalo@pldi.net
Canton	Canton Times	580/886-2221	580/886-3320	ctimes@pldi.net
Carnegie	Carnegie Herald	580/654-1443	580/654-1608	news@carnegieherald.com
Catoosa	Catoosa Independent	918/543-3134		inolanewsaper@tds.net
Chandler	Lincoln County News	405/258-1818	405/258-1824	lcnchandler@sbcglobal.net
Chelsea	Chelsea Reporter	918/789-2331	918/789-2333	chelsea_reporter@sbcglobal.net
Cherokee	Cherokee Messenger & Republican	580/596-3344	580/596-2959	chermessenger@att.net
Cheyenne	Cheyenne Star	580/497-3324	580/497-3516	cheystar@dobsonteleco.com
Chickasha	Express-Star	405/224-2600	405/224-2604	chickashaeditor@gmail.com
Claremore	Claremore Progress	918/341-1101	918/341-1131	editor@claremoreprogress.com
Clayton	Clayton Today	918/569-4741	918/569-4741	tricountypubinc@sbcglobal.net
Cleveland	Cleveland American	918/358-2553	918/358-2182	clevelandnews@sbcglobal.net
Clinton	Clinton Daily News	580/323-5151	580/323-5154	cdnews@swbell.net

City	Newspaper	Telephone	FAX	E-mail
Coalgate	Coalgate Record-Register	580/927-2355	580/927-3800	coalgaterec@aol.com
Comanche	Comanche Times	580/439-6500	580/439-6500	comanchetimes@pldi.net
Cordell	Cordell Beacon	580/832-3333	580/832-3335	thebeacon@cordellbeacon.com
Cushing	Cushing Citizen	918/285-5555	918/285-5556	editor@cushingcitizen.com
Davis	Davis News	580/369-2807	580/369-2807	davispaper@sbcglobal.net
Drumright	Drumright Gusher	918/352-2284		news@drumrightgusher.com
Duncan	Duncan Banner	580/255-5354	580/255-8889	editor@duncanbanner.com
Durant	Durant Daily Democrat	580/924-4388	580/924-0962	mswearengin@civitasmedia.com
Eakly	Country Connection	405/797-3648	405/797-3663	countrycollectionnews@yahoo.com
Edmond	Edmond Sun	405/341-2121	405/340-7363	news@edmondsun.com
El Reno	El Reno Tribune	405/262-5180	405/262-3541	1stinitiallastname@elrenotribune.com
Elk City	Elk City Daily News	580/225-3000	580/243-2414	ecdn@ecdailynews.com
Enid	Enid News & Eagle	580/233-6600	580/548-8147	editor@enidnewscom
Eufaula	Eufala Indian Journal	918/689-2191	918/689-2377	ijnews@bighasinllc.com
Fairfax	Fairfax Chief	918/642-3814	918/642-1376	
Fort Gibson	Fort Gibson Times	918/684-2828	918/684-2965	news@muskogeephoenix.com
Frederick	Frederick Leader	580/335-2188	580/335-2047	pressled@pldi.net
Freedom	Freedom Call	580/621-3578		thecall1906@pldi.net
Garber	Garber-Billings News	580/863-2240		gbnews@pldi.net
Geary	Geary Star	405/884-2424	405/884-2424	thegearystar@pldi.net
Grove	Grove Sun	918/786-2228	918/786-2156	news@grovesun.com
Guthrie	Guthrie News Leader	405/282-2222	405/282-7378	bramsey@guthrienewsleader.net
Guymon	Guymon Daily Herald	580/338-3355	580/338-5000	editor@ptsi.net
Haskell	Haskell News	918/482-5619	918/482-5619	hasnews@valornet.com
Healdton	Healdton Herald	580/229-0147	580/229-0132	healdtonherald@att.net
Heavener	Heavener Ledger	918/653-2425	918/653-7305	heavenerledger@windstream.net
Hennessey	Hennessey Clipper	405/853-2988	405/853-4890	barb@hennesseyclipper.com
Henryetta	Henryetta Free-Lance	918/652-3311	918/652-7347	reporter@henryettafreelance.com
Hinton	Hinton Record	405/542-6644	405/542-3120	hinton_record@hintonnet.net
Hobart	Hobart Democrat-Chief	580/726-3333	580/726-3431	dcnews@att.net
Holdenville	Holdenville News	405/379-5411	405/379-5413	holdenvillenews@sbcglobal.net
	Holdenville Tribune	405/379-5124	405/379-2336	robpublishing@sbcglobal.com
Hollis	Hollis News	580/688-3376	580/688-2261	hollisnews@pldi.net
Hominy	Hominy News-Progress	918/885-2101	918/885-4596	hominynews2@gmail.com
Hooker	Hooker Advance	580/652-2476		advance@ptsi.net
Hugo	Hugo Dailey News	580/326-3311	580/326-6397	news@sbcglobal.net

City	Newspaper	Telephone	FAX	E-mail
Idabel	McCurtain County Gazette	580/286-3321	580/286-2208	paper@mccurtain.com
	Southeast Times	580/286-2628	580/286-3818	thellis@valliant.net
Jay	Delaware County Journal	918/253-4322	918/253-4380	news@delcojournal.com
Kingfisher	Kingfisher Times & Free Press	405/375-3220	405/375-3222	kfrtimes@pldi.net
Laverne	Laverne Leader Tribune	580/921-3391		hcjbuffalo@pldi
Lawton	Lawton Constitution	580/353-0620	580/585-5140	firstinitiallastname@swoknews.com
Lindsay	Lindsay News	405/756-4461	405/756-2729	thelindsaynews@cableprinting.com
Lone Grove	Lone Grove Ledger	580/657-6492	580/657-2822	lgledger@cableone.net
Madill	Madill Record	580/795-3355	580/795-3530	recordeditorial@sbcglobal.net
Mangum	Mangum Star-News	580/782-3321	580/782-2198	mangumstarnews@sbcglobal.net
Marietta	Marietta Monitor	580/276-3255	580/276-2118	monitorok@sbcglobal.net
Marlow	Marlow Review	580/658-6657	580/658-6659	meview@cableone.net
Maysville	Garvin County News Star	405/867-4457	405/867-5115	news@gcnews-star.com
McAlester	McAlester News-Capital	918/423-1700	918/426-3081	firstinitiallastname@mcalesternews.com
Medford	Medford Patriot-Star/ Grant County Journal	580/395-2212	580/395-2907	mps@kanokla.net
	Pond Creek Herald	580/395-2212	580/395-2907	mps@kanokla.net
Miami	Miami News-Record	918/542-5533	918/542-1903	news@miaminewsrecord.com
Mnt. View	Mountain View News	580/347-2231	580/347-2231	lhobbs@westok.net
Mooreland	Mooreland Leader	580/994-5410	580/994-5409	leader2@pldi.net
Morris	Morris News	918/733-4898	888/701-3188	morrisnews@windstream.net
Muskogee	Muskogee Phoenix	918/684-2828	918/684-2865	news@muskogeephoenix.com
Mustang	Mustang News	405/376-4571	405/376-5312	bjones@mustangnews.info
Newcastle	Newcastle Pacer	405/387-5277	405/387-9863	news@newcastlepacer.com
Newkirk	Newkirk Herald Journal	580/362-2140	580/362-2348	news@newkirkherald.com
Norman	Norman Transcript	405/321-1800	405/366-3516	editor@normantranscript.com
Nowata	Nowata Star	918/273-2446	918/273-0537	nowatastar@sbcglobal.net
Okeene	Okeene Record	580/822-4401	580/822-3051	bcpub@pldi.net
Okemah	Okemah News Leader	918/623-0123	918/623-0124	office@okemanewsleader.com
Oklahoma City	Baptist Messenger	405/942-3000	405/942-3075	baptistmessenger@okbaptist.net
	Black Chronicle	405/424-4695	405/424-6708	alindsey@theblackchronicle.com
	City Sentinel	405/605-6062		news@city-sentinel.com
	El Nacional	405/632-4531	405/632-4533	jvega.nacional@coxinet.net
	Friday	405/755-3311	405/755-3315	roseokcfriday@aol.com
	Journal Record	405/235-3100	405/278-2890	news@journalrecord.com
	Oklahoma Banker	405/424-5252	405/424-4518	jeremy@oba.com

City	Newspaper	Telephone	FAX	E-mail
Oklahoma City	Oklahoma City Herald	405/842-7817	405/842-7276	news@okcherald.org
	Oklahoma Gazette	405/528-6000	405/528-4600	pbacharach@okgazette.com
	Oklahoman	405/475-3311	405/475-3183	rgreen@opubco.com
Okmulgee	Okmulgee Times	918/756-3600	918/756-8197	herman@bigbasinllc.com
Oologah	Oologah Lake Leader	918/443-2428	918/443-2429	lakeleader@sbcglobal.net
Owasso	Owasso Reporter	918/272-1155	918/272-0642	joshb@owassoreporter.com
Pauls Valley	Pauls Valley Democrat	405/238-6464	405/238-3042	firstinitiallastname@pvdemocrat.com
Pawhuska	Pawhuska Journal-Capital	918/287-1590	918/287-1804	mawlse@pawhuskajournalcapital.com
Pawnee	Pawnee Chief	918/762-2552	918/762-2554	news@pawneechief.net
Perkins	Perkins Journal	405/547-2411	405/547-2419	news@TheJournalOK.com
Perry	Perry Daily Journal	580/336-2222	580/336-3222	gloriapdjnews@yahoo.com
Piedmont	Piedmont-Surrey Gazette	405/373-1616	405/373-1636	editor@piedmontnewsonline.com
Ponca City	Ponca City News	580/765-3311	580/765-7800	news@poncacitynews.com
Poteau	Poteau Daily News	918/647-3188	918/647-8198	editor@poteaudailynews.com
Prague	Prague Times-Herald	405/567-3933	405/567-3934	praguetimes@brightok.net
Pryor	Pryor Daily Times	918/825-3292	918/825-1965	prynews@swbell.net
Purcell	Purcell Register	405/527-2126	405/527-3299	purcellregister@gmail.com
Ringling	Ringling Eagle	580/662-2221		ringlingeagle@sbcglobal.net
Rush Springs	Rush Springs Gazette	580/476-2525		rsgazette@sbcglobal.net
Sallisaw	Sequoyah County Times	918/775-4433	918/775-3023	news@seqcotimes.com
Sand Springs	Sand Springs Leader	918/245-6634	918/241-3610	news@sandspringsleader.com
Sapulpa	Sapulpa Daily Herald	918/224-5185	918/224-5196	editor@sapulpadailyherald.com
Sayre	Sayre Record & Beckham County Democrat	580/928-5540	580/928-5547	sayrerecord@cableone.net
Seiling	Dewey County Publisher	580/922-4296	580/922-7777	dcpub@pldi.net
Seminole	Konowa Leader	580/925-3187		news@seminoleproducer.com
	Seminole Producer	405/382-1100	405/382-1104	news@seminoleproducer.com
Sentinel	Sentinel Leader	580/393-4348	580/393-4349	sleader@pldi.net
Shattuck	NW Oklahoman & Ellis County News	580/938-2533	580/938-5240	nwopaper@pldi.net
Shawnee	Potawatomie County Democrat	405/273-8888	405/275-6473	demcop@sbcglobal
	Shawnee County Democrat	405/273-8888	405/275-6473	demcop@sbcglobal.net
	Shawnee News-Star	405/273-4200	405/273-4207	newsroom@news-star.com
Shidler	Shidler Review	918/793-3841	918/793-3842	thereview08@gmail.com
Skiatook	Skiatook Journal	918/396-1616	918/396-3921	news@skiatookjournal.com
Snyder	Kiowa County Democrat	580/569-2684	580/569-2640	kiowacountydemocrat@gmail.com
Spiro	Spiro Graphic	918/962-2075	918/962-3531	spirographic@sbcglobal.net

City	Newspaper	Telephone	FAX	E-mail
Stigler	Stigler News-Sentinel	918/967-4655	918/967-4289	editor@stiglernews.com
Stillwater	Stillwater NewsPress	405/372-5000	405/372-3112	editor@stwnewspress.com
Stilwell	Stilwell Democrat Journal	918/696-2228	918/696-7064	stilwelldj@windstream.nett
Stroud	Stroud American	918/968-2581	918/967-3864	stroudamerican@cotc.net
Sulphur	Sulphur Times-Democrat	580/622-2102	580/622-2937	jcjohn@sulphurtimes.com
Tahlequah	Tahlequah Daily Press	918/456-8833	918/456-2019	news@tahllequahdailypress.com
Talihina	Talihina American	918/567-2390	918/567-2390	tricountypubinc@sbcglobal.net
Tecumseh	Countywide Sun	405/598-3793	405/598-3891	editor@countywidenews.com
Thomas	Thomas Tribune	580/661-3525	580/661-3324	thethomastribune@yahoo.com
Tishomingo	Johnston County Capital-Democrat	580/371-2356	580/371-9648	capital_democrat@yahoo.com
Tonkawa	Tonkawa News	580/628-2532	580/628-4044	news@tonkawanews.com
	Oklahoma Eagle	918/582-7124	918/589-0250	news@theoklahomaeagle.net
Tulsa	Tulsa Business & Legal News	918/585-6655	918/295-4890	firstnamelastinitial@tulsabusiness.com
	Tulsa World	918/581-8300	918/581-8353	news@tulsaworld.com
Valliant	Valliant Leader	580/933-4579	580/933-4900	valeader@valliant.net
Vian	Vian Tenkiller News	918/773-8000	918/773-8745	news@bigbasinllc.com
Vici	Vici Vision	580/995-3425	580/995-4987	vicichamber@vicihorizon.com
Vinita	Vinita Daily Journal	918/256-6422	918/256-7100	
Wagoner	Wagoner Tribune	918/485-5505	918/485-8442	news@wagonertribune.com
Walters	Walters Herald	580/875-3326	580/875-3150	wherald@sbcglobal.net
Watonga	Watonga Republican	580/623-4922	580/623-4925	editor@thewatongarepublican.com
Waynoka	Woods County Enterprise	580/824-2171	580/824-2172	wcepaper@plidi.net
Weatherford	Weatherford Daily News	580/772-3301	580/772-7329	wdn@wdnonline.com
Westville	Westville Reporter	918/723-5445	918/696-7066	westvillereporter@yahoo.com
Wetumka	Hughes County Times	405/452-3294	405/452-3574	hugescountytimes@sbcglobal.net
Wewoka	Wewoka Times	405/257-3341	405/257-3342	news@seminoleproducer.com
Wilburton	Latimer Co. News-Tribune			lcnt@cwis.net
Woodward	Woodward News	580/256-2200	580/254-2159	editor@woodwardnews.net
Wynnewood	Wynnewood Gazette	405/665-4333	405/665-4334	wynnewoodgazette@sbcglobal.net
Yale	Phoenix			yalephoenix@yahoo.com
Yukon	Yukon Review	405/354-5264	405/350-3044	conrad@yukonreviewl.net

Oklahoma Television Stations

License City	Calls	Affiliate/Network	Phone	Contact E-mail
Ada	KTEN	NBC	903/337-4000	amaisel@kten.com
Bartlesville	KDOR	TBN		
Cheyenne	KWET	PBS	405/848-8501	dschiedel@oeta.tv
Claremore	KRSU		918/343-7649	
Eufaula	KOET	PBS	405/848-8501	dschiedel@oeta.tv
Lawton	KSWO	ABC	580/355-7000	lpatton@kswo.com
Muskogee	KQCW	The CW	918/732-6000	rob.krier@griffincommunications.net
Norman	KOCM	Daystar		
Oklahoma City	KAUT	Independent	405/424-4444	wes.milbourn@kfor.com
	KETA	PBS	405/848-8501	dschiedel@oeta.tv
	KFOR	NBC	405/424-4444	wes.milbourn@kfor.com
	KOCB	The CW	405/478-3434	
	KOCO	ABC	405/478-3000	bhensley@hearst.com
	KOKH	FOX	405/843-2525	
	KOPX	ION	405/751-6800	aishafigilis@ionmedia.com
	KSBI	MyNetworkTV	405/843-6641	rob.krier@griffincommunications.net
	KTBO	TBN		
	KWTV	CBS	405/843-6641	rob.krier@griffincommunications.net
Okmulgee	KTPX	ION	918/664-1044	aishafigilis@ionmedia.com
Shawnee	KTUZ	Telemundo	405/616-5500	armando.r@tylermedia.com
Tulsa	KGEB	Golden Eagle	918/488-5300	acalvert@oru.edu
	KJRH	NBC	918/743-2222	dwilson@kjrh.com
	KMYT	MyNetworkTV	918/388-5100	gbilte@fox23.com
	KOED	PBS	405/848-8501	dschiedel@oeta.tv
	KOKI	FOX	918/388-5100	gbilte@fox23.com
	KOTV	CBS	918/732-6000	rob.krier@griffincommunications.net
	KTUL	ABC	918/445-8888	pbaldwin@ktul.com
	KWHB	LeSEA	918/254-4701	dsmith@lesea.com
Woodward	KUOK	Univision	405/616-5500	armando.r@tylermedia.com

Note: Check your local channel guides for regular, cable, satellite, and high definition listings

Oklahoma Radio Stations

License City	Calls	Contact E-mail or Website	Phone
	KADA AM/FM	kada@wilnet1.com	580/332-1212
	KAJT-FM	www.sonliferadio.org	225/768-3288
Ada	KAKO-FM	www.afa.net	580/332-1212
	KCNP-FM	brian.brashier@chickasaw.net	580/332-1212
	KTGS-FM	email@thegospelstation.com	580/332-1212
	KEYB-FM	firstname@keyb.net	580/482-1555
	KKVO-FM	www.klove.com	919/251-1600
Altus	KOCU-FM	www.kccu.org	888/454-7800
	KTHL-FM	www.thehousefm.com	580/767-1400
	KWHW-AM/FM	cameron@kwhw.com	580/482-1450
Alva	KALV-AM		580/327-1430
	KPAK-FM	www.kpak.net	888/251-8427
Anadarko	KVSP-FM	kperry@kvsp.com	405/427-5877
Antlers	KDOE-FM	www.kdoe1023.com	580/326-2555
	KMAC-FM	okcatholicbroadcasting.com	405/255-7348
Apache	KACO-FM	anadarkospots@perrybroadcasting.net	405/247-6682
	KLCU-FM	www.kccu.org	888/454-7800
Ardmore	KQPD-FM	www.afa.net	662/844-8888
	KVSO-AM	michael@sokradio.com	580/226-0421
Atoka	KHKC-FM	khkc103@yahoo.com	580/889-3392
	KWON-AM	charlie@bartlesvilleradio.com	918/336-1400
Bartlesville	KWRI-FM	www.air1.com	916/251-1600
	KYFM-FM	charlie@bartlesvilleradio.com	918/336-1400
Beaver	KLDB-FM		724/516-8885
Bennington	KZRC-FM	www.mix961.net	580/745-5961
Bethany	KKWD-FM	1stname.lastname@cumulus.com	405/848-0100
Bixby	KJMM-FM	mvaughan@kjmm.com	918/494-9886
Blackwell	KOKB-AM	www.eteamradio.com	580/765-2485
Blanchard	KKNG-FM	okcatholicbroadcasting.com	405/255-7348
Boise City	KJHL-FM	www.kjil991.com	620/873-2991
Bristow	KREK-FM	www.sonliferadio.com	225/-768-3288
Broken Arrow	KNYD-FM	www.oasisnetwork.org	918/455-5693
	KTBT-FM	firstnamelastname@clearchannel.com	918/388-5100
Broken Bow	KBWW-FM		580/420-6687
	KKBI-FM	kkbi@pine-net.com	580/584-3388
Byng	KYKC-FM	score@cableone.net	580/332-1212

License City	Calls	Contact E-mail or Website	Phone
Cache	KARU-FM	www.air1.com	916/251–1600
	KJMZ-FM	joyc@kjmz.com	580/355–1050
Caney	KWEZ-FM	www.ebenezertv.com	972/840–9274
Carnegie	KJCC-FM	www.csnradio.com	800/357–4226
Catoosa	KETU-AM	www.radiovictory.org	918/491–7880
	KZLI-AM	krut@krut.com	918/254–7556
Chelsea	KTFR-FM	thekross.fm	918/369–5444
Chickasha	KFXU-FM		580/658–9292
	KWCO-FM	www.kool1055fm.com	405/224–1560
Claremore	KRSC-FM	requestline@rsuradio.edu	918/343–7669
	KTUZ-FM	firstname.lastinitial@tylermedia.com	405/616–5500
Clinton	KCLI-AM	www.newstalkcli.com	580/323–5234
	KWEY-AM	news@wrightwradio.com	580/772–5939
	KYCU-FM	www.kccu.org	888/454–7800
Coalgate	KXFC-FM	score@cableone.net	580/332–1212
Collinsville	KIZS-FM	firstnamelastname@clearchannel.com	918/664–2810
Comanche	KDDQ-FM	kperry@kvsperry.com	580/255–1350
Cordell	KCLI-FM	www.newstalkcli.com	580/323–5234
Coweta	KDIM-FM	www.oasisnetwork.org	918/455–5693
Cushing	KUSH-AM	kushradio@yahoo.com	918/225–0922
Davis	KKAJ-FM	michael@sokradio.com	580/226–0421
Del City	KEBC-AM	firstname.lastinitial@tylermedia.com	405/616–5500
Dickson	KTRX-FM	www.texomarocks.com	580/226–0421
Duncan	KKEN-FM	kperry@kvsperry.com	580/255–1350
	KPNS-AM	kperry@kvsperry.com	580/255–1350
Durant	KAYC-FM	www.afa.net	662/844–8888
	KLBC-FM	firstname@klbcfm.com	580/924–3100
	KSEO-AM	firstname@klbcfm.com	580/924–3100
	KSSU-FM	homepages.se.edu/kssu	580/745–2906
Edmond	KOKF-FM	www.air1.com	916/251–1600
	KUCO-FM	kucofm@uco.edu	405/974–3333
El Reno	KZUE-AM	kzue@aol.com	405/262–1460
Elk City	KADS-AM	www.thesportsanimal.com	580/225–9696
	KECO-FM	www.kecofm.com	580/225–9696
	KTIJ-FM	thezone@itlnet.ne	580/726–5656
	KXOO-FM	keproduction@cableone.net	580/225–9696
Enid	KCRC-AM	www.ctbsports.com	580/237–1390
	KGWA-AM	www.kgwanews.com	580/234–4230

License City	Calls	Contact E-mail or Website	Phone
Enid	KKRD-FM	www.air1.com	916/251-1600
	KNID-FM	www.knid.com	580/237-1390
	KOFM-FM	www.kofm.com	580/234-4230
	KQOB-FM	firstname.lastname@cumulus.com	405/848-0100
	KZLS-AM	radio.securenetsystems.net/v5/KZLS	405/456-0760
Eufaula	KTNT-FM	www.kfoxradio.com	918/689-3663
Fairview	KHEV-FM	www.khymfm.org	620/873-2991
Frederick	KCBK-FM	www.kcbi.ort	817/792-3800
	KTAT-AM	www.coyotenews.com	580/335-5923
	KYBE-FM	www.coyotenews.com	580/335-5923
Glenpool	KTSO-FM	www.941breeze.com	918/492-2660
Goltry	KGVV-FM	www.mypraisefm.com	580/767-1400
Goodwell	KPSU-FM	kpsu@opsu.edu	580/349-2414
Grandfield	KWKL-FM	www.klove.com	916/251-1600
Granite	KHEB-FM	www.thegospelstation.com	580/332-0902
	KZBA_FM	www.thegospelstation.com	580/332-0902
Grove	KGVE-FM	kgve@sbcglobal.net	918/786-2211
	KWXC-FM	www.kwxcradio.com	918/854-3496
Guthrie	KMFS-AM	www.sonliferadio.org	225/768-3288
Guymon	KBIJ-FM		806/202-0933
	KGUY-FM	www.hppr.org	620/275-7444
	KGYN-AM	www.kgynradio.com	580/338-1210
	KJDR-FM	www.kingdomkeysradio.org	806/359-8855
	KKBS-FM	kkbs@kkbs.com	580/338-5493
	KNGM-FM	www.kjil.com	620/873-2991
Haileyville	KQIK-FM	www.kfoxradio.com	918/689-3663
Hammon	KTHF-FM	www.thehousefm.com	580/767-1400
Healdton	KAZC-FM	www.kcnpradio.org	580/272-5267
	KICM-FM	bill@kicm.com	580/226-9393
Heavener	KPRV-FM	www.kprvradio.com	918/647-3221
Henryetta	KVAZ-FM	www.thegospelstation.com	580/332-0902
	KXBL-FM	www.bigcountry995.com	918/743-7814
Hobart	KQTZ-FM	cameron@kwhw.com	580/482-1450
	KTJS-AM	thezone@itlnet.net	580/726-5656
Holdenville	KTLS-FM	www.ktlsradio.com	580/332-1212
Hollis	KJOK-FM	www.keyb.net	580/482-1555
	KKRE-FM	www.keyb.net	580/482-1555
Hugo	KITX-FM	955@netv.com	580/326-2555

License City	Calls	Contact E-mail or Website	Phone
Idabel	KBEL-AM	kbel967@yahoo.com	580/286–6642
	KBEL-FM	kbel967@yahoo.com	580/286–6642
Idabel	KQIB-FM	kkbi@pine-net.com	580/584–3388
	KXRT-FM	www.afa.net	662/844–8888
Ketchum	KOSN-FM	www.kosu.org	405/744–6352
Kingfisher	KINB-FM		405/621–9094
Kiowa	KYOA-FM	www.kfoxradio.com	918/689–3663
Lahoma	KXLS-FM		580/237–1390
Langston	KALU-FM		405/466–2924
	KBZQ-FM	kbzq@sbcglobal.net	580/357–9950
	KCCU-FM	dcole@cameron.edu	580/581–2472
	KJRF-FM	www.thechristian-center.org	580/357–4498
	KKRX-AM	joyc@kjmz.com	580/355–1050
	KLAW-FM	www.klaw.com	580/581–3600
Lawton	KMGZ-FM	gm@kmgz.com	580/536–9530
	KVRS-FM	www.afa.net	662/844–8888
	KVRW-FM	www.my1073fm.com	580/581–3600
	KXCA-AM	joyc@kjmz.com	580/355–1050
	KZCD-FM	www.z94.com	580/581–3600
Lindsay	KBLP-FM	charliej@kblpradio.com	405/756–4438
Locust Grove	KEMX-FM	thekross.fm	918/369–5444
Lone Grove	KYNZ-FM	michael@sokradio.com	580/226–0421
Lone Wolf	KHWL-FM	www.khowl.fm	580/482–5495
Loyal	KIEL-FM	www.newlifemission1986.org	580/822–4848
Madill	KMAD-AM	kmad1550@yahoo.com	580/795–2345
Mangum	KHIM-FM		580/726–5656
Marlow	KFXH-FM		580/658–9292
	KFXI-FM	www.kfxi.com	580/658–9292
	KBCW-FM	www.kucofm.com	405/974–3333
	KNED-AM	www.mcalesterradio.com	918/426–1050
McAlester	KTMC-AM	www.mcalesterradio.com	918/426–1050
	KTMC-FM	www.mcalesterradio.com	918/426–1050
Miami	KGLC-FM	kglc.kvis@yahoo.com	918/542–1818
	KVIS-AM	kglc.kvis@yahoo.com	918/542–1818
Midwest City	KGHM-AM	www.1340thegame.com	405/840–5271
	KTLV-AM	www.ktlv1220.com	405/672–3886
Moore	KMSI-FM	www.oasisnetwork.org	918/455–5693
	KWPN-AM	www.thesportsanimal.com	405/848–0100

License City	Calls	Contact E-mail or Website	Phone
Mooreland	KLSI-FM		580/256-0935
Mooreland	KZZW-FM	www.kzzw.net	580/256-3692
Muldrow	KXMX-FM	www.kxmx.com	918/790-4444
Muskogee	KBIX-AM	studio@sportsanimaltulsa.com	918/682-9700
	KHTT-FM	www.khits.com	918/743-7814
	KYAL-FM	www.sportsanimaltulsa.com	918/492-2660
Mustang	KNAH-FM	www.crankhank.com	405/456-0760
Newcastle	KJKE-FM	www.933jakefm.com	405/616-5500
Norman	KGOU-FM	calendar@kgou.org	405/325-3388
	KREF-AM	production@kref.com	405/321-1400
	KSSO-FM	www.sonliferadio.org	225/768-3288
Nowata	KRIG-FM	charlie@bartlesvilleradio.com	918/336-1400
Okarche	KTUZ-FM	www.ktuz.com	405/616-5500
Okemah	KYLK-FM	www.klove.com	916/251-1600
Oklahoma City	KATT-FM	1stname.lastname@cumulus.com	405/848-0100
	KBRU-FM	firstnamelastname@clearchannel.com	405/840-5271
	KJYO-FM	1stnamelastname@heartradio.com	405/840-5271
	KMGL-FM	firstname.lastinitial@tylermedia.com	405/616-5500
	KOKC-AM	jwilliston@rendabroadcasting.com	405/478-5104
	KOMA-FM	firstname.lastinitial@tylermedia.com	405/478-5104
	KQCV-AM	kqcv@bottradionetwork.com	405/521-0800
	KRMP-AM	www.okcheartandsoul.com	405/427-5877
	KRXO-FM	firstname.lastinitial@tylermedia.com	405/478-5104
	KTLR-AM	www.ktlr.com	405/601-6380
	KTOK-AM	firstnamelastname@clearchannel.com	405/840-5271
	KTST-FM	firstnamelastname@clearchannel.com	405/840-5271
	KXXY-FM	firstnamelastname@clearchannel.com	405/840-5271
	KYIS-FM	firstname.lastname@cumulus.com	408/848-0100
	KYLV-FM		916/251-1600
	WKY-AM	jeff.couch@cumulus.com	405/848-1000
Okmulgee	KOKL-AM	brooks@kokl.net	918/756-3646
Owasso	KTGX-FM	www.1061thetwister.com	918/388-5100
Pawhuska	KOSG-FM	www.thegospelstation.com	580/332-0902
	KPGM-FM	charlie@bartlesvilleradio.com	918/336-1400
Perry	KOKP-AM	www.eteamradio.com	580/765-2485
	KOSB-FM	www.eteamradio.com	580/765-2485
Piedmont	KZTH-FM	www.thehousefm.com	580/767-1400
Pocola	KKRI-FM	www.air1.com	916/251-1600

License City	Calls	Contact E-mail or Website	Phone
Ponca City	KJTH-FM	mail@thehousefm.com	580/767-1400
	KLOR-FM	bill@eteamradio.com	580/765-2485
	KLVV-FM	mail@thehousefm.com	580/767-1400
	KPNC-FM	bill@eteamradio.com	580/765-2485
	KQSN-FM	www.sunny1047.com	580/765-5491
	WBBZ-AM	wbbz@wbbz.com	580/765-6607
Poteau	KARG-FM	www.afa.net	662/844-8888
	KOMS-FM	www.bigcountry1073.com	479/452-0681
	KPRV-AM	kprv@windstream.net	918/647-3221
	KZBB-FM	www.kzbb.com	479/782-8888
Prague	KIOP-FM	okcatholicbroadcasting.com	405/255-7348
Pryor	KMYZ-FM	www.edgetulsa.com	918/492-2660
Rattan	KZDV-FM		580/326-2555
Red Oak	KWLB-FM		918/465-6000
Roland	KREU-FM	www.laraza923.com	479/785-2526
Sallisaw	KKBD-FM	www.bigdog959.com	479/782-8888
Sand Springs	KJMU-AM		248/557-3500
	KRMG-FM	www.krmg.com	918/493-3434
Sapulpa	KXOJ-FM	www.kxoj.com	918/492-2660
	KYAL-AM	www.sportsanimaltulsa.com	918/492-2660
Sayre	KKZU-FM	www.kkzufm.com	580/225-5598
Seminole	KIRC-FM	kirc1059@aol.com	405/878-1803
	KXTH-FM	www.thehousefm.com	580/767-1400
Shawnee	KGFF-AM	www.kgff.com	405/273-4390
	KQCV-FM	www.bottradionetwork.com	405/521-0800
Snyder	KJCM-FM		580/726-5656
Soper	KMMY-FM	www.myrock965.com	580/326-2555
Spencer	KROU-FM	www.kgou.org	405/325-3388
Sperry	KMUS-AM	www.lasamericas1380am.com	918/794-0720
Stigler	KTKL-FM	www.klove.com	916/251-1600
Stillwater	KGFY-FM		405/372-7800
	KOSR-FM	www.kosu.org	405/744-6352
	KOSU-FM	www.kosu.org	405/744-6352
	KSPI-AM	stillwaterradio@coxinet.net	405/372-7800
	KSPI-FM	stillwaterradio@coxinet.net	405/372-7800
	KVRO-FM		405/372-7800
Stuart	KSTQ-FM	www.kfoxradio.com	918/689-3663
Sulphur	KFXT-FM		580/658-9292

License City	Calls	Contact E-mail or Website	Phone
Sulphur	KIXO-FM	kixoradio.com	580/658-9292
Taft	KCXR-FM	thekross.fm	918/369-5444
	KEOK-FM	www.lakescountry1021.com	918/456-2511
Tahlequah	KLRC-FM	www.klrc.com	479/238-8600
	KTLQ-AM	www.ktlq1350.com	918/456-2511
Tishomingo	KBBC-FM		580/924-3100
	KTGS-FM	www.thegospelstation.com	580/332-0902
Tonkawa	KAYE-FM	dean.pearcy@noc.edu	580/628-6446
	KAKC AM	firstname.lastname@coxinc.com	918/664-2810
	KBEZ-FM	firstinitiallastname@jrn.com	918/743-7814
	KCFO-AM	am970@kcfo.com	918/622-0970
	KFAQ-AM	firstinitiallastname@jrn.com	918/743-7814
	KGTO-AM	thetouch1050.com/	918/494-9886
	KJSR-FM	www.1033theeagle.com	918/493-3434
	KMOD-FM	firstnamelastname@clearchannel.com	918/388-5100
Tulsa	KMYZ-FM	studio@sportsanimalradio.com	918/492-2660
	KRAV-FM	firstname.lastname@coxinc.com	918/493-3434
	KRMG-AM	irstname.lastname@coxinc.com	918/493-3434
	KTBZ-AM	firstnamelastname@clearchannel.com	918/388-5100
	KVOO-FM	firstnamelastname@jrn.com	918/743-7814
	KWEN-FM	firstinitiallastname@coxinc.com	918/494-9500
	KWGS-FM	public@publicmediatulsa.org	918/631-2577
	KWTU-FM	public@publicmediatulsa.org	918/631-2577
Valliant	KYHD-FM		580/326-2555
The Village	WWLS-FM	www.thesportsanimal.com	405/848-0100
Vinita	KGND-FM	kito@kitofm.com	918/256-2255
	KITO-FM	kito@kitofm.com	918/256-2255
Wagoner	KXTD-AM	www.quebuenatulsa.com	918/254-7556
Walters	KOEG-FM	okcatholicbroadcasting.com	405/255-7348
Wapanucka	KZIG-FM	www.khkc1021.com	580/889-3392
Warner	KTFX-FM	www.okiecountry1017.com	918/684-1022
Watonga	KIMY-FM	www.thegospelstation.com	580/332-0902
Weatherford	KAYM-FM	www.afa.net	662/844-8888
	KWEY-AM		580/323-5254
Wewoka	KSLE-FM	kirc1059@aol.com	405/878-1803
	KWSH-FM	kirc1059@aol.com	405/878-1803
Wilburton	KMCO-FM	www.mcalesterradio.com	918/426-1050
Woodward	KCSC-FM	www.kucofm.com	405/974-3333

License City	Calls	Contact E-mail or Website	Phone
	KJOV-FM	www.kjil991.com	620/873-2991
	KMZE-FM	www.z92online.com	580/256-3692
	KSIW-AM	www.thesportsanimal.com	580/256-0935
Woodward	KWDQ-FM	www.woodwardradio.com	580/256-0935
	KWFX-FM	www.woodwardradio.com	580/256-0935
	KWOU-FM	www.kgou.org	405/325-3388
	KWOX-FM	www.k101online.com	580/256-4101

Howard House, Fort Gibson, from *Historic American Buildings Survey* of 1934, Fred Q. Casler, photographer.
Built in 1818 by Dr. R. B. Howard, one of the area's first doctors, the house was used as officers' quarters while the fort was being constructed in 1824.

FEDERAL GOVERNMENT

United States Senate

Jim Inhofe—Republican. Born in Des Moines, Iowa, on November 17, 1934, Inhofe grew up in Tulsa, Oklahoma, and graduated from Tulsa's Central High School. He received a bachelor's degree in economics from the University of Tulsa in 1973, after serving in the U.S. Army from 1954 to 1956. Inhofe has been a small businessman (working in aviation, real estate, and insurance) for over thirty years.

Elected to the Oklahoma House of Representatives in a special election in 1966, Inhofe was later elected to the Oklahoma Senate in 1968 and 1972. In 1978 he was elected mayor of Tulsa, winning re-election to that post in 1980 and 1982. Elected to the U.S. Congress in 1986, he was re-elected in 1988, 1990, and 1992. Inhofe relinquished his congressional seat in 1994 to run for the U.S. Senate, and was elected to fill an unexpired term. He was re-elected to full six -year terms in 1996, 2002, 2008, and 2014. He is a senior member of the Committee on Armed Services, and serves as chair of the Committee on Environment and Public Works. Active in aviation, Inhofe became the only member of Congress to fly around the world, when he recreated Wiley Post's famous trip around the globe. The conservative publication *Human Events*, in editorializing on a recent "Top 10 Most Outstanding Conservative Senators," ranked Inhofe number one saying he is an "unabashed conservative," and noted "he is unafraid to speak his mind." In 2013 *National Journal* magazine ranked him among the top most conservative members of the U.S. Senate. Inhofe, and his wife, Kay, have been married fifty-five years. They have four children and sixteen grandchildren.

Washington Address: 205 Russell Senate Office Building, Washington, DC, 20510-3603, or call 202/224-4721, or FAX 202/228-0380; Oklahoma City: 1900 Northwest Expressway, Suite 1210, Oklahoma City, OK 73118, or call 405/608-4381, or FAX 405/608-4120; Tulsa: 1924 S Utica, Suite 530, Tulsa, OK 74104-6511, or call 918/748-5111, or FAX 918/748-5119; McAlester: 215 E Choctaw, Suite 106, McAlester, OK 74501, or call 918/426-0933, or FAX 918/426-0935; Enid: 302 N Independence, Suite 104, Enid, OK 73701, or call 580/234-5105, or FAX 580/234-5094; Internet: inhofe.senate.gov

James Lankford—Republican. After serving four years in the United States House of Representatives, Lankford was elected to the U.S. Senate on November 4, 2014, to finish the remaining two years of retiring Senator Tom Coburn's term, which will end January 2017. Lankford serves on the Committee on Appropriations, the Committee on Homeland Security and Governmental Affairs, the Select Committee on Intelligence, and the Indian Affairs Committee. Within the Committee on Homeland Security and Governmental Affairs, he is the chair of the Subcommittee on Regulatory Affairs and Federal Management. He also serves on the Senate Republican Whip Team for the 114th Congress.

Lankford is committed to protecting America's freedom, establishing an efficient and transparent government, and ensuring America remains the world leader. His priorities include addressing the national debt and restoring a responsible federal budget, eliminating duplicative and excessive federal regulations.

Prior to Lankford's time in the U.S. Congress, he served as the director of Falls Creek Youth Camp and director of student ministry at the Baptist Convention of Oklahoma from 1995 to 2009. Falls Creek is the largest youth camp in the U.S., with more than 51,000 students and adults attending each summer.

Lankford lives in Edmond with his wife, Cindy. They have been married for over twenty years. Together, they have two daughters—Hannah and Jordan. He enjoys spending time with his family, sport shooting, and reading.

Washington Address: 316 Hart Senate Office Building, Washington, DC 20002, or call 202/224-5754; Oklahoma City: 1015 N Broadway, Suite 310, Oklahoma City, OK 73102, or call 405/231-4941; Tulsa: 5810 East Skelly Drive, Suite 1000, Tulsa, OK 74135, or call 918/581-7651; Internet: lankford.senate.gov

Longhorn at Fort Sill. Apache Prisoners of War engaged in farming and cattle-raising.

United States Congress

Jim Bridenstine—First District, Republican. Bridenstine was elected in 2012 to represent Oklahoma's First District, which covers Washington, Tulsa, and Wagoner counties plus portions of Rogers and Creek counties. He currently serves on the House Armed Services Committee and the Science, Space, and Technology Committee. From the start, Bridenstine has been widely recognized in the House for his integrity, commitment to principles, and willingness to uphold the rule of law. He has become an effective member of Congress by focusing on three specific areas: national security, economic freedom, and constitutional integrity. He supports moving toward a balanced budget through spending control, tax reform, and financial measures and policies promoting free markets. Bridenstine has focused on the elimination of Obamacare and reform of laws and regulations that present a huge burden on the economy. He has introduced legislation and supported a strong national defense, religious freedom, protection of life, free speech, and restoration of the balance of power within the branches of the federal government consistent with the U.S. Constitution.

Bridenstine became the first freshman on the Science, Space, and Technology Committee to author and pass legislation. The Weather Forecasting Act enables technology development to save lives and property from severe weather, including tornadoes, without adding to the budget or debt. The measure received tremendous bipartisan support and passed on a voice vote.

Bridenstine's background includes a triple major at Rice University, a Master of Business Administration degree from Cornell University, and nine years active duty in the United States Navy. He is an Eagle Scout. He began his naval aviation career flying the E-2C Hawkeye off the aircraft carrier *USS Abraham Lincoln*. It was there that he flew combat missions in Iraq and Afghanistan, and gathered most of his 1,900 flight hours and 333 carrier-arrested landings. While on active duty, he transitioned to the F-18 Hornet and flew at the Naval Strike and Air Warfare Center, the parent command to TOPGUN. He is currently a Lieutenant Commander in the U.S. Navy Reserve, where he flew the E2-C Hawkeye in America's war on drugs before becoming a member of Congress. He and his wife, Michelle, live in Tulsa with their three children, ages seven, five, and two.

Washington Address: 216 Cannon House Office Building, Washington, DC, 20515, or call 202-225-2211; Tulsa: 2448 E 81 Street, Suite 5150, Tulsa, OK 74137, or call 918/935-3222, or FAX 918-935-2716; Internet: bridenstine.house.gov

Markwayne Mullin—Second District, Republican. Mullin was elected to serve the people of Oklahoma's 2nd Congressional District in November 2012. He is currently serving his second term in office. The youngest of seven children, Mullin was raised in the small Adair County community of Westville. Mullin is an eastern Oklahoma native, successful businessman, rancher, and family man.

Shortly after Mullin graduated from Stilwell High School, his father fell ill and the family's small plumbing company encountered financial troubles. Markwayne was only twenty years old, but he and his wife, Christie, took over with only six employees. They had never run a business, but Mullin's dad had taught him the value of hard work and discipline. He stabilized the company and grew it into one of the largest service companies

Oklahoma Congressional Districts   2012–2020

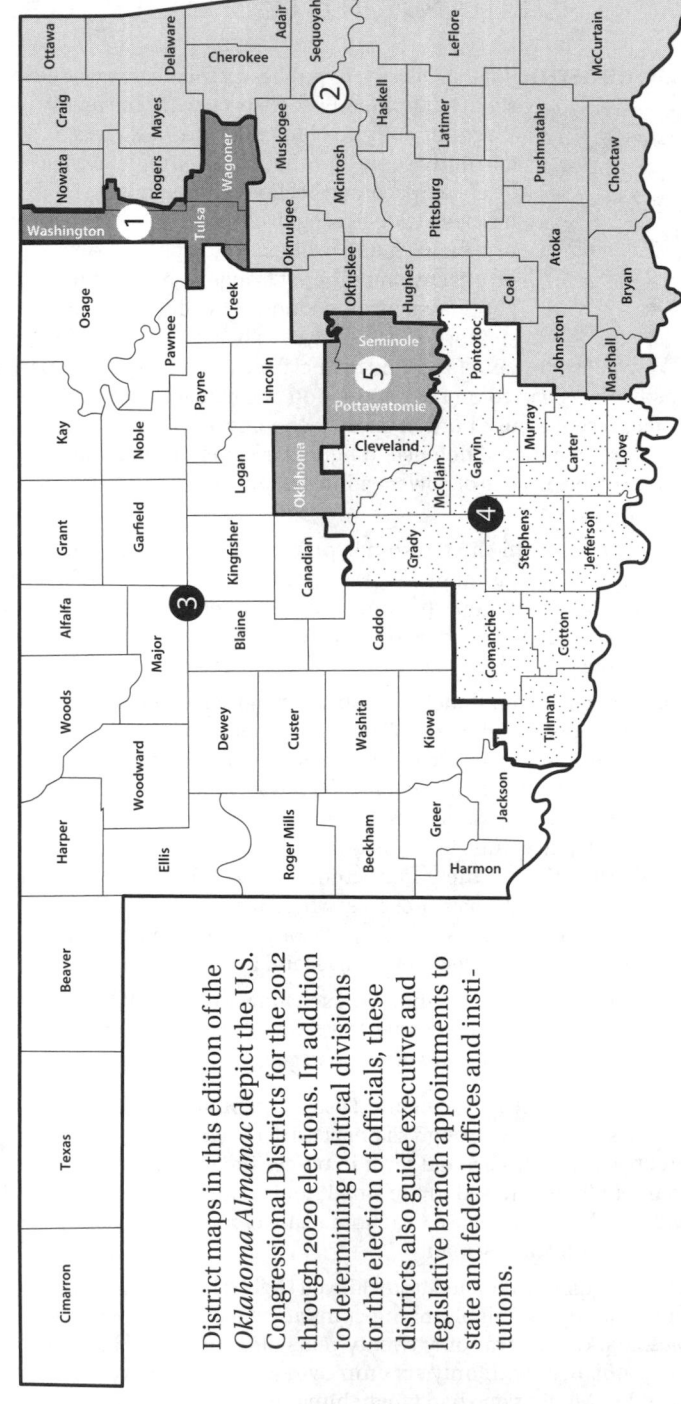

District maps in this edition of the *Oklahoma Almanac* depict the U.S. Congressional Districts for the 2012 through 2020 elections. In addition to determining political divisions for the election of officials, these districts also guide executive and legislative branch appointments to state and federal offices and institutions.

in the tri-state area. Today, it is only one of several successful companies they own and operate. Mullin is proud to have turned a family trade into a thriving business that employs over 120 Oklahomans. He also continues to run his cattle ranch in Westville.

Mullin was a high school athlete and went to college on a wrestling scholarship before returning home to run the family business. He is also a rodeo and a martial arts enthusiast and an avid hunter. He and Christie have been married for fifteen years, and they have three children—Jim, Andrew, and Larra.

When the 113th Congress convened in January 2013, Mullin's electorial victory put him in rare territory. As a citizen of the Cherokee Nation, he became the second Native American in the House; the other being Fourth District Representative Tom Cole, a citizen of the Chickasaw Nation. Mullin currently serves on the House Energy and Commerce Committee.

Washington Address: 1113 Longworth House Office Building, Washington, DC, 20515, or call 202/225-2701, or FAX 202-225-3038; Muskogee: 3109 Azelea Park, Muskogee, OK 74401, or call 918/687-2533, or FAX 918/686-0128; McAlester: 1 E Choctaw, Suite 175, McAlester, OK 74501; or call 918/423-5951, or FAX 918/423-1940; Internet: mullin.house.gov

Frank Lucas—Third District, Republican. Lucas is a fifth generation Oklahoman whose

family has lived and farmed in Oklahoma for over 100 years. Born on January 6, 1960, in Cheyenne, Oklahoma, Lucas graduated from Oklahoma State University in 1982 with a degree in agricultural economics. He was first elected to the United States House of Representatives in a special election in 1994, and is currently serving his twelfth term as a member of Congress.

Lucas proudly represents Oklahoma's Third Congressional District including all or portions of thirty-two counties in northern and western Oklahoma, stretching from the Oklahoma panhandle to parts of Tulsa, and from Yukon to Altus in the southwest. It takes up almost half the state's land mass and is one of the largest agricultural regions in the nation. Lucas has been a crusader for the American farmer since being elected to Congress in 1994 as well as working to protect Oklahoma values.

Lucas serves on the House Committee on Agriculture. In addition, he serves on the House Committee on Financial Services, and the House Committee on Science, Space, and Technology. He also serves as a member of the Republican Whip Team. The representatives, who are members of the team, serve as leaders in their party and work with the Republican leadership team to ensure every American's voice is heard in Congress.

Prior to his service in the U.S. Congress, Lucas served for five and a half years in the Oklahoma House of Representatives, where he tirelessly defended the rights of private property owners and focused on promoting agriculture issues. Frank and his wife, Lynda, have three children and two grandchildren. The Lucas family belongs to the First Baptist Church in Cheyenne.

Washington Address: 2405 Rayburn House Office Building, Washington, D.C. 20515, or call 202/225-5565, or FAX 202/225-8698; Canadian County Address: 10952 NW Expressway, Suite B, Yukon, OK 73099, or call 405/373-1958, or FAX 405/373-2046; Internet: lucas.house.gov

Tom Cole—Fourth District, Republican. Currently serving in his seventh term, Tom Cole was elected to Congress in 2002. Identified by *Time* magazine as "one of the sharpest minds in the House," Cole is an advocate for a strong national defense, a tireless advocate for taxpayers and small businesses, and a leader on issues dealing with Native Americans and tribal governments. Cole was named as one of "Five Freshmen to Watch" by *Roll Call* at the outset of his congressional career.

Since 2009, Cole has served on the powerful House Appropriations Committee, where he is chair of the Subcommittee on Labor, Health, and Human Services, Education, and Related Agencies. He also has been assigned to the subcommittees on Defense, and Interior.

Cole has a significant background of service to his home state of Oklahoma. He has served as the state chairman of the Oklahoma Republican Party, as district director to former Congressman Mickey Edwards, as a member of the Oklahoma State Senate, and as Oklahoma's Secretary of State. As secretary of state, he served as former Governor Frank Keating's chief legislative strategist and liaison to the state's federal delegation. Keating tapped Cole to lead Oklahoma's successful effort to secure federal funds to assist in the rebuilding of Oklahoma City in the wake of the 1995 bombing of the Alfred P. Murrah Federal Building.

Cole is widely regarded as one of the GOP's top political strategists. He served as executive director of the National Republican Congressional Committee in the 1992 cycle. He also served as the chief of staff of the Republican National Committee during the historic 2000 cycle in which Republicans won the presidency, the Senate, and the House for the first time in forty-eight years. In the 2008 cycle, Cole served as chairman of the National Republican Congressional Committee.

Cole is a founding partner and past president of CHS & Associates, a nationally recognized political consulting and survey research firm based in Oklahoma City. The firm has been named one of the top twenty in its field and has literally dozens of past and current clients scattered across the country.

A former college instructor in history and politics, Cole holds a bachelor's from Grinnell College, a master's degree from Yale University, and a Ph.D. from the University of Oklahoma. Cole has been a Thomas Watson Fellow and a Fulbright Fellow at the University of London. He serves on the Smithsonian Institute Board of Regents, as well as the national board of the Fulbright Association. He is also a member of the Congressional Advisory Board to the Aspen Institute.

Cole is a fifth generation Oklahoman, and an enrolled member of the Chickasaw Nation. He is currently one of only two Native Americans serving in Congress. He was awarded the Congressional Leadership Award by the National Congress of American Indians in 2007 and 2011. He was inducted in the Chickasaw Hall of Fame in 2004. Tom and his wife, Ellen, have one son, Mason, and reside in Moore.

Washington Address: 2467 Rayburn House Office Building, Washington, D.C. 20515, or call 202/225-6165, or FAX 202/225-3512; Norman Address: 2420 Springer Dr., Suite 120, Norman, OK 73069, or call 405/329-6500, or FAX 405/321-7369; Lawton Address: 711 SW "D" Avenue, Suite 201, Lawton, OK 73501, or call 580/357-2131, or FAX 580/357-7477; Ada: 100 E 13ww, Suite 213, Ada, OK 74820, or call 580/436-5375, or FAX 580/436-5451; Internet: cole.house.gov

Steve Russell—Fifth District, Republican.

A native Oklahoman, Russell graduated from Del City High School, where he was voted senior class president and the person most likely to succeed. He completed college through the United States Army ROTC program at Ouachita Baptist University in Arkadelphia, Arkansas. Upon earning his bachelor's degree in public speaking, he was commissioned a second lieutenant, army infantry, beginning his twenty-one year career with the U.S. Army. He completed the rigorous U.S. Army Ranger School in Class 11-87, and was deployed to assignment in the Arctic, the desert, the Pacific, Europe, and continental U.S. stations. Operationally, he was deployed to

Kosovo, Kuwait, Afghanistan, and Iraq. During Operation Iraqi Freedom, Russell commanded the First Battalion, Twenty-second Infantry, and conducted combat in Tikrit, Iraq. His unit was a key component in the hunt and capture of Saddam Hussein. He completed a master's degree in history from the Command and General Staff College. Highly decorated, Russell's military awards include the Legion of Merit, the Bronze Star with Valor Device, and Oak Leaf Cluster. Turning down a promotion and a fellowship to Queen's University in Kingston, Canada, he retired as a lieutenant colonel. He returned to Oklahoma with his wife, Cindy, and their five children.

Elected to the Oklahoma State Senate in 2008, Russell led efforts to pass legislation protecting the unborn, fight against human trafficking, support veterans benefits and exemptions, and accomplish adoption reform. He is the author of *We Got Him! A Memoir of the Hunt and Capture of Saddam Hussein*, published by Simon and Schuster. He is the founder and owner of Two Rivers Arms, a small rifle manufacturing business.

Elected to the United House of Representatives in 2014, Russell currently serves on the House Committee on Education and the Workforce and the House Committee on Government Oversight and Reform. Russell and Cindy make their home in Choctaw, Oklahoma. They are members of the First Southern Baptist Church of Del City.

Washington Address: 128 Cannon House Office Building, Washington D.C. 20515, or call 202/225–2132, or FAX 202/226–1463; Del City Address: 4600 SE 29 Street, Suite 400, Del City, OK 73115, or call 405/602–3074, or FAX 405/602–3953; Internet: russell.house.gov

"Comanche Town, near Fort Sill, I.T." (Indian Territory), circa 1880's.

United States District Judges

Robin J. Cauthron—U.S. District Judge for the Western District of Oklahoma. Born on July 14, 1950, in Edmond, Oklahoma, Cauthron graduated from Edmond High School. She received a bachelor's degree in language arts in 1970 from the University of Oklahoma, a master's degree in education from Central State University in 1974, and a Juris Doctor degree from the University of Oklahoma in 1977. She served as an editor of the *Oklahoma Law Review* from 1975 to 1977 and was elected to the Order of the Coif. Cauthron was a teacher at Harding Middle School from 1971 to 1974, and upon graduating from law school, became a law clerk to U.S. District Judge Ralph G. Thompson. In 1981 she and her family moved to Hugo, where she served as a staff attorney for Legal Services of Eastern Oklahoma. In February 1983 Cauthron was appointed special judge for McCurtain County, and served until October 1986, when she was sworn in as the first woman, full-time U.S. magistrate in the Tenth Circuit. In April 1991 she became the first woman U.S. district judge in Oklahoma. Cauthron is a member of the American, Oklahoma, and Oklahoma County bar associations, where she has served in several elected positions. She served as president and member of the Luther Bohanon American Inn of Court; as an officer in the National Council of U.S. Magistrates; the National Association of Women Judges; and the Federal Bar Association. She has served on the faculty of Continuing Legal Education programs, has published legal articles, and received the Maurice Merrill Golden Quill Award in 1991 for outstanding contributions to the *Oklahoma Bar Journal*. She served as a delegate to the National Conference on State-Federal Judicial Relationships in 1992, and attended the Second National Conference on Gender Bias in the Courts in 1993. She and her husband, Henry A. Meyer III, have four children. To contact Cauthron write 200 NW 4 Street, Oklahoma City, OK 73102, or call 405/609-5200.

Timothy D. DeGiusti—U.S. District Judge for the Western District of Oklahoma. Born in 1962 in Oklahoma City, Oklahoma, DeGiusti received a bachelor's degree with distinction from the University of Oklahoma in 1985. He is a 1988 graduate of the University of Oklahoma College of Law. DeGiusti practiced with the firm Andrews, Davis, Legg, Bixler, & Price in Oklahoma City, from 1988 to 1990, and again from 1993 to 2000. He was a founding partner of the Oklahoma City firm Holladay, Chilton & DeGiusti PLLC, where he practiced from 2000 to 2007. He was appointed to the federal bench in 2007. From 1990 to 1993 DeGiusti was a prosecutor in the United States Army Judge Advocate General's Corps, and in 2003 he retired from the Oklahoma Army National Guard after

twenty-two years of combined active and reserve service. He was an adjunct professor of law at the University of Oklahoma College of Law from 1998 to 2003, where he taught courses in military law and trial techniques. He was appointed by Governor Brad Henry as a commissioner with the National Conference of Commissioners on Uniform State Laws, and served from 2003 to 2007. DeGiusti is a Master of the Bench with the Luther Bohanon American Inn of Court, and is a past president of the Inn. He served as director of the Oklahoma County Bar Association from 2007 to 2010, and is a director of the Federal Bar Association's Oklahoma City chapter. In 2012 DeGiusti received the Oklahoma City Public Schools Foundation Wall of Fame Award. He and his wife, Elaine, have four children. To contact DeGiusti write 200 NW 4 Street, Oklahoma City, OK 73102, or call 405/609-5120.

John E. Dowdell—U.S. District Judge for the Northern District of Oklahoma. Born in

1955 in Tulsa, Oklahoma, Dowdell graduated from Wake Forest University in 1978, where he was a member of the Demon Deacon football team. Dowdell received his Juris Doctor degree from the University of Tulsa in 1981. Following law school, he served as a law clerk for Judge William J. Holloway, Jr. of the United States Court of Appeals for the Tenth Circuit from 1981 to 1983. In 1983, he joined the law firm of Norman, Wohlgemuth, & Chandler in Tulsa, where he practiced law until December 2012, when he was appointed to the United States District Court. During his twenty-nine year tenure at the law firm his practice consisted primarily of commercial and complex litigations, as well as an extensive criminal defense practice. Dowdell was repeatedly recognized as an Oklahoma Super Lawyer, and was rated among the top commercial litigation lawyers by *The American Litigation* magazine. From 1999 to 2012, he served on a pro bono basis as an adjunct settlement judge in the U.S. District Court for the Northern District of Oklahoma. He also served as a mediator in over forty matters from 2000 to 2012. Dowdell is admitted to the Oklahoma and Tulsa county bar associations, where he has served in a variety of capacities. He is also admitted to practice law before the United States Supreme Court, the Tenth Circuit Court of Appeals, and Oklahoma's federal district courts. He is past president of the Council Oak Chapter of the American Inns of Court (2000–2001), and is president elect of the Council Oak/Johnson-Songtag Chapter (2015–2016). Dowdell is an alumnus of Bishop Kelley High School, from which he graduated in 1973, and was inducted into the school's Hall of Fame in 2007, and its Athletic Hall of Fame in 2011. He and his wife, Rochelle, have four sons. To contact Dowdell, write 333 W 4 Street, Room 411, Tulsa, OK 74103, or call 918/699-4130.

Claire V. Eagan—U.S. District Judge for the Northern District of Oklahoma. Born October 9, 1950, in Bronx, New York, Eagan graduated cum laude from Trinity College in Washington, DC, in 1972. She also had undergraduate studies at University of Fribourg, Switzerland, and graduate studies at University of Paris Institute of Comparative Law. She received her Juris Doctor degree cum laude from Fordham University School of Law in New York City, in 1976. Following law school, Eagan served as a law clerk for Chief U.S. District Judge Allen E. Barrow and practiced with the Tulsa law firm of Hall, Estill, Hardwick, Gable, Golden and Nelson, P.C. until 1998. During her twenty-year tenure at the law firm, Eagan became a senior attorney in the litigation section, shareholder,

director, and executive committee member. Eagan has taught legal assistants courses at Adelphi University in New York and Tulsa Junior College. She served as an adjunct professor at the University of Tulsa College of Law in 1989, 1999, and 2001. From January 27, 1998, until October 24, 2001, Eagan served as the first female full-time U.S. magistrate judge for the Northern District of Oklahoma. She was appointed the first female U.S. district judge for the Northern District of Oklahoma on October 25, 2001. She served as chief judge from 2005 to 2012. From 2002–2012, Eagan became a member, and then chair, of the Judicial Conference Committee on Defender Services. Eagan is admitted to the bar in Oklahoma and New York, U.S. Supreme Court, Fifth, Eighth, Tenth, and Federal Circuit Courts of Appeals, and Oklahoma Federal District Courts. Eagan is past chair of the Admissions and Grievances Committee for the Northern District of Oklahoma. She is past president and current member of the American Inns of Court, Council Oak Chapter. Eagan is a member of the American, Oklahoma, and Tulsa County bar associations, and a fellow of the American Bar Foundation. Eagan is former president of the Tulsa Women Lawyers Association. She is also a trustee of the Oklahoma Medical Research Foundation. Eagan and her husband, Anthony J. Loretti

Jr., have been married since 1988. To contact Eagan write 333 W Fourth Street, Room 411, Tulsa, OK 74103, or call 918/699-4795.

Stephen P. Friot—U.S. District Judge for the Western District of Oklahoma. Friot

received a bachelor's degree in political science from the University of Oklahoma in 1969, and a juris doctor degree from the University of Oklahoma College of Law in 1972. Friot practiced civil trial and appellate law in Oklahoma City for twenty-nine years before his appointment to the bench by President George W. Bush in 2001. Friot was selected by the Oklahoma Chapter of the American Board of Trial Advocates as that organization's judge of the year for 2004. In 2012 he received the Oklahoma Bar Association's Award of Judicial Excellence. Friot served as the president of the Oklahoma County Bar Association from 1991 to 1992 and of the Ruth Bader Ginsburg American Inn of Court from 2001 to 2002. Friot also served on the Board of Directors of Legal Aid of Western Oklahoma, Inc., from 1999 to 2001. From 1992 to 2011, he served as a member of the Central Oklahoma Habitat for Humanity Board of Directors, which recognized him with its Outstanding Service Award in 1995. Governor Frank Keating appointed Friot in 1995 and again in 2000 to serve on the Oklahoma Housing Finance Agency Board of Trustees. Friot's publications include "Legal and Practical Aspects of Employee and Vendor Fraud in the Oil and Gas Industry," *Texas Oil and Gas Law Journal*, Vol. 4, Nos. 4 and 5 (March, 1990), as well as continuing legal education publications involving trial practice, legal ethics, discovery of electronic documents, real property law and conflict of laws. Friot was the U.S. judicial delegate to the Tenth International Forum on Constitutional Review (2007), in Moscow, sponsored by the Institute for Law and Public Policy. The *Comparative Constitutional Review* (*Sravnitelnoe Konstitutsionnoe Obozrenie*), a publication of the Institute for Law and Public Policy, has published the following articles by Judge Friot: "Social and Economic Rights in U.S. Constitutions: Where to Look," 62 CCR 100 (2008 No. 1), "Judicial Independence: A Time for Patience, Persistence and Public Awareness," 64 CCR 4 (2008 No. 3) and "Boumediene v. Bush: The Latest Chapter in the U.S. Supreme Court's Jurisprudence at the Intersection of the War on Terror and the Constitutional Doctrine of Separation of Powers," 66 CCR 147 (2008 No. 5). Friot is the recipient of the 2008 Global Vision Award, presented by the Oklahoma City affiliate of Sister Cities International. Friot has served as the president of the Last Frontier Council, Boy Scouts of America. He is a recipient of the 2002 Silver Beaver Award, scouting's highest council-level award for service to youth. Friot is married and has one son. To contact Friot write 200 NW 4 Street, Oklahoma City, OK 73102, or call 405/609-5500.

Joe Heaton—U.S. District Judge for the Western District of Oklahoma. Born in Alva,

Oklahoma, Heaton graduated from Northwestern State College at Alva in 1973 and received his law degree from the University of Oklahoma College of Law in 1976. Following his graduation from law school, Heaton worked in private law practice for approximately eighteen years with the Fuller, Tubb, & Pomeroy law firm in Oklahoma City. Heaton also worked in the U.S. Attorney's Office for six years, where he served as U.S. attorney and first assistant U.S. attorney. He served in the Oklahoma House of Representatives from 1984 to 1992, and was minority leader from 1988 to 1991. On December 13, 2001, he was sworn in as U.S. district judge. Heaton and his wife, Dee Anne, have two children. To contact Heaton write 200 NW 4 Street, Oklahoma City, OK 73102, or call 405/609-5600.

Gregory K. Frizzell—Chief Judge for the Northern District of Oklahoma. Born December 13, 1956, in Wichita Kansas, Frizzell attended the University of  Virginia, followed by two years working on construction of the Alaska Pipeline in Valdez and Prudhoe Bay, Alaska. In 1981 he graduated summa cum laude with a bachelor's degree in history from the University of Tulsa, where he received the William A. Settle Award in History and served as student association president. He received a Juris Doctor degree from the University of Michigan in 1984. From 1986 to 1995 Frizzell served as a law clerk in Tulsa for U.S. District Judge Thomas R. Brett. He practiced civil trial law in Tulsa from 1986 to 1995. In April 1995 he was appointed as general counsel for the Oklahoma Tax Commission. In May 1997 Governor Frank Keating appointed him as a state district judge for Tulsa and Pawnee counties. He was re-elected without opposition in 1998 and 2002, and served as chief judge of the Civil Division in 2003, presiding judge elect in 2004–2005, and presiding judge in 2006. In February 2007 Frizzell was appointed to the federal bench by President George W. Bush. His professional and civic involvement includes serving as president of Hudson, Hall, Wheaton Chapter of the American Inns of Court from 1999–2000, and 2011–2012; gubernatorial appointee to the Oklahoma Task Force on Judicial Selection; trustee of the Tulsa County Law Library from 1999–2005; and vice chair of the Oklahoma Bar Association Professionalism Committee from 2006–2007. He is a member of the Rotary Club of Tulsa, where he served on the board of directors in 2006–2007. Frizzell and his wife have six children, including two sets of twins. To contact Frizzell write Room 411, U.S. Courthouse, 333 W Fourth Street, Tulsa, OK 74103, or call 918/699-4780.

Vicki Miles-LaGrange—Chief U.S. District Judge for the Western District of Oklahoma. Born on September 30, 1953, in Oklahoma City, Oklahoma, Miles-LaGrange received a bachelor's degree from Vassar College in 1974. She later obtained a Juris Doctor degree from Howard University. Upon graduating from law school, she became a law clerk to U.S. District Judge Woodrow Seals in Houston, Texas, and a congressional aide for Speaker of the United States House of Representatives Carl Albert. She worked at the U.S. Department of Justice in Washington, DC, and served as an assistant district attorney in Oklahoma County from 1983 to 1986. From 1986 to 1993, she practiced law with Miles-LaGrange & Associates and served as a member of the Oklahoma  Senate, where she chaired the Senate Judiciary Committee for five years. From 1993 to 1994, she served as U.S. attorney in Oklahoma City. In 1994 President William Jefferson Clinton nominated Miles-LaGrange as a U.S. district judge for the Western District of Oklahoma. Upon approval by the U.S. Senate, she became the first African American judge ever appointed in Oklahoma or to the Tenth Judicial District. Miles-LaGrange served as a member of the International Judicial Relations Committee of the Judicial Conference of the United States from 1999–2005. She was appointed by the late Chief Justice William Rehnquist of the U.S. Supreme Court and chaired the committee's Africa Working Group. In that capacity, she worked with judges and courts on matters related to the establishment and expansion of the rule of law and administration of justice around the world consistent with the national policy of the United States. She has been the recipient of numerous awards including induction into the Oklahoma Women's Hall of Fame, the Oklahoma African-American Hall of Fame, the Child Advocates Hall of Fame, the 2006 Wall of Fame Humanitarian Award of the Oklahoma City Public School Foundation, the 2006 Fern Holland Courageous Lawyer Award for Rule of Law Work in Rwanda, and the 2008 Mid-America Education Hall of Fame. She is also an invited instructor to train new federal prosecutors at the Attorney General's

National Advocacy Center in Columbia, South Carolina. She has one daughter, Johnna. To contact Miles-LaGrange write 200 NW 4 Street, Oklahoma City 73102, or call 405/609-5400.

James H. Payne—Chief U.S. District Judge for the Eastern District. Born on March 5,

1941, In Lubbock, Texas, Payne received a bachelor's degree in 1963 from the University of Oklahoma, and a Juris Doctor degree in 1966 from the University of Oklahoma College of Law. He is admitted to practice before the U.S. Supreme Court, Tenth Circuit Court of Appeals, and the Eastern, Northern, and Western districts of Oklahoma. Payne also completed the National ADR Institute for Federal Judges at Harvard Law School in 1993. He served on active duty with the U.S. Air Force JAG Corps from 1966 to 1970, achieving the rank of captain. He served with the USAF Reserve from 1972 to 1992, attaining the rank of lieuten-ant colonel. From 1970 to 1973, he served as U.S. attorney for the East-ern District of Oklahoma. From 1973 to 1988, he worked in private law practice with the firm of Sandlin & Payne in Muskogee. From 1988 to 2001, Payne served as U.S. magistrate judge for the Eastern District of Oklahoma. He became U.S. district judge for the Eastern District of Oklahoma on October 24, 2001. Payne is a member of the American, Oklahoma, and Muskogee County bar associations. He is also a member of the Fellows of the ABA, and formerly served as a member of the Judicial Branch Committee for the Judicial Conference of the United States. He is a member of the Varsity O Club. Payne's civic involvements include pro bono work for establishing the Kelly B. Todd Cerebral Palsy Foundation Inc., Muskogee Crime Stoppers, and the Muskogee Public School Foundation. To contact Payne write U.S. Courthouse, 101 N 5 Street, Muskogee, OK 74401, or call 918/684-7940.

Ronald A. White—District Judge for the Eastern District of Oklahoma. Born on Janu-ary 27, 1961, in Sapulpa, Oklahoma, White graduated from Sapulpa High School in 1979. A member of Phi Beta Kappa, he graduated cum laude from the University of Oklahoma in 1983 with a bachelor's degree in Letters. In 1986 he received his Juris Doctor degree, cum laude, from the University of Oklahoma School of Law. During law school, White was a member of the Order of the Coif Honor Society, and worked as a law clerk for the Jones Givens law firm and the Boone, Smith, Davis & Hurst law firm in Tulsa. Following law school, from 1986 to 2003, he worked as an attorney with the law firm of Hall, Estill, Hardwick, Gable, Golden, & Nelson. As one of the senior attorneys in the Litigation Sec-

tion, he specialized in property damage, personal injury and insurance disputes, ERISA, employee benefits, and general commercial law. President George W. Bush appointed White to be U.S. district judge for the Eastern District of Oklahoma, and he was sworn in on Octo-ber 6, 2003. He is admitted to the bar in Oklahoma, the Tenth Federal Circuit Court of Appeals, and the Eastern, Northern, and Western Districts of Oklahoma Federal District Courts. White is a former member of the American Inns of Court, and the Council Oak Chapter of Tulsa, at the master level. He also is a member of the Federalist Society and the Oklahoma Bar Association. He is former member of the Judicial Conference Committee on Codes of Con-duct. His community activities have included the Indian Nations Council of Boy Scouts of America Executive Board; Margaret Hudson Program Board of Directors, member of the Human Resources Committee; district chair of the Neosho District of the Indian Nations Council of Boy Scouts of America; the Philbrook Museum of Art Masters' Society, member of the Steering Committee; the Tulsa Ballet Founders' Society; and the Tulsa Route 66 Asso-ciation Board of Directors. White was pre-deceased by his wife, Leah. To contact White write 101 N Fifth Street, Muskogee, OK 74401, or call 918/684-7965.

United States District Judges
Senior Judges

Terence C. Kern—Senior District Judge for the Northern District of Oklahoma. Born on September 25, 1944, in Clinton, Oklahoma, Kern received a Bachelor of Science degree from Oklahoma State University in 1966, a Juris Doctor degree from the University of Oklahoma College of Law, and an L.L.M. from the University of Virginia School of Law in 2004. Kern worked as an attorney at the Federal Trade Commission, Division of Compliance, Bureau of Deceptive Practices from 1969 until 1970. He was a partner in the law firm of Fischl, Culp, McMillin, Kern, & Chaffin from 1970 to 1986. Until appointment to the U.S. District Court on June 9, 1994, he also served as president and shareholder in Kern, Mordy, & Sperry. He served as the court's chief judge from 1996 to 2003. He has served as a member of the Judicial Conference of the United States, Committee on Space and Facilities from 2000–2006; a member of the Tenth Circuit Judicial Council; member of the American Bar Association; fellow of the American Bar Association; member of the American Board of Trial Advocates; member of the American Inns of Court, Council Oak/Sontag-Johnson Chapter, president 2008–2009; and sustaining fellow of the Oklahoma Bar Foundation. Kern received the Distinguished Alumni Award and the Leadership Legacy Award, both from Oklahoma State University in 2001; Judge of the Year Award from the Oklahoma Gang Investigators Association in 2007; Lion of the Bar Award from the American Inns of Court in 2013; Judge of the Year Award from the Oklahoma Association for Justice in 2014. He and his wife, Jeanette, live in Tulsa. He has three adult children—Lauren, Suzanne, and Justin. To contact Kern write Federal Building, Room 241, 224 S Boulder Avenue, Tulsa, OK 74103, or call 918/699-4770.

Tim Leonard—U.S. Senior District Judge. Born on January 22, 1940, in Beaver, Oklahoma, Leonard received a bachelor's degree in 1962 and a Juris Doctor degree in 1965, both from the University of Oklahoma. He served in the United States Navy from 1965 to 1968. While in the navy, he was stationed in the Office of the Judge Advocate General in the Pentagon, and also served as a White House military aide. Leonard served as an assistant to Oklahoma's attorney general from 1969 to 1971. He also was a partner in a law firm in Beaver from 1971 to 1988. From 1979 to 1988, Leonard served as a state senator from District 49, and served as the senate minority leader from 1985-86. In 1986 he was the Republican nominee for lieutenant governor. Leonard served as counsel with an  Oklahoma City firm until he was appointed U.S. attorney for the Western District of Oklahoma by President George H. W. Bush in October 1989. He was appointed to the Attorney General's Advisory Committee for the U.S. Attorneys in November 1990. He was appointed U.S. district judge for the Western District on August 21, 1992. He has served as a member of the Judicial Conference of the United States, Committee on Financial Disclosure from 1998 to 2005, and the Tenth Circuit Advisory Committee from 2002 to 2005. Leonard is a member of the Fellow of the American Bar Association, and the Oklahoma, Oklahoma County, and federal bar associations. He and his wife, Nancy, have three children—Kirstin, Ryan, and Tyler. To contact Leonard write 200 NW 4 Street, Oklahoma City, OK 73102, or call 405/609-5300.

David L. Russell—U.S. District Judge for Western District of Oklahoma, and he assumed senior status in 2014. Born in Sapulpa, Oklahoma, on July 7, 1942, Russell graduated from Oklahoma Baptist University in 1962, and the University of Oklahoma Law School in 1965. From 1965 to 1968, he served on active duty in the JAG Corps of the United States Navy, attaining the rank of lieutenant commander in the Naval Reserve. He served as an assistant attorney general for Oklahoma prior to his serving as a legal advisor to Dewey Bartlett, both when Bartlett was governor and in the U.S. Senate. Russell has twice served as U.S. attorney for the Western District of Oklahoma. He served from 1975 to 1977, and from June 1981 to January 1982. On January 12, 1982, he was sworn in as U.S. district judge for the Western District of Oklahoma. In 1988 the Oklahoma Trial Lawyers Association named him Outstanding Federal Trial Judge. In 2013 he was awarded the Rogers State Constitution Award. Russell is a member of the county, federal, and state bar associations. He served as chief judge of the Western District from 1995 to 2001. He is an alumnus member of Order of the Coif. In 2005 he received the Journal Record Award. Russell and his wife, Dana, have two daughters—Lisa and Sarah. To contact Russell write Room 3309, U.S. Courthouse, Oklahoma City, OK 73102, or call 405/609-5100.

Frank H. Seay—U.S. Senior District Judge. Born on September 5, 1938, in Shawnee, Oklahoma, Seay attended public schools in Seminole. He studied at Southern Methodist University and the University of Oklahoma, earning his Bachelor of Arts degree in 1961, and a Bachelor of Laws degree in 1963. Seay began private practice in Seminole, where he became Seminole County attorney in 1963. In 1966 he became first assistant district attorney for the twenty-second Judicial District of Oklahoma, and in 1974, he was elected district judge of the same district, where he served until his appointment as a U.S. district judge for the Eastern District of Oklahoma in November 1979. Seay is a member of the American and Oklahoma bar associations. He served as president of

the Seminole County Bar Association, and as a member of the Oklahoma Uniform Criminal Jury Instruction Committee. He and his wife, Janet, have two daughters—Trudy and Laura. To contact Seay write PO Box 828, Muskogee, OK 74402, or call 918/684-7950.

Lee R. West—U.S. Senior District Judge. Born in Clayton, Oklahoma, on November 26, 1929, West graduated from Antlers High School, in Antlers, Oklahoma, in 1948. He received a bachelor's degree in 1952 and a Juris Doctor degree in 1956, both from the University of Oklahoma. He also received a Master of Laws degree from Harvard University in 1963, and in 1966, attended the National College of State Trial Judges at the University of Nevada. Serving twenty-eight months active duty with the United States Marine Corps from 1952–1955, West spent six years on inactive duty from 1954–1960, achieving the rank of captain. West practiced law in Ada, Oklahoma, until he joined the law faculty at the University of Oklahoma in 1961. He attended Harvard Law School on a Ford Foundation Fellowship in Law Teaching from 1962 to 1963. Returning to practice law in Ada, he served as labor arbitrator for the National Mediation Board. In 1965 he was appointed district judge for the twenty-second Judicial District of Oklahoma, serving also as special justice of the Oklahoma Supreme Court and Oklahoma Court of Criminal Appeals. He was appointed to the Civil Aeronautics Board in Washington, DC, in 1973 by President Richard M. Nixon, and was acting chairman in 1977. He was in private practice in Tulsa, Oklahoma, until appointed U.S. district judge for the Western District of Oklahoma on November 5, 1979. In

2000 he received the National Conference for Community and Justice Humanitarian Award and the Oklahoma Bar Association Judicial Excellence Award. In 2006 he received the E.T. Dunlap Medal and Lectureship Award as well as the Rogers State University Constitution Day Award. On November 11, 2012, West was inducted into the Oklahoma Hall of Fame. On October 30, 2013, he was inducted into the Order of the Owl, the University of Oklahoma College of Law Hall of Fame. *Law & Laughter: The Life of Lee West* by Bob Burke and David L. Russell has been published by the Oklahoma Heritage Association. He and his wife, Mary Ann, have two children—Kimberly Ellis and Jennifer Lee. To contact West write 200 NW 4 Street, Oklahoma City, OK 73102, or call 405/609-5140.

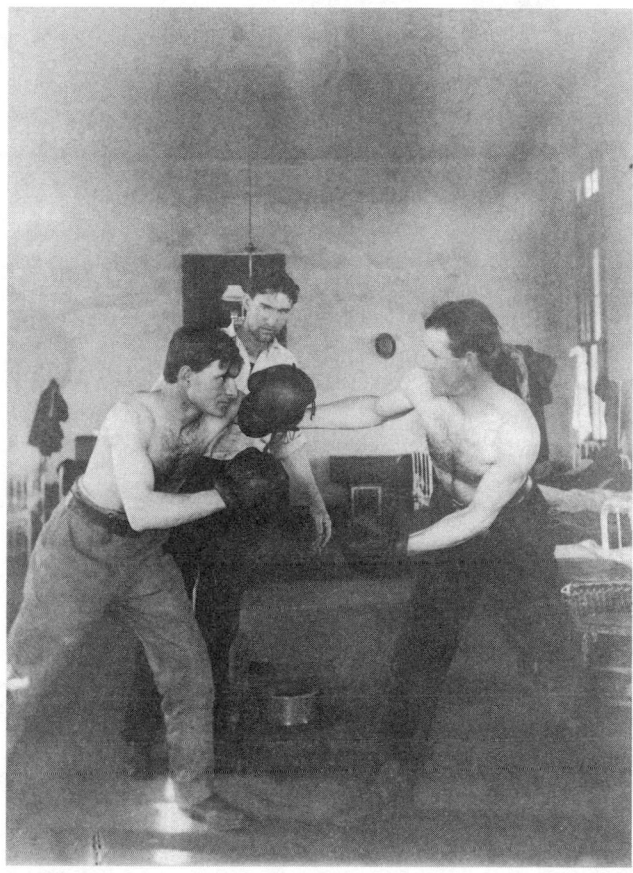

Boxing in the Fort Reno barracks.

United States Bankruptcy Judges

Western District

Sarah Hall, 215 Dean A. McGee Avenue, Oklahoma City, OK 73102 • 405/609-5660

Janice Loyd, 215 Dean A. McGee Avenue, Oklahoma City, OK 73102 • 405/609-5678

Northern District

Dana L. Rasure, 224 S Boulder, Room 122, Tulsa, OK 74103 • 918/699-4085

Terrence L. Michael, 224 S Boulder, Room 123, Tulsa, OK 74103 • 918/699-4065

Eastern District

Tom R. Cornish, Federal Building, 111 W 4 Street, Second Floor, Okmulgee, OK 74447 • 918/549-7205

United States Bankruptcy Clerks

Western District

Grant Price, 215 Dean A. McGee Avenue, Oklahoma City, OK 73102 • 405/609-5700

Northern District

Michael Williams, 224 S Boulder Avenue, Tulsa, OK 74103 • 918/699-4000

Eastern District

Therese Buthod, PO Box 1347, Okmulgee, OK 74447 • 918/549-7221

United States
District Court Magistrates

Western District

Shon T. Erwin, 200 NW 4 Street, Oklahoma City, OK 73102 • 405/609–5280
410 SW 5 Street, Lawton, OK 73501 • 580/355 6340
Charles P. Goodwin, 200 NW 4 Street, Oklahoma City, OK 73102 • 405/609–5440
Suzanne Mitchell, 200 NW 4 Street, Oklahoma City, OK 73102 • 405/609–5220
Gary M. Purcell, 200 NW 4 Street, Rm. 1423, Oklahoma City, OK 73102 • 405/609–5260

Northern District

Paul Cleary, 333 W 4 Street, OK Tulsa, 74103 • 918/699–4890
T. Lane Wilson, 333 W 4 Street, Tulsa, OK 74103 • 918/699–4760
Frank H. McCarthy, 333 W 4 Street, Tulsa, OK 74103 • 918/699–4765

Eastern District

Kimberly E. West, PO Box 2999, McAlester, OK 74402 • 918/684–7930
Stephen P. Shreder, PO Box 7002, Muskogee, OK 74402 • 918/684–7960

United States District Court Clerks

Western District

Robert D. Dennis, 200 NW 4 Street, Oklahoma City, OK 73102 • 405/609–5050

Northern District

Phil Lombardi, Room 333, W 4 Street, 411 U.S. Courthouse, Tulsa, OK 74103 •
918/699–4700

Eastern District

Patrick Keaney, 101 N 5 Street, Room 208, Muskogee, OK 74402 • 918/684–7920

United States Attorneys

Sanford C. Coats—U.S. Attorney for the Western District of Oklahoma. Sanford C.

Coats was nominated by President Barack Obama to become United States attorney for the Western District of Oklahoma on September 30, 2009. The nomination was confirmed by the United States Senate on December 24, 2009. Coats has been a practicing attorney since 1999, after receiving a Juris Doctorate from the University of Oklahoma College of Law in 1998. Prior to law school, Coats attended Tulane University of Louisiana, where he received a Bachelor of Arts degree in 1994. Coats became an assistant United States attorney in the Western District of Oklahoma in 2004. He has worked in all areas of the criminal division, where he has prosecuted a variety of cases, including child prostitution, child pornography, banking fraud, tax evasion, crimes in Indian Country, illegal immigration, complex drug conspiracies, firearm crimes, and violence associated with illegal street gangs. His responsibilities include managing investigations, over a dozen jury trials, and arguing appeals before the Tenth Circuit. In 2007 Coats volunteered for short-term assignment to the U.S. attorney's office in New Orleans as part of a special initiative by the Department of Justice following the devastation of Hurricane Katrina to assist in the prosecution of violent, firearm, and drug crime. Coats received a national Director's Award for Superior Performance as an assistant U.S. attorney for his work in the prosecution of multiple child prostitution cases. Prior to joining the U.S. attorney's office, Coats was in private practice with the Oklahoma City firm of Fellers, Snider, Blankenship, Bailey & Tippens, representing corporations and individuals in litigation. Coats also served as a legal intern for U.S. District Judge Tim Leonard, and as a law clerk for Oklahoma Supreme Court Justice Marian P. Opala. In addition to his work as a federal prosecutor, Coats has served on the board of directors of the Oklahoma City Chapter of the Federal Bar Association from 2004–08, serving as president from 2006–07 and co-chairman of the Federal Bar Association Annual Meeting and Convention in Oklahoma City in 2009. Coats also served on the board of directors of the Harding Fine Arts Academy, a charter high school in Oklahoma City, from 2004 to 2009, and the Oklahoma Bar Association Law School Committee from 2003 to 2005. From 2010–2011, Coats served on the Attorney General's Advisory Committee (AGAC), meeting regularly with Attorney General Eric Holder to address Department of Justice issues. Coats also currently serves on the Native American Issues Subcommittee of the AGAC, the Office of Management and Budget Subcommittee of the AGAC, and the Resource Allocation Working Group. Coats and his wife, Danielle, reside in Oklahoma City with their three children. To contact Coats write to 210 Park Avenue, Suite 400, Oklahoma City, OK 73102, or 405/553-8700.

Mark Green—U.S. Attorney for the Eastern District of Oklahoma. Born in 1953, Green

is a native Oklahoman. Green graduated from Sallisaw High School in 1971, and then attended the University of Oklahoma where he received a bachelor's degree in finance in 1975. Green then attended the University of Oklahoma College of Law where he graduated in December 1977. After graduation from law school and passing the bar exam, Green joined the staff of Michael C. Turpen in the district attorney's office of Muskogee County, Oklahoma. He thereafter served as assistant United States attorney from October 1978 through January 1983. He was in private practice in Muskogee, practicing primarily in state and federal courts in the Eastern District of Oklahoma, through October

2010 when he was officially appointed as the U.S. attorney for the Eastern District of Oklahoma. Green currently lives in Muskogee with his wife, Jan. They have two children—Kristin Carr, who is a high school counselor in Broken Arrow, and Phillip Green, who currently resides in Germany. To contact Green write to 1200 W Okmulgee, Suite 201, Muskogee, OK 74401, or 918/684-5100.

Danny C. Williams—U.S. Attorney for the Northern District of Oklahoma. President Barack Obama nominated Williams on March 29, 2012, to serve as the top federal law enforcement official in the Northern District of Oklahoma. He was confirmed by the United States Senate on August 2, 2012, and took the oath of office on August 7, 2012.

Williams graduated from Dillard University in New Orleans, Louisiana, with honors in 1988. He attended the University of Tulsa School of Law and earned his Juris Doctor degree in 1991. After graduating from law school, Williams served as an assistant district attorney for Tulsa County until 1993. In 1993 he joined the firm of Riggs, Abney, Neal, Turpin, Orbison, & Lewis, where he served as an associate and shareholder until 2000. In 2000 he joined the firm of Bodenheimer & Levinson, where he served as a partner until 2003. In 2003 Williams started his own law firm, Charney, Buss, and Williams, where he served as senior partner and president from 2003 until his confirmation on August 2, 2012. Williams lives in Tulsa, Oklahoma, with his wife of 24 years and their two children. To contact Williams write 110 W Seventh Street, Suite 300, Tulsa, OK 74119, or 918/382-2700.

For Further Information

Eastern District—520 Denison Avenue, Muskogee, OK 74401, 918/684-5100

Northern District—110 W 7 Street, Suite 300, Tulsa, OK 74119, 918/382-2700

Western District—210 W Park Avenue, Suite 400, Oklahoma City, OK 73102, 405/553-8700

Federal Installations and Agencies

This list includes only a part of federal operations in Oklahoma. For further information, call the Federal Information Center 800/688-9889 or 800/fed-info (800/333-4636).

General Services Administration
Federal Information Center

The Federal Information Center program, administered by the General Services Administration, was established to provide ready access to program and service information about federal agencies.

Federal Information Center—1800 F Street, NW, Washington, DC, 20405 • 844/872-4681 • www.info.gov

U.S. Office of Personnel Management

Regional Service Center—San Antonio, TX 210/805-2423 • www.opm.gov

Military
Department of the Air Force

Altus Air Force Base—Base located 3 miles northeast of Altus, Jackson County, 73523 • 580/482-8100 • www.altus.af.mil

Tinker Air Force Base (Oklahoma City Air Logistics Center)—3000 S Douglas Blvd., Midwest City 73145 • 405/732-7321 • www.tinker.af.mil

Vance Air Force Base—Base located 3 miles southwest of Enid, Garfield County, 73705 • 580/213-5000 • www.vance.af.mil

Department of the Army

U.S. Corps of Engineers—1645 S 101 East Ave., Tulsa 74128 • 918/669-7366 • www.swt.usace.army.mil

Fort Sill—Base located immediately northwest of Lawton, Comanche County, 73503 • 580/442-8111 • sill-www.army.mil

U.S. Army Ammunition Plant—Depot located nine miles south of McAlester, Pittsburg County, 74501-9002 • 918/420-6591 • mcalestr-www.army.mil

Department of the Navy

Naval Reserve Center—5316 S Douglas Blvd., Oklahoma City 73150 • 405/733-1052.

Naval and Marine Corps Reserve Center, Tulsa Armed Forces Reserve Center—Suite 5, 1101 N 6 St., Broken Arrow 74012 • 918/258-7576.

National Guard

Air—Oklahoma City—2136 West I-240 Service Road, Oklahoma City, 73159 • 800/528-2231 **Tulsa**—4200 N 93 East Avenue, Tulsa, 74115 • 800/333-7000

Army—3501 Military Circle, Oklahoma City, OK 73111 • 405/228-5000 • www.ok.ngb.army.mil

Department of Agriculture

Cooperative Extension Service—Oklahoma State University, as a Land Grant University, has the responsibility of providing state citizens educational programs in Agriculture, 4-H, Home Economics, and Rural Development. This effort is provided by the Cooperative Extension Services with offices usually in the county seat of the seventy-seven counties. State Headquarters are located in the Dean of Agriculture office, 102 Agricultural Hall, Oklahoma State University, Stillwater 74078 • 405/744-5398, FAX 405/744-5339 • www.oces.okstate.edu

Risk Management Division—Regional Office, 205 NW 63 Street, Suite 170, Oklahoma City 73116 • 405/879-2700, FAX 405/879-2741 • www.rma.usda.gov

Department of Commerce
National Oceanic and Atmospheric Administration

National Weather Service—NWS Forecast Office, 120 David L. Boren Blvd., Suite 2400, Norman 73072 • 405/325-3816 • www.srh.noaa.gov/oun
Tulsa Office—10159 E 11 Street, Suite 300, Tulsa 74128 • 918/838-7838 • www.srh.noaa.gov/tulsa

Federal Corrections Centers

El Reno Correctional Institution—P.O. Box 1500, 4201 Highway 66 West, El Reno, 73036 • 405/262-4875, FAX 405/319-7626

Federal Transfer Center—P.O. Box 898801, 7410 S MacArthur Blvd., Oklahoma City 73189 • 405/682-4075, FAX 405/680-4043

U.S. Forest Service

Ouachita National Forest—Embraces more than 1,575,000 acres from Central Arkansas into Southeastern Oklahoma, with 300,000 acres in LeFlore and McCurtain counties. • P.O. Box 1270, Hot Springs, Arkansas 71902 • 501/321-5202 • www.fs.usda.gov/ouachita

Choctaw District—HC 63, Box 5184, Hodgen 74939 • 918/653-2991

Kiamichi District—P.O. Box 577, Talihina 74571 • 918/567-2326.

Tiak District—Route 4, Box 2900, Broken Bow OK 74728 • 580/494-6402.

National Grasslands—National grasslands have been under supervision of the Forest Service since the 1950s functioning under authority of the Bankhead-Jones Farm Tenant Act of 1937. The Soil Conservation Service originally administered the program designed to demonstrate and promote sound principles in grassland agriculture. Districts are responsible for issuing grazing permits and managing the national grasslands under the principles of multiple-use management.

    Black Kettle District, Roger Mills County—supervising 31,000 acres
      18555 HWY 47A, Suite B, Cheyenne, OK 73628 • 580/497-2143

    Rita Blanca District, Cimarron County—supervising 15,000 acres
      2113 Osuna Road NE, Albuquerque, NM 87113 • 505/346-3900

Department of Health and Human Services

Indian Health Service—701 Market Drive, Oklahoma City, OK 73114 • 405/951-3820, FAX 405/951-3780 • www.ihs.gov

Department of Housing and Urban Development

Oklahoma City Field Office—301 NW 6 Street, Suite 200, Oklahoma City 73102 • 405/609-8400, FAX 405/609-8982 • www.hud.gov

Tulsa Field Office—Williams Center Tower II, 2 W Second Street, Suite 400, Tulsa 74103 • 918/292-8900, FAX 918/292-8993 • www.hud.gov

Department of Interior
National Park Service

Chickasaw National Recreation Area—(formerly Platt National Park) Area located adjacent to the City of Sulphur, Murray County, 1008 W Second Street, Sulphur 73086 • 580/622-7234. Area established March 17, 1976, by combining Platt National Park and Arbuckle Recreation Area with authorized acreage not to exceed 10,000 acres. • www.nps.gov/chic

U.S. Fish and Wildlife Service

Wichita Mountains Wildlife Refuge—32 Refuge Headquarters, Indiahoma 73552 • 580/429-3222. The refuge covers 59,020 acres in northwest Comanche County and was established as a game preserve in 1907, and made part of the national wildlife system in 1935. Buffalo, longhorn cattle, elk, and white-tail deer are the big game animals found in the refuge, along with other animals of resident species and migratory birds. There are ten recreational areas in the refuge with one designated for environmental education. • www.fws.gov/refuges

Department of Justice

Federal Bureau of Investigation—Oklahoma City Field Office—3301 W Memorial Road, Oklahoma City 73134 • 405/290-7770, FAX 405/290-3885 • oklahomacity.fbi.gov

U.S. Citizenship and Immigration Services—Oklahoma City Field Office—4400 SW 44 Street, Suite A, Oklahoma City 73119-2800 • 800/375-5283 • www.uscis.gov

U.S. Marshal, Western District—U.S. Courthouse, 200 NW 4 Street, Room 1210, Oklahoma City 73102 • 405/609-5000 • www.justice.gov/marshals

U.S. Marshal, Northern District—333 W 4, Room 4411 U.S. Courthouse, Tulsa 74103 • 918/699-4700 • www.justice.gov/marshals

U.S. Marshal, Eastern District—U.S. Courthouse, Room 208, 101 N 5 Street, Muskogee 74402 918/684-7920 • www.justice.gov/marshals

Department of Labor

Occupational Safety and Health Administration (OSHA)—55 North Robinson, Suite 315, Oklahoma City, 73102 • 405/278-9560, FAX 405/278-9572 • www.osha.gov

Department of Transportation

Mike Monroney Aeronautical Center (Federal Aviation Administration) 6500 S MacArthur Blvd., Oklahoma City 73169 • 405/954-4521 • www.ffa.gov

Coast Guard Institute—5900 SW 64 St., Room 235, Oklahoma City, 73169-6990 • 405/954-0072

Federal Highway Administration—5801 N Robinson, Suite 300, Oklahoma City, 73118 • 405/254-3300 • www.fhwa.dot.gov/okdiv

Transportation Safety Institute—6500 S MacArthur Blvd., Oklahoma City, 73169 • 405/954-3153 • www.tsi.dot.gov

Department of Treasury

Internal Revenue Service

Oklahoma City office—IRS Building, 55 N Robinson, Oklahoma City 73102 • 405/297-4057 • www.irs.gov

Tulsa office—1645 S 101 East Ave., Tulsa 74128 • 918/622-8482 • www.irs.gov

Enid office—601 S Harding, 73703. 580/234-5417 • www.irs.gov

Lawton office—2202 SW A Avenue, 73501. 580/357-5492 • www.irs.gov

Social Security Administration

Oklahoma City office—12301 N Kelley Avenue, Oklahoma City 73131 • Local Calls: 866/331-2207 • www.ssa.gov

Tulsa office—4750 S Garnett Road, Tulsa 74146 • 866/931-7106 • www.ssa.gov

Veterans Affairs

Veterans Administration Regional Office—125 S Main Street, Muskogee 74401 • 800/827-1000 • www.vba.va.gov/ro/muskogee/

Veterans Administration Hospitals
Muskogee—1011 Honor Heights Drive, 74401 • 918/577-3000
Oklahoma City—921 Northeast 13 Street, 73104 • 405/456-1000

Veterans Employment and Training Service—2401 Lincoln Blvd., Room 304-2, Oklahoma City, 73105 • 405/231-5088

Ft. Gibson National Cemetery—1423 Cemetery Road, Ft. Gibson 74434 • 918/478-2334

Ft. Sill National Cemetery—2648 NE Jake Dunn Road, Elgin, 73538 • 580/492-3200

COUNTY
GOVERNMENT

Sources for County Statistics were: Property Valuations—*Estimates of Need Table* from the State Board of Equalization • Per Capita Income—Bureau of Economic Analysis, U.S. Department of Commerce, 2013 figures • All Population Statistics, for Births and Deaths, for Marriage and Divorce—2013 & 2014 statistics from the State Health Department • Unemployment Rate and Labor Force—*Oklahoma Labor Force Data 2013*, Oklahoma Employment Security Commission • Number of Establishments and Number of Manufacturers—*2013 County Business Patterns*, U.S. Census Bureau • Public Assistance Payments—*Fiscal Year 2014 Annual Report*, Oklahoma Department of Human Services • Vehicle Registrations—*2014 Annual Vehicle Registration Report*, Oklahoma Tax Commission • Higher Learning—*2013 Annual Report*, Oklahoma State Regents for Higher Education • Crime Statistics—*2013 Uniform Crime Report*, Oklahoma State Bureau of Investigation • Number of Farms and Land (Acres) in Farms—*2012 Census of Agriculture*, U.S. Department of Agriculture • Information received from county clerks, librarians, and chambers of commerce, historical societies, and museum staff members was used to supplement the narrative portion of the county reports. • County road maps courtesy of Oklahoma Department of Transportation.

County Government in Oklahoma

At the time of Oklahoma's land opening in 1889, county lines were not designated, although county seats had been named at Guthrie, Oklahoma City, Norman, El Reno, Kingfisher, and Stillwater. Territorial Governor George Steele laid out the counties designated as First, Second, and so on through the Sixth County. Counties resulting from other land openings were given letters of the alphabet, later assuming their present names.

Oklahoma entered the Union in 1907 with seventy-five counties named for territorial leaders, eminent Americans or Indian tribes or leaders. Bryan County was named for William Jennings Bryan, the "cross of gold" orator who campaigned vigorously for the populist constitution written at the convention. Rogers County honors Clem Rogers, father of humorist Will Rogers and a leading member of the Oklahoma Constitutional Convention. Cherokee, Choctaw, Creek, Osage, Seminole, and Pottawatomie are named for Indian tribes or nations who were removed to the area. Osage, the state's largest county, was the Osage Indian Reservation during territorial days. Congress required separate county status for the Reservation in the 1906 Enabling Act. Shortly after statehood, two more counties were created under state constitutional provisions, raising the number to the present seventy-seven. Harmon County was created from a portion of giant Greer County in May 1909. Cotton County was carved from Comanche County in August 1912.

According to the Oklahoma Constitution, a new county must have at least 400 square miles of taxable area, 15,000 in population, and $2.5 million in taxable wealth. Furthermore, the boundary of a new county cannot be closer than ten miles from the seat of an existing county. These constitutional standards have been made more stringent by legislative enactment and now require 500 square miles of taxable area, 20,000 in population, and $4 million taxable wealth. Creation of any county requires a vote of the area's residents. The constitution provides for county dissolution if the taxable wealth drops below the minimum amount. A petition signed by a fourth or more of the county's qualified electors requires an election on de-organization. If a majority of voters approve, the county will be dissolved and attached to the adjoining county with the lowest taxable property valuation.

Although county powers are delegated by the state and are almost entirely for the administration of state law, county officers are locally elected. Every county elects three county commissioners, a county clerk, assessor, treasurer, and sheriff. (Formerly, a county superintendent of schools was elected, but this position was abolished in 1993.) County attorneys were elected in each county until a 1967 law created a district attorney system. Courts also have been reorganized, substituting a district system for the previous county-elected judiciary.

County general government is supported by tax levies on real estate, personal property, and aircraft registration fees. Counties may levy a sales tax on some products and services and may also impose an occupation tax on liquor establishments when those establishments are located outside municipal boundaries. County road, bridge, and highway funds are derived from a formula distribution of state collected fees.

Source: Association of Central Oklahoma Governments

County Clerk Addresses and Phone Numbers

County	Mailing Address	Phone Number
Adair	PO Box 169, Stilwell 74960	918/696-7198
Alfalfa	300 S Grand, Cherokee 73728	580/596-3158
Atoka	200 E Court Street, Ste. 203, Atoka 74525	580/889-5157
Beaver	PO Box 338, Beaver 73932	580/625-3141
Beckham	PO Box 67, Sayre 73662	580/928-3383
Blaine	PO Box 138, Watonga 73772	580/623-5890
Bryan	402 W Evergreen, Durant 74701	580/924-2202
Caddo	PO Box 10, Anadarko 73005	405/247-3394
Canadian	301 N Choctaw El Reno 73036	405/262-1070
Carter	PO Box 1236, Ardmore 73402	580/223-8162
Cherokee	213 W Delaware, Tahlequah 74464	918/456-4121
Choctaw	300 E Duke, Hugo 74743	580/326-3778
Cimarron	PO Box 145, Boise City 73933	580/544-2251
Cleveland	201 S Jones, Ste. 210, Norman 73069-6099	405/366-0240
Coal	4 N Main, Ste. 1, Coalgate 74538	580/927-2103
Comanche	Box 65, Lawton 73501	580/355-5214
Cotton	301 N Broadway, Walters 73572	580/875-3026
Craig	PO Box 397, Vinita 74301	918/256-2507
Creek	Box 1010, Sapulpa 74066	918/224-4084
Custer	PO Box 300, Arapaho 73620	580/323-1221
Delaware	PO Drawer 309, Jay 74346	918/253-4520
Dewey	PO Box 368, Taloga 73667	580/328-5361
Ellis	Box 197, Arnett 73832	580/885-7301
Garfield	100 W Broadway, Enid 73702	580/237-0225
Garvin	PO Box 926, Pauls Valley 73075	405/238-5596
Grady	PO Box 1009, Chickasha 73023	405/224-5211
Grant	112 E Guthrie, RM 102, Medford 73759	580/395-2274
Greer	PO Box 207, Mangum 73554	580/782-3664
Harmon	114 W Hollis, Hollis 73550	580/688-3658
Harper	PO Box 369, Buffalo 73834	580/735-2012
Haskell	105 SE 3 Street, Unit C, Stigler 74462	918/967-2884
Hughes	200 N Broadway, Suite 5, Holdenville 74848	405/379-5487

County	Mailing Address	Phone Number
Jackson	PO Box 515, Altus 73522	580/482–4070
Jefferson	220 N Main, Room 103, Waurika 73573	580/228–2029
Johnston	403 W Main, Tishomingo 73460	580/371–3184
Kay	PO Box 450, Newkirk 74647	580/362–3116
Kingfisher	101 S Main, Room 3, Kingfisher 73750	405/375–3887
Kiowa	PO Box 73, Hobart 73651	580/726–5286
Latimer	109 N Central, Rm. 103, Wilburton 74578	918/465–3543
LeFlore	PO Box 218, Poteau 74953	918/647–5738
Lincoln	PO Box 126, Chandler 74834	405/258–1264
Logan	301 E Harrison, Suite 102, Guthrie 73044	405/282–0266
Love	405 W Main, Suite 203, Marietta 73448	580/276–3059
Major	PO Box 379, Fairview 73737	580/227–4732
Marshall	PO Box 824, Madill 73446	580/795–3220
Mayes	1 Court Place, Ste. 120, Pryor 74361	918/825–2426
McClain	PO Box 629, Purcell 73080	405/527–3360
McCurtain	PO Box 1078, Idabel 74745	580/286–2370
McIntosh	PO Box 110, Eufaula 74432	918/689–2741
Murray	PO Box 442, Sulphur 73086	580/622–3920
Muskogee	PO Box 1008, Muskogee 74402	918/682–7781
Noble	300 Courthouse Drive, #11, Perry 73077	580/336–2141
Nowata	229 N Maple, Nowata 74048	918/273–2480
Okfuskee	PO Box 108, Okemah 74859	918/623–1724
Oklahoma	320 Robert S Kerr, Oklahoma City 73102	405/713–7184
Okmulgee	PO Box 904, Okmulgee 74447	918/756–0788
Osage	PO Box 87, Pawhuska 74056	918/287–3136
Ottawa	102 E Central Avenue, Ste. 103, Miami 74354	918/542–3332
Pawnee	500 Harrison, Room 202, Pawnee 74058	918/762–2732
Payne	315 W 6 Street, Suite 202, Stillwater 74074	405/747–8347
Pittsburg	115 E Carl Albert Parkway, McAlester 74501	918/423–6865
Pontotoc	PO Box 1425, Ada 74821	580/332–1425
Pottawatomie	325 N Broadway, Shawnee 74801	405/273–8222
Pushmataha	302 SW "B" Street, Antlers 74523	580/298–3626
Roger Mills	PO Box 708, Cheyenne 73628	580/497–3395
Rogers	219 S Missouri, Room 1–104, Claremore 74017	918/341–2518
Seminole	PO Box 1180, Wewoka 74884	405/257–2501
Sequoyah	120 E Chickasaw, Ste. 105, Sallisaw 74955	918/775–5539

County Clerk • Addresses and Phone Numbers

County	Mailing Address	Phone Number
Stephens	101 S 11, Room 203, Duncan 73533	580/255-0977
Texas	PO Box 197, Guymon 73942	580/338-3141
Tillman	PO Box 992, Frederick 73542	580/335-3421
Tulsa	500 S Denver, Suite 120, Tulsa 74103	918/596-5801
Wagoner	PO Box 156, Wagoner 74477	918/485-2216
Washington	400 S Johnstone, Bartlesville 74003	918/337-2840
Washita	PO Box 380, Cordell 73632	580/832-2284
Woods	PO Box 386, Alva 73717	580/327-0942
Woodward	1600 Main, Suite 8, Woodward 73801	580/256-3625

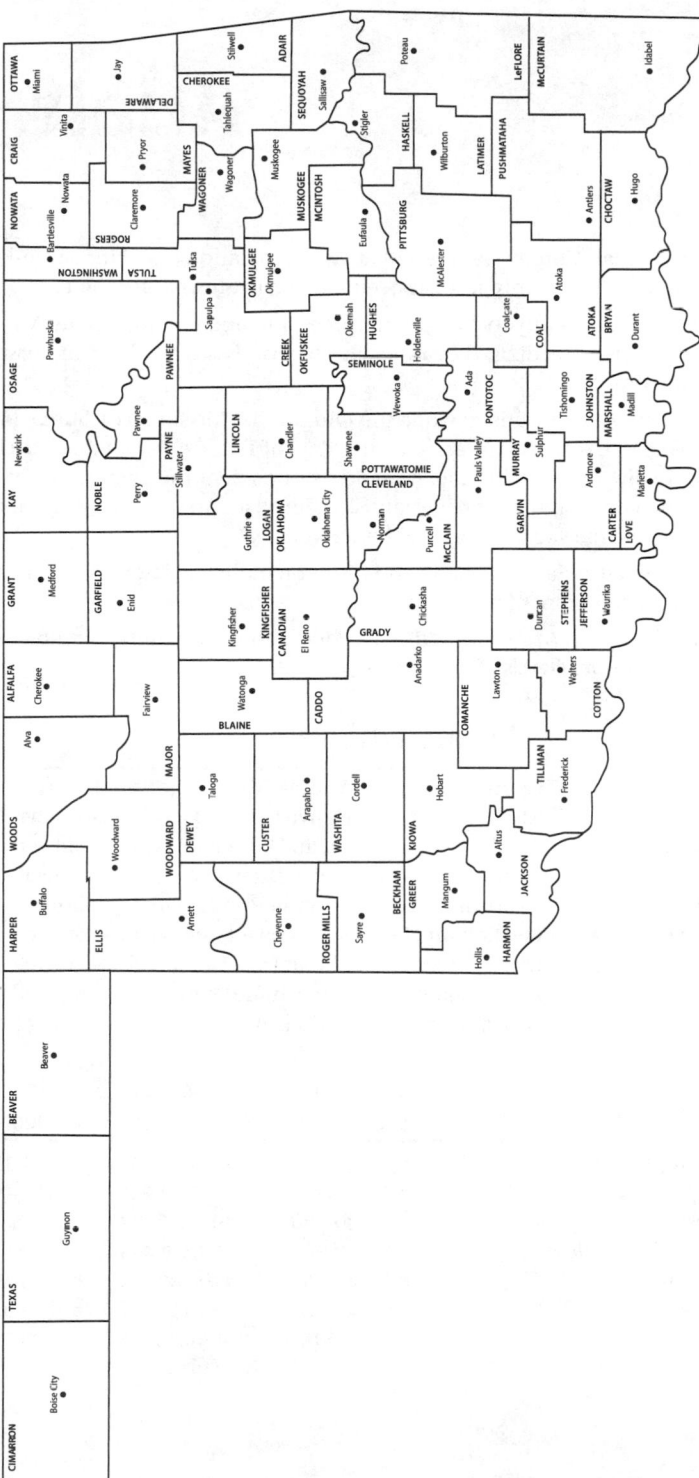

Oklahoma Counties with County Seats

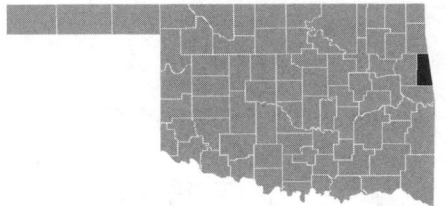

Adair

Bordering Arkansas, Adair County was created at statehood and named for a well-known Cherokee Indian family. The county seat has been located in Stilwell since 1910.

Primary industries of the county include food processing and canning, poultry raising, cattle ranching, and horse breeding. The Annual Strawberry Festival is held on the second Saturday in May in Stilwell.

Sites of interest within Adair County include the Old Baptist Missionary Church, built in 1836 by the Cherokee Indians, who traversed on the Trail of Tears to Oklahoma. The church is located north of Stilwell near Westville. A marker stands near the community of Watts recognizing Fort Wayne, a military post established in 1838. Abandoned in 1842, it was reactivated and became the site of a Civil War battle in 1862.

Professional football player Sam Claphan and Wilma Mankiller, former principal chief of the Cherokee Nation, hail from Adair County.

The *Adair County History Book* provides additional facts about the county. For more county information, call the county clerk's office at 918/696-7198.

Districts

Congress 2
State Senate.....................3
State Rep. 86
District Attorney 27
Court of Appeals. 2
Ct. of Crim. Appeals........2
Supreme Ct. Jud. 7
E. Cent. Jud. Adm.......... 15
   (Div. III)

County Officials

Court Clerk	Andrea Nicole Cooper (D)	Stilwell
Clerk	Danya Curtis (D)	Westville
Sheriff	David Harden (D)	Stilwell
Treasurer	Janice Brewer (D)	Stilwell
Assessor	Rhonda Pritchett (D)	Bunch
Election Brd. Sec.	Marilyn Hill Russell (D)	Stilwell
Dist. 1 Comm.	Clifton Dale Dandridge (D)	Stilwell
Dist. 2 Comm.	Sam Chandler (D)	Stilwell
Dist. 3 Comm.	Keith Davis (D)	Watts

Property Valuations

	2013–2014 Assessment	2014–2015 Assessment	Increase or Decrease
Real Estate and Improvement	$60,146,248	$63,806,182	$1,659,934
Personal Subject to Tax	$18,290,720	$17,550,535	($740,185)
Total Locally Assessed	$80,436,968	$81,356,717	$919,749
Homestead Exemptions Allowed	$5,112,966	$5,129,295	$16,329
Net Assessed Locally	$75,324,002	$76,227,422	$903,420
Public Service Assessment	$5,542,135	$5,432,140	($109,995)
Net Assessed Valuation	$80,866,137	$81,659,562	$793,425

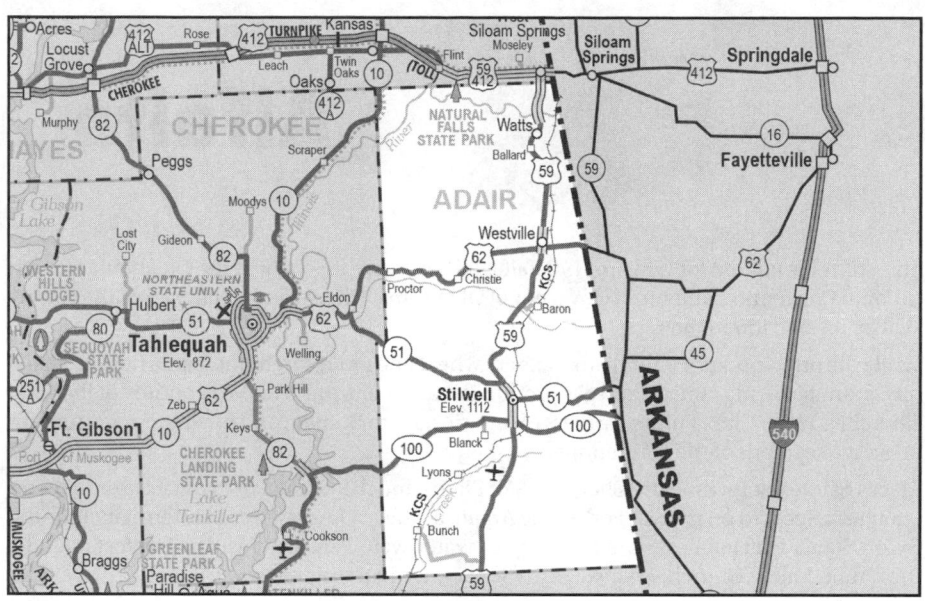

County Population

County Seat—Stilwell (Pop. 4,017) 2013 Estimate

Area (Land & Water)—577.3 square miles

Per Capita Income (2013)—$22,964 (Ranks 77th of 77 counties)

Population Statistics (2013)—Female-11,228; Male-11,199; Ethnicity—Wh.-13,641; Bl.-162; Am. Ind.-11,757; As.-152; Other-284; Pacific Is.-3; Two or more races-3,383; Hisp.-1,249

Births (2014)—342 • **Deaths** (2014)—229

Marriages (2013)—122 • **Divorces** (2013)—116

Unemployment Rate (2013)—7.6%

Labor Force (2013)—10,062

Number of Establishments (2013)—219

Number of Manufacturers (2013)—16

Public Assistance Payments
(FY2014) Total—$19,876,214 • TANF—$178,448 • Supplements—Aged-$74,100; Blind-$262; Disabled-$338,786

Vehicle Registration (2014)—
Automobiles-10,366; Farm Trucks-959; Comm. Trucks, Tractors, Trailers-918; Motor Homes and Travel Trailers-355; Motorcycles-348; Manufactured Homes-36; Tax Exempt Licenses-75; Boats-413

Crime Incidents (2013)—Murder-1; Rape-6; Robbery-3; Felony Assault-60; Breaking and Entering-109; Larceny-259; Motor Vehicle Theft-25; Arson-13 • Total Crime Index-463; Crime Rate per 1,000-20.82

Farms (2012)—1,129

Land in Farms (2012)—252,140

Recreation Area—Golda's Bidding Springs

Major Stream Systems—Illinois River, Sallisaw, and Little Lee creeks

Museums or Historic Sites—Golda's Bidding Springs Gristmill

Minerals—oil and gas

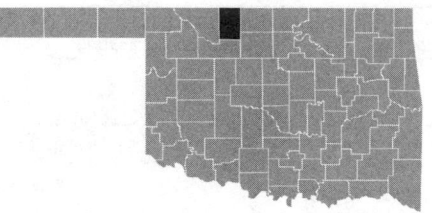

Alfalfa

This county is named for William H. "Alfalfa Bill" Murray, president of the Oklahoma Constitutional Convention and ninth Governor of Oklahoma. Cherokee was chosen as the county seat by an election in 1909.

While the principal agricultural products are wheat and grain sorghums, cattle raising, alfalfa hay, manufacturing, and oil and gas production also contribute to the economy of the area. Churches, Lions Club, Future Farmers of America, Farm Bureau, and other groups represent an active segment of the community.

Places of interest include the Cherokee Salt Plains and the Great Salt Plains Lake and recreation area, located on the Salt Fork of the Arkansas River. Other points of interest include the Byron State Fish Hatchery, and the artesian water well. Places of historic interest include: the Union Valley Church, Locust Grove School, and an original sod house, all more than one hundred years old.

Cherokee hosts the Selenite Crystal and Birding Festival in May each year. It is also home to the Alfalfa County Historical Society Museum. Cherokee celebrated its centennial in 2001. The Cherokee Chamber of Commerce also serves as a tourist center. For more information, call the county clerk's office at 580/596-3158.

Districts

Congress 3
State Senate...................19
State Rep. 58
District Attorney 26
Court of Appeals. 6
Ct. of Crim. Appeals........5
Supreme Ct. Jud..............4
E. Cent. Jud. Adm............4
　(Div. I)

County Officials

Court Clerk	Lori Irwin (R)	Aline
Clerk	Laneta Unruh (R)	Cherokee
Sheriff	Rick Wallace (R)	Cherokee
Treasurer	Valerie Vetter (R)	Cherokee
Assessor	Donna Price (R)	Amorita
Election Brd. Sec.	Kelly Stein (D)	Cherokee
Dist. 1 Comm.	Doug Murrow (R)	Cherokee
Dist. 2 Comm.	Chad Roach (R)	Cherokee
Dist. 3 Comm.	Ray Walker (R)	Helena

Property Valuations

	2013–2014 Assessment	2014–2015 Assessment	Increase or Decrease
Real Estate and Improvement	$35,703,004	$37,272,753	$1,569,749
Personal Subject to Tax	$47,978,095	$63,155,788	$15,177,693
Total Locally Assessed	$83,681,099	$100,428,541	$16,747,442
Homestead Exemptions Allowed	$1,280,344	$1,253,249	($27,095)
Net Assessed Locally	$82,400,755	$99,175,292	$16,774,537
Public Service Assessment	$9,919,340	$15,243,546	$5,324,206
Net Assessed Valuation	$92,320,095	$114,418,838	$22,098,743

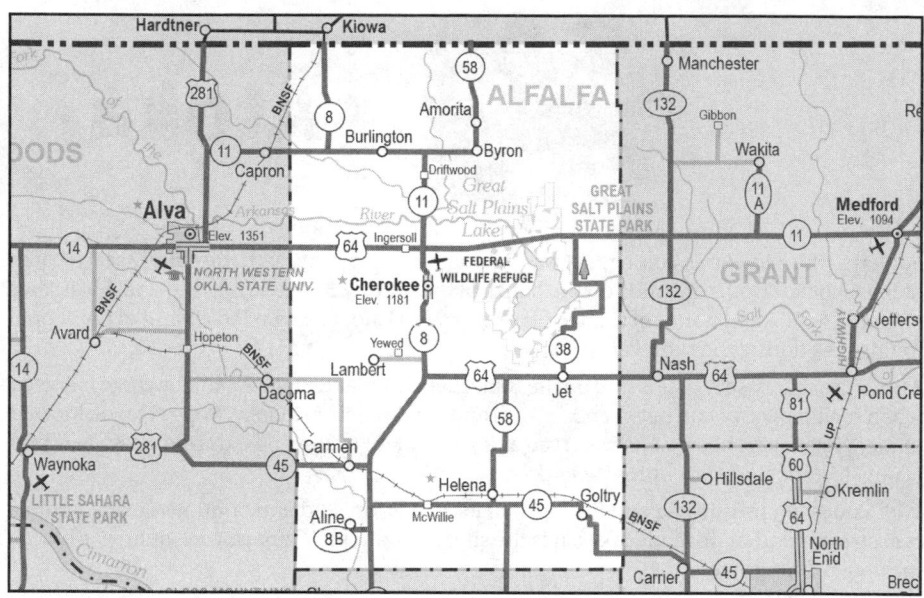

County Seat—Cherokee (Pop. 1,558) 2013 Estimate

County Seat—Cherokee (Pop. 1,558) 2013 Estimate

Area (Land & Water)—881.44 square miles

Per Capita Income (2013)—$41,497 (Ranks 23rd of 77 counties)

Population Statistics (2013)—Female-2,302; Male-3,372;
Ethnicity—Wh.-5,281; Bl.-162; Am. Ind.-654; As.-11;
Other-149; Pacific Is.-0; Two or more races-581; Hisp.-258

Births (2014)—57 • **Deaths** (2014)—57

Marriages (2013)—51 • **Divorces** (2013)—10

Unemployment Rate (2013)—3.9%

Labor Force (2013)-2,875

Number of Establishments (2013)—130

Number of Manufacturers (2013)—4

Public Assistance Payments (FY2014)
Total—$1,565,214 • TANF—$0 •
Supplements—Aged-$3,596; Blind-0;
Disabled-$23,668

Vehicle Registration (2014)—
Automobiles-2,665; Farm Trucks-1,289;
Comm. Trucks, Tractors, Trailers-224;
Motor Homes and Travel Trailers-144;
Motorcycles-136; Manufactured Homes-5; Tax
Exempt Licenses-10; Boats-73

Crime Incidents (2013)—Murder-0; Rape-0;
Robbery-0; Felony Assault-3 Breaking and
Entering-21; Larceny-26; Motor Vehicle

County Population	
1907 (Okla. Terr.)	16,070
1910	18,138
1920	16,253
1930	15,228
1940	14,129
1950	10,699
1960	8,445
1970	7,224
1980	7,077
1990	6,416
2000	6,105
2010	5,642
2014 Estimate	5,790

Theft-1; Arson-0 • Total Crime Index-51;
Crime Rate per 1,000-8.94

Farms (2012)—645

Land in Farms (2012)—545,223

Recreation Area—Great Salt Plains

Major Lake—Great Salt Plains

Major Stream Systems—Salt Fork of
Arkansas, Turkey Creek, Eagle Chief Creek

Museums or Historic Sites—Sod House
Museum, Aline; Alfalfa County Museum,
Cherokee

Minerals—oil and gas

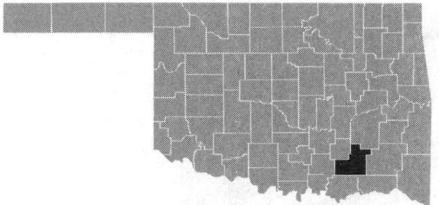

Atoka

Settled in the mid–1800s, this county was first called Shappaway, with the county seat located at the Choctaw Court grounds on the banks of the Muddy Boggy River. The name was later changed to Atoka in honor of Captain Atoka, a noted Choctaw who led a band of his people to this area during the removal.

Atoka, the county seat, was a stop on the Butterfield Overland Stage Road, the route followed when mail service began between Missouri and San Francisco in 1857. Boggy Depot, located in the western part of the county, served as an important trading post during early years and is now historic Boggy Depot State Park.

Well known for its hunting and fishing, half its area is forested and contains several mountain streams and man-made lakes. It is the site of Oklahoma's largest rock quarry, which is located at Stringtown.

The county claims many firsts including Oklahoma's first Masonic Lodge, first chapter of Eastern Star, and first Catholic Church in Indian Territory. Country entertainer Reba McEntire is from the county. Tales of Atoka County Heritage and Atoka County Museum offer more information. The Chamber of Commerce serves as a tourist center, and the Confederate Memorial Museum and Cemetery is also an information and rest area, located on HWY 69 north of Atoka. For more information, call the Atoka Chamber of Commerce at 580/889-2410.

Districts

Congress............................2
State Senate.................5, 6
State Rep....................19, 22
District Attorney 19
Court of Appeals. 3
Ct. of Crim. Appeals........3
Supreme Ct. Jud. 2
SE Jud. Adm...................25

County Officials

Court Clerk	April Maxey (D)	Atoka
Clerk	Christie Henry (D)	Atoka
Sheriff	Tony Head (D)	Caney
Treasurer	Richard Lillard (D)	Atoka
Assessor	Nancy Hill (D)	Atoka
Election Brd. Sec.	Racheal Feuerhelm (D)	Lane
Dist. 1 Comm.	Marvin Dale (D)	Atoka
Dist. 2 Comm.	Cliff Ridgeway (D)	Lane
Dist. 3 Comm.	Phillip Culbreath (D)	Caney

Property Valuations

	2013–2014 Assessment	2014–2015 Assessment	Increase or Decrease
Real Estate and Improvement	$47,977,487	$49,294,498	$1,316,876
Personal Subject to Tax	$11,912,253	$12,310,646	$398,393
Total Locally Assessed	$59,889,875	$61,605,144	$1,715,269
Homestead Exemptions Allowed	$4,190,029	$4,255,902	$65,873
Net Assessed Locally	$55,699,846	$57,349,242	$1,649,396
Public Service Assessment	$17,288,432	$23,866,630	$6,578,198
Net Assessed Valuation	$72,988,278	$81,215,872	$8,227,594

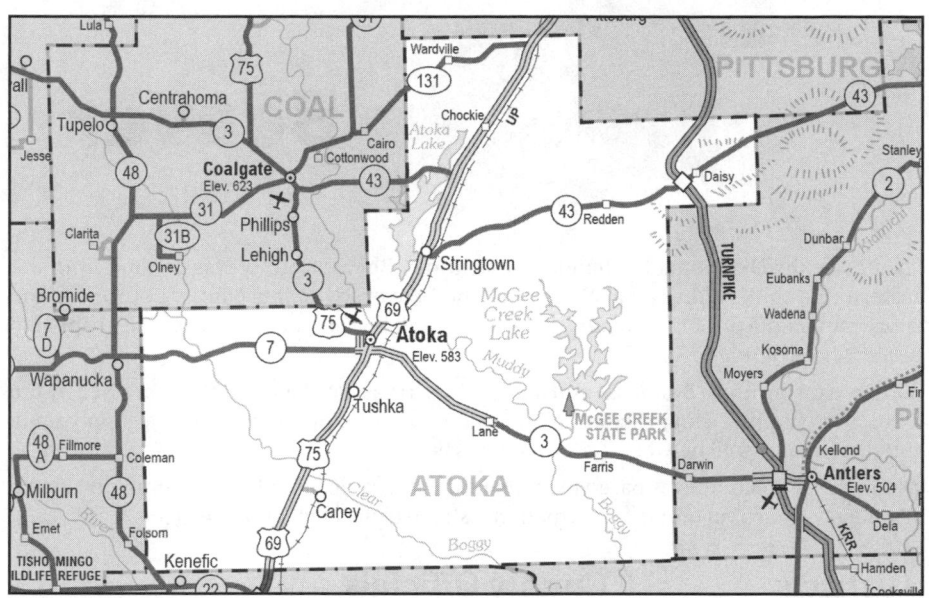

County Seat—Atoka (Pop. 3,098) 2013 Estimate

Area (Land & Water)—990 square miles

Per Capita Income (2013)—$29,389 (Ranks 72nd of 77 counties)

Population Statistics (2013)—Female–6,710; Male–7,360; Ethnicity—Wh.-11,697; Bl.-727; Am. Ind.-2,779; As.-81; Other-117; Pacific Is.-0. Two or more races-1,261; Hisp.-446

Births (2014)—169 • **Deaths** (2014)—159

Marriages (2013)—96 • **Divorces** (2013)—65

Unemployment Rate (2013)—6.0%

Labor Force (2013)—5,933

Number of Establishments (2013)—270

Number of Manufacturers (2013)—16

Public Assistance Payments (FY2014) Total—$8,779,868 • TANF—$87,036 • Supplements—Aged-$47,044; Blind-$964; Disabled-$189,514

Vehicle Registration (2014)—Automobiles-7,860; Farm Trucks-1,852; Comm. Trucks, Tractors, Trailers-314; Motor Homes and Travel Trailers-487; Motorcycles-301; Manufactured Homes-16; Tax Exempt Licenses-39; Boats-467

Crime Incidents (2013)—Murder-0; Rape-3; Robbery-2; Felony Assault-10; Breaking and Entering-78; Larceny-124; Motor Vehicle

Theft-12; Arson-4 • Total Crime Index-229; Crime Rate per 1,000-16.33

Farms (2012)—1,103

Land in Farms (2012)—353,158

Recreation Area—Boggy Depot

Major Lakes—Atoka, McGee Creek Reservoir

Major Stream Systems—Muddy Boggy and Clear Boggy

Museums or Historic Sites—Boggy Depot and Confederate Cemetery Museum

Minerals—oil and gas, crushed stone

County Population	
1907 (Okla. Terr.)	12,113
1910	13,808
1920	20,862
1930	14,533
1940	18,702
1950	14,269
1960	10,352
1970	10,972
1980	12,748
1990	12,778
2000	13,879
2010	14,182
2014 Estimate	13,796

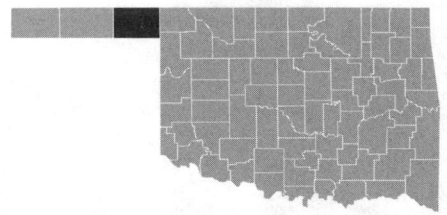

Beaver

Located in the Oklahoma Panhandle, present-day Beaver County was created from the eastern one-third of that area. Named for the Beaver River, this county comprised the entire panhandle prior to statehood. Its county seat, Beaver, was at one time the capital of Cimarron Territory.

Bordered on the north by Kansas and the south by Texas, Beaver County was crossed by the Jones and Plummer Trail. Established around 1874, this trail served first as a supply route and then a cattle trail between Texas and Kansas.

While the local economy is based on agriculture and cattle, it is also supplemented by the oil and gas industry. For more information, call the county clerk's office at 580/625-3141.

Districts

Congress..........................3
State Senate...................27
State Rep.......................61
District Attorney.............1
Court of Appeals............6
Ct. of Crim. Appeals........5
Supreme Ct. Jud..............4
NW Jud. Adm. 1

County Officials

Court Clerk	Tammie Patzkowsky (R)	Beaver
Clerk	Tammy Millikan (R)	Beaver
Sheriff	Reuben Parker Jr. (R)	Beaver
Treasurer	Albert Rodriguez (R)	Beaver
Assessor	Darlene Lansden (R)	Balko
Election Brd. Sec.	Christi Lansden (D)	Beaver
Dist. 1 Comm.	Brad Raven (R)	Beaver
Dist. 2 Comm.	C. J. Rose (R)	Beaver
Dist. 3 Comm.	Frank King (R)	Turpin

Property Valuations

	2013–2014 Assessment	2014–2015 Assessment	Increase or Decrease
Real Estate and Improvement	$46,047,681	$46,928,322	$880,641
Personal Subject to Tax	$50,308,204	$56,075,56	$5,767,359
Total Locally Assessed	$96,355,885	$103,003,885	$6,648,000
Homestead Exemptions Allowed	$1,433,977	$1,413,581	($20,396)
Net Assessed Locally	$94,921,908	$101,590,304	$6,668,396
Public Service Assessment	$37,705,730	$44,462,762	$6,757,032
Net Assessed Valuation	$132,627,638	$146,053,066	$13,425,428

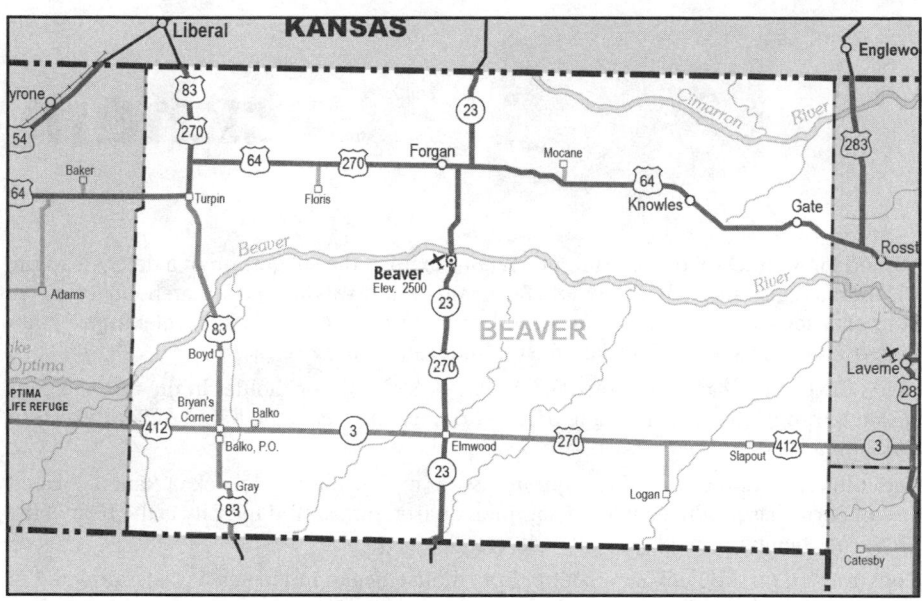

County Seat—Beaver (Pop. 1,496) 2013 Estimate

Area (Land & Water)—1,817.58 square miles

Per Capita Income (2013)—$47,943 (Ranks 6th of 77 counties)

Population Statistics (2013)—Female-2,782; Male-2,823;
Ethnicity—Wh.-5,011; Bl.-56; Am. Ind.-91; As.-80; Other-281;
Pacific Is.-0; Two or more races-120, Hisp.-1,164

Births (2014)—66 • **Deaths** (2014)—54

Marriages (2013)—21 • **Divorces** (2013)—16

Unemployment Rate (2013)—3.1%

Labor Force (2013)—3,502

Number of Establishments (2013)—167

Number of Manufacturers (2013)—3

Public Assistance Payments
(FY2014) Total—$979,130 • TANF—
$14,809 • Supplements—Aged-$45,262;
Blind-$0; Disabled-$12,543

Vehicle Registration (2014)—
Automobiles-5,442; Farm Trucks-1,383;
Comm., Trucks, Tractors, Trailers-893;
Motor Homes and Travel Trailers-350;
Motorcycles-285; Manufactured Homes-10;
Tax Exempt Licenses-9; Boats-140

Crime Incidents (2013)—Murder-0; Rape-0;
Robbery-0; Felony Assault-12; Breaking

County Population	
1907 (Okla. Terr.)	13,364
1910	13,631
1920	14,048
1930	11,452
1940	8,648
1950	7,411
1960	6,965
1970	6,282
1980	6,806
1990	6,023
2000	5,857
2010	5,636
2014 Estimate	5,486

and Entering-21; Larceny-54; Motor Vehicle
Theft-3; Arson-2 • Total Crime Index-90;
Crime Rate per 1,000-16.07

Farms (2012)—965

Land in Farms (2012)—1,115,852

Recreation Area—Beaver State Park

Major Stream Systems—North Canadian
(Beaver), and Cimarron rivers

Museums or Historic Sites—Jones and
Plummer Trail Museum, Beaver

Minerals—oil and gas, pumice

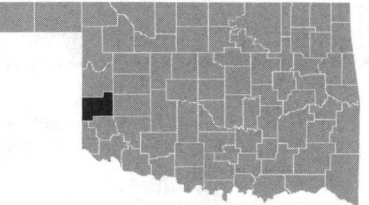

Beckham

Named for Kentucky Governor John C. W. Beckham at the suggestion of a delegate to the Oklahoma Constitutional Convention, Beckham County was formed at statehood from portions of Greer and Roger Mills counties and is the site of the Oklahoma Traveler Information Center for persons entering Oklahoma on Interstate 40 from Texas.

Sayre, the county seat, was named for Robert H. Sayre, a stockholder in the railroad constructed through Sayre at the time of its founding. The city is the home of Southwestern Oklahoma State University, Sayre campus.

Agriculture, oil, and gas are the major industries of the county. Merrick 14 Ranch, located east of Sayre, has produced world champion quarter horses and Elk City is the host of the Rodeo of Champions held each September.

Construction on the Beckham County Courthouse began in 1907 and was completed in 1911. Originally, four clocks were to be installed in the courthouse dome. Yet, due to a lack of funding the clocks were never installed. However, Beckham County residents raised the necessary funds, and the clocks were installed in the dome in time for the state's centennial celebration. For more information, call the county clerk's office at 580/928-3383.

Districts

Congress..........................3
State Senate...................26
State Rep.................. 55, 57
District Attorney 2
Court of Appeals 6
Ct. of Crim. Appeals........5
Supreme Ct. Jud..............4
NW Jud. Adm. 2

County Officials

Court Clerk	Donna Howell (D)	Sayre
Clerk	Leasa Hartman (R)	Sayre
Sheriff	Scott Jay (D)	Elk City
Treasurer	Janette Cornelius (D)	Willow
Assessor	Gayla Gillie (D)	Sayre
Election Brd. Sec.	Deidre O'Briant (D)	Sayre
Dist. 1 Comm.	Carl Don Campbell (D)	Sayre
Dist. 2 Comm.	Buddy Carnes (D)	Elk City
Dist. 3 Comm.	Johnny Davis (D)	Erick

Property Valuations

	2013–2014 Assessment	2014–2015 Assessment	Increase or Decrease
Real Estate and Improvement	$121,740,942	$129,125,922	$7,384,980
Personal Subject to Tax	$99,016,287	$115,722,631	$16,706,344
Total Locally Assessed	$220,757,229	$244,848,553	$24,091,324
Homestead Exemptions Allowed	$4,252,543	$4,282,950	$30,407
Net Assessed Locally	$216,504,686	$240,565,603	$24,060,917
Public Service Assessment	$35,433,505	$30,655,804	($4,777,701)
Net Assessed Valuation	$251,938,191	$271,221,407	$19,283,216

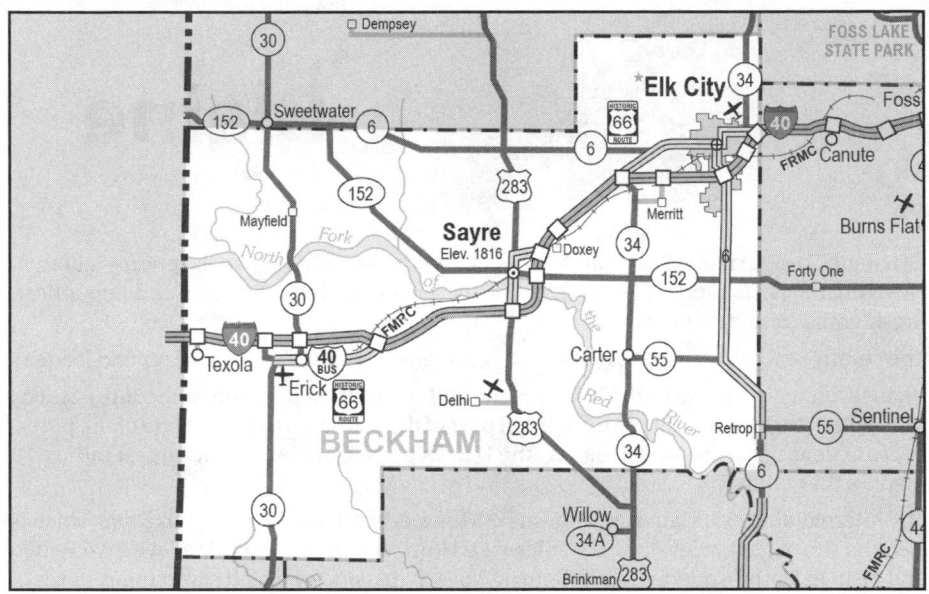

County Seat—Sayre (Pop. 4,631) 2013 Estimate

Area (Land & Water)—904.14 square miles

Per Capita Income (2013)—$44,707 (Ranks 15th of 77 counties)

Population Statistics (2013)—Female-10,530; Male-12,185; Ethnicity—Wh.-20,900; Bl.-1,106; Am. Ind.-1,656; As.-81, Other-905; Pacific Is.-24; Two or more races-1,118; Hisp.-2,852

Births (2014)—361 • **Deaths** (2014)—257

Marriages (2013)—174 • **Divorces** (2013)—122

Unemployment Rate (2013)—3.1%

Labor Force (2013)—14,812

Number of Establishments (2013)—894

Number of Manufacturers (2013)—18

Public Assistance Payments
(FY2014) Total—$11,972,619 • TANF—$88,436 • Supplements—Aged-$45,262; Blind-$2,911; Disabled-$222,854

Vehicle Registration (2014)—
Automobiles-22,006; Farm Trucks-3,818; Comm., Trucks, Tractors, Trailers-4,134; Motor Homes and Travel Trailers-1,321; Motorcycles-1,303; Manufactured Homes-120; Tax Exempt Licenses-84; Boats-585

Institutions of Higher Learning—
Southwestern Oklahoma State University, Sayre

Crime Incidents (2013)—Murder 0; Rape-1;

County Population	
1907 (Okla. Terr.)	17,758
1910	19,699
1920	18,989
1930	28,991
1940	22,169
1950	21,627
1960	17,782
1970	15,754
1980	19,243
1990	18,812
2000	19,799
2010	22,119
2014 Estimate	23,691

Robbery-4; Felony Assault-45; Breaking and Entering-117; Larceny-327; Motor Vehicle Theft-50; Arson-3 • Total Crime Index-544; Crime Rate per 1,000-23.10

Farms (2012)—1,016

Land in Farms (2012)—567,886

Major Stream Systems—North Fork of Red River, Elm Fork of Red River, and Washita River

Museums or Historic Sites—Old Town Museum at Elk City, RS & K Railroad Museum at Sayre, and the Shortgrass Country Museum at Sayre

Minerals—oil and gas

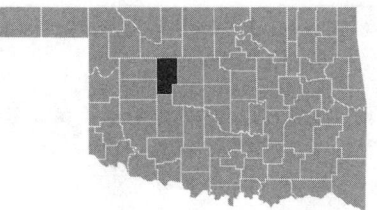

Blaine

Originally designated as "C" County in 1890, Blaine was adopted as the county name in November 1892, in honor of James G. Blaine, U.S. Senator, House Speaker, and Republican presidential candidate in 1884.

The county seat, Watonga, was named for Watangaa, or Black Coyote, an Arapaho leader.

Blaine County is the site of the first gypsum mill in Oklahoma Territory, the Ruby Stucco Mill. Southard, located in the north central part of the county, is the site of one of the purest gypsum deposits in the United States. The U.S. Gypsum Company is the largest industrial plant in the county.

The International Association of Rattlesnake Hunters has headquarters in Okeene, which is also the site of its Jaycees Annual Rattlesnake Hunt. The Canton Lake Walleye Pike Rodeo and Fishing Derby occur annually. Roman Nose State Park is located seven miles north of Watonga. For more information, call the Watonga Chamber of Commerce at 580/623-5452, or the county clerk's office at 580/623-5890.

Districts

Congress...........................3
State Senate...................26
State Rep.................. 57, 59
District Attorney 4
Court of Appeals............ 6
Ct. of Crim. Appeals........5
Supreme Ct. Jud. 4
NW Jud. Adm. 4
   (Div. II)

County Officials

Court Clerk	Christy Matli (R)	Watonga
Clerk	Della Wallace (R)	Watonga
Sheriff	Margarett Parman (R)	Watonga
Treasurer	Donna Hoskins (R)	Watonga
Assessor	Rian Parker (R)	Watonga
Election Brd. Sec.	Brenda Rice (D)	Watonga
Dist. 1 Comm.	Mike Allen (R)	Geary
Dist. 2 Comm.	Jonathon Cross (D)	Okeene
Dist. 3 Comm.	Raymond Scheffler (D)	Hitchcock

Property Valuations

	2013–2014 Assessment	2014–2015 Assessment	Increase or Decrease
Real Estate and Improvement	$48,443,284	$49,906,762	$1,463,478
Personal Subject to Tax	$48,060,587	$45,961,223	($2,099,364)
Total Locally Assessed	$96,503,871	$95,867,985	($635,886)
Homestead Exemptions Allowed	$2,354,654	$2,325,853	($28,801)
Net Assessed Locally	$94,149,217	$93,542,132	($607,085)
Public Service Assessment	$11,242,596	$12,602,861	$1,360,265
Net Assessed Valuation	$105,391,813	$106,144,993	$753,180

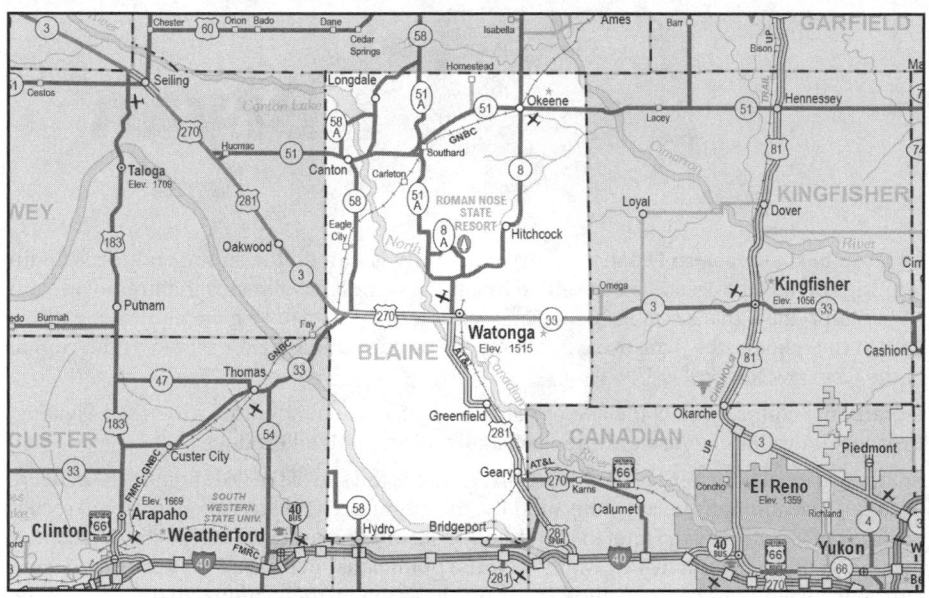

County Seat—Watonga (Pop. 2,986) 2013 Estimate

Area (Land & Water)—938.88 square miles

Per Capita Income (2013)—$37,038 (Ranks 36th of 77 counties)

Population Statistics (2013)—Female-4,660; Male-5,538; Ethnicity—Wh.-8,470; Bl.-686; Am. Ind.-966; As.-25, Other-502; Pacific Is.-0; Two or more races-678; Hisp.-1,234

Births (2014)—170 • **Deaths** (2014)—126

Marriages (2013)—34 • **Divorces** (2013)—53

Unemployment Rate (2013)—4.7%

Labor Force (2013)—4,537

Number of Establishments (2013)—289

Number of Manufacturers (2013)—8

Public Assistance Payments (FY2014) Total—$6,875,488 • TANF—$57,809 • Supplements—Aged-$18,709; Blind-$0; Disabled-$90,436

Vehicle Registration (2014)—Automobiles-7,246; Farm Trucks-2,473; Comm., Trucks, Tractors, Trailers-723; Motor Homes and Travel Trailers-407; Motorcycles-467; Manufactured Homes-11; Tax Exempt Licenses-74; Boats-225

Crime Incidents (2013)—Murder-0; Rape-1; Robbery-2; Felony Assault-25; Breaking and Entering-63; Larceny-109; Motor Vehicle

Theft-9; Arson-2 • Total Crime Index-209; Crime Rate per 1,000-21.47

Farms (2012)—798

Land in Farms (2012)—521,986

Recreation Area—Roman Nose State Park

Major Lake—Canton Lake

Major Stream Systems—North Canadian, Canadian, Cimarron rivers

Museums or Historic Sites—Fort Watonga (military supply fort), and T.B. Ferguson Home, Watonga

Minerals—oil and gas, gypsum

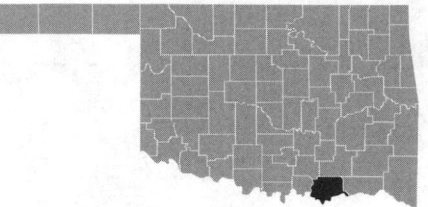

Bryan

Located in southeastern Oklahoma, Bryan County is named for famous orator William Jennings Bryan. The area was first settled by Choctaw Indians following their removal from Mississippi. The Indians established several schools in the area during the mid-to-late 1800s. One of the schools, the Armstrong Academy for Boys in Durant, later served as the capital of the Choctaw Nation.

Durant, the county seat, is the site of many manufacturers including American Packing, Bryan County Manufacturing, Potter Sausage, and Stahl Metal Products.

Southeastern Oklahoma State University in Durant is the site of the Oklahoma Shakespeare Festival. Held annually during June and July, this popular event has gained national recognition. The historic Bryan Hotel in Durant once served as southeastern Oklahoma's center for social and political activities. Many national politicians such as Robert Kerr, Carl Albert, and William Jennings Bryan included the hotel as a stop on their campaign trails. The hotel has been restored, and tours are available.

Lake Texoma Resort provides a variety of recreational facilities including a golf course, marina, and camping facilities. For information, call the county clerk at 580/924-2202.

Districts

Congress.........................2
State Senate...................6
State Rep..................19, 21
District Attorney...........19
Court of Appeals.............3
Ct. of Crim. Appeals........3
Supreme Ct. Jud..............2
SE Jud. Adm...................19

County Officials

Court Clerk	Sandy Stroud (D)	Durant
Clerk	Tammy Reynolds (D)	Durant
Sheriff	Kenneth Golden (D)	Hendrix
Treasurer	Nancy Conner (D)	Durant
Assessor	Glendel Rushing (D)	Durant
Election Brd. Sec.	Linda Fahrendorf (D)	Durant
Dist. 1 Comm.	Monty Montgomery (D)	Meade
Dist. 2 Comm.	Tony Simmons (D)	Calera
Dist. 3 Comm.	Jay Perry (D)	Bennington

Property Valuations

	2013–2014 Assessment	2014–2015 Assessment	Increase or Decrease
Real Estate and Improvement	$201,483,054	$208,246,663	$6,763,609
Personal Subject to Tax	$31,134,817	$32,648,274	$1,513,457
Total Locally Assessed	$232,617,871	$240,894,937	$8,277,066
Homestead Exemptions Allowed	$10,090,074	$10,103,164	$13,090
Net Assessed Locally	$222,527,797	$230,791,773	$8,263,976
Public Service Assessment	$57,849,662	$75,077,500	$17,227,838
Net Assessed Valuation	$280,377,459	$305,869,273	$25,491,814

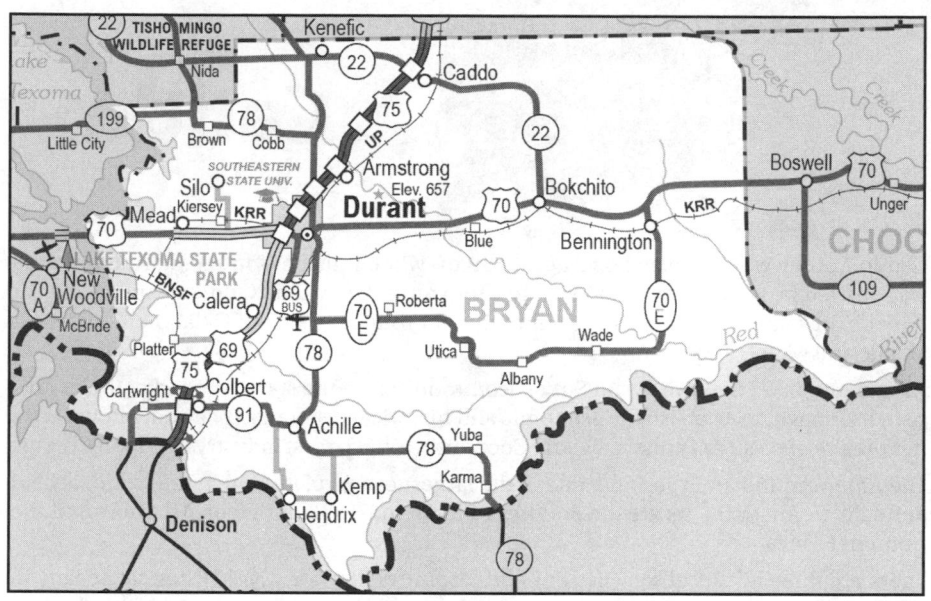

County Seat—Durant (Pop. 16,891) 2013 Estimate

Area (Land & Water)—943.43 square miles

Per Capita Income (2013)—$31,514 (Ranks 63rd of 77 counties)

Population Statistics (2013)—Female–22,032; Male–21,047; Ethnicity—Wh.-36,088; Bl.-956; Am. Ind.-8,274; As.-296 m; Other-1,161; Pacific Is.-14; Two or more races-3,847; Hisp.-2,212

Births (2014)—587 • **Deaths** (2012)—419

Marriages (2013)—487 • **Divorces** (2014)—501

Unemployment Rate (2013)—4.9%

Labor Force (2013)—20,285

Number of Establishments (2013)—750

Number of Manufacturers (2013)—36

Public Assistance Payments (FY2014) Total—$23,027,545 • TANF-$143,372 • Supplements—Aged-$86,425; Blind-$1,318; Disabled-$541,117

Vehicle Registration (2014)—Automobiles-34,744; Farm Trucks-3,997; Comm., Trucks, Tractors, Trailers-9,698; Motor Homes and Travel Trailers-2,020; Motorcycles-1,776; Manufactured Homes-110; Tax Exempt Licenses-180; Boats-1,713

Institutions of Higher Learning—Southeastern Oklahoma State University, Durant.

Crime Incidents (2013)—Murder-2; Rape-20; Robbery-10; Felony Assault-170; Breaking and Entering-426; Larceny-1,064; Motor Vehicle Theft-77; Arson-7 • Total Crime Index-1,769; Crime Rate per 1,000-40.35

Farms (2012)—1,484

Land in Farms (2012)—441,289

Major Lakes—Arbuckle and Texoma

Major Stream Systems—Blue, Island Boggy, Washita, Muddy Boggy, and Red rivers

Museums or Historic Sites—Fort Washita, Durant; Three Valley Museum, Durant; Fairchilds Gallery, Durant; and Fort Washita Military Park, Durant

Minerals—oil and gas, crushed stone

County Population	
1907 (Okla. Terr.)	27,865
1910	29,854
1920	40,700
1930	32,277
1940	38,138
1950	28,999
1960	24,252
1970	25,552
1980	30,535
1990	32,089
2000	36,534
2010	42,416
2014 Estimate	44,486

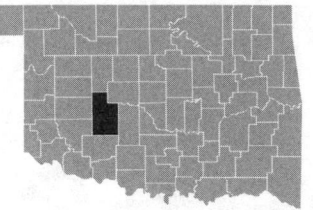

Caddo

Caddo County was organized on August 6, 1901, when much of southwestern Oklahoma was opened by land lottery. Caddo comes from an Indian word, Kaddi, meaning "life" or "chief." The county is primarily agricultural and produces much of Oklahoma's peanuts, alfalfa, and wheat.

As one of the original five "Main Street" communities in the state, Anadarko, the county seat, has sought to establish the economic and historical restoration of its downtown area. It is the site of Western Farmers Electric Cooperative, the largest industry in Caddo County.

The American Indian Exposition, one of the largest events of its kind in the world, is held annually in Anadarko, as are the Southern Plains Indian Rendezvous Art Show and the Autumn Festival.

There are three historical societies in Caddo County. They are: Cyril Historical Society in Cyril, Hinton Historical Society in Hinton, and the Philomathic Museum in Anadarko. The National Hall of Fame for American Indians and Tourist Information Center is located on Highway 62 in Anadarko. For more information, call the county clerk's office at 405/247-6609.

Districts

Congress..........................3
State Senate...................26
State Rep...... 56, 57, 60, 65
District Attorney 6
Court of Appeals. 6
Ct. of Crim. Appeals........5
Supreme Ct. Jud..............9
SW Jud. Adm. 6

County Officials

Court Clerk	Patti Barger (D)	Anadarko
Clerk	Patrice Dolch (D)	Anadarko
Sheriff	Gene Cain (D)	Anadarko
Treasurer	Regina Moser (D)	Gracemont
Assessor	Edward Whitworth (D)	Carnegie
Election Brd. Sec.	Sue Hobbs (D)	Anadarko
Dist. 1 Comm.	Benny Bowling (D)	Binger
Dist. 2 Comm.	Randy McLemore (D)	Gracemont
Dist. 3 Comm.	Brent Kinder (D)	Carnegie

Property Valuations

	2013–2014 Assessment	2014–2015 Assessment	Increase or Decrease
Real Estate and Improvement	$75,015,525	$77,036,007	$2,020,482
Personal Subject to Tax	$73,794,130	$70,647,296	$3,146,834
Total Locally Assessed	$148,809,655	$147,683,303	$1,126,352
Homestead Exemptions Allowed	$6,696,648	$6,669,527	($27,121)
Net Assessed Locally	$142,113,007	$141,013,776	($1,099,231)
Public Service Assessment	$40,612,1481	$34,268,695	($6,343,453)
Net Assessed Valuation	$182,725,155	$175,282,471	($7,442,684)

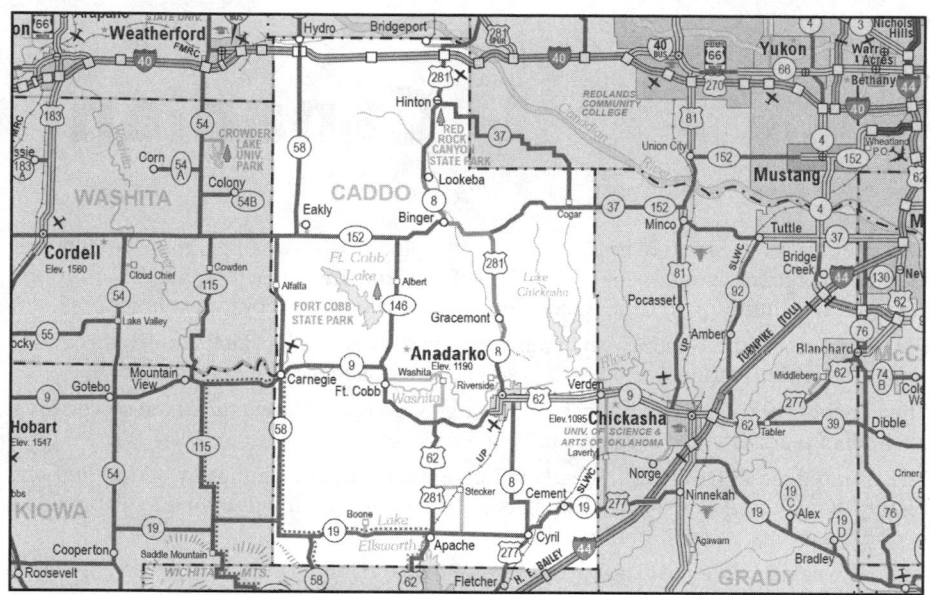

County Seat—Anadarko (Pop. 6,804) 2013 Estimate

Area (Land & Water)—1,290.31 square miles

Per Capita Income (2013)—$29,859 (Ranks 70th of 77 counties)

Population Statistics (2013)—Female–14,292; Male–15,313; Ethnicity—Wh.–18,552; Bl.–818; Am. Ind.–6,940; As.–123; Other–1,266; Pacific Is.–0; Two or more races–1,562; Hisp.–3,125

Births (2014)—415 • **Deaths** (2014)—341

Marriages (2013)—168 • **Divorces** (2013)—100

Unemployment Rate (2013)—6.0%

Labor Force (2013)—12,562

Number of Establishments (2013)—458

Number of Manufacturers (2013)—9

Public Assistance Payments
(FY2014) Total—$19,187,405 • TANF–$172,626 • Supplements—Aged-$72,132; Blind-$1,664; Disabled-$297,216

Vehicle Registration (2014)—
Automobiles–19,933; Farm Trucks–3,901; Comm., Trucks, Tractors, Trailers–2,169; Motor Homes and Travel Trailers–992; Motorcycles–981; Manufactured Homes–29; Tax Exempt Licenses–108; Boats–893

Crime Incidents (2013)—Murder–1; Rape–1; Robbery–4; Felony Assault–84; Breaking and Entering–216; Larceny–294; Motor Vehicle Theft–34; Arson–7; • Total Crime Index–634; Crime Rate per 1,000–21.08

County Population	
1907 (Okla. Terr.)	30,241
1910	35,685
1920	34,207
1930	50,799
1940	41,567
1950	34,913
1960	28,621
1970	28,931
1980	30,905
1990	29,550
2000	30,150
2010	29,600
2014 Estimate	29,317

Farms (2012)—1,461

Land in Farms (2012)—707,669

Recreation Areas—Ft. Cobb and Red Rock Canyon state parks

Major Lakes—Ft. Cobb, Ellsworth

Major Stream Systems—Washita and Canadian rivers, Cache Creek

Museums or Historic Sites—Anadarko Museum, Indian City USA, National Hall of Fame for Famous American Indians, So. Plains Indian Museum & Crafts Center, Delaware Tribal Museum, Anadarko

Minerals—oil and gas, crushed stone, gypsum

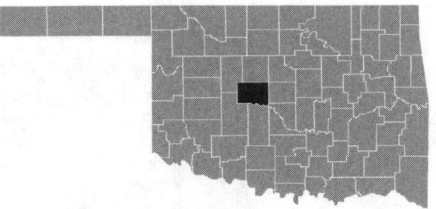

Canadian

This county was once part of the Cheyenne and Arapaho reservation, administered by the Darlington Agency. It was opened by the Run of 1889 and the Run of 1892, but the southwest corner of the county, part of the Caddo Reservation, was opened by lottery in 1901.

Fort Reno, established in 1874 to maintain order on the reservation, later served as a cavalry remount station. During World War II, it served as a prisoner-of-war camp.

The economy of Canadian County is based largely on agriculture, and Yukon served for a number of years as a major regional milling center.

The county seat, El Reno, was an early railroad center, and headquarters of the southern district of the Rock Island Railroad until its demise in 1981. Railroad service is still provided by the Oklahoma, Kansas, and Texas line.

Annual events include '89er Days in April, Fort Reno and Indian Territory Days in Fort Reno, Chisholm Trail Festival (Yukon) in June, and Czech Festival (Yukon) in October. Historical information is available in the *History of Canadian County* and *Family Histories of Canadian County*. Both books are available for purchase. For more county information, call the county clerk's office at 405/262-1070, or visit www.canadiancounty.org on the web.

Districts

Congress......................3, 4
State Senate..22, 23, 44, 45
State Rep.. 41, 43, 47, 57,59, 60
District Attorney 4
Court of Appeals 6
Ct. of Crim. Appeals........4
Supreme Ct. Jud. 9
Canad. Jud. Adm...........26

County Officials

Court Clerk	Marie Ramsey -Hirst(R)	El Reno
Clerk	Shelly Dickerson (R)	El Reno
Sheriff	Randall Edwards (R)	Yukon
Treasurer	Carolyn M. Leck (R)	El Reno
Assessor	Matt Wehmuller (R)	Okarche
Election Brd. Sec.	Wanda Armold (R)	El Reno
Dist. 1 Comm.	Marc Hader (R)	Piedmont
Dist. 2 Comm.	David Anderson (R)	Mustang
Dist. 3 Comm.	Jack Stewart (R)	Yukon

Property Valuations

	2013–2014 Assessment	2014–2015 Assessment	Increase or Decrease
Real Estate and Improvement	$794,092,745	$844,261,936	$50,169,191
Personal Subject to Tax	$256,496,944	$296,900,098	$40,403,154
Total Locally Assessed	$1,050,589,689	$1,141,162,034	$90,572,345
Homestead Exemptions Allowed	$34,354,592	$35,819,604	$1,465,012
Net Assessed Locally	$1,016,235,097	$1,105,342,430	$89,107,333
Public Service Assessment	$56,209,124	$55,226,823	($982,301)
Net Assessed Valuation	$1,072,444,221	$1,160,569,253	$88,125,032

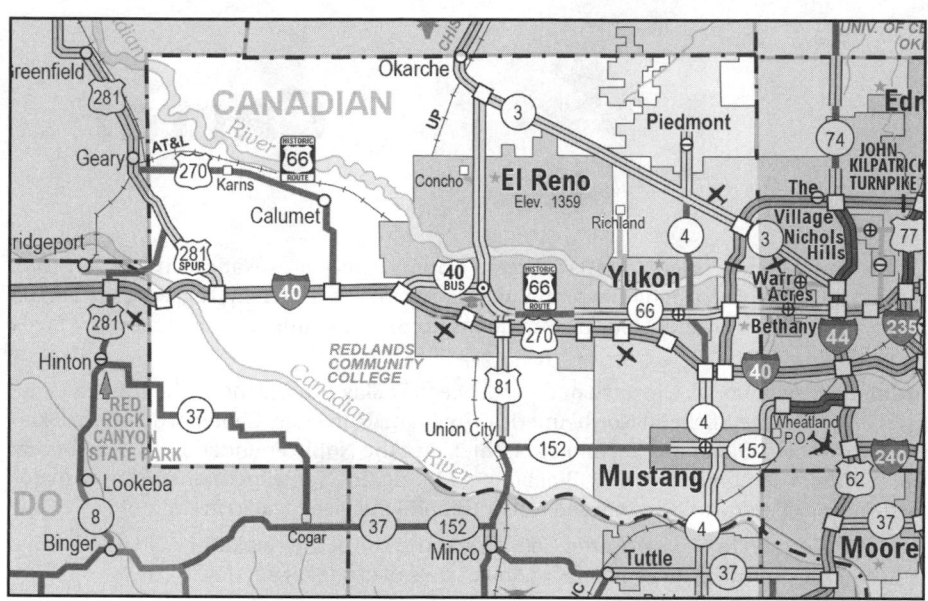

County Seat—El Reno (Pop. 17,857) 2013 Estimate

Area (Land & Water)—905.17 square miles

Per Capita Income (2013)—$42,296 (Ranks 20th of 77 counties)

Population Statistics (2013)—Female-60,267; Male-59,279;
Ethnicity—Wh.-99,039; Bl.-2,689; Am. Ind.-5,080; As.-3,537;
Other-3,056; Pacific Is.-11; Two or more races-5,257; Hisp.-8,589

Births (2014)—1,736 • Deaths (2014)—915

Marriages (2013)—778 • Divorces (2013)—549

Unemployment Rate (2013)—4.6%

Labor Force (2013)—59,810

Number of Establishments (2013)—2,458

Number of Manufacturers (2013)—68

Public Assistance Payments
(FY2014) Total—$43,285,615 • TANF—
$429,318 • Supplements—Aged-$79,208
Blind-$932; Disabled-$357,073

Vehicle Registration (2014)—
Automobiles-85,670; Farm Trucks-3,280;
Comm., Trucks, Tractors, Trailers-7,681;
Motor Homes and Travel Trailers-2,643;
Motorcycles-4,465; Manufactured Homes-109;
Tax Exempt Licenses-123; Boats-2,643

Institutions of Higher Learning—Redlands
Community College, El Reno

Crime Incidents (2013)—Murder-2; Rape-16;
Robbery-11; Felony Assault-126; Breaking
and Entering-346; Larceny-1,265; Motor

County Population	
1907 (Okla. Terr.)	20,110
1910	23,501
1920	22,288
1930	28,115
1940	27,329
1950	25,644
1960	24,727
1970	32,245
1980	56,452
1990	74,409
2000	87,697
2010	115,541
2014 Estimate	129,582

Vehicle Theft-82; Arson-21 • Total Crime
Index-1,858; Crime Rate per 1,000-24.15

Farms (2012)—1,307

Land in Farms (2012)—500,776

Recreation Area—Lake El Reno, Lake
Overholser

Major Stream Systems—North Canadian,
Canadian, Washita, and tributaries to the
Cimarron

Museums or Historic Sites—In El Reno,
Canadian County Historical Society, Fort
Reno, Darlington Game Bird Hatchery

Minerals—oil and gas, clay

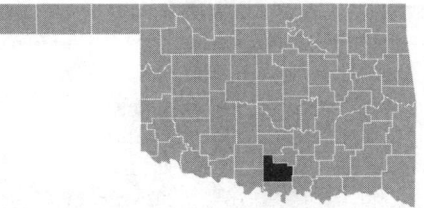

Carter

Carter County was formerly a part of Pickens County, Chickasaw Nation, Indian Territory. Named for a prominent early-day family, the county ranges from hilly, rugged terrain in the north, exemplified by the Arbuckle Mountains, to rolling plains with productive oil fields in the south.

Ardmore, the county seat, located midway between Dallas and Oklahoma City on Interstate 35, is the site of the Michelin North America Tire Plant, University Center of Southern Oklahoma, Southern Oklahoma Technology Center, and the Noble Foundation. The Joe Brown Co., Ultimar Diamond Shamrock, Bluebonnet Milling Co., Sunshine Industries, and major distribution centers for Best Buy and Dollar General are also located in Ardmore.

Healdton, located in western Carter County, was the site of the Healdton Field which, at its peak in 1916, produced an estimated 95,000 barrels of crude oil per day.

Lake Murray Resort, located seven miles south of Ardmore, offers recreational and conference facilities on a year-round basis. For additional county information, call the county clerk's office at 580/223-8162.

Districts

Congress..........................4
State Senate...................14
State Rep.................48, 49
District Attorney...........20
Court of Appeals.............3
Ct. of Crim. Appeals........3
Supreme Ct. Jud..............5
S. Cent. Jud. Adm..........20
    (Div. I)

County Officials

Court Clerk	Karen Volino (D)	Ardmore
Clerk	Cynthia Harmon (D)	Ardmore
Sheriff	Ken Grace (D)	Ardmore
Treasurer	Marsha Collins (D)	Ardmore
Assessor	Kim Cain (D)	Wilson
Election Brd. Sec.	Helen McReynolds (D)	Ardmore
Dist. 1 Comm.	Bill McLaughlin (D)	Ardmore
Dist. 2 Comm.	Kevin Robinson (D)	Lone Grove
Dist. 3 Comm.	Dale Ott (D)	Ardmore

Property Valuations

	2013–2014 Assessment	2014–2015 Assessment	Increase or Decrease
Real Estate and Improvement	$221,844,546	$227,705,376	$5,860,830
Personal Subject to Tax	$145,444,595	$177,649,033	$32,204,438
Total Locally Assessed	$367,289,141	$405,354,409	$38,065,268
Homestead Exemptions Allowed	$12,864,273	$12,757,751	($106,522)
Net Assessed Locally	$354,424,868	$392,596,658	$38,171,790
Public Service Assessment	$52,252,170	$60,254,533	$8,002,363
Net Assessed Valuation	$406,677,038	$452,851,191	$46,174,153

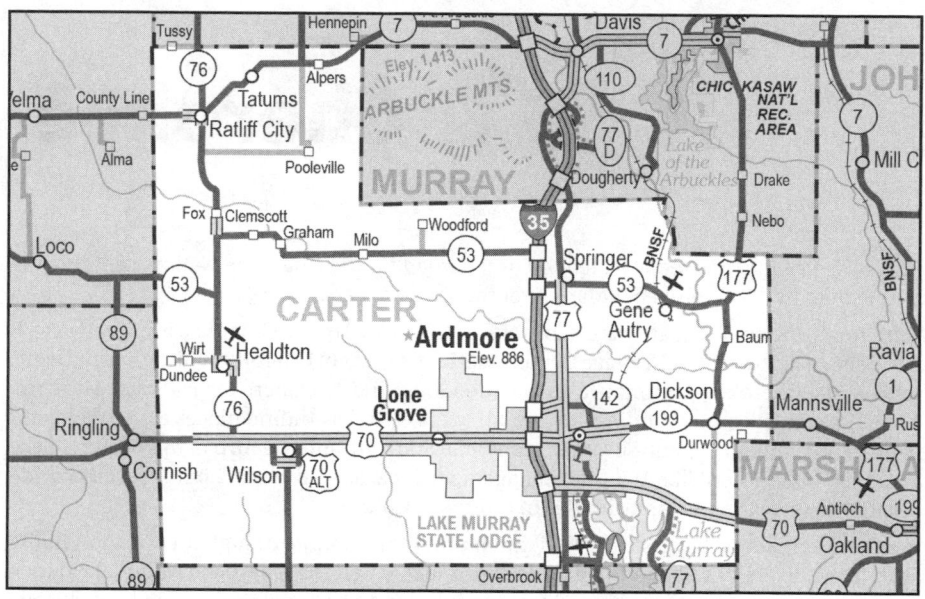

County Seat—Ardmore (Pop. 24,950) 2013 Estimate

Area (Land & Water)—833.72 square miles

Per Capita Income (2013)—$42,189 (Ranks 21st of 77 counties)

Population Statistics (2013)—Female-24,600; Male-23,304; Ethnicity—Wh.-36,210; Bl.-3,420; Am. Ind.-4,234; As.-452; Other-737; Pacific Is.-73; Two or more races-2,619; Hisp.-2,755

Births (2014)—689 • **Deaths** (2014)—598

Marriages (2013)—391 • **Divorces** (2013)—180

Unemployment Rate (2013)—4.1%

Labor Force (2013)—28,768

Number of Establishments (2013)—1,560

Number of Manufacturers (2013)—43

Public Assistance Payments
(FY2014) Total—$29,243,238 • TANF—$324,057 • Supplements—Aged-$64,715; Blind-$1,507; Disabled-$561,151

Vehicle Registration (2014)—
Automobiles-30,934; Farm Trucks-1,303; Comm., Trucks, Tractors, Trailers-2,339; Motor Homes and Travel Trailers-1,175; Motorcycles-1,383; Manufactured Homes-38; Tax Exempt Licenses-158; Boats-1,439

Crime Incidents (2013)—Murder-2; Rape-34; Robbery-31; Felony Assault-367; Breaking and Entering-535; Larceny-1,530; Motor Vehicle Theft-138; Arson-10 • Total Crime Rate-2,637; Crime Rate per 1,000-54.43

County Population	
1907 (Okla. Terr.)	26,402
1910	25,358
1920	40,247
1930	41,419
1940	43,292
1950	36,455
1960	39,044
1970	37,349
1980	43,610
1990	42,919
2000	45,621
2010	47,557
2014 Estimate	48,821

Farms (2012)—1,321

Land in Farms (2012)—456,594

Recreation Area—Murray State Park

Major Lakes—Lake Murray

Major Stream Systems—Washita River, Walnut Bayou, Caddo Creek

Museums or Historic Sites—Eliza Cruce Hall Doll House, Charles B. Goddard Center for Visual and Performing Arts, Ardmore; Carter County Museum, Ardmore; Military Memorial Museum, Ardmore; Healdton Oil Museum, Healdton

Minerals—oil and gas, crushed stone

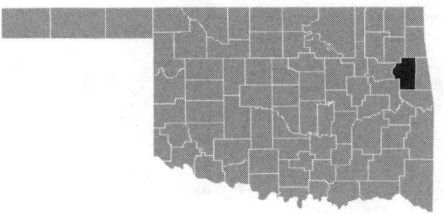

Cherokee

Cherokee County, created at statehood and named for the Cherokee Nation, is part of the area settled by the Cherokee Indians after the Trail of Tears.

Tahlequah, the county seat, was established as the capital of the Cherokee Nation in 1839. It is the site of the Cherokee Heritage Center; Tsa-La-Gi Ancient Cherokee Village, an authentic replica of a Cherokee community during the 1600s; and the Cherokee National Museum. The Cookson Hills, surrounding Tahlequah, were noted as hiding places for outlaws and bandits, including the James Brothers and Belle Starr, around the turn of the century. Lake Tenkiller and the Tenkiller Wildlife Management Area, as well as the Illinois River, provide additional recreational opportunities in Cherokee County.

Northeastern State University in Tahlequah provides a source of higher education in the area. The university's beginning dates back to 1846 when the Cherokee National Council authorized the creation of a National Male Seminary and a National Female Seminary. In 1909 the Oklahoma Legislature authorized the purchase of the building, land, and equipment of the Cherokee Female Seminary to form the Northeastern State Normal School at Tahlequah.

For more county information, call the county clerk's office at 918/456-4121.

Districts

Congress 2
State Senate 3, 9, 18
State Rep. 4, 14, 86
District Attorney 27
Court of Appeals 2
Ct. of Crim. Appeals........2
Supreme Ct. Jud. 7
E. Cent. Jud. Adm.......... 15
  (Div. I)

County Officials

Court Clerk	Shelly Kissinger (D)	Tahlequah
Clerk	Cheryl Trammel (D)	Tahlequah
Sheriff	Norman Fisher (D)	Tahlequah
Treasurer	Inez Peace (D)	Tahlequah
Assessor	Marsha Trammel (D)	Tahlequah
Election Brd. Sec.	Mary Kay Smith (D)	Tahlequah
Dist. 1 Comm.	Doug Hubbard (D)	Tahlequah
Dist. 2 Comm.	Bobby Botts (D)	Hulbert
Dist. 3 Comm.	Cliff Hall (D)	Park Hill

Property Valuations

	2013–2014 Assessment	2014–2015 Assessment	Increase or Decrease
Real Estate and Improvement	$160,542,099	$167,300,313	$6,758,214
Personal Subject to Tax	$19,423,785	$20,186,192	$762,407
Total Locally Assessed	$179,965,884	$187,486,505	$7,520,621
Homestead Exemptions Allowed	$9,230,457	$9,349,953	$119,496
Net Assessed Locally	$170,735,427	$178,136,552	$7,401,125
Public Service Assessment	$6,286,009	$6,378,047	$92,038
Net Assessed Valuation	$177,021,436	$184,514,599	$7,493,163

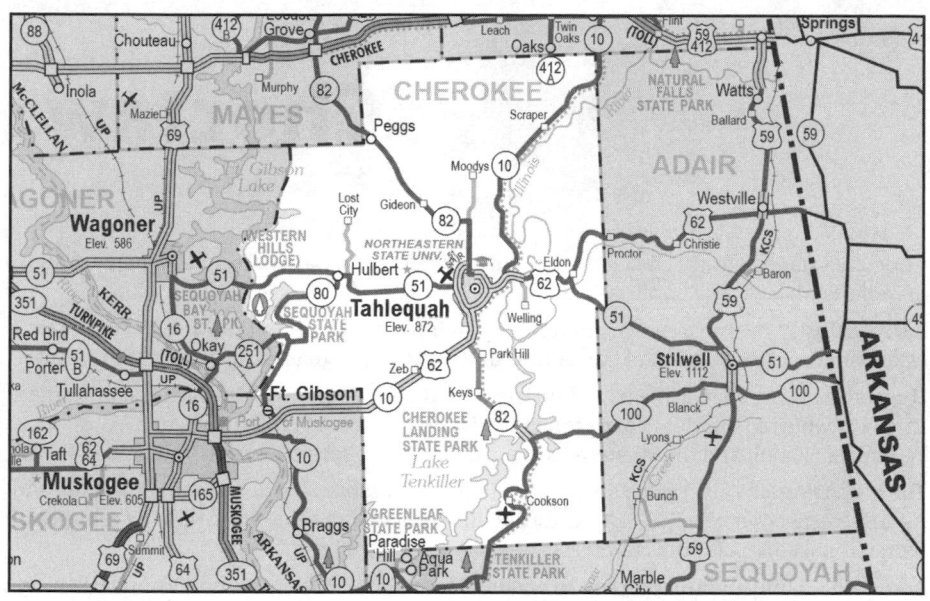

County Seat—Tahlequah (Pop. 16,359) 2013 Estimate

Area (Land & Water)—776.40 square miles

Per Capita Income (2013)—$30,536 (Ranks 68th of 77 counties)

Population Statistics (2013)—Female-24,155; Male-23,333;
Ethnicity-Wh.-31,732; Bl.-1,000; Am. Ind.-20,322; As.-355;
Other-1,083; Pacific Is.-71; Two or more races-6,976; Hisp.-3,035

Births (2014)—556 • Deaths (2012)—477

Marriages (2013)—299 • Divorces (2014)—496

Unemployment Rate (2013)—5.5%

Labor Force (2013)—24,167

Number of Establishments (2013)—728

Number of Manufacturers (2013)—17

Public Assistance Payments
(FY2014)Total—$29,243,238 • TANF—
$198,340 • Supplements—Aged-$119,826;
Blind-$2,917; Disabled-777,685

Vehicle Registration (2014)—
Automobiles-18,528; Farm Trucks-825;
Comm., Trucks, Tractors, Trailers-643;
Motor Homes and Travel Trailers-666;
Motorcycles-780; Manufactured Homes-49;
Tax Exempt Licenses-223; Boats-1,244

Institutions of Higher Learning—
Northeastern State University, Tahlequah

Crime Incidents (2013)—Murder-2; Rape-12;
Robbery-13; Felony Assault-89; Breaking and
Entering-332; Larceny-888; Motor Vehicle
Theft-82; Arson-6 • Total Crime Index-1,418;

County Population	
1907 (Okla. Terr.)	14,274
1910	 16,778
1920	 19,872
1930	 17,470
1940	 21,030
1950	 18,989
1960	17,762
1970	23,174
1980	 30,684
1990	34,049
2000	 42,521
2010	46,987
2014 Estimate	 48,341

Crime Rate
per 1,000-29.13

Farms (2012)—1,233

Land in Farms (2012)—236,042

Recreation Area—Rocky Ford, Sequoyah,
Tenkiller state parks

Major Lakes—Ft. Gibson, Tenkiller

Major Stream Systems—Illinois and Grand
rivers, tributaries to the Arkansas between the
mouth of the Canadian and Cimarron rivers

Museums or Historic Sites—Ft.
Chickamauga at Cookson; Cherokee National
Museum, Tsa-La-Gi Village, Tahlequah;
Adams Corner Rural Village, Tahlequah

Minerals—oil and gas, crushed stone

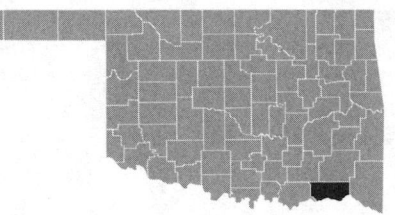

Choctaw

Choctaw County was created at the time of statehood and named for the Choctaw Nation of Indians whose tribal name is Chahta.

Early industry in the area was limited to patch farming, but agriculture became more established with the advent of the railroad and resulting increase of immigrants to the area.

Hugo, the county seat, is the winter quarters for the Carson and Barnes Circus, the largest truck-drawn circus under the big top in the United States. The Kiamichi Area Vocational-Technical School, and the Western Farmers Electric Cooperative are also located in Hugo.

The PRCA Professional Rodeo and Grant's Bluegrass Festival are held annually in June and August, respectively. Hugo Lake and Lake Raymond Gary State Park provide additional recreational outlets for the county.

Additional county information can be obtained from the Choctaw County Historical Society. *Smoke Signals* is a history book about the county. For more information, call the county clerk's office at 580/326-3778.

Districts

Congress	2
State Senate	5
State Rep.	19
District Attorney	17
Court of Appeals	3
Ct. of Crim. Appeals	3
Supreme Ct. Jud.	2
SE Jud. Adm	17

County Officials

Court Clerk	Laura Sumner (D)	Hugo
Clerk	Emily VanWorth (D)	Hugo
Sheriff	Terry Park (D)	Hugo
Treasurer	Arlene Minchey (D)	Soper
Assessor	Rhonda Cahill (D)	Hugo
Election Brd. Sec.	Cathy Davidson (D)	Grant
Dist. 1 Comm.	Ronnie Thompson (D)	Hugo
Dist. 2 Comm.	Randy Robertson (D)	Hugo
Dist. 3 Comm.	Roger Vandever (D)	Ft. Towson

Property Valuations

	2013–2014 Assessment	2014–2015 Assessment	Increase or Decrease
Real Estate and Improvement	$40,757,587	$42,034,988	$1,277,401
Personal Subject to Tax	$8,596,305	$10,016,043	$1,419,738
Total Locally Assessed	$49,353,892	$52,051,031	$2,697,139
Homestead Exemptions Allowed	$3,902,896	$3,827,576	($75,320)
Net Assessed Locally	$45,450,996	$48,223,455	$2,772,459
Public Service Assessment	$17,193,442	$17,618,683	$425,241
Net Assessed Valuation	$62,644,438	$65,842,138	$3,197,700

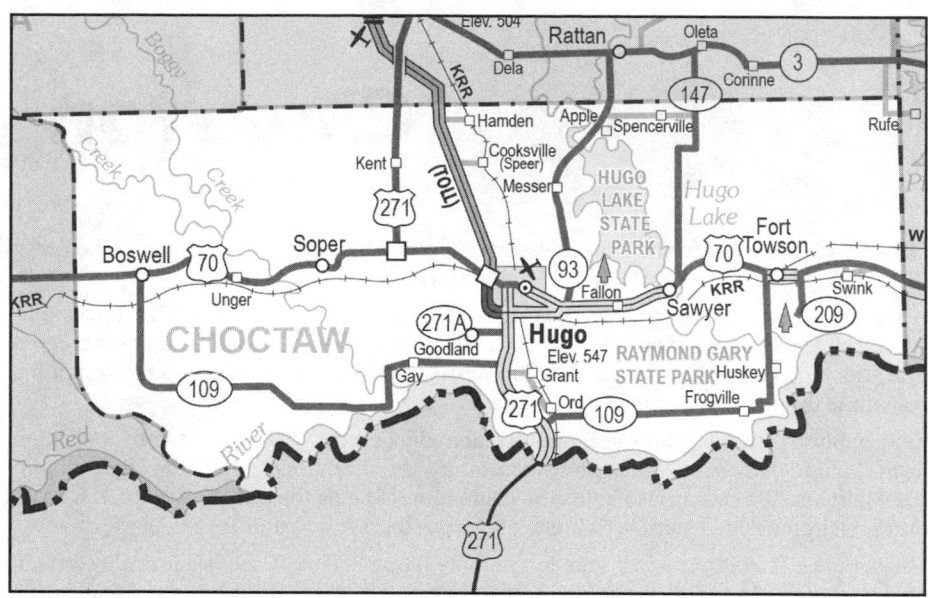

County Seat—Hugo (Pop. 5,257) 2013 Estimate

Area (Land & Water)—800.68 square miles

Per Capita Income (2013)—$30,816 (Ranks 66th of 77 counties)

Population Statistics (2013)—Female-7,875; Male-7,292; Ethnicity—Wh.-11,660; Bl.-1,974; Am. Ind.-3,286; As.-75; Other-350; Pacific Is.-0; Two or more races-2,129; Hisp.-479

Births (2014)—182 • **Deaths** (2014)—233

Marriages (2013)—144 • **Divorces** (2013)—33

Unemployment Rate (2013)—7.0%

Labor Force (2013)—7,192

Number of Establishments (2013)—261

Number of Manufacturers (2013)—12

Public Assistance Payments
(FY2014) Total—$14,623,978 • TANF—$290,729 • Supplements—Aged-$74,714; Blind-$644; Disabled-$297,365

Vehicle Registration (2014)—
Automobiles-11,266; Farm Trucks-1,392; Comm., Trucks, Tractors, Trailers-279; Motor Homes and Travel Trailers-623; Motorcycles-302; Manufactured Homes-5; Tax Exempt Licenses-133; Boats-532

Crime Incidents (2013)—Murder-0; Rape-1; Robbery-2; Felony Assault-14; Breaking and Entering-74; Larceny-99; Motor Vehicle Theft-8; Arson-0 • Total Crime Index-198; Crime Rate per 1,000-13.00

County Population	
1907 (Okla. Terr.)	17,340
1910	21,862
1920	32,144
1930	24,142
1940	28,358
1950	20,405
1960	15,637
1970	15,141
1980	17,203
1990	15,302
2000	15,342
2010	15,205
2014 Estimate	15,161

Farms (2012)—965

Land in Farms (2012)—330,410

Recreation Areas—Hugo Lake and Lake Raymond Gary state parks

Major Lake—Hugo

Major Stream Systems—Kiamichi and Muddy Boggy rivers and minor tributaries to the Red River

Museums or Historic Sites—Fort Towson, Goodland Presbyterian Children's Home, Hugo Depot Museum, Old Choctaw Chief's Home, Choctaw County Historical Museum

Minerals—oil and gas, crushed stone

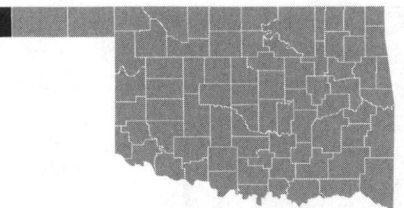

Cimarron

Cimarron County was formed at statehood and named for the Cimarron River. The name Cimarron is a Mexican-Apache word meaning "wanderer."

For many years, present-day Cimarron County was a part of "No Man's Land," an area populated with few settlers and regulated by virtually no law. Sheep and cattle ranchers entered this area long before it was opened to homesteaders, and today, farming and ranching constitute the economic base of the county.

In 1943, Boise City, the county seat, was accidentally bombed by United States servicemen from Dalhart Army Base. Cimarron County is also the site of Black Mesa, the highest point in Oklahoma. The county also holds the distinction of being the only one in the U.S. to be bordered by four other states—Colorado, Kansas, New Mexico, and Texas.

The Santa Fe Trail is a tourist attraction and the Santa Fe Trail Daze is a four-day festival held during the first weekend of June. The Cimarron Heritage Center Museum sponsors a tour of the Santa Fe Trail on the first Saturday in October annually. Cimarron County was once home to Hollywood stars Vera Miles and Jack Hoxie (featured in the museum). Several books have been published about Cimarron County. Contact the Cimarron Heritage Center Museum at 580/544-3479.

Districts

Congress..........................3
State Senate..................27
State Rep........................ 61
District Attorney 1
Court of Appeals............ 6
Ct. of Crim. Appeals........5
Supreme Ct. Jud..............4
NW Jud. Adm. 1

County Officials

Court Clerk	Debbie Kincannon (D)	Boise City
Clerk	Coleen Allen (D)	Boise City
Sheriff	Leon Apple (D)	Boise City
Treasurer	Jenny Richardson (D)	Boise City
Assessor	Charlene Collins (R)	Boise City
Election Brd. Sec.	Courtney Menefee (R)	Boise City
Dist. 1 Comm.	Danny Bass (D)	Felt
Dist. 2 Comm.	John Freeman (D)	Boise City
Dist. 3 Comm.	Mitchell Harriman (R)	Keyes

Property Valuations

	2013–2014 Assessment	2014–2015 Assessment	Increase or Decrease
Real Estate and Improvement	$20,245,482	$20,360,440	$114,958
Personal Subject to Tax	$17,183,189	$17,720,225	$537,036
Total Locally Assessed	$37,428,671	$38,080,665	$651,994
Homestead Exemptions Allowed	$687,199	$663,176	($24,023)
Net Assessed Locally	$36,741,472	$37,417,489	$676,017
Public Service Assessment	$12,065,072	$16,379,523	$4,314,451
Net Assessed Valuation	$48,806,544	$53,797,012	$4,990,468

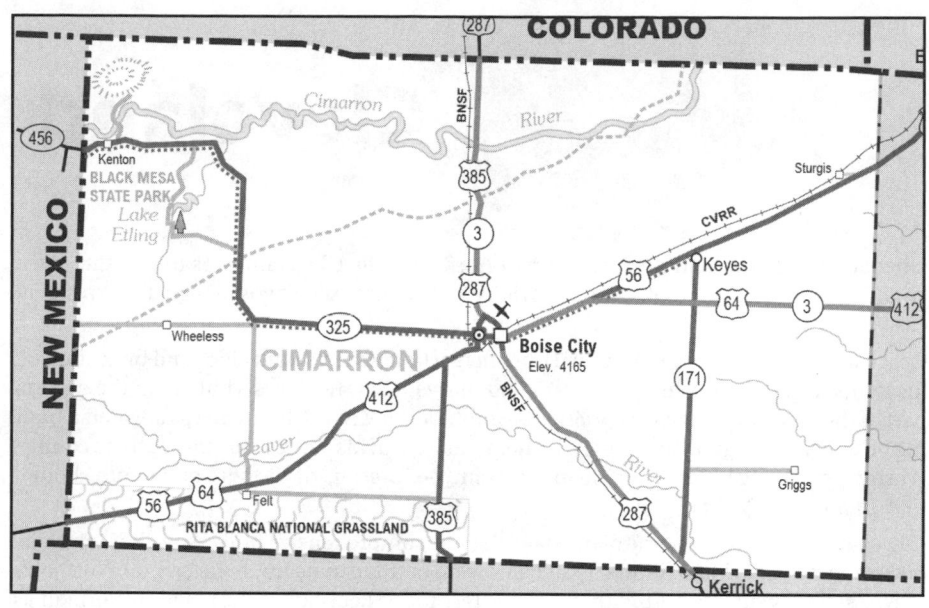

County Seat—Boise City (Pop. 1,189) 2013 Estimate

Area (Land & Water)—1,841.17 square miles

Per Capita Income (2013)—$42,320 (Ranks 19th of 77 counties)

Population Statistics (2013)—Female-1,211; Male-1,221; Ethnicity—Wh.-2,044; Bl.-17; Am. Ind.-46; As.-6; Other-354; Pacific Is.-0; Two or more races-35; Hisp.-494

Births (2014)—26 • **Deaths** (2014)—28

Marriages (2013)—18 • **Divorces** (2013)—10

Unemployment Rate (2013)—3.9%

Labor Force (2013)—1,061

Number of Establishments (2013)—73

Number of Manufacturers (2013)—1

Public Assistance Payments (FY2014) Total—$598,567 • TANF—$10,112 • Supplements—Aged-$5,640; Blind-$0; Disabled-$5,601

Vehicle Registration (2014)—Automobiles-2,281; Farm Trucks-1,424; Comm., Trucks, Tractors, Trailers-436; Motor Homes and Travel Trailers-130; Motorcycles-128; Manufactured Homes-1; Tax Exempt Licenses-9; Boats-43

Crime Incidents (2013)—Murder-1; Rape-0; Robbery-0; Felony Assault-0; Breaking and Entering-5; Larceny-8; Motor Vehicle Theft-2;

County Population	
1907 (Okla. Terr.)	5,927
1910	4,553
1920	3,436
1930	5,408
1940	3,654
1950	4,589
1960	4,496
1970	4,145
1980	3,648
1990	3,301
2000	3,148
2010	2,475
2014 Estimate	2,294

Arson-0 • Total Crime Index-16; Crime Rate per 1,000-6.75

Farms (2012) 554

Land in Farms (2012) 1,157,186

Recreation Area—Black Mesa State Park

Major Lakes—Carl Etling

Major Stream Systems—Cimarron and North Canadian (Beaver) rivers

Museums or Historic Sites—Autograph Rock, Cimarron Heritage Center

Minerals—oil and gas

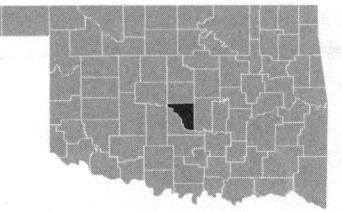

Cleveland

Opened to settlement in the Land Run of April 22, 1889, Cleveland was one of the seven counties organized as the Oklahoma Territory in 1890. Its first citizens named it for President Grover Cleveland.

Osage Indians had fought the Plains Tribes here where settlers built cities and broke the sod for farms. Explorers pushing westward had marveled at the Cross Timbers in the eastern part of the county and the vast prairies beyond. Colonel A. P. Chouteau established a trading post near Lexington, and Jesse Chisholm ran one of his cattle trails through the county. Washington Irving killed a buffalo in the vicinity of present-day Moore and wrote about it in *A Tour on the Prairies*.

Cleveland County is the home of the state's largest comprehensive university, the University of Oklahoma in Norman. While other cities were battling to become the capital, Norman's mayor skillfully directed a bill through the Territorial Legislature designating Norman as the site for the first institution of higher learning.

Although Cleveland County is the eighth smallest Oklahoma county in area, it has the third largest population and two of the state's largest cities, Norman and Moore. Farming, oil production and horse breeding are important industries. For more information, call the county clerk's office at 405/366-0240.

Districts

Congress 4
State Senate 15, 16, 24, 45
State Rep.. 20, 27, 44, 45, 46, 53,
                    54, 90, 91
District Attorney 21
Court of Appeals 4
Ct. of Crim. Appeals 2
Supreme Ct. Jud. 5
S. Cent. Jud. Adm. 21
    (Div. I)

County Officials

Court Clerk	Rhonda Hall (D)	Moore
Clerk	Tammy Belinson (R)	S. OKC
Sheriff	Joe Lester (R)	Norman
Treasurer	Jim Reynolds (R)	Norman
Assessor	David Tinsley (R)	Norman
Election Brd. Sec.	Jim Williams (R)	Norman
Dist. 1 Comm.	Rod Cleveland (R)	Norman
Dist. 2 Comm.	Darry Stacy (R)	Norman
Dist. 3 Comm.	Harold Haralson (R)	Norman

Property Valuations

	2013–2014 Assessment	2014–2015 Assessment	Increase or Decrease
Real Estate and Improvement	$1,654,321,108	$1,720,928,963	$66,607,855
Personal Subject to Tax	$128,998,130	$127,882,149	($1,115,981)
Total Locally Assessed	$1,783,319,238	$1,848,811,112	$65,491,874
Homestead Exemptions Allowed	$63,548,946	$63,717,968	$169,022
Net Assessed Locally	$1,719,770,292	$1,785,093,144	$65,322,852
Public Service Assessment	$63,621,834	$60,116,611	($3,505,223)
Net Assessed Valuation	$1,783,392,126	$1,845,209,755	$61,817,629

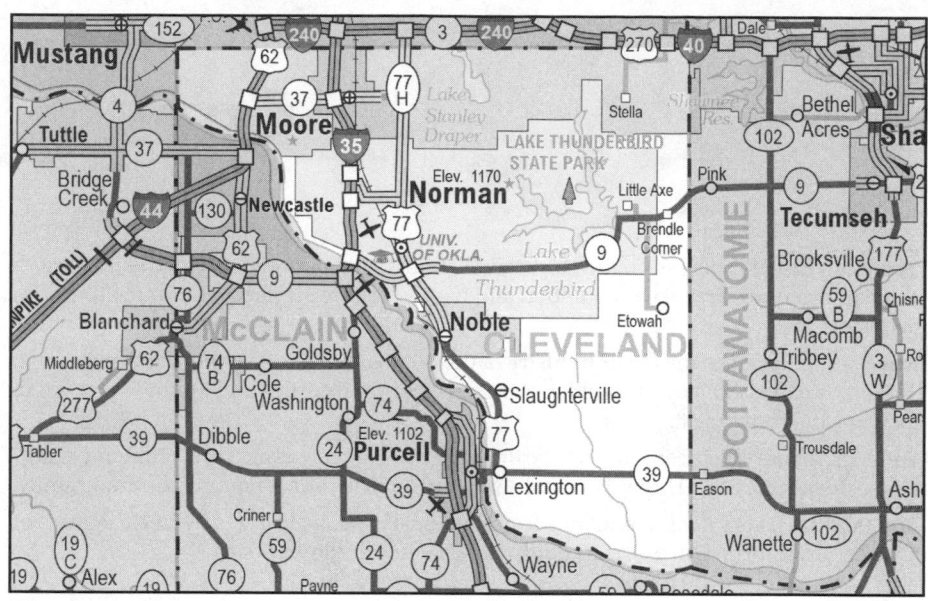

County Seat—Norman (Pop. 118,197) 2013 Estimate

Area (Land & Water)—558.34 square miles

Per Capita Income (2013)—$39,078 (Ranks 28th of 77 counties)

Population Statistics (2013)—Female-130,619; Male-130,428; Ethnicity—Wh.-224,116; Bl.-15,460; Am. Ind.-21,159; As.-12,958; Other-5,341; Pacific Is.-609; Two or more races-17,058; Hisp.-19,096

Births (2014)—3,051 • **Deaths** (2014)—1,805

Marriages (2013)—1,918 • **Divorces** (2013)—1,415

Unemployment Rate (2013)—4.6%

Labor Force (2013)—131,303

Establishments (2013)—5,529 • **Manufacturers** (2013)—134

Public Assistance Payments (FY2014)
Total—$106,049,104 • TANF—$555,766 • Supplements—Aged-$165,170; Blind-$5,196; Disabled-$1,230,678

County Population	
1907 (Okla. Terr.)	18,460
1910	18,843
1920	19,389
1930	24,948
1940	27,728
1950	41,443
1960	49,600
1970	81,839
1980	133,173
1990	174,253
2000	208,016
2010	255,755
2014 Estimate	269,908

Vehicle Registration (2014)—
Automobiles-185,147; Farm Trucks-1,795; Comm., Trucks, Tractors, Trailers-17,005; Motor Homes and Travel Trailers-3,784; Motorcycles-8,439; Manufactured Homes-171; Tax Exempt Licenses-306; Boats-4,997

Institutions of Higher Learning—
University of Oklahoma, Norman

Crime Incidents (2013)—Murder-5; Rape-72; Robbery-75; Felony Assault-152; Breaking and Entering-1,201; Larceny-4,156; Motor Vehicle Theft-366; Arson-25 • Total Crime Index-6,027; Crime Rate per 1,000-29.62

Farms (2012)—1,081

Land in Farms (2012)—133,729

Rec. Area—Little River State Park

Major Lakes—Draper and Thunderbird

Major Stream Systems—Little and Canadian rivers

Museums or Historic Sites—Fred Jones, Jr. Museum of Art, Oklahoma Museum of Natural History, University of Oklahoma; Norman and Cleveland County Historical Museum, Firehouse Art Center, Norman

Minerals—oil and gas

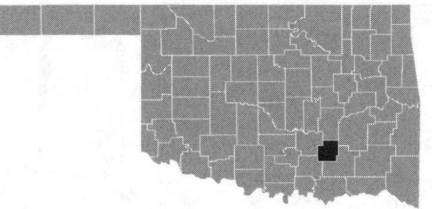

Coal

Formerly a part of Tobucksy County, Choctaw Nation, Coal County is located in southeastern Oklahoma and was created at statehood and named for the primary economic product of the region.

Coal mining was once the major industry of the county, but has been dormant since 1958. Mementos of this era may be found in the Coal County Historical and Mining Museum in Coalgate, the county seat.

While agriculture is now considered to be the primary economic mainstay of the county, businesses such as the Mary Hurley Hospital also contribute to the economy of the community.

Coal County History Book is available from the local genealogical society in Coalgate. For more county information, call the county clerk's office at 580/927-2103.

Districts

Congress...........................2
State Senate.................... 6
State Rep........................ 18
District Attorney 19
Court of Appeals.............3
Ct. of Crim. Appeals........3
Supreme Ct. Jud. 8
SE Jud. Adm....................25

County Officials

Court Clerk	Rachel Fuller (D)	Lehigh
Clerk	Eugina Loudermilk (D)	Coalgate
Sheriff	Bryan Jump (D)	Coalgate
Treasurer	Gina McNutt (D)	Coalgate
Assessor	Cherry Hefley (D)	Clarita
Election Brd. Sec.	Vicky Salmon (D)	Coalgate
Dist. 1 Comm.	Alvin Pebworth (D)	Coalgate
Dist. 2 Comm.	Johnny D. Ward (D)	Coalgate
Dist. 3 Comm.	Mike Hensley (D)	Lehigh

Property Valuations

	2013–2014 Assessment	2014–2015 Assessment	Increase or Decrease
Real Estate and Improvement	$17,856,867	$18,348,320	$491,453
Personal Subject to Tax	$44,485,396	$47,238,519	$2,753,123
Total Locally Assessed	$62,342,263	$65,586,839	$3,244,576
Homestead Exemptions Allowed	$1,759,599	$1,709,161	($50,438)
Net Assessed Locally	$60,582,664	$63,877,678	$3,295,014
Public Service Assessment	$21,286,520	$27,916,286	$6,629,766
Net Assessed Valuation	$81,869,184	$91,793,964	$9,924,780

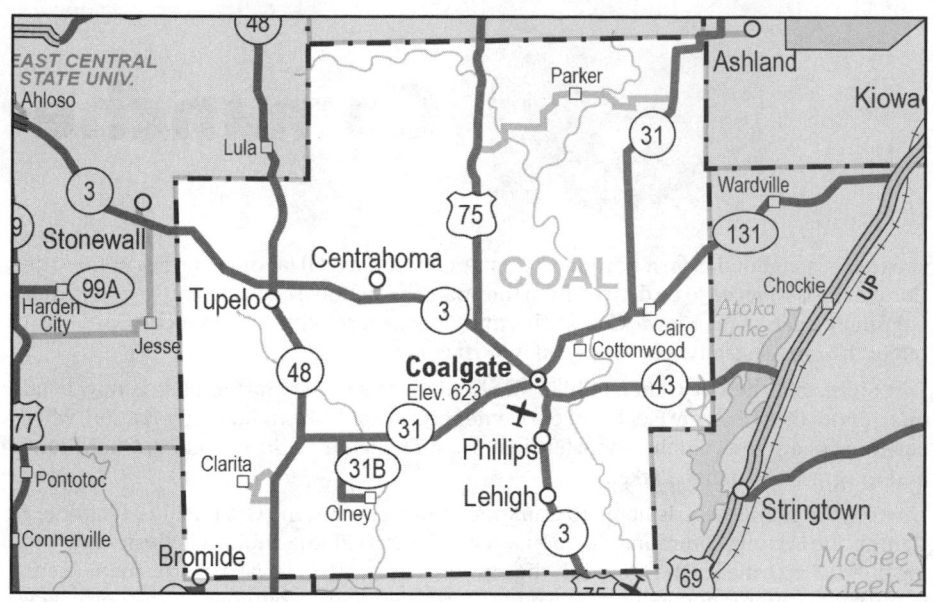

County Seat—Coalgate (Pop. 1,943) 2013 Estimate

Area (Land & Water)—521.30 square miles

Per Capita Income (2013)—$30,722 (Ranks 67th of 77 counties)

Population Statistics (2013)—Female-3,013; Male-2,914;
Ethnicity—Wh.-5,351; Bl.-102; Am. Ind.-1,317; As.-158;
Other-76; Pacific Is.-0; Two or more races-1,077; Hisp.-182

Births (2014)—63 • **Deaths** (2014)—87

Marriages (2013)—31 • **Divorces** (2013)—22

Unemployment Rate (2013)—6.8%

Labor Market (2013)—2,570

Number of Establishments (2013)—84

Number of Manufacturers (2013)—6

Public Assistance Payments
(FY2014) Total—$3,831,525 • TANF—
$33,828 • Supplements—Aged-$24,751;
Blind-$502; Disabled-$89,582

Vehicle Registration (2014)—
Automobiles-3,242; Farm Trucks-868; Comm.,
Trucks, Tractors, Trailers-194; Motor Homes
and Travel Trailers-178; Motorcycles-137;
Manufactured Homes-5; Tax Exempt
Licenses-6; Boats-130

Crime Incidents (2013)—Murder-0; Rape-2;
Robbery-0; Felony Assault-2; Breaking and
Entering-15; Larceny-31; Motor Vehicle
Theft-1; Arson-3 • Total Crime Index-49;
Crime Rate per 1,000-8.15

County Population	
1907 (Okla. Terr.)	15,585
1910	15,817
1920	18,406
1930	11,521
1940	12,811
1950	8,056
1960	5,546
1970	5,525
1980	6,041
1990	5,780
2000	6,031
2010	5,925
2014 Estimate	5,807

Farms (2012)—571

Land in Farms (2012)—273,616

Major Lakes—Atoka

Major Stream Systems—Muddy Boggy River

Museums or Historic Sites—Coal County
Historical and Mining Museum, Coalgate

Minerals—oil and gas

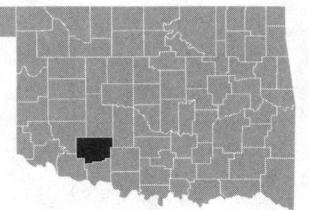

Comanche

Created at statehood from a portion of Comanche County, Oklahoma Territory. The word Comanche is believed to be derived from the Spanish Camino Ancho, meaning "broad trail." Originally a part of the Kiowa, Comanche, and Apache reservation, Comanche County was opened for homesteading by lottery on August 6, 1901.

Fort Sill, established by General Philip H. Sheridan as a cavalry fort in 1869, is now headquarters for the U.S. Army Field Artillery Center and School. The military reservation, which covers 95,000 acres, contains some fifty historic sites, including the Geronimo Guardhouse and the grave of Quanah Parker.

Lawton, the county seat, is home to Cameron University and the Great Plains Technology Center. The Lawton Community Theater and the Lawton Philharmonic Orchestra are leading cultural activities of the area, as is the annual Arts for All Festival in April. The Museum of the Great Plains is both educational and entertaining with its outdoor prairie dog village, depot, and trading post.

The Wichita Mountains Wildlife Refuge attracts more than a million visitors annually. It is also the site of the Holy City of the Wichitas where the annual Wichita Mountains Easter Sunrise Service is presented.

Call the county clerk's office at 580/355-5214 for more information.

Districts

Congress..........................4
State Senate..............31, 32
State Rep...... 62, 63, 64, 65
District Attorney.............5
Court of Appeals.............4
Ct. of Crim. Appeals........5
Supreme Ct. Jud..............9
SW Jud. Adm. 5
  (Div. I.)

County Officials

Court Clerk	Robert Morales (D)	Lawton
Clerk	Carrie Tubbs (R)	Lawton
Sheriff	Kenny Stradley (D)	Lawton
Treasurer	Rhonda Brantley (D)	Lawton
Assessor	Grant Edwards (R)	Lawton
Election Brd. Sec.	Amy Sims (R)	Lawton
Dist. 1 Comm.	Gail Turner (R)	Elgin
Dist. 2 Comm.	Johnny Owens (D)	Lawton
Dist. 3 Comm.	Don Hawthorne (R)	Cache

Property Valuations

	2013–2014 Assessment	2014–2015 Assessment	Increase or Decrease
Real Estate and Improvement	$589,236,191	$583,890,802	($5,345,389)
Personal Subject to Tax	$110,618,057	$105,508,091	($5,109,966)
Total Locally Assessed	$699,854,248	$689,398,893	$10,455,355
Homestead Exemptions Allowed	$44,405,249	$47,197,178	($2,791,929)
Net Assessed Locally	$655,448,999	$624,201,715	$13,247,284
Public Service Assessment	$44,628,705	$40,946,521	($3,682,184)
Net Assessed Valuation	$700,077,704	$683,148,236	$16,929,468

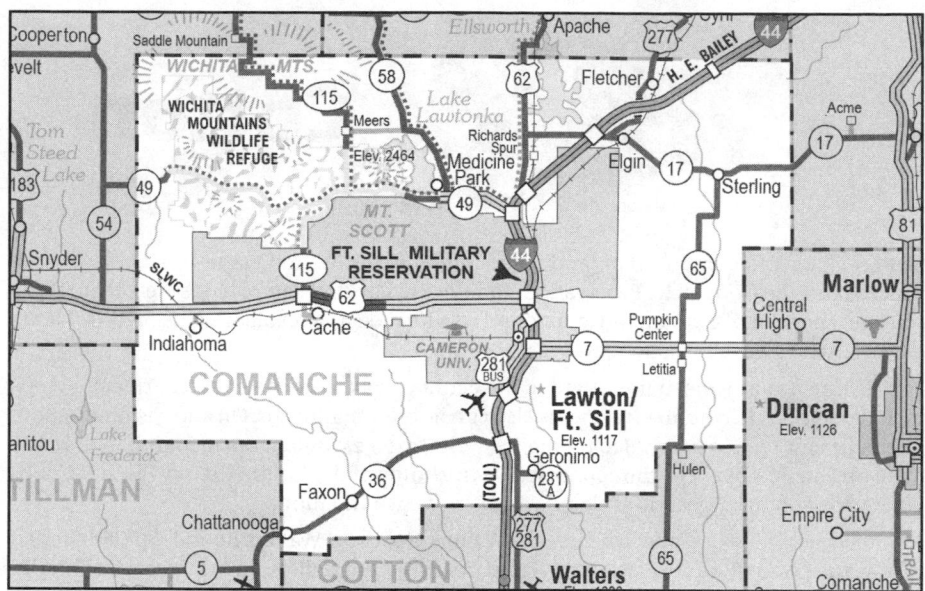

County Seat—Lawton (Pop. 97,151) 2013 Estimate

Area (Land & Water)—1,083.82 square miles

Per Capita Income (2013)—$38,052 (Ranks 31ˢᵗ of 77 counties)

Population Statistics (2013)—Female-60,163; Male-64,428
Ethnicity—Wh.-89,078; Bl.-25,185; Am. Ind.-10,932; As.-4,890;
Other-4,143; Pacific Is.-1,057; Two or more races-9,627; Hisp.-
14,638

Births (2014)—1,897 • **Deaths** (2014)—1,015

Marriages (2013)—1,237 • **Divorces** (2010)—982

Unemployment Rate (2013)—6.7%

Labor Force (2013)—48,197

Number of Establishments (2013)—2,180

Number of Manufacturers (2013)—45

Public Assistance Payments
(FY2014) Total—$67,967,979 • TANF—
$528,495 • Supplements—Aged-$151,433;
Blind-$5,120; Disabled-$1,069,033

Vehicle Registration (2014)—
Automobiles-80,587; Farm Trucks-2,995;
Comm., Trucks, Tractors, Trailers-3,988;
Motor Homes and Travel Trailers-1,916;
Motorcycles-4,160; Manufactured Homes-38;
Tax Exempt Licenses-311; Boats-1,961

Institutions of Higher Learning—Cameron
University, Lawton

Crime Incidents (2013)—Murder-13; Rape-81;
Robbery 170; Felony Assault-684; Breaking
and Entering-1,659; Larceny-3,593; Motor
Vehicle Theft-254; Arson-34 • Total Crime

County Population	
1907 (Okla. Terr.)	31,738
1910	41,489
1920	26,629
1930	34,317
1940	38,988
1950	55,165
1960	90,803
1970	108,144
1980	112,456
1990	111,486
2000	114,996
2010	124,098
2014 Estimate	125,033

Index-6,454;
Crime Rate per 1,000-50.71

Farms (2012)—1,107

Land in Farms (2012)—462,992

Recreation Area—Great Plains Major Lakes—
Ellsworth, Elmer Thomas, Lawtonka

Major Stream Systems—Cache and Beaver
creeks, Washita River and North Fork of the
Red River

Museums or Historic Sites—Eagle Park
Old West Ghost Town, Cache; U.S. Army Field
Artillery and Fort Sill Museum, Museum of the
Great Plains, Lewis Museum, and Mattie Beal
Home, Lawton

Minerals—oil and gas, crushed stone, and
gypsum

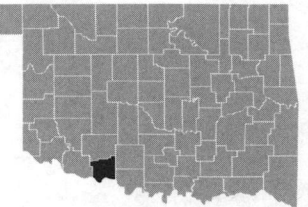

Cotton

Cotton County is composed of land belonging at one time to Quapaws, Choctaws, and Chickasaws, the Comanche Reservation, and the Big Pasture. Part of it was created from the southern portion of Comanche County, and was formed as a result of a vote of its residents on August 22, 1912, after statehood.

Agriculture has long been important to the economic base of the county. Principal crops include wheat and cotton. Livestock is also considered significant. Oil and gas production, begun in 1917, rose to nearly 800 producing wells by 1952, when it ranked ninth in the state in oil production. Walters, the county seat, is the home of the Cotton County Electric Cooperative, one of the largest rural electric cooperatives in Oklahoma.

Annual events held in Walters include the Walters Car Cruz, Walters Round-Up Club Rodeo in July, the Cotton County Free Fair in September, and the Gallery on the Green Art Show in May. Sultan Park, north of Walters, is a recreational area and is the site of Comanche Indian powwows that are also held in July.

For additional county information, call the county clerk's office at 580/875-3026.

Districts

Congress	4
State Senate	31
State Rep.	65
District Attorney	5
Court of Appeals	4
Ct. of Crim. Appeals	5
Supreme Ct. Jud.	9
SW Jud. Adm.	5
(Div. I)	

County Officials

Court Clerk	Debra Hodnefield (D)	Devol
Clerk	Janey Shively (D)	Walters
Sheriff	Kent Simpson (D)	Walters
Treasurer	Tammy Spence (D)	Walters
Assessor	Debbie Sturdivant (D)	Temple
Election Brd. Sec.	Shellie Hart (D)	Walters
Dist. 1 Comm.	Edward Eschiti (D)	Walters
Dist. 2 Comm.	Chris Lipscomb (D)	Walters
Dist. 3 Comm.	Greg Powell (D)	Devol

Property Valuations

	2013–2014 Assessment	2014–2015 Assessment	Increase or Decrease
Real Estate and Improvement	$28,876,861	$29,458,372	$581,511
Personal Subject to Tax	$3,523,039	$3,909,214	$386,175
Total Locally Assessed	$32,399,900	$33,367,586	$967,686
Homestead Exemptions Allowed	$1,779,766	$1,910,862	$131,096
Net Assessed Locally	$30,620,134	$31,456,724	$836,590
Public Service Assessment	$5,753,067	$5,705,502	($47,565)
Net Assessed Valuation	$36,373,201	$37,162,226	$789,025

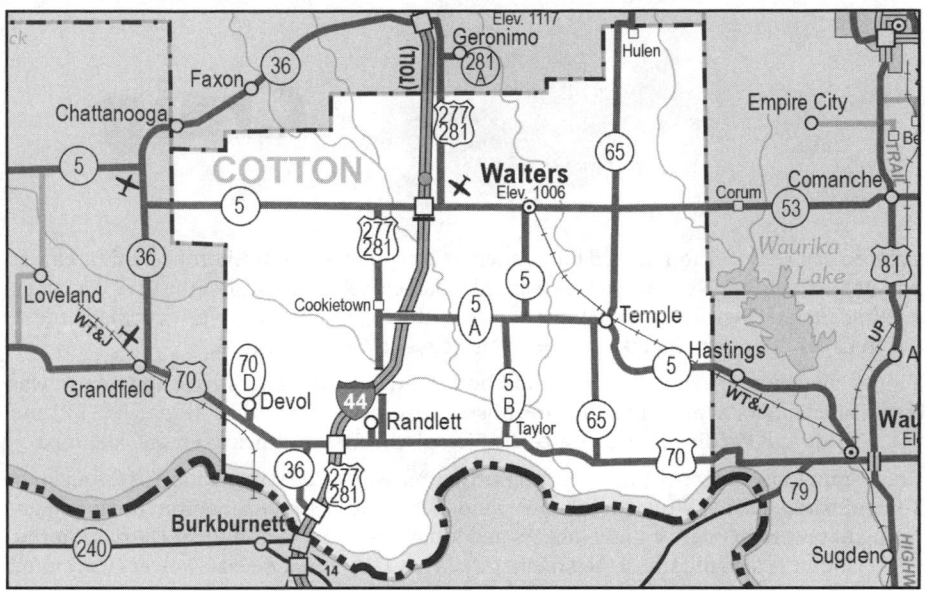

County Seat—Walters (Pop. 2,574) 2013 Estimate

Area (Land & Water)—641.94 square miles

Per Capita Income (2013)—$38,515 (Ranks 29th of 77 counties)

Population Statistics (2013)—Female-3,099; Male-3,067; Ethnicity—Wh.-5,365; Bl.-205; Am. Ind.-803; As.-78; Other-130; Pacific Is.-7; Two or more races-422; Hisp.-383

Births (2014)—70 • **Deaths** (2014)—81

Marriages (2013)—35 • **Divorces** (2013)—23

Unemployment Rate (2013)—4.9%

Labor Force (2013)—3,341

Number of Establishments (2013)—75

Number of Manufacturers (2013)—1

Public Assistance Payments (FY2014) Total—$3,477,212 • TANF—$14,272 • Supplements—Aged-$11,995; Blind-$119; Disabled-$51,240

Vehicle Registration (2014)—Automobiles-3,289; Farm Trucks-860; Comm. Trucks, Tractors, Trailers-100; Motor Homes and Travel Trailers-176; Motorcycles-132; Manufactured Homes-1; Tax Exempt Licenses-56; Boats-150

Crime Incidents (2013)—Murder-0; Rape-0; Robbery-0; Felony Assault-3; Breaking and Entering-18; Larceny-24; Motor Vehicle Theft-1; Arson-0 • Total Crime Index-46; Crime Rate per 1,000-7.45

County Population	
1907 (Okla. Terr.)	N/A
1910	N/A
1920	16,679
1930	15,442
1940	12,884
1950	10,180
1960	8,031
1970	6,832
1980	7,338
1990	6,651
2000	6,614
2010	6,193
2014 Estimate	6,150

Farms (2012)—500

Land in Farms (2012)—399,818

Recreation Area—Great Plains Major Lakes—Ellsworth, Elmer Thomas, Lawtonka

Major Stream Systems—Cache and Beaver creeks, Washita River and North Fork of the Red River

Museums or Historic Sites—Eagle Park Old West Ghost Town, Cache; U.S. Army Field Artillery and Fort Sill Museum, Museum of the Great Plains, Lewis Museum, and Mattie Beal Home, Lawton

Minerals—oil and gas, crushed stone, and gypsum

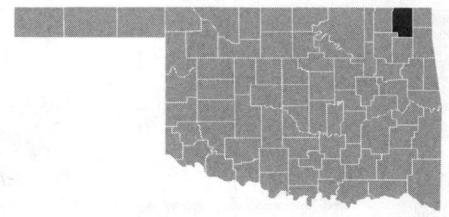

Craig

Created at statehood and named for Granville Craig, a prominent Cherokee, this area was part of the Cherokee Nation. The area was only sparsely settled until after the Civil War when a few scattered Cherokees made their homes in the region. Every three years the Battle of Cabin Creek Reenactment takes place; the next event will be Fall 2010.

Vinita, the county seat, was once called both Downingville and The Junction and was established in 1891 at the junction of the Missouri, Kansas, and Texas Railroad (KATY) and the Atlantic and Pacific Railroad, (later the Frisco), the first rail lines to enter Oklahoma.

Craig County has long been a livestock producing area with cattle ranches located throughout. The industrial base of Vinita has been expanded to include everything from the manufacturing of towers to micro connectors. As headquarters of the Grand River Dam Authority, Craig County is also the site of the Kansas, Arkansas, Oklahoma Electric Power Distributor, and the Northeast Oklahoma Electric Cooperative.

Annual events include the original Will Rogers Memorial Rodeo in August, the Calf Fry Festival in September, and Oktoberfest.

The *Craig County Book* and others offer more information, or call the county clerk's office at 918/256-2507.

Districts

Congress	2
State Senate	1
State Rep.	6
District Attorney	12
Court of Appeals	2
Ct. of Crim. Appeals	1
Supreme Ct. Jud.	1
NE Jud. Adm.	12

County Officials

Court Clerk	Mary Denny (D)	Bluejacket
Clerk	Tammy Malone (D)	Vinita
Sheriff	Jimmie L. Sooter (D)	Vinita
Treasurer	Lisa Washam (D)	Vinita
Assessor	Kelli Beisly-Minson (D)	Vinita
Election Brd. Sec.	Debbie Davenport (D)	Vinita
Dist. 1 Comm.	Roy Bible (D)	Vinita
Dist. 2 Comm.	Hugh Gordon (D)	Bluejacket
Dist. 3 Comm.	Dan Peetoom (D)	Vinita

Property Valuations

	2013–2014 Assessment	2014–2015 Assessment	Increase or Decrease
Real Estate and Improvement	$60,443,782	$62,227,846	$1,784,064
Personal Subject to Tax	$10,110,226	$9,623,516	($486,710)
Total Locally Assessed	$70,554,008	$71,851,362	$1,297,354
Homestead Exemptions Allowed	$4,177,466	$4,037,479	($139,987)
Net Assessed Locally	$66,376,542	$67,813,883	$1,437,341
Public Service Assessment	$13,025,865	$13,200,924	$175,059
Net Assessed Valuation	$79,402,407	$81,014,807	$1,612,400

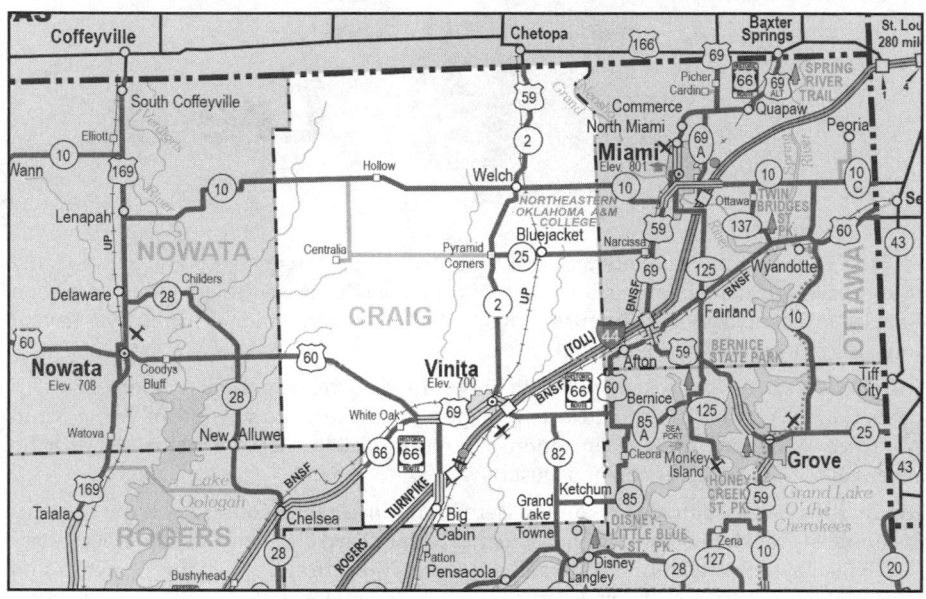

County Population

1907 (Okla. Terr.)	14,955
1910	17,404
1920	19,160
1930	18,052
1940	21,083
1950	18,263
1960	16,303
1970	14,722
1980	15,014
1990	14,104
2000	14,950
2010	15,029
2014 Estimate	14,582

County Seat—Vinita (Pop. 5,594) 2013 Estimate

Area (Land & Water)—762.71 square miles

Per Capita Income (2013)—$34,235 (Ranks 48th of 77 counties)

Population Statistics (2013)—Female-7,362; Male-7,507; Ethnicity—Wh.-11,943; Bl.-657; Am. Ind.-3,986; As.-131; Other-181; Pacific Is.-171; Two or more races-2,149; Hisp.-408

Births (2014)—184 • **Deaths** (2014)—174

Marriages (2013)—86 • **Divorces** (2013)—82

Unemployment Rate (2013)—6.1%

Labor Force (2013)—6,940

Number of Establishments (2013)—341

Number of Manufacturers (2013)—15

Public Assistance Payments (FY2014) Total—$9,481,843 • TANF—$57,904 • Supplements—Aged-$27,951; Blind-$2,505; Disabled-$221,147

Vehicle Registration (2014)—Automobiles-10,498; Farm Trucks-1,524; Comm. Trucks, Tractors, Trailers-1,612; Motor Homes and Travel Trailers-448; Motorcycles-487; Manufactured Homes-7; Tax Exempt Licenses-292; Boats-1,538

Crime Incidents (2013)—Murder-1; Rape-0; Robbery-1; Felony Assault-17; Breaking and Entering-37; Larceny-118; Motor Vehicle Theft-16; Arson-4 • Total Crime Index-190; Crime Rate per 1,000-12.92

Farms (2012)—1,263

Land in Farms (2012)—462,205

Major Stream Systems—Grand and Verdigris rivers

Museums or Historic Sites—Eastern Trails Museum at Vinita

Minerals—oil and gas; crushed stone

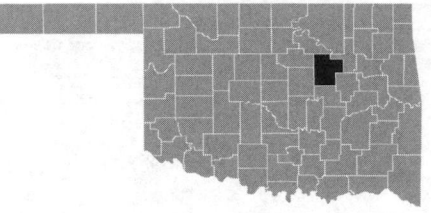

Creek

Located in east central Oklahoma, Creek County was created at statehood. Sapulpa, the county seat, was named for Sus pul ber, a Creek leader. It was so designated following an election by county residents August 12, 1908, after statehood and reaffirmed by a United States Supreme Court decision August 1, 1913.

The discovery of oil at the Red Fork Field in 1901 marked the beginning of boom times for Creek County, yet they were not to last. As oil production began to subside following World War I, economic hard times became more and more a reality and were intensified with the advent of the Great Depression and Dust Bowl eras.

For decades Creek County and Sapulpa were known across the country and the world as the home of Frankhoma Pottery. The factory, which utilized clay deposits from local Sugar Loaf Hill, manufactured dinnerware and art objects that are still sought by collectors and treasured by aficionados. Today, Frankhoma is no longer located in Creek County, but it survives as an online business in the Tulsa area.

Districts

Congress	1, 3
State Senate	12
State Rep.	29, 30, 35
District Attorney	24
Court of Appeals	1, 2
Ct. of Crim. Appeals	2
Supreme Ct. Jud.	7
E. Cent. Jud. Adm. (Div. I)	24

County Officials

Court Clerk	Amanda Vanorsdol (R)	Sapulpa
Clerk	Jennifer Mortazavi (R)	Sapulpa
Sheriff	John Davis (R)	Bristow
Treasurer	Byron Davis (R)	Sapulpa
Assessor	JaNell Enlow Gore (R)	Sapulpa
Election Brd. Sec.	Joy Naifeh (D)	Sapulpa
Dist. 1 Comm.	Newt Stephens (R)	Sapulpa
Dist. 2 Comm.	Rick Stewart (R)	Drumright
Dist. 3 Comm.	Lane Whitehouse (R)	Depew

Property Valuations

	2013–2014 Assessment	2014–2015 Assessment	Increase or Decrease
Real Estate and Improvement	$313,623,021	$319,331,813	$5,708,792
Personal Subject to Tax	$79,340,782	$83,954,841	$4,614,059
Total Locally Assessed	$392,963,803	$403,286,654	$10,322,851
Homestead Exemptions Allowed	$19,381,657	$19,319,990	($61,667)
Net Assessed Locally	$373,582,146	$383,966,664	$10,384,518
Public Service Assessment	$56,117,152	$56,117,934	$782
Net Assessed Valuation	$429,699,298	$440,084,598	$10,385,300

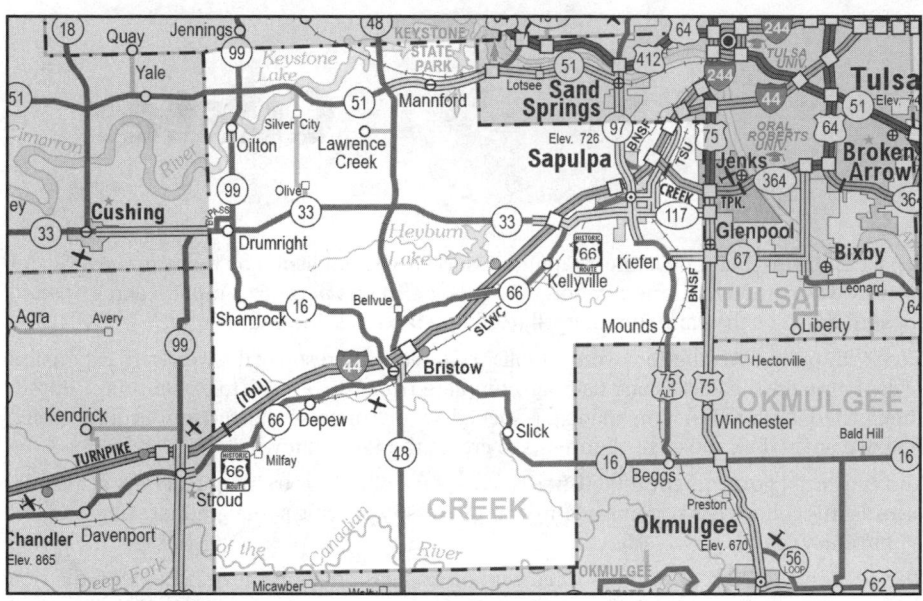

County Seat—Sapulpa (Pop. 20,836) 2013 Estimate

Area (Land & Water)—969.77 square miles

Per Capita Income (2013)—$35,587 (Ranks 42nd of 77 counties)

Population Statistics (2013)—Female-35,416; Male-34,830;
Ethnicity—Wh.-61,583; Bl.-2,294 Am. Ind.-11,081; As.-405;
Other-971; Pacific Is.-12; Two or more races: 5,910; Hisp.-2,370

Births (2014)—884 • Deaths (2014)—815

Marriages (2013)—555 • Divorces (2013)—290

Unemployment Rate (2013)—6.3%

Labor Force (2013)—31,152

Number of Establishments (2013)—1,382

Number of Manufacturers (2013)—122

Public Assistance Payments
(FY2014 Total—$43,225,281 • TANF—
$152,937 • Supplements—Aged-$92,299;
Blind-$1,652; Disabled-$706,012

Vehicle Registration (2014)—
Automobiles-43,324; Farm Trucks-1,411;
Comm. Trucks, Tractors, Trailers-2,880;
Motor Homes and Travel Trailers-2,079;
Motorcycles-2,340; Manufactured Homes-69;
Tax Exempt Licenses-139; Boats-2,340

Crime Incidents (2013)—Murder-0; Rape-23;
Robbery-9; Felony Assault-124; Breaking and
Entering-402; Larceny-886; Motor Vehicle
Theft-149; Arson-9 • Total Crime Index-1,593

County Population	
1907 (Okla. Terr.)	18,365
1910	26,223
1920	62,480
1930	64,115
1940	55,503
1950	43,143
1960	40,495
1970	45,532
1980	59,016
1990	60,915
2000	67,367
2010	69,967
2014 Estimate	70,632

Crime Rate per 1,000-22.36

Farms (2012)—1,777

Land in Farms (2012)—347,003

Recreation Area—Keystone State Park,
Heyburn Lake

Major Lakes—Heyburn, Keystone

Major Stream Systems—Tributaries to main
stem of Arkansas River below confluence of
Cimarron and Canadian rivers, tributaries of
Deep Fork and Cimarron rivers

Museums or Historic Sites—Drumright Oil
Field Museum, Sapulpa Memorial Museum

Minerals—oil and gas, crushed stone, clays

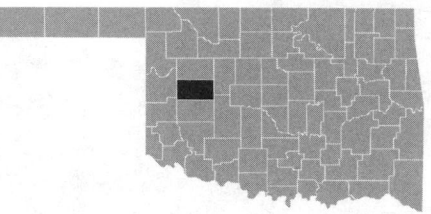

Custer

A part of the original Cheyenne-Arapaho Reservation established by treaty in 1867, Custer County was named for General George A. Custer and was part of 3.5 million acres opened for settlement by the Land Run of April 19, 1892. Arapaho is the county seat.

Both Clinton and Weatherford were established largely as a result of the westward expansion of the railroads. The Rock Island Railroad completed its east-west line to present-day Clinton, then called Washita Junction, in 1903. A special act of Congress allowed four Indians to sell half of each of their 160-acre allotments to create the Clinton townsite.

The territorial government established a two-year college for training teachers at Weatherford. This college has become a four-year university offering some graduate degrees and a pharmacy school.

The economy of Custer County is allied with oil and gas prices as the area lies atop the rich Anadarko Basin. Foss State Park and a wildlife refuge near Butler as well as Freightliner and Doane's PetCare facilities in Clinton also contribute to the economy of the county.

For additional county information, call the county clerk's office at 580/323-1221.

Districts

Congress...........................3
State Senate.............26, 38
State Rep........................57
District Attorney 2
Court of Appeals........... 6
Ct. of Crim. Appeals........5
Supreme Ct. Jud..............4
NW Jud. Adm. 2

County Officials

Court Clerk	Staci Hunter (D)	Arapaho
Clerk	Karen Fry (D)	Clinton
Sheriff	Bruce Peoples (R)	Weatherford
Treasurer	Janet Roulet (D)	Clinton
Assessor	Brad Rennels (D)	Arapaho
Electn Brd. Sec.	Ann Brown (R)	Clinton
Dist. 1 Comm.	Wade Anders (D)	Clinton
Dist. 2 Comm.	Kurt Hamburger (D)	Weatherford
Dist. 3 Comm.	Lyle Miller (R)	Clinton

Property Valuations

	2013–2014 Assessment	2014–2015 Assessment	Increase or Decrease
Real Estate and Improvement	$129,958,000	$129,766,814	$6,808,814
Personal Subject to Tax	$77,767,611	$89,345,707	($11,578,096)
Total Locally Assessed	$200,725,611	$219,112,521	$18,386,910
Homestead Exemptions Allowed	$5,604,908	$5,599,348	($5,560)
Net Assessed Locally	$195,120,703	$213,513,173	$18,392,470
Public Service Assessment	$23,490,805	$20,700,476	($2,790,329)
Net Assessed Valuation	$218,611,508	$234,213,649	($15,602,141)

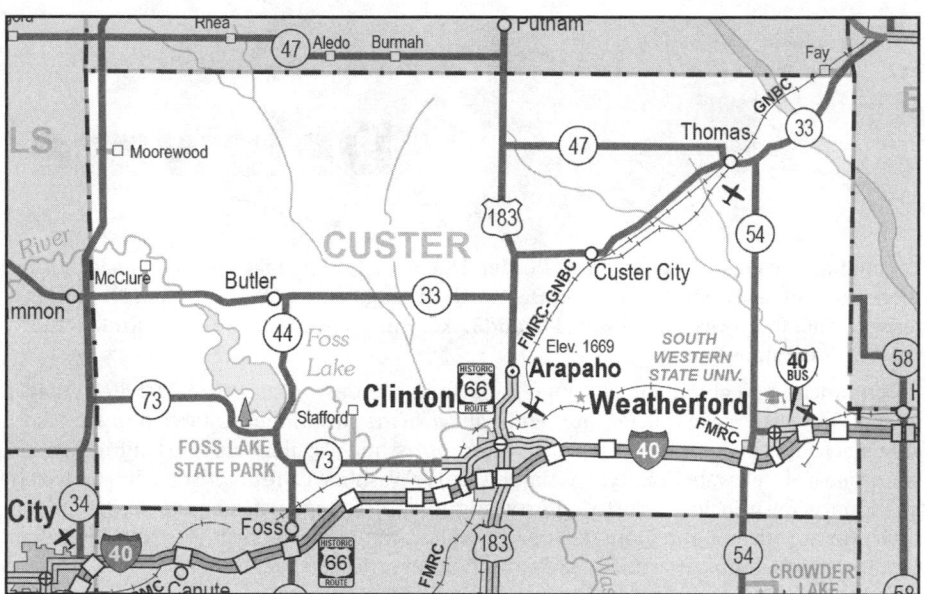

County Seat—Arapaho (Pop. 829) 2013 Estimate

Area (Land & Water)—1,002 square miles

Per Capita Income (2013)—$41,876 (Ranks 22nd of 77 counties)

Population Statistics (2013)—Female-14,141; Male-13,941;
Ethnicity—Wh.-25,128; Bl.-960; Am. Ind.-2,463; As.-398;
Other-650; Pacific Is.-119; Two or more races-1,613; Hisp.-4,185

Births (2014)—456 • Deaths (2014)—296

Marriages (2013)—185 • Divorces (2013)—119

Unemployment Rate (2013)—3.5%

Labor Force (2013)—16,606

Number of Establishments (2013)—920

Number of Manufacturers (2013)—34

Public Assistance Payments
(FY2014) Total—$7,947,868 • TANF—
$27,325 • Supplements—Aged-$14,436;
Blind-$630; Disabled-$79,527

Vehicle Registration (2014)—
Automobiles-22,370; Farm Trucks-2,947;
Comm. Trucks, Tractors, Trailers-2,481;
Motor Homes and Travel Trailers-834;
Motorcycles-1,133; Manufactured Homes-9;
Tax Exempt Licenses-96; Boats-510

Institutions of Higher Learning—
Southwestern Oklahoma State University,
Weatherford

Crime Incidents (2013)—Murder-2; Rape-12;

County Population	
1907 (Okla. Terr.)	18,478
1910	23,231
1920	18,736
1930	27,517
1940	23,068
1950	21,097
1960	21,040
1970	22,665
1980	25,995
1990	26,897
2000	26,142
2010	27,469
2014 Estimate	29,500

Robbery-3; Felony Assault-52; Breaking and
Entering-133; Larceny-427; Motor Vehicle
Theft-45; Arson-5 • Total Crime Index-674;
Crime Rate per 1,000-23.23

Farms (2012)—877

Land in Farms (2012)—622,947

Recreation Area—Foss State Park

Major Stream Systems—Washita and
Canadian rivers

Museums or Historic Sites—Western Trails
Museum, and Oklahoma Route 66 Museum,
Clinton

Minerals—oil and gas; clays

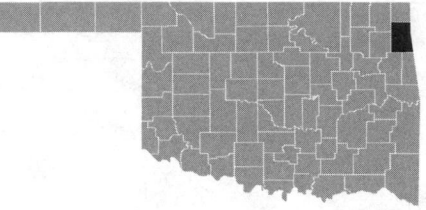

Delaware

Located on the Oklahoma-Arkansas border, Delaware County takes pride in its lakes and recreation areas. Grove, situated on the northern edge of the Old Cherokee Nation, is a resort center for the eastern shore of Grand Lake, which covers 46,500 acres, and includes 1,300 miles of shoreline.

Cattle ranches are abundant, although the principal industry is tourism. Har-Ber Village, west of Grove, is a reconstructed, authentic village of the past. Honey Creek, a popular resort area just south of Grove, has all types of water sports, and excellent crappie fishing. Jay, the county seat of Delaware County, was named for Jay Washburn, the grandson of an early-day missionary. The principal industry is the raising and processing of chickens. Green beans and soybeans are raised throughout the area, as well as cattle. East of Jay is the Oak Hill Indian Center, where Cherokees weave blankets and other articles on hand looms.

Beck's Mill, northeast of the town of Kansas, supplied meal for whites and Indians, and was built in 1835. It was once used as a Union prison camp.

Annual events in Delaware County include the Pelican Festival held in Grove every autumn, and the Huckleberry Festival located in Jay during July.

For more county information, call the county clerk's office at 918/253-4520.

Districts

Congress...........................2
State Senate..................1, 3
State Rep................ 5, 7, 86
District Attorney 13
Court of Appeals..............2
Ct. of Crim. Appeals........ 1
Supreme Ct. Jud. 7
NE Jud. Adm.................. 13

County Officials

Court Clerk	Caroline Weaver (D)	Jay
Clerk	Barbara Barnes (D)	Eucha
Sheriff	Harlan Moore (D)	Eucha
Treasurer	Susan Duncan (D)	Jay
Assessor	Larena Ellis-Cook(D)	Grove
Election Brd. Sec.	Dixie F. Smith (D)	Colcord
Dist. 1 Comm.	Doug Smith (R)	Afton
Dist. 2 Comm.	Tom Sanders (D)	Grove
Dist. 3 Comm.	Martin Kirk (R)	Rose

Property Valuations

	2013–2014 Assessment	2014–2015 Assessment	Increase or Decrease
Real Estate and Improvement	$308,006,209	$315,643,266	$7,637,057
Personal Subject to Tax	$24,222,300	$24,398,428	$176,128
Total Locally Assessed	$332,228,509	$340,041,694	$7,813,185
Homestead Exemptions Allowed	$12,969,315	$13,176,229	$206,914
Net Assessed Locally	$319,259,194	$326,865,465	$7,606,271
Public Service Assessment	$11,449,766	$10,241,353	$1,208,413
Net Assessed Valuation	$330,708,960	$337,106,818	$6,397,858

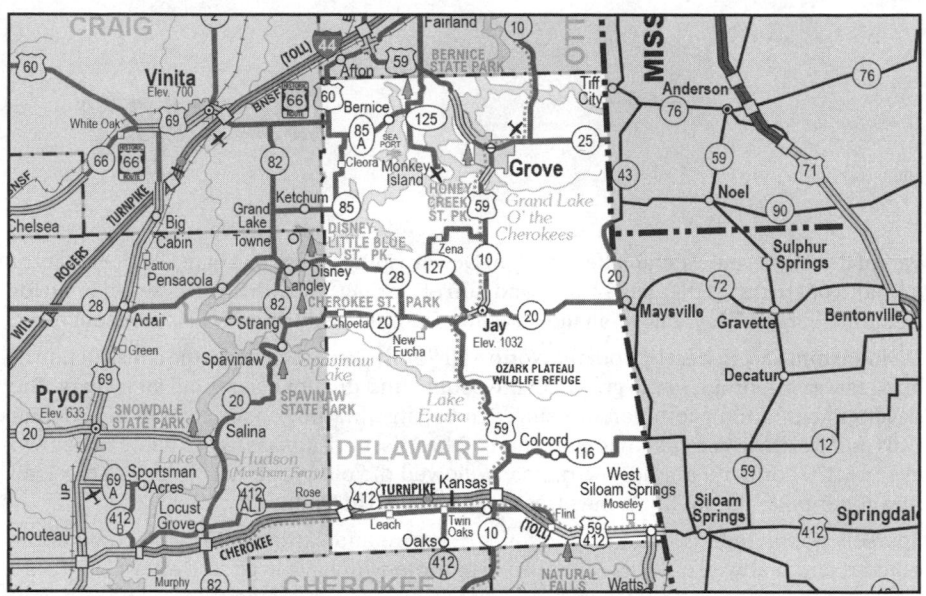

County Seat—Jay (Pop. 2,482) 2013 Estimate

Area (Land & Water)—792.33 square miles

Per Capita Income (2013)—$33,185 (Ranks 54th of 77 counties)

Population Statistics (2013)—Female–20,988; Male–20,406; Ethnicity—Wh.–31,227; Bl.–303; Am. Ind.–12,479; As.–562; Other–453; Pacific Is.–85; Two or more races–3,603; Hisp.–12,078

Births (2014)—401 • **Deaths** (2014)—488

Marriages (2013)—201 • **Divorces** (2013)—198

Unemployment Rate (2013)—6.2%

Labor Force (2013)—19,364

Number of Establishments (2013)—730

Number of Manufacturers (2013)—27

Public Assistance Payments
(FY2014) Total—$23,161,389 • TANF—$177,523 • Supplements—Aged–$60,687; Blind–$521; Disabled–$496,147

Vehicle Registration (2014)—
Automobiles–24,815; Farm Trucks–1,343; Comm. Trucks, Tractors, Trailers–956; Motor Homes and Travel Trailers–1,037; Motorcycles–1,146; Manufactured Homes–50; Tax Exempt Licenses–178; Boats–3,583

Crime Incidents (2013)—Murder–1; Rape–5; Robbery–4; Felony Assault–46; Breaking and Entering–138; Larceny–375; Motor Vehicle Theft–29; Arson–13 • Total Crime Index–598;

County Population	
1907 (Okla. Terr.)	9,876
1910	11,469
1920	13,868
1930	15,370
1940	18,592
1950	14,734
1960	13,198
1970	17,767
1980	23,946
1990	28,070
2000	37,077
2010	41,487
2014 Estimate	41,446

Crime Rate per 1,000–14.38

Farms (2012)—1,345

Land in Farms (2012)—283,317

Recreation Area—Honey Creek, Bernice, Upper Spavinaw

Major Lakes—Grand Lake O' the Cherokees, Eucha, Spavinaw

Major Stream Systems—Grand and Illinois rivers

Museums or Historic Sites—Thunderbird Frontier, Delaware County Historical Museum, Jay

Minerals—oil and gas

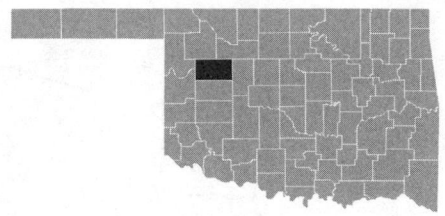

Dewey

Part of the Cheyenne-Arapaho Reservation, Dewey County was designated by the Treaty of 1867 and opened to settlement by the Land Run of April 19, 1892. The county was named for Admiral George Dewey. Taloga, an Indian word meaning "beautiful valley," is the county seat.

Divided from east to west by both the North and South Canadian rivers, the construction of bridges was important to the growth of the county and did not occur until later years. The development of transportation was slow and began with the construction of the Wichita Falls and Northwestern Railroad (later part of the Missouri-Kansas-Texas Railroad, known as the MKT—or Katy) in 1910. The railroad followed the old Western or Dodge Cattle Trail that cut through the county in the 1870s to the railhead at Dodge City.

Sparsely populated, the land is used for agriculture and cattle raising with some horse ranches and many oil and gas wells. People of note who have lived in Dewey County are former Oklahoma Supreme Court Justice Pat Irwin, TV climatologist Gary England, and prohibitionist Carry Nation.

For additional information, contact the Dewey County Historical Society in Taloga or call the county clerk's office at 580/328-5361.

Districts

Congress..........................3
State Senate...................27
State Rep........................59
District Attorney 26
Court of Appeals............ 6
Ct. of Crim. Appeals........5
Supreme Ct. Jud. 4
NW Jud. Adm. 4
    (Div. I)

County Officials

Court Clerk	Rachelle Rogers (R)	Seiling
Clerk	Gayla Holsapple (D)	Taloga
Sheriff	Lanny Clay Snder (R)	Seiling
Treasurer	Cindy Farris (D)	Leedy
Assessor	Julie Louthan (D)	Seiling
Election Brd. Sec.	Barbara Squires (D)	Taloga
Dist. 1 Comm.	Stacy King (D)	Putnam
Dist. 2 Comm.	Rupert Irving (R)	Seiling
Dist. 3 Comm.	M.W. Junior Salisbury (D)	Vici

Property Valuations

	2013–2014 Assessment	2014–2015 Assessment	Increase or Decrease
Real Estate and Improvement	$25,610,649	$26,980,074	$1,369,425
Personal Subject to Tax	$72,255,917	$67,830,368	$4,425,549
Total Locally Assessed	$97,866,566	$94,810,442	($3,056,124)
Homestead Exemptions Allowed	$1,213,047	$1,213,140	$93
Net Assessed Locally	$96,653,519	$93,597,302	$3,056,217
Public Service Assessment	$56,359,192	$53,313,007	($3,046,185)
Net Assessed Valuation	$153,012,711	$146,910,309	($6,102,402)

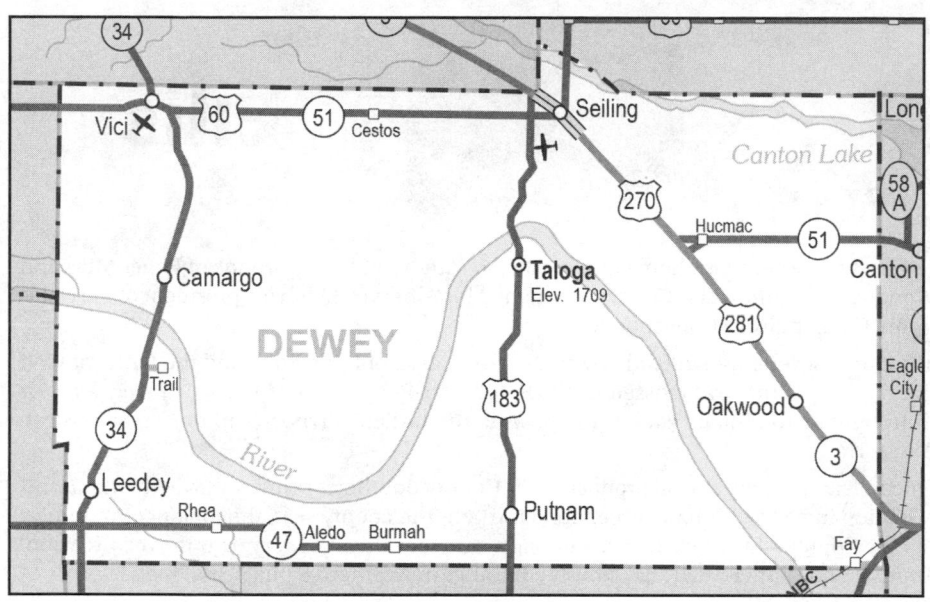

County Seat—Taloga (Pop. 305) 2013 Estimate

Area (Land & Water)—1,008.26 square miles

Per Capita Income (2013)—$53,445 (Ranks 2nd of 77 counties)

Population Statistics (2013)—Female-2,366; Male-2,434;
Ethnicity—Wh.-4,606; Bl.-38; Am. Ind.-483; As.-13; Other-27;
Pacific Is.-2; Two or more races-354; Hisp.-261

Births (2014)—50 • **Deaths** (2014)—73

Marriages (2013)—32 • **Divorces** (2013)—15

Unemployment Rate (2013)—2.9%

Labor Force (2013)—3,258

Number of Establishments (2013)—148

Number of Manufacturers (2013)—4

Public Assistance Payments
(FY2014) Total—$1,272,428 • TANF—
$10,478 • Supplements—Aged-$3,448;
Blind-0; Disabled-$15,436

Vehicle Registration (2014)—
Automobiles-4,096; Farm Trucks-1,668;
Comm. Trucks, Tractors, Trailers-489;
Motor Homes and Travel Trailers-310;
Motorcycles-195; Manufactured Homes-30;
Tax Exempt Licenses-17; Boats-185

Crime Incidents (2013)—Murder-0; Rape-0;
Robbery-0; Felony Assault-2; Breaking and

County Population	
1907 (Okla. Terr.)	13,329
1910	14,132
1920	12,434
1930	13,250
1940	11,981
1950	8,789
1960	6,051
1970	5,656
1980	5,922
1990	5,551
2000	4,743
2010	4,810
2014 Estimate	4,914

Entering-19; Larceny-34; Motor Vehicle
Theft-9; Arson-1 • Total Crime Index-64
Crime Rate per 1,000-13.36

Farms (2012)—743

Land in Farms (2012)—624,827

Major Lake—Canton

Major Stream Systems—Canadian, North
Canadian, and Washita rivers

Museums or Historic Sites—Boswell
Museum, Leedy; Jail House Museum, Taloga

Minerals—oil and gas

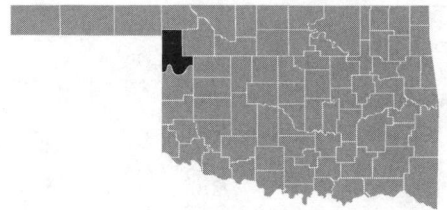

Ellis

Located in western Oklahoma and created at statehood from portions of Roger Mills and Woodward counties, Ellis County was named for Albert H. Ellis, vice president of the Oklahoma Constitutional Convention.

The site of several Indian battles including the Battle of Little Robe and the Battle of Wolf Creek, Ellis County was crossed by the Fort Elliott-Fort Supply Military Crossing, a major thoroughfare to military camps and posts in the Indian Territory and the Great Western Cattle Trail.

Once a leading dairy and oil producer, Ellis County now hosts primarily an agricultural and ranching industry. With the exception of Arnett, the county seat, the major communities of Ellis County—Shattuck, Fargo, and Gage—are located on or very near the old Atchison, Topeka, and Santa Fe Railroad, now the Burlington Northern Santa Fe Railroad.

Ellis County Heritage Volumes I and II, *A Pioneer History of Shattuck, Oklahoma; The 1910 Ellis County Plat Book,* and others offer historical information about the area. Call the county clerk's office at 580/885-7301 for more information.

Districts

Congress..........................3
State Senate..................27
State Rep........................ 61
District Attorney 2
Court of Appeals 6
Ct. of Crim. Appeals........5
Supreme Ct. Jud..............4
NW Jud. Adm. 2

County Officials

Court Clerk	Sally Wayland (R)	Gage
Clerk	Lynn Smith (D)	Arnett
Sheriff	DeWayne Miller (R)	Gage
Treasurer	Kathy Holloway (R)	Arnett
Assessor	Karen Mackey Perkins (D)	Gage
Election Brd. Sec.	Glenda Martin (D)	Arnett
Dist. 1 Comm.	Michael W. Latta (R)	Fargo
Dist. 2 Comm.	Frankie Stevens (R)	Gage
Dist. 3 Comm.	Blake Suthers (D)	Arnett

Property Valuations

	2013–2014 Assessment	2014–2015 Assessment	Increase or Decrease
Real Estate and Improvement	$26,063,044	$27,154,056	$1,091,012
Personal Subject to Tax	$47,237,412	$43,247,720	($3,989,692)
Total Locally Assessed	$73,300,456	$70,401,776	($2,898,680)
Homestead Exemptions Allowed	$1,218,492	$1,198,246	($20,246)
Net Assessed Locally	$72,081,964	$69,203,530	($2,878,434)
Public Service Assessment	$10,113,834	$11,625,775	$1,511,941
Net Assessed Valuation	$82,195,798	$80,829,305	$1,366,493

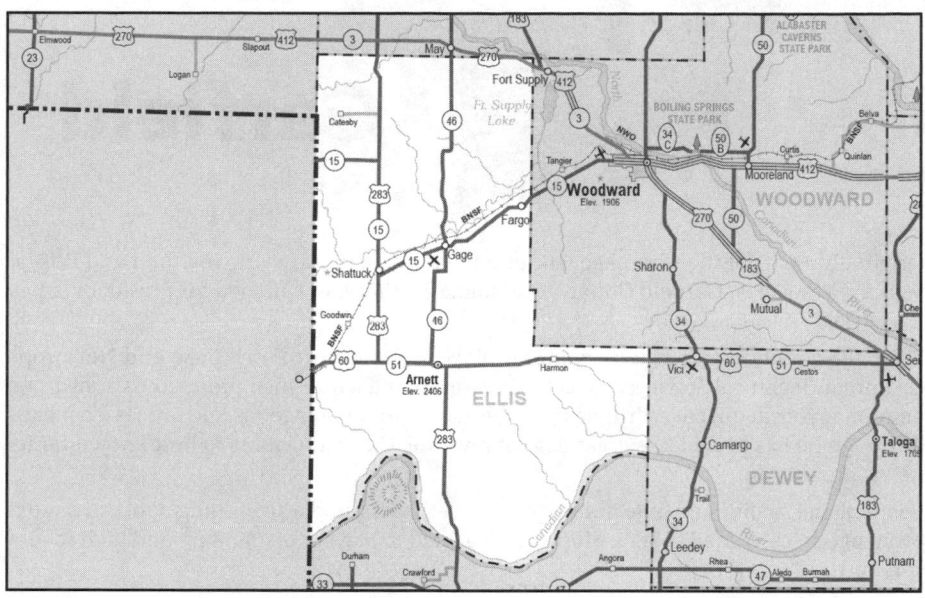

County Population

County Seat—Arnett (Pop. 527) 2013 Estimate

Area (Land & Water)—1,231.84 square miles

Per Capita Income (2013)—$54,357 (Ranks 1st of 77 counties)

Population Statistics (2013)—Female–2,069; Male–2,051; Ethnicity—Wh.–4,040; Bl.–12; Am. Ind.–123; As.–39; Other–47; Pacific Is.–0; Two or more races–141; Hisp.–279

Births (2014)—52 • **Deaths** (2014)—62

Marriages (2013)—37 • **Divorces** (2013)—13

Unemployment Rate (2013)—2.6%

Labor Force (2013)—2,856

Number of Establishments (2013)—103

Number of Manufacturers (2013)—1

Public Assistance Payments (FY2014) Total—$351,342 • TANF—$0 • Supplements—Aged–$0; Blind–$0; Disabled–$82

Vehicle Registration (2014)—Automobiles–3,235; Farm Trucks–1,134; Comm. Trucks, Tractors, Trailers–335; Motor Homes and Travel Trailers–226; Motorcycles–159; Manufactured Homes–7; Tax Exempt Licenses–7; Boats–122

Crime Incidents (2013)—Murder–0; Rape–0; Robbery–1; Felony Assault–3; Breaking and Entering–19; Larceny–33; Motor Vehicle Theft–3; Arson–3 • Total Crime Index–59; Crime Rate per 1,000–14.37

Farms (2012)—760

Land in Farms (2012)—758,323

Major Stream Systems—North Canadian and Canadian rivers

Museums or Historic Sites—Log Cabin, Arnett

Minerals—oil and gas

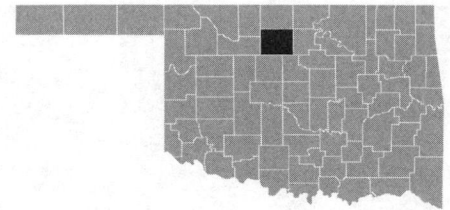

Garfield

Originally a part of the Cherokee Outlet opened for settlement during the Land Run of September 16, 1893, Garfield County, Oklahoma Territory, was named for President James A. Garfield.

Enid, the county seat, has two major employers—Vance Air Force Base and Northrop-Grumman Technical Services. Local businesses manufacture such products as anhydrous ammonia, petroleum coke, drilling rigs, steel fabricators, dairy goods and processed meats. Although oil has provided a great deal of revenue, Garfield County is best known for its wheat production.

Recreational facilities include public golf courses, parks, and a swimming pool. An annual event of interest is the Tri-State Music Festival held in May for elementary and high school students.

The Garfield County Historical Society and *Garfield County Oklahoma 1893–1982* (in two volumes) are sources for more information. The Retired Senior Volunteer Program Information Center is open from 8 AM to 4 PM, Monday through Friday. Call the county clerk at 580/237-0225 or the Greater Enid Chamber of Commerce at 580/237-2494 for additional information.

Districts

Congress...........................3
State Senate...................19
State Rep.............38, 40, 41
District Attorney 4
Court of Appeals............ 6
Ct. of Crim. Appeals........5
Supreme Ct. Jud..............4
NW Jud. Adm. 4
   (Div II)

County Officials

Court Clerk	Margaret F. Jones (R)	Enid
Clerk	Kathy R. Hughes (R)	Breckinridge
Sheriff	Jerry Niles (R)	Enid
Treasurer	Kevin R. Postier (R)	Breckinridge
Assessor	L. Wade Patterson (R)	Enid
Elect. Brd. Sec.	Cheryl Patterson (R)	Enid
Dist. 1 Comm.	Marc Bolz (R)	Covington
Dist. 2 Comm.	Reese Wedel (R)	Garber
Dist. 3 Comm.	James C. Simunek (R)	Waukomis

Property Valuations

	2013–2014 Assessment	2014–2015 Assessment	Increase or Decrease
Real Estate and Improvement	$310,532,521	$320,219,774	$9,687,253
Personal Subject to Tax	$179,818,977	$176,484,065	$3,334,912
Total Locally Assessed	$490,351,498	$496,703,839	$6,352,341
Homestead Exemptions Allowed	$14,730,328	$14,644,059	($86,269)
Net Assessed Locally	$475,621,170	$482,059,780	$6,438,610
Public Service Assessment	$43,763,138	$53,340,685	($9,577,547)
Net Assessed Valuation	$519,384,308	$535,400,465	$16,016,157

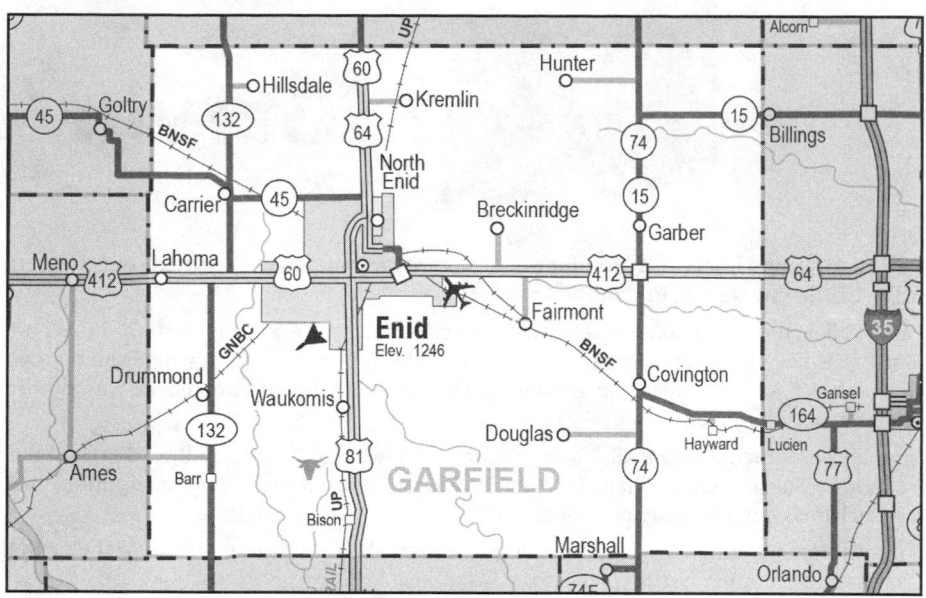

County Seat—Enid (Pop. 50,725) 2013 Estimate

Area (Land & Water)—1,059.94 square miles

Per Capita Income (2013)—$45,812 (Ranks 12th of 77 counties)

Population Statistics (2013)—Female-30,792; Male-30,164; Ethnicity—Wh.-52,877; Bl.-2,563; Am. Ind.-2,606; As.-960; Other-3,267; Pacific Is.-1,344; Two or more races-2,447; Hisp.-5,750

Births (2014)—978 • **Deaths** (2014)—649

Marriages (2013)—558 • **Divorces** (2013)—277

Unemployment Rate (2013)—3.7%

Labor Force (2013)—34,217

Number of Establishments (2013)—1,710

Number of Manufacturers (2013)—62

Public Assistance Payments
(FY2014) Total—$48,078,185 • TANF—$157,367 • Supplements—Aged-$58,930; Blind-$1,004; Disabled-$484,307

Vehicle Registration (2014)—
Automobiles-54,978; Farm Trucks-4,086; Comm. Trucks, Tractors, Trailers-10,502; Motor Homes and Travel Trailers-1,795; Motorcycles-3,273; Manufactured Homes-16; Tax Exempt Licenses-179; Boats-1,659

Institutions of Higher Learning—
Northwestern Oklahoma State University, Enid Campus

Crime Incidents (2013)—Murder-3; Rape-26;

County Population	
1907 (Okla. Terr.)	28,300
1910	33,050
1920	37,500
1930	45,588
1940	45,484
1950	52,820
1960	52,975
1970	55,365
1980	62,820
1990	56,735
2000	57,813
2010	60,580
2014 Estimate	63,091

Robbery-16; Felony Assault-198; Breaking and Entering-632; Larceny-1,770; Motor Vehicle Theft-99; Arson-20 • Total Crime Index-2,744; Crime Rate per 1,000-44.54

Farms (2012)—1,098

Land in Farms (2012)—666,373

Major Stream Systems—Cimarron River, Red Rock and Black Bear Creek and tributaries of the Salt Fork of the Arkansas River

Museums or Historic Sites—Museum of the Cherokee Strip at Enid, George's Antique Auto Museum, Midgley Museum, and the Railroad Museum of Oklahoma, Enid

Minerals—oil and gas

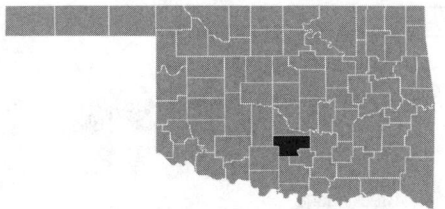

Garvin

Named for Samuel Garvin, a prominent Chickasaw Indian, Garvin County was once a part of the Chickasaw Nation, Indian Territory.

Pauls Valley, the county seat, was named for Smith Paul, the first white settler in this part of the Washita River Valley. In 1847 he described the area as "a section where the bottom land was rich and the blue stem grass grew so high that a man on horseback was almost hidden in its foliage."

Annual events include the Pauls Valley Junior Livestock Show in March, Brick Fest and the Jackpot Pig Sale in May, Heritage Days and Rodeo in June, Fourth of July Celebration, and the Christmas Parade of Lights in December.

For additional county information, call the county clerk's office at 405/238-5596 or the Chamber of Commerce at 405/238-2335.

Districts

Congress..........................4
State Senate..............13, 43
State Rep............ 20, 22, 42
District Attorney 21
Court of Appeals..............4
Ct. of Crim. Appeals........3
Supreme Ct. Jud..............5
S. Cent. Jud. Adm. 21
  (Div. II)

County Officials

Court Clerk	Cindy Roberts (D)	Pauls Valley
Clerk	Lori Fulks (D)	Stratford
Sheriff	Larry K. Rhodes (R)	Paoli
Treasurer	Sandy Goggans (D)	Pauls Valley
Assessor	Beverly Strickland (D)	Pauls Valley
Election Brd. Sec.	Doylene Cunningham (D)	Pauls Valley
Dist. 1 Comm.	Stan Spivey (D)	Lindsay
Dist. 2 Comm.	Shon Richardson (D)	Pauls Valley
Dist. 3 Comm.	Johnny Mann (D)	Stratford

Property Valuations

	2013–2014 Assessment	2014–2015 Assessment	Increase or Decrease
Real Estate and Improvement	$91,899,961	$95,085,907	$2,210,357
Personal Subject to Tax	$95,439,686	$114,363,999	$18,924,313
Total Locally Assessed	$187,339,647	$209,449,906	$22,110,259
Homestead Exemptions Allowed	$7,647,209	$7,550,657	($96,552)
Net Assessed Locally	$179,692,438	$201,899,249	$22,206,811
Public Service Assessment	$26,991,884	$31,874,944	$4,883,060
Net Assessed Valuation	$206,684,322	$233,774,193	$27,089,871

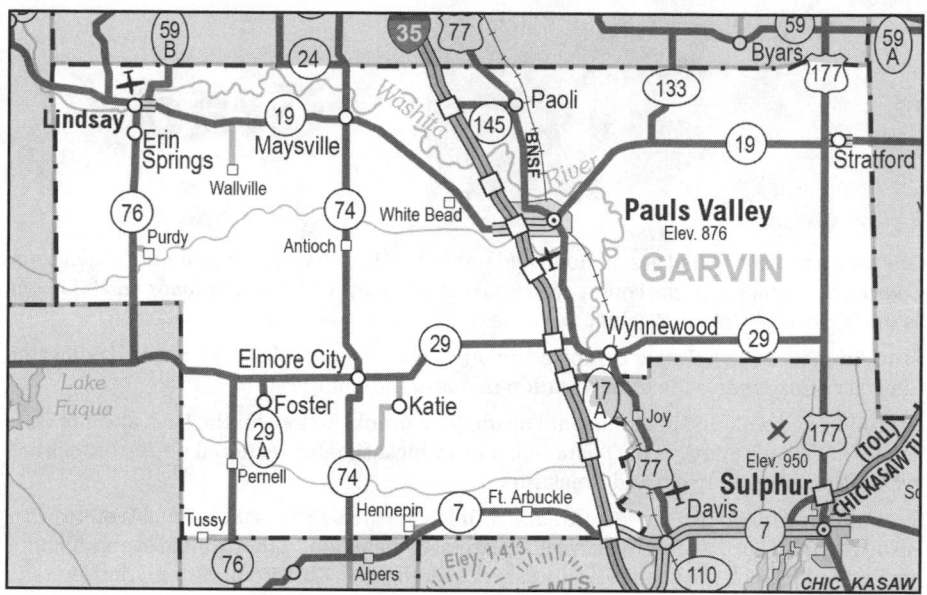

County Seat—Pauls Valley (Pop. 6,027) 2013 Estimate

Area (Land & Water)—813.66 square miles

Per Capita Income (2013)—$38,321 (Ranks 30th of 77 counties)

Population Statistics (2013)—Female-13,994; Male-13,416; Ethnicity—Wh.-24,143; Bl.-897; Am. Ind.-3,295; As.-176; Other-547; Pacific Is.-37; Two or more races-1,645; Hisp.-1,814

Births (2014)—389 • **Deaths** (2014)—339

Marriages (2013)—204 • **Divorces** (2013)—140

Unemployment Rate (2013)—4.3%

Labor Force (2013)—15,016

Number of Establishments (2013)—706

Number of Manufacturers (2013)—31

Public Assistance Payments (FY2014) Total—$30,346,289 • TANF—$87,131 • Supplements—Aged-$51,972; Blind-$2,501; Disabled-$274,790

Vehicle Registration (2014)—
Automobiles-26,163; Farm Trucks-4,109; Comm. Trucks, Tractors, Trailers-2,658; Motor Homes and Travel Trailers-1,292; Motorcycles-1,351; Manufactured Homes-34; Tax Exempt Licenses-158; Boats-1,151

Crime Incidents (2013)—Murder-2; Rape-10; Robbery-6; Felony Assault-61; Breaking and Entering-238; Larceny-424; Motor Vehicle

County Population	
1907 (Okla. Terr.)	22,787
1910	26,545
1920	32,445
1930	31,401
1940	31,150
1950	29,500
1960	28,290
1970	24,874
1980	27,856
1990	26,605
2000	27,210
2010	27,576
2014 Estimate	27,561

Theft-40; Arson-7 • Total Crime Index-781; Crime Rate per 1,000-28.56

Farms (2012)—1,498

Land in Farms (2012)—463,183

Major Stream Systems—Washita River and tributaries to the Canadian River

Museums or Historic Sites—Murray-Lindsey Mansion, Erin Springs; Washita Valley Museum, Santa Fe Depot Museum, and the Washita Valley Museum, Pauls Valley; Eskridge Hotel, Wynnewood

Minerals—oil and gas

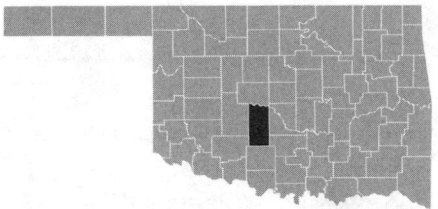

Grady

Grady County was created at statehood and named for Henry W. Grady, editor of the *Atlanta Constitution*. Chickasha, the county seat, was named for the Chickasaw Indians and is known as the "Queen City of the Washita" because of its strategic location.

In addition to the H. E. Bailey Turnpike and other highways, the Union Pacific and Stillwater Central railroads serve the transportation needs of the county.

Specialized educational needs are met by the Jane Brooks School for the Deaf and the University of Science and Arts of Oklahoma, all in Chickasha. Recreational opportunities are available at Lakes Burtschi and Chickasha.

Summer rodeos and swap meets attract visitors to the area, as does the annual Watermelon Festival at Rush Springs, the "Watermelon Capital of the World." Other annual events include the Festival of Light, the Grady County Fair, the Firefighters Chili Cook-off, and the Veterans Parade.

Contact the Grady County Historical Society and the chamber of commerce for more information, or call the county clerk's office at 405/224-7388.

Districts

Congress...........................4
State Senate............. 23, 43
State Rep....... 47, 51, 56, 65
District Attorney 6
Court of Appeals 4
Ct. of Crim. Appeals........3
Supreme Ct. Jud. 5
SW Jud. Adm. 6

County Officials

Court Clerk	Lisa Hannah (R)	Chickasha
Clerk	Sharon Shoemake (D)	Chickasha
Sheriff	Jim Weir (R)	Tuttle
Treasurer	Robin Burton (R)	Alex
Assessor	Bari Firestone (R)	Chickasha
Election Brd. Sec.	Susan Turner (D)	Tuttle
Dist. 1 Comm.	Windle Hardy (R)	Tuttle
Dist. 2 Comm.	Mike Lennier (D)	Chickasha
Dist. 3 Comm.	Ralph Beard (D)	Rush Springs

Property Valuations

	2013–2014 Assessment	2014–2015 Assessment	Increase or Decrease
Real Estate and Improvement	$231,942,124	$244,889,839	$12,947,715
Personal Subject to Tax	$112,899,096	$134,017,259	$21,118,163
Total Locally Assessed	$344,841,220	$378,907,098	$34,065,878
Homestead Exemptions Allowed	$15,996,430	$16,273,377	$276,947
Net Assessed Locally	$328,844,790	$362,633,721	$33,788,931
Public Service Assessment	$33,949,143	$29,791,278	($4,157,865)
Net Assessed Valuation	$362,793,933	$392,424,999	$29,631,066

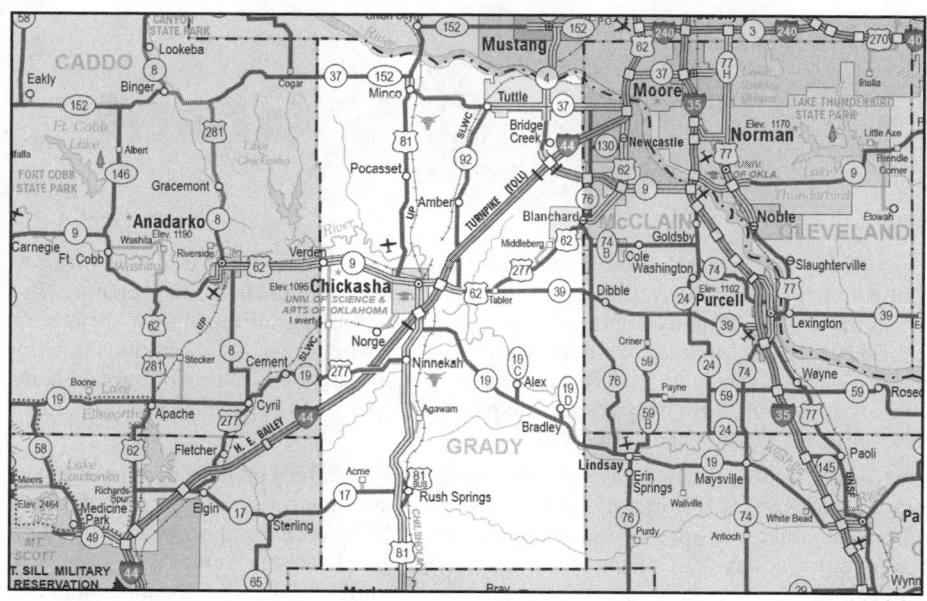

County Seat—Chickasha (Pop. 16,374) 2013 Estimate

Area (Land & Water)—1,105.30 square miles

Per Capita Income (2013)—$35,240 (Ranks 45th of 77 counties)

Population Statistics (2013)—Female–26,689; Male–26,166;
Ethnicity—Wh.–47,874 Bl.–1,941; Am. Ind.–4,595; As.–354;
Other–992; Pacific Is.–116; Two or more races–2,741; Hisp.–2,555

Births (2014)—601 • **Deaths** (2014)—544

Marriages (2013)—302 • **Divorces** (2013)—297

Unemployment Rate (2013)—5.2%

Labor Force (2013)—23,670

Number of Establishments (2013)—1,101

Number of Manufacturers (2013)—61

Public Assistance Payments
(FY2014) Total—$23,989,990 • TANF—
$216,924 • Supplements—Aged–$67,915;
Blind–$2,047; Disabled–$430,261

Vehicle Registration (2014)—
Automobiles–28,425; Farm Trucks–2,526;
Comm. Trucks, Tractors, Trailers–1,841;
Motor Homes and Travel Trailers–1,279;
Motorcycles–1,481; Manufactured Homes–29;
Tax Exempt Licenses–146; Boats–990

Institutions of Higher Learning—
University of Science and Arts of Oklahoma,
Chickasha

Crime Incidents (2013)—Murder 1; Rape–22;

County Population	
1907 (Okla. Terr.)	23,420
1910	30,309
1920	33,943
1930	47,638
1940	41,116
1950	34,872
1960	29,590
1970	29,354
1980	39,490
1990	41,747
2000	45,516
2010	52,431
2014 Estimate	53,854

Robbery–11; Felony Assault–164; Breaking
and Entering–362; Larceny–607; Motor Vehicle
Theft–75; Arson–8 • Total Crime Index–1,242;
Crime Rate per 1,000–24.08

Farms (2012)—1,666

Land in Farms (2012)—583,322

Major Stream Systems—Washita and
Canadian rivers and tributaries to Beaver
Creek

Museums or Historic Sites—Grady County
Historical Society, Antique Car Museum,
Muscle Car Ranch

Minerals—oil and gas

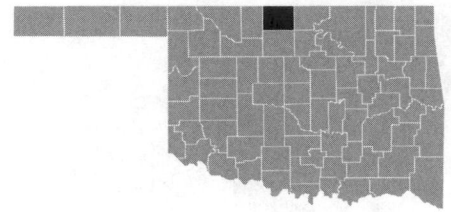

Grant

Located in north central Oklahoma, Grant County was named for President Ulysses S. Grant. Originally "L" county, this area was organized as a part of Oklahoma Territory. The economy of Grant County is basically agricultural, with Clyde Cooperative Association's general offices in Medford, the county seat. Conoco and Koch Hydrocarbon Company are two major businesses in the county. Lamont is home to one of five world Atmospheric Radiation Measurement Program sites, part of the Department of Energy's Global Climate Change Research Project of 1992.

The Grant County Museum, located in Medford, offers visitors a glimpse of pioneer life in the "Cherokee Strip." Historic Jefferson Park, Sewell's Stockade and a watering station for the Chisholm Trail cattle drive are located in Jefferson. The recording station for area weather, temperature, and rainfall for one hundred years is also in Jefferson. Grant County Free Fair and Fair Grounds are located at Pond Creek; the Community Health Center, a pioneer in rural health, is in Wakita. The county's celebration of the Run of 1893, "Old Settlers Day," is held in Wakita.

The Grant County Historical Society and Grant County Museum are sources of information, or call the county clerk's office at 580/395-2274.

Districts

Congress..........................3
State Senate...................19
State Rep.......................38
District Attorney.............4
Court of Appeals............ 6
Ct. of Crim. Appeals........5
Supreme Ct. Jud..............1
NW Jud. Adm. 4
  (Div. II)

County Officials

Court Clerk	Deana Killian (D)	Medford
Clerk	Sherri Eulberg (R)	Pond Creek
Sheriff	Scott Sterling (R)	Medford
Treasurer	Penny Dowell (D)	Lamont
Assessor	Robin Herod (R)	Medford
Election Brd. Sec.	Harvey Bush (R)	Medford
Dist. 1 Comm.	Max L. Hess (R)	Manchester
Dist. 2 Comm.	Cindy Bobbitt (R)	Lamont
Dist. 3 Comm.	Nathan Shaffer(D)	Pond Creek

Property Valuations

	2013–2014 Assessment	2014–2015 Assessment	Increase or Decrease
Real Estate and Improvement	$41,773,447	$42,739,183	$965,736
Personal Subject to Tax	$80,440,428	$84,493,329	($4,052,901)
Total Locally Assessed	$122,213,875	$127,232,512	($5,018,637)
Homestead Exemptions Allowed	$1,225,546	$1,229,914	4,368
Net Assessed Locally	$120,988,329	$126,002,598	$5,014,269
Public Service Assessment	$24,434,092	$32,037,856	$7,603,764
Net Assessed Valuation	$145,422,421	$158,040,454	$12,618,033

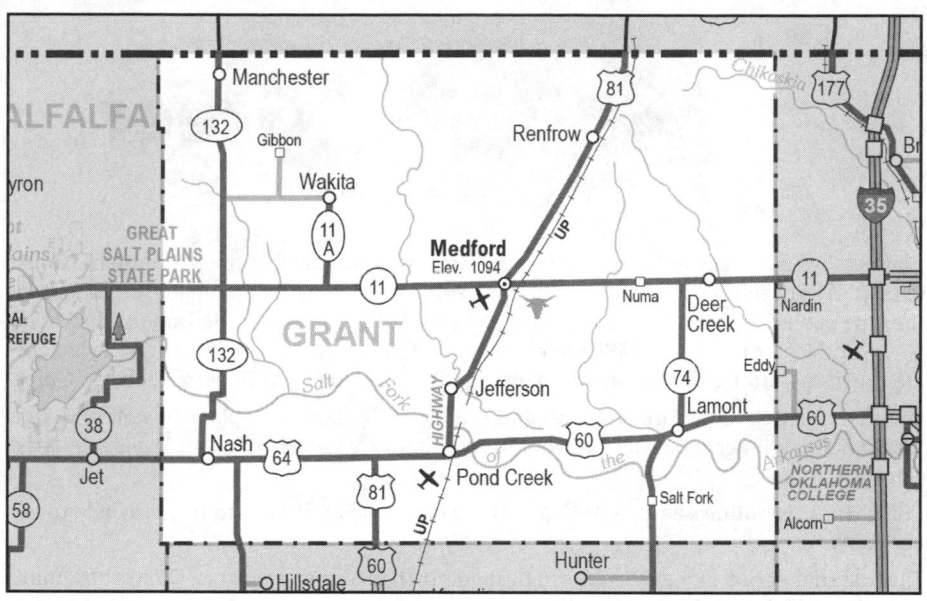

County Population

1907 (Okla. Terr.)	17,638
1910	18,760
1920	16,072
1930	14,150
1940	13,128
1950	10,461
1960	8,140
1970	7,117
1980	6,518
1990	5,689
2000	5,144
2010	4,527
2014 Estimate	4,501

County Seat—Medford (Pop. 991) 2013 Estimate

Area (Land & Water)—1,003.61 square miles

Per Capita Income (2013)—$48,067 (Ranks 4th of 77 counties)

Population Statistics (2013)—Female-2,268; Male-2,254; Ethnicity—Wh.-4,363; Bl.-58; Am. Ind.-242; As.-19; Other-81; Pacific Is.-0; Two or more races-233; Hisp.-167

Births (2014)—51 • **Deaths** (2014)—68

Marriages (2013)—24 • **Divorces** (2013)—14

Unemployment Rate (2013)—3.3%

Labor Force (2013)—2,790

Number of Establishments (2013)—123

Number of Manufacturers (2013)—3

Public Assistance Payments
(FY2014) Total—$1,089,953 • TANF—$175 • Supplements—Aged-$2,080; Blind-$262; Disabled-$18,942

Vehicle Registration (2014)—
Automobiles-3,047; Farm Trucks-1,716; Comm. Trucks, Tractors, Trailers-751; Motor Homes and Travel Trailers-186; Motorcycles-237; Manufactured Homes-6; Tax Exempt Licenses-8; Boats-108

Crime Incidents (2013)—Murder-1; Rape-0; Robbery-0; Felony Assault-0; Breaking and Entering-9; Larceny-16; Motor Vehicle Theft-5; Arson-0 • Total Crime Index-31; Crime Rate per 1,000-6.84

Farms (2012)—802

Land in Farms (2012)—582,216

Major Stream Systems—Salt Fork of Arkansas River and Chikaskia River

Museums or Historic Sites—Grant County Museum at Medford

Minerals—oil and gas

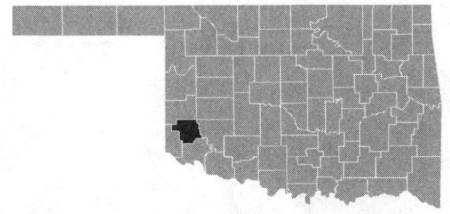

Greer

Claimed by both Texas and the United States, Greer was adjudged by the U.S. Supreme Court to be part of Indian Territory in 1896 and was soon attached and opened for settlement. At the time of the Oklahoma Constitutional Convention, the area was divided among Beckham, Greer, and Jackson counties. Following statehood, Greer County was further divided to create Harmon County. The county was named for Texas Lieutenant Governor John A. Greer.

The first meeting of the United States and the Plains Indians took place July 21, 1834, in a local Wichita village in Devil's Canyon. In attendance were Lt. Jefferson Davis and artist George Catlin.

Willis Granite Products and the Mangum Brick Plant, located in the county seat, add to the economy.

The first shelter belt in the U.S. was established north of Mangum in 1936. Quartz Mountain State Park, the Sandy Sanders Wildlife Area (founded in 1986 and containing 16,000 acres), and Lake Altus provide recreational opportunities. The Oklahoma Summer Arts Institute takes place each June at Quartz Mountain Lodge, while the last weekend in April offers a rattlesnake derby and flea market at Mangum.

For more county information, call the county clerk's office at 580/782-3664.

Districts

Congress	3
State Senate	38
State Rep.	52, 55
District Attorney	2
Court of Appeals	6
Ct. of Crim. Appeals	5
Supreme Ct. Jud.	9
SW Jud. Adm.	3

County Officials

Court Clerk	Rhonda Henry (D)	Mangum
Clerk	Jackie Cloyd (D)	Mangum
Sheriff	Devin Huckabay (D)	Mangum
Treasurer	Donna Bull (D)	Mangum
Assessor	Juanita Reeves (D)	Mangum
Election Brd. Sec.	Debbie Davis (D)	Mangum
Dist. 1 Comm.	Brent York (D)	Mangum
Dist. 2 Comm.	Terry Nickell (D)	Granite
Dist. 3 Comm.	Steven Fite (D)	Willow

Property Valuations

	2013–2014 Assessment	2014–2015 Assessment	Increase or Decrease
Real Estate and Improvement	$22,725,404	$22,829,737	$104,333
Personal Subject to Tax	$4,039,435	$4,008,325	$31,110
Total Locally Assessed	$26,764,839	$26,838,062	$73,223
Homestead Exemptions Allowed	$1,510,815	$1,511,304	$489
Net Assessed Locally	$25,254,024	$25,326,758	$72,734
Public Service Assessment	$2,271,468	$1,974,859	($296,609)
Net Assessed Valuation	$27,525,492	$27,301,617	($223,875)

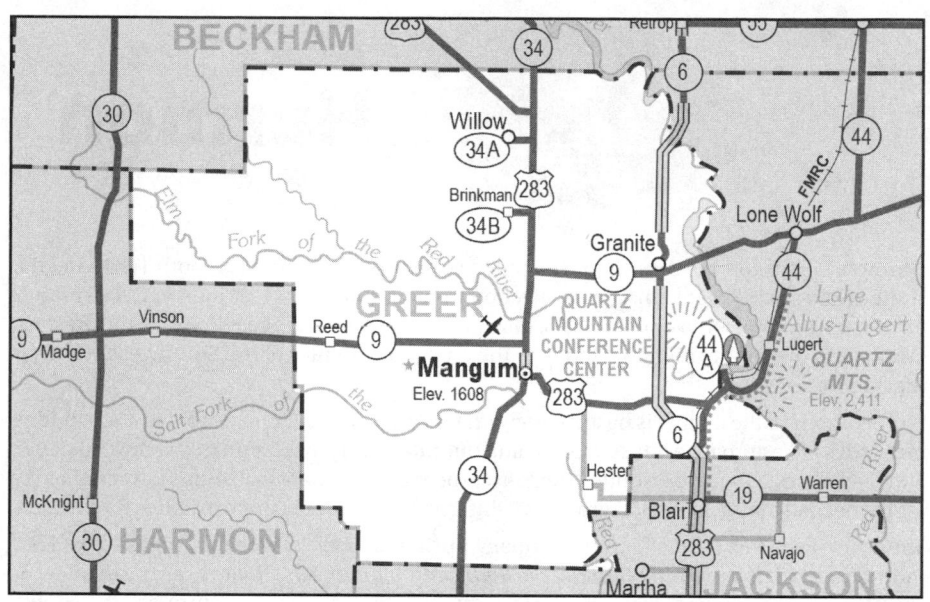

County Seat—Mangum (Pop. 2,974) 2013 Estimate

Area (Land & Water)—643.66 square miles

Per Capita Income (2013)—$28,673 (Ranks 74ᵗʰ of 77 counties)

Population Statistics (2013)—Female-2,677; Male-3,501;
Ethnicity—Wh.-5,129; Bl.-518; Am. Ind.-334; As.-2; Other-414;
Pacific Is.-0; Two or more races-199; Hisp.-635

Births (2014)—77 • Deaths (2014)—88

Marriages (2013)—35 • Divorces (2013)—48

Unemployment Rate (2013)—6.8%

Labor Force (2013)—1,826

Number of Establishments (2013)—94

Number of Manufacturers (2013)—2

Public Assistance Payments
(FY2014) Total—$3,730,903 • TANF—
$14,384 • Supplements—Aged-$14,578;
Blind-$0; Disabled-$57,403

Vehicle Registration (2014)—
Automobiles-3,999; Farm Trucks-1,101;
Comm. Trucks, Tractors, Trailers-132;
Motor Homes and Travel Trailers-166;
Motorcycles-173; Manufactured Homes-3; Tax
Exempt Licenses-16; Boats-104

Crime Incidents (2013)—Murder-0; Rape-2;
Robbery-0; Felony Assault-1; Breaking and
Entering-27; Larceny-30; Motor Vehicle
Theft-2; Arson-0 • Total Crime Index-62;

County Population	
1907 (Okla. Terr.)	23,624
1910	16,449
1920	15,836
1930	20,282
1940	14,550
1950	11,749
1960	8,877
1970	7,979
1980	7,028
1990	6,559
2000	6,061
2010	6,239
2014 Estimate	6,151

Crime Rate per 1,000-10.22

Farms (2012)—498

Land in Farms (2012)—401,551

Recreation Area—Quartz Mountain State
Park

Major Lake—Altus

Major Stream Systems—Elm Fork, Salt Fork
and North Fork of Red River

Museums or Historic Sites—Ford's
Museum, Granite; Old Greer County Museum,
Mangum

Minerals—oil and gas; stone (dimension) clays

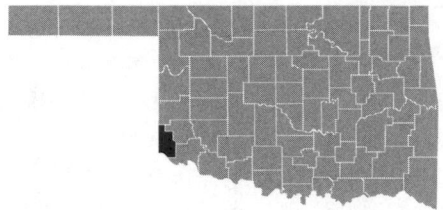

Harmon

Harmon County, part of the original disputed Greer County claimed by both Texas and the United States, was created by special election in 1909, and named for Judson C. Harmon, a former governor of Ohio and later U.S. attorney general. Located in extreme southwestern Oklahoma, the county is known today as the "Irrigation Center of the Southwest." Hollis is the county seat.

The economy of the county is based largely on farming and ranching, with two contributing industries—Western Fibers Insulation Plant, manufacturing insulation from recycled paper, and Buck Creek "Honey" Mesquite Company, processing mesquite for use as a flavor enhancer for barbecued meats. Lake Hall provides fishing and recreational opportunities for the area.

The Black-Eyed Pea Festival is held annually during the second week in August. Two Harmon County history books, *Planning the Route* and *Planning the Route 2*, are available. For more county information, contact the Harmon County Historical Society or call the county clerk's office at 580/688-3658.

Districts

Congress.........................3
State Senate..................38
State Rep.......................52
District Attorney.............2
Court of Appeals............ 6
Ct. of Crim. Appeals........5
Supreme Ct. Jud..............9
SW Jud. Adm. 3

County Officials

Court Clerk	Stacy Macias (D)	Hollis
Clerk	Kara Gollihare (D)	Hollis
Sheriff	Joe Johnson (D)	Hollis
Treasurer	David Seigrist (R)	Hollis
Assessor	Kendra Tillman (D)	Hollis
Election Brd. Sec.	Dana Aguilar (R)	Hollis
Dist. 1 Comm.	Gary Lewis (D)	Hollis
Dist. 2 Comm.	Nicky Boone (D)	Hollis
Dist. 3 Comm.	James Stegall (D)	Hollis

Property Valuations

	2013–2014 Assessment	2014–2015 Assessment	Increase or Decrease
Real Estate and Improvement	$14,168,420	$14,347,950	$179,530
Personal Subject to Tax	$2,663,296	$2,737,706	$74,410
Total Locally Assessed	$16,831,716	$17,085,656	$253,940
Homestead Exemptions Allowed	$662,075	$637,083	($24,992)
Net Assessed Locally	$16,169,641	$16,448,573	$278,4932
Public Service Assessment	$3,220,445	$2,998,001	$222,444
Net Assessed Valuation	$19,390,086	$19,446,574	$56,488

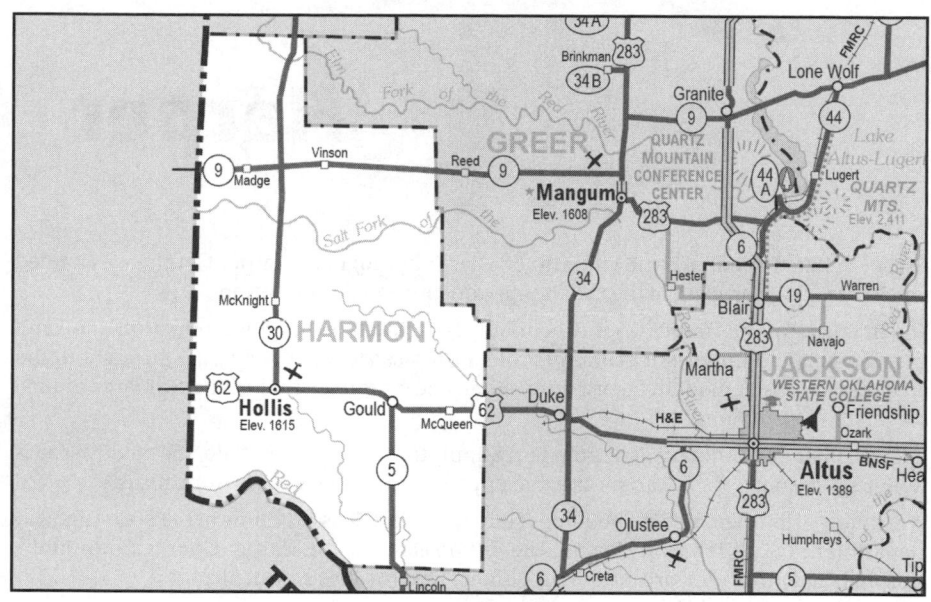

County Seat—Hollis (Pop. 2,025) 2013 Estimate

Area (Land & Water)—538.56 square miles

Per Capita Income (2013)—$36,896 (Ranks 37th of 77 counties)

Population Statistics (2013)—Female-1,563; Male-1,331; Ethnicity—Wh.-2,107; Bl.-245; Am. Ind.-104; As.-35; Other-504; Pacific Is.-0; Two or more races-101; Hisp.-752

Births (2014)—34 • **Deaths** (2014)—39

Marriages (2013)—20 • **Divorces** (2013)—14

Unemployment Rate (2013)—4.3%

Labor Force (2013)—1,403

Number of Establishments (2013)—52

Number of Manufacturers (2013)—3

Public Assistance Payments (FY2014) Total—$1,318,991 • TANF—$12,930 • Supplements—Aged-$7,485; Blind-$0; Disabled-$41,765

Vehicle Registration (2014)—Automobiles-2,015; Farm Trucks-673; Comm. Trucks, Tractors, Trailers-74; Motor Homes and Travel Trailers-93; Motorcycles-107; Manufactured Homes-2; Tax Exempt Licenses-18; Boats-46

Crime Incidents (2013)—Murder-0; Rape-3; Robbery-0; Felony Assault-1; Breaking and Entering-66; Larceny-64; Motor Vehicle Theft-2; Arson-1 • Total Crime Index-136; Crime Rate per 1,000-46.66

Farms (2012)—366

Land in Farms (2012)—340,599

Major Stream Systems—Salt Fork and Prairie Dog Town Fork of Red River

Museums or Historic Sites—Harmon County Historical Museum, Hollis

Minerals—oil and gas, salt

County Population	
1907 (Okla. Terr.)	N/A
1910	11,328
1920	11,261
1930	13,834
1940	10,019
1950	8,079
1960	5,852
1970	5,136
1980	4,519
1990	3,793
2000	3,283
2010	2,922
2014 Estimate	2,798

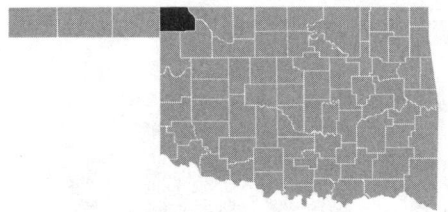

Harper

Part of the area opened in the land run of September 16, 1893, Harper County was named for Oscar G. Harper, clerk of the Oklahoma Constitutional Convention.

The mainstay of the Harper County economy is agriculture, but the production of oil and gas also plays an important economic role. Prime cattle are in evidence throughout the area's feed yards. A modern veterinarian clinic and hospital with facilities for large animal surgery is close at hand.

Located on the old Military Trail from Fort Supply to Fort Dodge, Buffalo, the county seat, is twelve miles south of the Kansas line and approximately thirty miles from Texas.

With many of its original stone buildings still in use, Buffalo is the home of the State Highway Department's Sixth Division Headquarters. Two schools, the Harper County Community Hospital, and an airport, are located in Buffalo. Laverne also has an airport.

Famous county residents include Roy Dunn, world champion wrestler; Mel Harpe, who recommended Knute Rockne as football coach for Notre Dame; and Jane Jayroe, Miss America, 1967. Annual events include the County Fair during early fall and the Laverne Trade Show. The Old Settler's Picnic has been held on the third Sunday in August annually since 1940. For more information, call the county clerk: 580/735-2012.

Districts

Congress..........................3
State Senate..................27
State Rep.......................61
District Attorney.............1
Court of Appeals...........6
Ct. of Crim. Appeals........5
Supreme Ct. Jud..............4
NW Jud. Adm. 1

County Officials

Court Clerk	Rae-Jean Burke (D)	Buffalo
Clerk	Karen Hickman (R)	Buffalo
Sheriff	Marty L. Drew (R)	Buffalo
Treasurer	Peggy Tillery (D)	Laverne
Assessor	Lynette Ingraham (D)	Buffalo
Election Brd. Sec.	Pauletta Roberts (R)	Buffalo
Dist. 1 Comm.	Cody Hickman (R)	Buffalo
Dist. 2 Comm.	Carl Laverty (R)	Laverne
Dist. 3 Comm.	Steven D. Myatt (D)	Buffalo

Property Valuations

	2013–2014 Assessment	2014–2015 Assessment	Increase or Decrease
Real Estate and Improvement	$20,252,640	$20,713,178	$460,538
Personal Subject to Tax	$36,819,624	$33,270,319	($3,549,305)
Total Locally Assessed	$57,072,264	$53,983,497	($3,088,767)
Homestead Exemptions Allowed	$944,267	$943,794	($473)
Net Assessed Locally	$56,127,997	$53,039,703	($3,088,294)
Public Service Assessment	$25,269,038	$25,539,299	$270,261
Net Assessed Valuation	$81,397,035	$78,579,002	($2,818,033)

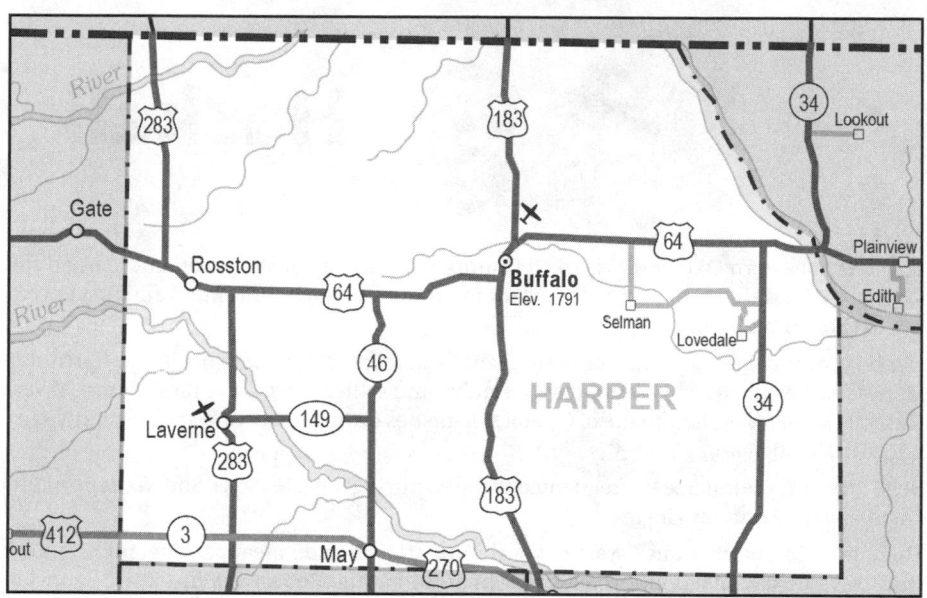

County Seat—Buffalo (Pop. 1,336) 2013 Estimate

Area (Land & Water)—1,040.96 square miles

Per Capita Income (2013)—$37,098 (Ranks 35th of 77 counties)

Population Statistics (2013)—Female-1,876; Male-1,834;
Ethnicity—Wh.-3,621; Bl.-28; Am. Ind.-74; As.-5; Other-85;
Pacific Is.-0; Two or more races-92; Hisp.-679

Births (2012)—51 • **Deaths** (2014)—43

Marriages (2014)—43 • **Divorces** (2013)—47

Unemployment Rate (2013)—3.3%

Labor Force (2013)—1,979

Number of Establishments (2013)—103

Number of Manufacturers (2013)—1

Public Assistance Payments
(FY2014) Total—$956,514 • TANF—
$16,110 • Supplements—Aged-$3,322;
Blind-$803; Disabled-$15,595

Vehicle Registration (2014)—
Automobiles-4,350; Farm Trucks-1,470;
Comm. Trucks, Tractors, Trailers-241;
Motor Homes and Travel Trailers-313;
Motorcycles-227; Manufactured Homes-5; Tax
Exempt Licenses-13; Boats-96

Crime Incidents (2013)—Murder-0; Rape-0;
Robbery-0; Felony Assault-1; Breaking and

County Population	
1907 (Okla. Terr.)	8,089
1910	8,189
1920	7,623
1930	7,761
1940	6,454
1950	5,977
1960	5,956
1970	5,151
1980	4,715
1990	4,063
2000	3,562
2010	3,685
2014 Estimate	3,812

Entering-1; Larceny-4; Motor Vehicle Theft-1;
Arson-0 • Total Crime Index-7; Crime Rate
per 1,000-1.90

Farms (2012)—532

Land in Farms (2012)—617,812

Major Stream Systems—North Canadian
and Cimarron rivers

Museums or Historic Sites—Harper County
Historical Society Museum, Laverne; Buffalo
Museum, Buffalo

Minerals—oil and gas

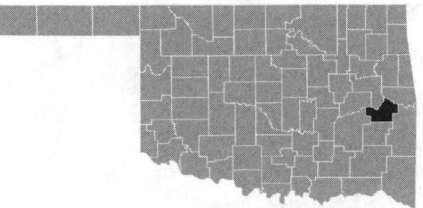

Haskell

Located in eastern Oklahoma, Haskell County was created at statehood and named for Charles N. Haskell, a member of the Oklahoma Constitutional Convention and first governor of Oklahoma.

Haskell County was one of the first permanent Choctaw settlements in the Indian Territory. Many Choctaws arrived by steamboat at Tamaha, and settled there along the Arkansas River. Haskell County was also the site of several skirmishes during the Civil War. The county seat is located at Stigler.

Belle Starr, the bandit queen, frequented the area during the late 1800s. She was reportedly killed near present-day Hoyt.

There is an in-county transit system. Local industries include meat packing, milling, and trucking. Recreational opportunities may be found at the Robert S. Kerr Lake, Sequoyah Wildlife Refuge and the Haskell County Recreation Club. Annual events include Reunion Days during the third week in June, the Christmas Parade on the first Saturday in December, and the Antique Car Show during late October.

Haskell County History: Indian Territory through 1988 is available from the Haskell County Historical Society. For more information, call the county clerk's office at 918/967-2884.

Districts

Congress 2
State Senate 7,
State Rep. 15
District Attorney 18
Court of Appeals 2
Ct. of Crim. Appeals 3
Supreme Ct. Jud. 2
SE Jud. Adm 16

County Officials

Court Clerk	Robin Rea (D)	Keota
Clerk	Karen McClary (D)	Keota
Sheriff	Brian Hale (D)	Stigler
Treasurer	Gale Dixon(D)	Kinta
Assessor	Roger Ballard (D)	Keota
Election Brd. Sec.	Marcia Goff (D)	Stigler
Dist. 1 Comm.	Kenny Short (D)	Keota
Dist. 2 Comm.	Marvin Nolen (D)	Stigler
Dist. 3 Comm.	Paul Storie (D)	Enterprise

Property Valuations

	2013–2014 Assessment	2014–2015 Assessment	Increase or Decrease
Real Estate and Improvement	$36,292,655	$37,385,230	$1,092,575
Personal Subject to Tax	$12,356,495	$13,143,820	$787,325
Total Locally Assessed	$48,649,150	$50,529,050	$1,879,900
Homestead Exemptions Allowed	$3,848,180	$3,894,475	$46,295
Net Assessed Locally	$44,800,970	$46,634,575	$1,833,605
Public Service Assessment	$8,684,450	$7,684,414	($1,000,036)
Net Assessed Valuation	$53,485,420	$54,318,989	$833,569

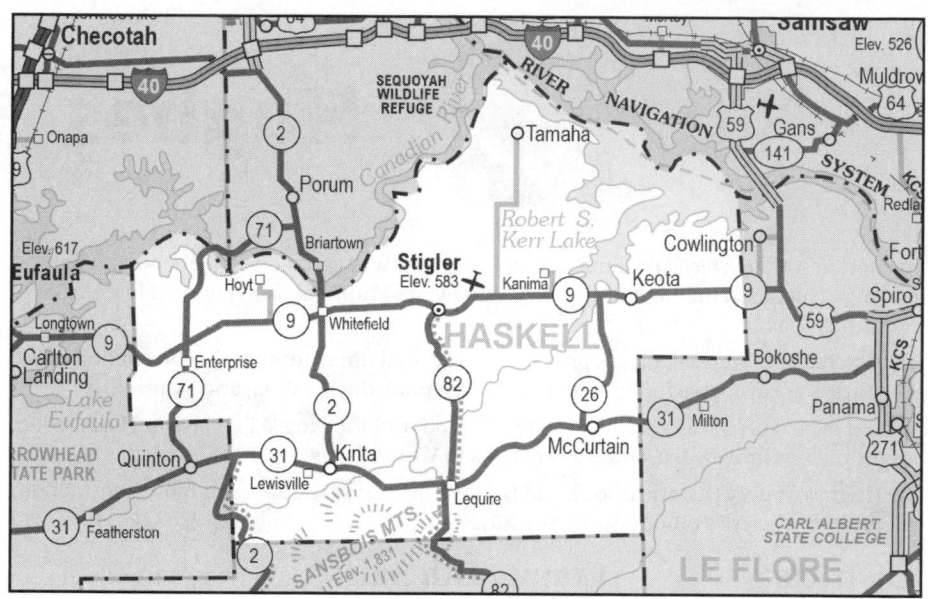

County Seat—Stigler (Pop. 2,764) 2013 Estimate

Area (Land & Water)—625.27 square miles

Per Capita Income (2013)—$33,804 (Ranks 50th of 77 counties)

Population Statistics (2013)—Female-6,511; Male-6,338; Ethnicity—Wh.-10,720; Bl.-131; Am. Ind.-2,916; As.-103; Other-218; Pacific Is.-7; Two or more races-1,240; Hisp.-454

Births (2014)—168 • **Deaths** (2014)—130

Marriages (2013)—87 • **Divorces** (2013)—73

Unemployment Rate (2013)—7.2%

Labor Force (2013)—5,533

Number of Establishments (2013)—225

Number of Manufacturers (2013)—8

Public Assistance Payments (FY2014) Total—$11,522,444 • TANF—$249,366 • Supplements—Aged-$36,401; Blind-$1,250; Disabled-$196,969

Vehicle Registration (2014)—Automobiles-8,387; Farm Trucks-1,536; Comm. Trucks, Tractors, Trailers-655; Motor Homes and Travel Trailers-405; Motorcycles-295; Manufactured Homes-8; Tax Exempt Licenses-386; Boats-557

Crime Incidents (2013)—Murder-2; Rape-2; Robbery-0; Felony Assault-21; Breaking and Entering-43; Larceny-135; Motor Vehicle Theft-21; Arson-2 • Total Crime Index-224; Crime Rate per 1,000-17.15

Farms (2012)—864

Land in Farms (2012)—256,026

Major Lakes—Eufaula, Webbers Falls, Robert S. Kerr lakes

Major Stream Systems—Tributaries of Arkansas between state line and mouth of Canadian River, and the Poteau River

Minerals—oil and gas, coal

County Population	
1907 (Okla. Terr.)	16,865
1910	18,875
1920	19,397
1930	16,216
1940	17,324
1950	13,313
1960	9,121
1970	9,578
1980	11,010
1990	10,940
2000	11,792
2010	12,769
2014 Estimate	12,896

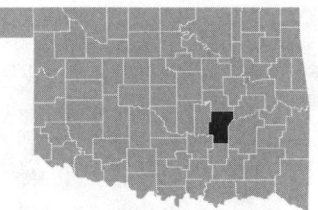

Hughes

Located in southeastern Oklahoma, Hughes County was created at statehood and named for W. C. Hughes, a member of the Oklahoma Constitutional Convention. Holdenville is the county seat.

Holdenville and Wetumka lakes provide recreational opportunities for the county, while other areas are available for hunting deer, dove, quail, duck, rabbit, and squirrel.

Annual events of interest include the IRA Rodeo and the Hog Wild Days in Holdenville, Sorghum Days in Wewoka, and Suckers Days in Wetumka.

The Hughes County Historical Society in Holdenville serves the area. For more information, call the county clerk's office at 405/379-5487.

Districts

Congress..........................2
State Senate................7, 13
State Rep...................18, 24
District Attorney 22
Court of Appeals 3
Ct. of Crim. Appeals........3
Supreme Ct. Jud. 8
S. Cent. Jud. Adm. 22
   (Div. III)

County Officials

Court Clerk	Patty Tilley (D)	Holdenville
Clerk	Joquita Walton (D)	Holdenville
Sheriff	Marcia Maxwell (D)	Holdenville
Treasurer	Dawn Lindsey (D)	Holdenville
Assessor	Jamie Foster (D)	Holdenville
Elect. Brd. Sec.	Brandy Davis (D)	Holdenville
Dist. 1 Comm.	Gary Phillips (D)	Holdenville
Dist. 2 Comm.	Gary Gray (D)	Dustin
Dist. 3 Comm.	Joe Moore (D)	Calvin

Property Valuations

	2013–2014 Assessment	2014–2015 Assessment	Increase or Decrease
Real Estate and Improvement	$47,898,565	$48,733,201	$834,636
Personal Subject to Tax	$43,824,953	$60,549,167	$16,724,214
Total Locally Assessed	$91,723,518	$109,282,368	$17,558,850
Homestead Exemptions Allowed	$3,823,988	$3,752,171	($71,817)
Net Assessed Locally	$87,899,530	$105,530,197	$17,630,667
Public Service Assessment	$33,428,352	$39,708,577	$6,280,225
Net Assessed Valuation	$121,327,882	$145,238,774	$23,910,892

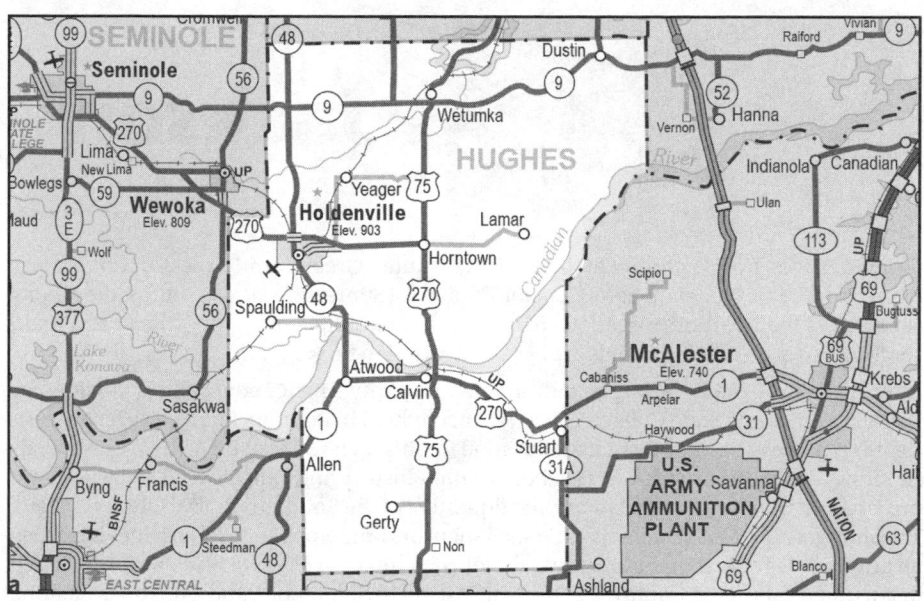

County Population

1907 (Okla. Terr.)	19,945
1910	24,040
1920	26,045
1930	30,334
1940	29,189
1950	20,664
1960	15,144
1970	13,228
1980	14,338
1990	13,023
2000	14,154
2010	14,003
2014 Estimate	13,806

County Seat—Holdenville (Pop. 5,795) 2013 Estimate

Area (Land & Water)—814.64 square miles

Per Capita Income (2013)—$31,747 (Ranks 60th of 77 counties)

Population Statistics (2013)—Female-6,429; Male-7,409; Ethnicity—Wh.-10,427; Bl.-954; Am. Ind.-3,338; As.-18; Other-287; Pacific Is.-4; Two or more races-1,184; Hisp.-551

Births (2014)—143 • **Deaths** (2014)—177

Marriages (2013)—84 • **Divorces** (2013)—47

Unemployment Rate (2013)—8.2%

Labor Force (2013)—5,982

Number of Establishments (2013)—226

Number of Manufacturers (2013)—5

Public Assistance Payments (FY2014) Total—$8,517,928 • TANF—$58,105 • Supplements—Aged-$36,063; Blind-$897; Disabled-$135,135

Vehicle Registration (2014)—Automobiles-11,907; Farm Trucks-2,761; Comm. Trucks, Tractors, Trailers-1,324; Motor Homes and Travel Trailers-665; Motorcycles-591; Manufactured Homes-27; Tax Exempt Licenses-56; Boats-536

Crime Incidents (2013)—Murder-2; Rape-2; Robbery-0; Felony Assault-12; Breaking and Entering-31; Larceny-63; Motor Vehicle Theft-21; Arson-6 • Total Crime Index-131; Crime Rate per 1,000-9.56

Farms (2012)—921

Land in Farms (2012)—436,121

Major Stream Systems—Canadian, North Canadian rivers and tributaries to the Little River

Minerals—oil and gas

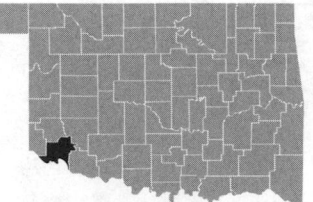

Jackson

Formed in 1907 from a portion of the original disputed Greer County, Jackson County was named for the Confederate hero, General Thomas J. (Stonewall) Jackson. Altus, the county seat, lies in the heart of "irrigation country." Primary crops are cotton, wheat, and grain sorghum. Cattle and greyhounds are bred and raised in this area.

Altus Air Force Base is the largest industry in the county. Higher education is provided by Western Oklahoma State College, a two-year accredited institution. Southwest Technology Center provides vocation-technical education for this region. Museum of the Western Prairie shows life in early southwest Oklahoma. Other history and genealogical collections are preserved at the Altus Public Library, headquarters of the Southern Prairie Library System. The Shortgrass Arts and Humanities Council sponsors numerous cultural activities including an annual arts festival in the fall. Annual events include the Great Plains Stampede Rodeo in late August, Jackson County Fair, the Fall Festival in September, and Christmas Lighting Display the month of December. Recreational opportunities are available fifteen miles north of Altus at Quartz Mountain State Park and Lake Altus-Lugert.

Local historical societies include Jackson County Historical Society and Western Trails Historical Society. For more information, call the Altus Chamber of Commerce at 580/482-0210.

Districts

Congress	3
State Senate	38
State Rep.	52
District Attorney	3
Court of Appeals	4
Ct. of Crim. Appeals	5
Supreme Ct. Jud.	9
SW Jud. Adm.	3

County Officials

Court Clerk	Rhonda Stepanovich (D)	Altus
Clerk	Robin Booker (R)	Altus
Sheriff	Roger Levick (R)	Altus
Treasurer	Renee Howard (R)	Headrick
Assessor	Lisa Roberson (D)	Duke
Election Brd. Sec.	Jennifer Wilson (R)	Blair
Dist. 1 Comm.	Marty R. Clinton (R)	Altus
Dist. 2 Comm.	Kirk Butler (D)	Altus
Dist. 3 Comm.	Cary Carrell (D)	Olustee

Property Valuations

	2013–2014 Assessment	2014–2015 Assessment	Increase or Decrease
Real Estate and Improvement	$108,142,956	$110,392,421	$2,249,465
Personal Subject to Tax	$16,840,852	$16,543,866	($296,986)
Total Locally Assessed	$124,983,808	$126,936,287	$1,952,479
Homestead Exemptions Allowed	$5,840,427	$5,916,332	$75,905
Net Assessed Locally	$119,143,381	$121,019,955	$1,876,574
Public Service Assessment	$12,459,796	$12,467,479	$7,683
Net Assessed Valuation	$131,603,177	$133,487,434	$1,884,257

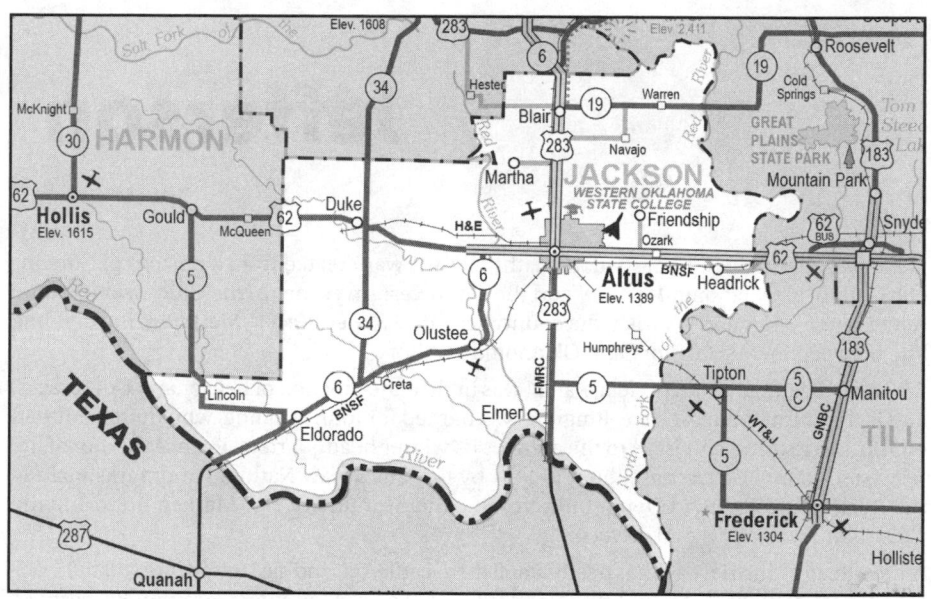

County Seat—Altus (Pop. 19,591) 2013 Estimate

Area (Land & Water)—804.15 square miles

Per Capita Income (2013)—$36,126 (Ranks 39th of 77 counties)

Population Statistics (2013)—Female-13,253; Male-13,027; Ethnicity—Wh.-21,875; Bl.-2,429; Am. Ind.-1,842; As.-460; Other-1,741; Pacific Is.-110; Two or more races-1,976; Hisp.-5,637

Births (2014)—405 • Deaths (2014)—266

Marriages (2013)—178 • Divorces (2013)—137

Unemployment Rate (2013)—5.2%

Labor Force (2013)—11,759

Number of Establishments (2013)—535

Number of Manufacturers (2013)—11

Public Assistance Payments (FY2014) Total—$15,950,498 • TANF—$123,620 • Supplements—Aged-$57,389; Blind-$2,390; Disabled-$256,814

Vehicle Registration (2014)—Automobiles-20,403; Farm Trucks-2,098; Comm. Trucks, Tractors, Trailers-780; Motor Homes and Travel Trailers-653; Motorcycles-1,053; Manufactured Homes-4; Tax Exempt Licenses-185; Boats-420

Institutions of Higher Learning—Western Oklahoma State College, Altus

County Population	
1907 (Okla. Terr.)	17,087
1910	23,737
1920	22,141
1930	28,910
1940	22,708
1950	20,082
1960	29,736
1970	30,902
1980	30,356
1990	28,764
2000	28,439
2010	26,446
2014 Estimate	25,998

Crime Incidents (2013)—Murder-0; Rape-7; Robbery-10; Felony Assault-37; Breaking and Entering-286; Larceny-531; Motor Vehicle Theft-24; Arson-5 • Total Crime Index-895; Crime Rate per 1,000-34.06

Farms (2012)—694

Land in Farms (2012)—478,878

Major Stream Systems—North Fork, Salt Fork and Prairie Dog Town Fork of Red River

Museums or Historic Sites—Museum of the Western Prairie at Altus

Minerals—oil and gas

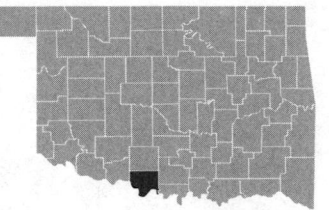

Jefferson

Named for President Thomas Jefferson, this county was created from a portion of Comanche County in Oklahoma Territory and the southwestern corner of the Chickasaw Nation. A marker on S.H. 70 in Waurika, the county seat, designates the 98th Meridian, the dividing line between Indian Territory and Oklahoma Territory.

Waurika, meaning "camp of clear water," was built at the junction of Beaver and Cow creeks, and is the site of Waurika Lake. Ringling was named for John Ringling, who built a railroad on this site to bring his circus to the area for its winter headquarters. Ryan is the site of the Jefferson County Courthouse, built in 1894 by the Chickasaw Nation. Landmarks include the Rock Island Railroad Depot built in 1912, and Monument Hill Marker, honoring the Chisholm Trail and its trail drivers.

Although an industrial base has been established, cattle, oil, and agriculture are still the leading sources of income. Annual events include the Waurika Volunteer Firemen Rattlesnake Hunt, the Waurika Art Show, and the Terral Melon Jubilee.

The Chisholm Trail Historical Association is located in Waurika, and two publications, *A History of Jefferson County* and *Post Offices in Jefferson County*, offer written historical accounts. For more information, call the county clerk's office at 580/228-2029.

Districts

Congress............................4
State Senate..................31
State Rep.......................50
District Attorney............6
Court of Appeals.............4
Ct. of Crim. Appeals........3
Supreme Ct. Jud..............5
SW Jud. Adm. 5
    (Div. II)

County Officials

Court Clerk	Kim Berry (D)	Waurika
Clerk	Traci Smith (D)	Waurika
Sheriff	Michael Bryant (D)	Waurika
Treasurer	Ann Medlinger (D)	Hastings
Assessor	Sandra Watkins (D)	Waurika
Election Brd. Sec.	Tammy Richardson (D)	Waurika
Dist. 1 Comm.	Billy Kidd (D)	Addington
Dist. 2 Comm.	Ty Phillips (D)	Ringling
Dist. 3 Comm.	Ricky Martin (D)	Terral

Property Valuations

	2013–2014 Assessment	2014–2015 Assessment	Increase or Decrease
Real Estate and Improvement	$22,278,657	$23,192,886	$914,229
Personal Subject to Tax	$2,763,967	$2,934,734	$170,767
Total Locally Assessed	$25,042,624	$26,127,620	$1,084,996
Homestead Exemptions Allowed	$1,522,708	$1,493,358	($29,350)
Net Assessed Locally	$23,519,916	$24,634,262	$1,114,346
Public Service Assessment	$10,777,930	$12,246,888	$1,468,958
Net Assessed Valuation	$34,297,846	$36,881,150	$2,583,304

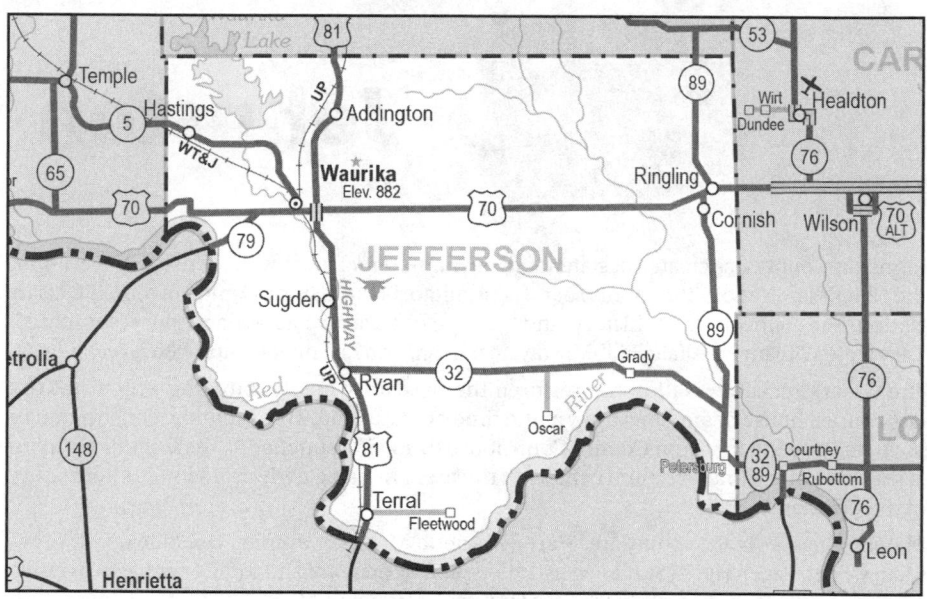

County Population

1907 (Okla. Terr.)	13,439
1910	17,430
1920	17,664
1930	17,392
1940	15,107
1950	11,122
1960	8,192
1970	7,125
1980	8,294
1990	7,010
2000	6,818
2010	6,472
2014 Estimate	6,292

County Seat—Waurika (Pop. 2,043) 2013 Estimate

Area (Land & Water)—773.83 square miles

Per Capita Income (2013)—$28,323 (Ranks 75th of 77 counties)

Population Statistics (2013)—Female-3,199; Male-3,258; Ethnicity—Wh.-5,732; Bl.-59; Am. Ind.-730; As.-20; Other-249; Pacific Is.-2; Two or more races-319; Hisp.-560

Births (2014)—71 • **Deaths** (2014)—110

Marriages (2013)—35 • **Divorces** (2013)—30

Unemployment Rate (2013)—6.0%

Labor Force (2013)—2,336

Number of Establishments (2013)—105

Number of Manufacturers (2013)—6

Public Assistance Payments
(FY2014) Total—$4,319,433 • TANF-- $66,107 • Supplements—Aged-$21,587; Blind-$101; Disabled-$97,197

Vehicle Registration (2014)— Automobiles-3,509; Farm Trucks-863; Comm. Trucks, Tractors, Trailers-93; Motor Homes and Travel Trailers-154; Motorcycles-156; Manufactured Homes-2; Tax Exempt Licenses-17; Boats-105

Crime Incidents (2013)—Murder-0; Rape-1; Robbery-1; Felony Assault-6; Breaking and Entering-17; Larceny-45; Motor Vehicle Theft-5; Arson-2 • Total Crime Index-75; Crime Rate per 1,000-11.75

Farms (2012)—417

Land in Farms (2012)—475,462

Major Lake—Waurika

Major Stream Systems—Mud and Beaver creeks and tributaries to Red River

Museums or Historic Sites—Chisholm Trail Museum at Waurika; Rock Island Depot, Waurika

Minerals—oil and gas

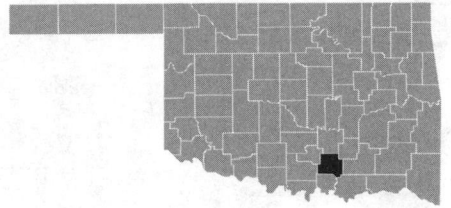

Johnston

Johnston County was created at statehood and named for Douglas H. Johnston, governor of the Chickasaw Nation. The county seat, Tishomingo, is the historic Capitol of the Chickasaw Nation. The county is rich in history, and the state has had two governors from Tishomingo. They were William H. "Alfalfa Bill" Murray, 1931–1935, and his son Johnston Murray, 1951–1955.

The Great Chickasaw Nation has restored the two-story granite building which was the last council house of the Chickasaw at the time of statehood. That building, constructed in 1898, became the Johnston County Courthouse following statehood. The Capitol Building is now one of the finest cultural centers of the area, housing early artifacts and the history of the Chickasaw Nation.

Major industries in the county are: Martin Marietta Material, Unimin, U.S. Silica, TXI, Tape-Matics, Scott Pet Products, Sundowner Trailers, and agriculture and cattle operations. Wildlife and recreational areas include the Tishomingo National Wildlife Refuge, The Federal Fish Hatchery and Catfish Research Center near Reagan, and the Blue River Public Hunting and Fishing area. *Johnston County History* and other books by the Johnston County Historical Society document the history of the area. For additional information, call the county clerk at 580/371-3184.

Districts

Congress..........................2
State Senate.............. 6, 14
State Rep........................22
District Attorney 20
Court of Appeals 3
Ct. of Crim. Appeals........3
Supreme Ct. Jud. 2
S. Cent. Jud. Adm. 20
   (Div. II)

County Officials

Court Clerk	Cassandra Slover (D)	Tishomingo
Clerk	Kathy Ross (D)	Tishomingo
Sheriff	Jon Smith (D)	Ravia
Treasurer	Rana Gilpin Smith (D)	Tishomingo
Assessor	Guyla Hart (D)	Tishomingo
Election Brd. Sec.	Janis Stewart (D)	Tishomingo
Dist. 1 Comm.	Roy Wayne Blevins (D)	Connerville
Dist. 2 Comm.	Mike Thompson (D)	Wapanucka
Dist. 3 Comm.	Melvin Farmer (D)	Mill Creek

Property Valuations

	2013–2014 Assessment	2014–2015 Assessment	Increase or Decrease
Real Estate and Improvement	$35,429,676	$36,216,818	$787,142
Personal Subject to Tax	$23,454,010	$20,051,683	($3,402,327)
Total Locally Assessed	$58,883,686	$56,268,501	($2,615,185)
Homestead Exemptions Allowed	$3,107,275	$3,091,931	($15,344)
Net Assessed Locally	$55,776,411	$53,176,570	($2,599,841)
Public Service Assessment	$15,205,166	$22,120,083	$6,914,017
Net Assessed Valuation	$70,981,577	$75,296,653	$4,315,076

County Seat—Tishomingo (Pop. 3,068) 2013 Estimate

Area (Land & Water)—658.29 square miles

Per Capita Income (2013)—$32,619 (Ranks 57th of 77 counties)

Population Statistics (2013)—Female-5,623; Male-5,359; Ethnicity—Wh.-9,862; Bl.-324; Am. Ind.-2,462; As.-52; Other-277; Pacific Is.-0; Two or more races-1,966; Hisp.-450

Births (2014)—141 • **Deaths** (2014)—127

Marriages (2013)—65 • **Divorces** (2013)—53

Unemployment Rate (2013)—6.1%

Labor Force (2013)—4,802

Number of Establishments (2013)—180

Number of Manufacturers (2013)—9

Public Assistance Payments (FY2014) Total—$7,063,606 • TANF—$36,446 • Supplements—Aged-$31,519; Blind-$247; Disabled-$153,991

Vehicle Registration (2014)—Automobiles-7,370; Farm Trucks-1,481; Comm. Trucks, Tractors, Trailers-233; Motor Homes and Travel Trailers-423; Motorcycles-353; Manufactured Homes-6; Tax Exempt Licenses-105; Boats-288

Institutions of Higher Learning—Murray State College, Tishomingo

Crime Incidents (2013)—Murder-0; Rape-2; Robbery-0; Felony Assault-49; Breaking

and Entering-23; Larceny-49; Motor Vehicle Theft-5; Arson-3 • Total Crime Index-128; Crime Rate per 1,000-11.58

Farms (2012)—645

Land in Farms (2012)—283,645

Major Lake—Texoma

Major Stream Systems—Washita and Blue rivers and tributaries to Muddy Boggy Creek

Museums or Historic Sites—Chickasaw Council House, and the Chickasaw National Bank Museum, Tishomingo

Minerals—sand and stone

County Population	
1907 (Okla. Terr.)	18,672
1910	16,734
1920	20,125
1930	13,082
1940	15,960
1950	10,608
1960	8,517
1970	7,870
1980	10,356
1990	10,032
2000	10,513
2010	10,957
2014 Estimate	11,103

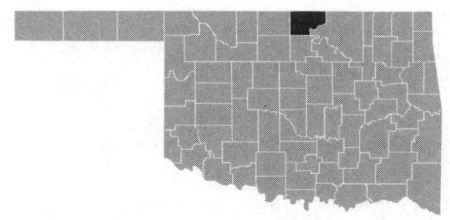

Kay

Located in north central Oklahoma bordering Kansas, Kay County was formed from the "Cherokee Strip" or "Cherokee Outlet." Originally designated as county "K," its name means simply that.

Newkirk, the county seat, is home of the Kay County Courthouse, originally built in 1894 and replaced with the current stone courthouse in 1926. The economy of the county is based on petroleum wealth as well as productive agricultural land. Blackwell, the second largest city, is located in the midst of the rich Chikaskia River farmland.

Kaw Dam and Reservoir, part of the $1.2 billion plan for the Arkansas River in Oklahoma and Arkansas, is located in Kay County. Other attractions include the 101 Ranch site, Pioneer Woman Statue and Museum, the Chilocco Indian School, Ponca City Cultural Center and Indian Museum, and the Marland Mansion, all in Ponca City, the county's largest community. Annual events include the Iris Festival in April and the 101 Ranch Rodeo in August.

Kay County was once home to Territorial Governor William M. Jenkins and infamous outlaw Belle Starr. Three history books have been written about the county. They are: *Diamond Jubilee*, *The Last Run*, and *Keepsakes and Yesteryears*. Historical societies are located in Newkirk and Tonkawa. For more info, call the county clerk at 580/362-2537.

Districts

Congress	3
State Senate	10, 19
State Rep.	37, 38
District Attorney	8
Court of Appeals	5
Ct. of Crim. Appeals	2
Supreme Ct. Jud.	1
N. Cent. Jud. Adm.	8

County Officials

Court Clerk	Marilee Thornton (R)	Ponca City
Clerk	Tammy Reese (R)	Nardin
Sheriff	Everett Van Hoesen (R)	Ponca City
Treasurer	Christy Kennedy (D)	Ponca City
Assessor	Susan Keen (D)	Newkirk
Election Brd. Sec.	Cheryl Howard (R)	Tonkawa
Dist. 1 Comm.	Vance Johnson (R)	Ponca City
Dist. 2 Comm.	Jason Shanks(R)	Newkirk
Dist. 3 Comm.	Paul Skidmore (R)	Blackwell

Property Valuations

	2013–2014 Assessment	2014–2015 Assessment	Increase or Decrease
Real Estate and Improvement	$175,578,304	$179,246,233	$3,667,929
Personal Subject to Tax	$149,679,958	$162,732,232	$13,052,274
Total Locally Assessed	$325,258,262	$341,978,465	$16,720,203
Homestead Exemptions Allowed	$10,610,946	$10,460,619	($150,327)
Net Assessed Locally	$314,467,316	$331,517,846	$16,870,530
Public Service Assessment	$52,703,858	$48,550,208	($4,153,650)
Net Assessed Valuation	$367,351,174	$380,068,054	$12,716,880

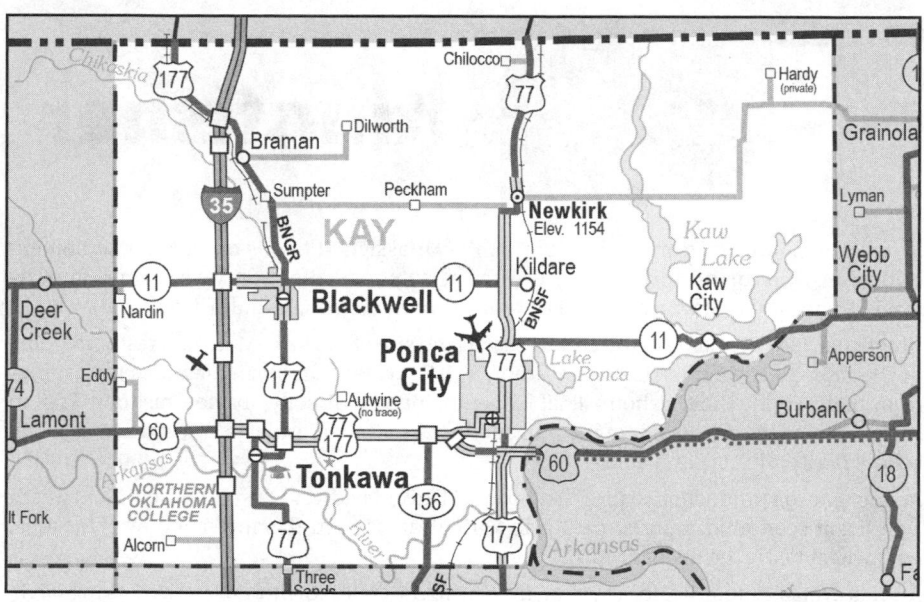

County Seat—Newkirk (Pop. 2,271) 2013 Estimate

Area (Land & Water)—945.12 square miles

Per Capita Income (2013)—$39,146 (Ranks 27th of 77 counties)

Population Statistics (2013)—Female-23,344; Male-22,778; Ethnicity—Wh.-40,021; Bl.-1,340; Am. Ind.-6,317; As.-339; Other-1,409; Pacific Is.-53; Two or more races-3,233; Hisp.-3,113

Births (2014)—590 • **Deaths** (2014)—565

Marriages (2013)—363 • **Divorces** (2013)—215

Unemployment Rate (2013)—6.4%

Labor Force (2013)—22,113

Number of Establishments (2013)—1,129

Number of Manufacturers (2013)—63

Public Assistance Payments
(FY2014) Total—$33,532,701 • TANF—$396,344 • Supplements—Aged-$43,829; Blind-$1,411; Disabled-$403,4537

Vehicle Registration (2014)—
Automobiles-34,645; Farm Trucks-2,986; Comm. Trucks, Tractors, Trailers-2,001; Motor Homes and Travel Trailers 1,741; Motorcycles-1,804; Manufactured Homes-15; Tax Exempt Licenses-109; Boats-2,588

Institutions of Higher Learning—Northern Oklahoma College, Tonkawa

Crime Incidents (2013)—Murder-1; Rape-29; Robbery-22; Felony Assault-137; Breaking and Entering-398; Larceny-1,162; Motor Vehicle Theft-52; Arson-8 • Total Crime Index-1,801;

County Population	
1907 (Okla. Terr.)	24,757
1910	26,999
1920	34,907
1930	50,186
1940	47,084
1950	48,892
1960	51,042
1970	48,791
1980	49,852
1990	48,056
2000	48,080
2010	46,562
2014 Estimate	45,470

Crime Rate per 1,000-39.29

Farms (2012)—993

Land in Farms (2012)—484,179

Major Lake—Kaw

Major Stream Systems—Chikaskia and Arkansas rivers, Salt Fork of the Arkansas, tributaries to the main stem of the Arkansas

Museums or Historic Sites—Top of Oklahoma Historical Society Museum, Blackwell; Newkirk Community Historical Museum; Marland Estate, Pioneer Woman Statue, and Rose Garden Museum, Ponca City; A.D. Buck Museum of Science and History, Tonkawa

Minerals—oil and gas

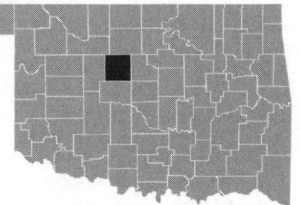

Kingfisher

Kingfisher County was originally a part of the Unassigned Lands opened for settlement during the land run on April 22, 1889. Created at statehood, the county was named for King David Fisher, a settler who operated a trading station on the Chisholm Trail.

Kingfisher, also the name of the county seat, is the site of the Seay Mansion, restored home of Oklahoma's second territorial governor, A. J. Seay. Built in 1892, it features furnishings from that period. The Chisholm Trail Museum, located directly on the Chisholm Trail in Kingfisher, traces the history of the trail and features Indian artifacts, a restored log cabin, school house, church, and bank.

At one time, oil production in the Cashion area, Dover Field, and East Columbia Field was of significant economic importance. Today, agriculture is central to the economy of the area, with wheat being the major crop.

Annual events include living history on the Chisholm Trail with fifty encampments in March, Pat Hennessey Days during late August, PRCA sanctioned rodeo in June, Chisholm Trail Museum Barbecue on April 22, German Fest at Okarche in October, and Kingfisher in Lights at Oklahoma Park opening the Saturday after Thanksgiving and running until December 30. For additional information, call the county clerk's office at 405/375-3887.

Districts

Congress............................3
State Senate..............20, 26
State Rep....................41, 59
District Attorney..............4
Court of Appeals............ 6
Ct. of Crim. Appeals........5
Supreme Ct. Jud..............4
NW Jud. Adm. 4
   (Div. II)

County Officials

Court Clerk	Lisa Markus (R)	Kingfisher
Clerk	Teresa Wood (R)	Hennessey
Sheriff	Dennis L. Banther (D)	Kingfisher
Treasurer	Karen Mueggenborg (R)	Kingfisher
Assessor	Carolyn Mulherin (R)	Kingfisher
Elect. Brd. Sec.	Shawna Butts (R)	Kingfisher
Dist. 1 Comm.	Jeff Moss (R)	Kingfisher
Dist. 2 Comm.	Ray Shimanek (R)	Hennessey
Dist. 3 Comm.	Keith Schroder (R)	Okarche

Property Valuations

	2013–2014 Assessment	2014–2015 Assessment	Increase or Decrease
Real Estate and Improvement	$83,968,554	$88,071,527	$4,102,973
Personal Subject to Tax	$43,383,152	$48,163,848	$4,780,696
Total Locally Assessed	$127,351,706	$136,235,375	$8,883,669
Homestead Exemptions Allowed	$3,168,876	$3,125,416	($43,460)
Net Assessed Locally	$124,182,830	$133,109,959	$8,927,129
Public Service Assessment	$26,605,154	$30,016,477	$3,411,323
Net Assessed Valuation	$150,787,984	$163,126,436	$12,338,452

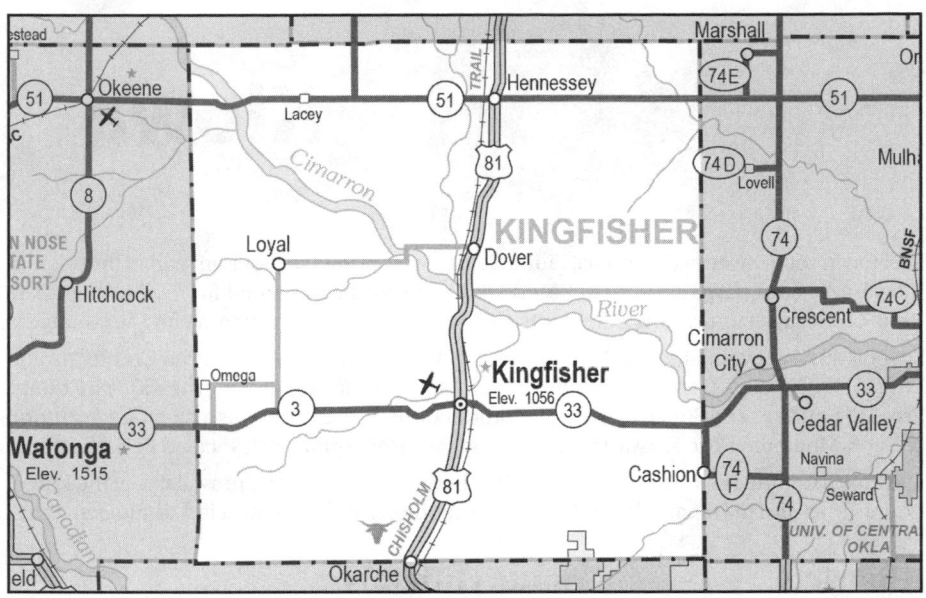

County Seat—Kingfisher (Pop. 4,739) 2013 Estimate

Area (Land & Water)—905.96 square miles

Per Capita Income (2013)—$44,903 (Ranks 13th of 77 counties)

Population Statistics (2013)—Female-7,621; Male-7,448; Ethnicity—Wh.-13,393; Bl.-218; Am. Ind.-811; As.-9; Other-960; Pacific Is.-19; Two or more races-341; Hisp.-2,075

Births (2014)—227 • **Deaths** (2014)—167

Marriages (2013)—116 • **Divorces** (2013)—66

Unemployment Rate (2013)—3.3%

Labor Force (2013)—8,215

Number of Establishments (2013)—476

Number of Manufacturers (2013)—17

Public Assistance Payments (FY2014) Total—$4,706,013 • TANF—$48,815 • Supplements—Aged-$12,031; Blind-$502; Disabled-$40,453

Vehicle Registration (2014)—Automobiles-12,799; Farm Trucks-2,874; Comm. Trucks, Tractors, Trailers-2,426; Motor Homes and Travel Trailers-518; Motorcycles-675; Manufactured Homes-36; Tax Exempt Licenses-44; Boats-428

Crime Incidents (2013)—Murder-0; Rape-2; Robbery-0; Felony Assault-11; Breaking and Entering-52; Larceny-152; Motor Vehicle Theft-13; Arson-1 • Total Crime Index-230; Crime Rate per 1,000-15.07

Farms (2012)—1,021

Land in Farms (2012)—567,621

Major Stream Systems—Cimarron River

Museums or Historic Sites—Chisholm Trail Museum and Governor A.J. Seay Mansion, Kingfisher

Minerals—oil and gas

County Population	
1907 (Okla. Terr.)	18,010
1910	18,825
1920	15,671
1930	15,960
1940	15,617
1950	12,860
1960	10,635
1970	12,857
1980	14,187
1990	13,212
2000	13,926
2010	15,034
2014 Estimate	15,532

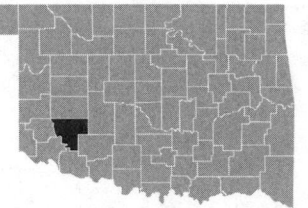

Kiowa

Located in southwestern Oklahoma, Kiowa County was formed in 1901 from part of the original Kiowa-Comanche-Apache Indian Reservation area, and was named for the Kiowa Indian tribe. Cattle, agriculture, and cash crops are the major sources of income for the county.

Special annual events held in Hobart, the county seat, include the Kiowa County Junior Livestock Show, the Arts-Crafts Festival, the Hobart Birthday Celebration, the Kiowa County Free Fair, and several Shortgrass Theater productions. The county was also home to author N. Scott Momaday. The Kiowa Tribal Museum and Headquarters is located in Carnegie.

The Kiowa County Historical Society has published six books, which are available at the Kiowa County Museum in Hobart. For additional information, call the county clerk at 580/726-5286.

Districts

Congress..........................3
State Senate..................38
State Rep............ 52, 55, 56
District Attorney 3
Court of Appeals 6
Ct. of Crim. Appeals........5
Supreme Ct. Jud..............9
SW Jud. Adm 3

County Officials

Court Clerk	Chris Sanders (D)	Hobart
Clerk	Geanea Watson (D)	Hobart
Sheriff	William Lancaster (R)	Roosevelt
Treasurer	Deanna Miller (D)	Hobart
Assessor	Buddy Jones Jr. (D)	Hobart
Election Brd. Sec.	Lynne Morris (D)	Hobart
Dist. 1 Comm.	Tim Binghom (D)	Hobart
Dist. 2 Comm.	Stanley Funkhouser (R)	Hobart
Dist. 3 Comm.	Tom Anderson (D)	Snyder

Property Valuations

	2013–2014 Assessment	2014–2015 Assessment	Increase or Decrease
Real Estate and Improvement	$39,583,585	$40,546,063	$962,478
Personal Subject to Tax	$32,886,336	$28,230,094	($4,656,242)
Total Locally Assessed	$72,469,921	$68,776,1572	$3,693,764
Homestead Exemptions Allowed	$2,567,746	$2,519,942	($47,804)
Net Assessed Locally	$69,902,175	$66,256,215	$3,645,960
Public Service Assessment	$12,465,991	$11,911,315	($554,676)
Net Assessed Valuation	$82,368,166	$78,167,530	($4,200,636)

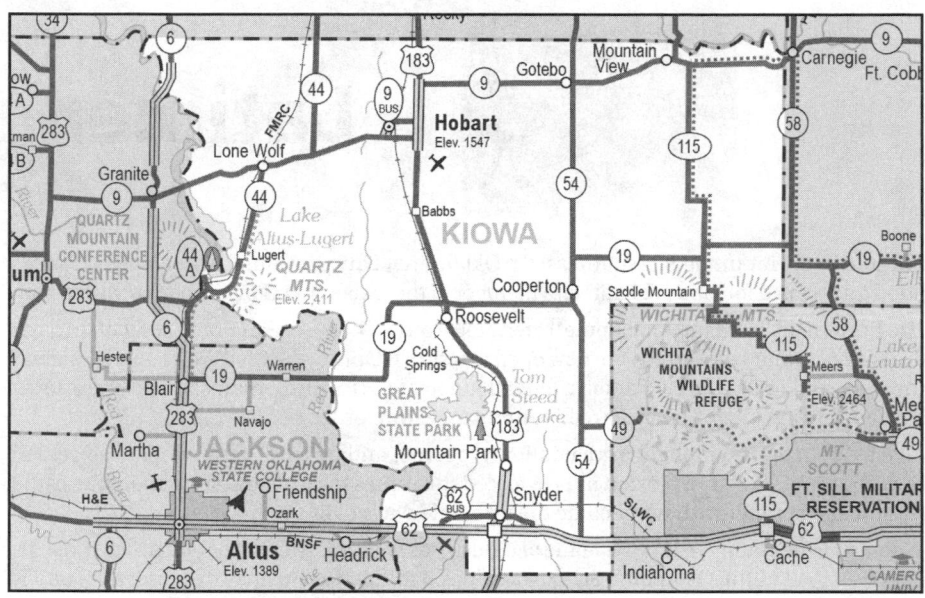

County Seat—Hobart (Pop. 3,705) 2013 Estimate

Area (Land & Water)—1,030.66 square miles

Per Capita Income (2013)—$33,197 (ranks 53rd of 77 counties)

Population Statistics (2013)—Female-4,766; Male-4,603; Ethnicity—Wh.-7,867; Bl.-486; Am. Ind.-861; As.-62; Other-516; Pacific Is.-40; Two or more races-415; Hisp.-885

Births (2014)—127 • **Deaths** (2014)—193

Marriages (2013)—56 • **Divorces** (2013)—42

Unemployment Rate (2013)—5.5%

Labor Force (2013)—3,818

Number of Establishments (2013)—208

Number of Manufacturers (2013)—5

Public Assistance Payments (FY2014) Total—$6,528,828 • TANF—$80,900 • Supplements—Aged-$31,196; Blind-$262; Disabled-$135,167

Vehicle Registration (2014)—Automobiles-6,633; Farm Trucks-1,964; Comm. Trucks, Tractors, Trailers-211; Motor Homes and Travel Trailers-318; Motorcycles-330; Manufactured Homes-7; Tax Exempt Licenses-43; Boats-304

Crime Incidents (2013)—Murder-0; Rape-3; Robbery-1; Felony Assault-6; Breaking and Entering-90; Larceny-94; Motor Vehicle

Theft-10; Arson-4 • Total Crime Index-204; Crime Rate per 1,000-21.90

Farms (2012)—667

Land in Farms (2012)—593,315

Recreation Area—Quartz Mountain State Park

Major Lakes—Altus-Lugert, Tom Steed

Major Stream Systems—North Fork of Red River, Washita River

Museums or Historic Sites—Kiowa County Museum, Hobart

Minerals—oil and gas

County Population	
1907 (Okla. Terr.)	22,247
1910	27,526
1920	23,094
1930	29,630
1940	22,817
1950	18,926
1960	14,825
1970	12,532
1980	12,711
1990	11,347
2000	10,227
2010	9,446
2014 Estimate	9,336

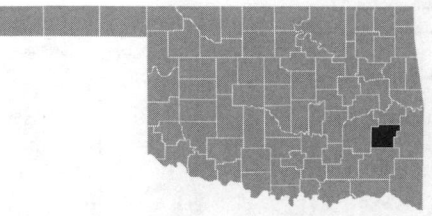

Latimer

Located in the mountains of southeastern Oklahoma, Latimer County was created at statehood and named for James S. Latimer, a member of the Oklahoma Constitutional Convention.

The Butterfield Overland Mail Route, extending from St. Louis to San Francisco, cut through the county at four stops which are now open to visitors. During the Civil War, outlaws roamed the area, and in 1875, Isaac Parker, a federal judge at Fort Smith, Arkansas, became known as the "hanging judge," because of his efforts to restore order.

A coal boom in 1870 brought a great influx of people, and by 1907 many people had settled in Wilburton. A tragic explosion in 1926 forced the mines to close and since that time cattle raising and agriculture have become the principle ways of life.

Wilburton, the county seat, is the home of industry as well as Eastern Oklahoma State College, begun in 1908 as the Oklahoma School of Mines. Latimer County has five reservoirs and is rich in minerals as well as forests, ranch land, and recreational opportunities.

For more county information, call the county clerk's office at 918/465-3543 or the chamber of commerce at 918/465-2759.

Districts

Congress..........................2
State Senate.....................7
State Rep........................ 17
District Attorney 16
Court of Appeals.............3
Ct. of Crim. Appeals........3
Supreme Ct. Jud. 2
SE Jud. Adm...................16

County Officials

Court Clerk	Melinda Brinlee (D)	Wilburton
Clerk	Erin Adams (D)	Wilburton
Sheriff	Jesse James (D)	Wilburton
Treasurer	Delana Moon (D)	Wilburton
Assessor	Chris Church (D)	Wilburton
Elect. Brd. Sec.	Barbara Helmert (D)	Wilburton
Dist. 1 Comm.	Jeremy W. Bullard (D)	Wilburton
Dist. 2 Comm.	John Medders (D)	Buffalo Valley
Dist. 3 Comm.	Roy Alford (D)	Red Oak

Property Valuations

	2013–2014 Assessment	2014–2015 Assessment	Increase or Decrease
Real Estate and Improvement	$22,889,408	$24,789,654	$900,246
Personal Subject to Tax	$22,654,603	$23,682,220	$1,027,617
Total Locally Assessed	$46,544,011	$48,471,674	$1,927,863
Homestead Exemptions Allowed	$2,746,517	$2,685,382	$61,135
Net Assessed Locally	$43,797,494	$45,786,492	$1,988,998
Public Service Assessment	$16,913,479	$12,265,062	($4,648,417)
Net Assessed Valuation	$60,710,973	$58,051,554	($2,659,419)

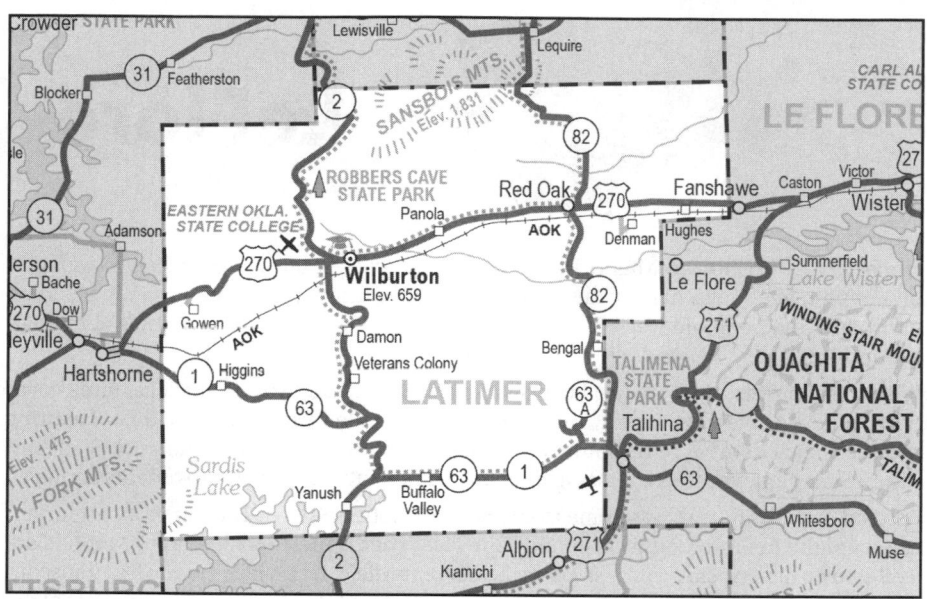

County Seat—Wilburton (Pop. 2,756) 2013 Estimate

Area (Land & Water)—729.12 square miles

Per Capita Income (2013)—$35,704 (Ranks 41st of 77 counties)

Population Statistics (2013)—Female–5,451; Male–5,583; Ethnicity—Wh.–9,268; Bl.–205; Am. Ind.–3,098; As.–58; Other–118; Pacific Is.–0; Two or more races–1,650; Hisp.–327

Births (2014)—125 • **Deaths** (2014)—123

Marriages (2013)—80 • **Divorces** (2013)—63

Unemployment Rate (2013)—9.6%

Labor Force (2013)—4,072

Number of Establishments (2013)—166

Number of Manufacturers (2013)—2

Public Assistance Payments (FY2014) Total—$5,656,583 • TANF—$12,289 • Supplements—Aged–$25,234; Blind–$513; Disabled–$104,323

Vehicle Registration (2014)—Automobiles–6,165; Farm Trucks–1,042; Comm. Trucks, Tractors, Trailers–615; Motor Homes and Travel Trailers–435; Motorcycles–292; Manufactured Homes–7; Tax Exempt Licenses–41; Boats–434

Institutions of Higher Learning—Eastern Oklahoma State College, Wilburton

Crime Incidents (2013)—Murder–0; Rape–2; Robbery–0; Felony Assault–20; Breaking and Entering–33; Larceny–36; Motor Vehicle Theft–6; Arson–2 • Total Crime Index–97; Crime Rate per 1,000–8.80

Farms (2012)—691

Land in Farms (2012)—220,552

Recreation Area—Robber's Cave State Park

Major Stream Systems—Poteau River and tributaries to the Canadian and the main stem of the Arkansas River

Museums or Historic Sites—Lutie Coal Miner's Museum and Robbers Cave Nature Center, Wilburton

Minerals—oil and gas, coal

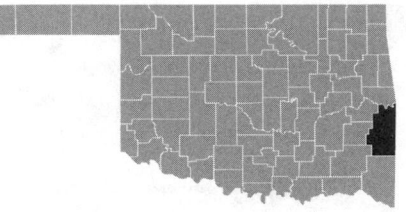

LeFlore

Once part of the Choctaw Nation, Indian Territory, LeFlore County is diverse in its topography. With rugged hills, narrow valleys and productive farmland, there is a gentle blending of modern days and old ways. Many of the towns were established as a result of railroad expansion.

Within its borders there are two hospitals, seven libraries, a two-year college, three vocational schools, five newspapers, a veteran's center, and numerous clinics. Manufacturing produces such items as refrigerator parts, instrument panels, crackers, and cattle feed. Carl Albert State College offers courses to more than 2,000 full and part-time students annually.

Poteau, the county seat, was home to late Senator Robert S. Kerr. Tourism is an important aspect of the LeFlore County economy. The Heavener Runestone and Spiro Mounds are well-known historic sites, as are stops on the old Butterfield Trail. Hailed as the first transcontinental link between East and West, several stops are still found in the northern part of the county. The Ouachita National Forest, including the Talimena Scenic Drive, dominates the southern half of the county. Annual events include the Cavanal Fall Festival and Auto Show in October near Poteau. For more information, call the county clerk's office at 918/647-5738.

Districts

Congress...........................2
State Senate......................4
State Rep............. 3, 5, 15, 17
District Attorney 16
Court of Appeals 3
Ct. of Crim. Appeals........3
Supreme Ct. Jud. 2
SE Jud. Adm................... 16

County Officials

Court Clerk	Melba Hall (D)	Poteau
Clerk	Kelli Ford (D)	Poteau
Sheriff	Rob Seale (D)	Poteau
Treasurer	Joe Wiles (D)	Poteau
Assessor	Brenda Cockburn (D)	Howe
Elect. Brd. Sec.	Sharon Steele (D)	Spiro
Dist. 1 Comm.	Derwin Gist (D)	Spiro
Dist. 2 Comm.	Lance Smith (D)	Monroe
Dist. 3 Comm.	Ceb Scott (D)	Heavener

Property Valuations

	2013–2014 Assessment	2014–2015 Assessment	Increase or Decrease
Real Estate and Improvement	$160,692,220	$164,320,018	$3,627,798
Personal Subject to Tax	$43,710,548	$43,301,105	($409,443)
Total Locally Assessed	$204,402,768	$207,621,123	$3,218,355
Homestead Exemptions Allowed	$13,801,686	$13,795,526	($6,160)
Net Assessed Locally	$190,601,082	$193,825,597	$3,224,515
Public Service Assessment	$34,133,067	$29,139,158	($4,993,909)
Net Assessed Valuation	$224,734,149	$222,964,755	($1,769,394)

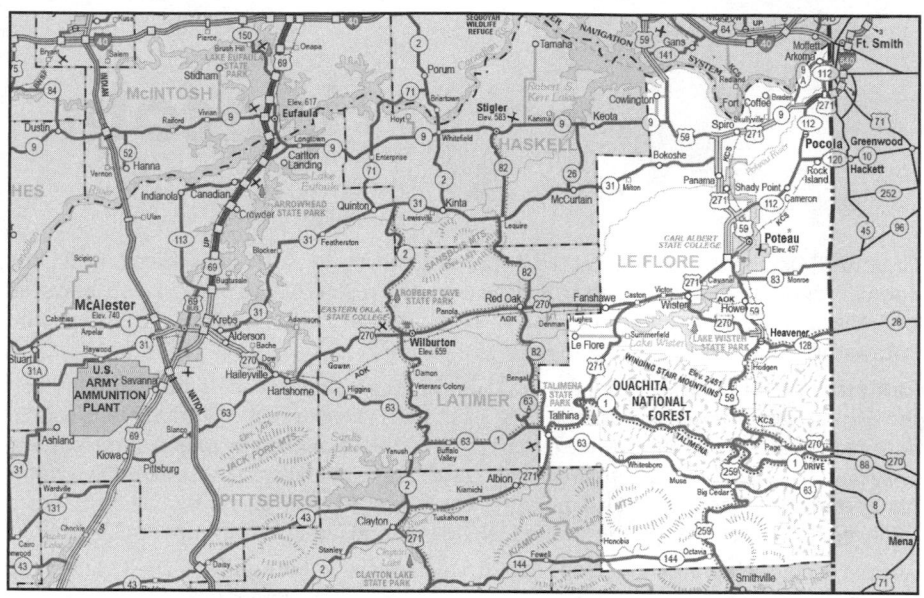

County Seat—Poteau (Pop. 8,590) 2013 Estimate

Area (Land & Water)—1,608.03 square miles

Per Capita Income (2013)—$29,250 (Ranks 73rd of 77 counties)

Population Statistics (2013)—Female-24,863; Male-25,199;
Ethnicity—Wh.-42,241; Bl.-1,405; Am. Ind.-8,702; As.-349;
Other-1,761; Pacific Is.-77; Two or more races-4,433; Hisp.-3,409

Births (2014)—660 • **Deaths** (2014)—553

Marriages (2013)—286 • **Divorces** (2013)—289

Unemployment Rate (2013)—8.8%

Labor Force (2013)—19,781

Number of Establishments (2013)—806

Number of Manufacturers (2013)—29

Public Assistance Payments
(FY2014) Total—$37,261,123 • TANF—
$474,991 • Supplements—Aged-$148,840;
Blind-$3,936; Disabled-$749,721

Vehicle Registration (2014)—
Automobiles-42,724; Farm Trucks-4,113;
Comm. Trucks, Tractors, Trailers-1,250;
Motor Homes and Travel Trailers-2,188;
Motorcycles-1,862; Manufactured Homes-74;
Tax Exempt Licenses-212; Boats-2,023

Institutions of Higher Learning—Carl
Albert State College, Poteau

Crime Incidents (2013)—Murder-1; Rape-6;
Robbery-4; Felony Assault-111; Breaking and
Entering-341; Larceny-729; Motor Vehicle
Theft-83; Arson-9 • Total Crime Index-1,275;

County Population	
1907 (Okla. Terr.)	24,678
1910	29,127
1920	47,765
1930	42,896
1940	45,866
1950	35,276
1960	29,106
1970	32,137
1980	40,698
1990	43,270
2000	48,109
2010	50,384
2014 Estimate	49,761

Crime Rate
per 1,000-25.55

Farms (2012)—1,843

Land in Farms (2012)—395,048

Recreation Area—Heavener Runestone,
Talimena, Wister

Major Lakes—Robert S. Kerr, Wister

Major Stream Systems—Poteau, Kiamichi,
and Arkansas rivers, tributaries to main stem
of Arkansas and Little rivers

Museums or Historic Sites—Runestone
Area, Peter Conser Home, Heavener; Robert S.
Kerr Museum and Caboose Museum, Poteau;
Spiro Mounds Interpretive Center, Spiro

Minerals—oil and gas, coal

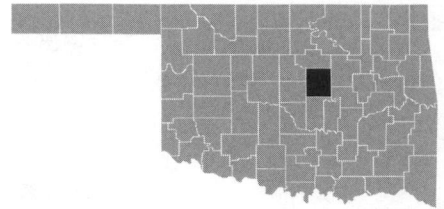

Lincoln

Organized October 1, 1891, and named by popular vote for President Abraham Lincoln, the county was originally a part of the Creek Nation. As a result of the Treaty of 1866, however, the area was ceded by the Creeks and settled by the Sac and Fox, Iowa, Kickapoo, and Potawatomie Indians.

Cattle trails began to appear after the Civil War, and the West Shawnee Trail passed through the area as Texas herds were driven to Kansas. After the Cherokee Commission secured allotment of these lands, they were opened September 22, 1891, with 20,000 homesteaders participating in this land run. Although cotton was the principal crop in the early days, castor beans and broom corn were also money crops. By 1915, oil was discovered near Chandler, followed by the discovery of the Stroud Field in 1923 and later the Davenport oil boom.

Annual county celebrations include an Ice Cream Festival in June and a July 4th Celebration, both in Chandler; Nettie Davenport Day held in Davenport; the International Brick Throwing Contest held in Stroud in July; and the Kolache Festival held in Prague each May. An Indian Summer Arts Festival on the last Saturday in September is held in Chandler.

The Lincoln County Historical Society published *Lincoln County, Oklahoma History*, in 1988. For more information, call the county clerk's office at 405/258-1264 or the Museum of Pioneer History at 405/258-2425.

Districts

Congress	3
State Senate	28
State Rep.	32
District Attorney	23
Court of Appeals	3
Ct. of Crim. Appeals	2
Supreme Ct. Jud.	8
N Cent. Jud. Adm.	23

County Officials

Court Clerk	Cindy Kirby (D)	Chandler
Clerk	Debbie Greenfield (D)	Chandler
Sheriff	Charlie Dougherty (D)	Wellston
Treasurer	Kathy Sherman (D)	Chandler
Assessor	Randy L. Wintz (D)	Stroud
Elect. Brd. Sec.	Melissa Stambaugh (R)	Davenport
Dist. 1 Comm.	Ted O'Donnell (D)	Perkins
Dist. 2 Comm.	Ricky Taylor (D)	Chandler
Dist. 3 Comm.	Lee Doolen (R)	McCloud

Property Valuations

	2013–2014 Assessment	2014–2015 Assessment	Increase or Decrease
Real Estate and Improvement	$106,423,310	$111,208,104	$4,785,794
Personal Subject to Tax	$68,020,946	$87,811,661	$19,790,715
Total Locally Assessed	$ 174,443,256	$199,019,765	$24,576,509
Homestead Exemptions Allowed	$9,431,823	$9,610,502	$178,679
Net Assessed Locally	$165,011,433	$189,409,263	$24,397,830
Public Service Assessment	$78,126,002	$136,822,062	$58,696,060
Net Assessed Valuation	$243,137,435	$325,231,325	$83,093,890

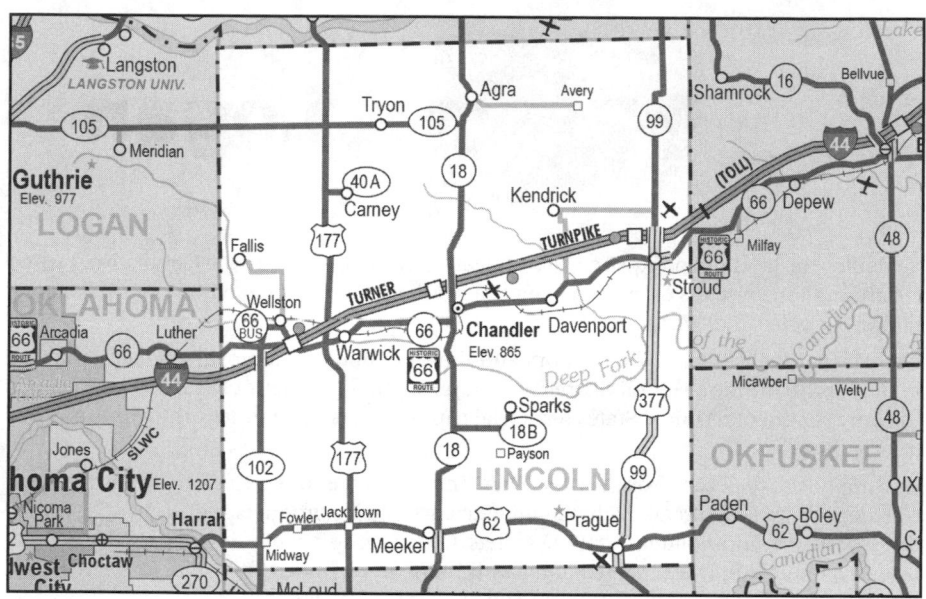

County Seat—Chandler (Pop. 3,126) 2013 Estimate

Area (Land & Water)—965.62 square miles

Per Capita Income (2013)—$33,699 (Ranks 51st of 77 counties)

Population Statistics (2013)—Female-17,268; Male-16,970; Ethnicity—Wh.-30,998; Bl.-784; Am. Ind.-3,641; As.-176; Other-251; Pacific Is.-33; Two or more races-1,622; Hisp.-892

Births (2014)—427 • **Deaths** (2014)—375

Marriages (2013)—195 • **Divorces** (2013)—116

Unemployment Rate (2013)—5.6%

Labor Force (2013)—14,687

Number of Establishments (2013)—571

Number of Manufacturers (2013)—31

Public Assistance Payments
(FY2014) Total—$16,544,728 • TANF— $101,046 • Supplements—Aged-$41,941; Blind-$1,528; Disabled-$260,580

Vehicle Registration (2014)— Automobiles-23,576; Farm Trucks-2,696; Comm. Trucks, Tractors, Trailers-1,822; Motor Homes and Travel Trailers-1,145; Motorcycles-1,196; Manufactured Homes-26; Tax Exempt Licenses-117; Boats-945

Crime Incidents (2013)—Murder-1; Rape-10; Robbery-4; Felony Assault-51; Breaking and Entering-256; Larceny-376; Motor Vehicle Theft-60; Arson-12 • Total Crime Index-758; Crime Rate per 1,000-22.10

Farms (2012)—2,121

Land in Farms (2012)—454,252

Major Stream Systems—Deep Fork, Cimarron, and North Canadian rivers

Museums or Historic Sites—Lincoln County Historical Society of Pioneer History, Chandler

Minerals—oil and gas

County Population	
1907 (Okla. Terr.)	37,293
1910	34,779
1920	35,406
1930	33,738
1940	29,529
1950	22,102
1960	18,783
1970	19,482
1980	26,601
1990	29,216
2000	32,080
2010	34,273
2014 Estimate	34,619

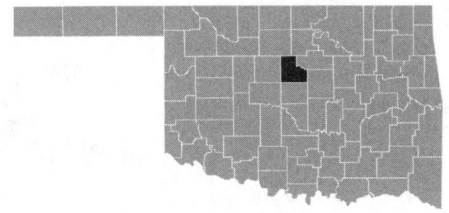

Logan

Settled by the land run on April 22, 1889, Logan County was designated County No. 1 when Oklahoma Territory was organized in 1890. It was later named for Senator John A. Logan of Illinois, popular Civil War general.

Guthrie was the capital of the territory and the state until the removal to Oklahoma City in June 1910. Guthrie's central district is on the National Register of Historic Places and is the only continental United States territorial capital that is substantially the same as it was during the 1890s.

Guthrie has easy access from I-35, S.H. 33, and S.H. 77, and is served by the Burlington Northern Santa Fe Railroad. Light manufacturing includes products such as hydraulic lifts, display islands, and wooden shipping pallets. Community facilities include two municipal lakes for water supply and recreation, a swimming pool, library, hospital, four city parks, three sports areas, two golf courses, and an airport for small planes.

Places of interest include the Oklahoma Territorial Museum, the Scottish Rite Masonic Temple, Pioneer Drugstore Museum, the historic downtown district, and the Lazy E Arena complex, all in Guthrie.

For more information, call the county clerk's office at 405/282-0266.

Districts

Congress	3
State Senate	20
State Rep.	31, 33, 38
District Attorney	9
Court of Appeals	5
Ct. of Crim. Appeals	2
Supreme Ct. Jud.	8
N. Cent. Jud. Adm.	9

County Officials

Court Clerk	ReJeania Zmek (R)	Guthrie
Clerk	Troy L. Cole (R)	Guthrie
Sheriff	Jim Bauman (R)	Guthrie
Treasurer	Sherri Longnecker (R)	Guthrie
Assessor	Tisha Hampton (R)	Guthrie
Elect. Brd. Sec.	Erin Dorio (D)	Guthrie
Dist. 1 Comm.	Mark Sharpton (R)	Guthrie
Dist. 2 Comm.	Mike Pearson (R)	Guthrie
Dist. 3 Comm.	Monty Piearcy (R)	Crescent

Property Valuations

	2013–2014 Assessment	2014–2015 Assessment	Increase or Decrease
Real Estate and Improvement	$241,005,943	$233,452,816	$7,553,127
Personal Subject to Tax	$38,539,481	$43,361,715	$4,822,234
Total Locally Assessed	$279,545,424	$276,814,531	($2,730,893)
Homestead Exemptions Allowed	$11,075,510	$11,091,113	$15,603
Net Assessed Locally	$268,469,914	$265,723,418	($2,746,496)
Public Service Assessment	$40,043,557	$50,231,682	$10,188,125
Net Assessed Valuation	$308,513,471	$315,955,100	$7,441,629

County Seat—Guthrie (Pop. 10,908) 2013 Estimate

Area (Land & Water)—748.92 square miles

Per Capita Income (2013)—$42,944 (Ranks 17th of 77 counties)

Population Statistics (2013)—Female-21,576; Male-21,295;
Ethnicity—Wh.-36,763; Bl.-4,363; Am. Ind.-2,701; As.-335;
Other-477; Pacific Is.-5; Two or more races-1,670; Hisp.-2,276

Births (2014)—505 • Deaths (2014)—348

Marriages (2013)—247 • Divorces (2013)—138

Unemployment Rate (2013)—4.9%

Labor Force (2013)—20,222

Number of Establishments (2013)—786

Number of Manufacturers (2013)—25

Public Assistance Payments
(FY2014) Total—$18,972,977 • TANF—
$113,573 • Supplements—Aged-$42,142;
Blind-$3,754; Disabled-$281,200

Vehicle Registration (2014)—
Automobiles-33,047; Farm Trucks-1,809;
Comm. Trucks, Tractors, Trailers-2,523;
Motor Homes and Travel Trailers-1,124;
Motorcycles-1,637; Manufactured Homes-45;
Tax Exempt Licenses-81; Boats-1,121

Institutions of Higher Learning—Langston
University, Langston

Crime Incidents (2013)—Murder-2; Rape-5;
Robbery-4; Felony Assault-44; Breaking and

County Population	
1907 (Okla. Terr.)	30,711
1910	31,740
1920	27,550
1930	25,761
1940	25,245
1950	22,170
1960	18,662
1970	19,645
1980	26,881
1990	29,011
2000	33,924
2010	41,848
2014 Estimate	45,276

Entering-284; Larceny-441; Motor Vehicle
Theft-27; Arson-5 • Total Crime Index-820;
Crime Rate per 1,000-18.55

Farms (2012)—1,023

Land in Farms (2012)—367,361

Major Stream Systems—Cimarron and Deep
Fork rivers

Museums or Historic Sites— Oklahoma
Territorial Museum Scottish Rite Temple,
State Capital Publishing Museum, Pioneer
Drugstore Museum, Olds House Museum,
National Lighter Museum, Guthrie

Minerals—oil and gas

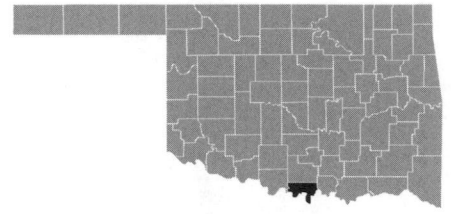

Love

Originally a part of Pickens County, Chickasaw Nation, Love County was named in honor of Overton Love, a prominent judge of the Chickasaws and landowner after the Civil War.

The county seat, according to some, was named Marietta by its first postmaster, Jerry C. Washington, for his wife, Mary, and his sister, Etta. Others contend the town was named for Marietta, Pennsylvania. The county courthouse, built in 1910, was the first courthouse built in Oklahoma after statehood.

Marietta is served by I-35, S.H. 32, and S.H. 77, and the Burlington Northern Santa Fe Railroad. Industries include Oktex Baking, Marietta Sportswear, Robertson Hams, Rapistan Systems, Earth Energy Systems, Dollar Tree, InnovationOne, and the Joe Brown Company. Texaco, Chevron, and Cimarron Transmission manufacture propane, butane, and natural gas. The *Marietta Monitor*, a weekly newspaper, has been owned and operated by the same family since 1896. Thackerville is home to the Windstar World Casino and Hotel, as well as the Windstar Golf Course.

Several famous horse ranches and cattle ranches are located in the county. The largest early-day ranch was operated by William E. Washington. Agricultural products include pecans, grains, hay, peanuts, and watermelons, while sheep and hogs are also raised.

Love County annually celebrates Frontier Days on the first Friday and Saturday of June. For more information, call the county clerk's office at 580/276-3059.

Districts

Congress..........................4
State Senate...................14
State Rep........................49
District Attorney 20
Court of Appeals.............3
Ct. of Crim. Appeals........3
Supreme Ct. Jud..............5
S. Cent. Jud. Adm. 20
  (Div. II)

County Officials

Court Clerk	Kim Jackson (D)	Courtney
Clerk	Shelly K. Russell (D)	Thackerville
Sheriff	Joe Russell (D)	Leon
Treasurer	Lorry Silley (D)	Marietta
Assessor	Cathy Carlile (D)	Marietta
Elect. Brd. Sec.	Cleta Willis (D)	Marietta
Dist. 1 Comm.	Jerry McGill (D)	Marietta
Dist. 2 Comm.	Linda Hyman (D)	Leon
Dist. 3 Comm.	Herschel Bub Perry (D)	Marietta

Property Valuations

	2013–2014 Assessment	2014–2015 Assessment	Increase or Decrease
Real Estate and Improvement	$49,402,317	$60,415,939	$11,013,622
Personal Subject to Tax	$12,272,711	$19,473,013	$7,200,302
Total Locally Assessed	$61,675,028	$79,888,952	$18,213,924
Homestead Exemptions Allowed	$2,672,142	$2,643,579	($28,563)
Net Assessed Locally	$59,002,886	$77,245,373	$18,242,487
Public Service Assessment	$5,916,252	$6,173,045	$256,793
Net Assessed Valuation	$64,919,138	$83,418,418	$18,499,280

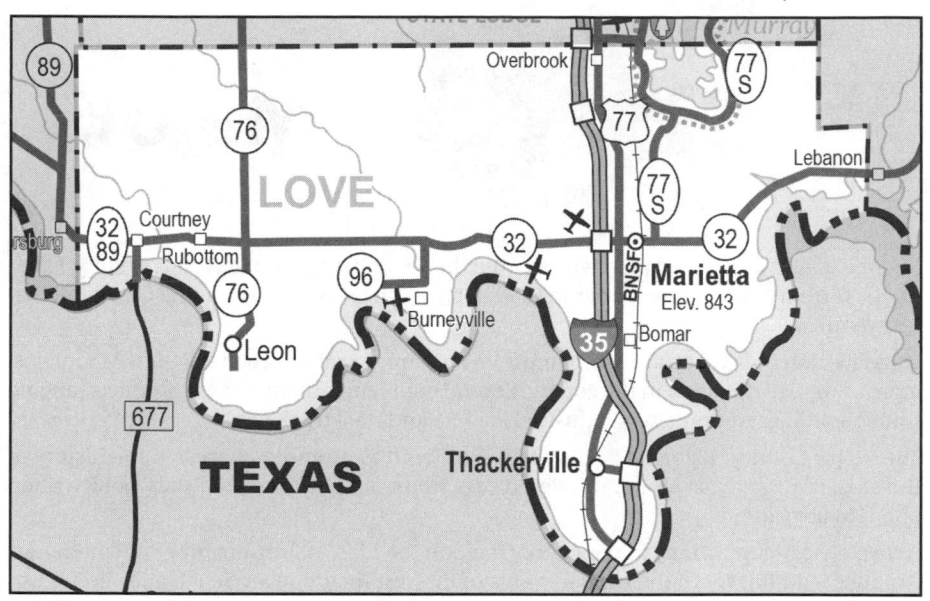

County Seat—Marietta (Pop. 2,706) 2013 Estimate

Area (Land & Water)—531.94 square miles

Per Capita Income (2013)—$42,383 (Ranks 18th of 77 counties)

Population Statistics (2013)—Female-4,827; Male-4,669; Ethnicity—Wh.-8,476; Bl.-255; Am. Ind.-967; As.-52; Other-135; Pacific Is.-8; Two or more races-388; Hisp.-1,216

Births (2014)—111 • **Deaths** (2014)—108

Marriages (2013)—155 • **Divorces** (2013)—49

Unemployment Rate (2013)—4.2%

Labor Force (2013)—5,972

Number of Establishments (2013)—157

Number of Manufacturers (2013)—5

Public Assistance Payments (FY2014) Total—$4,672,683 • TANF—$53,702 • Supplements—Aged-$21,998; Blind-$0; Disabled-$79,691

Vehicle Registration (2014)—Automobiles-11,587; Farm Trucks-893; Comm. Trucks, Tractors, Trailers-2,395; Motor Homes and Travel Trailers-465; Motorcycles-458; Manufactured Homes-23; Tax Exempt Licenses-45; Boats-353

Crime Incidents (2013)—Murder-3; Rape-1; Robbery-1; Felony Assault-12; Breaking and Entering-55; Larceny-98; Motor Vehicle

County Population	
1907 (Okla. Terr.)	11,134
1910	10,236
1920	12,433
1930	9,639
1940	11,433
1950	7,721
1960	5,862
1970	5,637
1980	7,469
1990	8,157
2000	8,831
2010	9,423
2014 Estimate	9,773

Theft-11; Arson-1 • Total Crime Index-181; Crime Rate per 1,000-18.78

Farms (2012)—621

Land in Farms (2012)—219,480

Recreation Area—Murray State Park

Major Lakes—Murray, Texoma

Major Stream Systems—Tributaries to Red River, Walnut Bayou, and Mud Creek

Museums or Historic Sites—Love County Military Museum and Love County Pioneer Museum, Marietta

Minerals—oil and gas

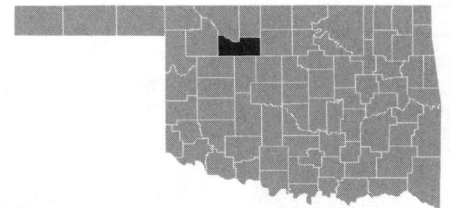

Major

Major County was created at statehood from the southern portion of Woods County, Oklahoma Territory, and named for John C. Major, a member of the Oklahoma Constitutional Convention.

Fairview, the county seat, takes its name from its scenic location east of the Glass Mountains, a major tourist attraction in the county. Several companies manufacture products ranging from oil drilling equipment to industrial loaders and steel truck bodies.

The Major County Historical Society Museum, built to promote interest in the history of the area, is located just east of Fairview. *Glass Mountain Country* is a history book written about Major County.

Active civic organizations in the county include the Lion's Club, chamber of commerce, Ambucs, and Rotary Club. Annual events of interest include Fairview Follies in August, Wranglers Rodeo in July, National John Deere Two Cylinder Show also in July, Major County Fair in September, and an Old Time Threshing Bee also in September.

For more county information, call the county clerk's office at 580/227-4732.

Districts

Congress	3
State Senate	27
State Rep.	58
District Attorney	26
Court of Appeals	6
Ct. of Crim. Appeals	5
Supreme Ct. Jud.	4
NW Jud. Adm.	4
(Div. I)	

County Officials

Court Clerk	Shauna N. Hoffman (R)	Fairview
Clerk	Kathy McClure (R)	Fairview
Sheriff	Steven P. Randolph (R)	Ringwood
Treasurer	Sandra K. Goss (R)	Cleo Springs
Assessor	Donise Rogers (R)	Fairview
Elect. Brd. Sec.	Mary Ann Lynch (D)	Fairview
Dist. 1 Comm.	John A. Haworth (D)	Ringwood
Dist. 2 Comm.	Kelly D. Wahl (R)	Fairview
Dist. 3 Comm.	Travis Rohla (R)	Chester

Property Valuations

	20133–2014 Assessment	2014–2015 Assessment	Increase or Decrease
Real Estate and Improvement	$43,287,266	$45,544,699	$2,257,433
Personal Subject to Tax	$36,928,780	$39,407,070	$2,478,290
Total Locally Assessed	$80,216,046	$84,951,769	$4,735,723
Homestead Exemptions Allowed	$2,107,962	$2,092,005	($15,957)
Net Assessed Locally	$78,108,084	$82,859,764	$4,751,680
Public Service Assessment	$10,264,967	$14,726,113	$4,461,146
Net Assessed Valuation	$88,373,051	$97,585,877	$9,212,826

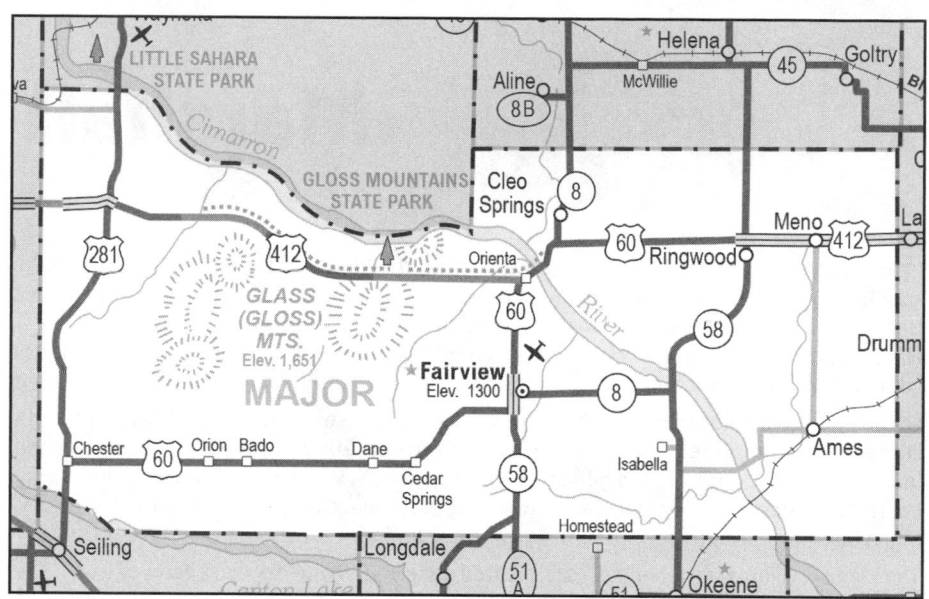

County Seat—Fairview (Pop. 2,635) 2013 Estimate

Area (Land & Water)—580.13 square miles

Per Capita Income (2013)—$44,839 (Ranks 14ᵗʰ of 77 counties)

Population Statistics (2013)—Female-3,772; Male-3,832; Ethnicity—Wh.-7,039; Bl.-53; Am. Ind.-476; As.-5; Other-277; Pacific Is.-0; Two or more races-197; Hisp.-612

Births (2014)—113 • **Deaths** (2014)—82

Marriages (2013)—56 • **Divorces** (2013)—26

Unemployment Rate (2013)—3.2%

Labor Force (2013)—4,459

Number of Establishments (2013)—260

Number of Manufacturers (2013)—6

Public Assistance Payments
(FY2014) Total—$2,668,621 • TANF—$4,792 • Supplements—Aged-$4,549; Blind-$0; Disabled-$34,186

Vehicle Registration (2014)—
Automobiles-7,040; Farm Trucks1,982; Comm. Trucks, Tractors, Trailers-1,080; Motor Homes and Travel Trailers-390; Motorcycles-432; Manufactured Homes-7; Tax Exempt Licenses-51; Boats-244

Crime Incidents (2013)—Murder-0; Rape-2; Robbery-2; Felony Assault-6; Breaking and Entering-46; Larceny-76; Motor Vehicle

County Population	
1907 (Okla. Terr.)	14,307
1910	15,248
1920	12,426
1930	12,206
1940	11,946
1950	10,279
1960	7,808
1970	7,529
1980	8,772
1990	8,055
2000	7,545
2010	7,527
2014 Estimate	7,750

Theft-4; Arson-0 • Total Crime Index-136; Crime Rate per 1,000-17.49

Farms (2012)—901

Land in Farms (2012)—537,111

Recreation Area—Glass Mountain State Park

Major Stream Systems—Cimarron and North Canadian rivers

Museums or Historic Sites—Charles L. Loomis Pioneer Museum, Major County Historical Society Museum at Fairview

Minerals—oil and gas, crushed stone, gypsum

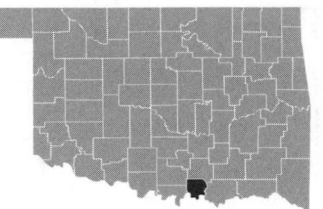

Marshall

Created at statehood from Pickens County in the Chickasaw Nation, Indian Territory, this smallest county in the state was settled by the Chickasaws beginning in 1837 with the removal from their eastern homes. A member of the Oklahoma Constitutional Convention, George A. Henshaw of Madill, succeeded in giving the county his mother's maiden name, Marshall. The county seat, Madill, is named for George A. Madill of St. Louis, an attorney for the railroad.

Oil has played a colorful part in the county's history. Leases along the Red River led to the United States Supreme Court's final decision in the boundary dispute with Texas. Principal industries in the county are: Oklahoma Steel and Wire, W. W. Trailer, Clint Williams–Texoma Peanut Co., Madill Equipment, S & H Trailer, J & I Manufacturing and Contract Manufacturing. Also important are oil, agriculture, livestock, and tourism.

The Denison Dam, completed in 1944, created Lake Texoma with 91,200 acres of water. This lake attracts some 500,000 visitors annually and has made tourism a major industry in the county.

Native son, Raymond D. Gary of Madill, brought the spotlight of attention to the county when he became the fifteenth governor of Oklahoma during the years 1955–1959. For more county information, call the county clerk's office at 580/795-3220.

Districts

Congress...........................2
State Senate....................6
State Rep.........................49
District Attorney 20
Court of Appeals 3
Ct. of Crim. Appeals........3
Supreme Ct. Jud. 2
S. Cent. Jud. Adm. 20
   (Div. II)

County Officials

Court Clerk	Wanda Pearce (D)	Madill
Clerk	Ann Hartin (D)	Madill
Sheriff	Ed Kent (R)	Kingston
Treasurer	Laura Larkin (D)	Madill
Assessor	Debbie Croasdale (D)	Kingston
Elect. Brd. Sec.	LaRue Wilhite (D)	Madill
Dist. 1 Comm.	Don Salty Melton (D)	Madill
Dist. 2 Comm.	Erin Lemons (D)	Kingston
Dist. 3 Comm.	Chris Duroy (D)	Kingston

Property Valuations

	2013–2014 Assessment	2014–2015 Assessment	Increase or Decrease
Real Estate and Improvement	$83,946,125	$86,340,968	$2,394,843
Personal Subject to Tax	$26,064,856	$29,655,304	$3,590,448
Total Locally Assessed	$110,010,981	$115,996,272	$5,985,291
Homestead Exemptions Allowed	$4,174,676	$4,191,484	$16,808
Net Assessed Locally	$105,836,305	$111,804,788	$5,968,483
Public Service Assessment	$7,638,349	$7,222,501	($415,848)
Net Assessed Valuation	$113,474,654	$119,027,289	$5,552,635

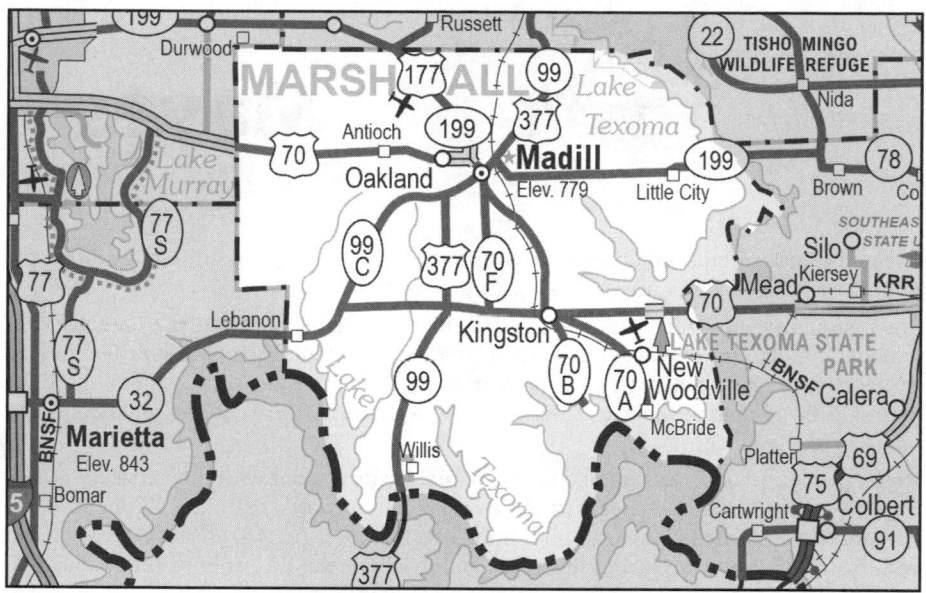

County Seat—Madill (Pop. 3,885) 2013 Estimate

Area (Land & Water)—426.95 square miles

Per Capita Income (2013)—$31,782 (Ranks 59th of 77 counties)

Population Statistics (2013)—Female-8,009; Male-7,851;
Ethnicity—Wh.-11,682; Bl.-237; Am. Ind.-685; As.-19;
Other-1,042; Pacific Is.-0; Two or more races-2,195; Hisp.-2,331

Births (2014)—181 • Deaths (2014)—197

Marriages (2013)—151 • Divorces (2013)—66

Unemployment Rate (2013)—6.0%

Labor Force (2013)—6,870

Number of Establishments (2013)—290

Number of Manufacturers (2013)—21

Public Assistance Payments
(FY2014) Total—$7,471,508 • TANF—
$61,634 • Supplements—Aged-$29,762;
Blind-$1,105; Disabled-$143,475

Vehicle Registration (2014)—
Automobiles- 15,269; Farm Trucks-1,300;
Comm. Trucks, Tractors, Trailers-918;
Motor Homes and Travel Trailers-881;
Motorcycles-808; Manufactured Homes-164;
Tax Exempt Licenses-57; Boats-1,572

Crime Incidents (2013)—Murder-0; Rape-2;
Robbery-1; Felony Assault-18; Breaking and
Entering-55; Larceny-151; Motor Vehicle

County Population	
1907 (Okla. Terr.)	13,144
1910	11,619
1920	14,674
1930	11,026
1940	12,384
1950	8,177
1960	7,263
1970	7,682
1980	10,550
1990	10,829
2000	13,184
2010	15,840
2014 Estimate	16,182

Theft-19; Arson-2 • Total Crime Index-246;
Crime Rate per 1,000-15.32

Farms (2012)—525

Land in Farms (2012)—191,836

Recreation Area—Texoma State Park

Major Lake—Texoma

Major Stream Systems—Tributaries to the
Red and Washita rivers

Museums or Historic Sites—Fort Washita,
11 miles east of Madill

Minerals—oil and gas, crushed stone

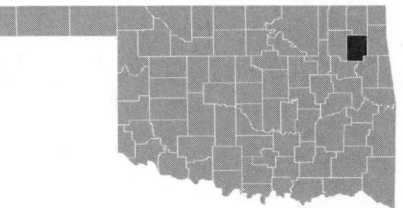

Mayes

Created at statehood from lands lying within the Cherokee Nation, Indian Territory, the county was named for Samuel H. Mayes, Cherokee chief.

The first permanent white settlement in Oklahoma was at Salina where the French established a trading post in 1769. Near Mazie is the site of Union Mission, established in 1820 by a Presbyterian missionary to the Osage Indians. The important Texas Trail followed the Grand River through the county, entering the state at the northeast corner and continuing south to the Red River.

Pryor, the county seat, was named for Nathaniel Pryor, a scout with the Lewis and Clark expedition who settled at Pryor's Creek, an Osage trading post a few miles southeast of the present town. Located forty-four miles from Tulsa, Pryor is on U.S. 69 and S.H. 20, and is twenty miles from the Arkansas River Navigation Channel. Mid-America Industrial Park, the largest in the state, has more than 7,000 acres of industrial real estate and is home to nearly 80 industries.

Industry includes beef production and dairying. Major crops are soybeans, hay, sorghum, wheat, and corn.

The Mayes County Historical Society published *Historical Highlights of Mayes County*.

Districts

Congress..........................2
State Senate..................1, 3
State Rep..................5, 6, 8
District Attorney 12
Court of Appeals.............2
Ct. of Crim. Appeals........1
Supreme Ct. Jud. 7
NE Jud. Adm..................12

County Officials

Court Clerk	Rita Harrison (D)	Pryor
Clerk	Brittney True-Howard (D)	Pryor
Sheriff	Mike Reed (D)	Pryor
Treasurer	Bobbie Martin (D)	Pryor
Assessor	Lisa Melchior (D)	Pryor
Elect. Brd. Sec.	Jill McCullah D)	Pryor
Dist. 1 Comm.	Kevin Whiteside (D)	Adair
Dist. 2 Comm.	Darrell Yoder (D)	Chouteau
Dist. 3 Comm.	Ryan Ball (R)	Salina

Property Valuations

	2013–2014 Assessment	2014–2015 Assessment	Increase or Decrease
Real Estate and Improvement	$203,790,259	$220,947,093	$17,156,834
Personal Subject to Tax	$90,967,746	$144,364,350	$53,396,604
Total Locally Assessed	$294,758,005	$365,311,443	$70,553,438
Homestead Exemptions Allowed	$11,649,772	$11,615,888	($33,884)
Net Assessed Locally	$283,108,233	$353,695,555	$70,587,322
Public Service Assessment	$20,923,495	$19,137,0472	($1,786,448)
Net Assessed Valuation	$304,031,728	$372,832,602	$68,800,874

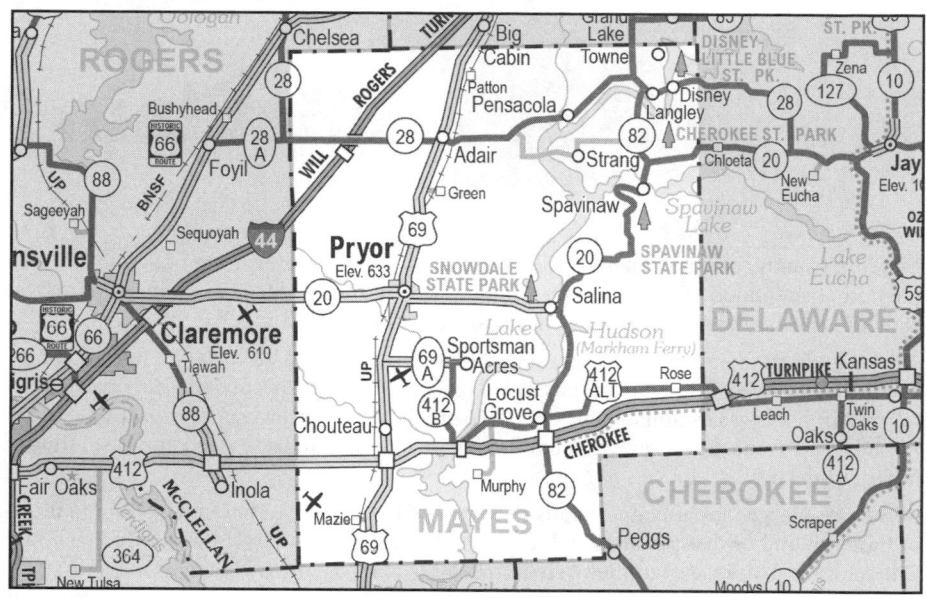

County Seat—Pryor (Pop. 9,469) 2013 Estimate

Area (Land & Water)—683.51 square miles

Per Capita Income (2013)—$31,653 (Ranks 62nd of 77 counties)

Population Statistics (2013)—Female-20,697; Male-20,413; Ethnicity—Wh.-37,237; Bl.-495; Am. Ind.-12,428; As.-201; Other-86; Pacific Is.-41; Two or more races-9,271; Hisp.-1,195

Births (2014)—496 • **Deaths** (2014)—457

Marriages (2013)—232 • **Divorces** (2013)—217

Unemployment Rate (2013)—5.9%

Labor Force (2013)—19,234

Number of Establishments (2013)—799

Number of Manufacturers (2013)—57

Public Assistance Payments
(FY2012) Total—$23,137,325 • TANF—$208,119 • Supplements—Aged-$39,718; Blind-$1,629; Disabled-$494,559

Vehicle Registration (2014)—Automobiles-29,864; Farm Trucks-1,746; Comm. Trucks, Tractors, Trailers-1,549; Motor Homes and Travel Trailers-1,267; Motorcycles-1,590; Manufactured Homes-24; Tax Exempt Licenses-125; Boats-2,549

Crime Incidents (2013)—Murder-0; Rape-13; Robbery-3; Felony Assault-94; Breaking and Entering-190; Larceny-346; Motor Vehicle Theft-55; Arson-8 • Total Crime Index-701 Crime Rate per 1,000-16.97

Farms (2012)—1,551

Land in Farms (2012)—285,102

Major Stream Systems—Grand Lake of the Cherokees, Hudson, Fort Gibson

Museums or Historic Sites—Saline County Courthouse, Rose; Chouteau Memorial, Salina; Coo-Y-Yah Museum, Pryor

Minerals—oil and gas

County Population	
1907 (Okla. Terr.)	11,064
1910	13,596
1920	16,829
1930	17,883
1940	21,668
1950	19,743
1960	20,073
1970	23,302
1980	32,261
1990	33,366
2000	38,369
2010	41,259
2014 Estimate	40,816

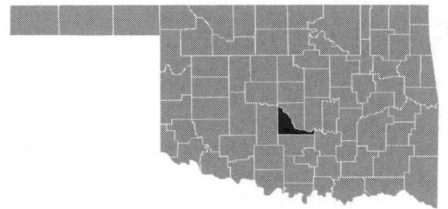

McClain

McClain County, originally part of Curtis County in the proposed state of Sequoyah, was created at statehood. The county was named for Charles M. McClain, a member of the Oklahoma Constitutional Convention and an early resident of Purcell.

Forty-niners on their way to the gold fields of California passed through southern McClain County on the California Trail that paralleled present S.H. 59. To protect travelers going west, Camp Arbuckle was established by the U.S. Army in 1850, northwest of present-day Byars. For health reasons, the camp was abandoned after a year for a site thirty miles southwest in the Arbuckles.

In the 1870s large ranching operations north of the Washita River belonged either to those of Indian blood or those related to Indians by marriage. Black slaves formerly owned by Choctaw and Chickasaw families were also eligible to own land. Cotton gins in many small towns prepared raw cotton for the cotton press in Purcell, the county seat. Broom corn growing was also productive in the 1920s and 1930s.

The McClain County Historical Society has published a three-volume history of the area, and sponsored the Morman microfilming of county records in 1998. For more information, call the county clerk's office at 405/527-3360, or the McClain County Museum at 405/527-5894 weekday afternoons.

Districts

Congress..........................4
State Senate...................43
St. Rep. 20, 42, 51
District Attorney 21
Court of Appeals 4
Ct. of Crim. Appeals........3
Supreme Ct. Jud. 5
S. Cent. Jud. Adm. 21
   (Div. II)

County Officials

Court Clerk	Lynda Baker (D)	Purcell
Clerk	Pam Beller (D)	Washington
Sheriff	Don Hewett (D)	Washington
Treasurer	Teresa Jones (D)	Washington
Assessor	Pam Irwin (D)	Purcell
Elect. Brd. Sec.	Karen Haley (R)	Purcell
Dist. 1 Comm.	Benny McGowen (D)	Wayne
Dist. 2 Comm.	Wilson Lyles (R)	Goldsby
Dist. 3 Comm.	Charles Shorty Foster (D)	Blanchard

Property Valuations

	2013–2014 Assessment	2014–2015 Assessment	Increase or Decrease
Real Estate and Improvement	$176,619,790	$187,103,306	$10,483,516
Personal Subject to Tax	$21,910,659	$23,898,532	$1,987,873
Total Locally Assessed	$198,530,449	$211,001,838	$12,471,389
Homestead Exemptions Allowed	$10,475,522	$10,859,600	$384,078
Net Assessed Locally	$188,054,927	$200,142,238	$12,087,311
Public Service Assessment	$47,445,620	$43,943,823	($3,501,797)
Net Assessed Valuation	$235,500,547	$245,086,061	$8,585,514

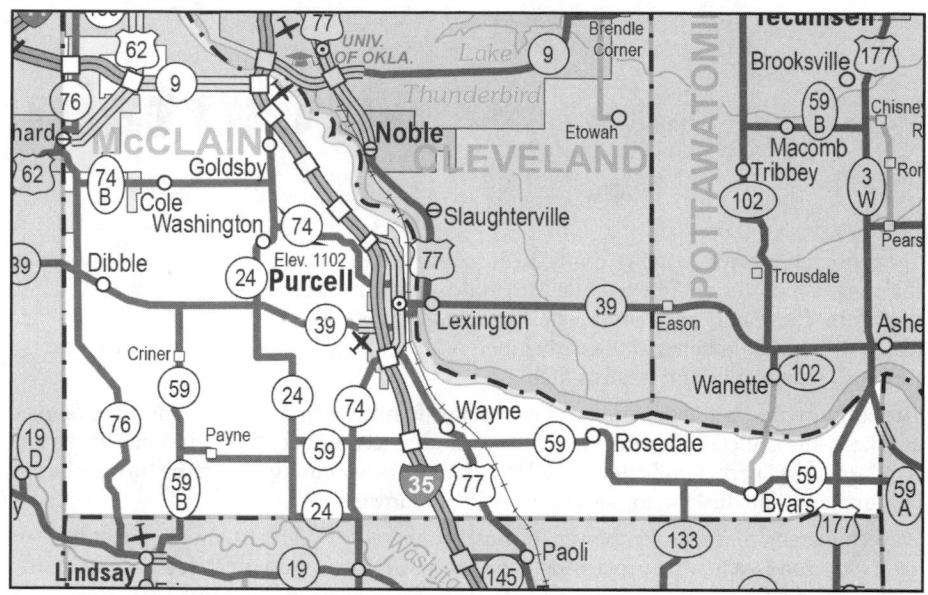

County Seat—Purcell (Pop. 6,339) 2013 Estimate

Area (Land & Water)—580.13 square miles

Per Capita Income (2013)—$47,087 (Ranks 8th of 77 counties)

Population Statistics (2013)—Female-17,696; Male-17,459; Ethnicity—Wh.-31,831; Bl.-396; Am. Ind.-3,742; As.-299; Other-961; Pacific Is.-190; Two or more races-2,251; Hisp.-2,524

Births (2014)—417 • **Deaths** (2014)—336

Marriages (2013)—219 • **Divorces** (2013)—152

Unemployment Rate (2013)—4.8%

Labor Force (2013)—16,347

Number of Establishments (2013)—803

Number of Manufacturers (2013)—24

Public Assistance Payments
(FY2014) Total—$14,951,677 • TANF—$87,263 • Supplements—Aged-$33,360; Blind-$1,004; Disabled-$215,586

Vehicle Registration (2014)—
Automobiles-35,122; Farm Trucks-1,981; Comm. Trucks, Tractors, Trailers-2,618; Motor Homes and Travel Trailers-1,731; Motorcycles-1,873; Manufactured Homes-55; Tax Exempt Licenses-89; Boats-1,544

Crime Incidents (2013)—Murder-0; Rape-8; Robbery-6; Felony Assault-44; Breaking and Entering-364; Larceny-737; Motor Vehicle Theft-94; Arson-8 • Total Crime Index-1,253;

County Population	
1907 (Okla. Terr.)	12,888
1910	15,659
1920	19,326
1930	21,575
1940	19,205
1950	14,681
1960	12,740
1970	14,157
1980	20,291
1990	22,795
2000	27,740
2010	34.506
2014 Estimate	37,313

Crime Rate per 1,000-32.93

Farms (2012)—1,239

Land in Farms (2012) 282,747

Recreation Area—Locust Grove State Park, Saline, Snowdale, Spavinaw, Disney, Cherokee I/II/III.

Major Stream Systems—Grand River, Canadian, and Washita rivers

Museums or Historic Sites—McClain County Historical Museum at Purcell

Minerals—oil and gas, cement, crushed stone, (dimension) clays

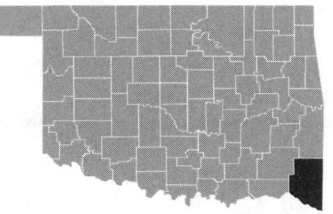

McCurtain

The topography of McCurtain County, in the southeastern corner of Oklahoma, varies from the rugged foothills of the Ouachita Mountains in the north to the fertile coastal plain in the south. The county has a unique heritage ranging from the Caddoan mound builders to the first white settlements in the early nineteenth century, including seventy-five years of Choctaw sovereignty, and finally statehood.

The county name is that of a prominent Choctaw family, several of whose members served as chiefs. The Choctaw period left such historic sites as the Wheelock Mission Church and Academy. The Dierks family developed large holdings beginning before the turn of the 20th century, and sold the land to Weyerhaueser Company in 1969.

Weyerhaueser is the largest employer and has a paper mill in Valliant. Other major employers are Tyson Foods, a poultry processing plant; and SETCO, a company that builds solid tires for heavy equipment and ships worldwide. Tourism is also a major industry with Beavers Bend State Resort, Museum of the Red River, hunting, fishing, and historic sites.

For more information, call the county clerk's office at 580/286-2370.

Districts

Congress..........................2
State Senate.....................5
State Rep..........................1
District Attorney 17
Court of Appeals 3
Ct. of Crim. Appeals........3
Supreme Ct. Jud..............2
SE Jud. Adm................... 17

County Officials

Court Clerk	Vickie Justus (D)	Idabel
Clerk	Karen S. Bryan (D)	Idabel
Sheriff	Scott McLain (D)	Idabel
Treasurer	Linda Laster (D)	Eagletown
Assessor	Stan Lyles (D)	Idabel
Elect. Brd. Sec.	Kelly Donaldson (D)	Idabel
Dist. 1 Comm.	Jim Freeny (D)	Broken Bow
Dist. 2 Comm.	Joe Coffman (D)	Idabel
Dist. 3 Comm.	Jimmy Westbrook (D)	Broken Bow

Property Valuations

	2013–2014 Assessment	2014–2015 Assessment	Increase or Decrease
Real Estate and Improvement	$104,866,377	$108,157,348	$3,290,971
Personal Subject to Tax	$48,934,126	$49,777,114	$842,988
Total Locally Assessed	$153,800,503	$157,934,462	$4,133,959
Homestead Exemptions Allowed	$8,328,702	$8,294,862	($33,840)
Net Assessed Locally	$145,471,801	$149,639,600	$4,167,799
Public Service Assessment	$26,798,250	$27,586,498	$788,248
Net Assessed Valuation	$172,270,051	$177,226,098	$4,956,047

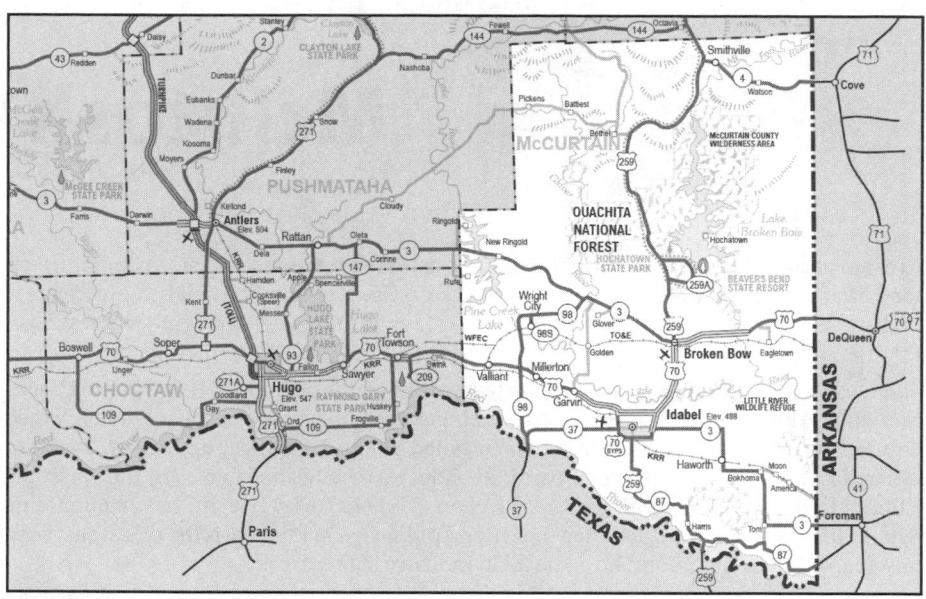

County Seat—Idabel (Pop. 7,007) 2013 Estimate

Area (Land & Water)—1,901.32 square miles

Per Capita Income (2013)—$29,934 (Ranks 69th of 77 counties)

Population Statistics (2013)—Female–17,698; Male–16,275; Ethnicity—Wh.–24,128; Bl.–3,317; Am. Ind.–7,343; As.–42; Other–514; Pacific Is.–6; Two or more races–2,161; Hisp.–1,620

Births (2014)—471 • **Deaths** (2014)—431

Marriages (2013)—234 • **Divorces** (2013)—159

Unemployment Rate (2013)—9.0%

Labor Force (2013)—15,043

Number of Establishments (2013)—573

Number of Manufacturers (2013)—29

Public Assistance Payments
(FY2014) Total—$29,540,519 • TANF—$267,961 • Supplements—Aged–$106,370; Blind–$1,389; Disabled–$567,788

Vehicle Registration (2014)—
Automobiles–26,111; Farm Trucks–3,492; Comm. Trucks, Tractors, Trailers–915; Motor Homes and Travel Trailers–1,758; Motorcycles–874; Manufactured Homes–38; Tax Exempt Licenses–122; Boats–1,786

Crime Incidents (2013)—Murder–1; Rape–8; Robbery–2; Felony Assault–87; Breaking and Entering–301; Larceny–607; Motor Vehicle Theft–39; Arson–13 • Total Crime Index–1,045; Crime Rate per 1,000–31.32

County Population	
1907 (Okla. Terr.)	13,198
1910	20,681
1920	37,905
1930	34,759
1940	41,318
1950	31,588
1960	25,851
1970	28,642
1980	36,151
1990	33,339
2000	34,402
2010	33,151
2014 Estimate	33,050

Farms (2012)—1,577

Land in Farms (2012)—316,606

Recreation Area—Beavers Bend, Hochatown, Pine Creek

Major Lakes—Pine Creek, Broken Bow

Major Stream Systems—Little River, Red River and minor tributaries to the Red River

Museums or Historic Sites—Wheelock Mission, Memorial Indian Museum, Broken Bow; Magnolia Mansion, Museum of the Red River, Forest Heritage Ctr., Barnes-Stevenson House

Minerals—oil and gas, crushed stone

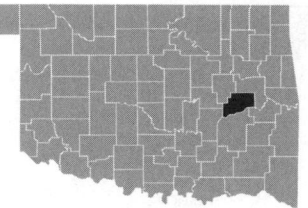

McIntosh

Created at statehood from lands in the southern part of the Cherokee Nation, Indian Territory, McIntosh County was named for a well-known Creek family. The chief physical feature of the county is Lake Eufaula, which is comprised of 105,000 acres and is the largest body of water in Oklahoma.

The county seat, Eufaula, is located thirteen miles south of I-40 on U.S. 69. The Creeks immigrated into the area in 1836 and their influence is seen in names such as Eufaula, which comes from an old Creek town in Alabama called Yufala, "they split up here and went to other places." The Asbury Mission Boarding School was established in 1849 by the Episcopal Church under a contract with the Creek Indian Council. Today it is the Eufaula Boarding School. The *Indian Journal*, founded in 1876 and published in Eufaula, is the oldest surviving newspaper in the state. Tourism is the main industry in this area.

Checotah, established by the KATY railroad station, was named for a principal chief of the Creek Indians, Samuel Checote. The town, once a battleground where the Creek and Little Osage fought, is now a trade center for northern McIntosh and southwest Muskogee counties.

For more county information, call the county clerk's office at 918/689-2741.

Districts

Congress	2
State Senate	8
State Rep.	15, 18
District Attorney	24
Court of Appeals	2
Ct. of Crim. Appeals	3
Supreme Ct. Jud.	2
E. Cent. Jud. Adm.	18

County Officials

Court Clerk	Carie Pittman (D)	Eufaula
Clerk	Ronda Prince (D)	Checotah
Sheriff	Kevin Ledbetter (D)	Checotah
Treasurer	Betty Whisenhunt (D)	Eufaula
Assessor	Trina Williams (D)	Checotah
Elect. Brd. Sec.	Carole Hayes (D)	Checotah
Dist. 1 Comm.	Bill Phillips (D)	Checotah
Dist. 2 Comm.	Tim Pendley (D)	Eufaula
Dist. 3 Comm.	Michael Burns (D)	Eufaula

Property Valuations

	2013–2014 Assessment	2014–2015 Assessment	Increase or Decrease
Real Estate and Improvement	$87,365,685	$91,435,480	$4,069,795
Personal Subject to Tax	$14,322,161	$14,598,669	$276,508
Total Locally Assessed	$101,687,846	$106,034,149	$4,346,303
Homestead Exemptions Allowed	$6,641,308	$7,214,483	$573,175
Net Assessed Locally	$95,046,538	$98,818,666	$3,773,128
Public Service Assessment	$8,931,751	$9,615,933	$684,182
Net Assessed Valuation	$103,978,289	$108,435,599	$4,457,310

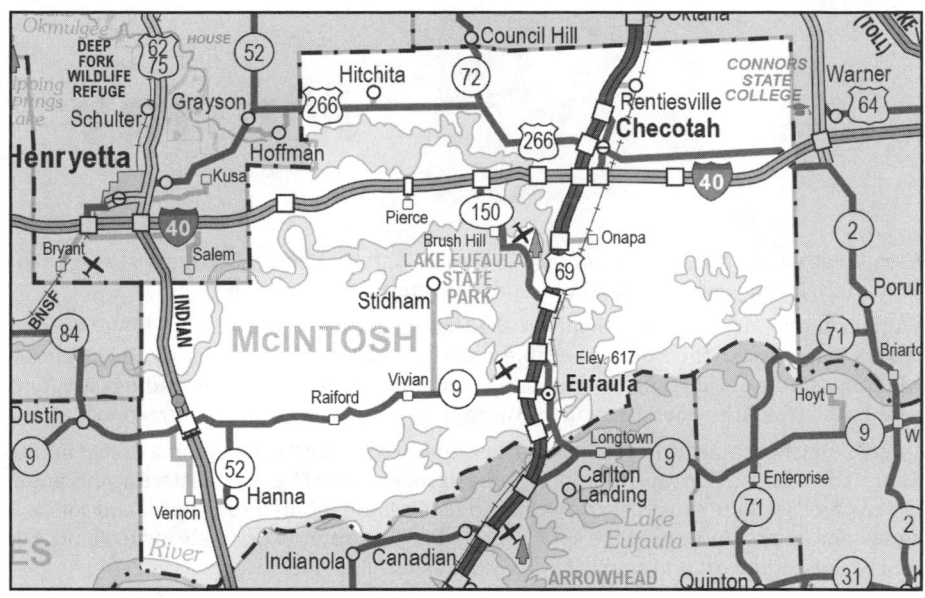

County Seat—Eufaula (Pop. 2,929) 2013 Estimate

Area (Land & Water)—712.48 square miles

Per Capita Income (2013)—$32,116 (Ranks 58th of 77 counties)

Population Statistics (2013)—Female–10,331; Male–10,027; Ethnicity—Wh.–16,439; Bl.–1,010; Am. Ind.–5,129; As.–115; Other–48; Pacific Is.–11; Two or more races–2,238; Hisp.–612

Births (2014)—199 • Deaths (2014)—307

Marriages (2013)—76 • Divorces (2013)—83

Unemployment Rate (2013)—7.8%

Labor Force (2013)—8,946

Number of Establishments (2013)—360

Number of Manufacturers (2013)—16

Public Assistance Payments (FY2014) Total—$14,374,579 • TANF—$92,602 • Supplements—Aged–$44,975; Blind–$1,161; Disabled–$253,699

Vehicle Registration (2014)—Automobiles–18,538; Farm Trucks–1,269; Comm. Trucks, Tractors, Trailers–637; Motor Homes and Travel Trailers–1,032; Motorcycles–887; Manufactured Homes–19; Tax Exempt Licenses–113; Boats–2,456

Crime Incidents (2013)—Murder–1; Rape–8; Robbery–5; Felony Assault–31; Breaking and Entering–145; Larceny–272; Motor Vehicle Theft–46; Arson–7 • Total Crime Index–508; Crime Rate per 1,000–24.46

Farms (2012)—1,018

Land in Farms (2012)—235,936

Recreation Area—Lake Eufaula State Park

Major Lake—Eufaula

Major Stream Systems—Canadian, North Canadian, Deep Fork rivers, and tributaries to the Arkansas River

Minerals—oil and gas, coal

County Population	
1907 (Okla. Terr.)	17,975
1910	20,961
1920	26,404
1930	24,924
1940	24,097
1950	17,829
1960	12,371
1970	12,472
1980	15,562
1990	16,779
2000	19,456
2010	20,252
2014 Estimate	20,088

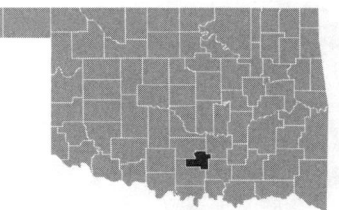

Murray

Created at statehood from part of the Chickasaw Nation, Murray County was named for William H. Murray, who eventually became the ninth governor of Oklahoma.

Sulphur, the county seat, was originally called Sulphur Springs for the bromide and sulphur waters that attracted thousands of people to the area early in the 20th century. The Arbuckle Mountains, Turner Falls, and the Chickasaw National Recreation Area, including the 2,400-acre Lake of the Arbuckles, have made Murray County a leading tourist attraction.

Initial Point, which determines the legal description of all land in Oklahoma except for the Panhandle, is located in Murray County some six miles west of Davis. Intersecting this point, the Indian Base Line runs east and west, and the Indian Meridian runs north and south. A sandstone marker indicating the spot is located in a pasture on privately owned land. For more information, call the county clerk's office at 580/622-3920.

Districts

Congress............................4
State Senate...................14
State Rep..................22, 48
District Attorney 20
Court of Appeals 3
Ct. of Crim. Appeals........3
Supreme Ct. Jud. 5
S. Cent. Jud. Adm. 20
    (Div. II)

County Officials

Court Clerk	Christie Pittman (D)	Sulphur
Clerk	David Thompson (D)	Sulphur
Sheriff	Darrel Richardson (D)	Sulphur
Treasurer	Judy Wells (D)	Sulphur
Assessor	Scott Kirby (D)	Sulphur
Elect. Brd. Sec.	Tommie Grimes (D)	Sulphur
Dist. 1 Comm.	Kent McKinley (D)	Sulphur
Dist. 2 Comm.	Jimmy Rackley (D)	Sulphur
Dist. 3 Comm.	Darrell Hudson (D)	Sulphur

Property Valuations

	2013–2014 Assessment	2014–2015 Assessment	Increase or Decrease
Real Estate and Improvement	$44,291,648	$46,683,408	$2,391,760
Personal Subject to Tax	$17,309,853	$14,851,190	($2,458,663)
Total Locally Assessed	$61,601,501	$61,534,598	$66,903
Homestead Exemptions Allowed	$3,735,795	$3,706,546	($29,249)
Net Assessed Locally	$57,865,706	$57,828,052	($37,654)
Public Service Assessment	$12,783,683	$14,480,170	$1,696,487
Net Assessed Valuation	$70,649,389	$72,308,222	$1,658,833

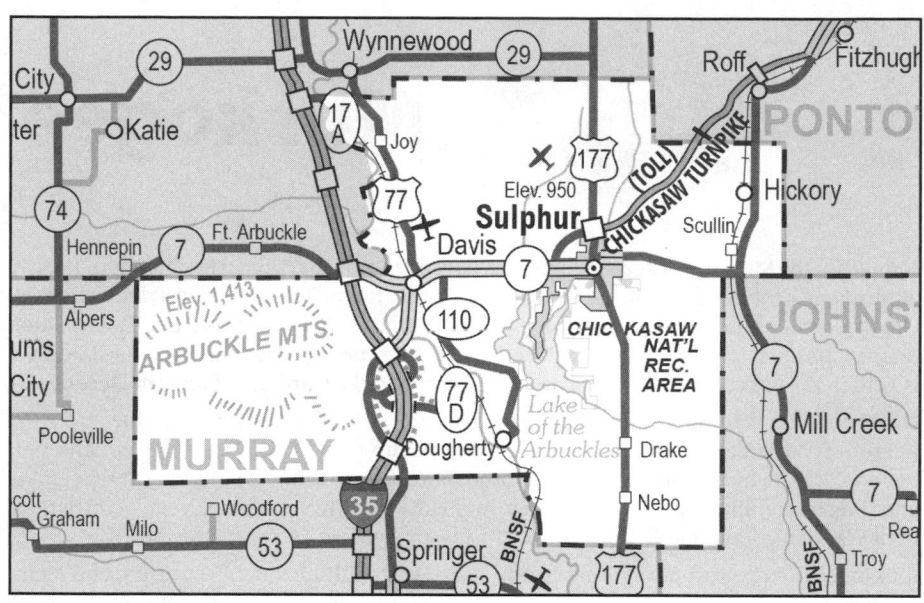

County Seat—Sulphur (Pop. 5,021) 2013 Estimate

Area (Land & Water)—424.92 square miles

Per Capita Income (2013)—$39,452 (Ranks 26th of 77 counties)

Population Statistics (2013)—Female-6,706; Male-6,865; Ethnicity—Wh.-11,826; Bl.-380; Am. Ind.-2,450; As.-88; Other-427; Pacific Is.-0; Two or more races-1,504; Hisp.-691

Births (2014)—157 • **Deaths** (2014)—184

Marriages (2013)—109 • **Divorces** (2013)—87

Unemployment Rate (2013)—3.7%

Labor Force (2013)—9,249

Number of Establishments (2013)—291

Number of Manufacturers (2013)—17

Public Assistance Payments
(FY2014) Total—$5,949,549 • TANF—$37,939 • Supplements—Aged-$17,662; Blind-$0; Disabled-$115,738;

Vehicle Registration (2014)—
Automobiles-12,083; Farm Trucks-1,390; Comm. Trucks, Tractors, Trailers-1,033; Motor Homes and Travel Trailers-521; Motorcycles-608; Manufactured Homes-4; Tax Exempt Licenses-54; Boats-615

Crime Incidents (2013)—Murder-0; Rape-5; Robbery-0; Felony Assault-32; Breaking and

County Population	
1907 (Okla. Terr.)	11,948
1910	12,744
1920	13,115
1930	12,410
1940	13,841
1950	10,775
1960	10,662
1970	10,669
1980	12,147
1990	12,042
2000	12,623
2010	13,488
2014 Estimate	13,803

Entering-75; Larceny-107; Motor Vehicle Theft-10; Arson-0 • Total Crime Index-229; Crime Rate per 1,000-16.63

Farms (2012)—470

Land in Farms (2012)—208,149

Major Lake—Arbuckle

Major Stream Systems—Washita River

Museums or Historic Sites—Travertine Nature Center, Arbuckle Historical Museum, and Chickasaw Cultural Center, all at Sulphur

Minerals—oil and gas, crushed stone

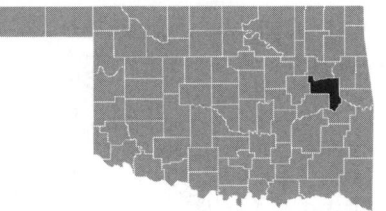

Muskogee

Named for the Muscogee Creek Indians, Muskogee County was created at statehood. The city of Muskogee, the county seat, became the focal point for the Five Civilized Tribes when the Union Agency established its headquarters in what is now Honor Heights Park. The old Union Agency Building is now the Five Civilized Tribes Museum and the famous Azalea Festival is held in the park each April. The park is also home to the Garden of Lights in December.

Other attractions to the county include: USS *Batfish*, a World War II submarine anchored at Port of Muskogee; Bacone College, established in 1879 as a university for Indians, and Bacone College Indian Museum; Fort Gibson Stockade, built in 1824 to protect area settlers and the oldest military post in Oklahoma; and Honey Springs Battlefield, site of the largest Civil War battle fought in Oklahoma.

Muskogee County's economy is based primarily on agriculture, but oil, industry, and recreation have also been part of the building of this county's economics. The city of Muskogee itself is within thirty minutes of five major lakes.

Historical Allies is a history book about Muskogee County and was written by John W. Morris and Edwin C. McReynolds. The Muskogee County Historical Society offers more information about the area, and a state tourist information center is located in Muskogee. For more information, call the county clerk's office at 918/682–7781.

Districts

Congress..........................2
State Senate............... 9, 18
State Rep.........13, 14, 15, 16
District Attorney 15
Court of Appeals 2
Ct. of Crim. Appeals........2
Supreme Ct. Jud. 7
E. Cent. Jud. Adm.......... 15
 (Div. II)

County Officials

Court Clerk	Paula Sexton (D)	Muskogee
Clerk	Dianna Cope (D)	Muskogee
Sheriff	Charles Pearson (D)	Muskogee
Treasurer	Kelly Garrett (D)	Muskogee
Assessor	Dan Ashwood (D)	Webbers Falls
Elect. Brd. Sec.	Kelley Beach (R)	Muskogee
Dist. 1 Comm.	Ken Doke (R)	Muskogee
Dist. 2 Comm.	Stephen Wright (D)	Porum
Dist. 3 Comm.	Kenny Payne (D)	Muskogee

Property Valuations

	2013–2014 Assessment	2014–2015 Assessment	Increase or Decrease
Real Estate and Improvement	$278,128,190	$285,231,990	$7,103,800
Personal Subject to Tax	$102,755,190	$100,596,775	($2,158,415)
Total Locally Assessed	$380,883,380	$385,828,765	($4,945,385)
Homestead Exemptions Allowed	$19,733,010	$19,760,796	$27,786
Net Assessed Locally	$361,150,370	$366,067,969	($4,917,599)
Public Service Assessment	$125,219,009	$126,150,599	$931,590
Net Assessed Valuation	$486,369,379	$492,218,568	$5,849,189

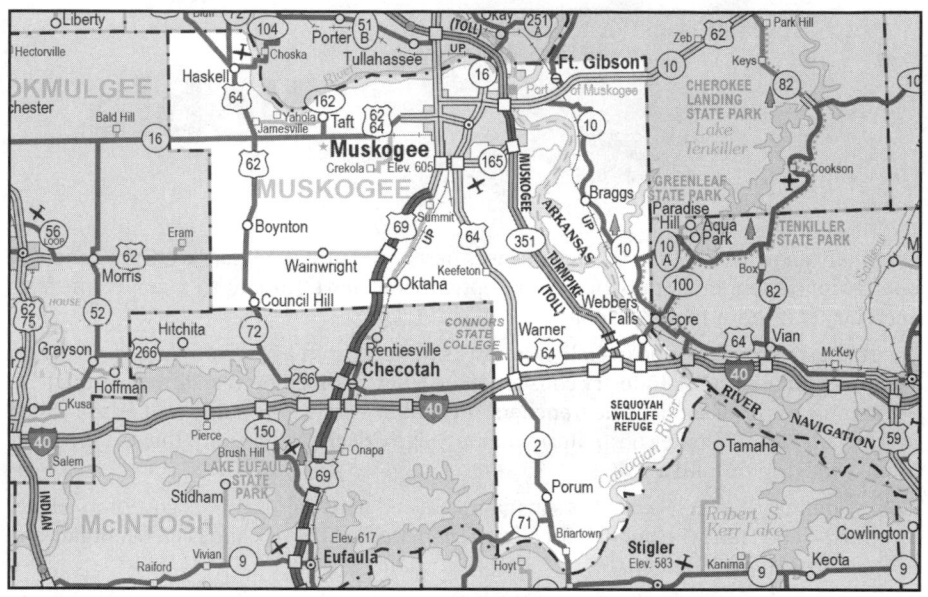

County Seat—Muskogee (Pop. 38,863) 2013 Estimate

Area (Land & Water)—838.99 square miles

Per Capita Income (2013)—$34,223 (Ranks 49th of 77 counties)

Population Statistics (2013)—Female-36,141; Male-34,516; Ethnicity—Wh.-51,221; Bl.-9,199; Am. Ind.-17,300; As.-581; Other-954; Pacific Is.-33; Two or more races 8,278; Hisp.-3,802

Births (2014)—927 • **Deaths** (2014)—906

Marriages (2013)—458 • **Divorces** (2013)—326

Unemployment Rate (2013)—6.5% • **Labor Force** (2013)—31,357

Establishments (2013)—1,436 • **Number of Manufacturers** (2013)—53

Public Assistance Payments
(FY2014) Total—$53,804,740 • TANF—$491,779 • Supplements—Aged-$113,081; Blind-$7,110; Disabled-$969,289

Vehicle Registration (2014)—
Automobiles-44,167; Farm Trucks-1,659; Comm. Trucks, Tractors, Trailers-2,318; Motor Homes and Travel Trailers-1,434; Motorcycles-1,939; Manufactured Homes-77; Tax Exempt Licenses-258; Boats-1,814

Institutions of Higher Learning—Connors State College, Warner; Bacone College, Muskogee; Northeastern State University, Muskogee Branch

Crime Incidents (2013)—Murder-3; Rape-34; Robbery-48; Felony Assault-341; Breaking and Entering-796; Larceny-1,340; Motor Vehicle Theft-152; Arson-35 • Total Crime Index-2,714; Crime Rate per 1,000-38.35

Farms (2012)—1,735

Land in Farms (2012)—350,119

Recreation Area—Greenleaf

Major Lakes—Webbers Falls, Greenleaf

Major Stream Systems—Arkansas and Grand rivers and minor tributaries to Deep Fork and Canadian rivers

Museums or Historic Sites—Five Civilized Tribes Museum, Thomas Foreman Home, USS *Batfish*, Ataloa Lodge, Muskogee; Bacone College Indian Museum, Bacone; Ft. Gibson Stockade, Ft. Gibson

Minerals—oil and gas, coal

County Population	
1907 (Okla. Terr.)	37,467
1910	52,743
1920	61,710
1930	66,424
1940	65,914
1950	65,573
1960	61,866
1970	59,542
1980	67,033
1990	68,078
2000	69,451
2010	70,990
2014 Estimate	69,966

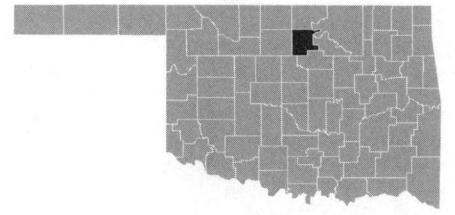

Noble

Originally known as County "P," the area was part of the original Cherokee Outlet and was opened for settlement by the land run on September 16, 1893. The county's name came from Secretary of Interior John W. Noble.

The main source of income in Noble County is derived from agriculture and its character remains primarily rural. Industry consists of the Charles Machine Works, the world's largest manufacturer of service line trenchers, located in Perry, the county seat. Also located in Perry are: the Cherokee Strip Museum, the Stage Coach Community Theater, the Perry Memorial Hospital, and a YMCA.

Noble County has seen several of its sons gain state and national office: two governors, Henry S. Johnston and Henry Bellmon; U.S. congressmen Manuel Herrick and Dick T. Morgan; and U. S. Senator Henry Bellmon.

Several books have been written about Noble County. They include *History of Noble County*, *First Generation*, *History of Perry*, and *Perry: Pride of the Prairie*. Two historical societies, Billings Historical Society and Noble County Cherokee Strip Historical Society, are located in the county. Annual events include the Cherokee Strip Celebration in September, Wheatheart Festival in September, and the Otoe Powwow in July. For more information, call the county clerk's office at 580/336-2141.

Districts

Congress	3
State Senate	20
State Rep.	35, 38
District Attorney	8
Court of Appeals	5
Ct. of Crim. Appeals	2
Supreme Ct. Jud.	8
N. Cent. Jud. Adm.	8

County Officials

Court Clerk	Hillary Vorndran (D)	Perry
Clerk	Sandra Richardson (R)	Perry
Sheriff	Charlie Hanger (D)	Perry
Treasurer	Rena Clark-Wheatley (R)	Perry
Assessor	Mandy Snyder (D)	Perry
Elect. Brd. Sec.	Pamela S. McBride (R)	Lucien
Dist. 1 Comm.	Jason Kienholz (R)	Perry
Dist. 2 Comm.	Larry Montgomery (D)	Perry
Dist. 3 Comm.	Lance West (I)	Perry

Property Valuations

	2013–2014 Assessment	2014–2015 Assessment	Increase or Decrease
Real Estate and Improvement	$51,661,099	$52,554,154	$893,055
Personal Subject to Tax	$21,732,554	$23,315,469	$1,582,915
Total Locally Assessed	$73,393,653	$75,869,623	$2,475,970
Homestead Exemptions Allowed	$2,963,749	$2,809,560	($154,189)
Net Assessed Locally	$70,429,904	$73,060,063	$2,630,159
Public Service Assessment	$94,904,322	$96,863,759	($1,959,437)
Net Assessed Valuation	$163,334,226	$169,923,822	($4,589,596)

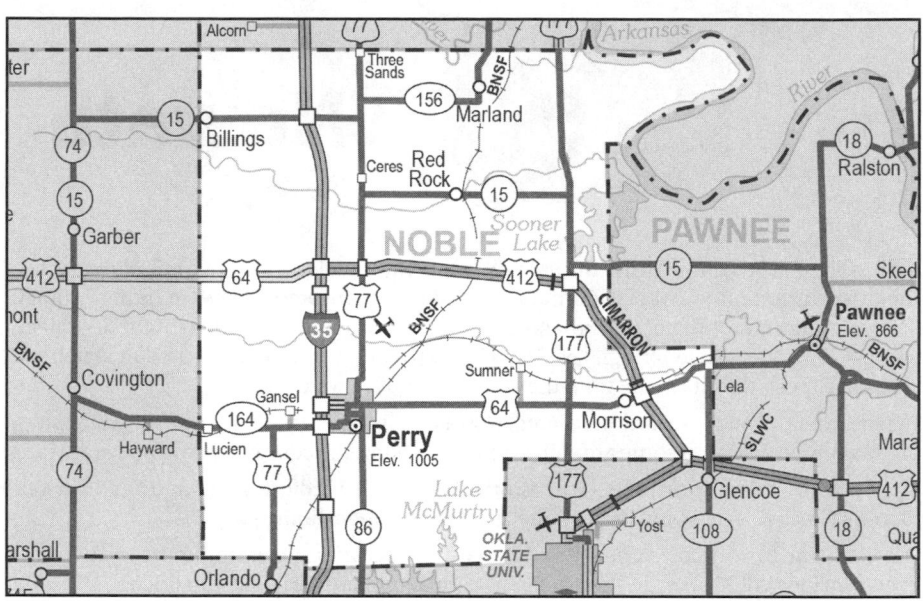

County Seat—Perry (Pop. 5,059) 2013 Estimate

Area (Land & Water)—742.44 square miles

Per Capita Income (2013)—$35,071 (Ranks 47th of 77 counties)

Population Statistics (2013)—Female-5,866; Male-5,663;
Ethnicity—Wh.-10,296; Bl.-289; Am. Ind.-1,393; As.-81;
Other-100; Pacific Is.-0; Two or more races-605; Hisp.-322

Births (2014)—130 • **Deaths** (2014)—131

Marriages (2013)—73 • **Divorces** (2013)—49

Unemployment Rate (2013)—4.1%

Labor Force (2013)—6,039

Number of Establishments (2013)—216

Number of Manufacturers (2013)—9

Public Assistance Payments
(FY2014) Total—$4,497,202 • TANF—
$21,907 • Supplements—Aged-$13,255;
Blind-$0; Disabled-$73,740

Vehicle Registration (2014)—
Automobiles-8,066; Farm Trucks-1,668;
Comm. Trucks, Tractors, Trailers-884;
Motor Homes and Travel Trailers-351;
Motorcycles-393; +Manufactured Homes-16;
Tax Exempt Licenses-21; Boats-345

Crime Incidents (2013)—Murder-0; Rape-0;
Robbery-0; Felony Assault-8; Breaking and
Entering-53; Larceny-110; Motor Vehicle
Theft-7; Arson-2 • Total Crime Index-178;
Crime Rate per 1,000-15.40

Farms (2012)—838

Land in Farms (2012828)—442,797

Major Stream Systems—Black Bear and Red
Rock creeks, Salt Fork of Arkansas River, and
some tributaries to the Cimarron

Museums or Historic Sites—Cherokee Strip
Museum, Henry S. Johnston Library, Perry

Minerals—oil and gas, crushed stone

County Population	
1907 (Okla. Terr.)	14,198
1910	14,495
1920	13,560
1930	15,119
1940	14,826
1950	12,156
1960	10,376
1970	10,043
1980	11,573
1990	11,045
2000	11,411
2010	11,561
2014 Estimate	11,494

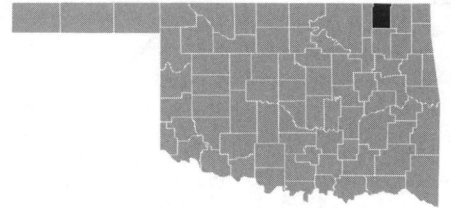

Nowata

Stories abound as to the origin of the name Nowata. One opinion is that two railroad surveyors took the suggestion of Roberta Campbell Lawson, an educated Delaware Indian woman: "Noweta" meaning "welcome." Others say a Georgian exploring the area found no water at some springs and posted a sign "No Wata" to warn other travelers. Created at statehood, Nowata County took its name from the county seat of Nowata.

In 1904, when oil and gas were discovered, Nowata County became known as the world's largest shallow oil field, and some are still producing. Today, the county is principally ranching.

The Nowata County Courthouse is a historic site and the Verdigris River and Oologah Lake Double Creek Cove provide recreational and fishing opportunities.

A Look at the History of Nowata by Robert W. DeMoss offers more about the area. Annual events include Wild Turkey Festival in May, Nowata Annual Championship Rodeo (ACRA and CRRA sanctioned) in July, the City-Wide Garage Sale in September and Christmas Open House in December at the Glass Mansion, a home designed and built by John Duncan Forsythe.

For additional information, call the county clerk's office at 918/273-2480 or the Nowata Area Chamber of Commerce at 918/273-2301.

Districts

Congress..........................2
State Senate...................29
State Rep.......................10
District Attorney 11
Court of Appeals 2
Ct. of Crim. Appeals........2
Supreme Ct. Jud. 1
NE Jud. Adm...................11

County Officials

Court Clerk	Sarah Webb (D)	Nowata
Clerk	Amber Wishall (D)	Nowata
Sheriff	James Hallett (D)	Nowata
Treasurer	Bonnie Workman (D)	Nowata
Assessor	Dave Neely (D)	Nowata
Elect. Brd. Sec.	Chris Freeman (R)	Nowata
Dist. 1 Comm.	Curtis Barnes (D)	Nowata
Dist. 2 Comm.	Doug Sonenberger (D)	Lenapah
Dist. 3 Comm.	Bud Frost (R)	Lenapah

Property Valuations

	2013–2014 Assessment	2014–2015 Assessment	Increase or Decrease
Real Estate and Improvement	$36,057,715	$36,797,915	$740,200
Personal Subject to Tax	$6,877,446	$7,228,360	$350,914
Total Locally Assessed	$42,935,161	$44,026,275	$1,091,114
Homestead Exemptions Allowed	$3,015,170	$2,920,846	($94,324)
Net Assessed Locally	$39,919,991	$41,105,429	$1,185,438
Public Service Assessment	$12,383,790	$12,091,669	($292,121)
Net Assessed Valuation	$52,303,781	$53,197,098	($893,317)

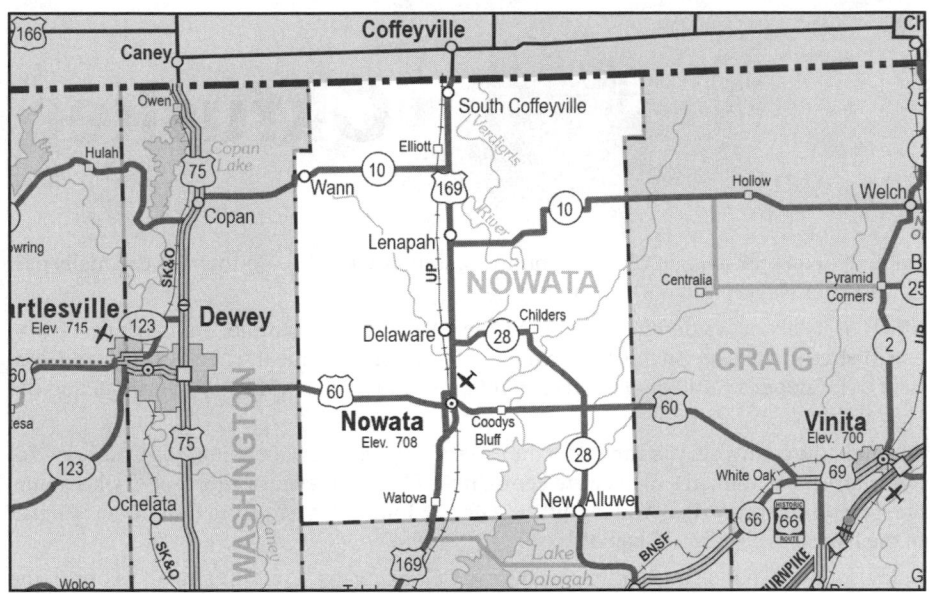

County Seat—Nowata (Pop. 3,736) 2013 Estimate

Area (Land & Water)—580.87 square miles

Per Capita Income (2013)—$31,699 (Ranks 61st of 77 counties)

Population Statistics (2013)—Female-5,281; Male-5,299;
Ethnicity—Wh.-8,202; Bl.-311; Am. Ind.-2,826; As.-24; Other-31;
Pacific Is.-89; Two or more races-903; Hisp.-274

Births (2014)—111 • **Deaths** (2014)—139

Marriages (2013)—39 • **Divorces** (2013)—47

Unemployment Rate (2013)—6.7%

Labor Force (2013)—5,018

Number of Establishments (2013)—160

Number of Manufacturers (2013)—12

Public Assistance Payments
(FY2014) Total—$6,067,298 • TANF—
$53,298 • Supplements—Aged-$15,235;
Blind-$0; Disabled-$88,098

Vehicle Registration (2014)—
Automobiles-6,097; Farm Trucks-888; Comm.
Trucks, Tractors, Trailers-322; Motor Homes
and Travel Trailers-284; Motorcycles-267;
Manufactured Homes-10; Tax Exempt
Licenses-101; Boats-399

Crime Incidents (2013)—Murder-0; Rape-2;
Robbery-0; Felony Assault-20; Breaking

and Entering-27; Larceny-58; Motor Vehicle
Theft-4; Arson-1 • Total Crime Index-111;
Crime Rate per 1,000-10.38

Farms (2012)—899

Land in Farms (2012)—292,122

Major Stream Systems—Verdigris River and
Big, Lightning, Salt, and Snow creeks

Museums or Historic Sites—Nowata
County Historical Museum, Post Office,
Glass House, Savoy Hotel, Nowata Lodge,
Presbyterian Church

Minerals—oil and gas, coal

County Population	
1907 (Okla. Terr.)	10,453
1910	14,223
1920	15,899
1930	13,611
1940	15,774
1950	12,734
1960	10,848
1970	9,773
1980	11,486
1990	9,992
2000	10,569
2010	10,536
2014 Estimate	10,524

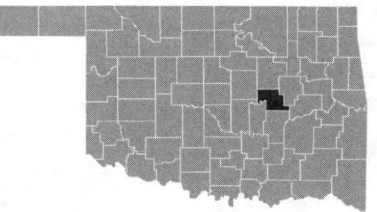

Okfuskee

Named for a Creek town in Cleburn County, Alabama, Okfuskee County was originally part of the Creek Nation, Indian Territory.

Much of its history is tied to that of the Creek Nation. For example, Thlopthlocco Town, established in the 1830s in this area in the Creek Nation, became the headquarters of Colonel D. H. Cooper's Confederate forces in 1861, prior to battles with Opothleyahola and the "Loyal Creeks."

Okemah, the county seat, is named for the Creek Chief Okemah, meaning "Big Chief." Two of Okemah's most noted residents were Leon Chase Phillips, eleventh governor of Oklahoma, and legendary songwriter Woody Guthrie. Glen D. Johnson, a two-term Oklahoma Speaker of the House, is also from Okemah.

Boley, founded in 1904 on eighty acres of land belonging to a Creek freedman, is one of the few black towns remaining in the United States. Established to show the ability of the black community to govern itself, it thrived for many years until, in 1932, George Birdwell, "chief lieutenant" of Pretty Boy Floyd, not only robbed the Farmer's State Bank, but in the process shot and killed D. J. Turner, bank president and mayor of Boley.

For more county information, call the county clerk's office at 918/623-1724.

Districts

Congress..........................2
State Senate.................7, 8
State Rep........................24
District Attorney 24
Court of Appeals.............2
Ct. of Crim. Appeals........2
Supreme Ct. Jud. 8
E. Cent. Jud. Adm..........24
    (Div. II)

County Officials

Court Clerk	Sherri Forman (D)	Okemah
Clerk	Dianne Flanders (D)	Okemah
Sheriff	Derrall Summers (D)	Weleetka
Treasurer	Lori Thomas (R)	Okemah
Assessor	Pam Parish (D)	Okemah
Elect. Brd. Sec.	Eric Swinford (R)	Pharoah
Dist. 1 Comm.	Danny Wilson (D)	Welty
Dist. 2 Comm.	Max Henry (D)	Okemah
Dist. 3 Comm.	Bruce Smith (D)	Weleetka

Property Valuations

	2013–2014 Assessment	2014–2015 Assessment	Increase or Decrease
Real Estate and Improvement	$31,241,088	$31,831,905	$590,817
Personal Subject to Tax	$16,553,805	$17,899,392	$1,345,587
Total Locally Assessed	$47,794,893	$49,731,297	$1,936,404
Homestead Exemptions Allowed	$2,956,069	$2,916,300	($39,769)
Net Assessed Locally	$44,838,824	$46,814,997	$1,976,173
Public Service Assessment	$15,871,410	$22,248,998	$6,377,588
Net Assessed Valuation	$60,710,234	$69,063,995	$8,353,761

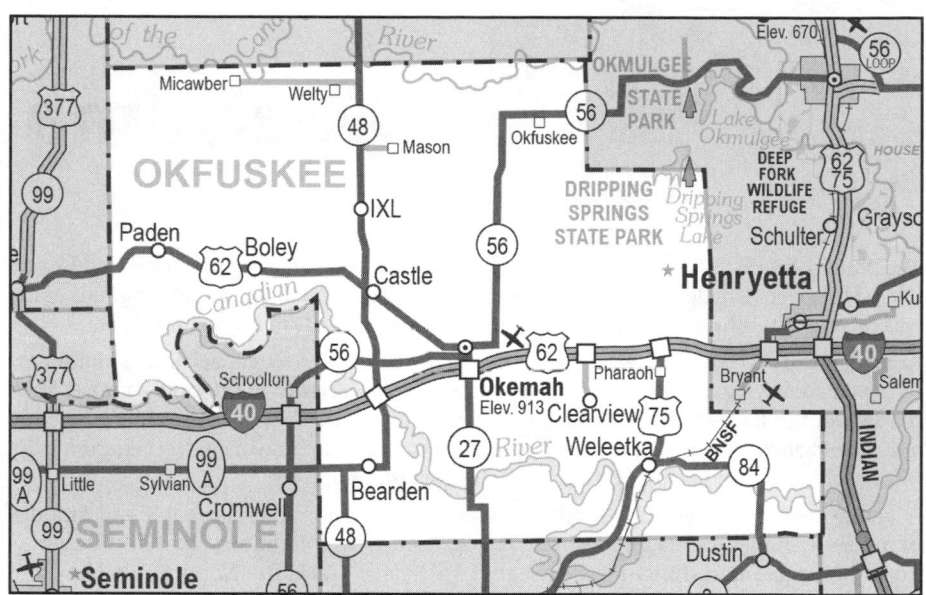

County Seat—Okemah (Pop. 3,314) 2013 Estimate

Area (Land & Water)—628.91 square miles

Per Capita Income (2013)—$26,426 (Ranks 76th of 77 counties)

Population Statistics (2013)—Female-5,675; Male-6,593;
Ethnicity—Wh.-9,224; Bl.-1,224; Am. Ind.-3,226; As.-41;
Other-91; Pacific Is.-0; Two or more races-1,505; Hisp.-424

Births (2014)—154 • Deaths (2014)—198

Marriages (2013)—56 • Divorces (2013)—49

Unemployment Rate (2013)—7.0%

Labor Force (2013)—4,739

Number of Establishments (2013)—165

Number of Manufacturers (2013)—6

Public Assistance Payments
(FY2014) Total—$7,990,530 • TANF—
$33,672 • Supplements—Aged-$38,523;
Blind-$41; Disabled-$188,022

Vehicle Registration (2014)—
Automobiles-4,051; Farm Trucks-904; Comm.
Trucks, Tractors, Trailers-259; Motor Homes
and Travel Trailers-195; Motorcycles-169;
Manufactured Homes-19; Tax Exempt
Licenses-39; Boats-233

Crime Incidents (2013)—Murder-0; Rape-2;
Robbery-1; Felony Assault-20; Breaking and

County Population	
1907 (Okla. Terr.)	15,595
1910	19,995
1920	15,051
1930	29,016
1940	26,279
1950	16,948
1960	11,706
1970	10,683
1980	11,125
1990	11,551
2000	11,814
2010	12,191
2014 Estimate	12,186

Entering-112; Larceny-220; Motor Vehicle
Theft-18; Arson-2 • Total Crime Index-373;
Crime Rate per 1,000-29.96

Farms (2012)—881 • Land in Farms (2012)—
319,725

Major Stream Systems—North Canadian
and Deep Fork rivers

Museums or Historic Sites—Territory Town
Museum and Okfuskee County Historical
Museum, Okemah

Minerals—oil and gas

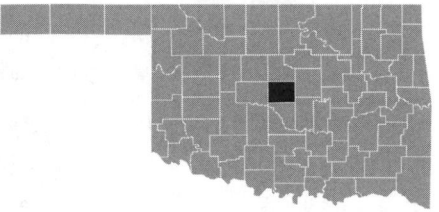

Oklahoma

The area that is now Oklahoma County was opened to settlement by the 1889 Land Run. A vote of the people made Oklahoma City the county seat. Although the state's original capital was located in Guthrie, the capital was eventually located in Oklahoma City.

In 1928, when oil was discovered in the county, petroleum products became a major part of the economy. Oklahoma County is now the economic center of the state. It is the chief market for the state's livestock and agricultural industries as well as the major wholesale and employment center for the area. The major sources of income in central Oklahoma are oil, agriculture, manufacturing, business, and government.

A leading medical center in the southwest, Oklahoma City is readily accessible by all modes of transportation. Cultural and recreational opportunities abound throughout the county. Local points of interest include Remington Park Race Track, the National Cowboy and Western Heritage Museum, the Oklahoma City Zoo, the Bricktown entertainment district and the Oklahoma City National Memorial site downtown.

For additional information, call the Greater Oklahoma City Chamber of Commerce at 405/297-8900.

Districts

Congress...................... 4, 5
State Senate 17, 22, 30,
              40-42, 44-48
State Rep. 31, 39, 41,
        81-85, 87-97, 99-101
District Attorney 7
Court of Appeals 4, 5, 6
Ct. of Crim. Appeals........4
Supreme Ct. Jud. 3
Okla. Jud. Adm. 7

County Officials

Court Clerk	Tim Rhodes (R)	Okla. City
Clerk	Carolynn Caudill (R)	Okla. City
Sheriff	John Whetsel (D)	Choctaw
Treasurer	Forrest Freeman (R)	Choctaw
Assessor	Leonard Sullivan (R)	Okla. City
Elect. Brd. Sec.	Doug Sanderson (D)	Edmond
Dist. 1 Comm.	Willa Johnson (D)	Okla. City
Dist. 2 Comm.	Brian Maughan (R)	Okla. City
Dist. 3 Comm.	Ray Vaughn (R)	Edmond

Property Valuations

	2013–2014 Assessment	2014–2015 Assessment	Increase or Decrease
Real Estate and Improvement	$4,925,1657,246	$5,153,046,172	$227,388,926
Personal Subject to Tax	$905,464,211	$925,808,735	$20,344,524
Total Locally Assessed	$5,831,121,457	$6,078,854,907	$247,733,450
Homestead Exemptions Allowed	$160,139,778	$160,079,710	($60,068)
Net Assessed Locally	$5,670,981,679	$5,918,775,197	$247,793,518
Public Service Assessment	$340,700,447	$324,447,133	($16,253,314)
Net Assessed Valuation	$6,011,682,126	$6,243,222,330	$231,540,204

County Seat—Oklahoma City (Pop. 610,613) 2013 Estimate

Area (Land & Water)—718.31 square miles

Per Capita Income (2013)—$47,533 (Ranks 7ᵗʰ of 77 counties)

Population Statistics (2013)—Female-373,944; Male-358,174; Ethnicity—Wh.-541,425; Bl.-126,485; Am. Ind.-55,690; As.-27,393; Other-30,887; Pacific Is.-1,566; Two or more races-48,000; Hisp.-112,705

Births (2014)—12,238 • **Deaths** (2014)—6,945

Marriages (2013)—5,461 • **Divorces** (2013)—3,428

Unemployment Rate (2013)—5.4% • **Labor Force** (2013)—339,146

Number of Establishments (2013)—22,949

Number of Manufacturers (2013)—591

Public Assistance Payments (FY2014) Total—$565,276,561 • TANF—$4,799,019 • Supplements—Aged-941,036; Blind-$21,734; Disabled-$6,601,745

Vehicle Registration (2014)—Automobiles 704,404; Farm Trucks-3,318; Comm. Trucks, Tractors, Trailers-96,323; Motor Homes and Travel Trailers-10,514; Motorcycles-24,200; Manufactured Homes-655; Tax Exempt Licenses-1,785; Boats-13,284

Institutions of Higher Learning— Oklahoma State University-Oklahoma City, University of Oklahoma Health Sciences Center, Oklahoma City Community College, Mid-America Bible College, Oklahoma Christian University of Science and Arts, Oklahoma City University, Oklahoma City; University of Central Oklahoma, Edmond; Rose State College, Midwest City; Southern Nazarene University, Southwestern College of Christian Ministries, Bethany

County Population	
1907 (Okla. Terr.)	55,849
1910	85,232
1920	116,307
1930	221,738
1940	244,159
1950	325,352
1960	439,506
1970	526,805
1980	568,933
1990	599,611
2000	660,448
2010	718,633
2014 Estimate	766,215

Crime
Incidents (2013)—Murder-68; Rape-553; Robbery-1,322; Felony Assault-3,868; Breaking and Entering-10,084; Larceny-26,317; Motor Vehicle Theft-4,725; Arson-153 • Total Crime Index-46,937; Crime Rate per 1,000-54.17

Farms (2012)—1,180

Land in Farms (2012)—144,188

Major Lakes—Arcadia, Hefner, Overholser

Major Stream Systems—North Canadian, Little & Deep Fork rivers, small tributaries to Canadian, Cimarron rivers

Museums or Historic Sites—Overholser House, 45ᵗʰ Infantry Museum, Cowboy and Western Heritage Museum, Softball Hall of Fame, OKC Museum of Art, Firefighters Museum, Heritage Center, State History Center, Harn Homestead, Kirkpatrick Center

Minerals—oil and gas, clays

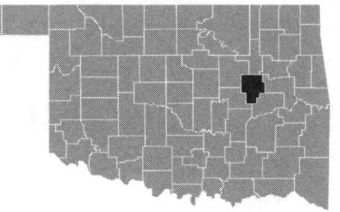

Okmulgee

The name Okmulgee comes from a Creek word meaning "boiling water." Created at statehood from lands in the Creek Nation, Indian Territory. The county seat, Okmulgee, has been the capital of the Creek Nation since the Civil War. The Indians chose the site in the belief that tornadoes would not strike the area.

Two local lakes furnish most of the water for the county. Major highways are I-40, east-west, and S.H. 75, north-south. Burlington Northern Santa Fe Railroad maintains a station for shipping.

Points of interest are: the Creek Council House Museum (former meeting place of the Intertribal Council of the Five Civilized Tribes), the Creek Tribal Complex, Samuel Checote grave site, Oklahoma State University–Okmulgee, Nuyaka Mission, and Okmulgee State Park. A Pecan Festival is held mid-June annually in Okmulgee and a Labor Day celebration is observed in Henryetta each year. Both cities support public libraries. The City of Okmulgee is a participant in the Oklahoma Department of Commerce's Main Street project.

History of Okmulgee County offers information about the area. For additional information, call the county clerk's office at 918/756-0788.

Districts

Congress	2
State Senate	8
State Rep.	16, 24
District Attorney	24
Court of Appeals	2
Ct. of Crim. Appeals	2
Supreme Ct. Jud.	7
E. Cent. Jud. Adm.	24
(Div. III)	

County Officials

Court Clerk	Linda Beaver (D)	Morris
Clerk	Becky Thomas (D)	Henryetta
Sheriff	Eddy Rice (D)	Beggs
Treasurer	Vonna Lampkins (D)	Beggs
Assessor	Lisa Smart (D)	Okmulgee
Elect. Brd. Sec.	Ava Ridgeway (D)	Okmulgee
Dist. 1 Comm.	J.W. Hill (R)	Mounds
Dist. 2 Comm.	Robert Hardridge (D)	Okmulgee
Dist. 3 Comm.	James Connors (D)	Dewar

Property Valuations

	2013–2014 Assessment	2014–2015 Assessment	Increase or Decrease
Real Estate and Improvement	$116,248,844	$120,387,809	$4,138,965
Personal Subject to Tax	$28,828,881	$29,579,383	$750,502
Total Locally Assessed	$145,077,725	$149,967,192	$4,889,467
Homestead Exemptions Allowed	$9,855,363	$9,967,010	$111,647
Net Assessed Locally	$135,222,362	$140,000,182	$4,777,820
Public Service Assessment	$23,992,205	$23,093,475	($898,730)
Net Assessed Valuation	$159,214,567	$163,093,657	$3,879,090

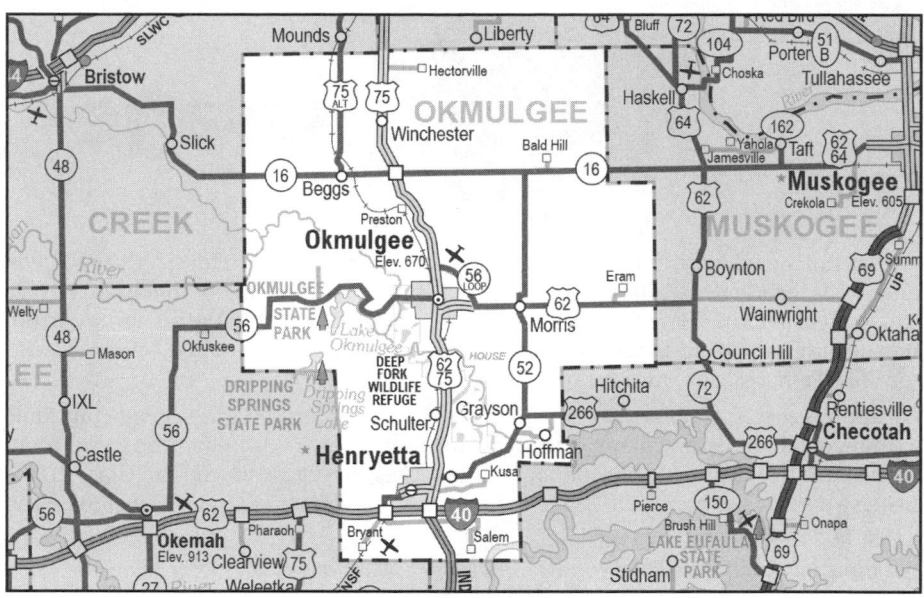

County Seat—Okmulgee (Pop. 12,373) 2013 Estimate

Area (Land & Water)—702.32 square miles

Per Capita Income (2013)—$31,498 (Ranks 64th of 77 counties)

Population Statistics (2013)—Female-19,879; Male-19,868;
   Ethnicity—Wh.-30,268; Bl.-4,273; Am. Ind.-9,291; As.-237;
   Other-221; Pacific Is.-81; Two or more races-4,515; Hisp.-1,366

Births (2014)—508 • Deaths (2014)—476

Marriages (2013)—266 • Divorces (2013)—205

Unemployment Rate (2013)—7.6%

Labor Force (2013)—15,959

Number of Establishments (2013)—679

Number of Manufacturers (2013)—36

Public Assistance Payments
   (FY2014) Total—$29,058,392 • TANF—
   $177,755 • Supplements—Aged-$80,683;
   Blind-$441; Disabled-$521,971

Vehicle Registration (2014)—
   Automobiles-23,740; Farm Trucks-1,615;
   Comm. Trucks, Tractors, Trailers-656;
   Motor Homes and Travel Trailers-1,082;
   Motorcycles-987; Manufactured Homes-189;
   Tax Exempt Licenses-111; Boats-1,302

Institutions of Higher Learning—
   Oklahoma State University-Okmulgee

Crime Incidents (2013)—Murder-1; Rape-16;
   Robbery-7; Felony Assault-63; Breaking

County Population	
1907 (Okla. Terr.)	14,362
1910	21,115
1920	55,072
1930	56,558
1940	50,101
1950	44,561
1960	36,945
1970	35,358
1980	39,169
1990	36,490
2000	39,685
2010	40,069
2014 Estimate	39,095

& Entering-226; Larceny-650; Motor
Vehicle Theft-64; Arson-16 • Total Crime
Index-1,027; Crime Rate per 1,000-25.92

Farms (2012)—1,329

Land in Farms (2012)—300,165

Recreation Area—Okmulgee

Major Stream Systems—Deep Fork and
   tributaries to the main stream of the Arkansas
   River

Museums or Historic Sites—Creek National
   Council House Museum and Nuyaka Mission
   Site, both at Okmulgee

Minerals—oil and gas, coal

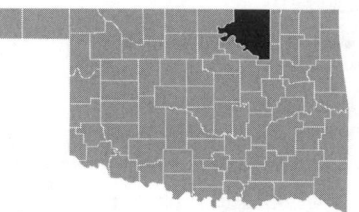

Osage

In 1872 the United States purchased land from the Cherokee Nation for the Osage Nation and it was then that the tribe moved to Indian Territory. At statehood in 1907, this Osage Reservation became Osage County, the largest county in Oklahoma. The name is a corruption by the French of the tribal name Wah-Sha-She. Pawhuska, the county seat, was named for Chief Pa-hue-Skah, which means "white hair."

Oil and gas as well as horse and cattle ranching on the famous bluestem grass contribute to the economy of Osage County. Attractions to the county include Indian and western cultural activities, museums, recreational facilities, lakes, creeks, rivers, the Tall Grass Prairie Reserve north of Pawhuska, the Osage Tribal Museum and Headquarters in Pawhuska, and Osage Hills State Park.

For more information, call the county clerk's office at 918/287-3136.

Districts

Congress..........................3
State Senate...............10, 11
State Rep..10, 35–37, 66, 73
District Attorney 10
Court of Appeals..........1, 5
Ct. of Crim. Appeals........2
Supreme Ct. Jud. 1
NE Jud. Adm..................10

County Officials

Court Clerk	Jennifer Burd (D)	Pawhuska
Clerk	Shelia Bellamy (D)	Pawhuska
Sheriff	Ty Koch (D)	Fairfax
Treasurer	Sally Hulse (D)	Pawhuska
Assessor	Gail Hedgcoth (D)	Pawhuska
Elect. Brd. Sec.	Andrea Conner (D)	Pawhuska
Dist. 1 Comm.	Bob Jackson (D)	Grainola
Dist. 2 Comm.	Scott Hilton (D)	Skiatook
Dist. 3 Comm.	Darren McKinney (D)	Fairfax

Property Valuations

	2013–2014 Assessment	2014–2015 Assessment	Increase or Decrease
Real Estate and Improvement	$224,057,338	$231,591,642	$7,534,304
Personal Subject to Tax	$39,551,114	$43,321,603	$3,770,489
Total Locally Assessed	$263,608,452	$274,913,245	$11,304,793
Homestead Exemptions Allowed	$9,695,288	$9,621,172	($74,116)
Net Assessed Locally	$253,913,164	$265,292,073	$11,378,909
Public Service Assessment	$37,068,809	$43,817,917	$6,749,108
Net Assessed Valuation	$290,981,973	$309,109,990	$18,128,017

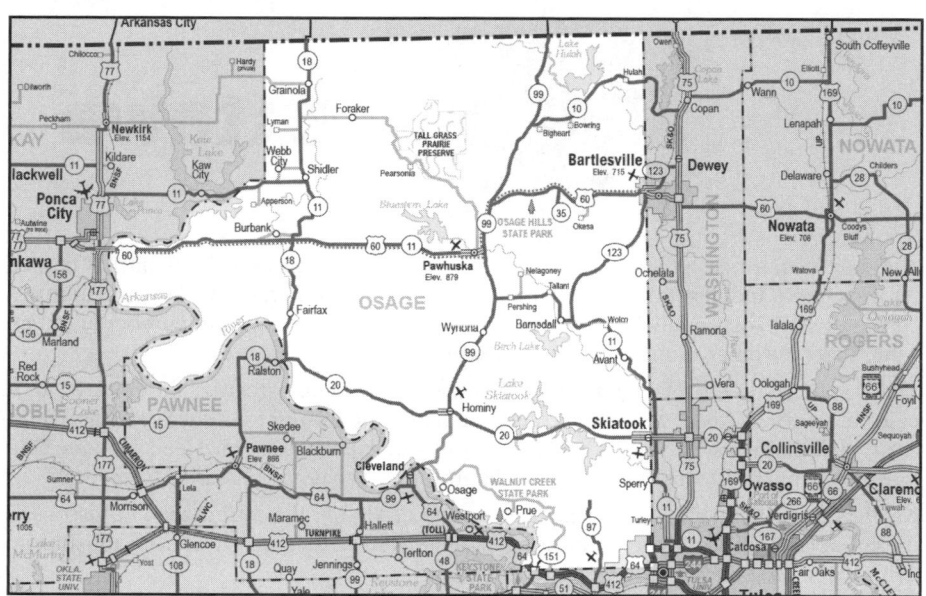

County Seat—Pawhuska (Pop. 3,666) 2013 Estimate

Area (Land & Water)—2,303.80 square miles

Per Capita Income (2013)—$40,312 (Ranks 25th of 77 counties)

Population Statistics (2013)—Female-23,763; Male-24,037;
Ethnicity—Wh.-34,490; Bl.-6,039; Am. Ind.-9,978; As.-227;
Other-496; Pacific Is.-177; Two or more races-3,412; Hisp.-1,447

Births (2014)—438 • **Deaths** (2014)—449

Marriages (2013)—105 • **Divorces** (2013)—118

Unemployment Rate (2013)—6.2%

Labor Force (2013)—20,869

Number of Establishments (2013)—580

Number of Manufacturers (2013)—25

Public Assistance Payments
(FY2014) Total—$17,665,773 • TANF—
$70,520 • Supplements—Aged-$61,736;
Blind-$1,620; Disabled-$378,772

Vehicle Registration (2014)—
Automobiles-32,684; Farm Trucks-2,262;
Comm. Trucks, Tractors, Trailers-1,920;
Motor Homes and Travel Trailers-1,545;
Motorcycles-1,839; Manufactured Homes-28;
Tax Exempt Licenses-128; Boats-1,984

Crime Incidents (2013)—Murder-2; Rape-4;
Robbery-4; Felony Assault-64; Breaking and
Entering 200; Larceny-317; Motor Vehicle
Theft-28; Arson-9 • Total Crime Index-619;
Crime Rate per 1,000-17.10

County Population	
1907 (Okla. Terr.)	15,332
1910	20,101
1920	36,536
1930	47,334
1940	41,502
1950	33,071
1960	32,441
1970	29,750
1980	39,327
1990	41,645
2000	44,437
2010	47,472
2014 Estimate	47,981

Farms (2012)—1,325

Land in Farms (2012)—1,216,673

Recreation Area—Osage Hills, Walnut Creek,
Wah-Sha-She

Major Lakes—Hulah, Kaw, Bluestern, Walnut
Creek, Birch, Skiatook

Major Stream Systems—Arkansas and its
tributaries, Bird Creek, Caney River

Museums or Historic Sites—Woolaroc
Museum, Osage County Historical Museum,
Osage Tribal Museum, Cathedral of the Osage,
Pawhuska

Minerals—oil and gas; crushed stone

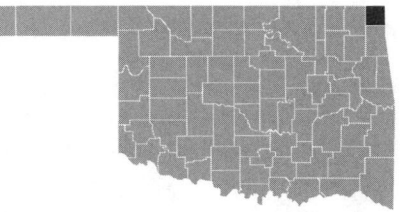

Ottawa

The extreme northeastern county of Oklahoma, bordering Kansas and Missouri, is named for the Ottawa Indians. But Ottawa comes from the Algonquian term adawe, meaning to "buy and sell." This county has been the home to members of a greater number of Indian tribes than any other county in the United States.

With 71 percent of the total land area in farms, as much as 60 percent of the county's agricultural income is from livestock and dairy products, and the rest from such crops as wheat, corn, grain sorghums, soybeans, and grass. The early existence of a vast lead and zinc field is evident from huge mountains of chat still present in the northern part of the county.

Northeastern Oklahoma A&M College is located at Miami, the county seat. Industries in the county include clothing, furniture, boat, metal, and leather manufacturing, mushroom cultivation, and concrete and block production.

Two books, *Pictorial Reflections of Ottawa County* and *History of Ottawa County*, have been written about the county. For additional information, contact the Ottawa County Historical Society or call the county clerk's office at 918/542-3332.

Districts

Congress	2
State Senate	1
State Rep.	7
District Attorney	13
Court of Appeals	2
Ct. of Crim. Appeals	1
Supreme Ct. Jud.	1
NE Jud. Adm.	13

County Officials

Court Clerk	Cassie Key (D)	Miami
Clerk	Reba Sill (D)	Miami
Sheriff	Terry Durborow (D)	Miami
Treasurer	Kathy Bowling (D)	Miami
Assessor	Becky Smith (D)	Miami
Elect. Brd. Sec.	Verna Ferris (D)	Miami
Dist. 1 Comm.	John Clarke (D)	Quapaw
Dist. 2 Comm.	Gary Wyrick (D)	Wyandotte
Dist. 3 Comm.	Russell Earls (D)	Fairland

Property Valuations

	2013–2014 Assessment	2014–2015 Assessment	Increase or Decrease
Real Estate and Improvement	$104,622,120	$107,578,923	$2,956,803
Personal Subject to Tax	$24,822,824	$25,346,182	$523,358
Total Locally Assessed	$129,444,944	$132,925,105	$3,480,161
Homestead Exemptions Allowed	$8,113,837	$8,037,268	($76,569)
Net Assessed Locally	$121,331,107	$124,887,837	$3,556,730
Public Service Assessment	$17,791,306	$19,040,072	$1,257,766
Net Assessed Valuation	$139,122,413	$143,936,909	$4,814,496

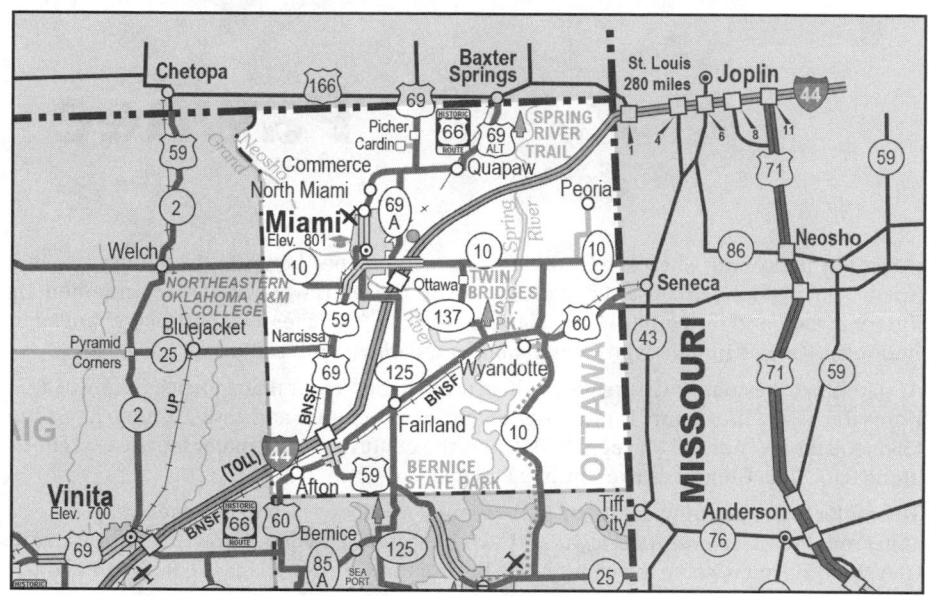

County Seat—Miami (Pop. 13,758) 2013 Estimate

Area (Land & Water)—484.73 square miles

Per Capita Income (2013)—$32,950 (Ranks 56th of 77 counties)

Population Statistics (2013)—Female-16,335; Male-15,694; Ethnicity—Wh.-25,492; Bl.-487; Am. Ind.-8,185; As.-284; Other-662; Pacific Is.-334; Two or more races-3,310; Hisp.-1,537

Births (2014)—447 • **Deaths** (2014)—419

Marriages (2013)—932 • **Divorces** (2013)—141

Unemployment Rate (2013)—6.4%

Labor Force (2013)—18,018

Number of Establishments (2013)—592

Number of Manufacturers (2013)—39

Public Assistance Payments
(FY2014) Total—$21,603,860 • TANF—$79,247 • Supplements—Aged-$56,534; Blind-$2,485; Disabled-$445,692

Vehicle Registration (2014)—
Automobiles-21,847; Farm Trucks-1,350; Comm. Trucks, Tractors, Trailers-853; Motor Homes and Travel Trailers-644; Motorcycles-1,106; Manufactured Homes-27; Tax Exempt Licenses-82; Boats-1,191

Institutions of Higher Learning—
Northeastern Oklahoma A&M College, Miami

Crime Incidents (2013)—Murder-1; Rape-5; Robbery-3; Felony Assault-75; Breaking and Entering 206; Larceny-422; Motor Vehicle

County Population	
1907 (Okla. Terr.)	12,827
1910	15,713
1920	41,108
1930	38,542
1940	35,849
1950	32,218
1960	28,301
1970	29,800
1980	32,870
1990	30,561
2000	33,194
2010	31,848
2014 Estimate	32,105

Theft-50; Arson-15 • Total Crime Index-762; Crime Rate per 1,000-23.44

Farms (2012)—1,020

Land in Farms (2012)—193,251

Recreation Area—Twin Bridges, Spring River Canoe Trails

Major Lake—Grand Lake o' the Cherokees

Major Stream Systems—Grand River and its tributaries

Museums or Historic Sites—Dobson Memorial Center, Dobson Museum, Intertribal Cultural Center at Miami

Minerals—oil and gas; crushed stone, abrasives

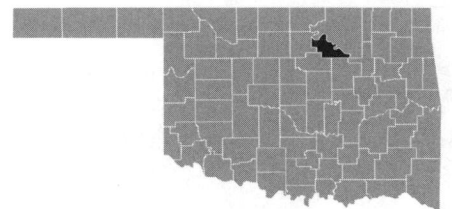

Pawnee

Originally part of the Cherokee Outlet, Pawnee County lies between the Cimarron River on the south and the Arkansas River on the north. The lands were opened to settlement by lottery in 1892, and the county was designated County "Q." Later the name was changed to honor the Pawnee Indians who located here in the nineteenth century.

At statehood, the county was created with an area slightly larger than Pawnee County, Oklahoma Territory. The county is primarily noted for agriculture and cattle. Today, Keystone Lake and the Pawnee Bill Museum in Pawnee, the county seat, are major tourist attractions along with Lone Chimney Lake south of Pawnee.

The major manufacturing company is Columbia Windows. Two newspapers, the *Pawnee Chief* and the *Cleveland American*, and two hospitals, Pawnee Municipal Hospital and Cleveland Hospital, serve the county. The Burlington Northern Santa Fe Railroad and the Cimarron Turnpike provide ready access to the county.

The Oklahoma Steam and Gas Engine Association holds its annual show in Steam Engine Park in Pawnee the first weekend in May for those interested in historical agricultural machinery.

For additional information, call the county clerk's office at 918/762-2732.

Districts

Congress...........................3
State Senate...................20
State Rep........................35
District Attorney 10
Court of Appeals 2
Ct. of Crim. Appeals........2
Supreme Ct. Jud. 1
Tulsa-Pawnee
    Jud. Adm..................... 14

County Officials

Court Clerk	Janet Dallas (D)	Pawnee
Clerk	Kristie Moles (D)	Pawnee
Sheriff	Mike Waters (D)	Pawnee
Treasurer	Carrie Tatum (D)	Pawnee
Assessor	Melissa Ryan (D)	Pawnee
Elect. Brd. Sec.	Tonda L. Miner (D)	Pawnee
Dist. 1 Comm.	Charles Brown (D)	Maramec
Dist. 2 Comm.	Jim McCormick (R)	Blackburn
Dist. 3 Comm.	Dale Carter(D)	Cleveland

Property Valuations

	2013–2014 Assessment	2014–2015 Assessment	Increase or Decrease
Real Estate and Improvement	$63,406,450	$65,189,917	$1,783,467
Personal Subject to Tax	$7,371,006	$8,262,008	$891,002
Total Locally Assessed	$70,777,456	$73,451,925	$2,674,469
Homestead Exemptions Allowed	$4,629,521	$4,663,770	$34,249
Net Assessed Locally	$66,147,935	$68,788,155	$2,640,220
Public Service Assessment	$17,697,058	$17,637,241	($59,817)
Net Assessed Valuation	$83,844,993	$86,425,396	$2,580,403

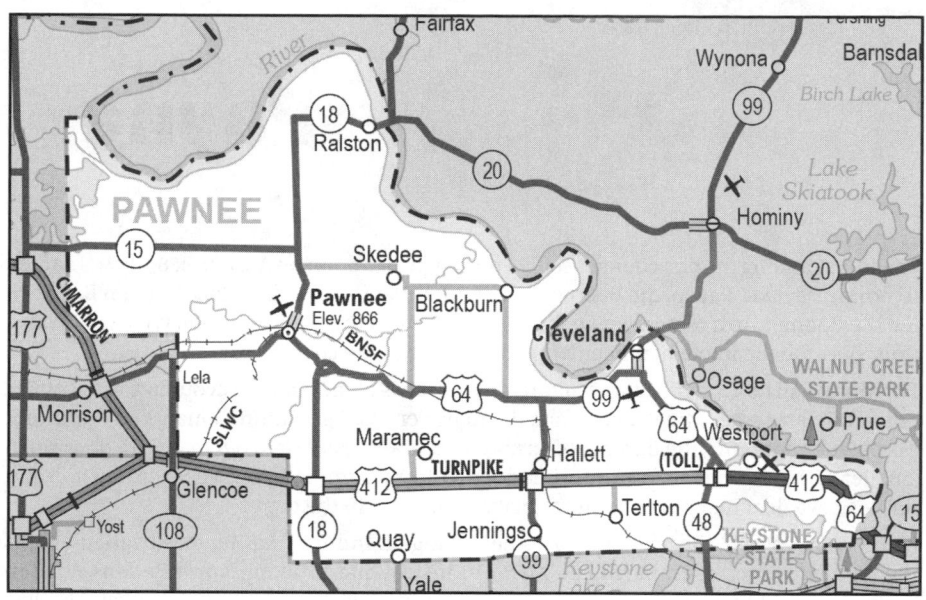

County Seat—Pawnee (Pop. 2,179) 2013 Estimate

Area (Land & Water)—594.87 square miles

Per Capita Income (2013)—$33,519 (Ranks 52nd of 77 counties)

Population Statistics (2013)—Female-8,330; Male-8,262; Ethnicity—Wh.-14,615; Bl.-209; Am. Ind.-2,863; As.-73; Other-104; Pacific Is.-56; Two or more races-1,322; Hisp.-388

Births (2014)—203 • **Deaths** (2014)—202

Marriages (2013)—72 • **Divorces** (2013)—78

Unemployment Rate (2013)—6.2%

Labor Force (2013)—7,243

Number of Establishments (2013)—268

Number of Manufacturers (2013)—17

Public Assistance Payments— (FY 2014) Total—$8,663,978 • TANF— $106,135 • Supplements—Aged-$18,835; Blind-$0; Disabled-$153,779

Vehicle Registration (2014)— Automobiles-11,390; Farm Trucks-1,206; Comm. Trucks, Tractors, Trailers-732; Motor Homes and Travel Trailers-547; Motorcycles-517; Manufactured Homes-19; Tax Exempt Licenses-225; Boats-689

Crime Incidents (2013)—Murder-1; Rape-3; Robbery-1; Felony Assault-25; Breaking and Entering-58; Larceny-114; Motor Vehicle Theft-14; Arson-5 • Total Crime Index-216; Crime Rate per 1,000-13.09

County Population	
1907 (Okla. Terr.)	17,112
1910	17,332
1920	19,126
1930	19,882
1940	17,395
1950	13,616
1960	10,884
1970	11,338
1980	15,310
1990	15,575
2000	16,612
2010	16,577
2014 Estimate	16,401

Farms (2012)—813

Land in Farms (2012)—285,982

Recreation Area—Feyodi Creek

Major Lake—Keystone

Major Stream Systems—Arkansas River, Black Bear Creek and tributaries to Cimarron River

Museums or Historic Sites—Pawnee Bill Museum & Ranch, Pawnee County Historical Society Museum at Pawnee

Minerals—oil and gas; crushed stone

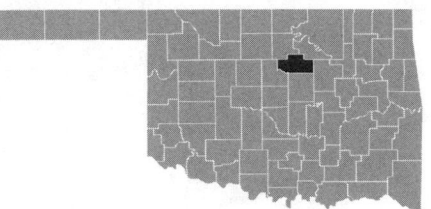

Payne

Payne was among the first counties settled during the land run on April 22, 1889. It was named to honor David L. Payne, the Boomer leader. After Payne's death in 1884, William L. Couch led the Boomers to a settlement on the banks of a creek they called the Still Water. Stillwater, thus, became the name of the settlement and later of the county seat.

For more than half a century, agriculture was the basis of the county's economy, with cotton, corn, and later oats, wheat, and alfalfa the major crops. Agriculture remains an important part of the economy. The number of farms has actually increased, but many are now much smaller. Livestock and hay are the primary agricultural commodities. Wheat production and dairies have declined but continue to make an impact in the county.

Since World War II, the economic base has changed. Industry has replaced agriculture as the leading source of employment. Major industrial plants along North Perkins Road in Stillwater employ more than 2,500 workers, many of whom commute from Yale, Ripley, Glencoe, Perkins, and Cushing. Oklahoma State University, which opened in 1891, is still the county's largest employer.

From 1913 to 1930, oil was a major economic factor in the county, but this, too, has declined except for massive facilities at Cushing, enhancing its status as "Pipeline Crossroads of the World." For more information, call the county clerk's office at 405/747-8310.

Districts

Congress...........................3
State Senate...................21
State Rep.............33, 34, 35
District Attorney 9
Court of Appeals 3
Ct. of Crim. Appeals........2
Supreme Ct. Jud. 8
N. Cent. Jud. Adm. 9

County Officials

Court Clerk	Lori Allen (D)	Stillwater
Clerk	Glenna Craig (R)	Stillwater
Sheriff	R.B. Hauf (R)	Stillwater
Treasurer	Bonita Stadler (R)	Stillwater
Assessor	James Cowan (R)	Stillwater
Elect. Brd. Sec.	Alyson Dawson (R)	Stillwater
Dist. 1 Comm.	Zachary Cavett (R)	Yale
Dist. 2 Comm.	Christofer Reding (R)	Stillwater
Dist. 3 Comm.	Kent Bradley (R)	Stillwater

Property Valuations

	2013–2014 Assessment	2014–2015 Assessment	Increase or Decrease
Real Estate and Improvement	$407,144,353	$424,685,744	$17,541,391
Personal Subject to Tax	$169,453,290	$200,984,152	$31,530,862
Total Locally Assessed	$576,597,643	$625,669,896	$49,072,253
Homestead Exemptions Allowed	$14,491,708	$14,507,538	$15,830
Net Assessed Locally	$562,105,935	$611,162,358	$49,056,423
Public Service Assessment	$93,658,888	$70,041,660	$23,617,228
Net Assessed Valuation	$655,764,823	$681,204,018	$25,439,195

County Seat—Stillwater (Pop. 47,186) 2013 Estimate

Area (Land & Water)—697.13 square miles

Per Capita Income (2013)—$37,146 (Ranks 34th of 77 counties)

Population Statistics (2013)—Female-38,266; Male-39,631;
Ethnicity—Wh.-68,330; Bl.-3,821; Am. Ind.-6,943; As.-3,503;
Other-653; Pacific Is.-72; Two or more races-5,289; Hisp.-3,131

Births (2014)—901 • **Deaths** (2014)—534

Marriages (2013)—478 • **Divorces** (2013)—239

Unemployment Rate (2013)—4.7%

Labor Force (2013)—36,329

Number of Establishments (2013)—1,761

Number of Manufacturers (2013)—71

Public Assistance Payments
(FY2014) Total—$27,356,256 • TANF—
$220,495 • Supplements—Aged-$45,949;
Blind-$1,893; Disabled-$488,740

Vehicle Registration (2014)—
Automobiles-54,378; Farm Trucks-2,530;
Comm. Trucks, Tractors, Trailers-5,362;
Motor Homes and Travel Trailers-1,703;
Motorcycles-2,677; Manufactured Homes-54;
Tax Exempt Licenses-231; Boats-1,284

Institutions of Higher Learning—
Oklahoma State University, Stillwater

Crime Incidents (2013)—Murder-3; Rape-40;
Robbery-48; Felony Assault-108; Breaking and
Entering-482; Larceny-1,729; Motor Vehicle

County Population	
1907 (Okla. Terr.)	22,022
1910	23,735
1920	30,180
1930	36,905
1940	36,057
1950	46,430
1960	44,231
1970	50,654
1980	62,435
1990	61,507
2000	68,190
2010	77,350
2014 Estimate	80,264

Theft-89;
Arson-10 • Total Crime Index-2,499; Crime
Rate per 1,000-31.63

Farms (2012)—1,466 • **Land in Farms**
(2012)—349,732

Major Lake—Carl Blackwell

Major Stream Systems—Cimarron River and
tributaries to Arkansas River

Museums or Historic Sites—Cimarron
Valley Railroad Museum, Cushing; Nat'l
Wrestling Hall of Fame, Sherrar Cultural and
Heritage Center, Gardiner Art Gallery, Okla.
Museum of Higher Education, Old Central,
Stillwater; Jim Thorpe Home, Yale

Minerals—oil and gas, crushed stone

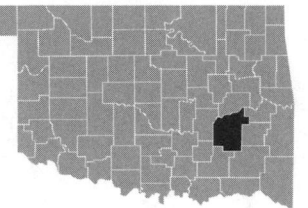

Pittsburg

Pittsburg County was created at statehood from Tobucksy County in the Choctaw Nation, Indian Territory. The new county took its name from Pittsburgh, Pennsylvania. Perryville, which no longer exists, was the place in Tobucksy County that court was held and elections were designated to take place. It was located a few miles south of present-day McAlester and was also an important military post and depot for Confederate forces. In September 1863 Perryville was burned to the ground by Union troops.

The largest city and the county seat of Pittsburg County is McAlester, which was originally developed as a rail center for the coal mining industry. Today, it is also the site of the Oklahoma State Penitentiary.

Agriculture is an important factor in the present-day economy of Pittsburg County. Peanuts, cotton, wheat, oats, and soybeans are among the major crops grown. McAlester Union Stockyard, which is one of the largest in the Southwest, and a large army ammunition plant are also vital to the county. Krebs is the largest Italian community in Oklahoma and is known for its fine food.

Annual events include the Italian Festival in McAlester in May, the Prison Rodeo in McAlester in September, and the Southeast Oklahoma Arts and Crafts Show during the first weekend in November. For more information, contact the county clerk at 918/423-6865.

Districts

Congress	2
State Senate	7
State Rep.	17, 18
District Attorney	18
Court of Appeals	3
Ct. of Crim. Appeals	3
Supreme Ct. Jud.	2
E. Cent. Jud. Adm.	18

County Officials

Court Clerk	Cindy Eller Smith(D)	McAlester
Clerk	Hope Trammell (D)	McAlester
Sheriff	Joel Kerns (D)	McAlester
Treasurer	Donna Scrivner (D)	McAlester
Assessor	Cathy L. Haynes (D)	Kiowa
Elect. Brd. Sec.	Cathy Thornton (D)	Hartshorne
Dist. 1 Comm.	Gene Rogers (D)	Crowder
Dist. 2 Comm.	Kevin Smith (D)	Blanco
Dist. 3 Comm.	Ronnie Young (D)	McAlester

Property Valuations

	2013–2014 Assessment	2014–2015 Assessment	Increase or Decrease
Real Estate and Improvement	$177,159,510	$183,332,182	$6,172,672
Personal Subject to Tax	$164,551,388	$163,145,762	($1,405,626)
Total Locally Assessed	$341,710,898	$346,477,944	$4,767,046
Homestead Exemptions Allowed	$13,708,575	$13,799,930	$91,355
Net Assessed Locally	$328,002,323	$332,678,825	$4,675,691
Public Service Assessment	$39,045,296	$33,719,095	($5,326,201)
Net Assessed Valuation	$367,047,619	$366,397,109	($650,510)

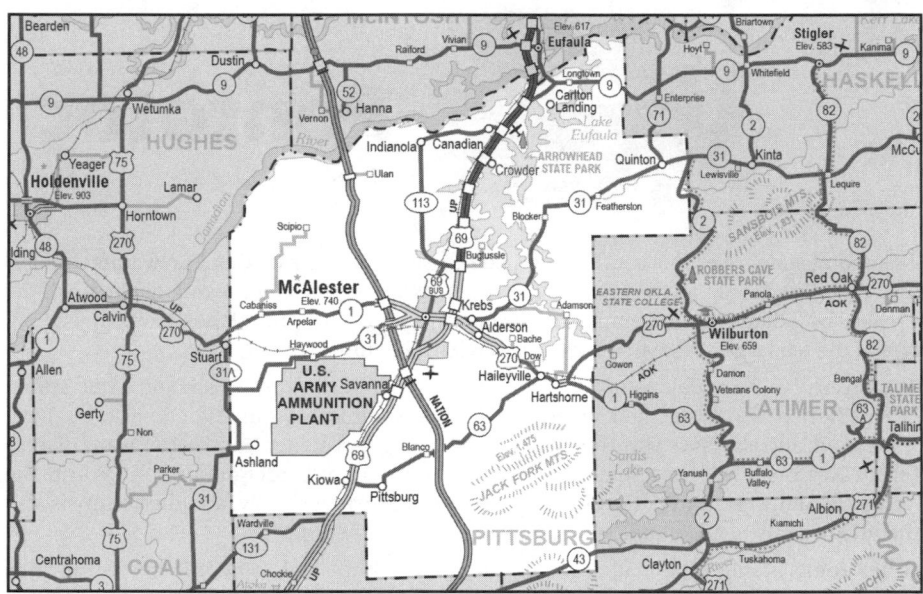

County Seat—McAlester (Pop. 18,301) 2013 Estimate

Area (Land & Water)—1,377.85 square miles

Per Capita Income (2013)—$35,430 (Ranks 44th of 77 counties)

Population Statistics (2013)—Female–22,289; Male–23,128; Ethnicity—Wh.-38,412; Bl.-1,954; Am. Ind.-9,380; As.-304; Other-985; Pacific Is.-36; Two or more races-5,573; Hisp.-1,892

Births (2014)—539 • **Deaths** (2014)—619

Marriages (2013)—324 • **Divorces** (2013)—195

Unemployment Rate (2013)—6.0%

Labor Force (2013)—22,750

Number of Establishments (2013)—963

Number of Manufacturers (2013)—27

Public Assistance Payments (FY2014) Total—$27,178,430 • TANF—$145,983 • Supplements—Aged-$61,608; Blind-$2,407; Disabled-$429,211

Vehicle Registration (2014)—Automobiles-28,680; Farm Trucks-2,828; Comm. Trucks, Tractors, Trailers-1,590; Motor Homes and Travel Trailers-1,266; Motorcycles-1,485; Manufactured Homes-17; Tax Exempt Licenses-128; Boats-1,624

Crime Incidents (2013)—Murder-1; Rape-10; Robbery-16; Felony Assault-73; Breaking and Entering-349; Larceny-875; Motor Vehicle Theft-83; Arson-7 • Total Crime Index-1,407; Crime Rate per 1,000-31.27

County Population	
1907 (Okla. Terr.)	37,677
1910	47,650
1920	52,570
1930	50,778
1940	48,985
1950	41,031
1960	34,360
1970	37,521
1980	40,524
1990	40,581
2000	45,953
2010	45,837
2014 Estimate	44,626

Farms (2012) 1,567

Land in Farms (2012) 523,627

Recreation Area—Arrowhead State Park

Major Stream Systems—Canadian River tributaries, and tributaries to the Poteau, Kiamichi and Muddy Boggy rivers

Museums or Historic Sites—Old Choate House, Indianola; Naval Ammunition Depot Museum, Scottish Rite Temple, International Order of Rainbow Girls and its Gardens with the "Temple of Silence," Oklahoma Prisons Historical Museum

Minerals—oil and gas, coal

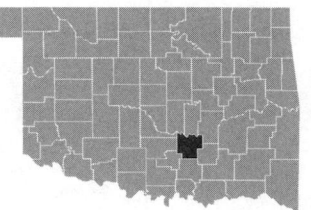

Pontotoc

Created at statehood, this south central county, Pontotoc, has a Chickasaw name meaning "cat tails growing on the prairie." The county was named after the original home of the Chickasaw Indians in Mississippi. Ada, the county seat, is the home of the Chickasaw Nation, one of the ten largest Native American tribes in the country.

The county has a rich blend of agriculture and industry. Quarter horses and cattle attract buyers from across the United States, and the area's natural resources of limestone, shale, silica sand, and clay have attracted manufacturers of glass, cement, and brick. Many diverse businesses, including LegalShield, are located in the county. Underground springs from the Arbuckle-Simpson Aquifer furnish an abundant pure water supply, and the county is also the hub of some of Oklahoma's richest oil and gas production.

Other points of interest include the log cabin in which the late Senator Robert S. Kerr was born, and the Kerr Environmental Research Laboratory, an EPA facility specializing in groundwater research. East Central University, a four-year institution of higher education, is located in Ada.

History of Pontotoc County gives a written account of the area's history. For additional information, call the county clerk's office at 580/332–1425.

Districts

Congress	4
State Senate	13
State Rep.	25
District Attorney	22
Court of Appeals	3
Ct. of Crim. Appeals	3
Supreme Ct. Jud.	8
S. Cent. Jud. Adm.	22
(Div. I)	

County Officials

Court Clerk	Karen Dunnigan (D)	Ada
Clerk	Pam Walker (D)	Ada
Sheriff	John Christian (D)	Ada
Treasurer	Glenda Gonderman (D)	Ada
Assessor	Debbie Byrd (D)	Ada
Elect. Brd. Sec.	Marilyn McDaniel (D)	Ada
Dist. 1 Comm.	Gary D. Starns (D)	Ada
Dist. 2 Comm.	Randy Floyd (D)	Ada
Dist. 3 Comm.	Justin Roberts (D)	Fitzhugh

Property Valuations

	2013–2014 Assessment	2014–2015 Assessment	Increase or Decrease
Real Estate and Improvement	$144,562,283	$150,694,547	$6,132,264
Personal Subject to Tax	$35,548,786	$38,750,675	$3,201,889
Total Locally Assessed	$180,111,069	$189,445,222	$9,334,153
Homestead Exemptions Allowed	$9,916,930	$9,797,610	($119,320)
Net Assessed Locally	$170,194,139	$179,647,612	$9,453,473
Public Service Assessment	$32,664,777	$44,990,237	$12,325,460
Net Assessed Valuation	$202,858,916	$224,637,849	$21,778,933

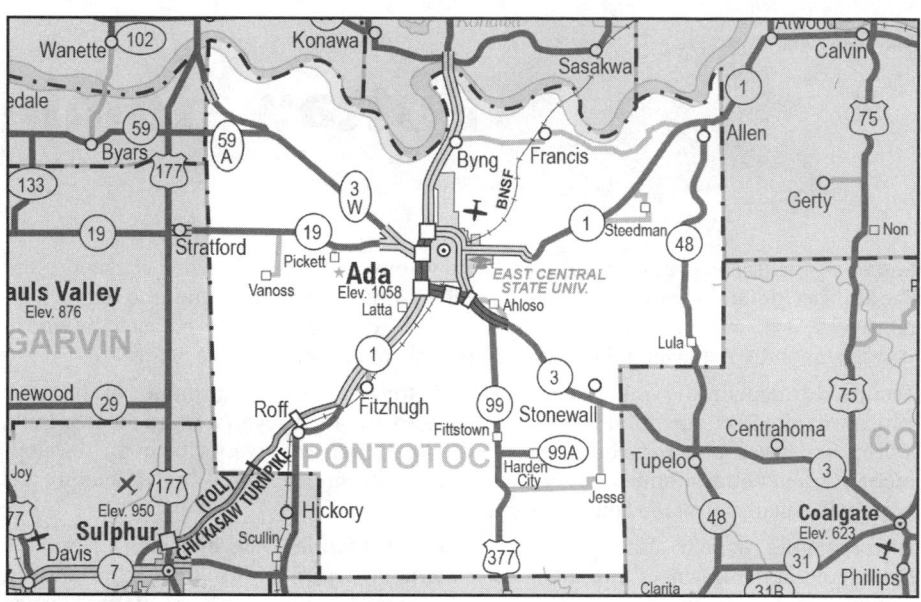

County Population

1907 (Okla. Terr.)	23,057
1910	24,331
1920	30,949
1930	32,469
1940	39,792
1950	30,875
1960	28,089
1970	27,867
1980	32,598
1990	34,119
2000	35,143
2010	37,492
2014 Estimate	38,005

County Seat—Ada (Pop. 17,140) 2013 Estimate

Area (Land & Water)—725.45 square miles

Per Capita Income (2013) $37,807 (Ranks 32nd of 77 counties)

Population Statistics (2013)—Female-19,359; Male-18,341; Ethnicity—Wh.-33,480; Bl.-1,542; Am. Ind.-8,983; As.-368; Other-75; Pacific Is.-181; Two or more races-6,536; Hisp.-1,586

Births (2014)—530 • **Deaths** (2014)—427

Marriages (2013)—360 • **Divorces** (2013)—182

Unemployment Rate (2013)—4.9%

Labor Force (2013)—20,511

Number of Establishments (2013)—978

Number of Manufacturers (2013)—31

Public Assistance Payments (FY2014) Total—$23,695,039 • TANF—$196,399 • Supplements—Aged-$59,838; Blind-$4,400; Disabled-$439,608

Vehicle Registration (2014)—Automobiles-27,505; Farm Trucks-2,824; Comm. Trucks, Tractors, Trailers-1,952; Motor Homes and Travel Trailers-990; Motorcycles-1,162; Manufactured Homes-55; Tax Exempt Licenses-138; Boats-783

Crime Incidents (2013)—Murder-0; Rape-14; Robbery-5; Felony Assault-195; Breaking and Entering-370; Larceny-686; Motor Vehicle Theft-72; Arson-6 • Total Crime Index-1,342; Crime Rate per 1,000-34.96

Farms (2012) 1,313

Land in Farms (2012) 324,584

Major Stream Systems—Canadian, Muddy Boggy, and Blue rivers and small tributaries to the Washita River

Museums or Historic Sites—East Central University Museum, Ada Arts & Heritage Center, both in Ada

Minerals—oil and gas, cement, crushed stone, and clays

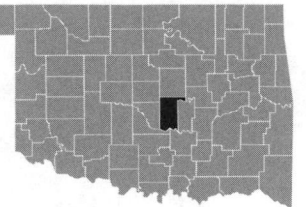

Pottawatomie

Settled by Seminole, Creek, Citizen Band Potawatomi, Absentee Shawnee, Kickapoo, and Sac and Fox Indian tribes, this area was opened to white settlement in the land run on September 22, 1891, and was designated County "B." The county name was changed by vote in 1892 to honor the Pottawatomi Indians and means "people of the place of fire."

Tecumseh, originally the county seat, soon lost to the fast growing community of Shawnee, which was also in competition for the state capitol. City fathers even went so far as to build a proposed governor's mansion. The oil and railroad industries were vital to the development of some Pottawatomie County towns and the decline of others, but agriculture has remained a mainstay of the county's economy.

History comes to life in annual celebrations such as Frontier Days in Tecumseh and the Heritage Fest in Shawnee. And the historic Santa Fe depot, built in 1903, still stands in Shawnee along with other early structures. Pottawatomie County is the site of the Shawnee Indian Reservation and has sixty-three "Ghost Towns."

Pottawatomie County has two institutions of higher education. Offices of the Shawnee, Potawatomi, and Sac and Fox tribes are located in the county.

For more information, call the county clerk's office at 405/273-8222.

Districts

Congress..........................5
State Senate.........13, 17, 28
State Rep.......20, 26, 27, 28
District Attorney 23
Court of Appeals 3, 4
Ct. of Crim. Appeals........2
Supreme Ct. Jud. 8
N. Cent. Jud. Adm. 23

County Officials

Court Clerk	Valerie Ueltzen (D)	Shawnee
Clerk	Raeshel Flewallen (D)	Shawnee
Sheriff	Mike Booth (D)	Shawnee
Treasurer	Wendy Magnus (D)	Shawnee
Assessor	Troyce King (D)	Shawnee
Elect. Brd. Sec.	Diana Knight (D)	Shawnee
Dist. 1 Comm.	Melissa Dennis (D)	Shawnee
Dist. 2 Comm.	Randy Thomas (R)	Norman
Dist. 3 Comm.	Eddie Stackhouse (D)	Maud

Property Valuations

	2013–2014 Assessment	2014–2015 Assessment	Increase or Decrease
Real Estate and Improvement	$246,951,963	$257,522,109	$10,570,146
Personal Subject to Tax	$49,560,879	$49,652,300	$91,421
Total Locally Assessed	$296,512,842	$307,174,4091	$10,661,567
Homestead Exemptions Allowed	$18,387,901	$18,683,279	$295,378
Net Assessed Locally	$278,124,941	$288,491,130	$10,366,189
Public Service Assessment	$34,668,965	$53,210,579	$18,541,614
Net Assessed Valuation	$312,793,906	$341,701,709	$28,907,803

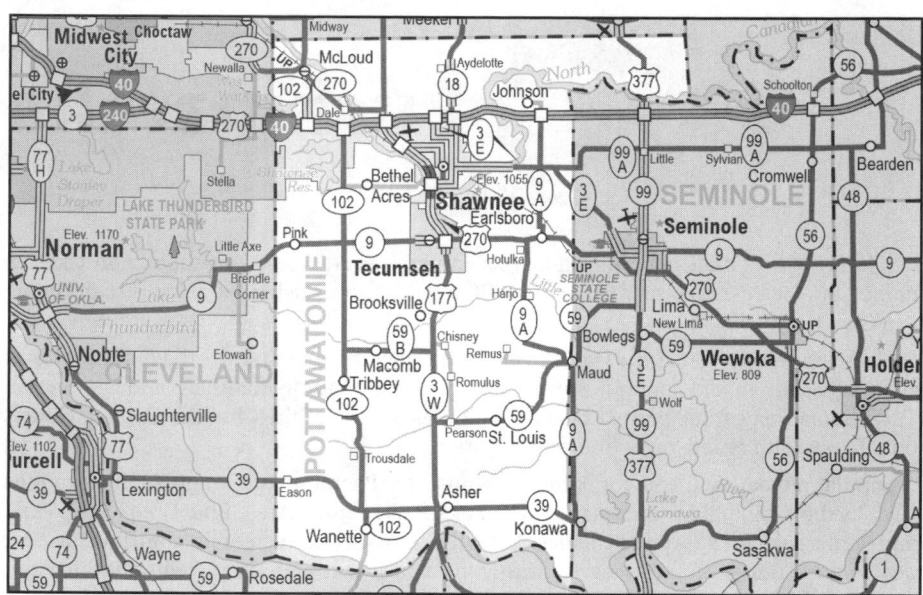

County Seat—Shawnee (Pop. 30,975) 2013 Estimate

Area (Land & Water)—793.26 square miles

Per Capita Income (2013)—$36,170 (Ranks 38th of 77 counties)

Population Statistics (2013)—Female-36,622; Male-33,522; Ethnicity—Wh.-58,145; Bl.-2,936; Am. Ind.-12,636; As.-684; Other-791; Pacific Is.-109; Two or more races-5,018; Hisp.-3,073

Births (2014)—939 • **Deaths** (2014)—815

Marriages (2013)—526 • **Divorces** (2013)—319

Unemployment Rate (2013)—5.2%

Labor Force (2013)—35,347

Number of Establishments (2013)—1,312

Number of Manufacturers (2013)—56

Public Assistance Payments
(FY2014) Total—$50,919,951 • TANF—$364,826 • Supplements—Aged-$80,492; Blind-$926; Disabled-$896,457

Vehicle Registration (2014)—
Automobiles-50,287; Farm Trucks-2,143; Comm. Trucks, Tractors, Trailers-3,231; Motor Homes and Travel Trailers-1,784; Motorcycles-2,832; Manufactured Homes-86; Tax Exempt Licenses-190; Boats-2,221

Institutions of Higher Learning—
Oklahoma Baptist University, St. Gregory's College, Shawnee

Crime Incidents (2013)—Murder-3; Rape-34; Robbery-23; Felony Assault-183; Breaking and Entering-827; Larceny-1,489; Motor Vehicle Theft-219; Arson-13

County Population	
1907 (Okla. Terr.)	43,272
1910	43,595
1920	46,028
1930	66,572
1940	54,377
1950	43,517
1960	41,486
1970	43,134
1980	55,239
1990	58,760
2000	65,521
2010	69,442
2014 Estimate	71,811

• Total Crime
Index-2,778; Crime Rate per 1,000-38.88

Farms (2012)—1,643

Land in Farms (2012)—335,240

Major Lake—Shawnee Reservoir

Major Stream Systems—North Canadian, Canadian, and Little rivers and minor tributaries to Deep Fork

Museums or Historic Sites—St. Gregory's College Gerrer Collection, Oklahoma Baptist University Museum, Santa Fe Depot Museum, Shawnee

Minerals—oil and gas

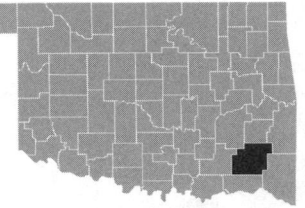

Pushmataha

Originally part of the Choctaw Nation, this county was created at statehood and takes its name from the Pushmataha District of the Choctaw Nation. Pushmataha was also the name of a Choctaw leader.

Antlers, the county seat, is the site of several manufacturing companies that produce items such as custom mixed concrete, lumber, roof trusses, building materials, and sportswear. Tuskahoma, last capital of the Choctaw Nation, is the site of the Choctaw Council House, built in 1884 and noted for its fine architecture.

A popular recreational area for outdoor enthusiasts, Pushmataha County offers locations such as the Kiamichi Mountains, Clayton Lake Recreational Area, Pine Creek State Park, and Sardis Lake for sporting activities. Although tourism and recreation contribute a great deal to the county's economy, agriculture is still a basic component, and wheat is the major crop. Ranching and timber are the main industries.

For additional information, call the county clerk's office at 580/298-3626 or the chamber of commerce at 580/298-2488.

Districts

Congress	2
State Senate	5
State Rep.	19
District Attorney	17
Court of Appeals	3
Ct. of Crim. Appeals	3
Supreme Ct. Jud.	2
SE Jud. Adm.	17

County Officials

Court Clerk	Tina Freeman (D)	Antlers
Clerk	Jane Dunlap (D)	Rattan
Sheriff	Terry Duncan (D)	Rattan
Treasurer	Jenny Beth Caraway (D)	Antlers
Assessor	Frances Joslin (D)	Snow
Elect. Brd. Sec.	Jack Matthews (D)	Antlers
Dist. 1 Comm.	Michael Brittingham (D)	Antlers
Dist. 2 Comm.	Jerry Duncan (D)	Antlers
Dist. 3 Comm.	Rickie Briggs (D)	Clayton

Property Valuations

	2013–2014 Assessment	2014–2015 Assessment	Increase or Decrease
Real Estate and Improvement	$35,356,349	$36,545,947	$1,189,598
Personal Subject to Tax	$5,725,541	$4,842,372	($883,169)
Total Locally Assessed	$41,081,890	$41,388,319	$306,429
Homestead Exemptions Allowed	$3,246,215	$3,212,035	($34,180)
Net Assessed Locally	$37,835,676	$38,176,284	$340,609
Public Service Assessment	$6,227,795	$6,589,559	$361,764
Net Assessed Valuation	$44,063,470	$44,765,843	$702,373

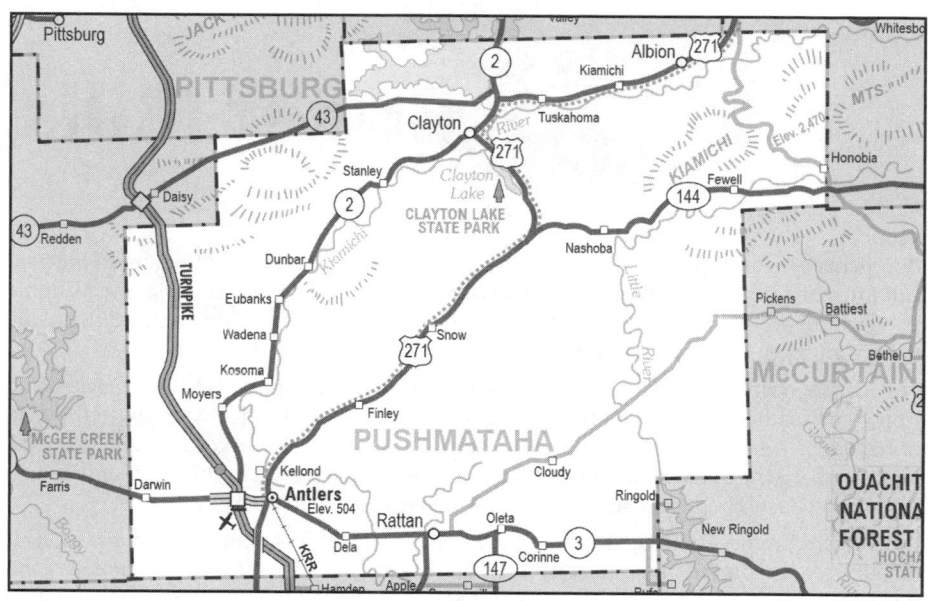

County Seat—Antlers (Pop. 2,374) 2013 Estimate

Area (Land & Water)—1,422.78 square miles

Per Capita Income (2013)—$30,826 (Ranks 65th of 77 counties)

Population Statistics (2013)—Female-5,802; Male-5,604; Ethnicity—Wh.-9,666; Bl.-160; Am. Ind.-2,602; As.-11; Other-89; Pacific Is.-6; Two or more races-1,116; Hisp.-316

Births (2014)—135 • **Deaths** (2014)—168

Marriages (2013)—75 • **Divorces** (2013)—28

Unemployment Rate (2013)—7.6%

Labor Force (2013)—5,338

Number of Establishments (2013)—190

Number of Manufacturers (2013)—7

Public Assistance Payments (FY2014) Total—$8,212,796 • TANF—$53,268 • Supplements—Aged-$54,566; Blind-$2,071; Disabled-$189,489

Vehicle Registration (2014)—Automobiles-8,782; Farm Trucks-1,512; Comm. Trucks, Tractors, Trailers-291; Motor Homes and Travel Trailers-574; Motorcycles-303; Manufactured Homes-12; Tax Exempt Licenses-43; Boats-551

Crime Incidents (2013)—Murder-0; Rape-2; Robbery-0; Felony Assault-17; Breaking and Entering-58; Larceny-70; Motor Vehicle

County Population	
1907 (Okla. Terr.)	8,295
1910	10,118
1920	17,514
1930	14,744
1940	19,446
1950	12,001
1960	9,088
1970	9,385
1980	11,773
1990	10,997
2000	11,667
2010	11,572
2014 Estimate	11,125

Theft-23; Arson-2 • Total Crime Index-170; Crime Rate per 1,000-15.27

Farms (2012)—732

Land in Farms (2012)—297,429

Recreation Area—Clayton Lake

Major Lakes—Hugo, Clayton

Major Stream Systems—Kiamichi, Little rivers and Muddy Boggy Creek

Museums or Historic Sites—Choctaw Council House, Pushmataha County Historical Museum, Antlers

Minerals—oil and gas

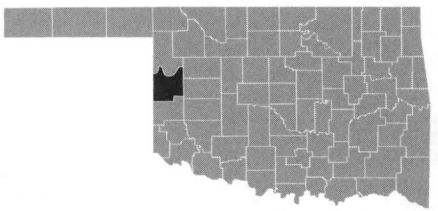

Roger Mills

Bordering the Texas panhandle, Roger Mills County was opened to settlement in the land run into the Cheyenne and Arapaho reservations in April 1892. It was designated County "F," and Cheyenne was the county seat. In November 1892, an election changed the name to honor Roger Q. Mills of Texas, a former United States senator.

The Antelope Hills once marked the international line between the U.S. and Mexico, and Coronado made mention of them as a campsite in 1541. The California Road to the gold mines of the West crossed the area in 1849, commemorated by a marker north of Roll. West of Cheyenne is the marker commemorating the Battle of the Washita, where General George Armstrong Custer raided a Cheyenne Indian village on November 27, 1868.

Roger Mills County lies atop the rich Anadarko Basin and has many oil and gas wells. It enjoyed a boom period in the late 1970s and early 1980s, but agriculture is the mainstay and most of the large ranches are still owned and operated by the same families that first settled them. The construction of the first series of upstream dams in the late 1940s at Sandstone followed the ruinous dust storms of the 1930s. These pioneering efforts helped develop land and water conservation projects throughout the U.S.

For more information, call the county clerk's office at 580/497-3395.

Districts

Congress	3
State Senate	26
State Rep.	55
District Attorney	2
Court of Appeals	6
Ct. of Crim. Appeals	5
Supreme Ct. Jud.	4
NW Jud. Adm.	2

County Officials

Court Clerk	Jan Bailey (D)	Cheyenne
Clerk	Jimmy Beavin (D)	Cheyenne
Sheriff	Joe Hay (D)	Cheyenne
Treasurer	Bab Coker (D)	Cheyenne
Assessor	Sarah Batterton (D)	Cheyenne
Elect. Brd. Sec.	Jana Maddux (D)	Cheyenne
Dist. 1 Comm.	Brian Hay (D)	Cheyenne
Dist. 2 Comm.	Justin Walker (D)	Hammon
Dist. 3 Comm.	Ron Burrows (R)	Claremore

Property Valuations

	2013–2014 Assessment	2014–2015 Assessment	Increase or Decrease
Real Estate and Improvement	$21,213,860	$21,834,335	$620,475
Personal Subject to Tax	$165,331,565	$167,850,470	$2,518,905
Total Locally Assessed	$186,545,425	$189,684,805	$3,139,380
Homestead Exemptions Allowed	$962,690	$966,715	$4,025
Net Assessed Locally	$185,582,735	$188,718,090	$3,135,355
Public Service Assessment	$7,981,671	$12,219,394	$4,237,723
Net Assessed Valuation	$193,564,406	$200,937,484	$7,373,078

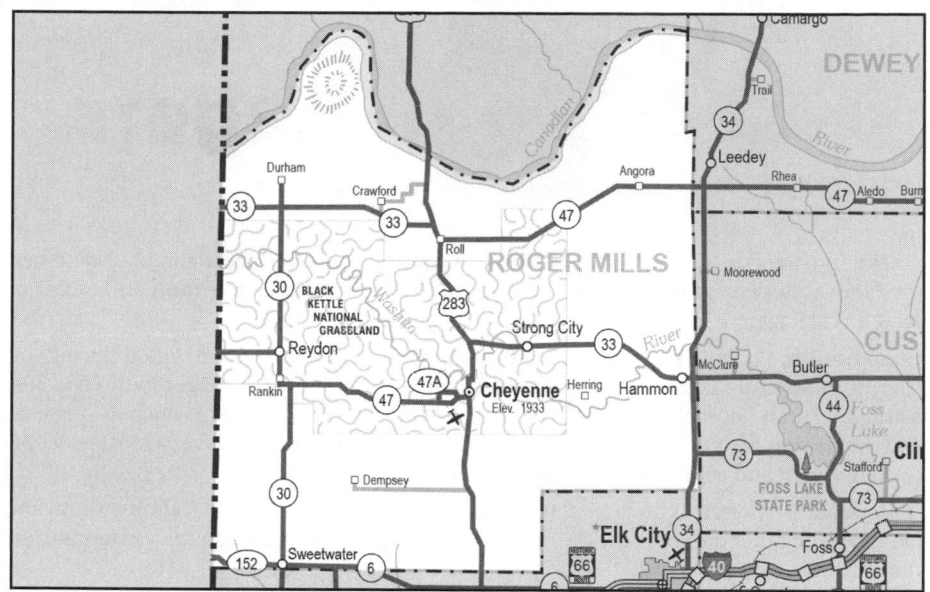

County Seat—Cheyenne (Pop. 815) 2013 Estimate

Area (Land & Water)—1,146.46 square miles

Per Capita Income (2013)—$46,789 (Ranks 9th of 77 counties)

Population Statistics (2013)—Female-1,860; Male-1,853; Ethnicity—Wh.-3,622; Bl.-5; Am. Ind.-318; As.-9; Other-12; Pacific Is.-7; Two or more races-258; Hisp.-194

Births (2014)—49 • **Deaths** (2014)—35

Marriages (2013)—19 • **Divorces** (2013)—15

Unemployment Rate (2013)—2.9%

Labor Force (2013)—2,114

Number of Establishments (2013)—86

Number of Manufacturers (2013)—2

Public Assistance Payments
(FY2014) Total—$468,102 • TANF—$921 • Supplements—Aged-$62; Blind-$101; Disabled-$1,069

Vehicle Registration (2014)—
Automobiles-1,676; Farm Trucks-888; Comm. Trucks, Tractors, Trailers-131; Motor Homes and Travel Trailers-105; Motorcycles-84; Manufactured Homes-5; Tax Exempt Licenses-6; Boats-32

Crime Incidents (2013)—Murder-0; Rape-0; Robbery-0; Felony Assault-3; Breaking and Entering-8; Larceny-36; Motor Vehicle Theft-3; Arson-0 • Total Crime Index-50; Crime Rate per 1,000-13.03

Farms (2012)—678

Land in Farms (2012)—719,291

Major Stream Systems—Washita and Canadian rivers and tributaries to the North Fork of the Red River

Museums or Historic Sites—Black Kettle Museum, Roll One-Room School Museum, Washita Battle Site, Cheyenne

Minerals—oil and gas

County Population	
1907 (Okla. Terr.)	13,239
1910	12,861
1920	10,638
1930	14,164
1940	10,736
1950	7,395
1960	5,090
1970	4,452
1980	4,799
1990	4,147
2000	3,436
2010	3,647
2014 Estimate	3,761

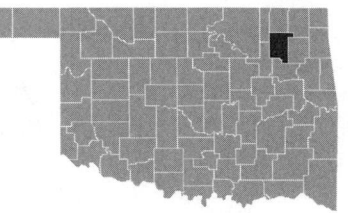

Rogers

Originally part of the Cherokee Nation, Rogers County was created at statehood, and named for Clem V. Rogers, member of the Oklahoma Constitutional Convention and father of famed Will Rogers.

Claremore, the county seat, was named for the Osage Chief Clermont, killed during the Clermont Mound Massacre. It claims as its own such notables as singer Patti Page and astronaut Stuart Roosa. Lynn Riggs, author of *Green Grow the Lilacs*, from which the musical *Oklahoma!* was adapted, was born three miles from Claremore. J.M. Davis, a local resident, owned a hotel and collected more than 20,000 guns in his lifetime.

Catoosa, now a port, was once a rail terminal which saw the likes of the Daltons, Youngers, Doolins, and other outlaws pass through its boundaries. The port's waterway extends from the Verdigris, Arkansas, and Mississippi rivers to the Gulf of Mexico.

While agriculture is still basic, the mining of coal and shale has also been important to the economy of Rogers County. Points of interest in the county include the Will Rogers Memorial Museum in Claremore, which attracts nearly one million visitors annually; the J.M. Davis Gun Museum; Totem Pole Historical Park located east of Foyil; and the Belvidere Mansion in Claremore. For more information, call the county clerk's office at 918/341-2518.

Districts

Congress	1, 2
State Senate	2, 29, 34
State Rep.	6, 8, 9, 11, 23, 74, 77
District Attorney	12
Court of Appeals	2
Ct. of Crim. Appeals	1
Supreme Ct. Jud.	1
NE Jud. Adm.	12

County Officials

Court Clerk	Kim Henry (R)	Claremore
Clerk	Robin Anderson (R)	Claremore
Sheriff	Scott Walton (R)	Inola
Treasurer	Cathy Pinkerton Baker (D)	Talala
Assessor	Scott Marsh (R)	Claremore
Elect. Brd. Sec.	Julie Dermody (R)	Oologah
Dist. 1 Comm.	Dan DeLozier (D)	Chelsea
Dist. 2 Comm.	Mike Helm (R)	Collinsville
Dist. 3 Comm.	Kirt Thacker (R)	Inola

Property Valuations

	2013–2014 Assessment	2014–2015 Assessment	Increase or Decrease
Real Estate and Improvement	$507,742,564	$531,776,046	$24,033,482
Personal Subject to Tax	$169,314,783	$181,590,855	$12,276,072
Total Locally Assessed	$677,057,347	$713,366,901	$36,309,554
Homestead Exemptions Allowed	$25,801,570	$26,503,121	$701,551
Net Assessed Locally	$651,255,777	$686,863,780	$35,608,003
Public Service Assessment	$116,361,602	$99,110,497	($17,251,105)
Net Assessed Valuation	$767,617,379	$785,974,277	$18,356,898

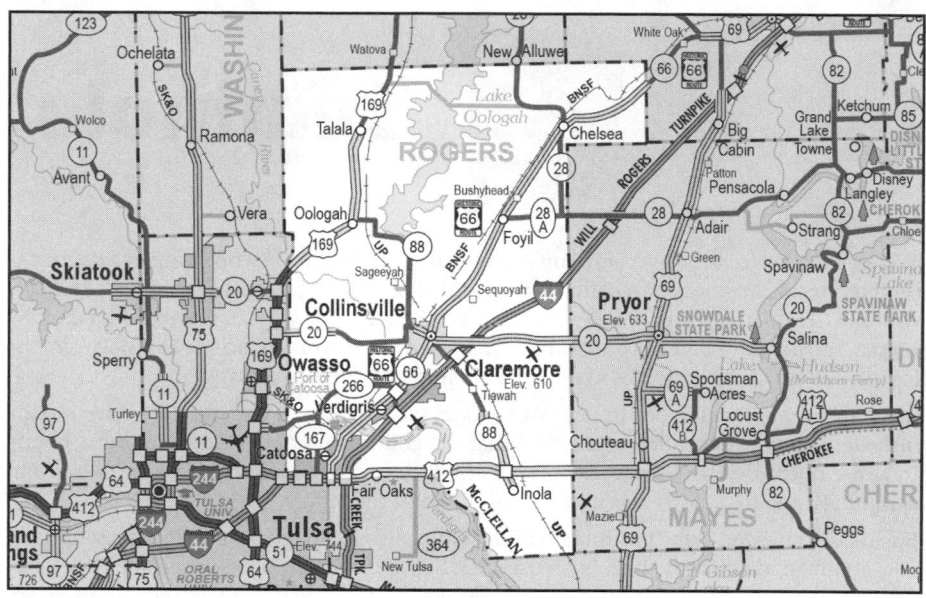

County Seat—Claremore (Pop. 19,032) 2013 Estimate

Area (Land & Water)—711.44 square miles

Per Capita Income (2013)—$41,106 (Ranks 24th of 77 counties)

Population Statistics (2013)—Female-44,126; Male-43,604;
Ethnicity—Wh.-74,039; Bl.-1,261; Am. Ind.-17,730; As.-1,424;
Other-1,237; Pacific Is.-65; Two or more races-7,885; Hisp.-3,396

Births (2014)—1,012 • **Deaths** (2014)—850

Marriages (2013)—515 • **Divorces** (2013)—373

Unemployment Rate (2013)—5.7%

Labor Force (2013)—41,667

Number of Establishments (2013)—1,702

Number of Manufacturers (2013)—152

Public Assistance Payments
(FY2014) Total—$39,129,402 • TANF—
$238,874 • Supplements—Aged-$57,907;
Blind-$2,439; Disabled-$532,174

Vehicle Registration (2014)—
Automobiles-56,123; Farm Trucks-1,704;
Comm. Trucks, Tractors, Trailers-4,438;
Motor Homes and Travel Trailers-2,314;
Motorcycles-3,024; Manufactured Homes-46;
Tax Exempt Licenses-204; Boats-3,234

Institutions of Higher Learning—Rogers
University, Claremore

Crime Incidents (2013)—Murder-0; Rape-38;
Robbery-5; Felony Assault-124; Breaking
and Entering-282; Larceny-769; Motor
Vehicle Theft-120; Arson-3 • Total Crime

County Population	
1907 (Okla. Terr.)	15,485
1910	17,736
1920	17,605
1930	18,956
1940	21,078
1950	19,532
1960	20,614
1970	28,425
1980	46,436
1990	55,170
2000	70,641
2010	86,905
2014 Estimate	89,815

Index-1,338;
Crime Rate per 1,000-15.19

Farms (2012)—1,733

Land in Farms (2012)—301,804

Recreation Area—Will RogersState Park

Major Lake—Oolagah

Major Stream Systems—Verdigris and Caney
rivers, Bird Creek and tributaries to Grand
River

Museums or Historic Sites—J.M. Davis
Gun Collection Museum, Belvidere Mansion,
Long's Historical Museum, Lynn Riggs
Memorial, Will Rogers Memorial, Claremore;
Will Rogers birthplace, Oolagah

Minerals—oil and gas; coal

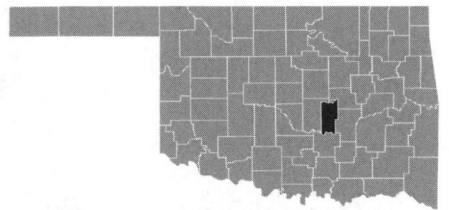

Seminole

Taking its name from a Creek word meaning "runaway" or "those who camp at a distance," this county was originally part of the Seminole Nation, Indian Territory. As a result of a treaty with the Creeks in 1856, the Seminoles received an estimated 2,169,080 acres of land in the Indian Territory where they could establish their own government and laws. They were the last of the Five Civilized Tribes to organize their government in this region.

Although oil exploration began near Wewoka as early as 1902, it was not until 1923 and the discovery of the Greater Seminole Field that the county experienced an economic boom. By September 1929, this became the premier high-gravity oil field in the United States. Now, agriculture and manufacturing also contribute to the economy.

Businesses engaged in the production of clothing, oil field chemicals and tanks, air blasting equipment, and others are located in the area. Seminole State College continues the tradition first exemplified by the founding of the Mekasukey Academy for Seminole boys in 1891 and the Emahaka Boarding School for Seminole girls in 1893.

Sources of recreational activities include area lakes as well as public golf courses in Seminole and Wewoka. For more information, call the county clerk's office at 405/257-2501.

Districts

Congress..........................5
State Senate..............13, 28
State Rep........................28
District Attorney 22
Court of Appeals 3
Ct. of Crim. Appeals........3
Supreme Ct. Jud. 8
S. Cent. Jud. Adm. 22
    (Div. II & Div. III)

County Officials

Court Clerk	Kim Davis (D)	Sasakwa
Clerk	Tahasha Wilcots (D)	Wewoka
Sheriff	Shannon Smith (D)	Wewoka
Treasurer	Lisa Turpin (D)	Wewoka
Assessor	Denise Bailey (D)	Sasakwa
Elect. Brd. Sec.	Mary Jo Rains (D)	Konawa
Dist. 1 Comm.	Gary Choate (D)	Sasakwa
Dist. 2 Comm.	Tommy Monks (D)	Seminole
Dist. 3 Comm.	John Kirby(D)	Wewoka

Property Valuations

	2013–2014 Assessment	2014–2015 Assessment	Increase or Decrease
Real Estate and Improvement	$66,847,481	$67,781,353	$933,872
Personal Subject to Tax	$22,057,245	$24,373,944	$2,316,699
Total Locally Assessed	$88,904,726	$92,155,297	$3,250,571
Homestead Exemptions Allowed	$6,438,319	$6,287,357	($150,96)
Net Assessed Locally	$82,466,407	$85,867,940	$3,401,533
Public Service Assessment	$46,287,938	$76,024,634	$29,736,696
Net Assessed Valuation	$128,754,345	$161,892,574	$33,138,229

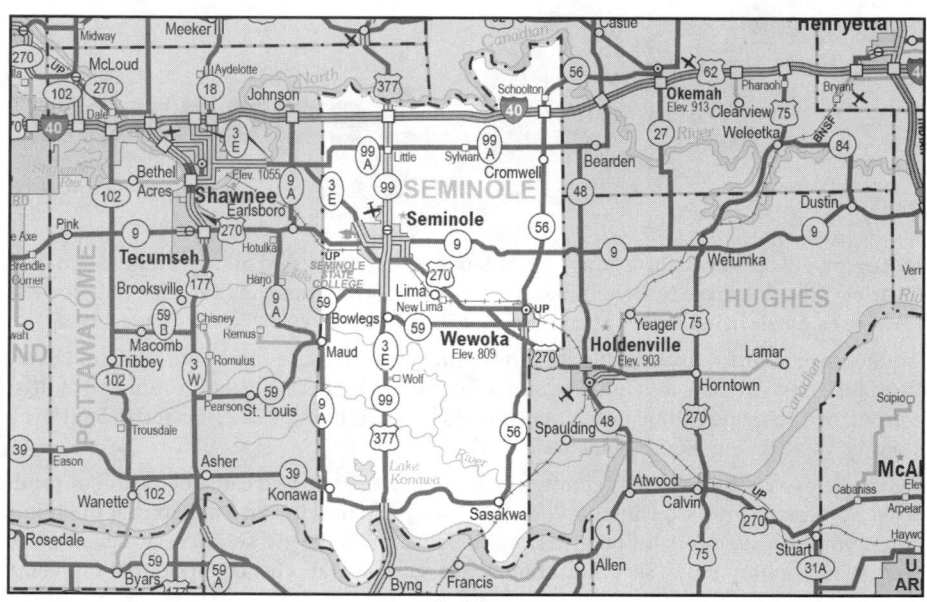

County Seat—Wewoka (Pop. 3,448) 2013 Estimate

Area (Land & Water)—640.57 square miles

Per Capita Income (2013)—$33,009 (Ranks 55th of 77 counties)

Population Statistics (2013)—Female-13,054; Male-12,389; Ethnicity—Wh.-19,153; Bl.-1,626; Am. Ind.-6,125; As.-144; Other-405; Pacific Is.-32; Two or more races-2,032; Hisp.-1,011

Births (2014)—318 • Deaths (2014)—365

Marriages (2013)—151 • Divorces (2013)—99

Unemployment Rate (2013)—7.4%

Labor Force (2013)—11,029

Number of Establishments (2013)—469

Number of Manufacturers (2013)—20

Public Assistance Payments (FY2014) Total—$20,680,841 • TANF—$255,563 • Supplements—Aged-$65,216; Blind-$201; Disabled-$372,596

Vehicle Registration (2014)—
Automobiles-15,658; Farm Trucks-1,350; Comm. Trucks, Tractors, Trailers-1,600; Motor Homes and Travel Trailers-674; Motorcycles-738; Manufactured Homes-28; Tax Exempt Licenses-58; Boats-578

Institutions of Higher Learning—Seminole State College, Seminole

Crime Incidents (2013)—Murder-1; Rape-2;

County Population	
1907 (Okla. Terr.)	14,687
1910	19,964
1920	23,808
1930	79,621
1940	61,201
1950	40,672
1960	28,066
1970	25,144
1980	27,473
1990	25,412
2000	24,894
2010	25,482
2014 Estimate	25,421

Robbery-2; Felony Assault-48; Breaking and Entering-193; Larceny-536; Motor Vehicle Theft-40; Arson-7 • Total Crime Index-823; Crime Rate per 1,000-32.20

Farms (2012)—1,054

Land in Farms (2012)—243,260

Major Stream Systems—North Canadian, Little, and Canadian rivers

Museums or Historic Sites—Seminole Nation Museum at Wewoka

Minerals—oil and gas, lime, crushed stone, clays

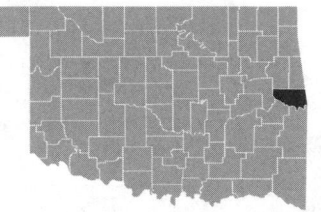

Sequoyah

Once a part of Arkansas, this county was created at statehood, and named for the Sequoyah District of the Cherokee Nation, Indian Territory. Sequoyah was the Cherokee linguist who developed an alphabet for his people. Sallisaw is the county seat.

In 1816 the land encompassing Sequoyah County was purchased by Major William Lovely from the Osage Indians as a hunting outlet for the Cherokees. During the removal of 1835, a group of Cherokees settled permanently in this area. Tahlonteeskee, located in Sequoyah County, was the Cherokee capital until 1839.

Agriculture is a mainstay of the county's economy, with grain and cattle being major products. Applegate Cove, Cowlington Point, and Short Mountain Cove are among the many campgrounds available in the county. Lake Tenkiller and Robert S. Kerr Reservoir also afford recreational opportunities. Sequoyah's home near Sallisaw is another county tourist attraction.

For more information, call the county clerk's office at 918/775-5539.

Districts

Congress	2
State Senate	4
State Rep.	2, 15
District Attorney	27
Court of Appeals	2
Ct. of Crim. Appeals	3
Supreme Ct. Jud.	2
E. Cent. Jud. Adm.	15
(Div. III)	

County Officials

Court Clerk	Vicki Beaty (D)	Roland
Clerk	Julie Haywood (D)	Sallisaw
Sheriff	Ronn Lockhart (D)	Sallisaw
Treasurer	Tricia Yates (D)	Sallisaw
Assessor	Donna Graham (D)	Sallisaw
Elect. Brd. Sec.	Cindy Osborn (R)	Roland
Dist. 1 Comm.	Ray Watts (D)	Muldrow
Dist. 2 Comm.	Steve Carter (D)	Gore
Dist. 3 Comm.	Jimmy Dale Rogers (D)	Sallisaw

Property Valuations

	2013–2014 Assessment	2014–2015 Assessment	Increase or Decrease
Real Estate and Improvement	$140,320,298	$145,839,306	$5,519,008
Personal Subject to Tax	$14,880,746	$15,494,294	$613,548
Total Locally Assessed	$155,201,044	$161,333,600	$6,132,556
Homestead Exemptions Allowed	$11,666,409	$11,969,588	$303,179
Net Assessed Locally	$143,534,635	$149,364,012	$5,829,377
Public Service Assessment	$18,419,218	$19,976,691	$1,557,473
Net Assessed Valuation	$161,953,853	$169,340,703	$7,386,850

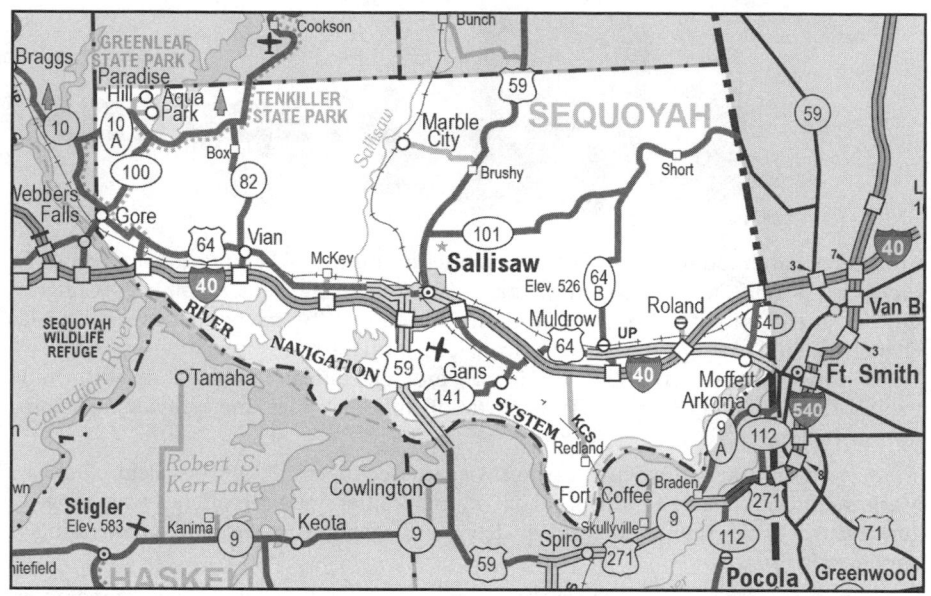

County Seat—Sallisaw (Pop. 8,623) 2014 Estimate

Area (Land & Water)—714.88 square miles

Per Capita Income (2013)—$29,827 (Ranks 71st of 77 counties)

Population Statistics (2013)—Female–21,172; Male–20,662;
Ethnicity—Wh.-35,091; Bl.-1,081; Am. Ind.-12,272; As.-339;
Other-523; Pacific Is.-33; Two or more races-7,374; Hisp.-1,486

Births (2014)—549 • **Deaths** (2014)—482

Marriages (2013)—235 • **Divorces** (2013)—174

Unemployment Rate (2013)—8.9%

Labor Force (2013)—16,791

Number of Establishments (2013)—572

Number of Manufacturers (2013)—19

Public Assistance Payments
(FY2014) Total—$31,891,702 • TANF—
$433,473 • Supplements—Aged-$112,241;
Blind-$3,238; Disabled-$700,315

Vehicle Registration (2014)—
Automobiles-26,752; Farm Trucks-1,499;
Comm. Trucks, Tractors, Trailers-26,382;
Motor Homes and Travel Trailers-1,088;
Motorcycles-1,127; Manufactured Homes-64;
Tax Exempt Licenses-197; Boats-1,845

Crime Incidents (2013)—Murder-0; Rape-9;
Robbery-7; Felony Assault-92; Breaking
and Entering-272; Larceny-646; Motor

County Population	
1907 (Okla. Terr.)	22,499
1910	25,005
1920	26,786
1930	19,505
1940	23,138
1950	19,773
1960	18,001
1970	23,370
1980	30,749
1990	33,828
2000	38,972
2010	42,391
2014 Estimate	41,358

Vehicle Theft-42; Arson-16 • Total Crime
Index-1,068; Crime Rate per 1,000-24.39

Farms (2012)—1,204

Land in Farms (2012)—215,116

Recreation Area—Tenkiller State Park

Major Lake—Tenkiller

Major Stream Systems—Arkansas and
Illinois rivers

Museums or Historic Sites—Sequoyah's
Home, Dwight Prebysterian Mission, Fourteen
Flags Museum, Sallisaw; Cherokee Courthouse

Minerals—oil and gas, crushed stone

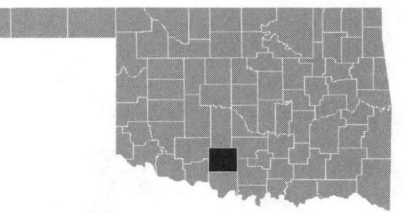

Stephens

Created at statehood from portions of Comanche County, Oklahoma Territory, and the Chickasaw Nation, Stephens County was named for John H. Stephens, a member of Congress from Texas and staunch advocate of Oklahoma statehood. The first permanent settler, Silas Fitzpatrick, sold his store to William Duncan, for whom the county seat was named in 1892. The county is served by U.S. 81 and S.H. 7, 29, and 53. Duncan Municipal Airport, Union Pacific Railroad, and Oklahoma Transportation-Jefferson Bus Lines provide additional transportation links.

The economy is based on agriculture (wheat, peanuts, cotton, cattle) and petroleum. Duncan, Marlow, and Comanche are the principal municipalities and each offers a wide range of goods and services. Halliburton Oil Field Services began in Duncan, and remains a major employer in the area.

Duncan maintains 144 acres of parks and playgrounds and two public swimming pools. There are golf courses in Duncan, Marlow, and Comanche. Boating, fishing, camping facilities, and 4,000 acres of recreational lands are found at Clear Creek, Duncan, Humphries, and Fuqua lakes.

The Stephens County Memorial Museum is located in Duncan. For more information, call the county clerk's office at 580/255-0977.

Districts

Congress	4
State Senate	31, 43
State Rep.	50, 51, 65
District Attorney	6
Court of Appeals	6
Ct. of Crim. Appeals	3
Supreme Ct. Jud.	5
SW Jud. Adm.	5
(Div. II)	

County Officials

Court Clerk	Margaret Cunningham	Duncan
Clerk	(D)	Duncan
Sheriff	Cindy Kaiser (D)	Marlow
Treasurer	Wayne McKinney (R)	Bray
Assessor	Janice Graham (D)	Duncan
Elect. Brd. Sec.	Cathy Hokit (D)	Duncan
Dist. 1 Comm.	Peggy Winton (D)	Marlow
Dist. 2 Comm.	Darrell Sparks (D)	Duncan
Dist. 3 Comm.	Lonnie Estes (D)	Comanche
	Dee Bowen (D)	

Property Valuations

	2013–2014 Assessment	2014–2015 Assessment	Increase or Decrease
Real Estate and Improvement	$193,453,900	$198,543,041	$5,089,141
Personal Subject to Tax	$121,691,866	$131,103,110	$9,411,244
Total Locally Assessed	$315,145,766	$329,646,151	$14,500,385
Homestead Exemptions Allowed	$13,424,568	$13,548,365	$123,797
Net Assessed Locally	$301,721,198	$316,097,786	$14,376,588
Public Service Assessment	$25,781,826	$25,612,630	($169,196)
Net Assessed Valuation	$327,503,024	$341,710,416	$14,207,392

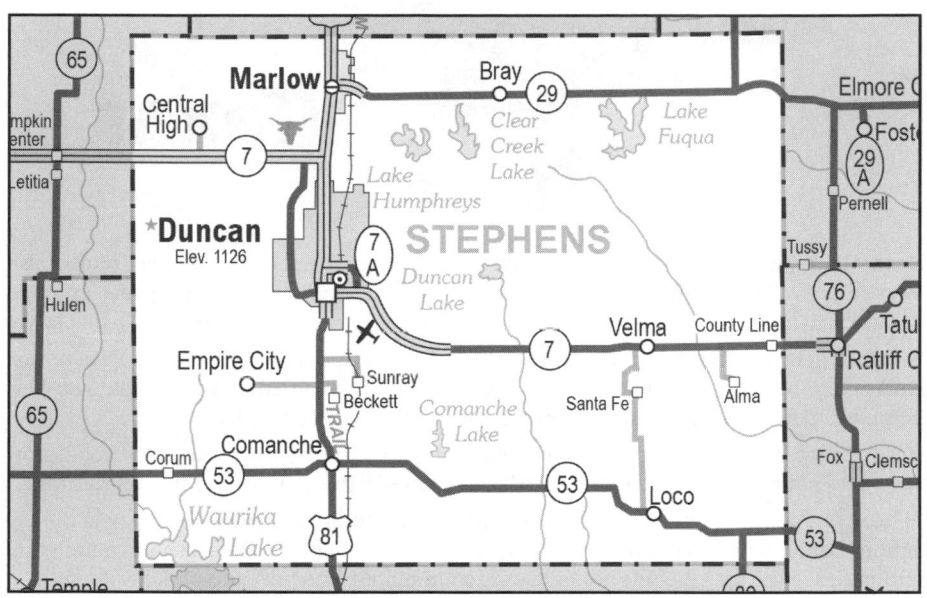

County Seat—Duncan (Pop. 23,400) 2013 Estimate

Area (Land & Water)—891.12 square miles

Per Capita Income (2013)—$46,376 (Ranks 10th of 77 counties)

Population Statistics (2013)—Female–23,014; Male–21,915; Ethnicity—Wh.-39,598; Bl.-1,342; Am. Ind.-3,817; As.-378; Other-1,176; Pacific Is.-36; Two or more races-1,722; Hisp.-2,881

Births (2014)—569 • **Deaths** (2014)—603

Marriages (2013)—258 • **Divorces** (2013)—251

Unemployment Rate (2013)—4.9%

Labor Force (2013)—23,369

Number of Establishments (2013)—1,080

Number of Manufacturers (2013)—58

Public Assistance Payments
(FY2014) Total—$21,946,661 • TANF—$173,368 • Supplements—Aged-$49,837; Blind-$1,165; Disabled-$375,368

Vehicle Registration (2014)—
Automobiles-40,049; Farm Trucks-2,848; Comm. Trucks, Tractors, Trailers-4,190; Motor Homes and Travel Trailers-1,699; Motorcycles-2,003; Manufactured Homes-30; Tax Exempt Licenses-183; Boats-1,634

Crime Incidents (2013)—Murder-2; Rape-17;

County Population	
1907 (Okla. Terr.)	20,148
1910	22,252
1920	24,692
1930	33,069
1940	31,090
1950	34,071
1960	37,990
1970	35,902
1980	43,419
1990	42,299
2000	43,182
2010	45,048
2014 Estimate	44,493

Robbery-21; Felony Assault-74; Breaking and Entering-450; Larceny-1,140; Motor Vehicle Theft-65; Arson-9 Total Crime Index-1,769; Crime Rate per 1,000-39.43

Farms (2012)—1,286

Land in Farms (2012)—480,668

Major Stream Systems—Beaver and Mud Creek and tributaries to Washita

Museums or Historic Sites—Stephens County Memorial Museum at Duncan

Minerals—oil and gas

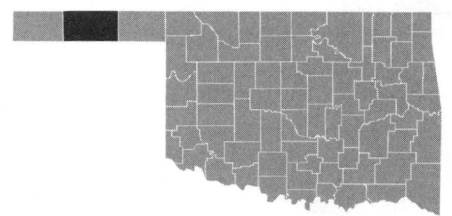

Texas

Texas County was formed at statehood from the central one-third of "Old Beaver County," also known as "No Man's Land." It took its name from the state of Texas. Its county seat is named for E. T. Guymon, uncle of George E. Ellison, who established the first business in that town.

The Beaver River is the principal stream in Texas County, rising in northeastern New Mexico and emptying into the Canadian River near Eufaula. It is joined by Wolf Creek near Fort Supply and from there becomes known as the North Canadian River.

Texas County consists of level plains and rolling hills. Many trees, especially cottonwood, grow along the streams. A large number of irrigation wells in the county help stabilize farming.

Wheat, grain sorghums, and cattle are the chief agricultural industries, ranking near the top among counties of the state in all three. The county ranks high in natural gas and petroleum. Industries in the area include gasoline extraction plants, and beef and pork production.

The county is served by three historical societies: Texhoma Historical Society, Beaver River Historical Society, and Daughters of the American Revolution. For more information, call the county clerk's office at 580/338-3141.

Districts

Congress	3
State Senate	27
State Rep.	61
District Attorney	1
Court of Appeals	6
Ct. of Crim. Appeals	5
Supreme Ct. Jud.	4
NW Jud. Adm.	1

County Officials

Court Clerk	M. Renee Ellis (R)	Texhoma
Clerk	Marcia Hollingshead (D)	Guymon
Sheriff	Rick Caddell (D)	Guymon
Treasurer	Lavena Chastine (D)	Guymon
Assessor	Judyth Campbell (R)	Guymon
Elect. Brd. Sec.	Glenda Williams (R)	Guymon
Dist. 1 Comm.	Ted Keeling (R)	Hooker
Dist. 2 Comm.	Richard Bryan (R)	Guymon
Dist. 3 Comm.	Jack Strain (D)	Goodwell

Property Valuations

	2013–2014 Assessment	2014–2015 Assessment	Increase or Decrease
Real Estate and Improvement	$112,455,742	$113,730,040	$1,274,298
Personal Subject to Tax	$120,785,443	$122,000,872	$1,215,429
Total Locally Assessed	$233,241,185	$235,730,912	$2,489,727
Homestead Exemptions Allowed	$3,824,512	$3,831,260	$6,748
Net Assessed Locally	$229,416,673	$231,899,652	$2,482,979
Public Service Assessment	$20,600,466	$21,854,666	$1,254,200
Net Assessed Valuation	$250,017,139	$253,754,318	$3,737,179

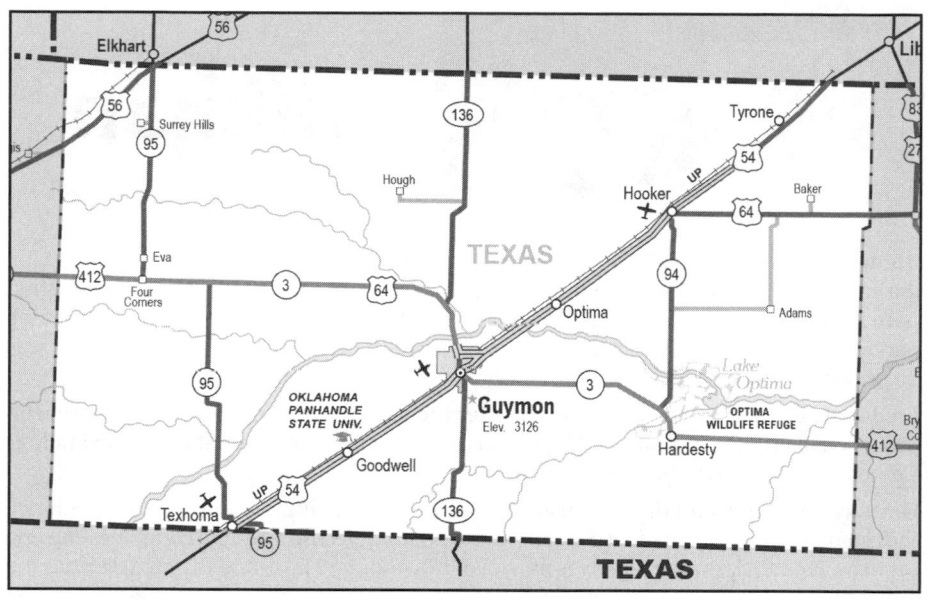

County Seat—Guymon (Pop. 12,272) 2013 Estimate

Area (Land & Water)—2,048.81 square miles

Per Capita Income (2013)—$37,505 (Ranks 33rd of 77 counties)

Population Statistics (2013)—Female-10,283; Male-10,874; Ethnicity—Wh.-14,643; Bl.-516; Am. Ind.-407; As.-770; Other-4,459; Pacific Is.-10; Two or more races-641; Hisp.-9,233

Births (2014)—395 • **Deaths** (2014)—175

Marriages (2013)—136 • **Divorces** (2013)—72

Unemployment Rate (2013)—5.1%

Labor Force (2013)—8,035

Number of Establishments (2013)—488

Number of Manufacturers (2013)—11

Public Assistance Payments
(FY2014) Total—$7,675,879 • TANF—$103,813 • Supplements—Aged-$18,582; Blind-$41; Disabled-$65,604

Vehicle Registration (2014)—
Automobiles-17,768; Farm Trucks-2,730; Comm. Trucks, Tractors, Trailers-1,255; Motor Homes and Travel Trailers-605; Motorcycles-703; Manufactured Homes-31; Tax Exempt Licenses-48; Boats-249

Institutions of Higher Learning—
Oklahoma Panhandle State University, Goodwell

County Population	
1907 (Okla. Terr.)	16,448
1910	14,249
1920	13,975
1930	14,100
1940	9,896
1950	14,235
1960	14,162
1970	16,352
1980	17,727
1990	16,419
2000	20,107
2010	20,640
2014 Estimate	21,853

Crime Incidents (2013)—Murder-0; Rape-3; Robbery-3; Felony Assault-34; Breaking and Entering-79; Larceny-219; Motor Vehicle Theft-12; Arson-1 • Total Crime Index-350; Crime Rate per 1,000-16.03

Farms (2012)—1,024

Land in Farms (2012)—1,286,834

Major Lake—Optima

Major Stream Systems—North Canadian (Beaver) and Cimarron rivers

Museums or Historic Sites—No Man's Land Historical Museum, Goodwell

Minerals—oil and gas

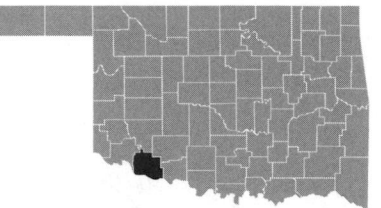

Tillman

Bordering Texas at the Red River, part of the county was in Comanche, Kiowa, and Apache grazing lands opened for settlement by lottery June 9, 1901, to August 6, 1901. The southeastern part, in the Big Pasture, was opened by sealed bids in December 1906. These lands became part of Comanche County, Oklahoma Territory, until statehood, when Tillman County was organized and named for South Carolina Senator Benjamin Tillman.

Frederick, the county seat, was named after the son of a Frisco Railway executive who promised to give the city an iron flagpole in return for the honor. Great Plains Technology Center has a campus in Frederick.

Farming, ranching, and dairies illustrate a variety of agricultural interests. The Frederick Industrial Park has a 6,000-foot concrete and asphalt lighted runway and complete refueling services. Frederick's water supply is provided by a 900-acre lake, and the area also has the Tom Steed Reservoir. Just east of Manitou, Deep Red Creek has been dammed to provide water and recreation. The Hackberry Flat Project has restored the area that was drained and farmed for years to provide a wildlife habitat for birds. The Oklahoma Historical Society completed a complex across from the Tillman County Courthouse depicting farm life in the early twentieth century. For more information, call the county clerk's office at 580/335-3421.

Districts

Congress	4
State Senate	31
State Rep.	63
District Attorney	3
Court of Appeals	4
Ct. of Crim. Appeals	5
Supreme Ct. Jud.	9
SW Jud. Adm.	3

County Officials

Court Clerk	Kevin Stevens (D)	Frederick
Clerk	Cacy Caldwell (D)	Frederick
Sheriff	Bobby Whittington (R)	Grandfield
Treasurer	Kim Lamb (D)	Davidson
Assessor	Matthew Smith (D)	Frederick
Elect. Brd. Sec.	Sherri Jacobs (D)	Frederick
Dist. 1 Comm.	Jimmie C. Smith (D)	Tipton
Dist. 2 Comm.	Joe Don Dickey (R)	Frederick
Dist. 3 Comm.	Kent Smith (D)	Loveland

Property Valuations

	2013–2014 Assessment	2014–2015 Assessment	Increase or Decrease
Real Estate and Improvement	$31,430,875	$32,004,390	$573,515
Personal Subject to Tax	$8,144,519	$8,498,406	$353,887
Total Locally Assessed	$39,575,394	$40,502,796	$927,402
Homestead Exemptions Allowed	$2,184,708	$2,196,279	$11,571
Net Assessed Locally	$37,390,686	$38,306,517	$915,831
Public Service Assessment	$6,671,349	$7,585,824	$914,475
Net Assessed Valuation	$44,062,035	$45,8892,341	$1,830,306

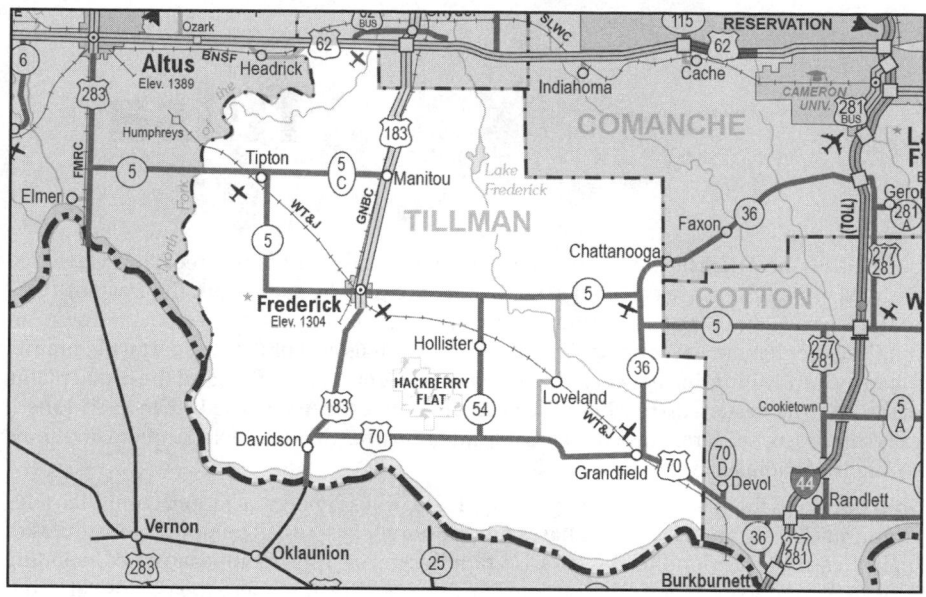

County Population

1907 (Okla. Terr.)	12,869
1910	18,650
1920	22,433
1930	24,390
1940	20,754
1950	17,598
1960	14,654
1970	12,901
1980	12,398
1990	10,384
2000	9,287
2010	7,992
2014 Estimate	7,628

County Seat—Frederick (Pop. 3,797) 2013 Estimate

Area (Land & Water)—879.21 square miles

Per Capita Income (2013)—$35,719 (Ranks 40th of 77 counties)

Population Statistics (2013)—Female-3,929; Male-3,969; Ethnicity—Wh.-6,520; Bl.-830; Am. Ind.-471; As.-82; Other-545; Pacific Is.-4; Two or more races-545; Hisp.-1,841

Births (2014)—106 • **Deaths** (2014)—98

Marriages (2013)—29 • **Divorces** (2013)—38

Unemployment Rate (2013)—5.5%

Labor Force (2013)—3,453

Number of Establishments (2013)—143

Number of Manufacturers (2013)—5

Public Assistance Payments (FY2014) Total—$5,167,303 • TANF—$50,252 • Supplements—Aged-$32,465; Blind-$344; Disabled-$108,769

Vehicle Registration (2014)—Automobiles-5,907; Farm Trucks-1,351; Comm. Trucks, Tractors, Trailers-194; Motor Homes and Travel Trailers-248; Motorcycles-212; Manufactured Homes-0; Tax Exempt Licenses-163; Boats-209

Crime Incidents (2013)—Murder-0; Rape-1; Robbery-1; Felony Assault-29; Breaking and Entering-55; Larceny-136; Motor Vehicle Theft-4; Arson-7 • Total Crime Index-226; Crime Rate per 1,000-28.95

Farms (2012)—556

Land in Farms (2012)—541,419

Major Stream Systems—Red River, North Fork of Red River and its tributaries, and tributaries to Cache Creek

Museums or Historic Sites—Tillman County Historic Museum at Frederick

Minerals—oil and gas

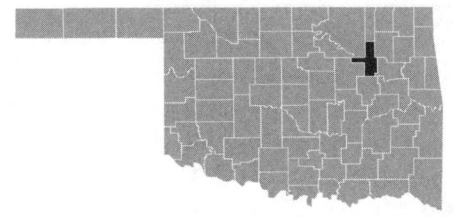

Tulsa

Located on the Arkansas River on lands that were once part of the Creek and Cherokee nations, Tulsa County was created at statehood and took its name from the town of Tulsa in the Creek Nation, Indian Territory. The name, Tulsa, is derived from Tulsey Town, an old Creek settlement in Alabama. The county is part hills and bluffs and part wide prairie, marking the dividing line between the ridges of the Ozarks in the East and the broad plains of the West. Its western tip reaches Lake Keystone, while the Arkansas River, in its wide bed, rolls southeastward across the county. Cattle and horse ranches and rich farmland lie almost within the shadow of urban buildings.

The county has the state's second largest city, Tulsa, whose energy, aviation, computer, tele-communications, and electronics bases are supported by a broad complex of institutes of higher learning. Surrounding this core, is a rapidly growing ring of suburban cities including Broken Arrow, Bixby, Jenks, Owasso, and Sand Springs. Beyond these areas, close at hand, there are still quiet, backwood areas.

History runs deep in Tulsa County, from the early Indian inhabitants to the cattlemen, the coming of the railroads, and the oil boom. Near downtown Tulsa lies the historic meeting place of the Creek, Cherokee, and Osage nations.

For more information, call the Tulsa Chamber of Commerce at 918/585-1201.

Districts

Congress.............................. 1
State Senate. 11, 12, 25, 33–37, 39
State Rep. 11, 23, 29, 30, 36, 66–80, 98
District Attorney 14
Court of Appeals 1, 2
Ct. of Crim. Appeals............ 1
Supreme Ct. Jud. 6
Tulsa-Pawnee Jud. Adm. 14

County Officials

Court Clerk	Sally Howe Smith (R)	Tulsa
Clerk	Pat Key (R)	Tulsa
Sheriff	Stanley Glanz (R)	Tulsa
Treasurer	Dennis Semler (R)	Tulsa
Assessor	Ken Yazel (R)	Tulsa
Elect. Brd. Sec.	Patricia Bryant (R)	Tulsa
Dist. 1 Comm.	John Smaligo (R)	Tulsa
Dist. 2 Comm.	Karen Keith (D)	Tulsa
Dist. 3 Comm.	Ron Peters (R)	Tulsa

Property Valuations

	2013–2014 Assessment	2014–2015 Assessment	Increase or Decrease
Real Estate and Improvement	$4,230,642,552	$4,371,576,746	$140,934,194
Personal Subject to Tax	$660,855,602	$698,773,293	$37,917,691
Total Locally Assessed	$4,891,498,154	$5,070,350,039	$178,851,885
Homestead Exemptions Allowed	$119,429,271	$118,055,977	($1,373,294)
Net Assessed Locally	$4,772,068,883	$4,952,294,062	$180,225,179
Public Service Assessment	$296,883,808	$256,915,186	($39,968,622)
Net Assessed Valuation	$5,068,952,691	$5,209,209,248	$140,256,557

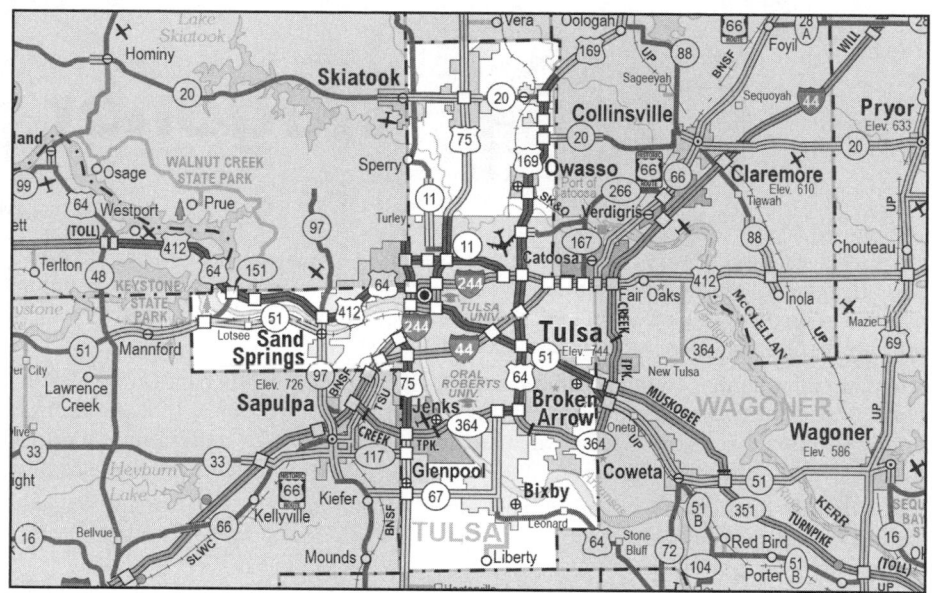

County Seat—Tulsa (Pop. 398,121s) 2013 Estimate

Area (Land & Water)—587.02 square miles

Per Capita Income (2013)—$52,843 (Ranks 3rd of 77 counties)

Population Statistics (2013)—Female-312,328; Male-297,282; Ethnicity—Wh.-487,651; Bl.-74,867; Am. Ind.-62,609; As.-18,208; Other-22,020; Pacific Is.-969; Two or more races-44,765; Hisp.-68,260

Births (2014)—9,356 • **Deaths** (2014)—5,666

Marriages (2013)—4,402 • **Divorces** (2013)—2,733

Unemployment Rate (2013)—5.5%

Labor Force (2013)—299,914

Number of Establishments (2013)—18,583

Number of Manufacturers (2013)—873

Public Assistance Payments (FY2014) Total—$312,124,202 • TANF—$2,665,785 • Supplements—Aged-$578,235; Blind-$14,877; Disabled-$4,857,972

Vehicle Registration (2014)— Automobiles-528,424; Farm Trucks-2,682; Comm. Trucks, Tractors, Trailers-32,558; Motor Homes and Travel Trailers 9,011; Motorcycles-19,986; Manufactured Homes-1,242; Tax Exempt Licenses-1,216; Boats-14,897

Institutions of Higher Learning—Tulsa Community College, Oral Roberts University, The University of Tulsa, Oklahoma State University-Tulsa

Crime Incidents (2013)—Murder-62; Rape-463; Robbery-1,066; Felony Assault-2,843;

County Population	
1907 (Okla. Terr.)	21,693
1910	34,995
1920	109,023
1930	187,574
1940	193,363
1950	251,686
1960	346,038
1970	401,663
1980	470,593
1990	503,341
2000	563,299
2010	603,403
2014 Estimate	629,598

Breaking and Entering-7,136; Larceny-16,507; Motor Vehicle Theft-2,842; Arson-181 • Total Crime Index-30,919; Crime Rate per 1,000-47.29

Farms (2012)—1,036

Land in Farms (2012)—106,222

Recreation Area—Keystone

Major Lake—Keystone

Major Stream Systems—Arkansas and Caney rivers, tributaries to Arkansas, south portion of Verdigris River, Bird Creek

Museums or Historic Sites—Gilcrease Institute of American History & Art, Philbrook Art Center, County Historical Society Museum, Tulsa Garden Center, Fenster Gallery of Jewish Art

Minerals—oil and gas; crushed stone

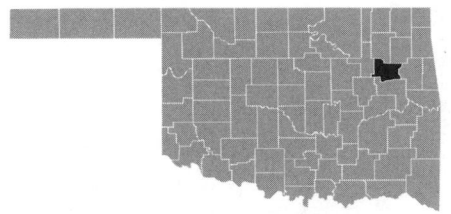

Wagoner

Created at statehood, Wagoner is named for its major city which is also the county seat. An early settler of the area was Nathan Pryor, a member of the Lewis and Clark expedition, which was originally based at Three Forks, now called Okay. Pryor later moved to what is now Mayes County, where he established a trading post.

The main thoroughfare of the county was the Osage Trace, which became known as the Texas Road in 1826. During the Civil War, this route was heavily traveled. In 1866 the Texas Road became known as the East Shawnee Trail, one of the first cattle trails to cross the area. In the early 1870s the Missouri, Kansas, and Texas (KATY) railroad extended into the county.

While Tulsa's industrial area and the Port of Catoosa provide employment for many Wagoner County citizens, agriculture remains a basic element in the economy, with grain and cattle being of major importance.

Two books, *Three Forks Country* and *History of Wagoner County*, are sources of county information. The Wagoner Historical Society also serves the area. For additional information, call the county clerk's office at 918/485-2216.

Districts

Congress	1
State Senate	18, 36
State Rep.	8, 12, 16, 23, 98
District Attorney	27
Court of Appeals	2
Ct. of Crim. Appeals	1
Supreme Ct. Jud.	7
E. Cent. Jud. Adm.	15
(Div. I)	

County Officials

Court Clerk	Jim Hight (R)	Broken Arrow
Clerk	Lori Hendricks (R)	Broken Arrow
Sheriff	Bob Colbert (R)	Wagoner
Treasurer	Dana Patten (R)	Coweta
Assessor	Sandy Hodges (R)	Coweta
Elect. Brd. Sec.	Larry Wilkinson (R)	Broken Arrow
Dist. 1 Comm.	James Hanning (R)	Broken Arrow
Dist. 2 Comm.	Chris Edwards (D)	Wagoner
Dist. 3 Comm.	Tim Kelley (R)	Coweta

Property Valuations

	2013–2014 Assessment	2014–2015 Assessment	Increase or Decrease
Real Estate and Improvement	$383,276,492	$390,870,147	$7,593,655
Personal Subject to Tax	$70,576,624	$68,367,064	($2,209,560)
Total Locally Assessed	$453,853,116	$459,237,211	$5,384,095
Homestead Exemptions Allowed	$23,387,196	$23,790,250	$403,054
Net Assessed Locally	$403,465,920	$435,446,961	$4,981,041
Public Service Assessment	$34,915,371	$35,014,320	$98,949
Net Assessed Valuation	$465,381,291	$470,461,281	$5,079,990

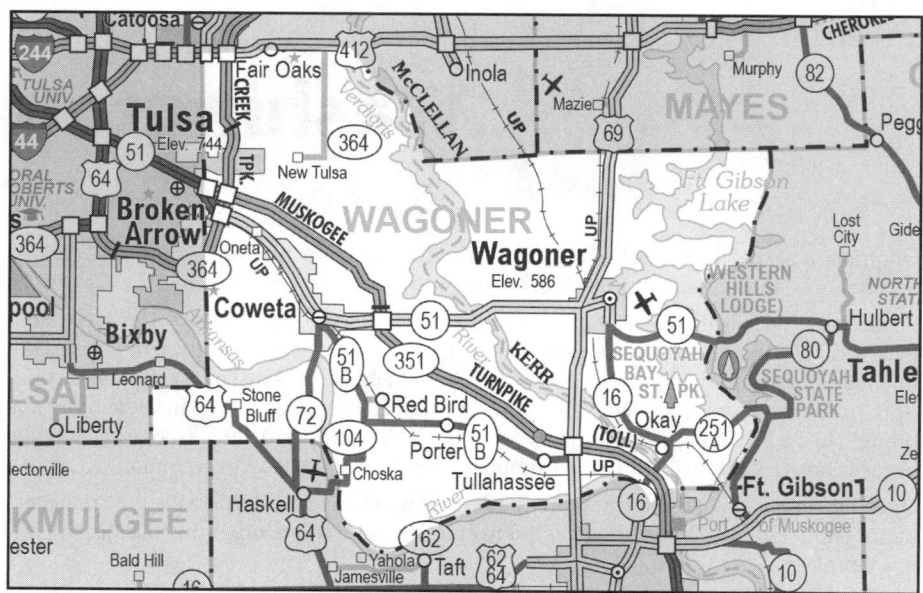

County Seat—Wagoner (Pop. 8,622) 2013 Estimate

Area (Land & Water)—590.99 square miles

Per Capita Income (2013)—$35,552 (Ranks 43rd of 77 counties)

Population Statistics (2013)—Female–37,441; Male–36,636; Ethnicity—Wh.–62,998; Bl.–3,470; Am. Ind.–12,019; As.–1,416; Other–1,210; Pacific Is.–90; Two or more races–6,786; Hisp.–3,676

Births (2014)—905 • **Deaths** (2014)—633

Marriages (2013)—266 • **Divorces** (2013)—166

Unemployment Rate (2013)—5.2%

Labor Force (2013)—35,530

Number of Establishments (2013)—919

Number of Manufacturers (2013)—60

Public Assistance Payments (FY2014) Total—$24,283,234 • TANF—$185,637 • Supplements—Aged–$35,336; Blind–$1,263; Disabled–$421,986

Vehicle Registration (2014)—Automobiles–41,947; Farm Trucks–1,571; Comm. Trucks, Tractors, Trailers–2,041; Motor Homes and Travel Trailers–1,885; Motorcycles–2,219; Manufactured Homes–36; Tax Exempt Licenses–119; Boats–3,007

Crime Incidents (2013)—Murder–3; Rape–10; Robbery–9; Felony Assault–105; Breaking and Entering–251; Larceny–807; Motor

County Population	
1907 (Okla. Terr.)	19,529
1910	22,086
1920	21,371
1930	22,428
1940	21,642
1950	16,741
1960	15,673
1970	22,163
1980	41,801
1990	47,883
2000	57,491
2010	73,085
2014 Estimate	75,702

Vehicle Theft–74; Arson–14 • Total Crime Index–1,259; Crime Rate per 1,000–23.00

Farms (2012)—1,090

Land in Farms (2012)—198,924

Recreation Area—Sequoyah Bay

Major Lake—Fort Gibson

Major Stream Systems—Verdigris, Grand, Caney, and Arkansas rivers and their tributaries

Museums or Historic Sites—Wagoner Indian Territory House Museum

Minerals—oil and gas; crushed stone

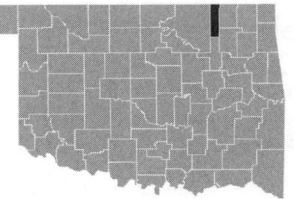

Washington

Originally a part of the Cherokee Nation, Indian Territory, Washington County was created at statehood, and named for President George Washington.

Bartlesville, the county seat, was the first oil-boom town in Indian Territory. George B. Keeler, a local fur trader, knew of the existence of oil in this area as early as 1875, but lacked the financial support and tribal permission necessary to exploit his discovery. It was not until April 15, 1897, that the No. 1 Nellie Johnstone, the first commercial oil well in Oklahoma, was brought in by the Cudahy Oil Company. W. W. "Bill" Keeler, grandson of George, eventually became head of Phillips Petroleum Company and chief of the Cherokee Nation.

Once headquarters of the former Phillips Petroleum Company, Bartlesville is also the site of the Frank Phillips Home, the restored twenty-six room mansion of the founder of Phillips Petroleum.

Dewey, the first town in Oklahoma to have electric lights, waterworks, and a telephone line, is the site of the Tom Mix Museum. Mix, one-time deputy sheriff and night marshal in Dewey, was an early-day silent film star.

The Bartlesville Historical Commission published two volumes of *History of Washington County* by Margaret Teague. For more information, call the county clerk's office at 918/337-2840.

Districts

Congress 1
State Senate 29
State Rep. 10, 11
District Attorney 11
Court of Appeals 1, 5
Ct. of Crim. Appeals 1
Supreme Ct. Jud. 1
NE Jud. Adm. 11

County Officials

Court Clerk	Jill Spitzer (R)	Bartlesville
Clerk	Marjorie Parrish (R)	Bartlesville
Sheriff	Rick Silver (R)	Bartlesville
Treasurer	Brad Johnson (R)	Bartlesville
Assessor	Todd Mathes (R)	Bartlesville
Elect. Brd. Sec.	Yvonne House (R)	Bartlesville
Dist. 1 Comm.	Gary Deckard (R)	Bartlesville
Dist. 2 Comm.	Michael Bouvier (R)	Bartlesville
Dist. 3 Comm.	Mike Dunlap (R)	Bartlesville

Property Valuations

	2013–2014 Assessment	2014–2015 Assessment	Increase or Decrease
Real Estate and Improvement	$262,718,025	$269,437,366	$6,719,341
Personal Subject to Tax	$39,107,431	$40,938,831	$1,831,400
Total Locally Assessed	$301,825,456	$310,376,197	$8,550,741
Homestead Exemptions Allowed	$13,940,268	$14,155,171	$214,903
Net Assessed Locally	$287,885,188	$296,221,026	$8,335,838
Public Service Assessment	$22,910,948	$24,623,301	$1,712,353
Net Assessed Valuation	$310,796,136	$320,844,327	$10,048,191

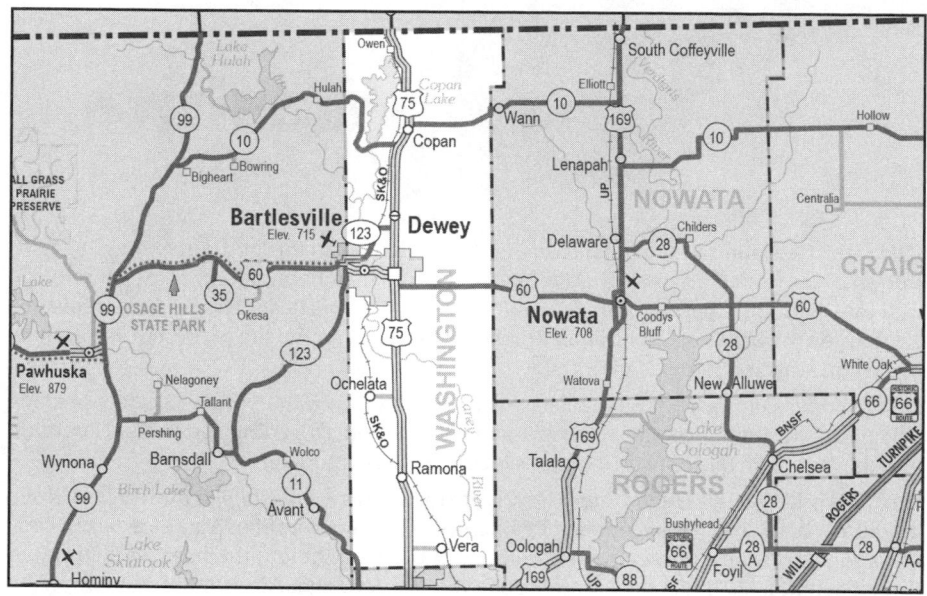

County Seat—Bartlesville (Pop. 36,258) 2013 Estimate

Area (Land & Water)—424.15 square miles

Per Capita Income (2013)—$46,702 (Ranks 11th of 77 counties)

Population Statistics (2013)—Female-26,779; Male-24,550; Ethnicity—Wh.-44,180; Bl.-1,791; Am. Ind.-7,769; As.-883; Other-494; Pacific Is.-32; Two or more races-3,805; Hisp.-2,677

Births (2014)—650 • **Deaths** (2014)—637

Marriages (2013)—420 • **Divorces** (2013)—212

Unemployment Rate (2013)—4.3%

Labor Force (2013)—29,145

Number of Establishments (2013)—1,192

Number of Manufacturers (2013)—36

Public Assistance Payments
(FY2014) Total—$23,593,322 • TANF—$172,739 • Supplements—Aged-$44,732; Blind-$0; Disabled-$421,377

Vehicle Registration (2014)—
Automobiles-34,569; Farm Trucks-871; Comm. Trucks, Tractors, Trailers-1,142; Motor Homes and Travel Trailers-1,217; Motorcycles-1,617; Manufactured Homes-8; Tax Exempt Licenses-137; Boats-1,234

Institutions of Higher Learning—
Oklahoma Wesleyan College, Rogers State University-Bartlesville

Crime Incidents (2013)—Murder-2; Rape-16; Robbery-13; Felony Assault-85; Breaking and Entering-298; Larceny-766; Motor Vehicle Theft-49; Arson-8

County Population	
1907 (Okla. Terr.)	12,813
1910	28,484
1920	27,002
1930	27,777
1940	30,559
1950	32,880
1960	42,347
1970	42,277
1980	48,113
1990	48,066
2000	48,996
2010	50,976
2014 Estimate	51,937

• Total Crime Index-1,229; Crime Rate per 1,000-23.61

Farms (2012)—811

Land in Farms (2012)—230,934

Major Lake—Copan

Major Stream Systems—Caney River and tributaries to Bird Creek

Museums or Historic Sites—Nellie Johnson Oil Well, Frank Phillips Home, Phillips Petroleum Co. Exhibit Hall, Price Tower, Bartlesville; Tom Mix Museum, Dewey Hotel at Dewey

Minerals—oil and gas, crushed stone, clays

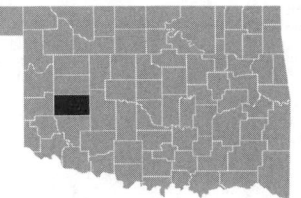

Washita

Part of the Cheyenne-Arapaho lands opened to settlement in the land run on April 19, 1892, this area was settled originally in 1886, when a white man named John M. Seger and 500 Indians left the old Cheyenne-Arapaho Agency at Darlington, near El Reno, and established a colony on the banks of Cobb Creek. This settlement was on the site of present-day Colony in eastern Washita County.

Designated as County "H," it was named after the Washita River. The word is Choctaw meaning "big hunt." Washita County has ranked as one of Oklahoma's leading agricultural counties, and the Anadarko Basin made it famous for oil and gas production.

During World War II, a United States Naval Air Station was established at Burns Flat. Closed after the war, the base was reopened in 1959 as the Clinton-Sherman Air Force Base. Many of its squadrons flew missions over Vietnam in the 1960s before the base was closed on December 31, 1969. It has since become the Clinton-Sherman Airport, used by Altus AFB pilots for practice landings and takeoffs. The Oklahoma Space Authority (now the Oklahoma Space Industry Development Authority) took title to the Clinton-Sherman Airpark on December 5, 2006.

Events include the Cheyenne-Arapahoe Celebration held on April 16 every five years, the Cordell Pumpkin Festival in October, and a city-wide garage sale in June. For more information, call the county clerk's office at 580/832-2284 or the Cordell Chamber of Commerce at 580/832-3538.

Districts

Congress	3
State Senate	38
State Rep.	55
District Attorney	3
Court of Appeals	6
Ct. of Crim. Appeals	5
Supreme Ct. Jud.	4
NW Jud. Adm.	2

County Officials

Court Clerk	Carol Corbett (D)	Cordell
Clerk	Kristen Dowell (R)	Cordell
Sheriff	Roger Reeve (D)	Cordell
Treasurer	Shari Giblet (D)	Cordell
Assessor	Clayton Twyman (D)	Cordell
Elect. Brd. Sec.	Leah Jones (D)	Cordell
Dist. 1 Comm.	Bart Gossen (R)	Colony
Dist. 2 Comm.	Leo Goeringer (R)	Bessie
Dist. 3 Comm.	Raydell Schneberger (D)	Dill City

Property Valuations

	2013–2014 Assessment	2014–2015 Assessment	Increase or Decrease
Real Estate and Improvement	$44,554,592	$46,311,167	$1,756,575
Personal Subject to Tax	$79,345,927	$80,213,561	$867,634
Total Locally Assessed	$123,900,519	$126,524,728	$2,624,209
Homestead Exemptions Allowed	$2,944,223	$2,924,641	($19,582)
Net Assessed Locally	$120,956,296	$123,600,087	$2,643,791
Public Service Assessment	$12,518,845	$10,875,101	($1,643,744)
Net Assessed Valuation	$133,475,141	$134,475,188	$1,000,047

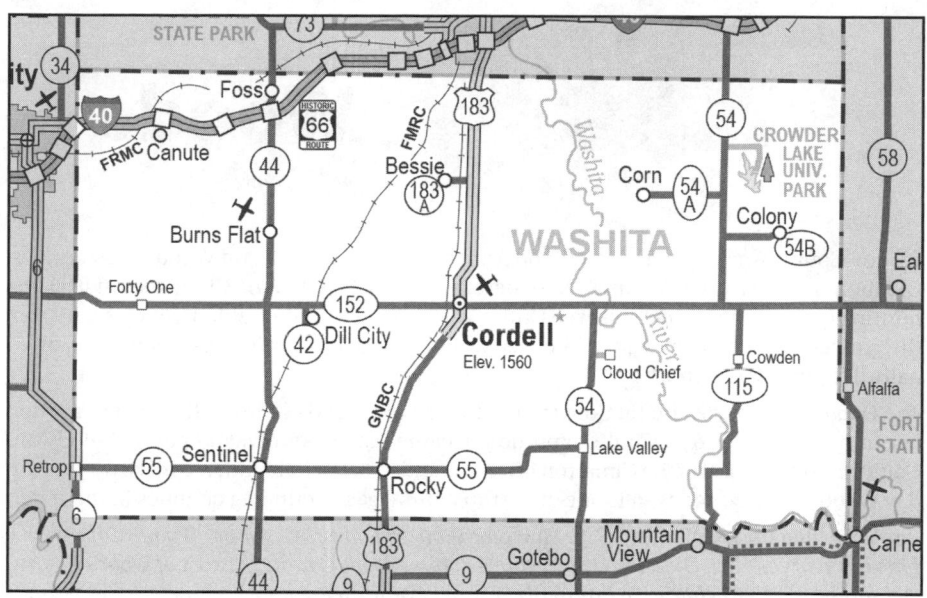

County Seat—New Cordell (Pop. 2,921) 2013 Estimate

Area (Land & Water)—1,009.07 square miles

Per Capita Income (2013)—$35,156 (Ranks 46th of 77 counties)

Population Statistics (2013)—Female-5,930; Male-5,701;
Ethnicity—Wh.-11,063; Bl.-186; Am. Ind.-621; As.-5; Other-276;
Pacific Is.-0; Two or more races-512; Hisp.-989

Births (2014)—170 • Deaths (2014)—136

Marriages (2013)—88 • Divorces (2013)—64

Unemployment Rate (2013)—3.8%

Labor Force (2013)—6,239

Number of Establishments (2013)—238

Number of Manufacturers (2013)—9

Public Assistance Payments
(FY2014) Total—$7,176,675 • TANF—
$90,182 • Supplements—Aged-$24,325;
Blind-$626; Disabled-$127,883

Vehicle Registration (2014)—
Automobiles-6,783; Farm Trucks-1,707;
Comm. Trucks, Tractors, Trailers-633;
Motor Homes and Travel Trailers-407;
Motorcycles-495; Manufactured Homes-9; Tax
Exempt Licenses-29; Boats-260

Crime Incidents (2013)—Murder-0; Rape-3;

County Population	
1907 (Okla. Terr.)	22,007
1910	25,034
1920	22,237
1930	29,435
1940	22,279
1950	17,657
1960	18,121
1970	12,141
1980	13,798
1990	11,441
2000	11,508
2010	11,629
2014 Estimate	11,547

Robbery-0; Felony Assault-12; Breaking
and Entering-62; Larceny-80; Motor Vehicle
Theft-13; Arson-5 • Total Crime Index-170;
Crime Rate per 1,000-14.56

Farms (2012)—973

Land in Farms (2012)—633,364

Major Stream Systems—Washita River and
tributaries to North Fork of Red River

Museums or Historic Sites—Washita
County Museum, Cordell

Minerals—oil and gas

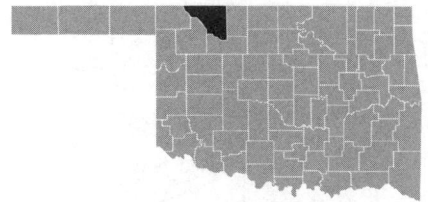

Woods

Woods County was created at statehood from portions of Woods and Woodward counties, Oklahoma Territory. It was part of the Cherokee Outlet, given to the Cherokees in 1828 as a hunting outlet. In 1893 the Cherokee Outlet was opened to white settlement by a land run, the greatest horserace in history. The area which was to become Woods County was originally designated as County "M."

The Oklahoma Constitutional Convention divided old Woods County. The eastern portion became Alfalfa County; a southern portion became Major County, and part of Woodward County north and east of the Cimarron River was added to the remainder to make up present-day Woods County. Today, it is one of the top natural gas-producing counties in the state.

Books written about Woods County include *Pioneer Footprints Across Woods County*; *The First 100 Years of Alva, Oklahoma*; *Reflections Across Woods County*; *History of Woods County, Oklahoma*; and *Ranchland to Railroads*. Annual events in the area include the Nescatunga Arts and Humanities Fair in June, the Rattlesnake Hunt the first weekend after Easter, and the Freedom Rodeo during the third week in August.

The county tourist center is located on the campus of Northwestern Oklahoma State University. For more information, call the county clerk's office at 580/327-0942.

Districts

Congress	3
State Senate	27
State Rep.	58
District Attorney	26
Court of Appeals	6
Ct. of Crim. Appeals	5
Supreme Ct. Jud.	4
NW Jud. Adm. (Div. I)	4

County Officials

Court Clerk	Staci Davey (R)	Alva
Clerk	Shelley Reed (R)	Dacoma
Sheriff	Rudy Briggs Jr. (D)	Alva
Treasurer	David Manning (R)	Alva
Assessor	Renetta Benson (R)	Alva
Elect. Brd. Sec.	Wylodean Linder (D)	Alva
Dist. 1 Comm.	David Hamil (R)	Alva
Dist. 2 Comm.	Randy McMurphy (R)	Alva
Dist. 3 Comm.	John Smiley (R)	Waynoka

Property Valuations

	2013–2014 Assessment	2014–2015 Assessment	Increase or Decrease
Real Estate and Improvement	$47,921,396	$51,850,759	$3,929,464
Personal Subject to Tax	$77,630,661	$97,053,276	$19,422,615
Total Locally Assessed	$125,552,057	$148,904,035	$23,351,978
Homestead Exemptions Allowed	$2,034,416	$1,984,806	($49,610)
Net Assessed Locally	$123,517,641	$146,919,229	$23,401,588
Public Service Assessment	$23,318,295	$26,307,900	($2,989,605)
Net Assessed Valuation	$146,835,936	$173,227,129	$26,391,193

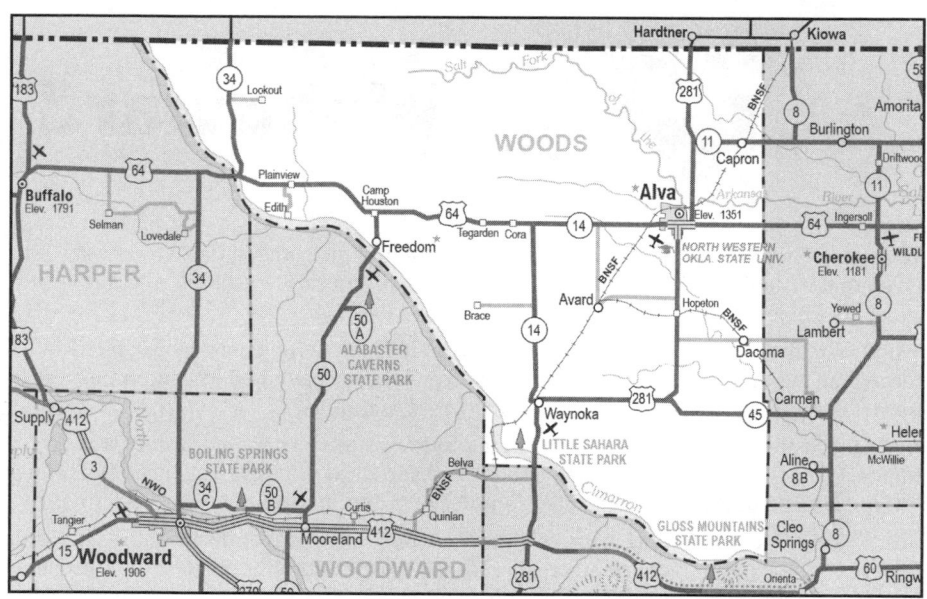

County Seat—Alva (Pop. 5,031) 2013 Estimate

Area (Land & Water)—1,290.07 square miles

Per Capita Income (2013)—$43,782 (Ranks 16th of 77 counties)

Population Statistics (2013)—Female-4,152; Male-4,697; Ethnicity—Wh.-8,138; Bl.-355; Am. Ind.-337; As.-116; Other-191; Pacific Is.-13; Two or more races-301; Hisp.-451

Births (2014)—122 • **Deaths** (2014)—95

Marriages (2013)—59 • **Divorces** (2013)—23

Unemployment Rate (2013)—3.3%

Labor Force (2013)—5,407

Number of Establishments (2013)—284

Number of Manufacturers (2013)—5

Public Assistance Payments (FY2014) Total—$3,315,775 • TANF—$50,263 • Supplements—Aged-$7,210; Blind-$0; Disabled-$37,959

Vehicle Registration (2014)—Automobiles-7,765; Farm Trucks-2,368; Comm. Trucks, Tractors, Trailers-746; Motor Homes and Travel Trailers-436; Motorcycles-528; Manufactured Homes-9; Tax Exempt Licenses-45; Boats-193

Institutions of Higher Learning—Northwestern Oklahoma State University, Alva

Crime Incidents (2013)—Murder-0; Rape-2; Robbery-0; Felony Assault-4; Breaking and Entering-36; Larceny-74; Motor Vehicle Theft-10; Arson-1

County Population	
1907 (Okla. Terr.)	15,517
1910	17,567
1920	15,939
1930	17,005
1940	14,915
1950	14,526
1960	11,932
1970	11,920
1980	10,923
1990	9,103
2000	9,089
2010	8,878
2014 Estimate	9,288

• Total Crime Index-126; Crime Rate per 1,000-14.23

Farms (2012)—751

Land in Farms (2012)—808,463

Recreation Area—Little Sahara

Major Stream Systems—Salt Fork of the Arkansas River, Cimarron River and its tributaries

Museums or Historic Sites—Cherokee Strip Museum and Northwestern Oklahoma State University Museum, Stevens-Carter Museum of Natural History, Alva

Minerals—oil and gas

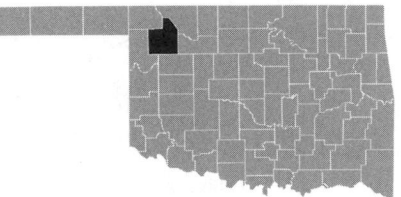

Woodward

When the Cherokee Outlet was opened to settlement in 1893, the name "Woodward" was given to the Atchison, Topeka, and Santa Fe station in central "N" County, Oklahoma Territory. The name was given later to the county.

Woodward, the county seat, became a shipping point for cattle, and in 1913, the United States located an agricultural research station there. Woodward celebrated its centennial year in 1987. It remains a hub for commerce in northwest Oklahoma.

Agriculture and petroleum have contributed to the county's economy. Today Woodward Iodine, Western Farmer's Electrical Cooperative, Bison Nitrogen, Terra Chemical, Deepwater Chemicals, and Mutual of Omaha are examples of the county's industrial development.

Scenic areas include Boiling Springs State Park northeast of Woodward, and Alabaster Caverns State Park in the northern section of the county. Fort Supply Reservoir provides hunting, fishing, camping, and swimming activities. Boiling Springs Golf Course is rated one of the top ten public courses in the state.

History books written about the county include *Below Devil's Gap*; *Woodward, First Century on Sand, Sage, and Prairie*; and *Sand In My Eyes*. A state tourism center is operated in Woodward. For additional information, call the county clerk's office at 580/256-3625 or the Plains Indians and Pioneers Museum at 580/256-6136.

Districts

Congress...........................3
State Senate...................27
State Rep.............58, 59, 61
District Attorney 26
Court of Appeals............ 6
Ct. of Crim. Appeals........5
Supreme Ct. Jud..............4
NW Jud. Adm. 4
　(Div. I)

County Officials

Court Clerk	Tammy Roberts (R)	Woodward
Clerk	Charolett Waggoner (D)	Woodward
Sheriff	Gary Stanley (R)	Woodward
Treasurer	Sonya Coleman (R)	Woodward
Assessor	Mistie Dunn (D)	Woodward
Elect. Brd. Sec.	Carol Carrell (D)	Woodward
Dist. 1 Comm.	Tommy Roedell (R)	Mooreland
Dist. 2 Comm.	Randy Johnson (R)	Mutual
Dist. 3 Comm.	Vernie R. Matt (D)	Fargo

Property Valuations

	2013–2014 Assessment	2014–2015 Assessment	Increase or Decrease
Real Estate and Improvement	$99,023,940	$106,399,060	$7,375,120
Personal Subject to Tax	$120,655,196	$120,768,928	$113,732
Total Locally Assessed	$219,679,136	$227,167,988	$7,488,852
Homestead Exemptions Allowed	$4,306,726	$4,151,301	($155,425)
Net Assessed Locally	$215,372,410	$223,016,687	$7,644,277
Public Service Assessment	$52,408,303	$58,575,070	$6,166,767
Net Assessed Valuation	$267,780,713	$281,591,757	$13,811,044

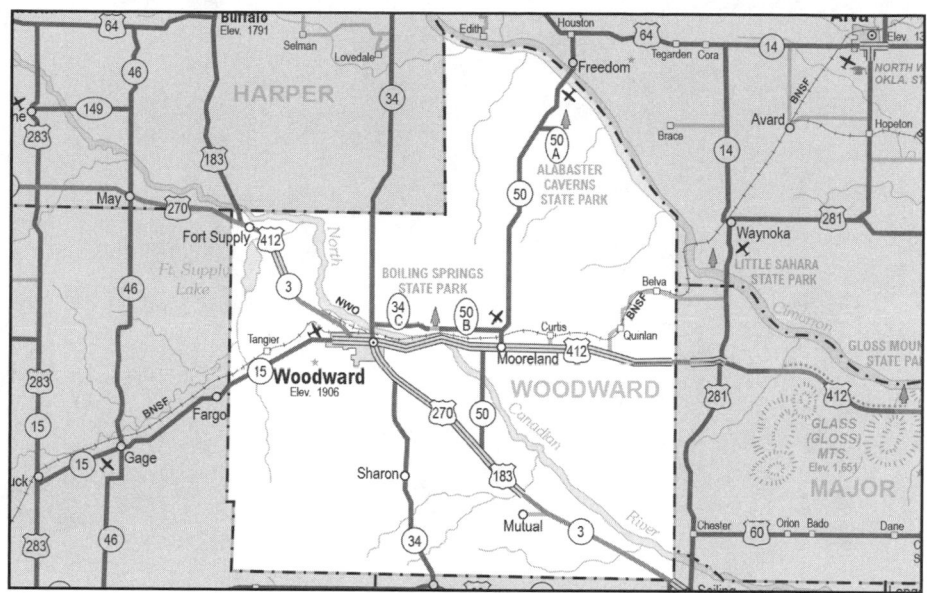

County Seat—Woodward (Pop. 12,758) 2013 Estimate

Area (Land & Water)—1,246.01 square miles

Per Capita Income (2013)—$47,972 (Ranks 5th of 77 counties)

Population Statistics (2013)—Female-9,668; Male-10,815;
Ethnicity—Wh.-19,361; Bl.-275; Am. Ind.-1,096; As.-109;
Other-362; Pacific Is.-3; Two or more races-702; Hisp.-2,198

Births (2014)—302 • **Deaths** (2014)—172

Marriages (2013)—155 • **Divorces** (2013)—104

Unemployment Rate (2013)—3.0%

Labor Force (2013)—13,295

Number of Establishments (2013)—809

Number of Manufacturers (2013)—22

Public Assistance Payments
(FY2014) Total—$7,772,028 • TANF—
$71,814 • Supplements—Aged-$14,801;
Blind-$0; Disabled-$113,169

Vehicle Registration (2014)—
Automobiles-18,608; Farm Trucks-2,239;
Comm. Trucks, Tractors, Trailers-2,860;
Motor Homes and Travel Trailers-1,052;
Motorcycles-1,186; Manufactured Homes-47;
Tax Exempt Licenses-61; Boats-618

Crime Incidents (2013)—Murder-0; Rape-9;
Robbery-3; Felony Assault-51; Breaking and
Entering-197; Larceny-398; Motor Vehicle
Theft-71; Arson-3 • Total Crime Index-729;
Crime Rate per 1,000-34.99

County Population	
1907 (Okla. Terr.)	14,595
1910	16,592
1920	14,663
1930	15,844
1940	16,270
1950	14,383
1960	13,902
1970	15,537
1980	21,172
1990	18,976
2000	18,486
2010	20,081
2014 Estimate	21,529

Farms (2012)—882

Land in Farms (2012)—714,706

Recreation Area—Alabaster Caverns, Boiling
Springs state parks

Major Lake—Fort Supply

Major Stream Systems—Cimarron and
North Canadian rivers and their tributaries

Museums or Historic Sites—Fort Supply
Museum and Plains Indians & Pioneers
Museum at Woodward

Minerals—oil and gas, iodine

OKLAHOMA
MUNICIPAL
GOVERNMENT

Except where otherwise noted, municipal government information was prepared by David Fudge, Executive Director-Emeritus of the Oklahoma Municipal League for the League's *Handbook for Oklahoma Municipal Officials*. To reflect changes in municipal law, the information has since been revised where necessary. All population figures are obtained from the U.S. Census Bureau at www.census.gov

Municipal Government History and Facts

The first towns in what we now call Oklahoma were officially incorporated by the Cherokee Nation—Fort Gibson and Downingville (now Vinita) in 1873; Webbers Falls in 1885; and Chelsea, Chouteau, and Claremore in 1889. Cherokee law, however, allowed sales of town lots only to members of the tribe. The only incorporated place outside the Indian Territory was Mangum, organized in 1886 under an 1860 act of the Texas Legislature, which claimed about 1.5 million acres in the southwestern part of Oklahoma. This area remained under Texas jurisdiction until a boundary dispute was decided by the United States Supreme Court in 1896.

The area outside that of the Five Civilized Tribes, known then as the "Oklahoma Lands" or simply as "Oklahoma," was offered to white settlement after a series of purchases by the federal government. A number of "runs" and lotteries, beginning in 1889 and continuing until 1901, were conducted.

The first run was held April 22, 1889, into some 3,000 square miles known as the "Unassigned Lands." This first run is of interest in its treatment of early municipal government in Oklahoma because it occurred before there was any kind of legal authority for the creation of towns, except for the size of town sites. It is reported 60,000 people had crowded into the area by the morning of April 23, more than enough to claim every foot of the quarter-sections of farmlands and the town sites. Federal law at that time limited town sites to 320 acres. Fortunately the 320-acre limit was increased to 1,280 acres by an act of Congress on May 14, 1890.

Considering the fact that not a line of valid law authorized town government at the time of the 1889 run, and those municipal officials, who were selected at public meetings, were without any enforceable authority, the provisional towns were relatively successful, not necessarily peaceful. As Professor John Alley of the University of Oklahoma puts it in his book, *Early City Beginnings*, it was a time of turbulence and confusion. "Oklahoma came into being with a bang." Probably more than one claim dispute was resolved at gunpoint, but there were no pitched battles and only one killing was recorded. By the fall of 1889, orderly, although still invalid, local governments prevailed in Oklahoma City and Guthrie, the most tumultuous of the overnight towns.

On May 2, 1890, Congress passed the Organic Act, giving legal status to municipal government in both Oklahoma and Indian territories. Section 14 of the act extended the laws of Nebraska in force on November 1, 1889, to "cities of the second class and villages" in the Oklahoma Territory. Section 31 extended the laws of Arkansas "as published in 1884 in the volume known as Mansfield's Digest ... to municipal corporations, chapter twenty-nine, division one" existing in the Indian Territory. By 1902, Indian Territory contained 147 towns, of which twenty-one had more than 1,000 inhabitants. The exact number actually carrying on municipal functions in Oklahoma Territory is not known, due to the fact that many original town sites failed. About one hundred towns might be a fair estimate.

The First Territorial Legislature met August 1890, and governed Oklahoma Territory until statehood. It enacted the first laws dealing with city and town government in Oklahoma Territory, but had no authority in Indian Territory. This resulted in the earliest municipal laws of Oklahoma coming from states with various backgrounds and differing philosophies of government.

The situation remained until enactment by Congress of the Enabling Act on June 16, 1906. The act authorized the Oklahoma and Indian territories to hold the Constitutional Convention. Its 112 members were elected November 6, 1906, and its first meeting was held November

20. It recessed March 15, 1907, met again from April 16 to April 22, again July 10, and finally adjourned July 16.

Its work was ratified by vote of the people on September 17, 1907, and President Theodore Roosevelt, on November 16, 1907, proclaimed Oklahoma the forty-sixth state.

The constitution's schedule enabled the government to operate in the interim between the change from the forms existing in the two territories to the new state government. Coupled with the Enabling Act, certain of the schedule's provisions are of municipal significance.

Section 10 provides: "Until otherwise provided by law, incorporated cities and towns, heretofore incorporated under the laws in force in the Territory of Oklahoma or in the Indian Territory, shall continue their corporate existence under the laws extended in force in the state and all officers of such municipal corporations at the time of admission of the state into the Union shall perform the duties of their respective offices under the laws extended in force in the state, until their successors are elected and qualified in the manner that is or may be provided by law: provided, that all valid ordinances now in force in such incorporated cities and towns shall continue in force until altered, amended, or repealed."

After statehood, the First Oklahoma Legislature re-enacted many of the municipal laws that had been previously passed by the Territorial Legislature, thus extending them throughout the new state. Many, particularly those relating to the mayor-council and the town forms of government, now found in Title II of the statutes, remained unchanged until a complete revision of the Municipal Code was enacted in 1977.

Cities and Towns as Governmental Entities

Both cities and towns in Oklahoma are bodies "corporate and politic," a term usually applied to the collective body of a nation, state, or municipality as politically organized or as exercising governmental and corporate powers. "A city has a legislative, public, and governmental power, in the exercise of which it is a sovereignty and governs its people, and a proprietary, corporate, or quasi-private power, for the private advantage of the inhabitants of the city and of the city itself as legal personality," (City of Tulsa v. Roberts, 107 P. 2d. 1006.) The same can be said of an incorporated town.

Cities and towns have a unique character that differs them from counties and school districts in that they have legislative and judicial powers. All, however, are "political subdivisions" of the state, and have only those powers that are conferred on them by the state constitution or the legislature. The constitution of the United States does not even mention cities or towns, although they may not, of course, violate any of its provisions. They are, in every way, "creatures" of the state.

Places that were incorporated as either cities or towns prior to statehood and all their ordinances not in conflict with the constitution or laws of the state were validated and declared to remain in force after statehood by an act of the First Oklahoma Legislature.

Under Oklahoma law, incorporated places of more than 1,000 population have a choice of forms of government—mayor-council, council-manager, strong-mayor—and if more than 2,000, they may become charter cities with any form, or combination of forms. Places of fewer than 1,000 are towns, with one exception: if a town has grown beyond that figure at some time in the past and adopted one of the forms allowed cities, a loss in population back to fewer than 1,000 does not change its status. In other words, it remains a city, although it may once again become a town by election of its voters.

Town Form of Government

The state statutes set out in detail how towns have been formed since statehood. Any person desiring to make application for incorporation should have a survey and map of the territory made by a surveyor. The map would have to show the boundaries and the amount of land to be contained and verified by affidavit of the surveyor. No territory within five miles of the corporate limits of a city of 200,000 or more population, or within three miles of the limits of any smaller city, may be included. A census of the resident population of the territory, showing the names and addresses of all people residing in the proposed town, must also be made and verified by those making it. The survey, map, and census shall be kept at some convenient place in the territory for public examination for not less than thirty days. A petition applying for incorporation, setting forth the contents of the survey, map, and census, must be signed by not fewer than one-third of the qualified voters residing in the territory or by at least twenty-five registered voters, whichever number is greater.

The petition, survey, map, and census are then submitted to the board of county commissioners, which shall hold a public hearing. If the board is satisfied that all requirements have been met, it shall order an election on the question of incorporation. If a majority of the votes are in favor, the territory shall from that time be deemed an incorporated town. In such case the county commissioners shall enter an order declaring that the town has been incorporated. Such order shall be conclusive and shall be given judicial notice in all courts of the state. Following the incorporation, another election is held for the purpose of electing officers for the newly incorporated town.

City Forms of Government

A town of 1,000 or more population, as shown by the last federal decennial census or other census recognized by the laws of the state, may become a city. It does so by petition signed by 35 percent of its voters, addressed to the board of county commissioners, which is required to issue a proclamation calling a local election on the question within thirty days. As an alternative, the town board of trustees, by its own resolution or ordinance, may call the election without petition. The resolution or ordinance shall divide the municipality into either four or six wards and shall designate which of the statutory forms is to be installed (aldermanic, council-manager, or strong-mayor).

All election expenses are to be paid by the city when fully organized. The secretary of the county election board, within five days after the canvass of the returns, must certify the vote to the board of county commissioners. If the vote is in favor, the board shall, within twenty days after receiving the certification, issue a proclamation that the municipality is now a city operating under the designated form of government and call an election to elect members of the city council and in the case of the mayor-council form, the mayor.

Cities operating under one of the statutory forms of government may change to one of the other statutory forms whenever the governing body directs the mayor to call an election, or upon petition signed by a number of legal voters equal to 20 percent of the total number of votes cast at the last preceding general state election in the city. When called by the governing body, the ordinance or resolution must be adopted at least four months prior to the next primary city election.

The election on the change may be held at the same time as another election. The secretary of the county election board certifies to the governing body the results of the election. Officials are to be elected at the next regular municipal election in the same manner as provided by law for other city elections. The change in forms goes into effect following the election of officers.

When a city changes from one statutory form of government to another, all appointed officers and employees under the previous form remain until their services terminate or are terminated in accordance with the law applicable to the new form.

Cities or towns of more than 2,000 population may adopt charters. The procedure is begun by election of a board of freeholders composed of two electors from each ward at any general or special election. The board shall, within ninety days, prepare the charter. The proposed charter shall be published for at least twenty-one days in a daily paper or in three consecutive issues of a weekly paper, and the first publication shall be made within twenty days after completion of the charter. The question of its adoption shall be submitted to the voters within thirty days, but not earlier than twenty days after the last publication. If approved by the voters, the charter is submitted to the governor, who is required to approve it unless it is in violation of the constitution or laws of the state. Once approved, the city charter is filed with the secretary of state, the county clerk, and in the archives of the city. It is given judicial notice by all courts.

Charters may be amended or abolished by election called by the city governing body or by petition. If by petition, it must be signed by a number of voters equal to 25 percent of the total number of votes cast in the city at the last preceding general election.

Amendments or revocations are submitted to the governor in the same manner as original charter adoptions. The proposal to revoke a charter must provide for the form of city government that is to be substituted.

Consolidation of Cities and Towns

The governing body of any city or town, by resolution or upon petition signed by at least 25 percent of the registered voters of the municipality, may ask to be consolidated with an adjacent city or town. The proposal is submitted to the adjacent municipality for its approval. If the proposal is approved, the governing bodies of both municipalities, or their representatives, prepare the terms and conditions of the consolidation, including provision for the transition of the officers and employees of each municipality. If each governing body approves the terms of consolidation, an election in each municipality is called on the question. If a majority of the votes cast in each municipality are in favor, the consolidation then takes place.

The books, records, evidences of debt to it and all property and effects of the requesting city or town become the property of the one accepting, but the debts or other obligations of each shall remain its own, unless otherwise expressly provided by the terms and conditions submitted at the election. Two or more cities and towns may be consolidated in this manner. The officers of the remaining municipality continue in office.

Municipal Revenues

Municipal government is supported by the following sources of direct revenue for operational funds in addition to bond issues for major expenditures such as capital improvements.

Cities and towns share in state tax revenues from gasoline and motor vehicle taxes based on population. Municipalities receive 1.875 percent of the sixteen-cent excise tax collections on gasoline and 3.10 percent of the motor vehicle collections. For the fiscal year ending June 30, 2014, these amounted to $5,655,241 and $23,493,800 respectively.

Cities and towns receive shares of alcoholic beverage tax on the basis of populations and land area. They are allocated one-third of 97 percent of alcoholic beverage tax collections. For the fiscal year ending June 30, 2014, this amounted to $12,512,092.

Source for municipal revenue data: Oklahoma Tax Commission

Top 40 Cities of Oklahoma

Cities are listed in descending order based on 2014 population.

City	U.S. Census 2014 Pop. Est.	2010 Pop.	% Pop. Change	Land Area Sq. Miles	Population Per Sq. Mile
Oklahoma City	620,602	579,999	7.0%	606.99	1,022
Tulsa	399,682	391,906	2.0%	182.65	2,188
Norman	118,040	110,925	6.4%	177.01	667
Broken Arrow	104,762	98,850	6.0%	44.99	2,333
Lawton	97,017	96,867	0.2%	75.14	1,211
Edmond	88,605	81,405	8.8%	85.14	1,041
Moore	59,196	55,081	7.5%	21.73	2,724
Midwest City	57,039	54,371	4.9%	24.59	2,320
Enid	51,386	49,379	4.1%	73.97	695
Stillwater	48,406	45,688	5.9%	27.85	1,738
Muskogee	38,616	39,223	-1.5%	37.34	1,034
Bartlesville	36,498	35,750	2.1%	21.11	1,729
Owasso	33,773	28,915	16.8%	10.03	3,367
Shawnee	31,254	29,857	4.7%	42.26	740
Yukon	25,349	22,709	11.6%	25.76	984
Ardmore	25,226	24,283	3.9%	49.12	514
Ponca City	24,766	25,387	-2.4%	18.11	1,368
Bixby	24,008	20,884	15.0%	24.05	998
Duncan	23,173	23,431	-1.1%	38.79	597
Del City	22,008	21,332	3.2%	7.54	2,919
Sapulpa	20,432	20,544	-0.5%	18.63	1,097
Jenks	19,951	16,924	17.9%	17.11	1,166
Mustang	19,638	17,395	12.9%	12.01	1,544
Bethany	19,580	19,051	2.8%	5.21	3,758
Sand Springs	19,553	18,906	3.4%	18.68	1,047
Altus	19,531	19,813	-1.4%	16.83	1,161
Claremore	18,971	18,581	2.1%	12.03	1,577
McAlester	18,247	18,383	-0.7%	15.69	1,163
El Reno	18,153	16,749	8.4%	79.98	227
Ada	17,130	16,810	1.9%	15.7	1,091
Durant	17,041	15,856	7.5%	19.03	895
Tahlequah	16,496	15,753	4.7%	12.02	1,372
Chickasha	16,334	16,036	1.9%	18.06	904
Miami	13,671	13,570	0.7%	9.71	1,408
Woodward	12,963	12,051	7.6%	13.12	988
Elk City	12,680	11,693	8.4%	14.62	867
Okmulgee	12,227	12,321	-0.8%	12.82	954
Guymon	12,128	11,442	6.0%	7.31	1,659
Choctaw	11,992	11,146	7.6%	27.32	439
Weatherford	11,989	10,833	10.7%	6.41	1,870

Oklahoma Cities with Populations Over 35,000

Oklahoma City

2010 Population, 579,999 • 2014 Est. Population, 620,602
Land Area, 606.99 sq. miles • Population Density, 1,022.4 people per sq. mile

www.okccvb.org • www.okc.gov

Oklahoma City is the capital of Oklahoma and the state's largest city. The city has a unique beginning, tracing its birth to a single hour of a single day—Noon, April 22, 1889—when the central part of what is now Oklahoma was opened for settlement by land run. Men and women from around the world gathered along the borders of the Unassigned Lands and raced into the area when the signal was given. By nightfall, more than 10,000 people had come to the town site for a new city and Oklahoma City was born.

The city was selected as the capital city in 1910. It has a mayor-city council form of government. As of July 2014, Oklahoma City ranked as the twenty-seventh largest city in the United States by population and the eighth largest in land area. Today, this metropolitan area of more than 1.3 million people is a center of commerce and industry. Its diversified economy includes major concentrations in telecommunications, government, aviation/aerospace, distribution, energy, and health care.

One of the city's largest employers is Tinker Air Force Base, a logistics depot for the U.S. Air Force and the U.S. Navy. Another major concentration of employment is at the Oklahoma Health Center, with its public, private, and non-profit research centers, specialized clinics, institutes, and state health care offices including the University of Oklahoma Health Sciences Center's seven colleges. In August 2010 Boeing announced it would relocate its C–130 Avionics Modernization Program from Long Beach, California, to Oklahoma City.

Located at the crossroads of the nation's largest interstate highways, I–40 and I–35, travelers visit Oklahoma City to go to the National Cowboy and Western Heritage Museum, Remington Park, Kirkpatrick Center Museum Complex, the Oklahoma City Zoo, the Oklahoma History Center, and to a host of arts festivals and events.

The dedication of the Ronald J. Norick Downtown Library on August 17, 2004, marked the completion of a more than $300–million renaissance development plan known as Metropolitan Area Projects, or MAPS. The nine MAPS projects, funded by a temporary one-cent sales tax approved by Oklahoma City voters in December 1993, constitute one of the most comprehensive municipal improvements ever done at one time by an American city. Projects include the 12,000–seat Bricktown Ballpark, the Chesapeake Arena, construction of a mile-long canal through the historic Bricktown Entertainment District, expansion of the City's convention center, enlarged and improved horse barns at the State Fairgrounds, complete renovation of the Civic Center Music Hall, and a trolley system to link the MAPS sites. In November 2001 citizens approved a MAPS for Kids project, which has brought in more than $500 million in tax revenue to improve metropolitan area schools. MAPS 3, a seven year project approved by citizen vote, began on April 1, 2010. The project will include development of a new downtown park, modern streetcars, construction of a new downtown convention center, fifty-seven miles of bicycling and walking trails, as well as other improvements.

On April 19, 2000, the Oklahoma City National Memorial opened on the site of the former Alfred P. Murrah Federal Building. Its huge bronze "Gates of Time," tranquil reflecting pool, 168 bronze and glass chairs, and "Survivor Tree" plaza honor those who were killed when the building was bombed in 1995, those who survived, and those whose lives were changed forever.

Following the devastation left by Hurricane Katrina, Oklahoma City became home to National Basketball Association team the New Orleans Hornets from 2005–2007. Oklahoma City proved it could support a major league team and local business leaders purchased the Seattle Supersonics and subsequently moved the team to Oklahoma City in 2008. The new team became the Oklahoma City Thunder.

(Also see "Welcome Back to the City" on page 58.)

Tulsa

2010 Population, 391,906 • 2014 Est. Population, 399,682
Land Area, 182.65 sq. miles • Population Density, 2,188.2 people per sq. mile

www.tulsachamber.com • www.vision2025.info • www.cityoftulsa.org

Fur traders, cattle rustlers, cowboys and Indians, oil barons, artists, and astronauts—Tulsa is indeed a city with a diverse history. In 1836 the first permanent settlement was founded here with the establishment of the village of Tallahassee, or Tulsa, in Indian Territory. A few years later, members of the Creek nation settled here after the Trail of Tears, which brought members of the Five Civilized Tribes to eastern Oklahoma. Tradition has it that these weary members of the Lochapoka band, led by Chief Archee Yahola, lit their council fire from the embers carried with them from their ancestral home in Alabama.

With the establishment of the first post office, the city's name changed officially to Tulsey Town. It became a convenient watering stop for cattlemen needing to rest and fatten their cattle on the long trail drive north from Texas to the slaughterhouses in Kansas City and Chicago. The Frisco Railroad reached Tulsa in 1882, and Tulsa's growth as a city really took hold. The railroads built the city's Union Station north of the modern downtown area. This was soon followed by a hotel and a general store—the beginnings of modern-day Tulsa.

Tulsa's population was about 200 when it was incorporated as a city in 1898. The oil boom brought many famous oil barons to the rapidly growing town during the next twenty or so years—men like J. Paul Getty, Harry Sinclair, William Skelly, and Waite Phillips. By 1920, the population was more than 72,000, and Tulsa was dubbed the "Oil Capital of the World." Today, more than 960,000 people live in the Tulsa Metropolitan area.

From the beginning, opportunities were present in Tulsa for people of every race and creed. The area known today as the Greenwood District flourished and was dubbed the "Black Wall Street" early in the twentieth century. This dream of opportunity died for many during a devastating 1921 race riot. A special commission was established by state legislation in 1998 to "gather information about the Tulsa Race Riot of 1921, to determine the essential facts concerning loss of life and property and to consider the larger issues of reparation, reconciliation, and memorialization." The John Hope Franklin Reconcilliation Park was dedicated on October 27, 2010.

Today, Tulsa is among the nation's most beautiful cities. Set beside the meandering Arkansas River in the northeastern quadrant of Oklahoma, the city boasts an abundance of trees and green rolling hills. For some, the uncommon beauty is symbolized in the unique feeling of "family" that pervades Tulsa's old and revered neighborhoods; or in the cultural and recreational assets of the community, including lush parks, outstanding museums, and the state's only professional opera company.

For others, the area's beauty is reflected in the ample opportunities for business success. Tulsa is a hub for aerospace, telecommunications, and financial services industries. In recent decades, the Creek and Cherokee Nations have become major players in the metro area's economic expansion. As of July 2014, the city ranked as the forty-seventh largest in the United States by population, and is often cited in the media for its high quality of life.

With their eye on the future, Tulsa County voters approved a one-penny, 13-year increase in the sales tax on September 9, 2003, to fund an ambitious capital improvements package called "Vision 2025." The money has funded dozens of projects throughout the county including high profile projects such as an advanced technology research center at OSU-Tulsa, the relocation of the Jazz Hall of Fame into the historic Union Depot, and the new BOK Center arena designed by internationally-renowned architect Cesar Pelli. Historic Route 66 passes through Tulsa. As part of the Vision 2025 project, funds were utilized to build the Cyrus Avery Plaza to pay homage to the man referred to as the Father of Route 66. Cities in Tulsa County are planning a renewal of Vision 2025 to keep momentum going.

(Also see "Welcome Back to the City" on page 58.)

Norman

2010 Population, 110,925 • 2014 Est. Population, 118,040
Land Area, 177.01 sq. miles • Population Density, 666.8 people per sq. mile

www.normanok.gov • www.ou.edu

Norman, founded at the time of the "Run of '89," was named for a Kentucky civil engineer and surveyor, Abner Ernest Norman. While the surveys were made, the survey parties encamped in a grove of trees at a spring near what is today the intersection of Classen Boulevard and East Lindsey Street. At this camp, the bark was removed from one side of a large elm tree, and the words "Norman's Camp" were burned into the tree. This was done by members of the survey party, somewhat in jest, to taunt their young supervisor.

History records that Andrew Kingkade, later owner of Kingkade Hotel in Oklahoma City, and a group of enterprising pioneers cooperated in organizing a town site company at Norman Switch. The town site was already platted when the '89ers hit town, so it was only a matter of hours before a provisional government was functioning the day of April 22, 1889.

T. R. Waggoner was selected as the provisional mayor, and Kingkade became one of four councilmen with a constituency of some 150 citizens. The new site became a village in 1890. While other cities were battling to become the capital, Norman's mayor skillfully directed a bill through the Territorial Legislature designating Norman as the site for the first institution of higher learning.

First classes at the University of Oklahoma began two years later. The original site for the university embraced only forty acres, but today it is a gigantic enterprise that includes an 18-hole golf course, the $5 million Oklahoma Center for Continuing Education, Lloyd Noble Center, University of Oklahoma Research Institute and Swearingen Research Park, Max Westheimer Airport, the $40 million Museum of Natural History, and a U.S. Postal

Service Training Center. Moreover, a $67 million National Weather Center has been completed and serves as the largest weather center in the nation, housing the school's world renown School of Meteorology as well as top federal weather research specialists of the National Oceanic and Atmospheric Administration, and a weather related museum. The university serves more than 27,000 students at its Norman campus.

Norman has a mayor-council form of government with the mayor elected by the people with a full vote on the eight-member council, nine members including the mayor.

Local annual events include the Chocolate Festival in February, Mayfair, Jazz in June, Midsummer Night's Fair in July, Taste of Norman and the Cleveland County Fair in September. The Medieval Fair in April is Norman's biggest festival.

Broken Arrow

2010 Population, 98,850 • 2014 Est. Population, 104,762
Land Area, 101 sq. miles • Population Density, 2,333.2 people per sq. mile
www.brokenarrowok.gov • brokenarrowchamber.com

Broken Arrow was given its name from the first group of Creek Indians, immigrating to Oklahoma from Georgia in 1828, who settled along the Arkansas, Verdigris, and Grand rivers, a few miles north of present Muskogee, Oklahoma. Traditionally, when a community became too big to gather around one campfire, the people divided and a new town would be established. When it came time to find a new town site, a group of Creeks decided on an area they had visited while gathering materials for making arrows. Because they had broken branches from the trees instead of cutting them to make their arrows, they named their new camp "Thlikachka" or "Broken Arrow." Also, the name Broken Arrow was from a community in the tribe's homelands in Georgia.

Among the early settlers were those families who were to play important roles in the Broken Arrow community: the McIntoshes, Perrymans, and Childers. A statue on Main Street in Veterans Park honors Lt. Col. Ernest Childers, a recipient of the Medal of Honor for heroic action in World War II.

Since 1954, Broken Arrow has operated under the statutory council-manager form of government, which consists of a five-member city council. The city council is elected by the community to four-year overlapping terms. The council is comprised of one representative from each of the four wards within the city as well as one member who represents the city at-large.

With some 300 manufacturing facilities, representing aerospace, machine tools, plastics, food processing, metal fabrication, furniture, and various other industries, Broken Arrow is the third largest manufacturing city in the state (after Tulsa and Oklahoma City). There are more than 2,000 support service companies to complement Broken Arrow's manufacturing operations. Tulsa International Airport and downtown Tulsa are within a fifteen-minute drive, and the South Loop Extension of the Creek Turnpike was completed in 2002, providing easy access to the Muskogee Turnpike and Interstate 44.

Broken Arrow's public school system and the Union School District operate within Broken Arrow city limits. Tulsa Technology Center has a campus in Broken Arrow, and there is a campus for Northeastern State University in Broken Arrow, completed August 20, 2001, and offering a wide range of bachelors and masters programs.

For sports enthusiasts, Broken Arrow offers seven championship-rated golf courses, thirty-three parks, seventeen tennis courts, and three swimming pools including two aquatic centers. Indian Springs Sports Complex offers twenty-five soccer fields along with two adult softball fields. There are sixteen lighted baseball fields, home to the Continental Amateur Baseball Association's 13–year-old World Series tournament and the USSSA World Series Tournament for the last several years. Arrowhead Softball Complex has eight lighted fields and has hosted some of the largest, most prestigious national tournaments for girl's softball.

Other festivals and points of interest include the Rooster Days Festival in May, Tuesdays in the Park in June, Farmer's Market, and Rhema Holiday Lights in November and December.

Lawton

2010 Population, 96,867 • 2014 Est. Population, 97,017
Land Area, 75.14 sq. miles • Population Density, 1,211.3 people per sq. mile

www.lawtonfortsillchamber.com • sill-www.army.mil

The town of Lawton was born August 6, 1901, when the Kiowa-Comanche-Apache Indian Reservation lands were opened to white settlement by the federal government. On June 6, 1901, President William H. McKinley signed a proclamation designating 9 AM, August 6 as the official time and date for auctioning lots in the new government town site four miles south of Fort Sill, Oklahoma Territory. Congress ratified the Jerome Treaty on June 6, 1900, after eight years of controversy involving the Indian leaders and the Jerome Commission over the lands. The Ratification Act, in addition to allotting each Indian man, woman, and child 160 acres from an area of 443,338 acres, provided that the federal government pay the Indians $2 million for the 2,033,583 acres to be opened for white settlement.

An official party composed of William M. Jenkins, Oklahoma's territorial governor, Dennis T. Flynn, territorial delegate to Congress, and a representative of the Interior Department toured the new country. There they met Ransome Payne, a pioneer of long standing, who had just returned from Washington, DC, where he attended the funeral of General Henry Ware Lawton, who had served in campaigns against the Indians. Payne suggested the new town be named Lawton, and this met with official approval.

Lawton city government was organized October 26, 1901. As many as 25,000 had come to the area for the land auction expecting a bonanza but instead found a pioneer city with many problems. Today, Lawton operates with the mayor-council form of government.

For higher education, Lawton points with pride to Cameron University, with a campus covering 350 acres. A modern municipal airport serves the daily scheduled airline flights and supplements training for the FAA School.

Just north of Lawton is Fort Sill, established by General Philip H. Sheridan as a cavalry fort on January 8, 1869. The post has been the home of the U.S. Army Field Artillery and is presently the headquarters of the Army's Field Artillery Center and School. The military reservation covers 95,000 acres.

Fort Sill has one of the finest military museums in the world and is a registered national historic landmark. More than fifty historic sites exist at the base.

The Wichita Mountains Wildlife Refuge was set aside from the Indian Reservation lands on July 4, 1901. The refuge is a sanctuary for buffalo, elk, deer, antelope, and longhorn cattle, along with native wildlife and more than 200 species of birds. The refuge is also the home of the Holy City of the Wichitas, site of Lawton's Easter Pageant founded by the Reverend Mark Wallock in 1926.

Edmond

2010 Population, 81,405 • 2014 Est. Population, 88,605 • Land Area, 85.14 sq. miles
Population Density, 1,040.7 people per sq. mile

www.edmondchamber.com • www.edmondok.com • www.uco.edu

After receiving a grant from Congress in 1887, the Santa Fe Railroad completed a north-south line between Arkansas City, Kansas, and Gainesville, Texas. At mile 103 on this line, a coaling and watering station was built due to the availability of a "good" water spring. The station was initially called "Summit" as the highest point of railroad grade between the Cimarron and North Canadian rivers, but later the name of Edmond was filed by Santa Fe with the government prior to July 14, 1887. The town was named for a traveling freight agent with the Santa Fe, Edmond Burdick, according to *The Edmond Sun*.

The town of Edmond sprang up overnight during the April 22, 1889, land run, when homesteads were staked around the Santa Fe station. The original plat for Edmond was prepared by the Seminole Town and Development Company, a newly formed syndicate with ties to the railroad. The University of Central Oklahoma is a notable feature of Edmond. One of the fastest growing universities in the state, with more than 16,000 students currently being served.

Other major sector employment in Edmond is in the areas of technology, manufacturing, construction, wholesale, and retail trade.

Edmond offers four eighteen-hole public golf courses, one nine-hole public course, a private club with thirty-six holes, and one championship course. Beautiful Arcadia Lake lies just east of I-35 and offers fishing, camping, boating, hiking, equestrian trails, and eagle viewing. Annual events include the Downtown Edmond Arts Festival, Canterbury Arts Festival, Jazz Festival, a Kid's Fishing Derby in the spring, and concerts in the park during June and July including LibertyFest, Oklahoma's premier 4th of July festival. Historic Route 66 also runs through Edmond. Located just east of Edmond on Route 66 in Arcadia is the famous Round Barn, and POPS, an iconic restaurant featuring a wide variety of classic, bottled soft drinks.

Moore

2010 Population, 55,0818 • 2014 Est. Population, 59,196 • Land Area, 21.73 sq. miles
Population Density, 2,724.1 people per sq. mile

www.cityofmoore.com • www.moorechamber.com

Settled first by participants in the 1889 Land Run, and originally called "Verbeck," the city of Moore is said to be named for a conductor of the Santa Fe Railway Company, who wrote his name on a board and nailed it to the boxcar in which he lived because he had trouble receiving his mail.

On March 23, 1893, an election of local residents resulted in a 22 to 0 vote to incorporate the town of Moore. It became a city March 2, 1962, under a council-manager form of government and created the Moore Public Works Authority.

Two council representatives are elected from each of three wards and the mayor is elected at large, all for four-year terms. Water is supplied solely by wells sunk into the Garber-Wellington Aquifer; thirty-two wells are in service with storage capacity of 7,600,000 gallons.

Approximately 23,000 students attend thirty-one school campuses within the Moore school district; Hillsdale Free Will Baptist College is also located in the city. Moore's business sector is primarily retail and service oriented, with limited industrial concerns. The bulk of the community is single-family residences with some multi-family dwellings, although retail development has taken off in recent years, especially along the I–35 corridor. There is a community center, library, swimming pool, senior citizen center, golf courses, tennis courts, and 179 acres of parks.

Moore has survived a series of tornadoes and severe storms during the past two decades. The resiliency of the people and their commitment to rebuilding their community in the face of adversity has inspired the slogan "Oklahoma Strong."

Midwest City

2010 Population, 54,371 • 2014 Est. Population, 57,039 • Land Area, 24.59 sq. miles
Population Density, 2,319.6 people per sq. mile

www.midwestcityok.com • www.tinker.af.mil • www.midwestcityok.org

On December 7, 1941, a sneak attack on Pearl Harbor brought the United States into nearly four years of conflict around the globe. To meet the challenge, the United States built new defense plants and military installations across the nation. At this time, W. P. "Bill" Atkinson learned that Oklahoma City was being considered as a plant site. The proposed air depot would employ 4,000 persons and would have to be located approximately ten miles from downtown Oklahoma City, available to railroads and highways, and no nearer than four miles to an oil field.

Atkinson, a former journalism professor who had turned to real estate development, saw an opportunity to build a planned city from scratch. He worked day and night for weeks and finally discovered a spot, nine miles from downtown Oklahoma City. He purchased 310 acres immediately north of Southeast 29 Street. Three weeks from the time he purchased the land, top military officials flew to Oklahoma City and selected the site across from his property.

Atkinson decided to gamble on building a city, provided he received the cooperation of the military. He hired Stewart Mott, one of the nation's master land planners, and within two weeks, Mott was on the job planning the community that was to become Midwest City. In just ten years, this "Dream City" was accorded national recognition by being named "America's Model City."

The mammoth Air Material Area Depot was first referred to as the "Midwest Air Depot," but it later became Tinker Air Force Base. It was named in honor of Maj. Gen. Clarence Tinker of Pawhuska, an ace World War II airman, who was killed in action. Tinker Air Force Base is now the largest, single site employer in Oklahoma.

As the service community for Tinker, Midwest City has attracted numerous, nationally recognized companies, such as Boeing, Rockwell International, and Northrop-Grumman.

Rose State College, located just north of Tinker Air Force Base, opened in 1970. Today it two-year college offers almost sixty degree and skilled-occupational programs.

Annual events in Midwest City include "Holiday Lights Spectacular," an animated drive through a holiday light display, and Global Oklahoma, a festival of cultures. Midwest City celebrated the state's centennial by constructing the Cascading Waters Fountain in Tinker Bicentennial Park, near downtown Midwest City.

Enid

2010 Population, 49,379 • 2014 Est. Population, 51,386 • Land Area, 73.97 sq. miles
Population Density, 694.7 people per sq. mile

www.enid.org • www.enidchamber.com

At noon September 16, 1893, a single gunshot marked the beginning of the land run into the Cherokee Outlet. Of the 100,000 people who participated in the run, 20,000 settled in an area designated as "O" County. This area, provided with a county seat reserve of 320 acres, a plot of four acres for a courthouse and one acre for a government land office, became Garfield County, with Enid as the county seat. From its beginnings, Enid has thrived, building on strong pioneer initiative.

Two Enid town sites were plotted—one by the Chicago, Rock Island, and Pacific Railroad and one by the government surveyors, and these two town sites were only three and one-half miles apart. There ensued a bitter struggle between North Town and South Town, but South Enid endured to become the Enid of today.

A board of commissioners/manager form of government is used in Enid. The medical facilities of Enid also serve much of northwestern Oklahoma. The City of Enid is a participant in the Main Street Program for promotion of downtown businesses and activities.

Enid has a diversified economy of agriculture, oil, and manufacturing. It is a leading retail and wholesale center for northwest Oklahoma and the center of the state's most prolific wheat farms. Oil has been an important factor in Enid's growth. It is surrounded by important fields—the Garber Pool, east of the city, which has had continuous production since its discovery in 1917; and the Ringwood Field, west of Enid, which was discovered in 1946. The city was the original headquarters for Continental Resources company, which has pioneered the use of hydraulic fracturing.

Vance Air Force Base, located three miles south of Enid, is a vital installation of the Air Education and Training Command. Other major employers include AdvancePierre Food Company and DynCorp, an aircraft/base maintenance company. In 1996 Northwestern Oklahoma State University-Enid opened its doors in a new multi-million dollar facility. In June 1999 Northern Oklahoma College purchased the former Phillips University campus and began offering classes in September 1999.

Enid's ninety churches represent twenty-seven denominations and are regularly attended. Enid and its immediate area have excellent recreational facilities, capitalizing on such nearby lakes as Great Salt Plains and Canton, and the Roman Nose State Park near Watonga.

The Enid area ranks high in quality of life surveys. *Progressive Farmer* magazine ranked Garfield County as the eighth best place to live in America in the magazine's 2007 survey. Good Morning America named the city one of the Five Hot Real Estate Markets in 2006. In 2004 Enid was named one of the top twenty-five small cities for business by *Industrial Market Trends* newsletter.

Stillwater

2010 Population, 45,688 • 2014 Population, 48,406 • Land Area, 27.85 sq. miles
Population Density, 1,738.1 people per sq. mile

www.stillwater.org • www.okstate.edu

Stillwater is located in what was once Indian Territory and was the scene for the first non-Indian settlement attempt in the area. In December 1884 colonists came from Kansas to establish a town at the junction of Stillwater and Boomer creeks. Less than a month later, the "Boomers" were forced to return to Kansas by federal troops.

In April 1889, the land was officially opened for settlement in the first great land run. At the end of the day, 240 acres were claimed in the Stillwater Township, and the population of the tent city numbered 300. Stillwater was selected county seat for Payne County. Two years later, the town approved a bond issue to build what would later become Oklahoma State University.

OSU's Stillwater campus now has an enrollment of more than 20,000 students and employs more than 4,900 persons. In addition, Stillwater is the home of the headquarters of the Oklahoma Department of Career and Technology Education, the only state agency with headquarters outside Oklahoma City. Ten major manufacturers also add to economic growth in the area.

Stillwater is home to Eskimo Joes, voted Best College Post-Game Hang-Out by *Sporting News*.

Annual events in Stillwater include the Arts and Heritage Festival in April, the Payne County Free Fair in late August/early September, the Juke-Joint Jog in the fall, and the Oklahoma Special Olympics in May.

Muskogee

2010 Population 39,223 • 2014 Est. Population 38,616 • Land Area, 37.34 sq. miles
Population Density, 1,034.2 people per sq. mile

www.muskogeechamber.org • www.cityofmuskogee.com

Named after the Muscogee or Creek Tribe of Indians, Muskogee was originally a terminus along the route of the Missouri, Kansas & Texas Railroad. The impetus for building a town on the site was due to the construction of a new agency building for the Creek Indians, begun on August 18, 1875. The agency building represented the consolidation of the different agencies of the Five Civilized Tribes into one "Union Agency," which established Indian administration at this place, and enabled Muskogee to become one of the most important cities in Indian Territory.

On March 3, 1893, Congress created a commission of three, known as the Dawes Commission, to introduce negotiations with several tribes of Indians for the purpose of creating a state in the Union embracing the lands within the Indian Territory. This commission had its headquarters at Muskogee.

From its rich, colorful past, Muskogee has developed into a commercial, industrial, and medical center. Its health and medical facilities include the Veterans Administration Hospital, Muskogee Regional Medical Center, City-Council Health Clinic, and numerous nursing homes. Muskogee also played a major role in the development of the McClellan-

Kerr Arkansas River Navigation System. Muskogee operates under the mayor-council system of government, with a city manager as the chief executive officer.

Muskogee is the home of three higher education campuses: Northeastern State University, Connors State College, and Bacone College, the oldest college in the state. Major sector employment is in construction, manufacturing, and retail trade.

Muskogee has many historical and recreational attractions nearby. Honor Heights Park has approximately 114 acres of natural beauty and attracts more than 600,000 visitors each year. Within a thirty-minute drive, there are five major recreational lake areas—Fort Gibson, Tenkiller, Greenleaf, Eufaula, and Webbers Falls.

Bartlesville

2010 Population, 35,750 • 2014 Population, 36,498 • Land Area, 21.11 sq. miles
Population Density, 1,728.9 people per sq. mile

www.cityofbartlesville.org • www.bartlesville.com

The Bartlesville area has a rich Indian and Western heritage. Three Indian tribes played a large role historically—the Cherokee, Delaware, and Osage. The Osage, who roamed, hunted, and fought over the vast Western Plains, were the first to live in the area. The Cherokee came next to establish settlements with the intent of staying permanently. The Delaware arrived in the area around 1856 to occupy lands in the Cherokee Nation area of eastern Oklahoma.

Taking its name from an early day settler, Jacob H. Bartles, the town was incorporated in 1897 as a part of Indian Territory. From its early days to the present, natural gas, oil, agriculture, and ranching have been the economic foundations of Bartlesville area business, industry, and commerce. For decades the city served as headquarters for the Phillips Petroleum Company. ConocoPhillips remains a major employer in the area.

The Price Tower is a nineteen story, 221 foot tower designed by Frank Lloyd Wright. It is the only realized skyscraper by Wright. Other points of interest in the area include Woolaroc, a 3,600–acre wildlife preserve, and Johnstone Park, an amusement park just for small children. Annual events include the OK Mozart Festival in June, Indian Summer in the fall, KidsFest in the summer, SunFest during the weekend after Memorial Day, and FantasyLand of Lights during the Christmas holiday season.

Oklahoma Chambers of Commerce

Oklahoma has more than 200 Chambers of Commerce that assist local companies with their business needs.

State Chamber of Commerce & Industry
330 NE 10 Street, Oklahoma City, OK 73104–3200
Telephone 405/235–3669, FAX 405/235–3670
www.okstatechamber.com

City	Address, Zip	Phone
Ada	209 W Main, 74820	580/332–2506
Altus	301 W Commerce, 73521	580/482–0210
Alva	502 Oklahoma Blvd., 73717	580/327–1647
American Indian	5103 S Sheridan Road, # 695 Tulsa, 74145	918/665–7087
Anadarko	106 E Broadway Street, 73005	405/247–6651
Antlers	119 W Main Street, 74523	580/298–2488
Ardmore	410 W Main, 73402	580/223–7765
Arnett	219 E Renfrow, 73832	580/885–7535
Atoka County	415 E Court Street, Atoka, 74525	580/889–2410
Barnsdall	PO Box 443, 74002	918/847–2202
Bartlesville	201 S Keeler, 74003	918/336–8708
Beaver	33 W 2, 73932	580/625–4726
Bixby	PO Box 158 74008	918/366–9445
Blackwell	120 S Main, 74631	580/363–4195
Blanchard	PO Box 1190, 73010	405/485–8787
Boise City	6 NE Square, 73933	580/544–3344
Boley	PO Box 31, 74829	918/667–9790
Bristow	1 Railroad Place, 74010	918/367–5151
Broken Arrow	210 N Main, Suite C, 74103	918/251–1518
Broken Bow	113 W Martin Luther King, 74012	580/584–3393
Buffalo	Box 439, 73834	580/735–6177
Cache	416 W "C" Avenue, 73527	580/429–4534
Canton	210 E Main Street, 73724	580/886–5387
Carnegie	Box 96, 73015	580/654–2121
Catoosa	PO Box 297, 74015	918/266–6042
Chandler	400 E 1 Street, 74834	405/258–0673
Checotah	201 N Broadway Street, 74426	918/473–2070
Chelsea	PO Box 392, 73728	918/789–2220
Cheyenne	PO Box 57, 73628	580/497–3318
Chickasha	221 W Chickasha Avenue, 73108	405/224–0787
Choctaw	2437 Main Street, 73020	405/390–3303

City	Address, Zip	Phone
Chouteau	Box 347, 74337	918/476-8222
Cimarron	6 NE Square, Boise City, 73933	580/544-3344
Claremore	419 W Will Rogers Blvd., 74017	918/341-2818
Clayton	PO Box 98, 74536	918/569-4776
Cleveland	PO Box 240, 74020	918/358-2131
Clinton	101 S 4 Street, 73601	580/323-2222
Coal County	6 S Main, Coalgate, 74538	580/927-2119
Coalgate	6 W Ohio, 74538	580/927-2119
Collinsville	1126 W Main, 74021	918/371-4703
Comanche	500 N Rodeo Drive, 73529	580/439-8852
Cordell	116 S College Street, 73632	580/832-3538
Coweta	117 W Cypress, 74429	918/486-2513
Crescent	PO Box 333, 73028	405/969-2814
Cushing	1301 E Main, 74023	918/225-2400
Davis	100 E Main, 73030	580/369-2402
Del City	5540 SE 15 Street, 73115	405/677-1910
Drumright	103 E Broadway Street, 74030	918/352-2204
Duncan	911 Walnut Avenue, 73534	580/255-3644
Durant	215 N 4 Street, 74701	580/924-0848
Edmond	825 E 2 Street, #100, 73034	405/341-2808
El Reno	206 N Bickford, 73036	405/262-1188
Elk City	PO Box 972, 73648	580/225-0207
Enid	210 Kenwood Blvd., 73701	580/237-2494
Erick	PO Box 1232, 73645	580/526-3332
Eufaula	321 N Main, 74432	918/689-2791
Fairfax	260 N 2 Street, 74637	918/642-5266
Fairview	624 N Main, 73737	405/227-2527
Fort Cobb	201 Main, 73038	405/643-2682
Fort Gibson	108 N Lee 74434	918/478-4780
Fort Sill/Lawton	302 Gore Boulevard, Lawton, 73501	580/355-3541
Frederick	100 S Main Street, 73542	580/335-2126
Freedom	Box 76, 73842	580/621-3276
Geary	106 E Main, 73040	405/884-2765
Glenpool	PO Box 767, 74033	918/322-3505
Gore	PO Box 943, 74435	n/a
Grand Lake Area (South)	PO Box 215, Langley, 74350	918/782-3214
Granite	PO Box 245, 73547	580/535-2184
Greater Muskogee Area	310 W Broadway, 74402	918/682-2401

City	Address, Zip	Phone
Greater Oklahoma City	123 Park Avenue, Oklahoma City, 73102	405/297-8900
Greater Tulsa Hispanic	14201 E 21 Street Tulsa, 74134	918/664-5326
Greenwood	131 N Greenwood #2, Tulsa, 74120	918/585-2084
Grove	9630 US HWY 69, 74344	918/786-9079
Guthrie	212 W Oklahoma Avenue, 73044	405/282-1947
Guymon	RR 5, Box 120, 73942	580/338-3376
Haskell	110 Commercial, 74436	918/482-1245
Healdton	PO Box 306, 73438	580/229-0900
Heavener	501 W First Street, 74937	918/653-4303
Hennessey	PO Box 306, 73742	405/853-2416
Henryetta	115 S 4 Street, 74437	918/652-3331
Hinton	PO Box 48, 73047	405/542-6428
Hobart	106 W 4 Street, 73651	580/726-2553
Holdenville	105 S Hinckley, 74848	405/592-4221
Hominy	113 W Main Street, 74035	918/261-0956
Hooker	102 HWY 54, 73945	580/652-2809
Hugo	200 S Broadway Street, 74743	580/326-7511
Idabel	7 NW Texas, 74745	580/286-3305
Jay	PO Box 806, 74346	918/253-8698
Jenks	PO Box 902, 74037	918/299-5005
Johnston County	106 W Main, Tishimingo, 73460	580/371-2175
Kaw City	PO Box 241, 74641	580/269-2276
Kingfisher	123 W Miles, 73750	405/375-4445
Konawa	PO Box 112, 74849	580/925-3775
Laverne	Box 634, Laverne, 73848	580/921-3612
Lawton	302 W Gore Boulevard, 73501-4301	580/355-3541
Lindsay	107 N Main Street, 73052	405/756-4312
Locust Grove	111 Harold Andrews Boulevard, 74352	918/479-6336
Love County	Box 422, Marietta, 73448	580/276-3102
Luther	PO Box 56, 73054	405/277-9965
Mangum	222 W Jefferson Street, 73554	580/782-2444
Mannford	PO Box 487, 74044	918/865-2000
Marlow	223 W Main Street, 73055	580/658-2212
Marshall County	PO Box 542, Madill, 73446	580/795-2431
McAlester	PO Box 759, 74502	918/423-2550
McLoud	PO Box 254, 74851	405/964-6566
Medford	PO Box 123, 73759	580/395-2823
Miami	111 N Main Street, 74354	918/542-4481

City	Address, Zip	Phone
Midwest City	5905 Trosper Road, 73140	405/733-3801
Minco	PO Box 451, 73059	405/352-0518
Moore	305 W Main, 73160	405/794-3400
Muskogee	310 W Broadway, 74402	918/682-2401
Mustang	1201 N Mustang Road, 73064	405/376-2758
Newcastle	820 N Main, 73065	405/387-3232
Newkirk	114 S Main Street, 74647	580/362-2155
Noble	114 S Main, 73068	405/872-5535
Norman	115 E Gray, 73069	405/321-7260
Nowata	126 S Maple Street, 74048	918/273-2301
Okeene	116 West "E", 73763	580/822-3005
Okemah	316 W Broadway, 74859	918/623-2440
Okmulgee	112 N Morton Avenue, 74447	918/756-6172
Oologah	PO Box 109, 74053	918/443-2790
Owasso	315 S Cedar, 74055	918/272-2141
Pauls Valley	112 E Paul Avenue, 73075	405/238-6491
Pawhuska	210 W Main Street, 74056	918/287-1208
Pawnee Community	613 Harrison, Pawnee, 74058	918/762-2108
Perkins	PO Box 502, 74059	405/747-6809
Perry	PO Box 426, 73077	580/336-4684
Piedmont	12 Monroe Avenue NW #E, 73078	405/373-2234
Pocola	n/a	918/436-2471
Ponca City	420 E Grand, 74601	580/765-4400
Poteau	201 S Broadway, 74953	918/647-9178
Prague	PO Box 111, 74864	405/567-2616
Pryor	PO Box 367, 74362	918/825-0157
Purcell	218 W Main, 73080	405/527-3093
Rogers Mills County & Tourism	PO Box 57, Cheyenne, 73628	580/497-3318
Sallisaw	301 E Cherokee, 74955	918/775-2558
Sand Springs	9 E Broadway, 74063	918/245-3221
Sapulpa	101 E Dewey Avenue, 74066	918/224-0170
Sayre	117 N 4 Street, 73662	580/928-3386
Seiling	PO Box 794, 73663	580/922-3110
Seminole	326 E Evans Avenue, 74868	405/382-3640
Sentinel	PO Box 131, 73664	580/393-2250
Shattuck	115 S Main, 73858	580/938-2818
Shawnee	131 N Bell, 74801	405/273-6092
Shidler	351 N Cosden Avenue, 74652	918/793-4171

City	Address, Zip	Phone
Skiatook	304 E Rogers Blvd., 74070	918/396-3702
Spencer	8606 Main, 73084	405/771-9933
Spiro	210 S Main Street, 74959	918/962-3816
Stigler	204 E Main Street, 74462	918/967-8681
Stillwater	409 S Main Street, 74074	405/372-5573
Stilwell	PO Box 845, 74960	918/696-7845
Stratford	PO Box 362, 74872	580/759-2326
Stroud	216 W Main Street, 74079	918/968-3321
Sulphur	717 W Broadway, 73086	580/622-2824
Tahlequah	123 E Delaware Street, 74464	918/456-3742
Talihina	900 2 Street #12, 74571	918/567-3434
Tecumseh	114 N Broadway, 74873	405/598-2188
Temple	PO Box 58, 73568	580/342-5115
Texhoma	112 2 Street, 73949	580/423-7112
Thomas	112 W Broadway, 73669	580/661-3689
Tipton	PO Box 403, 73570	580/667-5275
Tishomingo	106 W Main Street, 73460	580/371-2175
Tonkawa	100 E Grand, 74653	580/628-2220
Tulsa	1 W 3 Street, #100, 74103	918/585-1201
Tuttle	2422 E HWY 37, 73089	405/381-4600
Valliant	16 N Dalton, 74764	580/933-5050
Vinita	PO Box 882, 74301	918/256-7133
Wagoner Area	301 S Grant, Wagoner, 74467	918/485-3414
Walters	116 N Broadway, 73572	580/875-3335
Warner	PO Box 170, 74469	918/463-2696
Watonga	505 S Clarence Nash Boulevard, 73772	580/623-5452
Waurika	Box 366, 73573	580/228-2081
Waynoka	116 Main Street, 73860	580/824-4741
Weatherford	210 W Main, 73096	580/772-7744
Wellston	103 Key Drive, 74881	405/356-2476
Wetumka	202 N Main Street, 74883	405/452-3237
Wewoka	101 W Park Street, 74884	405/257-5485
Wilburton	302 W Main Street, 74578	918/465-2759
Woodward	1006 Oklahoma Avenue, 73801	580/256-7411
Wynnewood	PO Box 616, 73098	405/665-4466
Yale	209 N Main, 74085	918/387-2406
Yukon	510 Elm Street, 73099	405/354-3567

Incorporated Cities and Towns

1—Town • 2—Aldermanic • 3—Mayor • 4—Council–Manager • 5—Home–Rule Charter

City/Town–Gov't	Zip	County	Population 2000	2010	Phone Number
Achille–1	74720	Bryan	506	492	580/283-3734
Ada–4	74820	Pontotoc	15,691	16,810	580/436-6300
Adair–1	74330	Mayes	704	790	918/785-2432
Addington–1	73520	Jefferson	117	114	n/a
Afton–1	74331	Ottawa	1,118	1,049	918/257-4304
Agra–1	74824	Lincoln	356	339	918/375-2344
Albion–1	74521	Pushmataha	143	106	918/563-4200
Alderson–1	74522	Pittsburg	261	304	918/423-2260
Alex–1	73002	Grady	635	550	405/785-2393
Aline–1	73716	Alfalfa	214	201	580/463-2612
Allen–1	74825	Pontotoc	951	932	580/857-2461
Altus–2	73521	Jackson	21,447	19,813	580/481-2202
Alva–2	73717	Woods	5,288	4,945	580/327-1340
Amber–1	73004	Grady	490	419	405/222-2175
Ames–1	73718	Major	199	239	580/753-4624
Amorita–1	73719	Alfalfa	44	37	580/474-2280
Anadarko–4	73005	Caddo	6,645	6,762	405/247-2481
Antlers–4	74523	Pushmataha	2,552	2,453	580/298-3756
Apache–1	73006	Caddo	1,616	1,444	580/588-3505
Arapaho–1	73620	Custer	748	796	580/323-4376
Arcadia–1	73007	Oklahoma	279	247	405/396-2899
Ardmore–4	73402	Carter	23,711	24,283	580/223-2934
Arkoma–1	74901	LeFlore	2,180	1,989	918/875-3381
Armstrong–1	74726	Bryan	141	105	n/a
Arnett–1	73832	Ellis	520	524	580/885-7833
Asher–1	74826	Pottawatomie	419	393	405/784-2242
Ashland–1	74570	Pittsburg	53	66	918/867-2751
Atoka–4	74525	Atoka	2,988	3,107	580/889-3341
Atwood–1	74827	Hughes	113	74	580/986-2211
Avant–1	74001	Osage	372	320	918/263-3205
Barnsdall–2	74002	Osage	1,325	1,243	918/847-2795
Bartlesville–4	74003	Washington	34,748	35,750	918/338-4282
Bearden–1	74859	Okfuskee	140	133	n/a
Beaver–1	73932	Beaver	1,570	1,515	580/625-3331
Beggs–2	74421	Okmulgee	1,364	1,312	918/267-4935
Bennington–1	74723	Bryan	289	334	580/847-2311
Bernice–1	74331	Delaware	504	562	918/256-7777
Bessie–1	73622	Washita	190	181	580/337-6602

550   *Oklahoma Almanac*

1—Town • 2—Aldermanic • 3—Mayor • 4—Council–Manager • 5—Home–Rule Charter

City/Town–Gov't	Zip	County	Population 2000	2010	Phone Number
Bethany–4	73008	Oklahoma	20,307	19,051	405/789–2146
Bethel Acres–1	74802	Pottawatomie	2,735	2,895	405/275–4128
Big Cabin–1	74332	Craig	293	265	918/783–5704
Billings–1	74630	Noble	436	509	580/725–3610
Binger–1	73009	Caddo	708	672	405/656–2426
Bixby–4	74008	Tulsa	13,336	20,884	918/366–4430
Blackburn–1	74058	Pawnee	102	108	918/538–2271
Blackwell–4	74631	Kay	7,668	7,092	580/363–7250
Blair–1	73526	Jackson	894	818	580/563–2406
Blanchard–4	73010	McClain	2,816	7,670	405/485–9392
Bluejacket–1	74333	Craig	274	339	918/784–2382
Boise City–4	73933	Cimarron	1,483	1,266	580/544–2271
Bokchito–1	74726	Bryan	564	632	580/295–3775
Bokoshe–1	74930	LeFlore	450	512	918/969–2395
Boley–1	74829	Okfuskee	1,126	1,184	918/667–9790
Boswell–1	74727	Choctaw	703	709	580/566–2653
Bowlegs–1	74830	Seminole	371	405	405/398–4671
Boynton–1	74422	Muskogee	274	248	918/472–7232
Bradley–1	73011	Grady	182	130	405/462–7559
Braggs–1	74423	Muskogee	301	259	918/487–5952
Braman–1	74632	Kay	244	217	580/385–2169
Bray–1	73055	Stephens	1,035	1,209	580/658–2709
Breckenridge–1	73701	Garfield	239	245	580/977–8267
Bridgeport–1	73047	Caddo	109	116	405/524–6963
Bristow–3	74010	Creek	4,325	4,222	918/367–2237
Broken Arrow–4	74013	Tulsa	74,859	98,850	918/259–2400
Broken Bow–4	74728	McCurtain	4,230	4,120	580/584–2885
Bromide–1	74530	Johnston	163	165	580/638–2334
Brooksville–1	74873	Pottawatomie	90	63	405/598–5702
Buffalo–1	73834	Harper	1,200	1,299	580/735–2030
Burbank–1	74633	Osage	155	141	918/648–5383
Burlington–1	73722	Alfalfa	156	152	580/431–2550
Burns Flat–1	73624	Washita	1,782	2,057	580/562–3144
Butler–1	73625	Custer	345	287	580/664–3915
Byars–1	74831	McClain	280	287	405/783–4255
Byng–1	74820	Pontotoc	1,090	1,175	580/436–2545
Byron–1	73722	Alfalfa	45	35	n/a
Cache–2	73527	Comanche	2,371	2,796	580/429–3354
Caddo–1	74729	Bryan	944	997	580/367–2244
Calera–1	74730	Bryan	1,739	2,164	580/434–5420
Calumet–1	73014	Canadian	535	507	405/893–2323

1—Town • 2—Aldermanic • 3—Mayor • 4—Council-Manager • 5—Home-Rule Charter

City/Town–Gov't	Zip	County	Population 2000	2010	Phone Number
Calvin-1	74531	Hughes	279	294	405/645-2434
Camargo-1	73835	Dewey	115	178	580/926-3322
Cameron-1	74932	LeFlore	312	302	918/654-3591
Canadian-1	74425	Pittsburg	239	220	918/339-2517
Caney-1	74533	Atoka	199	205	580/889-8842
Canton-1	73724	Blaine	618	625	580/886-2212
Canute-1	73626	Washita	524	541	580/472-3111
Carmen-1	73726	Alfalfa	411	459	580/987-2321
Carnegie-1	73015	Caddo	1,637	1,723	580/654-1004
Carney-1	74832	Lincoln	649	647	405/865-2380
Carrier-1	73727	Garfield	77	85	580/855-2277
Carter-1	73627	Beckham	254	256	580/486-3205
Cashion-1	73016	Kingfisher	635	802	405/433-2243
Castle-1	74833	Okfuskee	122	106	n/a
Catoosa-3	74015	Rogers	5,449	7,151	918/266-2505
Cedar Valley-1	73044	Logan	58	288	405/282-4800
Cement-1	73017	Caddo	530	501	405/489-3222
Centrahoma-1	74534	Coal	110	97	580/845-2293
Central High-1	73055	Stephens	954	1,199	580/658-9372
Chandler-4	74834	Lincoln	2,842	3,100	405/258-3200
Chattanooga-1	73528	Comanche	432	461	580/597-3390
Checotah-2	74426	McIntosh	3,481	3,335	918/473-5411
Chelsea-1	74016	Rogers	2,136	1,964	918/789-2557
Cherokee-4	73728	Alfalfa	1,630	1,498	580/596-3052
Cheyenne-1	73628	Roger Mills	778	801	580/497-2455
Chickasha-4	73018	Grady	15,850	16,036	405/222-6020
Choctaw-4	73020	Oklahoma	9,377	11,146	405/390-8198
Chouteau-1	74337	Mayes	1,931	2,097	918/476-5902
Cimarron City-1	73028	Logan	110	150	n/a
Claremore-4	74018	Rogers	15,873	18,581	918/341-2365
Clayton-1	74536	Pushmataha	719	821	918/569-4126
Clearview-1	74880	Okfuskee	56	48	918/698-6037
Cleo Springs-1	73729	Major	326	338	580/438-2243
Cleveland-4	74020	Pawnee	3,282	3,251	918/358-3506
Clinton-4	73601	Custer	8,833	9,033	580/323-0217
Coalgate-4	74538	Coal	2,005	1,967	580/927-3914
Colbert-1	74733	Bryan	1,065	1,140	580/296-2560
Colcord-1	74338	Delaware	819	815	918/326-4200
Cole-1	73010	McClain	473	555	n/a
Collinsville-4	74021	Tulsa	4,077	5,606	918/371-1010
Colony-1	73021	Washita	163	147	405/929-7280

1—Town • 2—Aldermanic • 3—Mayor • 4—Council–Manager • 5—Home–Rule Charter

City/Town–Gov't	Zip	County	Population 2000	2010	Phone Number
Comanche–4	73529	Stephens	1,556	1,663	580/439-8832
Commerce–2	74339	Ottawa	2,645	2,243	918/675-4373
Cooperton–1	73564	Kiowa	20	16	580/639-2804
Copan–1	74022	Washington	796	733	918/532-4114
Cordell–2	73632	Washita	2,867	n/a	580/832-3825
Corn–1	73024	Washita	591	503	580/343-2255
Cornish–1	73456	Jefferson	172	163	580/662-2428
Council Hill–1	74428	Muskogee	129	158	918/474-3777
Covington–1	73730	Garfield	553	527	580/864-7428
Coweta–4	74429	Wagoner	7,139	9,943	918/486-2189
Cowlington–1	74941	LeFlore	133	155	918/966-3283
Coyle–1	73027	Logan	337	325	405/466-3741
Crescent–4	73028	Logan	1,281	1,411	405/969-2538
Cromwell–1	74837	Seminole	265	286	405/944-5333
Crowder–1	74430	Pittsburg	436	430	918/424-2873
Cushing–4	74023	Payne	8,371	7,826	918/225-2394
Custer City–1	73639	Custer	393	375	580/593-2312
Cyril–1	73029	Caddo	1,168	1,059	580/464-2411
Dacoma–1	73731	Woods	148	107	580/871-2250
Davenport–1	74026	Lincoln	881	814	918/377-2235
Davidson–1	73530	Tillman	375	315	580/568-2600
Davis–4	73030	Murray	2,610	2,683	580/369-3333
Deer Creek–1	74636	Grant	147	130	n/a
Del City–4	73155	Oklahoma	22,128	21,332	405/677-5741
Delaware–1	74027	Nowata	456	476	918/467-3218
Depew–1	74028	Creek	564	476	918/324-5251
Devol–1	73531	Cotton	150	151	n/a
Dewar–1	74431	Okmulgee	919	888	918/652-4042
Dewey–4	74029	Washington	3,179	3,432	918/534-2272
Dibble–1	73031	McClain	289	878	405/344-6659
Dickson–1	73401	Carter	1,139	1,207	580/223-5445
Dill City–1	73641	Washita	526	562	580/674-3376
Disney–1	74340	Mayes	226	311	918/435-8242
Dougherty–1	73032	Murray	224	215	580/993-2312
Douglas–1	73733	Garfield	32	32	580/862-7795
Dover–1	73734	Kingfisher	367	464	405/828-4212
Drummond–1	73735	Garfield	405	455	580/493-2900
Drumright–4	74030	Creek	2,905	2,907	918/352-2631
Duncan–4	73534	Stephens	22,505	23,431	580/252-0250
Durant–4	74702	Bryan	13,549	15,856	580/931-6600
Dustin–1	74839	Hughes	452	395	918/656-3220

1—Town • 2—Aldermanic • 3—Mayor • 4—Council–Manager • 5—Home–Rule Charter

City/Town–Gov't	Zip	County	Population 2000	2010	Phone Number
Eakly–1	73033	Caddo	276	338	405/797–3252
Earlsboro–1	74840	Pottawatomie	633	628	405/997–5560
East Duke–1	73532	Jackson	445	424	580/679–3400
Edmond–4	73033	Oklahoma	68,315	81,405	405/348–8830
Eldorado–1	73537	Jackson	527	446	580/633–2245
Elgin–2	73538	Comanche	1,210	2,156	580/492–5777
Elk City–4	73648	Beckham	10,510	11,693	580/225–3230
Elmer–1	73539	Jackson	96	96	580/687–4342
Elmore City–2	73433	Garvin	756	697	580/788–2345
El Reno–4	73036	Canadian	16,212	16,749	405/262–4070
Empire City–1	73533	Stephens	734	955	580/251–4727
Enid–4	73702	Garfield	47,045	49,379	580/234–0400
Erick–2	73645	Beckham	1,023	1,052	580/526–3924
Etowa–1	73068	Cleveland			n/a
Eufaula–2	74432	McIntosh	2,639	2,813	918/689–2534
Fair Oaks–1	74015	Wagoner	122	103	918/266–6740
Fairfax–1	74627	Osage	1,555	1,380	918/642–5211
Fairland–1	74343	Ottawa	1,025	1,057	918/676–3636
Fairmont–1	73736	Garfield	147	134	580/358–2282
Fairview–4	73737	Major	2,733	2,579	580/227–4416
Fallis–1	74881	Lincoln	28	27	n/a
Fanshawe–1	74935	LeFlore	384	419	918/659–2263
Fargo–1	73840	Ellis	326	364	580/698–2635
Faxon–1	73540	Comanche	134	136	580/597–3094
Fitzhugh–1	74843	Pontotoc	204	230	n/a
Fletcher–1	73541	Comanche	1,022	1,177	580/549–6550
Foraker–1	74638	Osage	23	19	n/a
Forest Park–1	73121	Oklahoma	1,066	998	405/424–1212
Forgan–1	73938	Beaver	532	547	580/487–3393
Fort Cobb–1	73038	Caddo	667	634	405/643–2682
Fort Coffee–1	74959	LeFlore	n/a	424	n/a
Fort Gibson–1	74434	Muskogee	4,054	4,154	918/478–3551
Fort Supply–1	73841	Woodward	328	330	580/766–3211
Fort Towson–1	74735	Choctaw	611	519	580/873–2628
Foss–1	73647	Washita	127	151	580/592–4513
Foyil–1	74031	Rogers	234	344	918/342–9525
Francis–1	74844	Pontotoc	332	315	580/332–3967
Frederick–4	73542	Tillman	4,637	3,940	580/335–7551
Freedom–1	73842	Woods	271	289	580/621–3302
Gage–1	73843	Ellis	429	442	580/923–7727
Gans–1	74936	Sequoyah	208	312	918/775–2411

1—Town • 2—Aldermanic • 3—Mayor • 4—Council-Manager • 5—Home-Rule Charter

City/Town–Gov't	Zip	County	Population 2000	2010	Phone Number
Garber–2	73738	Garfield	845	822	580/863–2254
Garvin–1	74736	McCurtain	143	256	580/286–7483
Gate–1	73844	Beaver	112	93	580/934–2202
Geary–2	73040	Blaine	1,258	1,280	405/884–5466
Gene Autry–1	73436	Carter	99	158	n/a
Geronimo–2	73543	Comanche	959	1,268	580/353–5511
Gerty–1	74531	Hughes	101	118	580/892–3836
Glencoe–1	74032	Payne	583	601	580/669–2271
Glenpool–4	74033	Tulsa	8,123	10,808	918/322–5409
Goldsby–1	73093	McClain	1,204	1,801	405/288–6675
Goltry–1	73739	Alfalfa	268	249	580/496–2441
Goodwell–1	73939	Texas	1,192	1,293	580/349–2566
Gore–1	74435	Sequoyah	850	977	918/489–2636
Gotebo–1	73041	Kiowa	272	226	580/538–5351
Gould–1	73544	Harmon	206	141	n/a
Gracemont–1	73042	Caddo	336	318	405/966–2201
Grainola–1	74652	Osage	31	31	n/a
Grand Lake–1	74301	Mayes	65	74	918/782–4436
Grandfield–4	73546	Tillman	1,110	1,038	580/479–5215
Granite–1	73547	Greer	1,844	2,065	580/535–2116
Grayson–1	74437	Okmulgee	134	159	918/652–4773
Greenfield–1	73043	Blaine	123	93	580/623–1281
Grove–4	74344	Delaware	5,131	6,623	918/786–6107
Guthrie–5	73044	Logan	9,925	10,191	405/282–2489
Guymon–4	73942	Texas	10,472	11,442	580/338–0137
Haileyville–2	74546	Pittsburg	891	813	918/297–2402
Hallet–1	74034	Pawnee	168	125	918/356–4335
Hammon–1	73650	Roger Mills	469	568	580/473–2281
Hanna–1	74845	McIntosh	133	138	918/657–2244
Hardesty–1	73944	Texas	277	212	580/888–4568
Harrah–4	73045	Oklahoma	4,719	5,095	405/454–2951
Hartshorne–2	74547	Pittsburg	2,102	2,125	918/297–2544
Haskell–1	74436	Muskogee	1,765	2,007	918/482–3933
Hastings–1	73548	Jefferson	155	143	580/228–2961
Haworth–1	74740	McCurtain	354	297	580/245–2369
Headrick–1	73549	Jackson	130	94	580/738–5723
Healdton–4	73438	Carter	2,786	2,788	580/229–1283
Heavener–4	74937	LeFlore	3,201	3,414	918/653–2217
Helena–1	73741	Alfalfa	443	1,403	580/852–3250
Hendrix–1	74741	Bryan	79	79	580/838–2270
Hennessey–1	73742	Kingfisher	2,058	2,131	405/853–2416

1—Town • 2—Aldermanic • 3—Mayor • 4—Council–Manager • 5—Home–Rule Charter

City/Town–Gov't	Zip	County	Population 2000	Population 2010	Phone Number
Henryetta–4	74437	Okmulgee	6,096	5,927	918/652–3348
Hickory–1	74865	Murray	87	71	580/456–7419
Hillsdale–1	73743	Garfield	101	121	580/635–2245
Hinton–1	73047	Caddo	2,175	3,196	405/542–3253
Hitchcock–1	73744	Blaine	141	121	580/825–3233
Hitchita–1	74438	McIntosh	113	88	918/466–3408
Hobart–4	73651	Kiowa	3,997	3,756	580/726–3100
Hoffman–1	74437	Okmulgee	148	127	n/a
Holdenville–2	74848	Hughes	4,732	5,771	405/379–3397
Hollis–4	73550	Harmon	2,264	2,060	580/688–9245
Hollister–1	73551	Tillman	60	50	n/a
Hominy–4	74035	Osage	2,584	3,565	918/885–2164
Hooker–2	73945	Texas	1,788	1,918	580/652–2885
Howe–1	74940	LeFlore	697	802	918/658–2459
Hugo–4	74743	Choctaw	5,536	5,310	580/326–7755
Hulbert–1	74441	Cherokee	543	590	918/772–2503
Hunter–1	73753	Garfield	173	165	n/a
Hydro–1	73048	Caddo	1,060	969	405/663–2531
Idabel–2	74745	McCurtain	6,952	7,010	580/286–7608
Indiahoma–1	73552	Comanche	374	344	580/246–3572
Indianola–1	74442	Pittsburg	191	162	918/823–4517
Inola–1	74036	Rogers	1,589	1,788	918/543–2430
IXL–1	74833	Okfuskee	60	51	918/668–3461
Jay–2	74346	Delaware	2,482	2,448	918/253–4148
Jefferson–1	73759	Grant	37	12	580/532–6278
Jenks–4	74037	Tulsa	9,557	16,924	918/299–5883
Jennings–1	74038	Pawnee	373	363	918/757–4250
Jet–1	73749	Alfalfa	230	213	580/626–4401
Johnson–1	74801	Pottawatomie	223	247	405/275–8562
Jones–1	73049	Oklahoma	2,517	2,692	405/399–5301
Kansas–1	74347	Delaware	685	802	918/868–2198
Katie–1	73433	Garvin	300	348	405/207–0951
Kaw City–2	74641	Kay	372	375	580/269–2525
Kellyville–1	74039	Creek	906	1,150	918/247–6160
Kemp–1	74747	Bryan	144	133	580/838–2606
Kendrick–1	74079	Lincoln	138	139	918/368–2219
Kenefic–1	74748	Bryan	192	196	580/367–2744
Keota–1	74941	Haskell	517	564	918/966–3655
Ketchum–1	74349	Craig	286	442	918/782–2244
Keyes–1	73947	Cimarron	410	324	580/546–7651
Kiefer–1	74041	Creek	1,026	1,685	918/321–5925

1—Town • 2—Aldermanic • 3—Mayor • 4—Council–Manager • 5—Home–Rule Charter

City/Town–Gov't	Zip	County	Population 2000	2010	Phone Number
Kildare–1	74604	Kay	92	100	580/716–6162
Kingfisher–4	73750	Kingfisher	4,380	4,633	405/375–3705
Kingston–1	73439	Marshall	1,390	1,601	580/564–3750
Kinta–1	74552	Haskell	243	297	918/768–3474
Kiowa–1	74553	Pittsburg	693	731	918/432–5621
Knowles–1	73844	Beaver	32	11	580/934–2643
Konawa–4	74849	Seminole	1,479	1,298	580/925–3775
Krebs–2	74554	Pittsburg	2,051	2,053	918/423–6519
Kremlin–1	73753	Garfield	240	255	580/874–2601
Lahoma–1	73754	Garfield	577	611	580/796–2600
Lake Aluma–1	73121	Oklahoma	97	88	n/a
Lamar–1	74850	Hughes	172	158	405/379–2114
Lambert–1	73728	Alfalfa	9	6	580/596–2850
Lamont–1	74643	Grant	465	417	580/388–4360
Langley–1	74350	Mayes	669	819	918/782–9850
Langston–1	73050	Logan	1,670	1,724	405/466–2271
Laverne–1	73848	Harper	1,097	1,344	580/921–5121
Lawrence Creek–1	74044	Creek	119	149	918/688–1203
Lawton–4	73501	Comanche	92,757	96,867	580/581–3305
Leedey–1	73654	Dewey	345	435	580/488–3616
LeFlore–1	74942	LeFlore	168	190	918/753–2287
Lehigh–3	74556	Coal	315	356	918/927–9953
Lenapah–1	74042	Nowata	298	293	918/468–2226
Leon–1	73441	Love	96	91	n/a
Lexington–4	73051	Cleveland	2,086	2,152	405/527–6123
Lima–1	74884	Seminole	74	53	n/a
Lindsay–4	73052	Garvin	2,889	2,840	405/756–2019
Loco–1	73442	Stephens	150	122	580/537–2283
Locust Grove–1	74352	Mayes	1,366	1,423	918/479–5102
Lone Chimney–1	74058	Pawnee	n/a	n/a	918/454–2448
Lone Grove–4	73443	Carter	4,631	5,054	580/657–3111
Lone Wolf–1	73655	Kiowa	500	438	580/846–9078
Longdale–1	73755	Blaine	310	262	580/274–3375
Lookeba–1	73053	Caddo	131	166	405/457–6361
Loveland–1	73553	Tillman	14	13	580/479–5788
Loyal–1	73756	Kingfisher	81	79	n/a
Luther–1	73054	Oklahoma	612	1,221	405/277–3833
Macomb–1	74852	Pottawatomie	61	32	405/598–6876
Madill–4	73446	Marshall	3,410	3,770	580/795–5586
Manchester–1	73758	Grant	104	103	580/694–2340
Mangum–4	73554	Greer	2,924	3,010	580/782–2256

1—Town • 2—Aldermanic • 3—Mayor • 4—Council–Manager • 5—Home–Rule Charter

City/Town–Gov't	Zip	County	Population 2000	2010	Phone Number
Manitou–1	73555	Tillman	278	181	580/397–2006
Mannford–1	74044	Creek	2,095	3,076	918/865–4314
Mannsville–1	73447	Johnston	587	863	580/371–3334
Maramec–1	74045	Pawnee	104	91	n/a
Marble City–1	74945	Sequoyah	242	263	918/775–3002
Marietta–2	73448	Love	2,445	2,626	580/276–5569
Marland 1	74644	Noble	280	225	580/268–3271
Marlow–4	73055	Stephens	4,592	4,662	580/658–5401
Marshall–1	73056	Logan	258	272	580/935–6624
Martha–1	73556	Jackson	205	162	580/266–3300
Maud–2	74854	Pottawatomie	1,136	1,048	405/374–2717
May–1	73851	Harper	33	39	580/689–2303
Maysville–1	73057	Garvin	1,313	1,232	405/867–5850
McAlester–4	74502	Pittsburg	17,783	18,383	918/423–9300
McCurtain–1	74944	Haskell	466	516	918/945–7209
McLoud–4	74851	Pottawatomie	3,548	4,044	405/964–5264
Mead–1	73449	Bryan	123	122	580/924–1872
Medford–4	73759	Grant	1,172	996	580/395–2823
Medicine Park–1	73557	Comanche	373	382	580/529–2825
Meeker–1	74855	Lincoln	978	1.144	405/279–3321
Meno–1	73760	Major	195	235	580/776–2275
Meridian–1	73058	Logan	54	1,531	405/586–2488
Miami–4	74355	Ottawa	13,704	13,570	918/542–6685
Midwest City–4	73110	Oklahoma	54,088	53,371	405/739–2281
Milburn–1	73450	Johnston	312	317	580/443–5702
Mill Creek–1	74856	Johnston	340	319	580/384–5757
Millerton–1	74750	McCurtain	359	320	580/746–2692
Minco–2	73059	Grady	1,672	1,632	405/352–4274
Moffett–1	74946	Sequoyah	179	128	918/875–3666
Moore–4	73160	Cleveland	41,138	55,081	405/793–5000
Mooreland–1	73852	Woodward	1,226	1,190	580/994–5924
Morris–2	74445	Okmulgee	1,294	1,479	918/733–4222
Morrison–1	73061	Noble	636	733	580/724–3531
Mounds–1	74047	Creek	1,153	1,168	918/827–6711
Mountain Park–1	73559	Kiowa	390	409	580/569–4234
Mountain View–1	73062	Kiowa	880	795	580/347–2711
Muldrow–1	74948	Sequoyah	3,104	3,466	918/427–3226
Mulhall–1	73063	Logan	239	225	405/649–2494
Muskogee–4	74402	Muskogee	38,310	39,223	918/682–6602
Mustang–4	73064	Canadian	13,156	17,395	405/376–4521
Mutual–1	73853	Woodward	76	61	n/a

1—Town • 2—Aldermanic • 3—Mayor • 4—Council-Manager • 5—Home-Rule Charter

City/Town–Gov't	Zip	County	Population 2000	Population 2010	Phone Number
Nash–1	73761	Grant	224	204	580/839-2829
Newcastle–4	73065	McClain	5,434	7,685	405/387-4427
Newkirk–4	74647	Kay	2,243	2,317	580/362-2117
New Alluwe–1	74016	Nowata	95	90	918/475-2257
Nichols Hills–4	73116	Oklahoma	4,056	3,710	405/843-6637
Nicoma Park–3	73066	Oklahoma	2,415	2,393	405/769-5673
Ninnekah–1	73067	Grady	994	1,002	405/222-0882
Noble–4	73068	Cleveland	5,260	6,481	405/872-9251
Norman–4	73070	Cleveland	95,694	110,925	405/366-5406
North Enid–1	73701	Garfield	796	860	580/234-5941
North Miami–1	74358	Ottawa	433	374	918/542-2718
Nowata–4	74048	Nowata	3,971	3,731	918/273-3538
Oakland–1	73446	Marshall	674	1,057	580/795-3467
Oaks–1	74359	Delaware	412	288	918/868-3370
Oakwood–1	73658	Dewey	72	65	918/891-3316
Ochelata–1	74051	Washington	494	424	918/535-2213
Oilton–2	74052	Creek	1,099	1,013	918/862-3202
Okarche–1	73762	Canadian	1,110	1,215	405/263-7290
Okay–1	74446	Wagoner	597	620	918/687-6585
Okeene–1	73763	Blaine	1,240	1,204	580/822-3035
Okemah–4	74859	Okfuskee	3,038	3,223	918/623-1050
Oklahoma City–4	73102	Oklahoma	506,132	579,999	405/297-2345
Okmulgee–4	74447	Okmulgee	13,022	12,321	918/756-4060
Oktaha–1	74450	Muskogee	327	390	918/682-3212
Olustee–1	73560	Jackson	680	607	580/648-2288
Oologah–1	74053	Rogers	883	1,146	918/443-2783
Optima–1	73945	Texas	266	356	580/338-0644
Orlando–1	73073	Logan	201	148	580/455-2403
Osage–1	74054	Osage	188	156	918/354-2301
Owasso–4	74055	Tulsa	18,502	28,915	918/376-1500
Paden–1	74860	Okfuskee	446	461	405/932-4441
Panama–1	74951	LeFlore	1,362	1,413	918/963-4116
Paoli–1	73074	Garvin	649	610	405/484-7844
Paradise Hill–1	74435	Sequoyah	100	85	918/213-9325
Pauls Valley–4	73075	Garvin	6,256	6,187	405/238-3308
Pawhuska–4	74056	Osage	3,629	3,584	918/287-3576
Pawnee–2	74058	Pawnee	2,230	2,196	918/762-2658
Pensacola–1	74301	Mayes	71	125	n/a
Peoria–1	74363	Ottawa	141	132	n/a
Perkins–4	74059	Payne	2,272	2,831	405/547-2445
Perry–2	73077	Noble	4,978	5,230	580/336-4241

1—Town • 2—Aldermanic • 3—Mayor • 4—Council–Manager • 5—Home–Rule Charter

City/Town–Gov't	Zip	County	Population 2000	2010	Phone Number
Phillips–1	74538	Coal	150	135	580/927-3372
Piedmont–4	73078	Canadian	3,650	5,720	405/373-2621
Pink–1	74873	Pottawatomie	1,165	2,058	405/598-2364
Pittsburg–1	74560	Pittsburg	280	207	918/432-5516
Pocasset–1	73079	Grady	192	156	405/459-6737
Pocola–1	74902	LeFlore	3,994	4,056	918/436-2388
Ponca City–4	74602	Kay	25,919	25,387	580/767-0301
Pond Creek–2	73766	Grant	896	836	580/532-4915
Porter–1	74454	Wagoner	574	566	918/483-8331
Porum–1	74455	Muskogee	725	727	918/484-5125
Poteau–2	74953	LeFlore	7,939	8,520	918/647-4191
Prague–4	74864	Lincoln	2,138	2,386	405/567-2270
Prue–1	74060	Osage	433	465	918/242-3613
Pryor Creek–3	74362	Mayes	8,659	9,539	918/825-0888
Purcell–4	73080	McClain	5,571	5,884	405/527-6561
Putnam–1	73659	Dewey	46	29	580/582-6248
Quapaw–1	74363	Ottawa	984	906	918/674-2525
Quinton–1	74561	Pittsburg	1,071	1,051	918/469-2652
Ralston–1	74650	Pawnee	355	330	918/738-4211
Ramona–1	74061	Washington	564	535	918/536-2245
Randlett–1	73562	Cotton	511	438	580/281-3370
Ratliff City–1	73481	Carter	131	120	580/856-3599
Rattan–1	74562	Pushmataha	241	310	580/587-2256
Ravia–1	73455	Johnston	459	528	580/371-3559
Red Bird–1	74458	Wagoner	153	137	918/483-4400
Red Oak–1	74563	Latimer	581	549	918/754-2832
Red Rock–1	74651	Noble	293	283	580/723-4474
Renfrow–1	73759	Grant	16	12	580/849-6500
Rentiesville–1	74459	McIntosh	102	128	918/473-1577
Reydon–1	73660	Roger Mills	177	210	580/655-4592
Ringling–1	73456	Jefferson	1,135	1,037	580/662-2264
Ringwood–1	73768	Major	424	497	580/883-5550
Ripley–1	74062	Payne	444	403	918/372-4287
Rock Island–1	74932	Le Flore	709	646	n/a
Rocky–1	73661	Washita	174	162	580/750/0590
Roff–1	74865	Pontotoc	734	725	580/456-7223
Roland–1	74954	Sequoyah	2,842	3,169	918/427-5779
Roosevelt–1	73564	Kiowa	280	248	580/639-2681
Rosedale–1	74831	McClain	66	68	n/a
Rosston–1	73855	Harper	66	31	580/921-5130
Rush Springs–1	73082	Grady	1,278	1,231	580/476-3277

1—Town • 2—Aldermanic • 3—Mayor • 4—Council–Manager • 5—Home–Rule Charter

City/Town–Gov't	Zip	County	Population 2000	2010	Phone Number
Ryan–1	73565	Jefferson	894	816	580/757–2277
Saint Louis–1	74866	Pottawatomie	206	158	n/a
Salina–1	74365	Mayes	1,422	1,396	918/434–5027
Sallisaw–4	74955	Sequoyah	7,989	8,880	918/775–6241
Sand Springs–4	74063	Tulsa	17,451	18,906	918/246–2500
Sapulpa–4	74067	Creek	19,166	20,544	918/224–3040
Sasakwa–1	74867	Seminole	150	150	580/941–3002
Savanna–1	74565	Pittsburg	730	686	918/548–3397
Sawyer–1	74756	Choctaw	274	321	580/326–5226
Sayre–2	73662	Beckham	4,114	4,375	580/928–2260
Schulter–1	74460	Okmulgee	600	509	918/652–3654
Seiling–1	73663	Dewey	875	860	580/922–4460
Seminole–4	74818	Seminole	6,899	7,488	405/382–4330
Sentinel–1	73664	Washita	859	901	580/393–2171
Shady Point–1	74956	LeFlore	848	1,026	918/963–4214
Shamrock–1	74068	Creek	125	101	918/352–4111
Sharon–1	73857	Woodward	122	135	n/a
Shattuck–1	73858	Ellis	1,274	1,356	580/938–2916
Shawnee–4	74802	Pottawatomie	28,692	29,857	405/878–1601
Shidler–2	74652	Osage	520	441	918/793–7171
Silo–1	74702	Bryan	282	331	580/931–9838
Skedee–1	74058	Pawnee	102	51	n/a
Skiatook–1	74070	Osage	5,396	7,397	918/396–2797
Slaughterville–1	73051	Cleveland	3,609	4,137	405/872–3000
Slick–1	74071	Creek	148	131	918/367–1800
Smith Village–1	73115	Oklahoma	40	34	405/672–0440
Snyder–3	73566	Kiowa	1,509	1,394	580/569–2119
Soper–1	74759	Choctaw	300	261	580/345–2630
So. Coffeyville–1	74072	Nowata	790	785	918/255–6045
Sparks–1	74869	Lincoln	137	169	918/866–2411
Spaulding–1	74848	Hughes	62	178	405/379–3668
Spavinaw–1	74366	Mayes	563	437	918/589–2278
Spencer–4	73084	Oklahoma	3,746	3,912	405/771–3226
Sperry–1	74073	Tulsa	981	1,206	918/288–7056
Spiro–1	74959	LeFlore	2,227	2,164	918/962–2477
Sportsman Acres–1	74361	Mayes	204	322	918/824–1000
Springer–1	73458	Carter	577	700	580/653–2500
Sterling–1	73567	Comanche	762	793	580/365–4445
Stidham–1	74432	McIntosh	23	18	918/689–2435
Stigler–4	74462	Haskell	2,731	2,685	918/967–2164
Stillwater–4	74076	Payne	39,065	45,688	405/372–0025

1—Town • 2—Aldermanic • 3—Mayor • 4—Council-Manager • 5—Home-Rule Charter

City/Town–Gov't	Zip	County	Population 2000	2010	Phone Number
Stilwell–2	74960	Adair	3,276	3,949	918/696–8111
Stonewall–1	74871	Pontotoc	465	470	580/265–4511
Strang–1	74367	Mayes	100	89	918/593–2222
Stratford–1	74872	Garvin	1,474	1,525	580/759–2371
Stringtown–1	74569	Atoka	396	410	580/346–7759
Strong City–1	73628	Roger Mills	42	47	580/497–3933
Stroud–4	74079	Lincoln	2,758	2,690	918/987–0224
Stuart–1	74570	Hughes	220	180	918/546–2249
Sugden–1	73573	Jefferson	59	43	n/a
Sulphur–4	73086	Murray	4,794	4,929	580/622–5096
Summit–1	74401	Muskogee	226	139	918/681–0100
Taft–1	74463	Muskogee	349	250	918/683–0568
Tahlequah–2	74464	Cherokee	14,458	15,753	918/456–0651
Talala–1	74080	Rogers	270	273	918/275–4203
Talihina–1	74571	LeFlore	1,211	1,114	918/567–2194
Taloga–1	73667	Dewey	372	299	580/328–5444
Tamaha–1	74462	Haskell	198	176	918/967–0817
Tatums–1	73087	Carter	172	151	580/856–3241
Tecumseh–4	74873	Pottawatomie	6,098	6,457	405/598–2188
Temple–1	73568	Cotton	1,146	1,002	580/342–6776
Terlton–1	74081	Pawnee	85	106	n/a
Terral–1	73569	Jefferson	386	382	580/437–2337
Texhoma–1	73949	Texas	935	926	580/423–7456
Texola–1	73668	Beckham	47	36	580/526–3778
Thackerville–1	73459	Love	404	445	580/276–4842
The Village–4	73120	Oklahoma	10,157	8,929	405/751–8861
Thomas–2	73669	Custer	1,238	1,181	580/661–3687
Tipton–1	73570	Tillman	916	847	580/667–5211
Tishomingo–4	73460	Johnston	3,162	3,034	580/371–2369
Tonkawa–4	74653	Kay	3,299	3,299	580/628–2508
Tribbey–1	74852	Pottawatomie	273	391	405/899–4178
Tryon–1	74875	Lincoln	448	491	918/374–2227
Tullahassee–1	74454	Wagoner	106	106	n/a
Tulsa–3	74103	Tulsa	393,049	391,906	918/596–2100
Tupelo–1	74572	Coal	377	329	580/845–2412
Tushka–1	74525	Atoka	345	312	580/889–3046
Tuttle–4	73089	Grady	4,294	6,019	405/381–2335
Tyrone–1	73951	Texas	880	762	580/854–6873
Union City–1	73090	Canadian	1,375	1,645	405/483–5509
Valley Brook–1	73129	Oklahoma	817	765	405/677–6948
Valliant–1	74764	McCurtain	771	754	580/933–4556

1—Town • 2—Aldermanic • 3—Mayor • 4—Council–Manager • 5—Home–Rule Charter

City/Town–Gov't	Zip	County	Population 2000	2010	Phone Number
Velma–1	73091	Stephens	664	620	580/444-3393
Vera–1	74082	Washington	188	241	918/371-5974
Verden–1	73092	Grady	659	530	405/453-7235
Verdigris–1	74018	Rogers	n/a	3,993	918/379-0142
Vernon–1	74845	McIntosh	56	n/a	n/a
Vian–1	74962	Sequoyah	1,362	1,466	918/773-8110
Vici–1	73859	Dewey	668	699	580/995-4442
Vinita–2	74301	Craig	6,472	5,743	918/256-6468
Wagoner–2	74477	Wagoner	7,669	7,669	918/485-4586
Wainwright–1	74468	Muskogee	197	165	918/616-0864
Wakita–1	73771	Grant	420	344	580/594-2200
Walters–4	73572	Cotton	2,657	2,551	580/875-3337
Wanette–1	74878	Pottawatomie	402	350	405/383-2246
Wann–1	74083	Nowata	132	125	918/531-2254
Wapanucka–1	73461	Johnston	445	438	580/937-4272
Warner–1	74469	Muskogee	1,430	1,641	918/463-2696
Warr Acres–3	73122	Oklahoma	9,375	10,043	405/789-2892
Warwick–1	74881	Lincoln	235	148	405/258-2882
Washington–1	73093	McClain	520	618	405/288-2578
Watonga–2	73772	Blaine	4,658	5,111	580/623-4669
Watts–1	74964	Adair	316	324	918/422-5924
Waukomis–1	73773	Garfield	1,261	1,286	580/758-3242
Waurika–4	73573	Jefferson	1,988	2,064	580/228-2713
Wayne–1	73095	McClain	714	688	405/449-3451
Waynoka–2	73860	Woods	993	927	580/824-2261
Weatherford–3	73096	Custer	9,859	10,833	580/772-7451
Webb City–1	74652	Osage	95	62	918/765-2431
Webbers Falls–1	74470	Muskogee	726	616	918/464-2920
Welch–1	74369	Craig	597	619	918/788-3616
Weleetka–1	74880	Okfuskee	1,014	998	405/786-2272
Wellston–1	74881	Lincoln	925	788	405/356-2476
W. Siloam Springs–1	74338	Delaware	877	846	918/422-5101
Westport–1	74020	Pawnee	264	298	918/243-7454
Westville–1	74965	Adair	1,596	1,639	918/723-3988
Wetumka–4	74883	Hughes	1,451	1,282	405/452-3153
Wewoka–4	74884	Seminole	3,562	3,430	405/257-2413
Whitefield–1	74472	Haskell	231	391	918/967-2217
Wilburton–2	74578	Latimer	2,972	2,843	918/465-5361
Willow–1	73673	Greer	114	149	580/287-3398
Wilson–2	73463	Carter	1,584	1,724	580/668-2106
Winchester–1	74421	Okmulgee	424	516	918/267-4142

1—Town • 2—Aldermanic • 3—Mayor • 4—Council–Manager • 5—Home–Rule Charter

City/Town–Gov't	Zip	County	Population 2000	2010	Phone Number
Wister–1	74966	LeFlore	1,002	1,102	918/655–7421
Woodlawn Park–1	73008	Oklahoma	161	153	405/789–8815
Woodward–4	73801	Woodward	11,853	12,051	580/256–2280
Wright City–1	74766	McCurtain	848	762	580/981–2100
Wyandotte–1	74370	Ottawa	363	333	918/678–2211
Wynnewood–2	73098	Garvin	2,367	2,212	405/665–2307
Wynona–1	74084	Osage	531	437	918/846–2526
Yale–4	74085	Payne	1,342	1,227	918/387–2405
Yeager–1	74848	Hughes	67	75	n/a
Yukon–4	73085	Canadian	21,043	22,709	405/354–1895

Total State Population—3,751,351   (2010 Census)

Source: 2013-2014 *Directory of City & Town Officials in Oklahoma* and the U.S. Census Bureau.

Fort Gibson commanding officer's quarters [top]
and enlisted men's barracks.

Communities Not Incorporated

Community Name (County)

Acme (Grady), Adams (Texas), Adamson (Pittsburg), Adel (Pushmataha), Agawan (Grady), Agnus Valley Acres (Tulsa), Ahloso (Pontotoc), Ahpeatone (Cotton), Albany (Bryan), Albert (Caddo), Alden (Caddo), Aledo (Dewey), Alfalfa (Caddo), Allison (Bryan), Alma (Stephens), Alpers (Carter), Alsuma (Tulsa), Altee (Jefferson), Altona (Kingfisher), Antioch (Garvin), Apperson (Osage), Apple (Choctaw), Arch (Pittsburg), Arlington (Lincoln), Arpelar (Pittsburg), Arrowhead Estates (Pittsburg), Avery (Lincoln), Aydelotte (Pottawatomie)

Babbs (Kiowa), Bache (Pittsburg), Bacone (Muskogee), Bailey (Grady), Baker (Texas), Baldhill (Okmulgee), Balko (Beaver), Ballard (Adair), Banner (Canadian), Banty (Bryan), Barber (Cherokee), Barnes (Logan), Baron (Adair), Barry (Bryan), Bartlett (Okmulgee), Battiest (McCurtain), Baum (Carter), Beachton (McCurtain), Beckett (Stephens), Bee (Johnston), Beland (Muskogee), Bellemont (Pottawatomie), Bellvue (Creek), Belzoni (Pushmataha), Bengal (Latimer), Bentley (Atoka), Berlin (Roger Mills), Bethel (Comanche), Bethel (McCurtain), Bidding Springs (Adair), Big Cedar (LeFlore), Big Creek (LeFlore), Big Spring (Hughes), Bison (Garfield), Blackgum (Sequoyah), Blanco (Pittsburg), Blocker (Pittsburg), Blue (Bryan), Bluff (Choctaw), Boatman (Mayes), Boehler (Atoka), Boggy Depot (Atoka), Bois D'Arc (Kay), Bokhoma (McCurtain), Bond (McIntosh), Boone (Caddo), Boss (McCurtain), Boulevard (Cleveland), Bowden (Creek), Bowlin Spring (Craig), Bowring (Osage), Box (Sequoyah), Boyd (Beaver), Braden (LeFlore), Brady (Garvin), Brentwood (Tulsa), Briartown (Muskogee), Brinkman (Greer), Brock (Carter), Brooken (Haskell), Brookside (Tulsa), Brown (Bryan), Broxton (Caddo), Bruner (Tulsa), Brush Hill (McIntosh), Bryant (Okmulgee), Buffalo (McCurtain), Buffalo Valley (Latimer), Bunch (Adair), Burmah (Dewey), Burneyville (Love), Burwell (McCurtain), Butner (Seminole)

Cade (Bryan), Cairo (Coal), Calhoun (LeFlore), Cambria (Latimer), Camp Houston (Woods), Canadian Shores (Pittsburg), Caney Ridge (Cherokee), Carleton (Blaine), Carpenter (Roger Mills), Carson (Hughes), Cartersville (Haskell), Cartwright (Bryan), Catale (Rogers), Catesby (Ellis), Cedar Lake (Canadian), Cedar Ridge (Pawnee), Center (Pontotoc), Center City (Oklahoma), Center Point (Atoka), Centerview (Pottawatomie), Centralia (Craig), Ceres (Noble), Cestos (Dewey), Chance (Adair), Chase (Muskogee), Chester (Major), Cheyenne Valley (Major), Chigley (Murray), Childers (Nowata), Chilli (Latimer), Chilocco (Kay), Chimney Hill (Tulsa), Chisney (Pottawatomie), Chitwood (Grady), Chloeta (Delaware), Choska (Wagoner), Christie (Adair), Cimarron (Oklahoma), Cimarron City (Logan), Cisco (McCurtain), Citra (Hughes), Clarita (Coal), Clarksville (Wagoner), Clayton Lake (Pushmataha), Clear Lake (Beaver), Clearview (Okfuskee), Clebit (McCurtain), Clemscot (Carter), Clothier (Cleveland), Cloud Chief (Washita), Cloudy (Pushmataha), Clyde (Grant), Coalton (Okmulgee), Cobb (Bryan), Cogar (Caddo), Coleman (Johnston), Connerville (Johnston), Conser (LeFlore), Cookietown (Cotton), Cookson (Cherokee), Corbett (Cleveland), Corinne (Pushmataha), Corum (Stephens), Cottonwood (Coal), Council (Oklahoma), Countyline (Stephens and Carter), Courtney (Love), Cove Acres (Comanche), Cowden (Washita), Cox City (Grady), Cravens (Latimer), Crawford (Roger Mills), Crekola (Muskogee), Creosote (Choctaw), Criner (McClain), Crossbow (Tulsa), Crystal (Atoka), Crystal Lakes (Major), Cumberland (Marshall)

Daisy (Atoka), Dale (Pottawatomie), Damon (Latimer), Dane (Major), Darwin (Pushmataha), Dawson (Tulsa), Degnan (Latimer), Dela (Pushmataha), Delhi (Beckham), Dempsey (Roger Mills), Dereco (Oklahoma), Dewright (Seminole), Dighton (Okmulgee), Dillard (Carter), Dixon (Seminole),

Donaldson (Tulsa), Dow (Pittsburg), Drake (Murray), Driftwood (Alfalfa), Drumb (Latimer), Dunbar (Love), Dunbar (Pushmataha), Dungee Park (Oklahoma), Durham (Roger Mills), Durwood (Carter)

Eagle City (Blaine), Eagletown (McCurtain), Earl (Johnston), Eastborough (Wagoner), East Jessie (Coal), Eastside (Custer), Eddy (Kay), Edgewater Park (Comanche), Edna (Creek), Elmwood (Beaver), Emerson Center (Cotton), Emet (Johnston), Enos (Marshall), Enterprise (Haskell), Enville (Love), Eram (Okmulgee), Estella (Craig), Ethel (Pushmataha), Etta (Cherokee), Eucha (Delaware), Eva (Texas), Ewing (Custer)

Falconhead (Love), Falfa (Latimer), Fame (McIntosh), Farmers Hill (McCurtain), Farris (Atoka), Fay (Dewey), Featherston (Pittsburg), Felker (McCurtain), Felt (Cimarron), Fewell (Pushmataha), Fillmore (Johnston), Finley (Pushmataha), Fisher (Tulsa), Fittstown (Pontotoc), Fleetwood (Jefferson), Floris (Beaver), Flynn (Oklahoma), Folsom (Johnston), Forest Hill (LeFlore), Forney (Choctaw), Forrester (LeFlore), Four Corners (Okmulgee), Four Corners (Texas), Fox (Carter), Fox Run (Tulsa), Franklin (Cleveland), Frisco (Pontotoc), Frogville (Choctaw), Fugate (Atoka), Fuller (Tulsa)

Garden City (Tulsa), Garr Corner (Pontotoc), Garden Grove (Pottawatomie), Garden View (Tulsa), Garland (Haskell), Garnett (Tulsa), Gay (Choctaw), Georgetown (Muskogee), Gibbon (Grant), Gibson (Wagoner), Gideon (Cherokee), Gilcrease (Tulsa), Gilmore (LeFlore), Glendale (LeFlore), Glover (McCurtain), Godner (Oklahoma), Golden (McCurtain), Goodland (Choctaw), Goodwater (McCurtain), Gould (Harmon), Gowen (Latimer), Grady (Jefferson), Graham (Carter), Grandview Heights (Muskogee), Grant (Choctaw), Gray (Beaver), Gray Horse (Osage), Greasy (Adair), Green Pastures (Oklahoma), Green Valley Estates (Cherokee and Sequoyah), Greenville (Love), Greenwood (Pushmataha), Griggs (Cimarron), Grimes (Roger Mills), Gulftown (Okmulgee), Gyp (Blaine), Gypsy (Creek)

Hall Addition (Tulsa), Hanson (Sequoyah), Happyland (Pontotoc), Harden City (Pontotoc), Hardy (Kay), Harjo (Pottawatomie), Harmon (Ellis), Harmony Star (Rogers), Harris (McCurtain), Harrison (Sequoyah), Haw Creek (LeFlore), Hawley (Grant), Hayward (Garfield), Haywood (Pittsburg), Hazel Del (Pottawatomie), Hennepin (Garvin), Herring (Roger Mills), Hess (Jackson), Hester (Greer), Hewitt (Carter), Hext (Beckham), Higgins (Latimer), Highland Park (Tulsa), Hill (LeFlore), Hill Top (Hughes), Hockerville (Ottawa), Hodgen (LeFlore), Hog Shooter (Washington), Holley Creek (McCurtain), Hollow (Craig), Hollywood Corners (Cleveland), Homer (Pontotoc), Homestead (Blaine), Honobia (LeFlore), Hontubby (LeFlore), Hopeton (Woods), Hough (Texas), Hoyt (Haskell), Hughes (Latimer), Hulen (Cotton), Humphreys (Jackson), Hyde Park (Muskogee)

Independence (LeFlore), Indian Meadows (Cherokee), Ingalls (Payne), Ingersoll (Alfalfa), Iona (Murray), Iron Post (Creek), Iron Stob Corner (McCurtain), Irving (Jefferson), Isabella (Major)

Jackson (Bryan), Jacktown (Lincoln), Jamestown (Rogers), Jesse (Pontotoc), Jimtown (Love), Jollyville (Murray), Joy (Murray), Jumbo (Pushmataha)

Keefeton (Muskogee), Keetonville (Rogers), Kellond (Pushmataha), Kellyville (Ottawa), Kendal Wood (Tulsa), Kent (Choctaw), Kenton (Cimarron), Kenwood (Delaware), Kiamichi (Pushmataha), Kiersey (Bryan), Kosoma (Pushmataha), Kulli/Kullituklo (McCurtain), Kusa (Okmulgee)

Lacey (Kingfisher), Lafayette (Haskell), Lake Creek (Greer), Lake Ellsworth Addition (Comanche), Lake Hiawasse (Oklahoma), Lake Humphreys (Stephens), Lakeside Village (Comanche), Lake Station (Tulsa), Lake Valley (Washita), Lake West (Bryan), Lane (Atoka), Lark (Marshall), Last Chance (Okfuskee), Latta (Pontotoc), La Mesa (Garfield), Leach (Delaware), Lebanon (Marshall), Lecox (Oklahoma), Lenna (McIntosh), Lenora (Dewey), Lenox (LeFlore), Leonard (Tulsa), Lequire

(Haskell), Lewisville (Haskell), Liberty (Bryan), Liberty (Sequoyah), Lighthouse (Tulsa), Lillard Park (Oklahoma), Limestone (Latimer), Lincolnville (Ottawa), Little (Seminole), Little Axe (Cleveland), Little Chief (Osage), Little City (Marshall), Little Ponderosa (Beaver), Lodi (Latimer), Logan (Beaver), Lona (Haskell), Lone Oak (Sequoyah), Lone View (Oklahoma), Lookout (Woods), Lovedale (Harper), Lovell (Logan), Loving (Le Flore), Lowrey (Cherokee), Lucien (Noble), Lugert (Kiowa), Lula (Pontotoc), Lutie (Latimer), Lynn Addition (Osage), Lynn Lane (Tulsa), Lyons (Adair)

MacArthur Park (Comanche), Madge (Harmon), Maguire (Cleveland), Mallard Bay (Wagoner), Manard (Cherokee), Maple (Sequoyah), Martin (Muskogee), Mason (Okfuskee), Matoy (Bryan), Maxwell (Pontotoc), Mayfield (Beckham), Mayhew (Choctaw), McBride (Marshall), McKiddyville (Cleveland), McKnight (Harmon), McLain (Muskogee), McMillan (Marshall), McWillie (Alfalfa), Meers (Comanche), Mehan (Payne), Mellette (McIntosh), Melvin (Cherokee), Merritt (Beckham), Messer (Choctaw), Micawber (Okfuskee), Middleberg (Grady), Midland (Bryan), Midlothian (Lincoln), Midway (Atoka and Coal), Milfay (Creek), Miller (Pushmataha), Milo (Carter), Milton (LeFlore), Mingo (Tulsa), Mocane (Beaver), Monroe (LeFlore), Montclair Addition (Le Flore), Moodys (Cherokee), Moon (McCurtain), Moorewood (Custer), Mound Grove (McCurtain), Mount Herman (McCurtain), Mount Zion (McCurtain), Mouser (Texas), Moyers (Pushmataha), Mudsand (Choctaw), Mule Barn (Pawnee), Muse (LeFlore)

Nani–Chito (McCurtain), Nardin (Kay), Nashoba (Pushmataha), Natura (Okmulgee), Navina (Logan), Nebo (Murray), Needmore (Cleveland), Neff (LeFlore), Nelagony (Osage), Newalla (Oklahoma), New Liberty (Beckham), New Lima (Seminole (New Oberlin (Choctaw), Newport (Carter), Nicut (Sequoyah), Nida (Johnston), Niles (Canadian), Nobletown (Seminole), Non (Hughes), Norris (Latimer), Northeast (Tulsa), North Heights (Tulsa), Northside (Tulsa), Northwest (Tulsa), North McAlester (Pittsburg), Nowhere (Caddo), Numa (Grant), Nuyaka (Okmulgee)

Oak Grove (Murray), Oak Grove (Pawnee), Oak Grove (Payne), Oak Hill (McCurtain), Oakhurst (Tulsa and Creek), Oakman (Pontotoc), Oak Park (Washington), Oakridge (Creek), Oakwood (Tulsa), Oberlin (Bryan), Octavia (LeFlore), Ogeechee (Ottawa), Oglesby (Washington), Oil Center (Pontotoc), Oil City (Carter), Okesa (Osage), Okfuskee (Okfuskee), Oleta (Pushmataha), Olive (Creek), Olney (Coal), Omega (Kingfisher), Onapa (McIntosh), Oneta (Wagoner), Oney (Caddo), Oowala (Rogers), Ord (Choctaw), Orienta (Major), Orion (Major), Orr (Love), Osage (Kay), Osage Hills Estates (Tulsa), Oscar (Jefferson), Oswalt (Love), Overbrook (Love)

Page (LeFlore), Panola (Latimer), Paradise View (Mayes), Park Hill (Cherokee), Parker (Coal), Parkland (Lincoln), Park Lane (Comanche), Park View (Tulsa), Patterson (Latimer), Patton (Mayes), Paw Paw (Sequoyah), Payne (McClain), Payson (Lincoln), Pearson (Pottawatomie), Pearsonia (Osage), Peckham (Kay), Peggs (Cherokee), Penn 89th (Oklahoma), Pernell (Garvin), Pershing (Osage), Petersburg (Jefferson), Petros (Le Flore), Pettit Bay (Cherokee), Pharoah (Okfuskee), Pickens (McCurtain), Pickett (Pontotoc), Pierce (McIntosh), Piney (Adair), Pin Oaks Acres (Mayes), Platter (Bryan), Pleasant Hill (McCurtain), Plucketville (McCurtain), Pollard (McCurtain), Pontotoc (Johnston), Pooleville (Carter), Porter Hill (Comanche), Powell (Marshall), Prattville (Tulsa), Preston (Okmulgee), Proctor (Adair), Pruitt (Carter), Pumpkin Center (Comanche), Pumpkin Center (Okmulgee), Purdy (Garvin), Pyramid Corners (Craig)

Qualls (Cherokee), Quinlan (Woodward)

Raiford (McIntosh), Reagan (Johnston), Reck (Carter), Red Hill (Haskell), Redland (Sequoyah), Reed (Greer), Reichert (LeFlore), Remus (Pottawatomie and Seminole), Retrop (Beckham and Washita), Rexroat (Carter), Reynolds (Atoka), Rhea (Dewey), Richards Spur (Comanche), Richland (Canadian), Richville (Pittsburg), Ringold (McCurtain), Roberta (Bryan), Rocky Point), Wagoner), Roll

(Roger Mills), Rose (Mayes), Rossville (Lincoln), Rubottom (Love), Rufe (McCurtain), Russell (Greer), Russellville, (Pittsburg), Russett (Johnston)

Sacred Heart (Pottawatomie), Saddle Mountain (Kiowa), Sageeyah (Rogers), Salem (McIntosh and Okmulgee), Salt Fork (Grant), Sams Point (Pittsburg), Sandbluff (Choctaw), Sand Creek (Grant), Sand Point (Bryan), Sans Bois (Haskell), Santa Fe (Stephens), Sardis (Pushmataha), Schlegal (Payne), Schoolton (Seminole), Scipio (Pittsburg), Scott (Caddo), Scraper (Cherokee), Scullin (Murray), Scullyville (LeFlore), Sedan (Kiowa), Selman (Harper), Seward (Logan), Shady Grove (Sequoyah), Shartel (Oklahoma), Shay (Marshall), Sheridan Plane (Comanche), Sheridan Place (Tulsa), Sherwood (McCurtain), Shinewell (McCurtain), Shults (McCurtain), Sickles (Caddo), Silver City (Creek), Silver Tree (Tulsa), Slapout (Beaver), Smith Lee (Bryan), Smithville (McCurtain), Snow (Pushmataha), Sobol (Pushmataha), Southard (Blaine), Speer (Choctaw), Spelter City (Okmulgee), Spencerville (Choctaw), Stafford (Custer), Stanley (Pushmataha), Stapp (LeFlore), Star (Haskell), Stealy (McClain), Stecker (Caddo), Steedman (Pontotoc), Steen (Garfield), Steel Junction (McCurtain), Stella (Cleveland), Stockyards (Oklahoma), Stonebluff (Wagoner), Stones Corner (Wagoner), Stony Point (Adair), Stony Point (LeFlore), Story (Garvin), Straight (Texas), Sullivan Village (Comanche), Summerfield (LeFlore), Sumner (Noble), Sungate (Comanche), Sunkist (Choctaw), Sunnybrook Estate (Tulsa), Sunray (Stephens), Sunshine Valley (Ottawa), Survey Hills (Texas), Swink (Choctaw)

Tabler (Grady), Tablerville (McCurtain), Tahona (LeFlore), Tailholt (Cherokee), Tallant (Osage), Tangier (Woodward), Taupa (Comanche), Taylor (Cotton), Teresita (Cherokee), The Meadows (Tulsa), Ti (Pittsburg), Tiajuana (Mayes), Tiawah (Rogers), Timber Brook (Wagoner), Timberlane (Pawnee), Tiner (McCurtain), Titanic (Adair), Tom (McCurtain), Topsy (Delaware), Townwest (Comanche), Trousdale (Pottawatomie), Troy (Johnston), Tucker (LeFlore), Turkey Ford (Delaware), Turner (Love), Turpin (Beaver), Tuskahoma (Pushmataha), Tuskegee (Creek), Tussy (Carter and Garvin), Tuxedo (Washington), Tyler (Marshall)

Ulan (Pittsburg), Ultima Thule (McCurtain), Unger (Choctaw), Union (Clevland), Union (Tulsa), Union Valley (Pontotoc), Utica (Bryan)

Vamoosa (Seminole), Vanoss (Pontotoc), Vernon (McIntosh), Victoria Pond (Tulsa), Victory (Jackson), Vinco (Payne), Vinson (Harmon), Virgil (Choctaw), Vista (Pottawatomie), Vivian (McIntosh)

Wade (Bryan), Wallville (Garvin), Ward Springs (Pittsburg), Warren (Jackson), Washita (Caddo), Waterloo (Logan), Watova (Nowata), Watson (McCurtain), Wauhillau (Adair), Weathers (Pittsburg), Webb (Dewey), Welty (Okfuskee), Wheeless (Cimarron), Whelon (Jackson), Westside (Muskogee), Westside (Oklahoma), West Tulsa (Tulsa), Wheatlan (Oklahoma), Whippoorwill (Osage), Whispering Creek (Tulsa), White Bead (Garvin), White Eagle (Kay), White Oak (Cherokee), White Oak (Craig), Whitesboro (LeFlore), Whittier (Tulsa), Wichita Mountain Estate (Comanche), Wildcat Point (Cherokee), Wild Horse (Osage), Williams (LeFlore), Willis (Marshall), Willow Springs (Oklahoma), Wilson (Okmulgee), Winganon (Rogers), Wirt (Carter), Wolco (Osage), Wolf (Seminole), Woodford (Carter), Woodland View (Tulsa), Woods (Oklahoma), Woody Chapel (McClain), Wybark (Muskogee and Wagoner), Wye (Pottawatomie)

Yanush (Latimer), Yarnaby (Bryan), Yewed (Alfalfa), Yost Lake (Payne), Yuba (Bryan)

Zafra (LeFlore), Zaneis (Carter), Zincville (Ottawa), Zoe (LeFlore)

Source: 2009 Rand McNally & Company *Commercial Atlas & Marketing Guide*

TRIBAL
GOVERNMENT

Tribal Political Organizations

Carol Mowdy Bond

Editor's Note—Few states have as unique a relationship with the continent's native political entities than Oklahoma. For thousands of years, the political organizations of native tribes provided the only law of the land that would become the forty-sixth state. Under United States policies of Indian removal, additional tribes came to the region, bringing with them a variety of governing structures. Even more tribes were moved into the territory following the Civil War. In the late nineteenth century, the U.S. Government set forth policies that no longer recognized the authority of tribal governments. This denial of tribal sovereignty would last less than 100 years, and indigenous governments once again became a force within the state and nation. We asked writer and historian Carol Mowdy Bond to provide a brief primer on the history of Native American populations and their governing structures, with an emphasis on tribes that call Oklahoma home.

North America's first people inhabited and shaped the continent thousands of years before the birth of Christ. There is no consensus on their numbers during the Pre-Columbian era, but consider today's southeastern Canada and northeastern United States. According to *Indian Nations of North America* (National Geographic Society, 2010) Europeans arriving in the area encountered a dense native population that included "more people per square mile and more diverse languages and cultures" than in all of Europe.

Historical Background

Following first contacts in the middle decades of the last millennium, word of the New World's abundant riches quickly spread through Europe. First on the scene, the Spanish plundered every native empire they encountered, and in one generation they acquired more territory in the New World than Rome had in 500 years. In European economies, gold and silver determined wealth and power. Thus, numerous European nations bolted into the Western Hemisphere.

The Spanish, French, and British were the most powerful contenders for the New World. North America became a stage for their military campaigns against each other. Their fight for resources and land caused major disruption for native groups.

North American natives self-governed their individual groups for thousands of years. Their governments involved tribal laws, cultural traditions, religious customs, and kinship systems such as clans and societies. They formed alliances and confederacies among themselves to defend against groups that aggressively sought to extend power over other groups. As well, native groups sometimes switched to different confederacies or absorbed other groups into their own.

Native confederacies sometimes aligned with European powers. Frequently a native group or confederacy aligned with a European power, and then switched and aligned with another. Europeans used native groups and confederacies as military troops, and as buffer zones to protect their interests from other European groups or hostile native groups. Such alliances sometimes brought about changes in native group political structures.

Various native groups adopted European ideas in an effort to shed the label of savage. In doing so, they hoped the Europeans, and later the Americans, would leave their groups in peace. For example, in the 1800s the Cherokees, Chickasaws, Choctaws, Creeks, and Seminoles earned the title Five Civilized Tribes when some among them adopted U.S. political structures and cultural changes, hoping to remain in their southeastern homelands.

Native groups often called themselves people, or human beings, in their own languages. As an example, the Delawares called themselves Lenni Lenape, meaning "original people." But Europeans assigned their own names to native groups—often multiple names to individual groups in numerous European languages—that did not necessarily relate to what they called themselves. During the 1600s, the five tribes of the Huron Confederacy resided in Canada. Although the French referred to these tribes as Hurons, they were actually the Wyandottes. The British and Americans called them Wendats and Wyandots.

Many native groups collectively owned and used land. Some groups fought over territorial rights, while others did not embrace any concept of boundaries. The Europeans created and assigned boundaries. The British Proclamation of 1763, for example, produced a dividing line between natives and British colonies on the Atlantic seaboard. The military removed natives who crossed the line, sending them west beyond the British colonial frontier line back to Indian Country, which sat east of Louisiana Territory.

The massive land grab by European invaders intensified. As a major part of this bloody contest for North America, the French and Indian Wars ended in 1763. The French troops withdrew, leaving the British with almost everything east of the Mississippi River. When British colonials declared their independence from the crown in 1776, a ferocious war ensued. In the process, various native groups sided with either the British or the Americans. In 1778, still engaged in the American Revolution, the U.S. signed its first Indian treaty to secure support from the Delaware tribe.

Victorious in their Revolutionary War, the young American nation faced the ongoing problem of native groups inhabiting the land. By 1786 the U.S. was already taking land from the Choctaws and Chickasaws to build military and trading posts.

With the U.S. purchase of the Louisiana Territory from France in 1803, native inhabitants of the 828,000-square-mile province were unknowingly living on U.S. soil. Louisiana doubled the young American republic's size. Serious U.S. plans emerged to create a boundary for American settlement in an area referred to by multiple names including Indian Territory, Indian country, Indian zone, and Indian colonization zone. The current states of Oklahoma, Kansas (statehood 1861), Nebraska (statehood 1867), and part of Iowa (statehood 1846) made up most of the colonization zone. But from the Louisiana Purchase, all or part of at least thirteen states emerged beginning in 1812. Of those states, Oklahoma was last, reaching statehood in 1907. Thus, by 1866 Indian Territory downsized to all of today's Oklahoma except the Panhandle.

As the frontier line moved west, problems between Americans and native groups aggressively worsened. Some native groups reluctantly relocated on their own into Indian Territory. The U.S. imposed treaties on other groups, including the infamous Indian Removal Act of 1830 which forced the Five Civilized Tribes into Indian Territory. Numerous native groups moved to their assigned Indian Territory lands along their individual trails of tears.

Oklahoma's First Tribes

Journals of European explorers give us a glimpse of some tribes that lived in, or hunted, or roamed through today's Oklahoma. From the 1500s through around 1821, the following Plains Indians were probably part of the area's landscape at some point: Caddos, Wichitas, Kaws, Osages, Shawnees, Cheyennes, Pawnees, Comanches, Kiowas, and Kiowa-Apaches a.k.a. Prairie Apaches.

Tribal Political Organizations Enter the Future Oklahoma

Categorizing political organizations that native groups brought into today's Oklahoma can lead to error and confusion. The concept of a tribe generally applies to groups with language, culture, kinship, territory, and history in common. Sometimes a tribe is made of bands (sub-tribes) or towns. A tribe often involves political and economic equality among its members. Even though the words tribe and chiefdom are used interchangeably, there is sometimes a difference between the two. A chiefdom usually refers to a tribe where a chief holds absolute power. Nation implies a political autonomy that is not always true of all native groups.

Native political organizations do not fit into neat categories. For example, a group labeled as a Plains Tribe might have ancestral homelands in subarctic forests of the Canadian Northwest Territory, with a migration and forced removal history throughout North America. As such, that group may have maintained original governmental traditions and merged them with Plains Indian leadership styles upon their settlement in the Plains. Then the U.S. snatched the group from the Plains, forcing its members into a specific area of Indian Territory, and labeled the group as Plains Indians. Thus, the following categories and political definitions are by no means authoritative descriptions for the listed tribes.

Fort Sill Apaches

The Fort Sill Apaches descended from the Chiricahua Apaches. Named after Arizona's Chiricahua Mountains in their homeland, they resided primarily in autonomous, kin-based bands that were widely scattered. But external pressure in the mid-nineteenth century caused powerful leaders to emerge from their bands.

Modocs

Modoc homelands were on the California-Oregon border. Today's Modocs describe their prehistoric era as a 10,000-year period when they were a culturally detached and unique band. Scholars debate their political history, though the Modocs had chiefs.

Northeastern Groups

Northeastern groups include the Absentee Shawnees, Shawnees, Eastern Shawnees, Pottawatomis, Wyandottes, Sacs (Sauks), Fox, Delawares, Senecas, Cayugas, Miamis, Ottawas, Kickapoos, and Peoria Tribe of Indians (a confederacy of Kaskaskias, Peorias, Piankeshaws, and Weas). These groups came from Canada, and the Great Lakes region. They had three primary types of political groups: bands, which came together and dispersed, contingent on the seasons; tribes, which were also called nations and were made up of numerous towns with a council of leaders governing each town and each town sending representatives to tribal councils; and confederacies. They often had leaders called sachems or sagamores.

Northeastern groups often organized into confederacies. During the 1600s, the British used the Iroquois Confederacy of upper New York, a.k.a. Iroquois League, or Five Nations (Mohawks, Oneidas, Onondagas, Cayugas, Senecas), or, after 1722, Six Nations as a buffer between their colonies and the French.

Plains Groups

Labeled as Plains Indians are the Pawnees, Apaches, Kaws (Kansa, Kansas, Kanza, Ko'za, or Konza), Wichitas, Comanches, Caddos, Cheyennes, Arapahos, Otoes, Missourias, Poncas, Quapaws, Iowas (Ioway), Tonkawas, Osages, and Kiowas. Often organized into tribes, their important political institutions consisted of chiefs and councils. When the men were absent, strong women often led. Some tribes had smaller political units—bands—led by headmen, with the bands congregating or breaking apart, depending on the season. Others lived along major rivers in fortified towns that were large and permanent. These tribes did not break apart into bands when the seasons changed.

Southeastern Groups

Southeastern U.S. groups include the Choctaws, Seminoles, Cherokees, United Keetoowah Band of Cherokees, Chickasaws, and Creeks (Muskogees, Muscogees, Maskogees, or Mvskokes). The Alabamas, Quassartes, Yuchis (Euchees), Kialegees, and Thlopthlocco Tribal Town were part of the Creek Confederacy. The Caddos, though considered Plains Indians, also fall into the Southeastern native grouping. Most Southeastern groups involved chiefdoms, but the brutality of sixteenth century Spanish conquerors heavily damaged or destroyed the native political structures. By 1750, each group maintained at least one town, sometimes enormous in size, and confederacies were common. Towns were quasi-independent, usually with councils composed of elite household leaders. Most political power rested in the hands of chiefs and occasionally women served as chiefs. As an example, Creek Confederacy towns were governed by a micco or meko (which means "king") with help from advisors. A checks-and-balances system existed.

Various tribes, including the Choctaws, embraced the American governmental style. The Choctaws wrote a constitution prior to their forced removal. After relocating into Indian Territory, the Choctaws reestablished their government by writing a new constitution. Their constitution probably represents the first constitution written in Indian Territory, and the first written west of the Mississippi River.

Loss of Tribal Sovereignty

At the Civil War's end, the U.S. Native American population was estimated at 340,000, with about 50,000 living in Indian Territory. But the 1866 Reconstruction Treaties required the Five Civilized Tribes, and those tribes living among them, to cede all their lands in the western half of Indian Territory. The U.S. then moved twelve to fifteen thousand more native people, from Kansas, Nebraska, and elsewhere into Indian Territory between 1867 and 1884. A Second Trail of Tears process, combined with military campaigns, made Indian Territory home to all or part of sixty-seven native groups.

In 1871, the U.S. ended the treaty-making process with native tribes, which began in 1778, and intiated the process of dissolving tribal governments and dividing up their lands. The 1887 Dawes Severalty Act ended tribal, communal ownership of land for all tribes except the Five Civilized Tribes, instead giving specified amounts of land, called allotments, to families and individuals. Surplus land was opened to settlement. In 1890, the western half of today's Oklahoma (previously the western half of Indian Territory) legally became Oklahoma Territory with today's Panhandle attached. In 1893, the allotment process was imposed on the Five Civilized Tribes. The 1896 Curtis Act stripped tribal governments in Indian Territory of their authority, giving it to Congress and/or the federal government. In 1905, the Five Civilized

Tribes moved to push Indian Territory, which was never a legal territory, toward statehood. But the U.S. House of Representatives stopped the bill to form the State of Sequoyah from the eastern half of today's Oklahoma. Hope for a separate Indian state ended in 1906, when President Theodore Roosevelt signed the Oklahoma Enabling Act that would create a single state from the Twin Territories.

Restoration of Tribal Sovereignty

Today's U.S. is home to about 700 tribes. The government offices of thirty-nine tribes are located in Oklahoma and thirty-eight are federally recognized. Many tribes organized as a result of the 1934 Indian Reorganization Act, which reversed the allotment policy, returned some unsold allotted lands to tribes, gave legal sanctions to tribal landholdings, and encouraged tribal restoration and constitutions. The 1936 Oklahoma Indian Welfare Act allowed for organization of native groups in Oklahoma. From the 1940s into the 1990s, the U.S. waffled numerous times on tribal restoration and sovereignty. But Native American activism, combined with innumerable new federal laws, fueled a stronger initiative toward tribal self-government, restoration of tribal economies, and the personal well-being of tribal members.

Two critical pieces of legislation embody the concepts of tribal self-determination and self-governance by giving tribes greater power over the development and implementation of federal programs and policies that directly impact the tribes. The 1975 Indian Self-Determination and Education Assistance Act and the 1994 Tribal Self-Governance Act give tribal governments two fundamental rights. They have the authority to administer U.S. Bureau of Indian Affairs programs and services to their own tribal members. They also must be consulted, and consent to any federal actions, policies, rules or regulations that directly impact them.

In the 1970s, the term Native American widely replaced the term American Indian. Contrary to a still-common belief, the descendants of North American indigenous people never unified as one united culture. They represent a plethora of groups with different political styles, languages, etc.

Tribal Sovereignty Today

A federally recognized tribe has a relationship with the U.S. where both are sovereign entities. The tribe holds a nationhood status and maintains inherent powers of self-government.

Tribal Citizenship Today

Native Americans are U.S. citizens, but may also enroll and become citizens of their tribes or villages. They are subject to federal, state, and local laws. However, those living on reservations are subject only to federal and tribal laws unless Congress provides otherwise.

Tribal Relationships with States

The political organization of a federally recognized tribe is generally not subordinate to that of the states. The tribe may maintain a relationship with a state in a government-to-government fashion. Unless Congress authorizes differently, states have no authority over tribal governments. Tribes often create compacts and agreements with states, especially on matters of mutual concern. Neither states nor tribes have power to print or issue currency, engage in foreign relations, or make war.

21st Century Tribal Political Organizations

Today's tribes may legally form their own governments and may adhere to their traditional systems of self-government whenever possible. Tribes may enforce both civil and criminal laws, levy taxes, establish and determine tribal membership, and administer justice.

A federal Indian reservation is a geographic area reserved for a specific tribe, though not all federally-recognized tribes have reservations. Tribes may license and regulate activities within their own jurisdictions, regulate property under tribal jurisdiction, and exclude persons from their tribal lands.

Tribal governments function in numerous manners. Some have constitutions, and some have other bodies of law. Many tribes combine their traditional ruling structures with modern governmental styles, while others do not function through any of these means.

Numerous tribal government structures consist of three branches: executive, legislative, and judicial. Chief executives and legislative bodies are often elected and have different names. The top executive of today's Choctaw Nation of Oklahoma is an elected chief. A governor heads the Chickasaw Nation's executive branch. The Osage Nation's legislative body is referred to as a congress, while the Shawnee Tribe has a business council. The Iowa Tribe of Oklahoma is governed by a five-person elected business committee which includes a chief.

Some tribes have established judicial branches that interpret tribal laws and administer justice. Tribal courts usually have civil jurisdiction over anyone who resides or does business on federal reservations and criminal jurisdiction over tribal members who violate tribal laws and reside or do business on the reservation.

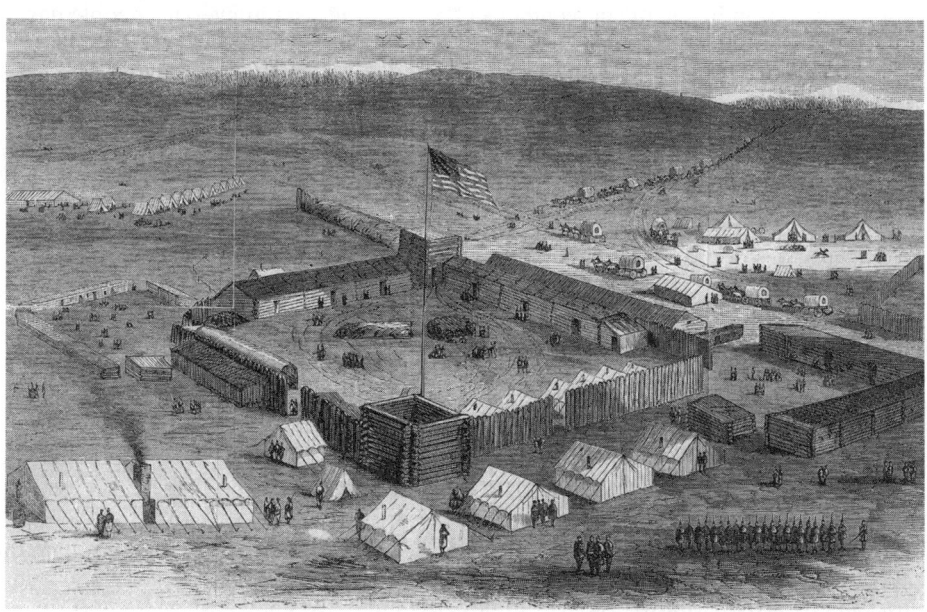

A drawing of Camp Supply in Indian Territory that appeared in *Harper's Weekly*.

Tribal Government Offices

There are thirty-nine Indian tribes in Oklahoma; thirty-eight tribes are recognized by the United States. Federally recognized Indian tribal government means the governing body or a governmental agency of any Indian tribe, band, nation, or other organized group or community is certified by the Secretary of the Interior as eligible for the special programs and services provided by the Secretary of the Interior through the Bureau of Indian Affairs. Some of Oklahoma's Indian tribal governments are self-governing. Self-governance returns decision-making authority and management responsibilities to tribes. It allows tribal control over federal funding available for tribal programs, services, functions, and activities. Tribes are accountable to their own people for resource management, service delivery, and development.

Absentee Shawnee Tribe*
Edwina Butler-Wolfe, Governor
2025 S Gordon Cooper
Shawnee 74801
405/275-4030, FAX 405/275-5637

Apache Tribe
Lyman Guy, Chair
511 E Colorado, Anadarko 73005
405/247-9493, FAX 405/247-2686

Cherokee Nation*
Bill John Baker, Principal Chief
PO Box 948, Tahlequah 74465
918/456-5000, FAX 918/458-5580

Chickasaw Nation*
Bill Anoatubby, Governor
PO Box 1548, Ada 74821
580/436-2603, FAX 580/436-4287

Citizen Potawatomi Nation*
John A. Barrett, Chair
1601 S Gordon Cooper Dr.
Shawnee 74801
405/275-3121, FAX 405/275-0198

Delaware Nation
C.J. Watkins, Acting President
PO Box 825, Anadarko 73005
405/247-2488, FAX 405/247 6329

Eastern Shawnee Tribe*
Glenna J. Wallace, Chief
PO Box 350, Seneca, MO 64865
918/666-2435, FAX 918/666-2186

Iowa Tribe of Oklahoma
Gary Pratt, Chair
RR 1, Box 721, Perkins 74059
405/547-2402, FAX 405/547-5294

Alabama Quassarte Tribal Town
Tarpie Yargee, Chief
PO Box 187
Wetumka 74883
405/452-3987, FAX 405/452-3968

Caddo Nation
Tamara Fourkiller, Chair
PO Box 487, Binger 73009
405/656-2344, FAX 405/656-2892

Cheyenne-Arapaho Tribes
Eddie Hamilton, Governor
PO Box 38, Concho 73022
800/247-4612, FAX 405/422-7424

Choctaw Nation*
Gary Batton, Principal Chief
PO Box 1210, Durant 74702
800/522-6170

Comanche Nation
Wallace Coffey, Chair
584 Binger Road
Lawton 73507
580/492-4988, FAX 580/492-6540

Delaware Tribe of Indians
Chester Brooks, Chief
170 NE Barbara, Bartlesville 74006
918/337-6590, FAX 337-6591

Ft. Sill Apache Tribe
Jeffrey Haozous, Chair
Rt. 2, Box 121, Apache 73006
580/588-2298, FAX 580/588-3133

Kaw Nation of Oklahoma*
Elaine Huch Chair
PO Box 50, Kaw City 74641
580/269-2552, FAX 580/269-2301

* "Self-governance" tribes   ** Non-federally recognized tribe

Kialegee Tribal Town
Jeremiah Hobia, Mekko
PO Box 332
Wetumka 74883
405/452-3262, FAX 405/452-3413

Kiowa Tribe
Amber C. Toppah, Chair
100 Kiowa Way
Carnegie 73015
580/654-2300, FAX 580/654-2188

Modoc Tribe*
Bill Follis, Chief
418 "G" SE
Miami 74354-8224
918/542-1190, FAX 918/542-5415

Osage Nation
Geoffrey M. Standing Bear, Principal Chief
PO Box 1449
Pawhuska 74056
918/287-5555, FAX 918/287-5562

Ottawa Tribe
Ethel E. Cook, Chief
PO Box 110
Miami 74355
918/540-1536, FAX 918/542-3214

Peoria Tribe of Indians of Oklahoma
John P. Froman, Chief
118 S Eight Tribes Trail, Miami 74354
918/540-2535
FAX 918/540-2538

Quapaw Tribe
John L. Berrey, Chair
PO Box 765, Quapaw 74363
918/542-1853
FAX 918/542-4694

Seminole Nation
Leonard Harjo, Principal Chief
PO Box 1498, Wewoka 74884
405/257-7200, FAX 405/257-7209

Shawnee Tribe
Ron Sparkman, Chair
PO Box 189, Miami 74355
918/542-2441, FAX 918/542-2922

Tonkawa Tribe
Donald Patterson, President
1 Rush Buffalo Road, Tonkawa 74653
580/628-2561, FAX 580/628-3375

Kickapoo Tribe of Oklahoma*
Gilbert Salazar, Chair
PO Box 70, McLoud 74851
405/964-7053
FAX 405/964-6211

Miami Nation*
Douglas Lankford, Chief
PO Box 1326
Miami 74355
918/542-1445, FAX 918/542-7260

Muscogee Creek Nation*
George Tiger, Principal Chief
PO Box 580
Okmulgee 74447
800/482-1979, FAX 918/756-2911

Otoe-Missouria Tribe
John R. Shotton, Chair
8151 Highway 177
Red Rock 74651
580/723-4466, FAX 580/723-4273

Pawnee Nation of Oklahoma
Marshall Gover, President
PO Box 470
Pawnee 74058
918/762-3621, FAX 918/762-6446

Ponca Nation*
Earl Howe, Chair
20 White Eagle Drive
Ponca City 74601
580/762-8104, FAX 580/762-2743

Sac & Fox Nation*
George Thurman, Principal Chief
920883 S HWY 99, Bldg. A
Stroud 74079
918/968-3526, FAX 918/968-1142

Seneca-Cayuga Tribes
William "Bill" Fisher, Chief
23701 S 655 Road, Grove 74344
918/787-5452, FAX 918/787-5521

Thlopthlocco Tribal Town
George Scott, Mekko
PO Box 188, Okemah 74859-0188
918/560-6198, FAX 918/560-6196

United Keetoowah Band of Cherokees
George Wickliffe, Chief
PO Box 746, Tahlequah 74465
918/431-1818, FAX 918/431-1873

* "Self-governance" tribes   ** Non-federally recognized tribe

Wichita & Affiliated Tribes
    Terri Parton, President
    PO Box 729, Anadarko 73005
    405/247-2425, FAX 405/247-2430

Yuchi (Euchee) Tribe of Indians **
    Andrew Skeeter, Chair
    PO Box 1086, Sapulpa 74067
    918/224-3065, FAX 918/512-6996

Wyandotte Nation*
    Billy Friend, Chief
    64700 E HWY 60
    Wyandotte 74370
    918/678-2297, FAX 918/678-2944

* "Self-governance" tribes   ** Non-federally recognized tribe

Geronimo and other Apache prisoners of war were moved to Fort Sill in 1895. In his later years, Geronimo was celebrated, appearing at the 1904 World's Fair in St. Louis and riding in President Theodore Roosevelt's 1905 inaugural parade.

ELECTION INFORMATION

Election Dates 2015

Election Date	Election Type	Resolution Due	Registration Deadline
Jan. 13, 2015*	Special Elections	Nov. 13, 2014[1]	Dec. 19, 2014
Feb. 10, 2015	Annual School Elections	Nov. 14, 2014[2]	Jan. 16, 2015
	Regular Municipal Primary	Nov. 14, 2014[2]	Jan. 16, 2015
	Primary Elections (partisan) Special Elections	Dec. 11, 2014[1]	Jan. 16, 2015
Mar. 3, 2015**	Special Elections	Dec. 31, 2014[1]	Feb. 6, 2015
Apr. 7, 2015**	Municipal General Elections (nonpartisan)	Jan. 16, 2015[2]	Mar. 13, 2015
	Annual School Runoff Elections		Mar. 13, 2015
	Special Elections	Feb. 5, 2015[1]	Mar. 13, 2015
May 12, 2015*	Special Elections	Mar. 12, 2015[1]	Apr. 17, 2015
Jun. 9, 2015*	Special Elections	Apr. 9, 2015[1]	May 15, 2015
Jul. 14, 2015*	Special Elections	May 14, 2015[1]	Jun. 19, 2015
Aug. 11, 2015*	Special Elections	Jun. 11, 2015[1]	Jul. 17, 2015
Sept. 8, 2015*	Special Elections	Jul. 9, 2015[1]	Aug. 14, 2015
Oct. 13, 2015*	Special Elections	Aug. 13, 2015[1]	Sep. 18, 2015
Nov. 10, 2015*	Special Elections	Sep. 10, 2015[1]	Oct. 16, 2015
Dec. 2015*	No Elections Allowed		

*Second Tuesday of the Month • **First Tuesday
[1]60 days before election • [2]15 days before

Contests of Candidacy and Election

Any candidate may contest the candidacy of any other candidate for the same office by filing a written petition with the Election Board where the Declaration of Candidacy was filed before 5:00 PM on the Friday following the close of the filing period.

A candidate for president or a candidate for a state or county office may contest an election in which he or she was a candidate by filing a written petition with the secretary of the Election Board where the Declaration of Candidacy was filed, before 5:00 PM on the Friday following the election.

Information for this chapter was supplied and verified by the staff of the State Election Board. Legislative districts provided by Tricia Dameron, Oklahoma House of Representatives.

Election Dates 2016

Election Date	Election Type	Resolution Due	Registration Deadline
Jan. 12, 2016*	Special Elections	Nov. 12, 2015[1]	Dec. 18, 2015
Feb. 9, 2016*	Annual School Elections	Nov. 20, 2016[2]	Jan. 15, 2016
	Special Elections	Dec. 10, 2015[1]	Jan. 15, 2016
Mar. 1, 2016**	Special Elections Presidential Preferential Primary Elections	Dec. 16, 2015[1]	Feb. 5, 2016
Apr. 5, 2016**	Annual School Runoff Elections		Mar. 11, 2016
	Special Elections	Feb. 4, 2016[1]	Mar. 11, 2016
May 2016	No Elections Allowed		
Jun. 28, 2016	Primary Elections Special Elections	April 13, 2016[3]	June 3, 2016
July 2016	No Elections Allowed		
Aug. 23, 2016	Special Elections Runoff Primary Election	Jun. 8, 2016[3]	July 29, 2016
Sep. 2016	No Elections Allowed		
Oct. 2016	No Elections Allowed		
Nov. 8, 2016**	General Election Special Elections	Aug. 24, 2016[3]	Oct. 14, 2016
Dec. 2016*	No Elections Allowed		

*Second Tuesday of the Month • **First Tuesday
[1]60 days before election • [2]15 days before • [3]75 days before

Changes in Voter Registration and Political Affiliation

Registration applications may be made any time. If an application is received twenty-four or fewer days preceding an election, it will not be processed until after the election. Changes in political affiliation may not be made during the period beginning at 5 PM on July 1 and ending at 5 PM on September 30 in any even-numbered year.

Total Votes Cast in General Elections—for President and Governor—1907–1964

	1907	1908	1910	1912	1914	1916	1918	1920	1922	1924	1926	1928	1930	1932	1934
Dem	134,162	122,362	120,218	119,143	100,597	148,123	104,117	215,798	280,206	255,798	213,167	219,174	301,921	516,468	365,992
Rep	106,507	110,473	99,527	90,726	95,904	97,233	82,985	243,465	230,469	225,756	170,714	394,046	208,575	188,165	243,841
Soc	9,740	21,425	24,707	41,630	52,703	45,091	7,428	25,698	3,941	5,134	1,350	3,924			16,688
Prog**					4,189	234				41,142					
Pop															
Prob			3,214	2,195		1,646									1,422
Ind					206						431		824		388
F-L*											1,646	1,283			
Total	250,409	254,260	247,666	253,694	253,599	292,327	194,530	484,961	514,616	527,830	387,308	618,427	511,320	704,633	628,331

	1936	1938	1940	1942	1944	1946	1948	1950	1952	1954	1956	1958	1960	1962	1964
Dem	501,069	355,740	474,313	196,565	401,549	259,491	452,782	329,308	430,939	357,386	385,581	399,504	370,111	315,357	519,834
Rep	245,122	148,861	348,872	180,454	319,424	227,426	268,817	313,205	518,045	251,808	473,769	107,495	533,039	392,316	412,665
Soc	2,211														
Prob**	1,328	2,579	3,027	1,762	1,663										
Ind		776				7,682		1,763				31,840			
Total	749,730	507,956	826,212	378,781	722,636	494,599	721,599	644,276	948,984	609,194	859,350	538,839	903,150	709,673	932,499

Dem= Democrat   Rep=Republican   Soc=Socialist   Prog=Progressive   Pop=Populist   Prob= Prohibition   Ind=Independent   F-L=Farm-Labor
Votes cast for Presidential Electors every four years, beginning in 1908.   Votes cast for Governor in 1907, and every four years beginning in 1910.
**No candidates since 1916 (Prog.), 1928 (F-L.), 1944 (Prob.), 1972 (Amer.).

Total Votes Cast in General Elections—for President and Governor—1966–2014

	1966	1968	1970	1972	1974	1976	1978	1980	1982	1984	1986	1988	1990	1992	1994
Dem	296,328	301,658	338,338	247,147	514,389	532,442	402,240	402,026	548,159	385,080	405,295	483,423	523,196	473,066	294,936
Rep	377,078	449,697	336,157	759,025	290,459	545,708	367,055	695,570	332,207	861,530	431,762	678,367	297,584	592,929	466,740
Amer**		191,731	24,295	23,728											
Lib								13,828		9,066		6,261		4,486	
Ind	3,852					14,101	8,119	38,284	2,764		60, 115		90,534	319,878	233,336
NA**												2,985			
Total	677,258	943,086	698,790	1,029,900	804,848	1,092,251	777,414	1,149,708	883,130	1,255,676	897,172	1,171,036	911,314	1,390,359	995,012

	1996	1998	2000	2002	2004	2006	2008	2010	2012	2014	2016	2018	2020	2022	2024
Dem	488,105	357,552	474,276	448,143	503,966	616,135	502,496	409,261	443,547	338,239					
Rep	582,315	505,498	744,337	441,277	959,792	310,327	960,165	625,506	891,325	460,298					
Lib	5,505		6,602												
Ind	130,788			146,200						26,294					
Rfm		10,535	9,014												
Total	1,206,713	873,585	1,234,229	1,035,620	1,463,758	926,462	1,462,661	1,034,766	1,334,872	824,831					

Dem= Democrat   Rep=Republican   Amer=American   Ind=Independent   Lib=Libertarian   NA=New Alliance   Rfm=Reform
Votes cast for Presidential Electors every four years, beginning in 1908.   Votes cast for Governor in 1907, and every four years beginning in 1910.
**No candidates since 1916 (Prog.), 1928 (F-L), 1944 (Prob.), 1972 (Amer.).

Oklahoma Vote: Presidential Elections

PR = Progressive S = Socialist F-L = Farmer-Labor P = Populist A = American
I = Independent L = Libertarian PH = Prohibition NA = New Alliance Rfm = Reform

Date	Democrat	Republican	Other			Total
1908	122,362	110,473	21,425 (S)			254,260
1912	119,143	90,726	41,630 (S)	2,195 (PH)		253,694
1916	148,123	97,233	45,091 (S)	1,646 (PH)	234 (PR)	292,327
1920	215,798	243,465	25,698 (S)			484,961
1924	255,798	225,756	5,134 (S)		41,142 (PR)	527,830
1928	219,174	394,046	3,924 (S)	1,283 (F-L)		618,427
1932	516,468	188,165				704,633
1936	501,069	245,122	2,211 (S)	1,328 (PH)		749,730
1940	474,313	348,872		3,027 (PH)		826,212
1944	401,549	319,424		1,663 (PH)		722,636
1948	452,782	268,817				721,599
1952	430,939	518,045				948,984
1956	385,581	473,769				859,350
1960	370,111	533,039				903,150
1964	519,834	412,665				932,499
1968	301,658	449,697		191,731 (A)		943,086
1972	247,147	759,025		23,728 (A)		1,029,900
1976	532,442	545,708		14,101 (I)		1,092,251
1980	402,046	695,570	13,828 (L)	38,284 (I)		1,149,708
1984	385,080	861,530	9,066 (L)			1,255,676
1988	483,423	678,367	6,261 (L)	2,985 (NA)		1,171,036
1992	473,066	592,929	4,486 (L)	319,878 (I)		1,390,359
1996	488,105	582,315	5,505 (L)	130,788 (I)		1,206,713
2000	474,276	744,337	6,602 (L)	9,014 (Rfm)		1,234,229
2004	503,966	959,792				1,463,758
2008	502,496	960,165				1,462,661
2012	443,547	891,325				1,334,872

Source: Presidential Elections Since 1789, 5th Edition *Congressional Quarterly*
and the State Election Board.

Registration by Party in Oklahoma Since 1960

As of January 15 of each year

Date	Democrat	Republican	Other	Independent	Total
1960	836,529	179,645		3,585	1,019,759
1961	940,702	215,344		4,469	1,160,515
1962	928,435	216,498		4,688	1,149,621
1963	978,115	227,144		4,763	1,210,022
1964	986,470	233,238		4,702	1,224,410
1965	953,243	231,673		4,110	1,189,026
1966	949,211	231,744		4,270	1,185,225
1967	927,853	232,881		4,244	1,164,978
1968	923,642	235,272		4,414	1,163,328
1969	929,749	269,051	5,289 (A)	6,903	1,210,992
1970	922,158	267,284	5,602 (A)	6,622	1,201,666
1971	887,540	262,056	5,486 (A)	7,445	1,162,527
1972	923,013	277,709	6,059 (A)	10,326	1,217,107
1973	977,380	320,923	3,601 (A)	18,604	1,320,508
1974	991,928	326,167	3,511 (A)	19,603	1,341,209
1975	802,619	233,003		11,513	1,047,135
1976	869,994	255,796		14,870	1,140,660
1977	1,050,142	323,852		27,100	1,401,094
1978	925,643	285,629		21,411	1,232,683
1979	1,022,228	314,621		24,345	1,361,194
1980	874,895	263,008		15,830	1,153,733
1981	1,045,316	380,702	875 (L)	31,731	1,458,624
1982	1,051,806	388,458		32,675	1,472,939
1983	1,141,796	429,601		37,140	1,608,537
1984	1,170,361	445,365	444 (L)	39,803	1,655,529
1985	1,304,454	574,135		50,049	1,928,638
1986	1,305,288	581,372		50,761	1,937,421
1987	1,352,780	608,775		53,023	2,014,578
1988	1,356,460	616,232		53,933	2,026,625
1989	1,427,144	699,032		57,018	2,183,194
1990	1,239,275	624,801		46,567	1,910,643

A =American Party   L = Libertarian Party

Please Note: Fluctuations in registrations occur, in part, because voter records are purged as specified in the National Voter Registration Act (NVRA) of 1993. In compliance with the NVRA, the Oklahoma voters' list was purged Jan. 31, 2003 for those voters who fell to inactive status in 1999.

Date	Democrat	Republican	Other	Independent	Total
1991	1,302,278	654,828		48,516	2,005,622
1992	1,337,196	688,159		51,759	2,077,114
1993	1,251,258	653,846		57,948	1,963,052
1994	1,250,247	657,267		58,759	1,966,273
1995	1,073,986	581,596		50,286	1,705,868
1996	1,112,560	624,240		86,948	1,823,748
1997	1,171,620	693,076	147 (Rfm)	122,139	1,986,982
1998	1,158,754	691,942	269 (Rfm)	139,626	1,990,591
1999	1,183,523	718,534		157,760	2,059,817
2000	1,189,332	734,382	267 (L) 120 (Rfm)	147,649	2,098,750
2001	1,233,481	803,908	770 (L) 256 (Rfm)	202,266	2,240,681
2002	1,079,298	729,393	171 (L) 10 (Rfm)	199,164	2,008,039
2003	1,099,458	758,275	299 (L) 16 (Rfm)	214,887	2,072,935
2004	1,101,072	816,933	31 (Rfm) 689 (L)	225,253	2,143,978
2005	1,100,263	822,131		227,163	2,149,557
2006	1,021,053	778,405		209,515	2,008,973
2007	1,045,490	805,607		224,464	2,008,973
2008	1,012,594	790,713		219,230	2,022,537
2009	1,077,616	860,378		246,002	2,183,996
2010	999,855	813,158		225,607	2,038,620
2011	999,943	849,332		240,855	2,090,130
2012	943,283	828,257		229,070	2,000,610
2013	962,072	897,663		256,450	2,116,186
2014	885,609	854,329		238,870	1,978,812
2015	882,686	886,153		261,429	2,030,277

A = American Party   L = Libertarian Party   Rfm = Reform Party

Please Note: Fluctuations in registrations occur, in part, because voter records are purged as specified in the National Voter Registration Act (NVRA) of 1993. In compliance with the NVRA, the Oklahoma voters' list was purged Jan. 31, 2003 for those voters who fell to inactive status in 1999.

County Registration by Party

Oklahoma State Election Board

as of January 15, 2015

County	Pcts.	Dem.	Rep.	Ind.	Other	Total
Adair	17	6,919	3,756	1,064	0	11,739
Alfalfa	7	830	1,859	249	0	2,938
Atoka	17	5,142	1,611	593	0	7,346
Beaver	7	627	2,307	280	0	3,214
Beckham	13	5,024	4,379	1,348	0	10,751
Blaine	9	2,135	2,728	467	0	5,330
Bryan	22	13,603	6,646	3,452	0	23,701
Caddo	20	8,378	3,653	1,328	0	13,359
Canadian	50	18,507	40,062	7,968	0	66,537
Carter	25	15,308	9,642	4,280	0	29,230
Cherokee	24	14,167	6,465	2,643	0	23,275
Choctaw	17	6,329	1,529	894		8,752
Cimarron	6	544	994	153	0	1,691
Cleveland	83	53,735	69,986	21,542	0	145,263
Coal	9	3,102	567	291	0	3,960
Comanche	39	25,455	18,389	8,173	1	52,018
Cotton	9	2,300	1,053	316	1	3,670
Craig	13	4,834	2,294	738	0	7,866
Creek	35	14,311	18,448	4,183	0	36,942
Custer	13	6,451	7,012	2,220	0	15,683
Delaware	22	10,686	8,922	2,545	0	22,153
Dewey	10	1,220	1,428	211	0	2,859
Ellis	7	744	1,527	250	0	2,521
Garfield	30	8,201	17,186	3,163	0	28,550
Garvin	17	8,395	4,750	1,668	0	14,813
Grady	28	12,209	14,182	4,185	0	30,576
Grant	7	941	1,692	258	0	2,891
Greer	8	2,030	661	216	0	2,907
Harmon	7	1,090	266	99	0	1,455

County	Pcts.	Dem.	Rep.	Ind.	Other	Total
Harper	6	654	1,164	174	0	1,992
Haskell	11	5,317	1,235	394	0	6,946
Hughes	16	4,675	1,367	585	0	6,627
Jackson	15	5,257	5,211	1,386	0	11,854
Jefferson	10	2,413	766	371	0	3,550
Johnston	14	4,287	1,467	549	0	6,303
Kay	28	8,370	12,688	3,097	0	24,155
Kingfisher	14	2,146	5,262	597	0	8,005
Kiowa	14	3,058	1,369	398	0	4,825
Latimer	12	5,032	978	394	0	6,404
Leflore	37	17,274	6,427	3,550	0	27,251
Lincoln	21	7,428	8,766	2,034	0	18,228
Logan	22	8,177	14,065	3,377	0	25,619
Love	12	3,722	1,261	696	0	5,679
Major	8	882	3,077	243	0	4,202
Marshall	11	4,430	2,291	876	0	7,597
Mayes	27	10,849	7,960	2,147	0	20,956
McClain	26	8,212	10,537	2,718	0	21,467
McCurtain	31	11,540	2,746	1,145	0	15,431
McIntosh	14	8,254	2,566	817	0	11,637
Murray	10	5,053	1,788	637	0	7,478
Muskogee	33	23,315	9,988	4,530	5	37,838
Noble	12	2,246	3,442	577	0	6,265
Nowata	11	2,871	2,453	699	0	6,023
Okfuskee	13	3,767	1,475	488	0	5,730
Oklahoma	256	158,011	175,804	59,960	1	393,776
Okmulgee	29	12,297	5,903	2,132	0	20,332
Osage	28	12,971	10,065	2,753	0	25,789
Ottawa	17	9,013	4,682	1,788	0	15,483
Pawnee	10	4,297	3,938	1,004	0	9,239
Payne	31	14,460	18,929	5,415	0	38,804
Pittsburg	41	16,668	6,098	3,293	0	26,059
Pontotoc	21	11,575	6,456	2,302	0	20,333
Pottawatomie	26	16,388	15,038	4,902	0	36,328
Pushmataha	16	5,226	1,002	498	1	6,727

County	Pcts.	Dem.	Rep.	Ind.	Other	Total
Roger Mills	9	1,387	796	138	0	2,321
Rogers	36	18,360	28,025	6,761	0	53,146
Seminole	14	7,009	3,371	1,154	0	11,534
Sequoyah	26	13,634	5,643	1,798	0	21,075
Stephens	28	11,941	10,511	2,665	0	25,117
Texas	11	2,512	5,339	1,614	0	9,465
Tillman	9	2,695	1,333	343	0	4,371
Tulsa	262	120,328	169,177	44,471	0	333,976
Wagoner	32	14,645	20,695	4,251	0	39,591
Washington	23	8,803	17,411	4,234	0	30,448
Washita	12	3,362	2,309	592	0	6,263
Woods	7	1,503	2,945	446	0	4,894
Woodward	15	3,155	6,340	1,659	0	11,154
County Totals	1,958	882,686	886,153	261,429	9	2,030,277

Troop L of the First U.S. Volunteer Cavalry regiment ("Rough Riders") that served during the Spanish-American War and participated in the Santiago campaign of June and July 1898. The troop was recruited from Indian Territory and commanded by Capt. Allyn K. Capron of the U.S. Seventh Cavalry, Fort Sill.

Election Results 1996–2014

For earlier results, please see previous editions of the Almanac, or contact the State Election Board at 405/521–2391

1996 Democratic Presidential Preferential Primary—March 12

Bill Clinton	279,454
Lyndon Larouche Jr.	46,392
Elvena E. Lloyd-Duffie	40,758

1996 Republican Presidential Preferential Primary—March 12

Patrick J. Buchanan	56,949
Lamar Alexander	3,436
Alan Keyes	6,306
Richard G. Lugar	538
Phil Gramm	1,490
Steve Forbes	37,213
Charles E. Collins	451
Bob Dole	156,829

1996 Democratic Nominations, Primary Elections—August 27/ September 17

	Regular	Runoff

Corporation Commissioner

Wando Jo Peltier	181,595
Charley T. Long	150,972

United States Senate

Don McCorkell	122,635
Jim Boren	186,611
David L. Annanders	26,794

United States Representative
District—Candidates

1–Randolph J. Amen (Unopposed)

2–Glen D. Johnson	57,948
Henry Flanders	3,170
Virginia Jenner	8,554
William S. Vardeman	4,890
James R. Wilson	9,103

3–Craig A. Seikel	3,847	
Darryl Roberts	49,628	41,478
Danny Williams	24,570	20,356
Mike Newport	23,217	

4–Ed Crocker (Unopposed)

5–James L. Forsythe	23,800
Cecil Pirrong	8,215

6–Paul M. Barby (Unopposed)

1996 Republican Nominations, Primary Elections—August 27

United States Senate

James M. Inhofe	116,241
Dan Lowe	38,044

United States Representative
District—Candidates

1–Steve Largent (Unopposed)

2–Tom Coburn (Unopposed)

3–Evelyn L. Rogers	1,262
Darrel D. Tallant	467
Wes Watkins	12,740
Ken B. Privett	1,045
Bill E. Henley	584

4–J.C. Watts Jr. (Unopposed)

5–Ernest Istook (Unopposed)

6–Frank Lucas (Unopposed)

1996 Libertarian Nominations, Primary Elections—August 27

United States Senate

Michael A. Clem	1,429
Agnes Marie Regier	1,511

1996 State Officers General Election—November 5

Total Vote Cast	1,206,713

Presidential Electors

Democrat—488,105
Bill Clinton—President
Al Gore—Vice President

Carl Albert	Julian J. Rothbaum
Thomas Dee Frasier	Lorray Dyson
George Lee Stidham	Betty J. McElderry
Elizabeth Whetsel	Marjean Mitchell

Republican—582,315
Bob Dole—President
Jack Kemp—Vice President

J. Michael Brown	Steven F. Garret
Skip Healey	Leo F. Herlacher
Dixie I. Galloway	Dale Switzer
Paul E. Thornbrugh	Gary W. Banz

Independent—130,788
Ross Perot—President
Pat Choate—Vice President

Dale Barlow	Grace Rayedelle Hill
Sylvia Suggs	H. Kelly Haynes
Emmy Butler	Vivian Winterman
Jack Newkirk	Patt Cameron

Libertarian—5,505
Harry Browne—President
Jo Jorgensen—Vice President

Randy Ashbrook	Sharon L. Atherton
Roger Bloxham	Charles Burris
Steven B. Galpin	C. Michael Todd
Chad Vanis	Robert Waldrop

Corporation Commissioner

Wanda Jo Peltier (D)	519,598
Ed Apple (R)	569,704

United States Senate

Jim Boren (D)	474,162
James M. Inhofe (R)	670,610
Chris Nedbalek (I)	8,691
Bill Maguire (I)	15,092
Agnes Marie Regier (L)	14,595

United States Representative

District—Candidates

1–Randolph J. Amen (D)	57,996
Steve Largent (R)	143,415

Karla Condray (I)	8,996
2–Glen D. Johnson (D)	90,120
Tom A. Coburn (R)	112,273
3–Darryl Roberts (D)	86,647
Wes Watkins (R)	98,526
Scott Demaree (I)	6,335
4–Ed Crocker (D)	73,950
J.C. Watts Jr. (R)	106,923
Robert T. Murphy (L)	4,500
5–James L. Forsythe (D)	57,594
Ernest Istook (R)	148,362
Ava Kennedy (I)	6,835
6–Paul M. Barby (D)	64,173
Frank D. Lucas (R)	113,499

Justices of the Supreme Court
Nonpartisan Retention Ballot

District—Judge	Yes	No
1–Robert E. Lavender	617,188	364,812
6–Robert D. Simms	617,318	357,110
9–Joseph M. Watt	608,009	364,042

Judges, Court of Criminal Appeals
Nonpartisan Retention Ballot

District—Judge	Yes	No
2–Charles A. Johnson	612,895	362,680
3–Gary L. Lumpkin	587,748	375,910

Justices of the Court of Civil Appeals
Nonpartisan Retention Ballot

District—Judge	Yes	No
District 1–Office 2		
Daniel J. Boudreau	595,248	367,808
District 2–Office 1		
John F. Reif	584,875	376,405
District 2–Office 2		
W. Keith Rapp	553,653	410,619
District 4–Office 2		
Larry E. Joplin	604,556	358,366
District 1–Office 1		
Jerry L. Goodman	618,199	351,398

1998 Democratic Nominations
Primary Elections—August 25/
September 15   Regular Runoff

Governor
Laura Boyd	171,121	
James Hager	112,941	

Lieutenant Governor
Dan Lowe	116,933	
Jack Morgan	145,705	

Commissioner of Labor
Virginia Jenner	52,895	
Jerry Morgan	90,486	77,879
J.C. Watts Sr.	141,118	81,731

Insurance Commissioner
Carroll Fisher	136,512	
Barry Hale	50,239	
John P. Spearman	84,092	

United States Senator
Don E. Carroll	120,759	117,442
Jerry Kobyluk	54,196	
Jacquelyn Ledgerwood	56,393	38,817
Arlie Nixon	31,860	

United States Representative
District—Candidates

1–Howard Plowman (Unopposed)		
2–Isabel K. Baker	19,138	18,799
Bryan J. Bigby	8,120	
Kent Pharaoh	19,846	19,977
James R. Wilson	16,551	
3–Bill Anoatubby	23,771	
James Litherland	4,430	
Darryl Roberts	29,067	28,195
Walt Roberts	34,382	31,274
4–Ben Odom (Unopposed)		
5–M.C. Smothermon (Unopposed)		
6–Paul M. Barby	24,950	
W.T. Dub Whalen	15,856	

1998 Republican Nominations
Primary Elections—August 25

Superintendent of Public Instruction
Linda D. Murphy	75,310
Tod Williams	40,633

Commissioner of Labor
Chris Brown	39,947
Brenda Reneau	79,430

Insurance Commissioner
John P. Crawford	64,377
Bill Maguire	20,520
Don Strong	34,723

Note: No Republican candidates filed for Attorney General or State Treasurer.

1998 State Officers General Election—November 3

Total Vote Cast	873,585

Note: There was no race for Attorney General or State Treasurer.

Governor
Laura Boyd (D)	357,552
Frank Keating (R)	505,498
H. Heidelberg (Rfm)	10,535

Lieutenant Governor
Jack Morgan (D)	281,379
Mary Fallin (R)	585,712

State Auditor and Inspector
Clifton H. Scott (D)	513,065
Allen M. Hart (R)	335,305

Superintendent of Public Instruction
Sandy Garrett (D)	520,270
Linda D. Murphy (R)	343,291

Commissioner of Labor
J.C. Watts Sr. (D)	273,043
Brenda Reneau (R)	591,636

Insurance Commissioner

Carroll Fisher (D)	427,961
John P. Crawford (R)	425,327

Corporation Commissioner

Charley Long (D)	338,676
Denise A. Bode (R)	510,910

United States Senator

Don E. Carroll (D)	268,898
Don Nickles (R)	570,682
Mike Morris (I)	15,516
Argus W. Yandell Jr. (I)	4,617

United States Representative

District—Candidates

1–Howard Plowman (D)	56,309
Steve Largent (R)	91,031
2–Kent Pharaoh (D)	59,042
Tom A. Coburn (R)	85,581
Albert Jones (I)	3,641
3–Walt Roberts (D)	55,163
Wes Watkins (R)	89,832
4–Ben Odom (D)	52,107
J.C. Watts Jr. (R)	83,272
5–M.C. Smothermon (D)	48,182
Ernest Istook (R)	103,217
6–Paul M. Barby (D)	43,555
Frank D. Lucas (R)	85,261
Ralph B. Finkle Jr. (I)	2,455

Justices of the Supreme Court
Nonpartisan Retention Ballot

District—Judge	Yes	No
2–Ralph B. Hodges	506,764	233,269
5–Alma Wilson	495,356	243,869
8–Rudolph Hargrave	487,920	236,428

Judges, Court of Criminal Appeals
Nonpartisan Retention Ballot

District—Judge	Yes	No
1–Charles S. Chapel	490,564	239,021

Justices of the Court of Civil Appeals
Nonpartisan Retention Ballot

District—Judge	Yes	No
District 3–Office 1		
Joe C. Taylor	492,655	232,125
District 3–Office 2		
Ron Stubblefield	476,636	245,878
District 4–Office 1		
Glenn D. Adams	488,301	232,119
District 4–Office 2		
Larry E. Joplin	483,425	236,475
District 5–Office 1		
Kenneth L. Buettner	482,217	238,740

2000 Democratic Presidential Preferential Primary—March 14

Bill Bradley	34,311
Al Gore	92,654
Lyndon H. Larouche Jr.	7,885

2000 Republican Presidential Preferential Primary—March 14

John McCain	12,973
Steve Forbes	1,066
George W. Bush	98,781
Alan L. Keyes	11,595
Gary Bauer	394

2000 Democratic Nominations, Primary Elections—August 22/ September 19

	Regular	Runoff

United States Representative

District—Candidates

	Regular	Runoff
1–Dan Lowe	25,985	
John Krymski	6,629	
2–James R. Wilson	13,949	
Brad Carson	39,837	35,410
Bill Settle	34,964	26,981
3–(No Candidate)		
4–Larry Weatherford (Unopposed)		
5–Garland McWatters (Unopposed)		

6–Randy Beutler   33,771
  Bob Mooneyham   15,173

2000 Republican Nominations, Primary Election—August 22

United States Representative
District—Candidates

1–Steve Largent   38,206
  Evelyn L. Rogers   5,355

2–Terry Gorham   468
  Tennie Rogers   266
  Mark Detro   197
  Steve Money   1,639
  Eric Troutt   815
  Jack Ross   7,758
  Andy Ewing   16,639

3–Wes Watkins (Unopposed)

4–J.C. Watts Jr.   21,960
  James Odom   5,163

5–Ernest Istook   39,976
  Phillip A. Hillian   7,179

6–Frank Lucas (Unopposed)

2000 Libertarian Nominations, Primary Election—August 22

Corporation Commission

Richard Prawdzienski   538
Roger Bloxham   652
Whitney L. Boutin Jr.   859

> Note: Whitney L. Boutin Jr. withdrew, therefore, no runoff primary was held.

2000 State Officers, General Election—November 7

Total Vote Cast   1,234,229

Presidential Electors

Democrat—474,276
Al Gore—President
Joseph Lieberman—Vice President

Obera Bergdall	Carma Lee Brock
George Nigh	Jay Parmley
Mary Jac Rauh	Edmund Synar
Beulah Vernon	Rhonda Walters

Republican—744,337
George W. Bush—President
Dick Cheney—Vice President

Steve Byas	James Cruson
Paul Hollroth	Kristol Markowitz
Bob McDowell	Donald O'Nesky
Tom Prince	George Wiland

Reform— 9,014
Pat Buchanan—President
Ezola Foster—Vice President

Robert K. Bell Jr.	Gregory D. Brown
Patrick B.J. Carmack	William B. Charles
Ivette Farmer	Isabel Faith Lyman
Earl David Shaffer	Mary P. Ziglinski

Libertarian—6,602
Harry Browne—President
Art Olivier—Vice President

Lyn Atherton	Charles Burris
Anne Fruits	Christine M. Kane
Mary Laurent	David Lewis
Jack Litherland	Agnes Regier

Corporation Commissioner

Gilbert S. Bigby (D)   380,108
Bob Anthony (R)   771,609
Roger Bloxham (L)   21,568

United States Representative
District—Candidates

1–Dan Lowe (D)   58,493
  Steve Largent (R)   138,528
  Michael A. Clem (L)   2,984

2–Brad Carson (D)   107,273
  Andy Ewing (R)   81,672
  Neil Mavis (L)   6,467

3–Wes Watkins (R)   137,826
  Argus W. Yandell Jr. (I) 14,660
  R.C. Sevier White (L)   6,730

Note: No Democrat filed for District 3 race.

4–Larry Weatherford (D)   54,808
  J.C. Watts Jr. (R)   114,000
  Keith B. Johnson (L)   1,979
  Susan Ducey (Rfm)   4,897

5-Garland McWatters (D)   53,275
  Ernest Istook (R)   134,159
  Bill Maguire (I)   5,930
  Robert T. Murphy (L)   2,658
6-Randy Beutler (D)   63,106
  Frank D. Lucas (R)   95,635
  Joseph V. Cristiano (L)   2,435

Justices of the Supreme Court Nonpartisan Retention Ballot

District—Judge	Yes	No
3-Marian P. Opala	695,216	317,818
4-Yvonne Kauger	673,273	328,540
6-Daniel J. Boudreau	674,402	320,181
7-Hardy Summers	670,458	322,430

Judges, Court of Criminal Appeals Nonpartisan Retention Ballot

District—Judge	Yes	No
4-Reta M. Strubhar	677,156	321,340
5-Steve Lile	675,234	317,318

Justices of the Court of Civil Appeals Nonpartisan Retention Ballot

	Yes	No
District 5-Office 1 Kenneth L. Beuttner	670,143	322,173
District 5-Office 2 Carl B. Jones	671,157	318,351
District 6-Office 1 James P. Garrett	685,054	308,763
District 6-Office 2 Carol M. Hansen	686,290	308,841

2001 Special Election—September 25

State Question 695 was the only item on the ballot.

2001 Special Democratic Primary Election—December 11

United States Representative

District—Candidates

1-James E. Lamkin   1,584
  Doug Dodd   12,516

2001 Special Republican Primary Election—December 11

United States Representative

District—Candidates

1-George E. Banasky   296
  Cathy Keating   12,737
  Scott Pruitt   9,513
  Evelyn L. Rogers   210
  John Sullivan   19,018

2002 Special General Election—January 8

United States Representative

District—Candidates

1-Doug Dodd (D)   50,850
  John Sullivan (R)   61,694
  David Fares (I)   388
  Neil Mavis (I)   1,758

2002 Democratic Nominations Primary Elections—August 27/September 17

	Regular	Runoff
Governor		
Kelly Haney	59,044	
Brad Henry	99,883	135,336
Vince Orza	154,263	122,855
James E. Lamkin	9,069	
Jim Dunegan	28,130	
State Auditor and Inspector		
Rod Dillard	69,651	
Jeff A. McMahan	197,308	
John K. Fodge	54,131	
Commissioner of Labor		
Lloyd L. Fields	218,686	
Virginia Jenner	110,489	
Corporation Commissioner		
Curtis Speaker	44,699	
Jeff Tomlin	116,276	91,779

Keith Butler   154,180   143,930

United States Senator

Tom Boettcher	118,986	111,067
David Walters	170,414	146,899
Jim Rogers	34,217	
George Gentry	22,770	

United States Representative
District—Candidates

1–Doug Dodd (Unopposed)

2–Mike Mass   34,450
    Brad Carson   72,612
    Dorothy Vandiver   6,040

3–No Democratic Candidate on the Ballot

4–Darryl Roberts   34,393
    Brandon Clabes   5,312
    Lance Compton   7,202
    Ben Odom   24,369

5–Lou Barlow (Unopposed)

Note: U.S. Congressional District 6 was eliminated as a result of the 2000 U.S. Census.

2002 Republican Nominations
Primary Elections—August 27/
September 17   Regular Runoff

Governor

Jim Denny	16,713
Andrew Marr Jr.	9,532
Steve M. Largent	179,631

Lieutenant Governor

Jim Clark	37,068
Mary Fallin	168,461

Attorney General

Denise A. Bode	119,245
Tim Green	81,912

Commissioner of Labor

Brenda Reneau Wynn	126,684
Tim Pope	70,511

Corporation Commission

Dana Murphy	77,449	35,740
Jeff Cloud	78,705	51,579
Mark Snyder	39,701	

United States Representative
District—Candidates

1–John Sullivan   39,992
    Evelyn L. Rogers   7,280

2–Kent Pharaoh (Unopposed)

3–Richard Hovis   5,330
    Frank D. Lucas   43,887

4–Terry Johnson   1,119
    Jerry J. Black   600
    Tom Cole   21,789
    Tennie Rogers   648
    Marc Nuttle   11,944
    Garlin Newton   426

5 Ernest Istook (Unopposed)

Note: U.S. Congressional District 6 was eliminated as a result of the 2000 U.S. Census.

2002 State Officers, General Election—November 5

Note: No race for State Treasurer, unopposed candidate in General Election.

Total Vote Cast   1,035,620

Governor

Brad Henry (D)	448,143
Steve Largent (R)	441,277
Gary L. Richardson (I)	146,200

Lieutenant Governor

Laura Boyd (D)	400,511
Mary Fallin (R)	584,990
Elmer Zen Million (I)	11,802
Billy Maguire (I)	31,053

State Auditor and Inspector

Jeff A. McMahan (D)	516,425
Gary Jones (R)	487,646

Attorney General

Drew Edmondson (D)	615,932
Denise A. Bode (R)	408,833

Superintendent of Public Instruction

Sandy Garrett (D)	609,851
Lloyd Roettger (R)	411,814

Commissioner of Labor

Lloyd L. Fields (D)	479,339
Brenda Reneau Wynn (R)	523,073

State Insurance Commissioner

Carroll Fisher (D)	586,871
Doug Barry (R)	422,713

Corporation Commissioner

Keith Butler (D)	415,355
Jeff Cloud (R)	540,751
Roger Bloxam (I)	51,155

United States Senator

David Walters (D)	369,789
Jim Inhofe (R)	583,579
James Germalic (I)	65,056

United States Representative

District—Candidates

1–Doug Dodd (D)	90,649
John Sullivan (R)	119,566
Joe Cristiano (I)	4,740
2–Brad Carson (D)	146,748
Kent Pharaoh (R)	51,234
3–Frank D. Lucas (R)	148,206
Robert T. Murphy (I)	47,884
4–Darryl Roberts (D)	91,322
Tom Cole (R)	106,452
5–Lou Barlow (D)	63,208
Ernest Istook (R)	121,374
Donna C. Davis (I)	10,469

6–Note: U.S. Congressional District 6 was eliminated as a result of the 2000 U.S. Census.

Justices of the Supreme Court Nonpartisan Retention Ballot

District—Judge	Yes	No
1–Robert E. Lavender	583,024	274,673
5–James R. Winchester	582,369	271,293
6–Daniel J. Boudreau	578,282	273,290
9–Joseph M. Watt	574,539	276,665

Judges, Court of Criminal Appeals Nonpartisan Retention Ballot

District—Judge	Yes	No
2–Charles A. Johnson	584,117	266,267
3–Gary L. Lumpkin	570,428	274,771

Justices of the Court of Civil Appeals Nonpartisan Retention Ballot

District—Judge	Yes	No
District 1–Office 1 Jerry L. Goodman	582,317	265,124
District 1–Office 2 Tom Colbert	587,088	262,910
District 2–Office 1 John F. Reif	568,771	276,545
District 2–Office 2 Keith Rapp	569,697	277,190

2004 Democratic Presidential Preferential Primary—February 3

Wesley K. Clark	90,526
Howard Dean	12,734
John Edwards	89,310
Dick Gephardt	1,890
John F. Kerry	81,073
Dennis J. Kucinich	2,544
Lyndon H. LaRouche Jr.	689
Joe Lieberman	19,680
Al Sharpton	3,939

2004 Republican Presidential Preferential Primary—February 3

George W. Bush	59,577
Bill Wyatt	6,621

2004 Democratic Nominations, Primary Elections—July 27

United States Senator

Brad Carson	280,026
Carroll Fisher	28,385
Monte E. Johnson	17,274
Jim Rogers	20,179
W.B.G. Woodson	6,932

United States Representative
District—Candidates

2–Bryan J. Bigby	5,328
Dan Boren	73,421
Vern L. Cassity	2,497
Kalyn Free	46,061
5–Bert Smith	26,903
Harley Venters	16,920

2004 Republican Nominations, Primary Election—July 27

United States Senator

Bob Anthony	29,596
Tom Coburn	145,974
Kirk Humphreys	59,877
Jay Richard Hunt	2,944

United States Representative
District—Candidates

1–Evelyn L. Rogers	2,779
John Sullivan	44,082
Bill Wortman	15,778
2–Damon Harris	6,664
Wayland Smalley	11,851
Raymond Wickson	4,321

2004 State Officers, General Election—November 2

Total Vote Cast	1,463,758

Presidential Electors

Democrat—503,966
John F. Kerry—President

John Edwards—Vice President

George Krumme	Edwynne Krumme
Maxine Horner	Jim Hamilton
Bernice Mitchell	Betty McElderry
Bob Lemon	

Republican—959,792
George W. Bush—President
Dick Cheney—Vice President

George Wiland III	Paul Hollrah
Colby Schwartz	Diana Gunther
Ken Bartlett	Donald Burdick
Bob Hudspeth	

Corporation Commissioner

John Wylie (D)	489,759
Denise A. Bode (R)	857,387

United States Senate

Brad Carson (D)	596,750
Tom Coburn (R)	763,433
Sheila Bilyeu (I)	86,663

United States Representative
District—Candidates

1–Doug Dodd (D)	116,731
John Sullivan (R)	187,145
John Krymski (I)	7,058
2–Dan Boren (D)	179,579
Wayland Smalley (R)	92,963
3–Frank D. Lucas (R)	215,510
Gregory M. Wilson (I)	46,621
4–Tom Cole (R)	198,985
Charlene Bradshaw (I)	56,869
5–Bert Smith (D)	92,719
Ernest Istook (R)	180,430

Justices of the Supreme Court
Nonpartisan Retention Ballot

District—Judge	Yes	No
5–James Winchester	886,987	344,301
8–Rudolph Hargrave	832,828	374,424

Judges, Court of Criminal Appeals
Nonpartisan Retention Ballot

District—Judge	Yes	No
1-Charles Chapel	855,934	369,223

Justices of the Court of Civil Appeals
Nonpartisan Retention Ballot

District—Judge	Yes	No
District 3–Office 1 Joe C. Taylor	854,691	362,294
District 3–Office 2 Ron Stubblefield	845,129	366,284
District 4–Office 1 Glenn D. Adams	853,183	356,955
District 4–Office 2 Larry E. Joplin	838,223	370,648
District 6–Office 1 E. Bay Mitchell III	851,118	361,485

2006 Democratic Nominations
Primary Elections—July 25/August 22

	Regular	Runoff
Governor		
Brad Henry	226,957	
Andrew W. Marr	37,510	
Lieutenant Governor		
Jari Askins	103,515	95,096
Cal Hobson	46,768	
Pete Regan	74,784	81,626
Jim Rogers	32,336	
Commissioner of Labor		
Lloyd L Fields	135,253	
Frank Shurden	109,678	
United States Representative		
District—Candidates		
3-Sue Barton	24,177	
John Coffee Harris	9,833	
Gregory M. Wilson	11,249	
5-David Hunter	24,660	
Bert Smith	14,455	

2006 Republican Nominations
Primary Elections—July 25/August 22

	Regular	Runoff
Governor		
Jim Evanoff	8,370	
Ernest Istook	99,650	
Bob Sullivan	56,347	
James A. Williamson	17,769	
Lieutenant Governor		
Todd Hiett	76,634	66,220
Scott Pruitt	60,367	63,817
Nancy Riley	41,984	
State Treasurer		
Howard Barnett	107,015	
Daniel Keating	71,170	
State Insurance Commissioner		
Bill Case	125,485	
Tahl Willard	35,278	
United States Representative		
District—Candidates		
1-Fran Moghaddam	1,895	
Evelyn L. Rogers	5,826	
John Sullivan	38,279	
2-Patrick K. Miller	9,941	
Raymond J. Wickson	3,829	
5-Denise A. Bode	9,139	
Kevin Calvey	4,870	
Mick Cornett	11,718	15,669
Mary Fallin	16,691	26,748
Fred Morgan	4,493	
Johnny B. Roy	1,376	

2006 State Officers, General
Election—November 7

Total Vote Cast	926,462

Governor

Brad Henry (D)	616,135
Ernest Istook (R)	310,327

Lieutenant Governor

Jari Askins (D)	463,753
Todd Hiett (R)	439,418
Elmer Zen Million (I)	21,684

State Auditor and Inspector

Jeff A. McMahan (D)	469,311
Gary Jones (R)	438,778

Attorney General

Drew Edmondson (D)	563,364
James Dunn (R)	357,267

State Treasurer

Scott Mecham (D)	542,347
Howard Barnett (R)	371,961

Superintendent of Public Instruction

Sandy Garrett (D)	576,304
Bill Crozier (R)	343,900

Commissioner of Labor

Lloyd L. Fields (D)	456,446
Brenda Reneau (R)	453,720

Insurance Commissioner

Kim Holland (D)	474,221
Bill Case (R)	437,081

Corporation Commissioner

Bob Anthony	536,341
Cody Graves	378,030

United States Representative
District—Candidates

1–Alan Gentges (D)	56,724
John Sullivan (R)	116,920
Bill Wortman (I)	10,085
2–Dan Boren (D)	122,347
Patrick K. Miller (R)	45,861
3–Sue Barton (D)	61,749
Frank D. Lucas (R)	128,042
4–Tom Cole (R)	118,266
Hal Spake (D)	64,775
5–Mary Fallin (R)	108,936

David Hunter (D)	67,293
Matthew Woodson (I)	4,196

2008 Democratic Presidential Preferential Primary—February 5

Hillary Clinton	228,480
Christopher J. Dodd	2,511
John Edwards	42,725
Dennis J. Kucinich	2,378
Barack Obama	130,130
Bill Richardson	7,078
Jim Rogers	3,905

2008 Republican Presidential Preferential Primary—February 3

Jerry R. Curry	387
Daniel Gilbert	124
Rudy Giuliani	2,412
Mike Huckabee	111,899
Duncan Hunter	317
Alan L. Keyes	817
John McCain	122,772
Ron Paul	11,183
Mitt Romney	83,030
Tom Tancredo	189
Fred Thompson	1,924

2008 Democratic Nominations, Primary Elections—July 29

United States Senator

Andrew Rice	113,795
Jim Rogers	76,981

United States Representatives
District—Candidates

1–Mark Manley	8,842
Georgianna W. Oliver	11,116
2–Dan Boren	66,041
Kevin Coleman	11,438
5–Steven L. Perry	12,902
Bert Smith	9,003

2008 Republican Nominations, Primary Elections—July 29

United States Senator

Jim Inhofe	116,371
Evelyn L. Rogers	10,770
Ted Ryals	7,306
Dennis Lopez	3,800

United States Representatives
District—Candidates

1–John Sullivan	33,563
Fran Mo-Ghaddam	3,025

Corporation Commissioner (Short Term)

Dana Murphy	68,757
Rob Johnson	65,947

2008 State Officers, General Election—November 4

Total Vote Cast	1,462,661

Presidential Electors

Democrat—502,496
Barack Obama—President
Joe Biden—Vice President

Sally Freeman Frasier	Robert Lemon
Gene A. Wallace	David Walters
Anita R. Norman	Walter W. Jenny Jr.
Tim Mauldin	

Republican—960,165
John McCain—President
Sarah Palin—Vice President

Virginia Chrisco	Gail Stice
Pete Katzdorn	Robert Cleveland
Mary Phyllis Gorman	Bunny Chambers
Diana Murphy Gunther	

Corporation Commissioner (Full Term)

Jeff Cloud (R)	856,879
Charles Gray (D)	548,190

Corporation Commissioner (Short Term)

Dana Murphy (R)	738,671
Jim Roth (D)	674,905

United States Senate

Jim Inhofe (R)	763,375
Andrew Rice (D)	527,736
Stephen P. Wallace (I)	55,708

United States Representative
District—Candidates

1–Georgianna Wallace (D)	98,890
John Sullivan (R)	193,404
2–Dan Boren (D)	173,757
Raymond Wickson (R)	72,815
3–Frank D. Lucas (R)	184,306
Forrest Michael (I)	17,756
Frankie Robbins (D)	62,297
4–Tom Cole (R)	180,080
Blake Cummings (D)	79,674
David E. Joyce (I)	13,027
5–Mary Fallin (R)	171,925
Steven L. Perry (D)	88,996

Justices of the Supreme Court Nonpartisan Retention Ballot

District—Judge	Yes	No
1–John F. Reif	778,524	453,015
6–Tom Colbert	829,450	425,291
9–Joseph M. Watt	778,002	443,036

Judges, Court of Criminal Appeals Nonpartisan Retention Ballot

District—Judge	Yes	No
2–Charles A. Johnson	804,532	425,954
3–Gary Lumpkin	783,652	429,211

Justices of the Court of Civil Appeals Nonpartisan Retention Ballot

District—Judge	Yes	No
District 1–Office 1		
Jerry L. Goodman	807,531	410,709
District 1–Office 2		
Jane P. Wiseman	803,906	413,889

District 2–Office 2

Keith Rapp	778,434	431,901

District 3–Office 2

John F. Fischer	793,573	422,448

2010 Democratic Nominations, Primary Elections—July 27

Governor

Jari Askins	132,591
Drew Edmondson	131,097

Superintendent of Public Instruction

Susan Paddack	183,550
Jerry Combrink	66,697

United States Senator

Jim Rogers	157,955
Mark Myles	83,715

United States Representative

District—Candidates

2–Dan Boren	66,439
Jim Wilson	21,496
5–Billy Coyle	21,143
Tom Guild	16,063

2010 Republican Nominations, Primary Elections—July 27/August 24

	Regular	Runoff

Governor

Mary Fallin	136,477
Randy Brogdon	98,170
Robert Hubbard	8,132
Roger L. Jackson	6,290

Lieutenant Governor

Todd Lamb	156,834
John A. Wright	41,177
Paul F. Nosak	13,941
Bill Crozier	12,177
Bernie Adler	10,515

State Auditor & Inspector

Gary Jones	151,712
David Hanigar	66,364

Attorney General

Scott Pruitt	134,355
Ryan Leonard	105,34

State Treasurer

Ken Miller	145,415
Owen Laughlin	85,240

Superintendent of Public Instruction

Janet Barresi	145,433
Brian S. Kelly	86,430

Commissioner of Labor

Mark Costello	127,413
Jason Reese	95,869

Insurance Commissioner

John P. Crawford	92,924	35,292
John Doak	87,274	84,573
Mark Croucher	42,772	

Corporation Commissioner

Dana Murphy	158,779
Tod Yeager	70,651

United States Representative

District—Candidates

1–John Sullivan	38,673	
Kenneth Rice	10,394	
Nathan Dahm	8,871	
Patrick K. Haworth	1,737	
Craig Allen	1,421	
Fran Moghaddam	1,213	
2–Charles Thompson	8,161	7,492
Daniel Edmonds	6,886	3,645
Daniel Arnett	3,863	
Howard Houchen	2,785	
Chester Clem Falling	1,527	
Raymond Wickson	1,095	
4–Tom Cole	32,589	
R. J. Harris	9,583	

5-James Lankford	18,760	29,817
Kevin Calvey	18,147	15,902
Mike Thompson	10,008	
Shane Jett	5,956	
Johnny B. Roy	1,548	
Rick Flanigan	762	
Harry Johnson	686	

2010 State Officers, General Election—November 2

| Total Vote Cast | 1,034,766 |

Governor

| Mary Fallin (R) | 625,506 |
| Jari Askins (D) | 409,261 |

Lieutenant Governor

Todd Lamb (R)	659,242
Kenneth Corn (D)	334,711
Richard Prawdzienski (I)	35,665

State Auditor and Inspector

| Gary Jones (R) | 570,174 |
| Steve Burrage (D) | 449,152 |

Attorney General

| Scott Pruitt (R) | 666,407 |
| Jim Priest (D) | 357,162 |

State Treasurer

| Ken Miller (R) | 675,515 |
| Stephen E. Covert (D) | 339,272 |

Superintendent of Public Instruction

Janet Barresi (R)	573,716
Susan Paddack (D)	387,007
Richard E. Cooper (I)	65,243

Commissioner of Labor

| Mark Costello (R) | 649,748 |
| Lloyd L. Fields (D) | 362,805 |

Insurance Commissioner

| John Doak (R) | 555,740 |
| Kim Holland (D) | 464,310 |

United States Senator

Tom Coburn (R)	718,482
Jim Rogers (D)	265,814
Stephen P. Wallace (I)	25,048
Ronald F. Dwyer (I)	7,807

United States Representative
District—Candidates

1-John Sullivan (R)	151,173
Angelia O'Dell (I)	45,656
2-Dan Boren (D)	108,203
Charles Thompson (R)	83,226
3-Frank D. Lucas (R)	161,927
Frankie Robbins (D)	45,689
5-James Lankford (R)	123,236
Billy Coyle (D)	68,074
Clark Duffe (I)	3,067
Dave White (I)	2,728

Justices of the Supreme Court Nonpartisan Retention Ballot

District—Judge	Yes	No
2-Steven W. Taylor	575,570	311,608
5-James R. Winchester	571,893	307,615

Justices of the Court of Civil Appeals Nonpartisan Retention Ballot

District—Judge	Yes	No
District 2-Office 1 Deborah Barnes	565,390	316,542
District 3-Office 1 Doug Gabbard II	539,326	336,136
District 3-Office 2 John F. Fischer	549,756	326,506
District 4-Office 2 Larry E. Joplin	548,247	329,520

2012 Democratic Presidential Preferential Primary—March 6

Bob Ely	5,323
Barack Obama	64,389
Darcy G. Richardson	7,201
Jim Rogers	15,546
Randall Terry	20,312

2012 Republican Presidential Preferential Primary—March 6

Michele Bachmann	951
Newt Gingrich	78,730
Jon Huntsman	750
Ron Paul	27,596
Rick Perry	1,291
Mitt Romney	80,356
Rick Santorum	96,849

2012 Democratic Nominations, Primary Elections—June 26

United States Representative
District—Candidates

3–Timothy Ray Murray	9,252
Frankie Robbins	8,429
4–Donna Marie Bebo	11,935
Bert Smith	8,532

2012 Republican Nominations, Primary Election—June 26

United States Representative
District—Candidates

1–Jim Bridenstine	28,055
John Sullivan	24,058
2–George Faught	6,582
Markwayne Mullin	12,008
Wayne Pettigrew	2,479
Dustin Rowe	2,871
Dwayne Thompson	901
Dakota Wood	3,479
3–Frank D. Lucas	33,454
William Craig Stump	4,492
4–Tom Cole	22,840
Gary D. Caissie	3,195

2012 General Election—November 6

Total Vote Cast	1,334,872

Presidential Electors

Democrat—443,547

Barack Obama—President
Joe Biden—Vice President

Isabel Baker	Doug Dodd
Carl Downing	Connie Johnson
Judy Eason McIntyre	Mack Miller
Martha Skeeters	

Republican—891,325
Mitt Romney—President
Paul Ryan—Vice President

David Holt	Lynn Windel
L. A. Williamson	Joe Peters
Mark Thomas	Jason Cowen
Duane Crumbacher	

United States Representative
District—Candidates

1–John Olsen (D)	91,421
Jim Bridenstine (R)	181,084
Craig Allen (I)	12,807
2–Rob Wallace (D)	96,081
Markwayne Mullin (R)	143,701
Michael G. Fulks (I)	10,830
3–Timothy R. Murray (D)	53,472
Frank D. Lucas (R)	201,744
William M. Sanders (I)	12,787
4–Donna Marie Bebo (D)	71,846
Tom Cole (R)	176,740
R.J. Harris (I)	11,745
5–Tom Guild (D)	97,504
James Lankford (R)	153,603
Pat Martin (I)	5,394
Robert T. Murphy (I)	5,176

2014 Democratic Nominations, Primary Elections—June 24/August 26

	Regular	Runoff

Superintendent of Public Instruction

	Regular	Runoff
John Cox	68,889	60,370
Freda Deskin	64,135	35,621
Jack C. Herron Jr.	22,335	
Ivan Holmes	12,504	

608

United States Senator
(Unexpired Term)

Patrick Michael Hayes	33,943	
Connie Johnson	71,462	54,762
Jim Rogers	57,598	39,664

United States Representative
District—Candidates

2-Earl E. Everett	33,119	
Joshua Harris-Till	19,813	
4-Tae Si	5,485	
Bert Smith	24,268	
5-Tom Guild	11,603	8,793
Leona Leonard	7,431	
Al McAffrey	8,507	10,417

2014 Republican Nominations,
Primary Elections—June 24 and August 26

	Regular	Runoff

Governor

Dax Ewbank	24,020
Mary Fallin	200,035
Chad Moody	40,839

Superintendent of Public Instruction

Janet Barresi	55,048
Joy Hofmeister	151,124
Brian Kelly	56,060

Insurance Commissioner

John Doak	189,893
Bill Viner	55,173

Corporation Commissioner

Cliff Branan	117,169
Todd Hiett	128,173

United States Senator

Jim Inhofe	231,291
Rob Moye	4,846
Evelyn Rogers	11,960
D. Jean McBride Samuels	3,965
Erick Paul Wyatt	11,713

United States Senator
(Unexpired Term)

Randy Brogdon	12,934
Andy Craig	2,427
Kevin Crow	2,828
James Lankford	152,749
T.W. Shannon	91,854
Jason Weger	1,794

United States Representative
District—Candidates

2-Markwayne Mullin	26,245	
Darrel Robertson	6,673	
3-Robbert Hubbard	7,925	
Frank D. Lucas	54,847	
Timothy Ray Murray	3,449	
4-Tom Cole	40,793	
Anna Flatt	7,511	
5-Patrice Douglas	13,445	13,319
Shane David Jett	7,022	
Clark Jolley	9,232	
Steve Russell	14,604	19,374
Harvey Sparks	2,898	
Mike Turner	7,760	

2014 General Election—November 4

Total Vote Cast	824,831

Governor

Mary Fallin (R)	460,298
Joe Dorman (D)	338,239
Kimberly Willis (I)	17,169
Richard Prawdzienski (I)	9,125

Lieutenant Governor

Todd G. Lamb (R)	562,088
Cathy Cummings (D)	258,564

Superintendent of Public Instruction

Joy Hofmeister (R)	457,053
John Cox (D)	361,878

Commissioner of Labor

Mark Costello (R)	504,307

Mike Workman (D)   299,284

United States Senator

Jim Inhofe (R)	558,166
Matt Silverstein (D)	234,307
Joan Farr (I)	10,554
Ray Woods (I)	9,913
Aaron DeLozier (I)	7,793

United States Senator
(Unexpired Term)

James Lankford (R)	557,002
Connie Johnson (D)	237,923
Mark T. Beard (I)	25,965

United States Representative
District—Candidates

2–Markwayne Mullin (R)	110,925
Earl E. Everett (D)	38,964
Jon Douthitt (I)	8,518
3–Frank D. Lucas (R)	133,335
Frankie Robbins (D)	36,270
4–Tom Cole (R)	117,721
Bert Smith (D)	40,998
Dennis B. Johnson (I)	7,549
5–Steve Russell (R)	95,632
Al McAffrey (D)	57,790
Tom Boggs (I)	2,065
Robert T. Murphy (I)	2,176
Buddy Ray (I)	1,470

Justices of the Supreme Court Nonpartisan Retention Ballot

District—Judge	Yes	No
1–John F. Reif	430,939	299,120
6–Tom Colbert	462,201	276,392
9–Joseph M. Watt	436,902	292,647

Justices of the Court of Criminal Appeals Nonpartisan Retention Ballot

District—Judge	Yes	No
District 3		
Gary L. Lumpkin	454,084	273,044

Justices of the Court of Civil Appeals Nonpartisan Retention Ballot

District—Judge	Yes	No
District 1–Office 1		
Jerry L. Goodman	440,731	282,929
District 1–Office 2		
Jane P. Wiseman	441,834	283,172
District 2–Office 1		
Deborah B. Barnes	448,020	274,279
District 2–Office 2		
Keith Rapp	426,667	293,299
District 6–Office 2		
Brian Jack Goree	439,192	280,790

Summary of State Questions By Topic

State Questions are listed in this summary by subject matter, and do not necessarily appear in numerical order. The questions are grouped within election years, following consecutively from the general election of 1908 until the current year. More information about state questions is available at www.sos.state.ok.us

Ad Valorem Taxation

SQ 68   **Method of assessments.** Rejected. Primary Election. August 4, 1914.

SQ 74   **Reducing maximum levy on assessments.** Rejected. General Election. November 3, 1914.

SQ 114   **Increasing maximum total taxes authorized.** Rejected. Primary Election. August 1, 1922.

SQ 124   **Limiting taxation to 31 1/2 mills.** Adopted. Special Election. October 2, 1923. (Supreme Court ruled act submitting proposal unconstitutional.)

SQ 138   **Method of ascertaining average tax rate.** Rejected. General Election. November 2, 1926.

SQ 168   **Limiting rate of taxation.** Rejected. Primary Election. July 5, 1932.

SQ 184   **Equalization of property assessments.** Law Vetoed. Special Election. August 15, 1933.

SQ 185   **Limiting tax for schools to 15 mills.** Adopted. Special Election. August 15, 1933.

SQ 201   **Exempting homesteads from Ad Valorem taxation.** Adopted. Special Election. September 24, 1935.

SQ 208   **Providing $1,500 exemption.** Rejected. Special Election. September 24, 1935.

SQ 379   **Assessment at 35 percent of fair cash value.** Adopted. Special Election. July 1, 1958.

SQ 443   **No situs on tangible personal property stored or in transit.** Adopted. Runoff Election. September 17, 1968.

SQ 460   **Prohibiting taxation of personal tangible property.** Adopted. Primary Election. August 27, 1968.

SQ 486   **Assessment at 35 percent for highest and best use.** Adopted. General Election. November 7, 1972.

SQ 575   **Additional Ad Valorem tax levy not to exceed 3 mills for health care.** Rejected. General Election. November 6, 1984.

SQ 588   **Exempting certain new or expanding manufacturing plants from Ad Valorem taxes for five years.** Adopted. Special Election. April 30, 1985.

SQ 669   **Limits the total amount of property tax that could be levied on a parcel of real property to 1993 levels and restricts future increases to no more than 3 percent per year with a 60 percent vote of county residents.** Rejected. Presidential Primary Election. March 12, 1996.

SQ 675   **Freezing assessment ratios at 1997 levels on all real property, including residences, agriculture property and business structures.** Adopted. General Election. November 5, 1996.

SQ 676   Limits annual increases placed on property values for tax purposes to five percent for any year in which the property is not transferred. Adopted. General Election. November 5, 1996.

SQ 677   Freezes property values on homes of homeowners 65 or older whose gross household income is no more than $25,000.00 annually. Adopted. General Election. November 5, 1996.

SQ 683   Exempts certain personal property from Ad Valorem tax, specifically "pollution control property" to be defined by the legislature. Rejected. General Election. November 3, 1998.

SQ 696   Exempts from property tax up to 100 square feet of storm shelters, added after January 1, 2002, including a safe room designed to protect against tornadoes. Adopted. General Election. November 5, 2002.

SQ 697   Allows county voters to decide to use a portion of property taxes from certain manufacturing facilities previously exempt from property tax for economic development purposes. Adopted. General Election. November 5, 2002.

SQ 702   Allows the legislature to enact laws for the abatement of property taxes under certain specified conditions. Adopted. General Election. November 5, 2002.

SQ 704   Allows school districts to use monies in their building fund for county assessor inspections for ad valorem revaluation purposes. Rejected. General Election. November 5, 2002.

SQ 758   The measure amends Section 8B of Article 10 of the Oklahoma Constitution. The measure changes the limits on fair cash value of property. Increases are limited to 5% of fair cash value in any taxable year. The measure also changes the cap on increases to 3% for homestead exempted property and agricultural land. Adopted. General Election. November 6, 2012.

SQ 766   The measure amends Oklahoma Constitution. The measure would exempt all intangible personal property from ad valorem property taxation. Adopted. General Election. November 6, 2012.

Affirmative Action

SQ 759   The measure does not allow affirmative action in employment, education, and contracting. The measure permits affirmative action: 1)When gender is a bona fide qualification; 2) Existing court orders and consent decrees that require preferred treatment will continue and can be allowed; 3) Affirmative action is allowed when needed to keep or obtain federal funds. The measure applies to the State and its agencies; counties, cities, and towns; school districts; and other State subdivisions. Adopted. General Election. November 6, 2012.

Agriculture

SQ 170   Limiting acreage on certain crops. Rejected. Primary Election. July 5, 1932.

Agriculture, Board of

SQ 38   **Membership and duties.** Adopted. General Election. November 5, 1912.

SQ 60   **Reducing membership from 11 to 5.** Adopted. Special Election. August 5, 1913.

SQ 158   **Relieving duties as board of A & M Colleges.** Rejected. General Election. November 4, 1930.

SQ 210   **Relieving duties as board of A & M Colleges.** Rejected. General Election. November 3, 1936.

Alcoholic Beverages (See also Beer)

SQ 1   **Dispensing by physicians' prescription.** Rejected. General Election. November 3, 1908.

SQ 22   **Local option for sale of liquor.** Rejected. General Election. November 8, 1910.

SQ 222   **Repeal of prohibition.** Rejected. General Election. November 3, 1936.

SQ 289   **Local option for sale of liquor.** Rejected. General Election. November 5, 1940.

SQ 343   **Legalizing sale and prohibiting open saloons.** Rejected. Special Election. September 27, 1949.

SQ 386   **Legalizing package sales.** Adopted. Special Election. April 7, 1959.

SQ 387   **County option sale of liquor.** Rejected. Special Election. April 7, 1959.

SQ 406   **Providing for franchising.** Rejected. General Election. November 6, 1962.

SQ 480   **Liquor by drink, franchising, and advertising.** Rejected. General Election. November 7, 1972.

SQ 515   **Authorizing sale of liquor by the drink.** Rejected. General Election. November 2, 1976.

SQ 563   **Retail sale of liquor by the drink at county option; repeal of Alcoholic Beverage Control Board.** Adopted. Primary Election. September 18, 1984.

SQ 591   **Requires winemakers to sell to licensed wholesale distributors. In-state winemakers could also sell to non-distributors.** Adopted. General Election. November 4, 1986.

SQ 637   **Allowing liquor stores to be open during certain elections such as city franchise elections with closure during other elections.** Rejected. General Election. November 6, 1990.

SQ 638   **Allowing the legislature to enact laws restricting state employees and certain agencies from being involved in alcoholic beverage business.** Adopted. Runoff Election, September 18, 1990.

SQ 663   **Would allow wineries to make wine with fruit grown outside Oklahoma.** Approved. General Election. November 8, 1994.

SQ 688   **Amends Section 3 of Article 28 of the Constitution. Allows winemakers to sell wine to retail package stores and restaurants.** Adopted. General Election. November 7, 2000.

SQ 733   The measure would amend Article 28 of the State Constitution to allow the sale of alcoholic beverages by package stores on election days. Adopted. General Election. November 7, 2006.

SQ 743   The measure amends Section 3 of Article 28 of the State Constitution. It requires a customer to be twenty-one and physically present to purchase wine at a winery, festival, or trade show. The measure changes the law to allow certain winemakers to sell directly to retail package stores and restaurants in Oklahoma. Adopted. General Election. November 4, 2008.

Auditor and Examiner, State

SQ 508   Removing as member of Board of Equalization. Adopted. Special Election. July 22, 1975.

SQ 510   Consolidating office of Auditor and Examiner and Inspector into office of Auditor and Examiner. Adopted. Special Election. July 22, 1975.

SQ 514   Changed membership of Commissioners of the Land Office. Adopted. Special Election. July 22, 1975.

SQ 508   Adding to membership on Board of Equalization. Adopted. Special Election. July 22, 1975.

SQ 510   Creating office by consolidation of Auditor and Examiner and Inspector. Adopted. Special Election. July 22, 1975.

Banks

SQ 125   Payment for claims against Depositors' Guaranty Fund. Rejected. Special Election. October 2, 1923.

Beer

SQ 183   Defining non-intoxicating beverages; providing for licensing, taxing. Adopted. Special Election. July 11, 1933.

SQ 376   County option on sale of beer. Rejected. Special Election. December 3, 1957.

SQ 530   Allowing marketing agreements between brewers and wholesalers. Rejected. General Election. November 7, 1978.

Bond Issues

SQ 100 $50 million for highway construction. Rejected. Special Election. May 6, 1919.

SQ 139   Method of issuance, sale, and payment. Rejected. General Election. November 2, 1926.

SQ 313   Use of surplus funds to retire bonded indebtedness. Adopted. Primary Election. July 11, 1944.

SQ 348 $36 million for construction of state buildings. Adopted. Special Election. September 27, 1949.

SQ 393   **$35.5 million for capital improvements at state institutions of higher education.** Adopted. Primary Election. July 5, 1960.

SQ 411   **$7 million for capital improvements at Medical Center.** Adopted. Special Election. December 3, 1963.

SQ 426   **$56.7 million for capital improvements for state government.** Rejected. Special Election. April 27, 1965.

SQ 427   **$60 million for highway construction.** Rejected. Special Election. April 27, 1965.

SQ 433   **$54.7 million for capital improvements at state institutions, departments.** Adopted. Special Election. December 14, 1965.

SQ 463   **$99.8 million for capital improvements at state institutions and departments.** Adopted. Special Election. December 10, 1968.

SQ 485   **$250 million for highway construction (Freeway '77).** Rejected. Special Election. March 7, 1972.

SQ 552   **Municipalities joint issuance, sale, and payment for public utilities.** Rejected. General Election. November 4, 1980.

SQ 616   **This measure expands the way certain city and town bond issues could be used.** Adopted. Primary Election, August 23, 1988.

SQ 647   **Measure would enact new laws to impose taxes on health care providers to pay for health care programs.** Rejected. General Election. November 3, 1992.

SQ 649   **Allows Legislature to authorize issuance of general obligation bonds to be used to build, remodel, and repair state buildings and make other capital improvements.** Adopted. General Election. November 3, 1992.

SQ 693   **Amends Constitution to allow expanding sources for payment of local bonds issued for economic/community development to include a sales tax not to exceed one cent or apportionment of tax increment financing revenues.** Adopted. General Election. November 5, 2002.

SQ 764   **Amends Constitution to allow the Oklahoma Water Resources Board to issue bonds.** Adopted. General Election. November 6, 2012.

Budget

SQ 298   **Appropriations not to exceed revenues.** Adopted. Special Election. March 11, 1941.

SQ 587   **Limits amount of tax money to be spent each year to 95 percent of estimated income. Limits how reserve funds can be spent.** Adopted. Special Election. April 30, 1985.

SQ 686   **Deals with the state budget, allowing state colleges and universities to make contracts with presidents for more than one (1) year but not more than three (3) years.** Adopted. General Election. November 7, 2000.

Budget Officer

SQ 173   **Creating state budget officer.** Rejected. Special Election. December 18, 1931.

Business Development

SQ 611 Would let state monies be used to make grants, loans, and investments to develop business in this state. Adopted. Runoff Election. September 20, 1988.

SQ 680 Would allow use of college or university property by a business to develop technology, defined as a product, process, or idea. Adopted. General Election. November 3, 1998.

SQ 681 Would allow colleges and universities and higher education employees to own technology (product, process, or idea) and/or interest in private business. Adopted. General Election. November 3, 1998.

SQ 693 Amends Constitution to allow expanding sources for payment of local bonds issued for economic/community development to include a sales tax not to exceed one cent or apportionment of tax increment financing revenues. Adopted. General Election. November 5, 2002.

SQ 697 Allows county voters to decide to use a portion of property taxes from certain manufacturing facilities previously exempt from property tax for economic development purposes. Adopted. General Election. November 5, 2002.

Charities and Corrections Commissioner

SQ 509 Abolishing office. Adopted. Special Election. July 22, 1975.

Children

SQ 636 Allowing the legislature to set the age at which children of this state would be required to attend school. Rejected. Special Election. June 26, 1990.

Chiropractors

SQ 94 Licensing and practice of chiropractic. Law Vetoed. General Election. November 2, 1920.

Cigarette Tax (See also Tobacco)

SQ 179 Levying 3-cent tax. Law vetoed. Special Election. August 15, 1933.

Cities and Towns

SQ 85 Limiting indebtedness. Rejected. Primary Election. August 1, 1916.

SQ 373 Increasing indebtedness for municipal water supply. Rejected. Primary Election. July 3, 1956.

SQ 380 Authorizing purchase of water supplies. Adopted. Special Election. July 1, 1958.

SQ 488 Removing requirement that voters be property taxpayers in public utility bond elections. Rejected. Primary Election. August 22, 1972.

SQ 489   **Indebtedness not to exceed ten percent of property valuations.** Adopted. Primary Election. August 22, 1972.

SQ 557   **Providing that constitutional limitation on borrowing for construction or maintenance on public buildings may be extended.** Rejected. General Election. November 2, 1982.

SQ 581   **Use of state monies to finance water resource and sewage treatment projects in cities and towns.** Adopted. August 28, 1984.

SQ 610   **Would allow the Oklahoma Development Finance Authority to issue general obligation bonds.** Adopted. Runoff Election, September 20, 1988.

SQ 626   **Allows cities and towns to borrow money for buying, building or improving public utilities without levying any additional tax.** Adopted. Primary Election. August 28, 1990.

SQ 641   **Permits cities and counties to give tax relief to certain areas in economic decline.** Adopted. General Election. November 6, 1990.

SQ 693   **Amends Constitution to allow expanding sources for payment of local bonds issued for economic/community development to include a sales tax not to exceed one cent or apportionment of tax increment financing revenues.** Adopted. General Election. November 5, 2002.

Coal Mines

SQ 47   **Health and safety regulations for coal miners.** Act vetoed. Special Election. August 5, 1913.

SQ 589   **Allowing males and females, at least eighteen years of age, to work in underground mines.** Adopted. General Election. November 4, 1986.

Cockfighting

SQ 687   **Proposes a statute making cockfighting illegal.** Adopted. General Election. November 5, 2002.

Colleges and Universities

SQ 159   **Creating Board of Regents for University of Oklahoma.** Rejected. General Election. November 4, 1930.

SQ 310   **Creating Board of Regents for A & M Colleges.** Adopted. Primary Election. July 11, 1944.

SQ 311   **Creating Board of Regents for University of Oklahoma.** Adopted. Primary Election. July 11, 1944.

SQ 328   **Creating Board of Regents for certain colleges.** Adopted. Primary Election. July 6, 1948.

SQ 371   **Creating Board of Regents for Oklahoma College for Women.** Rejected. Primary Election. July 3, 1956.

SQ 680   **Would allow use of college or university property by a business to develop technology, defined as a product, process, or idea.** Adopted. General Election. November 3, 1998.

SQ 681   **Would allow colleges and universities and higher education employees to own technology (product, process, or idea) and/or interest in private business.** Adopted. General Election. November 3, 1998.

SQ 686   **Deals with the state budget, allowing state colleges and universities to make contracts with presidents for more than one (1) year but not more than three (3) years.** Adopted. General Election. November 7, 2000.

Congress and Districts

SQ 357   **Creating six new districts.** Rejected. General Election. November 6, 1956.

SQ 437   **Fixing boundaries.** Rejected. Special Election. November 8, 1966.

SQ 556   **Repealing prior state legislation which established and fixed boundaries of congressional districts.** Rejected. General Election. November 2, 1982.

SQ 662   **Limits the terms of U.S. Representatives to three two-year terms and Senators to two six-year terms. No person could serve more than six years as a Representative and 12 years as a Senator, or combined 18 years total.** Approved. Runoff Election. September 20, 1994. (Note: This bill was nullified by the decision of the U.S. Supreme Court in U.S. Term Limits, Inc., et al., v. Ray Thornton, 514 U.S.779, 1995)

Conservation Commission

SQ 230   **Designating as agency for federal soil program.** Rejected. Primary Election. July 7, 1936.

Constitution, State

SQ 353   **No proposal shall embrace more than one general subject.** Adopted. Primary Election. July 1, 1952.

SQ 473   **Amendment by article as single question.** Rejected. Special Election. March 17, 1970.

SQ 495   **Eliminating provision that measures initiated directly by people need majority of total votes cast in that election ("Silent Vote").** Adopted. Primary Election. August 27, 1974.

SQ 496   **Eliminating provision that approval of constitutional amendment needs majority of total votes cast in that election ("Silent Vote").** Adopted. Primary Election. August 27, 1974.

SQ 603   **Would allow Senate or House alone to disapprove a rule made by a state entity.** Rejected. Presidential Preferential Primary Election, March 8, 1988.

SQ 660   **Would remove the requirement to hold a constitutional convention every twenty years.** Rejected. General Election. November 8, 1994.

Constitutional Convention

SQ 146   **Calling convention for November, 1927.** Rejected. General Election. November 2, 1926.

SQ 347   **Calling convention for September, 1951.** Rejected. General Election. November 7, 1950.

SQ 472   **Authorizing legislature to call convention.** Rejected. Special Election. March 17, 1970.

SQ 660   **Would remove the requirement to hold a constitutional convention every twenty years.** Rejected. General Election. November 8, 1994.

Convict Label Law

SQ 135   **Labeling of convict-made goods.** Referendum Rejected. Law Sustained. General Election. November 2, 1926.

Corporation Commission

(See also Oil Inspections and Public Service Corporations)

SQ 679   **Would allow salaries of Corporation Commissioners and members of the Oklahoma Tax Commission to be raised at any time so long as pay was equal.** Rejected. General Election. November 3, 1998.

Corporations

SQ 169   **Ownership of lands outside cities and towns.** Rejected. Special Election. December 18, 1931.

SQ 358   **Prohibiting corporate ownership of agriculture land.** Adopted. Primary Election. July 6, 1954.

SQ 375   **Ownership of stocks in competitive corporations.** Rejected. Primary Election. July 3, 1956.

SQ 455   **Eliminating filing of certain reports.** Adopted. Runoff Election. September 17, 1968.

SQ 458   **Restrictions for issuance of corporate stock.** Adopted. Runoff Election. September 17, 1968.

County Government

SQ 497   **Additional 2–mill levy for operational funds.** Rejected. Primary Election. August 27, 1974.

SQ 570   **Additional 3–mill levy to construct, maintain, improve county parks.** Rejected. General Election. November 6, 1984.

SQ 573   **Additional county ad valorem tax levy not to exceed 5 mills for roads and jails.** Rejected. General Election. November 6, 1984.

SQ 596   **Allowing for new tax levy not to exceed 3 mills to provide solid waste management services. Other sources of funding could be used.** Adopted. Primary Election. August 26, 1986.

SQ 625   **Allowing county to issue bonds to develop industry near the county with bond interest rates and issuance of bonds prescribed by law.** Adopted. Primary Election. August 28, 1990.

SQ 646   **Allowing annual property tax levy for county to maintain Oklahoma cooperative extension office.** Rejected. General Election. November 3, 1992.

SQ 647   **Measure would enact new laws to impose taxes on health care providers to pay for health care programs.** Rejected. General Election. November 3, 1992.

SQ 670   **Changes the number of signatures needed to call a county grand jury. Requires signatures equal to sixteen percent of the total vote cast at the last general election for the county office receiving the highest number of votes.** Adopted. General Election. November 5, 1996.

SQ 685   **Allows counties to increase property tax by up to two and one-half mills to support county health departments. The new tax will only be allowed in counties with more than 500,000 persons and must be approved by county voters.** Rejected. General Election. November 7, 2000.

SQ 693   **Amends Constitution to allow expanding sources for payment of local bonds issued for economic/community development to include a sales tax not to exceed one cent or apportionment of tax increment financing revenues.** Adopted. General Election. November 5, 2002.

SQ 697   **Allows county voters to decide to use a portion of property taxes from certain manufacturing facilities previously exempt from property tax for economic development purposes.** Adopted. General Election. November 5, 2002.

County Officers

SQ 377   **Four-year terms for county officers.** Rejected. General Election. November 6, 1956.

SQ 417   **Four-year terms for county officers.** Rejected. Special Election. December 3, 1963.

SQ 418   **Four-year terms for county judges.** Rejected. Special Election. December 3, 1963.

County Superintendent of Schools

SQ 424   **Authorized to conduct joint district program.** Rejected. General Election. November 3, 1964.

Courts

SQ 71   **Abolishing Court of Criminal Appeals.** Rejected. General Election. November 3, 1914.

SQ 84   **Appointment of Clerk of Supreme Court.** Rejected. Primary Election. August 1, 1916.

SQ 87   **Consolidation of Supreme Court and Criminal Court of Appeals.** Rejected. Primary Election. August 1, 1916.

SQ 89   **Abolishing county courts.** Rejected. Primary Election. August 1, 1916.

SQ 152   **Creating Court of Tax Review.** Adopted. Primary Election. August 7, 1928.

SQ 415   **Establishing Court on the Judiciary.** Rejected. General Election. November 3, 1964.

SQ 431   **Creating Court on the Judiciary.** Adopted. Primary Election. May 3, 1966.

SQ 441   **Creating Judicial Department.** Rejected. Runoff Election. September 17, 1968.

SQ 447   **Selection of judges on retention ballot and establishing Judicial Nominating Commission.** Adopted. Special Election. July 11, 1967.

SQ 448   **Establishing Judicial Department; election of judges on non-partisan ballot and appointment of clerk of Supreme Court.** Adopted. Special Election. July 11, 1967.

SQ 752   **The measure amends Section 3 of Article 7-B of the State Constitution regarding the Judicial Nominating Commission. The amendment adds two at-large members to the commission.** Adopted. General Election. November 2, 2010.

SQ 755   **The measure amends Article 7 Section 1 of the State Constitution. It requires courts to rely on federal and state law when deciding cases. It forbids courts from considering or using international law. It also forbids courts from considering or using Sharia Law.** Adopted. General Election. November 2, 2010.

Crime Victims

SQ 674   **Victims are to be given notice when an accused or convicted person is to be released from custody or escapes. Victims have a right to be present at proceedings where the defendant has a right to be present. Gives victims right to be heard at sentencing and parole hearings.** Adopted. General Election. November 5, 1996.

Criminal Prosecutions

SQ 401   **Trial in county where evidence indicates crime committed.** Adopted. Special Election. September 12, 1961.

SQ 612   **Expands the types of crimes for which bail may be denied.** Adopted. General Election. November 8, 1988.

Deaf and Mute

SQ 521   **Changing language relating to state care of deaf, dumb, and blind to read "deaf, deaf and mute, or blind."** Adopted. General Election. April 26, 1976.

Dual Office Holding

SQ 769   **Amends Section 12 of Article 2 of the State Constitution. Measure prohibits the holding of more than one office at the same time. It applies to certain offices. The measure would not allow the law to be construed to keep some people from holding two offices at the same time.** Adopted. General Election. November 4, 2014.

Education, State Board

SQ 172   Creating State Board of Education and Textbook Committee. Rejected. Special Election. December 18, 1931.

SQ 633   Providing for a State Board of Education with the School Superintendent being a member and president and the governor appointing the six other members. Rejected. Special Election. June 26, 1990.

Education, State System

SQ 300   Creating state system of higher education. Adopted. Special Election. March 11, 1941.

SQ 639   Replaces H.B. 1017 with law existing before bill's passage. Rejected. Special Election. October 15, 1991.

Educational Loans

SQ 481   Investing educational funds in student guaranteed loans. Adopted. Special Election. December 7, 1971.

Elderly

SQ 209   Authorizing legislation for old-age pensions. Rejected. Special Election. September 24, 1935.

SQ 214   Authorizing pensions, social security and creating Welfare Commission. Adopted. Special Election. September 24, 1935. (Supreme Court ruled amendment illegally submitted.)

SQ 215   Graduated tax on land for old-age security. Rejected. General Election. November 5, 1940.

SQ 220   Appropriating $2.5 million for welfare assistance. Adopted. Special Election. December 17, 1935.

SQ 225   Establishing welfare program and administration. Adopted. Primary Election. July 7, 1936.

SQ 226   Assistance for aged, blind, crippled children and dependent children. Adopted. Primary Election. July 7, 1936.

SQ 299   Repealing limitations on payments on providing taxation. Adopted. Special Election. March 11, 1941.

SQ 677   Freezes property values on homes of homeowners 65 or older whose gross household income is no more than $25,000.00 annually. Adopted. General Election. November 5, 1996.

Election Board, State

SQ 21   **Appointment of board and providing for elections.** Referendum Rejected. Law Sustained. General Election. November 8, 1910.

SQ 78   **Abolishing election boards and providing method of selecting State Election. Board.** Rejected. General Election. November 7, 1916.

Elections

SQ 312   **Providing for runoff primary election.** Adopted. Primary Election. July 11, 1944.

SQ 531   **Recodifying elector qualifications.** Adopted. General Election. November 7, 1978.

Emergency In Government

SQ 400   **Operation of government in case of disaster.** Adopted. Runoff Election. May 22, 1962.

Emergency Medical Districts (See Medical Service Districts)

Equalization Board, State

SQ 81   **Creating Tax Commission and abolishing Board of Equalization.** Rejected. Primary Election. August 1, 1916.

SQ 453   **Changing method of estimating revenues.** Adopted. Special Election. April 16, 1968.

SQ 461   **Changing method of estimating revenues.** Rejected. Primary Election. August 27, 1968.

SQ 506   **Changing method of estimating revenues.** Adopted. Special Election. July 22, 1975.

SQ 508   **Revising membership.** Adopted. Special Election. July 22, 1975.

Ethics Commission

SQ 627   **Creating a five-member Ethics Commission with the governor, chief justice, attorney general, president pro tempore and Speaker of the House each appointing one member.** Adopted. Runoff Election. September 18, 1990.

Examiner and Inspector, State

SQ 508   **Removed as member of Board of Equalization.** Adopted. Special Election. July 22, 1975.

SQ 510   **Consolidating office with State Auditor.** Adopted. Special Election. July 22, 1975.

Gambling (See also Lotteries, Cock Fighting, and Horse Racing)

SQ 61   **Repeal of law preventing gambling, bookmaking.** Rejected. Primary Election. August 4, 1914.

SQ 62   **Invalidating law penalizing gambling, slot machines.** Referendum Rejected. Law Sustained. Primary Election. August 4, 1914.

SQ 216   **Repeal of law legalizing slot machines, pinball machines.** Referendum Rejected. Law Sustained. General Election. November 8, 1938.

SQ 650   **Measure would enact new laws allowing and regulating charity games (bingo and break open ticket games).** Adopted. General Election. November 3, 1992.

SQ 658   **Would legalize a state lottery.** Rejected. Special Election. May 10, 1994.

SQ 672   **Would add a new Article to the Constitution legalizing slot machines, roulette, craps, keno, and video gambling. Only four non-Indian gambling facilities could be operated the first five years.** Rejected. Special Election. February 10, 1998.

SQ 687   **Proposes a statute making cockfighting illegal.** Adopted. General Election. November 5, 2002.

SQ 712   **The measure would enact a tribal gaming compact. Indian tribes agreeing to the compact could use new types of gaming machines. Gaming machines would be allowed at state racetracks.** Adopted. General Election. November 2, 2004.

Government Reorganization

SQ 505   **Reorganization of executive department of state government.** Rejected. Primary Election. August 27, 1974.

Governor

SQ 420   **Repealing authority of governor to appoint certain judges and U. S. Senators.** Rejected. General Election. November 3, 1964.

SQ 436   **Limits governor to two terms.** Adopted. Primary Election. May 3, 1966.

Grand Juries (See Juries, Grand)

Health Departments and Health Care

SQ 390   **Additional 2.5 mill levy for county health departments.** Adopted. Primary Election. July 5, 1960.

SQ 561   **Increase ad valorem tax to 5 mill levy for county health departments.** Rejected. Primary Election. August 28, 1984.

SQ 575   **Additional ad valorem tax levy not to exceed 3 mills for health care.** Rejected. General Election. November 6, 1984.

SQ 647   Measure would enact new laws to impose taxes on health care providers to pay for health care programs. Rejected. General Election. November 3, 1992.

SQ 667   Creates the Oklahoma Breast Cancer Act, creating a tax on places of entertainment, recreation or amusement. Rejected. General Election. November 8, 1994.

SQ 685   Allows counties to increase property tax by up to two and one-half mills to support county health departments. The new tax will only be allowed in counties with more than 500,000 persons and must be approved by county voters. Rejected. General Election. November 7, 2000.

SQ 756   The measure adds Section 37 to Article 2 of the State Constitution. It defines health care system. It prohibits making a person participate in a health care system. It prohibits making an employer participate in a health care system. It prohibits making a health care provider provide treatment in a health care system. It allows persons and employees to pay for treatment directly. It allows a health care provider to accept payment for treatment directly. It allows the purchase of health care insurance in private health care systems. It allows the sale of health insurance in private health care systems. Adopted. General Election. November 2, 2010.

Highway Commission

SQ 325   Creating four-member commission. Rejected. General Election. November 7, 1950.

SQ 396   Constitutional Highway Commission. Rejected. Special Election. September 20, 1960.

Highway Users Revenues

SQ 326   Prohibiting diversion of highway users' revenues. Rejected. General Election. November 7, 1950.

Homestead Exemptions

SQ 201   Exempting homesteads from ad valorem taxation. Adopted. Special Election. September 24, 1935.

SQ 208   Providing $1,500 exemption. Rejected. Special Election. September 24, 1935.

SQ 696   Exempts from property tax up to 100 square feet of storm shelters, added after January 1, 2002, including a safe room designed to protect against tornadoes. Adopted. General Election. November 5, 2002.

SQ 714   The measure would change the method for determining the fair cash value of the homestead of certain heads of household. The head of household must be at least 65 years old, and their gross income must meet income level requirements. Adopted. November 2, 2004.

SQ 770   The measure amends Section 8F to Article 10 of the State Constitution. The measure would create a homestead exemption for the surviving spouse of military personnel who die in the line of duty. Adopted. November 4, 2014.

SQ 771   The measure amends Section 8E to Article 10 of the State Constitution. The measure would provide a homestead exemption for certain qualifying disabled veterans. It also provides a homestead exemption to the surviving spouse of qualifying disabled veterans. Adopted. November 4, 2014.

Horse Racing

SQ 498   Pari-mutuel betting on horse racing; county option. Rejected. Primary Election. August 27, 1974.

SQ 553   Creating Horse Racing Commission. Adopted. Runoff Election. September 21, 1982.

Hospital Districts (See Medical Service Districts)

Human Services Department

SQ 765   The measure amends the Oklahoma Constitution. It abolishes the Oklahoma Department of Human Services, the Oklahoma Commission of Human Services, and the position of DHS director; authorizes legislature to create new department(s) to provide for public welfare. Adopted. General Election. November 6, 2012.

Impeachment

SQ 73   Drunkenness and intoxication grounds for impeachment. Adopted. Primary Election. August 4, 1914.

SQ 429   Provisions of impeachment for various state officers. Adopted. Primary Election. May 3, 1966.

Income Tax

SQ 167   Repeal of money and credits tax law and levying net income tax. Rejected. Special Election. December 18, 1931.

SQ 175   Reducing ad valorem taxes in lieu of income tax. Rejected. General Election. November 8, 1932.

SQ 395   Withholding by employer. Referendum Adopted. Law Vetoed. General Election. November 8, 1960.

SQ 539   Deduction state gross income amount equal to Federal Income Tax payable in same year. Rejected. Special Election. November 6, 1979.

Industrial Development

SQ 391   Creating Industrial Finance Authority; authorizing $10 million in bonds. Adopted. Runoff Election. July 26, 1960.

SQ 404   Cities and counties to issue industrial development bonds. Adopted. Primary Election. May 1, 1962.

SQ 465   Issuance of industrial finance bonds. Nullified.

SQ 468   Issuance of industrial finance bonds with full faith and credit of state. Rejected. Special Election. September 9, 1969.

SQ 474   Issuance of industrial finance bonds. Rejected. Special Election. March 17, 1970.

SQ 479   Limited tax bonds to obtain industry. Rejected. Special Election. December 7, 1971.

SQ 600   Increasing amount of bonds Industrial Finance Authority can sell to $90,000,000. Adopted. Primary Election. August 26, 1986.

Information Technology

SQ 703   Enables the legislature to enact laws limiting vendor liability to the state information technology contracts, provided that the liability is not less than the contract amount. Rejected. General Election. November 5, 2002.

Initiative Petition

SQ 698   Raises the petition signature requirement for abolishing certain animal-related activities from 8 percent to 15 percent of voters voting in the statewide office receiving the highest number of votes. Rejected. General Election. November 5, 2002.

SQ 750   Changes the number of required signatures on initiative petitions and referendums. The measure's basis only uses general elections with the governor on the ballot. The measure would have a lowering effect on the number of required signatures. Adopted. General Election. November 2, 2010.

Insurance

SQ 111   Nonprofit insurance organizations. Rejected. General Election. November 2, 1920.

Judicial Department (See Courts, SQ 441)

Judicial Nominating Commission (See Courts, SQ 447)

Judicial Reform (See Courts, SQ 448)

Juries

SQ 88 **Eight-man juries in certain courts.** Rejected. Primary Election. August 1, 1916.

SQ 354 **Women on juries.** Adopted. Primary Election. July 1, 1952.

SQ 449 **Providing exceptions to right of trial by jury.** (See SQ 459 below)

SQ 459 **Exceptions to right of trial by jury.** Adopted. Runoff Election. September 17, 1968.

SQ 623 **Changes in jury requirements in civil and criminal cases.** Adopted. Primary Election. August 28, 1990.

Juries, Grand

SQ 457 **Qualified electors eligible to sign petition.** Adopted. Primary Election. August 27, 1968.

SQ 483 **Attorney general to convene when multi-county crime involved.** Adopted. Special Election. December 7, 1971.

SQ 576 **Percentage of qualified electors signing petition increased from 1 percent to 2 percent of the county population.** Rejected. General Election. November 6, 1984.

SQ 670 **Changes the number of signatures needed to call a county grand jury. Requires signatures equal to sixteen percent of the total vote cast at the last general election for the county office receiving the highest number of votes.** Adopted. General Election. November 5, 1996.

Labor Commissioner, State

SQ 494 **Making office appointive.** Rejected. General Election. November 5, 1974.

SQ 512 **Making office appointive.** Adopted. Special Election. July 22, 1975.

SQ 613 **Making office elective.** Adopted. General Election, November 8, 1988.

Land Office, Commissioners of the

SQ 212 **Appointment by governor.** Rejected. Special Election. September 24, 1935.

SQ 514 **Change in membership.** Adopted. Special Election. July 22, 1975.

SQ 617 **This measure would allow the commissioners of the Land Office to grant commercial and agricultural leases in trust land.** Adopted. Primary Election, August 23, 1988.

Land Titles

SQ 2 **Torrens Registration System.** Rejected. General Election. November 3, 1908.

Lands, School and Public

SQ 5 **Sale of school and public lands.** Rejected. General Election. November 3, 1908.

SQ 490   **Increasing percentage on valuation.** Rejected. Primary Election. August 22, 1972.

SQ 624   **Taking private lands for public use will now involve more just compensation and consideration for injury to land not taken.** Adopted. Primary Election. August 28, 1990.

SQ 635   **Changing the way income from the leasing of public lands is distributed to common schools and the way interest is distributed to the schools. Now based on number of students, the legislature would henceforth decide distribution to common schools.** Rejected. Special Election. June 26, 1990.

SQ 684   **Changing the way the state can use the permanent school fund. The measure allows the state to use more than the fund's income to aid schools. The measure allows the state to diminish the fund itself to aid schools and universities.** Rejected. General Election. November 7, 2000.

Language

SQ 751   **The measure adds an amendment to the State Constitution. It requires that official state actions be in English. Native American languages could also be used.** Adopted. General Election. November 2, 2010.

Legislature

SQ 77   **Abolishing bicameral legislature.** Rejected. General Election. November 3, 1914.

SQ 112   **Pay of $6.00 per day.** Rejected. General Election. November 2, 1920.

SQ 119   **Investigation of state officers subject to impeachment.** Adopted. Special Election. October 2, 1923. **(Ruled inoperative by Supreme Court.)**

SQ 144   **Pay of legislators.** Rejected. General Election. November 2, 1926.

SQ 243   **Membership and salaries.** Rejected. General Election. November 8, 1938.

SQ 329   **$100 monthly salary.** Adopted. Primary Election. July 6, 1948.

SQ 389   **Monthly salary of $200.** Rejected. Primary Election. July 5, 1960.

SQ 394   **Calling itself into session.** Rejected. General Election. November 8, 1960.

SQ 397   **Apportionment by commission.** Rejected. Special Election. September 20, 1960.

SQ 405   **Limiting sessions and salary of $300 monthly.** Rejected. Runoff Election. May 22, 1962.

SQ 407   **Election. Board to apportion House.** Rejected. Special Election. September 12, 1961.

SQ 408   **Legislative apportionment commission.** Rejected. Special Election. November 6, 1962.

SQ 413   **Legislative compensation by law.** Rejected. Primary Election. May 5, 1964.

SQ 414   **Compensation of $25 per day for 75 days.** Rejected. General Election. November 3, 1964.

SQ 416   **Reapportionment.** Adopted. Runoff Election. May 26, 1963.

SQ 419   **Increasing terms.** Rejected. Special Election. December 3, 1963.

SQ 435   **Annual sessions with limit of 90 days.** Adopted. Runoff Election. May 24, 1966.

SQ 462 **Conflict of interest; creating Board on Legislative Compensation.** Adopted. Primary Election. August 27, 1968.

SQ 477 **Repealing certain provisions for legislative apportionment.** Rejected Primary Election. August 25, 1970.

SQ 523 **Increasing time limit for legislative apportionment.** Adopted. General Election. November 2, 1976.

SQ 540 **Special sessions called by joint order of the legislature.** Adopted. General Election. November 4, 1980.

SQ 551 **Apportionment within 45 days of 2nd session following decennial census.** Rejected. General Election. November 4, 1980.

SQ 620 **Setting new dates on which regular session of the Legislature can meet.** Adopted. Special Election. March 14, 1989.

SQ 632 **Limiting the term of office for both the Senate and House members to 12 years. Years served need not be consecutive, and service in either House of the legislature will be counted. When elected or appointed to serve less than a full term, those years shall not be counted. Effective January 1, 1991.** Adopted. Runoff Election. September 18, 1990.

SQ 662 **Limits the terms of U.S. Representatives to three two-year terms and Senators to two six-year terms. No person could serve more than six years as a Representative and 12 years as a Senator, or combined 18 years total.** Approved. Runoff Election. September 20, 1994. (Note: This was nullified by the decision of the U.S. Supreme Court in U.S. Term Limits, Inc., et al., v. Ray Thornton, 514 U.S.779, 1995)

SQ 724 **The measure would amend Article V, Section 21 of the State Constitution to restrict the pay of state legislators found guilty of a crime, or those legislators who plead guilty or no contest to a crime.** Adopted. General Election. November 7, 2006.

SQ 748 **The measure amends Sections 11A and 11B of Article 5 of the State Constitution. The measure changes the name of the Apportionment Commission. It removes all three existing commission members, with appointments made by the Governor, Senate President Pro Tempore, and House Speaker. The Lieutenant Governor chairs as a non-voting member.** Adopted. General Election. November 2, 2010.

Libraries

SQ 392 **Additional millage for county libraries.** Adopted. Runoff Election. July 26, 1960.

SQ 507 **Increasing millage for county libraries from 2 to 4 mills.** Adopted. General Election. November 2, 1976.

SQ 666 **Allows all counties the option of funding county library districts with ad valorem taxes approved by voters. Raises cap on the ad valorem tax levy for libraries from four (4) to six (6) mills in certain counties, based on population.** Approved. General Election. November 8, 1994.

Lieutenant Governor

SQ 508   **Added as member of Board of Equalization.** Adopted. Special Election. July 22, 1975.

SQ 514   **Added as member of the Commissioners of the Land Office.** Adopted. Special Election. July 22, 1975.

Loans and Lenders

SQ 454   **Classification of loans and licensing of lenders.** Adopted. Runoff Election. September 17, 1968.

Lotteries

SQ 658   **Would legalize a state lottery.** Rejected. Special Election. May 10, 1994.

SQ 705   **Would create the Oklahoma Education Lottery Act as well as create the Oklahoma Lottery Commission that would operate a state lottery.** Adopted. General Election. November 2, 2004.

SQ 706   **Would create the Oklahoma Education Lottery Trust Fund.** Adopted. General Election. November 2, 2004.

Marriage

SQ 711   **Would add a new section of law to the Constitution defining marriage to be between one man and one woman.** Adopted. General Election. November 2, 2004.

Medical Examiners, Board

SQ 241   **Composition of board and requiring hearings on license revocation.** Rejected. General Election. November 5, 1940.

Medical Service Districts

SQ 476   **Creation of hospital districts through bond issues.** Rejected. Runoff Election. September 15, 1970.

SQ 504   **4-mill levy to provide emergency service districts.** Rejected. Runoff Election. September 17, 1974.

SQ 522   **Providing for emergency medical service districts and election for issuance of bonds.** Adopted. Primary Election. August 24, 1976.

SQ 528   **Authorizing counties to create hospital districts.** Rejected. Primary Election. August 22, 1978.

SQ 678   **Would allow counties or parts of counties to withdraw from an existing ambulance service district if approved by the voters in the county.** Adopted. General Election. November 3, 1998.

Mine Inspector, Chief

SQ 513 **Appointment by governor.** Adopted. Special Election. July 22, 1975.

SQ 594 **Removes mention of Chief Mine Inspector from Constitution. Duties given to Department of Mines.** Adopted. Primary Election. August 26, 1986.

New Jerusalem District

SQ 6 **Centrally located land for model city, public buildings.** Rejected. General Election. November 8, 1910.

Oath of Office

SQ 445 **Oath of office for public officials.** Rejected. General Election. November 5, 1968.

SQ 466 **Form of oath of office for public officials.** Adopted. Special Election. September 9, 1969.

Oil Inspections

SQ 238 **State oil inspections supervised by Tax Commission instead of Corporation Commission.** Rejected. General Election. November 8, 1938.

Oklahoma Military Academy

SQ 346 **Proposing Board of Regents.** Rejected. General Election. November 7, 1950.

SQ 372 **Creating Board of Regents.** Rejected. Primary Election. July 3, 1956.

Oleomargarine

SQ 164 **Repeal of law regulating and taxing.** Referendum Rejected. Law Sustained. General Election. November 8, 1932.

SQ 236 **Regulating and collecting tax by Tax Commission.** Rejected. General Election. November 8, 1938.

Pardon and Parole Board

SQ 309 **Creating board and specifying duties of governor.** Adopted. Primary Election. July 11, 1944.

SQ 446 **Legislature to create new board.** Rejected. Primary Election. August 27, 1968.

SQ 502 **Creating full-time board.** Rejected. Runoff Election. September 17, 1974.

SQ 593 **Neither Pardon and Parole nor governor to grant paroles to convicts sentenced to death.** Adopted. General Election. November 4, 1986.

SQ 664   Would allow legislature to set minimum prison terms for felons. Approved. Primary Election. August 23, 1994.

SQ 762   The measure decreases the power and authority of the governor by removing the governor from the parole process for persons convicted of certain offenses defined as nonviolent offenses. Approved. General Election. November 6, 2102.

Pari-mutuel Betting (See Horse Racing)

Police Officers

SQ 187   Authorizing cities to provide pensions. Rejected. General Election. November 6, 1934.

SQ 207   Authorizing cities to provide pensions. Adopted. General Election. November 3, 1936.

Presidential Electors

SQ 388   Nomination of presidential electors by political parties. Adopted. Primary Election. July 5, 1960.

Prisons

SQ 682   Would allow the state to enter into contracts, up to 15-year terms, with counties and cities for housing of state inmates. Cities and counties could build or add to existing jails to participate. Adopted. General Election. November 3, 1998.

Public Service Corporations (See also Corporation Commission)

SQ 24   Transfer to or consolidation with foreign corporations. Rejected. General Election. November 8, 1910.

SQ 186   Transactions supervised by Corporation Commission. Rejected. General Election. November 6, 1934.

SQ 282   Approval of Corporation Commission for merger or sale. Rejected. General Election. November 5, 1940.

Racial Definitions

SQ 527   Repealing certain racial definitions. Adopted. General Election. November 7, 1978.

Railroad, Transportation, and Transmission Companies

SQ 16 Authorizing incorporation of out-of-state companies. Rejected. Special Election. June 11, 1910.

SQ 25 Same as SQ 16. Rejected. Special Election. April 25, 1911.

SQ 46 Purchase and sale of property or franchise. Adopted. Special Election. August 5, 1913.

SQ 545 Revenue funding for joint public transportation facilities. Rejected. General Election. November 4, 1980.

SQ 592 Allowing railroads to charge more than two cents per mile for any first-class passenger. Adopted. General Election. November 4, 1986.

SQ 643 Repeals necessity of railroad to pass through county seat and build depot when passing within 4 miles of same. Adopted. General Election. November 3, 1992.

Rainy Day Fund

SQ 708 The measure would change the amount which could be spent from the Rainy Day Fund. In the event of revenue failure, up to three-eights of the fund could be spent. The total amount spent from the fund could not exceed the amount of funds shortage predicted by the State Board of Equalization. Adopted. General Election. November 2, 2004.

SQ 725 The measure would allow money to be spent from the Rainy Day Fund to retain employment for state residents by helping at-risk manufacturers. Payments would be made to manufacturers to make investments in Oklahoma. Adopted. General Election. November 7, 2006.

SQ 757 The measure amends Article 10, Section 23 of the State Constitution. It increases the amount of surplus revenue which goes into the Rainy Day Fund. The amount would increase from 10 percent to 15 percent. Adopted. General Election. November 2, 2010.

Real Property, Delinquent Tax

SQ 361 Eliminating or reducing delinquent tax assessment charges. Adopted. General Election. November 2, 1954.

SQ 702 Allows the legislature to enact laws for the abatement of property taxes under certain conditions. Adopted. General Election. November 5, 2002.

Retirement System

SQ 645 Requires that proceeds, assets, and income of certain public retirement systems (state agencies) be held, invested or disbursed as in trust for a limited purpose only. Adopted. General Election. November 3, 1992.

Right-To-Work

SQ 409   Neither membership nor nonmembership in unions as condition of employment. Rejected. Primary Election. May 5, 1964.

SQ 695   Bans new employment contracts that require joining, remaining in, or quitting a labor organization to get or keep a job, and bans contracts requiring dues or other payments to labor organizations, or requiring labor organization approval of an employee to get or keep a job. Adopted. Special Election. September 25, 2002.

Roads and Highways

SQ 398   Transfer of county road construction to Highway Department. Rejected. Special Election. September 20, 1960.

Sales Tax

SQ 226   Increase from 1 to 2 cents for welfare. Adopted. Primary Election. July 7, 1936.

SQ 349   Increasing from 2 to 3 percent. Rejected. General Election. November 4, 1952.

SQ 425   Increase of one cent. Rejected. Special Election. April 27, 1965.

SQ 693   Amends Constitution to allow expanding sources for payment of local bonds issued for economic/community development to include a sales tax not to exceed one cent or apportionment of tax increment financing revenues. Adopted. General Election. November 5, 2002.

School Administration

SQ 671   Amends Constitution to allow school districts to make contracts with school superintendents for more than one year, but no more than three. Adopted. General Election. November 5, 1996.

School Annexation

SQ 423   For those not maintaining 12 years of instruction. Rejected. General Election. November 3, 1964.

School Financing

SQ 23   Statewide distribution of taxes from public service corporations. Rejected. General Election. November 8, 1910.

SQ 45   Legislature to levy taxes for school financing for five months of year. Rejected. General Election. November 5, 1912.

SQ 57   State distribution of taxes from public service corporations. Adopted. Special Election. August 5, 1913.

SQ 59   Tax levy by legislature for five months of year. Rejected. Primary Election. August 4, 1914.

SQ 83   Public service corporation taxation for common school funds. Rejected. Primary Election. August 1, 1916.

SQ 99   Taxing public service corporations for school purposes. Rejected. General Election. November 2, 1920.

SQ 109   Property tax of 6 to 10 mills for common schools. Rejected. General Election. November 2, 1920.

SQ 145   Creating Special Tax Apportionment Fund for common schools. Rejected. General Election. November 2, 1926.

SQ 314   Increasing ad valorem tax rate for school purposes. Adopted. General Election. November 5, 1946.

SQ 315   Appropriating funds on basis of $42 per capita statewide. Adopted. General Election. November 5, 1946.

SQ 316   Additional one mill for school construction. Adopted. General Election. November 5, 1946.

SQ 319   Levying one mill for construction of separate schools. Adopted. Primary Election. July 2, 1946.

SQ 327   Levying one mill for construction of separate schools. Adopted. Primary Election. July 6, 1948.

SQ 368   Ad valorem levies for public schools. Adopted. Special Election. April 5, 1955.

SQ 421   Local support levy for schools. Rejected. General Election. November 3, 1964.

SQ 422   Increasing minimum programs. Rejected. General Election. November 3, 1964.

SQ 430   Local support levy. Adopted. Special Election. September 14, 1965.

SQ 442   Deposit of school funds in banks insured by FDIC. Adopted. Primary Election. August 27, 1968.

SQ 487   Making certain local support levies permanent until repealed. Rejected. General Election. November 7, 1972.

SQ 546   Allowing up to 15 mills on emergency levy. Rejected. General Election. November 4, 1980.

SQ 548   Maximum indebtedness increased from 10 percent to 20 percent. Rejected. General Election. November 4, 1980.

SQ 549   Making emergency and local support levies uniform until repealed. Rejected. General Election. November 4, 1980.

SQ 572   Limit on debt a school district may incur for buildings and equipment increased from 10 to 15 percent. Rejected. General Election. November 6, 1984.

SQ 578   Amending wording and limits on Public Common Building Equalization Fund for school districts. Adopted. Primary Election. August 28, 1984.

SQ 580   Authorize local school district incentive tax levy. Up to 10 mills. Rejected. General Election. November 6, 1984.

SQ 582   Permit taxing of schools and colleges operating for profit. Remove tax for ex-Civil War soldiers and their widows. Adopted. General Election. November 6, 1984.

SQ 599   **Amends the way school funds can be invested.** Adopted. Primary Election. August 26, 1986.

SQ 634   **Changing the way local school property taxes on certain property are distributed with the legislature to decide how the fund is distributed to schools across the state.** Rejected. Special Election. June 26, 1990.

SQ 659   **Affecting the emergency school levy, local support levy and building fund levy, making them permanent until repealed by voters.** Rejected. Annual School election February 8, 1994.

SQ 665   **Allows for laws providing for use of permanent common school fund and other funds to guarantee bonds.** Approved. General Election. November 8, 1994.

SQ 684   **Changing the way the state can use the permanent school fund. The measure allows the state to use more than the fund's income to aid schools. The measure allows the state to diminish the fund itself to aid schools and universities.** Rejected. General Election. November 7, 2000.

SQ 690   **Changing the procedure for voter approval of emergency levy, local support levy and the building fund levy for school districts. Allows each school district to decide to eliminate the need for an annual election for those levies. Once levies are approved, the voters of the school district would also decide whether to allow them to continue from year to year. The vote on levies would change only if another election is held and the voters rescind their prior action.** Adopted. General Election. November 7, 2000.

SQ 704   **Allows school districts to use monies in their building fund for county assessor inspections for ad valorem revaluation purposes.** Rejected. General Election. November 5, 2002.

SQ 744   **The measure adds a new article to the Constitution. It sets a minimum average amount the state must annually spend on common schools. It requires the state to spend annually, no less than the average amount spent on each student by the surrounding states of Missouri, Texas, Kansas, Arkansas, Colorado, and New Mexico.** Rejected. General Election. November 2, 2010.

School Land (See Lands, School and Public)

Schools, County Superintendent of
(See County Superintendent of Schools)

Secretary of State

SQ 508   **Removal from Board of Equalization.** Adopted. Special Election. July 22, 1975.

SQ 511   **Appointment by governor.** Adopted. Special Election. July 22, 1975.

SQ 514   **Removal from Commissioners of the Land Office.** Adopted. Special Election. July 22, 1975.

Segregation

SQ 428   Repealing requirement for separate schools. Adopted. Primary Election. May 3, 1966.

SQ 475   Prohibiting segregation in public schools. Rejected. Runoff Election. September 15, 1970.

SQ 526   Prohibiting segregation in public schools. Adopted. General Election. November 7, 1978.

Senators, United States

SQ 41   Election by direct vote of people. Adopted. Primary Election. August 6, 1912.

Sentencing

SQ 525   Allowing legislature to prescribe minimum mandatory sentence for persons convicted of third felony. Adopted. General Election. November 7, 1978.

Silent Vote (See Constitution, State SQ 495 and 496)

Slot Machines (See Gambling, SQ 62 and 216)

State Appropriations

SQ 754   Adds a new section to the State Constitution. The measure would prohibit the Constitution from requiring the legislature from funding state functions based on predetermined constitutional formulas; how much others states spend on functions; and how much any entity spends on a function. Rejected. General Election. November 2, 2010.

State Capitol

SQ 3   Location of capitol by vote of people. Rejected. General Election. November 3, 1908.

SQ 4   Obtaining site for capitol. Rejected. General Election. November 3, 1908.

SQ 15   Locating capitol in Oklahoma City. Adopted. Special Election. June 11, 1910.

SQ 40   Location at Guthrie. Rejected. General Election. November 5, 1912.

State Offices

SQ 122   Qualifications for certain elective offices. Adopted. Special Election. October 2, 1923. (Supreme Court ruled election invalid.)

SQ 122   (Resubmitted) Qualifications for certain elective officers. Rejected. General Election. November 2, 1930.

SQ 281   Qualifications for elective offices. Rejected. General Election. November 5, 1940.

SQ 302   Qualifications for elective officers. Adopted. General Election. November 3, 1942.

SQ 436   Limiting governor to two terms; secretary of state, auditor, treasurer eligible to succeed self. Adopted. Primary Election. May 3, 1966.

SQ 456   Permitting change in salary of elected or appointive officer during terms. Rejected. Primary Election. August 27, 1968.

SQ 747   This measure amends sections 4 and 23 of Articles 6 and section 15 of Article 9 of the State Constitution. It limits the ability of voters to re-elect statewide elected officers by limiting how many years those officers can serve. It limits the number of years a person may serve in each statewide elected office. Service as governor is limited to eight years; lieutenant governor is limited to eight years; attorney general is limited to eight years; treasurer is limited to eight years; commissioner of labor is limited to eight years; auditor and inspector is limited to eight years; superintendent of public instruction is limited to eight years; insurance commissioner is limited to eight years; and corporation commissioner is limited to twelve years. Adopted. General Election. November 2, 2010.

Sunday Closing

SQ 478   Prohibiting sale of certain merchandise on consecutive days of Saturday and Sunday. Rejected. Special Election. December 7, 1971.

Superintendent of Public Instruction
(See Equalization Board, SQ 508)

Superintendent of Schools, County
(See County Superintendent of Schools)

Tax Commission

SQ 81   Creating Tax Commission and abolishing Board of Equalization. Rejected. Primary Election. August 1, 1916.

SQ 679   Would allow salaries of Corporation Commissioners and members of the Oklahoma Tax Commission to be raised at any time so long as pay was equal. Rejected. General Election. November 3, 1998.

Taxation (See also Ad Valorem, Income Tax, Sales Tax, School Financing)

SQ 75   Levy on mining, oil and gas. Rejected. General Election. November 3, 1914.

SQ 141   **Procedure for testing tax levy.** Adopted. Primary Election. August 3, 1926. (Supreme Court ruled unconstitutional.)

SQ 226   **Increasing motor vehicle excise tax from 1 to 2 percent.** Adopted. Primary Election. July 7, 1936.

SQ 253   **Apportionment of motor vehicle and gasoline taxes.** Rejected. General Election. November 5, 1940.

SQ 361   **Minimizing delinquent tax assessment charges against real property.** Adopted. General Election. November 2, 1954.

SQ 444   **Legislature to define amounts and imposition.** Adopted. Primary Election. August 27, 1968.

SQ 544   **Levying for public and private transportation systems.** Rejected. General Election. November 4, 1980.

SQ 590   **Poll tax to be removed because it is obsolete.** Adopted. General Election. November 4, 1986.

SQ 597   **Allowing tax to be placed on federal property obtained by foreclosure of bankruptcy, unless tax prohibited by federal law.** Adopted. General Election. November 4, 1986.

SQ 604   **Would allow cities to vote extra millage.** Adopted. Presidential Preferential Primary Election, March 8, 1988.

SQ 618   **This measure would require the legislature to define the term, "manufacturing facility," by law, for purposes of the property tax exemption.** Adopted. Primary Election, August 23, 1988.

SQ 640   **Would require approval of majority of voters before revenue bills could become law unless approved by three-fourths of each house of the legislature.** Adopted. Special Election. March 10, 1992.

SQ 648   **Would give counties the option of exempting household goods and certain livestock from ad valorem taxation.** Adopted. General Election. November 3, 1992.

SQ 685   **Allows counties to increase property tax by up to two and one-half mills to support county health departments. The new tax will only be allowed in counties with more than 500,000 persons and must be approved by county voters.** Rejected. General Election. November 7, 2000.

SQ 707   **The measure would allow cities, towns, or counties to use taxes and fees for specific public investments, development financing, or as an income source for other public bodies in the area.** Adopted. General Election. November 2, 2004.

SQ 715   **The measure would allow property tax exemptions for certain injured veterans or their surviving spouses. The exemption would be for the full fair cash value of the homestead.** Adopted. General Election. November 2, 2004.

SQ 723   **The measure would add Article XVI-A to the Oklahoma Constitution, creating a Bridge and Highway Trust Fund. The provision would levy new gasoline and diesel fuel taxes, of which 80 percent would go into the trust fund.** Rejected. Special Election. September 13, 2005.

SQ 734   **The measure would provide a property tax exemption to goods that are shipped into the state, but do not remain in the state for more than ninety days.** Adopted. General Election, November 7, 2006.

SQ 735   The measure amends the Oklahoma Constitution. It creates an exemption from personal property tax. The exemption would be for the full amount of taxes due on all household personal property. The exemption would apply to certain injured veterans. It would also apply to those veterans' surviving spouses. Adopted. General Election. November 4, 2008.

SQ 741   The measure amends the Oklahoma Constitution. It is related to exemptions from property taxes. It would require a person or business to file an application for an exemption. No exemption could be granted prior to filing an application. Adopted. General Election. November 4, 2008.

Teacher Retirement

SQ 242   Authorization legislature to provide retirement, death, and disability benefits. Rejected. General Election. November 8, 1938.

SQ 303   Authorizing legislature to provide retirement system. Rejected. General Election. November 3, 1942.

SQ 306   Creating state system. Adopted. Primary Election. July 14, 1942.

Textbooks

SQ 137   Repeal of free textbook bill. Referendum Rejected. Law Sustained. General Election. November 2, 1926.

SQ 172   Creating Board of Education, Textbook Committee and free textbooks. Rejected. Special Election. December 18, 1931.

SQ 318   Free textbooks for all school pupils. Adopted. General Election. November 5, 1946.

Tobacco

SQ 692   Creates the Tobacco Settlement Endowment Trust Fund. A percentage of payments received shall be deposited in the trust fund. The percentage goes from 50 percent for the fiscal year ending June 2002 to 75 percent for any fiscal year ending 2007 or after. Monies not deposited in the trust fund shall be subject to legislative appropriations. The trust fund would be managed by a board of directors consisting of members appointed by various state officials and chaired by the state treasurer. Adopted. General Election. November 7, 2000.

SQ 701   Limits the annual expenditure from the Tobacco Settlement Endowment Trust Fund to five and one-half percent of the Fund's average market value. Rejected. General Election. November 5, 2002.

SQ 713   The measure would end sales tax on cigarettes and other tobacco products. The measure places a new tax on cigarettes. The measure places a new tax on other tobacco products. Adopted. General Election. November 2, 2004.

Township Government

SQ 58   **Establishing or abolishing township government.** Adopted. Special Election. August 5, 1913.

Transportation

SQ 555   **Directing legislature to establish procedures for creation of transportation districts.** Rejected. Primary Election. August 24, 1982.

SQ 579   **Transportation service districts, formation, and funding.** Rejected. General Election. November 6, 1984.

Treasurer, State

SQ 469   **State Treasurer sole authority over deposit of state funds. Act** Rejected. General Election. November 3, 1970.

SQ 559   **Trust Fund.** Rejected. Primary Election. August 24, 1982.

SQ 692   **Creates the Tobacco Settlement Endowment Trust Fund. A percentage of payments received shall be deposited in the trust fund. The percentage goes from 50 percent for the fiscal year ending June 2002 to 75 percent for any fiscal year ending 2007 or after. Monies not deposited in the trust fund shall be subject to legislative appropriations. The trust fund would be managed by a board of directors consisting of members appointed by various state officials and chaired by the state treasurer.** Adopted. General Election. November 7, 2000.

Turnpikes

SQ 359   **Repealing Turnpike Projects in SB 454.** Act Adopted. Law Sustained. Special Election. January 26, 1954.

SQ 360   **Providing new turnpike routes.** Act Adopted. Law Sustained. Special Election. January 26, 1954.

Unemployment Relief

SQ 171   **Creating public works projects.** Rejected. Primary Election. July 5, 1932.

United Nations

SQ 344   **Supporting United Nations; urging world federal government.** Rejected. General Election. November 7, 1951.

Utilities, Public

SQ 205   **Government indebtedness to acquire public utilities.** Rejected. General Election. November 8, 1938.

SQ 574   **Indebtedness to finance public utilities.** Rejected. General Election. November 6, 1984.

Vehicle Registration

SQ 524   **Establishing staggered five-year tags and mail-order system.** Adopted. General Election. November 7, 1978.

SQ 691   **Changes vehicle registration fees and taxes. Annual registration fees change to a flat fee based on the number of years registered. The fee would be $85.00 for years one through four, $75 for years five through eight, $55 for years nine though twelve, and $35 for years thirteen through sixteen and $15 for years seventeen and over. The method of calculating vehicle excise tax would change, basing the excise tax on the actual sales price instead of the existing arbitrary formula. Also reduces tag costs for recreational vehicles.** Adopted. Primary Election. August 22, 2000.

Veterans

SQ 116   **Bonus for World War I.** Rejected. General Election. November 7, 1922.

SQ 123   **Benefits for World War I.** Rejected. Special Election. October 2, 1923.

SQ 355   **State veterans' bonus.** Rejected. General Election. November 4, 1952.

SQ 362   **Providing farm loans.** Adopted. Primary Election. July 6, 1954.

SQ 369   **Veterans Loan Authority for farm and home loans.** Rejected. Primary Election. July 3, 1956.

SQ 370   **Repealing authority for loans to veterans from school funds.** Rejected. Primary Election. July 3, 1956.

Victims and Victims' Rights (See Crime Victims)

Vocational-Technical Education

SQ 434   **Authorizing area school districts; five-mill levy.** Adopted. Runoff Election. May 24, 1966.

Voting

SQ 17   **Would prohibit voting unless voter is able to read and write any section of State Constitution. Further, any person who, prior to January 1, 1866, lived in a foreign nation, or any lineal descendent of such person, who was entitled to** vote under any form of government, would not be denied the right to register and vote because of his inability to read or write. Adopted. Primary Election. August 2, 1910. (Note: Found by U.S. Supreme Court in Guinn v. U.S., 238 U.S. 347, 1915, to be in violation of the 15ᵗʰ Amendment to U.S. Constitution.)

SQ 80 **Initiative measure only method to enact law for registration of electors.** Rejected. General Election. November 7, 1916.

SQ 82 **Literacy test for electors.** Rejected. Primary Election. August 1, 1916.

SQ 356 **Lowering voting age to 18.** Rejected. General Election. November 4, 1952.

SQ 412 **Residency requirements for voting.** Adopted. Primary Election. May 5, 1964.

SQ 432 **Waiving residency requirements in presidential elections.** Adopted. Primary Election. May 3, 1966.

SQ 484 **Providing 18–year-old vote.** Adopted. Special Election. December 7, 1971.

SQ 488 **Removing requirements voters be property taxpayers in municipal public utility bond elections.** Rejected. Primary Election. August 22, 1972.

SQ 503 **Removing durational residency requirements.** Rejected. Primary Election. August 27, 1974.

SQ 746 **The measure requires that each person appearing to vote present a document providing their identity. The document must have a name and photograph of the voter, and it must have been issued by the federal, state, or tribal government.** Adopted. General Election. November 2, 2010.

Voting Machines

SQ 464 **Eliminating straight-party voting in elections where there are nonpartisan and retention candidates.** Rejected. General Election. November 3, 1970.

Water

SQ 558 **Amending Article X of the Constitution to allow the legislature to incur indebtedness and make grants or gifts for water resource development and sewage treatment.** Rejected. General Election. November 2, 1982.

Welfare Assistance (See Elderly)

Wildlife Conservation Commission

SQ 374 **Creating commission and department.** Adopted. Primary Election. July 3, 1956.

SQ 742 **The measure adds a new section to the State Constitution. Allows all people of this state the right to hunt, trap, fish, and take game and fish. It allows the Wildlife Conservation Commission to approve methods and procedures for hunting, trapping, fishing, and taking of game and fish. It allows for taking of game and fish by traditional means.** Adopted. General Election. November 4, 2008.

Witnesses

SQ 482   **Immunity from prosecution.** Adopted. Special Election. December 7, 1971.

Women

SQ 8   **Women's right to vote.** Rejected. General Election. November 8, 1910.

SQ 97   **Universal suffrage.** Adopted. General Election. November 5, 1918.

SQ 211   **Eligible for elective state office.** Rejected. Special Election. September 24, 1935.

SQ 281   **Qualifications for elective officers, including allowing women to run for office.** Rejected. General Election. November 5, 1940.

SQ 302   **Qualifications for elective officers, including allowing women to run for office.** Adopted. General Election. November 3, 1942.

SQ 354   **Women on juries.** Adopted. Primary Election. July 1, 1952.

SQ 371   **Creating Board of Regents for Oklahoma College for Women.** Rejected. Primary Election. July 3, 1956.

SQ 517   **Repealing archaic provisions for women to vote only in school elections.** Adopted. General Election. November 2, 1976.

Worker's Compensation

SQ 86   **Legislation to provide death and injury benefits.** Rejected. Primary Election. August 1, 1916.

SQ 121   **Compulsory compensation in case of death or permanent, partial disability.** Rejected. Special Election. October 2, 1923.

SQ 304   **No statutory limit on amount recoverable.** Rejected. General Election. November 11, 1942.

SQ 345   **Compensation for death resulting from injuries during employment.** Adopted. Primary Election. July 4, 1950.

SQ 571   **Right to sue for damages resulting in death.** Rejected. General Election. November 6, 1984.

SQ 586   **Allowing legislature to set statutory limits on damages recovered from personal injuries resulting in death.** Adopted. Special Election. April 30, 1985.

County-by-County Vote for Governor
General Election, November 4, 2014

County	Joe Dorman (D)	Mary Fallin (R)	County	Joe Dorman (D)	Mary Fallin (R)
Adair	2,501	3,023	LeFlore	5,950	7,040
Alfalfa	737	1,301	Lincoln	3,838	6,976
Atoka	1,500	2,231	Logan	4,098	8,848
Beaver	321	1,564	Love	1,107	1,554
Beckham	1,994	3,471	Major	791	2,221
Blaine	1,100	2,061	Marshall	1,485	2,528
Bryan	4,346	6,115	Mayes	4,768	6,992
Caddo	3,602	3,723	McClain	3,817	7,248
Canadian	9,964	24,964	McCurtain	4,035	4,312
Carter	4,461	8,478	McIntosh	2,921	3,244
Cherokee	5,609	5,850	Murray	1,802	2,177
Choctaw	1,843	2,227	Muskogee	8,348	9,405
Cimarron	263	734	Noble	1,200	2,782
Cleveland	30,467	42,797	Nowata	1,300	1,981
Coal	958	1,052	Okfuskee	1,405	1,619
Comanche	10,950	10,827	Oklahoma	82,316	111,614
Cotton	1,007	818	Okmulgee	4,906	5,393
Craig	1,834	2,470	Osage	6,473	7,938
Creek	7,034	13,377	Ottawa	3,138	3,985
Custer	2,654	5,061	Pawnee	1,813	3,030
Delaware	4,127	7,304	Payne	8,258	11,633
Dewey	557	1,307	Pittsburg	5,671	6,808
Ellis	415	1,105	Pontotoc	4,412	5,365
Garfield	5,318	11,515	Pottawatomie	6,536	11,832
Garvin	3,641	5,254	Pushmataha	1,525	1,901
Grady	5,741	10,031	Roger Mills	413	923
Grant	613	1,199	Rogers	9,171	18,874
Greer	683	892	Seminole	2,689	3,637
Harmon	334	420	Sequoyah	4,497	5,659
Harper	331	899	Stephens	8,217	6,458
Haskell	1,525	1,901	Texas	889	3,545
Hughes	1,642	1,881	Tillman	1,020	1,083
Jackson	2,050	3,950	Tulsa	63,558	105,060
Jefferson	553	639	Wagoner	6,678	14,314
Johnston	1,231	1,713	Washington	5,039	11,548
Kay	4,970	8,656	Washita	1,333	2,265
Kingfisher	1,295	3,504	Woods	1,043	2,042
Kiowa	1,250	1,424	Woodward	1,523	4,082
Latimer	1,467	1,610	Total	338,239	460,298

County Election Tables
Vote for President and Governor

Presidential years are in bolder type.

Year	Dem	Rep	Other	Total
		Adair		
1907	922	718	6	1646
1908	825	782	26	1633
1910	753	693	35	1481
1912	916	850	162	1928
1914	1182	1028	183	2393
1916	1190	1010	221	2421
1918	1019	923	30	1972
1920	1560	2020	25	3605
1922	2470	1901	28	4399
1924	1942	2317	229	4488
1926	1796	1926	8	3730
1928	1944	2867	20	4831
1930	2658	2263	4	4925
1932	3812	1941	0	5753
1934	2793	3271	358	6099
1936	3257	2699	16	5972
1938	3573	2125	21	5719
1940	3203	3275	6	6484
1942	2368	2205	10	4583
1944	2760	2792	12	5564
1946	2684	1982	20	4686
1948	3067	2407	0	5474
1950	2834	2808	6	5648
1952	2725	3037	0	5762
1954	2988	1905	0	4893
1956	2418	3152	0	5570
1958	3136	1651	43	4830
1960	1903	3655	0	5558
1962	2419	2652	8	5079
1964	3003	2859	0	5862
1966	2484	2336	18	4838
1968	1549	2877	1000	5426
1970	2471	2204	158	4833
1972	1601	4720	134	6455
1974	3306	2165	0	5471
1976	3183	3013	63	6259
1978	2746	2223	116	5085
1980	2761	6429	151	9341
1982	4112	1965	10	6087
1984	2266	4423	56	6745
1986	2900	2745	176	5821
1988	2624	3558	58	6240
1990	2512	1168	314	3994
1992	2645	2994	944	6583
1994	1937	2063	918	4918
1996	2792	2956	773	6521
1998	2140	2111	61	4312
2000	2361	3503	113	5977

Year	Dem	Rep	Other	Total
2002	2803	2374	874	6051
2004	2562	4971	0	7533
2006	3253	1565	0	4818
2008	2052	4638	0	6690
2010	2501	3023	0	5524
2012	2127	4381	0	5524
2014	1737	2238	174	4149
		Alfalfa		
1907	1323	1698	122	3143
1908	1459	1732	179	3370
1910	1288	1883	369	3540
1912	1179	1714	484	3377
1914	954	1239	832	3025
1916	1390	1378	546	3314
1918	892	1393	173	2458
1920	1350	3004	348	4702
1922	1659	3025	50	4734
1924	1558	2967	656	5181
1926	1824	3017	38	4879
1928	1086	4224	107	5417
1930	2341	2428	7	4776
1932	3642	2037	0	5679
1934	2378	3399	120	5897
1936	3398	2573	55	6026
1938	2556	2644	84	5284
1940	2720	3675	60	6455
1942	1454	2414	33	3901
1944	1716	3434	32	5182
1946	1060	2318	114	3492
1948	1838	2765	0	4603
1950	1683	2858	7	4548
1952	1118	4155	0	5273
1954	1214	2445	0	3659
1956	1371	3251	0	4622
1958	1881	1268	397	3546
1960	1067	3332	0	4399
1962	977	3061	9	4047
1964	1730	2450	0	4180
1966	1018	2320	7	3345
1968	865	2672	310	3847
1970	1258	1949	77	3284
1972	641	3208	88	3937
1974	1761	1699	0	3460
1976	1725	2113	59	3897
1978	1215	1974	20	3209
1980	899	2628	115	3642
1982	1969	1012	2	2983
1984	866	2715	27	3608
1986	1147	1422	313	2882

Year	Dem	Rep	Other	Total
1988	1117	1960	55	3132
1990	1313	874	472	2659
1992	741	1567	737	3045
1994	550	1017	774	2341
1996	796	1504	363	2663
1998	726	1367	23	2116
2000	583	1886	38	2507
2002	782	964	297	2,043
2004	470	2201	0	2671
2006	1389	683	0	2072
2008	411	2023	0	2434
2010	737	1301	0	2038
2012	322	1761	0	2083
2014	530	972	46	1548

Atoka

Year	Dem	Rep	Other	Total
1907	1261	851	98	2210
1908	784	757	198	1739
1910	1005	630	208	1843
1912	1100	669	577	2346
1914	1135	900	954	2989
1916	1479	925	540	2944
1918	1346	1039	53	2438
1920	2103	2078	636	4817
1922	3623	2022	19	5664
1924	2204	1130	725	4059
1926	1700	1099	37	2836
1928	2056	1572	33	3661
1930	2544	592	0	3136
1932	3678	562	0	4240
1934	3273	1576	117	4966
1936	3173	1141	9	4323
1938	3192	546	8	3746
1940	3601	2218	13	5832
1942	1499	669	9	2177
1944	2172	1515	6	3693
1946	1993	792	21	2806
1948	3104	1033	0	4137
1950	2867	1131	2	4000
1952	2654	2004	0	4658
1954	3017	915	0	3932
1956	2424	1731	0	4155
1958	2068	271	86	2425
1960	1759	1892	0	3651
1962	1827	1632	19	3478
1964	2459	1424	0	3883
1966	1754	1166	14	2934
1968	1400	1131	1613	4144
1970	2381	905	260	3546
1972	933	2905	89	3927
1974	3207	579	0	3786
1976	3276	1098	28	4402
1978	2341	1079	31	3451
1980	2505	1613	98	4216
1982	3351	624	5	3980
1984	2047	2361	36	4444
1986	2520	1505	148	4173

Year	Dem	Rep	Other	Total
1988	2565	1971	34	4570
1990	2826	818	149	3793
1992	2336	1561	1270	5167
1994	761	839	2019	3619
1996	2281	1542	550	4373
1998	1746	1658	50	3454
2000	1906	2375	43	4324
2002	2429	1211	181	3821
2004	1946	3142	0	5088
2006	2372	806	0	3178
2008	1370	3511	0	4881
2010	1500	2231	0	3731
2012	1243	3538	0	4781
2014	1527	1825	135	3487

Beaver

Year	Dem	Rep	Other	Total
1907	1245	1235	109	2589
1908	1212	1362	197	2771
1910	963	1204	268	2435
1912	926	1070	520	2516
1914	791	940	429	2160
1916	1382	917	479	2778
1918	878	978	74	1930
1920	1068	1965	240	3273
1922	1408	1885	45	3338
1924	1195	1565	407	3167
1926	1134	1137	44	2315
1928	887	2596	41	3524
1930	1754	1226	10	2990
1932	2553	1358	0	3911
1934	1651	2278	64	3993
1936	2502	1340	21	3863
1938	1256	2087	14	3357
1940	2034	2219	29	4282
1942	1385	1160	24	2569
1944	1355	1913	27	3295
1946	1068	1040	43	2151
1948	1596	1420	0	3016
1950	1446	1502	5	2953
1952	819	2539	0	3358
1954	1299	1450	0	2749
1956	946	2046	0	2992
1958	788	585	107	1480
1960	887	2442	0	3329
1962	879	1901	3	2783
1964	1508	1982	0	3490
1966	1012	1333	11	2356
1968	624	2114	339	3077
1970	1254	1005	25	2284
1972	522	2562	102	3186
1974	1530	894	0	2424
1976	1213	1801	47	3061
1978	1125	1308	19	2452
1980	696	2430	92	3218
1982	1471	832	3	2306
1984	536	2689	27	3252
1986	599	1828	101	2528

Year	Dem	Rep	Other	Total
1988	777	2013	44	2834
1990	1025	1082	212	2319
1992	580	1699	571	2850
1994	416	1252	456	2124
1996	515	1893	203	2611
1998	466	1529	45	2040
2000	339	2092	25	2456
2002	561	1297	119	1977
2004	297	2272	0	2569
2006	857	990	0	1847
2008	265	2199	0	2464
2010	321	1564	0	1885
2012	244	2062	0	2306
2014	343	1110	63	1516

Beckham

Year	Dem	Rep	Other	Total
1907	2010	778	214	3002
1908	1807	866	498	3171
1910	1524	626	723	2873
1912	1566	648	892	3106
1914	964	719	1139	2822
1916	1850	527	898	3275
1918	1253	600	138	1991
1920	2343	1743	644	4730
1922	3109	1690	53	4852
1924	2496	1357	534	4387
1926	1929	764	41	2734
1928	2201	3810	101	6112
1930	3349	985	0	4334
1932	5979	892	7	6878
1934	3889	1861	294	6044
1936	5372	1352	56	6780
1938	2958	730	27	3715
1940	4598	2148	42	6788
1942	1279	773	15	2067
1944	3608	2034	15	5657
1946	2552	1148	108	3808
1948	4544	1310	0	5854
1950	3354	1863	14	5231
1952	3972	4504	0	8476
1954	3206	1767	0	4973
1956	3561	3194	0	6755
1958	2659	537	173	3369
1960	2721	4258	0	6979
1962	2483	3157	10	5650
1964	4115	2557	0	6672
1966	2223	2508	15	4746
1968	2354	2935	1550	6839
1970	2596	1687	110	4393
1972	1608	4472	155	6235
1974	4131	1262	0	5393
1976	4530	2351	54	6935
1978	2325	2441	17	4783
1980	3298	3637	178	7113
1982	3765	1439	1	5205
1984	2601	5005	48	7654
1986	4035	2038	260	6333

Year	Dem	Rep	Other	Total
1988	3388	3463	64	6915
1990	4041	1321	299	5661
1992	2947	2913	1960	7820
1994	1590	2235	1516	5341
1996	2797	2912	842	6551
1998	1641	2673	32	4346
2000	2408	4067	57	6532
2002	2105	2511	649	5265
2004	1931	5454	0	4421
2006	3423	1394	0	4817
2008	1625	5772	0	7397
2010	1994	3471	0	5465
2012	1417	5508	0	6925
2014	1701	2785	166	4652

Blaine

Year	Dem	Rep	Other	Total
1907	1469	1735	174	3378
1908	1317	1598	341	3256
1910	1286	1484	356	3126
1912	744	831	374	1949
1914	921	1260	702	2883
1916	1214	1339	715	3268
1918	831	1242	278	2351
1920	1292	2782	436	4510
1922	2314	2807	85	5206
1924	1488	2255	904	4647
1926	1639	1935	55	3629
1928	1543	3413	76	5032
1930	2426	2680	416	5522
1932	4719	1728	77	6524
1934	3362	3073	45	6480
1936	4242	2877	41	7160
1938	3060	2574	31	5665
1940	3095	4080	14	7189
1942	1112	2426	0	3538
1944	2097	3480	0	5577
1946	1507	2463	102	4072
1948	2595	2835	0	5430
1950	2186	3448	13	5647
1952	1826	4851	0	6677
1954	2139	2996	0	5135
1956	1844	3855	0	5699
1958	2459	1411	372	4242
1960	1725	3646	0	5371
1962	1371	3273	15	4659
1964	2384	2741	0	5125
1966	1371	2693	16	4080
1968	1285	3036	732	5053
1970	1517	2267	140	3924
1972	963	3958	171	5092
1974	2548	2043	0	4591
1976	2297	2682	77	5056
1978	1445	2886	15	4346
1980	1399	3708	157	5264
1982	2840	1736	4	4580
1984	1484	4037	33	5554
1986	1967	2120	463	4550

Year	Dem	Rep	Other	Total
1988	1775	2889	70	4734
1990	2517	1262	730	4509
1992	1564	2209	1279	5052
1994	1076	1803	1355	4234
1996	1832	2127	578	4537
1998	1052	2161	56	3269
2000	1402	2633	59	4094
2002	1554	1285	553	3392
2004	1222	3199	0	4421
2006	2192	961	0	3153
2008	1011	3101	0	4112
2010	1100	2061	0	3161
2012	992	2824	0	3816
2014	970	1589	84	2643

Bryan

Year	Dem	Rep	Other	Total
1907	2923	1234	264	4421
1908	2215	1044	462	3721
1910	2234	948	576	3758
1912	2278	711	823	3812
1914	2429	912	1427	4768
1916	2974	1267	766	5007
1918	2234	609	109	2952
1920	4502	3127	424	8053
1922	6545	1543	25	8113
1924	4593	1780	699	7072
1926	3440	1328	28	4796
1928	3885	3014	51	6950
1930	5355	1099	3	6457
1932	7681	825	0	8506
1934	6360	1892	111	8363
1936	8106	1362	20	9488
1938	5255	420	15	5690
1940	9095	2190	25	11310
1942	3194	767	10	3971
1944	7180	1677	17	8874
1946	4746	830	71	5647
1948	7748	1366	0	9114
1950	5633	1241	15	6889
1952	6739	3340	0	10079
1954	6013	1172	0	7185
1956	5729	2939	0	8668
1958	4253	352	48	4653
1960	4428	3845	0	8273
1962	3841	2355	14	6210
1964	5934	2652	0	8586
1966	3570	1694	9	5273
1968	3214	2727	2264	8205
1970	4483	1592	421	6496
1972	3144	5397	177	8718
1974	6965	919		7884
1976	7410	2848	35	10293
1978	4594	1475	33	6102
1980	6410	3980	192	10582
1982	6928	1234	9	8171
1984	5475	6246	48	11769
1986	5920	2757	129	8806

Year	Dem	Rep	Other	Total
1988	6849	4615	37	11501
1990	5805	1969	284	8058
1992	6259	3452	3757	13468
1994	2251	1683	5855	9789
1996	5962	3943	1430	11335
1998	3772	4476	83	8331
2000	5554	6084	108	11746
2002	6158	3422	383	9963
2004	5745	8615	0	14360
2006	6310	1671	0	7981
2008	4426	9307	0	13733
2010	4346	6115	0	10461
2012	3681	9520	0	13201
2014	4122	4337	299	8758

Caddo

Year	Dem	Rep	Other	Total
1907	3161	2873	202	6236
1908	2964	2860	423	6247
1910	2623	2734	629	5986
1912	2514	2413	1048	5975
1914	1934	2447	1167	5548
1916	2735	2272	1174	6181
1918	1949	2309	155	4413
1920	3581	4818	653	9052
1922	5075	4496	127	9698
1924	4211	4388	931	9530
1926	3985	4202	81	8268
1928	3885	7313	180	11378
1930	6647	4177	9	10833
1932	11001	2972	0	13973
1934	6396	5066	780	12242
1936	9358	5205	106	14669
1938	6492	2911	62	9465
1940	8280	6304	61	14645
1942	3444	3136	29	6609
1944	6850	5539	24	12413
1946	4681	3131	124	7936
1948	8110	3793	0	11903
1950	5925	4192	25	10142
1952	6153	6834	0	12987
1954	6064	3094	0	9158
1956	5884	5331	0	11215
1958	5138	1327	672	7137
1960	5115	5920	0	11035
1962	4740	4820	19	9579
1964	7447	3724	0	11171
1966	3845	3851	32	7728
1968	4212	4712	1858	10782
1970	4851	3681	182	8714
1972	2921	7683	308	10912
1974	6488	2456	0	8944
1976	7382	3854	91	11327
1978	4646	3957	57	8660
1980	4695	5945	355	10995
1982	5907	2204	11	8122
1984	4463	6811	67	11341
1986	5105	3345	538	8988

County Election for President and Governor

Year	Dem	Rep	Other	Total	Year	Dem	Rep	Other	Total
1988	5387	4689	101	10177	1988	7453	17872	205	25530
1990	5833	1846	723	8402	1990	10200	8721	2663	21584
1992	4861	3664	2963	11488	1992	7215	16756	9079	33050
1994	2705	2607	2618	7930	1994	5460	15004	4322	24786
1996	4844	3422	1404	9670	1996	8977	18139	3420	30536
1998	3077	3598	68	6743	1998	5292	15873	244	21409
2000	4272	4835	103	9210	2000	8367	22679	314	31360
2002	3948	2341	1463	7752	2002	9658	14422	4485	28565
2004	3916	6491	0	10407	2004	9712	33297	0	43009
2006	4990	1742	0	6732	2006	16188	11565	0	27753
2008	3404	6413	0	9817	2008	11426	36428	0	47854
2010	3602	3723	0	7325	2010	9964	24964	0	34928
2012	3164	5687	0	8851	2012	10537	35625	0	46162
2014	3082	2625	112	5819	2014	8708	18456	850	28014

Canadian / Carter

Year	Dem	Rep	Other	Total	Year	Dem	Rep	Other	Total
1907	2102	1790	95	3987	1907	2672	1543	252	4467
1908	2124	1931	157	4212	1908	2181	1305	587	4073
1910	1941	2144	318	4403	1910	2116	899	461	3476
1912	2047	1794	379	4220	1912	1860	652	713	3225
1914	1594	1749	468	3811	1914	1998	727	1152	3877
1916	2200	1590	469	4259	1916	2949	1013	946	4908
1918	1529	1362	120	3011	1918	2083	639	94	2816
1920	3268	3875	291	7434	1920	6003	3555	576	10134
1922	3680	3708	59	7447	1922	6149	3344	90	9583
1924	3065	3070	1262	7397	1924	7134	3164	564	10862
1926	2502	2233	110	4845	1926	5543	2392	58	7993
1928	2786	5011	78	7875	1928	5086	6538	92	11716
1930	3879	3029	9	6917	1930	6467	1865	11	8343
1932	6767	2549	0	9316	1932	9633	1733	0	11366
1934	4173	3078	325	7576	1934	7014	3706	237	10957
1936	6135	3325	48	9508	1936	9387	2247	35	11669
1938	4860	2746	49	7655	1938	6054	834	26	6914
1940	5506	4699	32	10237	1940	10441	3270	35	13746
1942	2201	3075	39	5315	1942	3627	1147	13	4787
1944	4800	4674	18	9492	1944	9184	2446	24	11654
1946	3706	3179	257	7142	1946	5363	1557	67	6987
1948	5568	3729	0	9297	1948	9474	2147	0	11621
1950	3706	4725	51	8482	1950	6928	2900	22	9850
1952	4203	7289	0	11492	1952	10276	5974	0	16250
1954	3622	3708	0	7330	1954	7043	2135	0	9178
1956	3896	5702	0	9598	1956	9341	5974	0	15315
1958	5055	1545	612	7212	1958	7364	713	215	8292
1960	4234	5697	0	9931	1960	8441	6288	0	14729
1962	3300	5081	32	8413	1962	6885	5,082	22	7620
1964	5747	5193	0	10940	1964	10645	4986	0	15631
1966	3485	5256	40	8781	1966	5903	4254	24	10181
1968	3577	5891	2525	11993	1968	5807	5127	3414	14348
1970	4030	4934	383	9347	1970	5829	4092	538	10459
1972	2751	11400	413	14564	1972	4577	9368	161	14106
1974	7996	5243	0	13239	1974	8071	2041	0	10112
1976	7288	9766	285	17339	1976	8319	6668	83	15070
1978	5432	8085	108	13625	1978	6044	4690	68	10802
1980	4889	15272	880	21041	1980	6509	9262	383	16154
1982	9290	7872	19	17181	1982	8404	3772	15	12191
1984	5245	20929	146	26320	1984	6161	11578	83	17822
1986	7761	9426	2633	19820	1986	6963	5658	576	13197

Year	Dem	Rep	Other	Total	Year	Dem	Rep	Other	Total
1988	7988	8430	117	16535	1988	6483	5838	103	12424
1990	8249	3557	906	12712	1990	6750	2180	947	9877
1992	7171	5947	5250	18368	1992	6794	4977	3340	15111
1994	3316	3788	5352	12456	1994	4569	3620	2265	10454
1996	6979	6769	2056	15804	1996	6817	5046	1833	13696
1998	5124	6978	112	12214	1998	5540	4083	123	9746
2000	6659	9667	132	16458	2000	7256	6918	294	14468
2002	7099	5458	900	13457	2002	6549	3731	2520	12800
2004	6466	12178	0	18644	2004	8623	9569	0	18192
2006	7348	3032	0	10380	2006	7903	2495	0	10398
2008	5603	13241	0	18844	2008	7194	9186	0	16380
2010	4461	8478	0	12939	2010	5609	5850	0	11459
2012	4908	12214	0	17122	2012	6144	8162	0	14306
2014	4241	5990	494	10725	2014	4655	4093	337	9085

	Cherokee					Choctaw			
1907	1248	1161	25	2434	1907	1554	1167	107	2828
1908	913	1040	47	2000	1908	1038	878	312	2228
1910	1291	1208	84	2583	1910	1202	764	579	2545
1912	1094	962	148	2204	1912	1392	692	723	2807
1914	1424	1325	426	3175	1914	1465	641	1071	3177
1916	1594	1379	282	3255	1916	1945	957	627	3529
1918	1256	1246	30	2532	1918	1097	356	114	1567
1920	1859	2522	86	4467	1920	2529	2088	282	4899
1922	3089	2489	35	5613	1922	3928	1566	26	5520
1924	2454	2622	185	5261	1924	2528	2013	737	5278
1926	2211	1972	13	4196	1926	2382	1480	29	3891
1928	2446	2963	29	5438	1928	2581	2541	30	5152
1930	2984	2279	10	5273	1930	3597	1344	44	4985
1932	4633	2275	0	6908	1932	4908	1040	0	5948
1934	3489	3518	55	7062	1934	4772	1587	59	6418
1936	3966	2917	21	6904	1936	4624	1269	17	5910
1938	4137	1939	16	6092	1938	3852	442	8	4302
1940	3952	4128	18	8098	1940	5177	2365	19	7561
1942	2740	2225	16	4981	1942	2138	624	12	2774
1944	3415	3336	12	6763	1944	4358	1404	13	5775
1946	3215	2288	20	5523	1946	2700	649	35	3384
1948	4249	2785	0	7034	1948	4750	1036	0	5786
1950	3113	2204	0	5317	1950	3563	1187	12	4762
1952	3234	3326	0	6560	1952	4260	2251	0	6511
1954	3693	2299	0	5992	1954	3942	730	0	4672
1956	2991	3277	0	6268	1956	3469	2206	0	5675
1958	3397	792	44	4233	1958	2544	197	41	2782
1960	2687	3571	0	6258	1960	2941	2531	0	5472
1962	3354	3156	4	6514	1962	2708	1615	5	4328
1964	4449	3467	0	7916	1964	3969	1718	0	5687
1966	3866	3110	20	6996	1966	2278	1232	10	3520
1968	2554	3971	1866	8391	1968	2268	1414	1751	5433
1970	3617	2526	188	6331	1970	2991	1000	389	4380
1972	2899	7080	227	10206	1972	1798	3399	81	5278
1974	5935	2894	0	8829	1974	3544	435	0	3979
1976	6006	4443	115	10564	1976	4269	1821	50	6140
1978	5143	2862	48	8053	1978	2920	998	60	3978
1980	5215	5594	499	11308	1980	3507	2394	108	6009
1982	5933	2645	20	8598	1982	3420	784	11	4215
1984	5307	7614	94	13015	1984	2801	3155	31	5987
1986	4609	5124	542	10275	1986	3022	1261	191	4474

Year	Dem	Rep	Other	Total
1988	3362	2217	20	5599
1990	3878	1086	120	5084
1992	3413	1641	1323	6377
1994	1127	652	2528	4307
1996	3198	1580	601	5379
1998	2091	1657	45	3793
2000	2799	2461	55	5315
2002	2472	1183	213	3868
2004	2639	3168	0	5807
2006	3139	704	0	3843
2008	1860	3730	0	5590
2010	1843	2227	0	4070
2012	1494	3572	0	5066
2014	1282	1743	104	3129

Cimarron

Year	Dem	Rep	Other	Total
1907	540	397	23	960
1908	449	371	38	858
1910	487	412	80	979
1912	342	263	817	1422
1914	280	253	94	627
1916	387	238	146	771
1918	373	289	36	698
1920	460	626	82	1168
1922	738	743	16	1497
1924	672	586	164	1422
1926	589	483	31	1103
1928	566	1139	20	1725
1930	1077	707	6	1790
1932	1895	571	0	2466
1934	1325	956	34	2315
1936	1342	555	13	1910
1938	808	779	23	1610
1940	989	841	0	1830
1942	632	485	0	1117
1944	746	822	0	1568
1946	214	176	3	393
1948	894	650	0	1544
1950	838	643	2	1483
1952	705	1438	0	2143
1954	1024	707	0	1731
1956	812	1053	0	1865
1958	758	294	74	1126
1960	696	1316	0	2012
1962	509	1284	5	1798
1964	878	1225	0	2103
1966	602	925	4	1531
1968	436	1122	527	2085
1970	822	544	85	1451
1972	323	1350	212	1885
1974	946	504	0	1450
1976	962	872	45	1879
1978	654	751	43	1448
1980	373	1404	44	1821
1982	937	729	5	1671
1984	359	1420	15	1794
1986	514	683	131	1328

Year	Dem	Rep	Other	Total
1988	470	1153	24	1647
1990	683	635	88	1406
1992	395	965	264	1624
1994	226	830	327	1383
1996	361	986	108	1455
1998	261	906	33	1200
2000	277	1230	27	1484
2002	298	909	74	1281
2004	184	1242	0	1426
2006	353	705	0	1058
2008	152	1119	0	1271
2010	263	734	0	997
2012	115	1082	0	1197
2014	137	576	52	765

Cleveland

Year	Dem	Rep	Other	Total
1907	1853	1188	213	3254
1908	1437	1092	414	2943
1910	1423	945	350	2718
1912	1471	938	453	2862
1914	1228	1167	705	3100
1916	1753	885	597	3235
1918	1323	625	85	2033
1920	2383	2280	304	4967
1922	3200	2185	54	5439
1924	2841	1672	495	5008
1926	2459	1337	145	3941
1928	2291	3738	64	6093
1930	3501	2157	17	5675
1932	5969	1868	0	7837
1934	4747	2567	164	7478
1936	6304	2643	75	9022
1938	3745	948	47	4740
1940	5833	3660	57	9550
1942	2351	1499	21	3871
1944	5240	3642	21	8903
1946	3511	2478	85	6074
1948	6556	3671	0	10227
1950	4328	4732	58	9118
1952	6190	8149	0	14339
1954	4994	3213	0	8207
1956	5987	7766	0	13753
1958	5734	1258	644	7636
1960	6397	9292	0	15689
1962	6043	6888	40	12971
1964	11599	9656	0	21255
1966	6060	10067	50	16177
1968	8617	12446	4711	25774
1970	8775	10596	563	19934
1972	8617	25777	615	35009
1974	18627	9447	0	28074
1976	20054	22098	1129	43281
1978	13501	16124	294	29919
1980	14536	31178	4687	50401
1982	21381	16080	70	37531
1984	16512	42806	387	59705
1986	16182	20186	4636	41004

Year	Dem	Rep	Other	Total	Year	Dem	Rep	Other	Total
1988	22067	36313	577	58957	**1988**	1365	891	14	2270
1990	24222	16802	5762	46786	1990	1621	429	131	2181
1992	24404	35561	20664	80629	**1992**	1448	714	638	2800
1994	17409	31459	9076	57944	1994	552	381	985	1918
1996	26038	36457	7288	69783	**1996**	1205	734	337	2276
1998	19460	30960	693	51113	1998	937	838	23	1798
2000	27792	47293	986	76171	**2000**	1148	1196	18	2362
2002	28112	29160	8022	65294	2002	1360	554	132	2046
2004	34007	65720	0	99727	**2004**	1203	1396	0	2599
2006	40641	21707	0	62348	2006	1627	380	0	2007
2008	39681	64749	0	104430	**2008**	600	1672	0	2272
2010	30467	42979	0	73264	2010	958	1052	0	2010
2012	34771	59113	0	93887	**2012**	649	1710	0	2359
2014	27247	30989	1994	60227	2014	937	749	65	1751
		Coal					Comanche		
1907	1377	705	247	2329	1907	3133	2538	192	5863
1908	906	722	524	2152	**1908**	3481	2437	411	6329
1910	1166	610	404	2180	1910	3221	2381	733	6335
1912	1109	571	623	2303	**1912**	1931	1320	632	3883
1914	1017	769	701	2487	1914	1307	1418	861	3586
1916	1418	824	588	2830	**1916**	2130	1221	815	4166
1918	1033	454	101	1588	1918	1374	968	130	2472
1920	1797	1748	483	4028	**1920**	2988	3286	431	6705
1922	2793	1335	12	4140	1922	4131	2855	61	7047
1924	1772	800	607	3179	**1924**	3084	3084	841	7009
1926	1771	854	31	2656	1926	3365	2989	44	6398
1928	1681	1283	32	2996	**1928**	2956	5069	92	8117
1930	2239	510	1	2750	1930	4605	2938	11	7554
1932	2788	300	0	3088	**1932**	7586	2046	0	9632
1934	2347	651	158	3156	1934	5646	2839	342	8827
1936	2550	603	7	3160	**1936**	7026	3039	75	10140
1938	1690	243	6	1939	1938	5850	1521	46	7417
1940	2377	1148	10	3535	**1940**	6796	3703	36	10535
1942	969	295	4	1268	1942	2911	1379	16	4306
1944	1959	760	5	2724	**1944**	7342	4109	28	11479
1946	1502	308	18	1828	1946	4697	2294	155	7146
1948	2124	464	0	2588	**1948**	7955	2787	0	10742
1950	1717	497	2	2216	1950	5702	3290	28	9020
1952	1755	1106	0	2861	**1952**	9029	8756	0	17785
1954	1715	392	0	2107	1954	7131	2683	0	9814
1956	1596	920	0	2516	**1956**	8756	7532	0	16288
1958	1265	123	39	1427	1958	11053	997	572	12622
1960	1269	1019	0	2288	**1960**	9562	10691	0	20253
1962	1249	759	4	2012	1962	8274	6018	31	14323
1964	1613	721	0	2334	**1964**	13585	7936	0	21521
1966	997	678	4	1679	1966	8926	6607	41	15574
1968	963	669	625	2257	**1968**	8061	9225	5879	23165
1970	1173	457	121	1751	1970	8938	5828	481	15247
1972	680	1461	38	2179	**1972**	4559	19759	427	24745
1974	1582	292	0	1874	1974	13913	4689	0	18602
1976	1774	769	23	2566	**1976**	12910	13163	230	26303
1978	1091	478	14	1583	1978	12592	6761	94	19447
1980	1442	926	63	2431	**1980**	9972	16609	1329	27910
1982	1536	313	5	1854	1982	15111	5824	33	20968
1984	1284	1259	21	2564	**1984**	8890	21382	122	30394
1986	1320	721	109	2150	1986	11362	6892	851	19105

Year	Dem	Rep	Other	Total
1988	11441	17464	194	29099
1990	13159	7890	957	22006
1992	12237	15704	7579	35520
1994	9554	10032	4902	24488
1996	12841	14461	2976	30278
1998	8578	12621	193	21392
2000	11971	17103	259	29333
2002	8363	9077	4340	21780
2004	12022	21170	0	33192
2006	14941	5086	0	20027
2008	14120	20127	0	34247
2010	10950	10827	0	21777
2012	12521	17664	0	30185
2014	9299	10091	610	20000

Cotton

Year	Dem	Rep	Other	Total
1907	0	0	0	0
1908	0	0	0	0
1910	0	0	0	0
1912	1063	587	288	1938
1914	1036	855	466	2357
1916	1500	685	370	2555
1918	1011	611	49	1671
1920	2256	1815	172	4243
1922	2665	1434	22	4121
1924	1825	1581	299	3705
1926	1588	1244	24	2856
1928	1605	2419	24	4048
1930	3298	990	0	4288
1932	4426	758	0	5184
1934	3522	1372	285	5179
1936	3842	1181	17	5040
1938	2425	577	11	3013
1940	3121	1616	23	4760
1942	1302	649	11	1962
1944	2711	1266	17	3994
1946	1731	498	72	2301
1948	2613	738	0	3351
1950	1875	498	72	2445
1952	2117	1897	0	4014
1954	1988	510	27	2525
1956	1889	1398	0	3287
1958	1625	230	47	1902
1960	1634	1619	0	3253
1962	1449	1060	2	2511
1964	2216	1123	0	3339
1966	1557	864	7	2428
1968	1192	1016	905	3113
1970	1367	650	76	2093
1972	798	2050	71	2919
1974	1730	414	0	2144
1976	1911	1127	26	3064
1978	1297	772	15	2084
1980	1410	1702	31	3143
1982	1804	461	0	2265
1984	1264	1796	20	3080
1986	1372	628	0	2000

Year	Dem	Rep	Other	Total
1988	1482	1266	27	2775
1990	1777	524	54	2355
1992	1314	910	867	3091
1994	885	545	911	2341
1996	1258	1042	398	2698
1998	889	1182	31	2102
2000	1068	1388	26	2482
2002	799	717	333	1849
2004	898	1742	0	2640
2006	1660	355	0	2015
2008	690	1793	0	2483
2010	1007	818	0	1825
2012	657	1796	0	2453
2014	730	902	52	1684

Craig

Year	Dem	Rep	Other	Total
1907	1671	1479	27	3177
1908	1578	1296	56	2930
1910	1584	1234	82	2900
1912	1772	1391	123	3286
1914	1456	1545	100	3101
1916	1901	1647	196	3744
1918	1459	1276	34	2769
1920	2903	3091	87	6081
1922	3048	2417	22	5487
1924	3096	2519	171	5786
1926	2587	2300	26	4913
1928	2897	3511	36	6444
1930	3413	2270	5	5688
1932	4861	2124	0	6985
1934	3962	3473	42	7477
1936	4377	2964	13	7354
1938	4157	1744	27	5928
1940	4316	3582	19	7917
1942	2528	2076	16	4620
1944	3363	3111	11	6485
1946	3252	2807	70	6129
1948	4182	2807	0	6989
1950	3357	2684	9	6050
1952	3135	3830	0	6965
1954	3484	1942	0	5426
1956	3106	3543	0	6649
1958	3264	1120	135	4519
1960	2792	3770	0	6562
1962	2647	2709	3	5359
1964	3838	2541	0	6379
1966	2569	2311	8	4888
1968	2098	2686	1229	6013
1970	2402	1904	118	4424
1972	1642	4163	112	5917
1974	3228	2078	0	5306
1976	3577	2540	61	6178
1978	2903	1368	35	4306
1980	2801	2956	195	5952
1982	3417	976	9	4402
1984	2515	3629	46	6190
1986	2361	2127	174	4662

Year	Dem	Rep	Other	Total
1988	2940	2463	43	5446
1990	2862	1161	357	4380
1992	2780	2106	1333	6219
1994	1760	1561	1076	4397
1996	2649	2058	779	5486
1998	2787	1589	43	4419
2000	2568	2815	111	5484
2002	2253	1409	851	4513
2004	2504	3894	0	6398
2006	3319	1012	0	4331
2008	2073	3858	0	5931
2010	1834	2470	0	4304
2012	1747	3559	0	5306
2014	1491	1958	115	3564

Creek

Year	Dem	Rep	Other	Total
1907	1302	1551	88	2941
1908	1417	1761	335	3513
1910	1619	1910	344	3873
1912	1676	1902	996	4574
1914	1608	2179	1049	4836
1916	3496	2820	1323	7639
1918	2775	2422	116	5313
1920	5406	7936	614	13956
1922	6989	8075	102	15166
1924	7969	8894	851	17714
1926	6292	6230	68	12590
1928	5693	12254	95	18042
1930	6931	7933	6	14870
1932	12963	6786	0	19749
1934	9218	7412	1225	17855
1936	12540	7257	106	19903
1938	10030	4878	62	14970
1940	10976	9468	51	20495
1942	4532	5538	42	10112
1944	8342	7549	41	15932
1946	5413	6630	294	12337
1948	9198	6532	0	15730
1950	6755	7410	21	14186
1952	8818	9257	0	18075
1954	7106	4729	0	11835
1956	7102	8295	0	15397
1958	6966	1898	385	9249
1960	6205	8785	0	14990
1962	5115	5838	11	10964
1964	9836	6355	0	16191
1966	5543	6179	44	11766
1968	5151	6934	3913	15998
1970	6050	5507	517	12074
1972	3705	12396	402	16503
1974	8028	6332	0	14360
1976	8964	8458	169	17591
1978	7363	5044	82	12489
1980	7339	11749	641	19729
1982	10088	5583	20	15691
1984	7465	15011	152	22628
1986	7430	7932	1622	16984

Year	Dem	Rep	Other	Total
1988	9512	11308	162	20982
1990	8904	4176	1771	14851
1992	9118	10055	6065	25238
1994	6476	7825	4020	18321
1996	9674	9861	2922	22457
1998	8114	8431	226	16771
2000	9753	13580	408	23741
2002	8385	7497	4132	20014
2004	9929	18848	0	28777
2006	12936	6519	0	19455
2008	8318	20187	0	28505
2010	7034	13377	0	20411
2012	7128	18986	0	26114
2014	5210	9618	509	15337

Custer

Year	Dem	Rep	Other	Total
1907	1930	1523	161	3614
1908	1721	1579	333	3633
1910	1817	1765	427	4009
1912	1774	1693	543	4010
1914	1173	1815	530	3518
1916	1771	1507	638	3916
1918	1031	1181	83	2295
1920	2263	3224	340	5827
1922	3006	3116	81	6203
1924	2473	2409	747	5629
1926	2435	1872	58	4365
1928	1995	4576	103	6674
1930	3434	2484	5	5923
1932	6573	1684	0	8257
1934	4226	2662	332	7220
1936	5093	2386	46	7525
1938	4452	931	39	5422
1940	4612	3419	40	8071
1942	1609	1407	14	3030
1944	3928	3349	25	7302
1946	3015	2021	57	5093
1948	4618	2568	0	7186
1950	3773	2882	44	6699
1952	3226	5667	0	8893
1954	3030	2264	0	5294
1956	3026	4182	0	7208
1958	3025	911	282	4218
1960	2743	5050	0	7793
1962	2527	3777	37	6341
1964	4464	3362	0	7826
1966	2366	3676	6	6048
1968	2717	4709	936	8362
1970	2887	3040	103	6030
1972	2298	7267	215	9780
1974	5014	2373	0	7387
1976	4597	4847	102	9546
1978	3083	4302	28	7413
1980	3008	6469	377	9854
1982	5208	2546	1	7755
1984	2700	8191	49	10940
1986	3886	4019	482	8387

Year	Dem	Rep	Other	Total
1988	3697	6735	95	10527
1990	5516	2475	748	8739
1992	3540	5362	2792	11694
1994	2098	3857	2171	8126
1996	4027	4723	1129	9879
1998	2451	4616	47	7114
2000	1068	1388	26	2482
2002	3426	3438	1179	8043
2004	2801	7839	0	10640
2006	4681	2148	0	6829
2008	2660	7842	0	10502
2010	2654	5061	0	7715
2012	2359	7446	0	9805
2014	2124	4210	184	5924

Delaware

Year	Dem	Rep	Other	Total
1907	1003	589	25	1617
1908	974	625	52	1651
1910	924	705	76	1705
1912	983	732	186	1901
1914	1080	783	206	2069
1916	1227	837	233	2297
1918	1021	817	43	1881
1920	1280	2059	141	3480
1922	2167	1657	22	3846
1924	1729	1563	263	3555
1926	1338	1404	95	2837
1928	1706	2603	51	4360
1930	2415	1488	5	3908
1932	3684	1469	0	5153
1934	2753	2990	42	5785
1936	3398	2632	15	6045
1938	3397	1971	30	5398
1940	3417	3305	17	6739
1942	2107	1909	23	4039
1944	2373	2660	93	5126
1946	2454	1943	33	4430
1948	3157	2343	0	5500
1950	3003	2644	5	5652
1952	2686	3399	0	6085
1954	3177	2211	0	5388
1956	2679	3078	0	5757
1958	3157	1285	94	4536
1960	2282	3639	0	5921
1962	2742	2737	8	5487
1964	3702	2743	0	6445
1966	2378	2422	15	4815
1968	2129	3168	1402	6699
1970	3141	3188	195	6524
1972	2135	5476	178	7789
1974	2865	2359	0	5224
1976	4924	3642	91	8657
1978	4514	2268	67	6849
1980	4244	5302	273	9819
1982	6167	2320	16	8503
1984	3789	6690	63	10542
1986	4237	3929	264	8430

Year	Dem	Rep	Other	Total
1988	4889	5248	75	10212
1990	4581	2132	675	7388
1992	4842	4840	2744	12426
1994	3619	4050	1732	9401
1996	5094	5230	1615	11939
1998	4635	5160	139	9934
2000	5514	7618	221	13353
2002	4845	4253	1728	10826
2004	5591	10017	0	15608
2006	6807	3098	0	9905
2008	5085	10277	0	15362
2010	4127	7304	0	11431
2012	4196	10080	0	14276
2014	3126	5614	250	8990

Dewey

Year	Dem	Rep	Other	Total
1907	1171	1137	342	2650
1908	1075	1210	486	2771
1910	983	1208	616	2807
1912	1075	1086	791	2952
1914	729	915	813	2457
1916	992	796	923	2711
1918	643	794	304	1741
1920	987	1734	623	3344
1922	1786	1638	148	3572
1924	1126	1539	799	3464
1926	1331	1168	52	2551
1928	1175	2486	143	3804
1930	2373	1412	6	3791
1932	3855	1051	0	4906
1934	1980	2326	654	4960
1936	2980	1846	37	4863
1938	2235	1642	30	3907
1940	2391	2613	34	5038
1942	1491	1534	25	3050
1944	1808	2166	13	3987
1946	1307	1202	51	2560
1948	2049	1494	0	3543
1950	1615	1800	9	3424
1952	1281	2583	0	3864
1954	1400	1639	0	3039
1956	1448	1896	0	3344
1958	1557	746	135	2438
1960	1082	2115	0	3197
1962	1007	1713	6	2726
1964	1617	1438	0	3055
1966	1127	1443	15	2585
1968	773	1508	540	2821
1970	1240	952	61	2253
1972	626	2106	84	2816
1974	1564	956	0	2520
1976	1540	1230	55	2825
1978	958	1374	14	2346
1980	826	1943	107	2876
1982	1472	794	4	2270
1984	664	2098	15	2777
1986	1035	1004	212	2251

Year	Dem	Rep	Other	Total
1988	963	1543	45	2551
1990	1459	637	315	2411
1992	845	1244	693	2782
1994	472	870	894	2236
1996	816	1179	306	2301
1998	523	1171	23	1717
2000	599	1607	14	2220
2002	820	744	283	1847
2004	408	1843	0	2251
2006	1291	562	0	1853
2008	346	1857	0	2203
2010	557	1307	0	1864
2012	301	1792	0	2093
2014	454	996	46	1496

Year	Dem	Rep	Other	Total
1988	786	1422	36	2244
1990	1078	623	280	1981
1992	594	1072	641	2307
1994	365	784	650	1799
1996	619	1090	287	1996
1998	463	1108	26	1597
2000	468	1513	32	2013
2002	633	739	270	1642
2004	395	1685	0	2080
2006	972	569	0	1541
2008	282	1627	0	1909
2010	415	1105	0	1520
2012	226	1575	0	1801
2014	316	888	43	1247

Ellis

Year	Dem	Rep	Other	Total
1907	1326	1328	104	2758
1908	1260	1379	224	2863
1910	1085	1417	379	2881
1912	918	1373	508	2799
1914	659	1012	665	2336
1916	960	983	620	2563
1918	494	835	202	1531
1920	842	1786	380	3008
1922	1266	1637	104	3007
1924	879	1499	700	3078
1926	1017	1282	44	2343
1928	1122	1953	35	3110
1930	1681	1455	2	3138
1932	2795	1089	0	3884
1934	1840	2158	116	4114
1936	2493	1324	30	3847
1938	1622	1576	13	3211
1940	1657	2162	17	3836
1942	703	916	19	1638
1944	1104	1939	8	3051
1946	929	1060	51	2040
1948	1420	1522	0	2942
1950	1140	1884	2	3026
1952	717	2583	0	3300
1954	771	1616	0	2387
1956	920	1916	0	2836
1958	1318	824	175	2317
1960	709	2085	0	2794
1962	615	1879	2	2496
1964	1120	1452	0	2572
1966	866	1204	7	2077
1968	533	1601	426	2560
1970	966	1099	89	2154
1972	473	2059	116	2648
1974	1373	1033	0	2406
1976	1256	1429	61	2746
1978	862	1373	43	2278
1980	561	1908	81	2550
1982	1254	712	2	1968
1984	562	1881	17	2460
1986	761	1128	87	1976

Garfield

Year	Dem	Rep	Other	Total
1907	2219	3237	175	5631
1908	2618	2924	254	5796
1910	2343	3436	348	6127
1912	2353	2900	466	5719
1914	1639	2989	619	5247
1916	2347	2854	694	5895
1918	1513	3176	140	4829
1920	3656	6615	569	10840
1922	5324	7267	107	12698
1924	3791	7524	2054	13369
1926	4356	5092	36	9484
1928	3503	12748	141	16392
1930	5582	6839	25	12446
1932	10773	6837	0	17610
1934	7353	7811	270	15434
1936	11142	7457	124	18723
1938	8419	6391	164	14974
1940	9544	10792	166	20502
1942	3736	8308	75	12119
1944	7879	11211	65	19155
1946	3978	8677	300	12955
1948	8217	10352	0	18569
1950	6273	11609	40	17922
1952	7047	17589	0	24636
1954	6308	10774	0	17082
1956	6769	15348	0	22117
1958	10181	4389	1322	15892
1960	6582	14860	0	21442
1962	5181	13413	62	18656
1964	10175	12297	0	22472
1966	5605	12364	43	18012
1968	5802	14370	3011	23183
1970	6973	9949	459	17381
1972	4557	19348	564	24469
1974	9937	8926	0	18863
1976	8969	14202	303	23474
1978	6771	10643	111	17525
1980	5718	17989	1121	24828
1982	9956	8265	8	18229
1984	5730	19642	162	25534
1986	7341	9287	1476	18104

Year	Dem	Rep	Other	Total	Year	Dem	Rep	Other	Total
1988	8067	15248	223	23538	1988	5438	5109	109	10656
1990	9543	5806	2843	18192	1990	5335	2313	931	8579
1992	6720	13095	5670	25485	1992	4811	3983	3069	11863
1994	5131	11120	3843	20094	1994	2677	2795	2983	8455
1996	7504	11712	2625	21841	1996	4639	3745	1383	9767
1998	5837	11191	178	17206	1998	3056	3597	82	6735
2000	6543	14902	238	21683	2000	4189	5536	118	9843
2002	6421	8381	2767	17569	2002	4525	3064	1275	8864
2004	5586	17685	0	23271	2004	3707	7610	0	11317
2006	10760	5351	0	16111	2006	5745	2304	0	8049
2008	5545	17067	0	22612	2008	3028	7710	0	10738
2010	5318	11515	0	16833	2010	3641	5254	0	8895
2012	4733	15177	0	19910	2012	2559	6925	0	9484
2014	4906	7247	530	12683	2014	2428	3417	189	6034

Garvin / Grady

Year	Dem	Rep	Other	Total	Year	Dem	Rep	Other	Total
1907	2772	1239	55	4066	1907	2981	1243	70	4294
1908	2391	1290	336	4017	1908	2826	1491	258	4575
1910	2055	959	385	3399	1910	2566	1287	513	4366
1912	2114	740	1066	3920	1912	2577	1121	776	4474
1914	1886	848	1435	4169	1914	1855	1073	1291	4219
1916	2697	804	1023	4524	1916	3243	1272	841	5356
1918	1798	651	52	2501	1918	2231	810	116	3157
1920	4096	2915	274	7285	1920	4320	3412	476	8208
1922	4825	1768	52	6645	1922	5236	2891	53	8180
1924	4758	1863	312	6933	1924	5091	2640	855	8586
1926	3244	1095	129	4468	1926	3861	2136	27	6024
1928	3589	3321	91	7001	1928	3667	6332	110	10109
1930	5535	1474	7	7016	1930	5160	2375	9	7544
1932	7834	1034	0	8868	1932	9247	2034	0	11281
1934	4151	1805	237	6193	1934	5184	2431	652	8267
1936	6276	1700	58	8034	1936	9025	3013	61	12099
1938	3810	896	31	4737	1938	5076	1451	37	6564
1940	7001	2958	40	9999	1940	8075	4299	43	12417
1942	2602	1137	10	3749	1942	2730	1946	13	4689
1944	5328	2086	7	7421	1944	7689	4069	20	11778
1946	3614	1082	52	4748	1946	4399	2341	96	6836
1948	6779	1681	0	8460	1948	8136	2882	0	11018
1950	5005	2114	6	7125	1950	5788	3590	16	9394
1952	6844	4402	0	11246	1952	7710	6348	0	14058
1954	5157	1468	0	6625	1954	5376	2472	0	7848
1956	6451	3850	0	10301	1956	6773	5191	0	11964
1958	4020	521	232	4773	1958	4917	733	405	6055
1960	4795	5125	0	9920	1960	5446	5913	0	11359
1962	4320	3828	17	8165	1962	4410	4208	28	8646
1964	7013	3470	0	10483	1964	7593	3569	0	11162
1966	3963	3531	89	7583	1966	4340	3784	35	8159
1968	3845	3786	2670	10301	1968	4760	4242	2117	11119
1970	4284	3261	295	7840	1970	4864	3372	232	8468
1972	2685	7245	315	10245	1972	3440	7762	297	11499
1974	6752	2096	0	8848	1974	6647	2539	0	9186
1976	6797	3905	83	10785	1976	7155	4686	114	11955
1978	4525	3352	44	7921	1978	4976	4114	46	9136
1980	5033	5520	307	10860	1980	5330	8131	510	13971
1982	6690	2833	4	9527	1982	7059	3707	10	10776
1984	4215	7505	91	11811	1984	4846	11042	72	15960
1986	5042	3355	696	9093	1986	6088	4532	1404	12024

Year	Dem	Rep	Other	Total
1988	6689	7994	165	14848
1990	7387	3817	1214	12418
1992	6177	6997	4583	17757
1994	3921	5822	3545	13288
1996	6256	7228	2114	15598
1998	4606	7345	180	12131
2000	6037	10040	199	16276
2002	6291	5583	2509	14383
2004	5970	14136	0	20106
2006	9151	4587	0	13738
2008	5520	15195	0	20715
2010	5741	10031	0	15772
2012	4786	14833	0	19619
2014	5568	7027	317	12912

Grant

Year	Dem	Rep	Other	Total
1907	1799	1729	87	3615
1908	1866	1796	105	3767
1910	1642	1886	216	3744
1912	1559	1729	362	3650
1914	1214	1610	337	3161
1916	1700	1517	368	3585
1918	1091	1449	64	2604
1920	1879	3205	206	5290
1922	1971	3161	29	5161
1924	1990	2800	622	5412
1926	1857	18/83	20	3760
1928	1449	4371	63	5883
1930	2920	2174	17	5111
1932	4432	1902	0	6334
1934	2951	2815	83	5849
1936	3955	2307	32	6294
1938	2769	2607	51	5427
1940	2970	3394	38	6402
1942	1456	2321	38	3815
1944	2045	3021	13	5079
1946	1257	2311	61	3629
1948	2126	2471	0	4597
1950	2211	2746	6	4963
1952	1521	3996	0	5517
1954	2005	2519	0	4524
1956	1953	2788	0	4741
1958	2385	1065	262	3712
1960	1723	2810	0	4533
1962	1194	2751	6	3951
1964	2120	1992	0	4112
1966	1265	2050	9	3324
1968	1047	2403	437	3887
1970	1434	1553	60	3047
1972	805	2829	121	3755
1974	1863	1289	0	3152
1976	1853	1685	50	3588
1978	1468	1520	25	3013
1980	927	2411	134	3472
1982	1834	967	1	2802
1984	825	2470	29	3324
1986	1175	1330	278	2783

Year	Dem	Rep	Other	Total
1988	1249	1690	41	2980
1990	1317	786	532	2635
1992	864	1311	881	3056
1994	596	1004	851	2451
1996	867	1382	404	2653
1998	800	1295	42	2137
2000	709	1762	32	2503
2002	875	941	325	2141
2004	571	1950	0	2521
2006	1302	589	0	1891
2008	514	1836	0	2350
2010	613	1199	0	1812
2012	393	1675	0	2068
2014	558	979	61	1598

Greer

Year	Dem	Rep	Other	Total
1907	2151	864	173	3188
1908	2149	708	472	3329
1910	1409	414	375	2198
1912	1334	351	404	2089
1914	946	406	590	1942
1916	1675	369	483	2527
1918	996	376	22	1394
1920	1850	1009	226	3085
1922	2208	862	14	3084
1924	1982	551	293	2826
1926	1423	540	8	1971
1928	1645	2262	28	3935
1930	2529	735	0	3264
1932	4240	418	0	4658
1934	2850	1078	73	4001
1936	3745	766	11	4522
1938	1852	304	6	2162
1940	3524	1195	21	4740
1942	1010	377	8	1395
1944	2984	1075	5	4064
1946	2260	556	51	2867
1948	3044	713	0	3757
1950	2469	838	6	3313
1952	2321	2147	0	4468
1954	1709	584	0	2293
1956	1907	1499	0	3406
1958	1367	292	111	1770
1960	1698	2158	0	3856
1962	2046	1192	3	3241
1964	2671	1247	0	3918
1966	1672	1117	11	2800
1968	1419	1225	830	3474
1970	1770	861	88	2719
1972	1004	2154	86	3244
1974	1978	519	0	2497
1976	2113	1164	31	3308
1978	1353	1084	9	2446
1980	1492	1535	72	3099
1982	1927	586	1	2514
1984	1220	1664	17	2901
1986	1348	764	78	2190

Year	Dem	Rep	Other	Total
1988	1256	1225	22	2503
1990	1745	608	171	2524
1992	1162	964	653	2779
1994	847	609	574	2030
1996	1240	905	372	2517
1998	757	1042	16	1815
2000	839	1287	26	2152
2002	957	651	331	1939
2004	719	1529	0	2248
2006	1085	460	0	1545
2008	566	1548	0	2114
2010	683	892	0	1575
2012	417	1344	0	1832
2014	616	820	52	1488

Harmon

Year	Dem	Rep	Other	Total
1907	0	0	0	0
1908	0	0	0	0
1910	852	174	135	1161
1912	895	197	291	1383
1914	628	248	343	1219
1916	1091	147	256	1494
1918	766	140	21	927
1920	1120	635	116	1871
1922	1578	502	28	2108
1924	1049	339	68	1456
1926	821	164	15	1000
1928	1060	1431	26	2517
1930	1828	354	2	2184
1932	3042	189	0	3231
1934	1809	449	102	2360
1936	2570	331	11	2912
1938	1102	130	8	1240
1940	2292	731	18	3041
1942	623	199	0	822
1944	1933	503	10	2446
1946	1059	215	30	1304
1948	2340	266	0	2606
1950	1772	372	7	2151
1952	1904	1057	0	2961
1954	1074	154	0	1228
1956	1743	837	0	2580
1958	972	84	22	1078
1960	1265	1142	0	2407
1962	1123	621	4	1748
1964	1665	602	0	2267
1966	866	524	3	1393
1968	1097	644	403	2144
1970	1075	355	45	1475
1972	568	1319	42	1929
1974	1318	114	0	1432
1976	1371	666	8	2045
1978	903	407	6	1316
1980	961	676	33	1670
1982	1189	279	0	1468
1984	785	1009	11	1805
1986	823	344	118	1285

Year	Dem	Rep	Other	Total
1988	890	611	3	1504
1990	1116	300	55	1471
1992	783	496	332	1611
1994	460	252	403	1115
1996	729	448	150	1327
1998	417	471	8	896
2000	507	692	6	1205
2002	446	310	133	889
2004	354	838	0	1192
2006	559	192	0	751
2008	333	757	0	1090
2010	334	420	0	754
2012	264	659	0	923
2014	269	404	13	686

Harper

Year	Dem	Rep	Other	Total
1907	729	735	91	1555
1908	746	876	201	1823
1910	701	810	177	1688
1912	523	679	303	1505
1914	443	612	545	1600
1916	798	662	427	1887
1918	482	647	67	1196
1920	751	1404	182	2337
1922	1199	1203	14	2416
1924	824	1226	365	2415
1926	906	979	12	1897
1928	872	1844	59	2775
1930	1368	1215	6	2589
1932	2139	783	0	2922
1934	1455	1575	64	3094
1936	1836	1068	7	2911
1938	1246	1093	15	2354
1940	1419	1616	38	3073
1942	874	964	11	1849
1944	1056	1394	23	2473
1946	923	936	54	1913
1948	1281	1221	0	2502
1950	1184	1669	7	2860
1952	736	2057	0	2793
1954	940	1484	0	2424
1956	736	1596	0	2332
1958	742	579	118	1439
1960	744	2057	0	2801
1962	685	1575	7	2267
1964	1240	1379	0	2619
1966	829	1248	7	2084
1968	518	1483	353	2354
1970	902	954	89	1945
1972	385	1976	114	2475
1974	1064	928	0	1992
1976	978	1303	39	2320
1978	687	1143	17	1847
1980	517	1652	61	2230
1982	1186	664	3	1853
1984	373	1748	25	2146
1986	578	1065	157	1800

Year	Dem	Rep	Other	Total	Year	Dem	Rep	Other	Total
1988	593	1281	24	1898	1988	2963	1822	44	4829
1990	901	597	308	1806	1990	3137	750	254	4141
1992	486	1038	511	2035	1992	3069	1461	1016	5546
1994	385	722	590	1697	1994	1220	736	1357	3313
1996	511	1036	231	1778	1996	2762	1442	601	4805
1998	570	904	33	1507	1998	1837	1108	37	2982
2000	374	1296	13	1683	2000	2510	2039	79	4628
2002	594	642	186	1422	2002	2516	1165	509	4190
2004	268	1397	0	1665	2004	2378	2946	0	5324
2006	746	410	0	1156	2006	2426	790	0	3216
2008	221	1342	0	1563	2008	1474	3207	0	4681
2010	331	899	0	1230	2010	1525	1901	0	3426
2012	173	1261	0	1434	2012	1175	3069	0	4244
2014	289	750	38	1077	2014	1176	1254	57	2487

Haskell					Hughes				
1907	1804	1319	91	3214	1907	1965	1256	89	3310
1908	1401	1139	363	2903	1908	1649	1459	380	3488
1910	1417	1176	304	2897	1910	1715	1204	442	3361
1912	1688	902	685	3275	1912	1769	1228	1004	4001
1914	1218	893	942	3053	1914	1396	1074	1129	3599
1916	1486	976	484	2946	1916	2187	1219	800	4206
1918	1108	774	74	1956	1918	1591	982	33	2606
1920	2201	2673	201	5075	1920	3481	3046	150	6677
1922	3516	1869	13	5398	1922	4067	2105	38	6210
1924	2480	1935	401	4816	1924	3996	1994	210	6200
1926	2526	2312	7	4845	1926	2846	1703	29	4578
1928	2172	2580	30	4782	1928	3169	3937	29	7135
1930	3069	1735	1	4805	1930	4792	2075	11	6878
1932	4357	1439	0	5796	1932	6485	1114	0	7599
1934	3737	2543	22	6302	1934	4068	2317	123	6508
1936	3961	2182	1	6144	1936	5990	2032	8	8030
1938	3744	1216	11	4971	1938	4286	9271	14	13571
1940	3896	2661	9	6566	1940	6005	3168	21	9194
1942	2231	1345	3	3579	1942	2764	1556	6	4326
1944	2924	2102	15	5041	1944	5009	2484	13	7506
1946	2337	1126	22	3485	1946	3545	1474	45	5064
1948	3206	1390	0	4596	1948	5492	1676	0	7168
1950	2275	1000	130	3405	1950	3770	1791	6	5567
1952	2619	1872	0	4491	1952	4639	3012	0	7651
1954	2764	907	0	3671	1954	3345	1020	0	4365
1956	2381	1758	0	4139	1956	4278	2783	0	7061
1958	1581	244	24	1849	1958	2865	362	102	3329
1960	1712	1858	0	3570	1960	3057	3117	0	6174
1962	1815	1161	3	2979	1962	2970	1986	9	4965
1964	2542	1355	0	3897	1964	4477	1692	0	6169
1966	1850	907	9	2766	1966	2578	1756	17	4351
1968	1563	1516	1013	4092	1968	2578	1897	1170	5645
1970	2032	710	144	2886	1970	2751	1298	126	4175
1972	1408	2815	0	4223	1972	1787	3497	108	5392
1974	2977	768	0	3745	1974	3856	793	0	4649
1976	3388	1401	29	4818	1976	4185	1715	56	5956
1978	2302	983	23	3308	1978	2659	1416	42	4117
1980	2874	2024	113	5011	1980	3211	2170	196	5577
1982	3123	855	5	3983	1982	3501	1002	9	4512
1984	2535	2417	29	4981	1984	2901	2663	34	5598
1986	2758	1199	133	4090	1986	2971	1356	180	4507

County Election for President and Governor

Year	Dem	Rep	Other	Total	Year	Dem	Rep	Other	Total
1988	3259	2037	31	5327	**1988**	3542	4423	36	8001
1990	3008	900	483	4391	1990	4310	1796	414	6520
1992	2850	1522	1182	5554	**1992**	3273	3893	2254	9420
1994	1119	805	2501	4425	1994	2180	2604	2089	6873
1996	2748	1510	754	5012	**1996**	3245	4422	915	8582
1998	2007	1682	42	3731	1998	1862	4438	35	6335
2000	2334	2196	55	4595	**2000**	2515	5591	53	8159
2002	2355	1173	578	4106	2002	2363	3156	785	6304
2004	2283	3066	0	5349	**2004**	2232	7024	0	9256
2006	2526	803	0	3329	2006	3673	1952	0	5625
2008	1709	3134	0	4843	**2008**	2264	6719	0	8983
2010	1642	1881	0	3523	2010	2050	3950	0	6000
2012	1370	2838	0	4208	**2012**	1954	5965	0	7919
2014	1262	1555	105	2922	2014	1018	3071	118	4207

Year	Dem	Rep	Other	Total	Year	Dem	Rep	Other	Total
		Jackson					**Jefferson**		
1907	2143	604	94	2841	1907	1543	594	72	2209
1908	1905	635	220	2760	**1908**	1435	604	288	2327
1910	2089	613	406	3108	1910	1446	563	458	2467
1912	1819	588	687	3094	**1912**	1118	361	673	2152
1914	1123	597	862	2582	1914	1198	566	821	2585
1916	2096	409	698	3203	**1916**	1739	493	630	2862
1918	1392	364	78	1834	1918	1079	389	32	1500
1920	2694	1340	415	4449	**1920**	2281	1728	379	4388
1922	2820	1371	56	4247	1922	2636	1139	42	3817
1924	2342	941	521	3804	**1924**	2441	1108	214	3763
1926	2114	558	29	2701	1926	2136	1003	22	3161
1928	2493	3440	27	5960	**1928**	1916	2251	18	4185
1930	3070	771	2	3843	1930	2830	627	5	3462
1932	5759	603	0	6362	**1932**	3566	485	0	4051
1934	3613	1227	273	5113	1934	2409	1340	251	4000
1936	5435	1095	41	6571	**1936**	3719	1032	22	4773
1938	2588	411	16	3015	1938	2505	349	11	2865
1940	4832	1540	36	6408	**1940**	3814	1226	20	5060
1942	1324	452	7	1783	1942	1534	580	18	2132
1944	4866	1313	13	6192	**1944**	2948	974	15	3937
1946	3278	649	54	3981	1946	1727	473	58	2258
1948	5450	923	0	6373	**1948**	3326	55	0	3381
1950	4055	1103	8	5166	1950	2382	608	5	2995
1952	4921	2627	0	7548	**1952**	2872	1384	0	4256
1954	3194	614	0	3808	1954	1968	351	0	2319
1956	4435	2343	0	6778	**1956**	2539	1186	0	3725
1958	3820	403	229	4452	1958	1471	152	23	1646
1960	3761	3375	0	7136	**1960**	1945	1343	0	3288
1962	3573	1610	7	5190	1962	1595	719	6	2320
1964	5894	2366	0	8260	**1964**	2555	811	0	3366
1966	3538	1855	12	5405	1966	1561	515	5	2081
1968	3371	2248	1786	7405	**1968**	1628	780	701	3109
1970	4191	1586	181	5958	1970	1410	471	62	1943
1972	2054	5519	134	7707	**1972**	969	1709	73	2751
1974	4913	874	0	5787	1974	1743	318	0	2061
1976	4914	3189	60	8163	**1976**	2303	26	956	3285
1978	3798	2072	45	5915	1978	1383	609	7	1999
1980	4031	4327	196	8554	**1980**	1812	1440	80	3332
1982	5153	1583	2	6738	1982	1823	465	3	2291
1984	2996	5773	26	8795	**1984**	1496	1656	27	3179
1986	3611	2480	400	6491	1986	1373	636	67	2076

County Election for President and Governor

Year	Dem	Rep	Other	Total	Year	Dem	Rep	Other	Total
1988	1767	1063	16	2846	**1988**	2042	1518	21	3581
1990	1831	470	86	2387	1990	2015	599	166	2780
1992	1580	671	768	3019	**1992**	2096	1191	1052	4339
1994	972	408	996	2376	1994	620	505	1874	2999
1996	1430	865	351	2646	**1996**	1998	1229	540	3767
1998	811	930	15	1756	1998	1450	1350	27	2827
2000	1245	1320	28	2593	**2000**	1809	2072	49	3930
2002	1057	756	155	1968	2002	2280	990	141	3411
2004	1057	1546	0	2603	**2004**	1713	2635	0	4348
2006	1402	343	0	1745	2006	2253	515	0	2768
2008	805	1652	0	2457	**2008**	1249	2708	0	3957
2010	943	881	0	1824	2010	1231	1713	0	2944
2012	605	1635	0	2239	**2012**	1137	2649	0	3786
2014	553	639	44	1236	2014	1119	1133	104	2356

		Johnston					Kay		
1907	1944	757	213	2914	1907	2651	2562	87	5300
1908	1274	693	602	2569	**1908**	2511	2754	138	5403
1910	1314	641	490	2445	1910	2400	2635	228	5263
1912	1289	506	758	2553	**1912**	2380	2508	382	5270
1914	1154	591	989	2734	1914	1857	2238	468	4563
1916	1727	756	678	3161	**1916**	2340	2482	496	5318
1918	1044	630	66	1740	1918	1682	2274	108	4064
1920	2119	1945	392	4456	**1920**	4543	5949	222	10714
1922	3617	1003	26	4646	1922	4582	5841	47	10470
1924	2122	923	676	3721	**1924**	6049	7392	1007	14448
1926	1536	929	19	2484	1926	5213	5076	47	10336
1928	1766	1294	36	3096	**1928**	4196	13829	136	18161
1930	3368	418	5	3791	1930	5250	7080	26	12356
1932	3277	329	0	3606	**1932**	12841	5884	0	18725
1934	2894	914	103	3911	1934	10578	5426	209	16213
1936	3099	743	23	3865	**1936**	11846	6671	132	18649
1938	2754	358	21	3133	1938	7704	6469	136	14309
1940	2955	1362	12	4329	**1940**	10725	10003	156	20884
1942	1110	443	10	1563	1942	4210	6060	101	10371
1944	2339	925	14	3278	**1944**	8656	9498	88	18242
1946	2089	530	32	2651	1946	4959	8360	156	13475
1948	2936	584	0	3520	**1948**	10119	8982	0	19101
1950	2668	580	6	3254	1950	7341	10100	33	17474
1952	2495	1349	0	3844	**1952**	8382	16460	0	24842
1954	2350	618	0	2968	1954	7678	8933	0	16611
1956	2232	1157	0	3389	**1956**	8071	14837	0	22908
1958	1812	155	47	2014	1958	12126	4201	867	17194
1960	1822	1441	0	3263	**1960**	8249	15156	0	23405
1962	1599	1302	6	2907	1962	6025	12719	45	18789
1964	2370	1065	0	3435	**1964**	11296	12033	0	23329
1966	1450	936	11	2397	1966	6127	11277	53	17457
1968	1216	1048	974	3238	**1968**	6031	12751	2809	21591
1970	1701	644	245	2590	1970	6898	8252	408	15558
1972	983	2205	68	3256	**1972**	4246	17244	494	21984
1974	2246	377	0	2623	1974	9877	7844	0	17721
1976	2765	1127	42	3934	**1976**	9371	12441	274	22086
1978	1654	928	13	2595	1978	7323	9459	115	16897
1980	2066	1701	90	3857	**1980**	6449	15004	884	22337
1982	2648	573	9	3230	1982	10283	7526	20	17829
1984	1820	2195	23	4038	**1984**	6044	16731	136	22911
1986	1675	1091	83	2849	1986	6880	9588	1267	17735

Year	Dem	Rep	Other	Total	Year	Dem	Rep	Other	Total
1988	7751	12646	167	20564	1988	1777	4011	64	5852
1990	7737	5439	1878	15054	1990	2306	2087	683	5076
1992	6643	9115	7070	22828	1992	1379	3479	1553	6411
1994	5243	8652	3938	17833	1994	974	2628	1790	5392
1996	6882	9741	2891	19514	1996	1626	3423	630	5679
1998	5004	9030	215	14249	1998	1001	3375	52	4428
2000	6122	11768	272	10162	2000	1304	4693	59	6056
2002	6071	7264	2279	15614	2002	1767	2426	708	4901
2004	5957	14121	0	20078	2004	1022	5630	0	6652
2006	9054	4096	0	13150	2006	2921	1939	0	4860
2008	5463	13230	0	18693	2008	1009	5372	0	6381
2010	4970	8656	0	13626	2010	1295	3504	0	4799
2012	4627	11499	0	16126	2012	898	4870	0	5768
2014	3551	6131	307	9989	2014	948	2662	96	3706

	Kingfisher					Kiowa			
1907	1688	2204	94	3986	1907	2610	1529	130	4269
1908	1541	2106	226	3873	1908	2354	1591	301	4246
1910	1339	1901	258	3498	1910	1414	1054	287	2755
1912	1235	1527	354	3116	1912	1831	1167	948	3946
1914	968	1721	497	3186	1914	1018	1230	1302	3550
1916	1364	1728	442	3534	1916	2279	1017	1130	4426
1918	791	1527	145	2463	1918	1218	1121	46	2385
1920	1743	3214	249	5206	1920	2512	2638	442	5592
1922	2545	2864	26	5435	1922	3554	2477	85	6116
1924	1644	2834	617	5095	1924	2635	1688	531	4854
1926	1471	2631	37	4139	1926	1857	1052	48	2957
1928	1780	4063	39	5882	1928	2270	4116	92	6478
1930	2151	2648	6	4805	1930	3692	1565	3	5260
1932	3986	2103	0	6089	1932	5204	966	0	6170
1934	2947	3380	27	6354	1934	3514	1729	587	5830
1936	4081	2539	32	6652	1936	5624	1684	53	7361
1938	3145	2632	36	5813	1938	2924	892	27	3843
1940	2865	3718	25	6608	1940	4679	2539	34	7252
1942	1440	2509	25	3974	1942	1383	831	16	2230
1944	2175	3417	17	5609	1944	4175	2081	24	6280
1946	1298	2435	145	3878	1946	2212	1030	60	3302
1948	2488	2931	0	5419	1948	4263	1530	0	5793
1950	1785	3701	14	5500	1950	3117	2048	10	5175
1952	1459	4873	0	6332	1952	3489	4100	0	7589
1954	1828	3069	0	4897	1954	3349	1303	0	4652
1956	1668	3935	0	5603	1956	3371	2713	0	6084
1958	2064	1636	354	4054	1958	2092	971	1149	4212
1960	1821	3501	0	5322	1960	2638	3515	0	6153
1962	1363	3753	13	5129	1962	2471	2348	8	4827
1964	2512	3117	0	5629	1964	3686	2206	0	5892
1966	1326	3221	13	4560	1966	2307	2114	6	4427
1968	1226	3558	720	5504	1968	2219	2418	957	5594
1970	1961	2729	136	4826	1970	2922	1714	153	4789
1972	912	4861	162	5935	1972	1495	3711	110	5316
1974	2752	2515	0	5267	1974	3367	897	0	4264
1976	2372	3443	82	5897	1976	3403	1971	46	5420
1978	1958	3209	45	5212	1978	2094	1752	15	3861
1980	1282	4962	174	6418	1980	2372	1737	116	4225
1982	3127	2455	9	5591	1982	3119	917	3	4039
1984	1125	5528	33	6686	1984	2016	2951	28	4995
1986	2026	2934	560	5520	1986	2351	1383	191	3925

Year	Dem	Rep	Other	Total	Year	Dem	Rep	Other	Total
1988	2296	2030	32	4358	1988	2365	1830	38	4233
1990	2805	923	220	3948	1990	2245	608	234	3087
1992	2143	1635	1132	4910	1992	2606	1212	1067	4885
1994	1490	1357	985	3832	1994	1121	509	1398	3028
1996	1973	1638	517	4128	1996	2222	1189	592	4003
1998	1369	1787	30	3186	1998	1774	991	34	2799
2000	1544	2173	33	3750	2000	1865	1739	65	3669
2002	1742	1000	373	3115	2002	1984	914	377	3275
2004	1413	2610	0	4023	2004	1945	2535	0	4480
2006	2148	630	0	2778	2006	2019	630	0	2649
2008	1226	2537	0	3763	2008	1313	2860	0	4173
2010	1250	1424	0	2674	2010	1467	1610	0	3077
2012	1106	2316	0	3422	2012	1170	2628	0	3798
2014	1090	1305	63	2458	2014	1266	1016	78	2360

Year	Dem	Rep	Other	Total	Year	Dem	Rep	Other	Total
		Latimer					LeFlore		
1907	969	629	68	1666	1907	2162	1715	83	3960
1908	720	616	197	1533	1908	1872	1771	230	3873
1910	690	527	199	1416	1910	1843	1529	229	3601
1912	722	482	349	1553	1912	2009	1538	528	4075
1914	759	570	382	1711	1914	1646	1220	1122	3988
1916	950	663	346	1959	1916	2576	1944	656	5176
1918	748	539	59	1346	1918	2101	1630	83	3814
1920	1200	1410	333	2943	1920	3757	4928	387	9072
1922	2245	1282	14	3541	1922	5820	3325	41	9186
1924	1457	971	274	2702	1924	4069	3326	852	8247
1926	1159	1103	16	2278	1926	3500	2845	54	6399
1928	1583	1368	38	2989	1928	4622	5168	57	9847
1930	1979	1038	6	3023	1930	5403	2665	15	8083
1932	3119	728	0	3847	1932	8680	2363	0	11043
1934	2897	1333	38	4268	1934	7717	4071	60	11848
1936	2923	1344	19	4286	1936	8061	3894	14	11969
1938	3023	773	22	3818	1938	6739	1865	41	8645
1940	3138	1600	28	4766	1940	8379	4664	44	13087
1942	1625	670	18	2313	1942	3345	1499	13	4857
1944	1948	1296	11	3255	1944	5660	3667	22	9349
1946	1574	662	10	2246	1946	4560	1777	21	6358
1948	2536	919	0	3455	1948	6786	2821	0	9607
1950	1805	910	3	2718	1950	5117	2278	7	7402
1952	2283	1668	0	3951	1952	6349	4631	0	10980
1954	2348	649	0	2997	1954	5826	1843	0	7669
1956	1994	1387	0	3381	1956	5276	4310	0	9586
1958	1678	235	37	1950	1958	4859	772	95	5726
1960	1534	1454	0	2988	1960	4844	5302	0	10146
1962	1756	1094	8	2858	1962	5064	2636	18	7718
1964	2297	849	0	3146	1964	7105	3904	0	11009
1966	1381	702	4	2087	1966	4293	2325	15	6633
1968	1350	1091	892	3333	1968	4020	3600	3345	10965
1970	2163	836	152	3151	1970	5123	2029	279	7431
1972	1239	2520	130	3889	1972	3433	7932	394	11759
1974	2562	529	0	3091	1974	7179	1862	0	9041
1976	2661	1312	55	4028	1976	8033	4907	145	13085
1978	2123	827	27	2977	1978	6859	2045	59	8963
1980	2105	1737	124	3966	1980	6668	6807	284	13759
1982	2364	679	2	3045	1982	9552	2058	19	11629
1984	1858	2210	32	4100	1984	5990	8604	104	14698
1986	2125	1094	110	3329	1986	6864	3364	416	10644

Year	Dem	Rep	Other	Total		Year	Dem	Rep	Other	Total
1988	6594	6964	83	13641		1988	4225	6409	106	10740
1990	8602	2622	293	11517		1990	4995	2860	1180	9035
1992	7843	5850	3070	16763		1992	3904	5315	3204	12423
1994	3529	2699	3854	10082		1994	2250	3777	3538	9565
1996	6831	5689	1729	14249		1996	4332	5243	1606	11181
1998	5910	5446	136	11492		1998	3211	5621	131	8963
2000	6536	8215	234	14985		2000	4140	7387	174	11701
2002	6941	4468	499	11908		2002	4935	4251	2103	11289
2004	6741	10683	0	17424		2004	4041	10149	0	14190
2006	7963	3100	0	11063		2006	7023	3369	0	10392
2008	5136	11605	0	16741		2008	3504	10470	0	13974
2010	5950	7040	0	12990		2010	3838	6976	0	10814
2012	4662	11177	0	15839		2012	3273	9553	0	12826
2014	4074	5281	465	9820		2014	3001	5377	337	8715

Lincoln · Logan

Year	Dem	Rep	Other	Total		Year	Dem	Rep	Other	Total
1907	3432	3562	220	7214		1907	2179	3831	84	6094
1908	3030	3515	534	7079		1908	2183	3768	203	6154
1910	2298	2662	784	5744		1910	1300	2761	257	4318
1912	2137	2459	971	5567		1912	1700	2546	565	4811
1914	1488	2557	1324	5369		1914	1026	2567	535	4128
1916	2258	2387	1081	5726		1916	1701	2270	626	4597
1918	1555	2461	152	4168		1918	1275	1933	137	3345
1920	2968	5254	635	8857		1920	2210	4606	278	7094
1922	3812	4269	62	8143		1922	3099	4992	57	8148
1924	3283	4220	739	8242		1924	2366	4445	751	7562
1926	2888	3353	74	6315		1926	2442	2838	44	5324
1928	2405	6118	126	8649		1928	2251	6277	104	8632
1930	4286	3868	10	8164		1930	2527	4600	21	7148
1932	7641	3505	0	11146		1932	5773	3959	0	9732
1934	4863	6097	221	11181		1934	4385	5023	134	9542
1936	5903	5452	52	11407		1936	5425	4609	61	10095
1938	5613	4232	50	9895		1938	5201	3213	118	8532
1940	5271	6269	34	11574		1940	4752	5427	46	10225
1942	3048	4377	36	7461		1942	2261	3190	35	5486
1944	3910	4801	28	8739		1944	3795	4586	36	8417
1946	3240	3555	134	6929		1946	2550	3634	243	6427
1948	4913	3898	0	8811		1948	4109	3817	0	7926
1950	3778	4306	10	8094		1950	2884	4771	18	7673
1952	4071	5778	0	9849		1952	3444	6172	0	9616
1954	4245	3552	0	7797		1954	3100	3871	0	6971
1956	3909	4993	0	8902		1956	2875	5326	0	8201
1958	5179	1927	384	7490		1958	4199	1614	740	6553
1960	3255	5528	0	8783		1960	2820	5121	0	7941
1962	3083	4924	19	8026		1962	2310	4560	15	6885
1964	5046	3854	0	8900		1964	4279	3787	0	8066
1966	2863	3928	23	6814		1966	2613	4081	34	6728
1968	2304	3855	1969	8128		1968	2508	3960	1689	8157
1970	3272	3302	273	6847		1970	2900	3385	307	6592
1972	1919	6512	254	8685		1972	2760	6543	200	9503
1974	5298	2660	0	7958		1974	4601	2898	0	7499
1976	4988	4429	133	9550		1976	4594	4382	160	9136
1978	3307	3506	41	6854		1978	3345	3763	65	7173
1980	3231	6064	290	9585		1980	3246	6311	435	9992
1982	5436	3665	13	9114		1982	4722	3391	20	8133
1984	3020	8088	81	11189		1984	3551	8356	71	11978
1986	3956	3795	1435	9186		1986	3905	3903	1465	9273

Year	Dem	Rep	Other	Total	Year	Dem	Rep	Other	Total
1988	4603	6947	154	11704	**1988**	1889	1361	17	3267
1990	5247	3446	1068	9761	1990	1804	471	143	2418
1992	4453	6071	3282	13806	**1992**	1708	922	1049	3679
1994	2526	5020	2223	9769	1994	545	366	1562	2463
1996	4854	5949	1419	12222	**1996**	1675	1224	392	3291
1998	2743	5564	113	8420	1998	1084	1176	19	2279
2000	4510	8187	173	12870	**2000**	1530	1807	35	3372
2002	4245	5048	1964	11257	2002	1753	884	95	2732
2004	4869	11474	0	16343	**2004**	1538	2295	0	3833
2006	6408	4280	0	10688	2006	1797	447	0	2244
2008	5717	12556	0	18273	**2008**	1257	2589	0	3846
2010	4098	8848	0	12946	2010	1107	1554	0	2661
2012	4724	12314	0	17038	**2012**	1034	2436	0	2470
2014	3462	6864	363	10689	2014	877	1177	93	2147

	Love					Major			
1907	1199	491	87	1777	1907	968	1296	302	2566
1908	835	413	253	1501	**1908**	877	1446	463	2786
1910	815	308	224	1347	1910	704	1379	506	2589
1912	750	199	412	1361	**1912**	987	321	556	1864
1914	1046	233	691	1970	1914	474	671	1007	2152
1916	1125	266	365	1756	**1916**	762	946	674	2382
1918	856	159	35	1050	1918	474	863	352	1689
1920	1660	711	152	2523	**1920**	780	1920	483	3183
1922	2112	301	7	2420	1922	1181	1774	132	3087
1924	1713	479	536	2728	**1924**	649	1781	614	3044
1926	1018	440	15	1473	1926	1053	1260	50	2363
1928	1268	843	0	2111	**1928**	674	2891	107	3672
1930	1778	195	3	1976	1930	1427	1405	7	2839
1932	2426	187	0	2613	**1932**	2525	1374	0	3899
1934	1574	641	154	2369	1934	1165	2798	237	4200
1936	2227	440	20	2687	**1936**	1929	2230	45	4204
1938	1606	154	7	1767	1938	1782	2010	40	3832
1940	2485	687	11	3183	**1940**	1404	3453	34	4891
1942	861	168	5	1034	1942	607	2096	20	2723
1944	1955	446	4	2405	**1944**	965	3019	21	4005
1946	1357	145	8	1510	1946	730	2144	79	2953
1948	2191	249	0	2440	**1948**	3054	798	5	3857
1950	1530	334	3	1867	1950	1170	2409	4	3583
1952	1972	806	0	2778	**1952**	845	2495	0	3340
1954	1892	240	0	2132	1954	888	2033	0	2921
1956	1756	731	0	2487	**1956**	951	2826	0	3777
1958	1311	66	17	1394	1958	1294	974	319	2587
1960	1443	932	0	2375	**1960**	716	2892	0	3608
1962	1255	481	4	1740	1962	672	2862	3	3537
1964	1863	663	0	2526	**1964**	1291	2436	0	3727
1966	1044	446	4	1494	1966	742	2295	11	3048
1968	931	677	766	2374	**1968**	594	2550	357	3501
1970	1151	460	129	1740	1970	1009	1776	119	2904
1972	671	1407	30	2108	**1972**	512	3203	103	3818
1974	1461	177	0	1638	1974	1517	1766	0	3283
1976	1923	846	9	2778	**1976**	1357	2282	58	3697
1978	1205	531	12	1748	1978	858	2011	14	2883
1980	1578	1449	48	3075	**1980**	584	3059	96	3739
1982	2717	452	7	3176	1982	1799	1164	3	2966
1984	1359	1833	17	3209	**1984**	619	3385	31	4035
1986	1384	1036	92	2512	1986	1020	1873	354	3247

Year	Dem	Rep	Other	Total	Year	Dem	Rep	Other	Total
1988	982	2638	51	3671	1988	2730	1911	28	4669
1990	1581	1120	563	3264	1990	2880	930	216	4026
1992	731	2154	870	3755	1992	2519	1478	1501	5498
1994	579	1588	1061	3228	1994	1075	831	1909	3815
1996	900	2188	424	3512	1996	2624	1605	684	4913
1998	707	1997	32	2736	1998	1670	2252	34	3956
2000	635	2672	45	3352	2000	2210	2641	49	4900
2002	907	1490	398	2795	2002	2694	1402	172	4268
2004	537	3122	0	3659	2004	2088	3363	0	5451
2006	1603	1191	0	2794	2006	2650	882	0	3532
2008	515	2956	0	3471	2008	1643	3730	0	5373
2010	791	2221	0	3012	2010	1485	2528	0	4013
2012	446	2700	0	3146	2012	1396	3744	0	5140
2014	693	1417	90	2200	2014	1494	1792	133	3419

Marshall / Mayes

Year	Dem	Rep	Other	Total	Year	Dem	Rep	Other	Total
1907	1248	467	218	1933	1907	1215	908	8	2131
1908	842	406	406	1654	1908	1186	1021	44	2251
1910	845	389	526	1760	1910	1454	1137	61	2652
1912	958	315	702	1975	1912	1391	1079	215	2685
1914	1037	399	1006	2442	1914	1362	1186	239	2787
1916	1352	449	623	2424	1916	1574	1229	228	3031
1918	841	365	90	1296	1918	1127	955	42	2124
1920	1589	1487	269	3345	1920	1989	2447	163	4599
1922	2416	664	34	3114	1922	2764	2172	24	4960
1924	1935	866	545	3346	1924	2246	2317	325	4888
1926	1298	778	43	2119	1926	1824	1941	27	3792
1928	1358	1063	80	2501	1928	2161	3004	49	5214
1930	1829	287	0	2116	1930	3098	1889	4	4991
1932	3236	319	0	3555	1932	4444	1596	0	6040
1934	2015	528	175	2718	1934	3345	3356	49	6750
1936	2840	415	23	3278	1936	3920	2690	13	6623
1938	1488	193	5	1686	1938	3874	1897	21	5792
1940	2723	1032	15	3770	1940	4057	3631	21	7709
1942	992	315	7	1314	1942	2052	1895	12	3959
1944	2261	752	11	3024	1944	3830	3822	19	7671
1946	1662	300	9	1971	1946	3371	2714	40	6125
1948	2455	469	0	2924	1948	4201	2854	0	7055
1950	1848	471	0	2319	1950	3756	3745	12	7513
1952	2288	1204	0	3492	1952	3837	4704	0	8541
1954	2971	288	0	3259	1954	4368	2765	0	7133
1956	2100	1151	0	3251	1956	3760	4677	0	8437
1958	1952	106	38	2096	1958	4603	1524	166	6293
1960	1793	1325	0	3118	1960	3721	5194	0	8915
1962	1060	1668	8	2736	1962	3802	4272	13	8087
1964	2318	1101	0	3419	1964	5421	4157	0	9578
1966	1220	1149	6	2375	1966	3613	3490	25	7128
1968	1191	1209	986	3386	1968	2855	4360	2431	9646
1970	1370	601	909	2880	1970	4279	3649	247	8175
1972	1113	2273	91	3477	1972	2656	7535	263	10454
1974	2694	300	0	2994	1974	5099	3541	0	8640
1976	2939	1358	27	4324	1976	6298	5040	81	11419
1978	1690	1237	21	2948	1978	4934	3355	43	8332
1980	2157	1961	77	4195	1980	5344	6633	381	12358
1982	3246	843	6	4095	1982	7002	3034	14	10050
1984	2039	2488	33	4560	1984	5154	8585	99	13838
1986	2395	1494	100	3989	1986	4820	4917	834	10571

Year	Dem	Rep	Other	Total	Year	Dem	Rep	Other	Total
1988	6691	6115	95	12901	1988	3594	4771	88	8453
1990	6539	2702	1037	10278	1990	4389	2177	831	7397
1992	6432	5445	3294	15171	1992	3378	4377	3021	10776
1994	4453	3902	2345	10700	1994	2421	3545	2248	8214
1996	6377	5268	1663	13308	1996	3753	4363	1323	9439
1998	5871	4000	117	9988	1998	2614	4385	119	7118
2000	6618	7132	251	14001	2000	3679	6750	110	10539
2002	6460	4025	1981	12466	2002	4102	4115	1536	9753
2004	6933	9946	0	16879	2004	3742	10041	0	13783
2006	8300	2940	0	11240	2006	6622	3527	0	10149
2008	5749	10243	0	15983	2008	3551	11193	0	14744
2010	4768	6992	0	11760	2010	3817	7248	0	11065
2012	4823	9637	0	14460	2012	3194	11112	0	14306
2014	4016	5158	337	9511	2014	3210	5593	260	9063

	McClain					McCurtain			
1907	1465	723	111	2299	1907	1287	955	61	2303
1908	1234	780	363	2377	1908	565	482	148	1195
1910	1292	671	344	2307	1910	1130	650	183	1963
1912	1273	583	420	2276	1912	1059	704	848	2611
1914	940	594	620	2154	1914	1645	512	1263	3420
1916	1541	680	495	2716	1916	1763	795	654	3212
1918	994	469	41	1504	1918	955	305	36	1296
1920	2310	1728	249	4287	1920	2598	1959	315	4872
1922	2623	1273	13	3909	1922	3483	1048	23	4554
1924	2519	1233	259	4011	1924	3279	1669	237	5185
1926	1980	809	26	2815	1926	2637	1011	42	3690
1928	1913	2399	44	4356	1928	2877	1915	21	4813
1930	3098	1102	7	4207	1930	3253	760	2	4015
1932	5087	818	0	5905	1932	5886	587	0	6473
1934	3367	1518	67	4952	1934	4238	1509	0	5747
1936	4092	1191	17	5300	1936	5089	1119	13	6221
1938	2063	433	2	2498	1938	3566	358	7	3931
1940	3768	1862	11	5641	1940	6994	2225	29	9248
1942	1353	697	6	2056	1942	2548	439	12	2999
1944	3301	1492	8	4801	1944	5322	1419	10	6751
1946	2057	764	47	2868	1946	2951	475	14	3440
1948	3451	908	0	4359	1948	6223	1091	0	7314
1950	2544	1193	4	3741	1950	5246	916	16	6178
1952	3201	2326	0	5527	1952	5793	2748	0	8541
1954	2418	874	0	3292	1954	4960	997	0	5957
1956	2981	2081	0	5062	1956	4761	2707	0	7468
1958	2435	235	111	2781	1958	3913	263	48	4224
1960	2365	2547	0	4912	1960	4202	3562	0	7764
1962	1941	1942	11	3894	1962	4246	2144	4	6394
1964	3638	1638	0	5276	1964	5982	2981	0	8963
1966	1844	1775	12	3631	1966	3857	2368	23	6248
1968	1842	2047	1647	5536	1968	2944	2795	2880	8619
1970	2263	1593	134	3990	1970	3433	1438	147	5018
1972	1350	4241	206	5797	1972	2568	6441	166	9175
1974	3465	1329	0	4794	1974	5899	628	0	6527
1976	4048	2444	80	6572	1976	7560	3423	97	11080
1978	2604	2123	53	4780	1978	4937	1517	89	6543
1980	2990	4284	259	7533	1980	5953	5189	230	11372
1982	4099	2230	5	6334	1982	4562	1641	9	6212
1984	2549	6056	67	8672	1984	3994	6381	41	10416
1986	3170	2753	793	6716	1986	4498	2412	110	7020

County Election for President and Governor

Year	Dem	Rep	Other	Total
1988	4928	4920	63	9911
1990	5584	1434	218	7236
1992	5082	3519	2893	11494
1994	2461	1553	4348	8362
1996	4350	3892	1532	9774
1998	3587	2926	255	6768
2000	3752	6601	129	10492
2002	5187	3035	427	8649
2004	3684	7472	0	11156
2006	4485	1926	0	6411
2008	2794	7745	0	10539
2010	4035	4312	0	8347
2012	2440	7635	0	10075
2014	2917	3445	361	6723

McIntosh

Year	Dem	Rep	Other	Total
1907	1666	1607	43	3316
1908	1236	1606	141	2983
1910	1256	1000	152	2408
1912	1325	970	540	2835
1914	1252	1009	842	3103
1916	1743	898	561	3202
1918	1185	725	65	1975
1920	2635	2353	258	5246
1922	2969	1519	10	4498
1924	2723	1675	97	4495
1926	1582	1274	10	2866
1928	2044	2742	35	4821
1930	3081	1797	9	4887
1932	4533	1077	0	5610
1934	3854	2951	66	6871
1936	3898	2470	16	6384
1938	3739	1106	26	4871
1940	3771	487	17	4275
1942	1633	1406	6	3045
1944	3190	2569	12	5771
1946	2144	1166	73	3383
1948	3674	1442	0	5116
1950	2401	1599	14	4014
1952	3007	2295	0	5302
1954	2634	1046	0	3680
1956	2728	2149	0	4877
1958	2587	366	45	2998
1960	2185	2221	0	4406
1962	2184	1319	8	3511
1964	3497	1428	0	4925
1966	2173	1288	7	3468
1968	1759	1532	1254	4545
1970	2174	1069	107	3350
1972	1686	3216	132	5034
1974	3607	1209	0	4816
1976	4145	1822	48	6015
1978	2884	1465	28	4377
1980	3654	2925	184	6763
1982	4310	1454	5	5769
1984	3479	3646	40	7165
1986	3292	2067	217	5576

Year	Dem	Rep	Other	Total
1988	4041	2665	36	6742
1990	4466	1229	473	6168
1992	4184	2225	1484	7893
1994	2990	1931	2057	6978
1996	4219	2400	1072	7691
1998	3698	2437	110	6245
2000	4206	3444	131	7781
2002	3631	1809	1357	6797
2004	4488	4692	0	9180
2006	4626	1404	0	6030
2008	3320	4903	0	8223
2010	2921	3244	0	6165
2012	2779	4509	0	7288
2014	2098	2361	150	4609

Murray

Year	Dem	Rep	Other	Total
1907	1356	502	93	1951
1908	1111	574	280	1965
1910	987	445	498	1930
1912	987	321	556	1864
1914	890	459	536	1885
1916	1305	458	356	2119
1918	903	336	20	1259
1920	1747	1359	119	3225
1922	2220	936	9	3165
1924	2083	784	148	3015
1926	1419	868	20	2307
1928	1498	1631	36	3165
1930	2920	697	1	3618
1932	3086	532	0	3618
1934	2902	1099	98	4099
1936	3181	823	23	4027
1938	2378	339	20	2737
1940	3126	1238	17	4381
1942	1425	452	7	1884
1944	2602	1005	9	3616
1946	2123	615	28	2766
1948	3054	798	0	3852
1950	2514	898	5	3417
1952	2868	1885	0	4753
1954	2279	788	0	3067
1956	2482	1809	0	4291
1958	2106	213	98	2417
1960	2129	1993	0	4122
1962	2059	1641	8	3708
1964	3083	1236	0	4319
1966	1665	1325	11	3001
1968	1773	1454	1027	4254
1970	1980	1036	141	3157
1972	1294	2983	95	4372
1974	2903	653	0	3556
1976	2932	1563	41	4536
1978	2039	1257	15	3311
1980	2384	2494	189	5067
1982	2903	1033	2	3938
1984	2229	3073	45	5347
1986	2440	1619	338	4397

Year	Dem	Rep	Other	Total
1988	2697	2056	41	4794
1990	2824	987	461	4272
1992	2594	1536	1458	5588
1994	1188	1011	1734	3933
1996	2620	1712	736	5068
1998	1740	1763	43	3546
2000	2263	2609	50	4922
2002	2662	1325	463	4450
2004	2130	3665	0	5795
2006	3015	916	0	3931
2008	1592	3746	0	5338
2010	1802	2177	0	3979
2012	1540	3606	0	5146
2014	1251	1606	95	2952

Muskogee

Year	Dem	Rep	Other	Total
1907	3479	3789	63	7331
1908	2793	3592	168	6553
1910	3241	2367	200	5808
1912	3681	2385	536	6602
1914	2866	2736	549	6151
1916	4004	2532	340	6876
1918	2692	1473	35	4200
1920	6378	5159	96	11633
1922	7471	5652	18	13141
1924	6895	6158	644	13697
1926	5644	5280	24	10948
1928	6343	9972	54	16369
1930	6690	5752	16	12458
1932	12621	5351	0	17972
1934	10485	7180	152	17817
1936	13344	6452	33	19829
1938	9762	2573	35	12370
1940	12917	9585	49	22551
1942	5137	3825	15	8977
1944	11679	8280	31	19990
1946	8218	5384	95	13697
1948	13860	6592	0	20452
1950	9183	7340	31	16554
1952	13040	11810	0	24850
1954	9860	4682	0	14542
1956	10413	11057	0	21470
1958	11596	1840	246	13682
1960	11082	12403	0	23485
1962	9612	8042	23	17677
1964	16330	8508	0	24838
1966	10004	8117	30	18151
1968	9377	8707	4596	22680
1970	9896	6246	436	16578
1972	7380	15101	551	23032
1974	13587	5101	0	18688
1976	14678	10287	190	25155
1978	12167	6255	120	18542
1980	13341	11511	863	25715
1982	13781	5984	26	19791
1984	12343	14652	188	27183
1986	9155	8772	781	18708

Year	Dem	Rep	Other	Total
1988	13760	11147	161	25068
1990	11525	4526	1691	17742
1992	13619	8782	5531	27932
1994	8515	6728	4587	19830
1996	12963	8974	3243	25180
1998	10265	7761	230	18256
2000	12520	11820	353	24693
2002	9867	6132	4275	20274
2004	12585	15124	0	27709
2006	12885	4117	0	17002
2008	11294	15289	0	26583
2010	8348	9405	0	17753
2012	9952	13404	0	23556
2014	7039	6822	469	14330

Noble

Year	Dem	Rep	Other	Total
1907	1459	1494	61	3014
1908	1364	1476	125	2965
1910	1258	1447	208	2913
1912	1188	1266	293	2747
1914	958	1352	279	2589
1916	1346	1243	234	2823
1918	916	1239	82	2237
1920	1553	2494	147	4194
1922	1950	2523	43	4516
1924	1927	2680	633	5240
1926	2611	2164	26	4801
1928	1777	3067	64	4908
1930	2529	2360	13	4902
1932	4414	1635	0	6049
1934	3077	2738	59	5874
1936	3901	2461	13	6375
1938	2800	2339	40	5179
1940	3226	3441	7	6674
1942	1381	2227	15	3623
1944	2300	3060	13	5373
1946	1547	2476	80	4103
1948	2770	2430	0	5200
1950	2071	3113	13	5197
1952	1803	4422	0	6225
1954	2134	2558	0	4692
1956	2017	3536	0	5553
1958	2727	1276	246	4249
1960	1910	3198	0	5108
1962	1366	3333	9	4708
1964	2713	2157	0	4870
1966	1643	2524	12	4179
1968	1412	2911	618	4941
1970	1697	2206	108	4011
1972	999	4085	128	5212
1974	2455	2058	0	4513
1976	2278	2634	53	4965
1978	1616	2393	21	4030
1980	1398	3663	179	5240
1982	2579	1834	7	4420
1984	1238	4018	23	5279
1986	1734	2161	422	4317

Year	Dem	Rep	Other	Total	Year	Dem	Rep	Other	Total
1988	1661	3015	50	4726	1988	2203	2000	31	4234
1990	2144	1417	689	4250	1990	1996	920	336	3252
1992	1333	2474	1476	5283	1992	1912	1531	1081	4524
1994	840	1865	1631	4336	1994	1195	1148	841	3184
1996	1756	2318	717	4791	1996	1788	1457	609	3854
1998	1234	2180	60	3474	1998	1546	1641	45	3232
2000	1416	3230	51	4697	2000	1703	2069	77	3849
2002	1757	1767	704	4228	2002	1718	1241	709	3668
2004	1335	3993	0	5328	2004	1660	2805	0	4465
2006	2460	1210	0	3670	2006	2026	840	0	2866
2008	1174	3881	0	5055	2008	1411	3031	0	4442
2010	1200	2782	0	3982	2010	1300	1981	0	3281
2012	1143	3488	0	4631	2012	1244	2832	0	4076
2014	927	1901	90	2918	2014	953	1656	96	2705

Nowata / Okfuskee

Year	Dem	Rep	Other	Total	Year	Dem	Rep	Other	Total
1907	1068	992	23	2083	1907	1125	878	181	2184
1908	923	1086	61	2070	1908	872	1297	402	2571
1910	1077	1070	105	2252	1910	957	749	371	2077
1912	1012	1087	172	2271	1912	952	651	740	2343
1914	1044	1300	236	2580	1914	990	810	744	2544
1916	1355	1322	184	2861	1916	1337	670	525	2532
1918	933	1180	25	2138	1918	887	557	52	1496
1920	1699	2678	75	4452	1920	1643	1764	241	3648
1922	2247	2240	19	4506	1922	3020	1522	33	4575
1924	2049	2296	154	4499	1924	2654	1431	264	4349
1926	1588	1578	29	3195	1926	2517	1748	107	4372
1928	1763	2930	19	4712	1928	2513	3612	76	6201
1930	2104	2216	8	4328	1930	3788	1764	4	5556
1932	3773	1900	0	5673	1932	5126	1415	0	6541
1934	2374	2647	51	5072	1934	3806	2142	865	6813
1936	3512	2552	20	6084	1936	4843	2162	47	7052
1938	3195	2100	27	5322	1938	4298	867	10	5175
1940	3615	3406	39	7060	1940	4574	3001	24	7599
1942	1691	2117	34	3842	1942	1939	1235	11	3185
1944	2581	2730	15	5326	1944	3291	2177	9	5477
1946	1814	2171	145	4130	1946	2061	1359	80	3500
1948	2688	2119	0	4807	1948	3335	1624	0	4959
1950	2136	2678	16	4830	1950	2234	1733	2	3969
1952	2657	3226	0	5883	1952	2775	2469	0	5244
1954	2573	2069	0	4642	1954	2398	1186	0	3584
1956	2268	3168	0	5436	1956	2331	2299	0	4630
1958	3021	1075	260	4356	1958	2336	357	142	2835
1960	2125	3014	0	5139	1960	1968	2510	0	4478
1962	2033	2409	7	4449	1962	1966	1594	2	3562
1964	2644	2142	0	4786	1964	2905	1629	0	4534
1966	1950	1844	8	3802	1966	1610	1548	11	3169
1968	1314	2116	1080	4510	1968	1777	1686	981	4444
1970	1659	1753	164	3576	1970	1774	1313	83	3170
1972	1096	3293	146	4535	1972	1328	2862	99	4289
1974	1830	1905	0	3735	1974	2763	985	0	3748
1976	2195	2077	39	4311	1976	2663	1630	32	4325
1978	1778	1529	14	3321	1978	1663	1248	22	2933
1980	1694	2640	136	4470	1980	2177	2126	98	4401
1982	2756	1122	5	3883	1982	2295	985	8	3288
1984	1687	3030	44	4761	1984	1684	2443	18	4145
1986	1867	1528	128	3523	1986	1832	1176	213	3221

Year	Dem	Rep	Other	Total
1988	2209	1851	38	4098
1990	2390	794	340	3524
1992	2141	1580	909	4630
1994	1253	1018	1327	3598
1996	2074	1380	556	4010
1998	1632	1432	64	3128
2000	1714	1910	64	3788
2002	1932	976	602	3510
2004	1743	2542	0	4285
2006	2147	726	0	2873
2008	1480	2643	0	4123
2010	1405	1619	0	3024
2012	1256	2335	0	3591
2014	1116	1290	91	2635

Oklahoma

Year	Dem	Rep	Other	Total
1907	5038	5944	337	11319
1908	4833	5317	498	10648
1910	6140	5051	913	12104
1912	6963	5706	905	13574
1914	3858	6478	1183	11519
1916	7971	5291	1302	14564
1918	5461	4332	222	10015
1920	17797	15314	1212	34323
1922	20397	23701	156	44254
1924	21708	17504	3873	43085
1926	17796	12549	203	30548
1928	16073	36608	272	52953
1930	15569	18965	44	34578
1932	41130	21238	0	62368
1934	30372	14150	879	45401
1936	50946	24312	373	75631
1938	31585	10828	352	42765
1940	53649	35639	329	89617
1942	19085	15605	133	34823
1944	57812	42464	116	100392
1946	28626	29772	1067	59465
1948	59954	40161	0	100115
1950	38679	49717	271	88667
1952	70199	95492	0	165691
1954	47928	42314	0	90242
1956	57512	85395	0	142907
1958	52472	16012	8477	76961
1960	64648	102992	0	167640
1962	52779	74470	682	127931
1964	90641	83660	0	174301
1966	43989	73817	1338	119144
1968	60395	93212	33834	187441
1970	49625	68272	4297	122194
1972	46986	156437	4502	207925
1974	85625	57770	0	143395
1976	87185	119120	3808	210113
1978	58348	79092	3575	141015
1980	58765	139538	12970	211273
1982	83706	74087	1704	159497
1984	60235	159974	3052	223261
1986	59176	75811	19309	154296

Year	Dem	Rep	Other	Total
1988	75812	135376	1703	212891
1990	85019	69514	16239	170772
1992	76271	126788	56864	259923
1994	50589	107489	26785	184863
1996	80438	120429	19386	220253
1998	50977	102216	1817	155010
2000	81590	139078	2443	223111
2002	73236	91270	24570	189076
2004	97298	174741	0	272039
2006	110726	64987	0	175713
2008	116182	163172	0	279354
2010	82316	111614	0	193930
2012	106982	149728	0	256710
2014	71431	79853	4356	155640

Okmulgee

Year	Dem	Rep	Other	Total
1907	1287	1502	140	2929
1908	1103	1400	295	2798
1910	1183	1246	358	2787
1912	1243	1140	567	2950
1914	1559	1101	752	3412
1916	2406	1860	773	5039
1918	1809	1550	114	3473
1920	4492	5368	588	10448
1922	5579	6542	68	12189
1924	5927	6015	896	12838
1926	4717	4714	62	9493
1928	5834	9149	73	15056
1930	7405	5128	10	12543
1932	11287	4762	0	16049
1934	9246	5740	250	15236
1936	12061	4975	57	17093
1938	8032	3166	53	11251
1940	11016	6696	84	17796
1942	4862	4081	27	8970
1944	9737	5430	25	15192
1946	6446	4294	230	10970
1948	10467	4368	0	14835
1950	6137	5247	25	11409
1952	10115	6717	0	16832
1954	7717	3482	0	11199
1956	7626	6703	0	14329
1958	6465	1157	246	7868
1960	7262	7107	0	14369
1962	6180	4852	15	11047
1964	10195	4704	0	14899
1966	6236	4493	37	10766
1968	6089	4709	2728	13526
1970	5767	3703	304	9774
1972	4494	8706	447	13647
1974	8131	3265	0	11396
1976	8499	5333	131	13963
1978	6800	3072	51	9923
1980	7236	6652	397	14285
1982	8140	3052	11	11203
1984	7380	8704	105	16189
1986	5581	5198	787	11566

Year	Dem	Rep	Other	Total
1988	8262	5674	60	13996
1990	6811	2432	1192	10435
1992	7767	4586	3068	15421
1994	4718	3335	2626	10679
1996	7555	4246	1536	13337
1998	5291	3428	82	8801
2000	7186	5797	195	13178
2002	5823	3341	1974	11138
2004	7367	8363	0	15730
2006	7321	2378	0	9699
2008	6191	8727	0	14918
2010	4906	5393	0	10299
2012	5432	7731	0	13163
2014	3780	4165	256	8201

Osage

Year	Dem	Rep	Other	Total
1907	1693	1357	50	3100
1908	1584	1528	159	3271
1910	1872	1651	223	3746
1912	1900	1713	488	4101
1914	1771	1555	527	3853
1916	2052	1524	430	4006
1918	1443	1184	63	2690
1920	3801	4567	254	8622
1922	4427	4842	73	9342
1924	7070	6363	769	14202
1926	4434	4475	54	8963
1928	5010	10555	67	15632
1930	6324	5461	15	11800
1932	10833	4775	0	15608
1934	7500	3964	229	11693
1936	10090	4917	49	15056
1938	5647	2468	74	8189
1940	9019	6419	43	15481
1942	2971	3482	48	6501
1944	6846	5557	7	12410
1946	3668	4107	157	7932
1948	7156	3951	0	11107
1950	4708	5198	24	9930
1952	6714	7731	0	14445
1954	4991	3538	0	8529
1956	5939	7296	0	13235
1958	6237	1519	488	8244
1960	5801	7508	0	13309
1962	4126	5382	15	9523
1964	7395	5695	0	13090
1966	4408	4794	24	9226
1968	3919	5499	2407	11825
1970	4654	4300	268	9222
1972	2968	9288	335	12591
1974	6240	4087	0	10327
1976	6832	6398	118	13348
1978	5912	4105	46	10063
1980	5687	8044	515	14246
1982	7576	3667	16	11259
1984	6095	10083	79	16257
1986	5764	5369	672	11805

Year	Dem	Rep	Other	Total
1988	7778	7162	115	15055
1990	7249	2829	1299	11377
1992	6894	5891	4537	17322
1994	5040	4863	2518	12421
1996	7342	5827	2014	15183
1998	6166	4700	154	11020
2000	7540	8138	231	15909
2002	6843	4696	2347	13886
2004	8068	11467	0	19535
2006	8833	3507	0	12340
2008	7498	12160	0	19658
2010	6473	7938	0	14411
2012	6704	11242	0	17946
2014	5009	5861	383	11253

Ottawa

Year	Dem	Rep	Other	Total
1907	1305	1245	43	2593
1908	1296	1174	94	2564
1910	1410	1274	123	2807
1912	1384	1315	173	2872
1914	1369	1435	19	2823
1916	1875	1642	228	3745
1918	2222	1808	96	4126
1920	3922	5269	368	9559
1922	4179	4086	60	8325
1924	4522	5197	658	10377
1926	4231	3553	57	7841
1928	4488	8144	88	12720
1930	5904	4156	20	10080
1932	8175	3210	0	11385
1934	6313	4665	264	11242
1936	7658	4697	57	12412
1938	6544	3237	48	9829
1940	7873	5738	35	13646
1942	3098	2983	22	6103
1944	5876	5056	13	10945
1946	3914	3605	72	7591
1948	7243	4304	0	11547
1950	5420	4304	15	9739
1952	6692	7211	0	13903
1954	5889	4100	0	9989
1956	5721	6730	0	12451
1958	5239	1688	176	7103
1960	5705	6520	0	12225
1962	5229	3830	13	9072
1964	7589	4090	0	11679
1966	4441	3549	15	8005
1968	4820	5000	1421	11241
1970	4707	3500	133	8340
1972	3657	8348	158	12163
1974	6328	2371	0	8699
1976	7446	4985	84	12515
1978	5619	2642	42	8303
1980	6143	6362	414	12919
1982	7497	2069	9	9575
1984	5781	7666	58	13505
1986	5819	3865	222	9906

Year	Dem	Rep	Other	Total
1988	6658	5026	45	11729
1990	5854	2014	417	8285
1992	6304	4141	2764	13209
1994	4325	2985	1312	8622
1996	5844	4127	1533	11504
1998	4464	3555	115	8134
2000	5647	5625	139	11411
2002	4508	3018	1136	8662
2004	5086	7443	0	12529
2006	5211	1929	0	7140
2008	4268	6905	0	11173
2010	3138	3985	0	7123
2012	3509	6466	0	9975
2014	2066	2950	202	5218

Pawnee

Year	Dem	Rep	Other	Total
1907	1714	1599	167	3480
1908	1500	1556	299	3355
1910	1394	1495	373	3262
1912	1316	1332	474	3122
1914	1134	1512	474	3120
1916	1491	1396	565	3452
1918	1123	1205	112	2440
1920	1948	2982	371	5301
1922	2481	3140	64	5685
1924	2376	3093	552	6021
1926	2260	2650	43	4953
1928	1949	4489	85	6523
1930	2804	3002	9	5815
1932	5000	2280	0	7280
1934	2887	3821	548	7256
1936	4031	2961	72	7064
1938	3252	2798	31	6081
1940	3435	3991	38	7464
1942	1900	2843	23	4766
1944	2460	3310	16	5786
1946	1682	2965	127	4774
1948	2721	2651	0	5372
1950	2028	3668	7	5703
1952	2274	3975	0	6249
1954	2420	2311	0	4731
1956	2264	3390	0	5654
1958	2576	1147	236	3959
1960	1639	3153	0	4792
1962	1369	2516	6	3891
1964	2389	2278	0	4667
1966	1533	2307	7	3847
1968	1343	2437	990	4770
1970	1716	2140	97	3953
1972	1135	4280	122	5537
1974	2547	2344	0	4891
1976	3031	3111	59	6201
1978	2590	2117	37	4744
1980	2020	3902	229	6151
1982	2905	2007	11	4923
1984	2165	4699	64	6928
1986	2288	2705	407	5400

Year	Dem	Rep	Other	Total
1988	2781	3324	57	6162
1990	2703	1372	620	4695
1992	2612	2675	1686	6973
1994	1889	2038	1399	5326
1996	2663	2560	783	6006
1998	1990	1969	64	4023
2000	2435	3386	94	5925
2002	2251	1814	904	4969
2004	2564	4412	0	6976
2006	3049	1373	0	4422
2008	2063	4533	0	6596
2010	1813	3030	0	4843
2012	1813	4232	0	6045
2014	1346	2191	138	3673

Payne

Year	Dem	Rep	Other	Total
1907	2261	2093	189	4543
1908	1980	2244	390	4614
1910	1699	1834	590	4123
1912	1534	1669	808	4011
1914	1367	1391	1223	3981
1916	2140	1767	902	4809
1918	1484	1808	165	3457
1920	3240	4576	543	8359
1922	4368	5356	75	9799
1924	4342	4817	774	9933
1926	2646	3098	66	5810
1928	2904	7864	125	10893
1930	4388	5025	16	9429
1932	7819	3874	0	11693
1934	5207	5128	302	10637
1936	8081	4783	57	12921
1938	6051	2876	58	8985
1940	7704	6772	63	14539
1942	3470	3919	34	7423
1944	5624	6048	30	11702
1946	4065	4325	139	8529
1948	7390	5799	0	13189
1950	5768	6387	47	12202
1952	6490	10605	0	17095
1954	5599	4951	0	10550
1956	6320	9381	0	15701
1958	6309	2180	656	9145
1960	5694	9943	0	15637
1962	4996	7541	22	12559
1964	8906	7936	0	16842
1966	4881	8036	32	12949
1968	5772	9577	2475	17824
1970	5982	7782	371	14135
1972	5644	17019	407	23070
1974	9992	7317	0	17309
1976	9987	13481	420	23888
1978	8531	8366	115	17012
1980	7466	15955	2270	25691
1982	10804	7093	39	17936
1984	7653	20811	184	28648
1986	7119	10317	1544	18980

Year	Dem	Rep	Other	Total
1988	10568	16027	310	26905
1990	9921	5803	2220	17944
1992	9886	13032	7962	30880
1994	3455	7518	9374	20347
1996	9985	11686	2637	24308
1998	6418	10283	165	16866
2000	9319	15256	372	24947
2002	8714	8697	2595	20006
2004	10101	19560	0	29661
2006	12006	5529	0	17535
2008	10601	18435	0	29036
2010	8258	11633	0	19891
2012	9198	16481	0	25679
2014	7088	7954	438	15480

Pittsburg

Year	Dem	Rep	Other	Total
1907	3366	2602	232	6200
1908	2893	2735	629	6257
1910	2901	2049	668	5618
1912	2767	1574	1478	5819
1914	2651	1530	1498	5679
1916	3441	1879	889	6209
1918	2602	1222	116	3940
1920	5364	5363	683	11410
1922	7855	4639	49	12543
1924	6062	3554	1149	10765
1926	5269	3125	76	8470
1928	5960	5875	107	11942
1930	7054	2751	4	9809
1932	10536	2396	0	12932
1934	8738	3569	129	12436
1936	9974	3651	43	13668
1938	7378	1144	22	8544
1940	10169	4484	23	14676
1942	3123	1097	11	4231
1944	8535	4068	23	12626
1946	5872	2195	44	8111
1948	9576	2893	0	12469
1950	6719	4008	12	10739
1952	9546	5909	0	15455
1954	8697	2225	0	10922
1956	8382	5239	0	13621
1958	7970	673	140	8783
1960	7310	5834	0	13144
1962	7600	3300	12	10912
1964	9903	3555	0	13458
1966	6594	3242	28	9864
1968	6112	3978	3726	13816
1970	6722	3054	339	10115
1972	4748	9989	303	15040
1974	9823	2050	0	11873
1976	10743	4807	142	15692
1978	8389	3427	75	11891
1980	8292	7062	503	15857
1982	9352	2480	19	11851
1984	6860	9778	122	16760
1986	7604	4721	702	13027

Year	Dem	Rep	Other	Total
1988	8623	7594	125	16342
1990	8797	3010	911	12718
1992	8523	5659	4645	18827
1994	4558	3352	5903	13813
1996	8475	5966	2325	16766
1998	7339	5437	140	12916
2000	7627	8514	216	16357
2002	8557	4987	1977	15521
2004	7452	11134	0	18586
2006	8076	2808	0	10884
2008	5457	11752	0	17209
2010	5671	6808	0	12479
2012	4831	10841	0	15672
2014	4599	5163	408	10170

Pontotoc

Year	Dem	Rep	Other	Total
1907	2328	855	244	3427
1908	1841	860	579	3280
1910	1893	711	578	3182
1912	1842	642	939	3423
1914	1626	720	1285	3631
1916	2418	913	957	4288
1918	1785	567	50	2402
1920	3800	2365	204	6369
1922	4692	2643	24	7359
1924	4268	1859	493	6620
1926	2168	1842	39	4049
1928	3203	3356	38	6597
1930	4619	1235	4	5858
1932	7227	1207	0	8434
1934	4580	1706	126	6412
1936	8079	2015	42	10136
1938	4128	815	22	4965
1940	9310	3449	35	12794
1942	3530	1282	18	4830
1944	6552	2960	21	9533
1946	4527	2116	46	6689
1948	7750	2289	0	10039
1950	5655	2840	14	8509
1952	7208	5389	0	12597
1954	5289	1856	0	7145
1956	5950	4814	0	10764
1958	4707	626	224	5557
1960	4654	5863	0	10517
1962	4994	4133	12	9139
1964	7449	4166	0	11615
1966	4111	3974	20	8105
1968	4291	4161	2425	10877
1970	4486	3025	334	7845
1972	3160	8762	240	12162
1974	8613	2250	0	10863
1976	7466	4895	125	12486
1978	5260	3986	72	9318
1980	5942	6232	457	12631
1982	7481	2953	5	10439
1984	5526	8301	80	13907
1986	6347	5340	1025	12712

Year	Dem	Rep	Other	Total
1988	6484	6609	146	13239
1990	5785	3605	1495	10885
1992	6350	5206	3965	15521
1994	2377	2456	7201	12034
1996	6470	5366	1777	13613
1998	5083	6297	128	11508
2000	5387	7299	150	12836
2002	5447	3904	1107	10458
2004	5165	9647	0	14812
2006	7313	2592	0	9905
2008	4512	9750	0	14262
2010	4412	5365	0	9777
2012	3947	8945	0	12892
2014	4051	3664	257	7972

Pottawatomie

Year	Dem	Rep	Other	Total
1907	4210	2911	232	7353
1908	3561	2609	555	6725
1910	2694	2451	822	5967
1912	3082	2075	1062	6219
1914	2161	2526	1226	5913
1916	3276	2042	1155	6473
1918	2086	1592	143	3821
1920	5314	5357	591	11262
1922	6558	5308	159	12025
1924	5072	4040	1297	10409
1926	4888	2577	55	7520
1928	3797	8478	89	12364
1930	7782	4993	14	12789
1932	12013	4063	0	16076
1934	8657	5533	269	14459
1936	12187	4703	27	16917
1938	11178	2574	230	13982
1940	12058	6776	78	18912
1942	4311	3478	32	7821
1944	9130	6486	43	15659
1946	5336	4283	134	9753
1948	10220	4760	0	14980
1950	7389	5609	76	13074
1952	9455	10099	0	19554
1954	7821	4303	0	12124
1956	8895	8496	0	17391
1958	8007	1408	550	9965
1960	8067	9421	0	17488
1962	6733	7226	39	13998
1964	10884	6841	0	17725
1966	6006	6741	33	12780
1968	6721	6899	3873	17493
1970	7197	5986	388	13571
1972	4822	13308	534	18664
1974	11261	3665	0	14926
1976	11255	9090	226	20571
1978	8072	6106	76	14254
1980	8526	12466	858	21850
1982	11508	5920	16	17444
1984	6966	16143	152	23261
1986	8889	7010	1791	17690

Year	Dem	Rep	Other	Total
1988	8873	12099	197	21169
1990	10141	5823	1913	17877
1992	8616	10350	6706	25672
1994	4967	7458	5730	18155
1996	9141	9802	2810	21753
1998	6291	10336	238	16865
2000	8763	13265	318	22316
2002	10740	6674	2125	19539
2004	8638	17215	0	25853
2006	12257	5073	0	17330
2008	7910	17753	0	25663
2010	6536	11832	0	18368
2012	7188	16250	0	23438
2014	5237	8909	475	14621

Pushmataha

Year	Dem	Rep	Other	Total
1907	864	520	45	1429
1908	625	484	125	1234
1910	691	535	239	1465
1912	747	479	490	1716
1914	874	524	640	2038
1916	1059	645	453	2157
1918	793	534	68	1395
1920	1364	1862	267	3493
1922	2546	1005	25	3576
1924	1647	1084	275	3006
1926	1494	998	25	2517
1928	3184	1616	56	4856
1930	2834	895	53	3782
1932	3419	490	0	3909
1934	2972	1182	62	4216
1936	3389	1097	19	4505
1938	3628	709	52	4389
1940	3952	1709	9	5670
1942	1344	404	7	1755
1944	2848	1181	11	4040
1946	2505	573	28	3106
1948	2977	789	0	3766
1950	2469	818	7	3294
1952	2578	1640	0	4218
1954	2496	678	0	3174
1956	2273	1499	0	3772
1958	2358	214	20	2592
1960	1630	1728	0	3358
1962	2095	1115	4	3214
1964	2563	1332	0	3895
1966	1707	960	7	2674
1968	1232	1225	1287	3744
1970	1841	642	176	2659
1972	1016	2456	127	3599
1974	2824	510	0	3334
1976	2987	1360	29	4376
1978	2348	1116	55	3519
1980	2666	1989	120	4775
1982	2785	678	6	3469
1984	2079	2499	36	4614
1986	2404	1170	135	3709

Year	Dem	Rep	Other	Total		Year	Dem	Rep	Other	Total
1988	2430	1841	30	4301		1988	866	1132	14	2012
1990	3121	749	112	3982		1990	1304	459	207	1970
1992	2553	1319	1025	4897		1992	767	890	516	2173
1994	1115	760	2299	4174		1994	479	705	645	1829
1996	2270	1458	613	4341		1996	733	959	241	1933
1998	1987	1724	52	3763		1998	466	949	19	1434
2000	1969	2331	48	4348		2000	441	1234	12	1687
2002	2336	1119	321	3776		2002	614	632	185	1431
2004	1934	2863	0	4797		2004	382	1388	0	1770
2006	2330	563	0	2893		2006	983	479	0	1462
2008	1265	3208	0	4473		2008	287	1502	0	1789
2010	1525	1901	0	3426		2010	413	923	0	1336
2012	1043	3087	0	4130		2012	272	1402	0	1674
2014	1085	1319	117	2575		2014	409	778	32	1219

Roger Mills / Rogers

Year	Dem	Rep	Other	Total		Year	Dem	Rep	Other	Total
1907	1290	854	241	2385		1907	1759	1116	31	2906
1908	1168	839	403	2410		1908	1599	1134	131	2864
1910	1014	673	478	2165		1910	1638	1195	210	3043
1912	902	716	572	2190		1912	1637	1258	451	3346
1914	636	657	749	2042		1914	1525	1344	517	3386
1916	1148	538	575	2261		1916	1900	1435	546	3881
1918	695	516	176	1387		1918	1425	1190	70	2685
1920	930	1189	426	2545		1920	2450	2850	212	5512
1922	1542	1005	134	2681		1922	3087	2330	47	5464
1924	1318	946	519	2783		1924	2901	2207	237	5345
1926	1232	743	170	2145		1926	2186	1870	44	4100
1928	986	1948	133	3067		1928	2147	3477	41	5665
1930	2637	835	5	3477		1930	3072	1995	1	5068
1932	3648	511	0	4159		1932	5347	1879	0	7226
1934	1801	1239	311	3351		1934	3130	3437	309	6876
1936	3383	989	57	4429		1936	4290	3119	42	7451
1938	2380	513	20	2913		1938	4019	1621	136	5776
1940	2580	1504	22	4106		1940	4028	4086	25	8139
1942	1258	660	18	1936		1942	1870	2046	17	3933
1944	2015	1148	13	3176		1944	3209	3739	8	6956
1946	1746	575	58	2379		1946	2358	2360	79	4797
1948	2176	509	0	2685		1948	4197	2849	0	7046
1950	1396	862	5	2263		1950	3125	2943	11	6079
1952	1479	1667	0	3146		1952	3830	4873	0	8703
1954	1305	594	0	1899		1954	3856	2475	0	6331
1956	1367	1072	0	2439		1956	3185	4487	0	7672
1958	920	233	67	1220		1958	3553	845	207	4605
1960	809	1463	0	2272		1960	3167	5412	0	8579
1962	841	1328	13	2182		1962	3334	4106	109	7549
1964	1345	926	0	2271		1964	5449	4202	0	9651
1966	979	1138	13	2130		1966	3353	3604	25	6982
1968	720	1102	610	2432		1968	2665	4631	3141	10437
1970	1158	680	56	1894		1970	4428	3858	484	8770
1972	420	1696	54	2170		1972	2607	9697	424	12728
1974	1267	588	0	1855		1974	5535	5108	0	10643
1976	1346	873	24	2243		1976	7368	7318	129	14815
1978	845	881	13	1739		1978	6390	4510	64	10964
1980	877	1221	73	2171		1980	6399	11581	662	18642
1982	1154	484	6	1644		1982	8775	5441	15	14231
1984	680	1550	13	2243		1984	6013	16137	138	22288
1986	904	828	96	1828		1986	6341	8458	1201	16000

Year	Dem	Rep	Other	Total		Year	Dem	Rep	Other	Total
1988	8771	12940	140	21851		1988	4911	4078	84	9073
1990	9517	5075	2061	16653		1990	5157	2135	727	8019
1992	8257	12455	7180	27892		1992	4624	3253	2363	10240
1994	6106	9991	3751	19848		1994	1943	2049	3507	7499
1996	9544	12883	3127	25554		1996	4225	2935	1069	8229
1998	8253	9766	286	18305		1998	3394	3159	70	6623
2000	10713	17713	425	28951		2000	3783	4011	72	7866
2002	10508	10265	4184	24957		2002	4260	2307	882	7449
2004	11918	24976	0	36894		2004	3648	5624	0	9272
2006	15674	8278	0	23952		2006	4384	1834	0	6218
2008	10772	27743	0	38515		2008	2977	5600	0	8577
2010	9171	18874	0	28045		2010	2689	3637	0	6326
2012	9148	27553	0	36701		2012	2600	4856	0	7456
2014	7167	14048	830	21945		2014	1955	2663	151	4769

Seminole

Year	Dem	Rep	Other	Total
1907	1396	1101	192	2689
1908	945	1168	452	2565
1910	1064	964	409	2437
1912	1172	715	766	2653
1914	1086	763	993	2842
1916	1444	872	935	3251
1918	1151	987	93	2231
1920	1870	3388	316	5574
1922	3352	2392	20	5764
1924	3007	2326	475	5808
1926	2446	1535	36	4017
1928	4423	8072	0	12495
1930	7721	3616	14	11351
1932	12154	3348	0	15502
1934	7257	3618	476	11351
1936	11695	4001	72	15768
1938	7148	1886	64	9098
1940	11167	6880	36	18083
1942	3782	2512	22	6316
1944	7116	4560	16	11692
1946	4819	3352	87	8258
1948	8122	3423	0	11545
1950	5617	4065	17	9699
1952	7076	6668	0	13744
1954	5737	2468	0	8205
1956	5897	5230	0	11127
1958	4489	865	286	5640
1960	4256	5505	0	9761
1962	3949	3842	19	7810
1964	6582	3676	0	10258
1966	3916	3990	18	7924
1968	3889	3711	2142	9742
1970	3618	3134	190	6942
1972	2746	6879	199	9824
1974	8236	1041	0	9277
1976	5874	4237	91	10202
1978	4513	2985	48	7546
1980	4726	5067	352	10145
1982	5447	2036	11	7494
1984	3957	6009	64	10030
1986	4788	2900	437	8125

Sequoyah

Year	Dem	Rep	Other	Total
1907	1927	1940	35	3902
1908	1648	2037	131	3816
1910	1596	1238	91	2925
1912	1416	1115	232	2763
1914	1517	1171	549	3237
1916	1632	1179	527	3338
1918	1395	1082	42	2519
1920	2503	3192	113	5808
1922	3689	2652	29	6370
1924	3429	2875	70	6374
1926	2714	2022	12	4748
1928	2692	3296	0	5988
1930	3207	2344	9	5560
1932	4704	1833	0	6537
1934	3767	3378	16	7161
1936	4281	2609	0	6890
1938	4240	1568	15	5823
1940	4469	3803	9	8281
1942	2963	1691	8	4662
1944	3571	2893	8	6472
1946	3243	1670	17	4930
1948	4449	2077	0	6526
1950	4159	2472	57	6688
1952	4072	3288	0	7360
1954	3656	1435	0	5091
1956	3560	3330	0	6890
1958	3241	530	34	3805
1960	2942	3862	0	6804
1962	3714	1837	5	5556
1964	4304	2846	0	7150
1966	3369	1676	17	5062
1968	2618	2797	2158	7573
1970	4318	1796	172	6286
1972	2519	6842	190	9551
1974	5881	1822	0	7703
1976	5873	3938	73	9884
1978	5409	2031	68	7508
1980	4983	5987	226	11196
1982	5889	1473	12	7374
1984	4202	7042	56	11300
1986	5673	3504	430	9607

Year	Dem	Rep	Other	Total
1988	4951	5710	68	10729
1990	7250	1970	395	9615
1992	6092	4925	2539	13556
1994	3911	2827	1333	8071
1996	5665	4733	1726	12124
1998	4141	4007	129	8277
2000	5425	6614	215	12254
2002	5158	3391	865	9414
2004	5910	8865	0	14775
2006	5882	2342	0	8224
2008	4454	9466	0	13920
2010	4497	5659	0	10156
2012	4193	9578	0	13771
2014	3649	4676	315	8640

Stephens

Year	Dem	Rep	Other	Total
1907	2205	710	331	3246
1908	1761	725	290	2776
1910	1802	819	721	3342
1912	1738	598	901	3237
1914	1279	875	1047	3201
1916	2343	607	1098	4048
1918	1337	461	97	1895
1920	2814	2038	348	5200
1922	7756	2566	145	10467
1924	4745	2377	412	7534
1926	3186	1301	46	4533
1928	2982	5192	105	8279
1930	5635	1703	19	7357
1932	7706	1012	0	8718
1934	3797	1713	590	6100
1936	6390	1636	45	8071
1938	4129	799	31	4959
1940	6149	2989	34	9172
1942	3073	1723	38	4834
1944	6189	2766	19	8974
1946	3358	1666	49	5073
1948	6702	1909	0	8611
1950	5292	2486	20	7798
1952	8029	6461	0	14490
1954	4951	1938	0	6889
1956	7524	6324	0	13848
1958	5601	935	366	6902
1960	6899	8084	0	14983
1962	5653	5152	22	10827
1964	9272	5323	0	14595
1966	5106	4404	43	9553
1968	5249	5508	3566	14323
1970	6119	3468	555	10142
1972	3623	10309	464	14396
1974	9161	2281	0	11442
1976	9795	7099	126	17020
1978	7118	5459	49	12626
1980	7191	10199	462	17852
1982	9827	4123	8	13958
1984	6359	12871	103	19333
1986	8935	5036	1101	15072

Year	Dem	Rep	Other	Total
1988	7833	9844	118	17795
1990	8556	4784	907	14247
1992	7644	7085	5742	20471
1994	4931	5556	4704	15191
1996	7248	8144	2384	17776
1998	4763	9355	136	14254
2000	6467	10860	161	17488
2002	5484	6290	2482	14256
2004	5515	13646	0	19161
2006	9168	4076	0	13244
2008	4538	14394	0	18932
2010	8217	6458	0	14675
2012	3939	12908	0	16847
2014	4613	6393	362	11368

Texas

Year	Dem	Rep	Other	Total
1907	1576	1353	86	3015
1908	1470	1315	239	3024
1910	1143	1130	333	2606
1912	764	683	280	1727
1914	745	642	285	1672
1916	1349	807	313	2469
1918	947	743	70	1760
1920	1397	1751	135	3283
1922	1884	1962	36	3882
1924	1812	1745	405	3962
1926	1583	1269	36	2888
1928	1240	2890	49	4179
1930	2326	1686	7	4019
1932	4033	1372	0	5405
1934	2918	1707	108	4733
1936	3229	1223	19	4471
1938	1313	2485	11	3809
1940	2831	1918	28	4777
1942	1523	852	10	2385
1944	2119	1731	20	3870
1946	1129	887	43	2059
1948	2693	1676	0	4369
1950	2265	1902	12	4179
1952	1915	4196	0	6111
1954	2224	1676	0	3900
1956	1886	3320	0	5206
1958	2296	839	221	3356
1960	1549	4314	0	5863
1962	1588	2991	8	4587
1964	2500	3339	0	5839
1966	1856	2361	10	4227
1968	1176	3729	954	5859
1970	2592	1833	77	4502
1972	924	5726	287	6937
1974	3327	1148	0	4475
1976	2591	3919	70	6580
1978	2787	2069	47	4903
1980	1451	5503	145	7099
1982	2852	2254	10	5116
1984	1033	5968	38	7039
1986	1756	3147	230	5133

Year	Dem	Rep	Other	Total	Year	Dem	Rep	Other	Total
1988	1717	4971	64	6752	**1988**	2148	1754	26	3928
1990	2063	2585	294	4942	1990	2166	743	107	3016
1992	1487	4059	1434	6980	**1992**	1749	1377	1052	4178
1994	792	2668	1052	4512	1994	1215	766	753	2734
1996	1408	4139	544	6091	**1996**	1827	1346	486	3659
1998	1035	3222	57	4314	1998	1131	1127	22	2280
2000	1084	4964	40	6088	**2000**	1400	1920	29	3349
2002	1424	3208	282	4914	2002	1263	1034	338	2635
2004	1016	5450	0	6466	**2004**	1175	2273	0	3448
2006	1642	2262	0	3904	2006	2185	459	0	2644
2008	923	5336	0	6259	**2008**	1042	2195	0	3237
2010	889	3545	0	4434	2010	1020	1003	0	2103
2012	862	4930	0	5792	**2012**	906	1815	0	2721
2014	639	2466	123	3228	2014	644	991	58	1693

	Tillman					Tulsa			
1907	1472	557	47	2076	1907	2163	1951	111	4225
1908	1661	732	109	2502	**1908**	2292	2150	226	4668
1910	1758	735	194	2687	1910	2594	2193	360	5147
1912	1801	638	374	2813	**1912**	2747	2029	571	5347
1914	1325	616	577	2518	1914	2432	3217	770	6419
1916	2250	625	382	3257	**1916**	4497	3857	886	9240
1918	1203	360	48	1611	1918	4011	3456	138	7605
1920	2640	1540	151	4331	**1920**	9994	14484	638	25116
1922	2728	1804	27	4559	1922	10467	13481	56	24004
1924	2653	1326	184	4163	**1924**	14377	19537	1265	35179
1926	1903	518	10	2431	1926	10095	14160	46	24301
1928	2141	3331	25	5497	**1928**	16062	38769	167	54998
1930	2746	681	0	3427	1930	14528	19468	79	34075
1932	4960	523	0	5483	**1932**	35330	25541	0	60871
1934	3854	935	48	4837	1934	23900	18128	983	43011
1936	5268	1126	16	6410	**1936**	41256	28759	328	70343
1938	2701	475	18	3194	1938	22903	11253	123	34279
1940	4920	1564	24	6508	**1940**	33098	40342	135	73575
1942	1329	462	8	1799	1942	14767	24982	63	39812
1944	3902	1496	12	5410	**1944**	33436	42663	89	76188
1946	2423	648	57	3128	1946	19859	40734	539	61132
1948	4071	1058	0	5129	**1948**	38548	42892	0	81440
1950	3080	1184	2	4266	1950	25679	49059	227	74965
1952	3639	2657	0	6296	**1952**	46728	73862	0	120590
1954	2683	593	0	3276	1954	36209	41415	0	77624
1956	3366	1810	0	5176	**1956**	42805	83219	0	126024
1958	2473	351	111	2935	1958	66564	19185	3953	89702
1960	2736	2678	0	5414	**1960**	52725	89899	0	142624
1962	2430	1474	3	3907	1962	32826	62387	319	95532
1964	3354	2001	0	5355	**1964**	61484	76770	0	138254
1966	2171	1296	18	3485	1966	30310	70462	1039	101811
1968	1771	1748	1376	4895	**1968**	32748	81476	28443	142667
1970	2295	1114	216	3625	1970	40289	65756	3233	109278
1972	1256	3331	110	4697	**1972**	32779	125278	3069	161126
1974	3045	493	0	3538	1974	60697	64492	0	125189
1976	2852	1802	41	4695	**1976**	65298	108653	2349	176300
1978	2018	1165	22	3205	1978	57482	61375	900	119757
1980	2144	2450	93	4687	**1980**	53438	124643	10067	188148
1982	2742	821	2	3565	1982	71098	67784	310	139192
1984	1674	2637	15	4326	**1984**	58274	159549	1049	218872
1986	2010	1017	109	3136	1986	47911	88096	10333	146340

Year	Dem	Rep	Other	Total	Year	Dem	Rep	Other	Total
1988	69044	127512	1207	197763	1988	7378	10219	121	17718
1990	72730	49403	15710	137843	1990	7334	3911	1372	12617
1992	71165	117465	50438	239068	1992	7041	9053	5435	21529
1994	45549	99606	21044	166199	1994	5167	7319	2972	15458
1996	76924	111243	19189	207356	1996	7749	9392	2417	19558
1998	59346	81938	1394	142678	1998	7067	7425	223	14715
2000	81656	134152	2883	218691	2000	8244	12981	292	21517
2002	65383	84187	25158	174728	2002	7320	7595	3676	18591
2004	90220	163452	0	253672	2004	9157	19081	0	28238
2006	90459	57060	0	147519	2006	10977	6464	0	17441
2008	96133	158363	0	254496	2008	8810	21441	0	30251
2010	63558	105060	0	168618	2010	6678	14314	0	20992
2012	82744	145062	0	227806	2012	7791	20900	0	28691
2014	53073	74867	3709	131649	2014	5500	10675	566	16741

Wagoner / Washington

Year	Dem	Rep	Other	Total	Year	Dem	Rep	Other	Total
1907	1200	1723	60	2983	1907	1404	1442	48	2894
1908	1151	2107	167	3425	1908	1409	1528	124	3061
1910	1182	828	171	2181	1910	1517	1484	221	3222
1912	888	555	281	1724	1912	1561	1447	340	3348
1914	953	714	467	2134	1914	1427	1922	359	3708
1916	1040	749	303	2092	1916	1839	1727	359	3925
1918	820	595	90	1505	1918	1130	1227	55	2412
1920	1373	1428	150	2951	1920	2800	4102	186	7088
1922	2226	1370	47	3643	1922	2478	3929	12	6419
1924	1985	1646	272	3903	1924	2487	4579	234	7300
1926	1791	1522	13	3326	1926	2755	2770	22	5547
1928	1745	2726	26	4497	1928	2563	7258	56	9877
1930	2644	1826	4	4474	1930	2536	3869	18	6423
1932	4015	1505	0	5520	1932	6863	4713	0	11576
1934	2667	2349	175	5191	1934	5062	4249	141	9452
1936	2977	2119	21	5117	1936	6202	5201	26	11429
1938	2929	1384	17	4330	1938	5370	3413	54	8837
1940	2946	4647	25	7618	1940	6289	7347	40	13676
1942	2114	2944	91	5149	1942	6249	4327	33	10609
1944	2373	3467	8	5848	1944	6090	6533	18	12641
1946	2056	2527	48	4631	1946	2886	5063	270	8219
1948	3389	2666	0	6055	1948	5508	6036	0	11544
1950	2494	3228	26	5748	1950	4496	7698	51	12245
1952	2966	3321	0	6287	1952	6238	11334	0	17572
1954	2968	1994	0	4962	1954	5344	7246	0	12590
1956	2544	3537	0	6081	1956	5529	12488	0	18017
1958	3591	1213	122	4926	1958	9345	3321	582	13248
1960	2707	3570	0	6277	1960	5479	13700	0	19179
1962	2652	2903	15	5570	1962	5267	11925	35	17227
1964	3957	2840	0	6797	1964	8571	12382	0	20953
1966	2586	2800	17	5403	1966	5819	11252	73	17144
1968	2183	3187	2262	7632	1968	4641	12812	3091	20544
1970	3219	2531	116	5866	1970	4904	9588	391	14883
1972	2257	6569	281	9107	1972	3658	16347	495	20500
1974	4975	3152	0	8127	1974	8210	8720	0	16930
1976	5879	5071	107	11057	1976	6898	14560	212	21670
1978	4841	3478	43	8362	1978	7275	8645	66	15986
1980	5235	8969	523	14727	1980	5854	16563	1086	23503
1982	7142	4303	10	11455	1982	9946	7722	18	17686
1984	5271	12534	108	17913	1984	5476	19043	148	24667
1986	5166	6344	974	12484	1986	6182	9967	526	16675

Year	Dem	Rep	Other	Total
1988	6971	14613	129	21713
1990	8072	6419	1707	16198
1992	6593	11342	5728	23663
1994	4401	10319	2544	17264
1996	6732	11605	2357	20694
1998	5438	8907	156	14501
2000	6644	13788	312	20744
2002	5801	8700	2687	17188
2004	6862	16551	0	23413
2006	8995	6265	0	15260
2008	6308	16457	0	22765
2010	5039	11548	0	16587
2012	5532	15668	0	21200
2014	3912	8795	528	13235

Washita

Year	Dem	Rep	Other	Total
1907	2100	1152	230	3482
1908	1867	1118	409	3394
1910	1723	1081	531	3335
1912	1663	1100	770	3533
1914	1187	1161	885	3233
1916	2107	958	719	3784
1918	1304	580	291	2175
1920	2122	2065	320	4507
1922	2853	1754	67	4674
1924	2325	1357	372	4054
1926	1561	774	35	2370
1928	2024	3572	49	5645
1930	3512	1469	4	4985
1932	6049	887	0	6936
1934	3107	1719	408	5234
1936	5205	1792	32	7029
1938	2680	867	16	3563
1940	4256	2978	11	7245
1942	1218	1009	9	2236
1944	3524	2706	18	6248
1946	2311	1143	65	3519
1948	4326	1637	0	5963
1950	2799	1722	4	4525
1952	3177	3914	0	7091
1954	2429	1220	0	3649
1956	3191	2552	0	5743
1958	1890	479	324	2693
1960	2414	3209	0	5623
1962	2151	2317	8	4476
1964	3339	2147	0	5486
1966	1948	1935	13	3896
1968	1771	2592	858	5221
1970	2233	1628	104	3965
1972	1305	3578	125	5008
1974	3143	1144	0	4287
1976	3304	2165	62	5531
1978	1702	2247	61	4010
1980	2044	3206	123	5373
1982	2848	1245	2	4095
1984	1547	3847	36	5430
1986	2750	1311	240	4301

Year	Dem	Rep	Other	Total
1988	2290	2402	53	4745
1990	3175	800	357	4332
1992	1929	1912	1498	5339
1994	1293	1645	1167	4105
1996	1913	1994	768	4675
1998	1173	2012	44	3229
2000	1564	2850	54	4468
2002	1810	1440	554	3804
2004	3705	1340	0	5045
2006	2766	1108	0	3874
2008	1052	3724	0	4776
2010	1333	2265	0	3598
2012	822	3494	0	4316
2014	1039	1943	82	3064

Woods

Year	Dem	Rep	Other	Total
1907	1276	1424	163	2863
1908	1421	1557	228	3206
1910	1327	1510	612	3449
1912	1247	1679	543	3469
1914	1030	1531	500	3061
1916	1417	1358	526	3301
1918	936	1365	113	2414
1920	1524	2815	330	4669
1922	2217	2469	71	4757
1924	1533	2615	840	4988
1926	1847	1930	52	3829
1928	1550	3941	109	5600
1930	2679	2405	7	5091
1932	4279	2008	0	6287
1934	3068	2795	196	6059
1936	4179	2346	44	6569
1938	3332	2384	65	5781
1940	3506	3440	61	7007
1942	1764	2198	37	3999
1944	2426	3226	23	5675
1946	1678	2381	89	4148
1948	2882	2871	0	5753
1950	2221	3444	13	5678
1952	1999	4892	0	6891
1954	2002	3053	0	5055
1956	2123	3787	0	5910
1958	2513	1304	395	4212
1960	1902	4064	0	5966
1962	1673	3465	14	5152
1964	2750	2886	0	5636
1966	1706	2851	27	4584
1968	1439	3449	517	5405
1970	2076	2460	130	4666
1972	1234	4413	142	5789
1974	2794	2086	0	4880
1976	2530	2788	103	5421
1978	1683	2753	12	4448
1980	1364	3592	5208	10164
1982	2630	1670	5	4305
1984	1231	3741	46	5018
1986	1697	2262	326	4285

Year	Dem	Rep	Other	Total	Year	Dem	Rep	Other	Total
1988	1735	2835	81	4651	1988	2408	4996	89	7493
1990	2215	1259	494	3968	1990	3741	2089	810	6640
1992	1361	2225	1191	4777	1992	2063	4006	2457	8526
1994	830	1648	1225	3703	1994	1336	3120	1798	6254
1996	1431	2151	520	4102	1996	2403	4093	1002	7498
1998	1099	2341	27	3467	1998	1805	3482	64	5351
2000	1235	2774	37	4046	2000	1950	5067	83	7100
2002	1471	1339	353	3163	2002	2339	2695	801	5835
2004	932	3166	0	4098	2004	1458	6193	0	7651
2006	2009	896	0	2905	2006	3517	1850	0	5367
2008	873	3043	0	3916	2008	1350	6404	0	7754
2010	1043	2042	0	3085	2010	1523	4082	0	5605
2012	671	2727	0	3398	2012	1133	5945	0	7078
2014	916	1440	98	2454	2014	1126	3029	125	4280

Woodward

Year	Dem	Rep	Other	Total
1907	1327	1416	232	2975
1908	1308	1614	371	3293
1910	1200	1524	420	3144
1912	1083	1403	596	3082
1914	754	1050	758	2562
1916	1130	1092	702	2924
1918	842	1076	125	2043
1920	1440	2482	288	4210
1922	1897	2112	40	4049
1924	1418	1831	763	4012
1926	1611	1578	51	3240
1928	1347	3188	81	4616
1930	2103	2276	14	4393
1932	3988	1614	0	5602
1934	2494	2930	156	5580
1936	3361	2430	40	5831
1938	2466	2232	67	4765
1940	2806	3403	34	6243
1942	1460	1930	24	3414
1944	2152	3055	18	5225
1946	1481	1855	44	3380
1948	2180	2391	0	4571
1950	2046	2796	8	4850
1952	1690	1463	0	3153
1954	1177	3720	0	4897
1956	1618	3405	0	5023
1958	2013	1766	313	4092
1960	1487	4185	0	5672
1962	1434	3770	7	5211
1964	2934	3094	0	6028
1966	1811	2863	22	4696
1968	1444	3748	663	5855
1970	1942	2899	126	4967
1972	1104	5350	229	6683
1974	3172	2250	0	5422
1976	2807	3782	102	6691
1978	1651	3082	55	4788
1980	1703	5318	268	7289
1982	3549	2142	2	5693
1984	1647	6376	40	8063
1986	2686	3600	644	6930

County Election Boards

Adair	PO Box 6, Stilwell 74960	918/696-7221
Alfalfa	300 S Grand, Cherokee 73728	580/596-2718
Atoka	200 E Court Street, Suite 106E, Atoka 74525	580/889-5297
Beaver	PO Box 639, Beaver 73932	580/625-4742
Beckham	306 E Main, Sayre 73662	580/928-3314
Blaine	212 N Weigle, Suite 6, Watonga 73772	580/623-5518
Bryan	402 W Evergreen, Suite A2, Durant 74701	580/924-3228
Caddo	PO Box 277, Anadarko 73005	405/247-5001
Canadian	PO Box 307, El Reno 73036	405/422-2422
Carter	106 Hinkle Street SW, Ardmore 73401	580/223-5290
Cherokee	914 S College Ave., Tahlequah 74464	918/456-2261
Choctaw	PO Box 517, Hugo 74743	580/326-5164
Cimarron	PO Box 331, Boise City 73933	580/544-3377
Cleveland	641 E Robinson, Suite 200, Norman 73071	405/366-0210
Coal	18 N Michigan Street, Coalgate 74538	580/927-3456
Comanche	315 SW 5 Street, Room 206 Lawton 73501	580/353-1880
Cotton	301 N Broadway, Room 2, Walters 73572	580/875-3403
Craig	210 W Delaware Ave., Suite 108, Vinita 74301	918/256-7559
Creek	PO Box 990, Sapulpa 74067	918/224-3529
Custer	PO Box 1326, Clinton 73601	580/323-5124
Delaware	PO Box 589, Jay 74346	918/253-8762
Dewey	PO Box 115, Taloga 73667	580/328-5668
Ellis	PO Box 492, Arnett 73832	580/885-7721
Garfield	PO Box 1872, Enid 73702	580/237-6016
Garvin	210 W Grant Avenue, Room 8, Pauls Valley 73075	405/238-3303
Grady	PO Box 1226, Chickasha 73023	405/224-1430
Grant	PO Box 68, Medford 73759	580/395-2862
Greer	106 E Jefferson, Room 1, Mangum 73554	580/782-2307
Harmon	114 W Hollis, 2nd Floor, Room 5, Hollis 73550	580/688-2460
Harper	PO Box 541, Buffalo 73834	580/735-2313
Haskell	PO Box 300, Stigler 74462	918/967-8792
Hughes	200 N Broadway, Suite 3, Holdenville 74848	405/379-2174
Jackson	101 N Main, Room 105, Altus 73522	580/482-2370
Jefferson	220 N Main, Room 203, Waurika 73521	580/228-3150

Johnston	705 W Main, Tishomingo 73460	580/371–3670
Kay	PO Box 331, Newkirk 74647	580/362–2130
Kingfisher	101 S Main, Room 8, Kingfisher 73750	405/375–3895
Kiowa	215 N Lincoln Street, Hobart 73651	580/726–2509
Latimer	109 N Central, Rm. 102, Wilburton 74578	918/465–3703
LeFlore	PO Box 249, Poteau 74953	918/647–3701
Lincoln	PO Box 97, Chandler 74834	405/258–1349
Logan	224 E Vilas Ave., Guthrie 73044	405/282–1900
Love	405 W Main, Suite 103, Marietta 73448	580/276–2242
Major	500 E Broadway, Suite 8, Fairview 73737	580/227–4520
Marshall	PO Box 9, Madill 73446	580/795–5460
Mayes	1 Court Place, Suite 130,, Pryor 74362	918/825–1826
McClain	PO Box 759, Purcell 73080	405/527–3121
McCurtain	104 N Central, Idabel 74745	580/286–7405
McIntosh	PO Box 1022, Eufaula 74432	918/689–2452
Murray	PO Box 556, Sulphur 73086	580/662–3800
Muskogee	PO Box 216, Muskogee 74402	918/687–8151
Noble	300 Courthouse Drive, Suite 2, Perry 73077	580/336–3527
Nowata	228 N Maple, Nowata 74048	918/273–0710
Okfuskee	209 N 3 Street, Okemah 74859	918/623–0105
Oklahoma	4201 N Lincoln Blvd., Oklahoma City 73105	405/713–1515
Okmulgee	314 W 7 Street, Room 102, Okmulgee 74447	918/756–2365
Osage	PO Box 929, Pawhuska 74056	918/287–3036
Ottawa	123 E Central Ave., Suite 104, Miami 74354	918/542–2893
Pawnee	PO Box 38, Pawnee 74058	918/762–2125
Payne	315 W 6 Street, Suite 207, Stillwater 74074	405/747–8350
Pittsburg	109 E Carl Albert Pkwy, Room 101, McAlester 74501	918/423–3877
Pontotoc	PO Box 302, Ada 74821	580/332–4534
Pottawatomie	14101 Acme Road, Shawnee 74804	405/273–8376
Pushmataha	204 SW 4th Street, Suite A, Antlers 74523	580/298–3292
Roger Mills	PO Box 147, Cheyenne 73628	580/497–3330
Rogers	415 W 1st Street, Claremore 74017	918/341–2965
Seminole	110 S Wewoka Ave., Suite 101, Wewoka 74884	405/257–2786
Sequoyah	110 E Creek Avenue, Sallisaw 74955	918/775–2614
Stephens	101 S 11 Street, Room 100, Duncan 73533	580/255–8782
Texas	PO Box 607, Guymon 73942	580/338–7644

Tillman	201 N Main, Suite Room 5, Frederick 73542	580/335–2287
Tulsa	555 N Denver, Tulsa 74103	918/596–5780
Wagoner	PO Box 714, Wagoner 74477	918/485–2124
Washington	420 S Johnstone, Room 101, Bartlesville 74003	918/337–2850
Washita	1116 S College Avenue, Cordell 73632	580/832–3658
Woods	PO Box 184, Alva 73717	580/327–1452
Woodward	PO Box 613, Woodward 73802	580/256–3609

SIGNAL TOWER

FORT RENO

D.C.

Voting Districts of Cities and Towns
2012–2020 Elections

Municipality	County	Congress	Senate	House
Achille	Bryan	2	6	21
Ada	Pontotoc	4	13	25
Adair	Mayes	2	1	6
Addington	Jefferson	4	31	50
Afton	Ottawa	2	1	7
Agra	Lincoln	3	28	32
Albion	Pushmataha	2	5	19
Alderson	Pittsburg	2	7	17
Alex	Grady	4	23	51
Aline	Alfalfa	3	19	58
Allen	Hughes/Pontotoc	2, 4	7, 13	18, 25
Altus	Jackson	3	38	52
Alva	Woods	3	27	58
Amber	Grady	4	23	56
Ames	Major	4	27	58
Amorita	Alfalfa	3	19	58
Anadarko	Caddo	3	26	56
Antlers	Pushmataha	2	5	19
Apache	Caddo	3	26	65
Arapaho	Custer	3	26	57
Arcadia	Oklahoma	5	41	96
Ardmore	Carter	4	14	48, 49
Arkoma	LeFlore	2	4	3
Armstrong	Bryan	2	6	21
Arnett	Ellis	3	27	6
Asher	Pottawatomie	5	13	20, 27
Ashland	Pittsburg	2	7	18
Atoka	Atoka	2	6	22
Atwood	Hughes	2	13	18
Avant	Osage	3	10	36
Avard	Woods	3	49	58
Barnsdall	Osage	3	10	36
Bartlesville	Osage/Washington	1, 3	10	10, 36
Bearden	Okfuskee	2	7	24
Beaver	Beaver	3	27	61
Beggs	Okmulgee	2	8	24

Municipality	County	Congress	Senate	House
Bennington	Bryan	2	6	19
Bernice	Delaware	2	1	5
Bessie	Washita	3	38	55
Bethany	Oklahoma	5	30, 40, 47	84, 100
Bethel Acres	Pottawatomie	5	28	26, 27
Big Cabin	Craig	2	1	6
Billings	Noble	3	20	38
Binger	Caddo	3	26	56
Bixby	Tulsa/Wagoner	1	12, 18, 25, 33	16, 30, 67, 69, 80
Blackburn	Pawnee	3	20	35
Blackwell	Kay	3	19	38
Blair	Jackson	3	38	52
Blanchard	Grady/McClain	4	23	51
Bluejacket	Craig	2	1	6
Boise City	Cimarron	3	27	61
Bokchito	Bryan	2	6	19
Bokoshe	LeFlore	2	4	15
Boley	Okfuskee	2	8	24
Boswell	Choctaw	2	5	19
Bowlegs	Seminole	5	28	28
Boynton	Muskogee	2	18	16
Bradley	Grady	4	43	51
Braggs	Muskogee	2	9	14
Braman	Kay	3	19	38
Bray	Stephens	4	43	51
Breckenridge	Garfield	3	19	38
Bridge Creek	Grady	4	23	51
Bridgeport	Caddo	3	26	60
Bristow	Creek	3	12	29
Broken Arrow	Tulsa/Wagoner	1	18, 25, 33, 36	12, 67, 75, 76, 80, 98
Broken Bow	McCurtain	2	5	1
Bromide	Coal/Johnston	2	6, 14	18, 22
Brooksville	Pottawatomie	5	28	27
Buffalo	Harper	3	27	61
Burbank	Osage	3	10	37
Burlington	Alfalfa	3	19	58
Burns Flat	Washita	3	38	55
Butler	Custer	3	26	57
Byars	McClain	4	43	20

Municipality	County	Congress	Senate	House
Byng	Pontotoc	4	13	25
Byron	Alfalfa	3	19	58
Cache	Comanche	4	32	63
Caddo	Bryan	2	6	21
Calera	Bryan	2	6	21
Calumet	Canadian	3	7	18
Calvin	Hughes	2	13	24
Camargo	Dewey	3	27	59
Cameron	LeFlore	2	4	3
Canadian	Pittsburg	2	7	18
Caney	Atoka	2	6	22
Canton	Blaine	3	26	59
Canute	Washita	3	38	55
Capron	Woods	3	27	58
Cardin	Ottawa	2	1	7
Carmen	Alfalfa	3	19	58
Carnegie	Caddo	3	26	60
Carney	Lincoln	3	28	32
Carrier	Garfield	3	20	41
Carter	Beckham	3	26	55
Cashion	Kingfisher/Logan	3	20	31, 41
Castle	Okfuskee	2	8	24
Catoosa	Rogers	1, 2	2	23, 77
Cedar Valley	Logan	3	20	31
Cement	Caddo	3	26	65
Centrahoma	Coal	2	6	18
Central High	Stephens	4	31, 43	51, 65
Chandler	Lincoln	3	28	32
Chattanooga	Comanche	4	31	63
Chattanooga	Tillman	4	31	63
Checotah	McIntosh	2	8	13
Chelsea	Rogers	2	29	6
Cherokee	Alfalfa	3	20	58
Cheyenne	Rogers Mills	3	26	55
Chickasha	Grady	4	23	51,56
Choctaw	Oklahoma	4, 5	17, 42, 48	96, 101
Chouteau	Mayes	2	3	8
Cimarron City	Logan	3	20	38
Claremore	Rogers	2	2, 29	6, 8, 9
Clayton	Pushmataha	2	5	19

Municipality	County	Congress	Senate	House
Clearview	Okfuskee	2	8	24
Cleo Springs	Major	4	27	58
Cleveland	Pawnee	3	20	35
Clinton	Custer/Washita	3	38	55, 57
Coalgate	Coal	2	6	18
Colbert	Bryan	2	6	21
Colcord	Delaware	2	3	86
Cole	McClain	4	43	20, 42
Collinsville	Rogers/Tulsa	1, 2	2, 34	9, 11, 36
Colony	Washita	3	38	55
Comanche	Stephens	4	31, 43	50
Commerce	Ottawa	2	1	7
Cooperton	Kiowa	3	38	56
Copan	Washington	1	29	10
Cordell	Washita	3	38	55
Corn	Washita	3	38	55
Cornish	Jefferson	4	31	50
Council Hill	Muskogee	2	18	16
Covington	Garfield	3	19	38
Coweta	Wagoner	1	18	12, 16, 80
Cowlington	LeFlore	2	4	15
Coyle	Logan	3	20	32, 33
Crescent	Logan	3	20	38
Cromwell	Seminole	5	28	28
Crowder	Pittsburg	2	7	17, 18
Cushing	Payne	3	21	33
Custer City	Custer	3	26	57
Cyril	Caddo	3	26	65
Dacoma	Woods	3	27	58
Davenport	Lincoln	3	28	32
Davidson	Tillman	4	31	63
Davis	Garvin/Murray	4	13, 14	22, 48
Deer Creek	Grant	3	19	38
Del City	Oklahoma	5	42	94
Delaware	Nowata	2	29	10
Depew	Creek	3	12	29
Devol	Cotton	4	31	65
Dewar	Okmulgee	2	8	16
Dewey	Washington	1	29	10
Dibble	McClain	4	43	42

Municipality	County	Congress	Senate	House
Dickson	Carter	4	14	49
Dill City	Washita	3	38	55
Disney	Mayes	2	1	5
Dougherty	Murray	4	14	22
Douglas	Garfield	3	19	38
Dover	Kingfisher	3	19	59
Drummond	Garfield	3	20	41
Drumright	Creek/Payne	3	12, 21	33, 35
Duncan	Stephens	4	31, 43	50, 51, 65
Durant	Bryan	2	6	20, 21
Dustin	Hughes	2	7	24
Eakly	Caddo	3	26	60
Earlsboro	Pottawatomie	5	28	26, 27
East Duke	Jackson	3	38	52
Edmond	Oklahoma	5	22, 41, 47	31, 39, 81, 82, 83, 96
El Reno	Canadian	3	23	59, 60
Eldorado	Jackson	3	38	52
Elgin	Comanche	4	31	65
Elk City	Beckham	3	26	55, 57
Elmer	Jackson	3	38	52
Elmore City	Garvin	4	13	42
Empire City	Stephens	4	31, 43	50, 65
Enid	Garfield	3	19	38, 40, 41
Erick	Beckham	3	26	55
Erin Springs	Garvin	4	43	42
Etowah	Cleveland	4	15	20
Eufaula	McIntosh	2	8	15, 18
Fair Oaks	Rogers/Wagoner	1, 2	2	23
Fairfax	Osage	3	10	36
Fairland	Ottawa	2	1	7
Fairmont	Garfield	3	19	38
Fairview	Major	3	27	58
Fallis	Lincoln	3	28	32
Fanshawe	Latimer/LeFlore	2	4, 5, 7	3, 17
Fargo	Ellis	3	27	61
Faxon	Comanche	4	31	63
Fitzhugh	Pontotoc	4	13	25
Fletcher	Comanche	4	31	65
Foraker	Osage	3	10	37
Forest Park	Oklahoma	5	48	97

Municipality	County	Congress	Senate	House
Forgan	Beaver	3	27	61
Fort Cobb	Caddo	3	26	56
Fort Coffee	LeFlore	2	4	3
Fort Gibson	Muskogee	2	9, 18	14
Fort Sill	Comanche	4	31, 32	65
Fort Supply	Woodward	3	27	61
Fort Towson	Choctaw	2	5	19
Foss	Washita	3	38	55
Foyil	Rogers	2	29	6
Francis	Pontotoc	4	13	25
Frederick	Tillman	4	31	63
Freedom	Woods	3	27	58
Gage	Ellis	3	27	61
Gans	Sequoyah	2	4	2
Garber	Garfield	3	19	38
Garvin	McCurtain	2	5	1
Gate	Beaver	3	27	61
Geary	Blaine/Canadian	3	23, 26	57, 60
Gene Autry	Carter	4	14	48
Geronimo	Comanche	4	31	63
Gerty	Hughes	2	7	18
Glencoe	Payne	3	21	35
Glenpool	Tulsa	1	12, 35, 37	30, 68
Goldsby	McClain	4	15, 43	20, 42, 46
Goltry	Alfalfa	3	19	58
Goodwell	Texas	3	27	61
Gore	Sequoyah	2	3, 4	15
Gotebo	Kiowa	3	38	56
Gould	Harmon	3	38	52
Gracemont	Caddo	3	26	56
Grainola	Osage	3	10	37
Grand Lake Towne	Mayes	2	1	5
Grandfield	Tillman	4	31	63
Granite	Greer	3	38	52
Grayson	Okmulgee	2	8	16
Greenfield	Blaine	3	26	59
Grove	Delaware	2	3	5, 7
Guthrie	Logan	3	20	31, 38
Guymon	Texas	3	27	61
Haileyville	Pittsburg	2	7	17

Municipality	County	Congress	Senate	House
Hallet	Pawnee	3	20	35
Hammon	Custer/Roger Mills	3	26	55, 57
Hanna	McIntosh	2	8	18
Hardesty	Texas	3	27	61
Harrah	Oklahoma	5	17	96, 101
Hartshorne	Pittsburg	2	7	17
Haskell	Muskogee	2	18	16
Hastings	Jefferson	4	31	50
Haworth	McCurtain	2	5	1
Headrick	Jackson	3	38	52
Healdton	Carter	4	14	48
Heavener	LeFlore	2	5	3
Helena	Alfalfa	3	19	58
Hendrix	Bryan	2	6	21
Hennessey	Kingfisher	3	19	59
Henryetta	Okmulgee	2	8	16, 24
Hickory	Murray	4	14	22
Hillsdale	Garfield	3	19	41
Hinton	Caddo	3	26	60
Hitchcock	Blaine	3	26	59
Hitchita	McIntosh	2	8	18
Hobart	Kiowa	3	38	55, 56
Hoffman	Okmulgee	2	8	16
Holdenville	Hughes	2	13	24
Hollis	Harmon	3	38	52
Hollister	Tillman	4	31	63
Hominy	Osage	3	10	36
Hooker	Texas	3	27	61
Hoot Owl	Mayes	2	1	5
Horntown	Hughes	2	7	18, 24
Howe	LeFlore	2	5	3
Hugo	Choctaw	2	5	19
Hulbert	Cherokee	2	18	4, 14
Hunter	Garfield	3	19	38
Hydro	Blaine/Caddo	3	26	57
Idabel	McCurtain	2	5	1
Indiahoma	Comanche	4	32	63
Indianola	Pittsburg	2	7	18
Inola	Rogers	2	3	8
IXL	Okfuskee	2	8	24

Municipality	County	Congress	Senate	House
Jay	Delaware	2	1	5
Jefferson	Grant	3	19	38
Jenks	Tulsa	1	25, 37	68, 69
Jennings	Pawnee	3	20	35
Jet	Alfalfa	3	19	58
Johnson	Pottawatomie	5	17, 28	26, 28
Jones	Oklahoma	5	48	96, 97
Kansas	Delaware	2	3	86
Kaw City	Kay	3	10	37
Kellyville	Creek	3	12	29
Kemp	Bryan	2	6	21
Kendrick	Lincoln	3	28	32
Kenefic	Bryan	2	6	21
Keota	Haskell	2	7	15
Ketchum	Craig	2	1	6
Keyes	Cimarron	3	27	61
Kiefer	Creek	1	12	30
Kildare	Kay	3	10	37
Kingfisher	Kingfisher	3	20, 26	59
Kingston	Marshall	2	6	49
Kinta	Haskell	2	7	15
Kiowa	Pittsburg	2	7	18
Knowles	Beaver	3	27	61
Konawa	Seminole	5	13	28
Krebs	Pittsburg	2	7	17
Kremlin	Garfield	3	19	38
Lahoma	Garfield	3	19	41
Lake Aluma	Oklahoma	5	48	97
Lamar	Hughes	2	7	18, 24
Lambert	Alfalfa	3	19	58
Lamont	Grant	3	19	38
Langley	Mayes	2	1	5, 6
Langston	Logan	3	20	31, 32, 33
Laverne	Harper	3	27	61
Lawrence Creek	Creek	3	12	35
Lawton	Comanche	4	31, 32	62, 63, 64, 65
Leedey	Dewey	3	27	59
LeFlore	LeFlore	2	5	17
Lehigh	Coal	2	6	18
Lenapah	Nowata	2	29	10

Municipality	County	Congress	Senate	House
Leon	Love	4	14	49
Lexington	Cleveland	4	16	20
Liberty	Okmulgee/Tulsa	1, 2	8, 33	24, 30
Lima	Seminole	5	28	28
Lindsay	Garvin	4	43	42
Loco	Stephens	4	43	50
Locust Grove	Mayes	2	3	8
Lone Grove	Carter	4	14	48, 49
Lone Wolf	Kiowa	3	38	52, 55
Longdale	Blaine	3	26	59
Lookeba	Caddo	3	26	60
Lotsee	Tulsa	1	37	29
Loveland	Tillman	4	31	63
Loyal	Kingfisher	3	20	59
Luther	Oklahoma	5	17	96
Macomb	Pottawatomie	5	13	27
Madill	Marshall	2	6	49
Manchester	Grant	3	19	38
Mangum	Greer	3	38	52, 55
Manitou	Tillman	4	31	63
Mannford	Creek/Pawnee/Tulsa	1, 3	12, 20, 37	29, 35
Mannsville	Johnston	2	14	22
Maramec	Pawnee	3	20	35
Marble City	Sequoyah	2	4	2
Marietta	Love	4	14	49
Marland	Noble	3	20	38
Marlow	Stephens	4	43	51
Marshall	Logan	3	20	38
Martha	Jackson	3	38	52
Maud	Pottawatomie/ Seminole	5	13	27, 28
May	Harper	3	27	61
Maysville	Garvin	4	13	42
McAlester	Pittsburg	2	7	17, 18
McCurtain	Haskell	2	7	15
McLoud	Pottawatomie	5	17, 28	26, 27
Mead	Bryan	2	6	21
Medford	Grant	3	19	38
Medicine Park	Comanche	4	32	63
Meeker	Lincoln	3	28	32
Meno	Major	3	27	58

Municipality	County	Congress	Senate	House
Meridian	Logan/Stephens	3	20	32
Miami	Ottawa	2	1	7
Midwest City	Oklahoma	4, 5	17, 42, 48	95, 97, 101
Milburn	Johnston	2	6	22
Mill Creek	Johnston	2	14	22
Millerton	McCurtain	2	5	1
Minco	Grady	4	23	56
Moffett	Sequoyah	2	4	2
Moore	Cleveland	4	15, 24, 45	27, 53, 54
Mooreland	Woodward	3	27	58
Morris	Okmulgee	2	8	16
Morrison	Noble	3	20	35
Mounds	Creek	1	12	30
Mountain Park	Kiowa	3	38	52
Mountain View	Kiowa	3	38	56
Muldrow	Sequoyah	2	4	2
Mule Barn	Pawnee	3	10	35
Mulhall	Logan	3	20	38
Muskogee	Muskogee	2	9	13, 14
Mustang	Canadian	3, 4	45	47
Mutual	Woodward	3	27	59
Nardin	Kay	3	20	38
Nash	Grant	3	19	38
New Alluwe	Nowata	2	29	10
New Cordell	Washita	3	26	55
New Tulsa	Wagoner	1	18, 36	98
Newcastle	McClain	4	15, 43	20, 46, 51
Newkirk	Kay	3	10	38
Nichols Hills	Oklahoma	5	40, 48	83, 85, 99
Nicoma Park	Oklahoma	5	17, 48	97, 101
Ninnekah	Grady	4	23	51
Noble	Cleveland	4	16	20, 46
Norge	Grady	4	23	56
Norman	Cleveland	4	15, 16, 24	20, 27, 44, 45, 46, 53
North Enid	Garfield	3	19	40
North Miami	Ottawa	2	1	7
Nowata	Nowata	2	29	10
Oak Grove	Pawnee	3	20	35
Oakhurst	Creek/Tulsa	1, 3	12, 37	30, 68
Oakland	Marshall	2	6	49

Municipality	County	Congress	Senate	House
Oaks	Cherokee/Delaware	2	3	86
Oakwood	Dewey	3	27	59
Ochelata	Washington	1	29	10
Oilton	Creek	3	12	35
Okarche	Canadian/Kingfisher	3	23, 26	59
Okay	Wagoner	1	18	12
Okeene	Blaine	3	26	59
Okemah	Okfuskee	2	8	24
Oklahoma City	Canadian, Cleveland, Oklahoma, Pottawatomie	3, 4, 5,	15, 17, 22, 23, 24, 30, 40, 41, 42, 44, 45, 46, 47, 48, 48,	27, 39, 41, 43, 47, 53, 54, 59, 60, 81, 82, 83, 84, 85, 87, 88, 89, 90, 91, 92, 93, 94, 95, 96, 97, 99, 100, 101
Okmulgee	Okmulgee	2	8	16, 24
Oktaha	Muskogee	2	9	13
Olustee	Jackson	3	38	52
Oologah	Rogers	2	29	6
Optima	Texas	3	27	61
Orlando	Logan/Payne	3	20, 21	33, 38
Osage	Osage	3	10	35
Owasso	Rogers/Tulsa	1, 2	2, 34	9, 11, 74
Paden	Okfuskee	2	8	24
Panama	LeFlore	2	4	15
Paoli	Garvin	4	13	20, 42
Paradise Hill	Sequoyah	2	4	15
Pauls Valley	Garvin	4	13	20, 42
Pawhuska	Osage	3	10	36, 37
Pawnee	Pawnee	3	20	35
Peggs	Cherokee	2	3	86
Pensacola	Mayes	2	1	5
Peoria	Ottawa	2	1	7
Perkins	Payne	3	21	33
Perry	Noble	3	20	35, 38
Phillips	Coal	2	6	18
Picher	Ottawa	2	1	7
Piedmont	Canadian/Kingfisher	3	20, 22	41, 59
Pink	Pottawatomie	5	28	27
Pittsburg	Pittsburg	2	7	17
Pocasset	Grady	4	23	56
Pocola	LeFlore	2	4	3

Municipality	County	Congress	Senate	House
Ponca City	Kay/Osage	3	10	37, 38
Pond Creek	Grant	3	19	38
Porter	Wagoner	1	18	12
Porum	Muskogee	2	8	15
Poteau	LeFlore	2	4	3, 15
Prague	Lincoln	3	28	32
Prue	Osage	3	10	35
Pryor Creek	Mayes	2	2	8
Purcell	Cleveland/McClain	4	16, 43	20, 42
Putnam	Dewey	3	27	59
Quapaw	Ottawa	2	1	7
Quay	Payne/Pawnee	3	10	33, 35
Quinton	Pittsburg	2	7	17
Ralston	Pawnee	3	20	35
Ramona	Washington	1	29	10
Randlett	Cotton	4	31	65
Ratliff City	Carter	4	14	48
Rattan	Pushmataha	2	5	19
Ravia	Johnston	2	14	22
Red Oak	Latimer	2	7	17
Red Rock	Noble	3	20	38
Redbird	Wagoner	1	18	12
Renfrow	Grant	3	19	38
Rentiesville	McIntosh	2	8	13
Reydon	Roger Mills	3	26	55
Ringling	Jefferson	4	31	50
Ringwood	Major	3	27	58
Ripley	Payne	3	21	33
Rock Island	LeFlore	2	4	3
Rocky	Washita	3	38	55
Roff	Pontotoc	4	13	25
Roland	Sequoyah	2	4	2
Roosevelt	Kiowa	3	38	5
Rosedale	McClain	4	43	20
Rosston	Harper	3	27	61
Rush Springs	Grady	4	43	65
Ryan	Jefferson	4	31	50
Salina	Mayes	2	1	5, 8
Sallisaw	Sequoyah	2	4	2
Sand Springs	Osage/Tulsa	1, 3	10, 11, 37	29, 36, 66, 68

Municipality	County	Congress	Senate	House
Sapulpa	Creek/Tulsa	1, 3	12, 37	29, 30, 68
Sasakwa	Seminole	5	13	28
Savanna	Pittsburg	2	7	17, 18
Sawyer	Choctaw	2	5	19
Sayre	Beckham	3	26	55
Schulter	Okmulgee	2	8	16
Seiling	Dewey	3	27	59
Seminole	Seminole	5	28	28
Sentinel	Washita	3	38	55
Shady Grove	Sequoyah	3	20	35
Shady Point	LeFlore	2	4	15
Shamrock	Creek	3	12	29
Sharon	Woodward	3	27	59
Shattuck	Ellis	3	27	61
Shawnee	Pottawatomie	5	17, 28	26, 27, 28
Shidler	Osage	3	10	37
Silo	Bryan	2	6	21
Skedee	Pawnee	3	20	35
Skiatook	Osage/Tulsa	1, 3	10, 34	10, 36
Slaughterville	Cleveland	4	15, 16	20
Slick	Creek	3	12	29
Smith Village	Oklahoma	5	42	94
Smithville	McCurtain	2	5	1
Snyder	Kiowa	3	38	52
Soper	Choctaw	2	5	19
South Coffeyville	Nowata	2	29	10
Sparks	Lincoln	3	28	32
Spaulding	Hughes	2	13	24
Spavinaw	Mayes	2	1	5
Spencer	Oklahoma	5	48	97
Sperry	Tulsa	1, 3	10, 34	36, 72
Spiro	LeFlore	2	4	3, 15
Sportsman Acres	Mayes	2	3	8
Springer	Carter	4	14	48
St. Louis	Pottawatomie	5	13	27
Sterling	Comanche	4	31	65
Stidham	McIntosh	2	8	18
Stigler	Haskell	2	7	15
Stillwater	Payne	3	21	33, 34, 35
Stilwell	Adair	2	3	86

Municipality	County	Congress	Senate	House
Stonewall	Pontotoc	4	13	25
Strang	Mayes	2	1	5
Stratford	Garvin	4	13	22
Stringtown	Atoka	2	5, 6	19
Strong City	Roger Mills	3	26	55
Stroud	Creek/Lincoln	3	12, 28	29, 32
Stuart	Hughes	2	7	18
Sugden	Jefferson	4	31	50
Sulphur	Murray	4	14	22
Summit	Muskogee	2	9	13
Sweetwater	Beckham/Roger Mills	3	26	55
Taft	Muskogee	2	9	13
Tahlequah	Cherokee	2	9, 18	4
Talala	Rogers	2	29	6
Talihina	LeFlore	2	5	1, 17
Taloga	Dewey	3	27	59
Tamaha	Haskell	2	7	15
Tatums	Carter	4	14	48
Tecumseh	Pottawatomie	5	28	26, 27
Temple	Cotton	4	31	65
Terlton	Pawnee	3	20	35
Terral	Jefferson	4	31	50
Texhoma	Texas	3	27	61
Texola	Beckham	3	26	55
Thackerville	Love	4	14	49
The Village	Oklahoma	5	30, 40	83, 85
Thomas	Custer	3	26	57
Tipton	Tillman	4	31	63
Tishomingo	Johnston	2	14	22
Tonkawa	Kay	3	10	38
Tribbey	Pottawatomie	5	13	27
Tryon	Lincoln	3	28	32
Tullahassee	Wagoner	1	18	12
Tulsa	Osage/Rogers/Tulsa	1, 2	2, 10, 11, 18, 25, 33, 34, 35, 36, 37, 39,	23, 36, 66, 67, 68–73, 75–79, 98
Tupelo	Coal	2	6	18
Turley	Tulsa	1	11	72
Tushka	Atoka	2	6	22

Municipality	County	Congress	Senate	House
Tuttle	Grady	4	23	47, 51
Tyrone	Texas	3	27	61
Union City	Canadian	3	23	60
Valley Brook	Oklahoma	5	45	54, 74
Valley Park	Rogers	2	2	9
Valliant	McCurtain	2	5	1
Velma	Stephens	4	43	51
Vera	Washington	1	29	10, 11
Verden	Grady	4	23	56
Verdigris	Rogers	2	2	9, 23
Vian	Sequoyah	2	4	2, 15
Vici	Dewey	3	27	59
Vinita	Craig	2	1	6
Wagoner	Wagoner	1	18	12
Wainwright	Muskogee	2	18	13
Wakita	Grant	3	19	38
Walters	Cotton	4	31	65
Wanette	Pottawatomie	5	13	20
Wann	Nowata	2	29	10
Wapanucka	Johnston	2	6	22
Warner	Muskogee	2	8	13, 15
Warr Acres	Oklahoma	5	30, 40	84, 85, 87, 100
Warwick	Lincoln	3	28	32
Washington	McClain	4	46	42
Watonga	Blaine	3	23	59
Watts	Adair	2	3	86
Waukomis	Garfield	3	19	41
Waurika	Jefferson	4	31	50
Wayne	McClain	4	43	42
Waynoka	Woods	3	27	58
Weatherford	Custer	3	38	57
Webb City	Osage	3	10	37
Webbers Falls	Muskogee	2	8	14, 15
Welch	Craig	2	1	6
Weleetka	Okfuskee	2	7, 8	24
Wellston	Lincoln	3	28	32
West Siloam Springs	Delaware	2	3	86
Westport	Pawnee	3	20	35
Westville	Adair	2	3	86
Wetumka	Hughes	2	13	24

Municipality	County	Congress	Senate	House
Wewoka	Seminole	5	28	28
Whitefield	Haskell	2	7	15
Wilburton	Latimer	2	7	17
Willow	Greer	3	38	55
Wilson	Carter	4	14	48, 49
Winchester	Okmulgee	2	8	24
Wister	LeFlore	2	4, 5	3,
Woodlawn Park	Oklahoma	5	30	84
Woodville	Marshall	2	6	49
Woodward	Woodward	3	27	58, 59
Wright City	McCurtain	2	5	1
Wyandotte	Ottawa	2	1	7
Wynnewood	Garvin	4	13	22
Wynona	Osage	3	10	36
Yale	Payne	3	21	33
Yeager	Hughes	2	7	24
Yukon	Canadian	3	22, 23, 45	43, 60

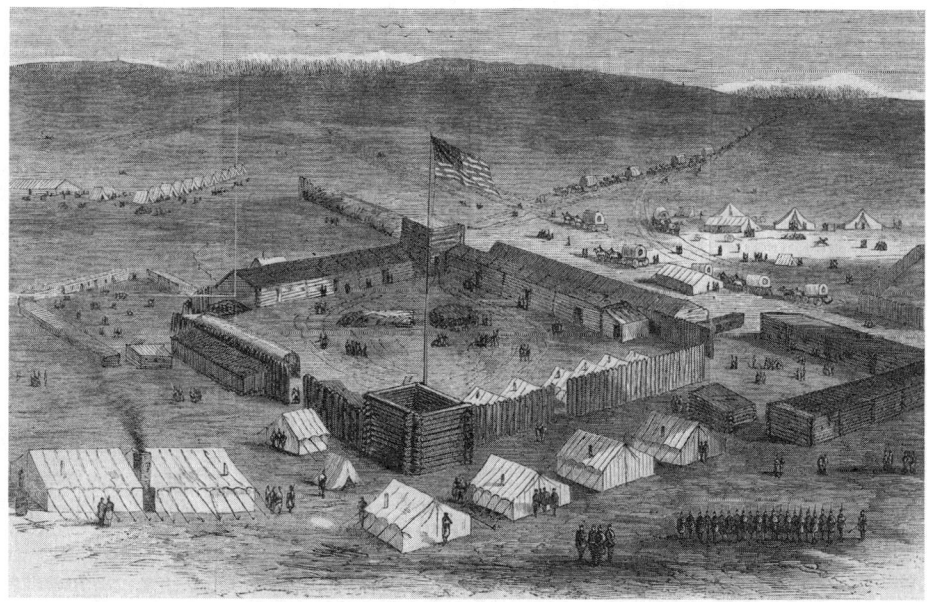

Illustration of Fort Supply, circa 1869.

EDUCATION

Information in this section was provided by the State Regents for Higher Education, and Judith Matthews at the Oklahoma Department of Libraries. • This section is also compiled from the websites of the State Department of Education (SDE) and the U.S. Department of Education. Specifically, *Profiles 2013 State Report*, (published by SDE). ACT test score data was obtained from the ACT report on National and State Scores, available online at www.act.org. • Information regarding higher education was obtained from the Oklahoma State Regents of Higher Education's *Educational and General Budgets Summary and Analysis Report 2013*. • Information about NAEP results is available through the National Center for Education Statistics (NCES) at www.ed.gov. Additional information was obtained from the Oklahoma State Department of Education website: www.ok.gov/sde

Public Schools In Oklahoma

Public schools in Oklahoma are operated by local boards of education, under accreditation standards established by the State Board of Education. Attendance is compulsory between the ages of five and eighteen, although schools are required to provide services for those three to twenty-one (U.S. Department of Education statistics). In addition, Oklahoma is implementing a variety of early childhood education and parental outreach programs. In most cases, the school year runs from early August to late May, although extended day and year programs are optional.

The total number of school districts in Oklahoma was 521 during the 2012-2013 academic year. The number of school districts has declined since 1914 when 5,889 school districts existed—the largest number since statehood—when schools were located within walking distance of every child. Between 1947 and 1965, almost 3,300 schools were annexed or consolidated. In 1967, 1,160 school districts operated in Oklahoma, and by 1987, that number had dropped to 615 districts. Incentives provided in 1990 fostered renewed interest in consolidation, contributing to additional reductions in the number of districts since that time.

Student Statistics

According to the State Department of Education (SDE), during the 2012–13 academic year, student enrollment (based upon average daily membership) reached 666,220, an increase of 6,624 (1.0%) students from the 2011–12 academic year. Oklahoma school enrollment by ethnic group for 2012–13 was White and Other, 52.6 percent; American Indian, 15.8 percent; Black, 9.4 percent; Hispanic, 14.1 percent; and Asian, 2.1 percent.

During the 2012–13 academic year, 97,509 students qualified for the Gifted/Talented program or 14.8 percent of all students in the state. That same year, 99,229 students qualified for the special education program which represented 15.0 percent of all students. There were 412,432 Oklahoma students eligible for the free and reduced-priced lunches. This equated to 61.9 percent of all students and was an increase of over 5,676 students or 1.4 percent from the 2011–12 school year.

Ethnic Group	1990	2010
White and Other	74%	54.5%
American Indian	12%	17.7%
Hispanic	3%	12.3%
Black	10%	10.2%
Asian	1%	2.1%

According to the 2000 Census Current Population Reports, in 1990, 74.6 percent of Oklahomans over age twenty-five had a high school diploma or higher, slightly less than the national average of 75.2 percent. By 2000, Oklahomans over the age of twenty-five with a high school diploma or higher grew to 86.1, exceeding the national average of 84.1 percent. In 2010, that percentage had declined to 85.4 percent, compared to the national average of 85.0 percent. In 1990, 20.3 percent of Oklahomans had a bachelor's degree or higher, and in 2000, that number had grown to 22.5 percent. In 2010 the percentage had slightly increased to 22.6, but remained below the national average of 27.9 percent.

Standardized Test Scores

The ACT exam is widely used in Oklahoma and other states as an assessment tool in college admissions and placement. The 2012–13 average composite score on the ACT for Oklahoma was 20.8, compared to the national average score of 20.9. Oklahoma's 20.8 score was an increase of 0.1 over the 2011–12 composite score of 20.7. Although Oklahoma's score was slightly below the national average, it was comparable to other states in the ACT's Southern region including Tennessee, (19.7), Texas, (20.8), Arkansas, (20.3), Georgia, (20.7), Alabama, (20.3), Louisiana, (20.3), and Mississippi, (18.7). Comparable states in the Midwest and Southwest region includes Kansas, (21.9), Missouri, (21.6), Colorado, (20.6), and New Mexico (19.9).

The SAT is another well-recognized college entrance test, although it is not widely taken in Oklahoma. In 2012–13 Oklahoma public school students' performance scores on critical reading was 571, math was 569, and writing was 549, out of 800 on each. National scores in these same areas were 496, 518, and 489, respectively. While Oklahoma's scores were well above the national average, this performance must be placed in proper perspective. According to the College Board, the company responsible for the SAT, only 5 percent or 1,879 of Oklahoma's students took the SAT in the 2012–13 year. This was down from the 1,996 students who took the SAT in 2011–12. Nationally, the SAT was taken by 54 percent of students during that same year. Most of the students who take the test in Oklahoma do so to compete for prestigious national-level scholarships or to attend out-of-state universities.

Dropout and Graduation Rates

According to the State Department of Education, Oklahoma's single year dropout rate for grades ninth through twelfth for the 2012–13 academic year was 2.3 percent, the same rate as 2010–11 and 2011–12. The rate was slightly up from the 2.2 percent rate in 2009–10. The number of students dropping out of school has consistently decreased in Oklahoma over the years. 2007-08 dropout rate was 2.9 percent; the 2006–07 dropout rate was 3.2 percent; the 2005–06 dropout rate was 3.3 percent; and the 2004–05 dropout rate was 3.2 percent. However, the four-year dropout rate for the 2012–13 academic year was 9.6 percent.

Oklahoma's freshmen graduation rates for the 2012–13 academic year was 78.8 percent, slightly down from 79.0 percent in 2011–12. The national graduation rate for the 2011–12 school year was 75.2 percent. For states in Oklahoma's region for the 2008–2009 year were: Oklahoma with 77.3 percent, Arkansas with 74.0 percent, Colorado with a 77.6 percent, Kansas with a 80.2 percent, New Mexico with a 64.8 percent, Missouri with a 83.1 percent, and Texas with a 75.4 percent. The national graduation rate in 2008–09 was 75.5 percent.

Teacher and Administrator Statistics

The *Profiles 2013 State Report* from the Office of Accountability reports that statewide the number of regular classroom teachers increased by 396 full-time employees (FTEs), for the 2012–13 academic year (37,104 in 2012–13 from 36,708 in 2011–12). The Average Daily Membership (ADM) increased by 6,624. Based on ADM of 662,220, the statewide gross student/teacher ratio for regular classroom teachers in 2012–13 was 17.8 students per teacher. This is one of the highest student teacher ratios in the last twenty years. The average teacher salary for the 2012–13 academic year was $44,118, a decrease of $27 from the previous year. The percent of teachers with an advance degree is 24.8 percent, compared to 25.8 percent the previous year. The current percentage of teachers with an advanced degree is well below the high 41 percent in 1989–90. Classroom teachers average 12.5 years of experience.

Similar to classroom teachers, the 2012–13 academic year saw an increase in the number of administrators from the previous year. There were 3,493 administrator FTEs at the 521 districts, an increase of 107 FTEs over the 2011–12 academic year count of 3,386 administrator FTEs. Statewide, there was an average of 6.7 administrators per school district, and each received an average salary of $76,424, an increase just over $500, or 0.7 percent over the last year. On average, each administrator supervised 11.9 teacher FTEs in 2012–13, and had 21.1 years of experience in public education.

Public School Funding

The three basic sources of school district revenue in Oklahoma are local and county, state, and federal. Total revenue for the 2012–13 academic year was $5,624,027,784. The largest portion of funding is provided by the state at 48 percent ($2.70 billion), followed by local and county with 39.6 percent ($2.23 billion), and federal at 12.5 percent ($701 million). Total revenues decreased for Oklahoma's districts by $21,519,046 or 0.4 percent over the 2012–13 revenues of $5,645,546,831. Each year, roughly one-third of Oklahoma's state budget goes to K–12 public education.

Historical Expenditures
Per Pupil in Average Daily Attendance
Unadjusted Dollars

Compiled from U.S. Dept. of Education, 2012 *Digest of Education Statistics*

Year	Oklahoma Average	National Average	Percent of Nat'l Average
1959	$311	$375	82.9%
1969	$604	$816	74.0%
1979	$1,926	$2,272	84.8%
1989	$3,508	$4,980	70.4%
1999	$5,684	$7,013	81.0%
2009	$7,878	$10,540	74.7%
2011	$7,631	$10,658	71.6%

Education expenditures are classified into eight categories: Instruction, Student Support, Instructional Support, District Administration, School Administration, District Support, Other, and Debt Service. The largest expenditure for the 2012–13 academic year was in the area of "Instruction" with 53.7 percent, a 0.3 percentage-point decrease from 2011–12, and is below a high mark of 58.6 percent of "All Funds" in 1995–96. "District Support" ran a distant second in 2012–13 at 17.9 percent of all expenditures. Statewide, total expenditures from "All Funds" were $5.6 billion, a $92 million increase over the 2011–12 academic year.

State appropriated revenues are distributed to school districts through a "State Aid Formula." While state tax revenues are collected geographically in a disproportionate manner, the formula strives to distribute tax dollars equitably to all districts. The formula attempts to assess the cost required to dispense education at each school district across the state, taking into account a district's wealth, then funds districts accordingly. The formula takes three costs differences into consideration: (1) differences in the cost of educating various types of students, (2) differences in transportation costs, and (3) differences in the salaries districts must pay teachers with varying credentials and years of experience. Additionally, the formula proportionately withholds state funds from districts that have a greater ability to raise money through local/county revenues.

Based on "All Funds," including "Debt Service," per student expenditures in 2012–13 ranged from a high of $22,926 per student in Taloga Public Schools in Dewey County to a low of $5,392 per student at Copan Public Schools in Washington County. Roger Mills County has the highest per student expenditure at $17,407, while Murray County has the lowest at $7,195.

State Expenditures Per Pupil,
2010–2011
Unadjusted Dollars

State	Expenditure per Pupil	Percentage of U.S. Total
Alabama	$8,726	81.8%
Arkansas	$9,496	89.1%
Colorado	$8,786	82.4%
Kansas	$9,802	91.9%
Louisiana	$10,799	101.3%
Mississippi	$7,926	74.3%
Missouri	$9,461	88.7%
Nebraska	$11,540	108.2%
New Mexico	$9,250	86.7%
Oklahoma	$7,631	71.6%
Texas	$8,685	81.4%
United States	$10,658	100.0%

Source: U.S. Dept. of Education
2012 Digest of Education Statistics

Public School District Index

From the State Department of Education • 10/2012 • www.ok.gov/sde

District (County)	Code	Superintendent	Telephone
Achille (Bryan)	07I003	Richard Beene	580/283-3775
Ada (Pontotoc)	62I019	Pat Harrison	580/310-7200
Adair (Mayes)	46I002	Tom P. Linihan	918/785-2424
Afton (Ottawa)	58I026	Randy Gardner	918/257-8303
Agra (Lincoln)	41I134	Jay Thomas	918/375-2261
Albion (Pushmataha)	64C002	C. Lynn Bullard	918/563-4331
Alex (Grady)	26I056	Jason James	405/785-2605
Aline-Cleo (Major)	44I004	Barry Nault	580/463-2255
Allen (Pontotoc)	62I001	Ty Harman	580/857-2417
Allen-Bowden (Creek)	19C035	Floyd Kirk	918/224-4440
Altus (Jackson)	33I018	Roger Hill	580/481-2100
Alva (Woods)	76I001	Steve Parkhurst	580/327-4823
Amber-Pocasset (Grady)	26I128	Chad Hance	405/224-5768
Anadarko (Caddo)	08I020	Cindy Hackney	405/247-6605
Anderson (Osage)	57C052	Brett Banker	918/245-0289
Antlers (Pushmataha)	64I013	Cary Ammons	580/298-5504
Arapaho-Butler (Custer)	20I005	James Edelen	580/323-3261
Ardmore (Carter)	10I019	Nathaniel Bates	580/226-7650
Arkoma (LeFlore)	40I091	John Turner	918/875-3351
Arnett (Ellis)	23I003	Danny Cochran	580/885-7811
Asher (Pottawatomie)	63I112	Terry Grissom	405/784-2332
Atoka (Atoka)	03I015	Jay McAdams	580/889-6611
Avant (Osage)	57C035	Michael Young	918/263-2135
Balko (Beaver)	04I075	Larry Mills	580/646-3385
Banner (Canadian)	09C031	Larry York	405/262-0598
Barnsdall (Osage)	57I029	Rick Loggins	918/847-2271
Bartlesville (Washington)	74I030	Gary Quinn	918/336-8600
Battiest (McCurtain)	48I071	Stace Ebert	580/241-7810
Bearden (Okfuskee)	54C029	Danielle Deere	918/623-0156
Beaver (Beaver)	04I022	Scott Kinsey	580/625-3444
Beggs (Okmulgee)	56I004	Cindy Swearingen	918/267-3628
Belfonte (Sequoyah)	68C050	Paul Pinkerton	918/427-3522
Bennington (Bryan)	07I040	Pamela Reynolds	580/847-2737
Berryhill (Tulsa)	72I010	Mike Campbell	918/446-1966
Bethany (Oklahoma)	55I088	Kent Shellenberger	405/789-3801

District (County)	Code	Superintendent	Telephone
Bethel (Pottawatomie)	63I003	Jerry Johnson	405/273-0385
Big Pasture (Cotton)	17I333	Nat Lunn	580/281-3831
Billings (Noble)	52I002	Rodney Vollmer	580/725-3271
Binger-Oney (Caddo)	08I168	Kirk Wilson	405/656-2304
Bishop (Comanche)	16C049	Howard J. Hampton	580/353-4870
Bixby (Tulsa)	72I004	Kyle Wood	918/366-2200
Blackwell (Kay)	36I045	Richard Riggs	580/363-2570
Blair (Jackson)	33I054	Jimmy Smith	580/563-2632
Blanchard (McClain)	47I029	Jim Beckham	405/485-3391
Bluejacket (Craig)	18I020	Shellie Baker	918/784-2365
Boise City (Cimarron)	13I002	Ira Harris	580/544-3110
Bokoshe (LeFlore)	40I026	Dennis Shoup	918/969-2491
Boone-Apache (Caddo)	08I056	Don Schneberger	580/588-3369
Boswell (Choctaw)	12I001	Keith Edge	580/566-2558
Bowlegs (Seminole)	67I003	Tommy Eaton	405/398-4172
Bowring (Osage)	57C007	Nicole Hinkle	918/336-6892
Braggs (Muskogee)	51I046	Michael Broyles	918/487-5265
Braman (Kay)	36I018	Rustin Clark	580/385-2191
Bray-Doyle (Stephens)	69I042	David Wayne Eads	580/658-5076
Bridge Creek (Grady)	26I095	David Morrow	405/387-4880
Briggs (Cherokee)	11C044	Stephen Haynes	918/456-4221
Bristow (Creek)	19I002	Jeanene Barnett	918/367-5555
Broken Arrow (Tulsa)	72I003	Jarod Mendenhall	918/259-5700
Broken Bow (McCurtain)	48I074	Carla Ellisor	580/584-3306
Brushy (Sequoyah)	68C036	Greg Reynolds	918/775-4458
Buffalo (Harper)	30I004	Martin Adams	580/735-2448
Buffalo Valley (Latimer)	39I003	Justin Kennedy	918/522-4426
Burlington (Alfalfa)	02I001	Glen Elliott	580/431-2501
Burns Flat-Dill (Washita)	75I010	Ron G. Hughes	580/562-4844
Butner (Seminole)	67I015	Bobbette Hamilton	405/944-5530
Byars (McClain)	47C004	David Powell	405/783-4366
Byng (Pontotoc)	62I016	Todd Crabtree	580/310-6751
Cache (Comanche)	16I001	Randy Batt	580/429-3266
Caddo (Bryan)	07I005	Richard Thomas	580/367-2208
Calera (Bryan)	07I048	Gerald Parks	580/434-5700
Calumet (Canadian)	09I076	Keith Weldon	405/893-2222
Calvin (Hughes)	32I048	Christopher Karch	405/645-2411
Cameron (LeFlore)	40I017	Jim Caughern	918/654-3225

District (County)	Code	Superintendent	Telephone
Canadian (Pittsburg)	61I002	Rodney Karch	918/339-7251
Caney (Atoka)	03I026	Lori Boehme	580/889-1996
Caney Valley (Washington)	74I018	Rick Peters	918/536-2500
Canton (Blaine)	06I105	Carl Baker	580/886-3516
Canute (Washita)	75I011	Larry Parrish	580/472-3295
Carnegie (Caddo)	08I033	Mark Batt	580/654-1470
Carney (Lincoln)	41I105	Dewayne Osborn	405/865-2344
Cashion (Kingfisher)	37I089	Sammy Jackson	405/433-2741
Catoosa (Rogers)	66I002	Rick Kibbe	918/266-8603
Cave Springs (Adair)	01I030	Geary Brown	918/775-2346
Cement (Caddo)	08I160	Daniel Pittman	405/489-3216
Central (Sequoyah)	68I007	Larry G. Henson	918/775-5525
Central High (Stephens)	69I034	Bennie Newton	580/658-6858
Chandler (Lincoln)	41I001	Wayland Kimble	405/258-1450
Chattanooga (Comanche)	16I132	Jerry Brown	580/597-3347
Checotah (McIntosh)	49I019	Janet Blocker	918/473-5610
Chelsea (Rogers)	46I003	Rich McSpadden	918/789-2528
Cherokee (Alfalfa)	02I046	Cory Ellis	580/596-3391
Cherokee Immersion Charter School (Cherokee)	N/A	Rita Bunch	918/453-5400
Cheyenne (Roger Mills)	65I007	Rick Garrison	580/497-2666
Chickasha (Grady)	26I001	David Cash	405/222-6500
Chisholm (Garfield)	24I042	Roydon Tilley	580/237-5512
Choctaw/Nicoma Park (Okla.)	55I004	Jim McCharen	405/769-4859
Chouteau-Mazie (Mayes)	46I032	Kenny Mason	918/476-8376
Cimarron (Major)	44I092	Steve Walker	580/796-2204
Claremore (Rogers)	66I001	J. Michael McClaren	918/923-4200
Clayton (Pushmataha)	64I010	Randall Erwin	918/569-4492
Cleora (Delaware)	21C006	Kenny Guthrie	918/256-6401
Cleveland (Pawnee)	59I006	Aaron Espolt	918/358-2210
Clinton (Custer)	20I099	Kevin Hime	580/323-1800
Coalgate (Coal)	15I001	Jim Girten	580/927-2351
Colbert (Bryan)	07I004	Jarvis Dobbs	405/296-2624
Colcord (Delaware)	21I004	Bud Simmons	918/326-4116
Coleman (Johnston)	35I035	James Dominick	580/937-4418
Collinsville (Tulsa)	72I006	Lance West	918/371-2326
Comanche (Stephens)	69I002	Terry Davidson	580/439-2900
Commerce (Ottawa)	58I018	Jim Haynes	918/675-4316
Copan (Washington)	74I004	Rick Ruckman	918/532-4344

District (County)	Code	Superintendent	Telephone
Cordell (Washita)	75I078	Brad Overton	580/832-3420
Cottonwood (Coal)	15C004	John Daniel	580/927-2937
Covington-Douglas (Garfield)	24I094	Darren Sharp	580/864-7481
Coweta (Wagoner)	73I017	Jeff Holmes	918/486-6506
Coyle (Logan)	42I014	Josh Sumrall	405/466-2242
Crescent (Logan)	42I002	H.T. Gee	405/969-3738
Crooked Oak (Oklahoma)	55I053	Brad Richards	405/677-5252
Crowder (Pittsburg)	61I028	Robert Florenzano	918/334-3203
Crutcho (Oklahoma)	55C074	Teresa McAfee	405/427-3771
Cushing (Payne)	60I067	Koln Knight	918/225-3425
Cyril (Caddo)	08I064	Jamie Mitchell	580/464-2419
Dahlonegah (Adair)	O1C029	Jeff Limore	918/696-7807
Dale (Pottawatomie)	63I002	Charles Dickinson	405/964-5558
Darlington (Canadian)	09C070	Cheryl Garrison	405/262-0137
Davenport (Lincoln)	41I003	Danny Acord	918/377-2277
Davidson (Tillman)	71I009	Phillip Ratcliff	580/568-2423
Davis (Murray)	50I010	Mike Martin	580/369-2386
Deborah Brown Comm. (Tulsa)	72G001	Deborah Brown	918/425-1407
Deer Creek (Oklahoma)	55I006	Ranet Tippens	405/348-6100
Deer Creek-Lamont (Grant)	27I095	James Lewis	580/388-4335
Denison (McCurtain)	48C037	Jordan Hill	580/286-3319
Depew (Creek)	19I021	Leon Hiett	918/324-5466
Dewar (Okmulgee)	56I008	Todd Been	918/652-9625
Dewey (Washington)	74I007	David Wilkins	918/534-2241
Dibble (McClain)	47I002	Chad Clanton	405/344-6375
Dickson (Carter)	10I077	Larry Case	580/223-9557
Discovery Schools of Tulsa (Tulsa)	72G003	Kaan Camuz	918/960-3131
Dover (Kingfisher)	37I002	Shannon Grimes	405/828-4206
Drummond (Garfield)	24I085	Mike Woods	580/493-2216
Drumright (Creek)	19I039	Robby Dorsey	918/352-2492
Duke (Jackson)	33I014	Kevin Brown	580/679-3014
Duncan (Stephens)	69I001	Glenda Cobb	580/255-0686
Durant (Bryan)	07I072	Duane Merideth	580/924-1276
Dustin (Hughes)	32I009	Brian Armstrong	918/656-3239
Eagletown (McCurtain)	48I013	Kent Hendon	580/835-2242
Earlsboro (Pottawatomie)	63I005	Mark Maloy	405/997-5616
Edmond (Oklahoma)	55I012	David Goin	405/340-2828
El Reno (Canadian)	09I034	Craig McVay	405/262-1703

District (County)	Code	Superintendent	Telephone
Eldorado (Jackson)	33I025	Dr. Harold Hayes	580/633-2219
Elgin (Comanche)	16I016	Tom Crimmins	580/492-3663
Elk City (Beckham)	05I006	Buddy Wood	580/225-0175
Elmore City-Pernell (Garvin)	25I072	Donny Darrow	580/788-2566
Empire (Stephens)	69I021	Vicki Davison	580/252-5392
Enid (Garfield)	24I057	Darrell Floyd	580/366-7000
Erick (Beckham)	05I051	Jeff Kelly	580/526-3476
Eufaula (McIntosh)	49I001	Jeanette Smith	918/689-2152
Fairland (Ottawa)	58I031	Mark Alexander	918/676-3811
Fairview (Major)	44I084	Rocky Burchfield	580/227-2531
Fanshawe (LeFlore)	40C039	Jerry Carpenter	918/659-2341
Fargo (Ellis)	23I002	Terry Stevens	580/698-2298
Farris (Atoka)	03C023	Wes Watson	580/889-5542
Felt (Cimarron)	13I010	Lewetta Hefley	580/426-2220
Fletcher (Comanche)	16I009	Randy Harris	580/549-3016
Flower Mound (Comanche)	16C048	Diana Jackson	580/353-4088
Forest Grove (McCurtain)	48C001	John Smith	580/286-3961
Forgan (Beaver)	04I123	Travis Smalts	580/487-3366
Ft. Cobb-Broxton (Caddo)	08I167	Kyle Lierle	405/643-2336
Fort Gibson (Muskogee)	51I003	Derald Glover	918/478-2474
Fort Supply (Woodward)	77I005	Pat Howell	580/766-2611
Fort Towson (Choctaw)	12I002	Jason Price	580/873-2712
Fox (Carter)	10I074	Brent Phelps	580/673-2081
Foyil (Rogers)	66I007	Rodney Carter	918/341-1113
Frederick (Tillman)	71I158	Shannon Vanderburg	580/335-5516
Freedom (Woods)	76I006	Danny McCuiston	580/621-3271
Friend (Grady)	26C037	Alton Rawlins	405/224-3822
Frink-Chambers (Pittsburg)	61C029	Charles Peckio Jr.	918/423-2434
Frontier (Noble)	52I004	Tracy Kincannon	580/723-4361
Gage (Ellis)	23I039	Greg Gregory	580/923-7909
Gans (Sequoyah)	68I004	Larry Calloway	918/775-2236
Garber (Garfield)	24I047	Jim Lamer	580/863-2220
Geary (Blaine)	06I080	Todd Glasgow	405/884-2989
Geronimo (Comanche)	16I004	Bill Pascoe	580/355-3801
Glencoe (Payne)	60I101	John Lazenby	580/669-4003
Glenpool (Tulsa)	72I013	Jerry Olansen	918/322-9500
Glover (McCurtain)	48C023	Joel Nichols	580/420-3232
Goodwell (Texas)	70I060	Frieda Burgess	580/349-2271

District (County)	Code	Superintendent	Telephone
Gore (Sequoyah)	68I006	Lucky McCrary	918/489-5587
Gracemont (Caddo)	08I086	Mike Jones	405/966-2236
Graham (Okfuskee)	54I032	Dusty D. Chancey	918/652-8935
Grand View (Cherokee)	11C034	Ed Kennedy	918/456-5131
Grandfield (Tillman)	71I249	Eva Spaulding	580/479-5237
Grandview (Stephens)	69C082	Gary Wade	580/439-2467
Granite (Greer)	28I003	Rodney Calhoun	580/535-2104
Grant (Choctaw)	12I003	Buck Hammers	580/326-8315
Greasy (Adair)	01C032	Jim Bynum	918/696-7768
Greenville (Love)	43C003	Jason Midkiff	580/276-2968
Grove (Delaware)	21I002	Sandy Jo Coaly	918/786-3003
Grove (Pottawatomie)	63C027	Sheril Payne	405/275-7435
Guthrie (Logan)	42I001	Dr. Mike Simpson	405/282-8900
Guymon (Texas)	70I008	Douglas Melton	580/338-4340
Gypsy (Creek)	19C012	Rachel Collins	918/324-5365
Haileyville (Pittsburg)	61IO11	Roger Hemphill	918/297-2626
Hammon (Roger Mills)	65I066	Robert Stafford	580/473-2221
Hanna (McIntosh)	49I064	Richard Boatright	918/657-2523
Hardesty (Texas)	70I015	Greg Faris	580/888-4258
Harmony (Atoka)	03C021	Brian Walker	580/889-3687
Harrah (Oklahoma)	55I007	Paul Blessington	405/454-6244
Hartshorne (Pittsburg)	61I001	Mark Ichord	918/297-2534
Haskell (Muskogee)	51I002	Sharon Herrington	918/482-5221
Haworth (McCurtain)	48I006	Ted Brewer	580/245-1406
Haywood (Pittsburg)	61C088	Richard Quaid	918/423-6265
Healdton (Carter)	10I055	Terry Shaw	580/229-0566
Heavener (LeFlore)	40I003	Edward Wilson	918/653-7223
Hennessey (Kingfisher)	37I016	Joe A. McCulley	405/853-4321
Henryetta (Okmulgee)	56I002	Dwayne Noble	918/652-6523
Hilldale (Muskogee)	51I029	Dr. Kaylin Coody	918/683-0273
Hinton (Caddo)	08I161	Richard Brownen	405/542-3257
Hobart (Kiowa)	38I001	Cathy Hunt	580/726-5691
Hodgen (LeFlore)	40C014	Ward Brown	918/653-4476
Holdenville (Hughes)	32I035	Randy Davenport	405/379-5483
Hollis (Harmon)	29I066	Jennifer McQueen	580/688-3450
Holly Creek (McCurtain)	48C072	Harvey Brumley	580/420-6961
Hominy (Osage)	57I038	Russell Hull	918/885-6511
Hooker (Texas)	70I023	Dan Faulkner	580/652-2162

District (County)	Code	Superintendent	Telephone
Howe (LeFlore)	40I067	Scott L. Parks	918/658-3666
Hugo (Choctaw)	12I039	Tod Harrison	580/326-6483
Hulbert (Cherokee)	11I016	Marilyn Dewoody	918/772-2501
Hydro-Eakly (Caddo)	08I011	Bill Derryberry	405/663-2774
Idabel (McCurtain)	48I005	Doug Brown	580/286-7639
Indiahoma (Comanche)	16I002	Deanna Voegeli	580/246-3448
Indianola (Pittsburg)	61I025	Mark Baumann	918/823-4231
Inola (Rogers)	66I005	Kent Holbrook	918/543-2255
Jay (Delaware)	21I001	Charles D. Thomas	918/253-4293
Jenks (Tulsa)	72I005	Stacey Butterfield	918/299-4411
Jennings (Pawnee)	59C002	Chris Ballenger	918/757-2536
Jones (Oklahoma)	55I009	Carl Johnson	405/399-9215
Justice (Seminole)	67C054	Chris Ballenger	405/257-2962
Justus-Tiawah (Rogers)	66C009	Carl Johnson	918/341-3626
Kansas (Delaware)	21I003	Chris Bryan	918/868-2562
Kellyville (Creek)	19I031	David Garroutte	918/247-6133
Kenwood (Delaware)	21C030	Billy Taylor	918/434-5799
Keota (Haskell)	31I043	Kelly Husted	918/966-3950
Ketchum (Craig)	18I006	Pete Hiseley	918/782-5091
Keyes (Cimarron)	13I011	Sherri Hitchings	580/546-7231
Keys (Cherokee)	11C006	Billie Jordan	918/485-1835
Keystone (Tulsa)	72C015	Della Jones	918/363-8711
Kiefer (Creek)	19I018	Mary Murrell	918/321-3421
Kildare (Kay)	36C050	Bruce Shelley	580/362-2811
Kingfisher (Kingfisher)	37I007	Jason Sternberger	405/375-4194
Kingston (Marshall)	45I003	Ron Whipkey	580/564-9033
Kinta (Haskell)	31I013	Patricia DeVille	918/768-3338
Kiowa (Pittsburg)	61IO14	Rick Pool	918/432-5631
Konawa (Seminole)	67I004	Robert Neel	580/925-3244
Krebs (Pittsburg)	61C009	Patrick Turner	918/426-4700
Kremlin-Hillsdale (Garfield)	24I018	Jim Patton	580/874-2284
Lane (Atoka)	03C022	Roland Smith	580/889-2743
Latta (Pontotoc)	62I024	Cliff Johnson	580/332-2092
Laverne (Harper)	30I001	Eddie K. Thomas	580/921-3362
Lawton (Comanche)	16I008	Tom Deighan	580/357-6900
Leach (Delaware)	21C014	John Long	918/868-2277
Leedey (Roger Mills)	65I003	Andrea Sealock	580/488-3424
LeFlore (LeFlore)	40I016	Cory Wood	918/753-2345

District (County)	Code	Superintendent	Telephone
Lexington (Cleveland)	14I057	Denny Prince	405/527-7236
Liberty (Sequoyah)	68C001	Jeff Ransom	918/427-3808
Liberty (Tulsa)	72I014	Donna J. Campo	918/366-8496
Lindsay (Garvin)	25I009	Dan Chapman	405/756-3131
Little Axe (Cleveland)	14I070	Tony Smith	405/329-7691
Locust Grove (Mayes)	46I017	Lori Helton	918/479-5243
Lomega (Kingfisher)	37I003	Karen Castonguay	405/729-4215
Lone Grove (Carter)	10I032	Todd Garrison	580/657-3131
Lone Star (Creek)	19C008	Tracie Hale	918/224-0201
Lone Wolf (Kiowa)	38I002	James W. Sutherland	580/846-9091
Lookeba-Sickles (Caddo)	08I012	Mike Davis	405/457-6623
Lowrey (Cherokee)	11C010	Bryan Hix	918/456-4053
Lukfata (McCurtain)	48C009	Kurt Neal	580/584-6834
Luther (Oklahoma)	55I003	Sheldon Buxton	405/277-3233
Macomb (Pottawatomie)	63I004	Matthew Riggs	405/598-3892
Madill (Marshall)	45I002	Jon Tuck	580/795-3303
Mangum (Greer)	28I001	Mike Southall	580/782-3371
Mannford (Creek)	19I003	Steve Waldvogel	918/865-4062
Mannsville (Johnston)	35C007	David Herron	580/371-2892
Maple (Canadian)	09C162	Arthur Eccard	405/262-5647
Marble City (Sequoyah)	68C035	Bill London	918/775-2135
Marietta (Love)	43I016	Joel K. Neely	580/276-9444
Marlow (Stephens)	69I003	George E. Coffman Jr.	580/658-2719
Maryetta (Adair)	01C022	Lori Means	918/696-2285
Mason (Okfuskee)	54I002	Jerry Bogle	918/623-0231
Maud (Pottawatomie)	63I117	Jerry McCormick	405/374-2416
Maysville (Garvin)	25I007	Shelly Hildebrand-Beach	888/806-5220
McAlester (Pittsburg)	61I080	Marsha Gore	918/423-4771
McCord (Osage)	57C077	Boyd Braden	580/765-8806
McCurtain (Haskell)	31I037	Dart Drummonds	918/945-7237
McLoud (Pottawatomie)	63I001	Doran Smith	405/964-3314
Medford (Grant)	27I054	Mickey Geurkink	580/395-2392
Meeker (Lincoln)	41I095	Rita Palmer	405/788-4540
Merritt (Beckham)	05I002	Jeff Daugherty	580/225-5460
Miami (Ottawa)	58I023	Loretta R. Robinson	918/542-8455
Middleberg (Grady)	26C096	Randy Hughes	405/485-3612
Midway (McIntosh)	49I027	Bob Grier	918/474-3434
MWCity-Del City (Okla.)	55I052	Pam Deering	405/737-4461

District (County)	Code	Superintendent	Telephone
Milburn (Johnston)	35I029	Joey McBride	580/443-5522
Milfay (Creek)	19C001	Paul D. Allee	918/968-2802
Mill Creek (Johnston)	35I002	Lorinda Chancellor	580/384-5514
Millwood (Oklahoma)	55I037	Cecilia Robinson	405/478-1336
Minco (Grady)	26I002	Kevin Sims	405/352-4867
Moffett (Sequoyah)	68C068	John D. Gordon	918/875-3668
Monroe (LeFlore)	40C011	Karen LaRosa	918/658-3516
Moore (Cleveland)	14I002	Robert Romines	405/735-4200
Mooreland (Woodward)	77I002	Terry Kellner	580/994-5388
Morris (Okmulgee)	56I003	James Lyons	918/733-9072
Morrison (Noble)	52I006	Jay Vernon	580/724-3341
Moseley (Delaware)	21C034	Charlene Carter	918/422-5927
Moss (Hughes)	32I001	Gil Turpin	405/379-2273
Mounds (Creek)	19I005	Alfred Gaches	918/827-6100
Moyers (Pushmataha)	64I022	Sam Belcher	580/298-5549
Mt. View-Gotebo (Kiowa)	38I003	Donna Dudley	580/347-2211
Muldrow (Sequoyah)	68I003	Ronal Flanagan	918/427-7406
Mulhall-Orlando (Logan)	42I003	Michael Parson	405/649-2000
Muskogee (Muskogee)	51I020	Mike Garde	918/684-3700
Mustang (Canadian)	09I069	Sean McDaniel	405/376-2461
Nashoba (Pushmataha)	64C015	Charles Caughern Jr.	918/755-4343
Navajo (Jackson)	33I001	Vicki Nance	580/482-7742
New Lima (Seminole)	67I006	Gil Turpin	405/257-5771
Newcastle (McClain)	47I001	Tony O'Brien	405/387-2890
Newkirk (Kay)	36I029	Steve Stanley	580/362-2388
Ninnekah (Grady)	26I051	Todd Bunch	405/224-4092
Noble (Cleveland)	14I040	Ronda Bass	405/872-3452
Norman (Cleveland)	14I029	Joseph Siano	405/364-1339
N. Rock Creek (Pottawatomie)	63C010	Blake Moody	405/275-3473
Norwood (Cherokee)	11C014	Diana Garnatz	918/478-3092
Nowata (Nowata)	53I040	Kathy Berry	918/273-3425
Oak Grove (Payne)	60C104	Krista Burden	918/352-2889
Oakdale (Oklahoma)	55C029	Kim Lanier	405/771-3373
Oaks-Mission (Delaware)	21I005	John Sheridan	918/868-2183
Oilton (Creek)	19I020	Matt Posey	918/862-3954
Okarche (Kingfisher)	37I105	Robert Friesen	405/263-7300
Okay (Wagoner)	73I001	Charles McMahan	918/682-2548
Okeene (Blaine)	06I009	Ron W. Pittman	580/822-3268

District (County)	Code	Superintendent	Telephone
Okemah (Okfuskee)	54I026	Tony Dean	918/623-1874
Okla. City (Oklahoma)	55I089	Robert Neu	405/587-0000
Okla. Union (Nowata)	53I003	Kevin Stacy	918/255-6550
Okmulgee (Okmulgee)	56I001	Tod Williams	918/758-2000
Oktaha (Muskogee)	51I008	Jerry Needham	918/687-7556
Olive (Creek)	19I017	Jimmy Reynolds	918/352-9567
Olustee (Jackson)	33I035	Gaylene Freeman	580/648-2243
Oologah-Talala (Rogers)	66I004	Max Tanner	918/443-6079
Optima (Texas)	70C009	Rex Hale	580/338-6712
Osage (Mayes)	46C043	Melinda Fink	918/825-2550
Osage Hills (Osage)	57C003	Jeannie O'Daniel	918/336-6804
Owasso (Tulsa)	72I011	Clark Ogilvie	918/272-5367
Paden (Okfuskee)	54I014	Lee Northcutt	405/932-5053
Panama (LeFlore)	40I020	Grant Ralls	918/963-2215
Panola (Latimer)	39I004	Brad Corcoran	918/465-3298
Paoli (Garvin)	25I005	Rick Worden	405/484-7336
Pauls Valley (Garvin)	25I018	Darsha Huckabaa	405/238-6453
Pawhuska (Osage)	57I002	Landon Berry	918/287-1265
Pawnee (Pawnee)	59I001	Ned Williams	918/762-3676
Peavine (Adair)	01C019	Jack Ritchie	918/696-7818
Peckham (Kay)	36C027	Gary Young	580/362-2633
Peggs (Cherokee)	11C031	John Cox	918/598-3412
Perkins-Tryon (Payne)	60I056	James Ramsey	405/547-5703
Perry (Noble)	52I001	Scott Chenoweth	580/336-4511
Pickett-Center (Pontotoc)	62C020	Daniel Pittman	580/332-7800
Piedmont (Canadian)	09I022	James White	405/373-2311
Pioneer (Grady)	26C131	Tyler Locke	405/224-2700
Pioneer/Pleasant Vale (Garfield)	24I056	Brent Koontz	580/758-3282
Pittsburg (Pittsburg)	61I063	Chad Graham	918/432-5062
Plainview (Carter)	10I027	Karl Stricker	580/223-6319
Pleasant Grove (Pottawatomie)	63C029	Alicia O'Donnell	405/275-6092
Pocola (LeFlore)	40I007	Monty Guthrie	918/436-2424
Ponca City (Kay)	36I071	David Pennington	580/767-8000
Pond Creek-Hunter (Grant)	27I090	Joel Quinn	580/532-4242
Porter Cons. (Wagoner)	73I365	Mark Fenton	918/483-2401
Porum (Muskogee)	51I088	Curtis Curry	918/484-5121
Poteau (LeFlore)	40I029	Don Sjoberg	918/647-7700
Prague (Lincoln)	41I103	Andy Evans	405/567-4455

District (County)	Code	Superintendent	Telephone
Preston (Okmulgee)	56I005	Mark Hudson	918/756-3388
Pretty Water (Creek)	19C034	Jeff Taylor	918/224-4952
Prue (Osage)	57I050	Tom Scully	918/242-3351
Pryor (Mayes)	46I001	Don Raleigh	918/825-1255
Purcell (McClain)	47I015	Kathy Adams	405/527-2146
Putnam City (Oklahoma)	55I001	Fred Rhodes	405/495-5200
Quapaw (Ottawa)	58I014	Bruce Chrz	918/674-2501
Quinton (Pittsburg)	61I017	Don Cox	918/469-3100
Rattan (Pushmataha)	64I001	Shari Pillow	580/587-2546
Ravia (Johnston)	35C010	David Duncan	580/371-9163
Red Oak (Latimer)	39I002	Bryan Deatherage	918/754-2426
Reydon (Roger Mills)	65I006	Phil Drouhard	580/655-4375
Ringling (Jefferson)	34I014	Rick Hatfield	580/662-2385
Ringwood (Major)	44I001	Wade Detrick	580/883-2202
Ripley (Payne)	60I003	Kenny R. Beams	918/372-4567
Riverside (Canadian)	09C029	Jeff Goure	405/262-2907
Robin Hill (Cleveland)	14C016	Brandon Voss	405/321-4186
Rock Creek (Bryan)	07I002	Preston Burns	580/295-3137
Rocky Mountain (Adair)	01C024	Margaret Carlile	918/696-7509
Roff (Pontotoc)	62I037	Scott Morgan	580/456-7663
Roland (Sequoyah)	68I005	Paul R. Wood	918/427-4601
Rush Springs (Grady)	26I068	Mike Zurline	580/476-3929
Ryal (McIntosh)	49C003	Lynn Maxwell	918/652-7461
Ryan (Jefferson)	34I001	Larry Ninman	580/757-2308
Salina (Mayes)	46I016	Tony Thomas	918/434-5091
Sallisaw (Sequoyah)	68I001	Scott Farmer	918/775-5544
Sand Springs (Tulsa)	72I002	Lloyd Snow	918/246-1400
Santa Fe S. ES Charter (Oklahoma)	55G001	Chris Brewster	405/631-6100
Sapulpa (Creek)	19I033	Kevin Burr	918/224-3400
Sasakwa (Seminole)	667I010	Kyle Wilson	405/941-3250
Savanna (Pittsburg)	61I030	Gary Reeder	918/548-3777
Sayre (Beckham)	05I031	Todd Winn	580/928-5531
Schulter (Okmulgee)	56I006	Allen Callahan	918/652-8219
Seiling (Dewey)	22I008	Randy Seifried	580/922-7383
Seminole (Seminole)	67I001	Jeff Pritchard	405/382-5085
Sentinel (Washita)	75I001	Jason Goostree	580/393-2101
Sequoyah (Rogers)	66I006	Terry Saul	918/341-5472
Shady Grove (Cherokee)	11C026	Emmett Thompson	918/772-2511

District (County)	Code	Superintendent	Telephone
Shady Point (LeFlore)	40C004	Bruce Gillham	918/963-2595
Sharon-Mutual (Woodward)	77I003	Jeff Thompson	580/989-3210
Shattuck (Ellis)	23I042	Randy Holley	580/938-2586
Shawnee (Pottawatomie)	63I093	Marc Moore	405/273-0653
Shidler (Osage)	57I011	John R. Herzig	918/793-2021
Silo (Bryan)	07I001	Bill Caruthers	580/924-7000
Skelly (Adair)	01C001	Emmett Thompson	918/723-5572
Skiatook (Tulsa)	72I007	Donna Anderson	918/396-5702
Smithville (McCurtain)	48I014	Rick Thomas	918/396-1792
Snyder (Kiowa)	38I004	Robert Trammell	580/569-2773
Soper (Choctaw)	12I004	Scott Van Worth	580/345-2757
S. Coffeyville (Nowata)	53I051	Clemo Haddox	918/255-6202
S. Rock Creek (Pottawatomie)	63C032	Michael Crawford	405/273-6072
Spavinaw (Mayes)	46C021	Christine Midgley	918/589-2228
Sperry (Tulsa)	72I008	Brian Beagles	918/288-6258
Spiro (LeFlore)	40I002	Don J. Atkinson	918/962-2463
Springer (Carter)	10I021	Cynthia Hunter	580/653-2656
Sterling (Comanche)	16I003	Julie Poteete	580/365-4307
Stidham (McIntosh)	49C016	Danny Williams	918/689-5241
Stigler (Haskell)	31I020	Clayton Edwards	918/967-2805
Stillwater (Payne)	60I016	Ann Caine	405/743-6300
Stilwell (Adair)	01I025	Geri Gilstrap	918/696-7001
Stonewall (Pontotoc)	62I030	Kevin Flowers	580/265-4241
Straight (Texas)	70C080	Steve Baird	580/652-2232
Stratford (Garvin)	25I002	Michael Blackburn	580/759-3615
Stringtown (Atoka)	03I007	Tony W. Potts	580/346-7423
Strother (Seminole)	67I014	Chad Broughton	405/382-4014
Stroud (Lincoln)	41I054	Joe van Tuyl	918/968-2541
Stuart (Hughes)	32I054	Bill San Millan	918/546-2476
Sulphur (Murray)	50I001	Gary Jones	580/622-2061
Sweetwater (Roger Mills)	65I015	Casey Reed	580/534-2272
Swink (Choctaw)	12C021	Mark Bush	580/873-2695
Tahlequah (Cherokee)	11I035	Lisa Presley	918/458-4100
Talihina (LeFlore)	40I052	Jason Lockhart	918/567-2259
Taloga (Dewey)	22I010	Darci Brown	580/328-5577
Tannehill (Pittsburg)	61C056	John Wilcox	918/423-6393
Tecumseh (Pottawatomie)	63I092	Tom Wilsie	405/598-3739
Temple (Cotton)	17I101	Kolby Johnson	580/342-6230

District (County)	Code	Superintendent	Telephone
Tenkiller (Cherokee)	11C066	Randy Roundtree	918/457-5996
Terral (Jefferson)	34C003	Greg Fouse	580/437-2244
Texhoma (Texas)	70I061	Tom Schroeder	580/423-7433
Thackerville (Love)	43I004	Greg Raper	580/276-2630
Thomas-Fay-Custer (Custer)	20I007	Rob Royalty	580/661-3527
Timberlake (Alfalfa)	02I093	Brent Rousey	580/852-3307
Tipton (Tillman)	71I008	Shane Boothe	580/667-5268
Tishomingo (Johnston)	35I020	Kevin Duncan	580/371-9190
Tonkawa (Kay)	36I087	Lori Simpson	580/628-3597
Tulsa (Tulsa)	72I001	Keith Ballard	918/746-6800
Tupelo (Coal)	15I002	Jerry Romines	580/845-2460
Turkey Ford (Ottawa)	58C010	Tamara D. Larson	918/786-4902
Turner (Love)	43I005	Jerry Garrett	580/276-1307
Turpin (Beaver)	04I128	Bret Rider	580/778-3333
Tushka (Atoka)	03I019	Billy Pingleton	580/889-7355
Tuskahoma (Pushmataha)	64C004	Barry R. Simpson	918/569-7737
Tuttle (Grady)	26I097	Bobby Waitman	405/381-2605
Twin Hills (Okmulgee)	56C011	Gary McElroy	918/733-2531
Tyrone (Texas)	70I053	Joshua E. Bell	580/854-6298
Union (Tulsa)	72I009	Kirtis Hartzler	918/357-4321
Union City (Canadian)	09I057	Todd Carel	405/483-3531
Valliant (McCurtain)	48I011	Craig Wall	580/933-7232
Vanoss (Pontotoc)	62I009	Marjana Tharp	580/759-2251
Varnum (Seminole)	67I007	David Brewer	405/382-1448
Velma-Alma (Stephens)	69I015	Raymond Rice	580/444-3355
Verden (Grady)	26I099	David Davidson	405/453-7247
Verdigris (Rogers)	66I008	Mike Payne	918/266-7227
Vian (Sequoyah)	68I002	Victor Salcedo	918/773-5798
Vici (Dewey)	22I005	Coby Nelson	580/995-4744
Vinita (Craig)	18I065	Kelly Grimmitt	918/256-6778
Wagoner (Wagoner)	73I019	Monte Thompson	918/485-4046
Wainwright (Muskogee)	51C009	Jim Ogden	918/474-3484
Walters (Cotton)	17I001	Jimmie Dedmon	580/875-2568
Wanette (Pottawatomie)	63I115	Crystal Shaw	405/383-2656
Wapanucka (Johnston)	35I037	Stanley Williams	580/937-4466
Warner (Muskogee)	51I074	Davis Vinson	918/463-5171
Washington (McClain)	47I005	A. J. Brewer	405/288-6190
Watonga (Blaine)	06I042	Bill Deitter	580/623-7364

District (County)	Code	Superintendent	Telephone
Watts (Adair)	01I004	Lisa Weaver	918/422-5311
Waukomis (Garfield)	24I001	Shawn Tennyson	580/758-3247
Waurika (Jefferson)	34I023	Roxie D. Terry	580/228-3373
Wayne (McClain)	47I010	David Powell	405/449-3646
Waynoka (Woods)	76I003	Loren Tackett	580/824-6561
Weatherford (Custer)	20I026	Matt Holder	580/772-3327
Webbers Falls (Muskogee)	51I006	Dixie Swearingen	918/464-2334
Welch (Craig)	18I017	R. Clark McKeon	918/788-3129
Weleetka (Okfuskee)	54I031	Chris Carter	405/786-2203
Wellston (Lincoln)	41I004	Dwayne Danker	405/356-2534
Western Heights (Okla.)	55I041	Joe Kitchens	405/350-3410
Westville (Adair)	01I011	Terry Heustis	918/723-3181
Wetumka (Hughes)	32I005	Donna McGee	405/452-5150
Wewoka (Seminole)	67I002	Sam McElvany	405/257-5475
White Oak (Craig)	18I001	David J. Money	918/256-4484
White Rock (Lincoln)	41C005	Travis Gates	405/964-3428
Whitebead (Garvin)	25C016	Mary E. Smith	405/238-3021
Whitefield (Haskell)	31C010	Scott Shepherd	918/967-8572
Whitesboro (LeFlore)	40I062	Katie Blagg	918/567-2556
Wickliffe (Mayes)	46C035	Teresia Knott	918/434-5558
Wilburton (Latimer)	39I001	Beatrice Butler	918/465-2100
Wilson (Carter)	10I043	Eric Smith	580/668-2306
Wilson (Okmulgee)	56I007	Andrea James	918/652-3374
Wister (LeFlore)	40I049	Jerry F. Carpenter	918/655-7381
Woodall (Cherokee)	11C021	Linda Clinkenbeard	918/458-5444
Woodland (Osage)	57I090	Todd Kimrey	918/642-3297
Woodward (Woodward)	77I001	Kyle Reynolds	580/256-6063
Wright City (McCurtain)	48I039	David Hawkins	580/981-2824
Wyandotte (Ottawa)	58I001	Troy Gray	918/678-2255
Wynnewood (Garvin)	25I038	Raymond Cole	405/665-2004
Wynona (Osage)	57I030	Dixie Hurd	918/846-2467
Yale (Payne)	60I103	Dale Bledsoe	918/387-2434
Yarbrough (Texas)	70I001	Jim Wiggin	580/545-3329
Yukon (Canadian)	09I027	W. Jason Simeroth	405/354-2587
Zaneis (Carter)	10C072	Ryan Cole	580/668-2955
Zion (Adair)	01C028	Charles Benham	918/696-7866

Oklahoma Public Education Statistics

Average Daily Attendance, (ADA), 2012–2013	630,766.00
Average Daily Membership, (ADM), 2012–2013	667,982,65
Weighted ADM, Used for 2012–2013 State Aid	1,072,547.19

School District Net Valuations
(as certified by the State Board of Equalization)

Valuation of Real Property	$19,697,353,037
Valuation of Personal Property	$5,946,307,955
Valuation of Public Services	$2,883,673,762
Total Net Valuation	$26,516,232,670
Per Capita Valuation basis ADA	$45,198

Number of School Districts Voting Millage

Levies: General Fund @ 35 Mills	517
Building Fund Mills @ 5 Mills	517
Sinking Fund Mills	393
General Fund Balance, as of June 30, 2013	$623,553,690

Total General Fund Revenue Received
By School Districts, 2012–2013

Local and County Revenue	$1,221,828,538
State Dedicated Revenue	$427,625,481
State Appropriated Revenue	$2,268,055,209
Federal Revenue	$508,059,275
Total Revenue Received	$4,425,568,503
Per Capita Revenue Basis Actual 2012–2013 Weighted ADM	$4,173
Per Capita Revenue Basis Weighted ADM, Used for 2012–2013 State Aid	$4,126

Total General Fund Expenditures
By Function

As Reported By School Districts, 2012–2013

Instructional Salaries	$1,915,415,001
Instructional Employee Benefits	$613,171,226
Instructional Purchased Services	$43,788,530
Instructional Tuition	$11,416,353
Instructional Supplies	$123,870,994
Instructional Property	$10,883,933
Instructional Other	$2,888,340
Guidance and Health	$286,309,312
Support Services Instructional Staff	$198,967,258
Support Services General Administration	$155,113,811
Support Services Operation & Maintenance	$434,781,213
Support Services Student Transportation	$183,413,394
Operation of Non-Instructional Services	$98,876,332
Facilities Acquisition and Construction	$13,595,216
Total General Fund Expenditures	**$4,612,524,731**
Per Capita Expenditure basis Weighted ADM	**$4,349**

State Department of Education—History of Comparative Data

Year	Dist. No.	No. of Teachers	Average Salary ($)	Local or County Revenue ($)		State Dedicated Revenue ($)		State Appropriated Revenue ($)		Federal Revenue ($)		Total ($)
1973	634	32,191	8,534	173,704,610	40%	62,822,909	14%	160,435,896	36%	45,052,128	10%	422,015,544
1974	628	32,861	9,322	187,061,554	38%	67,544,296	14%	188,747,537	38%	48,754,811	10%	492,108,200
1975	624	33,738	10,105	200,113,479	36%	70,343,511	13%	231,908,642	42%	50,817,883	9%	553,183,517
1976	623	34,577	10,963	215,275,228	34%	87,089,065	13%	279,398,348	44%	56,909,326	9%	638,671,967
1977	622	35,510	11,993	228,550,520	32%	95,994,728	13%	320,022,144	45%	68,680,708	10%	713,248,102
1978	620	36,551	12,746	249,639,348	32%	103,812,327	13%	362,814,336	46%	74,902,530	9%	791,168,543
1979	619	37,751	13,668	274,093,902	30%	121,229,330	13%	424,744,065	47%	86,610,715	10%	906,678,015
1980	618	38,464	15,170	310,296,818	29%	138,393,361	13%	510,318,203	49%	93,192,880	9%	1,052,201,263
1981	616	38,894	16,992	343,862,483	28%	177,411,415	14%	634,985,119	51%	86,486,907	7%	1,242,745,925
1982	616	39,901	19,163	383,813,883	27%	195,656,087	14%	736,821,427	52%	93,577,617	7%	1,409,869,016
1983	615	39,950	19,503	410,205,551	29%	207,169,948	15%	698,357,985	50%	90,048,175	6%	1,405,781,661
1984	615	39,903	19,974	450,847,993	31%	212,206,148	14%	703,121,908	48%	97,795,571	7%	1,463,971,621
1985	613	40,889	22,458	467,757,401	29%	214,749,343	13%	841,434,389	52%	98,093,045	6%	1,622,034,181
1986	613	39,653	22,563	485,846,910	32%	187,648,011	12%	760,464,577	50%	95,973,238	6%	1,529,932,736
1987	611	39,281	22,773	503,381,931	32%	194,883,148	12%	769,052,093	49%	104,479,690	7%	1,572,296,862
1988	609	40,052	23,521	509,304,315	31%	195,983,635	12%	838,017,039	50%	117,938,690	7%	1,661,743,679
1989	604	40,649	24,306	518,945,584	30%	205,209,653	12%	878,709,875	51%	123,156,389	7%	1,726,021,501
1990	578	42,034	25,580	516,219,483	27%	212,521,583	11%	1,069,733,53	56%	119,176,242	6%	1,917,650,841

Year	Dist. No.	No. of Teachers	Average Salary ($)	Local or County Revenue ($)		State Dedicated Revenue ($)		State Appropriated Revenue ($)		Federal Revenue ($)		Total ($)
1991	569	44,164	26,604	530,889,053	26%	225,794,957	11%	1,183,596,190	57%	117,059,757	6%	2,057,339,957
1992	554	45,123	27,726	504,450,974	23%	229,722,597	11%	1,263,197,753	59%	149,327,280	7%	2,146,698,604
1993	551	45,949	29,011	487,737,799	22%	240,473,964	11%	1,351,608,671	60%	166,274,335	7%	2,246,094,769
1994	550	46,630	30,246	510,503,458	22%	242,129,146	11%	1,394,524,110	60%	173,859,578	7%	2,321,016,292
1995	549	46,558	30,584	534,648,996	22%	251,180,232	11%	1,436,789,060	60%	176,669,418	7%	2,399,287,706
1996	549	46,882	30,217	571,251,265	23%	261,521,748	10%	1,500,153,663	60%	178,956,547	7%	2,511,883,223
1997	547	47,655	30,570	589,564,361	22%	268,884,609	10%	1,574,605,894	60%	198,100,211	8%	2,631,155,075
1998	547	48,659	31,105	635,222,233	23%	274,947,489	10%	1,688,884,818	60%	210,530,061	7%	2,809,584,601
1999	544	49,607	31,254	692,910,789	23%	301,334,889	11%	1,728,878,659	58%	252,205,081	8%	2,975,329,418
2000	544	49,920	34,381	702,148,649	22%	327,300,583	10%	1,919,440,079	59%	288,818,121	9%	3,237,707,432
2001	543	50,536	34,640	744,865,965	23%	309,094,758	9%	1,890,111,529	57%	362,303,789	11%	3,306,376,041
2002	541	49,346	34,807	765,279,135	23%	321,135,114	10%	1,814,164,728	55%	400,254,939	12%	3,300,833,916
2003	541	48,042	34,980	789,287,511	23%	331,591,482	10%	1,897,033,733	55%	405,342,810	12%	3,423,255,576
2004	540	56,536	35,148	833,686,766	23%	335,627,014	10%	1,968,531,914	54%	474,985,641	13%	3,612,831,345
2005	540	58,310	36,231	893,134,458	23%	365,867,442	10%	2,058,554,505	54%	490,872,098	13%	3,808,428,503
2006	540	59,592	39,300	957,526,284	23%	360,909,686	9%	2,262,968,539	56%	485,104,243	12%	4,066,508,752
2007	539	52,008	40,264	1,022,228,211	24%	386,264,039	9%	2,402,014,144	56%	470,717,215	11%	4,281,223,609
2008	533	52,167	40,535	1,034,442,306	23%	399,275,281	9%	2,446,462,840	55%	581,796,423	13%	4,461,976,850
2009	527	52,901	40,576	1,090,455,417	25%	391,287,866	9%	2,139,346,386	49%	776,987,924	17%	4,398,077,593
2010	524	51,388	40,370	1,129,890,923	25%	415,385,677	9%	2,144,838,504	49%	775,184,295	17%	4,465,299,399

Year	Dist. No.	No. of Teachers	Average Salary ($)	Local or County Revenue ($)		State Dedicated Revenue ($)		State Appropriated Revenue ($)		Federal Revenue ($)		Total ($)
2011	522	51,719	40,496	1,187,398,989	27%	438,091,210	10%	2,242,453,017	50%	573,894,692	13%	4,441,837,908
2012	520	52,380	40,681	1,221,828,538	28%	427,625,481	10%	2,268,055,209	51%	508,059,275	11%	4,425,568,503

Fort Sill, Indian Territory, December 1889, frcm the southeast

County-by-County Education
Revenue and Expenditures 2013–2014 Estimated

County	Total Net Valuation ($)	Per Capita Valuation ($)	County	Total Net Valuation ($)	Per Capita Valuation ($)
Adair	78,229,068	17,862	LeFlore	220,228,277	23,621
Alfalfa	92,731,773	128,780	Lincoln	228,939,299	42,451
Atoka	61,595,122	28,470	Logan	185,468,142	42,577
Beaver	121,420,487	117,030	Love	62,637,650	38,067
Beckham	237,094,903	62,759	Major	84,493,584	57,948
Blaine	128,681,940	71,763	Marshall	113,474,654	40,587
Bryan	280,973,674	39,982	Mayes	277,722,524	40,531
Caddo	199,031,491	35,552	McClain	224,133,091	32,234
Canadian	1,083,602,719	47,123	McCurtain	176,970,813	27,503
Carter	406,118,277	46,603	McIntosh	106,265,549	32,342
Cherokee	167,772,105	23,855	Murray	65,738,232	26,945
Choctaw	61,952,622	24,595	Muskogee	491,440,460	39,078
Cimarron	47,787,591	114,676	Noble	175,369,441	85,976
Cleveland	1,851,986,672	45,082	Nowata	51,936,908	29,274
Coal	81,512,536	71,806	Okfuskee	66,402,073	32,789
Comanche	694,296,,304	33,664	Oklahoma	6,000,393,305	54,019
Cotton	34,615,431	32,850	Okmulgee	150,475,471	23,148
Craig	123,765,524	45,597	Osage	162,119,902	44,983
Creek	411,049,384	33,569	Ottawa	150,662,661	26,295
Custer	240,392,623	48,519	Pawnee	70,911,599	28,651
Delaware	309,057,402	49,717	Payne	655,807,402	65,006
Dewey	110,679,583	137,699	Pittsburg	364,853,542	49,477
Ellis	104,033,298	124,728	Pontotoc	214,478,100	32,067
Garfield	475,314,494	47,378	Pottawatomie	325,841,997	26,484
Garvin	221,333,010	43,647	Pushmataha	44,223,010	20,430
Grady	345,370,457	39,368	Roger Mills	243,953,711	250,150
Grant	171,991,773	224,085	Rogers	654,594,917	49,075
Greer	25,790,862	28,931	Seminole	133,193,777	27,672
Harmon	18,705,924	36,017	Sequoyah	163,807,974	20,061
Harper	65,089,947	87,268	Stephens	338,303,201	43,814
Haskell	52,266,067	23,522	Texas	234,974,691	53,768
Hughes	121,122,943	53,505	Tillman	39,163,451	26,433
Jackson	133,832,029	27,694	Tulsa	5,616,542,303	52,436
Jefferson	34,773,846	31,831	Wagoner	179,499,190	28,466
Johnston	74,451,789	40,494	Washington	315,744,158	38,437
Kay	364,083,110	46,541	Washita	112,855,046	53,088
Kingfisher	197,576,610	59,990	Woods	162,705,801	131,837
Kiowa	85,761,477	54,713	Woodward	269,830,650	75,444
Latimer	57,333,331	39,202	Total	28,509,334,754	45,198

Oklahoma Public Schools, Attendance and Teacher Information, Since 1924

School Year	Total Average Daily Attendance	No. of Teachers	Annual Salary ($)	Per Capita Expenditure (ADA) ($)	State Total Net Valuation ($)*
1924	457,413	18,390	1,001	62.32	1,674,826,952
1925	444,905	18,393	1,032	62.68	1,697,364,213
1926	432,086	18,813	1,022	68.37	1,729,432,830
1927	457,983	19,130	991	68.26	1,791,424,587
1928	461,808	19,565	1,041	51.04	1,829,674,641
1929	470,090	20,146	1,096	68.06	1,851,602,103
1930	492,864	19,978	1,120	64.3	1,753,690,249
1931	493,244	19,842	1,071	57.32	1,409,663,561
1932	491,464	19,510	901	47.01	1,232,731,121
1933	492,022	19,300	784	42.84	1,258,686,473
1934	501,890	19,617	860	46.14	1,232,928,286
1935	497,974	19,858	982	56.38	1,221,659,918
1936	498,753	20,459	976	58.21	1,099,735,872
1937	492,907	20,874	1,061	65.76	1,103,189,782
1938	502,561	20,938	1,083	66.28	1,070,560,468
1939	484,290	20,980	1,040	64.93	1,054,067,835
1940	463,763	20,276	1,069	67.59	1,061,983,422
1941	439,238	19,391	1,140	72.89	1,092,050,565
1942	413,205	18,084	1,284	76.95	1,248,906,651
1943	368,061	17,272	1,418	89.84	1,302,573,500
1944	383,028	16,931	1,506	94.21	1,315,052,379
1945	391,337	17,863	1,815	113.06	1,391,238,021
1946	405,667	18,312	1,837	113.84	1,423,516,463
1947	399,966	18,097	2,209	143.43	1,554,090,583
1948	395,631	18,447	2,306	158.37	1,402,276,751
1949	401,931	18,885	2,776	186.04	1,485,096,011
1950	409,191	19,244	2,808	192.66	1,547,017,095
1951	404,767	19,477	3,113	215.99	1,647,726,019
1952	411,430	19,411	3,237	219.42	1,724,215,669
1953	425,425	19,695	3,502	228.99	1,806,078,557

*Does not include fringe benefits, includes real property, personal property and public services.

School Year	Total Average Daily Attendance	No. of Teachers	Annual Salary ($)	Per Capita Expenditure (ADA) ($)	State Total Net Valuation ($)*
1954	447,394	20,075	3,570	224.37	1,854,873,584
1955	453,173	20,512	3,768	239.73	1,930,985,725
1956	460,146	20,683	3,943	251.94	2,009,607,374
1957	460,385	20,698	4,272	270.09	2,082,262,809
1958	476,489	20,858	4,646	287.32	2,147,193,171
1959	485,559	21,530	4,792	298.31	2,234,900,180
1960	495,123	21,983	4,904	306	2,355,709,113
1961	503,671	22,466	5,069	315.56	2,497,133,560
1962	518,872	23,026	5,257	324.76	2,597,915,409
1963	532,781	23,687	5,302	331.66	2,681,355,608
1964	541,367	24,377	5,312	337.56	2,803,158,819
1965	545,611	25,380	5,894	422.16	3,053,210,944
1966	554,860	27,062	6,103	466.71	3,180,768,156
1967	559,350	27,979	6,258	483.11	3,293,792,497
1968	555,675	28,567	6,818	521.88	3,399,734,049
1969	560,993	29,355	7,257	566.71	3,524,525,761
1970	565,028	30,272	7,697	623.29	3,665,785,809
1971	566,857	31,231	7,905	677.94	3,923,053,356
1972	558,034	31,186	8,074	716.47	4,141,854,992
1973	549,561	32,191	8,534	794.6	4,411,743,890
1974	548,337	32,861	9,322	894.47	4,677,187,259
1975	548,538	33,738	10,105	996.52	4,962,487,286
1976	547,990	34,577	10,963	1,129.16	5,290,312,617
1977	544,539	35,510	11,993	1,284.18	5,689,221,932
1978	540,288	36,551	12,746	1,456.45	6,086,031,912
1979	538,454	37,751	13,668	1,654.27	6,729,290,252
1980	542,701	38,464	15,170	1,894.93	7,261,448,618
1981	547,385	38,894	16,992	2,177.02	8,132,632,233
1982	556,115	39,901	19,163	2,472.47	8,575,194,619
1983	553,237	39,950	19,503	2,513.83	9,286,241,257
1984	552,857	39,903	19,974	2,624.86	9,883,760,839
1985	553,365	40,889	22,458	2,948.65	10,239,980,098
1986	550,949	39,653	22,563	2,817.00	10,581,857,546
1987	547,149	39,281	22,773	2,883.00	10,531,835,114

*Does not include fringe benefits, includes real property, personal property and public services.

School Year	Total Average Daily Attendance	No. of Teachers	Annual Salary ($)	Per Capita Expenditure (ADA) ($)	State Total Net Valuation ($)*
1988	542,693	40,052	23,521	3,068.00	10,788,840,570
1989	543,170	40,659	24,306	3,199.00	10,689,818,434
1990	548,387	42,034	25,580	3,503.00	10,794,646,025
1991	556,609	44,164	26,604	3,659.00	10,747,271,580
1992	560,744	45,123	27,726	3,847.00	10,918,556,773
1993	565,489	45,949	29,011	3,964.00	11,260,140,502
1994	570,358	46,630	30,246	4,084.00	11,746,744,181
1995	574,440	46,558	30,584	4,103.00	12,171,204,097
1996	580,571	46,882	30,217	4,306.00	12,728,293,110
1997	582,459	47,655	30,570	4,459.00	13,256,227,025
1998	586,323	48,659	31,105	4,782.00	13,988,867,783
1999	586,266	49,607	31,254	4,992.00	14,821,788,968
2000	580,744	49,920	34,381	5,583.00	15,858,340,953
2001	580,795	50,536	34,807	5,780.00	16,714,244,199
2002	581,766	49,346	34,807	5,642.00	17,316,186,582
2003	583,932	48,042	34,980	5,706.75	18,370,844,741
2004	599,296	56,536	34,148	5,995.81	19,577,126,984
2005	591,486	58,310	36,231	6,440.61	20,749,243,920
2006	596,172	59,592	39,300	6,859.97	22,048,236,282
2007	596,450	52,008	40,264	7,130.97	23,385,539,557
2008	603,409	52,167	40,535	7,194.92	24,793,308,707
2009	616,018	52,901	40,576	6,683.06	25,562,147,421
2010	616,774	51,388	40,370	6,374.55	26,516,232,670
2011	624,409	51,719	40,496	7,158.62	27,411,093,738
2012	630,766	52,380	40,681	7,312.58	28,509,334,754

*Does not include fringe benefits, includes real property, personal property and public services.

Consolidations of School Districts by County, 1946 and 2013

County	Districts in 1946	Districts in 2013	County	Districts in 1946	Districts in 2013
Adair	39	11	LeFlore	86	17
Alfalfa	78	3	Lincoln	107	9
Atoka	60	6	Logan	74	4
Beaver	87	4	Love	22	4
Beckham	32	4	Major	88	4
Blaine	68	4	Marshall	34	2
Bryan	57	8	Mayes	64	8
Caddo	97	11	McClain	38	7
Canadian	81	10	McCurtain	68	13
Carter	34	9	McIntosh	47	6
Cherokee	74	11	Murray	22	2
Choctaw	51	6	Muskogee	69	10
Cimarron	28	3	Noble	73	4
Cleveland	58	6	Nowata	36	3
Coal	38	3	Okfuskee	47	6
Comanche	64	10	Oklahoma	51	15
Cotton	55	3	Okmulgee	39	9
Craig	72	5	Osage	63	12
Creek	56	15	Ottawa	43	7
Custer	64	4	Pawnee	55	3
Delaware	63	9	Payne	69	7
Dewey	64	3	Pittsburg	91	14
Ellis	69	4	Pontotoc	54	7
Garfield	108	8	Pottawatomie	91	14
Garvin	61	8	Pushmataha	57	7
Grady	73	12	Roger Mills	32	5
Grant	112	3	Rogers	41	9
Greer	19	2	Seminole	41	10
Harmon	10	1	Sequoyah	58	12
Harper	44	2	Stephens	59	8
Haskell	56	5	Texas	55	9
Hughes	45	6	Tillman	53	4
Jackson	19	6	Tulsa	25	14
Jefferson	29	4	Wagoner	61	4
Johnston	31	7	Washington	23	4
Kay	100	6	Washita	63	4
Kingfisher	77	6	Woods	105	3
Kiowa	56	4	Woodward	84	4
Latimer	33	4	State	4,450	520

Higher Education

According to the 2010 Census Current Population Reports, in 2010, 85.4 percent of Oklahomans over age twenty-five had a high school diploma or higher, slightly less than the national average of 85.2 percent. In 2000, Oklahomans over the age of twenty-five with a high school diploma or higher grew to 86.1, exceeding the national average of 84.1 percent. In 1990, 20.3 percent of Oklahomans had a bachelor's degree or higher; in 2000, that number had grown to 22.5 percent; and in 2010 it was 22.6 percent, but remained below the national average of 27.9 percent. According to the 2010 US Census, 22.6 percent of Oklahomans had a bachelor's degree or higher, or 81.1 percent of the national total of 27.9.

Percent of State Populations Older Than 25 Years Holding Bachelor's Degrees

2010, U.S. Bureau of the Census

State	Percentage of Adults With College Degree	Each State's Percentage of National Total
Colorado	35.90%	128.70%
Kansas	29.30%	105.10%
Nebraska	27.70%	99.30%
Texas	25.80%	92.50%
New Mexico	24.50%	91.40%
Missouri	25.00%	89.90%
Oklahoma	22.60%	81.70%
Alabama	21.70%	77.80%
Louisiana	20.90%	75.00%
Mississippi	19.50%	70.00%
Arkansas	19.10%	68.50%
U.S. Total	27.9%	100.0%

Enrollment

In the academic year 2011–2012, Oklahoma ranked twenty-seventh in the nation in the percentage of the state's population enrolled in public higher education. In 2001 Oklahoma ranked fourteenth.

During the 2011–2012 academic year at Oklahoma's public institutions, females outnumbered males by 56 percent to 44 percent. The white population comprised 60.4 percent of higher education enrollment, while minority enrollments made up 39.6 percent. The African American population had the highest minority enrollment with 9.6 percent, followed by 9.4 percent Native American enrollment, 5.1 percent Hispanic enrollment, and 2.3 percent Asian-American enrollment.

The median age of students was twenty-two for those enrolled at public institutions. Sixty-one percent of students were age twenty-four and under, and 23 percent were thirty years of age or older. Sixty-seven percent were twenty-four or younger at research universities, and 60 percent of students studying at regional universities were twenty-four or younger, while 24 percent were thirty or older.

Oklahoma (35,484), Tulsa (31,730), and Cleveland (11,910) counties were the top three counties of origin for students studying at public institutions in the 2011–2012 academic year. Texas, California, Kansas, Arkansas, and Missouri were the top five states of origin for out-of-state students at Oklahoma public institutions..

For the 2011–2012 academic year, institutions reported the most popular studies among students receiving bachelor's degrees were business and education. Health services, business, and liberal arts were the programs most frequently selected by the students earning associate degrees. Students earned master's degrees mostly in education and business. The most popular areas of study for professional degrees were medicine (M.D.) and law.

Retention rates for higher education students who enrolled at the same or another Oklahoma public college or university the following year have increased, with the exception of a decrease at regional universities. From 2002–2003 to 2011–2012, retention rates for new freshmen decreased slightly from 90.8 percent to 89.7 percent at research universities, decreased from 79.7 percent to 70.0 percent at regional universities, and decreased from 68.6 percent to 58.6 percent at community colleges.

From 2002–2003 to 2011–2012, six-year graduation rates (within the state) for new freshmen increased from 60.3 percent to 67.0 percent at research universities and deceased from 38.3 percent to 35.1 percent at the regional universities. At community colleges, three-year graduation rates (within the state) for new freshmen decreased from 19.9 percent to 13.6 percent.

During 2011–2012, public institutions granted 32,935 degrees. Of those, 9,872 were associate degrees; 15,807 were bachelor's degrees; and master's and doctoral degrees totaled 5,398.

2011–2012
Annual Student Enrollments by Field of Study

Oklahoma State Regents of Higher Education *Annual Report*

Field of Study	Students Enrolled
Health Professions	34,629
Business Management	33,426
Education	22,889
Engineering Tech	10,195
Engineering	9,743
Biological Sciences	8,826
Social Sciences	8,341
Psychology	7,777
Fine and Applied Arts	6,609
Protective Services	6,420
Communication and Journalism	5,964
Physical Sciences	5,891
Computer Science	5,667
Family and Consumer/Human Science	5,049
Multi/Interdisciplinary Studies	4,301
Parks/Recreation/Leisure/Fitness	3,873
Agriculture	3,290
Public Administration/Social Services	2,544
Letters	2,004
History	1,709
Mathematics	1,276
Foreign Languages/Literature	1,240
Mechanic/Repair Tech	1,195
Legal Professions	989
Transportation/Materials Moving	715
Architecture	610
Natural Resources/Conservation	521
Personal/Culinary Services	473
Library Science	321
Philosophy/Religious Studies	297

Fiscal Year 2015 Operating Budget

The Fiscal Year 15 Education and General Budget (E&G) Part I, (the primary budget) consisting of public funding sources such as appropriations and student fees, shows an increase of $85.9 million (3.9 percent), and is comprised of 37.8 percent in state support and 62.2 percent in self-generated revolving funds, primarily from tuition and fee revenue. Student tuition and fees increased $54.8 million or 5.4 percent.

The Educational and General Budget (E&G) Part II (the sponsored budget) is funded from external sources including federal awards, grants, and training contracts; private contracts; and contracts from other state agencies. The E&G Part II for FY 15 is $528.4 million, an increase of $5.2 million (1.0 percent) over the $511 million in FY14.

Federal funds continue to be the largest source of revenue for the FY15 sponsored budget at $268.5 million or 50.8 percent of the total, down slightly from 53.1 percent in FY14. The State of Oklahoma provides 17.5 percent of the sponsored revenue. Uses of sponsored revenue funds are substantial for research and public service, 46.6 percent, and 22.7 percent of the total sponsored budget respectfully.

Since FY 96, sponsored research in Oklahoma's higher education institutions has shown an increase of 188.8 percent. Research has become a target area for improvement with investments in the Oklahoma EPSCoR program, incentive programs, and in large research investments with multiple funding sources. Sponsored research was $239.1 million in FY14, compared to $246.5 million in FY 15, and increase of $7.4 million or 3.1 percent.

It is noteworthy that, in general, at the research universities, the sponsored budget for research is considerably larger than the Primary (E&G Part I) budget for research, totaling $246.5 million or 46.6 percent, compared to $110.1 million or 4.8 percent.

State System of Higher Education

Comprehensive and Regional Universities

Cameron University

University of Central Oklahoma

East Central University

Langston University

Northeastern State University

Northwestern Oklahoma State University

University of Oklahoma
  (including School of Dentistry,
  Geological Survey, Health Sciences
  Center, Law Center, Oklahoma City;
  College of Medicine, Tulsa)*

OU/OSU Graduate Education Center,
  Tulsa

Oklahoma Panhandle State University

Oklahoma State University
  (including Agricultural Experiment
  Station, Agricultural Extension
  Division, College of Osteopathic
  Medicine, College of Veterinary
  Medicine, Veterinary Medicine
  Teaching Hospital and Technical
  Branches in Okmulgee and
  Oklahoma City)*

Rogers State University

University of Science and Arts of
  Oklahoma

Southeastern Oklahoma State University

Southwestern Oklahoma State University

Two-Year Colleges

Carl Albert State College

Connors State College

Eastern Oklahoma State College

Murray State College

Northeastern Oklahoma A&M College

Northern Oklahoma College

Oklahoma City Community College

Redlands Community College

Rose State College

Seminole State College

Tulsa Community College

Western Oklahoma State College

State Higher Education Centers

University Center of Southern
  Oklahoma

---

*Constituent entities of the System cited by
statute (see 70:3103, 3201.1, 3308, 3312, 3423).

Oklahoma State Regents/Trustees for Higher Education

(Constitution, Article 13 § A:2; 70 § 3202)

655 Research Parkway, Suite 200, Oklahoma City 73104-6266
PO Box 108850, Oklahoma City 73101-8850
405/225-9100, FAX 405/225-9230
Student Information Hotline 800/858-1840

Administration: Glen D. Johnson, Chancellor

Six chancellors have headed The Oklahoma State System of Higher Education over the 65-year history of the Oklahoma State Regents for Higher Education. Chancellor Mel Nash served from 1943-61, Chancellor E.T. Dunlap served from 1961-81, Chancellor Joe Leone served from 1982-87, Interim Chancellor Dan S. Hobbs served in 1987, and Chancellor Hans Brisch served from 1987 to 2003. Paul Risser served from 2003 to 2006. Phil Moss became Interim Chancellor in 2006. Chancellor Glen D. Johnson began serving in January 2007.

Carl Albert State College, Board of Regents (70 § 4423[C])

1507 South McKenna, Poteau 74953-5208 • 918/647-1200, FAX 918/647-1216

Eastern Oklahoma State College, Board of Regents (70 § 3512)

1301 West Main, Wilburton 74578-4999 • 918/465-1767

Murray State College, Board of Regents (70 § 3407.2)*

One Murray Campus Road, Tishomingo 73460-3130 • 580/387-7000

Northern Oklahoma College, Board of Regents (70 § 3702)

1220 East Grand, Tonkawa 74653-0310 • 580/628-6200

Oklahoma Agricultural and Mechanical Colleges, Board of Regents

(Constitution, Article 7 § 31a; 70 § 3409)

2800 N Lincoln Boulevard, Oklahoma City 73105-4224 • 580/521-2411

Oklahoma City Community College, Board of Regents [70 § 4423(C)]

7777 South May Avenue, Oklahoma City 73159-4444 • 405/682-1611

Redlands Community College, Board of Regents (70 § 4423[C])

1300 S Country Club Road, El Reno 73036-5304 • 405/262-2552

Rose State College, Board of Regents (70 § 4423[C])

6420 Southeast 15 Street, Midwest City 73110-2799 • 405/733-7673

---

*70 § 3407.2 identifies this board as the Board of Regents of Murray State College of Technology. However, pursuant to 70 § 3407, the name is Murray State College.

Seminole State College, Board of Regents (70 § 4423[C])

2701 Boren Boulevard, Seminole 74868–0361 • 405/382–9950

Tulsa Community College, Board of Regents (70 § 4413[b])

6111 East Skelly Drive, Suite 200, Tulsa 74135–6198 • 918/595–7000

University Center of Southern Oklahoma, Board of Trustees (70 § 3213[B])

611 Veterans Boulevard, Ardmore 73401–1443 • 405/223–1441

University of Oklahoma, Board of Regents (Constitution, Article 8 § 8; 70 § 3302)

660 Parrington Oval, Room 119, Norman 73019–0390 • 405/321–0311

University of Science and Arts of Oklahoma, Board of Regents (70 § 3602)*

1727 W. Alabama Avenue, Chickasha 73018 • 405/224–3140

Western Oklahoma State College, Board of Regents (70 § 4418)

2801 North Main Street, Altus 73521–1397 • 580/477–2000

---

*70 § 3602 identifies this board as the Board of Regents of the Oklahoma College of Liberal Arts. However, pursuant to 70 § 3601.1, the school's name was changed in 1974 to the University of Science and Arts of Oklahoma.

Apache at Fort Sill.

Institutions of Higher Education

Comprehensive and Regional Universities

Cameron University [70 § 3404; 3404.1]—2800 Gore Boulevard, Lawton 73505-6377, 580/581-2200. John McArthur, President. Governing board: Board of Regents of the University of Oklahoma (Former Governing board: Board of Regents for the University of Oklahoma). Formerly: Cameron State Agricultural College

University of Central Oklahoma [70 § 3501, 3501.1, 3518]—100 North University Drive, Edmond 73034-0170, 405/974-2000. Dr. Don Betz, President. Governing board: Board of Regents of Oklahoma Colleges. Formerly: Central State College, Central State University.

East Central University [70 § 3502, 3515]—1100 East 14 Street, Ada 74820-6899, 580/332-8000. Dr. John R. Hargrave, President. Governing board: Board of Regents of Oklahoma Colleges. Formerly: East Central State College, East Central Oklahoma State University.

Langston University [70 § 3403]—701 Sammy Davis Jr. Drive, Langston 73050, 405/466-2231. Dr. Kent J. Smith Jr., President. Governing board: Board of Regents for Okla. Agricultural & Mechanical Colleges.

Northeastern State University [70 § 3513]—600 N Grand Ave. Tahlequah 74464-7099, 918/456-5511. Campuses also in Broken Arrow and Muskogee. Dr. Steve Turner, President. Governing board: Board of Regents of Oklahoma Colleges. Formerly: Northeastern State College, Northeastern Oklahoma State University.

Northwestern Oklahoma State University [70 § 3517]—709 Oklahoma Boulevard, Alva 73717-2799, 580/327-1700. Campuses also in Enid and Woodward. Dr. Janet Cunningham, President. Governing board: Board of Regents of Oklahoma Colleges. Formerly: Northwestern State College.

University of Oklahoma [70 § 3301]—660 Parrington Oval, Norman 73019-0390, 405/325-0311. David L. Boren, J.D., President. Governing board: Board of Regents of the University of Oklahoma.

> **University of Oklahoma School of Dentistry** [70 § 3308]—1201 N Stonewall, Oklahoma City 73117, 405/271-6326. Stephen Young, D.D.S., Dean, College of Dentistry.

> **Oklahoma Geological Survey** [70 § 3103]—Sarkeys Energy Center, 100 E Boyd, Room N-131, Norman 73019-0628, 405/325-3031, FAX 405/325-7069. Richard D. Andrews, Interim Director.

> **Health Sciences Center (University of Oklahoma Medical Center)** [70 § 3103, 3301, 3307]—1100 N Lindsay, Oklahoma City 73104, 405/271-4000. M. Dewayne Andrews, M.D., Senior V.P/Provost.

> **University of Oklahoma College of Community Medicine—Tulsa** [70 § 3312]—4502 E 41 Street, Tulsa 74135-2512, 918/660-3000. Ondria C. Gleason, M.D., Interim Dean.

> **Law Center** [70 § 3103]—300 W Timberdell Road, Norman 73019, 405/325-4699. Joseph Harroz Jr., J.D., Dean of the Law School.

Oklahoma State University [70 § 3401]—107 Whitehurst Hall, Stillwater 74078-0999, 405/744-5000. Dr. Burns Hargis, President. Governing board: Board of Regents for the Oklahoma Agricultural and Mechanical Colleges. Formerly: Oklahoma Agricultural and Mechanical College.

> **Agricultural Experiment Station** [70 § 3103]—139 Agricultural Hall, Oklahoma State University, Stillwater 74078, 405/744-5000. Dr. Thomas Coon, DASNR, Dean and Director; Keith Woods, Interim Director, Agricultural Experiment Station.

> **Agricultural Cooperative Extension Division** (70 § 3103, 3418[4])—139 Agricultural Hall, Oklahoma State University, Stillwater 74078, 405/744-5398. Dr. Thomas Coon,

DASNR, Dean and Director of the Agricultural Cooperative Extension Service.

Oklahoma State University College of Osteopathic Medicine [70 § 3423]—1111 West 17 Street, Tulsa 74107-1898, 918/582-1972. Kayse M. Shrum, D.O., President and Dean.

Oklahoma State University—Tulsa [70 § 4673]—700 North Greenwood Ave. Tulsa, OK 74106-0700, 918/594-8000. Howard Barnett JD, President. Formerly: University Center at Tulsa.

Oklahoma State University—Oklahoma City [70 § 3103]—900 North Portland, Oklahoma City 73107-6187, 405/947-4421, FAX 405/945-3325. Natalie Shirley, President.

Oklahoma State University—Okmulgee [70 § 3103]—1801 East 4 Street, Okmulgee 74447, 800/722-4471. Dr. Bill Path, President/Provost.

College of Veterinary Medicine [70 § 3103]—Oklahoma State University, 205 McElroy Hall, Stillwater 74078, 405/744-6651. Jean Sander, DVM, Dean

Oklahoma State Veterinary Medicine Teaching Hospital [70 § 3201.1]—Boren Veterinary Medical Teaching Hospital, 2113 W Farm Road, Stillwater 74078, 405/744-7000. T. Mark Neer, Director.

Oklahoma Panhandle State University [70 § 3402]—323 Eagle Boulevard, Goodwell 73939, 580/349-2611. Dr. David Bryant, President. Governing board: Board of Regents for the University of Oklahoma. Formerly: Panhandle State College of Agriculture and Applied Science, Panhandle A&M College, Panhandle State College.

Rogers State University (70 § 3802, O.S.L. 1996, Ch. 276:11)—1701 West Will Rogers Boulevard, Claremore, OK 74017-3252, 918/343-7777. Campus also in Bartlesville. Dr. Larry Rice, President. Governing board: Board of Regents of Oklahoma Colleges. Formerly: Rogers State College.

University of Science and Arts of Oklahoma [70 § 3601.1]—1727 W Alabama, Chickasha 73018, 405/224-3140. Dr. John Feaver, President. Governing board: Board of Regents of the University of Science and Arts of Oklahoma. Formerly: Oklahoma College for Women, Oklahoma College of Liberal Arts.

Southeastern Oklahoma State University [70 § 3514]—1405 N 4 Street, Durant 74701, 580/745-2000. Dr. Larry Minks, President. Governing board: Board of Regents of Oklahoma Colleges.

Southwestern Oklahoma State University [70 § 3516]—100 Campus Drive, Weatherford 73096-3098, 580/774-3063. Dr. Randy Beutler, President. Governing board: Board of Regents of Oklahoma Colleges. Branch Campus in Sayre. Formerly: Southwestern State College.

Two-Year Colleges

Carl Albert State College [70 § 4423]—1507 South McKenna, Poteau 74953-5208, 918/647-1200. Garry M. Ivey, President. Governing board: Board of Regents of Carl Albert State College. Branch Campus in Sallisaw.

Connors State College [70 § 3405]—700 College Road, Warner 74469, 918/463-2931. Dr. Tim Faltyn, President. Governing board: Board of Regents for the Oklahoma Agricultural and Mechanical Colleges. Branch Campus in Muskogee. Formerly: Connors State Agriculture College.

Eastern Oklahoma State College [70 § 3511]—1301 West Main, Wilburton 74578-4999, 918/465-2361. Dr. Steven Smith, President. Governing board: Board of Regents of Eastern Oklahoma State College. Branch Campus in McAlester.

Murray State College [70 § 3407]—1 Murray Campus Road,, Tishomingo 73460-3130, 580/371-2371. Joy McDaniel, President. Governing board: Board of Regents of Murray State College of Technology.

Northeastern Oklahoma Agricultural and Mechanical College [70 § 3408]—200 "I" Street, NE, Miami 74354-6497, 918/542-8441. Dr. Jeff Hale President. Governing board: Board of Regents for the Oklahoma Agricultural and Mechanical Colleges.

Northern Oklahoma College [70 § 3701]—1220 East Grand, Post Office Box 310, Tonkawa 74653-0310, 580/628-6200. Dr. Cheryl Evans, President. Governing board: Board of Regents of Northern Oklahoma College.

Oklahoma City Community College [70 § 4423]—7777 South May Avenue, Oklahoma City 73159-4444, 405/682-1611. Dr. Paul W. Sechrist, President. Governing board: Board of Regents of Oklahoma City Community College.

Redlands Community College [70 § 4423]—1300 S Country Club Dr., El Reno 73036-5304, 405/262-2552. Jack Bryant, President. Governing board: Board of Regents of Redlands Community College.

Rose State College [70 § 4423]—6420 Southeast 15 Street, Midwest City 73110-2799, 405/733-7673. Dr. Jeanie Webb, President. Governing board: Board of Regents of Rose State College.

Seminole State College [70 § 4423]—2701 Boren Boulevard, Seminole 74868-0361, 405/382-9950. Dr. James Utterback, President. Governing board: Board of Regents of Seminole State College.

Tulsa Community College [70 § 4413]—6111 East Skelly Drive, #200, Tulsa 74135-6198, 918/595-7000. Dr. Leigh B. Goodson, President. Governing board: Board of Regents of Tulsa Community College.

Western Oklahoma State College [70 § 4417]—2801 North Main Street, Altus 73521-1397, 580/477-2000. Dr. Phil Birdine, President. Governing board: Board of Regents of Western Oklahoma State College.

State Higher Education Centers/Programs

University Center of Southern Oklahoma [70:3213]—611 Veterans Boulevard, Ardmore 73401-1443, 580/223-1441, Oklahoma City 405/521-6139. Dr. Steven C. Mills, Director and CEO. Governing board: Board of Trustees for the Ardmore Higher Education Program.

Oklahoma Department of Career and Technology Education

Autry Technology Center—1201 W Willow, Enid 73703-2506, Telephone 580/242-2750. Dr. Jim Strate, Superintendent.

Caddo-Kiowa Technology Center—Post Office Box 190, Fort Cobb 73038-0190, Telephone 405/643-5511. Dennis Ruttman, Superintendent.

Canadian Valley Technology Center—6505 East Highway 66, El Reno 73036-9117, Telephone 405/262-2629. Greg Winters, Superintendent.

> **Grady County** 1401 Michigan Ave., Chickasha 73018-2136, Telephone 405/224-7220. George Tiner, Asst. Supt.

> **Cowan Campus**—1701 S Czech Hall Road, Yukon 73099, Telephone 405/354-3333. Greg Taylor, Director.

Central Technology Center ("Central Tech")—3 CT Circle, Drumright 74030-9613, Telephone 918/352-2551. Phil Waul, Superintendent.

> **Sapulpa Campus**—1720 S Main, Sapulpa 74066-6453, Telephone 918/224-9300. Dr. Kim Howard, Director.

Chisholm Trail Technology Center—Rural Route 1, Box 60, Omega 73764-9720, Telephone 405/729-8324. Max Thomas, Superintendent.

Eastern Oklahoma County Technology Center—4601 North Choctaw Road, Choctaw 73020-9017, Telephone 405/390-9591. Dr. Terry Underwood, Superintendent.

Francis Tuttle Technology Center—12777 North Rockwell, Oklahoma City 73142-2789, Telephone 405/717-7799. Tom Friedmann, Superintendent

> **Portland Campus**—3500 Northwest 150 Street. Mailing Address: 12777 North Rockwell, Oklahoma City 73142-2789, Telephone 405/717-7799. Malcom Fowler, Asst. Supt.

> **Reno Campus**—7301 W Reno. Mailing Address: 12777 North Rockwell, Oklahoma City 73142-2789, Telephone 405/717-7799. Marie Howard, Director.

Gordon Cooper Technology Center—One John C. Bruton Blvd., Shawnee 74804, Telephone 405/273-7493. Marty Lewis, Superintendent.

Great Plains Technology Center—4500 Southwest Lee Boulevard, Lawton 73505-8399, Telephone 580/355-6371. Clarence Fortney, Deputy Superintendent.

> **Tillman County**—2001 E Gladstone, Frederick 73542-4600, Telephone 580/335-5525. Gary Tyler, Assistant Superintendent.

Green Country Technology Center—PO Box 1217, Okmulgee 74447-1217, Telephone 918/758-0840. Brady McCullough, Superintendent.

High Plains Technology Center—3921 34 Street, Woodward 73801-7000, Telephone 580/256-6618. Dwight Hughes, Superintendent.

Indian Capital Technology Center—2403 North 41 Street East, Muskogee 74403-1799, Telephone 918/686-7565. Tom Stiles, Superintendent.

> **Adair County**—Route 6, Box 3320, Stilwell 74960-0192, Telephone 918/696-3111. Dan Collins, Director.

> **Cherokee County**—240 VoTech Road, Tahlequah 74464, Telephone 918/456-2594. Robin Roberts, Director.

> **Muskogee County)** 2403 North 41 Street East, Muskogee 74403-1799, Telephone 918/687-6383. Randy Craven, Director.

Sequoyah County—HC 61 Box 12, Sallisaw 74955-9401, Telephone 918/775-9119. Curtis Shumaker, Director.

Kiamichi Technology Center, Post Office Box 548, Wilburton 74578-0548, Telephone 918/465-2323. Eddie Coleman, Superintendent.

Atoka County—Post Office Box 240, Atoka 74525-0240, Telephone 580/889-7321. Elaine Gee, Director.

Bryan County—810 Waldron, Durant, 74701-1904, Telephone 580/924-7081. Michael Goodwin, Director.

Choctaw County—Post Office Box 699, Hugo 74743-0699, Telephone 580/326-6491. Debbie Golden, Director.

Haskell County—1410Kiamichi Technology Center, Old Military Road, Stigler 74462, Telephone 918/967-2801. Joe Carrick, Director.

Latimer County—RR 2, Box 1800, Talihina 74571-9518, Telephone 918/567-2264. Larry Brooks, Director.

LeFlore County—Post Office Box 825, Poteau 74953-0825, Telephone 918/647-4525. Doug Hall, Director.

LeFlore County—610 SW Third, Spiro 74959-2502, Telephone 918/962-3722. Doug Hall, Director.

McCurtain County—R.R. 3, Box 177, Idabel 74745-9534, Telephone 580/286-7555. Johnnie Meredith, Director.

Pittsburg County—301 Kiamichi Drive, McAlester 74501, Telephone 918/426-0940. April Murray, Director.

Meridian Technology Center—1312 South Sangre Road, Stillwater 74074-1899, Telephone 405/377-3333. Dr. Doug Major, Superintendent.

Metro Technology Centers ("Metro Tech")—1900 Springlake Drive, Oklahoma City 73111-5238, Telephone 405/424-8324. Elaine Stith, Superintendent.

Springlake Campus—1900 Springlake Drive, Oklahoma City 73111-5238, Telephone 405/424-8324. Danene Vincent, Asst. Superintendent.

Aviation Career Center—5600 S MacArthur, Oklahoma City 73179-8205, Telephone 405/595-5501. Peter Lee, Director.

South Bryant Campus—4901 S Bryant, Oklahoma City 73129-8801, Telephone 405/424-8324. Ed Mellott, Director.

Mid-America Technology Center—Post Office Box H, Wayne 73095-0210, Telephone 405/449-3391. Dusty Ricks, Superintendent.

Mid-Del Technology Center—1621 Maple Drive, Midwest City 73110-4825, Telephone 405/739-1707. Seve Allen, Assistant Superintendent.

Mid-Del Tinker Careertech Training Center—Building 1 D Avenue, Tinker Air Force Base 73145, Telephone 405/734-7266. Jefferson Tarver, Director.

Moore Norman Technology Center—4701 12 Avenue NW, Norman 73069-8399, Telephone 405/364-5763. Jane Bowen, Superintendent.

Northeast Technology Centers—Post Office Box 487, Pryor 74362-0487, Telephone 918/825-5555. Fred Probis, Superintendent.

Northeast-East Campus—Post Office Box 30, Kansas (OK) 74347, Telephone 918/868-3535. Greg Mitchell, Asst. Supt.

Northeast-North Campus—Post Office Box 219, Afton 74331-0219, Telephone 918/257-8324. Patty Tipton, Asst. Supt.

Northeast-South Campus—Post Office Box 825, Pryor 74362-0825, Telephone 918/825-5555. Debbie Peaster, Asst. Supt.

Northwest Technology Center—1801 South 11 Street, Alva 73717-9600, Telephone 580/327-0344. Dr. Gerald Harris, Superintendent.

Northwest, Major County—801 VoTech Drive, Fairview 73737, Telephone 580/227-3708. Colt Shaw, Asst. Supt.

Pioneer Technology Center—2101 North Ash, Ponca City 74601-1110, Telephone 580/762-8336. Dr. Steve Tiger, Superintendent.

Pontotoc Technology Center—601 West 33 Street, Ada 74820-9791, Telephone 580/310-2200. David Lassiter, Superintendent.

Red River Technology Center—Post Office Box 1807, Duncan 73534-1807, Telephone 580/255-2903. Ken Layn, Superintendent.

Southern Oklahoma Technology Center—2610 Sam Noble Parkway, Ardmore 73401-2100, Telephone 580/223-2070. David Powell, Superintendent.

Southwest Technology Center—711 W Tamarack Rd., Altus 73521-1527, Telephone 580/477-2250. Dale Latham, Superintendent.

Tri-County Technology Center—6101 Southeast Nowata Road, Bartlesville 74006-6029, Telephone 918/333-2422. Anita Risner, Superintendent.

Tulsa Technology Center—Post Office Box 477200, Tulsa 74147-7200, Telephone 918/828-5000. Dr. Steve Tiger, Superintendent.

Broken Arrow Campus—4600 South Olive, Broken Arrow 74011-1740, Telephone 918/828-3000. Brad Wayman, Director.

Lemley Campus—3420 South Memorial, Tulsa 74145-1390, Telephone 918/828-1000. Randy Dean, Director.

Peoria Campus—3850 North Peoria, Tulsa 74106-1600, Telephone 918/828-2000. John Robinson, Director.

Riverside Campus—801 East 91 Street, Tulsa 74132-4008, Telephone 918/828-4000. Brad Hanselman, Director.

Wes Watkins Technology Center—7892 Highway 9, Wetumka 74883-6155, Telephone 405/452-5500. Wade Walling, Superintendent.

Western Technology Center—Post Office Box 1469, Burns Flat 73624-1469, Telephone 580/562-3181. Gene Orsack, Superintendent.

Western, Beckham County—RR 4, Box 132, Sayre 73662-9301, Telephone 580/928-2097. Andy Humble, Director.

OKLAHOMA

HISTORY

The following information was excerpted from the work of Arrell Morgan Gibson, specifically, *The Oklahoma Story*, (University of Oklahoma Press 1978), and *Oklahoma: A History of Five Centuries* (University of Oklahoma Press 1989). *Oklahoma: A History of the Sooner State* (University of Oklahoma Press 1964) by Edwin C. McReynolds was also used, along with Muriel Wright's *A Guide to the Indian Tribes of Oklahoma* (University of Oklahoma Press 1951), and Don G. Wyckoff's *Oklahoma Archeology: A 1981 Perspective* (University of Oklahoma, Archeological Survey 1981). • Additional information was provided by Jenk Jones Jr., Tulsa • David Hampton, Tulsa • Office of Archives and Records, Oklahoma Department of Libraries • Oklahoma Historical Society. *Guide to Oklahoma Museums* by David C. Hunt (University of Oklahoma Press, 1981) was used as a reference.

A Brief History of Oklahoma

The Prehistoric Age

Substantial evidence exists to demonstrate the first people were in Oklahoma approximately 11,000 years ago and more than 550 generations of Native Americans have lived here. More than 10,000 prehistoric sites are recorded for the state, and they are estimated to represent about 10 percent of the actual number, according to archaeologist Don G. Wyckoff. Some of these sites pertain to the lives of Oklahoma's original settlers—the Wichita and Caddo, and perhaps such relative latecomers as the Kiowa Apache, Osage, Kiowa, and Comanche. All of these sites comprise an invaluable resource for learning about Oklahoma's remarkable and diverse Native American heritage.

> The Clovis people lived in Oklahoma at the end of the last Ice Age, some 11,500 years ago.

Given the distribution and ages of studies sites, Oklahoma was widely inhabited during prehistory. Among the earliest people were those who came and resided here at the end of the last Ice Age, some 11,500 years ago. These earliest cultures are: Clovis, 11,500 to 10,900 years ago; Folsom, 10,600 to 10,200 years ago; and Plainview, 10,000 to 9,500 years ago. Named after the Southern Plains locations where their distinctive artifacts were first discovered, these cultures are the material goods of Native American bands that occupied adjacent parts of Oklahoma, Texas, and New Mexico in different ways. All are so far back in prehistory that they cannot be linked directly to any historically known tribes. Oklahoma archaeologists have discovered good examples of places once occupied by these earliest people. At the Domebo Site in Caddo County, three Clovis-type spear points were found among the ribs and vertebrae of a Colombian mammoth. In Harper County, a major Folsom-age bison kill recently was uncovered near Fort Supply. Called the Cooper site, this location resulted from Folsom hunters trapping and spearing bison herds in a deep gully on three separate occasions. Perhaps a thousand years later, Native American hunters using the Plainview-style spear point killed a small herd at what is now called the Parry Ranch site in Jackson County.

Approximately 8,000 years ago, Oklahoma was undergoing drastic environmental changes, and warm, dry weather was becoming prevalent. Bison herds became fewer, and people increasingly turned to hunting smaller game and gathering plants. Band territories became smaller as groups developed seasonal hunting-gathering patterns in favored localities. Among Oklahoma's notable sites that bear witness to this lifeway are the 5,500–year-old Gore Pit site in Comanche County, the equally old Scott site in LeFlore County, and the 4,500–year-old Lawrence site in Nowata County. These sites have yielded a diverse array of chipped or ground stone tools along with remains of roasting ovens made from stones. Currently, professional and avocational archaeologists are documenting a previously unknown hunting-gathering people who lived here 5,000 years ago. Called the Calf Creek culture, these people left important camps in Murray, Garvin, Caddo, Kay, Tulsa, Muskogee, and Haskell counties.

About 2,500 years ago, Oklahoma's climate began to become more like that of today. As plant and animal communities like those in the 1800s emerged, Oklahoma's Native Americans began to become farmers and important traders. The bow and arrow was in use 2,500 years ago, and 1,800–to–2,000-year-old clues to pottery making and farming are known from small villages studied in Delaware, Kay, Osage, and Ottawa counties. About 1,000 years ago, Oklahoma had major populations of farming villagers in the Panhandle, along the Washita River in Garvin and Caddo counties, along the Arkansas and Grand rivers in Wagoner,

Muskogee, Sequoyah, and LeFlore counties, and along Little River and its tributaries in McCurtain County. Some of these villagers constructed ceremonial centers that vied for power with other southeastern chiefdoms. Between 1,000 and 800 years ago, the Spiro site in LeFlore County was one of the most important political-religious centers known north of the Valley of Mexico. By 500 years ago, all of Oklahoma's village societies were undergoing rapid change, in part due to climatic fluctuations, and out of this turmoil came the Wichita and Caddo people who were observed by the first Spanish and French explorers of the area.

The Historic Age

Whites first came to Oklahoma as explorers. Europeans discovered Oklahoma and its people in 1541, when Francisco Vasquez de Coronado led a gold expedition through western Oklahoma. Members of the expedition hunted buffalo and visited the camps of the Plains Apaches, the first Indian tribe the Spaniards met in Oklahoma. Coronado left a small group of missionaries who wished to work among the tribes teaching Christianity, putting Oklahoma under the Spanish flag.

Another Spanish explorer, Hernando de Soto, introduced some of the eastern tribes to firearms, tools, and other European ways, although he only traveled as far as Little Rock, Arkansas. De Soto encountered the Chickasaws, Choctaws, Creeks, and other tribes then living in the southeastern United States, and who were later removed to Oklahoma.

About 1700, two tribes from the North, the Comanches and Kiowas, migrated to Oklahoma. They settled in the Wichita Mountains where they adopted the horse; hunted buffalo; and raided Spanish settlements in Texas, northern Mexico, and New Mexico. Spaniards from New Mexico often came to Oklahoma to trade with the Comanches and Kiowas, and although they did not establish settlements in Oklahoma, they claimed Oklahoma as a part of their territory in North America.

Next came the French from the North and the East. Robert Cavelier, Sieur de la Salle led an expedition down the Mississippi River to the Gulf of Mexico. The territory on the west bank of the Mississippi River he named Louisiana. Fur traders and other French expeditions moved inland from New Orleans, which the French founded in 1718. The first Frenchman to actually visit Oklahoma was Juchereau de St. Denis. He explored land drained by the Red River, searching for places to establish settlements for trading with the tribes. In 1718 Bernard de la Harpe led an expedition to the Canadian River in eastern Oklahoma, that was inhabited by the Wichitas and Caddoes. The French established towns and lived with the tribal people. Oklahoma was under the French flag until the 1760s.

The largest conflicts to take place during the 1700s were the battles between the Spanish and the Comanches and Kiowas in the West. The French, who wished to trade for the buffalo hides of the Comanches and Kiowas, sent members of the eastern tribes to trade and avoided conflict with them. In 1762 French and Spanish leaders signed a treaty. It required France to return Louisiana (which included the area of Oklahoma) to Spain. However, in 1800 a treaty between the French and Spanish governments required the return of Louisiana, including Oklahoma, to France. In 1803 ownership of Louisiana changed once again, when the United States government purchased it for $15 million. Oklahoma was now under the American flag.

Soon after 1803, explorers, soldiers, and private citizens entered Oklahoma. Explorers came to study the land and resources and to map Oklahoma. Soldiers came to build forts and to guard the Oklahoma frontier. Spain still owned Texas and New Mexico, and were not very friendly neighbors at this time. Citizens included settlers, who came to establish farms and towns, and trappers and traders, who came to hunt fur-bearing animals and to supply tribes with goods. These pioneers found several tribes living here: Osages in northeastern

Oklahoma's tall grass prairies; Quapaws in eastern Oklahoma, ravaged by measles, small-pox, and other European diseases; the Wichitas and Caddoes in the southwest; and the Plains Apaches and Comanches living in western Oklahoma. The Osages, Comanches, and Kiowas fiercely resisted American pioneers. The western boundary of the territory was not established until 1806 and was the result of an expedition led by Captain Richard Sparks, the first American official to reach Oklahoma. His expedition was turned back by the Spanish. Another expedition that same year, led by Captain Zebulon M. Pike explored the Arkansas River and reached Oklahoma's eastern border on New Year's Day in 1807. Other explorers who visited the state: George C. Sibley accompanied by Osage scouts, explored northern Oklahoma along the Arkansas River and its tributaries; Stephen H. Long in 1817 established Fort Smith, Arkansas, between the Poteau and Arkansas rivers; and Thomas Nuttall, a sci-entist, came to Oklahoma in 1819 to study the geology, plants, and animals along the Grand, Verdigris, Cimarron, Poteau, and Arkansas rivers. Nuttall also wrote Journal of Travels in the Arkansas Territory, one of the earliest scientific books about Oklahoma.

Through these early expeditions, maps, and reports prepared by the explorers assisted Ameri-can officials to make agreements about the southern and western boundaries separating the territory of the United States and Spain. Portions of this boundary line—the Red River and the 100th Meridian—later became the southern and western boundaries of Oklahoma.

Soldiers were assigned to explore Oklahoma and were expected to protect the area against foreign invasion. Fort Smith, as mentioned, was established in 1817; Fort Gibson in northeast-ern Oklahoma and Fort Towson in the southeast were erected in 1824; and by 1861, several other posts were constructed, including Camp Arbuckle, Camp Holmes, and Camp Washita and Fort Coffee in 1834, and Fort Cobb in 1859. Soldiers surveyed and mapped the territory, built roads, and were some of the first law enforcement officers, farmers, and builders in the territory. Some leading men of the nation served as officers at the Oklahoma forts, including Zachary Taylor, a general in the Mexican War and later president of the United States; Jef-ferson Davis, later United States secretary of war and president of the Confederate States of America; and Robert E. Lee, later commander in chief of Confederate armies in the Civil War.

Territorial Days

Settlement of the territory by American pioneers ended, temporarily, when the United States government changed the use of Oklahoma: it became the area to which all Indian tribes from east of the Mississippi River would be removed. It would be called Indian Territory until 1906. The federal government resettled many tribes to Oklahoma from the eastern U.S., Kansas and Texas, Arizona, California, Idaho, and Washington. The tribes were relocated to remove them from American expansion. Tribes living in the territory south of the Ohio River were among the first to be colonized in Oklahoma. These included the Cherokees, Choctaws, Creeks, Seminoles, and Chickasaws who came from Georgia, Florida, Alabama, and Mississippi. These tribes were moving to an area already inhabited by the Wichita, Caddo, Kiowa, Plains Apache, Comanche, Osage, and Quapaw tribes.

Many tribes resisted removal, both those being relocated and those already inhabiting the territory. In 1830, under President Andrew Jackson, Congress passed the Indian Removal Act, which increased the federal government's power with respect to removal of the tribes. Jackson appointed a three-man group called the Stokes Commission to prepare Oklahoma for the arrival of the Southern tribes.

The Stokes group assigned reservations for the Senecas, Quapaws, and others. The removal of the Southern tribes began in 1820 when the Choctaws signed a removal treaty. In 1826 the Lower Creek leaders signed a treaty, giving up a large portion of their eastern lands in return

Indian Territory—1830–1855

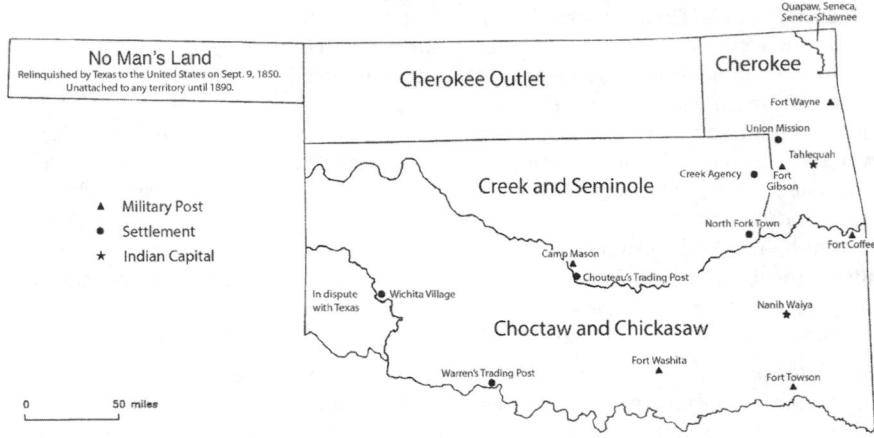

Indian Territory—1855–1866

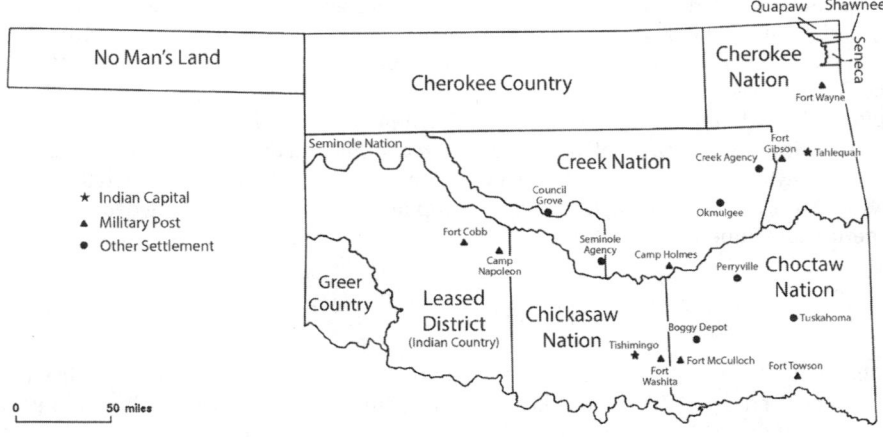

Indian Territory—1866–1889

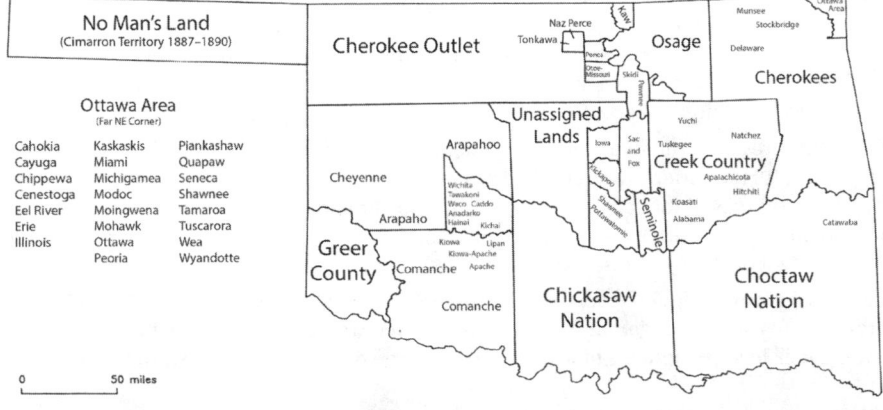

for a part of Indian Territory, and in 1832, the Upper Creeks made an agreement and moved onto the same reservation with the Lower Creeks. The Seminole tribe signed a treaty soon after requiring emigration to Indian Territory, as did the Chickasaw tribe.

Although the most famous removal was that of the Cherokee tribe, known as the "Trail of Tears," many other tribes, including the Choctaws, were removed by the same method. Most of the removals were completed in the 1830s. The tribal people, however, had been forced to walk all the way to Oklahoma across the South suffering cholera, smallpox, and measles epidemics, often in winter. Each tribe lost about one-fourth of its population on the westward march. Once established in the territory, the Choctaws, Cherokees, Creeks, Seminoles, and Chickasaws became known as the Five Civilized Tribes, due to their having adopted many European and American ways. They were well educated, and operated businesses, plantations, farms, and ranches. Many were slaveholders. The 1830 map of Indian Territory divided Oklahoma into three Indian nations: Cherokee, Creek, and Choctaw. In 1833 the Seminoles accepted a home with the Creeks, and in 1837, the Chickasaws agreed to settle among the Choctaws. Upon arrival in Oklahoma, these tribes also established towns, businesses, and schools including institutions of higher education for men and women years before similar institutions were established by white men in Oklahoma Territory. Very quickly the tribes became nations, establishing governments with written constitutions.

Already established in the western part of the territory were the Wichitas and Caddoes, basically agricultural tribes, and the Kiowas, Comanches, and Plains Apaches, primarily buffalo hunters who roamed the western half of Oklahoma, into Texas and New Mexico. Before the Civil War, several battles were fought in western Oklahoma between Americans and Plains tribes. The intrusion of Americans was depleting their hunting range and the size of herds, and these tribes actively resisted being assigned to a small area of the territory as the other tribes had done. The Civil War delayed the conquest of these tribes for nearly fifteen years.

By 1861 Indian Territory was prosperous. The tribes had tamed much of the wilderness and had established farms, plantations, schools, ranches, and businesses as mentioned. Their towns were, by now, busy commercial centers. Confederate leaders saw Indian Territory as a good supply of meat, horses, lead, salt, and grains. Since many tribes owned slaves, and their loss would be severe, the Five Civilized Tribes supported the Confederacy. Albert Pike was selected by Confederate officials as the commissioner in charge of the Indians of Oklahoma. He came to Indian Territory during the spring of 1861 and signed a Confederate treaty of alliance with each of the Five Civilized Tribes. Other tribes also sided with the Confederacy, while some remained neutral.

Many battles were fought in Oklahoma during the Civil War, and by the time the war ended in 1865, Oklahoma was a wasteland. Battles were fought between the soldiers of the Union and Confederate armies, but also between Confederate and neutral tribes. By 1863 the Union army controlled the northern half of Indian Territory. The Confederacy was led by Stand Watie, a Cherokee, and while he had many victories over Union troops, they had little effect on the outcome of the war. On April 9, 1865, Robert E. Lee surrendered to Ulysses S. Grant at Appomattox Courthouse in Virginia. Confederate commanders in the West then began to surrender. In Oklahoma, Watie and the Confederacy surrendered to Union officials at Doaksville in the Choctaw Nation on June 23, 1865.

During Reconstruction, the tribes were punished for helping the Confederacy; the most severe punishment was loss of tribal land. The Plains tribes were assigned to reservations. The Five Civilized Tribes lost much of their territory, and their governments were weakened. The year 1866 marked the beginning of the end for Indian Territory.

The war further reduced a population already diminished by removal, and smallpox and cholera epidemics infected Union and Confederate refugee camps. Both armies had burned most of the buildings owned by the tribes. The Cherokee, Creek, and Seminole nations were wastelands. The Choctaw and Chickasaw nations had escaped total destruction, but most of their livestock and food had been used to feed the Confederate army and refugees.

In the chaos, many outlaws passed through and hid in Indian Territory due to the lack of law enforcement. Belle Starr; the Younger brothers; the James brothers; and Ned Christie, the Cherokee bandit, were among the robbers and cattle rustlers living in Indian Territory after the war. Eventually the tribes asked the federal government for help and it cooperated by sending a large number of deputy U.S. marshals to Indian Territory. A further complication for the tribes was the arrival of more and more tribes from other parts of the country. In 1867 the Wyandots, Peorias, Miamis, and Ottawas began to arrive in Oklahoma. In 1873 the Modocs were removed from their original homeland and forced to Oklahoma, along with the Delawares and Shawnees. Additionally, many all-black towns were established in Oklahoma during this period due to segregation laws passed by the Five Civilized Tribes. Boley, Foreman, Red Bird, and Rentiesville are examples of all-black towns in Oklahoma.

> Lack of law enforcement attracted notorious outlaws to Indian Territory.

By 1869 prosperity had returned to Oklahoma. Farming, ranching, mining, and railroad building helped the Indian nations. Before the railroads were opened in Oklahoma, the territory was a great highway for Texas cattle moving to railroad yards in Kansas. The first of these trails was the East Shawnee Trail. It crossed the Red River at Colbert's Ferry, to Baxter Springs, Kansas. The West Shawnee Trail branched toward Abilene (Kansas) at Boggy Depot. Abilene was the most important Kansas cow town. The Chisholm Trail was the greatest cattle highway in the West. It crossed central Indian Territory. Most of the Texas cattle marketed in the Kansas cow towns moved along the Chisholm Trail. The fourth cattle highway was the Dodge City, or Great Western Cattle Trail. After rail lines were built across Indian Territory, ranchmen used trains to ship their cattle to market.

Coal mining was another important industry in this period. Most of the early-day coal mining was in the Choctaw Nation near McAlester. Railroad companies operated the mines since coal was ideal for firing the locomotives' steam boilers. Miners and their families came to Oklahoma from Italy, Greece, Germany, Russia, Poland, and England.

Since many people who came to work in Indian Territory wished to live in the territory, tribes began selling permits, because only members of tribes could officially live in an Indian nation. By 1900 more permit holders were living in Indian Territory than tribal members. The demands of the permit holders led to the end of tribal governments.

In western Oklahoma, conditions were quite different than in the East. The federal government had taken the western half of Indian Territory from the Five Civilized Tribes and planned to carve this area into reservations for other tribes from other parts of the U. S. The Kaws, Osages, Sac and Fox, Potawatomis, Iowas, and Kickapoos came to Oklahoma after the war, along with Ponca, Otoe and Missouria, Pawnee, Nez Perce, Tonkawa, Keechi, Anadarko, Ioni, and Waco people. The Comanches, Kiowas, Cheyennes, and Arapahos left their reservations to hunt buffalo and raid settlements. Between 1868 and 1874, there were many battles in western Oklahoma between Indian tribes and American soldiers. In one of the most famous of these battles, in late November 1868, Colonel George Custer led the Seventh Cavalry from Fort Supply, and at daybreak on November 27, Custer and his troops reached the Washita River. Scouts found a Cheyenne camp led by Chief Black Kettle. Custer ordered a surprise attack, and the Seventh Cavalry killed more than one hundred warriors, including Black Kettle. They took fifty women and children prisoners. Known as the "Battle of the Washita," it was the first of many campaigns against the Plains tribes. By 1874 the U.S.

War Department decided to conquer these tribes. General Nelson Miles was placed in command of a large army. He defeated many warrior bands; others came in to the reservations and surrendered. Cheyenne and Arapaho bands that surrendered, did so at the Darlington Agency near El Reno; Kiowa and Comanche bands at Fort Sill in Lawton. The last warriors to be captured were the Quahada Comanches, led by Quanah Parker, on June 24, 1875. In 1894 Geronimo and his followers were captured and settled on the Comanche-Kiowa reservation.

Once the Plains tribes had been conquered, Congress began removing the obstacles to white settlement. The railroad companies also worked to open Oklahoma to settlement. The Katy, Frisco, Rock Island, and Santa Fe lines crossed Indian Territory. The railroad companies wanted more settlement to induce more freight, passengers, and profits. In addition to the railroad interests, a group of promoters called "Boomers" also worked to open Indian Territory to settlement. Boomers described Oklahoma's rich land and resources to large audiences in the East. They wrote newspaper articles describing Oklahoma as a "Garden of Eden." Leading Boomers were Charles C. Carpenter, Elias C. Boudinot, David L. Payne, and William L. Couch. They led settlers to the border of Indian Territory and set up camps, waiting for Oklahoma to be opened. Boomer raids and the related publicity put pressure on Congress, but before Indian Territory could be opened to homesteaders, tribal title to the land had to be removed.

The tribes held their land in common, with ownership of the land vested in the tribe and not in its individual members. During the 1880s, leaders in Congress decided the reservation system was a failure. They wished to change Indian culture, and Congress became convinced the only way to do this was to destroy tribal governments and tribal land ownership. They decided to break up the reservations, giving each tribal member an allotment of 160 acres. Government leaders believed making tribal members landowners would change their culture. In 1887 Congress passed the Dawes Allotment Act, which provided for dividing the reservations. Government agents were to assign each tribal member a 160-acre homestead-an allotment. Any land remaining was declared surplus, and this surplus land was to be opened to settlement by homesteaders. At this time the Dawes Act did not apply to the Five Civilized Tribes. By 1906 all of Oklahoma west of the territory of the Five Civilized Tribes had been opened to settlement. The Indian reservations had been changed to counties in the new Oklahoma Territory.

Homesteaders received farms in Oklahoma Territory by land runs and a lottery. The first portion of Indian Territory opened to settlement was the Unassigned Lands, a 2 million-acre tract in the center of Indian Territory. Only about 10,000 claims of 160 acres each remained, so in order to give all homeseekers an equal chance, officials decided to open the Unassigned Lands by a land run. On April 22, 1889, more than 50,000 homeseekers ran to stake their claim, and by evening, every homestead had been staked and town lots in Guthrie, Kingfisher, Oklahoma City, and Norman were claimed. Nearly 1,000 blacks made the Run of 1889. Most were from the South and many obtained homesteads. Langston was an all-black town established by these pioneers. Other land runs were held in 1891 in central Indian Territory; in 1892 in the Cheyenne and Arapaho reservations; and in 1893, the largest land run in history opened the Cherokee Outlet. The final land run was in 1895 when the Kickapoo reservation was opened for settlement.

For the next land opening, federal officials used the lottery. The surplus lands of the Kiowa, Comanche, Apache, Wichita, and Caddo reservations were opened. In 1906 the Osage reservation was allotted, and no surplus land for settlers existed. In addition, the Osage tribe held mineral rights in common, which later contributed to their being some of the wealthiest people on earth during the oil boom in the decades following statehood in 1907. After each reservation was allotted and settled, it was shifted from Indian Territory to Oklahoma Territory. Once a dispute with Texas about the ownership of Greer County was settled by the U.S. Supreme Court in 1906, which denied Texas's claim to the land, western Oklahoma had reached its present area and shape.

The newly arrived Oklahoma pioneers suffered great hardship. Money was scarce, and the environment was often cruel. Families lived in sod houses or dugouts due to shortages of timber. Much of Oklahoma was grassland, and wood-when it was available-was used for fuel. Otherwise, dried buffalo or cattle dung, known as "cowchips," fueled the pioneers' stoves.

During the pioneer period, most Oklahomans lived in the country on homesteads. However, several towns grew with the spread of the railroads. Guthrie, Oklahoma City, Norman, Enid, Woodward, El Reno, Lawton, and other towns developed into regional trade centers. Pioneer farmers marketed grain, cotton, and livestock. Guthrie was the territorial capital with a population of about 6,000 people in 1890, at that time the largest town in Oklahoma Territory.

Statehood

Oklahoma's present state government had its beginning during the territorial period. The guide for forming a government for Oklahoma Territory was a law passed by Congress in 1890, the Oklahoma Organic Act. This law provided for a governor, a secretary, and a supreme court of three judges. The president of the United States appointed these officials. The act provided for a legislature and a congressional delegate to be elected by the voters of Oklahoma Territory.

Land Openings in Oklahoma—1889 to 1906

The act also divided Oklahoma Territory into temporary counties and provided for county and town governments, and required the territorial capital be located at Guthrie. President Benjamin Harrison appointed George W. Steele of Indiana to be governor. Other territorial governors were Robert Martin (1891-92), Abraham J. Seay (1892-93), William C. Renfrow (1893-97), Cassius M. Barnes (1897-1901), William Miller Jenkins (1901), William C. Grimes (Acting, 10 days in 1901), Thompson B. Ferguson (1901-1906), and Frank Frantz (1906-07). All of these men were Republicans except Governor Renfrow, a Democrat appointed by President Grover Cleveland, also a Democrat.

During the territorial period, the Oklahoma Legislature established the foundation of future state government. Laws adopted by the territorial legislature created counties and courts, established the system of public schools, and began formation of the Oklahoma university and college system. The first territorial legislature created three institutions of higher learning: the University of Oklahoma at Norman, the Oklahoma Agricultural and Mechanical College at Stillwater, and the Oklahoma Normal School at Edmond. The normal school was to train teachers for the public schools of Oklahoma Territory.

White settlers were eager for statehood and held conventions each year. However, Congress did not act on Oklahoma statehood because most congressmen believed Oklahoma Territory should be joined with Indian Territory to form a single, larger state. Until this was done, Congress refused to take any final action on Oklahoma statehood. In 1893 Congress passed a law that extended the Dawes Allotment Act to the Five Civilized Tribes. By 1902 the Dawes Commission had signed allotment agreements with all of the Five Civilized Tribes and began to assign allotment. There were no surplus lands for homesteaders.

The Curtis Act, passed by Congress in 1898, ended tribal rule. The Curtis Act substituted federal law for the laws of the Indian governments. It provided for surveying of townsites and it extended voting rights to more than half a million non-Indians-the permit holders. The Curtis Act abolished tribal courts and made Indian citizens subject to federal courts.

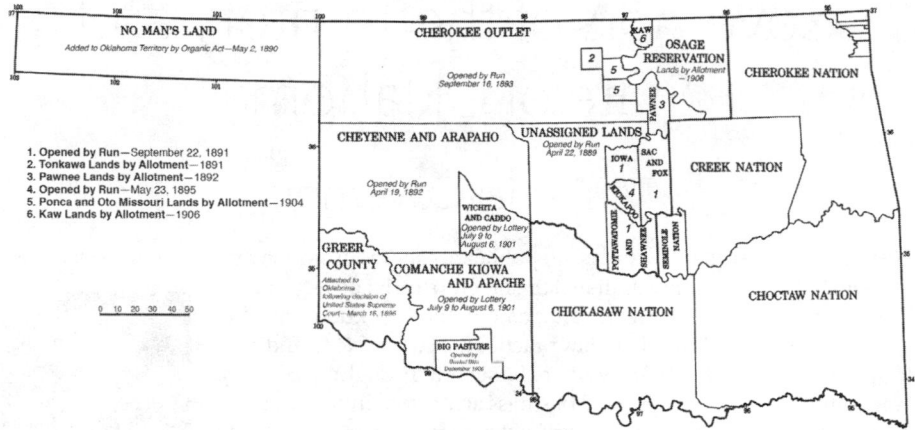

Land Openings in Oklahoma, 1889–1906

With allotment completed and tribal governments abolished, statehood was possible. However, leaders of the Five Civilized Tribes opposed joining Oklahoma Territory. They wanted to form an all-Indian state named "Sequoyah." Leaders of the Five Civilized Tribes met at Muskogee in 1905 where Creek Chief Pleasant Porter was elected president of the Sequoyah Convention. Alexander Posey, Creek poet and journalist, was elected secretary. The delegates wrote a constitution for the proposed state of Sequoyah. It was approved by the voters of Indian Territory, but Congress refused to consider it. They were preparing to join the Twin Territories to form the state of Oklahoma.

On June 16, 1906, Congress passed the Oklahoma Enabling Act. It permitted the people of Oklahoma Territory and Indian Territory to join and write a constitution. The Constitutional Convention was to meet in Guthrie, and was to consist of 112 delegates. Fifty-five delegates were to be elected from Oklahoma Territory, fifty-five from Indian Territory, and two delegates were to be elected from the Osage Nation. During the summer of 1906, voters in the Twin Territories elected convention delegates. Democratic delegates won one hundred of the convention seats, while Republicans won twelve. Democrat William H. Murray was elected president of the convention. His majority floor leader was Charles N. Haskell. The Republican leader in the convention was Henry Asp.

Delegates worked through the winter and drafted a constitution that created three departments for the new government. The executive branch consisted of a governor and eleven other executive officials. The legislative branch consisted of a house of representatives and a senate. The judicial branch was to be made up of a supreme court, district courts, county courts, and municipal courts. The constitution included provisions for initiative and referendum. Citizens could propose laws and could vote on laws submitted to them by the legislature. Social reforms included the eight-hour workday in mines and on public works. Child labor was forbidden. Prohibition, banning the sale of alcoholic beverages, was included.

An election in the Twin Territories was held on September 17, 1907, and the people approved the constitution and elected Charles N. Haskell as the state's first governor, upon approval of the U.S. Congress. The constitution was sent to Washington, D.C., and after some study, Congress approved it on November 16, 1907, making Oklahoma the forty-sixth state.

Governors of the Territory and State of Oklahoma

Territorial Governors

George Washington Steele—Republican—served from 1890 to 1891. Born December 13, 1839, in Fayette County, Indiana, the first territorial governor read law and was admitted to the bar after completing his studies at Ohio Wesleyan University. He left his law practice in Hartford City, Indiana, to volunteer in the Union Army where he served throughout the Civil War. Returning home, he entered business at Marion, Indiana, and as a Republican, served his locality in Congress from March 4, 1883, to March 3, 1889. His experience in Congress and as an army officer may have influenced President William Henry Harrison to select him as the initial governor of Oklahoma Territory. He took the oath of office in Guthrie on May 22, 1890, and found his hands full trying to bring order out of the chaotic legislative fights that he encountered. The school systems, plus three colleges, and the state library were all established in the course of his term. He resigned effective October 18, 1891, and returned to Indiana where he continued in public service until shortly before his death in Marion on July 12, 1922. Steele is buried in the I.O.O.F. Cemetery in Marion.

Robert Martin—Republican—served from 1891 to 1892. As the secretary of the territory, Martin served as acting governor from October 18, 1891, when George W. Steele left for Indiana, until February 2, 1892, when Governor Abraham J. Seay took office. Martin was born in Frankfort Springs, Pennsylvania, in 1833. After a law career in Ohio, Martin moved to Wichita, Kansas, and then to Harrison, Oklahoma Territory, in April 1889. He was involved in activity leading to adoption of the Organic Act, and, after moving to El Reno, he was named secretary of the territory. In later political life, he became mayor of Guthrie. He died there on March 2, 1897, and was buried in Summit View Cemetery just northeast of Guthrie.

Abraham Jefferson Seay—Republican—served from 1892 to 1893. A native of Amherst County, Virginia, Seay was born on November 28, 1832. Three years later his family moved to Osage County, Missouri, where he eventually helped to educate himself while assisting in the care of his ten brothers and sisters. He read law and was admitted to the bar in 1861. He also served in the Civil War, attaining the rank of colonel in the Union Army at the end of the conflict. He returned to Missouri and alternated between private practice and serving as a district judge. Later, he became president of the First National Bank of Rolla, Missouri, an office he held until his death. In the course of that time he served as an associate justice of the Supreme Court of Oklahoma Territory, from which office he was advanced to the governorship. He took office on February 2, 1892, and served until May 7, 1893. After his death on December 22, 1915, he was buried at Kingfisher.

William Cary Renfrow—Democrat—served from 1893 to 1897. Born March 15, 1845, at

Smithfield, North Carolina, Renfrow left the public schools at seventeen to serve in the Confederate Army until 1864. Returning from war he moved to Russellville, Arkansas, in 1865. He was a deputy county official until he entered the banking business in Norman, Oklahoma. He became governor of Oklahoma Territory on May 7, 1893, the only Democrat to serve. During his term, the Cherokee Outlet opened and the Oklahoma Historical Society formed. Four years later he returned to business, operating lead and zinc mines, and promoting oil and gas discoveries in Oklahoma, Kansas, and Texas. He died on January 31, 1922, and is buried in Russellville, Arkansas.

Cassius McDonald Barnes—Republican—served from 1897 to 1901. Born on August 25, 1845, in Livingston County, New York, Barnes moved in his early life to Michigan where he completed his secondary education. After his Civil War service as a Union soldier he moved to Arkansas. In 1876 he became chief deputy United States marshal, holding that position for ten years. In 1890 he went to Guthrie to become receiver of the United States Land Office. There he read law and in 1893 was admitted to the practice. He served in the third and fourth Oklahoma Territorial Legislatures, and became governor on May 24, 1897. At the end of his tenure he became president of a bank and later was mayor of Guthrie. Later he moved to Kansas, then to New Mexico for his health. He died in Albuquerque, New Mexico, on February 19, 1925, and is buried in Guthrie.

William Miller Jenkins—Republican—served from May 1901 to November 1901, when

he was removed from office by President Theordore Roosevelt on November 30. Born on April 25, 1856, in Alliance, Ohio, he received his education there. In Shelby County, Louisiana, he was admitted to the bar in 1893, before moving to Arkansas City, Kansas, to begin his law practice. He made the race into the Cherokee Outlet on September 16, 1893, and secured a homestead in Kay County. He served as secretary of the territory from June 1897 until he became governor on May 12, 1901. Criticism about his involvement with stock purchases in the Oklahoma Sanitarium Company in Norman as well as the death of President William McKinley led to his removal from office in 1901. After a few years in California, he returned to Oklahoma and lived in Sapulpa until his death on October 19, 1941. He is buried in Southern Heights Cemetery in Sapulpa. Thompson B. Ferguson was appointed successor.

William C. Grimes—Republican—served as acting governor from November 30, 1901 to December 9, 1901—a period of ten days. Grimes was born near Lexington, Ohio, on November 6, 1857, but at age twenty moved to Nebraska where he became a newspaper publisher and owner of a mercantile business. He also served as sheriff of Johnson County, Nebraska, and then moved to Oklahoma just prior to the 1889 Land Run, settling northeast of Kingfisher. He became a strong Republican leader in Oklahoma Territory and served as a U.S. marshal and laid the foundation for establishing a system of law and order in the territory. He later served as secretary of the territory under appointment of President William McKinley. Grimes moved to Oregon and then to

California. He died in Santa Monica, California, on April 8, 1931, and is buried there.

Thompson Benton Ferguson—Republican—served from 1901 to 1906. Born on March 17, 1857, near Des Moines, Iowa, he spent his early years in Kansas where he was educated as a teacher and a Methodist minister. In 1889 he made the run into Oklahoma and secured a claim near Oklahoma City, but returned to Kansas where he was an editor and author. He was a recognized leader in the Republican Party in the territory and state, serving as postmaster and territorial governor under that party. His term was from December 9, 1901, to January 13, 1906. In 1892 he moved to Watonga where he established the newspaper that he continued to publish until his death on February 14, 1921. He is buried in the I.O.O.F. Cemetery in Watonga.

Frank Frantz—Republican—served from 1906 to 1907, the last territorial governor. He was born on May 7, 1872, at Roanoke, Illinois, and educated there. He made his home in Medford shortly after the opening of the Cherokee Outlet. He served with the "Rough Riders" under Colonel Theodore Roosevelt. After the Spanish-American War he moved to Enid, Oklahoma, where he was named postmaster from 1901 to 1903. He served as Indian agent of the Osage Agency until he assumed the office of governor on January 13, 1906, and remained in office until statehood on November 16, 1907. He lost as the Republican candidate in the first state gubernatorial election. Until his death on March 9, 1941, he was in the oil business. He is buried in Memorial Park Cemetery in Tulsa.

Governors Since Statehood

Charles Nathaniel Haskell—Democrat—served from 1907 to 1911. Oklahoma's first state governor was born on March 13, 1860, in Putman County, Ohio. He was educated as a lawyer, admitted to the Ohio Bar in 1881, and began practice in Ottawa, Ohio. In 1901 he moved to Muskogee, Indian Territory, where he added to his law practice the promotion of railroads. He was a leader in the Oklahoma Constitutional Convention in 1906. After his term as governor, from November 16, 1907, to January 9, 1911, he engaged in the oil business. He died on July 5, 1933, and is buried in Green Hill Cemetery in Muskogee.

Lee Cruce—Democrat—served from 1911 to 1915. He was born on July 8, 1863, near Marion, Kentucky. Although he was admitted to the Kentucky Bar in 1887, he never practiced until he joined his older brother's law firm in 1891, at Ardmore, Indian Territory. Ten years later he became cashier of the Ardmore National Bank. In time he advanced to be its president. He served as Oklahoma's second governor from January 9, 1911, to January 11, 1915. In 1930 he was defeated in the primary for the United States Senate. He died on January 16, 1933, in Los Angeles, California. He is buried in Rose Hill Cemetery in Ardmore.

Robert Lee Williams—Democrat—served from 1915 to 1919. Oklahoma's third governor was born on December 20, 1868, at Brundidge, Alabama. He earned a number of college degrees including LL.D., was admitted to the Alabama Bar in 1891, and began his practice in Troy,

Alabama. In 1896 he went to Atoka, Indian Territory. His long years of public service included member of the Oklahoma Constitutional Convention, 1906 to 1907; chief justice of the Oklahoma Supreme Court, 1907 to 1914; governor of Oklahoma, January 11, 1915 to January 13, 1919; United States district judge, Eastern District of Oklahoma, 1919 to 1937; and United States circuit judge, Tenth Circuit, 1937 to 1939. He retired in 1939, but continued to serve as needed. He died at his home in Durant, Oklahoma, on April 10, 1948. He is buried in City Cemetery in Durant.

James Brooks Ayers Robertson—Democrat—Served 1919 to 1923. Robertson was born on March 15, 1871, in Keokuk County, Iowa, and educated in the public schools. In 1893 he moved to Oklahoma and was admitted to the Oklahoma Bar in 1898. He held the following political offices: Lincoln County attorney, 1900 to 1902; Tenth Judicial District of Oklahoma judge, 1909 to 1910; State Capitol Commission member, 1911; Supreme Court Commission member, 1911 to 1914; governor of Oklahoma, January 13, 1919, to January 8, 1923; Democratic Presidential Elector-at-Large, 1932. He died at his home in Oklahoma City, on March 7, 1938. He is buried in Oak Park Cemetery in Chandler.

Jack Callaway Walton—Democrat—served from January 1923 to November 1923, when he was impeached and convicted. He was born on March 6, 1881, on a farm near Indianapolis, Indiana. After a ten-year stay in Lincoln, Nebraska, he joined the army in 1897. Although he saw no foreign service during the Spanish-American War, he did live in Mexico before coming to Oklahoma City in 1903, as a sales engineer. He was commissioner of public works in 1917; mayor of Oklahoma City, 1919 to 1923; elected governor in 1922, and impeached within the year, serving from January 8, to November 19, 1923; served on the State Corporation Commission from 1933 until 1939, when he retired to enter

private law practice. He died on November 25, 1949, and is buried in Rose Hill Cemetery in Oklahoma City.

Martin Edwin Trapp—Democrat—served from 1923 to 1927. Born on April 18, 1877, in Robinson, Kansas, he was educated almost entirely by association and studied with Mr. McDaniel, a neighbor. He served as Logan County clerk, 1905 to 1907; state auditor, 1907 to 1911; lieutenant governor, 1915 to 1923. After the ouster of Governor Jack Walton, he served as governor from November 19, 1923, until January 10, 1927. He was a dealer in investment securities until his death on July 26, 1951, in Oklahoma City. He is buried in Fairlawn Cemetery in Oklahoma City.

Henry Simpson Johnston—Democrat—served from January 1927 to March 20, 1929, when he was impeached and convicted. Born on December 30, 1867, near Evansville, Indiana, he migrated to Colorado at the age of twenty-four where he studied law and was admitted to the Colorado Bar in 1891. Later he came to Perry, Oklahoma, to practice. He was a member, and temporary presiding officer of the Oklahoma Constitutional Convention in 1906. He was elected governor in 1926 and took office on January 10, 1927. He served as president pro tempore of the first Oklahoma Senate, and returned to the Senate from 1933 to 1937. He maintained a law practice in his hometown of Perry until his death on January 7, 1965. He is buried in Perry.

William Judson Holloway—Democrat—served from 1929 to 1931. He succeeded Governor Henry Johnston in office and completed the term. A native of Arkadelphia, Arkansas, he was born on December 15, 1888. After graduation from Ouachita College in 1910, he attended the University of Chicago for a time. While he was living in Hugo and working as a high school principal he began to read law. He later completed his course at Cumberland University and was admitted to the practice of law at Hugo. He was elected county attorney in 1916, and was a state senator from 1920 to 1926, serving as president pro tempore. In 1926 he was elected lieutenant governor and advanced to the governor's office upon the impeachment and removal of Governor Johnston. He practiced law in Oklahoma City until his death on January 28, 1970, and is buried in Rose Hill Cemetery in Oklahoma City.

William Henry Murray—Democrat—served from 1931 to 1935. Probably Oklahoma's most colorful political figure, William Murray was born on November 21, 1869, in Collinsville, Texas. At age twenty, he graduated from College Hill Institute in Springtown, Texas. For the next six years he held various jobs, including day laborer, teacher, editor of a Dallas farm magazine, and of a Corsicana daily newspaper. Admitted to the bar in 1895, he practiced at Fort Worth before moving to Tishomingo, Indian Territory, in 1898. There he became legal advisor to the governor of the Chickasaw Nation. He served as president of the Oklahoma Constitutional Convention in 1906; Speaker of the House of Representatives, 1907 to 1908; member of the Sixty-third and Sixty-fourth United States

Congresses; and governor of Oklahoma from January 12, 1931, to January 15, 1935. At his urging, the Oklahoma Tax Commission was created. His ranching interests spread to Bolivia, where he established a colony. He wrote articles and books dealing with constitutional rights. He died on October 15, 1956, and is buried in Tishomingo.

Ernest Whitworth Marland—Democrat—served from 1935 to 1939. A native of Pittsburgh, Pennsylvania, Marland was born on May 8, 1874. He was educated at Park Institute of that city and received his LL.B. from the University of Michigan in 1893. He began his law practice at Pittsburgh, but engaged in the oil production business after moving to Oklahoma. He was president of the Marland Oil Company. Marland was a member of the Seventy-third United States Congress from 1933 to 1935, and served as governor of Oklahoma from January 15, 1935, to January 9, 1939. Before Marland left office, nearly 90,000 Oklahomans were working on 1,300 WPA projects. Marland provided leadership in the development of the Oklahoma Highway Patrol and the Interstate Oil Compact. He died on October 3, 1941. His civic contributions to Ponca City included the Pioneer Woman Statue. He is buried in Ponca City.

Leon Chase Phillips—Democrat—served from 1939 to 1943. Born on December 9, 1890, in Worth County, Missouri, Phillips moved to Oklahoma at an early age. While a student at Epworth University in Oklahoma City, he studied for the ministry, but changed to law and received his LL.B. from the University of Oklahoma in 1916. He was admitted to the Oklahoma Bar in that year, and later practice before the United States Supreme Court. After service in World War I, he returned to Okemah where he practiced law. He was a member of the

Oklahoma Legislature from 1933 to 1938, serving as Speaker of the House in 1935. He served as governor from January 9, 1939, to January 11, 1943. He lived in Okemah until his death on March 27, 1958, and is buried in Weleetka.

Robert Samuel Kerr—Democrat—served from 1943 to 1947. Oklahoma's first native-born governor, Kerr was born near Ada, Indian Territory, on September 11, 1896. He attended college at East Central Normal School, and Oklahoma Baptist University. He was admitted to the Oklahoma Bar in 1922, and practiced in Ada. Beginning as a drilling contractor in 1926, he built up a large oil producing company and at the time of his death was president of the Kerr-McGee Oil Industries, Inc. He served as governor of Oklahoma from January 13, 1943, to January 13, 1947. He was elected to the U.S. Senate on November 2, 1948, and served until his death on January 1, 1963. While governor, Kerr's administration liquidated the state debt. During his tenure in the U.S. Senate, he worked to get the McClellan-Kerr Arkansas River Navigation System developed, changing much of Oklahoma's landscape. He is buried at his birthplace near Ada.

Roy Joseph Turner—Democrat—served from 1947 to 1951. Turner was born on November 6, 1894, in Lincoln County, Oklahoma Territory. Upon completion of his high school education, he attended Hill's Business College in Oklahoma City. He was a bookkeeper for Morris Packing Company in Oklahoma City from 1911 to 1915; a salesman for the Goodyear Tire and Rubber Company; and after his service in World War I, he was a dealer in real estate, principally in Oklahoma, Florida, and Texas. By 1928 he had become an independent oil producer. In 1933 he established the Turner Ranch at Sulphur, but he maintained a residence in Oklahoma City where he served on the board of education from 1939 to 1946. He served as governor of Oklahoma from January 13, 1947, to

January 8, 1951. He lived in Oklahoma City until his death on June 11, 1973. He is buried in Rose Hill Cemetery in Oklahoma City.

Johnston Murray—Democrat—served from 1951 to 1955. He was born on July 21, 1902, in the mansion of the Chickasaw Nation's governor at Emet, Johnston County, Indian Territory. His early education was governed by the location of the work of his famous father, former Governor William H. Murray. After graduation from the Murray State School of Agriculture in 1924, he went to Bolivia where he lived for four years trying to make a success of his father's colonization expedition there. He received his law degree in 1946, having studied and worked at other things for a number of years. He served as governor from January 8, 1951, to January 1955. He served as an attorney with the State Department of Welfare until his death on April 16, 1974. He is buried at Tishomingo along with his father.

Raymond Dancel Gary—Democrat—served from 1955 to 1959. He was the first governor to be born in Oklahoma since statehood. Born on January 21, 1908, his birthplace was a farm midway between Madill and Kingston. He was educated in the local schools and Southeastern State College. After five years of teaching he was elected county superintendent of schools and served for four years. In 1936 he began his business career, first in school and office supplies, and later as president of the Sooner Oil Company. He was a state senator from

1941 until he became governor of Oklahoma on January 10, 1955. He died on December 11, 1993, and is buried in Madill.

James Howard Edmondson—Democrat—served from 1959 to 1963. The youngest

governor in the history of the state, Edmondson was born in Muskogee, Oklahoma, on September 27, 1925. He attended elementary and secondary schools in that city and enrolled in the University of Oklahoma after high school graduation. He enlisted in the U.S. Air Force in March 1942, and served until December 5, 1945. He completed his law degree in August 1948. After practicing law in Muskogee, he moved to Tulsa to become the chief prosecutor in the office of the county attorney of Tulsa County. He was elected county attorney in 1954 and was re-elected in 1956. Edmondson was inaugurated governor of Oklahoma on January 8, 1959, after having been elected to that post by the largest majority ever given a gubernatorial candidate in the state. He resigned the office on January 6, 1963, and was appointed to the United States Senate to fill the position left vacant by the death of Robert S. Kerr. At the time of his death on November 17, 1971, he was a practicing attorney in Oklahoma City, where he is buried.

Lieutenant Governor **George Nigh** served from January 6 until January 14, 1963, when Bellmon assumed office.

Henry Louis Bellmon—Republican—served from 1963 to 1967. The first Republican governor of Oklahoma was born in Tonkawa, Oklahoma, on September 3, 1921. He is the son of George and Edith Caskey Bellmon. He attended Colorado State University, later transferring to Oklahoma State University where he was granted the degree of Bachelor of Science in Agriculture. Henry Bellmon served with the U.S. Marine Corps from 1942 through 1946, received the Silver Star for action on Saipan and the Legion of Merit for action on Iwo Jima. He was a member of the Oklahoma House of Representatives during the Twenty-first Oklahoma Legislature in 1947. He was a farmer in Billings, Oklahoma, at the time of his election as governor. He served from January 14, 1963,

to January 9, 1967. He was elected to the U. S. Senate in 1968 and again in 1974, the first Republican in state history to be re-elected to the U. S. Senate. He chose not to run in 1980.

Dewey Follett Bartlett—Republican—served from 1967 to 1971. The second Republican

governor of Oklahoma, Bartlett was born in Marietta, Ohio, on March 28, 1919. He was the son of David A. and Jessie Follett Bartlett. He attended Princeton University where he was granted a BSE degree in Geological Engineering. Dewey Bartlett served in the Marine Corps during World War II as a combat dive-bomber pilot. He received the Air Medal. He was a partner in Keener Oil Company, one of Oklahoma's oldest, small independent oil companies. He was first elected to the Oklahoma Senate in 1962 and was re-elected in 1964. He served as governor from January 9, 1967, to January 11, 1971, and was elected to the U. S. Senate on November 7, 1972. He did not seek re-election because of failing health, and died on March 1, 1979. He is buried in Tulsa.

David Hall—Democrat—served from 1971 to 1975. Hall was born on October 20, 1930, in Oklahoma City. He is the son of Mr. and Mrs. William A. "Red" Hall. He was Phi Beta Kappa at the University of Oklahoma, where he received a Bachelor of Arts degree in 1952. Hall served in the U.S. Air Force from 1952 to 1954. He continued his education at the University of Tulsa, earning his law degree in 1959. He served as assistant county attorney of Tulsa County from 1959 to 1962, and as county attorney from 1962 to 1966. In 1968 he returned to the University of Tulsa where he served as professor of law. He was inaugurated governor of Oklahoma on January 11, 1971, following the closest gubernatorial election in the state's history. Hall was indicted by a federal grand jury three days after leaving office. He later served nineteen months of a three-year sentence for extortion and conspiracy convictions.

David Lyle Boren—Democrat—served from 1975 to 1979. Boren was born in Washington, D.C., on April 21, 1941, the son of Congressman Lyle H. and Christine McKown Boren. He graduated from Yale University summa cum laude, receiving a BA degree in 1963, graduated with honors with a MA degree from Oxford University, England, in 1965, and received his JD degree in 1968 from the University of Oklahoma, where he was class president of the College of Law. He was an outstanding law graduate and scholar and was selected as a Rhodes Scholar. In addition to his profession as an attorney, he was chairman of the Division of Social Sciences and professor of political science at Oklahoma Baptist University, and also company commander of the Oklahoma Army National Guard. He was elected to the Oklahoma House of Representatives in 1967 and served until his election as governor of Oklahoma in November 1974. He was inaugurated on January 13, 1975, and made his home in Seminole before moving into the Governor's Mansion. He is the father of two children, Carrie Christine and David Daniel. He was elected to the U.S. Senate in 1978, and served successive terms until he became president of the University of Oklahoma in Norman in November 1994.

George Patterson Nigh—Democrat—served from 1979 to 1987. Nigh was born in McAlester, Oklahoma, on June 9, 1927, the son of Wilbur R. and Irene Crockett Nigh. He attended public schools in McAlester and Eastern Oklahoma Agricultural and Mechanical College at Wilburton, Oklahoma. From June 1945 through September 1946, he served in the U.S. Navy. He was granted a Bachelor of Arts degree from East Central State College, Ada, Oklahoma, in 1950. From 1952 to 1958, he taught at McAlester High School. Nigh served in the House of Representatives from the Twenty-third through the Twenty-sixth Oklahoma Legislatures. He was elected lieutenant governor, the youngest in the state's history, in 1958. In 1963 Nigh became the seventeenth governor of Oklahoma, filling an unexpired 9-day term following the resignation of Governor J. Howard Edmondson. He was elected lieutenant governor again in 1966, 1970, and 1974. He was elected governor on November 7, 1978, and was sworn in on January 3, 1979. Nigh became the twenty-second governor of Oklahoma, serving five days to fill an unexpired term following the resignation of Governor David Boren. He began his regular term as twenty-second governor of Oklahoma on January 8, 1979, and was re-elected in 1982. Nigh was most recently president of the University of Central Oklahoma in Edmond, a position from which he retired in 1997.

Henry Louis Bellmon—Republican—served from 1987 to 1991. Bellmon was elected the first Republican governor of Oklahoma in November 1962 and then was elected November 4, 1986, to his second term as governor. Bellmon is the first governor to be elected to non-consecutive terms. He chose not to run in 1990. Bellmon died September 29, 2009, after a long battle with Parkinson's disease. He is buried at Union Cemetery in Billings, Oklahoma.

David Lee Walters—Democrat—served from 1991 to 1995. Born on November 20, 1951, near Canute, Oklahoma, in Washita County, Walters is the son of Harold and Evelyn Walters. He graduated as valedictorian from Canute High School in 1969, and from the University of Oklahoma in 1973, with a bachelor's degree in Industrial Engineering. In 1977 he earned a Master of Business Administration from Harvard University. Walters worked as a project manager in the administration of Governor David Boren, and later served as assistant and associate provost at the OU Health Sciences Center where, at age twenty-nine, he became the youngest executive officer in the university's history. He joined the Burks Group, a commercial real estate company in 1982, and became  president of American Fidelity Property Company in 1985. He served on the Commission for the Oklahoma State Department of Human Services in 1983, and was appointed co-chairman of the Governor's 100-member Commission on Government Reform in 1984. On November 6, 1990, Walters was elected governor of Oklahoma, carrying seventy-five of the state's seventy-seven counties. During Walters's term, education funding increased by approximately 30 percent, and a $350-million bond issue for higher education, the first in twenty-five years, brought construction and renovation to every state college campus. While in office, Walters pleaded guilty to a misdemeanor election violation. He did not run for re-election in 1994. He and his wife, Rhonda, have three daughters; a son died in 1991.

Francis Anthony Keating—Republican—elected November 1994 and re-elected in 1998.  Born in St. Louis, Missouri, on February 10, 1944, Keating's family moved to Tulsa before he was six months old. He received a Bachelor of Arts in history from Georgetown University in 1966 and earned a Juris Doctor degree from the University of Oklahoma College of Law in 1969. Keating served as an FBI agent and as an assistant district attorney in Tulsa. From 1972 to 1974, he served in the Oklahoma House of Representatives, and from 1974 to 1981, he served in the Oklahoma Senate and was unanimously elected Republican leader of the Senate. From 1981 to 1986, Keating was the U.S. attorney for the Northern District of Oklahoma and was national chair of the United States Attorneys. He served in both the Reagan and Bush administrations: as assistant secretary of the U.S. Treasury (1988–1989), where he presided over the U.S. prison system, U.S. Marshals, the Immigration and Naturalization Service, and all ninety-four U.S. Attorneys; and as acting deputy secretary and general counsel of Housing and Urban Development (1990 to 1993). Keating and his wife, Cathy, are the parents of three children: daughters Carrie and Kelly, and son, Chip.

Brad Henry—Democrat—elected November 2002 and re-elected in 2006. Born in Shawnee, Oklahoma, on July 10, 1963. Henry attended public schools in Shawnee and graduated from Shawnee High School. He attended the University of Oklahoma as a President's Leadership Scholar and earned a bachelor's degree in economics in 1985. In 1988 Henry was awarded his Juris Doctor degree from the University of Oklahoma College of Law, where he served as managing editor of the

Law Review. Henry served in the Oklahoma Senate from 1992 to 2002, and as chairman of the Senate Judiciary Committee. Governor Henry and his wife, Kim, have three daughters—Leah, Laynie, and Baylee.

Mary Fallin—Republican—elected November 2, 2010, and re-elected in 2014. The 2010 election was an historic election in which she became the first female governor of Oklahoma. After a successful career in the private sector as a manager for a national hotel chain, Fallin made her first foray into public service in 1990 when she was elected to the Oklahoma House of Representatives. This began her long and distinguished career of public service. In 1994 Fallin would first make history by becoming the first woman and first Republican to be elected lieutenant governor of Oklahoma, an office she would hold for twelve years. Fallin was elected to the U.S. Congress in 2006 where she represented the Fifth District of Oklahoma. Fallin is married to Wade Christensen, an Oklahoma City attorney who is the state's first "First Gentleman." The couple have six children between them. They attend Crossings Community Church in northwest Oklahoma City.

During World War II, Fort Reno housed over thirteen hundred prisoners of war, guarded by the U.S. Army's 435th Military Police Escort Guard Company. Sixty-two German and eight Italian POWs are interred in the west side of the Fort Reno Military Cemetery (most of the dead came from other POW camps in Oklahoma and Texas).

First Ladies of Oklahoma

As with all of the state's women, Oklahoma's first ladies represent a great range of personalities, interests, and backgrounds. Some first ladies were highly visible, while others have been reclusive. They had one common goal—a desire to make a contribution to their state. These contributions varied greatly, especially considering the continuum of history. For the past several decades, first ladies have adopted banner causes to support by increasing awareness and motivating Oklahoma citizens to action.

The following is a list of Oklahoma's first ladies and the years they served:

Lillian Elizabeth Gallup Haskell, 1907–1911

Oklahoma did not have a first lady from 1911 until 1919. Chickie LeFlore Cruce died before her husband, Lee Cruce, became Governor. Governor Robert Lee Williams never married.

Isabell Butler Robertson, 1919–1923

Madeleine Orrick Walton, 1923

Lula C. Strang Trapp, 1923–1927

Ethel L. Littleton Johnston, 1927–1929

Amy Arnold Holloway, 1929–1931

Mary Alice Hearrell Murray, 1931–1935

Lydie Roberts Marland, 1935–1939

Myrtle Ellenberger Phillips, 1939–1943

Grayce Breene Kerr, 1943–1947

Jessica Grimm Turner, 1947–1951

Willie Emerson Murray, 1951–1955

Emma Mae Purser Gary, 1955–1959

Jeannette Barleson Edmondson, 1959–1963

Shirley Osborn Bellmon, 1963–1967

Ann Smith Bartlett, 1967–1971

Jo Evans Hall, 1971–1975

Janna Lou Little Boren, 1975

Molly Shi Boren, 1977–1979

Donna Skinner Nigh, 1979–1987

Shirley Osborn Bellmon, 1987–1991

Rhonda Walters, 1991–1995

Cathy Keating, 1995–2003

Kim Henry, 2003–2011

And Gentleman

Wade Christensen, 2011–present

Many of the inaugural gowns worn by Oklahoma's first ladies are displayed at the Kirkpatrick Center in Oklahoma City. *Oklahoma's First Ladies*, a book by LuCelia Wise, (Evans Publications, Perkins, Oklahoma, 1983) provides some additional information.

Secretaries of State, Since Statehood

The office of the Secretary of State was an elective office from statehood until 1975 when the Oklahoma Constitution was amended and it became an appointive office, running concurrent with the governor and effective January 8, 1979. Passage of State Question 436, on May 3, 1966, made it possible for secretaries of state to succeed themselves.

Secretary of State	Term of Office Beginning
Bill Cross (D)	November 16, 1907
Thomas Smith (D)	Appt. Aug. 6, 1910, after Cross's death.
B. F. Harrison (D)	January 9, 1911
H. G. Oliver (D)	Appt. Jan. 2, 1915, after Harrison resigned.
S. L. Lyon (D)	January 11, 1915
Joe Morris (D)	January 13, 1919
R. A. Sneed (D)	January 8, 1923
Graves Leeper (D)	January 10, 1927
R. A. Sneed (D)	January 6, 1931
Frank C. Carter (D)	January 15, 1935
C. C. Childers (D)	January 9, 1939
Frank C. Carter (D)	January 11, 1943
Katherine Manton (D)	Appt. Nov. 8, 1946, after Carter resigned.
Wilburn Cartwright (D)	January 13, 1947
John D. Conner (D)	January 8, 1951
Andy Anderson (D)	January 10, 1955
John D. Conner (D)	January 12, 1959
Wm. N. Christian (D)	Appt. Aug. 31, 1959, after Conner's death.
James M. Bullard (D)	January 14, 1963
John Rogers (D)	January 9, 1967
John Rogers (D)	January 11, 1971
John Rogers (D)	January 13, 1975
Jerome Byrd (D)	Appt. July 1, 1975 after Rogers resigned.
Jeannette B. Edmondson (D)	January 18, 1979
Jeannette B. Edmondson (D)	January 13, 1983
Hannah D. Atkins (D)	October 8, 1987
John Kennedy (D)	January 14, 1991
Glo Henley (D)	Appt. after Kennedy resigned January 31, 1994
Tom J. Cole (R)	January 9, 1995
Mike Hunter (R)	Appt. March 15, 1999, after Cole resigned
Kay Dudley (R)	Appt. October 16, 2002
Susan Savage (D)	Appt. January 16, 2003

Secretary of State	Term of Office Beginning
Glenn Coffee (R)	Appt. January 4, 2011
Larry V. Parman (R)	Appt. March 1, 2013
Chris Benge (R)	Appt. November 8, 2013

Eagle Nest, 94 (in 1948, when the photograph was taken), believed to have been the longest living survivor of the Battle of the Washita.

Elective State Officers
Since Statehood

Office	Term 1—1907	Term 2—1911	Term 3—1915
Governor	C. N. Haskell (D)	Lee Cruce (D)	R. L. Williams (D)
Lieutenant Governor	Geo. W. Bellamy (D)	J. J. McAlester (D)	M. E. Trapp (D)
Secretary of State	Bill Cross (D) [1]	B. F. Harrison (D) [4]	S. L. Lyon (D)
State Auditor	M. E. Trapp (D)	Leo Meyers (D) [5]	E. B. Howard (D)
Attorney General	Chas. West (D)	Chas. West (D)	S. P. Freeling (D)
Treasurer	J. A. Menefee (D)	Robt. Dunlop (D)	W. L. Alexander (D)
Supt. Public Instruction	E. D. Cameron (D)	R. H. Wilson (D)	R. H. Wilson (D)
Examiner and Inspector	Chas. A. Taylor (D)	Chas. A. Taylor (D) [6]	Fred Parkinson (D)
Commissioner of Labor	C. L. Daugherty (D)	C. L. Daugherty (D)	W. G. Ashton (D) [9]
Charities and Corrections	Kate Barnard (D)	Kate Barnard (D)	W. D. Matthews (D)
Pres. Bd. of Agriculture	J. P. Connors (D)	G. T. Bryan (D)	F. M. Gault (D)
Clerk Supreme Court	W. H. L. Campbell (D)	W. H. L. Campbell (D)	W. M. Franklin (D)
Insurance Commissioner	T. J. McCombs (D) [2]	P. A. Ballard (D) [7]	A. L. Welch (D)
State Printer	Clint Worrell (D) [3]	Giles Farris (D) [8]	
Chief Mine Inspector	Pete Hanraty (D)	Ed Boyle (D)	Ed Boyle (D)
Asst. Mine Insp. D. 1		John O'Brien (D)	Tom Scott (D)
Asst. Mine Insp. D. 2		Martin Clark (D)	W. T. Williams (D)
Asst. Mine Insp. D. 3		Frank Haley (D)	Frank Haley (D)
	Term 4—1919	Term 5—1923	Term 6—1927
Governor	J. B. A. Robertson (D)	J. C. Walton (D) [12]	H. S. Johnston (D) [15]
Lieutenant Governor	M. E. Trapp (D)	M. E. Trapp (D)	W. J. Holloway (D)
Secretary of State	Joe Morris (D)	R. A. Sneed (D)	Graves Leeper (D)
State Auditor	Frank Carter (D)	C. C. Childers (D)	A. S. J. Shaw (D)
Attorney General	S. P. Freeling (D) [10]	Geo. Short (D)	Ed Dabney (D) [16]
Treasurer	A. N. Leecraft (D)	A. S. J. Shaw (D)	R. A. Sneed (D)
Supt. Public Instruction	R. H. Wilson (D)	M. A. Nash (D)	M. A. Nash (D) [17]
Examiner and Inspector	Fred Parkinson (D)	Fred Parkinson (D) [13]	John Rogers (D)
Commissioner of Labor	Claude Connally (D)	Claude Connally (D)	W. A. Pat Murphy (D)
Charities and Corrections	W. D. Matthews (D)	Mabel Bassett (D)	Mabel Bassett (D)
Pres. Bd. of Agriculture	J. A. Whitehurst (D)	J. A. Whitehurst (D)	Harry B. Cordell (D)
Clerk Supreme Court	W. M. Franklin (D)	W. M. Franklin (D)	Jessie E. Moore (D)
Insurance Commissioner	A. L. Welch (D) [11]	E. W. Hardin (D) [14]	Jess G. Read (D)
Chief Mine Inspector	Ed Boyle (D)	Ed Boyle (D)	Miller D. Hay (D)

Asst. Mine Insp. D. 1	Tom Scott (D)	Robert H. Brown (D)	Robert H. Brown (D)
Asst. Mine Insp. D. 2	W. T. Williams (D)	W. G. Roberts (D)	W. G. Roberts (D)
Asst. Mine Insp. D. 3	Miller D. Hay (D)	John Almond (D)	W. R. Rutherford (D)
Asst. Mine Insp. D. 4			Riley Clark (D)
	Term 7—1931	**Term 8—1935**	**Term 9—1939**
Governor	Wm. H. Murray (D)	E. W. Marland (D)	Leon C. Phillips (D)
Lieutenant Governor	Robert Burns (D)	James E. Berry (D)	James E. Berry (D)
Secretary of State	R. A. Sneed (D)	Frank C. Carter (D)	C. C. Childers (D)
State Auditor	Frank C. Carter (D)	C. C. Childers (D)	Frank C. Carter (D)
Attorney General	J. Berry King (D)	Mac Q. Williamson (D)	Mac Q. Williamson (D)
Treasurer	Ray Weems (D)	Hugh L. Harrell (D)[18]	Carl B. Sebring (D)
Supt. Public Instruction	John Vaughan (D)	John Vaughan (D)[19]	A. L. Crable (D)
Examiner and Inspector	John Rogers (D)	John Rogers (D)	John Rogers (D)
Commissioner of Labor	W. A. Pat Murphy (D)	W. A. Pat Murphy (D)	W. A. Pat Murphy (D)
Charities and Corrections	Mabel Bassett (D)	Mabel Bassett (D)	Mabel Bassett (D)
Pres. Bd. of Agriculture	Harry B. Cordell (D)	Harry B. Cordell (D)[20]	Joe C. Scott (D)
Clerk Supreme Court	Gus Pool (D)	Andy Payne (D)	Andy Payne (D)
Insurance Commissioner	Jess G. Read (D)	Jess G. Read (D)	Jess G. Read (D)
Chief Mine Inspector	Robert H. Brown (D)	Robert H. Brown (D)	Robert H. Brown (D)
Asst. Mine Insp. D. 1	James Jones (D)	James Jones (D)	James Jones (D)
Asst. Mine Insp. D. 2	W. C. Robbins (D)	Tom Woods (D)	John W. Moore (D)
Asst. Mine Insp. D. 3	Charles E. Bailey (D)	Charles E. Bailey (D)	Joe Johnson (D)
Asst. Mine Insp. D. 4	Ivan Fisher (D)	Ivan Fisher (D)	Ivan Fisher (D)
	Term 10—1943	**Term 11—1947**	**Term 12—1951**
Governor	Robert S. Kerr (D)	Roy J. Turner (D)	Johnston Murray (D)
Lieutenant Governor	James E. Berry (D)	James E. Berry (D)	James E. Berry (D)
Secretary of State	Frank C. Carter (D)[21]	Wilburn Cartwright (D)	John D. Conner (D)
State Auditor	C. C. Childers (D)	A. S. J. Shaw (D)	Wilburn Cartwright (D)[27]
Attorney General	Mac Q. Williamson (D)[22]	Mac Q. Williamson (D)	Mac Q. Williamson (D)
Treasurer	A. S. J. Shaw (D)	John D. Conner (D)	A. S. J. Shaw (D)
Supt. Public Instruction	A. L. Crable (D)	Oliver Hodge (D)	Oliver Hodge (D)
Examiner and Inspector	John Rogers (D)[23]	Charles G. Morris (D)	Charles Morris (D)[28]
Commissioner of Labor	W. A. Pat Murphy (D)	Jim Hughes (D)	Jim Hughes (D)
Charities and Corrections	Mabel Bassett (D)	Buck Cook (D)	Buck Cook (D)
Pres. Bd. of Agriculture	Joe C. Scott (D)	Joe C. Scott (D)[26]	No longer elective
Clerk Supreme Court	Andy Payne (D)[24]	Andy Payne (D)	Andy Payne (D)
Insurance Commissioner	Jess G. Read (D)[25]	Donald F. Dickey (D)	Donald Dickey (D)[29]
Chief Mine Inspector	Robert H. Brown (D)	John M. Malloy (D)	John M. Malloy (D)

Asst. Mine Insp. D. 1	Otto H. Sandmann (D)	Sam C. Wells (D)	Sam C. Wells (D)
Asst. Mine Insp. D. 2	John W. Moore (D)	John W. Moore (D)	John W. Moore (D)
Asst. Mine Insp. D. 3	Joe Johnson (D)	Joe Johnson (D)	Joe Johnson (D)
Asst. Mine Insp. D. 4	Joe Hobson (D)	Joe Hobson (D)	Joe Hobson (D)

	Term 13—1955	Term 14—1959	Term 15—1963
Governor	Raymond Gary (D)	J. Howard Edmondson (D) [30]	Henry Bellmon (R)
Lieutenant Governor	Cowboy Pink Williams (D)	George Nigh (D)	Leo Winters (D)
Secretary of State	Andy Anderson (D)	John D. Conner (D) [31]	James M. Bullard (D)
State Auditor	A. S. J. Shaw (D)	Andy Anderson (D) [32]	A. F. Shaw (D)
Attorney General	Mac Q. Williamson (D)	Mac Q. Williamson (D)	Charles Nesbitt (D)
Treasurer	John D. Conner (D)	William A. Burkhart (D)	Cowboy Pink Williams (D)
Supt. Public Instruction	Oliver Hodge (D)	Oliver Hodge (D)	Oliver Hodge (D)
Examiner and Inspector	Scott Burson (D)	John M. Rogers (D)	John M. Rogers (D)
Commissioner of Labor	Jim Hughes (D)	Jim Hughes (D)	W. T. Bill Hughes (D)
Charities and Corrections	Buck Cook (D)	Buck Cook (D)	Buck Cook (D)
Clerk Supreme Court	Andy Payne (D)	Andy Payne (D)	Andy Payne (D)
Insurance Commissioner	Joe B. Hunt (D)	Joe B. Hunt (D)	Joe B. Hunt (D)
Chief Mine Inspector	John M. Malloy (D)	John M. Malloy (D)	John M. Malloy (D) [33]
Asst. Mine Insp. D. 1	Sam C. Wells (D)	Sam C. Wells (D)	Paul H. Scroggins (D)
Asst. Mine Insp. D. 2	John W. Moore (D)	John W. Moore (D)	John W. Moore (D)
Asst. Mine Insp. D. 3	Joe Johnson (D)	Buck Perry (D)	Buck Perry (D)
Asst. Mine Insp. D. 4	Joe Hobson (D)	Joe Hobson (D)	C. R. Hall (D)

	Term 16—1967	Term 17—1971	Term 18—1975
Governor	Dewey F. Bartlett (R)	David Hall (D)	David Boren (D)
Lieutenant Governor	George Nigh (D)	George Nigh (D)	George Nigh (D)
Secretary of State	John Rogers (D)	John Rogers (D)	John Rogers (D) [37]
State Auditor	Joe Bailey Cobb (D)	Joe Bailey Cobb (D)	Joe Bailey Cobb (D) [38]
Attorney General	G. T. Blankenship (R)	Larry Derryberry (D)	Larry Derryberry (D)
Treasurer	Leo Winters (D)	Leo Winters (D)	Leo Winters (D)
Supt. Public Instruction	Oliver Hodge (D) [34]	Leslie R. Fisher (D)	Leslie R. Fisher (D)
Examiner and Inspector	John M. Rogers (D)	John M. Rogers (D)	John M. Rogers (D)
Commissioner of Labor	L. E. Bailey (R)	Wilbur Wright (D) [36]	Wilbur Wright (D) [39]
Charities and Corrections	Jim Cook (D)	Jim Cook (D)	Jim Cook (D) [40]
Clerk Supreme Court	Andy Payne (D)	No longer elective	No longer elective
Insurance Commissioner	Joe B. Hunt (D)	Joe B. Hunt (D)	Joe B. Hunt (D) [41]
Chief Mine Inspector	Ward Padgett (D)	Ward Padgett (D)	Ward Padgett (D) [42]
Asst. Mine Insp. D. 1	Paul H. Scroggins (D)	No longer elective	No longer elective

Asst. Mine Insp. D. 2	John Moore (D)	No longer elective	No longer elective
Asst. Mine Insp. D. 3	Buck Perry (D)[35]	No longer elective	No longer elective
Asst. Mine Insp. D. 4	C. R. Hall (D)	No longer elective	No longer elective
	Term 19—1979	**Term 20—1983**	**Term 21—1987**
Governor	George Nigh (D)	George Nigh (D)	Henry Bellmon (R)
Lieutenant Governor	Spencer Bernard (D)	Spencer Bernard (D)	Robert S. Kerr III (D)
State Auditor and Inspector	Tom Daxon (R)	Clifton Scott (D)	Clifton Scott (D)
Attorney General	Jan Eric Cartwright (D)	Michael C. Turpen (D)	Robert H. Henry (D)
Treasurer	Leo Winters (D)	Leo Winters (D)	Ellis Edwards (D)
Supt. Public Instruction	Leslie Fisher (D)	Leslie Fisher (D)[43]	John Folks (D)[44]
Insurance Commissioner	Gerald Grimes (D)	Gerald Grimes (D)	Gerald Grimes (D)
	Term 22—1991	**Term 23—1995**	**Term 24—1999**
Governor	David Walters (D)	Frank Keating (R)	Frank Keating (R)
Lieutenant Governor	Jack Mildren (D)	Mary Fallin (R)	Mary Fallin (R)
State Auditor and Inspector	Clifton Scott (D)	Clifton Scott (D)	Clifton Scott (D)
Attorney General	Robert H. Henry (D)[45]	W. A. Drew Edmondson (D)	W. A. Drew Edmondson (D)
Treasurer	Claudette Henry (R)	Robert Butkin (D)	Robert Butkin (D)
Supt. Public Instruction	Sandy Garrett (D)	Sandy Garrett (D)	Sandy Garrett (D)
Insurance Commissioner	Gerald Grimes (D)[46]	John P. Crawford (R)	Carroll Fisher (D)
Commissioner of Labor	Dave Renfro (D)[47]	Brenda Reneau (R)	Brenda Reneau Wynn (R)
	Term 25—2003	**Term 26—2007**	**Term 27—2011**
Governor	Brad Henry (D)	Brad Henry (D)	Mary Fallin (R)
Lieutenant Governor	Mary Fallin (R)	Jari Askins (D)	Todd Lamb (R)
State Auditor and Inspector	Jeff McMahan (D)	Jeff McMahan (D)	Gary Jones (R)
Attorney General	W. A. Drew Edmondson (D)	W.A. Drew Edmondson (D)	Scott Pruitt (R)
Treasurer	Robert Butkin (D)[48]	Scott Meacham (D)	Ken Miller (R)
Supt. Public Instruction	Sandy Garrett (D)	Sandy Garrett (D)	Janet Barresi (R)
Insurance Commissioner	Carroll Fisher (D)[49]	Kim Holland (D)	John Doak (R)
Commissioner of Labor	Brenda Reneau (R)	Lloyd Fields (D)	Mark Costello (R)
	Term 28—2015	**Term 29—2019**	**Term 30—2023**
Governor	Mary Fallin (R)		
Lieutenant Governor	Todd Lamb (R)		
State Auditor and Inspector	Gary Jones (R)		
Attorney General	Scott Pruitt (R)		

Treasurer	Ken Miller (R)
Supt. Public Instruction	Joy Hofmeister (R)
Commission of Labor	Mark Costello (R)

Footnotes

1 Died. Thos. P. Smith (D) appointed August 6, 1910.

2 Resigned. Milas Lasater (D) appointed November 30, 1909.

3 Office created by 1st Legislature. Clint Worrell (D) appointed.

4 Resigned. H. G. Oliver (D) appointed January 2, 1915.

5 Resigned. Jos. C. McClelland (D) appointed February 12, 1913.

6 Died. Fred Parkinson (D) appointed July 31, 1912.

7 Resigned. A. L. Welch (D) appointed April 29, 1913.

8 Removed. Office abolished.

9 Resigned. Claude Connally (D) appointed August 8, 1917.

10 Resigned. George Short (D) appointed February 7, 1922.

11 Resigned. E. W. Hardin (D) appointed January 1, 1920.

12 Removed. Succeeded by M. E. Trapp (D).

13 Resigned. George J. Mechling (D) appointed.

14 Resigned. J. G. Read (D) appointed January 17, 1924.

15 Removed. Succeeded by W. J. Holloway (D).

16 Resigned. J. Berry King (D) appointed.

17 Resigned. John S. Vaughan (D) appointed April 9, 1927.

18 Resigned. Hubert L. Bolen (D) appointed February 13, 1935.

19 Resigned. A. L. Crable (D) appointed August 19, 1936.

20 Died. Joe C. Scott (D) appointed February 23, 1937.

21 Resigned. Katherine Manton (D) appointed November 8, 1946.

22 Resigned. Randell S. Cobb (D) appointed September 15, 1943; Cobb resigned and Mac Q. Williamson (D) appointed after returning from military service.

23 Died. Charles G. Morris (D) appointed June 20, 1946.

24 Resigned. Vivian S. Payne (D) appointed December 31, 1943; Vivian Payne resigned and Andy Payne (D) appointed after returning from military service.

25 Died. Donald F. Dickey (D) appointed July 25, 1946.

26 Resigned. Harold P. Hutton (D) appointed December 1, 1948. President of State Board of Agriculture became an appointive office in 1949.

27 Resigned. Gladys Warren (D) appointed July 10, 1954.

28 Died. Scott Burson (D) appointed June 8, 1954.

29 Resigned. Robert L. Birdwell (D) appointed March 20, 1954.

30 Resigned January 6, 1963. Succeeded by Lt. Governor George Nigh (D) who served until January 14, 1963.

31 Died. William N. Christian (D) appointed August 31, 1959.

32 Died. Imogene Holmes (D) appointed August 28, 1962.

33 Died. Ward Padgett (D) appointed April 1, 1963.

34 Died. D. D. Creech (R) appointed April 16, 1968, serving until December 31, 1969, when he resigned and Scott Tuxhorn (R) was appointed to finish term.

35 Resigned. James F. Leonard (D) appointed December 1, 1968.

36 Resigned. L. P. Williams (D) appointed March 21, 1973.

37 Resigned. Jerome W. Byrd (D) appointed July 1, 1975.

38 Resigned. Ray Parr (D) appointed September 30, 1977.

39 Resigned. William E. Foster (D) appointed November 1, 1975.

40 Resigned. November, 1977. Jack Stamper (D) appointed January 1978. Office eliminated, State Question No. 509 (1975) effective 1–8–79.

41 Died. Gerald Grimes (D) appointed February 15, 1975.

42 Resigned. April 30, 1980. Otis English (D) appointed May 1, 1980, resigned October 31, 1980.

43 Resigned. June 30, 1984. John Folks (D) appointed July 2, 1984.

44 Resigned. June 30, 1988. Gerald Hoeltzel (R) appointed August 2, 1988.

45 Resigned. June, 1991. Susan Loving (D) appointed June 21, 1991.

46 Resigned. Sept. 30, 1991. Cathy Weatherford (D) appointed Oct. 1, 1991.

47 Commissioner of Labor was restored to election ballot in 1990.

48 Resigned May 1, 2005. Scott Meachum appointed May 2005.

49 Resigned. September 24, 2004. Kim Holland (D) appointed January 21, 2005

Corporation Commissioners
Since Statehood

The Oklahoma Corporation Commission comprises three commissioners who are elected to six-year terms. The terms are staggered so one commissioner vacancy occurs every two years. This pattern was established by lot after election of the first three commissioners in 1907. In-term vacancies are filled by gubernatorial appointment. Appointed commissioners serve until the next regularly scheduled election.

Forty-one different persons have served on the commission since statehood. All commissioners have been Democrats except Robert H. (Bob) Anthony, E. R. Hughes, J. C. Watts Jr., Ed Apple, Denise Bode, Jeff Cloud, Dana Murphy, Patrice Douglas, and Todd Heitt, all Republicans.

Anthony, elected in 1988 and again in 1994 and 2000, was the first Republican commissioner in sixty years. Hughes held the distinction of being the only commissioner to serve two non-successive terms. He was elected in 1920, but lost a 1926 re-election bid. He was elected again in 1928.

The commission panel with longest tenure was the twentieth, when Harold Freeman, Wilburn Cartwright and Ray C. Jones sat together for 13 years (1955–68). No other Commission sat longer than eight years without a membership change. The average tenure for a Commission panel is 3.8 years. Commissioners in order of succession are:

Seat One

Andrew P. Watson (D), elected 1907, 1908, 1914, impeached and removed 1915; W.D. Humphrey (D), appointed 1915, elected 1916, resigned 1919; R.E. Echols (D), appointed 1919; E.R. Hughes (R), elected 1920; C.C. Childers, (D), elected 1926; J.C. (Jack) Walton (D), elected 1932; Ray O. Weems (D), elected 1938, 1944, 1950, resigned 1955; Harold Freeman (D), appointed 1955, elected 1956, 1962; Charles Nesbitt (D), elected 1968; Hamp Baker (D), elected 1974, 1980; Bob Hopkins (D), elected 1986, resigned 1991; Cody L. Graves (D), appointed 1991, elected 1992, resigned 1997; Denise Bode (R) appointed 1997, elected 1998, 2004, resigned 2007; Jim Roth (D), appointed 2007; Dana Murphy (R), elected 2008, re-elected 2010.

Seat Two

J.J. McAlester (D), elected 1907; George Henshaw (D), elected 1910; Campbell Russell (D), elected 1916; Frank Carter (D), elected 1922; E.R. Hughes (R), elected 1928; A.S.J. Shaw (D), elected 1934; William J. Armstrong (D), elected 1940; Ray C. Jones (D), elected 1946, 1952, 1958, 1964, 1970, resigned 1975; Jan Eric Cartwright (D), appointed 1975, elected 1976, resigned 1979; Norma Eagleton (D), appointed 1979, elected 1980, 1982; Bob Anthony (R), elected 1988, 1994, 2000, 2006, 2012.

Seat Three

J.E. (Jack) Love (D), elected 1907, 1912, died in office, 1918; Art L. Walker (D), appointed 1918, elected 1918, resigned 1923; Joe B. Cobb (D), appointed 1923; Fred Capshaw (D), elected 1924; Paul A. Walker (D), elected 1930, resigned 1934; Reford Bond (D), appointed 1934, elected 1936, 1942, 1948, died in office, 1954; Wilburn Cartwright (D), appointed 1954, elected 1954, 1960, 1966; Rex Privett (D), elected 1972; Bill Dawson (D), elected 1978, resigned 1982; James B. Townsend (D), appointed 1982, elected 1982, 1984; J.C. Watts Jr. (R), elected 1990, resigned 1995; Ed Apple (R), appointed 1995, elected 1996. Jeff Cloud (R), elected 2002, 2008; Patrice Douglas (R), appointed 2011; Todd Heitt (R), elected 2014.

---

* In 1995, J.C. Watts Jr. resigned as commissioner after his election to the U.S. Congress, but didn't vacate this office until 1/9/95, the day Governor Keating was sworn in. Departing Governor Walters attempted to appoint Charles Nesbitt to the commission in December 1994 to fill the vacancy left by Watts. Walters contended the position would be vacant 1/4/95, when Congress convened. Walter's appointment of Nesbitt was denied by the Oklahoma Supreme Court, allowing Keating to appoint Ed Apple.

House of Representatives Since Statehood
First to Fourth Legislatures

County	1907 • 1st	1909 • 2nd	1911 • 3rd	1913 • 4th
Speakers	Wm. H. Murray (D)	Ben F. Wilson (D)	W. A. Durant (D) W. B. Anthony (D) elected Speaker for short Special Session.	J. Harvey Maxey (D)
Adair	T. L. Rider (D)	T. L. Rider (D)	Geo. W. Smith (D)	T. L. Rider (D)
Alfalfa	Dan G. Murley (D) [1]	A. J. Butts (D) [2]	G. N. Kneeland (R) [3]	Chas. B. Parkhurst (R)
Atoka	R. M. Rainey (D) [1]	J. M. Humphreys (R) [2]	J. W. Clark (D) [3]	I. L. Cook (D)
Beaver	Abel J. Sands (R)	A. W. Tooley (R)	A. W. Tooley (R)	
Beaver/Harper				R. B. Rutherford (D)
Beckham	G. C. Whitehurst (D)	G. W. Lewis (D)	Geo. W. Lewis, Sr. (D)	H. V. Joseph (D)
Blaine	Wm. H. Bowdre (R)	A. L. Edgington (R)	Geo. Jamison (R)	Geo. Jamison (R)
Bryan	J. H. Baldwin (D) [1] A. F. Ross (D) [1]	Wm. F. Semple (D) [2] A. E. Ewell (D) [2]	J. H. Baldwin (D) [3] Wm. F. Semple (D) [3]	W. A. Durant (D) R. R. Halsell (D)
Caddo	Chas. C. Fisher (D) [1] Frank Stevens (D) [1]	Joe Smith (D) [2] J. S. Bell (D) [2]	H. N. Christian (D) [3] G. M. Fuller (D) [3]	H. N. Christian (D) Theo. Pruett (D)
Canadian	Milton B. Cope (D) [1]	Milton B. Cope (D) [2]	U. S. Brown (R) [3]	R. J. Thompson (D)
Carter	Leo Harris (D) J. F. McCants (D)	Wm. F. Gilmer (D) John R. Whayne (D)	J. B. Champion (D) U. T. Rexroat (D)	U. T. Rexroat (D)
Cherokee	Jos. L. Manus (D)	Henry Ward (R)	Houston B. Teehee (D)	Houston B. Teehee (D)
Choctaw	W. H. Armstrong (D)	Lyman W. White (D)	M. L. Webb (D)	Thos. W. Hunter (D)
Cimarron	Frank L. Casteel (D)	Frank L. Casteel (D)	O. Marshall (D)	
Cimarron/Texas				W. L. Roberts (D)
Cleveland	J. Vandeveer (D) [1]	S. W. Hutchins (D) [2]	Oliver H. Aikin (D) [3]	N. E. Sharp (D)
Coal	Geo. W. O'Neal (D) [1]	Geo. E. Jahn (D) [2]	Geo. T. Searcy (D) [3]	Geo. T. Searcy (D)
Comanche	J. Roy Williams (D) [1]	Leslie P. Ross (D) [2]	J. Roy Williams (D) [3]	
Comanche/Cotton				J. Roy Williams (D) J. M. Haynes (D)
Craig	E. J. Hobdy (D) [1]	E. N. Ratcliff (D) [2]	Pete Coyne (D) [3]	Pete Coyne (D)
Creek	W. B. Stone (D) [1]	Geo. O'Heim (R) [2]	S. J. Smith (R) [3]	H. H. Sherman (R)
Custer	Howell Smith (D) [1]	Howell Smith (D) [2]	J. M. Thrash (R) [3]	W. S. Dearing (D)
Delaware	Lee B. Smith (D)	Lee B. Smith (D)	O. W. Killam (D)	Lee Howe (D)
Dewey	W. G. Smith (R)	R. C. Brownlee (R)	H. O. Devereaux (R)	Howell Smith (D)
Ellis	Elmer V. Jessee (D)	H. P. Covey (R)	Flavius P. Rose (R)	Flavius P. Rose (R)
Garfield	A. H. Ellis (D) [1] Jos. M. Porter (R) [1]	Jos. M. Porter (R) [2] Arthur A. Stull (R) [2]	Jos. M. Porter (R) [3] J. B. Campbell (R) [3]	Geo. M. Dizney (R) C. C. Childers (D)
Garvin	W. M. Lindsey (D) Wm. Tabor (D)	J. J. Rotenberry (D) Robt. Wallace (D)	O. W. Patchell (D) Wm. Tabor (D)	Joe A. Edwards (D) W. B. M. Mitchell (D)

First to Fourth Legislatures

County	1907 • 1st	1909 • 2nd	1911 • 3rd	1913 • 4th
Grady	Robt. M. Johnson (D) Albert S. Riddle (D)	Henry Ireton (D) R. L. Glover (D)	E. W. Frey (D) R. L. Glover (D)	T. J. Brown (D) Albert S. Riddle (D)
Grant	Jos. W. Smith (D) [1]	Jos. W. Smith (D) [2]	W. T. Clark (R) [3]	I. E. Lemon (D)
Greer	Geo W. Briggs (D) W. C. Pendergraft (D)	G. L. Wilson (D) Jas. J. Savage (D)	K. C. Cox (D)	O. L. Cummings (D)
Harmon			C. H. Madden (D)	H. L. Russell (D)
Harper	John W. Durst (D)	Henry L. Vogle (R)	Henry L. Vogle (R)	See Beaver & Harper
Haskell	Ed Boyle (D) [1]	Ed Boyle (D) [2]	H. H. Edwards (D)	H. M. Moore (D)
Hughes	Ed Swengel (D) [1]	N. J. Johnson (D) [2]	N. J. Johnson (D)	J. B. Griggs (D)
Jackson	Wm. A. Banks (D)	S. G. Ashby (D)	S. G. Ashby (D)	R. J. Morgan (D)
Jefferson	Chas. M. London (D)	Alex C. Savage (D)	Cham Jones (D)	A. McCrory (D)
Johnston	Wm. H. Murray (D) [1]	J. M. Ratliff (D) [2]	W. J. Milburn (D) [3]	Andrew A. Veatch (D)
Kay	Q. T. Brown (D) Logan Hawkins (D)	Lester A. Maris (R) Chas. M. Compton (R)	T. O. Williams (D) W. H. Clarke (R)	C. L. Pinkham (D) W. C. Baum (R)
Kingfisher	Harvey Utterback (R) [1]	Harvey Utterback (R) [2]	Geo. L. King (R) [3]	Geo. L. King (R)
Kiowa	J. T. Armstrong (D) J. V. Faulkner (D)	J. E. Terral (D) J. V. Faulkner (D)	O. J. Logan (D)	Leonard D. Lewis (D)
Latimer	J. E. Stivers (D)	Lon Lovelace (D)	W. H. New (D)	Cliff V. Peery (D)
LeFlore	C. W. Broome (D) [1]	C. C. Mathies (D) [2]	C. W. Broome (D) [3]	T. G. McMahan (D) J. L. Spengler (D)
Lincoln	H. M. Jarrett (D) [1] Jas. H. Lockwood (R) [1]	John B. Charles (R) [2] Jas. H. Lockwood (R) [2]	John B. Charles (R) [3] C. R. Blackburn (R) [3]	John B. Charles (R) Fred B. Hoyt (R)
Logan	Will H. Chappell (R) John S. Shearer (R) Geo. H. Stagner (R)	O. B. Acton (R) John S. Shearer (R) A. C. Hamlin (R)	G. E. Clayton (D) O. B. Acton (R) John S. Shearer (R)	Frank H. McGuire (R) Walter H. Matthews (D)
Love	John R. McCalla (D)	John R. McCalla (D)	W. H. Brooks (D)	W. H. Brooks (D)
Major	J. R. Sherman (R)	J. R. Sherman (R)	S. S. Davidson (R)	W. T. Ruby (R)
Marshall	H.S.P. Ashby (D)	J. W. McDuffee (D)	J. W. McDuffee (D)	C. H. Thomas (D)
Mayes	Henry M. Butler (D)	D. C. Hughes (D)	R. W. Lindsey (R)	Gideon Morgan (D)
McClain	Thos. C. Whitson (D)	Thos. C. Whitson (D)	E. L. Green (D)	E. E. Glasco (D)
McCurtain	Wm. H. Harrison (D)	C. M. Anderson (D)	Jas. R. Knight (D)	W. S. Davis (D) Tom G. Taylor (D)
McIntosh	Wm. B. Beck (D)	A. J. Milsap (R)	J. W. Steen (D)	R. H. Berry (D)
Murray	M. Turner (D)	M. Turner (D)	Chas. B. Emanuel (D)	Chas. B. Emanuel (D)
Muskogee	Fred Branson (D) [1] A. J. Snelson (D) [1]	James Knox (R) [2] Edward Merrick (R) [2]	W.C. Jackson (D) [3] W. P. Miller (D) [3]	Wm. O. Carr (D) J. H. Maxey (D) J. E. Wyand (D)
Noble	Chas. A. Fraser (R)	R. F. Howe (R)	E. T. Testerman (R)	E. T. Testerman (R)
Nowata	J. A. Tillotson (D)	J. A. Tillotson (D)	C. L. Miller (D)	W. A. Chase (D)
Okfuskee	Thomas Wortman (D)	Robert J. Dixon (R)	J. J. Roland (D)	George Harvison (D) W. H. Case (D)

First to Fourth Legislatures

County	1907 • 1st	1909 • 2nd	1911 • 3rd	1913 • 4th
Oklahoma	Curtis R. Day (R) C. G. Jones (R) I. M. Putnam (D) A. T. Earley (D)	I. M. Putnam (D) E. L. Dunn (D) C. G. Jones (R) S. W. Murphy (R)	R. L. Peebly (D) Hubert L. Bolen (D) John H. Wright (D) C. H. DeFord (R)	C. H. DeFord (R) Hugh A. Randall (D) John H. Wright (D) Hubert L. Bolen (D) D. B. Welty (D)
Okmulgee	Wm. C. McAdoo (R)	J. H. Lincoln (R)	J. M. Lenox (D)	J. M. Lenox (D)
Osage	John B. Deyerle (D)	Prentiss Price (D)	Charles B. Peters (D)	Charles B. Peters (D) M. B. Prentiss (R)
Ottawa	A. G. Martin (D)	J. F. Tucker (D)	James K. Moore (D)	J. S. Mabon (R)
Pawnee	Wm. Murdock (D) [1]	John Bonar (R) [2]	Ross Brubaker (D) [3]	S. C. Edmister (R)
Payne	P. A. Ballard (D) [1]	C. E Sexton (R) [2]	T. H. Stockton (R) [3]	J. W. Reece (D)
Pittsburg	J. Hendrickson (D) [1] H. McElhaney (D) [1]	H. McElhaney (D) [2] Wm. S. Rogers (D) [2]	H. McElhaney (D) [3] S. F. Whitman (D) [3]	R. I. Bond (D) E. P. Hill (D) S. F. Whitman (D)
Pontotoc	Frank Huddleston (D) [1]	Frank Huddleston (D) [2]	J. P. Crawford (D) [3]	J. P. Crawford (D)
Pottawatomie	Milton Bryan (D) [1] Wm. S. Carson (D) [1] Wm. F. Durham (D) [1]	Milton Bryan (D) [2] Wm. S. Carson (D) [2] Wm. F. Durham (D) [2]	C. F. Barrett (D) [3] Wm. S. Carson (D) [3] B. F. Nesbitt (D) [3]	James T. Farrall (D) Harvey H. Smith (D) H. O. Tener (D)
Pushmataha	Ben T. Williams (D)	Ben T. Williams (D)	H.S.P. Ashby (D)	H.S.P. Ashby (D)
Roger Mills	Jos. L. Paschall (D)	Jos. L. Paschall (D)	Perry Madden (D)	Thomas Joyner (D)
Rogers	J. F. Fandy (D) [1]	C. S. Wortman (D) [2]	Joe Chambers (D) [3]	Archibald Bonds (D)
Seminole	J. B. Chastain (D) [1]	H. M. Tate (R) [2]	E. E. Jayne (D) [3]	W. A. Bishop (D)
Sequoyah	G. W. Allen (D) [1]	Isaac Jacobs (R) [2]	J. W. Breedlove (D) [3]	Wm. L. Curtis (D)
Stephens	W. B. Anthony (D) [1]	W. B. Anthony (D) [2]	W. B. Anthony (D) [3]	O. M. Morris (D)
Texas	E. J. Earle (D)	E. J. Earle (D)	T. O. James (D)	See Cimarron & Texas
Tillman	Henry R. King (D)	Henry R. King (D)	Walter L. Coughlin (D)	Harry B. Cordell (D)
Tulsa	Ciceero L. Holland (D) [1]	F. L. Haynes (D) [2]	J. I. Gillespie (D) [3]	W. B. Williams (D) Frank Z. Curry (D)
Wagoner	A. D. Orcutt (R)	J. P. Calhoun (R)	John S. Moss (D)	John O. Baker (D)
Washington	A. F. Vandeventer (D)	Clint Moore (R)	Lon Fisher (D)	R. F. Stilwell (D)
Washita	David L. Smith (D) [1]	S. C. Burnette (D) [2]	Eckles L. Harris (D) [3]	C. C. Hill (D)
Woods	Wm. T. Abbott (D)	H. T. Parsons (R)	D. S. Woodson (D)	W. H. Olmstead (R)
Woodward	Irving W. Hart (D)	John H. Bridges (R)	E. G. Vosburgh (R)	E. G. Vosburgh (R)

[1, 2, & 3] See Flotorial Districts listed separately on following pages.

Flotorial Districts

Original apportionment of the House of Representatives, as provided by the Constitution, authorized at least one representative for each county. In addition, 14 two-county districts and one tri-county district (known as flotorial districts) were created, each of which was to elect one representative. These multi-county districts were superimposed over the single county districts, and were created to provide for population in excess of the minimum specified in the Constitution. This arrangement continued until 1911 when a reapportionment was made on the basis of the 1910 census.

Counties	First Legislature	Second Legislature
Atoka and Bryan	W. A. Durant (D)	W. A. Durant (D)
Alfalfa and Grant	John R. Evans (R)	Geo. W. Partridge (R)
Caddo, Canadian, and Cleveland	Ben F. Wilson (D)	Ben F. Wilson (D)
Coal and Johnston	C. A. Skeen (D)	John M. Moore (D)
Comanche and Stephens	Amil H. Japp (D)	Amil H. Japp (D)
Craig and Rogers	John T. Ezzard (D)	Peter J. Coyne (D)
Creek and Tulsa	Woodson E. Norvell (D)	J. H. Simmons (R)
Custer and Washita	L. L. Reeves (D)	L. L. Reeves (D)
Garfield and Kingfisher	Eugene Watrous (R)	Eugene Watrous (R)
Haskell and Muskogee	J. B. Crouch (D)	Chas. A. Cook (R)
Hughes and Pittsburg	Ben F. Harrison (D)	Ben F. Harrison (D)
LeFlore and Sequoyah	E. A. Moore (D)	J. J. Sullivan (R)
Lincoln and Pottawatomie	H. G. Stettmund (D)	J. H. Maxey Jr. (D)
Pawnee and Payne	George D. Hudson (D)	E. M. Clark (R)
Pontotoc and Seminole	Edgar S. Ratliff (D)	E. S. Ratliff (D)

Counties	Third Legislature
Atoka and Bryan	W. A. Durant (D)
Alfalfa and Grant	A. J. Renfrow (R)
Caddo, Canadian, and Cleveland	Dan W. Perry (D)
Coal and Johnston	John M. Moore (D)
Comanche and Stephens	J. W. Leftwich (D)
Craig and Rogers	W. L. Jeffords (D)
Creek and Tulsa	W. V. Pryor (D)
Custer and Washita	Geo W. Cornell (D)
Garfield and Kingfisher	Eugene A. Watrous (R)
Haskell and Muskogee	Eugene M. Kerr (D) Jas. A. Cullop (D)
Hughes and Pittsburg	William A. Hammond (D)
LeFlore and Sequoyah	S. J. Folsom (D)
Lincoln and Pottawatomie	J. H. Maxey Jr. (D)
Pawnee and Payne	Ed M. Clark (R)
Pontotoc and Seminole	J. S. Barham (D)

Fifth to Eighth Legislatures

County	1915 • 5th	1917 • 6th	1919 • 7th	1921 • 8th
Speakers	A. McCrory (D)	Paul Nesbitt (D)	Tom C. Waldrep (D)	Geo. B. Schwabe (R)
Adair	Thos. J. Welch (D)	D. B. Collums (D)	D. B. Collums (D)	W. A. Scofield (R)
Alfalfa	J. C. Smith (R)	J. C. Smith (R)	W. S. David (R)	Leslie E. Salter (R)
Atoka		J. A. Thurmond (D)	Wm. Gill (D)	F. C. Johnson (D)
Beaver/Harper	Howard M. Drake (R)	E. Lee Adams (D)	J. W. Steffen (R)	J. W. Steffen (R)
Beckham	Thos. H. McElmore (S)	A. Mansur (D)	W. A. Hornbeck (D)	W. A. Hornbeck (D)
Blaine	L. A. Everhart (R)	L. A. Everhart (R)	L. A. Everhart (R)	L. A. Everhart (R)
Bryan	W. A. Durant (D) G. A. Ramsey (D)	W. A. Durant (D) Porter Newman (D)	Porter Newman (D) J. B. Smith (D)	Porter Newman (D) J. B. Smith (D)
Caddo	Jos. A. Baker (D) Frank Carpenter (D)	S. C. Kelly (D) Newt Dickinson (D)	J. W. Hollarn (R) J. E. Thirsk (R)	T. F. Cummings (R) T. C. Ottinger (R)
Canadian	T. F. Hensley (D)	Jack Barker (D) T. F. Hensley (D)	Jack Barker (D) J. L. Trevathan (R)	J. L. Trevathan (R)
Carter	Kelly Brown (D)	Roy Shores (D) Thad Baker (D)	D. S. Hoover (D) J. L. Galt (D)	D. S. Hoover (D)
Cherokee	J. D. Cox (D)	Roy C. Hinds (D)	S. M. Redburn (R)	Bruce L. Keenan (R)
Choctaw	Thos. W. Hunter (D) W. L. Garner (D)	R. K. Warren (D)	D. A. Stovall (D)	D. A. Stovall (D)
Cimarron/Texas	Chas. Williams (D)	M. W. Pugh (D)	S. L. Portwood (D)	John Q. Denney (R)
Cleveland	H. O. Miller (D)	H. O. Miller (D)	J. B. Phillips (D)	Ralph C. Hardie (R)
Coal	Wilburn Cartwright (D)	Wilburn Cartwright (D)	F. Brinkworth (D)	Austin H. Rice (R)
Comanche			R. B. Thomas (D)	Thornton Clark (R)
Comanche/Cotton	Wm. T. Powell (D) Lewis Hunter (D)	Lewis Hunter (D) Fletcher Riley (D) Wm. T. Powell (D)	J. B. McTaggart (D)	
Cotton			Lon Morris (D)	Leroy Elmore (D)
Craig	Bryant Cash (D)	J. H. Butler (R)	G. R. Hill (D)	P. Z. Newman (R)
Creek	Wm. J. Ladd (R)	J. M. Morgan (D) W. L. Cheatham (D)	J. M. Morgan (D) W. L. Cheatham (D)	Eli L. Admire (R)
Custer	John A. Simpson (D)	E. J. Meacham (D) O. E. Houston (D)	E. A. Olmstead (R) W. D. Crane (R)	W. D. Crane (R)
Delaware	Lee Howe (D)	John H. Gibson (D)	John H. Gibson (D)	J. P. Butler (R)
Dewey	D. C. Kirkpatrick (S)	M. L. Jones (D)	G. W. Trimble (D)	Otto Smith (R)
Ellis	C. H. Holmes (R)	Bert E. Hill (R)	Bert E. Hill (R)	G. E. Davison (R)
Garfield	Marvin M. McCord (R) C. C. Childers (D)	J. A. Eakins (R) J. B. Campbell (R)	H. O. Glasser (R) J. B. Campbell (R)	L. G. Gossett (R) J. B. Campbell (R)
Garvin	Cicero I. Murray (D) L. D. Abney (D)	Alfred Stevenson (D) E. O. Northcutt (D)	Alfred Stevenson (D)	J. S. Garrison (D)
Grady	Bert Jackson (D) L. N. Barbee (D)	Bert Jackson (D) Ed Sheegog (D)	Bert Jackson (D) M. I. Stokes (D)	M. B. Louthan (D) A. L. Davis (D)
Grant	J. E. Lemon (D)	T. E. Beck (R)	T. E. Beck (R)	T. E. Beck (R)
Greer	J. O. McCollister (D)	J. O. McCollister (D)	H. D. Henry (D)	J. H. Simpson (D)

Fifth to Eighth Legislatures

County	1915 • 5th	1917 • 6th	1919 • 7th	1921 • 8th
Harmon	H. Treadway (D)	H. Treadway (D)	L. A. Pearson (D)	L. A. Pearson (D)
Harper	See "Beaver & Harper" (on previous page)			
Haskell	A. H. Huggins (D)	J. L. Hendrickson (D)	A. A. Webb (D)	J. H. Ogle (R)
Hughes	B. F. Harrison (D)	H. A. Hicks (D) Silas M. Shirley (D)	B. F. Harrison (D) Tom Anglin (D)	B. F. Harrison (D)
Jackson	R. J. Morgan (D)	Everett Petry (D) R. J. Morgan (D)	Edwin Dabney (D) W. D. Ballard (D)	Edwin Dabney (D)
Jefferson	A. McCrory (D)	G. M. Bond (D)	C. S. Storms (D)	J. M. Robberson (D)
Johnston	J. J. Clark (D)	B. N. Hultzman (D)	S. E. Cummings (D)	Hugh C. Jones (D)
Kay	C. L. Pinkham (D) H. W. Headley (R)	H. W. Headley (R) S. M. Elder (R)	S. M. Elder (R)	F. A. Heberling (R)
Kingfisher	J. A. Marsh (R)	J. A. Marsh (R)	W. P. Kimerer (R)	W. P. Kimerer (R)
Kiowa	R. R. Fitzgerald (D) N. D. Pritchett (S)	R. R. Fitzgerald (D) W. G. Woodard (D)	R. R. Fitzgerald (D) W. G. Woodard (D)	G. E. Mitchell (R) S. D. Bailey (R)
Latimer	Cliff V. Peery (D)	L. P. Bobo (D)	L. P. Bobo (D)	J. A. Smallwood (R)
LeFlore	T. G. McMahan (D) G. L. Council (D)	Tom W. Neal (D) J. B. Harper (D)	J. B. Harper (D) M. W. Romine (D)	S. A. Neely (D) J. T. White (R)
Lincoln	Jake Zabloudil (R) Ed G. Keegan (R)	W. F. Pardoe (R) Ed G. Keegan (R)	B. Taylor (R) Ed. B. Ambler (R)	B. Taylor (R) M. M. Watson (R)
Logan	Amos A. Ewing (R) O. B. Acton (R)	Amos A. Ewing (R) O. B. Acton (R)	Amos A. Ewing (R) John O'Neill (D)	E. G. Sharp (R) William Dodd (R)
Love	Asa E. Walden (D)	Asa E. Walden (D)	Asa E. Walden (D)	J. C. Graham (D)
McClain	E. E. Glasco (D)	G. H. A. Thomas (D)	E. E. Glasco (D)	M. F. Gibbons (D)
McCurtain	Tom G. Taylor (D)	J. E. Rowland (D)	John W. Schott (D)	J. Dyer Jr. (D)
McIntosh	W. M. Duffy (D)	R. H. Berry (D) S. S. Mayfield (D)	W. M. Duffy (D)	Chas. Whitaker (D)
Major	C. H. Ingham (S)	S. J. Bardsley (R)	J. R. Haley (R)	Roy V. Harp (R)
Marshall	O. G. Rollins (D)	S. J. Wheeler (D)	Syd J. Wheeler (D)	Marvin F. Shilling (D)
Mayes	Johnson Crawford (D)	D. C. Hughes (D)	Gideon Morgan (D)	W. A. Crockett (R)
Murray	George W. Pullen (D)	Jas. Draughon (D)	H. W. Broadbent (D)	Jess L. Pullen (D)
Muskogee	N. B. Maxey (D) R. L. Disney (D) Walter Eaton (D)	R. L. Disney (D) Robt. E. West (D) L. E. Neff (D)	W. E. Disney (D) Robt. E. West (D) L. E. Neff (D)	W. E. Disney (D) W. P. Miller (D) J. F. Strayhorn (D)
Noble	E. T. Testerman (R)	Roy Harvey (R)	Roy Harvey (R)	H. E. Keim (R)
Nowata	Eldon E. Sams (R)	A. R. Garrett (R)	Geo. B. Schwabe (R)	Geo. B. Schwabe (R)
Okfuskee	W. H. Berry (D)	W. N. Barry (D)	W. N. Barry (D)	T. W. Harman (R)
Oklahoma	J. T. Dickerson (R) R. L. Peebly (D) John H. Wright (D) Jesse B. Norton (R) James A. Young (D)	I. L. Harris (R) S. S. Butterfield (D) Rollin E. Gish (D) W. W. Robertson (D) Tom Dolan (D)	I. L. Harris (R) S. S. Butterfield (D) Allen Street (D) W. W. Robertson (D) Chas. H. Ruth (D)	W. W. Robertson (D) John T. Jerkins (D) John F. Martin (D) T. F. Gorman (D) I. L. Harris (R)
Okmulgee	S. L. Johnson (D)	H. R. Christopher (D) Bert C. Hodges (D)	Bert C. Hodges (D)	Clarence L. Tylee (R)

Fifth to Eighth Legislatures

County	1915 • 5th	1917 • 6th	1919 • 7th	1921 • 8th
Osage	Loris E. Bryant (D)	L. A. Wismeyer (R)	L. A. Wismeyer (R)	L. A. Wismeyer (R)
Ottawa	James K. Moore (D)	John N. Scott (D)	J. S. Mabon (R)	Jas. Miller (R)
Pawnee	G. W. Goodwin (D)	Millard F. Grubb (R)	Millard F. Grubb (R)	W. S. Caldwell (R)
Payne	J. L. McKeown (D)	A. J. Hartenbower (D) Chas. C. Platt (R)	Chas. C. Platt (R) J. F. Vaughan (R)	Chas. C. Platt (R)
Pittsburg	Paul Nesbitt (D) T. G. Wilkes (D) Tom G. Haile (D)	S. J. Fitzgerald (D) Paul Nesbitt (D) Tom G. Haile (D)	Paul Nesbitt (D) S. Z. Fitzgerald (D) T. W. Smith (D)	Chas. S. Brice (D) R. H. Matthews (R)
Pontotoc	Sam H. Hargis (D)	J. W. Vaden (D) Robt. Wimbish (D)	W. H. Ebey (D) Date Crawford (D)	W. O. Pratt (D)
Pottawatomie	Tom C. Waldrep (D) R. R. Hendon (D) W. K. Dunn (D)	Tom C. Waldrep (D) N. A. J. Ticer (D) W. L. Chapman (D)	Tom C. Waldrep (D) N. A. J. Ticer (D)	C. A. Knight (D) W. S. Pendently (D)
Pushmataha	J. H. Reigner (D)	C. A. Welch (D)	G. T. Johnson (D)	Victor M. Locke Jr. (R)
Roger Mills	S. W. Hill (S)	J. T. Nicholson (D)	J. T. Nicholson (D)	B. McColgin, Mrs. (R)
Rogers	A. E. Ball (D)	E. E. Woods (R)	H. T. Kight (D)	Harry Jennings (R)
Seminole	Luther Harrison (D)	A. S. Norvell (D) M. M. Turlington (D)	W. W. Pryor (D)	D. O. Jennings (R)
Sequoyah	J. N. Davis (D)	C. B. Johnson (D) J. V. Blackard Jr. (D)	J. H. Dodson (D) L. C. McNabb (D)	R. A. Ballance (R)
Stephens	Henry W. Sitton (D) J. P. Speer (D)	J. P. Speer (D)	L. Akers (D)	James C. Nance (D)
Texas	See "Cimarron/Texas"			
Tillman	A. North (D)	Squire Humble (D)	J. E. Williams (D)	H. R. King (D)
Tulsa	Jas. H. Sykes (D) Wash Hudson (D)	Glenn Condon (R) Harry H. Rogers (R)	W. V. Biddison (D) Joe W. Kenton (D)	Bailey E. Bell (R) Remington Rogers (R)
Wagoner	Wm. E. Long (D)	P. A. Fox (D) J. C. Hamilton (D)	T. A. Parkinson (D)	W. T. Drake (R)
Washington	M. W. Bovee (D)	A. E. Craver (R)	A. E. Craver (R)	A. E. Craver (R)
Washita	C. C. Hill (D)	W. T. Graves (D) I. B. Hurst (D)	W. T. Graves (D) J. H. Hay (D)	W. T. Graves (D)
Woods	W. H. Olmstead (R)	W. H. Olmstead (R)	Marion Clothier (R)	E. A. Herod (R)
Woodward	E. O. McCance (D)	B. H. Beatte (D)	Jerry Coover (R)	Jerry Coover (R)

Ninth to Twelfth Legislatures

County	1923 • 9th	1925 • 10th	1927 • 11th	1929 • 12th
Speakers	Murray Gibbons (D) W. D. McBee (D) elected Speaker for Special Session, 1923–24.	J.B. Harper (D)	D.A. Stovall (D) E. P. Hill (D) served as Speaker of Special Session, Dec. 6, 1927.	James Nance (D) Allen Street (D) was the first Speaker for this session. He resigned Jan. 8, 1929 and was replaced by Nance.
Adair	K. G. Comfort (D)	J. D. Bouyear (R)	Frank C. Adair (D)	John Bunch (R)
Alfalfa	Leslie E. Salter (R)	O. W. T. Henderson (D)	O. W. T. Henderson (D)	E. D. Immell (R)

Ninth to Twelfth Legislatures

County	1923 • 9th	1925 • 10th	1927 • 11th	1929 • 12th
Atoka	H. G. Eastridge (D)	P. R. Crowley (D)	P. R. Crowley (D)	Ferman Phillips (D)
Beaver/Harper	Leslie I. Ray (R)	Roy O. Coppock (R)	C. E. Baggerly (D)	R. O. Allen (R)
Beckham	Ira M. Finley (D)	Ira M. Finley (D)	Frank Carmichael (D)	Frank Carmichael (D)
Blaine	L. A. Everhart (R)	Elias Smith (D)	Elias Smith (D)	Elmer L. Kenison (R)
Bryan	E. P. White (D) O. E. Thornley (D)	O. E. Thornley (D) E. P. White (D)	A. N. Leecraft (D) J. B. Smith (D)	A. N. Leecraft (D) J. B. Smith (D)
Caddo	J. L. Montgomery (D) F. B. Jones (D)	Harry Jolly (D) Roy F. Hangar (R)	Harry Jolly (D) Lewis G. Ware (R)	W. L. Mauk (D)
Canadian	Price Thompson (D)	Price Thompson (D)	J. B. Deardorff (D)	Herman Dittmer (R)
Carter	Guy F. Sigler (D) T. J. Pollock (D)	J. W. Murphy (D) Lloyd Noble (R)	Earl A. Brown (D) Arleigh David (D)	Earl A. Brown (D) Louis A. Fischl (D)
Cherokee	J. D. Gulager (D)	J. A. Morgan (R)	Chas. L. Rogers (D)	Bruce L. Keenan (R)
Choctaw	D. A. Stovall (D)	D. A. Stovall (D)	D. A. Stovall (D) O. A. Brewer (D)	D. A. Stovall (D) R. H. Stanley (D)
Cimarron & Texas	I. M. Lightner (D)	Wm. A. Strong (D)	Frank A. Sewell (D)	C. W. Ferguson (R)
Cleveland	J. B. Phillips (D)	E. V. George (D)	C. T. Lane (D)	Richard H. Cloyd (D)
Coal	W.H. Thornsbrough (D)	J. R. Hickman (D)	C. Leslie Cardwell (D)	Walter E. Jacobs (D)
Comanche	L. E. Goodrich (D) [1]	A. M. Reinwand (D) H. P. Wettengel (D)	J. A. Johnson (D)	Owen Black (D)
Cotton	Fred Hansen (D)	J. M. Hooper (D)	James C. Nance (D)	James C. Nance (D)
Craig	Joe L. Williams (D)	O. E. Odell (D)	Bryant Cash (D)	Clay M. Roper (D)
Creek	Lulu D. Anderson (D) W. I. Cunningham (D) C. T. Hutson (D) [2]	W. I. Cunningham (D) Ida L. Robertson (D) Edward F. White (R)	W. G. Beatty (D) Sebe A. Christian (D) J. A. Watson (D)	B. E. Drake (R) H. G. Matherly (R) Grady Lewis (R)
Custer	J. W. Bremer (D)	Thos. P. Stone (D)	Thos. P. Stone (D)	E. E. Fry (R)
Delaware	A. V. Harlin (D) [3]	Isaiah H. Long (R)	James P. Butler (R)	James P. Butler (R)
Dewey	M. R. Payne (D)	C. R. Flint (R)	V. D. McArthur (D)	Fred Langley (R)
Ellis	E. M. Beum (D)	G. E. Davison (R)	George H. Baldwin (D)	Harry H. Dunning (R)
Garfield	Wm. J. Otjen (R) V. L. Headrick (R)	Wm. J. Ryan (D) O. R. Miller (R)	Arthur J. Strauss (R) J. B. Campbell (R)	Geo. A. Hutchinson (R) J. B. Campbell (R)
Garvin	J. M. Thompson (D)	J. M. Thompson (D)	J. M. Thompson (D) Homer Paul (D)	Homer Paul (D) W. B. Gibson (D)
Grady	A. L. Davis (D) Gordon Gray (D)	A. L. Davis (D) D. C. Roberts Jr. (D)	David C. Hybarger (D) Frank Manning (D)	Geo. W. Thomas (R)
Grant	L. E. Watkins (D)	Wm. A. Thornhill (R)	T. E. Beck (R)	C. E. Herschberger (R)
Greer	J. G. H. Windle (D)	J. G. H. Windle (D)	J. G. H. Windle (D)	Will C. Jones (D)
Harmon	H. Treadway (D)	E. C. Abernathy (D)	R. B. Bryant (D)	S. W. Carmack (D)
Harper	See Beaver & Harper	See Beaver & Harper	See Beaver & Harper	See Beaver & Harper
Haskell	Newt Sanders (D)	Newt Sanders (D)	O. P. Nash (D)	Ben W. Belew (D)
Hughes	C. W. Miller (D) C. T. Edwards (D)	N. J. Johnson (D)	W. F. Gilmer (D)	Ralph L. Busey (D)
Jackson	L. R. Lowry (D)	A. E. Bilbrey (D)	A. E. Bilbrey (D)	L. R. Lowry (D)

Ninth to Twelfth Legislatures

County	1923 • 9th	1925 • 10th	1927 • 11th	1929 • 12th
Jefferson	A. C. Burger (D)	Guy Green (D)	J. T. Daniel (D)	J. T. Daniel (D)
Johnston	John F. Garner (D)	John F. Garner (D)	Kenneth Clark (D)	J. R. Cartwright (D)
Kay	Walter H. Franks (D) John M. Bell (D)	G. A. Chappell (R) Joe W. Morris (R)	G. A. Chappell (R) John M. Bell (D)	G. A. Chappell (R)
Kingfisher	Henry L. Cloud (R)	Robt. McClintock (R)	Robt. McClintock (R)	Robt. McClintock (R)
Kiowa	James R. Tolbert (D)	C. F. Fawks Jr. (D)	J. E. Watson (D)	Raymond Harvey (D)
Latimer	J. W. Callahan (D)	E. M. Cooper (D)	Claud Briggs (D)	Claud Briggs (D)
LeFlore	Burton Kidd (D) J. B. Harper (D)	Burton Kidd (D) J. B. Harper (D)	F. W. Bird (D) John J. Thomas (D)	James Babb (D) Burton Kidd (D)
Lincoln	B. Taylor (R) M. M. Watson (R)	B. Taylor (R) M. M. Watson (R)	B. Taylor (R) J. B. Pomeroy (R)	M. M. Watson (R)
Logan	O. B. Acton (R)	O. B. Acton (R)	O. B. Acton (R)	J. H. Farr (R) V. G. Houston (R)
Love	J. Woody Dixon (D)	J. Woody Dixon (D)	J. Woody Dixon (D)	J. Woody Dixon (D)
McClain	M. F. Gibbons (D) [2]	C. C. Hester (D)	J. Nealy Forehand (D)	C. C. Hester (D)
McCurtain	Paul Stewart (D) James Dyer (D)	Paul C. Thorn (D) Paul Stewart (D)	E. E. Cochran (D) James Dyer (D)	John Head (D) James Dyer (D)
McIntosh	E. F. Saltsman (D) D. A. Brumley (D)	L. D. Ogden (D)	L. D. Ogden (D)	Joe M. Whitaker (D)
Major	John N. Voorhees (R)	John N. Voorhees (R)	John N. Voorhees (R)	Joe Sherman (R)
Marshall	D. T. Wooten (D)	David L. Faulk (D)	David L. Faulk (D)	David L. Faulk (D)
Mayes	J. C. Lindsey (D)	Fred S. Lee (D)	A. Lee Battenfield (D)	Babe Howard (D)
Murray	Jess L. Pullen (D)	H. W. Broadbent (D)	Oscar K. Lowrance (D)	Oscar K. Lowrance (D)
Muskogee	W. E. Disney (D) Albert K. Berry (D) W. P. Miller (D) [2]	Tom B. O'Bryan (D) J. F. Strayhorn (D) F. L. Walton (D)	Tom B. O'Bryan (D) Albert K. Berry (D) Charles A. Moon (D)	W. H. Harrower (D) Charles A. Moon (D) Q. B. Boydstun (D)
Noble	R. F. Howe (R)	R. F. Howe (R)	W. R. Fry (R)	A. Duff Tillery (D)
Nowata	C. H. Baskin (D) [2]	W. T. Bluejacket (R)	James Nairn (D)	Eldon E. Sams (R)
Okfuskee	T. H. Wren (D) W. H. Case (D)	T. H. Wren (D)	Joe L. Dukes (D)	W. N. Barry (D)
Oklahoma	W. S. Burleson (D) Anna Laskey (D) Allen Street (D) W. W. Robertson (D) Joe O'Brien (D) [2] R. A. Singletary (D)	Henry L. Cloud (R) Anna Laskey (D) Allen Street (D) H. S. Caldwell (R) Robt. C. Graham (D) R. A. Singletary (D)	C. R. Reeves (D) Anna Laskey (D) R. A. Billups Jr. (D) Ben F. Davis (D) Robt. C. Graham (D) R. A. Singletary (D)	Mrs. Elma Eylar (R) Wm. P. Hoover (R) Allen Street (D) Jerry R. Marker (R) Robt. C. Graham (D)
Okmulgee	A. H. Culp (D) Joseph P. Rossiter (D) Chas. D. Lewis (D)	S. M. Hufstedler (D) David M. Logan (D) Chas. D. Lewis (D)	Tom Payne (D) David M. Logan (D) Virgil E. Riddle (D)	David M. Logan (D) W. O. McAdoo (R)
Osage	Richard Elam (D) Marshall L. Smith (D)	H. M. Curnutt (D) Frank V. Shaw (D)	Martin C. Fraley (D) Clarence Lohman (D)	A. S. Perryman (R) W. R. Mitchell (R)
Ottawa	J. S. Mabon (R) G.W. Moothart (D)	Perry Porter (D) R. W. Skinner (D)	Perry Porter (D) R. W. Skinner (D)	R. W. Skinner (D) Ralph M. Chambers (D)
Pawnee	E. M. Funkhouser(D)	W. S. Caldwell (R)	C. D. Webber (R)	C. D. Webber (R)

Ninth to Twelfth Legislatures

County	1923 • 9th	1925 • 10th	1927 • 11th	1929 • 12th
Payne	Edith Mitchell (D)	Geo. A. Hoke (D)	Guy L. McLaury (D) J. W. Reece (D)	Frank C. Orner (R) B. H. Schiegel (R)
Pittsburg	T. D. Taylor (D) Chas. S. Brice (D) Frank Watson (D)	E. P. Hill (D) Fletcher Davis (D) Pres S. Lester (D)	E. P. Hill (D) D. L. Roe (D)	O. H. Whitt (D) D. L. Roe (D)
Pontotoc	Fred F. Brydia (D)	Otto Strickland (D) Will H. Thompson (D)	W. H. Ebey (D) Otto Strickland (D)	Robt. J. Wimbish (D)
Pottawatomie	L. C. Watson (D) N. A. J. Ticer (D)	Gladys Whittett (D) M. M. Henderson (D) Sam F. Bailey (D)	Joe B. Cobb (D) F. H. Reily (D)	J. Knox Byrum (D) Geo. W. Noble (R)
Pushmataha	G. T. Johnson (D)	L. W. Weaver (D)	Tom Johnson (D)	Clark Wasson (R)
Roger Mills	W. A. Adams (D)	John Simpler (D)	W. R. Trent (R)	W. R. Trent (R)
Rogers	Wayne W. Bayless (D)	E. H. Lightner (D)	H. Tom Kight (D)	H. Tom Kight (D)
Seminole	Wilbur F. Varnum (D)	Bart Aldridge (D)	Bart Aldridge (D)	J. A. Patterson (R)
Sequoyah	J. L. Watson (D)	T. M. McCombs (D) W. A. Carlile (D)	T. M. McCombs (D)	C. H. Orendorff (D)
Stephens	W. D. McBee (D) James C. Nance (D) [2]	P. D. Sullivan (D)	P. D. Sullivan (D)	Cham Jones (D)
Texas	See Cimarron & Texas			
Tillman	H. R. King (D)	H. R. King (D)	R. L. Christian (D)	H. R. King (D)
Tulsa	W. Warren Ferrell (D) J. W. Simpson (D) Frank M. Boyer (D) John H. Miller (D) G. S. Long (D) [2]	John H. Miller (D) Phillip J. Kramer (D) Thos. I. Munroe (D) Frank M. Boyer (D) O. H. Terwilleger (R)	L. O. Maxwell (R) O. O. Owens (R) G. C. Thomas (R) D. A. Wilson (R) Hugh Webster (R)	L. O. Maxwell (R) D. A. Wilson (R) Chas. B. Parker (R) O. O. Owens (R) Clyde L. Sears (R) Horace J. Newberry (R)
Wagoner	W. S. Vernon (D)	Horace S. Foster (D)	Horace S. Foster (D)	Bob Wagner (D)
Washington	G. I. Van Dall (D)	Wm. M. Rupard (D) A. C. Easter (R)	A. C. Easter (R)	W. B. Allen (R)
Washita	Ed W. Hines (D)	Ed W. Hines (D)	Ed W. Hines (D)	Ed W. Hines (D)
Woods	Marion Clothier (R)	Marion Clothier (R)	E. W. Snoddy (R)	E. W. Snoddy (R)
Woodward	Jerry Coover (R)	Jerry Coover (R)	Willis James (D)	Willis C. Odell (R)

[1] Resigned. J. E. Thomas (D) elected at Special Election, Jan. 26, 1924 to fill unexpired term.
[2] Resigned. No interim successor elected.
[3] Resigned. W. D. Gibson (D) elected at Special Election, Jan. 29, 1923 to fill unexpired term.

Thirteenth to Sixteenth Legislatures

County	1931 • 13th	1933 • 14th	1935 • 15th	1937 • 16th
Speakers	Carlton Weaver (D)	Tom Anglin (D)	Leon C. Phillips (D)	J. T. Daniel (D)
Adair	F. C. Adair (D)	D. W. Bushyhead (D)	Howard Morton (R)	E. B. Arnold (D)
Alfalfa	E. D. Immell (R)	D. S. Collins (D)	Webster Wilder Jr. (R)	Webster Wilder Jr. (R)
Atoka	Ferman Phillips (D)	Ferman Phillips (D)	Rowe Cook (D)	Ira Stephenson (D)
Beaver		Thomas Z. Wright (R)	Thomas Z. Wright (R)	Floyd Harrington (D)

Thirteenth to Sixteenth Legislatures

County	1931 • 13th	1933 • 14th	1935 • 15th	1937 • 16th
Beaver/Harper	W. D. Batman (D)			
Beckham	A. D. Jones (D)	A. D. Jones (D)	R. W. Brewer (D) Cecil A. Myers (D)	R. W. Brewer (D)
Blaine	Elmer L. Kenison (R)	John R. Hankla (D)	John R. Hankla (D)	E. Blumhagen (D)
Bryan	A. N. Leecraft (D) E. O. White (D)	A. N. Leecraft (D) Sam Sullivan (D)	O. K. Campbell (D) Sam Sullivan (D)	A. N. Leecraft (D) Ceph Shoemake (D)
Caddo	W. L. Mauk (D)	J. H. Mallory (D) G. H. Wingo (D)	W. L. Mauk (D) G. H. Wingo (D)	J. Kenneth Hogue (D) D. L. Kelly (D)
Canadian	Herbert M. Palmer (D)	Herbert M. Palmer (D)	Ellis V. Gregory (D)	Ellis V. Gregory (D)
Carter	Louis A. Fischl (D) Charles P. Jones (D)	Arthur Grunert (D) Bob Cavins (D)	Arleigh Davis (D) Alvin Bruce (D)	Charles P. Jones (D) Wilson Wallace (D)
Cherokee	Iredelle Hinds (D)	Iredelle Hinds (D)	Percy Wyly II, (D)	Floyd H. Norris (D)
Choctaw	R. H. Stanley (D)	T. J. Hutchings (D)	Lucien C. Spear (D)	Lucien C. Spear (D)
Cimarron		Julius W. Cox (D)	Julius W. Cox (D)	Frank Conner (D)
Cimarron/Texas	Charles Williams (D)			
Cleveland	Richard H. Cloyd (D)	Richard H. Cloyd (D)	Ben Huey (D)	Ben Huey (D)
Coal	Ed King (D)	Ed King (D)	Dale Brown (D)	Dale Brown (D)
Comanche	A. M. Reinwand (D)	Merton Munson (D) J. A. Johnson (D)	Merton Munson (D) J. A. Johnson (D)	Roy B. Hooper (D) Ted Fraser (D)
Cotton	J. C. Nance (D)	Bob Mooney (D)	Bob Mooney (D)	Charles Flanagan (D)
Craig	S. F. Parks (D)	S. F. Parks (D)	Frank Bailey (D)	Francis Goodpaster (D)
Creek	Jimmie Wilson (D) Don W. Walker (D) D. A. McDougal (D)	Henry Clay King (D) E. Landingham (D) J. A. Watson (D)	Henry Clay King (D) Homer O'Dell (D) Joe Brewster (D)	Roy H. Page (D) Homer O'Dell (D) Wm. L. Cheatham (D)
Custer	Carl W. Remund (D)	Carl W. Remund (D)	W. R. Dunn (D)	W. R. Dunn (D)
Delaware	Claude Keith (D)	L. V. Beaman (D)	L. V. Beaman (D)	Lee Howe (D)
Dewey	Orley Hart (D)	Fred N. Burnham (D)	Tupper Jones (D)	Tupper Jones (D)
Ellis	George H. Baldwin (D)	H. R. Allen (R)	Bert Larason (D)	Bert Larason (D)
Garfield	Geo. A. Hutchinson (R) C. W. Burton (R)	T. W. Eason (D) F. B. O'Neill (R)	T. W. Eason (D) F. B. O'Neill (R)	Paul Edwards (R) Floyd E. Carrier (R)
Garvin	Homer Paul (D)	Mason Hart (D) W. M. Lindsey (D)	Sam J. Goodwin (D) Harold Freeman (D)	Harold Freeman (D) E. W. Foley (D)
Grady	Sidney L. Chapman (D)	David C. Roberts (D) Sam E. Neill (D)	David C. Roberts (D) J. D. Carmichael (D)	David C. Roberts (D) J. D. Carmichael (D) Dutch Hill (D)
Grant	W. A. Thornhill (R)	Ed Brazell (D)	J. W. McCollom (D)	George Streets (D)
Greer	W. W. Paxton (D)	W. W. Paxton (D)	Marvin Byrom (D)	H. W. Worthington (D)
Harmon	Oscar H. Abernethy (D)	Oscar H. Abernethy (D)	Oscar H. Abernethy (D)	Elmer Willingham (D)
Harper	See "Beaver/Harper"	M. W. Wilmont (R)	George Pauls (D)	George Pauls (D)
Haskell	Nat Henderson (D)	Nat Henderson (D)	D. C. Cantrell (D)	D. C. Cantrell (D)
Hughes	Robert Stilwell (D)	Tom Anglin (D) Herman Darks (D)	O. S. Huser (D)	George W. Oliphant (D)

Thirteenth to Sixteenth Legislatures

County	1931 • 13th	1933 • 14th	1935 • 15th	1937 • 16th
Jackson	Wm. E. Allen (D)	Burr Speck (D) Jack Sutherland (D)	Burr Speck (D)	Burr Speck (D) Drew B. Thomas (D)
Jefferson	J. T. Daniel (D)	J. T. Daniel (D)	G. J. Williams (D)	J. T. Daniel (D)
Johnston	J. R. Cartwright (D)	Clarence Rawls (D)	Clarence Rawls (D)	Ed Gill (D)
Kay	L. A. Shaw (R)	Andrew Fraley (D) William H. Cline (D)	Walter M. Doggett (D) Ralph C. Haynes (D)	H. N. Andrews (D) Ralph C. Haynes (D)
Kingfisher	Robert McClintock (R)	Arthur W. Ulmark (D)	Arthur W. Ulmark (D)	Elbert S. Stoner (D)
Kiowa	R. L. Rickerd (D)	Bob Fitzgerald (D)	Ed. E. Corson (D)	F. C. Gillespie Jr. (D)
Latimer	Carlton Weaver (D)	R. C. Garland (D)	H. O. Boggs (D)	J. A. Harwell (D)
LeFlore	James Babb (D) John J. Thomas (D)	M. A. Stewart (D) James Babb (D)	Roy Coleman (D) B. J. Traw (D)	Earl F. Johnson (D) B. J. Traw (D)
Lincoln	Robert Biles (D)	J. I. Gibson (D)	Lester D. Hoyt (D) Darwin Frayer (D)	Lester D. Hoyt (D)
Logan	Ralph M. Davis (D)	Ralph M. Davis (D) [1]	C. W. Allen (D)	C. W. Allen (D)
Love	John Steele Batson (D)	John Steele Batson (D)	Virgil L. Stokes (D)	Virgil L. Stokes (D)
McClain	Austin Beaver (D)	Austin Beaver (D)	Louie W. Beck (D)	James C. Nance (D)
McCurtain	R. C. Blocker (D) G. B. Massey (D)	R. C. Blocker (D) G. B. Massey (D)	Ira Rone (D) J. A. Standridge (D)	Bascom Coker (D) Carl Dees (D)
McIntosh	Joe M. Whitaker (D)	Dyton Bennett (D)	Carl Twidwell (D)	Milam M. King (D)
Major	J. C. Major (D)	L. D. Armstrong (I)	L. D. Armstrong (I)	J. C. Major (D) [4]
Marshall	D. L. Faulk (D)	Rex Strickland (D)	Don Welch (D)	Don Welch (D)
Mayes	Ernest R. Brown (D)	D. C. Hughes (D)	D. E. Martin (D)	C. J. Howard (D)
Murray	Luther E. Green (D)	Oscar K. Lowrance (D)	Ewing C. Sadler (D)	Malcolm Baucum (D)
Muskogee	Rex C. Robertson (D) Benj. Martin (D) J. M. Brooks (D)	Bower Broaddus (D) Benj. Martin (D) F. N. Shoemake (D)	Herbert L. Branan (D) Murrell H. Thornton (D) F. N. Shoemake (D)	Herbert L. Branan (D) Murrell H. Thornton (D) F. N. Shoemake (D)
Noble	Walter D. Sullins (D)	A. Duff Tillery (D) [2]	Thos. O. Munger (D)	Thos. O. Munger (D)
Nowata	F. D. Stevick (R)	Chas. A. Whitford (D)	Penn Couch (D)	Penn Couch (D)
Okfuskee	W. N. Barry (D)	Leon C. Phillips (D) T. H. Ottesen (D)	Leon C. Phillips (D)	Leon C. Phillips (D)
Oklahoma	Sloan Childers (D) Ira M. Finley (D) Allen Street (D) Clay M. Roper (D) Bob Graham (D)	Leslie Connor (D) Bryan Billings (D) Ben F. Ellis (D) William O. Coe (D) Bob Graham (D) Geo. H. Copeland (D) W. J. Marshall (D)	C. W. Schwoerke (D) Bryan Billings (D) Ben F. Ellis (D) William O. Coe (D) LaVerne Carleton (D) Chester A. Keys (D) Murray F. Gibbons (D)	C. W. Schwoerke (D) Bryan Billings (D) Ben F. Ellis (D) William O. Coe (D) LaVerne Carleton (D) B. B. Kerr (D) Murray F. Gibbons (D)
Okmulgee	David M. Logan (D) W. J. Peterson (D)	Dan C. Kenan (D) James M. Hays (D) Wilbur L. Morse (D)	W. A. Barnett (D) W. J. Peterson (D) Wilbur L. Morse (D)	S. E. Hammond (D) W. J. Peterson (D) [5] J. Harry Swan (D)
Osage	H. M. Curnutt (D) Martin C. Fraley (D)	G. B. Sturgell (D) Walter B. Johnson (D)	Harry G. Hunt (D) Walter Johnson (D)	Harry G. Hunt (D) Frank Mahan (D)
Ottawa	R. W. Skinner (D) C. A. Douthat (D)	Jesse A. Harp (D) C. A. Douthat (D)	R. W. Skinner (D) William E. Poteet (D)	Jesse A. Harp (D) E. E. Shipley (D)
Pawnee	J. D. Turner (D)	J. D. Turner (D)	Emerson R. Phillips (R)	Noel Duncan (D)

Thirteenth to Sixteenth Legislatures

County	1931 • 13th	1933 • 14th	1935 • 15th	1937 • 16th
Payne	J. T. Gray (D)	J. T. Gray (D)	V. A. Doty (R) Geo. H. David [3]	Elbert R. Weaver (D)
Pittsburg	C. M. Surry (D) W. E. Hailey (D)	M. L. Misenheimer (D) Tom G. Haile (D) H. M. McElhaney (D)	W. B. McAlester (D) George H. Hunt (D) O. H. Whitt (D)	W. B. McAlester (D) [7] George H. Hunt (D) Huby Jordan (D)
Pontotoc	Otto Strickland (D)	Otto Strickland (D) W. H. Ebey (D)	Austin R. Deaton (D) Aubrey M. Kerr (D)	Austin R. Deaton (D) Aubrey M. Kerr (D)
Pottawatomie	B. B. Wyatt (D) [6] Scott Glen (D)	Kenneth Abernathy (D) Scott Glen (D) Joe H. Smalley (D)	Kenneth Abernathy (D) Ralph Spencer (D) Leonard Carey (D)	Mead Norton (D) Ralph Spencer (D) Clarence Tankersley (D)
Pushmataha	Wayland Childers (D)	Wayland Childers (D)	R. W. Frazier (D)	Louie Gossett (D)
Roger Mills	Nat Taylor (D)	T. J. Hogg (D)	T. J. Hogg (D)	Edgar L. McVicker (D)
Rogers	H. Tom Kight (D)	H. Tom Kight (D)	W. P. Johnston (D)	H. Tom Kight (D)
Seminole	W. D. Grisso (D)	C. L. Hill (D) W. D. Grisso (D) Marvin Wooten (D)	Robert N. Chase (D) V. L. Kiker (D) Con Long (D) Marvin Wooten (D)	V. L. Kiker (D) Con Long (D) Marvin Wooten (D)
Sequoyah	Roy Cheek (D)	Fred Spear (D)	J. A. Morrow (D)	J. A. Morrow (D)
Stephens	Cham Jones (D)	A. F. Duke (D) Sandy H. Singleton (D)	Samuel G. Whitaker (D) Sandy H. Singleton (D)	Samuel C. Whitaker (D) Sandy H. Singleton (D)
Texas	See "Cimarron/Texas"	Charles Williams (D)	Vernon Howell (D)	Wallace G. Hughes (D)
Tillman	Harry P. Warhurst (D)	M. C. Worthington (D)	M. C. Worthington (D)	M. C. Worthington (D)
Tulsa	Robert Galbreath (D) Joe Chambers (D) Henry C. Timmons (D) Mat X. Beard (D) Ben O. Kirkpatrick (D)	Krit Logsdon (D) Joe Chambers (D) Henry C. Timmons (D) Mat X. Beard (D) Ben O. Kirkpatrick (D) Seth G. Eby Jr. (D) Frank M. Boyer (D)	A. E. Montgomery (D) Joe Chambers (D) Ed B. Moffett (D) L. M. Poe (D) G. R. Kirkpatrick (D) Seth G. Eby Jr. (D) Edw. P. O'Brien (D)	A. E. Montgomery (D) Joe Chambers (D) Ed B. Moffett (D) Mat X. Beard (D) G. R. Kirkpatrick (D) Seth G. Eby Jr. (D) Herbert Gibson (D)
Wagoner	Bob Wagner (D)	Bob Wagner (D)	Jean R. Reed (D)	W. B. Lumpkin (D)
Washington	C. E. Bailey (D)	John M. Holliman (D)	John M. Holliman (D)	John M. Holliman (D)
Washita	B. W. Todd (D)	B. W. Todd (D)	J. Carl Wright (D) F. E. Raasch (D)	F. E. Raasch (D)
Woods	E. W. Snoddy (R)	Chas. Albright (D)	M. T. Pugh (D)	M. T. Pugh (D)
Woodward	L. A. Jessee (D)	L. A. Jessee (D)	Jesse E. Taylor (D)	Jesse E. Taylor (D)

[1] Died Jan. 23, 1933. Ella M. Davis (D) elected at Special Election, Feb. 22, 1933, to fill unexpired term.
[2] Died Nov. 15, 1932. R. A. Cavitt (D) elected at Special Election Dec. 13, 1932, to fill unexpired term.
[3] Died Jan. 14, 1935. No interim successor elected.
[4] Died Jan. 30, 1937. C. H. Carey (D) elected at Special Election, March 9, 1937 to fill unexpired term.
[5] Resigned. No interim successor elected.
[6] Died May 7, 1931. No interim successor elected.
[7] Died April 19, 1937. No interim successor elected.

Seventeenth to Twentieth Legislatures

County	1939 • 17th	1941 • 18th	1943 • 19th	1945 • 20th
Speakers	Don Welch (D)	E. Blumhagen (D)	Harold Freeman (D) Resigned as Speaker after 1943 session. Merle Lansden (D) elected Speaker for First Extraordinary Session of the 19th Legislature, 4/10/1944.	Johnson Davis Hill (D) Resigned as Speaker, 2/19/1945. H.I. Hinds (D) elected as successor.
Adair	E. B. Arnold (D)	W. H. Langley (D)	C. W. Waters (R)	W. H. Langley (D)
Alfalfa	S. J. Carrier (R) [1]	D. S. Collins (D)	W. E. Cordray (R)	W. E. Cordray (R)
Atoka	Henry Cooper (D)	Henry Cooper (D)	Harold A. Toaz (D)	Harold A. Toaz (D)
Beaver	Floyd Harrington (D)	Merle Lansden (D)	Merle Lansden (D)	Merle Lansden (D)
Beckham	Cecil A. Myers (D)	R. F. Estes (D) H. F. Carmichael (D)	H. F. Carmichael (D)	H. F. Carmichael (D) H. C. Hathcoat (D)
Blaine	E. Blumhagen (D)	E. Blumhagen (D)	E. B. Grennell (R)	Jack Dillon (R)
Bryan	A. N. Leecraft (D) Sam Sullivan (D)	Ebenezer Hotchkin (D) William Parrish (D)	W. H. Underwood (D) William Parrish (D)	W. H. Underwood (D) William Parrish (D)
Caddo	J. Kenneth Hogue (D) Amos Stovall (D)	Dan T. Hunter (D) Amos Stovall (D)	Harold Plummer (D) Amos Stovall (D)	Don Baldwin (D) Walter Morris (D)
Canadian	A. Francis Porta (D)	Claude W. Cherry (D)	J. L. Trevathan (R) [2]	E. R. Barnhart (D)
Carter	Wm. M. Selvidge (D) Wilson Wallace (D)	Wm. M. Selvidge (D) Ernest W. Tate (D)	R. Rhys Evans (D) Ernest W. Tate (D)	R. Rhys Evans (D) Wilson Wallace (D)
Cherokee	Dan D. Draper (D)	Dan D. Draper (D)	H. I. Hinds (D)	H. I. Hinds (D)
Choctaw	Paul E. Webb (D)	Paul E. Webb (D)	Bayless Irby (D)	Hal Welch (D)
Cimarron	Frank Conner (D)	C. R. Board (D)	C. R. Board (D)	C. R. Board (D)
Cleveland	Ben Huey (D)	Richard T. Pendleton (D)	Ben Huey (D)	Ben Huey (D)
Coal	Dale Brown (D)	Henry D. Binns (D)	Henry D. Binns (D)	T. K. Klinglesmith (D)
Comanche	C. S. McCuistion (D) Bill Logan (D)	Dick Riggs (D) Charles G. Ozmun (D)	W. J. Johnson (D) W. H. McKenzie (D)	W. J. Johnson (D) Lewis F. Oerke (D)
Cotton	Charles Flanagan (D)	Thos. J. Huff (D)	Charles Flanagan (D)	Charles Flanagan (D)
Craig	Jack L. Rorschach (D)	Craig Goodpaster (D)	Walter W. Bailey (D)	Walter W. Bailey (D)
Creek	Streeter Speakman (D) Homer O'Dell (D) Wm. L. Cheatham (D)	Streeter Speakman (D) A. Dean Scott (D) Lawrence Jones (D)	Streeter Speakman (D) Orange W. Starr (D) Fletcher M. Johnson (D)	Streeter Speakman (D) Orange W. Starr (D) Fletcher M. Johnson (D)
Custer	Earl D. Duncan (D)	W. R. Dunn (D)	W. R. Dunn (D)	W. R. Dunn (D)
Delaware	H. C. Shackelford (R)	George A. Wilson (D)	W. Hendrix Wolf (D)	LeRoy O. Fields (D)
Dewey	T. J. Hussey (R)	John W. Wilcox (D)	T. J. Hussey (R)	T. J. Hussey (R)
Ellis	G. E. Davison (R)	G. E. Davison (R)	George E. Davison (R)	W. S. Sibley (R)
Garfield	O. R. Whiteneck (D) Floyd E. Carrier (R)	O. R. Whiteneck (D) Robert Crews (R)	Earl Coldiron (R) John N. Camp (R)	Martin Garber (R) John N. Camp (R)
Garvin	Harold Freeman (D) Herbert Hope (D)	Harold Freeman (D) Herbert Hope (D)	Harold Freeman (D) [3] Russell Farmer (D) [4]	Ike Tolbert (D) E. W. Foley (D)
Grady	Dutch Hill (D) C. D. Van Dyck (D)	Dutch Hill (D) C. D. Van Dyck (D) Tommie Jelks (D)	Bill Wallace (D) C. D. Van Dyck (D)	A. L. Davis (D) C. D. Van Dyck (D) [5]
Grant	K. T. Trout (R)	J. C. Hoffsommer (R)	J. C. Hoffsommer (R)	J. C. Hoffsommer (R)
Greer	H. W. Worthington (D)	W. L. Jordan (D)	H. W. Worthington (D)	Wade H. Shumate (D)

Seventeenth to Twentieth Legislatures

County	1939 • 17th	1941 • 18th	1943 • 19th	1945 • 20th
Harmon	W. T. Cunningham (D)	T. N. Crow (D)	T. N. Crow (D)	Raymond Barry (D)
Harper	George Pauls (D)	Elizie S. Spicer (D)	Elzie S. Spicer (D)	C. F. Miles (D)
Haskell	D. C. Cantrell (D)	D. C. Cantrell (D)	D. C. Cantrell (D)	D. C. Cantrell (D)
Hughes	Frank Grayson (D)	Frank Grayson (D) Paul Ballinger (D)	Frank Crane (D)	Frank Crane (D) Fred Treadwell (D)
Jackson	Burr Speck (D)	Burr Speck (D) Woodie Snider (D)	D. L. Jones (D)	D. L. Jones (D)
Jefferson	Otto G. Bound (R)	J. T. Daniel (D)	Dick Coleman (D)	Ewell Sam Singleton (D)
Johnston	Ed Gill (D)	T. Bone King (D)	T. Bone King (D)	Karl V. Wright (D) [6]
Kay	David M. LeMarr (R) W. E. Knapp (R)	Leonard G. Geb (D) William H. Cline (D)	J. R. Dorsett (R) W. E. Knapp (R)	J. R. Dorsett (R) Floyd D. Focht (D)
Kingfisher	Robert L. Barr (D)	Robert L. Barr (D)	Robert L. Barr (D)	Robert L. Barr (D)
Kiowa	F. C. Gillespie Jr. (D)	J. Robin Field (D) W. B. McDonald (D)	W. B. McDonald (D)	W. B. McDonald (D)
Latimer	M. B. Patterson (D)	Jack Bradley (D)	Jack Bradley (D)	Jack Bradley (D)
LeFlore	Earl F. Johnson (D) Raymond H. Lucas (D)	Baysul T. Balentine (D) Raymond H. Lucas (D)	Arthur Reed (D) Raymond H. Lucas (D)	Arthur Reed (D) Edd C. Hawthorne (D)
Lincoln	L. D. Hoyt (D) Clyde L. Andrews (D)	Clarence Hall (D) C. L. Mills (R)	C. L. Mills (R)	C. L. Mills (R) S. J. Thompson (R)
Logan	Carl Morgan (R)	Carl Morgan (R)	Carl Morgan (R)	Carl Morgan (R)
Love	Owen Townsend (D)	John Steele Batson (D)	John Steele Batson (D)	John Steele Batson (D)
McClain	Purman Wilson (D)	Purman Wilson (D)	Purman Wilson (D)	Purman Wilson (D)
McCurtain	Bascom Coker (D) Carl Dees (D)	Herbert D. Flowers (D) Guy B. Massey (D)	Herbert D. Flowers (D) Guy B. Massey (D)	Herbert D. Flowers (D) Carl Dees (D)
McIntosh	Kirksey M. Nix (D)	Kirksey M. Nix (D)	Kirksey M. Nix (D)	Milam M. King (D)
Major	A. L. McFadden (R)	A. L. McFadden (R)	Joe Story (R)	Joe Story (R)
Marshall	Don Welch (D)	J. Horace Harbison (D)	J. Horace Harbison (D)	Roy Biles (D)
Mayes	Lincoln Battenfield (D)	Cicero J. Howard (D)	W. T. Bill Gooldy (D)	Earl Ward (D)
Murray	Malcolm Baucum (D)	D. C. Matthews (D)	J. A. Arms (D)	J. A. Arms (D)
Muskogee	Herbert L. Branan (D) George A. Coffey (D) Will Rogers (D)	Chester Norman (D) R. M. Mountcastle (D) Will Rogers (D)	Robert P. Chandler (D) R. M. Mountcastle (D) J. M. Wiley (D)	Carl Frix (D) R. M. Mountcastle (D) J. M. Wiley (D)
Noble	Merle D. Allen (D)	Merle D. Allen (D)	Leon Hicks (D)	Robt. R. McCubbins (R)
Nowata	LaRue Rush (D)	Chas. A. Whitford (D)	Chas. A. Whitford (D)	Chas. A. Whitford (D)
Okfuskee	Bennie F. Hill (D)	Glen D. Johnson (D)	Roger E. Standley (D) W. O. Black (D)	Roger E. Standley (D)
Oklahoma	George Miskovsky (D) Bryan Billings (D) Ben F. Ellis (D) Creekmore Wallace (D) LaVerne Carleton (D) B. B. Kerr (D) Murray F. Gibbons (D)	George Miskovsky (D) J. D. McCarty (D) Ben F. Ellis (D) Creekmore Wallace (D) Ila Huff (D) B. B. Kerr (D) Paul Washington (D)	Ben Gullett (D) J. D. McCarty (D) Robert H. Sherman (D) Creekmore Wallace (D) Ila Huff (D) B. B. Kerr (D) Paul Washington (D)	Ben Gullett (D) J. D. McCarty (D) Robert H. Sherman (D) Creekmore Wallace (D) Harold Carey (D) B. B. Kerr (D) Paul Washington (D)

Seventeenth to Twentieth Legislatures

County	1939 • 17th	1941 • 18th	1943 • 19th	1945 • 20th
Okmulgee	S. E. Hammond (D) James M. Hays (D)	F. C. Helm (D) Bill Shipley (D)	F. C. Helm (D) Bill Shipley (D) C.B. McMahan (D)	B. L. Williams (D) Bill Shipley (D) Q. D. Gibbs (D)
Osage	Charles Bacon (D) Frank Mahan (D)	Charles Bacon (D) Frank Mahan (D)	Charles Bacon (D) L. C. Sullivan (D)	Charles Bacon (D) Bill Burkhart (D)
Ottawa	Walter Miller (D) C. A. Douthat (D)	Percy M. Smith (D) C. A. Douthat (D)	Percy M. Smith (D) C. A. Douthat (D)	Grace Mitchelson (D) Mona Jean Russell (D)
Pawnee	Harry Fischer (R)	Roy Berry (D)	Ward Guffy (R)	Prentiss E. Rowe (D)
Payne	Elbert R. Weaver (D)	Elbert R. Weaver (D) Robert L. Hert (D)	Elbert R. Weaver (D) J. H. Arrington (D)	Elbert R. Weaver (D) J. H. Arrington (D)
Pittsburg	Elmer Tompkins (D) Jay Basolo (D) Andy Banks (D)	Elmer Tompkins (D) E. P. Hill (D) Andy Banks (D)	C. Plowboy Edwards (D) Aiden E. Allen (D) [7] Andy Banks (D)	C. Plowboy Edwards (D) Hiram Impson (D) Ben P. Choate (D)
Pontotoc	Moss Wimbish (D) Fred McCabe (D)	Moss Wimbish (D) Virgil B. Medlock (D)	Joe Tom McKinley (D) Virgil B. Medlock (D)	Thomas P. Holt (D) Virgil B. Medlock (D)
Pottawatomie	Bill High (D) Ralph Spencer (D) Clarence Tankersley (D)	Bill High (D) [6] John T. Levergood (D) Tom Wyatt (D)	Scott Glen (D) [8] John T. Levergood (D) Burke Larch-Miller (D)	Clarence Tankersley (D) John T. Levergood (D) A. J. Ownby (D)
Pushmataha	Louie Gossett (D)	Claud Thompson (D)	Claud Thompson (D)	Claud Thompson (D)
Roger Mills	Edgar L. McVicker (D)	Wesley B. Hunt (D)	Wesley B. Hunt (D)	Wesley B. Hunt (D) [6]
Rogers	H. Tom Kight (D)	Dennis Bushyhead (D)	H. Tom Kight (D)	E. W. Meads (D)
Seminole	V. L. Kiker (D) Dick Bell (D) J. T. Means (D)	Walter Billingsley (D) Con Long (D) F. M. Streetman (D)	Walter Billingsley (D) Con Long (D) F. M. Streetman (D)	Walter Billingsley (D) Con Long (D) F. M. Streetman (D)
Sequoyah	Paul V. Carlile (D)	Carl Frix (D)	Carl Frix (D) [6]	Owen B. Taylor (D)
Stephens	James M. Bullard (D) Pat Fitzgerald (D)	M. W. Pugh (D) Pat Fitzgerald (D)	M. W. Pugh (D) James M. Bullard (D)	D. A. Segrest (D) James M. Bullard (D)
Texas	Wallace G. Hughes (D)	Wallace G. Hughes (D)	Wallace G. Hughes (D)	Wallace G. Hughes (D)
Tillman	James B. Witt (D)	James B. Witt (D)	E. H. Shelton (D)	E. H. Shelton (D)
Tulsa	A. E. Montgomery (D) A. F. Sweeney (D) Wm. F. Latting (D) D. E. Temple (D) Glade Kirkpatrick (D) Holly L. Anderson (D) Wm. J. Melton (D)	A. E. Montgomery (D) Joe Chambers (D) Wm. F. Latting (D) D. E. Temple (D) Glade Kirkpatrick (D) Holly L. Anderson (D) Wm. J. Melton (D)	A. E. Williams (R) Joe E. Musgrave (R) Arthur L. Price (R) Horace Newberry (R) D. M. Madrano (R) Johnson D. Hill (D) Joe Harshbarger (R)	A. E. Montgomery (D) Joe E. Musgrave (R) Arthur L. Price (R) Harmon G. Bellamy (R) Dan M. Madrano (R) Johnson D. Hill (D) [6] Joe Harshbarger (R)
Wagoner	Bob Wagner (D)	W. B. Lumpkin (D)	W. B. Carr (R)	W. B. Carr (R)
Washington	John M. Holliman (D)	John M. Holliman (D)	John M. Holliman (D)	Laton L. Doty (R)
Washita	Ripley S. Greenhaw (D)	Jesse Stovall (D)	Ed W. Hines (D)	Ed W. Hines (D) A. R. Ash (D)
Woods	J. G. Powers (R)	J. G. Powers (R)	R. W. McNally (R)	R. W. McNally (R)
Woodward	Dick Houston (D)	Dick Houston (D)	Frank Durant (R)	Frank Durant (R) [9]

Seventeenth to Twentieth Legislatures

County	1939 • 17th	1941 • 18th	1943 • 19th	1945 • 20th

[1] Died July 31, 1939. No interim successor elected.

[2] Died July 12, 1943. J. A. Wheatley (R) elected at Special Election, April 4, 1944, to fill unexpired term.

[3] Resigned as Member and Speaker after 1943 session. Ike Tolbert (D) elected member at Special Election April 4, 1944 to fill unexpired term.

[4] Failed to qualify. E. W. Foley (D) elected at Special Election, April 4, 1944.

[5] Died Nov. 26, 1946. A. E. Hennings (D) elected at Special Election Dec. 31, 1946.

[6] Resigned. No interim successor elected.

[7] Resigned. Hiram Impson (D) elected at Special Election April 4, 1944, to fill unexpired term.

[8] Died Jan. 30, 1943. Clarence Tankersley (D) elected at Special Election, April 4, 1944, to fill unexpired term.

[9] Died Jan. 27, 1945. No interim successor elected.

Twenty-First to Twenty-Fourth Legislatures

County	1947 • 21st	1949 • 22nd	1951 • 23rd	1953 • 24th
Speakers	C.R. Board (D)	Walther Billingsley (D)	James M. Bullard (D)	J.C. Nance (D)
Adair	W. H. Langley (D)	W. H. Langley (D)	W. H. Langley (D)	W. H. Langley (D)
Alfalfa	W. E. Cordray (R)	W. E. Cordray (R)	Vernon J. Collins (D)	Tom H. Morford (R)
Atoka	Harold A. Toaz (D)	Bob A. Trent (D)	Floyd Mason (D)	Floyd Mason (D)
Beaver	W. T. Quinn (R)	Floyd Sumrall (D)	Floyd Sumrall (D)	Floyd Sumrall (D)
Beckham	H. C. Hathcoat (D) [1]	H. F. Carmichael (D)	J. L. Edgecomb (D) Charles M. Wilson (D)	H. F. Carmichael (D)
Blaine	Jack Dillon (R)	Jack Dillon (R)	H. G. Tolbert (R)	H. G. Tolbert (R)
Bryan	Clark E. White (D) [1] Keith Cartwright (D)	James E. Douglas (D) Jack E. McGahey (D)	James E. Douglas (D) Joe Engler (D)	James E. Douglas (D) Raney Arnold (D)
Caddo	Don Baldwin (D) Walter Morris (D)	Wayne L. Brewer (D) Walter Morris (D)	F. H. Moorehead (D) Charley W. Long (D)	F. H. Moorehead (D) Charley W. Long (D)
Canadian	Jean L. Pazoureck (D)	Jean L. Pazoureck (D)	Jean L. Pazoureck (D)	Jean L. Pazoureck (D)
Carter	R. Rhys Evans (D) Wilson Wallace (D)	R. Rhys Evans (D) Ernest W. Tate (D)	James D. Payne (D) Ernest W. Tate (D)	James D. Payne (D) Ernest W. Tate (D)
Cherokee	Richard Smith (D)	Richard Smith (D)	Richard Smith (D)	Richard Smith (D)
Choctaw	Hal Welch (D)	Hal Welch (D)	Lucien C. Spear (D)	Lucien C. Spear (D)
Cimarron	C. R. Board (D)	Roy T. Nall (D)	Roy T. Nall (D)	Carl G. Etling (R)
Cleveland	Joe A. Smalley (D)	Joe A. Smalley (D)	Virgil Young (D)	Virgil Young (D) Leland Wolf (D)
Coal	Owen Summers (D)	T. K. Kinglesmith (D)	T. K. Klinglesmith (D)	T. K. Klinglesmith (D)
Comanche	Dick Riggs (D) Charles G. Ozmun (D)	Dick Riggs (D) Charles G. Ozmun (D)	Jim Taliaferro (D) Charles G. Ozmun (D)	Jim Taliaferro (D) Charles G. Ozmun (D) Githen K. Rhoads (D)
Cotton	G. G. Upchurch (D)	Luther B. Eubanks (D)	Luther B. Eubanks (D)	W. B. Nelson (D)
Craig	W. Walter Bailey (D)	W. Walter Bailey (D)	George P. Pitcher (D)	George P. Pitcher (D)
Creek	Streeter Speakman (D) [2] Lou S. Allard (D) William Shibley (D)	Streeter Speakman Jr. (D) Lou S. Allard (D) William Shibley (D)	Streeter Speakman Jr. (D) Lou S. Allard (D) William Shibley (D)	L. A. Hudgins (D) Lou S. Allard (D) William Shibley (D)
Custer	William R. Dunn (D)	Wayne Wallace (D)	Wayne Wallace (D)	Clarence Sweeney (D)

Twenty-First to Twenty-Fourth Legislatures

County	1947 • 21st	1949 • 22nd	1951 • 23rd	1953 • 24th
Delaware	Mattison E. Sparkman (D)	A. B. Johnston (D)	Wiley Sparkman (D)	Wiley Sparkman (D)
Dewey	Jim Kouns (D)	Jim Kouns (D)	Jack Wilcox (D)	J. B. Graybill (D)
Ellis	A. R. Larason (D)	A. R. Larason (D)	A. R. Larason (D)	A. R. Larason (D)
Garfield	Martin Garber (R) John N. Camp (R)	Richard E. Romang (R) John N. Camp (R)	Richard E. Romang (R) John N. Camp (R)	Richard E. Romang (R) Dan Mitchell (R) John N. Camp (R)
Garvin	Ike Tolbert (D) Easter Brown (D)	Ike Tolbert (D) J. Cecil Long (D)	Ike Tolbert (D) Glen Ham (D)	Jesse C. Daniel (D) Glen Ham (D)
Grady	Laverne Sumner (D) A. E. Hennings (D) C. C. Chastain (D)	Bill Wallace (D) A. J. Lance (D)	Ira D. Humphreys (D) Jeff Davis (D) James F. Renegar (D)	Ira D. Humphreys (D) [3] Jeff Davis (D)
Grant	J. C. Hoffsommer (R)	William L. Card (D)	William L. Card (D)	William L. Card (D)
Greer	Wade H. Shumate (D)	Wade H. Shumate (D)	Basil R. Wilson (D)	Elmo B. Hurst (D)
Harmon	Wilburn H. Medaris (D)	Valdhe F. Pitman (D)	Valdhe F. Pitman (D)	Valdhe F. Pitman (D)
Harper	C. F. Miles (D)	Ben W. Douglas (R)	Boyce Stinson (D)	J. E. Bouse (D)
Haskell	D. C. Cantrell (D)	D. C. Cantrell (D)	Howard Young (D)	Folsom M. Scott (D)
Hughes	Paul Ballinger (D) Jimie Scott (D)	Tom Anglin (D)	Frank Grayson (D)	Frank Grayson (D) Hugh M. Sandlin (D)
Jackson	D. L. Jones (D) Guy K. Horton (D)	Guy K. Horton (D)	William J. Ivester (D)	William J. Ivester (D) Guy K. Horton (D)
Jefferson	Jack Coleman (D)	Jack Coleman (D)	Jack Coleman (D)	W. D. Bradley (D)
Johnston	Marvin F. Brannon (D)	Marvin F. Brannon (D)	Jack Gilliam (D)	Jack Gilliam (D)
Kay	C. B. McClean (R) James A. McNeese (R)	Guy O. Bailey (D) H. Evertt Black (D)	Guy O. Bailey (D) Raymond O. Craig (R)	T. D. Harris (R) Raymond O. Craig (R)
Kingfisher	W. A. Burton Jr. (R)	W. A. Burton Jr. (R)	Wm. A. Burton Jr. (R)	Wm. A. Burton Jr. (R)
Kiowa	Ralph Farrar (D)	Lloyd Reeder (D)	Lloyd Reeder (D) C. L. Krieger (D)	C. L. Krieger (D)
Latimer	E. T. Dunlap (D)	E. T. Dunlap (D)	E. T. Dunlap (D)	Jim Cook (D)
LeFlore	Dual Autry (D) Edd C. Hawthorne (D)	Dual Autry (D) Edd C. Hawthorne (D)	Dual Autry (D) [1] Ralph Vandiver (D)	James E. Fesperman (D) Ralph Vandiver (D)
Lincoln	C. L. Mills (R)	Jesse Berry (R) John E. Wagner (R)	Jesse Berry (R) Richard James (R)	Richard James (R)
Logan	Lloyd H. McGuire (R)	Lewis F. Wolfe (R)	Lewis F. Wolfe (R)	Lewis F. Wolfe (R)
Love	Joe Thompson (D)	Thomas S. Anderson (D)	Clint G. Livingston (D)	Clint G. Livingston (D)
McClain	Purman Wilson (D)	James R. Williams (D)	James R. Williams (D)	J. C. Nance (D)
McCurtain	Paul Harkey (D) James Dyer (D)	Paul Harkey (D) James Dyer (D)	Paul Harkey (D) Mort A. Welch (D)	Paul Harkey (D) Mort A. Welch (D)
McIntosh	Clinton White (D)	Wilford E. Bohannon (D)	Wilford E. Bohannon (D)	Lonnie P. McPeak (D)
Major	Sam L. Alexander (R)	J. Howard Lindley (R)	J. Howard Lindley (R)	J. Howard Lindley (R)
Marshall	Roy Biles (D)	Roy Biles (D)	Don E. Welch (D)	Jay E. Payne (D)
Mayes	J. Gus Bethell (D)	J. Gus Bethell (D)	G. A. Sampsel (D)	G. A Sampsel (D)
Murray	Jack Barron (D)	L. B. Peak (D)	Bruce L. Frazier (D)	Bruce L. Frazier (D)

Twenty-First to Twenty-Fourth Legislatures

County	1947 • 21st	1949 • 22nd	1951 • 23rd	1953 • 24th
Muskogee	Carl Frix (D) David Wood (D) H. P. Watkins (D)	Edwin Langley (D) Bill Haworth (D) Joe R. Cannon (D)	Edwin Langley (D) Bill Haworth (D) Louis Smith (D)	Charles O. Hammers (D) Bill Haworth (D) Louis Smith (D)
Noble	Henry Bellmon (R)	F. C. Seids (D)	Robert S. Taylor (R)	Robert S. Taylor (R)
Nowata	James M. Staten (D)	Otis Munson (D)	Otis Munson (D)	Otis Munson (D)
Okfuskee	Dwight Tolle (D)	William L. Jones (D)	William L. Jones (D)	Bennie F. Hill (D) Harlon S. Avey (D)
Oklahoma	Ben Gullett (D) J. D. McCarty (D) John H. Jarman Jr. (D) Dwain D. Box (D) Harold R. Carey (D) B. B. Kerr (D) Paul Washington (D)	R.O. Cunningham (D) J. D. McCarty (D) Robert H. Sherman (D) Dwain D. Box (D) Ben Brickell (D) N.E. Reynolds Jr. (D) W. R. Wallace Jr. (D)	R.O. Cunningham (D) J. D. McCarty (D) Robert H. Sherman (D) B. E. Bill Harkey (D) Eddie G. Kessler (D) N.E. Reynolds Jr. (D) W. R. Wallace Jr. (D)	R.O. Cunningham (D) J. D. McCarty (D) Cleeta John Rogers (D) B. E. Bill Harkey (D) Red Andrews (D) N.E. Reynolds Jr. (D) G. M. Fuller (D)
Okmulgee	B. L. Williams (D) Bill Shipley (D) John W. Russell Jr. (D)	Edgar R. Boatman (D) John W. Russell Jr. (D)	Manuel Furr (D) John W. Russell Jr. (D)	Porter R. Lee (D) K. D. Bailey (D) Tom Payne Jr. (D)
Osage	Chas. Bacon (D) William A. Burkhart (D)	Chas. Bacon (D) William A. Burkhart (D)	Shockley T. Shoemake (D) William Burkhart Jr. (D) [4]	Shockley T. Shoemake (D) William Burkhart Jr. (D)
Ottawa	Grace Mitchelson (D) Mona Jean Russell (D)	Robert H. Reynolds Jr. (D) Jess L. Fronterhouse (D)	C. D. Wilson (D) J. R. Hall Jr. (D)	C. D. Wilson (D) J. R. Hall Jr. (D)
Pawnee	D. Jo Ferguson (R)	Ray D. Henry (D)	Ray D. Henry (D)	Ray D. Henry (D)
Payne	J. H. Arrington (D)	Robert L. Hert (D)	Robert L. Hert (D)	J. H. Arrington (D) Chilton Swank (D)
Pittsburg	C. Plowboy Edwards (D) Lonnie W. Brown (D) Garland Jordan (D)	Gene Stipe (D) Lonnie W. Brown (D) Kirksey M. Nix (D)	Gene Stipe (D) George P. Nigh (D) C. Plowboy Edwards (D)	Gene Stipe (D) George P. Nigh (D) C. Plowboy Edwards (D)
Pontotoc	Thomas P. Holt (D) H. P. Sugg (D)	J. W. Huff (D) H. P. Sugg (D)	J. W. Huff (D) George R. Collins (D)	J. W. Huff (D) George R. Collins (D)
Pottawatomie	William E. Tiffany (D) John T. Levergood (D) James W. Densford Jr. (D)	William E. Tiffany (D) Frank E. Brown (D) A. J. Ownby (D)	Tom Stevens (D) John T. Levergood (D) George Defenbaugh (D)	Tom Stevens (D) John T. Levergood (D) George Defenbaugh (D)
Pushmataha	Claud Thompson (D)	Curtis Roberson (D)	Lee Welch (D)	Lee Welch (D)
Roger Mills	S. S. McColgin (D)	S. S. McColgin (D)	Jodie S. Moad (D)	S. S. McColgin (D)
Rogers	E. W. Meads (D)	Dave L. Smith (D)	Dave L. Smith (D)	Robert L. Wadley (D)
Seminole	Walter Billingsley (D) Con Long (D) N. Blaylock (D)	Walter Billingsley (D) Charles A. Sims (D) N. Blaylock (D) [5]	Glen C. Collins (D) Charles A. Sims (D) James F. Haning (D)	Glen C. Collins (D) Con Long (D) James F. Haning (D)
Sequoyah	Owen Taylor (D)	Owen Taylor (D)	M. Shawnee Stewart (D)	M. Shawnee Stewart (D)
Stephens	D. A. Segrest (D) James M. Bullard (D)	Harold Garvin (D) James M. Bullard (D)	Val R. Miller (D) James M. Bullard (D)	Val R. Miller (D) James M. Bullard (D)
Texas	Leon B. Field (D)	Leon B. Field (D)	Don Dale (D)	Don Dale (D)
Tillman	E. H. Shelton (D)	D. H. Laing Jr. (D)	Arthur A. Kelly (D)	Arthur A. Kelly (D)

Twenty-First to Twenty-Fourth Legislatures

County	1947 • 21st	1949 • 22nd	1951 • 23rd	1953 • 24th
Tulsa	A. E. Williams (R) Joe E. Musgrave (R) Robert N. Alexander (R) George Campbell (R) C. R. Nixon (R) Richard B. McDermott (R) Joe Harshbarger (R)	S. H. Andrews (D) Al Jennings (D) James G. Davidson (D) Grant G. Forsythe (D) Wesley V. Disney (D) Richard T. Oliver (D) Harvey F. Allen (D)	C. R. Nixon (R) Joe E. Musgrave (R) Robert N. Alexander (R) Dean H. Smith (R) Russell C. Reynolds (R) Dale J. Briggs (R) Wendell B. Barnes (R)	C. R. Nixon (R) Joe E. Musgrave (R) Robert N. Alexander (R) Dean H. Smith (R) Paul V. Beck (R) Glenn J. Twist (R) H. Everett Pope Jr. (R)
Wagoner	John Waggoner (D)	Carlisle Duke (D)	Carlisle Duke (D)	Fred W. Martin (D)
Washington	Laton L. Doty (R)	Laton L. Doty (R)	Laton L. Doty (R)	C. W. Staats (R) Clinton Beard (R)
Washita	A. R. Ash (D)	Dale Griffin (D)	Dale Griffin (D)	Harold Witcher (D)
Woods	Ben B. Easterly (D)	Ben B. Easterly (D)	Ben B. Easterly (D)	Ben B. Easterly (D)
Woodward	Clarence W. Meigs (R)	Clarence W. Meigs (R)	Clarence W. Meigs (R)	J. Don Williams (D)

[1] Resigned. No interim successor elected.
[2] Died July 31, 1948. No interim successor elected.
[3] Died Nov. 18, 1953. No interim successor elected.
[4] Died March 11, 1951. William A. Burkhart Jr. (D) elected at Special Election, May 1, 1951, to fill unexpired term.
[5] Died Sept. 29, 1949. No interim successor elected.

Twenty-Fifth to Twenty-Eighth Legislatures

County	1955 • 25th	1957 • 26th	1959 • 27th	1961 • 28th
Speakers	B.E. Bill Harkey (D)	B.E. Bill Harkey (D)	Clint G. Livingston (D)	J.D. McCarty (D)
Adair	W. H. Langley (D)	W. H. Langley (D)	W. H. Langley (D)	Bill T. Harper (D)
Alfalfa	Tom H. Morford (R)	Tom H. Morford (R)	Frank Reneau (D)	Frank Reneau (D)
Atoka	Joseph Payton (D)	Otto Strickland (D)	Robert I. Cooksey (D)	Harold Thomas (D)
Beaver	Floyd Sumrall (D)	Floyd Sumrall (D) [1]	G. H. Karnes (D)	G. H. Karnes (D)
Beckham	H. F. Carmichael (D) J. L. Edgecomb (D)	H. F. Carmichael (D) [2]	Holland Meacham (D)	Homer R. Holcomb (D) O. R. Wilhelm (D)
Blaine	Lewis H. Bohr (R)	Lewis H. Bohr (R) [3]	James F. Burnham (D)	James F. Burnham (D)
Bryan	J. H. Belvin (D) Raney Arnold (D)	J. H. Belvin (D) Earl Cartwright (D)	J. H. Belvin (D) Earl Cartwright (D)	John Massey (D) Earl Cartwright (D) [6]
Caddo	R. L. Goodfellow (D) Charley W. Long (D)	R. L. Goodfellow (D) Charley W. Long (D) [4]	R. L. Goodfellow (D) J. M. Kardokus (D)	R. L. Goodfellow (D) J. M. Kardokus (D)
Canadian	Jean L. Pazoureck (D)	Jean L. Pazoureck (D)	Ralph Watkins (D)	Ralph Watkins (D)
Carter	John T. Tipps (D) Harley E. Venters (D)	Robert Price (D) Rex Sparger (D)	Martin E. Dyer (D) Rex Sparger (D)	Martin E. Dyer (D) James W. Williams (D)
Cherokee	Jack Bliss (D)	Jack Bliss (D)	William P. Willis (D)	William P. Willis (D)
Choctaw	Lucien C. Spear (D)	Lucien C. Spear (D)	Lucien C. Spear (D)	Wayne Sanguin (D)
Cimarron	Carl G. Etling (R)	Carl G. Etling (R)	Carl G. Etling (R)	Carl G. Etling (R)
Cleveland	Robert L. Bailey (D) Leland Wolf (D)	Robert L. Bailey (D) Leland Wolf (D)	Kenneth J. Poynor (D) Leland Wolf (D)	Kenneth J. Poynor (D) Leland Wolf (D)
Coal	Delbert Inman (D)	Delbert Inman (D)	Delbert Inman (D)	Delbert Inman (D)

Twenty-Fifth to Twenty-Eighth Legislatures

County	1955 • 25th	1957 • 26th	1959 • 27th	1961 • 28th
Comanche	Jim Taliaferro (D) Charles G. Ozmun (D) Githen K. Rhoads (D)	Jim Taliaferro (D) Charles G. Ozmun (D) Earl L. Simmons (D)	Jim Taliaferro (D) Charles G. Ozmun (D)	Jim Taliaferro (D) Manville Redman (D)
Cotton	W. B. Nelson (D)	Tracy Daugherty (D)	Tracy Daugherty (D)	James B. Witt (D)
Craig	George P. Pitcher (D)	George P. Pitcher (D)	R. L. Wheatley Jr. (D)	Harold D. Morgan (D)
Creek	Heber Finch Jr. (D) Lou S. Allard (D) William K. Shibley (D)	Heber Finch Jr. (D) Lou S. Allard (D) William K. Shibley (D)	Heber Finch Jr. (D) Lou S. Allard (D) William K. Shibley (D)	Heber Finch Jr. (D) Lou S. Allard (D) William K. Shibley (D)
Custer	Clarence Sweeney (D)	Clarence Sweeney (D) [5]	R. E. Lee Richardson (D)	M. A. Diel (D)
Delaware	Carl Thomas Mustain (D)	Wiley Sparkman (D)	Wiley Sparkman (D)	Wiley Sparkman (D)
Dewey	J. B. Graybill (D)	J. B. Graybill (D)	Roger S. Wilcox (D)	E. D. Nichols (D)
Ellis	A. R. Larason (D)	A. R. Larason (D)	A. R. Larason (D)	A. R. Larason (D)
Garfield	Richard E. Romang (R) John N. Camp (R)	Richard E. Romang (R) John N. Camp (R)	Richard E. Romang (R) John N. Camp (R)	Bert F. Page (R) John N. Camp (R)
Garvin	Jesse C. Daniel (D) Glen Ham (D)	Jesse C. Daniel (D) Glen Ham (D)	Jesse C. Daniel (D) Glen Ham (D)	Sam Richardson (D) Tom E. Strickland (D)
Grady	A. J. Lance (D) Jeff Davis (D)	A. J. Lance (D) Jeff Davis (D)	A. J. Lance (D) Jeff Davis (D) [8] Robert E. Clark (D)	A. J. Lance (D) Spencer T. Bernard (D) Robert E. Clark (D)
Grant	A. E. Green (D)	A. E. Green (D)	A. E. Green (D)	A. E. Green (D)
Greer	Elmo B. Hurst (D)	Elmo B. Hurst (D)	Elmo B. Hurst (D)	Elmo B. Hurst (D)
Harmon	Dale Kite (D)	Dale Kite (D)	R. H. Lynch (D)	J. B. Fowler (D)
Harper	J. E. Bouse (D)	J. E. Bouse (D)	J. E. Bouse (D)	Clayton H. Lauer (R)
Haskell	Edward L. Chunings (D)	Samuel M. Mitchell (D)	Sam'l M. Mitchell (D) [9]	Earl Bilyeu (D)
Hughes	Hugh M. Sandlin (D)	Stanley Huser Jr. (D) Bob Rives (D)	Stanley Huser Jr. (D)	Stona Fitch (D)
Jackson	Guy K. Horton (D)	Guy K. Horton (D) Bob Scarbrough (D)	Maurice L. Willis (D)	Maurice L. Willis (D)
Jefferson	W. D. Bradley (D)	W. D. Bradley (D)	W. D. Bradley (D)	W. D. Bradley (D)
Johnston	Charles J. Norris (D)	Charles J. Norris (D)	Kenneth Converse (D)	Kenneth E. Converse (D)
Kay	Guy O. Bailey (D) Raymond O. Craig (R)	Guy O. Bailey (D) [7] Raymond O. Craig (R)	John Howe (D) Raymond O. Craig (R)	John Howe (D) Raymond O. Craig (R)
Kingfisher	Wm. A. Burton Jr. (R)	Milton W. Priebe (R)	Milton W. Priebe (R)	Milton W. Priebe (R)
Kiowa	William W. Metcalf (D)	William W. Metcalf (D)	William W. Metcalf (D)	William W. Metcalf (D) Joyce Leon Holder (D)
Latimer	Jim Cook (D)	Jim Cook (D)	Jim Cook (D)	Jim Cook (D)
LeFlore	James E. Fesperman (D) Ralph Vandiver (D)	Tom Traw (D) Ralph Vandiver (D)	Tom Traw (D) Ralph Vandiver (D)	Tom Traw (D) Ralph Vandiver (D)
Lincoln	Jesse Berry (R) Barbour Cox (D)	Barbour Cox (D)	Barbour Cox (D) Clarence Hall (D)	Barbour Cox (D) Milton C. Craig (R)
Logan	Joe Carey (R)	Joe Carey (R)	Dick Fogarty (D)	Dick Fogarty (D)
Love	Rudolph Folsom (D)	Clint G. Livingston (D)	Clint G. Livingston (D)	John Steele Batson (D)
McClain	Henry H. Montgomery (D)	James C. Nance (D)	James C. Nance (D)	Norman A. Smith (D)

Twenty-Fifth to Twenty-Eighth Legislatures

County	1955 • 25th	1957 • 26th	1959 • 27th	1961 • 28th
McCurtain	Virgil Jumper (D) Mort A. Welch (D)	Virgil Jumper (D) Mort A. Welch (D)	Virgil Jumper (D) Kelsie Jones (D)	Garfield Settles (D) Kelsie Jones (D)
McIntosh	Milam M. King (D)	Milam M. King (D)	Martin Odom (D)	Martin Odom (D)
Major	J. Howard Lindley (R) [10]	Art F. Bower (R)	Art F. Bower (R)	Art F. Bower (R)
Marshall	Jay E. Payne (D)	William L. Bond (D)	William L. Bond (D)	Delmas L. Northcutt (D)
Mayes	G. A. Sampsel (D)	G. A. Sampsel (D)	John C. Wilkerson (D)	J. W. Bynum (D)
Murray	Lynn W. Norman (D)	Carl Williams (D)	Carl Williams (D)	Carl Williams (D)
Muskogee	Chas O. Hammers (D) David C. Reid (D) Russell Ruby (D)	Chas O. Hammers (D) Harold D. Smith (D) Russell Ruby (D)	George Dick Spraker (D) Bill Haworth (D) Russell Ruby (D)	George Dick Spraker (D) Bill Haworth (D) Russell Ruby (D)
Noble	Robert S. Taylor (R)	Henry Dolezal (R)	Henry Dolezal (R)	Henry Dolezal (R)
Nowata	Otis Munson (D)	Otis Munson (D)	Bill Shipley (D)	Bill Shipley (D)
Okfuskee	Bennie F. Hill (D)	Bennie F. Hill (D)	Harlon S. Avey (D)	Harlon S. Avey (D)
Oklahoma	R. O. Cunningham (D) J. D. McCarty (D) Cleeta John Rogers (D) B. E. Bill Harkey (D) Red Andrews (D) Earl Foster Jr. (D) G. M. Fuller (D)	R. O. Cunningham (D) J. D. McCarty (D) Cleeta John Rogers (D) B. E. Bill Harkey (D) Red Andrews (D) Earl Foster Jr. (D) G. M. Fuller (D)	Jack R. Skaggs (D) J. D. McCarty (D) Cleeta John Rogers (D) Bryce Baggett (D) Red Andrews (D) Earl Foster Jr. (D) G. M. Fuller (D)	Jack R. Skaggs (D) J. D. McCarty (D) J. Thomas Taggart (R) Bryce Baggett (D) Red Andrews (D) George C. Keyes (D) G. T. Blankenship (R)
Okmulgee	Bill Shipley (D) Tom Payne Jr. (D)	Ed Cole (D) O. E. Richeson (D) James Nevins (D)	Ed Cole (D) O. E. Richeson (D)	Ed Cole (D) O. E. Richeson (D)
Osage	Shockley T. Shoemake (D) Virgil B. Tinker (D)	Shockley T. Shoemake (D) Virgil B. Tinker (D)	Shockley T. Shoemake (D) Virgil B. Tinker (D)	Tom Tate (D) Virgil B. Tinker (D)
Ottawa	C. D. Wilson (D) J. R. Hall Jr. (D)	C. D. Wilson (D) Robert C. Lollar (D)	Joseph E. Mountford (D) Robert C. Lollar (D)	Joseph E. Mountford (D) Pat S. McCue (D)
Pawnee	Ray D. Henry (D)	Rex Privett (D)	Rex Privett (D)	Rex Privett (D)
Payne	J. H. Arrington (D) Joe E. Johnson (D)	J. H. Arrington (D) H. L. Sparks (D)	J. H. Arrington (D) H. L. Sparks (D)	Jake E. Hesser (D) H. L. Sparks (D)
Pittsburg	William H. Skeith (D) George P. Nigh (D) C. Plowboy Edwards (D)	William H. Skeith (D) George P. Nigh (D) Willard M. Gotcher (D)	William H. Skeith (D) Ray Van Hooser (D) Willard M. Gotcher (D)	William H. Skeith (D) Ray Van Hooser (D) Tom McChristian (D)
Pontotoc	J. W. Huff (D) George R. Collins (D)	J. W. Huff (D) Martin Clark (D)	Henry R. Roberts (D) Robert W. Ford (D)	Lonnie L. Abbott (D) Robert W. Ford (D)
Pottawatomie	Tom Stevens (D) John T. Levergood (D) Ralph W. Graves (D)	Tom Stevens (D) John T. Levergood (D) Ralph W. Graves (D)	Tom Stevens (D) John T. Levergood (D) Ralph W. Graves (D)	Tom Stevens (D) John T. Levergood (D) Charles T. Henry (D)
Pushmataha	Lee Welch (D)	Bob Hargrave (D)	Bob Hargrave (D)	Ray Tucker (D)
Roger Mills	Glenn E. Estes (D)	Jodie S. Moad (D)	Jodie S. Moad (D)	Jodie S. Moad (D)
Rogers	Robert L. Wadley (D)	Bill Briscoe (D)	Bill Briscoe (D)	Bill Briscoe (D)
Seminole	E. J. Evans (D) Con Long (D) Buck Cartwright (D)	Bucky Buckler (D) Con Long (D) Buck Cartwright (D)	Bucky Buckler (D) Laurence P. Howze (D) Allen G. Nichols (D)	A. F. Eidson (D) Laurence P. Howze (D) Allen G. Nichols (D)
Sequoyah	Noble R. Stewart (D)	Noble R. Stewart (D)	Noble R. Stewart (D)	Maynard E. Blackard (D)

Twenty-Fifth to Twenty-Eighth Legislatures

County	1955 • 25th	1957 • 26th	1959 • 27th	1961 • 28th
Stephens	Edward L. Bond (D)	Edward L. Bond (D)	Edward L. Bond (D)	Edward L. Bond (D)
	James M. Bullard (D)	James M. Bullard (D)	James M. Bullard (D)	James M. Bullard (D)
Texas	Frank Ogden (D)	Frank Ogden (D)	Frank Ogden (D)	Frank Ogden (D)
Tillman	Arthur A. Kelly (D)	Arthur A. Kelly (D)	Frank G. Patterson (D)	Frank G. Patterson (D)
Tulsa	C. R. Nixon (R)	C. R. Nixon (R)	Robert E. Hopkins (D)	Robert E. Hopkins (D)
	Joe E. Musgrave (R)	Joe E. Musgrave (R)	Jack E. McGahey (D)	David D. Atkinson (D)
	Robert N. Alexander (R)	Robert N. Alexander (R)	Alexander Johnston Jr. (D)	Alex Johnston (D)
	Dean H. Smith (R)	Gordon L. Patten (R)	Grant G. Forsythe (D)	Grant G. Forsythe (D)
	Paul V. Beck (R)	H. E. Chambers (R)	Gene C. Howard (D)	Gene C. Howard (D)
	Joe Chambers (D) [11]	John M. Slater (R) [3]	John W. McCune (D)	John W. McCune (D)
	Bernard E. Calkins (R)	Bernard E. Calkins (R)	Ed Bradley (D)	Ed Bradley (D)
Wagoner	J. Roy Cocke (R)	V. H. Odom (D)	V. H. Odom (D)	V. H. Odom (D)
Washington	Carl W. Staats (R)	Denzil D. Garrison (R)	Denzil D. Garrison (R)	C. W. Doornbos (R)
	Clinton Beard (R)	Lloyd M. Reudy (R)	Clyde W. Sare (D)	Clyde W. Sare (D)
Washita	Harold Lee Witcher (D)	Don R. Greenhaw (D)	Don R. Greenhaw (D)	Don R. Greenhaw (D)
	Don R. Greenhaw (D)			
Woods	Herbert D. Smith (D)	A. L. Murrow (R)	A. L. Murrow (R)	A. L. Murrow (R)
Woodward	J. Don Williams (D)	J. Don Williams (D)	J. Don Williams (D)	William R. Burkett (R)

[1] Died Oct. 28, 1958. No interim successor elected.
[2] Died Oct. 11, 1957. No interim successor elected.
[3] Resigned. No interim successor elected.
[4] Died June 19, 1957. No interim successor elected.
[5] Died Feb. 25, 1958. No interim successor elected.
[6] Died Nov. 17, 1960. Sam Sullivan (D) elected Dec. 13, 1960, to fill unexpired term.
[7] Died Aug. 22, 1957. No Interim successor elected.
[8] Died June 2, 1960. Spencer Bernard (D) substitute at General Election by Democratic Central Committee.
[9] Died June 5, 1959. No interim successor elected.
[10] Died June 20, 1956. No interim successor elected.
[11] Died Oct. 28, 1955. No interim successor elected.

Twenty-Ninth to Thirty-Second Legislatures

Beginning with the 30th Legislature, members were elected by district rather than by county.

County	1963 • 29th	Dist	1965 • 30th	1967 • 31st	1969 • 32nd
Speakers	J.D. McCarty (D)		J. D. McCarty (D)	Rex Privett (D)	Rex Privett (D)
Adair	Bill T. Harper (D)	1	Joe G. Hendrix (D)	Jimmie Lane (D)	Mike Murphy (D)
Alfalfa	Scott Edward Tuxhorn (R)	2	Ray Fine (D)	Ray Fine (D)	Ray Fine (D)
Atoka	Harold Thomas (D)	3	Rucker Blankenship (D)	Rucker Blankenship (D)	Mike Sullivan (D)
Beaver	Merle Lansden (D)	4	William P. Willis (D)	William P. Willis (D)	William P. Willis (D)
Beckham	Homer R. Holcomb (D)	5	Wiley Sparkman (D)	Wiley Sparkman (D)	Wiley Sparkman (D)
Blaine	James F. Burnham (D)	6	J. D. Witt (D)	J. D. Witt (D)	J. D. Witt (D)
Bryan	John Massey (D)	7	Joseph E. Mountford (D)	Joseph E. Mountford (D)	Joseph E. Mountford (D)
	Pauline Tabor (D)	8	J. W. Bynum (D)	J. W. Bynum (D)	J. D. Whorton (R)

Twenty-Ninth to Thirty-Second Legislatures

Beginning with the 30ᵗʰ Legislature, members were elected by district rather than by county.

County	1963 • 29th	Dist	1965 • 30th	1967 • 31st	1969 • 32nd
Caddo	R. L. Goodfellow (D)	9	Bill Briscoe (D)	Bill Briscoe (D)	Bill Briscoe (D)
	J. M. Kardokus (D)	10	James W. Connor (R)	James W. Connor (R)	James W. Connor (R)
Canadian	Ralph Watkins (D)	11	C. W. Doornbos (R)	C. W. Doornbos (R)	C. W. Doornbos (R)
	Paul G. Liebmann (D)	12	V. H. Odom (D)	V. H. Odom (D)	V. H. Odom (D)
Carter	Burke G. Mordy (D)	13	Mike Frix (D)	Mike Frix (D)	Jim L. Barker (D)
	R. B. Hammer (D)	14	William L. Nigh (D)	William L. Nigh (D)	John L. Monks (D)
Cherokee	William P. Willis (D)	15	Martin Odom (D)	Martin Odom (D)	Martin Odom (D)
Choctaw	Lucien C. Spear (D)	16	Ed Cole (D)	Ed Cole (D)	Ed Cole (D)
Cimarron	Carl G. Etling (R)	17	Jim Cook (D)	William G. Jones (D)	William G. Jones (D)
Cleveland	Ralph W. Hamilton (D)	18	William H. Skeith (D)	William H. Skeith (D)	William H. Skeith (D)
	Leland Wolf (D)	19	Wayne Sanguin (D)	Wayne Sanguin (D)	Wayne Sanguin (D)
	Jack Odom (D)	20	John D. Rushing (D)	John D. Rushing (D)	Gary Edison Payne (D)
Coal	Herman L. Baumert (D)	21	Pauline Tabor (D)	Pauline Tabor (D)	Pauline Tabor (D)
Comanche	Jim Taliaferro (D)	22	Kenneth E. Converse (D)	Kenneth E. Converse (D)	Kenneth E. Converse (D)
	Donald W. Beauchamp (D)	23	W. W. Burnett (D)	Charles W. Vann (D)	Charles W. Vann (D)
	Alfred Thomas (D)				
	Walter Hutchins (D)	24	Hugh M. Sandlin (D)	Hugh M. Sandlin (D)	Hugh M. Sandlin (D)
Cotton	Tracy Daugherty (D)	25	Lonnie L. Abbott (D)	Lonnie L. Abbott (D)	Lonnie L. Abbott (D)
Craig	Harold D. Morgan (D)	26	Tom Stevens (D) [1]	John T. Levergood (D)	John T. Levergood (D) [2]
Creek	Heber Finch Jr. (D)	27	James B. Townsend (D)	James B. Townsend (D)	James B. Townsend (D)
	William K. Shibley (D)	28	Raymond W. Reed (D)	David L. Boren (D)	David L. Boren (D)
Custer	M. A. Diel (D)	29	Lou S. Allard (D)	Lou S. Allard (D)	Lou S. Allard (D)
Delaware	Wiley Sparkman (D)	30	Heber Finch Jr. (D)	Heber Finch Jr. (D)	Heber Finch Jr. (D)
Dewey	E. D. Nichols (D)	31	Ruth M. Patterson (R)	Ruth M. Patterson (R)	Donald Coffin (D)
Ellis	Jack M. Harrison (D)	32	Barbour Cox (D)	Barbour Cox (D)	Barbour Cox (D)
Garfield	Bert F. Page (R)	33	H. L. Sparks (D)	Allen Williamson (D)	Allen Williamson (D)
	James H. Gungoll (R)	34	Jake E. Hesser (D)	Jake E. Hesser (D)	Jake E. Hesser (D)
	Harold V. Hunter (R)	35	Rex Privett (D)	Rex Privett (D)	Rex Privett (D)
Garvin	W. W. Burnett (D)	36	Virgil B. Tinker (D)	Lewis Bean (D)	Lewis Bean (D)
	Tom E. Strickland (D)	37	Ray L. Peterson (D)	Jerry B. Peterson (R)	Jerry B. Peterson (R) [3]
Grady	A. J. Lance (D)	38	Brian F. Conaghan (R)	Brian F. Conaghan (R)	Brian F. Conaghan (R)
	Spencer T. Bernard (D)	39	Lynn Thornhill (R)	Lynn Thornhill (R)	Lynn Thornhill (R)
Grant	Lynn Thornhill (R)	40	Bert Page (R)	Bert Page (R)	Tom Rogers (D)
Greer	Elmo B. Hurst (D)	41	Harold V. Hunter (R)	Harold V. Hunter (R)	Harold V. Hunter (R) [4]
Harmon	J. B. Fowler (D)	42	Robert L. Barr (D)	Robert L. Barr (D)	William J. Gooden (R)
Harper	Clayton H. Lauer (R)	43	Ralph Watkins (D)	Ralph Watkins (D)	Anna Belle Wiedemann (D)
Haskell	Earl W. Bilyeu (D)	44	Phil Smalley (D)	Lee Cate (D)	Lee Cate (D)
Hughes	Stona Fitch (D)	45	Leland Wolf (D)	Leland Wolf (D)	Leland Wolf (D)

Twenty-Ninth to Thirty-Second Legislatures

Beginning with the 30th Legislature, members were elected by district rather than by county.

County	1963 • 29th	Dist	1965 • 30th	1967 • 31st	1969 • 32nd
Jackson	Guy K. Horton (D)	46	Norman A. Smith (D)	Norman A. Smith (D)	Norman A. Smith (D)
	Larry Dale Derryberry (D)	47	Spencer T. Bernard (D)	Spencer T. Bernard (D)	Spencer T. Bernard (D)
Jefferson	W. D. Bradley (D)	48	Burke G. Mordy (D)	Harry L. Bickford (D)	Harry L. Bickford (D)
Johnston	C. D. Robertson Jr. (D)	49	W. D. Bradley (D)	W. D. Bradley (D)	W. D. Bradley (D)
Kay	James W. Burger (D)	50	Jerome Sullivan Jr. (D)	William R. Tarwater (D)	William R. Tarwater (D)
	Brian F. Conaghan (R)	51	Vernon Dunn (D)	Vernon Dunn (D)	Vernon Dunn (D)
	Ray Lewis Davis (R)	52	Larry Dale Derryberry (D)	Larry Dale Derryberry (D)	Larry Dale Derryberry (D)
Kingfisher	Milton W. Priebe (R)	53	Frank G. Patterson (D)	Frank G. Patterson (D)	Frank G. Patterson (D)
Kiowa	William W. Metcalf (D)	54	David Hutchens (D)	David Hutchens (D)	David Hutchens (D)
Latimer	Jim Cook (D)	55	Don R. Greenhaw (D)	Don R. Greenhaw (D)	Don R. Greenhaw (D)
LeFlore	Tom Traw (D)	56	Robert L. Goodfellow (D)	Robert L. Goodfellow (D)	Robert L. Goodfellow (D)
	Ralph Vandiver (D)	57	J. O. Dickey Jr. (D)	J. O. Dickey Jr. (D)	David Stratton (D)
Lincoln	Barbour Cox (D)	58	A. L. Murrow (R)	Lewis M. Kamas (R)	Lewis M. Kamas (R)
Logan	Dick Fogarty (D)	59	Jack M. Harrison (D)	Jack M. Harrison (D)	Jack M. Harrison (D)
Love	Willard O. Willis (D)	60	J. B. Fowler (D)	J. B. Fowler (D)	Carl Robinson (D)
McClain	Norman A. Smith (D)	61	Mike Grey (D)	Mike Grey (D)	Marvin E. McKee (D)
McCurtain	Garfield Settles (D)	62	D. W. Beauchamp (D)	D. W. Beauchamp (D)	D. W. Beauchamp (D)
	Mort A. Welch (D)	63	D. D. Raibourn (D)	D. D. Raibourn (D)	D. D. Raibourn (D)
McIntosh	Martin Odom (D)	64	Walter Hutchins (D)	Walter Hutchins (D)	Jack L. I. Lindstrom (D)
Major	Art F. Bower (R)	65	J. Fred Ferrell Jr. (D)	J. Fred Ferrell Jr. (D)	J. Fred Ferrell Jr. (D)
Marshall	Delmas L. Northcutt (D)	66	Tot Brown (D)	Tot Brown (D)	Clyde E. Browers (D)
Mayes	J. W. Bynum (D)	67	Douglas C. Wixson (R)	Douglas C. Wixson (R)	Douglas C. Wixson (R)
Murray	Carl Williams (D)	68	Robert E. Hopkins (D)	Robert E. Hopkins (D)	Robert E. Hopkins (D)
Muskogee	Bill Bull (D)	69	Joe E. Musgrave (R)	Joe E. Musgrave (R)	Joe E. Musgrave (R)
	Max Rust (D)				
	Russell Ruby (D)	70	Joseph R. McGraw (R) [5]	James M. Inhofe (R) [6]	Richard E. Hancock (R)
Noble	Henry Dolezal (R)	71	Warren E. Green (R)	Warren E. Green (R)	Warren E. Green (R)
Nowata	Bill Shipley (D)	72	John W. McCune (D)	John W. McCune (D)	John W. McCune (D)
Okfuskee	Harlon S. Avey (D)	73	Curtis L. Lawson (D)	Curtis L. Lawson (D)	Ben H. Hill (D)
Oklahoma	Jack R. Skaggs (D)	74	George Hargrave Jr. (D)	C. G. Hargrave (D)	C. G. Hargrave (D)
	J. D. McCarty (D)				
	J. Thomas Taggart (R)	75	Roger L. Smithey (D)	Roger L. Smithey (D)	Roger L. Smithey (D)
	Bryce Baggett (D)	76	Percy Butler (R)	Stephen C. Wolfe (R)	Stephen C. Wolfe (R)
	Red Andrews (D)				
	George C. Keyes (D)	77	William F. Poulos (D)	William F. Poulos (D)	William F. Poulos (D)
	G. T. Blankenship (R)	78	Howard D. Williams (R)	Howard D. Williams (R)	Howard D. Williams (R)
Okmulgee	Ed Cole (D)	79	Leslie Guy Ferguson (R)	Leslie Guy Ferguson (R)	Leslie Guy Ferguson (R)
	Tommie J. Yates (D)	80	Peyton A. Breckinridge (R)	Charles R. Ford (R)	Charles R. Ford (R)
Osage	Tom D. Tate (D)	81	C. H. Spearman Jr. (D)	C. H. Spearman Jr. (D)	C. H. Spearman Jr. (D)
	Virgil B. Tinker (D)	82	T. W. Bill Holaday (R)	T. W. Bill Holaday (R)	T. W. Bill Holaday (R)

Twenty-Ninth to Thirty-Second Legislatures

Beginning with the 30th Legislature, members were elected by district rather than by county.

County	1963 • 29th	Dist	1965 • 30th	1967 • 31st	1969 • 32nd
Ottawa	Joseph E. Mountford (D)	83	G. T. Blankenship (R)	Ralph G. Thompson (R)	Ralph G. Thompson (R)
	Pat S. McCue (D)	84	Nathan S. Sherman (D)	Texanna L. Hatchett (R)	Texanna L. Hatchett (R)
Pawnee	Rex Privett (D)	85	John Whitfield Drake (R)	George Camp (R)	George Camp (R)
Payne	H. L. Sparks (D)	86	J. Thomas Taggart (R)	J. Thomas Taggart (R)	J. Thomas Taggart (R)
	Jake E. Hesser (D)	87	George Camp (R)	Denton I. Howard (R)	Denton I. Howard (R)
Pittsburg	William H. Skeith (D)	88	Red Andrews (D)	Red Andrews (D)	Red Andrews (D)
	Tom McChristian (D)	89	L. H. Bengtson Jr. (D)	L. H. Bengtson Jr. (D)	L. H. Bengtson Jr. (D)
Pontotoc	Lonnie L. Abbott (D)	90	Thomas A. Bamberger (D)	Thomas A. Bamberger (D)	Thomas A. Bamberger (D)
	Clive Rigsby (D)	91	Joe L. Roselle (D)	Michael E. Fair (R)	Kenneth R. Nance (D)
Pottawatomie	Tom Stevens (D)	92	J. D. McCarty (D)	Vondel L. Smith (R)	Marvin B. York (D)
	John T. Levergood (D)	93	E. W. Smith (D)	E. W. Smith (D)	E. W. Smith (D)
Pushmataha	Ray Tucker (D)	94	Ray Trent (D)	Ray Trent (D)	Ray Trent (D)
Roger Mills	Jodie S. Moad (D)	95	A. J. Clemons (D)	A. J. Clemons (D)	A. J. Clemons (D)
Rogers	Bill Briscoe (D)	96	John Miskelly Jr. (D)	John Miskelly Jr. (D)	John Miskelly Jr. (D)
Seminole	Raymond W. Reed (D)	97	Jerry D. Sokolosky (D)	Jerry D. Sokolosky (D)	Hannah D. Atkins (D)
	Laurence P. Howze (D)	98	John B. White (D)	A. Visanio Johnson (D)	A. Visanio Johnson (D)
Sequoyah	Maynard E. Blackard (D)	99	Archibald B. Hill Jr. (D)	Archibald B. Hill Jr. (D)	Archibald B. Hill Jr. (D)
Stephens	Jerome Sullivan Jr. (D)				
	Wayne Holden (D)				
Texas	George Russell Gear (R)				
Tillman	Frank G. Patterson (D)				
Tulsa	Joe E. Musgrave (R)				
	W. Timothy Dowd (R)				
	Douglas C. Wixson (R)				
	Richard F. Taylor (R)				
	Ralph S. Rhoades (R)				
	John W. McCune (D)				
	Laurence W. Gunnison (R)				
Wagoner	V. H. Odom (D)				
Washington	James W. Connor (R)				
	C. W. Doornbos (D)				
Washita	Don R. Greenhaw (D)				
Woods	A. L. Murrow (R)				
Woodward	William R. Burkett (R)				

[1] Died Feb. 16, 1965. John T. Levergood (D) elected at Special Election, March 16, 1965, to fill unexpired term.

[2] Died March 7, 1969. Russell Wayland (D) elected at Special Election, April 15, 1969, to fill unexpired term.

[3] Resigned. Fred L. Boettcher (D) elected at Special Election, Jan. 13, 1970, to fill unexpired term.

[4] Resigned. Robert E. Anderson (R) elected at Special Election, July 22, 1969, to fill unexpired term.

[5] Resigned after winning re-election in Nov. 8, 1966, General Election and elected to State Senate at Special Election, Dec. 20, 1966.

[6] Elected to succeed Joseph McGraw (R) at Special Election, Dec. 20, 1966.

Thirty-Third to Thirty-Sixth Legislatures

District	1971 • 33rd	1973 • 34th	1975 • 35th	1977 • 36th
Speakers	Rex Privett (D)	William P. Willis (D)	William P. Willis (D)	William P. Willis (D)

Thirty-Third to Thirty-Sixth Legislatures

District	1971 • 33rd	1973 • 34th	1975 • 35th	1977 • 36th
1	Mike Murphy (D)	Mike Murphy (D)	Mike Murphy (D)	Mike Murphy (D)
2	Ray Fine (D)	Bob Parris (D)	Bob Parris (D)	Bob Parris (D)
3	Mike Sullivan (D)	Joe Johnson (D)	Joe Johnson (D)	Mick Thompson (D)
4	William P. Willis (D)	William P. Willis (D)	William P. Willis (D)	William P. Willis (D)
5	Wiley Sparkman (D)	Wiley Sparkman (D)	Wiley Sparkman (D)	Wiley Sparkman (D)
6	J. D. Witt (D)	J. D. Witt (D)²	George Vaughn (D)	George Vaughn (D)
7	Joseph E. Mountford (D)	Joseph E. Mountford (D)	Joseph E. Fitzgibbon (D)	Joseph E. Fitzgibbon (D)
8	J. D. Whorton (R)	J. D. Whorton (R)	J. D. Whorton (R)	J. D. Whorton (R)
9	Bill Briscoe (D)	Bill Briscoe D)	Bill Briscoe (D)	Bill J. Crutcher (D)
10	Jerry T. Pierce (R)	A. C. Holden (D)	A. C. Holden (D)	A. C. Holden (D)
11	C. W. Doornbos (R)	C. W. Doornbos (R)	Robert M. Kane (R)	Robert M. Kane (R)
12	V. H. Odom (D)	V. H. Odom (D)	V. H. Odom (D)⁵	Bill Lancaster (D)
13	Jan Eric Cartwright (D)	Jan Eric Cartwright (D)	Drew Edmondson (D)	Jim L. Barker (D)
14	John L. Monks (D)	John L. Monks (D)	John L. Monks (D)	John Monks (D)
15	Leo H. Wynn (D)	Leo H. Wynn (D)	Charles R. Peterson (D)	Charles R. Peterson (D)
16	Ed Cole (D)	Ed Cole (D)	J. B. Bennett (D)	J. B. Bennett (D)
17	Don Huddleston (D)	Don Huddleston (D)	E. A. Red Caldwell (D)	E. A. Red Caldwell (D)
18	William H. Skeith (D)	William J. Ervin (D)	William J. Ervin (D)	William J. Ervin (D)
19	Wayne Sanguin (D)	Wayne Sanguin (D)	Hollis E. Roberts (D)	Hollis E. Roberts (D)
20	Gary Edison Payne (D)	Gary Edison Payne (D)	Gary Edison Payne (D)⁶	Bob A. Trent (D)
21	Roy A. Boatner (D)	Roy A. Boatner (D)	Guy Davis (D)	Guy Davis (D)
22	Kenneth E. Converse (D)	Kenneth E. Converse (D)	Kenneth E. Converse (D)	Kenneth E. Converse (D)
23	A. L. Carlton (D)	Charles J. Prentice (R)	Charles J. Prentice (R)	Harold D. Monlux (R)
24	Hugh M. Sandlin (D)	Hugh M. Sandlin (D)³	Bill Robinson (D)	Bill Robinson (D)
25	Lonnie L. Abbott (D)	Lonnie L. Abbott (D)	Lonnie L. Abbott (D)	Lonnie L. Abbott (D)
26	Russell Wayland (D)	Charles T. Henry (D)	Charles T. Henry (D)	Robert H. Henry (D)
27	James B. Townsend (D)	James B. Townsend (D)	James B. Townsend (D)	James B. Townsend (D)
28	David L. Boren (D)	David L. Boren (D)	Jeff Johnston (D)	Jeff Johnston (D)
29	Harlon S. Avey (D)¹	Lou S. Allard (D)⁴	Oval Cunningham (D)	Oval Cunningham (D)
30	Heber Finch Jr. (D)	Heber Finch Jr. (D)	Donald D. Thompson (D)	Donald D. Thompson (D)
31	Donald L. Coffin (D)	James R. Cummings (R)	James R. Cummings (R)	James R. Cummings (R)
32	Barbour Cox (D)	Charlie O. Morgan (D)	Charlie O. Morgan (D)	Charlie O. Morgan (D)
33	Allen Williamson (D)	Allen Williamson (D)	Joe R. Manning Jr. (R)	Joe R. Manning Jr. (R)
34	Daniel D. Draper Jr. (D)	Daniel D. Draper Jr. (D)	Daniel D. Draper Jr. (D)	Daniel D. Draper Jr. (D)
35	Rex Privett (D)	Don Johnson (D)	Don Johnson (D)	Don Johnson (D)
36	Billy F. Kennedy (D)	Billy F. Kennedy (D)	Billy F. Kennedy (D)	Billy F. Kennedy (D)
37	Fred L. Boettcher (D)	Fred L. Boettcher (D)	James Doepel Holt (R)	James Doepel Holt (R)
38	Brian F. Conaghan (R)	Brian F. Conaghan (R)⁷	Dorothy D. Conaghan (R)	Dorothy D. Conaghan (R)

Thirty-Third to Thirty-Sixth Legislatures

District	1971 • 33rd	1973 • 34th	1975 • 35th	1977 • 36th
39	Lynn Thornhill (R)	Lynn Thornhill (R)	Lynn Thornhill (R)	Robert Milacek (R)
40	Tom Rogers (D)	Tom Rogers (D)	Tom Rogers (D)	Tom Rogers (D)
41	Robert E. Anderson (R)	Robert E. Anderson (R)	Robert E. Anderson (R)	Robert E. Anderson (R)
42	William J. Gooden (R)	William J. Gooden (R)	Tom R. Stephenson (D)	Tom R. Stephenson (D)
43	Anna Belle Wiedemann (D)	Mark Hammons (D)	Mark Hammons (D)	Mark Hammons (D)
44	Lee Cate (D)	Lee Cate (D)[8]	Mina Hibdon (R)	Cleta Deatherage (D)
45	Leland Wolf (D)	Leland Wolf (D)	Glenn Eldon Floyd (D)	Glenn Eldon Floyd (D)
46	Charles Elder (D)	Charles Elder (D)	Charles Elder (D)	Charles Elder (D)
47	Spencer T. Bernard (D)	Spencer T. Bernard (D)	Spencer T. Bernard (D)	Spencer T. Bernard (D)
48	Don Duke (D)	Don Duke (D)	Don Duke (D)	Don Duke (D)
49	W. D. Bradley (D)	W. D. Bradley (D)	W. D. Bradley (D)	W. D. Bradley (D)
50	William R. Tarwater (D)	Robert Wilson (D)	Robert Wilson (D)	Robert Wilson (D)
51	Vernon Dunn (D)	Vernon Dunn (D)	Vernon Dunn (D)	Vernon Dunn (D)
52	Howard Paul Cotner (D)	Howard Paul Cotner (D)	Howard Paul Cotner (D)	Howard Paul Cotner (D)
53	Bob E. Harper (D)	Bob E. Harper (D)	Bob E. Harper (D)	Bob E. Harper (D)
54	Victor E. Wickersham (D)	Ron Shotts (R)	Ron Shotts (R)	Kenneth P. Craig (D)
55	Don R. Greenhaw (D)	Jerry Weichel (D)	Jerry Weichel (D)	Jerry Weichel (D)
56	James M. Kardokus (D)	James M. Kardokus (D)	James M. Kardokus (D)	James M. Kardokus (D)
57	David Stratton (D)	David Stratton (D)	David Stratton (D)	Wayne Winn (D)
58	Lewis M. Kamas (R)	Lewis M. Kamas (R)	Lewis M. Kamas (R)	Lewis M. Kamas (R)
59	Jack M. Harrison (D)	Earnest Isch (R)	Mark Bradshaw (D)	Mark Bradshaw (D)[9]
60	Carl Robinson (D)	Victor E. Wickersham (D)	Victor E. Wickersham (D)	Victor E. Wickersham (D)
61	Marvin E. McKee (D)	Marvin E. McKee (D)	Marvin E. McKee (D)	Marvin E. McKee (D)
62	Don Davis (D)	Don Davis (D)	Don Davis (D)	Don Davis (D)
63	Gordon Beznoska (D)	Gordon Beznoska (D)	Gordon Beznoska (D)	Marvin L. Baughman (D)
64	Jack L. I. Lindstrom (D)	Jack L. I. Lindstrom (D)	Roy B. Hooper Jr. (D)	Roy B. Hooper Jr. (D)
65	J. Fred Ferrell Jr. (D)	J. Fred Ferrell Jr. (D)	J. Fred Ferrell Jr. (D)	Jim R. Glover (D)
66	David M. Riggs (D)	David M. Riggs (D)	David M. Riggs (D)	David M. Riggs (D)
67	Douglas C. Wixson (R)	Douglas C. Wixson (R)	Joan King Hastings (R)	Joan King Hastings (R)
68	Robert E. Hopkins (D)	Robert E. Hopkins (D)	Robert E. Hopkins (D)	Robert E. Hopkins (D)
69	Joe E. Musgrave (R)	William E. Foster (D)	William J. Wiseman Jr. (R)	William J. Wiseman Jr. (R)
70	Richard E. Hancock (R)	Frank Keating (R)	Paul D. Brunton (R)	Paul D. Brunton (R)
71	Warren E. Green (R)	Warren E. Green (R)	Warren E. Green (R)	Helen Arnold (R)
72	John W. McCune (D)	Mandell L. Matheson (D)	Mandell L. Matheson (D)	Mandell L. Matheson (D)
73	Ben H. Hill (D)[10]	Bernard J. McIntyre (D)	Bernard J. McIntyre (D)	Bernard J. McIntyre (D)
74	C. G. Hargrave (D)	Jerry Hargrave (D)	Robert V. Cullison (D)	Robert V. Cullison (D)
75	Rodger Allen Randle (D)	Jim W. Hardesty (D)	Jim W. Hardesty (D)	Jim W. Hardesty (D)[11]
76	Stephen C. Wolfe (R)	Jerry L. Smith (R)	Jerry L. Smith (R)	Jerry L. Smith (R)

Thirty-Third to Thirty-Sixth Legislatures

District	1971 • 33rd	1973 • 34th	1975 • 35th	1977 • 36th
77	William F. Poulos (D)	William F. Poulos (D)	William F. Poulos (D)	William F. Poulos (D)
78	Howard D. Williams (R)	Howard D. Williams (R)	Charles Cleveland (D)	Charles Cleveland (D)
79	Leslie Guy Ferguson (R)	Leslie Guy Ferguson (R)	Ted M. Cowan (R)	Ted M. Cowan (R)
80	Charles R. Ford (R)	Charles R. Ford (R)	Charles R. Ford (R)	Charles R. Ford (R)
81	C. H. Spearman Jr. (D)	Jan Turner (R)	Neal A. McCaleb (R)	Neal A. McCaleb (R)
82	T. W. Bill Holaday (R)	T. W. Bill Holaday (R)	T. W. Bill Holaday (R)	T. W. Bill Holaday (R)
83	Kent F. Frates (R)	Kent F. Frates (R)	Kent F. Frates (R)	Kent F. Frates (R)
84	Texanna L. Hatchett (R)	Francis D. Oakes (R)	Judy Swinton (D)	Judy Swinton (D)
85	George Camp (R)	George Camp (R)	George Camp (R)	George Camp (R)
86	J. Thomas Taggart (R)	J. Thomas Taggart (R)	David Craig Hood (D)	David Craig Hood (D)
87	E. C. Sandy Sanders (D)	E. C. Sandy Sanders (D)	E. C. Sandy Sanders (D)	E. C. Sandy Sanders (D)
88	Red Andrews (D)	Don Curry Denman (R)	Don Curry Denman (R)	Don Curry Denman (R)
89	L. H. Bengtson Jr. (D)	L. H. Bengtson Jr. (D)	L. H. Bengtson Jr. (D)	L. H. Bengtson Jr. (D)
90	Thomas A. Bamberger (D)	Thomas A. Bamberger (D)	Thomas A. Bamberger (D)	J. Mike Lawter (D)
91	Kenneth R. Nance (D)	Kenneth R. Nance (D)	Kenneth R. Nance (D)	Kenneth R. Nance (D)
92	Marvin York (D)	Marvin York (D)	Jim Fried (D)	Jim Fried (D)
93	Don W. Kilpatrick (D)	Don W. Kilpatrick (D)	Don W. Kilpatrick (D)	Jerry Steward (D)
94	Ray Trent (D)	Ray Trent (D)	Fred C. Joiner (D)	Fred C. Joiner (D)
95	A. J. Clemons (D)	David C. Craighead (D)	David C. Craighead (D)	David C. Craighead (D)
96	John Miskelly Jr. (D)	John Miskelly Jr. (D)	John Miskelly Jr. (D)	John Miskelly (D) [12]
97	Hannah D. Atkins (D)	Hannah D. Atkins (D)	Hannah D. Atkins (D)	Hannah D. Atkins (D)
98	A. Visanio Johnson (D)	Ross Duckett (D)	Ross Duckett (D)	Ross Duckett (D)
99	Archibald Hill (D)	A. Visanio Johnson (D)	A. Visanio Johnson (D)	A. Visanio Johnson (D)
100		Terry L. Campbell (R)	Terry L. Campbell (R)	Terry L. Campbell (R)
101		Carl Twidwell Jr. (D)	Carl Twidwell Jr. (D)	Carl Twidwell Jr. (D)

[1] Died June 15, 1972. No interim successor elected.
[2] Died May 23, 1973. George Vaughn (D) elected at Special Election, Aug. 21, 1973, to fill unexpired term.
[3] Died Sept. 10, 1974. No interim successor elected.
[4] Died Nov. 2, 1974. Oval Cunningham (D) elected at Special Election, Jan. 7, 1975, to fill unexpired term.
[5] Died Feb. 14, 1975. Bill Lancaster (D) elected at Special Election, April 29, 1975, to fill unexpired term.
[6] Resigned July 1, 1976. No interim successor elected.
[7] Died April 1, 1973. Dorothy Conaghan (R) elected at Special Election, May 29, 1973, to fill unexpired term.
[8] Resigned. Mina Hibdon (R) elected at Special Election, Oct. 2, 1973, to fill unexpired term.
[9] Died May 29, 1978. No interim successor elected.
[10] Died Sept. 17, 1971. Bernard McIntyre (D) elected at Special Election Dec. 7, 1971, to fill unexpired term.
[11] Died Jan. 7, 1978. Gene D. Combs (D) elected at Special Election, March 7, 1978, to fill unexpired term.
[12] Died June 9, 1977. James E. Briscoe (D) elected at Special Election, August 16, 1977, to fill unexpired term.

Thirty-Seventh to Fortieth Legislatures

District	1979 • 37th	1981 • 38th	1983 • 39th	1985 • 40th
Speakers	Daniel D. Draper Jr. (D)	Daniel D. Draper Jr. (D)	Daniel D. Draper Jr. (D)	Jim L. Barker (D) Jim L. Barker was elected Speaker Sept. 19, 1983.
1	Mike Murphy (D)	Mike Murphy (D)	Mike Murphy (D)	Mike Murphy (D)
2	Don Mentzer (D)	Don Mentzer (D)	Don Mentzer (D)	Don Mentzer (D)
3	Mick Thompson (D)	Mick Thompson (D)	Mick Thompson (D)	James E Hamilton (D)
4	William P. Willis (D)	William P. Willis (D)	William P. Willis (D)	William P. Willis (D)
5	Wiley Sparkman (D)	Wiley Sparkman (D)	Rick M. Littlefield (D)	Rick M. Littlefield (D)
6	George Vaughn (D)	George Vaughn (D)	George Vaughn (D)	George Vaughn (D)
7	Joseph E. Fitzgibbon (D)	Joseph Fitzgibbon (D)	Joseph Fitzgibbon (D) [1]	Larry D. Roberts (D)
8	J. D. Whorton (R)	J. D. Whorton (R)	J. D. Whorton (R)	J. D. Whorton (R)
9	Stratton Taylor (D)	Stratton Taylor (D)	Billy C. Boyd (D)	Bob L. Brown (R)
10	A. C. Holden (D)	A. C. Holden (D)	A. C. Holden (D)	A. C. Holden (D)
11	Robert M. Kane (R)	Donald T. Koppel (R)	Don T. Koppel (R)	Don T. Koppel (R)
12	Bill Lancaster (D)	Bill Lancaster (D)	Bill Lancaster (D)	Robert T. Harris (D)
13	Jim L. Barker (D)	Jim L. Barker (D)	Jim L. Barker (D)	Jim L. Barker (D)
14	John Monks (D)	John Monks (D)	John Monks (D)	John Monks (D)
15	Charles R. Peterson (D)	Charles R. Peterson (D)	Charles R. Peterson (D)	Walter R. McDonald (D)
16	Franklin D. Shurden (D)	Franklin D. Shurden (D)	Franklin D. Shurden (D)	Franklin D. Shurden (D)
17	E. A. Red Caldwell (D)	E. A. Red Caldwell (D)	E. A. Red Caldwell (D)	Gene Newby (D)
18	Frank Harbin (D)	Frank Harbin (D)	Frank Harbin (D)	Frank Harbin (D)
19	Hollis E. Roberts (D)	Gary L. Sherrer (D)	Gary L. Sherrer (D)	Gary L. Sherrer (D)
20	Bob A. Trent (D)	Bob A. Trent (D)	Kenneth E. Converse (D)	Kenneth E. Converse (D)
21	Guy Davis (D)	Guy Davis (D)	Guy Davis (D)	Guy Davis (D)
22	Jack Kelly (D)	Jack Kelly (D)	Jack Kelly (D)	Jack Kelly (D)
23	Harold D. Monlux (R)	Twyla Mason (D)	Twyla Mason Gray (D)	Kevin A. Easley (D)
24	Bill Robinson (D)	Bill Robinson (D)	Glen D. Johnson (D)	Glen D. Johnson (D)
25	Lonnie L. Abbott (D)	Lonnie L. Abbott (D)	Lonnie L. Abbott (D)	Lonnie L. Abbott (D)
26	Robert H. Henry (D)	Robert H. Henry (D)	Robert H. Henry (D)	Robert H. Henry (D)
27	James B. Townsend (D)	Steve Lewis (D)	Steve Lewis (D)	Steve Lewis (D)
28	Ronald G. Sheppard (D)	Enoch Kelly Haney (D)	Enoch Kelly Haney (D)	Enoch Kelly Haney (D)
29	Oval H. Cunningham (D)	Oval H. Cunningham (D)	Jim Formby (D)	Jim Formby (D)
30	Donald D. Thompson (D)	Benny F. Vanatta (D)	Benny F. Vanatta (D)	Benny F. Vanatta (D)
31	Frank W. Davis (R)	Frank W. Davis (R)	Frank W. Davis (R)	Frank W. Davis (R)
32	Charlie O. Morgan (D)	Charlie O. Morgan (D)	Charlie O. Morgan (D)	Charlie O. Morgan (D)
33	Joe R. Manning Jr. (R)	Joe R. Manning Jr. (R)	Tom Hall (D)	Michael D. Morris (R)
34	Daniel D. Draper Jr. (D)	Daniel D. Draper Jr. (D)	Daniel D. Draper Jr. (D) [2]	Larry Gish (D)
35	Don Johnson (D)	Don Johnson (D)	Don Johnson (D)	Don Johnson (D) [4]
36	Billy Kennedy (D)	Don Anderson (D)	Don Anderson (D)	Don Anderson (D)

Thirty-Seventh to Fortieth Legislatures

District	1979 • 37th	1981 • 38th	1983 • 39th	1985 • 40th
37	James Doepel Holt (R)	James Doepel Holt (R)	James Doepel Holt (R)	James Doepel Holt (R)
38	Dorothy D. Conaghan (R)	Dorothy D. Conaghan (R)	Dorothy D. Conaghan (R)	Dorothy D. Conaghan (R)
39	Robert Milacek (R)	Robert Milacek (R)	Steven Boeckman (R)	Steven Boeckman (R)
40	Homer Rieger (R)	Homer Rieger (R)	Homer F. Rieger (R)	Homer F. Rieger (R)
41	Robert E. Anderson (R)	Robert E. Anderson (R)	J. Bruce Harvey (R)	John McMillen (R)
42	Tom R. Stephenson (D)	Ralph J. Butch Choate (R)	Don Garrison (D)	Billy Joel Mitchell (D)
43	Donald D. Feddersen (D)	Donald D. Feddersen (D)	Harold Hale (D)	Harold Hale (D)
44	Cleta Deatherage (D)	Cleta Deatherage (D)	Cleta Deatherage (D)	Carolyn Thompson (D)
45	Cal Hobson (D)	Cal Hobson (D)	Cal Hobson (D)	Cal Hobson (D)
46	Charles Elder (D)	Jerry F. Smith (D)	Jerry F. Smith (D)	A. Joe Cunningham (R)
47	Denver Talley (D)	Denver Talley (D)	Denver Talley (D)	Denver Talley (D)
48	Don Duke (D)	Don Duke (D)	Don Duke (D)	Don Duke (D)
49	W. D. Bradley (D)	W. D. Bradley (D)	Bill K. Brewster (D)	Bill K. Brewster (D)
50	Robert Wilson (D)	J. D. Blodgett (D)	J. D. Blodgett (D)	J. D. Blodgett (D)
51	Vernon Dunn (D)	Vernon Dunn (D)	Bill Smith (D)	Bill Smith (D)
52	Howard Cotner (D)	Howard Cotner (D)	Howard Cotner (D)	Howard Cotner (D)
53	Bob E. Harper (D)	Bob E. Harper (D)	Nancy Virtue (D)	Nancy Virtue (D)
54	Helen G. Cole (R)	Helen G. Cole (R)	Helen G. Cole (R)	Kenneth McKenna (R)
55	Jerry Weichel (D)	Jerry Weichel (D)	Emil L. Grieser (D)	Emil L. Grieser (D)
56	James M. Kardokus (D)[3]	Tom J. Manar (D)	Tom J. Manar (D)	Tom J. Manar (D)
57	Wayne Winn (D)	Bill Widener (D)	Bill Widener (D)	Bill Widener (D)
58	Lewis M. Kamas (R)	Lewis M. Kamas (R)	Lewis M. Kamas (R)	Lewis M. Kamas (R)
59	Rollin D. Reimer (D)	Rollin D. Reimer (D)	Rollin D. Reimer (D)	Rollin D. Reimer (D)
60	Willie F. Rogers (D)	Willie F. Rogers (D)	Willie F. Rogers (D)	Danny B. George (D)
61	Walter E. Hill (R)	Walter E. Hill (R)	Walter E. Hill (R)	Walter E. Hill (R)
62	Don C. Davis (D)	Kenny D. Harris (D)	Kenny D. Harris (D)	Kenny D. Harris (D)
63	Marvin Baughman (D)	Marvin Baughman (D)	Marvin Baughman (D)[5]	Loyd Lee Benson (D)
64	Roy B. Hooper Jr. (D)	Roy B. Hooper Jr. (D)	Roy B. Hooper Jr. (D)	Roy B. Hooper Jr. (D)
65	Jim R. Glover (D)	Jim R. Glover (D)	Jim R. Glover (D)	Jim R. Glover (D)
66	David M. Riggs (D)	David M. Riggs (D)	David M. Riggs (D)	David M. Riggs (D)
67	Joan King Hastings (R)	Joan King Hastings (R)	Joan King Hastings (R)	H. Wayne Cozort (R)
68	Robert E. Hopkins (D)	Robert E. Hopkins (D)	Jay Logan (D)	Jay Logan (D)
69	William J. Wiseman Jr. (R)	Nelson Little (R)	Nelson Little (R)	Nelson Little (R)
70	Paul D. Brunton (R)	Penny Williams (D)	Penny Williams (D)	Penny Williams (D)
71	Helen Arnold (R)	Helen Arnold (R)	Bill Clark (R)	Bill Clark (R)
72	Don McCorkell Jr. (D)	Don McCorkell Jr. (D)	Don McCorkell Jr. (D)	Don McCorkell Jr. (D)
73	Bernard J. McIntyre (D)	Bernard J. McIntyre (D)	Don Ross (D)	Don Ross (D)
74	Rodney G. Hargrave (D)	Rodney G. Hargrave (D)	Gene D. Combs (D)	Gene D. Combs (D)

Thirty-Seventh to Fortieth Legislatures

District	1979 • 37th	1981 • 38th	1983 • 39th	1985 • 40th
75	Gene D. Combs (D)	Alene B. Baker (D)	Alene B. Baker (D)	Larry J. Schroeder (D)
76	Jerry L. Smith (R)	James A. Williamson (R)	James A. Williamson (R)	James A. Williamson (R)
77	William F. Poulos (D)	William F. Poulos (D)	Gary Stottlemyre (D)	Gary Stottlemyre (D)
78	Charles Cleveland (D)	Frank F. Pitezel (R)	Frank F. Pitezel (R)	Frank F. Pitezel (R)
79	Ted M. Cowan (R)	James E. Henshaw (R)	James E. Henshaw (R)	James E. Henshaw (R)
80	Charles R. Ford (R)	Charles R. Ford (R)[6]	Joe Gordon (R)	Joe Gordon (R)
81	Neal A. McCaleb (R)	Neal A. McCaleb (R)	Steve Sill (R)	Gaylon L. Stacy (R)
82	T. W. Bill Holaday (R)	George H. Osborne (R)	George H. Osborne (R)	George H. Osborne (R)
83	Stanley W. Alexander (R)	Gean Atkinson (R)	Gean Atkinson (R)	Joe L. Heaton (R)
84	Bill Graves (R)	Bill Graves (R)	Bill Graves (R)	Bill Graves (R)
85	George Camp (R)	George Camp (R)	Porter Davis (R)	Michael J. Hunter (R)
86	Bob Kerr (D)	Rick Stahl (R)	Larry E. Adair (D)	Larry E. Adair (D)
87	E. C. Sandy Sanders (D)	E. C. Sandy Sanders (D)	E. C. Sandy Sanders (D)	E. C. Sandy Sanders (D)
88	Don Denman (D)	Don Denman (D)	Don Denman (D)	Linda H. Larason (D)
89	L. H. Bengtson Jr. (D)	Rebecca Hamilton (D)	Rebecca Hamilton (D)	Rebecca Hamilton (D)
90	J. Mike Lawter (D)	J. Mike Lawter (D)	J. Mike Lawter (D)	J. Mike Lawter (D)
91	Charles Gray (D)	Charles Gray (D)	Keith C. Leftwich (D)	Keith C. Leftwich (D)
92	Jim Fried (D)	Jim Fried (D)	Jim Fried (D)	Dale Patrick (D)
93	Jerry Steward (D)	Ben Brown (D)	Ben Brown (D)	E. Jan Collins (R)
94	Fred C. Joiner (D)	Fred C. Joiner (D)	Fred C. Joiner (D)	Gary C. Bastin (R)
95	David C. Craighead (D)	David C. Craighead (D)	David C. Craighead (D)	David C. Craighead (D)
96	James E. Briscoe (D)	Maxine C. Kincheloe (R)	Maxine C. Kincheloe (R)	Maxine C. Kincheloe (R)
97	Hannah D. Atkins (D)	Kevin Cox (D)	Kevin Cox (D)	Kevin Cox (D)
98	Ross Duckett (D)	Ross Duckett (D)	Ross Duckett (D)	Ross Duckett (D)
99	A. Visanio Johnson (D)	Freddye H. Williams (D)	Freddye H. Williams (D)	Freddye H. Williams (D)
100	Mike Fair (R)	Mike Fair (R)	Mike Fair (R)	Mike Fair (R)
101	Carl Twidwell Jr. (D)	Carl Twidwell Jr. (D)	Carl Twidwell Jr. (D)	Susan M. Milton (R)

[1] Suspended Aug. 18, 1983. Reinstated May 23, 1984 (Art.VIII, Sec.1, Okla. Const.) Larry D. Roberts (D) elected Dec. 6, 1983 to serve during Fitzgibbon's suspension.

[2] Suspended August 18, 1983. Reinstated May 23, 1984 (Art.VIII, Sec.1, Okla. Const.) Larry Gish (D) elected December 6, 1983 to serve during Draper's suspension.

[3] Died Jan. 10, 1979. Tom J. Manar (D) elected at Special Election, Feb. 20, 1979, to fill unexpired term.

[4] Died Feb. 24, 1985. Larry R. Ferguson (R) elected April 30, 1985.

[5] Died Dec. 5, 1983. No interim.

[6] Resigned to run for the Senate. Jim Forrester elected July, 1981.

Forty-First to Forty-Fourth Legislatures

District	1987 • 41st	1989 • 42nd	1991 • 43rd	1993 • 44th
Speakers	Jim L. Barker (D)	Jim L. Barker (D) Steve Lewis (D) Jame L. Barker removed as Speaker of the House on May 17, 1989.	Glen D. Johnson (D)	Glen D. Johnson (D)
1	Mike Murphy (D)	Mike Murphy (D)	Terry J. Matlock (D)	Terry J. Matlock (D)
2	Don Mentzer (D)	Don Mentzer (D)	Don Mentzer (D) [3]	J. T. Stites (D)
3	James E. Hamilton (D)	James E. Hamilton (D)	James E. Hamilton (D)	James E. Hamilton (D)
4	Robert P. Medearis (D)	Benny F. Vanatta (D) [2]	Bob Ed Culver (D)	Bob Ed Culver (D)
5	Rick M. Littlefield (D)	Rick M. Littlefield (D)	Rick M. Littlefield (D)	Joe J. Hutchison (D)
6	George Vaughn (D)	Don Kinnamon (D)	George Vaughn (D)	George H. Vaughn (D)
7	Larry D. Roberts (D)	Larry D. Roberts (D)	Larry D. Roberts (D)	Larry D. Roberts (D)
8	Larry Rice (D)	Larry Rice (D)	Larry Rice (D)	Larry Dean Rice (D)
9	Dwayne Steidley (D)	Dwayne Steidley (D)	Dwayne Steidley (D)	Dwayne Steidley (D)
10	A.C. Holden (D)	James Hager (D)	Gary S. Taylor (D)	Gary S. Taylor (D)
11	Don Koppel (R)	James D. Holt (R)	James R. Dunlap (R)	James R. Dunlap (R)
12	Robert T. Harris (D)	Jim Reese (R)	Jerry W. Hefner (D)	Jerry W. Hefner (D)
13	Jim Barker (D)	Jim Barker (D)	Bill Settle (D)	Bill Settle (D)
14	John Monks (D)	Jeff Potts (D)	John Monks (D)	John Monks (D)
15	Chester Dusty Rhodes (D)	John McMillen (R)	Chester Dusty Rhodes (D)	Chester Dusty Rhodes (D)
16	M.C. Leist (D)	M.C. Leist (D)	M.C. Leist (D)	M.C. Leist (D)
17	Ronald F. Glenn (D)	Harold Hale (D)	Mike Mass (D)	Mike Mass (D)
18	Walt Roberts (D)	Walt Roberts (D)	Walt Roberts (D)	Walt Roberts (D)
19	Gary L. Sherrer (D)	Bart S. Bates (D)	Bart S. Bates (D)	Bart S. Bates (D)
20	Kenneth E. Converse (D)	Tommy Thomas (D)	Tommy Thomas (D)	Tommy Thomas (D)
21	Guy Davis (D)	Guy Davis (D)	James H. Dunegan (D)	James H. Dunegan (D)
22	Gary Coffee (D)	Gary Coffee (D)	Danny Hilliard (D)	Danny Hilliard (D)
23	Kevin A. Easley (D)	Bill K. Brewster (D)	Betty Boyd (D)	Betty Boyd (D)
24	Glen D. Johnson (D)	Ed Apple (R)	Glen D. Johnson (D)	Glen D. Johnson (D)
25	Lonnie L. Abbott (D)	Karroll G. Rhoads (R)	Karroll G. Rhoads (R)	Karroll G. Rhoads (R)
26	George D. Snider (D)	Robert E. Weaver (R)	Robert E. Weaver (R)	Robert E. Weaver (R)
27	Steve Lewis (D)	Steve Lewis (D)	Dale Smith (D)	Dale Smith (D)
28	Jim Morgan (D)	Danny Williams (D)	Danny Williams (D)	Danny Williams (D)
29	Bill Gurley (R)	Bill Gurley (R)	R.C. Lester (D)	David L. Thompson (D)
30	Benny F. Vanatta (D)	Robert P. Medearis (D)	Mike Tyler (D)	Mike Tyler (D)
31	Frank W. Davis (R)	Frank W. Davis (R)	Frank W. Davis (R)	Frank W. Davis (R)
32	Charlie O. Morgan (D)	George Vaughn (D)	Don Kinnamon (D)	Don Kinnamon (D)
33	Michael D. Morris (R)	Jessie Pilgrim (D)	Jessie Pilgrim (D)	Jessie Pilgrim (D) [1]
34	Larry Gish (D)	Larry Gish (D)	Larry Gish (D) [4]	Calvin J. Anthony (D)
35	Larry R. Ferguson (R)	Larry Ferguson (R)	Larry R. Ferguson (R)	Larry R. Ferguson (R)
36	Don Anderson (D)	Gary S. Taylor (D)	James Hager (D)	James Hager (D)

Forty-First to Forty-Fourth Legislatures

District	1987 • 41st	1989 • 42nd	1991 • 43rd	1993 • 44th
37	James D. Holt (R)	James R. Dunlap (R)	James D. Holt (R)	James D. Holt (R)
38	Jim Reese (R)	Jerry W. Hefner (D)	Jim Reese (R)	Jim Reese (R)
39	Steven Emil Boeckman (R)	Steven Emil Boeckman (R)	Steven Boeckman (R)	John A. Bass (D)
40	Homer F. Rieger (R)	James Sears Bryant (D)	Gary Maxey (D)	James Sears Bryant (D)
41	John McMillen (R)	Walter McDonald (D)	Sean Voskuhl (D)	Sean Voskuhl (D)
42	Billy Joel Mitchell (D)	Billy Joel Mitchell (D)	Billy J. Mitchell (D)	Bill Mitchell (D)
43	Harold Hale (D)	Ronald F. Glenn (D)	Tony Kouba (R)	Tony Kouba (R)
44	Carolyn A. Thompson (D)	Carolyn A. Thompson (D)	Carolyn A. Thompson (D)	Laura Boyd (D)
45	Cal Hobson (D)	Cal Hobson (D)	Ed Crocker (D)	Ed Crocker (D)
46	Vickie White (D)	Vickie White (D)	Gary R. York (D)	Gary R. York (D)
47	Denver Talley (D)	Denver Talley (D)	Todd Flake (D)	Todd Flake (D)
48	Don Duke (D)	Don Duke (D)	Al Sadler (D)	Al Sadler (D)
49	Bill K. Brewster (D)	Kevin A. Easley (D)	Fred Stanley (D)	Fred Stanley (D)
50	Ed Apple (R)	Glen D. Johnson (D)	Ed Apple (R)	Ed Apple (R)
51	Bill Smith (D)	Bill Smith (D)	Bill Smith (D)	Bill Smith (D)
52	Howard Cotner (D)	Howard Cotner (D)	Howard Cotner (D)	Howard Cotner (D)
53	John D. Lassiter (D)	John D. Lassiter (D)	Carolyn Coleman (R)	Carolyn Coleman (R)
54	Kenneth McKenna Jr. (R)	Joan Greenwood (R)	Joan Greenwood (R)	Joan Greenwood (R)
55	Emil L. Grieser (D)	Emil L. Grieser (D)	Emil L. Grieser (D)	Jack Bonny (D)
56	Tom J. Manar (D)	Tom J. Manar (D)	Tom J. Manar (D)	Ron Langmacher (D)
57	Bill Widener (D)	Bill Widener (D)	Bill Widener (D)	Bill Widener (D)[5]
58	Lewis Kamas (R)	Elmer Maddux (R)	Elmer Maddux (R)	Elmer Maddux (R)
59	Bert Russell (D)	Frank D. Lucas (R)	Frank D. Lucas (R)	Frank D. Lucas (R)
60	Danny Bruce George (D)[1]	Wendell Powell (D)	James D. Howard (D)	Randy Beutler (D)
61	Walter E. Hill (R)	Jack Begley (D)	Jack Begley (D)	Jack Begley (D)
62	Ken Harris (D)	Jim Maddox (D)	Jim Maddox (D)	Jim Maddox (D)
63	Loyd Lee Benson (D)	Loyd Lee Benson (D)	Loyd L. Benson (D)	Loyd Benson (D)
64	Sid Hudson (D)	Sid Hudson (D)	Sid Hudson (D)	Ron Kirby (D)
65	Jim R. Glover (D)	Jim R. Glover (D)	Jim Glover (D)	Jim R. Glover (D)
66	Russ Roach (D)	Russ Roach (D)	Russ Roach (D)	Russ Roach (D)
67	H. Wayne Cozort (R)	H. Wayne Cozort (R)	H. Wayne Cozort (R)	Wayne Cozort (R)
68	Jay Logan (D)	Jay Logan (D)	Shelby D. Satterfield (D)	Shelby Satterfield (D)
69	William A. Veitch (R)	William A. Veitch (R)	William A. Veitch (R)	David Smith (R)
70	Penny Williams (D)	John Bryant (R)	John Bryant (R)	John Bryant (R)
71	Bill Clark (R)	Rob Johnson (R)	Rob Johnson (R)	Rob Johnson (R)
72	Don McCorkell Jr. (D)	Don McCorkell Jr. (D)	Don McCorkell Jr. (D)	Don McCorkell (D)
73	Don Ross (D)	Don Ross (D)	Don Ross (D)	Don Ross (D)
74	Gene D. Combs (D)	Gene D. Combs (D)	Gene D. Combs (D)	Grover R. Campbell (R)

Forty-First to Forty-Fourth Legislatures

District	1987 • 41st	1989 • 42nd	1991 • 43rd	1993 • 44th
75	Grover Campbell (R)	Grover Campbell (R)	Grover Campbell (R)	Mike Thornbrugh (R)
76	Richard Williamson (R)	Richard Williamson (R)	Don Weese (R)	Don Weese (R)
77	Gary Stottlemyre (D)	Gary Stottlemyre (D)	Gary Stottlemyre (D)	Gary Stottlemyre (D)
78	Frank F. Pitezel (R)	Frank F. Pitezel (R)	Bruce E. Niemi (D)	Flint Breckenridge (R)
79	James E. Henshaw (R)	James E. Henshaw (R)	James E. Henshaw (R)	James E. Henshaw (R))
80	Joe Gordon (R)	Joe Gordon (R)	Bob Gates (R)	Bob Gates (R)
81	Gaylon L. Stacey (R)	Ray Vaughn (R)	Ray Vaughn (R)	Ray Vaughn (R)
82	Leonard E. Sullivan (R)	Leonard E. Sullivan (R)	Leonard E. Sullivan (R)	Leonard E. Sullivan (R)
83	Joe L. Heaton (R)	Joe L. Heaton (R)	Joe L. Heaton (R)	Tony Caldwell (R)
84	John Bumpus (R)	Bill Graves (R)	Bill Graves (R)	Bill Graves (R)
85	Michael J. Hunter (R)	Michael J. Hunter (R)	Mary Fallin (R)	Mary Fallin (R)
86	Larry E. Adair (D)	Larry E. Adair (D)	Larry E. Adair (D)	Larry E. Adair (D)
87	Robert D. Worthen (R)	Robert D. Worthen (R)	Robert D. Worthen (R)	Robert D. Worthen (R)
88	Linda H. Larason (D)	Linda H. Larason (D)	Linda H. Larason (D)	Linda H. Larason (D)
89	Kevin Hutchcroft (D)	Kevin Hutchcroft (D)	Kevin Hutchcroft (D)	Charles Gray (D)
90	Charles Key (R)	Charles Key (R)	Charles Key (R)	Charles Key (R)
91	Keith Leftwich (D)	Alice Musser (D)	Dan Webb (R)	Dan Webb (R)
92	Claudette Henry (R)	William R. Paulk (D)	William R. Paulk (D)	Bill Paulk (D)
93	Wanda Jo Peltier (D)	Wanda Jo Peltier (D)	Wanda Jo Peltier (D)	Wanda Jo Peltier (D)
94	Gary Bastin (D)	Gary Bastin (D)	Gary Bastin (D)	Gary Bastin (D)
95	David C. Craighead (D)	Jim L. Isaac (D)	Jim L. Isaac (D)	Jim L. Isaac (D)
96	Jim Zimmerman (D)	Mark Seikel (D)	Mark Seikel (D)	Mark Seikel (D)
97	Kevin Cox (D)	Kevin Cox (D)	Kevin Cox (D)	Kevin Cox (D)
98	Ross Duckett (D)	Tim Pope (R)	Tim Pope (R)	Tim Pope (R)
99	Freddye H. Williams (D)	Freddye H. Williams (D)	Angela Monson (D)	Angela Monson (D)
100	Ernest Jim Istook (R)	Ernest Jim Istook (R)	Ernest Jim Istook (R)	Richard Phillips (R)
101	Jeff Hamilton (D)	Jeff Hamilton (D)	Jeff Hamilton (D)	Jeff Hamilton (D)

[1] Resigned. Victor Wickersham (D) elected February 2, 1988; died March 15, 1988. No interim.

[2] Resigned December 31, 1988. Mike Tyler (D) elected March 14, 1989.

[3] Died prior to taking office. Special Election held Nov. 27, 1990, to fill vacancy resulted in election of J. T. Stites (D).

[4] Died in office Sept. 13, 1991. Larry Hansen elected in Special Election December 1991. Calvin J. Anthony elected Nov. 1993.

[5] Died March 16, 1996. No interim successor elected.

Forty-Fifth to Forty-Eighth Legislatures

District	1995 • 45th	1997 • 46th	1999 • 47th	2001 • 48th
Speakers	Glen D. Johnson (D)	Loyd Benson (D)	Loyd Benson (D)	Larry E. Adair (D)
1	Terry J. Matlock (D)	Terry J. Matlock (D)	Terry J. Matlock (D)	Terry J. Matlock (D)

Forty-Fifth to Forty-Eighth Legislatures

District	1995 • 45th	1997 • 46th	1999 • 47th	2001 • 48th
2	J. T. Stites (D)	J. T. Stites (D)	J. T. Stites (D)	J. T. Stites (D)
3	James E. Hamilton (D)	James E. Hamilton (D)	Kenneth Corn (D)	Kenneth Corn (D)
4	Bob Ed Culver (D)	Bob Ed Culver (D)	Bob Ed Culver (D)	Jim Wilson (D)
5	Joe J. Hutchison (D)	Joe J. Hutchison (D)	Joe J. Hutchison (D)	Joe J. Hutchison (D)
6	Joe Eddins (D)	Joe Eddins (D)	Joe Eddins (D)	Joe Eddins (D)
7	Larry D. Roberts (D)	Larry D. Roberts (D)	Larry D. Roberts (D)	Larry D. Roberts (D)
8	Larry D. Rice (D)	Larry D. Rice (D)	Larry D. Rice (D)	Larry D. Rice (D)
9	Dwayne Steidley (D)	Dwayne Steidley (D)	Tad Jones (R)	Tad Jones (R)
10	Gary S. Taylor (D)	Gary S. Taylor (D)	Gary S. Taylor (D)	Gary S. Taylor (D)
11	James R. Dunlap (R)	Mike Wilt (R)	Mike Wilt (R)	Mike Wilt (R)
12	Jerry W. Hefner (D)	Jerry W. Hefner (D)	Jerry W. Hefner (D)	Jerry W. Hefner (D)
13	Bill Settle (D)	Bill Settle (D)	Bill Settle (D)	Stuart Ericson (R)
14	Barbara Staggs (D)	Barbara Staggs (D)	Barbara Staggs (D)	Barbara Staggs (D)
15	Chester Dusty Rhodes (D)	Bobby Frame (D)	Bobby Frame (D)	Ray Miller (D)
16	M.C. Leist (D)	M.C. Leist (D)	M.C. Leist (D)	M.C. Leist (D)
17	Mike Mass (D)	Mike Mass (D)	Mike Mass (D)	Mike Mass (D)
18	Lloyd Fields (D)	Lloyd Fields (D)	Lloyd L. Fields (D)	Lloyd L. Fields (D)
19	Randall Lee Erwin (D)	Randall Lee Erwin (D)	Randall Lee Erwin (D)	Randall Lee Erwin (D)
20	Tommy Thomas (D)	Tommy Thomas (D)	Tommy Thomas (D)	Paul D. Roan (D)
21	James H. Dunegan (D)	James H. Dunegan (D)	James H. Dunegan (D)	James H. Dunegan (D)
22	Danny Hilliard (D)	Danny Hilliard (D)	Danny Hilliard (D)	Danny Hilliard (D)
23	Betty Boyd (D)	Betty Boyd (D)	Betty Boyd (D)	Sue Tibbs (R)
24	Glen D. Johnson (D)	Dale Turner (D)	Dale Turner (D)	Dale Turner (D)
25	Bob Plunk (D)	Bob Plunk (D)	Bob Plunk (D)	Bob Plunk (D)
26	Robert Weaver (D)	Robert Weaver (D)	Robert Weaver (D)	Kris Steele (R)
27	Dale Smith (D)	Dale Smith (D)	Dale Smith (D)	Dale Smith (D)
28	Mike Ervin (D)	Mike Ervin (D)	Mike Ervin (D)	Mike Ervin (D) [2]
29	Todd Hiett (R)	Todd Hiett (R)	Todd Hiett (R)	Todd Hiett (R)
30	Mike Tyler (D)	Mike Tyler (D)	Mike Tyler (D)	Mike Tyler (D)
31	Frank W. Davis (R)	Frank W. Davis (R)	Frank W. Davis (R)	Frank W. Davis (R)
32	Don Kinnamon (D)	Don Kinnamon (D)	Don Kinnamon (D)	Kent Friskup (R)
33	Dale W. Wells (D)	Dale W. Wells (D)	Dale W. Wells (D)	Dale W. Wells (D)
34	Calvin J. Anthony (D)	Terry Ingmire (R)	Terry Ingmire (R)	Terry Ingmire (R)
35	Larry Ferguson (R)	Larry Ferguson (R)	Larry Ferguson (R)	Larry Ferguson (R)
36	James Hager (D)	James Hager (D)	Joe Sweeden (D)	Joe Sweeden (D)
37	James D. Holt (R)	Jim Newport (R)	Jim Newport (R)	Jim Newport (R)
38	Jim Reese (R)	Jim Reese (R)	Jim Reese (R)	Jim Reese (R) [3]
39	Wayne Pettigrew (R)	Wayne Pettigrew (R)	Wayne Pettigrew (R)	Wayne Pettigrew (R)

Forty-Fifth to Forty-Eighth Legislatures

District	1995 • 45th	1997 • 46th	1999 • 47th	2001 • 48th
40	Mike O'Neal (R)	Mike O'Neal (R)	John Sellers (D)	Mike O'Neal (R)
41	Sean Voskuhl (D)	Sean Voskuhl (D)	Curt Roggow (R)	Curt Roggow (R)
42	Bill Mitchell (D)	Bill Mitchell (D)	Bill Mitchell (D)	Bill Mitchell (D)
43	Tony Kouba (R)	Tony Kouba (R)	Tony Kouba (R)	Ray Young (R)
44	Laura Boyd (D)	Laura Boyd (D)	Bill Nations (D)	Bill Nations (D)
45	Ed Crocker (D)	Wallace Collins (D)	Wallace Collins (D)	Thad Balkman (R)
46	Doug Miller (R)	Doug Miller (R)	Doug Miller (R)	Doug Miller (R)
47	Dan Ramsey (R)	Dan Ramsey (R)	Susan Winchester (R)	Susan Winchester (R)
48	Al Sadler (D)	Al Sadler (D)	Greg A. Piatt (R)	Greg A. Piatt (R)
49	Fred Stanley (D)	Fred Stanley (D)	Fred Stanley (D)	Fred Stanley (D)
50	Jari Askins (D)	Jari Askins (D)	Jari Askins (D)	Jari Askins (D)
51	Bill Smith (D)	Raymond G. McCarter (D)	Raymond G. McCarter (D)	Raymond G. McCarter (D)
52	Howard Cotner (D)	David B. Braddock (D)	David B. Braddock (D)	David B. Braddock (D)
53	Carolyn Coleman (R)	Carolyn Coleman (R)	Carolyn Coleman (R)	Carolyn Coleman (R)
54	Joan Greenwood (R)	Joan Greenwood (R)	Joan Greenwood (R)	Joan Greenwood (R)
55	Jack Bonny (D)	Jack Bonny (D)	Jack Bonny (D)	Jack Bonny (D)
56	Ron Langmacher (D)	Ron Langmacher (D)	Ron Langmacher (D)	Ron Langmacher (D)
57	Bill Widener (D)[1]	James E. Covey (D)	James E. Covey (D)	James E. Covey (D)
58	Elmer Maddux (R)	Elmer Maddux (R)	Elmer Maddux (R)	Elmer Maddux (R)
59	Clay Pope (D)	Clay Pope (D)	Clay Pope (D)	Clay Pope (D)
60	Randy Beutler (D)	Randy Beutler (D)	Randy Beutler (D)	Purcy D. Walker (D)
61	Jack Begley (D)	Jack Begley (D)	Jack Begley (D)	Jack Begley (D)
62	Abe Deutschendorf (D)	Abe Deutschendorf (D)	Abe Deutschendorf (D)	Abe Deutschendorf (D)
63	Loyd Benson (D)	Loyd Benson (D)	Loyd Benson (D)	Loyd Benson (D)
64	Ron Kirby (D)	Ron Kirby (D)	Ron Kirby (D)	Ron Kirby (D)
65	Jim R. Glover (D)	Jim R. Glover (D)	Jim R. Glover (D)	Jim R. Glover (D)
66	Russ Roach (D)	Russ Roach (D)	Russ Roach (D)	Russ Roach (D)
67	Wayne Cozort (R)	Hopper Smith (R)	Hopper Smith (R)	Hopper Smith (R)
68	Shelby Satterfield (D)	Shelby Satterfield (D)	Chris Benge (R)	Chris Benge (R)
69	Fred Perry (R)	Fred Perry (R)	Fred Perry (R)	Fred Perry (R)
70	John Bryant (R)	John Bryant (R)	John Bryant (R)	Ron Peters (R)
71	John Sullivan (R)	John Sullivan (R)	John Sullivan (R)	John Sullivan (R)[4]
72	Don McCorkell (D)	Darrell Gilbert (D)	Darrell Gilbert (D)	Darrell Gilbert (D)
73	Don Ross (D)	Don Ross (D)	Don Ross (D)	Don Ross (D)
74	John Smaligo (R)	Phil Ostrander (D)	Phil Ostrander (D)	John Smaligo (R)
75	Mike Thornbrugh (R)	Mike Thornbrugh (R)	Mike Thornbrugh (R)	Dennis Adkins (R)
76	Don Weese (R)	Don Weese (R)	John A. Wright (R)	John A. Wright (R)
77	Gary Stottlemyre (D)	Mark Liotta (R)	Mark Liotta (R)	Mark Liotta (R)

Forty-Fifth to Forty-Eighth Legislatures

District	1995 • 45th	1997 • 46th	1999 • 47th	2001 • 48th
78	Flint Breckenridge (R)	Mary Easley (D)	Mary Easley (D)	Mary Easley (D)
79	Chris Hastings (R)	Chris Hastings (R)	Chris Hastings (R)	Chris Hastings (R)
80	Scott Adkins (R)	Scott Adkins (R)	Scott Adkins (R)	Ron Peterson (R)
81	Ray Vaughn (R)	Ray Vaughn (R)	Ray Vaughn (R)	Raymond Vaughn (R)
82	Leonard E. Sullivan (R)	Leonard E. Sullivan (R)	Leonard E. Sullivan (R)	Leonard E. Sullivan (R)
83	Fred Morgan (R)	Fred Morgan (R)	Fred Morgan (R)	Fred Morgan (R)
84	Bill Graves (R)	Bill Graves (R)	Bill Graves (R)	Bill Graves (R)
85	Odilia Dank (R)	Odilia Dank (R)	Odilia Dank (R)	Odilia Dank (R)
86	Larry E. Adair (D)	Larry E. Adair (D)	Larry E. Adair (D)	Larry E. Adair (D)
87	Robert D. Worthen (R)	Robert D. Worthen (R)	Robert D. Worthen (R)	Robert D. Worthen (R)
88	Debbie Blackburn (D)	Debbie Blackburn (D)	Debbie Blackburn (D)	Debbie Blackburn (D)
89	Charles Gray (D)	Charles Gray (D)	Charles Gray (D)	Charles Gray (D)
90	Charles Key (R)	Charles Key (R)	John Nance (R)	John Nance (R)
91	Dan Webb (R)	Dan Webb (R)	Dan Webb (R)	Dan Webb (R)
92	Bill Paulk (D)	Bill Paulk (D)	Bill Paulk (D)	Bill Paulk (D)
93	Wanda Jo Peltier (D)	Al Lindley (D)	Al Lindley (D)	Al Lindley (D)
94	Gary Bastin (D)	Gary Bastin (D)	Kevin Calvey (R)	Kevin Calvey (R)
95	Bill Case (R)	Bill Case (R)	Bill Case (R)	Bill Case (R)
96	Mark Seikel (D)	Mark Seikel (D)	Mark Seikel (D)	Lance Cargill (R)
97	Kevin Cox (D)	Kevin Cox (D)	Kevin Cox (D)	Kevin Cox (D)
98	Tim Pope (R)	Tim Pope (R)	Tim Pope (R)	Tim Pope (R)
99	Opio Toure (D)	Opio Toure (D)	Opio Toure (D)	Opio Toure (D)
100	Richard Phillips (R)	Richard Phillips (R)	Richard Phillips (R)	Richard Phillips (R)
101	Forrest Claunch (R)	Forrest Claunch (R)	Forrest Claunch (R)	Forrest Claunch (R)

[1] Died March 16, 1996. No interim successor elected.
[2] Switched parties, from Democrat to Republican, in 2001.
[3] Resigned May 22, 2001. Dale DeWitt (R) elected August 14, 2001.
[4] Resigned after his election to US Congressional District 1 on January 8, 2002. Chad Stites (R) elected April 2, 2002.

Forty-Ninth to Fifty-Second Legislatures

District	2003 • 49th	2005 • 50th	2007 • 51st	2009 • 52nd
Speakers	Larry E. Adair (D)	Todd Hiett (R)	Lance Cargill (R)	Chris Benge (R)
1	Jerry Ellis (D)	Jerry Ellis (D)	Jerry Ellis (D)	Dennis R. Bailey (D)
2	Glen Bud Smithson (D)	Glen Bud Smithson (D)	Glen Bud Smithson (D)	Glen Bud Smithson (D)
3	Neil Brannon (D)	Neil Brannon (D)	Neil Brannon (D)	Neil Brannon (D)
4	Jim Wilson (D)	Mike Brown (D)	Mike Brown (D)	Mike Brown (D)
5	Joe J. Hutchison (D)	Doug Cox (R)	Doug Cox (R)	Doug Cox (R)
6	Joe Eddins (D)	Joe Eddins (D)	Chuck Hoskin (D)	Chuck Hoskin (D)

Forty-Ninth to Fifty-Second Legislatures

District	2003 • 49th	2005 • 50th	2007 • 51st	2009 • 52nd
7	Larry D. Roberts (D)	Larry Glenn (D)	Larry Glenn (D)	Larry Glenn (D)
8	Larry D. Rice (D)	Ben Sherrer (D)	Ben Sherrer (D)	Ben Sherrer (D)
9	Tad Jones (R)	Tad Jones (R)	Tad Jones (R)	Tad Jones (R)
10	Gary S. Taylor (D)	Steve Martin (R)	Steve Martin (R)	Steve Martin (R)
11	Mike Wilt (R)	Mike Wilt (R)	Earl Sears (R)	Earl Sears (R)
12	Jerry W. Hefner (D)	Wade Rousselot (D)	Wade Rousselot (D)	Wade Rousselot (D)
13	Stuart Ericson (R)	Jerry McPeak (D)	Jerry McPeak (D)	Jerry McPeak (D)
14	Barbara Staggs (D)	Barbara Staggs (D)	George Faught (R)	George Faught (R)
15	Ray Miller (D)	Ray Miller (D)	Ed Cannaday (D)	Ed Cannaday (D)
16	M.C. Leist (D)	Jerry Shoemake (D)	Jerry Shoemake (D)	Jerry Shoemake (D)
17	Richard Lerblance (D)[2]	Mike Mass (D)	Brian Renegar (D)	Brian Renegar (D)
18	Terry Harrison (D)	Terry Harrison (D)	Terry Harrison (D)	Terry Harrison (D)
19	Randall Lee Erwin (D)	R. C. Pruett (D)	R. C. Pruett (D)	R. C. Pruett (D)
20	Paul D. Roan (D)	Paul D. Roan (D)	Paul D. Roan (D)	Paul D. Roan (D)
21	John Carey (D)	John Carey (D)	John Carey (D)	John Carey (D)
22	Danny Hilliard (D)	Wes Hilliard (D)	Wes Hilliard (D)	Wes Hilliard (D)
23	Sue Tibbs (R)	Sue Tibbs (R)	Sue Tibbs (R)	Sue Tibbs (R)
24	Dale Turner (D)	Dale Turner (D)	Dale Turner (D)	Steve Kouplen (D)
25	Bob Plunk (D)	Bob Plunk (D)	Todd Thomsen (R)	Todd Thomsen (R)
26	Kris Steele (R)	Kris Steele (R)	Kris Steele (R)	Kris Steele (R)
27	Dale Smith (D)	Shane Jett (R)	Shane Jett (R)	Shane Jett (R)
28	David Daniel Boren (D)	Ryan Kiesel (D)	Ryan Kiesel (D)	Ryan Kiesel (D)
29	Todd Hiett (R)	Todd Hiett (R)	Skye McNiel (R)	Skye McNiel (R)
30	Mike Tyler (D)	Brian Bingman (R)	Mark McCullough (R)	Mark McCullough (R)
31	Frank W. Davis (R)	Dale DePue (R)	Jason Murphey (R)	Jason Murphey (R)
32	Danny Morgan (D)	Danny Morgan (D)	Danny Morgan (D)	Danny Morgan (D)
33	Dale W. Wells (D)	Lee Denney (R)	Lee Denney (R)	Lee Denney (R)
34	Terry Ingmire (R)	Terry Ingmire (R)	Terry Ingmire (R)	Cory T. Williams (D)
35	Larry Ferguson (R)	Rex Duncan (R)	Rex Duncan (R)	Rex Duncan (R)
36	Joe Sweeden (D)	Joe Sweeden (D)	Scott BigHorse (D)	Eddie Fields (R)
37	Jim Newport (R)	Jim Newport (R)	Ken Luttrell (D)	Ken Luttrell (D)
38	Dale DeWitt (R)[1]	Dale DeWitt (R)	Dale DeWitt (R)	Dale DeWitt (R)
39	Wayne Pettigrew (R)	Marian Cooksey (R)	Marian Cooksey (R)	Marian Cooksey (R)
40	Mike O'Neal (R)	Mike Jackson (R)	Mike Jackson (R)	Mike Jackson (R)
41	Curt Roggow (R)	Curt Roggow (R)	John Enns (R)	John Enns (R)
42	Bill Mitchell (D)	Lisa Billy (R)	Lisa Billy (R)	Lisa Billy (R)
43	Ray Young (R)	Ray Young (R)	Colby Schwartz (R)	Colby Schwartz (R)
44	Bill Nations (D)	Bill Nations (D)	Bill Nations (D)	Bill Nations (D)

Forty-Ninth to Fifty-Second Legislatures

District	2003 • 49th	2005 • 50th	2007 • 51st	2009 • 52nd
45	Thad Balkman (R)	Thad Balkman (R)	Wallace Collins (D)	Wallace Collins (D)
46	Doug Miller (R)	Doug Miller (R)	Scott Martin (R)	Scott Martin (R)
47	Susan Winchester (R)	Susan Winchester (R)	Susan Winchester (R)	Leslie Osborn (R)
48	Greg A. Piatt (R)	Greg A. Piatt (R)	Greg A. Piatt (R)	Pat Ownbey (R)
49	Fred Stanley (D)	Terry Hyman (D)	Terry Hyman (D)	Samson R. Buck (D)
50	Jari Askins (D)	Jari Askins (D)	Dennis Johnson (R)	Dennis Johnson (R)
51	Raymond G. McCarter (D)	Raymond G. McCarter (D)	Raymond G. McCarter (D)	Corey Holland (R)
52	David B. Braddock (D)	David B. Braddock (D)	David B. Braddock (D)	Charles Ortega (R)
53	Carolyn Coleman (R)	Randy Terrill (R)	Randy Terrill (R)	Randy Terrill (R)
54	Joan Greenwood (R)	Paul Wesselhoft (R)	Paul Wesselhoft (R)	Paul Wesselhoft (R)
55	Jack Bonny (D)	Ryan McMullen (D)	Ryan McMullen (D)	Ryan McMullen (D)
56	Ron Langmacher (D)	Phil Richardson (R)	Phil Richardson (R)	Phil Richardson (R)
57	James E. Covey (D)	James E. Covey (D)	James E. Covey (D)	Harold Wright (R)
58	Elmer Maddux (R)	Jeff Hickman (R)	Jeff Hickman (R)	Jeff Hickman (R)
59	Clay Pope (D)	Rob Johnson (R)	Rob Johnson (R)	Mike Sanders (R)
60	Purcy D. Walker (D)	Purcy D. Walker (D)	Purcy D. Walker (D)	Purcy D. Walker (D)
61	Gus Blackwell (R)	Gus Blackwell (R)	Gus Blackwell (R)	Gus Blackwell (R)
62	Abe Deutschendorf (D)	Abe Deutschendorf (D)	T.W. Shannon (R)	T.W. Shannon (R)
63	Don Armes (R)	Don Armes (R)	Don Armes (R)	Don Armes (R)
64	Ron Kirby (D)	Ann Coody (R)	Ann Coody (R)	Ann Coody (R)
65	Joe Dorman (D)	Joe Dorman (D)	Joe Dorman (D)	Joe Dorman (D)
66	Lucky Lamons (D)	Lucky Lamons (D)	Lucky Lamons (D)	Lucky Lamons (D)
67	Hopper Smith (R)[3]	Pam Peterson (R)	Pam Peterson (R)	Pam Peterson (R)
68	Chris Benge (R)	Chris Benge (R)	Chris Benge (R)	Chris Benge (R)
69	Fred Perry (R)	Fred Perry (R)	Fred Jordan (R)	Fred Jordan (R)
70	Ron Peters (R)	Ron Peters (R)	Ron Peters (R)	Ron Peters (R)
71	Roy McClain (D)	Daniel Sullivan (R)	Daniel Sullivan (R)	Daniel Sullivan (R)
72	Darrell Gilbert (D)	Darrell Gilbert (D)	Darrell Gilbert (D)	Seneca Scott (D)
73	Judy Eason McIntyre (D)	Jabar Shumate (D)	Jabar Shumate (D)	Jabar Shumate (D)
74	John Smaligo (R)	John Smaligo Jr. (R)	David Derby (R)	David Derby (R)
75	Dennis Adkins (R)	Dennis Adkins (R)	Dennis Adkins (R)	Dan Kirby (R)
76	John A. Wright (R)	John A. Wright (R)	John A. Wright (R)	John A. Wright (R)
77	Mark Liotta (R)	Mark Liotta (R)	Eric Proctor (D)	Eric Proctor (D)
78	Mary Easley (D)	Jeannie McDaniel (D)	Jeannie McDaniel (D)	Jeannie McDaniel (D)
79	Chris Hastings (R)	Chris Hastings (R)	Weldon Watson (R)	Weldon Watson (R)
80	Ron Peterson (R)	Ron Peterson (R)	Ron Peterson (R)	Mike Ritze (R)
81	Raymond Vaughn (R)	Kenneth Miller (R)	Kenneth Miller (R)	Kenneth Miller (R)
82	Leonard E. Sullivan (R)	Guy Liebmann (R)	Guy Liebmann (R)	Guy Liebmann (R)

Forty-Ninth to Fifty-Second Legislatures

District	2003 • 49th	2005 • 50th	2007 • 51st	2009 • 52nd
83	Fred Morgan (R)	Fred Morgan (R)	Randy McDaniel (R)	Randy McDaniel (R)
84	Bill Graves (R)	Sally Kern (R)	Sally Kern (R)	Sally Kern (R)
85	Odilia Dank (R)	Odilia Dank (R)	David Dank (R)	David Dank (R)
86	Larry E. Adair (D)	John Auffett (D)	John Auffett (D)	John Auffett (D)
87	Robert D. Worthen (R)	Trebor Worthen (R)	Trebor Worthen (R)	Jason Nelson (R)
88	Debbie Blackburn (D)	Debbie Blackburn (D)	Al McAffrey (D)	Al McAffrey (D)
89	Rebecca Hamilton (D)	Rebecca Hamilton (D)	Rebecca Hamilton (D)	Rebecca Hamilton (D)
90	John Nance (R)	John Nance (R)	Charles Key (R)	Charles Key (R)
91	Mike Reynolds (R)	Mike Reynolds (R)	Mike Reynolds (R)	Mike Reynolds (R)
92	Bill Paulk (D)	Richard Morrissette (D)	Richard Morrissette (D)	Richard Morrissette (D)
93	Al Lindley (D)	Al Lindley (D)	Al Lindley (D)	Mike Christian (R)
94	Kevin Calvey (R)	Kevin Calvey (R)	Scott Inman (D)	Scott Inman (D)
95	Bill Case (R)	Bill Case (R)	Charlie Joyner (R)	Charlie Joyner (R)
96	Lance Cargill (R)	Lance Cargill (R)	Lance Cargill (R)	Lewis H. Moore (R)
97	Kevin Cox (D)	Mike Shelton (D)	Mike Shelton (D)	Mike Shelton (D)
98	John Trebilcock (R)	John Trebilcock (R)	John Trebilcock (R)	John Trebilcock (R)
99	Opio Toure (D)	Opio Toure (D)	Anastasia Pittman (D)	Anastasia Pittman (D)
100	Richard Phillips (R)	Mike Thompson (R)	Mike Thompson (R)	Mike Thompson (R)
101	Forrest Claunch (R)	Gary Banz (R)	Gary Banz (R)	Gary Banz (R)

[1] Elected August 14, 2001 to fill seat vacated when Jim Reese resigned May 22, 2001.
[2] Elected to Oklahoma Senate June 10, 2003. Mike Mass (D) elected August 12, 2003.
[3] Resigned due to military orders, November 12, 2003. No interim successor elected.

Fifty-Third to Fifty-Sixth Legislatures

District	2011 • 53rd	2013 • 54th	2015 • 55th	2017 • 56th
Speaker	Kris Steele (R)	T. W. Shannon (R)	Jeffrey Hickman (R)	
1	Rusty Farley (R)	Curtis McDaniel (D)	Johnny Tadlock (D)	
2	John Bennett (R)	John Bennett (R)	John Bennett (R)	
3	James Lockhart (D)	James Lockhart (D)	James Lockhart (D)	
4	Mike Brown (D)	Mike Brown (D)	Mike Brown (D)	
5	Doug Cox (R)	Doug Cox (R)	Doug Cox (R)	
6	Chuck Hoskin (D)	Chuck Hoskin (D)	Chuck Hoskin (D)	
7	Larry Glenn (D)	Larry Glenn (D)	Ben Loring (D)	
8	Ben Sherrer (D)	Ben Sherrer (D)	Ben Sherrer (D)	
9	Marty Quinn (R)	Marty Quinn (R)	Mark Lepak (R)	
10	Steve Martin (R)	Steve Martin (R)	Travis Dunlap (R)	
11	Earl Sears (R)	Earl Sears (R)	Earl Sears (R)	
12	Wade Rousselot (D)	Wade Rousselot (D)	Wade Rousselot (D)	

Fifty-Third to Fifty-Sixth Legislatures

District	2011 • 53rd	2013 • 54th	2015 • 55th	2017 • 56th
13	Jerry McPeak (D)	Jerry McPeak (D)	Jerry McPeak (D)	
14	George Faught (R)	Arthur Hulbert (R)	George Faught (R)	
15	Ed Cannaday (D)	Ed Cannaday (D)	Ed Cannaday (D)	
16	Jerry Shoemake (D)	Jerry Shoemake (D)	Jerry Shoemake (D)	
17	Brian Renegar (D)	Brian Renegar (D)	Brian Renegar (D)	
18	Donnie Condit (D)	Donnie Condit (D)	Donnie Condit (D)	
19	R.C. Pruett (D)	R.C. Pruett (D)	R.C. Pruett (D)	
20	Paul D. Roan (D)	Bobby Cleveland (R)	Bobby Cleveland (R)	
21	Dustin Roberts (R)	Dustin Roberts (R)	Dustin Roberts (R)	
22	Wes Hilliard (D)	Charles A. McCall (R)	Charles A. McCall (R)	
23	Sue Tibbs (R)	Terry O'Donnell (R)	Terry O'Donnell (R)	
24	Steve Kouplen (D)	Steve Kouplen (D)	Steve Kouplen (D)	
25	Todd Thomsen (R)	Todd Thomsen (R)	Todd Thomsen (R)	
26	Kris Steele (R)	Justin F. Wood (R)	Justin F. Wood (R)	
27	Josh Cockroft (R)	Josh Cockroft (R)	Josh Cockroft (R)	
28	Tom Newell (R)	Tom Newell (R)	Tom Newell (R)	
29	Skye McNiel (R)	Skye McNiel (R)	James Leewright (R)	
30	Mark McCullough (R)	Mark McCullough (R)	Mark McCullough (R)	
31	Jason Murphey (R)	Jason Murphey (R)	Jason Murphey (R)	
32	Danny Morgan (D)	Jason Smalley (R)	Kevin Wallace (R)	
33	Lee Denney (R)	Lee Denney (R)	Lee Denney (R)	
34	Cory T. Williams (D)	Cory T. Williams (D)	Cory T. Williams (D)	
35	Dennis Casey (R)	Dennis Casey (R)	Dennis Casey (R)	
36	Sean Roberts (R)	Sean Roberts (R)	Sean Roberts (R)	
37	Steve Vaughan (R)	Steve Vaughan (R)	Steve Vaughan (R)	
38	Dale DeWitt (R)	Dale DeWitt (R)	John Pfeiffer (R)	
39	Marion Cooksey (R)	Marion Cooksey (R)	Marion Cooksey (R)	
40	Mike Jackson (R)	Mike Jackson (R)	Chad Caldwell (R)	
41	John Enns (R)	John Enns (R)	John Enns (R)	
42	Lisa J. Billy (R)	Lisa J. Billy (R)	Lisa J. Billy (R)	
43	Colby Schwartz (R)	Colby Schwartz (R)	John Paul Jordan (R)	
44	Emily Virgin (D)	Emily Virgin (D)	Emily Virgin (D)	
45	Aaron Stiles (R)	Aaron Stiles (R)	Claudia Griffith (D)	
46	Scott Martin (R)	Scott Martin (R)	Scott Martin (R)	
47	Leslie Osborn (R)	Leslie Osborn (R)	Leslie Osborn (R)	
48	Pat Ownbey (R)	Pat Ownbey (R)	Pat Ownbey (R)	
49	Tommy Hardin (R)	Tommy Hardin (R)	Tommy Hardin (R)	
50	Dennis Johnson (R)	Dennis Johnson (R)	Dennis Johnson (R)	
51	Corey Holland (R)	R. Scott Biggs (R)	Scott Biggs (R)	

Fifty-Third to Fifty-Sixth Legislatures

District	2011 • 53rd	2013 • 54th	2015 • 55th	2017 • 56th
52	Charles Ortega (R)	Charles Ortega (R)	Charles Ortega (R)	
53	Randy Terrill (R)	Mark McBride (R)	Mark McBride (R)	
54	Paul Wesselhoft (R)	Paul Wesselhoft (R)	Paul Wesselhoft (R)	
55	Todd Russ (R)	Todd Russ (R)	Todd Russ (R)	
56	Phil Richardson (R)	David L. Perryman (D)	David L. Perryman (D)	
57	Harold Wright (R)	Harold Wright (R)	Harold Wright (R)	
58	Jeffrey W. Hickman (R)	Jeffrey W. Hickman (R)	Jeffrey W. Hickman (R)	
59	Mike Sanders (R)	Mike Sanders (R)	Mike Sanders (R)	
60	Purcy D. Walker (D)	Dan Fisher (R)	Dan Fisher (R)	
61	Gus Blackwell (R)	Gus Blackwell (R)	Casey Murdock (R)	
62	T.W. Shannon (R)	T.W. Shannon (R)	John Montgomery (R)	
63	Don Armes (R)	Don Armes (R)	Jeff Coody (R)	
64	Ann Coody (R)	Ann Coody (R)	Ann Coody (R)	
65	Joe Dorman (D)	Joe Dorman (D)	Scooter Park (R)	
66	Jadine Nollan (R)	Jadine Nollan (R)	Jadine Nollan (R)	
67	Pam Peterson (R)	Pam Peterson (R)	Pam Peterson (R)	
68	Glen Mulready (R)	Glen Mulready (R)	Glen Mulready (R)	
69	Fred Jordan (R)	Fred Jordan (R)	Chuck Strohm (R)	
70	Ron Peters (R)	Ken Walker (R)	Ken Walker (R)	
71	Daniel Sullivan (R)	Katie Henke (R)	Katie Henke (R)	
72	Seneca Scott (D)	Seneca Scott (D)	Seneca Scott (D)	
73	Jabar Shumate (D)	Kevin Matthews (D)	Kevin Matthews (D)	
74	David Derby (R)	David Derby (R)	David Derby (R)	
75	Dan Kirby (R)	Dan Kirby (R)	Dan Kirby (R)	
76	David Brumbaugh (R)	David Brumbaugh (R)	Davide Brumbaugh (R)	
77	Eric Proctor (D)	Eric Proctor (D)	Eric Proctor (D)	
78	Jeannie McDaniel (D)	Jeannie McDaniel (D)	Jeannie McDaniel (D)	
79	Weldon Watson (R)	Weldon Watson (R)	Weldon Watson (R)	
80	Mike Ritze (R)	Mike Ritze (R)	Mike Ritze (R)	
81	Randy Grau (R)	Randy Grau (R)	Randy Grau (R)	
82	Guy Liebmann (R)	Mike Turner (R)	Kevin Calvey (R)	
83	Randy McDaniel (R)	Randy McDaniel (R)	Randy McDaniel (R)	
84	Sally Kern (R)	Sally Kern (R)	Sally Kern (R)	
85	David Dank (R)	David Dank (R)	David Dank (R)	
86	William Fourkiller (D)	William Fourkiller (D)	William Fourkiller (D)	
87	Jason Nelson (R)	Jason Nelson (R)	Jason Nelson (R)	
88	Al McAffrey (D)	Kay Floyd (D)	Jason Dunnington (D)	
89	Rebecca Hamilton (D)	Rebecca Hamilton (D)	Shane Stone (D)	

Fifty-Third to Fifty-Sixth Legislatures

District	2011 • 53rd	2013 • 54th	2015 • 55th	2017 • 56th
90	Charles Key (R)	Charles Key (R)	Jon Echols (R)	
91	Mike Reynolds (R)	Mike Reynolds (R)	Chris Kannady (R)	
92	Richard Morrissette (D)	Richard Morrissette (D)	Richard Morrissette (D)	
93	Mike Christian (R)	Mike Christian (R)	Mike Christian (R)	
94	Scott Inman (D)	Scott Inman (D)	Scott Inman (D)	
95	Charlie Joyner (R)	Charlie Joyner (R)	Charlie Joyner (R)	
96	Lewis H. Moore (R)	Lewis H. Moore (R)	Lewis H. Moore (R)	
97	Mike Shelton (D)	Mike Shelton (D)	Mike Shelton (D)	
98	John Trebilcok (R)	John Trebilcok (R)	Michael Rogers (R)	
99	Anastasia Pittman (D)	Anastasia Pittman (D)	George Young (D)	
100	Elise Hall (R)	Elise Hall (R)	Elise Hall (R)	
101	Gary W. Banz (R)	Gary W. Banz (R)	Gary W. Banz (R)	

Ruined barracks at Fort Gibson, circa 1934.

State Senate Since Statehood

First to Fourth Legislatures

From 1907 to 1963, Senators were elected from their districts at-large.
For Districts 13, 14, and 15, special nominating provisions existed.

District	1st · 1907	2nd · 1909	3rd · 1911	4th · 1913
Pres. Pro Tempore	Henry S. Johnston (D)	J. C. Graham (D)	J. Elmer Thomas (D)	C. B. Kendrick (D)
1	Joe S. Morris (D)	Joe S. Morris (D)	J. H. Langston (R)	Geo. L. Aycock (D)
2	A. E. Agee (D)	E. L. Mitchell (D)	E. L. Mitchell (D)	E. L. Mitchell (D)
2	R. E. Echols (D)	R. E. Echols (D)	R. E. Echols (D)	R. E. Echols (D)
3	A. G. Updegraff (R)	A. G. Updegraff (R)	Wm. A. Briggs (R)	Wm. A. Briggs (R)
4	Frank Mathews (D)	Henry J. Denton (D)	Henry J. Denton (D)	J. L. Carpenter (D)
5	Tom Moore (D)	Tom Moore (D)	Guy P. Horton (D)	Guy P. Horton (D)
6	J. J. Williams (D)	J. J. Williams (D)	J. J. Williams (D)	James L. Austin (D)
6	R. A. Billups (D)	R. A. Billups (D)	Geo. A. Coffey (D) [1]	J. V. McClintic (D)
7	R. S. Curd (R)	R. S. Curd (R)	J. W. McCully (R)	J. W. McCully (R)
8	P. J. Goulding (D)	P. J. Goulding (D)	P. J. Goulding (D)	Eugene Watrous (R)
9	S. J. Soldani (D)	S. J. Soldani (D)	Wm. R. Dutton (R)	Wm. R. Dutton (R)
9	Edmund Brazell (D)	E. B. Chapman (R)	E. B. Chapman (R)	J. E. Curran (R)
10	H. S. Johnston (D)	J. Q. Newell (D)	J. Q. Newell (D)	Geo. A. Waters (D)
11	Clarence Davis (D)	Clarence Davis (D)	Jos. J. Jones (R)	Jos. J. Jones (R)
12	H. S. Cunningham (R)	H. S. Cunningham (R)	Ben F. Berkey (R)	John H. Burford (R)
13	M. F. Eggerman (D)	M. F. Eggerman (D)	M. F. Eggerman (D)	Chas. F. Barrett (D)
13	S. A. Cordell (D)	S. A. Cordell (D)	Wm. Tilghman (D) [2]	C. L. Edmonson (D)
14	Roy E. Stafford (D)	Roy E. Stafford (D)	Tom F. McMechan (D)	Tom F. McMechan (D)
14	W. H. Johnson (D)	F. M. Colville (R)	Frank M. Colville (R)	Ben F. Wilson (D)
15	Geo. O. Johnson (D)	Geo. O. Johnson (D)	Geo. W. Barefoot (D)	Geo. W. Barefoot (D)
15	L. K. Taylor (D)	L. K. Taylor (D)	Joe Smith (D)	John D. Pugh (D)
16	E. D. Brownlee (R)	E. D. Brownlee (R)	E. D. Brownlee (R)	E. J. Warner (R)
17	D. M. Smith (D)	D. M. Smith (D)	F. W. Anderson (D)	F. W. Anderson (D)
17	J. Elmer Thomas (D)	J. Elmer Thomas (D)	J. Elmer Thomas (D)	J. Elmer Thomas (D)
18	J. C. Graham (D)	J. C. Graham (D)	C. B. Kendrick (D)	C. B. Kendrick (D)
18	J. C. Little (D)	Harry K. Allen (D)	Harry K. Allen (D)	Ben Franklin (D)
19	H. S. Blair (D)	H. S. Blair (D)	J. B. Thompson (D)	J. T. McIntosh (D)
19	R. P. Wynne (D)	R. P. Wynne (D)	R. P. Wynne (D)	Fred E. Tucker (D)
20	J. M. Hatchett (D)	J. M. Hatchett (D)	J. M. Hatchett (D)	J. B. Thompson (D)
20	T. F. Memminger (D)	T. F. Memminger (D)	T. F. Memminger (D)	T. F. Memminger (D)
21	E. T. Sorrels (D)	E. T. Sorrels (D)	E. T. Sorrels (D)	E. T. Sorrels (D)
22	H. H. Holman (D)	Frank L. Warren (R)	Frank L. Warren (R)	C. W. Board (D)

First to Fourth Legislatures

From 1907 to 1963, Senators were elected from their districts at-large.
For Districts 13, 14, and 15, special nominating provisions existed.

District	1st · 1907	2nd · 1909	3rd · 1911	4th · 1913
23	R. M. Roddie (D)	R. M. Roddie (D)	R. M. Roddie (D)	R. M. Roddie (D)
24	W. P. Stewart (D)	W. P. Stewart (D)	W. P. Stewart (D)	W. C. McAlister (D)
25	Wm. N. Redwine (D)	Wm N. Redwine (D)	Wm. N. Redwine (D)	Wm N. Redwine (D)
26	Wm. M. Franklin (D)	Wm. M. Franklin (D)	Wm. M. Franklin (D)	C. C. Shaw (D)
27	Campbell Russell (D)	Campbell Russell (D)	Sid Garrett (D)	Sid Garrett (D)
27	Eck E. Brook (D)	Harry B. Beeler (R)	Harry B. Beeler (R)	Campbell Russell (D)
28	P. C. Conn (D)	J. H. Cloonan (R)	J. H. Cloonan (R)	M. S. Blassingame (D)
29	J. M. Keys (D)	J. M. Keys (D)	E. C. Harlan (D)	E. C. Harlan (D)
30	E. M. Landrum (D)	E. M. Landrum (D)	E. M. Landrum (D)	Geo. W. Fields Jr.(D)
31	P. J. Yeager (D)	P. J. Yeager (D)	A. F. Vandeventer (D)	A. F. Vandeventer (D)
32	H. E. P. Standford (R)	R. T. Potter (R)	R. T. Potter (R)	Jas. H. Sutherlin (D)
33	J. H. Strain (D)	J. H. Strain (D)	Gid Graham (D)	Gid Graham (D)

[1] Resigned. J. V. McClintic (D) elected 11–5–1912 to fill unexpired term.
[2] Resigned. C. L. Edmonson (D) elected 11–5–1912 to fill unexpired term.

Fifth to Eighth State Senate

District	5th · 1915	6th · 1917	7th · 1919	8th · 1921
Pres. Pro Tempore	E. L. Mitchell (D)	C. W. Board (D)	R. L. Davidson (D)	T. C. Simpson (D)
1	W. J. Risen (D)	W. J. Risen (D)	M. W. Pugh (D)	M. W. Pugh (D)
2	E. L. Mitchell (D)	Arthur Leach (D)	Arthur Leach (D)	C. B. Leedy (R)
2	Geo. E. Wilson (S)	Geo. E. Wilson (S)	James Spurlock (D)	James Spurlock (D)
3	W. M. Bickel (D)	W. M. Bickel (D)	Wm. A. Briggs (R)	Wm. A. Briggs (R)
4	J. L. Carpenter (D)	G. L. Wilson (D)	G. L. Wilson (D)	Lamar Looney Mrs. (D)
5	Harry B. Cordell (D)	Harry B. Cordell (D)	Harry B. Cordell (D)	Harry B. Cordell (D)
6	James L. Austin (D)	R. L. Knie (D)	R. L. Knie (D)	James A. Land (R)
6	O. J. Logan (D)	O. J. Logan (D)	T. C. Simpson (D)	T. C. Simpson (D)
7	A. C. Beeman (R)	Walter Ferguson (R)	Joe Sherman (R)	Joe Sherman (R)
8	Eugene Watrous (R)	Eugene Watrous (R)	Eugene Watrous (R)	Harry O. Glasser (R)
9	Wm. S. Cline (D)	Wm. S. Cline (D)	W. T. Clark (R)	W. T. Clark (R)
9	J. E. Curran (R)	R. L. Hall (D)	R. L. Hall (D)	(2)
10	Geo. A. Waters (D)	Tom Testerman (R)	Tom Testerman (R)	Roy Harvey (R)
11	Clarence Davis (D)	Clarence Davis (D)	M. F. Ingraham (R)	M. F. Ingraham (R)
12	John H. Burford (R)	John Golobie (R)	John Golobie (R)	John Golobie (R)
13	Chas. F. Barrett (D)	T. B. Hogg (D)	T. B. Hogg (D)	Chas. E. Wells (R)
13	C. L. Edmonson (D)	C. L. Edmonson (D)	M. W. Lynch (R)	M. W. Lynch (R)

Fifth to Eighth State Senate

District	5th · 1915	6th · 1917	7th · 1919	8th · 1921
14	Tom F. McMechan (D) [1]	Robt. Burns (D)	T. F. Hensley (D)	T. F. Hensley (D)
14	Ben F. Wilson (D)	W. K. Snyder (D)	W. K. Snyder (D)	Ross N. Lillard (D)
15	Thos. J. O'Neill (D)	Thos. J. O'Neill (D)	C. A. Dearmon (D)	C. A. Dearmon (D)
15	John D. Pugh (D)	Frank Carpenter (D)	Frank Carpenter (D)	L. L. West (D)
16	S. W. Hogan (R)	H. Brown (R)	H. Brown (R)	H. Brown (R)
17	Frank Beauman (D)	Frank Beauman (D)	L. A. Morton (D)	L. A. Morton (D)
17	J. Elmer Thomas (D)	J. Elmer Thomas (D)	J. Elmer Thomas (D)	Jed J. Johnson (D)
18	R. A. Keller (D)	R. A. Keller (D)	James Draughon (D)	James Draughon (D)
18	Fred E. Tucker (D)	Fred E. Tucker (D)	Fred E. Tucker (D)	John H. Carlock (D)
19	Joe A. Edwards (D)	Joe A. Edwards (D)	W. R. Wallace (D)	W. R. Wallace (D)
19	Ben Franklin (D)	Jep Knight (D)	Jep Knight (D)	W. H. Woods (D)
20	J. T. McIntosh (D)	J. T. McIntosh (D)	J. T. McIntosh (D)	C. E. McPherren (D)
20	John R. Hickman (D)	John R. Hickman (D)	W. Cartwright (D)	W. Cartwright (D)
21	M. M. Ryan (D)	M. M. Ryan (D)	J. E. Fleming (D)	J. E. Fleming (D)
22	C. W. Board (D)	C. W. Board (D)	C. W. Board (D)	Tom Anglin (D)
23	R. H. Chase (D)	R. H. Chase (D)	Luther Harrison (D)	Luther Harrison (D)
24	W. C. McAlister (D)	W. C. McAlister (D)	W. C. McAlister (D)	W. J. Holloway (D)
25	W. V. Buckner (D)	W. V. Buckner (D)	E. P. Hill (D)	E. P. Hill (D)
26	C. C. Shaw (D)	John S. Vaughan (D)	John S. Vaughan (D)	Joe S. Ratliff (D)
27	T. H. Davidson (D)	T. H. Davidson (D)	S. S. Mayfield (D) [3]	Clark Nichols (D)
27	Campbell Russell (D)	Eugene M. Kerr (D)	Eugene M. Kerr (D)	S. M. Rutherford (D) [4]
28	M. S. Blassingame (D)	T. L. Rider (D)	T. L. Rider (D)	E. M. Frye (R)
29	O. W. Killam (D)	O. W. Killam (D)	Pete Coyne (D)	Pete Coyne (D)
30	Geo. W. Fields Jr. (D)	J. J. Smith (D)	J. J. Smith (D)	Horace B. Durant (R)
31	R. L. Davidson (D)	R. L. Davidson (D)	R. L. Davidson (D)	R. L. Davidson (D)
32	Jas. H. Sutherlin (D)	S. L. Johnson (D)	S. L. Johnson (D)	Glen R. Horner (R)
33	W. A. Chase (D)	W. A. Chase (D)	E. E. Woods (R)	E. E. Woods (R)
34				J. Corbett Cornett (R)

[1] Resigned. Robert Burns elected November 7, 1916 to fill unexpired term.
[2] Reapportionment Act of 1921.
[3] Resigned. Clark Nichols (D) elected November 2, 1920 for unexpired term.
[4] Died December 16, 1922. Clark Nichols elected in special election December 21, 1922 to fill unexpired term.

Ninth to Twelfth State Senate

District	9th · 1923	10th · 1925	11th · 1927	12th · 1929
Pres. Pro Tempore	Tom Anglin (D)	W. J. Holloway (D)	Mac Q. Williamson (D)	C. S. Storms (D)
1	Wallace G. Hughes (D)	Wallace G. Hughes (D)	W. H. Loofbourrow (D)	W. H. Loofbourrow (D)
2	C. B. Leedy (R)	Stanley Shepherd (D)	Stanley Shepherd (D)	Alvin Moore (D)

Ninth to Twelfth State Senate

District	9th · 1923	10th · 1925	11th · 1927	12th · 1929
2	E. M. Reed (D)	E. M. Reed (D)	E. M. Reed (D)	E. M. Reed (D)
3	L. R. Hughey (D)	L. R. Hughey (D)	D. H. Powers (R)	D. H. Powers (R)
4	Lamar Looney Mrs. (D)	Lamar Looney Mrs. (D)	Lamar Looney Mrs. (D)	H. D. Henry (D) [4]
5	Harry B. Cordell (D)	Harry B. Cordell (D)	W. C. Austin (D)	W. C. Austin (D)
6	James A. Land (R)	S. G. Thomas (D)	S. G. Thomas (D)	Grover Thomas (D)
6	A. E. Darnell (D)	A. E. Darnell (D)	A. E. Darnell (D)	A. E. Darnell (D)
7	Ira A. Hill (R)	Ira A. Hill (R)	Ira A. Hill (R)	Ira A. Hill (R)
8	Harry O. Glasser (R)	W. J. Otjen (R)	W. J. Otjen (R)	W. J. Otjen (R)
9	Wm. S. Cline (D)	Wm. S. Cline (D)	W. T. Clark (R)	W. T. Clark (R)
10	Roy Harvey (R)	Jo O. Ferguson (R)	Jo O. Ferguson (R)	Jo O. Ferguson (R)
11	Harry Jones (D)	Harry Jones (D)	Fletcher Johnson (D)	Fletcher Johnson (D)
12	John Golobie (R)	John S. Shearer (R)	John S. Shearer (R)	Amos A. Ewing (R)
13	Chas. E. Wells (R)	Tom C. Waldrep (D)	Tom C. Waldrep (D)	Clarence Johnson (R)
13	C. M. Feuquay (D)	C. M. Feuquay (D)	Geo. D. Peck (D)	George D. Peck (D)
14	Jack Barker (D)	Jack Barker (D)	John L. Rice (D)	John L. Rice (D)
14	Ross N. Lillard (D)	W. C. Fidler (D)	W. C. Fidler (D)	W. C. Fidler (D)
15	Ed F. Johns (D)	Ed F. Johns (D)	Gordon Gray (D)	Gordon Gray (D)
15	L. L. West (D)	Jed J. Johnson (D)	Jed J. Johnson (D)	Harry Jolly (D)
16	H. Brown (R)	W. P. Kimerer (R)	W. P. Kimerer (R)	W. P. Kimerer (R)
17	W. C. Lewis (D)	W. C. Lewis (D)	C. S. Storms (D)	C. S. Storms (D)
17	Jed J. Johnson (D)	Dave Boyer (D)	Dave Boyer (D)	Dave Boyer (D)
18	Earl A. Brown (D)	Earl A. Brown (D)	Jess Pullen (D)	Jess Pullen (D)
18	John H. Carlock (D)	U. T. Rexroat (D)	U. T. Rexroat (D)	U. T. Rexroat (D)
19	John E. Luttrell (D)	John E. Luttrell (D)	E. V. George (D)	E. V. George (D)
19	W. H. Woods (D)	Mac Q. Williamson (D)	Mac Q. Williamson (D)	Mac Q. Williamson (D)
20	C. E. McPherren (D)	J. H. McCurley (D)	J. H. McCurley (D)	John A. MacDonald (D)
20	T. F. Memminger (D)	T. F. Memminger (D)	J. N. Nesbitt (D)	J. N. Nesbitt (D)
21	L. P. Bobo (D)	L. P. Bobo (D)	D. A. Shaw (D) [3]	J. B. Harper (D)
22	Tom Anglin (D)	Tom Anglin (D)	Tom Anglin (D)	Tom Anglin (D)
23	Joseph C. Looney (D)	Joseph C. Looney (D)	Lester E. Smith (D)	Lester E. Smith (D)
24	W. J. Holloway (D)	W. J. Holloway (D) [1]	Paul Stewart (D)	Paul Stewart (D)
25	Carl Monk (D)	Carl Monk (D)	Guy L. Andrews (D)	Guy L. Andrews (D)
26	Joe S. Ratliff (D)	J. R. McClendon (D) [2]	Felix Simmons (D)	W. O. Ray (D)
27	W. M. Gulager (D)	W. M. Gulager (D)	W. M. Gulager (D)	W. M. Gulager (D)
27	Clark Nichols (D)	W. G. Stigler (D)	W. G. Stigler (D)	W. G. Stigler (D)
28	E. M. Frye (R)	John A. Goodall (D)	John A. Goodall (D)	G. J. Patton (R)
29	Harve N. Langley (D)	Harve N. Langley (D)	R. L. Wheatley (D)	R. L. Wheatley (D)
30	Horace B. Durant (R)	H. L. Marshall (R)	H. L. Marshall (R)	A. L. Commons (D)

Ninth to Twelfth State Senate

District	9th · 1923	10th · 1925	11th · 1927	12th · 1929
31	Wash E. Hudson (D)	Wash E. Hudson (D)	C. H. Terwilleger (R)	C. H. Terwilleger (R)
32	Glen R. Horner (R)	A. H. Culp (D)	A. H. Culp (D)	T. T. Blakely (R)
33	Floyd A. Calvert (D)	Floyd A. Calvert (D)	Gid Graham (D)	Gid Graham (D)
34	J. Corbett Cornett (R)	G. I. Van Dall (D)	G. I. Van Dall (D)	A. C. Easter (R)

[1] Resigned. Elected Lt. Governor. Paul Stewart (D) elected at Special Election November 23, 1926 to fill unexpired term.
[2] Resigned. Felix Simmons (D) elected at Special Election December 21, 1926 to fill unexpired term.
[3] Died January 2, 1927. J. B. Harper (D) elected at Special Election January 18, 1927.
[4] Died January 8, 1929. W. M. Williams (D) elected at Special Election January 29, 1929 to fill unexpired term.

Thirteenth to Sixteenth State Senate

District	13th · 1931	14th · 1933	15th · 1935	16th · 1937
Pres. Pro Tempore	W. G. Stigler (D)	Paul Stewart (D)	Claud Briggs (D)	Allen G. Nichols (D)
1	Ross Rizley (R)	Ross Rizley (R)	R. L. Howsley (D)	R. L. Howsley (D)
2	Alvin Moore (D)	Nat Taylor (D)	Nat Taylor (D)	Nat Taylor (D)
2	E. M. Reed (D)	E. M. Reed (D)	H. C. Ivester (D)	H. C. Ivester (D)
3	D. H. Powers (R)	D. H. Powers (R)	Chas. Albright (D)	Chas. Albright (D)
4	W. M. Williams (D)	S. W. Carmack (D)	S. W. Carmack (D)	W. F. Hearne (D)
5	C. R. Chamberlin (D)	C. R. Chamberlin (D)	C. R. Chamberlin (D)	C. R. Chamberlin (D)
6	Grover Thomas (D)	Grover Thomas (D)	Grover Thomas (D)	LeRoy Clayton (D)
6	Claude E. Liggett (D)	Claude E. Liggett (D)	DeRoy Burns (D)	DeRoy Burns (D)
7	Stanley Coppock (R)	Stanley Coppock (R)	H. W. Wright (D)	H. W. Wright (D)
8	W. J. Otjen (R)	Geo. A. Hutchinson (R)	Geo. A. Hutchinson (R)	James M. Wilson (D)
9	W. T. Clark (R)	W. T. Clark (R)	Chas. B. Duffy (D)	Charles B. Duffy (D)
10	Jo O. Ferguson (R)	Henry S. Johnston (D)	Henry S. Johnston (D)	John T. Sanford (D)
11	G. H. Jennings (D)	George H. Jennings (D)	Ray C. Jones (D)	Ray C. Jones (D)
12	Amos A. Ewing (R)	Louis H. Ritzhaupt (D)	Louis H. Ritzhaupt (D)	Louis H. Ritzhaupt (D)
13	Clarence Johnson (R)	Tom C. Waldrep (D)	Tom C. Waldrep (D)	Tom C. Waldrep (D)
13	Willard Sowards (D)	Willard Sowards (D)	Willard Sowards (D)	Willard Sowards (D)
14	W. P. Morrison (D)	W. P. Morrison (D)	J. A. Rinehart (D)	J. A. Rinehart (D)
14	W. C. Fidler (D)	W. C. Fidler (D)	W. C. Fidler (D)	W. C. Fidler (D)
15	William Stacey (D)	William Stacey (D)	Gerald Spencer (D)	Gerald Spencer (D)
15	Harry Jolly (D)	John D. Pugh (D)	John D. Pugh (D)	W. L. Mauk (D)
16	W. P. Kimerer (R)	Bert R. Willis (D)	Bert R. Willis (D)	Leslie Chambers (D)
17	Knox L. Garvin (D)	Knox L. Garvin (D)	Knox L. Garvin (D)	Knox L. Garvin (D) [1]
17	Dave Boyer (D)	Jim Nance (D)	Jim Nance (D)	Merton Munson (D)
18	J. Woody Dixon (D)	J. Woody Dixon (D)	Oscar K. Lowrance (D)	Oscar K. Lowrance (D)
18	U. T. Rexroat (D)	Louis A. Fischl (D)	Louis A. Fischl (D)	Joe B. Thompson (D)
19	Hardin Ballard (D)	Hardin Ballard (D)	E. V. George (D)	E. V. George (D)

Thirteenth to Sixteenth State Senate

District	13th · 1931	14th · 1933	15th · 1935	16th · 1937
19	Mac Q. Williamson (D)	Homer Paul (D)	Homer Paul (D)	Homer Paul (D)
20	John A. MacDonald (D)	John A. MacDonald (D)	John A. MacDonald (D)	John A. MacDonald (D)
20	C. B. Memminger (D)	C. B. Memminger (D)	Ed King (D)	Ed King (D)
21	Claud Briggs (D)	Claud Briggs (D)	Claud Briggs (D)	Claud Briggs (D)
22	Tom Anglin (D)	Don Wilbanks (D)	Don Wilbanks (D)	W. N. Barry (D) [2]
23	Allen G. Nichols (D)	Allen G. Nichols (D)	Allen G. Nichols (D)	Allen G. Nichols (D)
24	Paul Stewart (D)	Paul Stewart (D)	Paul Stewart (D)	Paul Stewart (D)
25	Pres. S. Lester (D)	Pres. S. Lester (D)	E. P. Hill (D)	E. P. Hill (D)
26	W. O. Ray (D)	W. O. Ray (D)	W. O. Ray (D)	W. O. Ray (D)
27	Charles A. Moon (D)	Charles A. Moon (D)	Bower Broaddus (D)	Bower Broaddus (D)
27	W. G. Stigler (D)	Joe M. Whitaker (D)	Joe M. Whitaker (D)	Joe M. Whitaker (D)
28	G. J. Patton (R)	W. A. Carlile (D)	W. A. Carlile (D)	R. O. Ingle (D)
29	Babe Howard (D)	Babe Howard (D)	Jack L. Rorschach (D)	Jack L. Rorschach (D)
30	A. L. Commons (D)	A. L. Commons (D)	A. L. Commons (D)	Felix Church (D)
31	S. M. Rutherford (D)	S. M. Rutherford (D)	Henry C. Timmons (D)	Henry C. Timmons (D)
32	T. T. Blakely (R)	David M. Logan (D)	David M. Logan (D)	W. A. Barnett (D)
33	H. P. Daugherty (D)	H. P. Daugherty (D)	Dennis Bushyhead (D)	Dennis Bushyhead (D)
34	A. C. Easter (R)	H. M. Curnutt (D)	H. M. Curnutt (D)	H. M. Curnutt (D)

[1] Died August 25, 1937. No interim successor elected.
[2] Died October 13, 1938. Tom Anglin (D) elected at Special Election November 8, 1938 to fill unexpired term.

Seventeenth to Twentieth State Senate

District	17th · 1939	18th · 1941	19th · 1943	20th · 1945
Pres. Pro Tempore	J. A. Rinehart (D)	H. M. Curnutt (D) [1]	Tom Anglin (D)	Homer Paul (D)
1	Julius W. Cox (D)	Julius W. Cox (D)	Dwight Leonard (D)	Dwight Leonard (D)
2	Nat Taylor (D)	E. F. Cornels (D)	E. F. Cornels (D)	A. E. Anderson (D)
2	T. J. Hogg (D)	T. J. Hogg (D)	E. S. Collier (D)	E. S. Collier (D)
3	Jesse Taylor (D)	Jesse Taylor (D) [2]	E. P. Williams (R)	E. P. Williams (R)
4	W. F. Hearne (D)	W. F. Hearne (D)	W. F. Hearne (D)	H. W. Worthington (D)
5	Robert B. Harbison (D)	Robert B. Harbison (D)	Burr Speck (D)	Burr Speck (D)
6	LeRoy Clayton (D)	L. E. Wheeler (D)	L. E. Wheeler (D)	L. E. Wheeler (D)
6	E. D. Walker (D)	E. D. Walker (D)	E. D. Walker (D) [3]	Byron Dacus (D)
7	O. M. Bill Ginder (R)	O. M. Bill Ginder (R)	O. M. Bill Ginder (R)	O. M. Bill Ginder (R)
8	James M. Wilson (D)	Floyd E. Carrier (R)	Floyd E. Carrier (R)	Floyd E. Carrier (R)
9	Charles B. Duffy (D)	Charles B. Duffy (D)	Charles B. Duffy (D)	Charles B. Duffy (D)
10	John T. Sanford (D)	John T. Sanford (D)	John T. Sanford (D)	Sherman J. Trussel (R)
11	Ray C. Jones (D)	Ray C. Jones (D)	Ray C. Jones (D)	Ray C. Jones (D)

Seventeenth to Twentieth State Senate

District	17th · 1939	18th · 1941	19th · 1943	20th · 1945
12	Louis H. Ritzhaupt (D)	Louis H. Ritzhaupt (D)	Louis H. Ritzhaupt (D)	Louis H. Ritzhaupt (D)
13	Tom C. Waldrep (D)	Mead Norton (D)	Mead Norton (D)	Mead Norton (D)
13	Boyd Cowden (D)	Boyd Cowden (D)	Boyd Cowden (D)	Boyd Cowden (D)
14	J. A. Rinehart (D)	J. A. Rinehart (D)	J. A. Rinehart (D)	J. A. Rinehart (D)
14	W. C. Fidler (D)	Robert Burns (D)	Robert Burns (D)	Robert Burns (D)
15	Gerald Spencer (D)	Gerald Spencer (D)	Jack Neill (D)	Jack Neill (D) [4]
15	W. L. Mauk (D)	Theodore Pruett (D)	Theodore Pruett (D)	Theodore Pruett (D)
16	Leslie Chambers (D)	George L. Bowman (D)	George L. Bowman (D)	E. B. Grennell (R)
17	Phil H. Lowery (D)	Phil H. Lowery (D)	Phil H. Lowery (D)	Phil H. Lowery (D)
17	Merton Munson (D)	Bill Logan (D)	Bill Logan (D)	Bill Logan (D)
18	Virgil L. Stokes (D)	Virgil L. Stokes (D)		
18	Joe B. Thompson (D)	Joe B. Thompson (D) [5]	Fred Chapman (D)	Fred Chapman (D)
19	James C. Nance (D)	James C. Nance (D)	James C. Nance (D)	James C. Nance (D)
19	Homer Paul (D)	Homer Paul (D)	Homer Paul (D)	Homer Paul (D)
20	John A. MacDonald (D)	H. V. Posey (D)	H. V. Posey (D)	Bayless Irby (D)
21	James Babb (D)	James Babb (D)	Clint Braden (D)	Clint Braden (D)
22	Tom Anglin (D)	Tom Anglin (D)	Tom Anglin (D)	Tom Anglin (D)
23	John B. McKeel (D)	John B. McKeel (D)	Allen G. Nichols (D)	Allen G. Nichols (D)
24	Paul Stewart (D)	Paul Stewart (D) [6]	Thomas D. Finney (D)	Thomas D. Finney (D)
25	John C. Monk (D)	John C. Monk (D)	M. O. Counts (D)	M. O. Counts (D)
26	W. O. Ray (D)	Raymond Gary (D)	Raymond Gary (D)	Raymond Gary (D)
27	Murrell H. Thornton (D)	Murrell H. Thornton (D)	Murrell H. Thornton (D)	Murrell H. Thornton (D)
27	Joe M. Whitaker (D)	Guy A. Curry (D)	Guy A. Curry (D)	Roy White (D)
28	R. O. Ingle (D)	Paul V. Carlile (D) [7]	Ray Fine (D)	Ray Fine (D)
29	R. H. Sibley (D)	R. H. Sibley (D)	Craig O. Goodpaster (D)	Craig O. Goodpaster (D)
30	Felix Church (D)	C. D. Wilson (D)	C. D. Wilson (D)	Perry Porter (D)
31	Henry C. Timmons (D)	Henry C. Timmons (D)	Clyde L. Sears (R)	Clyde L. Sears (R)
32	W. A. Barnett (D)	S. E. Hammond (D)	S. E. Hammond (D)	James A. Nevins (D)
33	Penn Couch (D)	Penn Couch (D)	H. Tom Brown (D)	H. Tom Brown (D)
34	H. M. Curnutt (D)	H. M. Curnutt (D) [8]	Frank Mahan (D)	Frank Mahan (D)
35	Ferman Phillips (D)	Ferman Phillips (D)	Ferman Phillips (D)	Ferman Phillips (D)
36			Joe Bailey Cobb (D)	Joe Bailey Cobb (D)

[1] Died September 21, 1941. Ray C. Jones (D) elected to fill unexpired term as Pres. Pro Tempore at Special Session, October 6, 1941.

[2] Died January 22, 1941. No interim successor elected.

[3] Died August 24, 1943. Byron Dacus (D) elected at Special Election April 4, 1944 to fill unexpired term.

[4] Resigned. No interim successor elected.

[5] Resigned. Fred Chapman (D) elected at Special Election December 31, 1942 to fill unexpired term.

[6] Resigned. Elected to U.S. Congress. Thomas D. Finney (D) elected at Special Election December 22, 1942 to fill unexpired term.

[7] Resigned. Ray Fine (D) elected at Special Election November 3, 1942 to fill unexpired term.

[8] Died September 21, 1941. Frank Mahan (D) elected at Special Election November 3, 1942 to fill unexpired term.

Twenty-First to Twenty-Fourth State Senate

District	21st · 1947	22nd · 1949	23rd · 1951	24th · 1953
Pres. Pro Tempore	J. C. Nance (D)	Bill Logan (D)	Boyd Cowden (D)	Raymond Gary (D)
1	Dwight Leonard (D)	Dwight Leonard (D)	Leon B. Field (D)	Leon B. Field (D)
2	A. E. Anderson (D)	A. E. Anderson (D)	A. E. Anderson (D)	Charles M. Wilson (D)
2	Orval Grim (D)	Orval Grim (D)	Lawrence L. Irwin (D)	Lawrence L. Irwin (D)
3	Claude E. Seaman (R)	Claude E. Seaman (R)	Claude E. Seaman (R)	Claude E. Seaman (R)
4	H. W. Worthington (D)	H. W. Worthington (D)	H. W. Worthington (D)	Basil R. Wilson (D)
5	Burr Speck (D)	Burr Speck (D)	D. L. Jones (D)	D. L. Jones (D)
6	L. E. Wheeler (D)	Carl Max Cook (D)	Carl Max Cook (D)	Carl Max Cook (D)
6	Byron Dacus (D)	Byron Dacus (D)	Byron Dacus (D)	Byron Dacus (D)
7	Bill Ginder (R)	Bill Ginder (R)	Stanley Coppock (R)	Stanley Coppock (R)
8	Floyd E. Carrier (R)	Floyd E. Carrier (R)	Floyd E. Carrier (R)	Floyd E. Carrier (R)
9	Perry Howell (R)	Perry Howell (R)	Roy E. Grantham (D)	Roy E. Grantham (D)
10	Sherman J. Trussel (R)	J. Val Connell (D)	J. Val Connell (D)	J. L. Maltsberger (R)
11	Everett S. Collins (D)	Everett S. Collins (D)	Everett S. Collins (D)	Everett S. Collins (D)
12	Louis H. Ritzhaupt (D)	Louis H. Ritzhaupt (D)	Louis H. Ritzhaupt (D)	Carl Morgan (R)
13	Mead Norton (D)	Oliver C. Walker (D)	Oliver C. Walker (D)	Oliver C. Walker (D)
13	Boyd Cowden (D)	Boyd Cowden (D)	Boyd Cowden (D)	Boyd Cowden (D)
14	Jim A. Rinehart (D)	Jim A. Rinehart (D)	Jim A. Rinehart (D)	Jim A. Rinehart (D)
14	Robert Burns (D)	John H. Jarman Jr. (D) [1]	George Miskovsky (D)	George Miskovsky (D)
15	Tom Jelks (D)	Tom Jelks (D)	Walt Allen (D)	Walt Allen (D)
15	Theodore Pruett (D)	Don Baldwin (D)	Don Baldwin (D)	Don Baldwin (D)
16	E. B. Grennell (R)	Roy C. Boecher (D)	Roy C. Boecher (D)	Roy C. Boecher (D)
17	Phil H. Lowery (D)	Phil H. Lowery (D)	Harold Garvin (D)	Harold Garvin (D)
17	Bill Logan (D)	Bill Logan (D)	Bill Logan (D)	Bill Logan (D)
18	Fred Chapman (D)	Joe B. Thompson (D)	Joe B. Thompson (D)	Fred Chapman (D)
19	James C. Nance (D)	James C. Nance (D)	Joe A. Smalley (D)	Joe A. Smalley (D) [4]
19	Homer Paul (D)	Herbert Hope (D)	Herbert Hope (D)	Herbert Hope (D)
20	Bayless Irby (D)	Keith Cartwright (D)	Keith Cartwright (D)	Keith Cartwright (D)
21	J. Gladston Emery (D)	J. Gladston Emery (D)	Clem M. Hamilton (D)	Clem M. Hamilton (D)
22	Tom Anglin (D)	Paul Ballinger (D)	Paul Ballinger (D)	Paul Ballinger (D)
23	Virgil B. Medlock (D)	Virgil B. Medlock (D)	Virgil B. Medlock (D)	Virgil B. Medlock (D)
24	Thomas D. Finney (D)	Leroy McClendon (D)	Leroy McClendon (D)	Leroy McClendon (D)
25	M. O. Counts (D)	M. O. Counts (D)	Kirksey M. Nix (D)	Kirksey M. Nix (D)
26	Raymond Gary (D)	Raymond Gary (D)	Raymond Gary (D)	Raymond Gary (D) [5]
27	Will Rogers (D)	Will Rogers (D) [2]	Harold R. Shoemake (D)	Harold R. Shoemake (D)
27	Roy White (D)	Roy White (D)	Roy White (D)	Howard Young (D)
28	Ray Fine (D)	Ray Fine (D)	Ray Fine (D)	Ray Fine (D)
29	W. T. Gooldy (D)	W. T. Gooldy (D)	Harold D. Morgan (D)	Harold D. Morgan (D)

Twenty-First to Twenty-Fourth State Senate

District	21st · 1947	22nd · 1949	23rd · 1951	24th · 1953
30	Perry Porter (D)	Perry Porter (D) [3]	Jess L. Fronterhouse (D)	Jess L. Fronterhouse (D)
31	Arthur L. Price (R)	Arthur L. Price (R)	Arthur L. Price (R)	Arthur L. Price (R)
32	James A. Nevins (D)	James A. Nevins (D)	James A. Nevins (D)	John W. Russell Jr. (D)
33	W. A. Waller (D)	W. A. Waller (D)	H. Tom Kight Jr. (D)	H. Tom Kight Jr. (D)
34	Frank Mahan (D)	Frank Mahan (D)	Frank Mahan (D)	Frank Mahan (D)
35	H. D. Binns (D)	H. D. Binns (D)	Henry Cooper (D)	Henry Cooper (D)
36	Joe Bailey Cobb (D)	Joe Bailey Cobb (D)	Joe Bailey Cobb (D)	Joe Bailey Cobb (D)

[1] Resigned. Won Democratic runoff same day as George Miskovsky (D) elected at Special Election to fill unexpired term: July 25, 1950. Jarman was elected to U.S. Congress later in the year.
[2] Died December 19, 1950. Harold R. Shoemake (D) elected at Special Election January 16, 1951 to fill unexpired term.
[3] Died December 1, 1949. Jess L. Fronterhouse (D) elected at Special Election July 4, 1950 to fill unexpired term.
[4] Died July 15, 1953. No interim successor elected.
[5] Resigned. Gene Herndon (D) elected at Special Election October 20, 1954 to fill unexpired term.

Twenty-Fifth to Twenty-Eighth State Senate

District	25th · 1955	26th · 1957	27th · 1959	28th · 1961
Pres. Pro Tempore	Ray Fine (D)	Don Baldwin (D)	Harold Garvin (D)	Everett S. Collins (D)
1	Leon B. Field (D)	Leon B. Field (D)	Leon B. Field (D)	Leon B. Field (D)
2	Charles M. Wilson (D)	Charles M. Wilson (D)	Charles M. Wilson (D)	Charles M. Wilson (D) [5]
2	S. S. McColgin (D)	S. S. McColgin (D)	S. S. McColgin (D)	S. S. McColgin (D)
3	Ben B. Easterly (D)	Ben B. Easterly (D)	Ben B. Easterly (D)	Ben B. Easterly (D)
4	Basil R. Wilson (D)	Basil R. Wilson (D)	Basil R. Wilson (D)	Basil R. Wilson (D)
5	D. L. Jones (D)	D. L. Jones (D)	Ryan Kerr (D)	Ryan Kerr (D)
6	Carl Max Cook (D)	K. C. Perryman (D) [2]	Ed Berrong (D)	Ed Berrong (D)
6	Byron Dacus (D)	Byron Dacus (D)	Byron Dacus (D)	Byron Dacus (D)
7	Stanley Coppock (R)	Stanley Coppock (D)	Tom H. Morford (R)	Tom H. Morford (R)
8	Floyd E. Carrier (R)	Floyd E. Carrier (R)	Floyd E. Carrier (R)	Richard E. Romang (R)
9	Roy E. Grantham (D)	Roy E. Grantham (D)	Roy E. Grantham (D)	Roy E. Grantham (D)
10	J. L. Maltsberger (R)	Robert H. Breeden (R)	Robert H. Breeden (R)	Robert H. Breeden (R)
11	Everett S. Collins (D)	Everett S. Collins (D)	Everett S. Collins (D)	Everett S. Collins (D)
12	Carl Morgan (R)	Louis H. Ritzhaupt (D)	Louis H. Ritzhaupt (D)	Louis H. Ritzhaupt (D)
13	Oliver C. Walker (D)	Oliver C. Walker (D)	Oliver C. Walker (D)	Ralph W. Graves (D)
13	Boyd Cowden (D)	Boyd Cowden (D)	Boyd Cowden (D)	Boyd Cowden (D)
14	Jim A. Rinehart (D)	Jim A. Rinehart (D)	Jean L. Pazoureck (D)	Jean L. Pazoureck (D)
14	George Miskovsky (D)	George Miskovsky (D)	George Miskovsky (D)	Cleeta John Rogers (D)
15	Walt Allen (D)	Walt Allen (D)	Walt Allen (D)	Walt Allen (D)
15	Don Baldwin (D)	Don Baldwin (D)	Don Baldwin (D)	Don Baldwin (D)
16	Roy C. Boecher (D)	Roy C. Boecher (D)	Roy C. Boecher (D)	Roy C. Boecher (D)

Twenty-Fifth to Twenty-Eighth State Senate

District	25th · 1955	26th · 1957	27th · 1959	28th · 1961
17	Harold Garvin (D)	Harold T. Garvin (D)	Harold T. Garvin (D)	Harold T. Garvin (D)
17	Bill Logan (D)	Fred R. Harris (D)	Fred R. Harris (D)	Fred R. Harris (D)
18	Fred Chapman (D)	Tom Tipps (D)	Tom Tipps (D)	Tom Tipps (D)
19	Virgil Young (D)	Virgil Young (D)	Robert L. Bailey (D)	Robert L. Bailey (D)
19	Herbert Hope (D)	Herbert Hope (D)	Herbert Hope (D)	Glen Ham (D)
20	Keith Cartwright (D)	Keith Cartwright (D)	Keith Cartwright (D)	J. H. Belvin (D)
21	Clem M. Hamilton (D)	Clem M. Hamilton (D)	Clem M. Hamilton (D)	Clem M. Hamilton (D)
22	Paul Ballinger (D)	Hugh M. Sandlin (D)	Hugh M. Sandlin (D)	Alfred Stevenson (D)
23	Glen C. Collins (D)	Glen C. Collins (D)	Buck Cartwright (D)	Buck Cartwright (D)
24	Leroy McCLendon (D)	Leroy McClendon (D)	Leroy McClendon (D)	Leroy McClendon (D)
25	Kirksey M. Nix (D) [1]	Gene Stipe (D)	Gene Stipe (D)	Gene Stipe (D)
26	Gene Herndon (D)	Gene Herndon (D)	Gene Herndon (D)	Charles E. Colston (D)
27	Harold R. Shoemake (D)	Harold R. Shoemake (D)	Harold R. Shoemake (D)	Harold R. Shoemake (D)
27	Howard Young (D)	Howard Young (D) [3]	Milam King (D)	Wilford E. Bohannon (D)
28	Ray Fine (D)	Ray Fine (D)	Ray Fine (D)	Ray Fine (D)
29	Buck Dendy (D)	Buck Dendy (D)	George P. Pitcher (D)	George P. Pitcher (D)
30	Jess L. Fronterhouse (D)	J. R. Hall Jr. (D)	J. R. Hall Jr. (D)	Robert C. Lollar (D)
31	Arthur L. Price (R)	Arthur L. Price (R)	Yates A. Land (D)	Yates A. Land (D)
32	John W. Russell Jr. (D)	Tom Payne Jr. (D) [4]	Tom Payne Jr. (D)	Tom Payne Jr. (D)
33	Clem McSpadden (D)	Clem McSpadden (D)	Clem McSpadden (D)	Clem McSpadden (D)
34	Frank Mahan (D)	Frank Mahan (D)	Frank Mahan (D)	Denzil D. Garrison (R)
35	Bob A. Trent (D)	Bob A. Trent (D)	Bob A. Trent (D)	Bob A. Trent (D)
36	Bruce L. Frazier (D)	Bruce L. Frazier (D)	Joe Bailey Cobb (D)	Joe Bailey Cobb (D)

[1] Resigned. Gene Stipe (D) elected at Special Election December 11, 1956 to fill unexpired term.

[2] Resigned. Ed Berrong (D) elected at Special Election November 4, 1958 to fill unexpired term.

[3] Died February 24, 1958. Milam King (D) elected at Special Election November 4, 1958 to fill unexpired term.

[4] John W. Russell Jr. won the Democratic nomination in the 1956 Democratic Runoff Primary Election after recount of absentee ballots. This was challenged in District Court by Tom Payne Jr., and the court ruled invalid all absentee ballots, thus giving the nomination to Payne. The State Supreme Court later ruled that the District Court had no jurisdiction in the election and declared Russell the winner. On November 23, 1956, Governor Raymond Gary declared the office vacant since neither candidate's name appeared on the General Election ballot and ordered a Special Election on December 22, 1956. This was won by Payne over his Republican opponent after Russell refused to be a candidate, maintaining the election was illegal. He contested the Governor's authority for such an election in the Supreme Court. Citing previous rulings, the Supreme Court said the Legislature was the sole judge of its membership and on January 15, 1957, the Senate voted unanimously to seat Payne.

[5] Resigned. Arthur G. McComas (D) elected at Special Election December 11, 1962 to fill unexpired term.

Twenty-Ninth to Thirty-Second State Senate

Even-numbered districts elected for two-year terms under reapportionment of 1964.

District	29th · 1963	30th · 1965	31st · 1967	32nd · 1969
Pres. Pro Tempore	Roy C. Boecher (D)	Clem McSpadden (D)	Clem McSpadden (D)	Finis Smith (D)

Twenty-Ninth to Thirty-Second State Senate

Even-numbered districts elected for two-year terms under reapportionment of 1964.

District	29th · 1963	30th · 1965	31st · 1967	32nd · 1969
1	Leon B. Field (D)	Robert S. Gee (D)	Robert S. Gee (D)	William Fred Phillips (D)
2	Arthur G. McComas (D)	Clem McSpadden (D)	Clem McSpadden (D)	Clem McSpadden (D)
2	S. S. McColgin (D) [1]	—	—	—
3	G. O. Williams (R)	Claude G. Berry (D)	Claude G. Berry (D)	Robert P. Medearis (D)
4	Basil R. Wilson (D)	Clem M. Hamilton (D)	Clem M. Hamilton (D) [3]	James E. Hamilton (D)
5	Ryan Kerr (D)	Leroy McClendon (D)	Leroy McClendon (D)	Jim E. Lane (D)
6	Ed Berrong (D)	John Massey (D)	John Massey (D)	John Massey (D)
6	Byron Dacus (D)	—	—	—
7	Roy Schoeb (R)	Gene Stipe (D)	Gene Stipe (D)	Gene Stipe (D)
8	Richard E. Romang (R)	Tom Payne (D)	Tom Payne (D)	Tom Payne (D)
9	Roy E. Grantham (D)	John D. Luton (D)	John D. Luton (D)	John D. Luton (D)
10	Robert H. Breeden (R) [2]	Raymond L. Horn (D)	Raymond L. Horn (D)	Raymond L. Horn (D)
11	Robert M. Murphy (D)	Allen G. Nichols (D)	Allen G. Nichols (D)	Allen G. Nichols (D)
12	Louis H. Ritzhaupt (D)	John W. Young (D)	John W. Young (D)	John W. Young (D)
13	Ralph W. Graves (D)	George A. Miller (D)	George A. Miller (D)	George A. Miller (D)
13	Boyd Cowden (D)	—	—	—
14	Jean L. Pazoureck (D)	Ernest D. Martin (D)	Ernest D. Martin (D)	Ernest D. Martin (D)
14	Cleeta John Rogers (D)	—	—	—
15	Walt Allen (D)	Glen Ham (D)	Glen Ham (D)	Glen Ham (D)
15	Don Baldwin (D)	—	—	—
16	Roy C. Boecher (D)	Hal L. Muldrow (D)	Phil Smalley (D)	Phil Smalley (D)
17	Harold T. Garvin (D)	Ralph W. Graves (D)	Ralph W. Graves (D)	Ralph W. Graves (D)
17	Fred R. Harris (D)	—	—	—
18	Tom Tipps (D)	Boyd Cowden (D)	Donald F. Ferrell (R)	Donald F. Ferrell (R)
19	Hal L. Muldrow (D)	Richard E. Romang (R)	Richard E. Romang (R)	Richard E. Romang (R) [4]
19	Glen Ham (D)	—	—	—
20	J. H. Belvin (D)	Roy E. Grantham (D)	Roy E. Grantham (D)	Roy E. Grantham (D)
21	Clem M. Hamilton (D)	Robert M. Murphy (D)	Robert M. Murphy (D)	Robert M. Murphy (D)
22	Alfred Stevenson (D)	Roy C. Boecher (D)	Roy C. Boecher (D)	Roy C. Boecher (D)
23	Allen G. Nichols (D)	Don Baldwin (D)	Don Baldwin (D)	Don Baldwin (D)
24	Leroy McClendon (D)	Wayne M. Holden (D)	Wayne M. Holden (D)	Wayne M. Holden (D)
25	Gene Stipe (D)	Anthony M. Massad (D)	Anthony M. Massad (D)	Herschal Crow (D)
26	Charles E. Colston (D)	Byron Dacus (D)	Byron Dacus (D)	Byron Dacus (D)
27	Bill Haworth (D)	Ed Berrong (D)	Ed Berrong (D)	Ed Berrong (D)
27	Wilford E. Bohannon (D)	—	—	—
28	Ray Fine (D)	G. O. Williams (R)	G. O. Williams (R)	G. O. Williams (R)
29	John C. Wilkerson Jr. (D)	Denzil D. Garrison (R)	Denzil D. Garrison (R)	Denzil D. Garrison (R)

Twenty-Ninth to Thirty-Second State Senate

Even-numbered districts elected for two-year terms under reapportionment of 1964.

District	29th · 1963	30th · 1965	31st · 1967	32nd · 1969
30	Robert C. Lollar (D)	Leon B. Field (D)	Leon B. Field (D)	Leon B. Field (D)
31	Dewey F. Bartlett (R)	Jim Taliaferro (D)	Jim Taliaferro (D)	Jim Taliaferro (D)
32	Tom Payne Jr. (D)	Al Terrill (D)	Al Terrill (D)	Al Terrill (D)
33	Clem McSpadden (D)	Ed W. Bradley (D)	Ed W. Bradley (D)	Ed W. Bradley (D)
34	Denzil D. Garrison (R)	Charles Pope (D)	George Hargrave Jr. (D)	George Hargrave Jr. (D)
35	Bob A. Trent (D)	L. Beauchamp Selman (D)	L. Beauchamp Selman (D)	James M. Inhofe (R)
36	Joe Bailey Cobb (D)	Gene C. Howard (D)	Gene C. Howard (D) [6]	Gene C. Howard (D)
37		Finis W. Smith (D)	Finis W. Smith (D)	Finis W. Smith (D)
38		Ralph S. Rhoades (R)	Peyton A. Breckinridge (R)	Peyton A. Breckinridge (R)
39		Dewey F. Bartlett (R) [5]	Joseph R. McGraw (R)	Joseph R. McGraw (R)
40		Richard D. Stansberry (R)	Richard D. Stansberry (R)	Richard D. Stansberry (R)
41		Bryce Baggett (D)	Bryce Baggett (D)	Bryce Baggett (D)
42		H. B. Atkinson (D)	H. B. Atkinson (D)	H. B. Atkinson (D)
43		John L. Garrett (D)	John L. Garrett (D)	John L. Garrett (D)
44		J. Lee Keels (D)	J. Lee Keels (D)	J. Lee Keels (D)
45		Jimmy Birdsong (D)	Jimmy Birdsong (D)	Jimmy Birdsong (D)
46		Cleeta John Rogers (D)	Jack M. Short (R)	Jack M. Short (R)
47		Ted C. Findeiss (R)	Ted C. Findeiss (R)	John R. McCune (R)
48		E. Melvin Porter (D)	E. Melvin Porter (D)	E. Melvin Porter (D)

[1] Died October 26, 1963. No interim successor elected.
[2] Resigned. No interim successor elected.
[3] Died May 30, 1967. James E. Hamilton (D) elected at Special Election July 11, 1967 to fill unexpired term.
[4] Resigned. Norman Lamb (R) elected at Special Election January 5, 1971 to fill unexpired term.
[5] Resigned. Elected governor. Joseph R. McGraw (R) elected at Special Election December 20, 1966 to fill unexpired term.
[6] Elected at Special Election February 14, 1967, to fill vacancy created by action of the Senate January 16, 1967.

Thirty-Third to Thirty-Sixth State Senate

District	33rd · 1971	34th · 1973	35th · 1975	36th · 1977
Pres. Pro Tempore	Finis Smith (D)	James E. Hamilton (D)	Gene C. Howard (D)	Gene C. Howard (D)
1	William Fred Phillips (D)	William M. Schuelein (D)	Willam M. Schuelein (D)	William M. Schuelein (D)
2	Clem McSpadden (D) [1]	Robert L. Wadley (D)	Robert L. Wadley (D)	Robert L. Wadley (D)
3	Robert P. Medearis (D)	Robert P. Medearis (D)	Robert P. Medearis (D)	Herbert Rozell (D)
4	James E. Hamilton (D)	James E. Hamilton (D)	James E. Hamilton (D) [5]	Joe Johnson (D)
5	Jim E. Lane (D)	Jim E. Lane (D)	Jim E. Lane (D)	Jim E. Lane (D)
6	Bob A. Trent (D)	Bob A. Trent (D)	Roy A. Boatner (D)	Roy A. Boatner (D)
7	Gene Stipe (D)	Gene Stipe (D)	Gene Stipe (D)	Gene Stipe (D)
8	Tom Payne (D)	Tom Payne (D) [2]	Kenneth Butler (D)	Kenneth Butler (D)

Thirty-Third to Thirty-Sixth State Senate

District	33rd · 1971	34th · 1973	35th · 1975	36th · 1977
9	John D. Luton (D)	John D. Luton (D)	John D. Luton (D)	John D. Luton (D)
10	John L. Dahl (D)	John L. Dahl (D)	John L. Dahl (D)	John L. Dahl (D)
11	Allen G. Nichols (D)	—[6]	—[6]	—[6]
12	John W. Young (D)	John W. Young (D)	John W. Young (D)	John W. Young (D)
13	George A. Miller (D)	George A. Miller (D) [3]	Wes Watkins (D)	James W. McDaniel (D)
14	Ernest D. Martin (D)	Ernest D. Martin (D)	Ernest D. Martin (D)	Ernest D. Martin (D)
15	Glen Ham (D)	Glen Ham (D)	Glen Ham (D)	Charles W. Vann (D)
16	Phil Smalley (D)	Phil Smalley (D) [4]	Lee Cate (D)	Lee Cate (D)
17	Ralph W. Graves (D)	Ralph Graves (D)	Ralph Graves (D)	John L. Clifton (D)
18	Donald F. Ferrell (R)	—[6]	—[6]	—[6]
19	Norman Lamb (R)	Norman Lamb (R)	Norman Lamb (R)	Norman Lamb (R)
20	Roy E. Grantham (D)	Roy E. Grantham (D)	Roy E. Grantham (D)	Roy E. Grantham (D)
21	Robert M. Murphy (D)	Robert M. Murphy (D)	Robert M. Murphy (D)	Robert M. Murphy (D)
22	Roy C. Boecher (D)	Roy C. Boecher (D)	Gideon Tinsley (D)	Gideon Tinsley (D)
23	Don Baldwin (D)	Don Baldwin (D)	Don Baldwin (D)	Ray Giles (D)
24	Wayne M. Holden (D)	Wayne M. Holden (D)	Wayne M. Holden (D)	Wayne M. Holden (D)
25	Herschal Crow (D)	Herschal Crow (D)	Herschal Crow (D)	Herschal H. Crow (D)
26	Gilmer N. Capps (D)	Gilmer N. Capps (D)	Gilmer N. Capps (D)	Gilmer N. Capps (D)
27	Ed Berrong (D)	Ed Berrong (D)	Ed Berrong (D)	Ed Berrong (D)
28	G. O. Williams (R)	—[6]	—[6]	—[6]
29	Denzil D. Garrison (R)	Jerry T. Pierce (R)	Jerry T. Pierce (R)	Jerry T. Pierce (R)
30	Leon B. Field (D)	—[6]	—[6]	—[6]
31	Jim Taliaferro (D)	Jim Taliaferro (D)	Jim Taliaferro (D) [7]	Paul Taliaferro (D)
32	Al Terrill (D)	Al Terrill (D)	Al Terrill (D)	Al Terrill (D)
33	Ed W. Bradley (D)	Rodger A. Randle (D)	Rodger A. Randle (D)	Rodger A. Randle (D)
34	George Hargrave Jr. (D)	George Hargrave Jr. (D)	Bob R. Shatwell (D)	Bob R. Shatwell (D)
35	James M. Inhofe (R)	James M. Inhofe (R)	James M. Inhofe (R)	Warren E. Green (R)
36	Gene C. Howard (D)	Gene C. Howard (D)	Gene C. Howard (D)	Gene C. Howard (D)
37	Finis W. Smith (D)	Finis W. Smith (D)	Finis W. Smith (D)	Finis W. Smith (D)
38	Peyton A. Breckinridge (R)	Peyton A. Breckinridge (R)	Frank Keating (R)	Frank Keating (R)
39	Joseph R. McGraw (R)	Stephen C. Wolfe (R)	Stephen C. Wolfe (R)	Stephen C. Wolfe (R)
40	Richard D. Stansberry (R)	Richard D. Stansberry (R)	Phillip E. Lambert (D)	Phillip E. Lambert (D)
41	Bryce Baggett (D)	Phil Watson (R)	Phil Watson (R)	Phil Watson (R)
42	James F. Howell (D)	James F. Howell (D)	James F. Howell (D)	James F. Howell (D)
43	John L. Garrett (D)	John L. Garrett (D)	John L. Garrett (D)	Don Kilpatrick (D)
44	J. Lee Keels (D)	J. Lee Keels (D)	Marvin York (D)	Marvin York (D)
45	Jimmy Birdsong (D)	Jimmy Birdsong (D)	Jimmy Birdsong (D)	Jimmy Birdsong (D)
46	Cleeta John Rogers (D)	Cleeta John Rogers (D)	Mary Helm (R)	Mary Helm (R)

Thirty-Third to Thirty-Sixth State Senate

District	33rd · 1971	34th · 1973	35th · 1975	36th · 1977
47	John R. McCune (R)	John R. McCune (R)	John R. McCune (R)	John R. McCune (R)
48	E. Melvin Porter (D)	E. Melvin Porter (D)	E. Melvin Porter (D)	E. Melvin Porter (D)
49	—⁶	Leon B. Field (D)	Leon B. Field (D)	Leon B. Field (D)
50	—⁶	Donald F. Ferrell (R)	Bill Dawson (D)	Bill Dawson (D)
52	—⁶	E. W. Keller (R)	E. W. Keller (R)	E. W. Keller (R)
54	—⁶	Bob Funston (D)	Bob Funston (D)	Bob Funston (D)

¹Resigned. Elected to U.S. Congress. Robert L. Wadley (D) elected at Special Election December 20, 1972 to fill unexpired term.
²Died April 17, 1974. Kenneth Butler (D) elected at Special Election June 4, 1974 to fill unexpired term.
³Resigned. Wes Watkins (D) elected at Special Election November 5, 1974 to fill unexpired term.
⁴Died August 9, 1973. Lee Cate (D) elected at Special Election October 2, 1973 to fill unexpired term.
⁵Resigned. Joe Johnson (D) elected at Special Election, August 24, 1976.
⁶Reapportionment Act of 1971 eliminated Senate Districts 11, 18, 28, and 30. It created Senate Districts 49, 50, 52, and 54 (14 O.S. §80.1 et seq).
⁷Died April 24, 1976. Paul Taliaferro (D) appointed November 5, 1976 to fill unexpired term. Elected for a full term November 2, 1976.

Thirty-Seventh to Fortieth State Senate

District	37th · 1979	38th · 1981	39th · 1983	40th · 1985
Pres. Pro Tempore	Gene C. Howard (D)	Marvin E. York (D)	Marvin E. York (D)	Rodger Randle (D)
1	William M. Schuelein (D)	William M. Schuelein (D)	William M. Schuelein (D)	William M. Schuelein (D)
2	Bill J. Crutcher (D)	Bill J. Crutcher (D) ⁵	Stratton Taylor (D)	Stratton Taylor (D)
3	Herbert Rozell (D)	Herbert Rozell (D)	Herbert Rozell (D)	Herbert Rozell (D)
4	Joe Johnson (D)	Joe Johnson (D)	Joe Johnson (D)	Joe Johnson (D)
5	Jim E. Lane (D)	Gerald C. Dennis (D)	Gerald C. Dennis (D)	Gerald C. Dennis (D)
6	Roy A. Boatner (D)	Roy A. Boatner (D)	Roy A. Boatner (D)	Roy A. Boatner (D)
7	Gene Stipe (D)	Gene Stipe (D)	Gene Stipe (D)	Gene Stipe (D)
8	Robert L. Miller (D)	Robert L. Miller (D)	Robert L. Miller (D)	Robert L. Miller (D)
9	John D. Luton (D)	John D. Luton (D)	John D. Luton (D)	John D. Luton (D)
10	John L. Dahl (D)	John Dahl (D)	John L. Dahl (D)	John L. Dahl (D)
11	—³&⁴	—³&⁴	Bernard J. McIntyre (D)	Bernard J. McIntyre (D)
12	John W. Young (D)	John W. Young (D)	John W. Young (D)	John W. Young (D)
13	James W. McDaniel (D)	James W. McDaniel (D)	James W. McDaniel (D)	Billie J. Floyd (D)
14	Ernest D. Martin (D)	Ernest D. Martin (D)	Darryl F. Roberts (D)	Darryl F. Roberts (D)
15	Charles W. Vann (D)	Bill Branch (D)	Bill Branch (D)	Bill Branch (D)
16	Lee Cate (D)	Lee Cate (D)	Lee Cate (D)	Lee Cate (D)
17	John L. Clifton (D)	John L. Clifton (D)	John L. Clifton Jr. (D)	Roy H. Sadler (D)
19	Norman Lamb (R)	Norman A. Lamb (R)	Norman A. Lamb (R)	Norman A. Lamb (R)
20	Don Nickles (R) ¹	William P. O'Connor (R)	William P. O'Connor (R)	William P. O'Connor (R)

Thirty-Seventh to Fortieth State Senate

District	37th · 1979	38th · 1981	39th · 1983	40th · 1985
21	Robert M. Murphy (D)	Bernice Shedrick (D)	Bernice Shedrick (D)	Bernice Shedrick (D)
22	Gideon Tinsley (D)	Gideon Tinsley (D)	Ralph J. Choate (R)	Ralph J. Choate (R)
23	Ray Giles (D)	Ray A. Giles (D)	Ray A. Giles (D)	Ray A. Giles (D)
24	Kenneth K. Landis (D)	Kenneth K. Landis (D)	Kenneth K. Landis (D)	Kenneth K. Landis (D)
25	Herschal H. Crow (D)	Herschal H. Crow (D)	—[9]	—[9]
26	Gilmer N. Capps (D)	Gilmer N. Capps (D)	Gilmer N. Capps (D)	Gilmer N. Capps (D)
27	Ed Berrong (D)	Wayne Winn (D)	—[9]	—[9]
29	Jerry T. Pierce (R)	Jerry T. Pierce (R)	Jerry T. Pierce (R)	Jerry T. Pierce (R)
31	Paul Taliaferro (D)	Paul Taliaferro (D)	Paul Taliaferro (D)	Paul Taliaferro (D)
32	Al Terrill (D)	Al Terrill (D)	Al Terrill (D)	Al Terrill (D)
33	Rodger A. Randle (D)	Rodger A. Randle (D)	Rodger A. Randle (D)	Rodger A. Randle (D)
34	Robert V. Cullison (D)	Robert V. Cullison (D)	Robert V. Cullison (D)	Robert V. Cullison (D)
35	Warren E. Green (R)	Warren E. Green (R)	Warren E. Green (R)	Warren E. Green (R)
36	Gene C. Howard (D)	Gene C. Howard (D)	Frank Rhodes (R)	Frank Rhodes (R)
37	Finis W. Smith (D)	Finis W. Smith (D)[7]	Robert E. Hopkins (D)	Robert E. Hopkins (D)[10]
38	Frank Keating (R)	Frank Keating (R)[8]	Wayne Winn (D)	Wayne Winn (D)
39	Stephen C. Wolfe (R)	Jerry L. Smith (R)	Jerry L. Smith (R)	Jerry L. Smith (R)
40	Mike Combs (D)	Mike Combs (D)	Mike Combs (D)	Mike Combs (D)
41	Phil Watson (R)	Phil Watson (R)	Phil Watson (R)	Phil Watson (R)
42	James F. Howell (D)	James F. Howell (D)	James F. Howell (D)	James F. Howell (D)
43	Don Kilpatrick (D)	Don Kilpatrick (D)	Don Kilpatrick (D)	Benjamin James Brown (D)
44	Marvin York (D)	Marvin York (D)	Marvin York (D)	Marvin York (D)
45	Jimmy Birdsong (D)	Ed Moore (R)	Ed Moore (R)	Helen G. Cole (R)
46	Bernest Cain (D)	Bernest Cain (D)	Bernest Cain (D)	Bernest Cain (D)
47	John R. McCune (R)	John R. McCune (R)	John R. McCune (R)	John R. McCune (R)
48	E. Melvin Porter (D)	E. Melvin Porter (D)	E. Melvin Porter (D)	E. Melvin Porter (D)
49	Leon B. Field (D)[2]	Tim Leonard (R)	Tim Leonard (R)	Tim Leonard (R)
50	Jeff Johnston (D)	Jeff Johnston (D)[6]	William Dawson Jr. (D)	William Dawson Jr. (D)
51	—[11]	—[11]	Charles R. Ford (R)	Charles R. Ford (R)
52	E. W. Keller (R)	E. W. Keller (R)	E. W. Keller (R)	E. W. Keller (R)
54	Don Cummins (D)	Don Cummins (D)[12]	Gerald "Ged" Wright (R)	Gerald "Ged" Wright (R)

[1] Resigned, November 17, 1980. Elected to U.S. Senate. Wm. P. O'Connor (R) elected to fill unexpired term at Special Election January 13, 1981.

[2] Resigned. Tim Leonard (R) elected at Special Election November 6, 1979.

[3] Reapportionment Act of 1971 eliminated Senate Districts 11, 18, 28, and 30. It created Senate Districts 49, 50, 52, and 54 (14 O.S. §80.1 et seq).

[4] District 11 was re-created in the Reapportionment Act of 1981 (O.S. 1991, § 80.20).

[5] Resigned September 30, 1982. No interim successor elected.

[6] Died January 22, 1982. Bill Dawson (D) elected at Special Election March 23, 1982.

[7] Resigned May 31, 1982. Robert E. Hopkins (D) elected, Special Election, August 24, 1982.

[8] Keating resigned to run for Federal office. Charles Ford elected, Special Election, June 6, 1981. Ford served in District 51 after reapportionment in 1981.

Thirty-Seventh to Fortieth State Senate

District	37th · 1979	38th · 1981	39th · 1983	40th · 1985

[9] Reapportionment Act of 1981. (14 O.S. §80.10 et seq.)
[10] Resigned January 5, 1987. David Riggs (D) elected at Special Election, March 23, 1987.
[11] No district 51 existed until the Reapportionment Act of 1981. (14 O.S. §80.10 et seq.).
[12] Died October 24, 1982. No interim successor elected.

Forty-First to Forty-Fourth State Senate

District	41st · 1987	42nd · 1989	43rd · 1991	44th · 1993
Pres. Pro Tempore	Rodger Randle (D)	Robert V. Cullison (D)	Robert V. Cullison (D)	Robert V. Cullison (D)
1	William M. Schuelein (D)	William M. Schuelein (D)	William M. Schuelein (D)	Rick Littlefield (D)
2	Stratton Taylor (D)	Stratton Taylor (D)	Stratton Taylor (D)	Stratton Taylor (D)
3	Herbert Rozell (D)	Herbert Rozell (D)	Herbert Rozell (D)	Herbert Rozell (D)
4	Larry Dickerson (D)	Larry Dickerson (D)	Larry Dickerson (D)	Larry Dickerson (D)
5	Gerald C. Dennis (D)	Rex W. Chandler (D)	Rex W. Chandler (D)	Jack Bell (D)
6	Roy A. Boatner (D) [1]	Billy A. Mickle (D)	Billy A. Mickle (D)	Billy A. Mickle (D)
7	Gene Stipe (D)	Gene Stipe (D)	Gene Stipe (D)	Gene Stipe (D)
8	Franklin D. Shurden (D)	Franklin D. Shurden (D)	Franklin D. Shurden (D)	Franklin D. Shurden (D)
9	John D. Luton (D)	Ben H. Robinson (D)	Ben H. Robinson (D)	Ben H. Robinson (D)
10	John L. Dahl (D)	John Dahl (D)	J. Berry Harrison (D)	J. Berry Harrison (D)
11	Maxine Horner (D)	Maxine Horner (D)	Maxine Horner (D)	Maxine Horner (D)
12	Ted V. Fisher (D)	Ted V. Fisher (D)	Ted V. Fisher (D)	Ted V. Fisher (D)
13	Billie Floyd (D)	Dick Wilkerson (D)	Dick Wilkerson (D)	Dick Wilkerson (D)
14	Darryl F. Roberts (D)	Darryl F. Roberts (D)	Darryl F. Roberts (D)	Darryl F. Roberts (D)
15	Bill Branch (D)	Patrica Weedn (D)	Patricia Weedn (D)	Patricia Weedn (D)
16	Gary Gardenhire (R)	Gary Gardenhire (R)	Cal Hobson (D)	Cal Hobson (D)
17	Roy H. Sadler (D)	Carl C. Franklin (D)	Carl C. Franklin (D)	Brad Henry (D)
18	—	—	Kevin Alan Easley (D) [5]	Kevin Alan Easley (D)
19	Norman A. Lamb (R)	Ed Long (D)	Ed Long (D)	Ed Long (D)
20	Olin Branstetter (R)	Olin Branstetter (R)	Paul Muegge (D)	Paul Muegge (D)
21	Bernice Shedrick (D)	Bernice Shedrick (D)	Bernice Shedrick (D)	Bernice Shedrick (D)
22	Ralph J. Choate (R)	Ralph J. Choate (R)	Bill Gustafson (R)	Bill Gustafson (R)
23	Ray A. Giles (D)	Ray A. Giles (D)	Ray A. Giles (D)	Bruce Price (D)
24	Cliff Marshall (D)	Cliff Marshall (D)	Larry Lawler (D)	Larry Lawler (D)
26	Gilmer N. Capps (D)	Gilmer N. Capps (D)	Gilmer N. Capps (D)	Gilmer N. Capps (D)
29	Jerry T. Pierce (R)	Jerry T. Pierce (R)	Jerry T. Pierce (R)	Jerry T. Pierce (R)
31	Paul Taliaferro (D)	Paul Taliaferro (D)	Sam Helton (D)	Sam Helton (D)
32	Roy B. Butch Hooper (D)	Roy B. Hooper (D)	Roy B. Hooper (D)	Roy B. Hooper (D)
33	Rodger A. Randle (D) [2]	Penny Williams (D)	Penny Williams (D)	Penny Williams (D)
34	Robert V. Cullison (D)	Robert V. Cullison (D)	Robert V. Cullison (D)	Robert V. Cullison (D)

Forty-First to Forty-Fourth State Senate

District	41st · 1987	42nd · 1989	43rd · 1991	44th · 1993
35	Warren E. Green (R)	Don Rubottom (R)	Don Rubottom (R)	Don Rubottom (R)
36	Frank Rhodes (R)	Frank Rhodes (R)	—³	—³
37	David Riggs (D)	Lewis Long Jr. (D)	Lewis Long Jr. (D)	Lewis Long Jr. (D)
38	Robert M. Kerr (D)	Robert M. Kerr (D)	Robert M. Kerr (D)	Robert M. Kerr (D)
39	Jerry L. Smith (R)	Jerry L. Smith (R)	Jerry L. Smith (R)	Jerry L. Smith (R)
40	Leo Kingston (R)	Leo Kingston (R)	Brooks Douglass (R)	Brooks Douglass (R)
41	Phil Watson (R)	Mark Snyder (R)	Mark Snyder (R)	Mark Snyder (R)
42	Dave Herbert (D)	Dave Herbert (D)	Dave Herbert (D)	Dave Herbert (D)
43	Benjamin J. Brown (D)	Ben Brown (D)	Ben Brown (D)	Ben Brown (D)
44	Kay Dudley (R)	Kay Dudley (R)	Keith C. Leftwich (D)	Keith C. Leftwich (D)
45	Helen G. Cole (R)	Tom Cole (R)	Helen G. Cole (R)	Helen G. Cole (R)
46	Bernest Cain (D)	Bernest Cain (D)	Bernest Cain (D)	Bernest Cain (D)
47	John R. McCune (R)	Mike Fair (R)	Mike Fair (R)	Mike Fair (R)
48	Vicki Miles-LaGrange (D)	Vicki Miles-LaGrange (D)	Vicki Miles-LaGrange (D)	Vicki Miles-LaGrange (D) ⁴
49	Tim Leonard (R)	Don Williams (D)	Don Williams (D)	Don Williams (D)
50	Enoch Kelly Haney (D)	Enoch Kelly Haney (D)	Enoch Kelly Haney (D)	Enoch Kelly Haney (D)
51	Charles R. Ford (R)	Charles R. Ford (R)	Charles R. Ford (R)	Charles R. Ford (R)
52	Howard H. Hendrick (R)	Howard H. Hendrick (R)	Howard H. Hendrick (R)	Howard H. Hendrick (R)
54	Gerald "Ged" Wright (R)	Gerald "Ged" Wright (R)	Gerald "Ged" Wright (R)	Gerald "Ged" Wright (R)

[1] Resigned October 19, 1987. Billy A. Mickel (D) elected January 12, 1988.
[2] Resigned May 2, 1988. No Interim filling term.
[3] Senate bill 14 O.S. 1991, § 80.21 eliminated District 36.
[4] Resigned. Named U.S. Attorney; sworn in December 16, 1994 as U.S. District Judge.
[5] Reapportionment Act of 1991 (14 O.S. § 80.20 et seq.)

Forty-Fifth to Forty-Eighth State Senate

District	45th · 1995	46th · 1997	47th · 1999	48th · 2001
Pres. Pro Tempore	Stratton Taylor (D)	Stratton Taylor (D)	Stratton Taylor (D)	Stratton Taylor (D)
1	Rick Littlefield (D)	Rick Littlefield (D)	Rick Littlefield (D)	Rick Littlefield (D)
2	Stratton Taylor (D)	Stratton Taylor (D)	Stratton Taylor (D)	Stratton Taylor (D)
3	Herbert Rozell (D)	Herbert Rozell (D)	Herbert Rozell (D)	Herbert Rozell (D)
4	Larry Dickerson (D)	Larry Dickerson (D)	Larry Dickerson (D)	Larry Dickerson (D) ¹
5	Jack Bell (D)	Jeff Rabon (D)	Jeff Rabon (D)	Jeff Rabon (D)
6	Billy A. Mickle (D)	Billy A. Mickle (D)	Billy A. Mickle (D)	Billy A. Mickle (D)
7	Gene Stipe (D)	Gene Stipe (D)	Gene Stipe (D)	Gene Stipe (D)
8	Franklin D. Shurden (D)	Franklin D. Shurden (D)	Franklin D. Shurden (D)	Franklin D. Shurden (D)
9	Ben H. Robinson (D)	Ben H. Robinson (D)	Ben H. Robinson (D)	Ben H. Robinson (D)
10	J. Berry Harrison (D)	J. Berry Harrison (D)	J. Berry Harrison (D)	J. Berry Harrison (D)

Forty-Fifth to Forty-Eighth State Senate

District	45th · 1995	46th · 1997	47th · 1999	48th · 2001
11	Maxine Horner (D)	Maxine Horner (D)	Maxine Horner (D)	Maxine Horner (D)
12	Ted V. Fisher (D)	Ted V. Fisher (D)	Ted V. Fisher (D)	Ted V. Fisher (D)
13	Dick Wilkerson (D)	Dick Wilkerson (D)	Dick Wilkerson (D)	Dick Wilkerson (D)
14	Darryl F. Roberts (D)	Darryl F. Roberts (D)	Johnnie C. Crutchfield (D)	Johnnie C. Crutchfield (D)
15	Patricia Weedn (D)	Patricia Weedn (D)	Patrica Weedn (D)	Jonathan Nichols (R)
16	Cal Hobson (D)	Cal Hobson (D)	Cal Hobson III (D)	Cal Hobson III (D)
17	Brad Henry (D)	Brad Henry (D)	Brad Henry (D)	Brad Henry (D)
18	Kevin Alan Easley (D)	Kevin Alan Easley (D)	Kevin A. Easley (D)	Kevin A. Easley (D)
19	Ed Long (D)	Robert V. Milacek (R)	Robert V. Milacek (R)	Robert V. Milacek (R)
20	Paul Muegge (D)	Paul Muegge (D)	Paul Muegge (D)	Paul Muegge (D)
21	Bernice Shedrick (D)	Mike Morgan (D)	Mike Morgan (D)	Mike Morgan (D)
22	Bill Gustafson (R)	Bill Gustafson (R)	Mike Johnson (R)	Mike Johnson (R)
23	Bruce Price (D)	Bruce Price (D)	Bruce Price (D)	Bruce Price (D)
24	Carol Martin (R)	Carol Martin (R)	Carol Martin (R)	Carol Martin (R)
26	Gilmer N. Capps (D)	Gilmer N. Capps (D)	Gilmer N. Capps (D)	Gilmer N. Capps (D)
29	Jerry T. Pierce (R)	Jim Dunlap (R)	Jim Dunlap (R)	Jim Dunlap (R)
31	Sam Helton (D)	Sam Helton (D)	Sam Helton (D)	Sam Helton (D)
32	Jim Maddox (D)	Jim Maddox (D)	Jim Maddox (D)	Jim Maddox (D)
33	Penny Williams (D)	Penny Williams (D)	Penny Williams (D)	Penny Williams (D)
34	Grover Campbell (R)	Grover Campbell (R)	Grover Campbell (R)	Grover Campbell (R)
35	Don Rubottom (R)	James A. Williamson (R)	James A. Williamson (R)	James A. Williamson (R)
37	Lewis Long Jr. (D)	Lewis Long Jr. (D)	Lewis Long Jr. (D)	Nancy Riley (R)
38	Robert M. Kerr (D)	Robert M. Kerr (D)	Robert M. Kerr (D)	Robert M. Kerr (D)
39	Jerry L. Smith (R)	Jerry L. Smith (R)	Jerry L. Smith (R)	Jerry L. Smith (R)
40	Brooks Douglass (R)	Brooks Douglass (R)	Brooks Douglass (R)	Brooks Douglass (R)
41	Mark Snyder (R)	Mark Snyder (R)	Mark Snyder (R)	Mark Snyder (R)
42	Dave Herbert (D)	Dave Herbert (D)	Dave Herbert (D)	Dave Herbert (D)
43	Ben Brown (D)	Ben Brown (D)	Ben Brown (D)	Jim Reynolds (R)
44	Keith C. Leftwich (D)	Keith C. Leftwich (D)	Keith C. Leftwich (D)	Keith C. Leftwich (D)
45	Helen G. Cole (R)	Kathleen Wilcoxson (R)	Kathleen Wilcoxson (R)	Kathleen Wilcoxson (R)
46	Bernest Cain (D)	Bernest Cain (D)	Bernest Cain (D)	Bernest Cain (D)
47	Mike Fair (R)	Mike Fair (R)	Mike Fair (R)	Mike Fair (R)
48	Angela Monson (D)	Angela Monson (D)	Angela Monson (D)	Angela Monson (D)
49	Don Williams (D)	Owen Laughlin (R)	Owen Laughlin (R)	Owen Laughlin (R)
50	Enoch Kelly Haney (D)	Enoch Kelly Haney (D)	Enoch Kelly Haney (D)	Enoch Kelly Haney (D)
51	Charles R. Ford (R)	Charles R. Ford (R)	Charles R. Ford (R)	Charles R. Ford (R)
52	Howard Hendrick (R)	Howard H. Hendrick (R)	Glenn Coffee (R)	Glenn Coffee (R)
54	Gerald "Ged" Wright (R)	Gerald "Ged" Wright (R)	Scott Pruitt (R)	Scott Pruitt (R)

[1]Died March 7, 2001. No interim successor named.

Forty-Ninth to Fifty-Second State Senate

District	49th · 2003	50th · 2005	51st · 2007	52nd · 2009
Pres. Pro Tempore	Cal Hobson III (D)	Mike Morgan (D)	Mike Morgan (D) Glenn Coffee (R) [1]	Glenn Coffee (R)
1	Rick Littlefield (D)	Charles Wyrick (D)	Charles Wyrick (D)	Charles Wyrick (D
2	Stratton Taylor (D)	Stratton Taylor (D)	Sean Burrage (D)	Sean Burrage (D)
3	Herbert Rozell (D)	Jim Wilson (D)	Jim Wilson (D)	Jim Wilson (D
4	Kenneth Corn (D)	Kenneth Corn (D)	Kenneth Corn (D)	Kenneth Corn (D)
5	Jeff Rabon (D)	Jeff Rabon (D)	Jeff Rabon (D)	Jerry Ellis (D)
6	Jay Paul Gumm (D)	Jay Paul Gumm (D)	Jay Paul Gumm (D)	Jay Paul Gumm (D)
7	Gene Stipe (D) [2]	Richard Lerblance (D)	Richard Lerblance (D)	Richard Lerblance (D)
8	Franklin D. Shurden (D)	Franklin D. Shurden (D)	Roger Ballenger (D)	Roger Ballenger (D)
9	Ben H. Robinson (D)	Earl Garrison (D)	Earl Garrison (D)	Earl Garrison (D)
10	J. Berry Harrison (D)	J. Berry Harrison (D)	Joe Sweeden (D)	Joe Sweeden (D)
11	Maxine Horner (D)	Judy Eason McIntyre (D)	Judy Eason McIntyre (D)	Judy Eason McIntyre (D)
12	Ted V. Fisher (D)	Ted V. Fisher (D)	Brian Bingman (R)	Brian Bingman (R)
13	Dick Wilkerson (D)	Susan Paddack (D)	Susan Paddack (D)	Susan Paddack (D)
14	Johnnie Crutchfield (D)	Johnnie Crutchfield (D)	Johnnie Crutchfield (D)	Johnnie Crutchfield (D)
15	Jonathan Nichols (R)	Jonathan Nichols (R)	Jonathan Nichols (R)	Jonathan Nichols (R)
16	Cal Hobson III (D)	Cal Hobson III (D)	John Sparks (D)	John Sparks (D)
17	Charlie Laster (D) [3]	Charlie Laster (D)	Charlie Laster (D)	Charlie Laster (D)
18	Kevin A. Easley (D)	Mary Easley (D)	Mary Easley (D)	Mary Easley (D)
19	Robert V. Milacek (R)	Patrick Anderson (R)	Patrick Anderson (R)	Patrick Anderson (R)
20	David Myers (R)	David Myers (R)	David Myers (R)	David Myers (R)
21	Mike Morgan (D)	Mike Morgan (D)	Mike Morgan (D)	Jim Halligan (R)
22	Mike Johnson (R)	Mike Johnson (R)	Mike Johnson (R)	Mike Johnson (R)
23	Bruce Price (D)	Ron Justice (R)	Ron Justice (R)	Ron Justice (R)
24	Daisy Lawler (D)	Daisy Lawler (D)	Anthony Sykes (R)	Anthony Sykes (R)
25	Charles R. Ford (R) [4]	Mike Mazzei (R)	Mike Mazzei (R)	Mike Mazzei (R)
26	Gilmer N. Capps (D)	Gilmer N. Capps (D)	Tom Ivester (D)	Tom Ivester (D)
27	Owen Laughlin (R) [5]	Owen Laughlin (R)	Owen Laughlin (R)	Bryce Marlatt (R)
28	Harry Coates (R) [6]	Harry Coates (R)	Harry Coates (R)	Harry Coates (R)
29	Jim Dunlap (R)	John W. Ford (R)	John W. Ford (R)	John W. Ford (R)
30	Glenn Coffee (R) [7]	Glenn Coffee (R)	Glenn Coffee (R)	Glenn Coffee (R)
31	Sam Helton (D)	Don Barrington (R)	Don Barrington (R)	Don Barrington (R)
32	Jim Maddox (D)	Randy Bass (D)	Randy Bass (D)	Randy Bass (D)
33	Penny Williams (D)	Tom Adelson (D)	Tom Adelson (D)	Tom Adelson (D)
34	Randy Brogdon (R)	Randy Brogdon (R)	Randy Brogdon (R)	Randy Brogdon (R)
35	James A. Williamson (R)	James A. Williamson (R)	James A. Williamson (R)	Gary Stanislawski (R)
36	Scott Pruitt (R) [8 & 11]	Scott Pruitt (R)	Bill Brown (R)	Bill Brown (R)
37	Nancy Riley (R)	Nancy Riley (R)	Nancy Riley (D) [9]	Dan Newberry (R)

Forty-Ninth to Fifty-Second State Senate

District	49th · 2003	50th · 2005	51st · 2007	52nd · 2009
38	Robert M. Kerr (D)	Robert M. Kerr (D)	Mike Schulz (R)	Mike Schulz (R)
39	Jerry L. Smith (R)	Brian A. Crain (R)	Brian A. Crain (R)	Brian A. Crain (R)
40	Cliff Branan (R)	Cliff Branan (R)	Cliff Branan (R)	Cliff Branan (R)
41	Mark Snyder (R)	Clark Jolley (R)	Clark Jolley (R)	Clark Jolley (R)
42	Cliff Aldridge (R)	Cliff Aldridge (R)	Cliff Aldridge (R)	Cliff Aldridge (R)
43	Jim Reynolds (R)	Jim Reynolds (R)	Jim Reynolds (R)	Jim Reynolds (R)
44	Keith Leftwich (D)	Debbe Leftwich (D)	Debbe Leftwich (D)	Debbe Leftwich (D)
45	Kathleen Wilcoxson (R)	Kathleen Wilcoxson (R)	Kathleen Wilcoxson (R)	Steve Russell (R)
46	Bernest Cain (D)	Bernest Cain (D)	Andrew Rice (D)	Andrew Rice (D)
47	Mike Fair (R)	Todd Lamb (R)	Todd Lamb (R)	Todd Lamb (R)
48	Angela Monson (D)	Angela Monson (D)	Constance N. Johnson (D)	Constance N. Johnson (D)
49	—[10]	—	—	—
50	—[10]	—	—	—
51	—[10]	—	—	—
52	—[10]	—	—	—
54	—[10]	—	—	—

[1] The tie in the Senate resulted in parties sharing power equally.
[2] Resigned March 11, 2003.
[3] Elected in Special Election February 11, 2003, to fill seat vacated by Brad Henry. Henry elected governor.
[4] For the 49th Legislature, District 51 became District 25.
[5] For the 49th Legislature, District 49 became District 27.
[6] For the 49th Legislature, District 50 became District 28.
[7] For the 49th Legislature, District 52 became District 30.
[8] For the 49th Legislature, District 54 became District 36.
[9] Nancy Riley switched parties in the summer of 2006.
[10] For the 49th Legislature, the following Senate District Number changes were made: District 49 became District 27, District 50 became District 28, District 51 became District 25, District 52 became District 30, and District 54 became District 36.
[11] Reapportionment Act of 1991 (14 O.S. § 80.20 et seq.)

Fifty-Third to Fifty-Sixth State Senate

District	53rd · 2011	54th · 2013	55th · 2015	56th · 2017
President Pro Tem	Brian Bingman (R)	Brian Bingman (R)	Brian Bingman (R)	
1	Charles Wyrick (D)	Charles Wyrick (D)	Charles Wyrick (D)	
2	Sean Burrage (D)	Sean Burrage (D)	Marty Quinn (R)	
3	Jim Wilson (D)	Wayne Shaw (R)	Wayne Shaw (R)	
4	Mark Allen (R)	Mark Allen (R)	Mark Allen (R)	
5	Jerry Ellis (D)	Jerry Ellis (D)	Joseph Silk (R)	
6	Josh Brecheen (R)	Josh Brecheen (R)	Josh Brecheen (R)	
7	Richard Lerblance (D)	Larry Boggs (R)	Larry Boggs (R)	
8	Roger Ballenger (D)	Roger Ballenger (D)	Roger Thompson (R)	
9	Earl Garrison (D)	Earl Garrison (D)	Earl Garrison (D)	
10	Eddie Fields (R)	Eddie Fields (R)	Eddie Fields (R)	
11	Judy Eason McIntyre (D)	Jabar Shumate (D)	Kevin Matthews (D)[1]	

Fifty-Third to Fifty-Sixth State Senate

District	53rd · 2011	54th · 2013	55th · 2015	56th · 2017
12	Brian Bingman (R)	Brian Bingman (R)	Brian Bingman (R)	
13	Susan Paddack (D)	Susan Paddack (D)	Susan Paddack (D)	
14	Frank Simpson (R)	Frank Simpson (R)	Frank Simpson (R)	
15	Jonathann Nichols (R)	Rob Standridge (R)	Rob Standridge (R)	
16	John Sparks (D)	John Sparks (D)	John Sparks (D)	
17	Charlie Laster (D)	Ron Sharp (R)	Ron Sharp (R)	
18	Kim David (R)	Kim David (R)	Kim David (R)	
19	Patrick Anderson (R)	Patrick Anderson (R)	Patrick Anderson (R)	
20	David Myers (R)	A.J. Griffin (R)	A.J. Griffin (R)	
21	Jim Halligan (R)	Jim Halligan (R)	Jim Halligan (R)	
22	Rob Johnson (R)	Rob Johnson (R)	Stephanie Bice (R)	
23	Ron Justice (R)	Ron Justice (R)	Ron Justice (R)	
24	Anthony Sykes (R)	Anthony Sykes (R)	Anthony Sykes (R)	
25	Mike Mazzei (R)	Mike Mazzei (R)	Mike Mazzei (R)	
26	Tom Ivester (D)	Tom Ivester (D)	Darcy Jech (R)	
27	Bryce Marlatt (R)	Bryce Marlatt (R)	Bryce Marlatt (R)	
28	Harry Coats (R)	Harry Coats (R)	Jason Smalley (R)	
29	John Ford (R)	John Ford (R)	John Ford (R)	
30	David Holt (R)	David Holt (R)	David Holt (R)	
31	Don Barrington (R)	Don Barrington (R)	Don Barrington (R)	
32	Randy Bass (D)	Randy Bass (D)	Randy Bass (D)	
33	Tom Adelson (D)	Nathan Dahm (R)	Natham Dahm (R)	
34	Rick Brinkley (R)	Rick Brinkley (R)	Rick Brinkley (R)	
35	Gary Stanislawski (R)	Gary Stanislawski (R)	Gary Stanislawski (R)	
36	Bill Brown (R)	Bill Brown (R)	Bill Brown (R)	
37	Dan Newberry (R)	Dan Newberry (R)	Dan Newberry (R	
38	Mike Schulz (R)	Mike Schulz (R)	Mike Schulz (R)	
39	Brian Crain (R)	Brian Crain (R)	Brian Crain (R)	
40	Cliff Branan (R)	Cliff Branan (R)	Ervin Yen (R)	
41	Clark Jolley (R)	Clark Jolley (R)	Clark Jolley (R)	
42	Cliff Aldridge (R)	Cliff Aldridge (R)	Jack Fry (R)	
43	Jim Reynolds (R)	Corey Brooks (R)	Corey Brooks (R)	
44	Ralph Shortey (R)	Ralph Shortey (R)	Ralph Shortey (R)	
45	Steve Russell (R)	Kyle Loveless (R)	Kyle Loveless (R)	
46	Andrew Rice (D)	Al McAffrey (D)	Kay Floyd (D)	
47	Greg Treat (R)	Greg Treat (R)	Greg Treat (R)	
48	Constance Johnson (D)	Constance Johnson (D)	Anastasia Pittman (D)	

Jabar Shumate (D) resigned on January 5. 2015. Matthews was elected in Special Election, April 7, 2015.

History of Oklahoma Congressmen

U.S. Senate

Seat #1—Thomas Pryor Gore (D) elected 1907; J.W. Harreld (R) elected 1920; Elmer Thomas (D) elected 1926; Mike Monroney (D) elected 1950; Henry Bellmon (R) elected 1968; Don Nickles (R) elected 1980; Tom Coburn (R) elected 2004; James Lankford (R) elected 2014.

Seat #2—Robert L. Owen (D) elected 1907; W.B. Pine (R) elected 1924; Thomas P. Gore (D) elected 1930; Josh Lee (D) elected 1936; E.H. Moore (R) elected 1942; Robert S. Kerr (D) elected 1948 (died 1963); J. Howard Edmondson (D) appointed 1-6-63 to fill office until General Election, 1964; Fred R. Harris (D) elected 1964 (for unexpired 2-year term), elected full term 1966; Dewey F. Bartlett (R) elected 1972; David Boren (D) elected 1978, resigned 1994; James Inhofe (R) elected to fill unexpired term at general election, November 1994, elected to full term in 1996.

U.S. Representatives

District 1—Bird S. McGuire (R) elected 1907; James S. Davenport (D) elected 1914; T.A. Chandler (R) elected 1916; E.B. Howard (D) elected 1918; T.A. Chandler (R) elected 1920; E.B. Howard (D) elected 1922; S.J. Montgomery (R) elected 1924; E.B. Howard (D) elected 1926; Charles O'Connor (R) elected 1928; Wesley E. Disney (D) elected 1930; George R. Schwabe (R) elected 1944; Dixie Gilmer (D) elected 1948; George R. Schwabe (R) elected 1950; Page Belcher (R) elected 1952; James R. Jones (D) elected 1972; James Inhofe (R) elected 1986; Steve Largent (R) elected 1994, resigned January 2002. John Sullivan (R) elected 2002; Jim Bridenstine (R) elected 2012.

District 2—Elmer L. Fulton (D) elected 1907; Dick T. Morgan (R) elected 1908; W.W. Hastings (D) elected 1914; Alice M. Robertson (R) elected 1920; W.W. Hastings (D) elected 1922; Jack Nichols (D) elected 1934 and resigned 1944; W.G. Stigler (D) elected 3-8-44 to fill unexpired term and elected full term 1944; Ed Edmondson (D) elected 1952; Clem Rogers McSpadden (D) elected 1972; Theodore M. Risenhoover (D) elected 1974; Mike Synar (D) elected 1978; Tom Coburn (R) elected 1994; Brad Carson (D) elected 2000; Dan Boren (D) elected 2004; Markwayne Mullin (R) elected 2012.

District 3—James S. Davenport (D) elected 1907; C. E. Creager (R) elected 1908; James S. Davenport (D) elected 1910; Charles D. Carter (D) elected 1914; Wilburn Cartwright (D) elected 1926; Paul Stewart (D) elected 1942; Carl Albert (D) elected 1946; Wes Watkins (D) elected 1976; Bill Brewster (D) elected 1990; Wes Watkins (R)[1] elected 1996. Redistricting eliminated district 6; Frank Lucas (R), previously 6th District congressman, elected in the new 3rd District, 2002.

District 4—Charles D. Carter (D) elected 1907; William H. Murray (D) elected 1914; Tom D. McKeown (D) elected 1916; J.C. Pringey (R) elected 1920; Tom D. McKeown (D) elected 1922; P.L. Gassaway (D) elected 1934; Lyle H. Boren (D) elected 1936; Glen

D. Johnson (D) elected 1946; Tom Steed (D) elected 1948; Dave McCurdy (D) elected 1980; J.C. Watts Jr. (R) elected 1994; Tom Cole (R) elected 2002.

District 5—Scott Ferris (D) elected 1907; Joe B. Thompson (D) elected 1914 (died 1918); J.W. Harreld (R) elected at special election 11–8–19 to fill unexpired term; F.B. Swank (D) elected 1920; U.S. Stone (R) elected 1928; F.B. Swank (D) elected 1930; Josh Lee (D) elected 1934; R.P. Hill (D) elected 1936, died; Gomer Smith (D) elected at special election 12–10–37 to fill unexpired term; Mike Monroney (D) elected 1938; John Jarman (D) elected 1950; Mickey Edwards (R) elected 1976; Ernest Jim Istook (R) elected 1992; Mary Fallin (R) elected 2006; James Lankford (R) elected 2010; Steve Russell (R) elected 2014.

[2] **District 6**—Scott Ferris (D) elected 1914; L.M. Gensman (R) elected 1920; Elmer Thomas (D) elected 1922; Jed J. Johnson (D) elected 1926; Toby Morris (D) elected 1946; Victor Wickersham (D) elected 1952; Toby Morris (D) elected 1956; Victor Wickersham (D) elected 1960; Jed Johnson Jr. (D) elected 1964; James V. Smith (R) elected 1966; John N. "Happy" Camp (R) elected 1968; Glenn English Jr. (D) elected 1974, resigned 1994; Frank Lucas (R) elected at special election (May 1994) to fill unexpired term, elected to full term at general election 1994.

[3] **District 7**—J.V. McClintic (D) elected 1914; Sam Massingale (D) elected 1934 (died 1940); Victor Wickersham (D) elected at special election 4–1–41 to fill unexpired term and elected 1942; Preston E. Peden (D) elected 1946; Victor Wickersham (D) elected 1948.

[3] **District 8**—Dick T. Morgan (R) elected 1914 (died 1920); Charles Swindall (R) elected 11–2–20 to fill unexpired term; Manuel Herrick (R) elected 1920; M.C. Garber (R) elected 1922; E.W. Marland (D) elected 1932; Phil Ferguson (D) elected 1934; Ross Rizley (R) elected 1940; George Howard Wilson (D) elected 1948; Page Belcher (R) elected 1950.

Congressmen-At-Large—In 1912, the state elected three Congressmen-at-Large: William H. Murray (D), Joe B. Thompson (D) and Claude Weaver (D). Beginning 1932 to 1940 inclusive, the state nominated and elected one Congressman-at-Large: Will Rogers (D) elected 1932.

---

[1] Watkins ran for governor in 1994 as an Independent, and ran as a Republican for Congress in 1996.

[2] District 6 eliminated in 2002 re-apportionment.

[3] Redistricting in 1950 eliminated Districts 7 and 8.

Party Affiliation of Governor, U.S. Delegation, and State Legislature, Since Statehood

Year	Political Party	Governor or President[1]	U.S. Senate	U.S. House	State Senate	State House
1907	Democrat	◉	2	4	39	92
1st	Republican			1	5	17
1909	Democrat	◉	2	2	34	68
2nd	Republican			3	10	41
1911	Democrat	◉	2	3	31	82
3rd	Republican			2	13	27
1913	Democrat	◉	2	5	36	80
4th	Republican			3	8	18
1915	Democrat	◉	2	7	38	75
5th	Republican			1	5	17
	Other				1	5
1917	Democrat	◉	2	6	38	85
6th	Republican			2	5	26
	Other				1	0
1919	Democrat	◉	2	8/7	34	74
7th	Republican			0/1	10	30
1921	Democrat		1	3	27	37
8th	Republican	◉	1	5	17	55
1923	Democrat	◉	1	7	32	93
9th	Republican		1	1	12	14
1925	Democrat	◉		6	38	81
10th	Republican		2	2	6	27
1927	Democrat	◉	1	7	35	87
11th	Republican		1	1	9	21
1929	Democrat		1	5	32	56
12th	Republican	◉	1	3	12	47
1931	Democrat	◉	2	7	32	88
13th	Republican			1	12	9
1933	Democrat	◉	2	9	39	113
14th	Republican			0	5	4
	Other				0	1

Year	Political Party	Governor or President[1]	U.S. Senate	U.S. House	State Senate	State House
1935	Democrat	⊙	2	9	43	112
15th	Republican			0	1	7
	Other				0	1
1937	Democrat	⊙	2	9	44	114
16th	Republican			0	0	3
1939	Democrat	⊙	2	9	43	102
17th	Republican			0	1	13
1941	Democrat	⊙	2	8	42	114
18th	Republican			1	2	7
1943	Democrat	⊙	1	7	40	93
19th	Republican		1	1	4	24
1945	Democrat	⊙	1	6	38	98
20th	Republican		1	2	6	22
1947	Democrat	⊙	1	6	37	95
21st	Republican		1	2	7	23
1949	Democrat	⊙	2	8	39	103
22nd	Republican			0	5	12
1951	Democrat	⊙	2	6	41	99
23rd	Republican			2	3	19
1953	Democrat		2	5	38	104
24th	Republican	⊙		1	6	20
1955	Democrat	⊙	2	5	39	102
25th	Republican			1	5	19
1957	Democrat		2	5	41	101
26th	Republican	⊙		1	3	20
1959	Democrat	⊙	2	5	41	110
27th	Republican			1	3	9
1961	Democrat		2	5	40	107
28th	Republican	⊙		1	4	14
1963	Democrat		2	5	38	96
29th	Republican	⊙		1	6	24
1965	Democrat	⊙	2	5	41	78
30th	Republican			1	7	21
1967	Democrat		2	4	39	74
31st	Republican	⊙		2	9	25
1969	Democrat		1	4	38	76
32nd	Republican	⊙	1	2	10	23
1971	Democrat	⊙	1	4	39	78

Year	Political Party	Governor or President[1]	U.S. Senate	U.S. House	State Senate	State House
33rd	Republican		1	2	9	21
1973	Democrat			5	38	75
34th	Republican	⊙	2	1	10	26
1975	Democrat	⊙		6[2]	39	76
35th	Republican		2	0	9	25
1977	Democrat			5	39	78
36th	Republican	⊙	2	1	9	23
1979	Democrat	⊙	1	5	39/38[3]	75
37th	Republican		1	1	9/10[3]	26
1981	Democrat		1	5	37	73
38th	Republican	⊙	1	1	11	28
1983	Democrat	⊙	1	5	34	76
39th	Republican		1	1	14	25
1985	Democrat		1	5	34	70
40th	Republican	⊙	1	1	14	31
1987	Democrat		1	4	31	70
41st	Republican	⊙	1	2	17	31
1989	Democrat		1	4	33	69
42nd	Republican	⊙	1	2	15	32
1991	Democrat	⊙	1	4	37	69
43rd	Republican		1	2	11	32
1993	Democrat		1	4	37	68
44th	Republican	⊙	1	2[4]	11	33
1995	Democrat			1	35	65
45th	Republican	⊙	2	5	13	36
1997	Democrat			0	33	65
46th	Republican	⊙	2	6	15	36
1999	Democrat			0	33	61
47th	Republican	⊙	2	6	15	40
2001	Democrat			1	30	53
48th	Republican	⊙	2	5	18	48[5]
2003	Democrat	⊙		1	28	53[6]
49th	Republican		2	4[7]	20	48
2005	Democrat			1	26	44
50th	Republican	⊙	2	4	22	57
2007	Democrat	⊙		1	24	44
51st	Republican		2	4	24	57
2009	Democrat	⊙		1	22	40

Year	Political Party	Governor or President [1]	U.S. Senate	U.S. House	State Senate	State House
52nd	Republican		2	4	26	61
2011	Democrat			1	16	31
53rd	Republican	◉	2	4	32	70
2013	Democrat				12	29
54th	Republican	◉	2	5	36	72
2014	Democrat				7	29
55th	Republican	◉	2	5	40	72

[1] Presidential candidate receiving Oklahoma's electoral votes.

[2] Jarman switched from Democrat to Republican early in this Congress, but was elected as a Democrat.

[3] Democrat was replaced by a Republican at a Special Election Nov. 6, 1979.

[4] Lucas (R) was elected May 1994; the delegation was then 3 Republicans and 3 Democrats.

[5] Ervin (D) switched parties in 2001, from Democrat to Republican, after which the ratio was 49–52.

[6] Gene Stipe (D) resigned March 11, 2003.

[7] A congressional district was eliminated in 2002 re-apportionment.

United States District Judges Since Statehood

Eastern District

Ralph E. Campbell, 1907–1918

Robert L. Williams, 1919–1937*

Eugene Rice, 1937–1967

Orville Edwin Langley, 1965–1973

James W. Morris, 1974–1978

Frank H. Seay, 1979–present

Michael Burrage, 1994–2001

James H. Payne, 2001–present

Ronald A. White, 2003–present

Northern District

Franklin E. Kennamer, 1924

Royce H. Savage, 1940–1961

Allen E. Barrow, 1962–1974

H. Dale Cook, 1974–2008

James O. Ellison, 1979–2005

Terry C. Kern, 1994–present

Sven Erik Holmes, 1995–2005

Claire V. Eagan, 2001–present

James H. Payne, 2001–present

Gregory K. Frizzell, 2008–present

John E. Dowdell, 2012–present

Western District

John Hazelton Cotteral, 1907–1928

Edgar Sullins Vaught, 1928–1959

Stephen S. Chandler, 1943–1989

Ross Rizley, 1956–1969

Luther Boyd Eubanks, 1965–1987

Ralph G. Thompson, 1975–2007

Lee R. West, 1979–present

David L. Russell, 1982–present

Wayne E. Alley, 1985–present

Layn R. Phillips, 1987–1991

Robin J. Cauthron, 1991–present

Tim Leonard, 1992–present

Vicki Miles-LaGrange, 1995–present

Stephen P. Friot, 2001–present

Joe Heaton, 2001–present

Timothy D. DeGiusti, 2008–present

Northern/Eastern/Western Districts

Alfred Paul Murrah, 1937–1940 *

Bower Broaddus, 1940–1949

William Robert Wallace, 1950–1960

Luther Lee Bohanon, 1961–2003

Frederick A. Daugherty, 1961–2006

James H. Payne, 2001–present

* Appointed Circuit Judge

United States Attorneys Since Statehood

District of Oklahoma

Horace Speed, 1890–1894
Caleb R. Brooks, 1894–1898
Samuel L. Overstreet, 1898–1899
John W. Scothorn, 1899–1900
Horace Speed, 1900–1900

Central District

John H. Wilkins, 1901–1906
Thomas B. Lathone, 1906–1906

Northern District

John M. Goldesberry, 1925–1933
Clarence E. Bailey, 1933–1937
Whitfield Y. Mauzy, 1937–1953
John S. Athens, 1953–1954
B. Hayden Crawford, 1954–1958
Robert S. Rizley, 1958–1961
Russell H. Smith, 1961–1961
John M. Imel, 1961–1967
Laurence A. McSoud, 1967–1969
Nathan G. Graham, 1969–1977
Hubert A. Marlow, 1977–1977
Hubert H. Bryant, 1977–1981
Francis A. Keating, 1981–1983
Layn R. Phillips, 1983–1987
Tony M. Graham, 1987–1993
Frederick L. Dunn, 1993–1993
Stephen C. Lewis, 1993–2000
Thomas Scott Woodward, 2000–2001
David O'Meilia, 2001–2009
Thomas Scott Woodward, 2009–2012
Danny C. Williams, 2012–present

Eastern District

William Gregg Jr., 1908–1913
D. Hayden Linebaugh, 1913–1917
W.P. McGinnis, 1917–1919
C.W. Miller, 1919–1919
Archibald Bonds, 1919–1920
C.W. Miller, 1920–1920
Berry J. King, 1920–1921
John T. Harley, 1921–1921
Frank Lee, 1921–1930
W.F. Rampendahl, 1930–1934
Cleon A. Summers, 1934–1952
E. Edwin A. Langley, 1952–1953
Frank D. McSherry, 1953–1961
E. Edwin A. Langley, 1961–1965
Robert B. Green, 1965–1969
William J. Settle, 1969–1974
Richard A. Pyle, 1974–1977
Julian Fite, 1977–1980
James E. Edmondson, 1980–1981
Betty O. Williams, 1981–1982
Gary L. Richardson, 1982–1984
Donn F. Barker, 1984–1985
Roger Hilfiger, 1985–1990
Sheldon J. Sperling, 1990–1990
John W. Raley Jr., 1990–1997
Robert Bruce Green, 1997–2000
Sheldon Sperling, 2000–2010
Mark F. Green, 2010–present

Western District

William M. Mellette, 1902–1907

John Embry, 1907–1912

Isaac D. Taylor, 1912–1912

Homer N. Boardman, 1912–1913

Isaac D. Taylor, 1913–1914

John A. Fain, 1914–1920

Frank E. Randall, 1920–1920

Robert M. Peck, 1920–1921

W. A. Maurer, 1921–1925

Ray St. Lewis, 1925–1931

Herbert K. Hyde, 1931–1934

William C. Lewis, 1934–1938

Charles E. Dierker, 1938–1947

Robert E. Shelton, 1947–1953

Fred M. Mack, 1953–1954

Paul W. Cress, 1954–1961

B. Andrew Potter, 1961–1969

William R. Burkett, 1969–1975

David L. Russell, 1975–1977

John E. Green, 1977–1978

Larry D. Patton, 1978–1981

David L. Russell, 1981–1982

John E. Green, 1982–1982

William S. Price, 1982–1989

Robert E. Mydans, 1989–1989

Timothy D. Leonard, 1989–1992

Joe L. Heaton, 1992–1993

John E. Green, 1993–1993

Vicki L. Miles-LaGrange, 1993–1994

Rozia McKinney-Foster, 1994–1995

Patrick M. Ryan, 1995–1999

Daniel G. Webber Jr., 1999–2001

Robert G. McCampbell, 2001–2005

John C. Richter, 2006–2009

Sanford C. Coats, 2009–present

United States Marshals Since Statehood

www.usdoj.gov/marshals

Eastern District

918/687–2523 • Created under Act of June 16, 1906,
effective upon admission of Oklahoma as a State November 16, 1907.

Grosvenor A. Porter, 1907–1908

Samuel G. Victor, 1908–1913

B.A. Enlow Jr., 1913–1921

Henry F. Cooper, 1921–1930

Clark B. Wasson, 1930–1934

Samuel E. Swinney, 1934–1936

Granville T. Norris, 1936–1949

Herbert I. Hinds, 1949–1951

Robert E. Boen, 1951–1953

Herbert I. Hinds, 1953–1953

Paul Johnson, 1953–1961

William L. Owen, 1961–1961

William M. Broadrick, 1961–1965

Jackie V. Robertson, 1965–1970

Laurence Beard, 1970–1977

Rex O. Presley, 1977–1981

Laurence Beard, 1981–1989

Richard Reynolds, 1989–1990

James L. Webb, 1990–1994

Robert B. Robertson, 1994–1998

(Vacant, 1998–2000)

Donald Abdallah, (acting) 2000–2001

John W. Loyd, 2001–2012

Patrick J. Wilkerson, 2012–present

Northern District

918/581–7738 • Created by Act of February 16, 1925

Henry G. Beard, 1925–1928

Samuel G. Victor, 1928–1929

John H. Vickrey, 1929–1933

John P. Logan, 1933–1949

Virgil B. Stanley, 1949–1953

James Y. Victor, 1953–1961

Doyle W. Foreman, 1961–1969

Harry Connolly, 1969–1977

Carl W. Gardner, 1977–1981

Harry Connolly, 1981–1989

J.D. Sink (acting), 1989

Raymond Van Putten, 1989–1990

Donald E. Crowl, 1990–1994

James M. Hughes, 1994–2002

Timothy D. Welch, 2002–2010

Clayton D. Johnson, 2011–present

Western District

405/231–4206 • Created under Act of June 16, 1906,
effective upon admission of Oklahoma as a State November 16, 1907.

John R. Abernathy, 1907–1910

Christian Madsen, 1910–1911

William S. Cade, 1911–1913

John Q. Newell, 1913–1921

Alva McDonald, 1921–1925

Ewers White, 1925–1926

Duke Stallings, 1926–1926

Richard B. Quinn, 1926–1933

Duke Stallings, 1933–1933

W. C. Geers, 1933–1933

Joe W. Ballard, 1933–1940

Roy Manley, 1940–1941

Dave E. Hilles, 1941–1949

Rex B. Hawks, 1949–1954

Kenner W. Greer, 1954–1961

Rex B. Hawks, 1961–1969

Floyd E. Carrier, 1969–1977

Floyd L. Park, 1977–1978

Coy W. Roger, 1978–1982

Stuart E. Earnest, 1982–1994

Patrick J. Wilkerson, 1994–2001

Michael W. Roach, 2001–2010

Charles T. Weeks II, 2011–present

Justices of the Supreme Court Since Statehood

The Constitution, Article VII, Section 1, established the Supreme Court of Oklahoma. Section 3 divided the state in five districts, creating the positions of five justices in the court and providing that the number could be changed by law.

The Sixth Legislature, R.S. (1917) enacted Senate Bill No. 252 that increased the number of justices from five to nine and redistricted the state into nine Supreme Court Judicial Districts. The act authorized the governor to appoint, by and with the advice and consent of the Senate, one justice from each of the four additional Supreme Court Judicial Districts created. The act further provided for the election of justices at the regular biennial election in 1918. The justices for District Six and Nine were elected for terms of six years, a justice for District Seven was elected for a term of four years and a justice for District Eight was elected for a term of two years, "and thereafter, three of the Justices of the Supreme Court shall be elected at each general biennial election to serve for a term of six years each..."

The Sixteenth Legislature, R.S. (1937) enacted Senate Bill No. 249 which authorized each justice of the Supreme Court to appoint a legal assistant, subject to confirmation by the court. Legal assistants were required to have the qualifications of a district judge. The act further authorized the court to appoint two Supreme Court referees having the qualifications of a district judge and one chief legal executive assistant to the chief justice. The chief legal executive assistant was directed to act as marshal.

At a Special Election, July 11, 1967, constitutional amendments were adopted to provide a complete reorganization of Oklahoma courts. Beginning in 1968, members of the Supreme Court ran on a nonpartisan statewide retention ballot at the general election only. If retained by the voters, they serve a six-year term. If rejected, the vacancy is filled by the governor.

District 1—J. B. Turner (D) elected 1907, 1912. John H. Pitchford (D) elected 1918 (died 3/2/23). C. W. Mason (D) appointed 4/4/23, elected 1924. J. H. Langley (D) elected 1930. Resigned 2/2/31. W. H. Kornegay (D) appointed 2/2/31. Wayne W. Bayless (D) elected 1932 for unexpired term, re-elected 1936, 1942. N. B. Johnson (D) elected 1948, 1954, 1960 (impeached by Special Court of Impeachment 5/13/65). Robert E. Lavender (R) appointed 6/24/65; elected 1966, retained in 1972, 1978, 1984, 1990, 1996, 2002. Resigned 08/01/2007. John F. Reif, appointed 10/22/2007, retained 2008, 2014.

District 2—R. L. Williams (D) elected 1907, 1908 (resigned 3/10/14). Stillwell H. Russell (D) appointed 3/11/14 (died 5/16/14). W. R. Bleakmore (D) appointed 5/26/14. Summers T. Hardy (D) elected 1914 for unexpired term. Resigned 5/1/19. R. W. Higgins (D) appointed 5/7/19. C. H. Elting (R) elected 1920 (died 12/3/22). Charles B. Cochran (D) appointed, 12/6/22. Resigned 5/1/24. James H. Gordon (D) appointed 5/1/24. E. F. Lester (D) elected 1924 for unexpired term, re-elected 1926. Earl Welch (D) elected 1932, 1938, 1944, 1950, 1956, 1962. Resigned. Ralph B. Hodges (D) appointed 4/20/65; elected 1966 for unexpired term; retained in 1968, 1974, 1980, 1986, 1992, 1998. Retired 2004. Steven W. Taylor appointed 9/23/2004, retained 2010.

District 3—Matthew J. Kane (D) elected 1907, 1910, 1918 (died 1/2/24). J. D. Lydick (D) appointed 1/7/24. James I. Phelps (D) elected 1924 for unexpired term. James B. Cullison (R) elected 1928. James I. Phelps (D) elected 1934. Resigned 12/1/38. Harris L. Danner (D) appointed 12/1/38. Resigned 10/10/40. Sam Neff (D) appointed 10/10/40. Ben Arnold (D) elected 1940, 1946, 1952 (died 9/30/55). Albert C. Hunt (D) appointed

10/14/55 (died 8/26/56). W. A. Carlile (D) appointed 9/17/56, elected 1956 for unexpired term. William A. Berry (D) elected 1958, 1964; retained 1970, 1976. Resigned 11/20/78. Marian Opala appointed 11/21/78, elected 1980 for unexpired term; retained 1982, 1988, 1994, 2000, 2006 (died 10/11/2010). Noma Gurich appointed 1/7/2011, retained 2012.

District 4—Jesse J. Dunn (D) elected 1907, 1910. Resigned 9/1/13. R. H. Loofbourrow (D) appointed 9/1/13. J. F. Sharp (D) elected 1914 (number of district changed from District No. 4 to District No. 5 in 1917). (See District No. 5). Charles M. Thacker (D) (See District No. 5) (died 2/17/18). B. L. Tisinger (D) appointed 3/5/18. John B. Harrison (D) elected 1918 for unexpired term, re-elected 1922. Charles Swindall (R) elected 1928. N. S. Corn (D) elected 1934, 1940, 1946, 1952. Pat Irwin (D) elected 1958, 1964; retained 1970, 1976, 1982. Retired December 1983. Yvonne Kauger appointed 3/22/1984; retained 1986, 1988, 1994, 2000, 2006, 2012.

District 5—Samuel W. Hayes (D) elected 1907, 1908 (resigned 4/7/14). F. E. Riddle (D) appointed 4/7/14. G. A. Brown (D) elected 1914 (died 10/25/15). Charles M. Thacker (D) appointed 11/2/15 (number of district changed from District No. 5 to District No. 4 in 1917. See District No. 4). J.F. Sharp (D) (See Dist. No. 4) (Resigned 10/1/19). Frank M. Bailey (D) appointed 10/1/19. George M. Nicholson (R) elected 1920. Robert A. Hefner (D) elected 1926. Monroe Osborn (D) elected 1932, 1938, 1944 (died 6/20/47). John E. Luttrell (D) appointed 7/1/47, elected 1948 for unexpired term, re-elected 1950. Resigned 8/13/51. George Bingaman (D) appointed 8/13/51. Ben T. Williams (D) elected 1952 for unexpired term, elected to full term 1956, 1962; retained 1968, 1974, 1980. Died 1/82. Alma Wilson appointed 2/9/82; retained 1986, 1992, 1998. Died 7/27/99. James R. Winchester appointed 1/4/2000; retained 2002, 2004, 2010.

District 6—J. H. Miley (D) appointed 3/31/l917. Neil E. McNeill (D) elected 1918. Albert C. Hunt (D) elected 1924. Edwin R. McNeill (D) elected 1930. Thurman S. Hurst (D) elected 1936, 1942. Harry L. S. Halley (D) elected 1948, 1954, 1960. Rooney McInerney (D) elected 1966. Resigned 9/1/72. Robert D. Simms appointed 10/2/72, retained 1974 for unexpired term; retained in 1978, 1984, 1990, 1996. Retired 9/30/99. Daniel Boudreau appointed 10/12/99; retained 2000 for unexpired term, 2002 for full term. Retired 2004. Tom Colbert appointed on 10/07/04; retained 2006, 2008, 2014.

District 7—Thomas H. Owen (D) appointed 3/31/17, elected 1918. Resigned 5/1/20. George S. Ramsey (R) appointed 5/1/20. Resigned 11/5/20. Wm. A. Collier (D) appointed 11/5/20. John R. Miller (R) elected 1920 for unexpired term. Fred P. Branson (D) elected 1922. Thomas G. Andrews (R) elected 1928. Thomas L. Gibson (D) elected 1934, 1940, 1946. W. H. Blackbird (D) elected 1952, 1958, 1964; retained 1970 (retired 12/1/71). Don Barnes appointed 1/4/72; retained 1974 for unexpired term; retained 1976, 1982. Retired 1/10/85. Hardy Summers appointed 2/1/85; retained 1986, 1988, and 1994, 2000. Retired 2003. James E. Edmondson appointed 12/02/2003; retained 2006, 2012.

District 8—Robert M. Rainey (D) appointed 3/31/17, elected 1918. F. E. Kennamer (R) elected 1920 (resigned 4/1/24). Frank L. Warren (D) appointed 4/1/24. J. W. Clark (D) elected 1924 for unexpired term, re-elected 1926. Orel Busby (D) elected 1932 (resigned 8/7/37). Denver N. Davison (D) appointed 8/7/37; elected 1938, 1944, 1950, 1956, 1962; retained 1968, 1974; Retired 8/8/78. Rudolph Hargrave appointed 10/10/78; retained 1980, 1986, 1992, 1998, 2004; Retired 12/31/2010. Douglas Combs appointed 11/05/2010, retained 2012.

District 9—Rutherford Brett (D) appointed 3/31/17. J. T. Johnson (D) elected 1918, Fletcher S. Riley (D) elected 1924, 1930, 1936, 1942. Cecil Talmage O'Neal (R) elected 1948. Floyd L. Jackson (D) elected 1954, 1960, 1966; retained 1972. Retired 1/8/73. John B. Doolin appointed 1/8/73, retained 1974 for unexpired term, 1978, 1984, 1990

Retired 5/1/1992. Joseph M. Watt appointed 6/1/92; retained 1994 to fill unexpired term, retained 1996, 2002, 2008, 2014.

Commissioners of the Supreme Court

(The legislation creating this commission expired 4/1/59)

The Third Legislature, R.S. (1911) enacted House Bill 75 to authorize the Oklahoma Supreme Court to appoint six persons, possessing the qualifications required for justice of the Supreme Court, one from each Supreme Court Judicial District and one from the state at large, to be Supreme Court commissioners. The commissioners were appointed for a two-year term and worked in two divisions known as Supreme Court Commissioners Divisions 1 and 2. The Fourth Legislature, R.S. (1913) enacted House Bill 25 to extend the commission for an additional two years. The provisions and requirements for commissioner were the same as in the previous act. The organization under the acts, the first effective September 1, 1911, was:

Division 1—C. B. Ames (resigned 3/1/1913). Charles M. Thacker, appointed 3/19/1913. J. F. Sharp, J. B. A. Robertson (resigned 2/1/1914). George Rittenhouse, appointed 2/2/1914.

Division 2—P. D. Brewer, J. B. Harrison (resigned 9/11/1915). C.L. Moore, appointed 1/11/1915. Malcolm E. Rosser (resigned 9/1/1915). C. A. Galbraith, appointed 9/1/1915.

The Fifth Legislature, R.S. (1915) enacted Senate Bill 204 authorizing the governor to appoint, with the consent of the Oklahoma Supreme Court, nine persons possessing the qualifications required for justice of the Supreme Court, as Supreme Court commissioners to serve two years; one to be selected from the state at large. The commissioners were divided into groups of three and were designated as Division 1, 2, and 3. The act further authorized the governor to designate not more than nine district judges to act as Supreme Court commissioners for a period of not less than four months at a time. District judges acting as Supreme Court commissioners were divided into groups of three. Each constituted a separate division known as Divisions 4, 5, and 6. All commissioners were subject to removal at any time by the governor. The assignments under Division 4, 5, and 6 are too complicated to show in a tabulation. Organization under Divisions 1, 2, and 3, which became effective April 1, 1915:

Division 1—Charles M. Thacker (resigned 11/2/1915). Nestor Rummons, appointed 11/2/1915. Wm. A Collier, P. D. Brewer (resigned 4/1/1916). Jean P. Day, appointed 4/1/1916 (resigned 10/24/1916). A. M. Stewart, appointed 10/24/1916.

Division 2—C. A. Galbraith, John Devereux (resigned 1/5/1916). Sam Hooker, appointed 1/5/1916, assigned to Division 3, 1/5/1916. Frank Burford, appointed 2/15/1916. Rutherford Brett (resigned 6/1/1916). D. D. Brunson, appointed 6/7/1916.

Division 3—George Rittenhouse (resigned 9/19/1916). Hunter L. Johnson, appointed 9/19/1916. W. R. Bleakmore, J. B. Dudley (resigned 2/15/1916). Sam Hooker, reassigned from Division 2 to Division 3, 2/15/1916.

The Sixth Legislature, R.S. (1917) enacted House Bill 19 to authorize the governor to appoint, with the consent of the Oklahoma Supreme Court, nine persons possessing the qualifications of the justice of the Supreme Court, as Supreme Court commissioners. The commissioners were divided into groups of three each and designated as Divisions 1, 2, and 3, and were subject to removal only in cases of impeachment as provided in impeachment of justices of the Supreme Court. The commissioners served until November 30, 1918. The following was the organization under the act effective March 31, 1917.

Division 1—Nester Rummons, A. M. Stewart, Wm. A. Collier.

Division 2—D. K. Pope, appointed 4/23/1917. A. T. West (resigned 6/1/1918). H. S. Davis, appointed 6/11/1918. C. A. Galbraith.

Division 3—W. V. Pryor appointed 4/23/1917. W. R. Bleakmore (resigned 2/16/1918). J. M. Springer, appointed 2/26/1918. Sam Hooker.

The Ninth Legislature, R.S. (1923) enacted Senate Bill 35 to authorize the governor to appoint, with the consent of the Oklahoma Supreme Court, fifteen persons possessing the qualifications required for justice of the Supreme Court, as Supreme Court commissioners, and to serve until December 31, 1926. The following was the organization under the act, effective March 16, 1923:

Division 1—N. B. Maxey, Presiding Comm., B. C. Logsdon, Robert Ray.

Division 2—J. S. Estes, Presiding Comm., J. H. Jarman, Thomas D. Lyons (resigned 11/28/1925). W. B. Williams, appointed.

Division 3—C. M. Threadgill, Presiding Comm., Charles H. Ruth. Cham Jones.

Division 4—A. S. Dickson, Presiding Comm., J. S. Shackelford, R. E. Stephenson.

Division 5—Wm. P. Thompson, Presiding Comm., Wm. E. Foster, C. L. Pinkham.

The Eleventh Legislature, R.S. (1927) enacted Senate Bill 38 to authorize the governor to appoint, with the consent of seven members of the Oklahoma Supreme Court, nine persons possessing qualifications for justice of the Supreme Court and one from each Supreme Court Judicial District, as Supreme Court commissioners. Commissioners were to hold office at the pleasure of the Supreme Court, but for a term not longer than December 31, 1930. The commissioners were divided into two divisions with one presiding commissioner over both divisions. The following was the organization under the Act effective March 25, 1927:

Division 1—Crawford D. Bennett, Presiding Commissioner. Houston B. Teehee, L. V. Reid. Arthur Leach, Dudley Monk (resigned 6/28/1927). Earl Foster, appointed 6/28/1927 (resigned 9/10/1930). No appointment made.

Division 2—J. A. Diffendaffer, A. L. Herr, A. L. Jeffrey (resigned 2/10/1930). W. L. Eagleton Jr., appointed 2/13/1930. W. C. Hall.

The Twenty-fifth Legislature, R.S. (1955) enacted House Bill 547 to authorize the governor to appoint, with the consent of the Oklahoma Supreme Court, three persons possessing the qualifications for justice of the Supreme Court, as Supreme Court commissioners. The commissioners were to hold office at the pleasure of the Supreme Court or until the expiration of the act, April 1, 1959, unless it was previously repealed. The following was the organization under the act, effective June 3, 1955:

J. W. Crawford (resigned 7/7/1957)—no appointment made.

James H. Nease

Jean R. Reed (resigned 4/30/1957)—no appointment made.

Court of Criminal Appeals History

The highest court in Oklahoma with exclusive appellate jurisdiction in criminal cases was established and named the Criminal Court of Appeals by the First Legislature, R.S. (1907–08) when it enacted House Bill 397. The act provided "If in any case appealed to the Criminal Court of Appeals, in which the construction of the Constitution of this State, or of the United States, or any Act of Congress is brought in question, the said Criminal Court of Appeals shall certify to the Supreme Court of the State, the question involving the construction of the Constitution of this State, or of the United States, or any Act of Congress for final determination of the question so certified." The act further provided that the judges should be appointed by the governor, by and with the consent and advice of the Senate. The judges appointed were to hold office until January 1, 1911, when the court was to terminate, unless continued by the legislature.

The Second Legislature, R.S. (1909) enacted House Bill 33 which perpetuated the Criminal Court of Appeals. The act repealed all prior laws in conflict and gave the court exclusive appellate jurisdiction. In case of a vacancy in the office of a judge of the court, the governor was authorized to fill the vacancy by appointment for the unexpired term, or until the first succeeding biennial election. The judges of the court who were in office at the time the act took effect were to continue in office until the expiration of their term of office under their appointment, and until their successors were duly elected and qualified. The act further provided for the first election of judges at the General Election in 1910. The state was divided into three Criminal Court of Appeals Judicial Districts, designated respectively as the Eastern, Northern and Southern Criminal Court of Appeals Judicial Districts.

The Twenty-seventh Legislature, R.S. (1959) enacted Senate Bill 36, which changed the name from Criminal Court of Appeals to Court of Criminal Appeals.

At a Special Election, July 11, 1967, constitutional amendments were adopted to provide a complete reorganization of Oklahoma courts. Beginning in 1968 judges of the Court of Criminal Appeals ran on a nonpartisan statewide retention ballot at the General Election only. If retained by the voters, judges serve a six-year term. If rejected, the vacancy is filled by appointment of the governor. In 1987 redistricting created two new positions on the court.

Judges of the Court of Criminal Appeals

District 1*—H. G. Baker (D) appointed 6/22/09. Thomas H. Owen (D) appointed, (resigned 3/31/10). D. A. Richardson (D) appointed, (term expired January 1911). James R. Armstrong (D) elected 1910, 1914. E. S. Bessey (R) elected 1920. James S. Davenport (D) elected 1926, 1932, 1938 (died 1/3/40). Dick Jones (D) appointed 1/20/40, elected 1944, 1950. Kirksey Nix (D) elected 1956, 1962, retained 1968. Retired 11/1/71. Robert D. Simms (D) appointed 12/1/71 (appointed to Supreme Court 10/2/72). C. F. June Bliss Jr. (D) appointed 11/27/72, retained 1974. Tom R. Cornish appointed 10/15/77; retained 1978, 1980; resigned 1/31/84. Ed Parks Jr. appointed 4/27/84, retained 1986. Resigned 12/31/92. Charles S. Chapel appointed 2/1/93, retained 1994, 1998, 2004. Retired 2/28/2010. Clancy Smith appointed 7/13/2010, retained 2012.

District 2*—Henry M. Furman (D) appointed, elected 1910, 1912 (died 4/10/16). Rutherford Brett (D) appointed 6/1/16. Resigned 4/10/17. Smith C. Matson (D) appointed 4/19/17, elected 1918. Thomas A. Edwards (D) elected 1924, 1930. Bert B. Barefoot (D) elected 1936, 1942, 1948 (died 6/28/49). John C. Powell (D) appointed 8/14/49, elected 1954. Hez J. Bussey (D) elected 1960, 1966; retained 1972, 1978, 1984 (retired). Charles

A. Johnson appointed 10/31/89, retained 1990, 1996, 2002, 2008. Retired 07/30/2014.

District 3—Gary L. Lumpkin appointed 11/15/88, retained 1990, 1996, 2002, 2008, 2014.

District 4*—Thomas H. Doyle (D) appointed, elected 1910, 1916, 1922. Will H. Chappell (R) elected 1928. Thomas H. Doyle (D) elected 1934, 1940. John A. Brett (D) elected 1946, 1952, 1958, (retired 1/14/63). Joe E. Johnson (D) appointed 1/14/63. Tom Brett (D) elected 1964; retained 1970, 1976, 1982, 1988. (died 1/23/93). Reta M. Strubhar appointed 8/11/93, retained 1994, 2000. Retired 11/01/04. Arlene Johnson appointed 2/18/05; retained 2006, 2012.

District 5—James F. Lane appointed 11/15/88, retained 1990, 1994. Retired 12/31/98. Stephen E. Lile appointed 1/4/99, retained 2000. Resigned 03/01/05. David B. Lewis appointed 8/04/2005; retained 2006, 2012.

---

*Redistricted by State Legislation. Laws 1987, Chapter 185.

Photograph courtesy of the Oklahoma Historical Society

Comanches camped at Fort Sill.

Oklahoma Museums

Information contained in the Oklahoma Travel Guide published by the Oklahoma Tourism and Recreation Department was used to compile this list of museums and important historical sites. To obtain a copy of the guide, call 1-800-652-6552. The guide gives hours of operation, admission prices and other information. Find out more about this and other tourism information at www.travelok.com.

For additional information about Oklahoma museums and historical sites and societies, contact the Oklahoma Museums Association • 405/424-7757 • www.okmuseums.org • 2100 NE 52 Street, Oklahoma City 73111. You may also wish to contact the Oklahoma History Center • 405/522-5248 • www.okhistorycenter.org • 2401 N Laird, Oklahoma City 73105.

Ada

Ada Arts and Heritage Center

400 S Rennie, Ada, Oklahoma 74820 • 580/332-7302
www.adaartsheritagecenter.com

Rotating exhibits—local, regional, and national artists, also historic photograph collection.

Chickasaw Nation Visitor Center

901 W 1 Street, Sulphur, Oklahoma 73086 • 580/622-8050 • www.chickasaw.net

Guided tours offer an educational look at modern tribal society, as well as tribal artifacts dating to the 1500s.

Adair

Cabin Creek Civil War Battle Site

9 miles east of city on SH-28 E, Adair, Oklahoma 74330 • 918/256-7133

The site features a granite monument, and markers tell the story of the 1862 Confederate victory. Periodic reenactments.

Aline

Sod House Museum

4628 SH-8 (between Aline and Cleo Springs)—Route 3, Box 28, Aline, Oklahoma 73716 • 580/463-244

Museum was built around an 1894 restored and furnished settler's sod house. Pioneer farm machinery, blacksmith shop, outbuildings, and cellar are displayed on the grounds.

Altus

Museum of the Western Prairie

1100 N Memorial Drive, Altus, Oklahoma 73522 • 580/482-1044

History of southwestern Oklahoma and Greer County, features an operating windmill, half dugout and old farm machinery.

Alva

Alva Municipal Airport Museum

2875 College Boulevard, Alva, Oklahoma 73717 • 580/327–2898
www.nwosu.edu/museum

Cherokee Strip Museum

901 14 Street, Alva, Oklahoma 73717 • 580/327–2030

Forty theme rooms in main building include a chapel, kitchen, living room, military room, Oklahoma room, gun room, clothes room, hat room and other exhibits dating from the mid-1800s to 1900s. Agricultural building displays small agricultural items and a one-room schoolhouse.

Northwestern Oklahoma State University Museum of Natural History

709 Oklahoma Boulevard, Alva, Oklahoma 73717 • 580/327–1700

Museum features fossils and geological and archaeological materials, including an endangered species collection and other natural history items.

Ames

Hajek Motorsports Museum

105 E Corporate Drive, Ames, Oklahoma 73718 • 580/753–4611 • hajekmotorsports.com

Museum features the biggest names in the sport of drag racing and Winston Cup including Dyno Don Nicholson, Bob Glidden, Dale Earnhardt, and Bill Elliott. By appointment only.

Anadarko

Delaware Nation Museum

31064 Highway 81, Building 100, Anadarko, Oklahoma 73005 • 405/247–2448

Displays of traditional clothing, beadwork, and artifacts of the Delaware Nation. Gift shop.

National Hall of Fame for Famous American Indians

851 E Central, Anadarko, Oklahoma 73005 • 405/247–5555

Outdoor displays feature bronze art and busts of famous American Indian leaders, along with an information center.

Philomathic Pioneer Museum

311 E Main Street, Anadarko, Oklahoma 73005 • 405/247–3240

Railroad memorabilia is displayed in ticket office. Military equipment and uniforms, American Indian doll collection, paintings, costumes, artifacts, photographic collection, pioneer physician's office and country store also are featured.

Southern Plains Indian Museum and Oklahoma Indian Arts & Crafts Center

81 E Central Boulevard, Anadarko, Oklahoma 73005 • 405/247–6221

Exhibits and galleries devoted to the creative achievements of Native American artists and craftsmen. Gift shop.

Antlers

Historic Frisco Depot Railroad Museum

119 W Main, Antlers, Oklahoma 74523 • 580/298–2488

Local genealogy research, area artifacts, memorial to victims of a catastrophic 1945 tornado.

Wildlife Heritage Museum

610 SW "D" Street, Antlers, Oklahoma 74523 • 580/298–9933
www.wildlifeheritagecenter.org

The museum features a hands on animal-hides petting zoo inside along with mounted deer, bobcats, and fox.

Apache

Apache Historical Museum

101 W Evans, Apache, Oklahoma 73006 • 580/588–3392

Housed in a frontier bank, built in 1901, the museum features original fixtures, records, photo gallery, and town history items. Listed on the National Register of Historic Sites.

Arcadia

Round Barn

107 E Highway 66, Arcadia, Oklahoma 73007 • 405/396–0824
www.arcadiaroundbarn.org

This restored 1898 landmark along old Route 66 is the only wooden round barn in Oklahoma. Exhibits and gift shop inside.

Ardmore

Eliza Cruce Hall Doll Museum

320 "E" Street, NW, Ardmore Public Library, Ardmore, Oklahoma 73401 • 580/223–8290

Three hundred of the world's finest dolls are featured, ranging from famed "Court Dolls" belonging to Marie Antoinette, to Italy's Lenci dolls as well as miniature tea sets of gold, silver, brass, pewter, wood, ivory, and glass.

Charles P. Goddard Center

401 First Avenue SW, Ardmore, Oklahoma 73402 • 580/226–0909
www.goddardcenter.org

Western gallery displays collection of contemporary paintings and features traveling art exhibits from national galleries.

Greater Southwest Historical Museum

35 Sunset Boulevard, Ardmore, Oklahoma 73402 • 580/226–3857 • www.gshm.org

Exhibits and artifacts from twenty states explore the region's history. Music, historic fashions, toys, early businesses, tools, and other displays.

Military Memorial Museum

35 Sunset Drive, Ardmore, Oklahoma 73402 • 580/226–5522 • www.gshm.org/miliary museum

Six thousand square feet of military artifacts, from the Civil War to Desert Storm. Located within the Greater Southwest Historical Museum.

Tucker Tower Museum and Nature Center

18407 Scenic Highway 77, Ardmore, Oklahoma 73401 • 580/223–2109

The museum pays tribute to one of the most unusual geological formations in the U.S. Exhibits include one of the world's largest known meteorites. Housed in 1930s governor's retreat built by the WPA, includes natural and cultural history of the Lake Murray area.

Arnett

Log Cabin Museum

211 E Barnes, Arnett, Oklahoma 73832 • 580/885–7680

Built in 1893, the museum features period furnishings. By appointment only.

Atoka

Confederate Memorial Museum, Cemetery, and Information Center

258 N Highway 69, Atoka, Oklahoma 74525 • 580/889–7192
www.civilwaralbum.com/atoka

Memorabilia from Civil War battle fought on February 13, 1864. Exhibits include stone artifacts, tableaux, clothing, and weapons.

Barnsdall

Bigheart Museum

616 W Main, Barnsdall, Oklahoma 74002 • 918/847–2397

Town was once named Bigheart in honor of a prominent Osage chief. Cherokee and Osage Nation artifacts and oil refinery items.

Bartlesville

Bartlesville Area History Museum

401 S Johnstone, Bartlesville, Oklahoma 74003 • 918/338–4290
www.bartlesvillehistory.com

Local history of a three-county area is presented with genealogy of Indians and pioneers.

Bartlesville Community Center

300 SE Adams, Bartlesville, Oklahoma 74003 • 918/337–2787
www.bartlesvillecommunitycenter.com

The $13 million center, designed by the Frank Lloyd Wright Foundation, features an art gallery, conference center and 1,700-seat auditorium.

Frank Phillips' Home

1107 SE Cherokee, Bartlesville, Oklahoma 74003 • 918/336–2491
www.frankphillipshome.com

The 26 room mansion of Frank Phillips, founder of Phillips Petroleum Company, was built in 1908 and is elaborately restored with 1930s furnishings and art.

Laquinta Foster Mansion

2201 Silverlake Road, Bartlesville, Oklahoma 74006 • 918/336–6234

Circa 1932 Spanish style 32-room mansion.

Nellie Johnstone Oil Well

200 N Cherokee, Bartlesville, Oklahoma 74003

Replica of Oklahoma's first commercial oil well.

Phillips Petroleum Company Museum

410 Keeler, Bartlesville, OK 74004 • 918/338-4116• www.phillips66museum.com

Exhibits explore the rich history of Phillips Petroleum and the popularity of the Phillips 66 brand in American culture.

Frank Lloyd Wright's Price Tower & Price Tower Arts Center

510 Dewey Avenue, Bartlesville, Oklahoma 74003 • 918/336–4949 • www.pricetower.org

This 1956 glass and copper skyscraper was designed by legendary architect Frank Lloyd Wright. It features an arts center, museum, restaurant, and hotel with rotating exhibitions on the ground floor.

Woolaroc Museum & Wildlife Preserve

1925 Woolaroc Ranch Road, Bartlesville, Oklahoma 74003 • 918/336–0307 • www.woolaroc.org

Getaway of oilman Frank Phillips includes Woolaroc Museum with western art, artifacts, and cultural history; wildlife preserve including buffalo trails.

Beaver

Jones and Plummer Trail Museum

11th and Douglas, Beaver, Oklahoma 74003 • 580/625–4439

Antiques of No Man's Land and disputed territory of surrounding states are exhibited. The items include clothing, saddles, old pictures and a special exhibit of antique medical supplies.

Bernice

Darryl Starbird Rod and Custom Car Hall of Fame Museum

55251 E SH–85A, Afton, Oklahoma 74331 • 918/257–4234 • www.darrylstarbird.com

Fifty custom built cars and street rods, hall of fame for famous custom designers, photographs, and memorabilia, all indoors.

Bethany

Bethany Historical Society Museum

6700 NW 36 Street, Bethany, Oklahoma 73008 • 405/789–2146

Artifacts detailing the history of Bethany are included.

Billings

Henry Bellmon Library and Museum

Main and Broadway, Billings, Oklahoma 74630 • 580/725–3411

Chronicles of the life of Oklahoma Governor and U.S. Senator Henry Bellmon. Housed in a circa 1900 sandstone building. By appointment.

Renfrow-Miller Museum

201 S Broadway, Billings, Oklahoma 74630 • 580/725–3258

Historic "Castle on the Prairie" built in 1901 was home/office of pioneer doctor who took part in the 1893 Cherokee Strip Land Run. By appointment.

Blackwell

Top of Oklahoma Museum

303 S Main, Blackwell, Oklahoma 74631 • 580/363–0209

Features the pioneer history of the Cherokee Outlet.

Boise City

Autograph Rock

Call for permission and directions—580/544–3344

Approximately 200 signatures, some from the 1840s, of travelers who crossed the Santa Fe Trail.

Bomb Memorial

Town Square, 580/544–3344

Display of one of several bombs mistakenly dropped on the city during testing in WWII.

Cimarron Heritage Center Museum & Information Center

1300 N Cimarron, Boise City, Oklahoma 73933 • 580/544–3479

History of Cimarron County from dinosaurs to present, and the Santa Fe Trail, with historic sites nearby.

Boley

Boley Historic District

Downtown—918/667–9790

Founded in 1893 as a camp for black railroad construction workers; billed as a haven where African Americans could govern themselves.

Boley Historical Museum

10 W Grant, Boley, Oklahoma, 74829 • 918/667–9790

Highlights the history of the "all-black" town in Oklahoma. By appointment only.

Bristow

Bristow Historical Museum

1 Railroad Place, Bristow, Oklahoma 74010 • 918/367–5151

Restored 1923 depot contains rotating exhibits about the city's history from Indian Territory days to the present.

Broken Arrow

Broken Arrow Historical Society Museum

400 S Main, Broken Arrow, Oklahoma 74012 • 918/258–2616
www.bahistoricalsociety.com

The city's history is shown through military displays, farming and pioneer items, photographs, and unusual belt buckle collection.

Broken Bow

Beavers Bend Wildlife Museum

7 miles north of Broken Bow on Highway 259 • 580/494–6193 • www.pine-net.com/nature

Museum features wildlife dioramas.

Forest Heritage Center and Museum

Beavers Bend State Park, Broken Bow, Oklahoma 74728 • 580/494–6497
www.forestry.ok.gov/fhc

History of forestry research is presented through dioramas depicting the evolution of the forest. A hand carved 22-foot-tall Indian statue decorates the center's entrance.

Gardner Mansion

Six miles east of Broken Bow on US–70 • 580/584–6588

The 1880s home of Jefferson Gardner, principal chief of the Choctaw tribe, houses prehistoric and historic Indian artifacts from eastern Oklahoma. Includes a 2,000–year-old cypress tree killed by lightning in 1982.

Buffalo

Buffalo Museum

108 S Hoy, Buffalo, Oklahoma 73834 • 580/735–6177

Local artifacts, Fort Dodge Trail crossing, furnished sod house and natural springs nearby. By appointment.

Cache

Holy City of the Wichitas

Inside Wichita Mountains Wildlife Refuge • 580/429–3361 • www.theholycitylawton.com

Natural amphitheater and structures built by WPA and the CCC in 1935 including chapel with murals and intricate ceramic brickwork. Site of annual pageant on Easter.

Quanah Parker Star House and Eagle Park Ghost Town

SH–15/US–62, Cache, Oklahoma 73527 • 580/429–3238

Collection of 15 historical buildings, with original furniture. Buildings include 1884 home of the Comanche Chief, which has stars painted on the roof to mimic those on uniforms of U.S. military.

Caddo

Caddo Indian Territory Museum and Library

110 Buffalo Street, Caddo, Oklahoma 74729 • 580/367–2787

The museum houses pioneer items, Indian artifacts and a library. Includes horse-drawn fire cart, blacksmith shop, and arrowhead collection.

Canton

Canton Area Museum

1 Block West of SH–51, Canton, Oklahoma 73726 • 580/886–2266

Historical memorabilia from surrounding areas.

Carmen

Carmen Depot

SH–45, Carmen, Oklahoma—580/987–2321

State's first Kansas City, Mexico & Orient depot. Local history and rail transportation items—1916 caboose.

Ralph Cain Jr. Memorial Newspaper Museum

SH–45, Carmen, Oklahoma—580/987–2321

Demonstrations of 1916 newspaper printing using handset type and vintage equipment. Civil War tent and artifacts.

Carnegie

Kiowa Tribal Museum and Resource Center

¼ mile west of Carnegie on SH–9, Carnegie, Oklahoma—580/654–2300

Artifacts, art work and resource materials of the Kiowa tribe are featured. Ten murals by Kiowa artists interpret the heritage of the Kiowa people, from pre-history to the present.

Catoosa

Blue Whale

2705 N SH–66, Catoosa, Oklahoma 74015 • 918/694–7390

Restored Route 66 landmark.

Catoosa Historical Society Museum & Depot

207 N Cherokee, Catoosa, Oklahoma 74015 • 918/266–7156

Tulsa Port of Catoosa-Arkansas Waterway Museum

US–169 north to 46 Street N, then east five miles to Port Authority Building
5350 Cimarron Road, Catoosa, Oklahoma 74015 • 918/266–2291 • www.arkansasriver.org

The head of navigation for the McClellan-Kerr Arkansas River Navigation System, Tulsa's port links the Arkansas River with 2,500 miles of inland waterways stretching from the Gulf of Mexico and the Mississippi River to the Great Lakes and St. Lawrence Seaway. Museum features artifacts and memorabilia representing development of the waterway.

Chandler

Museum of Pioneer History

719 Manvel Avenue, Chandler, Oklahoma 74834 • 405/258–2425
www.pioneermuseumok.org

Exhibits and displays highlight more than 4,000 artifacts representing pioneer life in Lincoln County. Collections of frontier marshal Bill Tilghman and pioneer movie news photographer Benny Kent are also included. Museum has a children's touring marionette theater.

Checotah

Honey Springs Battlefield Site

1863 Honey Springs Battlefield Road, Checotah, Oklahoma 74426 • 918/473–5572

Site of the territory's largest Civil War battle, this "Gettysburg of the West" involved Black, Hispanic, and Indian soldiers. Monuments and interpretive signs on site.

Katy Depot Center

US–69 and US–266, Paul Carr Drive, Checotah, Oklahoma 74426 • 918/473–6377

Wooden MKT depot from 1890 houses local artifacts, railroad memorabilia. Listed on the National Register of Historic Places.

Chelsea

Oklahoma's First Oil Well Historical Site

1 mile south and 4 miles west of Chelsea off US–66 • 918/789–2220

Replica of an old-fashioned oil well proclaimed as the state's first non-commercial oil well.

Cherokee

Alfalfa County Historical Society

117 W Main Street, Cherokee, Oklahoma 73728 • 580/596–2960

Early Alfalfa County life, from the Land Run of 1893. Former hotel houses Cherokee Strip memorabilia, old-fashioned kitchen, school room, printing press, and war items.

Cheyenne

Black Kettle Museum

US–283 and SH–47 • 101 South LL Males, Cheyenne, Oklahoma 73628 • 580/497–3929

Focus is on Custer and the 7th Cavalry attack on Cheyenne Chief Black Kettle's village in 1868. Cheyenne art and artifacts–7th Cavalry items, and gift shop.

Briggs Family Private Museum

305 S 3 Street, Cheyenne, Oklahoma 73628 • 580/497–3693

Pioneer memorabilia. By appointment only.

Pioneer/Community Museum Complex

Cheyenne City Park, S edge of town off US–283 • 580/497–3882

Museum features Santa Fe depot, chapel, pioneer artifacts, WW I and WW II cannons.

Roll One-Room School Museum

US–283, Route. 1, Box 34, Cheyenne, Oklahoma 73628 • 580/497–3882
rogermills.org/mueseums

Visitors are welcome to view classes for fourth graders taught 1910–style. Small fee for participating students.

Washita Battlefield

2 miles west and north of Cheyenne on SH–47, Cheyenne, Oklahoma 73628 • 580/497–2712

The monument and memorial were erected in remembrance of the November 1868 battle between Chief Black Kettle's tribe and General George Custer. The battlefield is listed on the National Register of Historic Places.

Chickasha

Grady County Historical Museum

415 W Chickasha Avenue, Chickasha, Oklahoma 73018 • 405/224–6480

Housed in the Dixie Building, a 1907 former grocery store with period rooms, featuring area history and Harvey House items.

Muscle Car Ranch

3609 S 16 Street, Chickasha, Oklahoma 73108　•　405/222–4910　•　www.musclecarranch.com

Open-air displays of classic autos and motorcycles, neon and porcelain signs, automotive folk art. Camping and fall swap meet.

Claremore

Belvidere Mansion

121 N Chickasaw, Claremore, Oklahoma 74017　•　918/342–1127
www.belvideremansion.com

Three-story Victorian home was built before statehood. Period furnishings, tour guides wear period clothing.

J.M. Davis Arms and Historical Museum

333 N Lynn Riggs Boulevard, Claremore, Oklahoma 74018　•　918/341–5707
www.thegunmuseum.com

The firearms exhibits cover a 700-year span of gunmaking including a collection of 20,000 guns and gun-related items—70 saddles, musical instruments—1,200 steins, edged weapons, John Rogers' statuary collection, more than 600 WW I posters and hundreds of animal horns, trophy heads, and Outlaw Gallery.

Lynn Riggs Memorial

121 N Weenonah, Claremore, Oklahoma 74017–2099　•　918/342–1127

A large collection of memorabilia is featured from Riggs' professional life as a writer and author of the play "Green Grow the Lilacs," from which the musical "Oklahoma!" was taken. Displays include the surrey used in the original production of "Oklahoma!"

Oklahoma Military Academy Memorial Museum

1701 Will Rogers Boulevard, Claremore, Oklahoma 74017–2099　•　918/343–7803

Listed on the National Register of Historic Places, the academy pays tribute to the corps of cadets who attended the prestigious Oklahoma Military Academy, now Rogers University.

Will Rogers Memorial

1720 W Will Rogers Boulevard, Claremore, Oklahoma 74017　•　918/341–0719

Rogers' burial site, and museum relating life and times of the famed humorist and film star, including a children's interactive center, theater, and gift shop. www.willrogers.org

Cleveland

Triangle Heritage Museum

512 W Delaware, Cleveland, Oklahoma—918/519–6251

Cleveland and Pawnee County history and memorabilia from brickyards to oilfields.

Clinton

Cheyenne Cultural Center

2250 NE Highway 66, Clinton, Oklahoma 73601 • 580/323–6224

Cheyenne cultural exhibits by award-winning artisans, seasonal special events, traveling exhibits throughout the year.

Mohawk Lodge Indian Store

1 mile east on SH–66, Clinton, Oklahoma 73601 • 580/323–2360

Established in 1892, features 1890s artifacts from Plains and Western tribes, plus American Indian art and crafts supplies.

Oklahoma Route 66 Museum

2229 W Gary Boulevard, Clinton, Oklahoma 73601 • 580/323–7866 • www.route66.org

Newly expanded showcase of the development of "The Mother Road" and transportation history. Self-guided audio tours.

Coalgate

Coal County Historical and Mining Museum, Inc.

212 S Broadway, Coalgate, Oklahoma 74538 • 580/927–2360

Museum houses mining equipment and maps, two model mines, county and cemetery records, oil lamps, drill bits, antique musical instruments, WWII uniforms, and antique household items.

Colbert

Colbert Historical Museum

100 N Burney, Colbert, Oklahoma 74733 • 580/296–2385

History of pioneers and early residents, photographs, documents, "Colbert's Ferry" historical marker.

Colcord

Talbot Library and Museum

500 S Colcord Avenue, Colcord, Oklahoma 74338 • 918/326–4532 • www.talbotlibrary.com

Farm machinery from 1900s though WWII. More than 9,000 historical items, including a genealogy library with more than 3,000 books. Collection includes Cherokee and other tribal artifacts and documents.

Collinsville

Collinsville Depot Museum

115 S 10 Street, Collinsville, Oklahoma 74021 • 918/371–3540
www.cvilleok.com/depot

Old train depot houses exhibits of turn-of-the-century living room and kitchen settings with mission-style furniture, player piano and railroad depot items. Caboose on site.

Newspaper Museum

1110 W Main, Collinsville, Oklahoma 74021 • 918/371–1901 • www.cvilleok.com

Features history and photos of the people and city of Collinsville, newspaper production equipment dating to 1899.

Cordell

Historic Washita Theatre

111 S Main, Cordell, Oklahoma 73632 • 580/832–5400

Theatre features art deco splendor with evening shows daily and Sunday matinee.

Washita County Museum

105 E First Street, Cordell, Oklahoma 73632 • 580/832–3681 or 580/832–2053

Chuckwagon and farm home displays, photographs, and numerous other items. Records of the settlement and development of Washita County from 1890 to present.

Coweta

Mission Bell Museum

204 S Bristow Avenue, Coweta, Oklahoma 74429 • 918/279-8408

Museum features Coweta history and Indian artifacts. The museum is located in the former First Presbyterian Church founded in 1907.

Crescent

Frontier Country Historical Museum

500 N Grand, Crescent, Oklahoma 73028 • 405/969–3660
www.frontiercountrymuseum.org

The museum features a one-room schoolhouse, an armed forces memorial, doctor's office, barbershop, and general store. Logan county exhibits are also on display.

Cushing

Dodrill's Museum of Rocks, Minerals, and Fossils

123 S Cleveland, Cushing, Oklahoma 74023 • 918/225–0662

Hand-hewn sandstone building features 7,000 square feet of rocks, minerals, fossils, artifacts regarding Oklahoma's history.

Cyril

Cyril Museum

US–77 and Main Street, Cyril, Oklahoma 73029 • 580/464–2547

Museum features Cyril's history and memorabilia.

Davis

Arbuckle Historical Museum
Old Santa Fe Railroad Depot—12 Main Street, Davis, Oklahoma 73030 • 580/369–2518

Museum features Indian artifacts—250-year-old loom, Fort Arbuckle artifacts, pictorial history, collection of books, pioneer and railroad artifacts.

Del City

Del City Preservation Center
4501 SE 15 Street, Del City, Oklahoma, 73115 • 405/677–1910

Exhibits relate the city's history.

Oklahoma Country/Western Museum
3925 SE 29 Street, Del City, Oklahoma, 73115 • 405/677–3174

A 10,000 square foot building dedicated to country and western music performers.

Dewey

Dewey Hotel Museum
801 N Delaware, Dewey, Oklahoma 74029 • 918/534–0215 • www.prairiesong.net

Restored 1899 hotel exhibits, period furnishings, vintage clothing, and rare photographs of early-day settlement. Victorian architecture, gaming room, and wrap-around porch.

Prairie Song Indian Territory
5 1/2 miles east of Highway 75 on Durham Road
402621 W 1600 Road, Dewey, Oklahoma 74029 • 918/534–2662

Replica of 1800s prairie village featuring more than 20 hand-hewn log buildings. The buildings include a schoolhouse, chapel, cowboy line shack, and trading post.

Tom Mix Museum and Western Theatre
721 N Delaware, Dewey, Oklahoma 74029 • 918/534–1555

The nation's most comprehensive collection of the silent movie star's clothing, saddles, trophies, pictures, and records are displayed. A theater shows his movies. Gift shop.

Drumright

Drumright Historical Museum
301 E Broadway, Drumright, Oklahoma 74030 • 918/352–3002
www.drumrighthistoricalsociety.org

Old oilfield equipment, tools, clothes, home furnishings, tapes from early day citizens and murals depict the history of the oilfield and area.

Duncan

Chisholm Trail Heritage Center

1000 Chisholm Trail Parkway, Duncan, Oklahoma 73533 • 580/252–6692
www.onthechisholmtrail.com

Bronze depiction of a cattle drive, Chisholm Trail artifacts and visible trail ruts, animated 3-D likeness of Jesse Chisholm, multi-sensory experience theater where individuals relive adventures of the West.

Prairie House Historic Site

814 W Oak, Duncan, Oklahoma 73533 • 580/255–7693 • www.theprairiehouse.com

Built in 1918, one of the earliest example of the Prairie Style that was made famous by Frank Lloyd Wright.

Stephens County Historical Society Museum

1402 W Beech Avenue, Fuqua Park—Duncan, Oklahoma 73534 • 580/252–0717

The Boomer Room–pioneer life from 1877 to 1920—includes Indian artifacts, Chisholm Trail displays, photographs and replicas of a surrey, covered wagon and blacksmith shop. The Sooner Room—life from 1920 to 1977—features the history of Halliburton Services and its impact on the oil industry from the innovation of cementing methods to the present off-shore drilling techniques. Gift shop.

Durant

Fort Washita Historic Site and Museum

3348 State Road 199, Durant, Oklahoma 74701 • 580/924–6502

The ruins of a U.S. fort constructed in 1842 features General Cooper's cabin and reconstructed south barracks. The fort provided protection for the civilized Chickasaw and Choctaw Indians against the Plains Indians in the mid-1800s.

Three Valley Museum

401 W Main Street, Durant, Oklahoma 74701 • 580/920–1907

Housed in the basement of 1909 building that serves as Choctaw Nation headquarters, features artifacts of early statehood.

Durham

Break O'Day Farms and Metcalfe Museum

9 miles north of Cheyenne, Oklahoma on SH–283; 12 miles west on SH–33, Durham, Oklahoma 73642 • 580/655–4467, www.metcalfemuseum.org

Five buildings of memorabilia, spinning wheels, historic photographs, guns, blacksmith items, farm equipment. Repository for the works of pioneer "Sage Brush" artist Augusta Metcalf.

Edmond

Edmond Historical Society Museum

431 S Boulevard, Edmond, Oklahoma 73034 • 405/340–0078 • www.edmondhistory.org

1936 Armory features artifacts, photographs, and documents relating to area development.

University of Central Oklahoma Museum of Art

Evans Hall, Room 103 • 100 N University Drive, Edmond, Oklahoma 73034 • 405/974–2000
www.uco.edu.com

Permanent collections include original graphics, paintings, prints, drawings, photographs, and political cartoons, as well as sculpture and artifacts from various world cultures.

El Reno

Canadian County Historical Museum

300 S Grand, El Reno, Oklahoma 73036 • 405/262–5121

The museum features an American Indian display, Darlington and Concho items, Fort Reno display, model trains, original ticket office for Rock Island Railroad. There are 1880s cattle brands, old schoolhouse, the El Reno Hotel built in 1892, and the first Red Cross canteen built in 1917.

Fort Reno

7107 W Cheyenne • 405/262–3987 • www.fortreno.org

Now a federal and state agricultural station, the fort was a cavalry outpost from 1875–1908. The grave of General Custer's head scout, Ben Clark, is located here, along with a WWII POW cemetery.

Elk City

National Route 66 Museum

2717 W 3 Street, Elk City, Oklahoma—580/225–6266

Spectacular national tribute to the "Mother Road."

Old Town Museum Complex & Farm and Ranch Museum

2717 W Highway 66, Elk City, Oklahoma 73648 • 580/225–0207

Turn-of-the-century, gingerbread-style home furnished in the late Victorian style includes rodeo and Indian rooms, a wagon yard, Rock Bluff schoolhouse, and replicas of a 1900s chapel and of the Katy Depot. The complex also features a town square with replicas of early-day businesses. The latest attraction, the National Route 66 Museum, opened in 1998.

Enid

Cherokee Strip Regional Heritage Center

507 S 4 Street, Enid, Oklahoma 73701 • 580/237–1907

Artifacts and materials pertaining to settlement of the Cherokee Outlet are displayed in the museum. The barn features farm exhibits.

Humphrey Heritage Village

507 S Fourth Street, Enid, Oklahoma 73701 • 580/237–1907

Includes an elaborate Victorian style home, original land office where pioneers filed their 1893 land run claims, Enid's oldest church building and original one-room school house.

Leonardo's Discovery Warehouse/Adventure Quest

200 E Maple, Enid, Oklahoma 73701 • 580/233–2787 • www.leonardos.org

Interactive science and art museum especially for children, housed in 1909 warehouse. Promoted as the "world's largest community-built playground and science park." Gift shop.

Midgley Museum

1001 Sequoyah Drive, Enid, Oklahoma 73703 • 580/234–7265

Furnished home built of petrified wood and rock. Rock and mineral collections, area items. Gift shop.

Railroad Museum of Oklahoma

702 N Washington, Enid, Oklahoma 73701 • 580/233–3051
www.railroadmuseumofoklahoma.org

Railroad memorabilia from across the nation, dining car china, telegraph equipment, history compiled on all railroads that ran though Oklahoma, more than 5,000 postcards from depots located all over the world.

Erick

100th Meridian Museum

Sheb Wooley Avenue and Roger Miller Boulevard, Erick, Oklahoma—580/526–3221

The museum relates the story of the 100th Meridian of longitude from prehistoric times to the present. Built as the First National Bank in 1907, the building is now on the National Register of Historic Places. An authentic replica of a First National Bank teller's cage is featured.

Roger Miller Museum

101 S Sheb Wooley Street, Erick Oklahoma 73645 • 580/526–3833
www.rogermillermuseum.com

Museum features memorabilia regarding Grammy Award winning singer/songwriter Roger Miller.

Fairview

Major County Historical Society Museum

1 ½ miles east of Fairview on SH–58 • 580/227–2265 • www.mchsok.com

Farming and related exhibits, seasonal exhibits, Major County memorabilia, genealogical library.

Fort Gibson

Fort Gibson Historic Site

110 Ash Avenue, Fort Gibson, Oklahoma 74434 • 918/478–4088

Originally built in 1824, these stockade houses were reconstructed in the 1930s with displays focusing on the Seventh Infantry. The Garrison Hill area has a reconstructed bakery and restored 1870s barracks with furnished period rooms. The first army post in Indian Territory operating from 1824–1890.

Fort Gibson National Cemetery

1423 Cemetery Road, Fort Gibson, Oklahoma 74434 • 918/478–2334 • www.cem.va.gov

Established as a national cemetery in 1861, burial place for veterans from the War of 1812 to Persian Gulf War. Self-guided walking tours.

Garrett Historic Home

504 E Coppinger Avenue, Fort Gibson, Oklahoma 73701 • 918/478–3747

Built in 1867 as the commanding officers residence. Renovated and restored in 1997. Original home contained a ballroom on the 3rd floor.

Fort Supply

Fort Supply Historic Site

1 mile east of Fort Supply on SH–270 and SH–3
PO 247, Fort Supply, Oklahoma 73841 • 580/256–6136

Five historic structures from the frontier military days (1868-1894), small museum with Army memorabilia.

Fort Towson

Fort Towson Historic Site

1 mile northeast of Fort Towson on Highway 70

HC 63, Box 1580, Fort Towson, Oklahoma 74735 • 580/873–2634

Ruins of the 1824–1854 army post with artifacts on display. Site of Civil War General Stand Watie's surrender in 1865.

Fort Towson Historical Society Museum

Adjacent to City Hall on US–70, Fort Towson, Oklahoma 74735 • 580/873–2458

The museum features artifacts and territorial memorabilia.

Foyil

Totem Pole Park

4 miles east of town on SH–28A—918/342–9149

Fantasy roadside park created by folk artist Ed Galloway in the 1940s as a tribute to the American Indians. Unique structures—90-foot concrete totem pole.

Frederick

Pioneer Heritage Townsite Center

200 N 9 Street, Frederick, Oklahoma 73542 • 580/335–5844

A one-room country schoolhouse, railroad depot and barn featuring antique farm implements and tools, household items and area artifacts.

Ramona Theatre

114 S 9 Street, Frederick, Oklahoma 73542 • 580/335–2881 • www.ramonatheatre.com

Restored Mediterranean-style theater.

Tillman County Historical Museum

201 N 9 Street, Frederick, Oklahoma 73542 • 580/335–7541

The museum features household items, horse drawn fire equipment and farming implements, wagons, and a 1916 Case tractor.

Freedom

Freedom Museum

505 Main Street, Freedom, Oklahoma 73842 • 580/621–3533

Restored Mediterranean-style theater.

Gate

Gateway to the Panhandle Museum

MKT Depot—Highway 64 and Oklahoma Street, Gate, Oklahoma 73844 • 580/934–2004

Farm and home items, Civil War memorabilia, ancient bones, prehistoric elephant tusks, Indian artifacts, newspapers of the area and other displays which depict life in the early days of the Oklahoma panhandle.

Geary

Canadian Rivers Historical Society Museum

100 E Main, Geary, Oklahoma—405/884–2765

Area's first log jail; train caboose.

Gene Autry

Gene Autry Oklahoma Museum

47 Prairie Street, Gene Autry, Oklahoma 74346 • 580/294–3047
www.geneautryokmuseum.com

Dedicated to the "Singing Cowboys of the 'B' Western Movies" offering memorabilia of Western film stars.

Goodwell

No Man's Land Historical Museum

Panhandle State University Campus—207 W Sewell Street
P.O. Box 278, Goodwell, Oklahoma 73939 • 580/349–2670

The history of No Man's Land and the Dust Bowl, as well as an art gallery, a library, William E. Baker archaeological collection and the Duckett alabaster carvings collection.

Gore

Cherokee Courthouse, Tahlonteeskee

3 miles southeast of Gore on US–64 • 918/489–5663

Reconstructed 1829 council house, courthouse, and original cabin; items related to the area's first Cherokee settlement. Gift shop.

Grove

Har-Ber Village

4404 W 20 Street, Grove, Oklahoma 74344 • 918/786–6646 • www.har-bervillage.com

Self-guided tours through 116 buildings furnished with items and artifacts that re-create all aspects of the area's early settlement. Ecology Center and Nature Trail program promote eco-tourism. Docent presentations on the area's ecology available.

Guthrie

Guthrie Historic District

Guthrie, Oklahoma 73044 • 800/299–1889

The 1400–acre site is the largest urban acreage on the National Register of Historic Places. The 14–block original downtown area also contains the largest collection of restored Victorian commercial buildings in the United States. The district has been restored to resemble 1910, the last year it served as Oklahoma's capital. www.guthrieok.com

Guthrie Scottish Rite Masonic Temple

900 East Oklahoma, Guthrie, Oklahoma 73044 • 405/282–1281

Located on the site designated in 1890 as land for the Oklahoma Capitol, the temple is one of the largest Masonic buildings in the world. It features 17 rooms including two elaborate theaters. All rooms are furnished with authentic decorations, furniture, and artifacts of ancient civilizations and cultures.

National Lighter Museum

107 S 2 Street, Guthrie, Oklahoma 73044 • 405/282–3025

Thousands of items in this 55–year collection of man's early fire-making devices. The only known museum of its kind in America.

Oklahoma Frontier Drug Store Museum

214 W Oklahoma, Guthrie, Oklahoma 73044 • 405/282–1895
www.drugmuseum.org

Site of Oklahoma Territory's first drug store, authentic restoration includes numerous turn-of-the-century items.

Oklahoma Territorial Museum

402 E Oklahoma, Guthrie, Oklahoma 73044 • 405/282–1889
www.okterritorialmuseum.org

The late Victorian-style museum is attached to the Carnegie Library building, which was the site of the inaugurations of the last territorial governor and the state's first governor. Displays of all phases of life in Oklahoma Territorial times—1889-1907, are featured including the artwork of Frederick A. Olds.

Harrah

Harrah Historical Society Museum

20881 E Main Street, Harrah, Oklahoma 73045 • 405/454–6911

Restored depot houses turn-of-the-century railroad artifacts and displays about early-day Harrah, caboose and two coal cars.

Healdton

Healdton Oil Museum

315 E Main, Healdton, Oklahoma 73438 • 580/229–0900 • www.healdtonok.org

Oil field equipment, photographs, and books relating to the oil industry. Site of what was once the richest oilfield in the world.

Heavener

Heavener Runestone State Park

2 miles east of Heavener on Morris Creek Road—918/653–2241

A 12-foot high monument-like stone bears Runic alphabet markings dating 600 to 800 AD. The inscriptions are believed to have been carved by Viking explorers 500 years before Columbus. An interpretive center is on the grounds as well as a gift shop and amphitheater.

Peter Conser Historic Home

4 miles south and 3 miles west of Heavener off US–59/270 • 918/653–2493

The restored—1894 home and barn of Peter Conser, outstanding leader of the Choctaw Lighthorsemen, features the original furnishings.

Henryetta

Henryetta Art Association Museum

606 W Division, Henryetta, Oklahoma 74437 • 918/652–4165

Permanent display of work by local artists, plus a gallery of local art available for purchase.

Henryetta Territorial Museum

410 W Moore, Henryetta, Oklahoma 74437 • 918/652–7112

Early-day area artifacts, housed in a 1905 one-room school. Items from Dallas Cowboy Troy Aikman and rodeo champion Jim Shoulders.

Hinton

Hinton Historical Museum

801 S Broadway, Hinton, Oklahoma 73047 • 405/542–3181

More than 3,000 articles relating to the Hinton area and its history. Museum is located in a house built before 1909. The 15,000–square foot facility houses one of the state's largest horse carriage collections, antique cars from Model T's to Edsels, and antique bicycles from 1910 to 1960s.

Hobart

Kiowa County Museum

518 S Main, Hobart, Oklahoma 73651 • 580/726–6202

1909 depot houses old post office window, quilts, clothing, farm implements, and American Indian artifacts.

Holdenville

Holdenville Historical Museum

Main and Creek, Holdenville, Oklahoma 74848 • 405/379–6723

Hollis

Harmon County Historical Museum

102 W Broadway, Hollis, Oklahoma 73550 • 580/688–9545

Area history with rotating displays and work of local artists, dinosaur bones, covered wagon and blacksmith shop.

Hominy

Field Historical Printing Museum

109 W Main, Hominy, Oklahoma 74035 • 918/885–2688

The museum features a 1930 linotype, presses, engravers, and printing equipment.

Fred Drummond Home

305 N Price, Hominy, Oklahoma 74035 • 918/885–2374

The 1905 Victorian-style home of a merchant/ranching family is listed on the National Register of Historic Places. It contains almost all of its original furnishings. Guided tours.

Marland Station Wall of Memories

East Main/South Wood, Hominy, Oklahoma 74035 • 918/885–4939

Circa 1925 Marland Oil Company Station and memorabilia. By appointment only.

MKT Caboose and Restored MKT Depot

300 W Main, Hominy, Oklahoma 74035 • 918/885–4939

New Territory Sculpture

West side of town, Hominy, Oklahoma 74035

Twenty-foot steel images top a hill on the west side of town.

Hugo

Frisco Depot Museum

307 North B Street, Hugo, Oklahoma 74743 • 580/326–6630
www.friscodepot.org

Restored Frisco depot converted to an expansive two floor historical museum.

Goodland Presbyterian Children's Home

2 miles south of Hugo on US–271 and 2 miles west on SH–271A—580/326–7568

Two structures available for viewing on the campus are the Presbyterian Church erected in 1850 and a log cabin, dating to 1837, that was occupied by a Choctaw chief. An 1848 building remains in use as an orphanage and school for Indian children.

Showmen's Rest/Mount Olivet Cemetery

Trice and 8 Streets, Hugo, Oklahoma 74743 • 580/326–7511

Unusual monuments of circus performers, burial place of Champion bull riders Freckles Brown and Lane Frost.

Idabel

Barnes-Stevenson House

302 SE Adams, Idabel, Oklahoma 74745 • 580/286–3305

Exhibits: A 1912 Victorian home featuring period furnishings.

Museum of the Red River

812 East Lincoln Road, Idabel, Oklahoma, 74745 • 580/286–3616
www.museumoftheredriver.org

Exhibits include archaeological artifacts of the Caddo and Choctaw, Precolumbian objects from Middle and South America, modern and contemporary native arts and crafts from throughout the Americas, and a cast skeleton of the dinosaur, Acrocanthosaurus atokensis, discovered nearby in McCurtain County. The museum also displays representative works from African, East Asian, and Pacific Island native cultures. The recently expanded museum now features a community conference center.

Indianola

Choate House Museum

403 W Walnut, Indianola, Oklahoma 74442 • 918/823–4421

The double log cabin with dogtrot was built in 1867 by George Choate, a leader of the Choctaw Nation. The house is filled with pre-statehood furniture and items, barn and outbuildings.

Jay

Delaware County Historical Society and Marie Wallace Museum

538 Krause Street, Jay, Oklahoma 74346 • 918/253–4345

Artifacts and exhibits from across the nation, including toy trains, buggies, wagons, and American Indian and Trail of Tears items.

Jenks

Oklahoma Aquarium

300 Aquarium Drive, Jenks, Oklahoma 74037 • 918/296–3474 • www.okaquarium.org

The Oklahoma Aquarium offers nearly 200 exhibits including ten major galleries with more than 4,000 creatures from the earth's waters.

Kaw City

Kanza Museum

746 Grandview, Kaw City, Oklahoma 74641 • 580/269–2552 • www.kanzamueum.org

Kaw Indian Nation museum and tribal headquarters.

Kaw City Museum

910 Washunga Drive, Kaw City, Oklahoma 74641 • 580/269–2366

Housed in 1902 depot, exhibits relate the history of the area. Indian artifacts are on display.

Kenton

Dinosaur Tracks

6 miles North of Kenton—580/544–3479

Preserved in sandstone creek bed.

Kenton Mercantile Museum

101 West Main, Oklahoma 73946 • 580/261–7447 • www.kentonmercantile.net

General store and eclectic museum, housed in an 1882 Studebaker wagon assembly plant. Dinosaur artifacts, jar and bottle collection.

Kingfisher

Chisholm Trail Museum

605 Zellers Avenue, Kingfisher, Oklahoma 73750 • 405/375–5176
www.kingfisher.org

The museum traces the history of the Chisholm Trail and features Indian artifacts, a restored log cabin, schoolhouse, church, and bank. Site is an original trade route opened by Jesse Chisholm in 1861.

Governor A.J. Seay Mansion

605 Zellers Avenue, Kingfisher, Oklahoma 73750 • 405/375–5176

The home of the second territorial governor, built in 1892, features period furnishings.

Krebs

Krebs Heritage Museum

85 S Main Street, Krebs, Oklahoma 74554—918/426–0377 • www.krebsmuseum.com

Area history and artifacts, coal mining history exhibits and equipment, military exhibits and artifacts dating from Revolutionary War period to present.

Langston

Beulah Land Cemetery

Off SH–33, northeast of Langston University • 405/466–2271

Markers of town founders and former slaves echo the town's early history as an all-black city in Oklahoma Territory.

Melvin B. Tolson Black Heritage Center

Langston University, Sanford Hall, West SH–33, Langston, Oklahoma 73050
405/466–3346 • www.lunet.edu/lib

African American art, books, records. The state's only resource center for the study of African and African American history.

Laverne

Laverne Museum

First and Broadway streets, Laverne, Oklahoma 73848 • 580/921–3612

Indian artifacts, glass shoe collection, Jayne Jayroe items, an art room and a Western room are displayed.

Lawton

Comanche National Museum and Cultural Center

701 NW Ferris Avenue, Lawton, Oklahoma 73507 • 580/353–0404
www.comanchenation.com

The center features Native American art and memorabilia.

Fort Sill National Historic Landmark and Museum

437 Quanah Road, Fort Sill, Oklahoma 73503 • 580/442–5123 • sill-www.army.mil/museum/home page.htm

The museum at Fort Sill is the largest in the U.S. Army. Of the 46 historic buildings in the National Historic Landmark, the museum occupies 26 structures where its vast collections are both stored and exhibited. Exhibits cover buffalo soldiers, Geronimo, Southern Plains tribes, and the world's largest collections of military memorabilia.

Mattie Beal Home

1006 SW 5 Street, Lawton, Oklahoma 73502 • 580/678–3156

This 14–room mansion–the first in Lawton–was built in 1901 and is listed on the National Register of Historic Sites.

Museum of the Great Plains

601 Ferris Avenue, Lawton, Oklahoma 74507 • 580/581–3460
www.museumofthegreatplains.org

The history, archaeology and anthropology of the Great Plains are detailed from prehistoric times through the early 1900s. Special attractions include an ancient mammoth skull and tusks, an outdoor prairie dog village and a rendition of an 1840s fortified trading post complete with living history interpretive programming.

Lindsay

Murray-Lindsay Mansion

410 SW 5 Street, Lindsay, Oklahoma 73052 • 405/756–6502

The 1881 mansion of Frank Murray, early-day rancher and farmer of the Chickasaw Nation. Period furniture, clothing, a 187–piece teapot collection are featured.

Locust Grove

Saline Courthouse

9 miles east on US–412, then ¾ mile south (Rose, OK)—918/479–6336

Only original remaining Cherokee courthouse.

Willard Stone Family Museum and Gallery

7980 E Highway 412, Locust Grove, Oklahoma 74352 • 918/479–6481

More than 40 examples of original work of nationally-known wood and bronze sculptor.

Mangum

Old Greer County Museum and Hall of Fame, Inc.

222 W Jefferson Street, Mangum, Oklahoma 73554 • 580/782–2851
www.oldgreercountymuseum.com

The museum features Indian artifacts and the history of old Greer County, which includes today's Beckham, Harmon, Greer, and Jackson counties. The Hall of Fame is an outdoor display of 114 granite monoliths bearing etched faces and biographies of pioneers who settled in the area prior to statehood. An authentic half-dugout has been erected on the grounds, with an old outhouse and windmill.

Mannford

Keystone Crossroads Museum

Corner of Coonrod Avenue and SH–51, Mannford, Oklahoma 74044 • 918/865–7206

Artifacts from Keystone Crossroads Lake area including Creek, Pawnee, Osage, and Tulsa counties. Indian artifacts and pioneer collections, photographs and video library. A 1200-square-foot map of prehistoric and historic sites from five counties.

Marietta

Love County Military Museum

408 1/2 W Chickasaw, Marietta, Oklahoma 73448 • 580/276–3192

Items from Revolutionary War to present, family military history, area law enforcement displays, two-story 1910 jailhouse.

Love County Pioneer Museum

409 W Chickasaw, Marietta, Oklahoma 73448 • 580/276–9020

Artifacts from early Love County history, including Civil War artillery, original barber chair and pole and genealogical research center.

Marlow

Marlow Area Museum

127 W Main, Marlow, Oklahoma, 73055 • 580/658–2212

Maud

Maud Historical Museum

127 W Main, Maud, Oklahoma 74854 • 405/374–6565

Items of city's early history are displayed within several rooms in an old drug store, still with its original soda fountain.

McAlester

Coal Miners Memorial Plaza

400 S Third, McAlester, Oklahoma 74501 • 918/421–2550

Documents the impact of the coal mining industry in early Pittsburg County. Coal Miners Wall of Memories, Carl Albert statue.

Garrard Ardeneum

500 N 5 Street, McAlester, Oklahoma 74502 • 918/423–1555

Complete collection of University of Oklahoma literary journals, other rare antiques and records. Garrard Ardeneum includes Puterbaugh Gardens.

International Order of Rainbow for Girls Temple
315 E Carl Albert, McAlester, Oklahoma 74502 • 918/423–1328

Memorabilia of Rainbow founder Reverend W. Mark Sexson. Gift Shop.

J.G. Puterbaugh House
Fifth and Adams streets, McAlester, Oklahoma 74502 • 918/423–0314

Opulent home of coal business founder.

J.J. McAlester Mansion
14 E Smith, McAlester, Oklahoma 74502 • 918/423–8620

Historic mansion with original cabin and trading post.

McAlester Building Foundation Inc.
220 E Adams, McAlester, Oklahoma 74502 • 918/423–2932

Themed rooms and hand-on displays in old high school contain Indian history, coal mining exhibit, and military hall of fame.

McAlester Scottish Rite Masonic Center
305 N Second, McAlester, Oklahoma 74501 • 918/423–6360

Lavish architecture houses a library/museum, costume room—1930 Kimball organ with more than 3,100 pipes.

Oklahoma Prisons Historical Museum
Oklahoma State Penitentiary, PO Box 97, McAlester, Oklahoma 74502 • 918/423–4700

The state's only museum about the history of prisons in Oklahoma. Numerous historical photographs, equipment, and related items.

Pittsburg County Genealogical and Historical Museum
113 E Carl Albert Parkway, McAlester, Oklahoma 74502 • 918/426–0388

Research and genealogical library, Dawes Indian rolls, mining, and Indian artifacts.

Tannehill Museum
500 W Stonewall, McAlester, Oklahoma 74501 • 918/423–5953

Firearms collection, Oklahoma State Penitentiary items, dolls, Coca Cola items, antique tools, Civil War documents.

Tobusky Indian Courthouse Museum
315 E Krebs, McAlester, Oklahoma 74502 • 918/423–8620

First courthouse in McAlester.

Medford

Grant County Museum and Historical Society

106 W Cherokee, Medford, Oklahoma 73759 • 580/395–2786

The museum features historic pictures, antique china, pioneer furniture, books, toys, and clothing found in Grant County since 1893.

Meeker

Meeker Historical Museum

510 W Carl Hubbell, Meeker, Oklahoma 74855 • 405/279–3321

Memorabilia of baseball great Carl Hubbell, hall-of-famer and left-handed "screwball" pitcher who played with the New York Giants from 1928–1943.

Meeker Historical Society and Museum

214 E Carl Hubbell, Meeker, Oklahoma 74855 • 405/279–3321

Meeker memorabilia.

Miami

Coleman Theatre

103 N Main, Miami, Oklahoma 74354 • 918/540–2425 • www.colemantheatre.org

Restored 1929 Vaudeville/movie theatre is still in operation. Lavish Spanish Mission Revival exterior and Louis XV interior.

Dobson Museum

110 "A" Street SW, Miami, Oklahoma 74354 • 918/542–5388
www.visitmiamiok.com

The museum contains Indian art, a mining display, tools, toys, and furniture.

Muskogee

Ataloa Lodge Museum

2299 Old Bacone Road, Muskogee, Oklahoma 74403 • 918/781–7283

Houses more than 20,000 pieces of traditional and contemporary Native American art, plus Civil War artifacts. Gift shop.

Five Civilized Tribes Museum

1101 Honor Heights Drive, Muskogee, Oklahoma 74401 • 918/683–1701 • www.fivetribes.org

The original Union Indian Agency building built in 1875, houses a trading post with beadwork and baskets made by members of the Five Civilized Tribes, a gallery of original art, library, print room, and artifacts from each of the tribes.

Muskogee War Memorial Park—USS Batfish

3500 Batfish Road, Muskogee, Oklahoma 74401 • 918/682–6294 • www.batfish.com

The 312-foot WWII submarine holds the record for sinking the greatest number of enemy submarines within a single patrol-three in a 72-hour period. An adjacent military museum houses artifacts from WWII through the Vietnam War.

Oklahoma Music Hall of Fame

401 S 3 Street, Muskogee, Oklahoma 74403 • 918/687–0800
www.oklahomamusichalloffame.com

The hall showcases and preserves the heritage of Oklahoma musicians.

Thomas-Foreman Home

1419 W Okmulgee, Muskogee, Oklahoma 74401 • 918/682–6938

The former home of Grant and Carolyn Foreman, two of Oklahoma's outstanding historians and world travelers, features the original furnishings, private collections, and souvenirs from trips abroad.

Three Rivers Museum

220 Elgin Street, Muskogee, Oklahoma 74401 • 918/686–6624 • www.3riversmuseum.com

The Midland Valley Depot, built in 1916, has been converted to a museum that tells the story of the settlement and development of the Three Rivers region of Northeastern Oklahoma. This eight-county area surrounds the confluence of three important rivers—the Arkansas, Grand, and Verdigris. The exhibits tell the stories of many cultures and events that shaped the history of this area.

Newkirk

Newkirk Community Historical Museum

101 S Maple, Newkirk, Oklahoma 74647 • 580/362–2377

Main emphasis of the museum is on Kay County and the Cherokee Outlet with Indian artifacts and display of an early-day frontier home.

Newkirk Heritage Center

116 N Main, Newkirk, Oklahoma 74647 • 580/362–2377

Noble

Timberlake Rose Rock Museum

419 South US–77, Noble, Oklahoma 73068 • 405/872–9838 • www.roserockmuseum.com

Dedicated to Oklahoma's official state rock, the barite rose. Rock displays, sculpture, and natural items. Gift shop.

Norman

Moore-Lindsay House Historical Museum

508 N Peters, Norman, Oklahoma 73070 • 405/321–0156 • www.normanhistorichouse.org

The 1899 Queen Anne style house contains period rooms and photographs. Special exhibits and events highlight the history of the county. Listed on National Register of Historic Places.

Firehouse Art Center

444 S Flood, Norman, Oklahoma 73069 • 405/329–4523 • www.normanfirehouse.com

A place for exploring the visual arts. Free exhibits, plus classes on pottery, painting, photography, sculpture, and jewelry-making. Housed in the remodeled and expanded Norman Firehouse #2, the Center also hosts special community events. The institution now has a second gallery: the Firehouse Interurban Campus in downtown Norman—105 W Main Street—405/292-9278.

Fred Jones Jr. Museum of Art

555 Elm Ave, Norman, Oklahoma 73019 • 405/325–3272 • www.ou.edu/fjjma

Permanent collections include American, Native American, and Contemporary art, as well as icons and photography. In 2000, the Weitzenhoffer Collection of French Impressionism was donated to the museum, including works by Degas, Monet, Renoir, and Van Gogh. The new Stuart Wing, built to house the Eugene B. Adkins Collection, opened in fall 2011.

Jacobson House Native American Arts Center

609 Chautauqua, Norman, Oklahoma 73069 • 405/366–1667 • www.jacobsonhouse.org

Home of the Native American fine arts movement, traditional and contemporary exhibitions, symposia, workshops, demonstrations, and seasonal markets.

Sam Noble Oklahoma Museum of Natural History

2401 Chautauqua, Norman, Oklahoma 73072 • 405/325–4712 • www.snomnh.ou.edu

This new 198,000 square-foot facility is home to six million artifacts, including the world's largest Apatosaurus, priceless Native American artifacts and exhibits describing Oklahoma's natural and cultural history.

Santa Fe Depot

200 S Jones, Norman, Oklahoma 73070 • 405/307–9320

Restored Santa Fe Railroad Station developed as a multi-use facility and downtown urban park. Available for rent. Listed in the National Register of Historic Places.

Sooner Theatre of Norman

101 E Main, Norman, Oklahoma 73069 • 405/321–9600 • www.soonertheatre.org

This 1929 Spanish Gothic theater was spared from the wrecking ball and is now on the National Register of Historic Places. Restored by volunteers, the theater hosts a variety of performances and films throughout the year, and is available for rent.

The Crucible LLC

110 E Tonhawa, Norman, Oklahoma 73069 • 405/579–2700 • www.thecruciblellc.com

Foundry, gallery, and sculpture garden.

Nowata

Diamond Point School

3 miles south of Nowata on SH–60 • 918/273–3146

One-room school built in 1919 and listed on the National Register of Historic Places.

J Wood Glass Mansion

324 W Delaware, Nowata, Oklahoma 74048 • 918/273–3514

Fully furnished turn-of-the-century four-story home of prominent resident. Designed by Ponca City's Marland Mansion architect.

Nowata County Courthouse

229 N Maple, Nowata, Oklahoma 74048 • 918/273–0127

Built in 1912 and listed on the National Register of Historic Places.

Nowata County Historical Museum

121 S Pine, Nowata, Oklahoma 74048 • 918/273–1191

Twenty-one rooms of Nowata County history, each with its own theme: Native American, oil boom, dental office, laundry room and more.

The Crucified Christ

208 W Delaware, Muskogee, Oklahoma 74403 • 918/273–1191

The church contains stained glass windows created in France between 1540 and 1590, and was once owned by millionaire William Randolph Hearst.

Okemah

Okfuskee County Historical Museum

407 W Broadway, Okemah, Oklahoma 74859 • 918/623–2027

Items depicting history of Okfuskee County, including tools, clothing, and utensils are housed in a 1926 Masonic Temple.

Territory Town Museum

5 miles west of Okemah on I–40, Exit 214 • 918/623–2599

Exhibits include Civil War relics, Wells Fargo items and pre-statehood artifacts.

Oklahoma City

45th Infantry Division Museum

2145 NE 36 Street, Oklahoma City, Oklahoma 73111 • 405/424–5313
www.45thdivisionmuseum.com

The history of Oklahoma's citizen-soldier is detailed from the relocation of the Five Civilized Tribes in Indian Territory through the 45th Infantry Division up to the present-day Oklahoma National Guard. It is the largest National Guard Museum in the United States. Includes outdoor exhibits of military vehicles, aircraft, and artillery pieces. Housed in a 1938 WPA armory.

American Banjo Museum

9 E Sheridan, Oklahoma City, OK 73104 • 405/604–2793 • www.americanbanjomuseum.com

This museum will soon be moving in the Spring of 2009 from downtown Guthrie to its new home in Oklahoma City's Bricktown district. Formerly known as the National Four-String Banjo Hall of Fame Museum, the museum outgrew its Guthrie quarters after the acquisition of 200 jazz age banjos from a private collection in Germany. Features the largest collection of vintage banjos on public display in the world.

99s Museum of Women Pilots

4300 Amelia Earhart Road, Oklahoma City • 405/685–9990
www.museumofwomenpilots.com

Exhibitions and archives focusing on the history of women in aviation.

Harn Homestead and 1889er Museum

1721 N Lincoln Blvd, Oklahoma City, Oklahoma 73105 • 405/235–4058
www.harnhomestead.com

Featured is a pre-statehood homestead restored by the 1889er Society, descendants of the men and women who made the Great Land Run. Located on the 10 acres is a three-story barn—an exact replica of the original—featuring a windmill piercing the roof. Hands-on programs for children. Listed on the National Register of Historic Places.

International Gymnastics Hall of Fame

Now located in the Omniplex/ Science Museum Oklahoma.
2100 NE 52 Street, Oklahoma City, OK 73111 • www.ighof.com
Omniplex number: 405–235–5600
Celebrating the athletic and artistic excellence of our gymnastics most accomplished athletes.

Jim Thorpe Museum and Oklahoma Sports Hall of Fame

4040 N Lincoln Boulevard, Oklahoma City—405/427–1400 • www.jimthorpeassoc.org

The museum encourages excellence through sports, academics, health and fitness. It also preserves the state's sports heritage, while building pride in Oklahoma in the spirit of Jim Thorpe.

Martin Park Nature Center

5000 W Memorial Road, Oklahoma City, Oklahoma 73142 • 405/755–0676

The center contains exhibits on wildlife, plants, and conservation. A 140-acre park has a total of 2 1/2 miles of self-guiding trails, some accessible to wheelchairs.

Myriad Botanical Gardens

301 W Reno, Oklahoma City, Oklahoma 73102 • 405/445–7080
www.myriadgardens.org

17–acre oasis in the heart of downtown Oklahoma City.

Museum of Osteology

10301 South Sunnylane, Oklahoma City, OK 73160 • 405/814–0006
www.museumofosteology.org

The Museum of Osteology is a unique educational experience. Focusing on the form and function of the skeletal system, this 7,000 square foot museum displays hundreds of skulls and skeletons from all corners of the world. The museum is the only one of its kind in America.

National Cowboy and Western Heritage Museum

1700 NE 63 Street, Oklahoma City, Oklahoma 73111 • 405/478–2250
www.nationalcowboymuseum.org

Showcase of the American West features renowned and rare art and artifacts. Numerous heroic-sized works on display. Contains Prosperity Junction, a 14,000 square-foot, turn-of-the-century western town, and three major exhibition galleries, museum store, and restaurant.

National Softball Hall of Fame

2801 NE 50 Street, Oklahoma City, Oklahoma 73111 • 405/424–5266 • www.asasoftball.com

The hall presents history, memorabilia, and displays on every aspect of softball. Home of the Amateur Softball Association.

Oklahoma City Museum of Art

415 Couch Drive, Oklahoma City, Oklahoma 73102 • 405/236–3100 • www.okcmoa.com

The museum features fifteen galleries, a 252-seat theater, gift shop, café, library, and education center. The museum's signature piece is the Eleanor Blake Kirkpatrick Memorial Tower created by renowned artist Dale Chihuly.

Oklahoma City National Memorial and Museum

601 N Harvey, Oklahoma City, Oklahoma 73102 • 405/235–3313 • 888/542–4673
www.oklahomacitynationalmemorial.org

The site honors the victims of the Alfred P. Murrah Federal Building bombing, and includes an Interactive Learning Museum and outdoor memorial.

Oklahoma City Zoological Park

NE 50 and Martin Luther King Avenue
2101 NE 50 Street, Oklahoma City, Oklahoma 73111 • 405/424–3344 • www.okczoo.com

Oldest zoo in the Southwest and one of the ten best in the nation. Exhibits include the Great EscApe primate habitat, Cat Forest/Lion Overlook and Oklahoma Trails exhibit. Picnic areas, rides, tours, and classes.

Oklahoma Firefighters Museum

2716 NE 50 Street, Oklahoma City, Oklahoma 73111 • 405/424–3440
www.osfa.info/muse.html

Displays relate firefighting through history, from 1730s bucket brigades to the present. Murrah Building bombing memorial is also featured.

Oklahoma Governor's Mansion

820 NE 23 Street, Oklahoma City, Oklahoma 73105 • 405/521–9211

The Dutch-Colonial style mansion, built in 1928, houses artifacts such as the silver service from the Battleship Oklahoma and a Victorian dresser and bed from Emperor Maximillian of Mexico.

Oklahoma Heritage Association—Oklahoma Hall of Fame and the Gaylord-Pickens Museum

1400 N Classen Boulevard, Oklahoma City, Oklahoma 73106 • 405/235–4458
www.oklahomaheritage.com

The association features the Oklahoma Hall of Fame, heritage galleria, and book center.

Oklahoma History Center

800 Nazh Zuhdi Drive, Oklahoma City, Oklahoma 73105 • 405/522–5248
www.okhistorycenter.org

The center includes the Oklahoma Historical Society, research library, five main exhibit halls, and the Red River Journey outdoor exhibits.

Oklahoma Railway Museum

3400 NE Grand Boulevard, Oklahoma City, OK 73111 • 405/424–8222
www.oklahomarailwaymuseum.org

The Oklahoma Railway Museum is the National Railway Historical Society's Central Oklahoma chapter. There is something for all ages, from freight cars and passenger cars to a real steam engine on display. The kids can also visit a red caboose, look forward to a visit from Thomas the Train, and see a Pullman car that once ferried earlier generations across the country.

Oklahoma State Capitol

2300 N Lincoln, Oklahoma City, Oklahoma 73105 • 405/521–3356

Neoclassic Greco-Roman architecture, murals, restored stained glass, tribal flag plaza, changing art exhibits. Only capitol in the world surrounded by working oil wells.

Science Museum Oklahoma

2100 NE 52 Street, Oklahoma City—405/602–6664 • www.science museumoklahoma.com

More than ten acres of science, technology, and education museums and attractions. Art and cultural galleries, planetarium, and OmniDome theater.

Overholser Mansion

405 NW 15 Street, Oklahoma City, Oklahoma 73103 • 405/525–5325
www.overholsermansion.org

The first mansion in Oklahoma City, built by early-day entrepreneur Henry Overholser, is of late nineteenth-century architecture with original furnishings and hand-painted, canvas-covered walls.

Red Earth Museum

6 Santa Fe Plaza, Oklahoma City, Oklahoma 73102 • 405/427–5228 • www.redearth.org

Unique educational programs and exhibitions focusing on the Native American way of life. Historical artifacts, art exhibits, hands-on exhibits, and research library.

World of Wings Pigeon Center

2300 NE 63 Street, Oklahoma City, Oklahoma 73111 • 405/478–5155
www.pigeoncenter.org

The museum houses an extensive collection of historic pigeon equipment clocks, bands, trophies, plaques, paintings, and photographs. Also included is World War I and World War II army pigeon corp equipment.

World Organization of China Painters Museum

2641 NW 10 Street, Oklahoma City, Oklahoma 73107 • 405/521–1234

Collection of hand-painted china, portraits, figurines, and other items from around the world, as well as local works. Gift shop.

Okmulgee

Orpheum Theatre

210 W 7 Street, Okmulgee, Oklahoma 74447 • 918/756–2270

A 1921 vaudeville/movie house.

Oologah

Bank of Oologah

202 Cooweescoowee Street, Oologah, Oklahoma 74053 • 918/443–2790

Restored historic 1906 bank that closed due to embezzlement. The interior and exterior are restored to the period between 1906 and 1932. All furnishings and equipment are from early statehood banking days. Original ceiling and vault.

Dog Iron Ranch and Will Rogers Birthplace

9501 E 380 Road—918/275–4201

Overlooking Lake Oologah, the relocated ranch house where Rogers was born in 1879 is elaborately restored with period furnishings. New Amish-built barn and Texas longhorn cattle. www.willrogers.com/birthplace

Oologah Historical Museum
Maple and Cooweescoowee streets, Oologah, Oklahoma 74053 • 918/443–2934
Antiques from the local area including a complete doctor's office.

Owasso
Owasso Historical Society Museum
26 S Main, Owasso, Oklahoma 74055 • 918/272–4966
Historical artifacts of local and statewide interest, periodic art displays and special exhibits.

Park Hill
Cherokee Heritage Center
21192 S Keeler Drive, Park Hill, Oklahoma 74451 • 918/456–6007
Story of the Cherokee people and the Trail of Tears related through a museum, living history villages, and summer amphitheater performances. www.cherokeeheritage.org
The Cherokee Heritage Center also features the following attractions:

Cherokee National Museum/Adams Corner
>The museum is one of the most modern facilities of its kind in America. Using state-of-the-art technology, multi-media exhibits and innovative displays, the entire Cherokee story is presented. Adams Corner is located adjacent to the museum and is a detailed reconstruction of a small crossroads community established in 1875. Gift shop.

Tsa-La-Gi Ancient Village
>A re-created 17th century Cherokee settlement is staffed by Cherokees to portray the village life of their ancestors.

George M. Murrell Home
19479 E Murrell Road, Park Hill, Oklahoma 74451 • 918/456–2751
Antebellum residence of prominent citizen George M. Murrell. Nature Trail.

Pauls Valley
Santa Fe Depot Museum
204 S Santa Fe, Pauls Valley, Oklahoma 73075 • 405/238–2244
The 1905 Depot contains railroad memorabilia, historic photos, area history items.

Toy and Action Figure Museum
111 S Chickasaw Street, Pauls Valley, Oklahoma 73075 • 405–238–6300
www.actionfiguremuseum.com
Features a comprehensive collection of pop culture toys, with an emphasis on the social and historic evolution of the action figure. The museum is also home to the Oklahoma Cartoonists Collection which salutes the state's published writers and artists from the comics field. Action Figure Hall of Fame, exhibit on toymaking, and gift shop.

Washita Valley Museum

Wacker Park, Ash Street, Building 101, Pauls Valley, Oklahoma 73075 • 405/238–3048

Items pertaining to the early pioneer lifestyle of the Garvin County people. Also included are the artifacts of the Washita River people.

Pawhuska

Cathedral of the Osage

1314 N Lynn Avenue, Pawhuska, Oklahoma 74056 • 918/287–1414

Church originally built in 1887, known for its rare stained glass windows. This French Gothic-style church was the principal church of the Osage tribe.

Historic Constantine Center

110 W Main, Pawhuska, Oklahoma—74056 • 918/287–1992

Greek-style theater.

Osage County Historical Museum

700 N Lynn Avenue, Pawhuska, Oklahoma 74056 • 918/287–9119
www.osagecohistoricalmuseum.com

Historical, Indian, pioneer, and Western artifacts include a monument to America's first Boy Scout troop established in 1909. Included are two railroad cars, a gazebo and schoolhouse.

Osage Tribal Museum

819 N Grandview Avenue, Pawhuska, Oklahoma 74056 • 918/287–5441
www.visittheosage.com

Osage culture from the 1600s to present is exhibited, Osage art and culture workshops, outreach programs, archives and photo collections. Gift shop.

Pawnee

Historic Indian Agency Monument

1 mile East on Agency Road, Pawnee, Oklahoma 74058 • 918/762–3621

Honors original tribal leaders.

Historic Pawnee Lake Bathhouse

1 mile North on SH–18, Pawnee, Oklahoma 74058 • 918/762–2658

Overlooks Pawnee lake, carved from native stone by the WPA in 1939.

Pawnee Bill Museum and Ranch

1141 Pawnee Bill Road, Pawnee, Oklahoma 74058 • 918/762–2513

Pawnee Bill's 1908 home and museum is filled with his personal effects and mementos from the famous Pawnee Bill Wild West Show. Added attractions are an enormous original billboard, a blacksmith shop, log cabin, picnic area, and a drive-through buffalo pasture.

Pawnee County Historical & Dick Tracy Museum

513 6 Street, Pawnee, Oklahoma 74058 • 918/762–4681 • www.pawneechs.org

Focuses on the Pawnee community and Pawnee Tribe as well as surrounding region. Artifacts from area ghost towns. Section dedicated to Chester Gould, Pawnee native and creator of Dick Tracy comic strip.

Pensacola

Civil War Monument/Second Battle of Cabin Creek

3 miles north of Pensacola off SH–28, Pensacola, Oklahoma 74301

Twelve-acre Civil War battle site features granite monument and markers that tell the story of this 1862 Confederate victory.

Perkins

Dave Sasser Memorial Museum

202 E Thomas, Perkins, Oklahoma 74059

Pioneer life in the Cimarron Valley.

Perry

Cherokee Strip Museum/Rose Hill School

2617 W Fir Avenue, Perry, Oklahoma 73077 • 580/336–2405 • cherokee-strip-museum.org

Located on five acres, the museum complex traces the history of the Cherokee Outlet and its people. The 1895 school offers 1910 curriculum classes September through May.

Heritage Center and Ditch Witch Museum

6 Street, Perry, Oklahoma 73077 • 580/336–4402

The museum showcases the history of Ditch Witch equipment.

IOOF Grand Lodge of Oklahoma

615 Delaware, Perry, Oklahoma 73077 • 580/336–4076

The state headquarters of the Independent Order of Odd Fellows. Built in 1894, the building is listed on the National Register of Historic Places.

Jim Franklin Studio

602 E Cedar, Perry, Oklahoma 73077 • 580/336–6572
www.jimfranklinsculpture.com

Award-winning sculptor shows the process involved in creating his art pieces.

Piedmont

Piedmont Historical Museum

101 Monroe, Piedmont, Oklahoma 73078 • 405/373–1424
www.piedmonthistoricalsociety.org

Artifacts of Piedmont, area families and businesses including Wiedemann's Old Store from the early 1900s.

Ponca City

Cann Memorial Botanical Gardens

1500 E Grand, Ponca City, Oklahoma 74604 • 580/767–0430

Winding paths guide visitors through herb gardens, native grasses, arbors, sundials, and a reflection pond, all surrounding a circa 1908 home.

Conoco Museum

501 W South Avenue, Ponca City, Oklahoma 74601 • 580/765–8687
www.conocomuseum.com

Covers the heritage of Conoco, the history of the Ponca City Refinery, and the award-winning marketing campaigns of the brand.

Marland Mansion/Marland Oil Museum

901 Monument Road, Ponca City, Oklahoma 74604 • 580/767–0420
www.marlandmansion.com

The home of pioneer oilman, philanthropist, Congressman, and 10th Governor of Oklahoma E.W. Marland, is listed on the National Register of Historic Places. The elegant 55-room mansion is copied from the Florentine estates of the Italian Renaissance and houses the National Petroleum Hall of Fame.

Matzene Art Collection

515 E Grand, Ponca City, Oklahoma 74604 • 580/767–0339

The collection features Chinese and Western art.

Pioneer Woman Statue and Museum

701 Monument Road, Ponca City, Oklahoma 74604 • 580/765–6108
www.pioneerwomanmuseum.com

This 17-foot bronze statue is a memorial to the courage of thousands of women who suffered hardships to create homes in untried lands. Adjacent to the statue is the museum which houses exhibits of antique household furniture, equipment, costumes, and memorabilia. Gift shop.

Ponca City Art Center

819 E Central Avenue, Ponca City, Oklahoma 74601 • 580/765–9746

Work of artists is housed in 1925 mansion with lavish walnut woodwork, beveled glass and terrazzo tile floor.

Poncan Theatre

104 E Grand, Ponca City, Oklahoma 74601 • 580/765–0943 • www.poncantheatre.org

Restored 1927 Vaudeville palace is one of the few remaining examples of once-famous "atmospheric theaters." Ornate interior, elaborate ceilings, stained glass.

Poteau

Robert S. Kerr Museum & Conference Center

6 miles southwest of Poteau on US–270 • 918/647–8221

Founder of the internationally known Kerr-McGee Corporation, first native governor of Oklahoma, powerful U.S. Senator and devout conservationist, Robert S. Kerr constructed this home to exemplify the unique blend of man-made materials with natural surroundings. It is divided into two sections–a conference center, available for public use, and a museum that depicts the history and development of eastern Oklahoma.

Prague

National Shrine of the Infant Jesus of Prague

4th & Jim Thorpe Boulevard, Prague, Oklahoma 74864 • 405/567–3080
www.shrineofinfantjesus.com

When the 300-year-old Shrine of the Divine Infant Jesus of Prague, Czechoslovakia, fell behind the Iron Curtain, this shrine was established in the Catholic church in Prague, Oklahoma.

Prague Historical Museum

1008 N Jim Thorpe Boulevard, Prague, Oklahoma 74864 • 405/567–4750

Shows the history of development of the Prague area and the Czechoslovakian people who started the city in 1902, also features a military room and memorabilia and information since the Land Run of 1891. Prague is the birthplace of Jim Thorpe.

Pryor

Coo-Y-Yah County Museum

847 S Mill, Pryor, Oklahoma 74361 • 918/825–2575

Katy Depot houses Cherokee and Osage artifacts and art, local history items, rare salt-glazed pottery collection, and 1800s printing press.

Purcell

McClain County Museum

203 W Washington Street, Purcell, Oklahoma 73080 • 405/527–5894

Eleven different theme rooms feature artifacts pertaining to McClain County history including family historical records, photographs, and genealogy rooms.

Ralston

White Hair Memorial

1/2 mile south of SH–20, Ralston, Oklahoma 74650 • 918/538–2417

Circa 1920s home of Osage Lillie Morrell Burkhart is now a resource learning center for Osage tribal culture and heritage.

Ripley

Washington Irving Trail Museum

3918 S Mehan Road, Ripley, Oklahoma 74062 • 405/624–9130

www.washintonirvingtrailmuseum.com

Chronicles area's heritage, including the 1832 tour by Washington Irving, who documented the journey in his book *A Tour on the Prairies*. Military exhibits, Billy McGinty exhibit, pioneer and American Indian artifacts.

Salina

Chouteau Memorial Museum

420 W Ferry Street, Salina, Oklahoma 74365 • 918/434–2224

History of the fur trade from the 1790s to 1830s is presented, emphasizing the Chouteau family and their impact on Indian Territory and the Three Forks of the Arkansas River.

Sallisaw

Dwight Presbyterian Mission

Northeast of Vian, I–40 and Dwight Mission Road Exit, Vian, Oklahoma 74962
918/775–2018

The 1829 cabin was first mission in Oklahoma, now on vocational school campus. Original items include printing equipment used by Sequoyah.

14 Flags Museum

400 E Cherokee, Sallisaw, Oklahoma 74955 • 918/775–2608

Oklahoma's history under 14 different nations. Recreated general store—1800s cabin, caboose, cattle brand collection. Log cabins built before 1845.

Sequoyah's Cabin

7 miles east of Sallisaw on SH–101, Sallisaw, Oklahoma 74955 • 918/775–2413

The home of Sequoyah, inventor of the Cherokee alphabet, was constructed in 1829 and is listed on the National Register of Historic Places. Cherokee history and the basics of Cherokee language are taught to visitors.

Sand Springs

Sand Springs Historical and Cultural Museum

Page Memorial Library—9 East Broadway, Sand Springs, Oklahoma 74063 • 918/246–2509

Housed in art deco 1930 library, rotating exhibits focus on area history, natural history, archaeology, and art.

Sapulpa

Sapulpa Historical Museum

100 E Lee, Sapulpa, Oklahoma 74066 • 918/224–4871

Displays housed in 1910 YWCA building include an 1890s kitchen, country school room, telephone exhibit, music room, Frisco railroad items and more.

Sayre

RS & K Railroad Museum

411 N 6 Street, Sayre, Oklahoma 73662 • 580/928–3525

More than 250 model trains in several gauges, operating model railroad accommodates more than 10 trains at once. Railroad memorabilia.

Shortgrass Country Museum

106 E Poplar, Sayre, Oklahoma 73662 • 580/928–5757

Changing displays of early-day life in western Oklahoma's shortgrass country.

Seminole

Jasmine Moran Children's Museum

1714 W Wrangler, Seminole, Oklahoma 74868 • 405/382–0950

Hands-on museum featuring an entire town including a courthouse, dentist's office, grocery store, fire department, a television studio and more. Geared for children ages three to 12.

Seminole Area Oil and Historical Museum

1800 Wrangler, Seminole, Oklahoma 74868 • 405/382–1500

Collection of antique woodworking tools, farm machinery and equipment—1926 dental x-ray machine, historic photographs, changing exhibits.

Shattuck

Ellis County Servicemen's Memorial

520 S Main, Shattuck, Oklahoma 73858 • 580/938–2025

The memorial pays tribute to Ellis County veterans.

Time Line Murals

101 S Main, Shattuck, Oklahoma 73858 • 580/938–5104

Located in the Stewart Memorial Building, these murals depict the history of Shattuck.

Windmill Museum and Park

120 E 11 Street, Shattuck, Oklahoma 73858 • 580/938–5291
www.shattuckwindmillmuseum.org

Outdoor display of rare and restored mills from 1850–1950 illustrate the impact of water and wind on the development of the high plains.

Shawnee

Citizen Potawatomi Nation Heritage Center

1901 S Gordon Cooper Drive, Shawnee, Oklahoma 74801 • 405/878–5830
www.potawatomi.org

Pictures, artifacts, including handmade items and paintings by Indian artists.

Mabee-Gerrer Museum of Art

1900 W MacArthur Drive, Shawnee, Oklahoma 74801 • 405/878–5300
www.mgmoa.org

European paintings from the year 1300 to present are on display, as well as 19th and 20th century American paintings and sculpture, Greco-Roman, Oriental, East African, Oceanic, Egyptian, and American Indian collections. Two mummies are displayed, as well as more than 500 artifacts from Egyptian tombs.

Pottawatomie County Museum

614 E Main, Shawnee, Oklahoma 74801 • 405/275–8412

Numerous artifacts housed in photogenic depot of Bedford stone. Unique architecture resembles a Scottish lighthouse.

Townsend's Classic and Antique Auto Museum

8901 N Harrison, Shawnee, Oklahoma 74801 • 405/275–0330

Antique and classic cars from 1906 to 1938, autos owned by Mae West, Elvis Presley, and Sammy Davis Jr. on display.

Skiatook

Skiatook Museum

115 S Broadway, Skiatook, Oklahoma 74070 • 918/396–7558

Housed in a 1912 home of a local physician, displays Civil War artifacts from the Bird Creek Basin and Quapaw Creek depict life in the area.

Spiro

Spiro Historical Society Museum

216 S Main Street, Spiro, Oklahoma 74959 • 918/962–5321 or 962–2708

First printing press from local newspaper, telephone switchboard, early electric appliances, horse-drawn farm implements and other memorabilia from the area.

Spiro Mounds Archaeological State Park

11 miles northeast of Spiro on Lock & Dam Road, Spiro, Oklahoma 74959 • 918/962–2062

The state's only archaeological park features artifacts from the lives and cultures of prehistoric Indians discovered through the excavation of burial mounds in the 1930s.

Stigler

Haskell County Historical Museum

204 E Main, Stigler, Oklahoma 74462 • 918/967–2161

Stillwater

National Wrestling Hall of Fame

405 W Hall of Fame Avenue, Stillwater, Oklahoma 74075 • 405/377–5243
www.wrestlinghalloffame.org

The nation's only museum dedicated to the sport of amateur wrestling. It contains the Wall of Champions and the Museum of Wrestling History as well as the national offices of USA Wrestling.

Pfeiffer Farm Collection

Payne County Fairgrounds—3 miles east of Stillwater on SH–51
4518 Expo Circle East, Stillwater, Oklahoma 74075 • 405/377–1275

The museum features a fascinating collection of antique farm machinery and equipment.

Sheerar Cultural and Historical Museum

702 S Duncan, Stillwater, Oklahoma 74074 • 405/377–0359 • www.sheerarmuseum.org

Permanent exhibits illustrate area history. Sheerar button collection contains some 4,000 buttons from the 1740s to 1930s.

Stillwater Airport Memorial Museum

2020 W Airport Road, Stillwater, Oklahoma 74075 • 405/372–7881

The museum features pictures and artifacts from the first plane landing in Stillwater in 1918 to present day.

Stilwell

Little Log Cabin on the Farm

2 miles west of city on SH–100W, Stilwell, Oklahoma 74960 • 918/696–2249

Pioneer-style cedar cabin, demonstrations of lye soap-making, cooking, needlework, and sewing.

Sulphur

Arbuckle Historical Museum

402 W Muskogee, Sulphur, Oklahoma 73086 • 580/622–5593 • www.ahsmc.org

Focuses on history of the Chickasaw, mineral springs, the former Platt National Park, and early ranch life.

Chickasaw Cultural Center

867 Charles Cooper Memorial Road, Sulphur, Oklahoma 73086 • 580/622–7130
www.chickasawculturalcenter.com

The center is nestled on 109 acres of beautiful Chickasaw territory in Sulphur. The sprawling campus features state-of-the-art exhibit buildings, outdoor gatherings, a theater, cafe, and a historically accurate village that takes you back in time to native Chickasaw villages.

National Museum of Horse Shoeing Tools

8 miles north of city on SH–7, Sulphur, Oklahoma 73086 • 580/622–4644
www.horseshoeingmuseum.com

The museum features tools and other products that make up the horse-shoer's world.

Tahlequah

Old Cherokee National Capitol

101 S Muskogee Avenue, Tahlequah, Oklahoma 74464

Listed on the National Register of Historic places, this building served as the meeting place for the Cherokee government. Built in 1870.

Taloga

Dewey County Jail House Museum

West Riggs and Cheney, Taloga, Oklahoma 73667 • 580/328–5558

Original circa 1920s jail, restored sheriff's office, photographs of Dewey County sheriffs since 1892, outlaw items. Appointment only.

Tecumseh

Tecumseh Historical Museum

114 S Broadway, Tecumseh, Oklahoma 74873 • 405/598–2397

The museum features artifacts relating to the town's history.

Tishomingo

Chickasaw Bank Museum

413 W Main, Tishomingo, Oklahoma 73460 • 580/371–3141

Interior has been restored to original bank facility used by the Chickasaw Tribe during the early 1900s.

Chickasaw Council House Museum

209 North Fisher, Tishomingo, Oklahoma 73460 • 580/371–3351

The original log council house, built in 1855, was the first capitol of the Chickasaws after their removal to Indian Territory. Exhibits highlight the culture of the Chickasaw tribe from 1540 to present, and features a genealogy research center.

Tonkawa

A.D. Buck Museum of Science and History

1220 E Grand Street, Tonkawa, Oklahoma 74653 • 580/628–3318

Photograph collections of oil field days and history of Northern Oklahoma College.

McCarter Museum of Tonkawa History

220 E Grand, Tonkawa, Oklahoma 74653 • 580/628–2895

The museum features photographs and other artifacts relating to pioneer living, World War III German POW camp and other historical events.

Tonkawa Tribal Museum

36 Cisco Drive, Tonkawa, Oklahoma 74653 • 580/628–5301

Artifacts, photographic history of the Tonkawa tribe, including original allotment records, items from Southwestern and Northern tribes. Nez Perce cemetery nearby.

Tulsa

Alexandre Hogue Gallery of Art

2905 E 5 Street, Tulsa, Oklahoma 74104 • 918/631–2202

The gallery presents showings of traveling art collections and featured works by local artists, including photography and design, cultural and ethnic exhibitions.

Creek Nation Council Oak Park

1750 S Cheyenne Avenue, Tulsa, Oklahoma 74114 • 918/596–7275

Known as "Tulsa's First City Hall," this historic landmark was the site in 1828 where the first contingent of Creek Indians, upon arriving in Indian Territory, spread their ashes from the fire of Tallassee, their mother town in Alabama, from which the modern name of Tulsa was derived.

Elsing Museum

7777 S Lewis, Tulsa, Oklahoma 74137 • 918/495–6262

Sixty-year collection of rare and beautiful precious gems, minerals, crystals, and stones. Four-foot jade sculpture, Indian relics.

Geoscience Center

610 S Main Street, Suite 300, Tulsa, Oklahoma 74137 • 918/392–4556

Educational learning center especially for children. More than 25 interactive exhibits encourage self-discovery.

Gilcrease Museum

1400 Gilcrease Museum Road, Tulsa, Oklahoma 74127 • 918/596–2700 • www.gilcrease.org

This national treasury is one of the world's outstanding museum and research facilities. Collections of art, artifacts, rare books, and documents illustrate the development of North America from the pre-Columbian era through the 19th century. The collection features paintings by major American artists Gilbert Stuart, Winslow Homer, John Singleton Copley, John Singer Sargent, Thomas Eakins, John James Audubon, James A.M. Whistler, Frederic Remington, Charles Russell, Albert Bierstad, George Catlin, William R. Leigh, Thomas Moran and Olaf Carl Seltzer.

Greenwood Cultural Center

322 N Greenwood Avenue, Tulsa, Oklahoma 74120 • 918/596–1020
www.greenwoodculturalcenter.com

Located in the historic Greenwood district, once known as the "Black Wall Street" of America. Location of the Jazz Hall of Fame and Mable B. Little Heritage Center, photographic exhibit of the tragic 1921 riot. Music, books, memorabilia, and gift shop.

Harwelden Mansion

2210 S Main Street, Tulsa, Oklahoma 74114 • 918/584–3333 • www.harweldenmansion.com

Once home to oil baron Earl Palmer Harwell, Harwelden is a 30-room, four-level Tudor Gothic mansion. It houses the Arts and Humanities Council of Tulsa. Situated in Maple Ridge, one of the National Historic Districts, Harwelden is listed on the National Register of Historic Places.

Ida Dennie Willis Museum

628 N Country Club, Tulsa, Oklahoma 74127 • 918/584–6654

The museum, housed in a 1910 Tudor-style mansion, features trains, robots, and more than 1,000 dolls.

International Linen Registry Museum

4107 S Yale, Promenade Mall, Tulsa, Oklahoma 74136 • 918/622–5223

Ancient linens from around the world are displayed. Demonstrations and seminars of various types of needle and textile arts available.

Municipal Rose Garden

2435 S Peoria, Tulsa, Oklahoma 74114 • 918/746–5125

The garden features over 9,000 rose bushes and the All-American Rose Society Test Garden.

Mac's Antique Car Museum

1319 E 4 Street, Tulsa, Oklahoma 74120 • 918/596–7400

Warehouse of more than fifty rare and vintage cars, including Rolls Royce, LaSalle, Packard, and the 1948 Hudson featured in "Driving Miss Daisy."

Oklahoma Jazz Hall of Fame

5 S Boston, Tulsa 74120 • 918/928–5299 • www.okjazz.org

Housed in historic Greenwood district, the state's only facility devoted to gospel, jazz, and blues musicians with Oklahoma ties.

Oxley Nature Center

6700 Mohawk Boulevard, Tulsa, Oklahoma 74115 • 918/669–6644
www.oxleynaturecenter.org

Houses numerous hands-on exhibits of area plants and animals and is situated on an 800-acre tract threaded with nature trails for exploring. Includes a working beehive.

Philbrook Museum of Art

2727 S Rockford Road, Tulsa, Oklahoma 74152 • 918/749–7941 • www.philbrook.org

The beautiful mansion, styled after an Italian Renaissance villa, was built in 1929 as the home of oilman Waite Phillips amid the 23 acres of formal landscaped gardens. Featured is the Samuel H. Kress collection of Italian Renaissance paintings and sculpture, a major collection of contemporary Indian paintings, collections of Indian pottery, basketry, and artifacts, and 20th century American art. The museum has opened a new downtown gallery at 116 East Brady Street.

Sherwin Miller Museum of Jewish Art

2021 E 71 Street, Tulsa, Oklahoma 74136 • 918/492–1818 • www.jewishmuseum.net

The Southwest's largest collection of Judaica is housed in this museum. It contains objects reflecting the history, art, and customs of the Jewish faith. The exhibits span the period from 2,000 B.C. to the present and have been collected from Poland, Germany, Spain, Russia, Morocco, India, and Persia, reflecting ethnic and national traditions. The facility also houses the Kaiser Museum of the Holocaust.

Tulsa Air and Space Center

3624 N 74 E Avenue, Tulsa, Oklahoma—918/834–9900
www.tulsaairandspacemuseum.org

A center for aviation and space discovery, educational and industry awareness that features flight simulators, exhibits, interactive displays, video presentations, library resources, NASA exhibits, rare aircraft displays and a Hall of Honor.

Tulsa Garden Center

2435 S Peoria, Tulsa, Oklahoma 74114 • 918/746–5125
www.tulsagardencenter.com

1919 mansion and conservatory is part of the Woodward Park complex, a forty-plus acre urban forest with WPA features and numerous gardens. Gift shop.

Tulsa Historical Society Museum

2445 S Peoria, Tulsa, Oklahoma, 74114–1326 • 918/712–9484 • www.tulsahistory.org

The historic Samuel Travis mansion in Woodward Park has been renovated and expanded to serve as the new home of this repository of the city's history. The museum features exhibits of early Tulsa history. The collections are open to researchers by appointment.

Tulsa Zoo and Living Museum

6421 E 36 Street North, Tulsa, Oklahoma 74115 • 918/669–6600 • www.tulsazoo.org

The Tulsa Zoo is located in Mohawk Park, a 2,800–acre tract of natural woodland representing one of the largest city-owned U.S. parks. Zoological park includes a zoo with 800 animals on display, the children's zoo, and the Robert J. LaFortune North American Living Museum. Voted America's Favorite Zoo.

Tuskahoma

Choctaw Nation Museum

2 miles north of US–271, Tuskahoma, Oklahoma 74574 • 918/569–4465

Built in 1884, the building was once the capitol of the Choctaw Nation and now houses Choctaw artifacts, paintings, and photographs. Gift shop.

Vinita

Cabin Creek Civil War Battle Site

918/256–7133 • www.vinita.com

Eastern Trails Museum

215 W Illinois, Vinita, Oklahoma 74301 • 918/256–2115

Re-created post office, general store, printing office, doctor's office, Indian history, train, and military items.

Wagoner

Wagoner City Historical Museum

122 S Main Street, Wagoner, Oklahoma 74467 • 918/485–9111

Historic fashions from pre-Civil War, Indian Territory items and local memorabilia.

Wakita

Twister Museum

101 W Main, Wakita, Oklahoma 73771 • 580/594–2312

The museum features behind-the-scenes photographs, debris, and other memorabilia from the 1996 hit movie Twister.

Walters

Cotton County Museum

116 N Broadway, Walters, Oklahoma 73572 • 580/875–3335

Donations from local residents, interesting tools, housewares, medical equipment, cook-stoves, typewriters, pianos, etc.

Walters 1920 Rock Island Depot

220 W Nevada, Walters, Oklahoma 73572 • 580/875–2384

Rock Island depot features Comanche artist's fresco paintings documenting the history of the area.

Warner

Wallis Museum at Connors State College

Route 1, Box 571, Warner, Oklahoma 74469 • 918/463–2931

Fossils, minerals, and other geological artifacts, WW I and frontier-era items. Some American Indian artifacts.

Watonga

T.B. Ferguson Home

519 N Weigel, Watonga, Oklahoma 73772 • 580/623–5069

The mansion of Thomas Benton Ferguson, pioneer newspaperman and Oklahoma's sixth Territorial Governor. Displays interpret the life and influence of Ferguson. Also includes an 1870 remount station and 1893 jail.

Waurika

Chisholm Trail Historical Museum

At Hwy 70 & 81, Waurika, Oklahoma 73573 • 580/228–2166

History of the Chisholm Trail featuring a Pioneer Room, full-size covered wagon and video.

Rock Island Depot

98 Meridian Street, Waurika, Oklahoma 73573 • 580/228–3274

Restored 1912 depot features Italian marble floors and original ticket office. Houses artifact room with railroad memorabilia.

Waynoka

Waynoka Historical Museum

1383 S Cleveland, Waynoka, Oklahoma 73860 • 580/824–1886 • www.waynoka.org

Transcontinental Air Transport exhibits, Santa Fe Railway and Harvey House memorabilia and numerous other historical items.

Weatherford

Stafford Air and Space Museum

3000 Logan Road, Weatherford, Oklahoma 73096 • 580/772–5871
www.staffordmuseum.com

General Thomas P. Stafford was commander of Apollo 10 in May 1969, first flight of the lunar module to the moon. Previously he piloted Gemini VI, the first space rendezvous. The museum also has full-size replicas of the Wright Flyer, Sprit of St. Louis, and more.

Wewoka

Seminole Nation Museum

524 S Wewoka Avenue, Wewoka, Oklahoma 74884 • 405/257–5580
www.theseminolenationmuseum.org

Focuses on the people of Seminole County, including American Indians and Freedmen. Pioneer wing, military room, art gallery, library, and gift shop.

The Whipping Tree

Wewoka Avenue, Seminole county Courthouse lawn.

The Seminoles punished their criminals at this spot from 1856 to statehood.

Wilburton

Lutie Coal Miner's Museum

2 1/2 miles east on US–270, Wilburton, Oklahoma 74578 • 918/465–2216

Displays of mining artifacts housed in coal mining house with furnishings dating from 1880 to 1930.

Robbers Cave Nature Center

SH–2, Robbers Cave State Park, Wilburton, Oklahoma 74578 • 918/465–2565

Refurbished CCC bathhouse and exhibits about Native American history, natural history, and the environment. Gift shop.

Veteran's Museum

9 miles south on SH–2, Wilburton, Oklahoma 74578 • 918/465–2607

The museum is housed in Hawk's Nest, the log cabin built by Col. Hawk who started a colony with veterans of the Spanish-American War.

Woodward

Fort Supply Historic Site

1 William Key Boulevard, Fort Supply, Oklahoma 73841 • 580/256–6136

Frontier Army fort from 1868–1895 includes five historic structures and visitor center with interpretive exhibits.

Plains Indians and Pioneers Museum

2009 Williams Avenue, Woodward, Oklahoma 73801 • 580/256–6136 • www.pipm1.org

Focuses on Plains Tribes, ranching, and homesteaders. Art gallery.

Wynnewood

Eskridge Hotel Museum

114 E Robert S. Kerr, Wynnewood 73098 • 405/665–0894

Constructed in 1907, the hotel is virtually unchanged in architecture.

Yale

Jim Thorpe Home

706 E Boston, Yale, Oklahoma 74085 • 918/387–2815 • www.jimthorpehome.com

Home of the legendary Olympian who lived here from 1917–1923. Track and field awards and family items are on display.

Yukon

Yukon's Best Railroad Museum

1020 West Oak, Third and Main, Yukon, Oklahoma 73099 • 405/354–5079

Static display of caboose and rail cars contains Rock Island antiques and artifacts, and general rail items. Also features a Route 66 exhibit. Old Interurban Depot nearby.

Yukon Historical Society Museum and Art Center

601 Oak, Yukon, Oklahoma 73099 • 405/350–7810

Museum is located in the Old Central School building, constructed in 1910. Exhibits include scale models of Dr. Goodman's office, old drug store and soda fountain with apothecary, and early day post office. Also featured: a "Yukon's Best" flour mill history, and Mulvey's Mercantile display built in 1903.

Historical Markers in Oklahoma

For a more complete listing of historical markers, go to www.okhistory.org/sites/markerresults.

Name	County	Name	County
Ardmore Air Crash	Carter	Bull Foot Station	Kingfisher
Ardmore Army Air Field	Carter	Burney Institute	Marshall
Atoka	Atoka	Butterfield Overland Mail Rt.	LeFlore
B.B. McKinney Cabin	Murray	Cabin Creek Battle Field	Mayes
Bake Oven	Muskogee	California Road	Roger Mills
Baker's Ranch	Kingfisher	California Trail	McClain
Baptist Mission	Adair	Camp Supply	Woodward
Barnes-Stevenson House	McCurtain	Camp Leavenworth	Marshall
Battle of Backbone Mountain	LeFlore	Camp Comanche	Caddo
Battle of Honey Springs	Muskogee	Camp Radziminski	Kiowa
Battle of Round Mountain	Tulsa	Camp Tonkawa POW Camp	Kay
Battle of the Washita	Roger Mills	Camp Arbuckle	McClain
Battle of Chusto-Talash	Tulsa	Cantonment	Blaine
Battle of Turkey Springs	Woods	Canute	Washita
Battle of Chustenahlah	Osage	Carl Albert	Pittsburg
Battle Wichita Village	Grady	Carnegie Library	Logan
Battle of Locust Grove	Mayes	Carr-Bartles Mill	Washington
Battle of Cabin Creek	Mayes	Carry A. Nation	Dewey
Beecham Cemetery Marker	Canadian	Civilian Conservation Corps (CCC)— Lake Murray State Park	Carter
Bernard de la Harpe 1719	Latimer	CCC—Osage Mountain	Osage
Big Pasture	Tillman	CCC—Quartz Mountain State Park	Kiowa
Bill Dalton Killing	Carter	CCC—Robbers Cave State Park	Latimer
Birthplace of Jim Thorpe	Lincoln	Central State College	Oklahoma
Birthplace of Univ. of Okla.	Cleveland	Chahta Tamaha	Bryan
Birthplace of the State of OK	McClain	Charleston	Harper
Black Beaver	Caddo	Cherokee Strip	Garfield
Black Iron Fountain	Kay	Cherokee National Cemetery	Muskogee
Blackburn's Station	Pittsburgh	Cherokee-Seneca Boundary	Delaware
Bloomfield	Bryan	Cheyenne-Arapaho Cattle Ranch	Custer
Blue Bell Bar	Logan	Chickasaw Council House	Johnston
Boggy Station	Atoka	Chickasaw Trail of Tears	McCurtain
Boley, Town of	Okfuskee	Chief Bugler's Grave	Kiowa
Booth No. One	Payne	Chief Joseph	Kay
Boudinot, Elias	Cherokee	Chief Mosholatubbee	LeFlore
Boundary Line 1889 & 1893	Payne	Chief Pushmataha	Wagoner
Brooks Opera House	Logan	Chief Roman Nose	Blaine
Buffalo Springs	Garfield		

Historical Markers in Oklahoma

Name	County	Name	County
Chief Stumbling Bear Pass	Comanche	Doaksville	Choctaw
Chief's Old House	Choctaw	Doan's Crossing	Tillman
Chilocco Indian School	Kay	Dodge City Trail	Dewey
Chisholm Trail	Kingfisher	Dorothy Jean Orton	Choctaw
Chisholm Trail	Canadian	Drummond Home	Osage
Chitto Harjo's Creek Patriot	McCurtain	Durant	Bryan
Choctaw Agency	LeFlore	Dwight Mission	Sequoyah
Choctaw Capitol	Pushmataha	Eagletown	McCurtain
Choctaw Nation Capitol Bldg.	Pushmataha	Eaves-Brady Log Cabin	Carter
Choctaw Chief's House	Choctaw	Edmond Pickens	Love
Chouteau's Post	Mayes	Edward's Store	Latimer
Civil War 10 Pounder	Oklahoma	Elias Boudinot	Cherokee
Claremore Mound	Rogers	Elliott Academy	McCurtain
Clear Creek Water Mill	McCurtain	Emahaka Mission	Seminole
Cleveland-Pioneer Oil City	Osage	Empire of Greer	Beckham
Cloud Chief Courthouse	Washita	Entering Indian Territory	Sequoyah
Cloud Creek Marker	Washita	Entering Indian Territory	Ottawa
Colbert Family	Bryan	Euchee	Creek
Colbert's Ferry	Bryan	Fairfield Mission	Adair
Coleman Theatre	Ottawa	First Military Road	LeFlore
Colony	Washita	First Rural Mail Route	Kingfisher
Comanche Indian Mission	Comanche	First Cultivated Tree	Oklahoma
Confederate Cemetery	Atoka	First Gas Processing Plant West of the Mississippi	Tulsa
Constitutional Convention	Logan	First Hospital/Tulsa County	Tulsa
Cordell Academy	Washita	First Shelterbelt	Greer
Corn	Washita	First Tornado Forecast	Oklahoma
Coronado	Beaver	First Town Site of Marshall	Logan
Council Grove School	Oklahoma	Fisher's Station	Osage
Cowboy Hill	Kay	Fort Cobb	Caddo
Creek Capitol	Okmulgee	Fort Arbuckle	Garvin
Creek Council Ground	McIntosh	Fort Davis	Muskogee
Creek Council Oak	Tulsa	Fort Coffee	LeFlore
Custer's Rendezvous	Kiowa	Fort Cobb	Caddo
Cutthroat Gap Massacre	Pittsburg	Fort Dodge-Camp Supply Trail	Harper
Dalton Cave	Creek	Fort Washita	Bryan
Darlington	Canadian	Fort Towson	Choctaw
Dave Blue Trading Post	Cleveland	Fort Arbuckle	Tulsa
Delaware Mount	Pontotoc	Fort Gibson	Muskogee
Delmar Gardens	Oklahoma	Fort Towson	Choctaw

Historical Markers in Oklahoma

Name	County	Name	County
Fort Washita	Bryan	Jabbok Orphange & School	Custer
Fort Wayne	Delaware	Jackson Barnett Well #11	Creek
Fort Sill Indian School	Comanche	James Bigheart	Osage
Ft.Smith/Ft. Towson Military Road	LeFlore	James C. Nance Bridge	McClain
Fort Holmes	Hughes	Jean Pierre Chouteau Bridge	Mayes
Fort McCulloch	Bryan	Jim Thorpe	Payne
Fort Nichols	Cimarron	Jim Thorpe Birthplace No.1	Lincoln
Fort Reno	Canadian	Joseph Bradfield Thoburn	Oklahoma
Fountain Church	Muskogee	Kiamichi Baptist Assembly	LeFlore
Frank A. Phillips Home	Washington	Kickingbird	Oklahoma
Friendship School	Jackson	King Charles II Charter	Oklahoma
Gardner Mansion	McCurtain	La Harpe's Council	Muskogee
Garland Cemetery	McCurtain	Lake Creek Marker	Greer
Geary's Station	Atoka	Lake Murray Lodge	Carter/Love
George C. Sibley Expedition	Alfalfa	Last Boomer Town	Payne
Gift of John Kirkpatrick	Canadian	Leroy Gordon Cooper	Pottawatomie
Glen Pool World Greatest Oil	Tulsa	Liberty Bell Replica	Oklahoma
Goodland Mission	Choctaw	Locomotive 1108	Carter
Goodwater Choctaw Mission	Choctaw	Locomotive 1615	Jackson
Governor Cyrus Harris	Murray	Love County Courthouse	Love
Grand	Ellis	Magnolia	McCurtain
Great Western Traill	Dewey	March of the Dragoons	Cleveland
Green Corn Dance	McIntosh	Marland's Grand Home	Kay
Guthrie	Logan	Massacre of Pat Hennessey	Kingfisher
Harris House	McCurtain	Millie Durgan	Kiowa
Harris Mill Cemetery	McCurtain	Million Dollar Elm	Osage
Healdton Oil Museum	Carter	Modoc Cemetery	Ottawa
Hillside Mission	Tulsa	Mormon Battalion	Cimarron
Historical Society Birthplace	Kingfisher	Mt. Zion Baptist Church	Tulsa
Holloway's Station	Latimer	Murray-Lindsay Mansion	Garvin
Home on the Range-Dr. Higley	Pottawatomie	Nail's Crossing	Bryan
Hochatown	McCurtain	Naked Head	McIntosh
Hughes Ranch	LeFlore	Nathan Boone	Woods
Hwy-OK	Beckham	Natural Mound	Pontotoc
Indian Baseline Monument	Stephens	No Man's Land	Beaver
Initial Point/Indian Meridian	Carter	Norman's Camp	Cleveland
International Oil Expedition	Tulsa	Oil in the Cushing-Drumright Area	Payne
Interstate Oil Co. Commission	Kay	Oklahoma City No.1	Oklahoma
Irving's Castle	Payne	Oklahoma War Chief	Kay

Historical Markers in Oklahoma

Name	County	Name	County
Oklahoma's First Baptist Church	Wagoner	Rentiesville	McIntosh
Old Boggy Depot	Atoka	Reynolds Castle	LeFlore
Old Greer County	Greer	Riddle's Station	Latimer
Old Military Trail	Stephens	Riley's Chapel/Station	Cherokee
Old Military Road	Craig	Riverside School	Caddo
Old Mountain View Townsite	Kiowa	Robert Rogers	Adair
Original No Man's Land	Texas	Rock Mary	Caddo
Osage Chief Fred Lookout	Osage	Will Rogers, Birthplace of	Rogers
Osage County Museum	Osage	Will Rogers Park	Oklahoma
Osage Village	Pontotoc	Ron School	Logan
Osage Agency	Osage	Rose Hill	Choctaw
Osage Hills State Park	Osage	Rough Rider	Logan
Otoe-Missouria Tribal Reserv.	Noble	Roxana	Logan
Outlaw Battle	Payne	Roy V. Cashion	Kingfisher
Overholser Mansion	Oklahoma	Run of '89-S. Boundary	Cleveland
Paden	Okfuskee	Run of '89-N. Boundary	Logan
Park Hill	Cherokee	Run of '92	Kingfisher
Park Hill Press	Cherokee	Run of '89-W. Boundary	Kingfisher
Payne Campsite	Oklahoma	Run of '89-W. Boundary	Canadian
Pawnee Agency	Pawnee	Run of '89-E. Boundary	Oklahoma
Peace on the Plains	Greer	Run of '89-N. Boundary	Kingfisher
Pecan Point	McCurtain	Rural Electrification	Kingfisher
Perryville	Pittsburgh	Sac & Fox Agency	Lincoln
Peter Conser Home	LeFlore	Sacred Heart Mission	Pottawatomie
Picher Mining Field	Ottawa	Saint Patrick's Church	Oklahoma
Pikey's Crossing	Canadian/ Grady	Same Old Moses Saloon	Logan
Pine Ridge Mission	Choctaw	Samuel Checote	Okmulgee
Platt National Park	Murray	San Bernardo	Jefferson
Pleasant Porter	Tulsa	Sandstone Creek Area	Roger Mills
Post Oak School	Love	Santa Fe Trail	Cimarron
Powder Magazine	Muskogee	Sasakwa	Seminole
Price's Falls	Murray	Seger Colony	Washita
Pusley's Station	Latimer	Seneca Agency	Ottawa
Quannah Parker	Kiowa	Sequoyah's Home	Sequoyah
Rainey Mountain Boarding School	Kiowa	Shade's Well	Texas
Red Fork Station	Kingfisher	Shawnee Milling Company	Pottawatomie
Red Bluffs Community	Washita	Shawnee Town	Hughes
Red River Bridge	Marshall	Shawneetown	McCurtain
Red Wheat	Custer	Sheridan	Kingfisher

Historical Markers in Oklahoma

Name	County	Name	County
Sheriff Died in Line of Duty	Stephens	Washington Irving's Camp	Oklahoma
Sherman House	Comanche	Washita School	Caddo
Sinking of the J.R. Williams	Haskell	Waterhole Cemetery	McCurtain
Skiatook	Osage	Watie & Ridge	Delaware
Skullyville	LeFlore	Waurika	Jefferson
Smithville	McCurtain	Webbers Falls	Muskogee
Sod House	Alfalfa	Western Cattle Trail	Jackson
Solomon, Andrew Layton	Oklahoma	Western Cattle Trail/Yelton Store	Harper
Southwestern State College	Custer	Wheelock Seminary Mission	McCurtain
Spanish Road Crossing	Beckham	Whipple Survey	Hughes
Spencer Academy	Choctaw	Wichita Agency	Caddo
Stand Waite Surrender	Choctaw	Wigwam Neosho	Wagoner
Stand Waite	Delaware	Wild Horse Creek-Washing Irv.	Payne
Star Springs	Adair	Wooster Mound	Osage
State's Earliest Oil Refinery	Muskogee	Wyandotte Tribe	Ottawa
Steen's Buttes	Caddo	Wyatt Cemetery	Grady
Stella Friends Academy	Alfalfa	Wynona	Osage
St. Johns School/Osage Indian Boys	Osage		
St. Louis School/Osage Indian Girls	Osage		
Sulphur	Garvin		
Tahlequah	Cherokee		
Tahlonteeskee	Sequoyah		
Tamaha Jail & Ferry Landings	Haskell		
Texas Road	Muskogee		
Texas Road	Wagoner		
The American Flag	Caddo		
The Great Wolf Hunt of 1905	Tillman		
Thomas-Foreman Home	Muskogee		
Tishomingo	Johnston		
Tom Mix Museum	Washington		
Trahern's Station	LeFlore		
Turkey Track Ranch	Payne		
Union Agency	Muskogee		
Union Mission	Mayes		
Waddell's Station	Atoka		
Wagoner	Wagoner		
Walker's Station	LeFlore		
Wapanucka Academy	Johnston		
Washington Irving's Camp	Tulsa		

Oklahoma Hall of Fame Members

Heritage Center, 1400 Classen Drive, Oklahoma City, OK 73106-6614 • 405/235-4458
www.oklahomaheritage.com/halloffame

The Oklahoma Hall of Fame was organized in 1928 by Anna B. Korn to annually recognize the achievements of Oklahomans. The Hall lists members by the year that they were inducted.

1928	Dennis T. Flynn and Elizabeth Fulton Hester.
1929	James Shannon Buchanan, Charles F. Colcord, Alice M. Robertson, and R.A. Sneed.
1930	David Ross Boyd, Alice Brown Davis, E.K. Gaylord, Annette Ross Hume, Graves Leeper, Frank Phillips, and Joseph Whitfield Scroggs.
1931	Charles F. Barrett, Laura Clubb, Gregory Gerrer, Roy A. Hoffman, Douglas H. Johnston, Ernest Whitworth Marland, Benjamin F. Nihart, and Joseph B. Thoburn.
1932	Frank Bailey, Joseph Blatt, Fowler Border, Fred S. Clinton, J.P. Connors, John Cotteral, John B. Doolin, William A. Durant, F.B. Fite, Frank Frantz, Thomas P. Gore, Charles Nathaniel Haskell, J.W. Hawley, William Miller Jenkins, W.A. Ledbetter, J.L. McBrien, John J. Methvin, J.S. Murrow, James F. Owens, Gabe Parker, D.P. Richardson, Will Rogers, Campbell Russell, Jasper Sipes, Sidney Suggs, Elmer Thomas, and C.P. Wickmiller.
1933	John A. Brown, Madaline Conklin, Edward Everett Dale, Eva Shartell Ferguson, Mrs. M.B. Gibbons, John A. Hatchett, John F. Kroutil, Dan Perry, Una Lee Roberts, Angie Russell, Angelo C. Scott, and Charles B. Stuart.
1934	Eugene M. Antrim, Maude Richman Calvert, Grant Foreman, Emma Estill Harbour, W.W. Hastings, Samuel W. Hayes, Travis F. Hensley, Thomas P. Howell, Charles William Kerr, Everett S. Lain, Gordon W. Lillie, Zack Miller, Francis F. Treadgill, and Clara C. Waters.
1935	Czarina Colbert Conlan, Etta D. Dale, Charles N. Gould, David W. Griffin, Edith Johnson, Roberta Campbell Lawson, Oscar J. Leherer, W.H. McFadden, Ida M. McFarlin, R.M. McFarlin, Lewis J. Moorman, Mell A. Nash, Jennie Harris Oliver, E.B. Ringland, Winnie M. Sanger, and Mary Frances Troy.
1936	William Bennett Bizzell, Alice M. David, Rachel Caroline Eaton, Annett Blackburn Ehler, S. Prince Freeling, Forney Hutchinson, William S. Key, W.H. Kornegay, LeRoy Long, James A. Maney, and M. Alice Miller.
1937	Mable Bassett, A.G.C. Bierer, Elmer E. Brown, Frank C. Carter, Dorothea B. Dale, James S. Davenport, Clarence B. Douglas, John F. Easley, Ida Ferguson, Lucia Loomis Ferguson, A.L. Kates, James R. Keaton, Lilah D. Lindsey, Margaret McVean, Mrs. Jessie E. Moore, Boss Neff, Minnie Shockley, and Ida Wright.
1938	Henry Garland Bennett, Mrs. Virgil Browne, Scott Ferris, Carolyn Thomas Foreman, Everett G. Fry, John W. Harreld, Walter M. Harrison, Abbie B. Hillerman, Patrick J. Hurley, William B. Johnson, Henry S. Johnston, Arthur Neal Leecraft, Bob Makovsky, John B. Nichols, G. Lee Phelps, Jane Gibson Phillips, William B. Pine, George Rainey, Scott Squyres, Martin Edwin Trapp, Edward A. Walker, and Anna L. Witteman.

Oklahoma Hall of Fame

1939	O.H.P. Brewer, Cassius M. Cade, Nannie K. Fite, George Riley Hall, John B. Harrison, Mrs. Charles N. Haskell, Blanche Lucas, Issac Newton McCash, James I. Phelps, Meta Chestnutt Sager, W.G. Skelly, Katherine VanLeuven, and A.M. Wallock.
1940	G. Walter Archibald, J.C. Bushyhead, Frank Buttram, Nannie Hutcheson Cleveland, Milton C. Garber, E.B. Howard, Mrs. W.A. Ledbetter, Anna Lewis, Eugene Lorton, Christian Madsen, Alma J. Neill, Mrs. Lute Walcott, and Muriel H. Wright.
1941	Mrs. Anton H. Classen, Julien C. Monnet, Robert Latham Owen, W. Mark Sexson, and Edgar S. Vaught.
1942	Walter S. Campbell (Stanley Vestal), Houston Benge Teehee, and Louis Wentz.
1943	Gladys Anderson Emerson, O.C. Newman, Waite Phillips, and Mrs. Oscar W. Stewart.
1944	John R. Abernathy, Kenneth Carlyle Kaufman, Burton Rascoe, and Paul B. Sears.
1945	Joseph P. Blickensderfer, Roy Gittinger, Raymond S. McLain, and Paul A. Walker.
1946	Robert Burns, Frances Dinsmore Davis, Charles Evans, and Mark R. Everett.
1947	William Green Beasley, Daniel Luther Edwards, John E. Mabee, and Yvonne Chouteau Terekhov.
1948	Roy Temple House, Mrs. Charles H. Kimes, Fred Lookout, E.H. Moore, and Lynn Riggs.
1949	Nina Kay Gore, Robert A. Hefner, Oscar Brouse Jacobson, Irene Bowers Sells, and Poe B. Vandament.
1950	Angie Debo, Norris Henthorne, J.G. Puterbaugh, Waldo Stephens, Jim Thorpe, and Louis Turley.
1951	Joseph H. Benton, Eugene S. Briggs, George L. Cross, Luther Harrison, Ernest Lachman, Perle Mesta, William Henry Murray, and C.I. Pontius.
1952	George Lynn Bowman, Joseph J. Clark, Everett Lee DeGolyer, Thomas Gilcrease, J. Raymond, Hinshaw Jr., Richard Lloyd Jones, and Savoie Lottinville.
1953	C.B. Bee, James E. Berry, William J. Holloway, Roy M. Johnson, James C. Nance, Pearle Sayre, Nan Sheets, and Gomer Smith Sr.
1954	Felix M. Adams, J.R. Hinshaw, Louis McMahon, Maud Lorton Myers, John L. Peters, and T.H. Steffens.
1955	Annetta A. Childs, F. Hiner Dale, Paul Harvey, Gaston Litton, James C. Penney, and Ross Rizley.
1956	William M. Franklin, C.B. Goddard, Robert Samuel Kerr, Jesse Lee Rader, Robert Terry Stuart, and Nora A. Talbot.
1957	Carl Albert, Robert H. Bayley, Stanley C. Draper, Te Ata Fisher, Erle P. Halliburton, Roy Harris, James A. Rinehart, Anna T. Scruggs, and Roy J. Turner.
1958	K.S. Adams, Willis Maxson Chambers, Dean A. McGee, Alice Lee Marriott, Mrs. Charles Page, John Wesley Raley, and Oliver S. Wilham.

Oklahoma Hall of Fame

1959	Charles R. Anthony, Mrs. John A. Brown, H.H. Herbert, H.C. Jones, Alfred P. Murrah, Bess B. Truitt, Mrs. William Kelly Warren, and Mac Q. Williamson.
1960	Stephen Chandler, Mrs. Patrick J. Hurley, Richard Kelvin Lane, Joe C. Scott, Ned Shepler, and Joseph R. Taylor.
1961	Virgil Browne, Anna B. Korn, Joe W. McBride, A.S. "Mike" Monroney, John Rogers, Fred E. Tarman, and William Kelly Warren.
1962	Jennie Dahlgren, J. Howard Edmondson, John E. Kirkpatrick, J.B. Perkey, and W. Angie Smith.
1963	W.P. Atkinson, Orel Busby, Gordon Cooper, Ben C. Henneke, Herschel H. Hobbs, Mrs. Paul Sutton, and Charles B. "Bud" Wilkinson.
1964	Mrs. Frank Buttram, Harvey P. Everest, Van Heflin, Mickey Mantle, Madame Ramon Vinay, and Clarence H. Wright.
1965	Page Belcher, T. Jack Foster, Henry Payne Iba, Jacob Johnson, Fred Jones, and Mabelle Kennedy.
1966	Mrs. Anita Bryant, W.W. Keeler, Donald S. Kennedy, Edwin W. Parker, William T. Payne, and Lloyd Edwin Rader.
1967	Henry B. Bass, Mrs. J.A. Chapman, Hicks Epton, Malcom E. Phelps, H. Milt Phillips, George M. Sutton, James E. Webb, and Raymond A. Young.
1968	Hayden H. Donahue, W.D. Finney, Jake L. Hamon, Floyd L. Jackson, Jenkin Lloyd Jones, Augusta I. Carson Metcalf, Hal L. Muldrow, and Grace Steele Woodward.
1969	Jack T. Conn, Fred A. Daugherty, Mrs. Clifford L. Frates, William T. Gossett, Morton R. Harrison, Mrs. Frank Johnson Hightower, and George H. Shirk.
1970	Mrs. George L. Bowman, Raymond Gary, Joseph A. LaFortune, Ward S. Merrick, Maurice H. Merrill, D.H. O'Donoghue, and Willard Stone.
1971	Jack Abernathy, Mildred Andrews Boggess, S.N. Goldman, E.L. "Mike" Massad, J. Rud Neilsen, Tom Steed, Mrs. Frederick P. Walter, H. Merle Woods, and John McLain Young.
1972	George S. Benson, Milo M. Brisco, B.D. Eddie, Mrs. Henry C. Hitch, Robert B. Kamm, Ph.D., Maria Tallchief Paschen, and Oral Roberts.
1973	Mrs. Frances Rosser Brown, Guy Frazer Harrison, Robert A. Hefner Jr., John M. Houchin, Paul Miller, Eugene Swearingen, Maj. Gen. Thomas P. Stafford, and Mrs. Fred Zahn.
1974	Armais Arutunoff, William H. Bell, Edward L. Gaylord, Sam Noble, Brig. Gen. Robinson Risner, J.B. Saunders, Cedomir M. Sliepcevich, Ph.D., and Mrs. Kathleen P. Westby.
1975	Alfred E. Aaronson, Eleanor Blake Kirkpatrick, Robert J. LaFortune, T. Howard McCasland, Lela O'Toole, Ph.D., Carl L. Reistle Jr., Holmes Tuttle, and Dolphus Whitten Jr., Ph.D.
1976	Harriet G. Barclay, Henry Louis Bellmon, Jerrie Cobb, James G. Harlow, J.W. McLean, Merle Montgomery, Kent Ruth, and Jim Shoulders.
1977	Lt. Gen. Ira C. Eaker, Bryce N. Harlow, Earnest Hoberecht, Ross H. Miller, M.D., Inez Lunsford Silberg, Earl Sneed, John H. Williams, and Charles Banks Wilson.

Oklahoma Hall of Fame

1978	Dewey Follett Bartlett, Woodrow "Woody" Crumbo, Mary Johnston Evans, John Hope Franklin, Ph.D., W.H. Helmerich, Mrs. Fred Jones, James Kilpatrick, and Morrison G. Tucker.
1979	Christine Anthony Brown, John Burns, Henry C. "Ladd" Hitch Jr., Moscelyne Larkin Jasinski, J.C. Kennedy, P.C. Lauinger, James C. Leake Sr., and Dale Robertson.
1980	Mrs. Marion Briscoe DeVore, Owen K. Garriott, Ph.D., Cluff Hopla, Ph.D., Patience Sewell Latting, W.P. Longmire, M.D., W.F. Martin, and M.A. Wright.
1981	J.W. Bates Jr., James D. Berry, Admiral William J. Crowe, E.T. Dunlap, Ed.D., Russell F. Hunt, Leonard D. McMurry, Walter F. Merrick, and Juanita Kidd Stout.
1982	Fred E. Brown Jr., Roy Clark, James D. Fellers, John T. Griffin, Charles C. Ingram, Ambassador Jeane J. Kirkpatrick, Roberta Knie, Lowe Runkle.
1983	William W. Caudill, Kenneth H. Cooper, M.D., Howard C. Kauffmann, Clarence E. Page, Patti Page, James Ralph Scales, Ph.D., Harold C. Stuart, and Robert E. Thomas.
1984	Johnny Bench, Jacqueline L. Carey, Gloria Twine Chisum, Ph.D., Tullos O. Coston, M.D., William C. Douce, Nolen J. Fuqua, James M. Hewgley Jr., and General (USAF/Ret.) James E. Hill.
1985	Vida Chenoweth, Ph.D., Arrell M. Gibson, Ph.D., Allan Houser, Edward C. Jollian III, Edwin Malzahn, F.M. Petree, Woodrow Richard Stubbs, and Charles E. Thorton.
1986	Lyle H. Boren, Charles P. Brown, Nancy Frantz Davies, James Garner, Julian J. Rothbaum, James E. Stewart, G. Rainey Williams, M.D., and Henry Zarrow.
1987	James G. Harlow Jr., Marilyn Harris, Robert Mayes Hart, Jeane Porter Hester, N. Scott Momaday, John W. Nichols, and Samuel Moore Walton.
1988	David Lyle Boren, Ed L. Calhoon, M.D., Richard D. Harrison, A.T. Stair Jr. Ph.D., Kay Starr, Patricia W. Wheeler, Joseph H. Williams, and Stanton L. Young.
1989	Virginia Thomas Austin, James R. Bellatti, Bennie L. Davis, William R. Howell, Tom P. McAdams Jr., George Nigh, C.J. "Pete" Silas, and John S. "Jack" Zink.
1990	Jim Hartz, Jack Van Doren Hough, M.D., John Kilpatrick Jr., Clem McSpadden, and Ray H. Siegfried II.
1991	Gene Autry, James E. Barnes, Glenn A. Cox, Jack N. Merritt, Allie P. Reynolds, and Marjorie Tallchief Skibine.
1992	J.M. "Jack" Graves, Allen E. Greer, M.D., Frank A. McPherson, Robert L. Parker Sr., Helen Robson Walton, and Martha Griffin White.
1993	Ray Ackerman, Jimmie Baker, Jane B. Harlow, John A. Sabolich, CPO, John F. Snodgrass, Warren Spahn, and Jack Zarrow.
1994	James R. Jones, Wilma Mankiller, Don Nickles, Lee Allan Smith, Max Weitzenhoffer, and Nazih Zuhdi, M.D.
1995	Clark Bass, Alan C. "Ace" Greenberg, Wilson Hurley, Stephen J. Jatras, Mary Jane Noble, and Ralph G. Thompson.
1996	Keith E. Bailey, William R. "Bill" Bright, Robert Lorton, Charles A. Rockwood Jr., M.D., G.W. "Bill" Swisher, and Alma Wilson

Oklahoma Hall of Fame

1997	W.W. Allen, Ann Simmons Alspaugh, Vince Gill, Tony Hillerman, Melvin Moran, and Gen. Dennis J. Reimer.
1998	W. French Anderson, M.D., Wanda L. Bass, Donald L. Cooper, M.D., Archie W. Dunham, Reba McEntire, and Herman Meinders.
1999	Larry Brummett, Jean G. Gumerson, Abe Lemons, Jay O'Meilia, H.E. "Gene" Rainbolt, Barry Switzer, Jimmy Webb.
2000	Hannah D. Atkins, Thomas R. Brett, Tom E. Love, John W. Montgomery, Samuel Lloyd Noble, Marian P. Opala, Darrell Royal, Charles Schusterman.
2001	G.T. Blankenship, John Brock, Luke Corbett, Howard Lester, Roxana Lorton, Larry Nichols, C.D. Northcutt.
2002	Chester Cadieux, Ralph Ellison, Josie Freede, John Massey, W. DeVier Pearson, Richard Sias, Wes Watkins.
2003	William Crawford, George Henderson, Roberts S. Kerr, Jr., William G. Paul, Boone Pickens, Milann Siegfried, William K. Warren, Jr.
2004	Bill Anoatubby, Molly Shi Boren, Frederick F. Drummond, William E. Durrett, Christine Gaylord Everest, Leona Mitchell, James Woolsey, Wiley Post.
2005	Andrew Coates, Nancy Payne Ellis, Gilbert Gibson, Frank Keating, Peter Meinig, Bobby Murcer, Edward Ruscha, Cyril Wagner.
2006	Bob Burke, Woody Guthrie, Glen D. Johnson Jr., King Kirchner, J. Philip Kistler, Tom McDaniel, Lynn Schusterman
2007	Clayton I. Bennett, Jane Jayroe, Toby Keith, David Kyle, Clara Luper, Aubrey McClendon, Gregory E. Pyle, Linda K. Twine.
2008	Bill W. Burgess Jr., Robert H. Henry, Donna Nigh, Ronald J. Norick, Carl R. Renfro, Charles C. Stephenson, Jordan J.N. Tang.
2009	C. Kendric Fergeson, Marlin G. "Ike" Glass, V. Burns Hargis, Polly Nichols, Lee Roy Selmon, Steven W. Taylor, Wayman Lawrence.
2010	Kristin Chenoweth, Robert A. Hefner III, Edward F. Keller, Judy Love, Michael C. Turpen, Lew O. Ward III.
2011	Tommy Franks, Harold Hamm, Marques Haynes, Cathy Keating, Steve Malcolm, Roger Miller, and Elizabeth Warren.
2012	Stan Clark, Bart Conner, Edith Kinney Gaylord, Tom L. Ward, Suzanne Warren, Lee R. West, and Ronald H. White.
2013	Michael D. Case, Gary A. England, John D. Groendyke, Timothy P. Headington, Vicki Miles-LaGrange, Russell M. Perry, and Reggie N. Whitten.
2014	Harold T. Holden, Wanda Jackson, Neal McCaleb, Thomas H. McCasland Jr., Blake Shelton, Peggy Clark Stephenson, and Alfre Woodard.

Oklahoma Women's Hall of Fame

The Oklahoma Women's Hall of Fame, created in 1982, is a project of the Oklahoma Commission on the Status of Women (www.ok.gov/ocsw).

Inductees are women who have lived in Oklahoma for a major portion of their lives or who are easily identified as Oklahomans and are a pioneer in her field or in a project that benefits Oklahoma, has made a significant contribution to the State of Oklahoma, serves or has served as a role model to other Oklahoma women, is an "unsung hero" who has made a difference in the lives of Oklahomans or Americans because of her action, has championed other women, women's issues, or served as a public policy advocate for issues important to women. Inductees exemplify the Oklahoma Spirit.

Year	Inductees
1982	Hannah Diggs Atkins, Kate Barnard, June Brooks, Gloria Stewart Farley, Aloysius Larch-Miller, Susie Ryan Peters, Christine Salmon, Edyth Thomas Wallace
1983	Zelia N. Breaux, Kate Frank, Leona Mitchell, Jean Pitts, Juanita Kidd Stout, Alma Wilson
1984	Angie Debo, Jeane Duane Kirkpatrick, Jewell Russell Mann, Zella J. Patterson
1985	Mae Boren Axton, June Tompkins Benson, Pam Olson, Betty Durham Price, Bertha Frank Teague
1986	Sara Ruth Cohen, Vinita Cravens, Rubye Hibler Hall, Elizabeth Ann McCurdy Holmes, Grace Elizabeth Hudlin, Wilma P. Mankiller, Edna Mae Phelps, Evelyn LaRue Pittman
1993	Marie Cox, Anita Faye Hill, Moscelyne Larkin, Jacquelyn C. Longacre, Shannon Lucid, Clara Luper, Opaline Deveraux Wadkins, Pat Woodrum
1995	Nancy Goodman Feldman, Barbara J. Gardner, Ruth Blalock Jones, Mona Salyer Lambird, Gloria Grace Langdon, Bernice Compton Mitchell, Donna Nigh
1996	Betty Boyd, Ada Lois Sipuel Fisher, Lela Foreman, Sandy Ingraham, Lorena Males, Bernice Shedrick, Valree Fletcher Wynn
1997	Isabel Keith Baker, Jessie Thatcher Bost, Norma Eagleton, Kay Goebel, Ruth Gilliland Kistler Hardman, Beverly Horse, Mazola McKerson, Penny Baldwin Williams
2001	Jari Askins, Shirley Bellmon, Dorothy Moses DeWitty, Sandy Garrett, Lynn Jones, Yvonne Kauger, Jill Zink Tarbel, Dana Tiger
2003	Esther Houser, Vicki Miles-LaGrange, Linda Morrissey, Lynn Schusterman, Donna Shirley
2005	Wanda Bass, Nancy Coats, Mary Fallin, Bessie McColgin, Stephanie Seymour, Jeanine Rhea
2007	Sherri Coale, Ginny Creveling, Joe Anna Hibler, Maxine Horner, Kay Martin, Terry Neese, Claudia Tarrington, Carolyn Taylor, and Della Warrior
2009	Rita Aragon, Suzanne Edmondson, Edna Miller Hennessee, Kim Henry, Mirabeau Lamar Cole Looney, Susan Savage, and Carolyn Whitner.
2011	Laura Boyd, Chloe L. Brown, Joy D. Culbreath, Marcia J. Mitchell, Ardina R. Moore, Cynthia S. Ross, Kathryn Taylor, and Helen Harrod Thompson.
2013	Ida Blackburn, Elaine Dodd, Linda Haneborg, Lou Kerr, Nancy Miller, and Terri Watkins.

Oklahoma Poets Laureate

The Oklahoma Poet Laureate Program is designed to honor outstanding poets and to promote the literary arts of the state. The honorary position of State Poet Laureate was established June 21, 1923. The position is appointed by the governor from a list provided by poetry societies and organizations and is coordinated by the Oklahoma Humanities Council (www.okhumanities.org).

1923	Violet McDougal
1931	Paul Kroeger
1940	Jenny Harris Oliver
1942	Della I. Young
1943	Anne R. Semple
1945	Bess Truitt
1963	Delbert Davis
1966	Rudolph Nelson Hill
1970	Leslie A. McRill
1970	Rudolph Nelson Hill (emeritus)
1977	Maggie Culver Fry
1995	Carol Hamilton
1997	Betty Shipley
1998	Joe Kreger
2001	Carl Sennhenn
2003	Francine Ringold
2005	Francine Ringold
2007	N. Scott Momaday
2009	Jim Barnes
2011	Eddie D. Wilcoxen
2013	Nathan Brown
2015	Benjamin Myers

Oklahoma Rhodes Scholars
University of Oxford, England

Name of Undergraduate	Oxford College/Hall	Attended
Kendall, William Leamon	Brassnosa, 1904	University of Oklahoma
Mahaffie, Charles Delahunt	St. John's, 1905	Kingfisher College.
Kline, Earl Kilburn	Pembroke, 1907	University of Oklahoma
Campbell, Walter Stanley	Merton, 1908	SW State Normal
Lange, Ray Loomis	St. John's, 1910	Kingfisher College.
Vogt, William Claude	Hertford, 1911	Kingfisher College.
Eagleton, Clyde	Worcester, 1914	Austin College
Moseley, John O.	Merton, 1917	Austin College
McLaughlin, Thomas Oscar	Merton, 1918	Phillips University
Holleman, Wilbur Jennings	Merton, 1920	University of Oklahoma
Brandt, Joseph August	Lincoln, 1921	University of Oklahoma
Burk, Robert Emmett	Merton, 1923	Cornell University
Robertson, Wallace Edward	Merton, 1924	University of Oklahoma
Ogle, Joseph W. *	St. Edmund Hall, 1926	Phillips University
Springer, Charles Eugene	Merton, 1927	University of Oklahoma
Lottinville, Savoie	St. Catherine's, 1929	University of Oklahoma
Van Meter, Rbt. E.	Magdalen, 1930	U.S. Naval Academy
Albert, Carl	St. Peter's, 1931	University of Oklahoma
Kendall, Willmoore	Pembroke, 1932	University of Oklahoma
Fischer, Jack	Lincoln, 1933	University of Oklahoma
St. Clair, David	Queen's, 1933	University of Oklahoma
Boorstin, Daniel J.	Balliol, 1934	Harvard University
McGhee, George C.	Queen's, 1934	University of Oklahoma
Carpenter, John R. W.	Lincoln, 1935	University of Illinois
Earley, LeRoy W.	Jesus, 1938	University of Oklahoma
Luttrell, Jack M.	Merton, 1938	University of Oklahoma
Hinshaw, J. Raymond	Hertford, 1947	University of Oklahoma
Howard, Wm. Lowry	University, 1948	University of Oklahoma
Slesnick, Wm. Ellis	Jesus, 1948	U.S. Naval Academy
Salter, Lewis S., Jr.	Jesus, 1949	University of Oklahoma
Bell, Aldon Duane	Hertford, 1951	University of Oklahoma
Revard, Carter	Merton, 1952	University of Tulsa

Name of Undergraduate	Oxford College/Hall	Attended
Kramer, Martin Alvord	Trinity, 1954	Harvard University
Dennis, Jack Stanley	Balliol, 1955	University of Oklahoma
Johns, Oliver D.	Balliol, 1956	Mass. Institute of Tech.
Womack, John Jr.	Merton, 1959	Harvard University
Gubser, Nicholas James	Magdalen, 1962	Yale University
Woolsey, Rbt. James Jr.	St. John's, 1963	Stanford University
Boren, David Lyle	Balliol, 1963	Yale University
Parkhurst, Guy Wm. II., Jr.	Lincoln, 1964	University of Oklahoma
McGrew, Wm. Clement III	Merton, 1965	University of Oklahoma
Malick, Terrence F.	Magdalen, 1966	Harvard University
McCarter, Pete Kyle, Jr. *	Christ Church, 1967	University of Oklahoma
von Kaenel, Howard Jackson	Magdalen, 1969	U.S. Military Academy
Rahe, Paul A., Jr.	Wadham, 1971	Yale University
Jackson, Phillip L.	Merton, 1973	University of Oklahoma
Griffin, Brian C.	Queen's, 1974	Harvard University
Tabor, Timothy Lee	St. John's, 1975	University of Oklahoma
Coiner, Nancy Lee	St. Hugh's, '77	St. John's College
Morishige, Nina T.	Wolfson, 1982	Johns Hopkins University
Noever, David A.	Magdalen, 1984	Princeton University
Lee, Vivian S.	Balliol, 1986	Radcliffe College
Pepin, Susan	St. John's, 1987	Yale University
Bednekoff, Peter	Wadham, 1988	University of Tulsa
Carson, Brad R.	Trinity, 1989	Baylor University
Rubenstein, Jay C.	St. John's, 1989	Carleton College
Turner, Deacon	New College, 1990	Harvard University
Trong, Germaine	Magdalen, 1994	Middlebury College
Greteman, Blaine	Merton, 1998	Oklahoma State University
Sanders, Jason Roe	Trinity, 2000	University of Oklahoma
Harris, Jennifer Michelle	Pembroke, 2004	Wake Forest University
DenHoed, Andrea	n/a, 2008	University of Oklahoma
Swenson, Sarah	n/a, 2011	University of Oklahoma
Mubeen A. Shakir	n/a, 2013	University of Oklahoma

* Did not take up scholarship.
www.rhodesscholar.org

COMMERCE &
AGRICULTURE

Commerce in Oklahoma

According to the Oklahoma Employment Security Commission's *Oklahoma Economic Indicators Report March 2015,* Oklahoma's real Gross Domestic Product (real GDP) increased in 2013 to $164.3 billion in constant 2009 dollars, growing at a rate of 4.2 percent from 2012. Real Gross Domestic Product (real GDP) is a macroeconomic measure of the value of economic output adjusted for price changes such as inflation or deflation. This adjustment transforms the money value measure, nominal GDP, into an index for quantity of total output. The United States unemployment rate remained at a 6½–year low in March 2015 at 5.5 percent, but that was mostly due to discouraged workers dropping out of the labor force. In February 2015, Oklahoma's seasonally adjusted unemployment rate was unchanged at 3.9 percent, ranking the state as the sixth lowest unemployment rate among all states and tied with New Hampshire and Vermont.

Gross Domestic Product

According to the Oklahoma Employment Security Commission's *Oklahoma Economic Indicators Report March 2015,* Gross Domestic Product (GDP)—the output of goods and services produced by labor and property located in the United States—is the broadest measure of economic activity. It is also the measure that is most indicative of whether the economy is in recession. In the post-World War II period, there has been no recession in which GDP did not decrease in at least two quarters, (the exceptions being during the recessions of 1960–61 and 2001). There are four major components to GDP: personal consumption expenditures, investment, net exports, and government.

United States economic growth slowed as 2014 came to a close. Gross Domestic Product (GDP) increased at an annual rate of 2.2 percent in the fourth quarter of 2014. Consumer spending increased to 4.4 percent in the fourth quarter of 2014, the biggest gain in consumer spending in eight years. Durable goods expenditures rose to 6.2 percent, while nondurable goods spending increased to 4.1 percent during the fourth quarter of 2014. Spending on services grew at a 4.3 percent pace during the fourth quarter of 2014, which was the fastest pace since the second quarter of 2000. Business accumulated $80 billion worth of inventory in the fourth quarter of 2014. After-tax corporate profits declined $57.1 billion, the largest drop since the first quarter of 2001. Residential construction increased 3.8 percent during the fourth quarter of 2014. Exports also rose to 4.5 percent, and import growth rose to 10.4 percent during the fourth quarter of 2014. Foreign trade subtracted 1.03 percentage points from the fourth quarter GDP growth. A stronger dollar made U.S. exports more expensive and imports cheaper. Government spending in the last three months of 2014 was slightly weaker than previously estimated. Real federal government consumption expenditures and gross investment decreased 7.3 percent in the fourth quarter. National defense spending plunged 12.2 percent.

In the fourth quarter of 2013, Oklahoma's real GDP was $165.7 billion in constant 2009 dollars, up from $164.5 billion in the third quarter. The state's fourth quarter real GDP increased by $1.19 billion, or 2.9 percent, ranking Oklahoma twenty-ninth among all other states and the District of Columbia.

For all of 2013, Oklahoma's real GDP was at a level of $164.3 billion in constant 2009 dollars, growing at a rate of 4.2 percent from 2012. That was the fourth-highest annual GDP growth rate among all other states and the District of Columbia. North Dakota was first with a 9.7 percent growth rate followed by Wyoming at 7.6 percent and West Virginia at 5.1 percent.

Fifteen Oklahoma industry sectors contributed to GDP growth in the fourth quarter of 2013, with six sectors subtracting from growth. The mining sector, which includes the oil and gas industry, was by far the largest contributor to Oklahoma's GDP growth in the fourth quarter, adding 2.39 percentage points to overall GDP growth, followed by non-durable goods manufacturing which contributed 0.94 percentage points. Agriculture, forestry, fishing and hunting was the biggest drag to state GDP growth subtracting 1.95 percentage points.

Unemployment

The United States unemployment rate remained at a 6½-year low in March 2015, but that was mostly due to discouraged workers dropping out of the labor force. The unemployment rate held at 5.5 percent in March 2015, according to the Bureau of Labor Statistics (BLS). It appears that some discouraged workers are returning to the labor force.

In February 2015, Oklahoma's seasonally adjusted unemployment rate was unchanged at 3.9 percent, ranking the sixth lowest unemployment rate among all states and tied with New Hampshire and Vermont. Over the year, the state's seasonally adjusted unemployment rate was down by 1.0 percentage point from 4.9 percent in February 2014. Kentucky and Rhode Island saw the largest drop in year-over-year change in jobless rates among states (-2.1 percentage points), while Louisiana had the largest over-the-year gain at 1.3 percentage points

Employment

United States employers added the fewest number of jobs in more than a year in March 2015, snapping a streak of twelve straight months of job gains above 200,000. Nonfarm payroll employment increased 126,000 in March 2015, after rising 264,000 in February, according to the Bureau of Labor Statistics (BLS). In March 2015, employment continued to trend up in professional and business services (+40,000), health care (+22,000), and retail trade (+26,000), while employment in mining declined (-11,000).

Oklahoma's nonfarm employment growth slowed a bit in 2013, adding 19,000 jobs for a 1.2 percent growth rate. In 2013, nine out of Oklahoma's eleven statewide supersectors recorded job growth. Leisure and hospitality led all other supersectors adding 4,700 jobs with the bulk of hiring occurring in accommodations and food services. Construction employment added 4,100 jobs with almost all of the growth coming from heavy and civil engineering construction and specialty trade contractors. The broad trade, transportation and utilities group added 4,000 employees with most of the growth in wholesale trade. Professional and business services employment grew by 2,100 driven by job gains in administrative and support and waste management and remediation services and employment services. Mining and logging and manufacturing employment growth both slowed significantly from the previous year. Education and health services added 1,000 jobs with nearly all the job growth in ambulatory health care services. Once again, over-the-year declines were seen in information (-700 jobs) and other services (-400 jobs).

Housing Construction

While home construction represents a small portion of the housing market, it has an outsize impact on the economy. Each home built creates an average of three jobs for a year and about $90,000 in taxes, according to the National Association of Home Builders. Overall, United States homebuilding fell to its lowest levels in fifty years in 2009, when builders began work on just 554,000 homes.

In February 2015, Oklahoma's total residential permitting was 181 permits, or 22.5 percent, less than February 2014. Single-family permits were down sixty-two permits, or 8.35 percent, less than a year ago, while the more volatile multi-family permitting was 153 more than the January 2014 level of eleven permits.

In 2014, total unadjusted residential building permitting was at a level of 14,024 or 12.7 percent greater than the 2013 total of 12,464 and the highest annual total since 2007. Multi-family permits were 1,127, or 51.8 percent more than 2013, while single-family permits were 447, or 4.1 percent less than 2013.

Personal Income

Personal income includes earnings, property income such as dividends, interest, and rent and transfer payments, such as retirement, unemployment insurance, and various other benefit payments. It is a measure of income that is available for spending and is seen as an indicator of the economic well-being of the residents of a state. Earnings and wages make up the largest portion of personal income.

Oklahoma's total personal income growth accelerated to 3.8 percent in 2014, from 2.0 percent in 2013, and ranked twenty-seventh among all states for income growth, according to the BEA. Total personal income was at a level of $167.3 billion for 2014. Oklahoma per capita personal income was $43,138 in 2014, based on an estimated 3.88 million residents.

Selected Oklahoma Indicators

	2009	2010	2011	2012	2013
Real Gross State Product ($Mil)	147,045	148,038	153,104	157,737	164,303
Real Personal Income ($Mil)	132,132	136,627	147,430	154,958	N/A
Wage and Salary Income ($Mil)	61,318	62,735	66,240	70,470	72,479
Ratio OK/US Per Cap Income (%)	89.7	89.7	92.0	93.7	93.5
Unemployment Rate (%)	6.6	7.0	5.5	5.2	5.0
Taxes on Production and Imports ($Mil)	8,775	9,278	9,866	10,527	N/A
Personal Current Taxes ($Mil)	10,439	10,584	13,249	14,418	15,881
Personal Property Taxes ($Thousands)	30,137	33,993	32,679	36,483	36,587

Source: U.S. Bureau of Economic Analysis

Oklahoma Gross State Product by Industrial Sector

Actual (2005, 2006, 2007, 2008, 2009, 2010, 2011, 2012, and 2013) in Millions

Major Industry	2005 Actual ($)	2006	2007	2008	2009	2010	2011	2012	2013
Agriculture	2,154	2,035	2,149	2,281	1,819	2,287	2,686	3,006	4,108
Mining	16,301	20,882	19,536	20,255	22,939	13,705	24,038	21,831	27,156
Construction	4,772	5,162	4,450	5,232	4,908	5,235	5,945	6,476	7,199
Manufacturing-Durable	7,964	9,090	9,554	10,008	9,211	8,840	8,956	10,014	10,415
Manufacturing-Nondurable	4,661	4,909	5,954	8,304	8,366	7,984	7,402	7,862	7,917
Wholesale and Retail Trade	14,370	15,397	15,940	16,428	16,050	16,740	18,245	19,624	20,477
Finance, Insurance, and Real Estate	16,442	18,327	17,473	17,473	21,224	21,578	22,465	24,019	23,774
Transportation and Utilities	6,668	7,238	8,415	8,764	8,865	8,414	11,977	12,662	11,258
Services	24,775	26,950	29,068	21,314	21,284	28,734	29,969	31,352	32,852
Government	19,392	20,551	21,811	24,902	26,403	26,098	26,889	27,332	27,793

Source: 2013 U.S. Department of Commerce, Bureau of Economic Analysis

Oklahoma Non-Farm Wage and Salary Disbursements

(In millions of dollars)

Major Industry	2002	2003	2004	2005	2006	2007	2008	2009	2010	2011	2012
Total	45,050	46,086	48,277	50,937	56,196	59,465	63,042	61,028	62,469	66,259	66,332
Mining	1,559	1,745	1,953	2,351	3,643	3,680	4,483	3,567	3,665	4,842	6,325
Construction	2,049	2,068	2,064	2,271	2,581	2,752	3,131	2,895	2,941	3,045	3,931
Manufacturing—Durable	4,076	3,789	3,844	3,994	4,440	4,666	4,895	4,151	4,054	4,527	6,324
Manufacturing—Nondurable	1,822	1,837	1,853	1,909	1,961	1,951	1,946	1,878	1,926	2,013	2,680
Wholesale and Retail Trade	5,799	5,776	5,978	6,290	6,774	7,080	7,375	7,099	7,138	7,560	9,560
Finance, Insurance, and Real Estate	2,713	2,882	3,066	2,504	3,448	3,625	3,706	3,622	3,297	3,909	5,021
Transportation and Utilities	2,264	2,276	2,397	2,672	2,709	3,022	3,065	3,033	3,032	3,220	4,477
Services	11,596	11,992	12,533	13,177	14,206	15,281	16,163	16,382	15,575	16,705	23,323
Government—All Levels	10,432	10,714	11,166	11,774	12,507	13,326	13,968	14,572	14,993	14,980	21,017

Source: 2012 U.S. Department of Commerce, Bureau of Economic Analysis

Fortune 500 Companies

Souce: Oklahoma Department of Commerce

Company Name	Business Type	Location	# Employees
Walmart Stores Inc.	Retail	Statewide	32,000
AMR	Retail	Tulsa	7,000
Community Health Systems	Health	Statewide	7,000
Chesapeake Energy	Petroleum	Statewide	4,500
Lowe's	Specialty Retailers	Statewide	4,000
Seaboard	Food Production	Statewide	3,400
HCA Holdings	Health	Oklahoma City/Edmond	3,000
Halliburton	Oil/Gas Equipment	Statewide	3,000
Dollar General	Retail	Statewide/Tulsa	3,000
Oneok	Pipelines	Statewide	3,000
Phillips 66	Petroleum Refining	Statewide	2,900
AT&T	Telecommunications	Statewide	2,500
Goodyear Tire & Rubber	Motor Vehicle Parts	Statewide/Lawton	2,500
Target	Retail	Statewide	2,000
Walgreen	Food/Drug Retail	Statewide	2,000
United Parcel Service	Mail/Package Delivery	Statewide	2,000
McDonald's	Food Services	Statewide	2,000
Baker Hughes	Oil/Gas Equipment	Statewide	2,000
Yum Brands	Food Services	Statewide	2,000
Marriott International	Hotels/Casinos/Resorts	Statewide	2,000
Devon Energy	Mining/Crude Oil Production	Statewide	2,000
Darden Restaurants	Food Services	Statewide	2,000
Health Management Associates	Health Care/Facilities	Oklahoma City/Midwest City/Durant/Choctaw	2,000
Home Depot	Specialty Retailers	Statewide	1,500
Best Buy	Specialty Retailers	Statewide	1,500
Coca-Cola	Beverages	Oklahoma City	1,500
Tyson Foods	Food Production	Statewide/Broken Bow	1,500
J.C. Penney	Retail	Statewide	1,500
Dillard's	Retail	Statewide	1,500
Williams	Energy	Statewide	1,400
O'Reilly Automotive	Specialty Retailers	Statewide	1,400
Dell	Computers/Office Equipment	Oklahoma City	1,250
Boeing	Aerospace/Defense	Altus/Oklahoma City	1,200
State Farm Insurance	Insurance	Statewide/Tulsa	1,200

Company Name	Business Type	Location	# Employees
Universal Health Services	Health Care/Facilities	Statewide	1,200
Kohl's	Retail	Statewide	
Berkshire Hathaway	Insurance	Statewide	1,000
International Business Machines	Information Technology Services	Tulsa	1,000
Sears Holding	Retail	Statewide	1,000
Sprint Nextel	Telecommunications	Statewide	1,000
Directv	Telecommunications	Statewide	1,000
American Electric Power	Energy	Statewide	1,000
National Oilwell Varco	Oil/Gas Equipment, Services	Statewide	1,000
GAP	Specialty Retailers	Statewide	1,000
Dish Network	Telecommunications	Statewide	1,000
Hertz Global Holdings	Automotive Retail Services	Statewide	1,000
Advance Auto Parts	Specialty Retailers	Statewide	1,000
Dollar Tree	Specialty Retailers	Statewide	900
Northrop Grumman	Aerospace/Defense	Lawton/Oklahoma City/Midwest City	850
Johnson Controls	Motor Vehicle Parts	Statewide	800
Southwest Airlines	Airlines	Oklahoma City/Tulsa	800
Navistar International	Motor Vehicles/Parts	Tulsa	800
Starbucks	Food Services	Statewide	800
Quest Dianostics	Health Care/Pharmacy	Statewide	800
Telephone & Data Systems	Telecommunications	Statewide	800
Autozone	Specialty Retailers	Statewide	775
Hewlett-Packard	Computers/Office Equipment	Tulsa	750
Macy's	Retail	Oklahoma City/Tulsa	750
Ross Stores	Specialty Retailers	Statewide	750
Family Dollar Stores	Retail	Statewide	750
Level 3 Communications	Telecommunications	Tulsa	750
Big Lots	Specialty Retailers	Statewide/Durant	750
Hartford Financial	Insurance	Oklahoma City/Tulsa	600
Whirlpool	Electronics/Electrical	Tulsa	600
Dover	Industrial Machinery	Statewide	600
Spectra Energy	Pipelines	Oklahoma City	600
Fidelity National	Financial Data	Oklahoma City	525
Gamestop	Specialty Retailers	Statewide	520
Exxon Mobil	Petroleum	Shawnee	500
CVS Caremark	Food/Drug Stores	Statewide	500

Company Name	Business Type	Location	# Employees
Verizon Communications	Telecommunications	Tulsa	500
J.P. Morgan Chase	Commercial Banks	Statewide	500
Bank of America	Commercial Banks	Statewide	500
Unitedhealth Group	Health Care/Insurance	Oklahoma City	500
Pepsico	Food Consumer Products	Statewide	500
International Paper	Forest/Paper Products	Fletcher/Oklahoma City/Tulsa/Valliant	500
Hollyfrontier	Petroleum	Tulsa	500
Genuine Parts	Wholesalers	Statewide	500
Limited Brands	Specialty Retailers	Statewide	500
Avis Budget Group	Automotive Retailers	Statewide	500
Toys "R" Us	Specialty Retailers	Norman/Oklahoma City/Tulsa	475
Kelly Services	Temporary Help	Oklahoma City/Tulsa	475
SAIC	Information Technology	Midwest City/Norman/Oklahoma City/Tulsa	475
KKR	Securities	Oklahoma City	450
Petsmart	Specialty Retailers	Statewide	450
Starwood Hotels/Resorts	Hotels/Casinos/Resorts	Midwest City/Oklahoma City/Tulsa	450
Hillshire Brands	Food Consumer Products	Broken Bow/Enid/Tulsa	425
Metlife	Insurance	Tulsa	400
Goldman Sachs Group	Commercial Banks	Statewide	400
Staples	Specialty Retailers	Statewide	400
Kimberly-Clark	Household/Personal Products	Jenks	400
Paccar	Motor Vehicle/Parts	Ardmore/Broken Arrow/Oklahoma City/Tulsa	400
VF	Apparel	Oklahoma City/Seminole	350
Sherwin-Williams	Chemicals	Statewide/Weatherford	350
Sonic Automotive	Automotive Retail/Services	Statewide	350
Coca-Cola Enterprises	Beverages	Statewide	350
Eaton	Industrial Machinery	Shawnee/Tulsa/Oklahoma City/Edmond	350
TJX	Specialty Retailers	Statewide	325
Office Depot	Specialty Retailers	Statewide	320
Sysco	Wholesalers/Food/Grocery	Statewide	300
Murphy Oil	Petroleum Refining	Statewide	300
Raytheon	Aerospace/Defense	Lawton/McAlester	300

Company Name	Business Type	Location	# Employees
Terex	Construction/Farm Equipment	Oklahoma City/Tulsa	300
Avaya	Network/Communications	Lawton/Oklahoma City	300
United Stationers	Wholesalers/Electronics/Office Equipment	Muskogee/Oklahoma City/Tulsa	300
CC Media Holdings	Entertainment	Oklahoma City/Tulsa	275
Valero Energy	Petroleum Refining	Statewide	250
URS	Engineering/Construction	Oklahoma City/Tulsa	250
Travelcenters of America	Specialty Retailers	Oklahoma City/Sayre	250
Officemax	Specialty Retailers	Norman	250
Barnes & Noble	Specialty Retailers	Statewide	250
Dick's Sporting Goods	Specialty Retailers	Statewide	250
Apache	Mining/Crude Oil Production	Chickasha/Elk City/Tulsa/Woodward	230
Waste Management	Waste Management	Oklahoma City/Muskogee	230
Manpower	Temporary Help	Lawton/Oklahoma City/Tulsa	225
McKesson	Wholesalers/Health Care	Lawton/Oklahoma City/Tulsa	200
Wells Fargo	Commercial Banks	Statewide	200
Enterprise Products	Pipelines	Cushing/Healdton/Oklahoma City	200
Honeywell International	Aerospace/Defense	Oklahoma City/Tulsa	200
Morgan Stanley	Commercial Banks	Statewide	200
Plains All American Pipeline	Pipelines	Statewide	200
Xerox	Computers/Office Equipment	Statewide	200
Illinois Tool Works	Industrial Machinery	Oklahoma City/Tulsa	200
Cummins	Construction/Farm Machinery	Duncan/Norman/Oklahoma City/Tulsa	200
Bed Bath & Beyond	Specialty Retailers	Edmond/Norman/Oklahoma City/Tulsa	200
Kindred Healthcare	Health Care/Medical Facilities	Statewide	200
Con-Way	Transportation/Logistics	Oklahoma City/Sapulpa	200
YRC Worldwide	Trucking/Truck Leasing	Oklahoma City/Tulsa	200
Sunoco	Petroleum Refining	Statewide	200
C.H. Robinson Worldwide	Transportation/Logistics	Oklahoma City	175
Carmax	Automotive Retailers/Services	Oklahoma City/Tulsa	175
Omnicare	Health Care/Pharmacy	Oklahoma City/Tulsa	175
SPX	Industrial Machinery	Norman/Tulsa	175

Company Name	Business Type	Location	# Employees
Marathon Petroleum	Petroleum Refining	Statewide	150
Lockheed Martin	Aerospace/Defense	Lawton/Oklahoma City	150
Allstate	Insurance	Statewide	150
Aramark	Diversified Outsourcing Services	Oklahoma City/ Shawnee/Tulsa	150
Dean Foods	Food Consumer Products	Oklahoma City/Tulsa	150
Whole Foods Market	Food/Drug Stores	Oklahoma City/Tulsa	150
Republic Services	Waste Management	Statewide	150
Weyerhaeuser	Forest/Paper Products	Broken Bow/Idabel/ Valliant	150
Harley-Davidson	Miscellaneous	Statewide	150
Susser Holdings	Specialty Retailers	Statewide	150
Marathon Oil	Mining/Crude Oil Production	Statewide	140
Lowes	Insurance	Oklahoma City	130
Mondelez International	Food Consumer Products	Oklahoma City/Tulsa	120
HD Supply	Wholesalers	Cherokee/ Oklahoma City	120
CF Industries Holdings	Chemical	Claremore/Catoosa/ Woodward	120
Foot Locker	Specialty Retailers	Statewide	120
Chevron Corporation	Petroleum Refining	Bartlesville/Pryor	100
Cardinal health	Wholesalers/Health Care	Mannford	100
Google	Internet Services/Retail	Pryor	100
Supervalu	Food/Drug Stores	Statewide	100
United States Steel	Metals	Catoosa/Tulsa	100
Union Pacific	Railroads	Statewide	100
AES	Utilities	Panama	100
Computers Sciences	Information Technology	Enid	100
Progressive	Insurance	Stillwater/Tulsa	100
Penske Automotive Group	Automotive Retail/Services	Oklahoma City/Tulsa	100
Enbridge Energy Partners	Pipelines	Statewide	100
Energy Transfer Equity	Pipelines	Statewide	100
W.W. Grainger	Wholesalers/Diversified	Oklahoma City/Tulsa	100
Cameron International	Oil/Gas Equipment Services	Statewide	100
Ryder Sysem	Trucking/Truck Leasing	Statewide	100
MRC Global	Oil/Gas Equipment Services	Statewide	100

Mining/Petroleum Overview

Non-fuel Mineral Production, 2009

Mineral	Quantity (in metric tons)	Value (in thousands)
Cement	w	w
Common Clay	572,000	$2,800
Gypsum	2,180,000	$15,900
Iodine	w	w
Sand & Gravel	13,010,000	$108,500
Stone	36,835,000	$312,330
Tripoli	w	w

w = data withheld to avoid disclosing company proprietary data

Note: Total value in table above does not equal the total value of nonfuel mineral production in Oklahoma for 2009. The difference is in mineral values not released for public distribution.

According the United States Geological Survey 2009 Minerals Yearbook, in 2009 Oklahoma's nonfuel raw mineral production was valued at $667 million. This was a $153 million, or 18 percent decrease from the state's total nonfuel mineral value of $820 million in 2008, which then had increased by $86 million, or almost 12 percent from the total of $734 million in 2007. The state decreased to twenty-eighth rank from twenty-seventh among the fifty states in total nonfuel mineral production value, accounting for 1.1 percent of the U.S. total value. In 2009, crushed stone continued to be Oklahoma's leading nonfuel commodity, based upon value, accounting for 46 percent of the state's total nonfuel mineral production value, an increase from 42 percent in 2008. Crushed stone was followed by portland cement, construction sand and gravel, crude iodine, industrial sand and gravel, and Grade-A helium (descending order of value). Four of Oklahoma's leading industrial minerals: crushed stone, construction sand and gravel, industrial sand and gravel, and crude gypsum accounted for 65 percent of the state's total production value, essentially unchanged from 63 percent and 62 percent in 2008 and 2007, respectively.

Oklahoma's enormous mineral reserve can be divided into three types of mineral products: mineral fuels, metals, and non-metals. Mineral fuels are materials that can be burned, such as petroleum (crude oil and natural gas), and coal. These account for more than 90 percent of Oklahoma's annual mineral output. Metals are substances that can be melted and molded into any shape desired and are usually hard and heat resistant. There presently are no metals mined in Oklahoma. Zinc and lead are the principal metals previously mined in Oklahoma, but copper, manganese, iron, and uranium also were produced. A non-metal (industrial mineral) is any rock, mineral or other select naturally occurring or synthetic material of economic value often used in combination with other materials, such as sand and crushed stone used in concrete. The principal industrial minerals produced in Oklahoma include crushed stone, Portland cement, construction sand and gravel, industrial sand and gravel, gypsum, and iodine. Other Oklahoma non-metals include tripoli, feldspar, helium, common clay, dimension stone, salt, volcanic ash, and lime.

Oklahoma's Crude Oil Production

Source: Oklahoma Employment Security Commission

According to the Oklahoma Employment Security Commission's *Oklahoma Economic Indicators Report March 2015,* crude oil is an important commodity in the global market. Prices fluctuate depending on supply and demand conditions in the world. Since oil is such an important part of the economy, it can also help determine the direction of inflation. In the United States, consumer prices have moderated whenever oil prices have fallen, but have accelerated when oil prices have risen. The U.S. Energy Information Administration (EIA) provides information on petroleum inventories in the U.S., whether produced here or abroad.

The Baker Hughes rig count is an important indicator for the energy industry and Oklahoma. When drilling rigs are active they consume products and services produced by the oil service industry. The active rig count acts as a leading indicator of demand for products used in drilling, completing, producing and processing hydrocarbons.

West Texas Intermediate (WTI-Cushing) is a light crude oil produced in Texas and southern Oklahoma which serves as a reference or "marker" for pricing a number of other crude streams and which is traded in the domestic spot market at Cushing, Oklahoma.

Oklahoma produces a substantial amount of oil, with annual production typically accounting for more than 3 percent of total U.S. production in recent years. Crude oil wells and gathering pipeline systems are concentrated in central Oklahoma. Two of the one hundred largest oil fields in the United States are found in Oklahoma.

The city of Cushing, in central Oklahoma, is a major crude oil trading hub connecting Gulf Coast producers to Midwest refining markets. In addition to Oklahoma crude oil, the Cushing hub receives supply from several major pipelines that originate in Texas. Traditionally, the Cushing Hub has pushed Gulf Coast and Mid-Continent crude oil supply north to Midwest refining markets. However, production from those regions is in decline, and an underused crude oil pipeline system has been reversed to deliver rapidly expanding heavy crude oil supply produced in Alberta, Canada, to Cushing, where it can access Gulf Coast refining markets.

Cushing is the designated delivery point for the New York Mercantile Exchange (NYMEX) crude oil futures contracts. Crude oil supplies from Cushing that are not delivered to the Midwest are fed to Oklahoma's five refineries, which have a combined distillation capacity of over 500 thousand barrels per day—roughly 3 percent of the total U.S. refining capacity.

Current Oil Trends

According to the Oklahoma Employment Security Commission's *Oklahoma Economic Indicators Report March 2015,* United States crude oil production increased during 2014 by 1.2 million barrels per day (bbl/d) to 8.7 million bbl/d, the largest volume increase since recordkeeping began in 1900, according to the U.S. Energy Information Administration (EIA). On a percentage basis, output in 2014 increased by 16.2 percent, the highest growth rate since 1940. Most of the increase during 2014 came from tight oil plays in North Dakota, Texas, and New Mexico where hydraulic fracturing and horizontal drilling were used to produce oil from shale formations.

Oklahoma's crude production in February 2015 was at 11,179,000 barrels, 79,000 barrels (or 6.0 percent) less than January 2015 level of 11,250,000 barrels. For 2014, Oklahoma's crude production was 127,730,000 barrels, 13,548,000 barrels or 11.9 percent more than the 114,182,000 barrels produced in 2013 and the highest annual crude production level since 1988.

North American crude oil poured into the country's main trading hub at Cushing, Oklahoma while oil prices remain on the decline. After increasing for fifteen consecutive weeks, crude oil storage at Cushing reached 54.4 million barrels on March 13, 2015.

West Texas Intermediate (WTI-Cushing) spot prices drifted down in March 2015 and remained at about half of the level seen just six months prior. The WTI-Cushing spot price stood at $48.68 per barrel for the week ending March 27, 2015. That's $4.29 above the previous week's price but $51.98, or 51.6 percent below a year ago.

The number of U.S. oil rigs (Baker-Hughes count) fell by eleven in March 2015 to 802, the lowest oil rig count in four years. The biggest declines came from North Dakota, which saw six rigs shut down, and Texas, which saw five rigs shut down. In March 2015, Oklahoma's active rotary rig count tumbled to its lowest level since July 2010. The number of active rigs in the state stood a 133. Of those 133 rigs, 124 were oil-directed and nine were natural gas-directed.

Oklahoma's Natural Gas Production

According to the Oklahoma Employment Security Commission's *Oklahoma Economic Indicators Report March 2015*, Oklahoma is one of the top natural gas producers in the United States with production typically accounting for almost one-tenth of the U.S. total. More than a dozen of the one hundred largest natural gas fields in the country are found in Oklahoma and proven reserves of conventional natural gas have been increasing in recent years.

Most natural gas in Oklahoma is consumed by the electricity generation and industrial sectors. About three-fifths of Oklahoma households use natural gas as their primary energy source for home heating. Nevertheless, only about one-third of Oklahoma's natural gas output is consumed within the state. The remaining supply is sent via pipeline to neighboring states, the majority to Kansas, including the natural gas trading hubs in Texas and Kansas.

Current Natural Gas Trends

Despite declining rig counts, the U.S. Energy Information Administration (EIA) forecasts continued growth in natural gas production. In the past, the number of gas-oriented drilling rigs in a particular region was a common metric for estimating the production of natural gas. However, over the last several years, natural gas production has steadily increased, while the number of active rigs characterized as targeting natural gas has fallen dramatically.

The EIA lists several reasons that have contributed to the breakdown of traditional methods of estimating natural gas production based principally on rig counts. First, with the development of shale resources, there is an increased integration of oil and gas production, and natural gas is often produced from rigs that are targeting oil. Additionally, there have been increases in drilling efficiency, or the number of wells drilled per rig each month.

Natural gas prices moved downward at most market locations through March 2015 with more seasonal temperatures. The Henry Hub spot price posted a .25 cent (8.2 percent) decline from $3.04/MMBtu for the week ending March 6, 2015, to $2.79/MMBtu for the week ending March 27, 2015.

The Baker Hughes rotary rig count for natural gas in Oklahoma gained a rig in March 2015. For the week ending March 27, 2015. Oklahoma's natural gas-directed drilling rig count was at a level of nine active rigs, the same rig count as the previous week but one more from the week ending March 6, 2015, and representing only six percent of total statewide drilling activity. Over the year, Oklahoma's natural gas-directed rotary rig count was down ten rigs from the nineteen rigs reported for the week ended March 28, 2014.

Agriculture Overview

Environmental conditions such as climate and soil type have a great influence on agriculture practices in the state. Oklahoma lies between the long growing season of the South and the shorter growing season of the North. The average length of this season, also called the freeze-free period, ranges from 168 days in the northwestern Panhandle to about 240 days along the Red River in south central and southern sections of the state.

In most circumstances, individual farming areas include more than one type of crop since it is more economical to grow a variety of crops within one area; however, wheat is planted on more acres than any other crop in Oklahoma. Wheat production is centered primarily in the northwestern and north central areas of the state. Oklahoma normally ranks second in winter wheat production, surpassed only by Kansas.

The Panhandle area of Oklahoma is a mixed area of rangeland and valuable irrigated cropland. Wheat, corn, and grain sorghum are grown to help support a large cattle feeding industry and a recent expansion in hog production.

Cotton and grain production is extensive in the southwestern corner of the state. The warm climate in this area is extremely hospitable to cotton production and provides an annual growing season in excess of 210 days. The area receives between twenty-two and thirty inches of rainfall annually.

A wide variety of crops are grown in the mixed-farming region in the eastern part of the state. While soybeans play an important role on farms within this zone, farmers supplement their income by growing crops such as corn, peanuts, strawberries, peaches, and assorted vegetables. Contract broiler operations, egg laying flocks, and hog production facilities are found in this area of the state, which also has a large number of cattle ranches and a significant number of dairy farms.

The range-grazing lands of Oklahoma are spread across the state. The six regions shown on the map generally have rich soils and plentiful supplies of water to support grasses. Ranches located in areas where soils are not as rich make up for the deficit by increasing the number of grazing acres per animal.

The years between 1879 and 1900 saw a rapid increase in farm production because of an expansion in the labor force and more efficient technology in the area of horse drawn plows, cultivators, and grain harvesters. During this period, the total acreage of cropland in the United States grew rapidly. This expansion period ended by 1920.

Between 1935 and 1960, agricultural output per man hour increased by more than

Information for Agriculture Overview was provided by the Agricultural Statistics Division, Oklahoma Department of Agriculture, and in particular, the *Oklahoma Agricultural Statistics 2014 Report*. The U.S. Department of Agriculture's *Trade and Agriculture: What's at Stake for Oklahoma* report for 2010 served as the source of information on Oklahoma's agricultural exports. Additional information (including maps) was found in the *Atlas of Oklahoma*, edited by Tom Wikle, published by Oklahoma State University, 1991.

four times, while crop production per acre nearly doubled. It was also during this time that many subsistence farms were eliminated by larger, more specialized farms. Although the number of farms in the U.S. in the mid-1930s was almost seven million, by the mid 1970s, that number had dropped to about two million.

According to the *2014 Oklahoma Agricultural Statistics Report*, in 2013 Oklahoma had a total of 80,100 farms. The total land area in farms equaled 34,400,000 acres. The average size farm was 429 acres.

As of January 1, 2014, Oklahoma's farms and ranches held 4,300,000 cattle and calves, down 800,000 from 2011. The cow inventory consisted of 1,800,000 beef cows and 45,000 milk cows. The annual average milk production per cow decreased slightly to 17,556 pounds, an average decrease of 132 pounds of milk per cow. The total milk production in 2013 was 790 millions pounds. As of December 1, 2013, Oklahoma held 1,980,000 hogs, and 7,064,000 pigs. As of January 1, 2014, the state held 65,000 sheep; the 2013 lamb crop was 44,000 lambs. As of December 1, 2013, total chickens (excluding broilers) in Oklahoma totaled 4.23 million. Hens and pullets of laying age, at 3 million, were down 3 percent from 2012.

Cash receipts for all Oklahoma commodities sold in 2012 totaled 7.04 billion, up 1.7 percent from 2011. Receipts from livestock and related products, which accounted for 78 percent of the total cash receipts, totaled $5.51 billion, a 4.8 percent decrease from 2011. Receipts for cattle and calves sold were down 5.1 percent to $3.56 billion, as were hog receipts, at $914 million, down 3.4 percent. The third largest livestock item, based on cash receipts, was broilers at $710 million, down 2.7 percent from 2011. Dairy product receipts decreased 16 percent from 2011 sales, at $169 million.

Crop sales for 2012, at $1.53 billion, were up 35 percent from 2011. Sales of wheat totaled $758 million, up 93 percent from 2011. All hay sales, at $170 million, were

Agricultural Regions

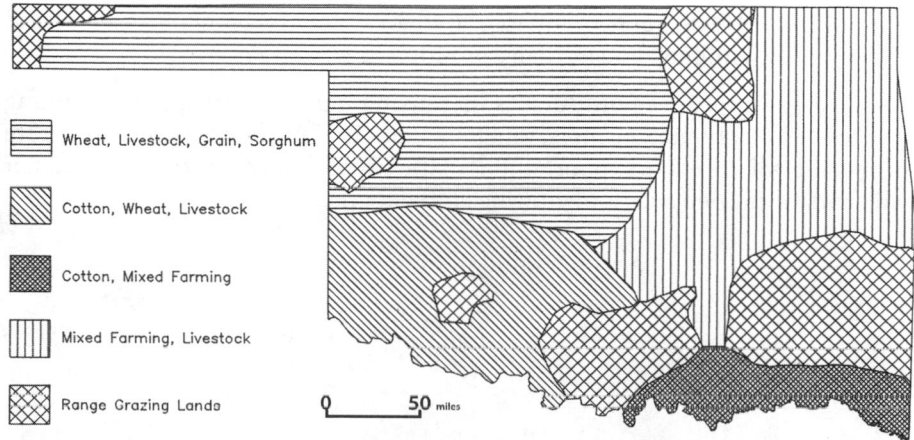

Wheat, Livestock, Grain, Sorghum

Cotton, Wheat, Livestock

Cotton, Mixed Farming

Mixed Farming, Livestock

Range Grazing Lands

0   50 miles

more than double 2011 receipts. Cash receipts for corn, sorghum, cotton, soybeans, and sunflowers all declined from 2011. Cash receipts for canola, oats, and rye all increased from the previous year.

The average value per head of all cattle and calves on January 1, 2104, was $1,110, up $60 from a year earlier. The total inventory value of all cattle and calves was $4.77 billion. The average value per head of all sheep and lambs on January 1, 2014, was $238, up $15 from 2013. The total inventory value was $15.5 million. There were 150 thousand pounds of wool produced in 2013, level the amount with 2012. The average price received for wool was .60 cents per pound, .10 cents less than 2012. The average value per head of all hogs and pigs on December 1, 2013, was $125, up $20 dollars from 2012. The total inventory value of all hog and pigs was $249 million. The average price per pound for broilers, at 60.5 cents, was up 10.5 cents from the 2012 price. The calculated price per dozen eggs increased .11 cents from a year earlier to $1.58 per dozen.

The 2013 Oklahoma winter wheat market year average price was $6.90 per bushel, a decrease of .55 cents from 2012. The average sorghum price was $7.45 per hundredweight, a decrease of $4.55 from the previous year. Corn, at $5.20 per bushel, decreased $1.84 from 2012. Soybeans were $12.60 per bushel for 2013, down $1.80 for 2012. The cotton lint market year average price was up from 2012 to .77 cents per pound. Peanut prices decreased to 29.7 cents per pound. The average price for all hay was $147 per ton in 2013, 16.6 percent higher than 2012. Oat prices decreased, while rye prices increased and canola was down $2.60 to $22.60 per hundredweight. The market year average price of native pecans decreased by .5 cents, while prices for improved pecans increased by .50 cents. Cash rent paid for cropland in Oklahoma in 2014 was unchanged from 2013, at $33.50 per acre. Cash rent paid for pasture land was also static, at $12.00 per acre in 2014.

Oklahoma produces agricultural products that are exported worldwide. In 2012, the state's farm cash receipts totaled $7.04 billion, and exports were an estimated $1.7 billion. Oklahoma's top ten agricultural exports in 2010 were (1) wheat products at $403.2 million, (2) beef and veal at $288.4 million, (3) pork at $260.5 million, (4) hides and skins at $145.3 million, (5) chicken meat at $131.1 million, (6) grain products at $65.7 million, (7) cotton at $51.7 million, (8) soybeans at $29.5 million, (9) feeds and fodders at $25.9 million, and (10) dairy products at $23.4 million.

World demand for these products is increasing, but so is competition among suppliers. If Oklahoma's farmers, ranchers, and food processors are to compete successfully for the export opportunities of the twenty-first century, they need fair trade and more open access to growing global markets.

2013 Crop Weather Review

January—Drought continued to afflict the state with the U.S. Drought Monitor reporting the entire state in a severe to exceptional drought, with nearly 40 percent of the state in exceptional drought, the worst condition. The state averaged just under one inch of rain for the month, and while the Southeast district received just over two inches it was still below average. Temperatures varied greatly throughout the month with a low of –10 in Kenton and a high of 80 in Hollis during the month. Over the month the average low temperature was below freezing. Both small grains and pasture conditions were rated as poor to very poor.

February—The drought continued throughout the month of February but was lessened slightly due to rain and snow during the later portion of the month. The moisture allowed for some crop improvements, however wheat, canola, and rye were rated mostly fair to poor and oats were rated mostly poor to very poor. Topsoil conditions improved somewhat with 2 percent being rated surplus, and 43 percent rated adequate.

March—The month was cool slowing small grain growth. There were reports of snow in the northern part of the state early in the month, and the month ended with severe thunderstorms, damaging winds, and hail. The state averaged 0.6 inches of rain in the last week of the month. Despite that six of the nine districts ended the month with less than half of the normal amount of rain, and none of the districts reported above average rainfall for the month of March.

April—The month of April began wet with an average of 1.44 inches of rain during the first week of the month and .86 in the second week. Freeze damage was reported with Boise City tying the previous record low on April 11th at 15 degrees and setting a state record on the 24th at the same temperature. Seventy-two percent of the state remained in drought conditions.

May—May began cold with Tulsa setting a new record for latest snowfall in that city. Drought conditions lessened in the eastern part of the state early in the month while the Panhandle deteriorated. The second half of the month was characterized by little rain in the western half of the state, and deadly storms, including the May 20th tornado in Moore that took twenty-four lives. Crop progress continued to lag behind the average, and only four districts reported above 90 percent average rainfall, with only two above average.

June— Rain during the month brought some districts closer to their normal rain accumulation, however, the Panhandle and West Central Oklahoma both ended the month with less than 60 percent of their normal rain accumulation for the period between March 1 and June 30. Grasshopper problems were reported throughout the month of June and crop progress was generally lagging behind normal. The exceptions to this were sorghum which was progressing normally, and peanuts and non-alfalfa hay, which were both slightly ahead of normal progress by the end of the month.

July— Small grain harvest ended in July, later that normal. Row crop progress generally was behind normal, however rain later in the month allowed for row crop conditions to improve. Precipitation since the beginning of March was at or above 90 percent of average in six districts, and the Southwest district was at 87 percent of average. The Panhandle and West Central districts were both below 70 percent of the average rainfall for the period.

August—By the second week of August only 23 percent of the state was in severe to exceptional drought. Cotton conditions improved substantially during the month ending mostly fair to good. Other row crops were rated mostly good. By the end of the month seven districts were at or above 80 percent of normal rain for the period between the first of March and the end of August, and five of those were above 100 percent. Only the Panhandle and West Central districts were below 80 percent at 58 and 68 percent of normal rainfall respectively.

September—After a dry start to the month, seedbed preparation and planting slowed on small grains. By the end of the month, rain had allowed preparation and planting to resume and was on par with normal progress. Despite late rains seven districts had less than average rainfall for the month; however, the West Central district was slightly above average, while the Panhandle district received 162 percent of normal rainfall for the period.

October— Rain was lacking throughout the state during October. Only the Panhandle and the Southeast district reported 100 percent or more of normal precipitation for the period between September 1 and the end of October. Pasture and range conditions were mostly fair to good as well. Crop progress was normal or ahead of normal except for rye, of which 6 percent less than normal had emerged, and cotton, which was also behind the five year average.

November— The month began with rainfall in the Northeast. Crops progressed normally for most of the month, although cotton lagged behind initially. Crops were mostly rated as being in good condition, with the exception of cotton with 50–48 percent rated as fair to good during the month. Topsoil moisture was rated as mostly adequate with approximately 60 percent of the soil in this moisture category. Subsoil was not as well off with just under 50 percent rated as adequate. The month ended with snow, freezing rain, and sleet throughout the state.

December— Temperatures in December were below normal due to multiple winter storms. Despite the winter storms, precipitation in the state was below normal for the period between September 1 and the end of December. Only two districts reported over 90 percent of normal precipitation while three districts were below 70 percent of normal. Soil moisture conditions deteriorated slightly. Despite ice and drought conditions small grain and pasture conditions were rated mostly good to fair in December allowing for more livestock grazing.

Agricultural and Livestock Production

Highlights of Oklahoma Agriculture

Source: 2012 Census of Agriculture, Oklahoma Department of Agriculture
This Census is published every five years by the U.S. Department of Agriculture.

Category	1997	2007	2012
Number of Farms	74,214	86,565	80,245
Land in Farms (acres)	33,218,677	35,087,269	34,356,110
Average Size of Farm (acres)	448	405	428

Value of Land and Buildings (based on sample of farms)

Average per farm ($)	$271,996	$468,809	$573,858
Average per acre ($)	$610	$1,157	$1,340

Estimated Market Value of All Machinery and Equipment
(based on sample of farms)

Average per farm ($)	$36,936	$63,642	$74,212
Farms by Size			
1 to 9 acres	2,505	3,802	3,724
10 to 49 acres	12,673	18,700	16,327
50 to 179 acres	24,681	29,719	27,418
180 to 499 acres	18,288	19,140	17,546
500 to 999 acres	8,155	7,484	7,401
1,000 acres or more	7,912	7,720	7,829

Total Cropland

Farms	58,741	59,040	49,150
Acres	14,843,823	13,007,625	11,279,031

Harvested Cropland

Farms	44,786	46,224	40,246
Acres	8,462,079	7,650,080	8,074,733

Irrigated Land

Farms	2,710	3,026	2,500
Acres	506,459	534,768	479,750

Category	1997	2007	2012
Market Value of Agricultural Products Sold ($)	$4,146,351	$5,806,061	$7,129,584
Average per farm ($)	$55,870	$67,072	$88,848
Crops, including nursery and greenhouse crops ($)	$907,865	$1,187,625	$1,875,569
Livestock, poultry and their products ($)	$3,238,485	$4,618,436	$5,254,015

Farms by Value of Sales

	1997	2007	2012
Less than $2,500	20,476	34,669	29,794
$2,500 to $4,999	11,713	9,059	8,032
$5,000 to $9,999	12,341	10,731	9,680
$10,000 to $24,999	12,869	13,494	12,437
$25,000 to $49,999	6,234	6,886	7,070
$50,000 to $99,999	4,285	4,563	5,198
$100,000 or more	5,296	7,163	8,034
Total Farm Production Expenses ($)	$3,576,456	$5,223,365	$6,682,769
Average per farm ($)	$48,186	$60,340	$83,280

Net Cash Return from Agricultural Sales for the Farm Unit

	1997	2007	2012
# of farms w/$1000 or more sales	74,222	86,565	80,245
Average per Farm	$6,145	$11,885	$11,899

Livestock and Poultry

	1997	2007	2012
Cattle and Calves Inventory			
Farms w/cattle	58,023	55,105	51,043
Number of head of cattle	5,321,161	5,391,337	4,245,970
Beef Cows			
Farms	49,281	47,059	44,106
Number	1,931,805	2,063,613	1,677,903
Milk Cows			
Farms	1,921	981	756
Number	87,647	66,023	45,885
Hogs and Pigs inventory			
Farms	3,002	2,702	1,947
Number	1,689,700	2,398,372	2,304,740

Category	1997	2007	2012
Hogs and Pigs sold			
Farms	2,082	2,274	1,456
Number	3,943,563	9,010,682	7,707,814
Sheep and Lambs inventory			
Farms	1,792	1,939	1,779
Number	74,596	76,243	53,738
Chickens 3 months old or older inventory			
Farms	3,293	5,235	6,760
Number	5,059,373	3,323,802	3,121,799
Broilers and other meat-type chickens sold			
Farms	632	636	606
Number	138,607,293	242,228,335	211,214,930

Selected Crops Harvested

Category	1997	2007	2012
Sorghum for Grain or Seed			
Farms w/sorghum	2,557	966	954
Acres in state	417,872	219,883	200,532
Bushels in state	18,863,920	11,682,402	5,132,364
Wheat for Grain			
Farms	13,935	8,744	9,946
Acres	4,825,074	3,421,098	4,291,939
Bushels	141,302,977	89,968,524	139,417,085
Cotton			
Farms	849	420	451
Acres	176,962	164,273	139,740
Bales	190,186	279,871	153,250
Soybeans for Beans			
Farms	1,921	813	1,039
Acres	323,082	180,878	259,921
Bushels	9,498,068	4,559,245	3,639,154
Peanuts for Nuts			
Farms	662	148	166
Acres	68,340	16,319	21,926
Pounds	163,572,035	55,039,635	76,491,464
Hay—Alfalfa, other wild silage			
Farms	35,751	38,897	32,781
Acres	2,478,944	3,250,005	2,705,150
Tons, dry	4,651,859	6,607,628	3,761,205

Agricultural Trade Statistics, 2012

Product	Oklahoma Exports (millions of $)	U. S. Exports (millions of $)
Beef and Veal	288.4	5,509
Pork	260.5	6,321
Hides and Skins	145.3	2,775
Chicken Meat	131.1	4,179
Dairy Products	23.4	5,124
Wheat	403.2	8,158
Grain Products	65.7	5,902
Cotton	51.7	6,255
Soybeans	29.5	24,606
Feeds and Fodder	25.9	6,417
Tree Nuts	21.8	6,506
Corn	18.2	9,338
Vegetable Oils	11.1	4,165
Soybean Meal	5.9	4,865
Vegetables, Processed	4.0	4,053
Fruits, Fresh	3.7	4,936
Fruits, Processed	2,2	2,883
Vegetables, Fresh	2.1	2,159
Planting Seeds	1.7	1,522
Other Products	298.9	20,406
Total	1,794.4	141,270

The above data are based on the assumption that each state's contribution to exports is equal to each state's share of production or marketing. They should not be interpreted as an actual measure of the state's export. Totals in this chart for U.S. exports include Tobacco, Rice, and Sunflower Seed and Sunflower Oil. These commodities are not listed, as Oklahoma has no exports in these categories.

WILDLIFE
& NATURE

Location and Size

Oklahoma is surrounded by six other states: Texas to the south and west, New Mexico to the west, Colorado and Kansas to the north, and Missouri and Arkansas to the east. Oklahoma City serves as the state's capital. It is located very near the geographic center of the state. Geographic center is approximately eight miles north of Oklahoma City.

Lines of longitude and latitude form a grid system on the earth's surface. These reference lines are used to pinpoint the position of any spot on Earth. Oklahoma extends across north latitudes and west longitudes.

Latitude is distance measured north and south of the equator. Lines of latitude, also called parallels, are established by the angle between a radius from a point at the center of the earth in relation to the equatorial plane. Latitude ranges from 90 degrees at each pole to zero degrees at the equator. For greater precision, degrees of latitude can be broken up into minutes and seconds. There are sixty minutes in a degree and sixty seconds in each minute. One degree of latitude equals roughly sixty-nine miles because the Earth is not a perfect sphere.

Longitude is the other component of the Earth's grid system. Lines of longitude, called meridians, run north and south and help to pinpoint locations east and west. Longitude is

Location of Oklahoma

This section was compiled using data from the following sources: *The Atlas of Oklahoma, Classroom Edition*, published by the Department of Geography, Oklahoma State University, October 1991, Tom Wikle, Editor • U.S. Government Information Division, Oklahoma Department of Libraries, Steve Beleu, Administrator • Geological Survey at the University of Oklahoma • State Geographer Bob Springer • Oklahoma Climatological Survey • Wayne Wyrick at the Kirkpatrick Planetarium • The Oklahoma Department of Wildlife Conservation • Forestry Services Division of the Oklahoma Department of Agriculture.

Longitude and Latitude

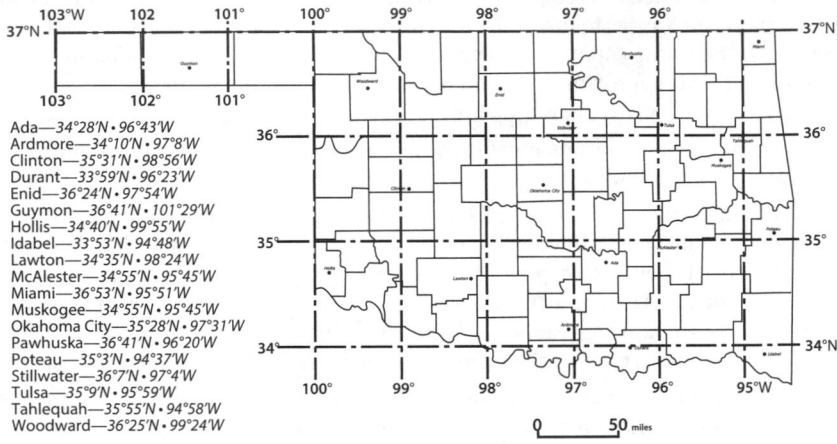

Ada—*34°28′N • 96°43′W*
Ardmore—*34°10′N • 97°8′W*
Clinton—*35°31′N • 98°56′W*
Durant—*33°59′N • 96°23′W*
Enid—*36°24′N • 97°54′W*
Guymon—*36°41′N • 101°29′W*
Hollis—*34°40′N • 99°55′W*
Idabel—*33°53′N • 94°48′W*
Lawton—*34°35′N • 98°24′W*
McAlester—*34°55′N • 95°45′W*
Miami—*36°53′N • 95°51′W*
Muskogee—*34°55′N • 95°45′W*
Oklahoma City—*35°28′N • 97°31′W*
Pawhuska—*36°41′N • 96°20′W*
Poteau—*35°3′N • 94°37′W*
Stillwater—*36°7′N • 97°4′W*
Tulsa—*35°9′N • 95°59′W*
Tahlequah—*35°55′N • 94°58′W*
Woodward—*36°25′N • 99°24′W*

also measured in degrees, minutes, and seconds. The most important reference line used for longitudinal reference is the Prime Meridian established in 1884 by international agreement. The Prime Meridian runs through the Royal Observatory at Greenwich, England, and represents a longitude of zero degrees. Longitudes to the east of the Prime Meridian are called east longitudes and those to the west, west longitudes. On the opposite side of the earth is the International Date Line that represents a longitude of 180 degrees.

Oklahoma is situated between ninety-four degrees, twenty-nine minutes, and 103 degrees west longitude; and thirty-three degrees, forty-one minutes, and thirty-seven degrees north latitude.

By the time Oklahoma was granted statehood in 1907, it had been divided into seventy-five counties. New counties were created when Harmon County was separated from Greer County,

Trends in County Populations

County	1991 Population	2014 Pop. Est.
Five Largest		
Oklahoma	636,539	766,215
Tulsa	548,296	629,598
Cleveland	203,449	269,908
Canadian	86,498	129,582
Comanche	106,621	125,033
Five Smallest		
Cimarron	2,922	2,294
Harmon	3,336	2,798
Roger Mills	3.593	3,761
Harper	3,580	3,812
Ellis	4,194	4,150

Source: U.S. Census Bureau data

and Cotton County broke away from Comanche County. With these additions in 1910, the number of counties was elevated to the present total of seventy-seven. Since statehood, only eight counties have relocated their county seats.

Osage is the state's largest county with an area of 2,293 square miles, while Marshall is the smallest county in the state with only 360 square miles. Cimarron County is the only state county in the nation that borders four other states (Kansas, Colorado, New Mexico, and Texas).

The five largest counties by population, according to the U.S. Census 2014 estimates are: Oklahoma (766,215), Tulsa (629,598), Cleveland (269,908), Canadian (129,582) and Comanche (125,033). In contrast, the five smallest counties by population are: Cimarron (2,294), Harmon (2,798), Roger Mills (3,812), Harper (3,761), and Ellis (4,150). For more information, visit www.census.gov

Locating property in Oklahoma can be accomplished by using a reference system known as Township and Range. The system was adopted by the federal government as a part of the Northwest Ordinance of 1785 to prevent conflicting titles of land as pioneers claimed irregularly shaped plots to acquire the most fertile lands. It was also initiated to assist in the orderly survey and sale of public land. The Township and Range System uses an initial point from which all locations are referenced. The primary initial point used for land in Oklahoma is located about one mile south of Fort Arbuckle in Murray County (in south central Oklahoma). This point was established by Ehud N. Darling in 1870 to aid in the dispersion of Indian lands. Running through the initial point are two lines: a base line that corresponds to an east/west parallel, and a north/south meridian. All areas to the north of this point are referred to as township north and areas to the south are called township south. The meridian associated with the initial point is called the "Indian Meridian" and is used to designate range east from range west.

The base line and meridian are divided into six-mile segments forming a grid of individual township/range units. These units are again divided into thirty-six, one-square-mile sections that are numbered consecutively beginning in the northeast corner of the township/range. These sections (640 acres each) are then divided into half-sections, quarter-sections, etc.

Townships and Ranges

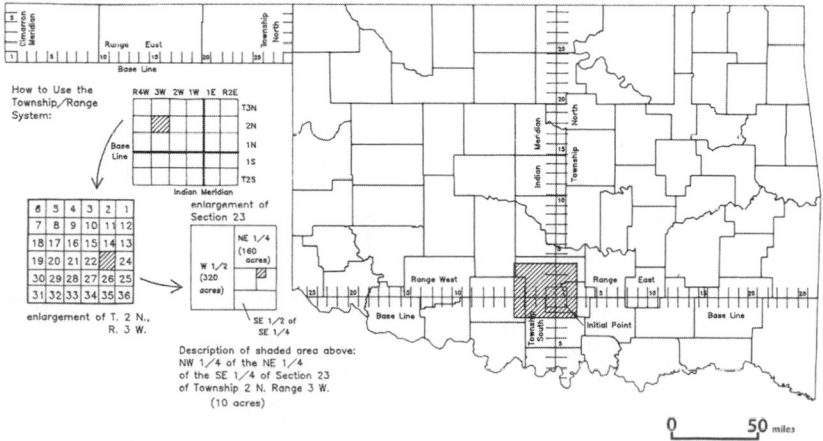

State Dimensions

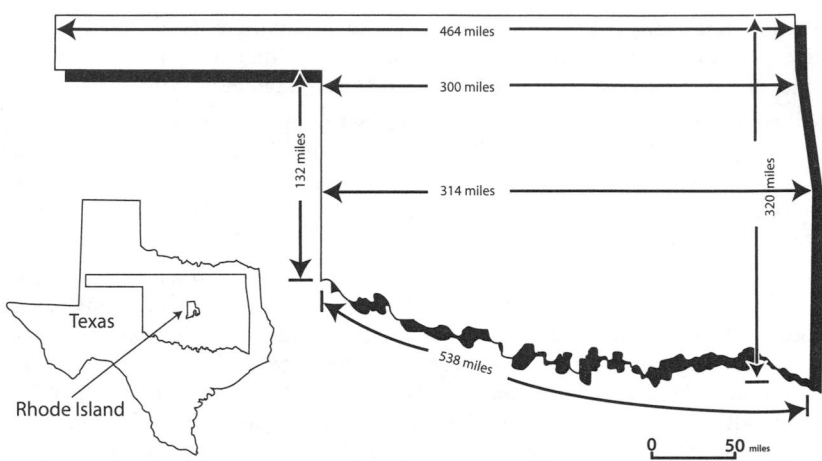

Excluding the Panhandle, there are thirty-eight township lines running east and west and fifty-three range lines running north and south. A separate initial point was used for the panhandle and is located at the southwest corner of Cimarron County.

Oklahoma is located farther west than any country in South America. Traveling due south from Oklahoma City, one would cross Texas and the country of Mexico before reaching the Pacific Ocean. All of South America would be located to the east. Oklahoma covers an area of 69,903 square miles (68,679 in land and 1,224 in water).

Oklahoma ranks eighteenth in size in the United States and is considered one of the larger states when compared to those of the East Coast. The combined area of Maine, Massachusetts, New Hampshire, Rhode Island, Vermont, and Connecticut are smaller than the area of Oklahoma. Oklahoma is more than fifty times larger than the state of Rhode Island and has about the same area as the South American country of Uruguay. Only Montana, Tennessee, Texas, and Alaska have greater east-west distances than Oklahoma. With 277,340 square miles, Texas is almost four times larger than Oklahoma. When compared to other states in the West, Oklahoma is larger than Washington and Hawaii.

Demographics

Population

According to the U.S. Census Bureau, Oklahoma's population for 2000 was 3,450,654. This represents an increase of 9.7 percent from 1990 to 2000, or 305,069 persons. For 2014, Oklahoma's population was estimated to be 3,878,051. In 1990, population density was 46.1 persons per square mile; in 2000, the density was 50.3. Trends in Oklahoma continue to show people leaving rural areas of the state in favor of urbanized areas. The two biggest concentrations of people in the state are in the metropolitan areas of Oklahoma City and Tulsa. U.S. Census Bureau population predictions state that Oklahoma's population is estimated to be 4,057,000 by 2025.

Vital Statistics

In 2014 Oklahoma had 53,230 live births, and 38,345 deaths (preliminary data). By comparison, in 2000, there were 49,782 births and 35,079 deaths. The number of births to unwed teenage mothers in Oklahoma in 2014 was 4,078 (preliminary data), a decrease from 4,353 in 2013.

The number of marriages in Oklahoma in 2013 was 27,275, a decrease from the 28,321 marriages in 2012. The number of divorces in Oklahoma decreased in 2013 with 17,227, down from 18,339 in 2012.

Vernacular and Cultural Regions

Vernacular regions are areas that have a unique cultural identity among their residents. R. Todd Zdorkowski and George O. Carney's map [below] was constructed using a survey of past and present Oklahoma place names that respondents had heard or used. The regions shown reflect local customs and economic histories. The area known as "Little Dixie" is dominated

Vernacular Regions

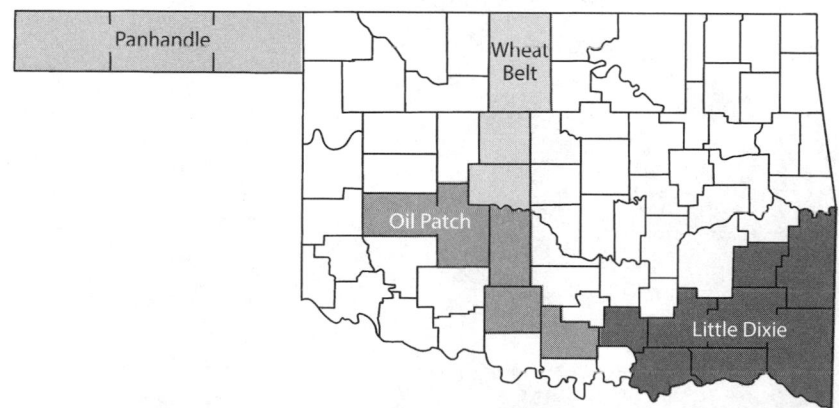

Zdorkowski and Carney, 1985

Cultural Regions

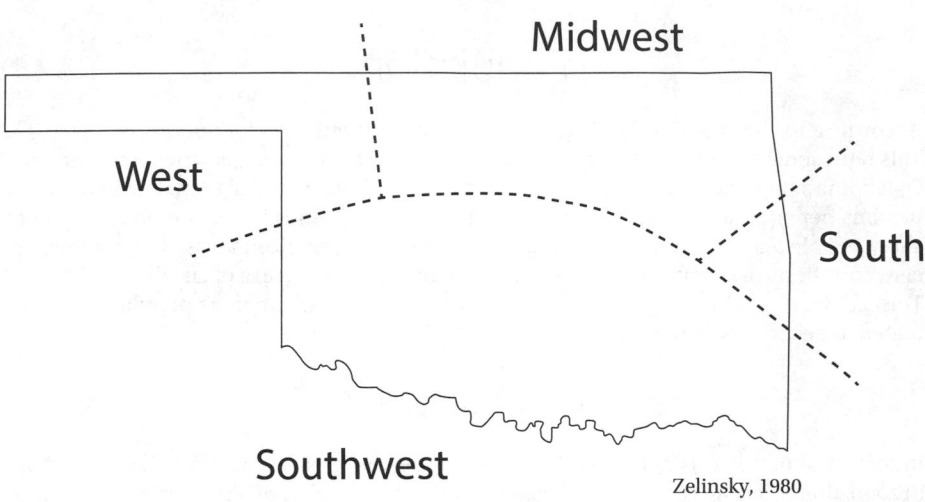

Midwest

West

South

Southwest

Zelinsky, 1980

by a non-Indian population; however, the Indian population of this region responded to the survey with the name "Kiamichi," which was once the Oklahoma Tourism Department's name for the area (although pronunciations differ). A uniformity among responses concerning the Panhandle region suggests it is the most widely accepted vernacular region. Other region names are derived from economic terms, suggesting local experience and public involvement may be the keys to regional perception.

Wilbur Zelinsky's map [above] is an excerpt from a national map of cultural geography. Oklahoma is at the center of three cultural regions of the nation: the Middle West, the South and the West. The influx of Indians from the East and the settlement of Europeans add to uncertainty in the national cultural identity of Oklahoma.

Climate

According to the Koppen climate classification, Oklahoma's climate ranges from humid subtropical in the east to semi-arid in the west. Warm, moist air moving northward from the Gulf of Mexico often exerts much influence, particularly over the southern and eastern portions of the state, where humidity, cloudiness, and precipitation are greater than in western and northern sections. Summers are long and usually quite hot. Winters are shorter and less severe than those of the more northern Plains states. Periods of extreme cold are infrequent, and those lasting more than a few days are rare.

Our knowledge of climate is based on the variables that we measure, typically with surface observing stations, weather radar, satellites, weather balloons, and other instrumentation. Some weather events cannot be measured easily by automated methods (e.g., tornadoes) and must be documented by human observers. Hence, as Oklahoma's population increased over the years, human observations of rare events became more prevalent. Even measurements of mundane variables such as temperature have become more common, with automated weather stations taking more measurements per day at more locations than in past decades. Climatologists know how to work with changes in observing intervals, sensors, techniques, and locations to provide decision makers with an historical record to better understand climate normals, extremes, and variability.

Precipitation

The dominant feature of the spatial distribution of rainfall across Oklahoma is a sharp decrease in rainfall from east to west. Although precipitation is quite variable on a year-to-year basis average annual precipitation ranges from about 17 inches in the far western panhandle to about 56 inches in the far southeast. Only the summer months of July and August see a substantial relaxation of this distribution. The greatest annual precipitation recorded at an official reporting station was 84.47 inches at Kiamichi Tower in the southeast in 1957. The least annual rainfall occurred during 1956, when Regnier, in the extreme northwestern panhandle, observed 6.53 inches.

Normal Annual Precipitation

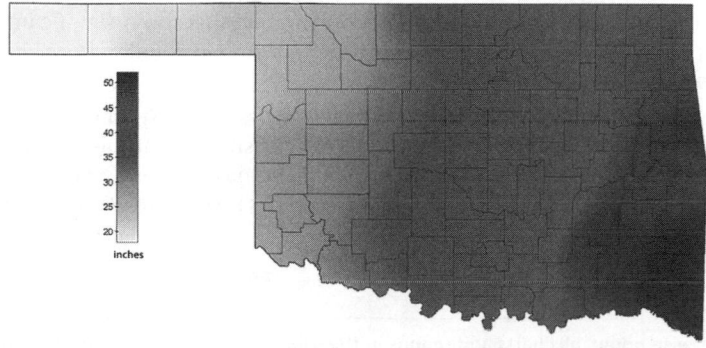

Calculated using normal data provided by NCDC. ©2011 Oklahoma Climatological Survey

Annual Precipitation History
with 5–year Tendencies

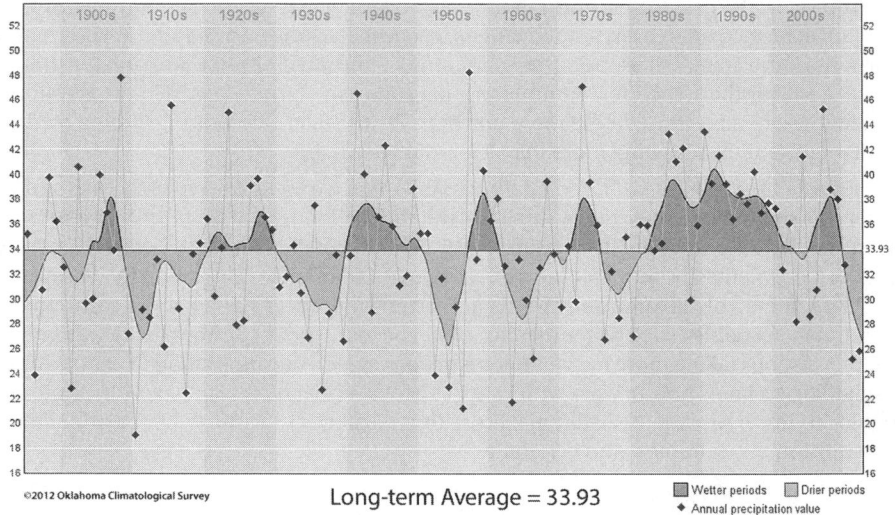

©2012 Oklahoma Climatological Survey

Long-term Average = 33.93

■ Wetter periods □ Drier periods
◆ Annual precipitation value

Graph of the statewide average annual precipitation (in inches) for Oklahoma using data from 1895 to 2009. Dark gray shading (above the horizontal line) highlights wetter periods and lighter gray shading (below the line) highlights drier periods than average.

The frequency of days with measurable precipitation follows the same gradient as the annual accumulation, increasing from forty-five days per year in western Oklahoma to 115 near the Arkansas border. On average, more precipitation falls during the nighttime hours, while greatest rainfall intensities occur during late afternoon. Excessive rainfall occurs at times. Amounts of 10 inches or more during 24 hours, while rare, have been recorded. The greatest official rainfall in a 24–hour period is 15.68 inches at Enid on October 11, 1973.

The character of precipitation also varies by season. Wintertime precipitation tends to be somewhat widespread, stratiform in nature, and tied almost exclusively to synoptic-scale systems. Rainfall is the dominant precipitation type during winter for all but the Oklahoma panhandle. Summertime precipitation is almost entirely convective in nature, produced by individual thunderstorms and thunderstorm complexes. The transition seasons of spring and autumn offer both convective and stratiform precipitation. A significant portion of the state's precipitation during the transition seasons is associated with systems of severe thunderstorms.

Average annual snowfall increases from less than 2 inches in the extreme southeast to nearly 30 inches in the western panhandle. The frequency of snow events also increases sharply along the same gradient. Locations in southeast Oklahoma have gone several years between events, while northwestern Oklahoma typically records several snow events in one winter.

Unless otherwise noted, all charts and graphs in the Climate section are courtesy of the Oklahoma Climatological Survey, and are based on statistics spanning from 1971 until 2011.

Other Climatic Features

Annual average relative humidity ranges from about 60 percent in the panhandle to just over 70 percent in the east and southeast. On average, cloudiness increases from west to east across Oklahoma. The annual fraction of possible sunshine observed ranges from about 45 percent in eastern Oklahoma to near 65 percent in the panhandle. These fractions are highest in the summer and lowest in the winter for all portions of the state.

Average annual lake evaporation varies from 48 inches in the extreme east to 65 inches in the southwest, numbers that far exceed the average yearly rainfall in those areas. Evaporation and percolation into the soil expend about 80 percent of Oklahoma's precipitation.

Prevailing winds are from the south to southeast throughout most of the state from the spring through autumn months. These prevailing winds typically are from the south to southwest in far western Oklahoma, including the panhandle. The winter wind regime is roughly equally split between northerly and southerly winds.

Temperatures

The mean annual temperature over the state ranges from 62 degrees along the Red River to about 58 degrees along the northern border. It then decreases westward to 56 degrees in Cimarron County. Temperatures of 90 degrees or greater occur, on average, about 60–65 days per year in the western panhandle and the northeast corner of the state. The average is about 115 days in southwest Oklahoma and about eighty-five days in the southeast. Temperatures of 100 degrees or higher occur, frequently during some years, from May through September, and very rarely in April and October. With thirty to forty days at or above 100 degrees, western Oklahoma experiences more extreme summer temperatures than elsewhere in the state. Both the Panhandle and eastern Oklahoma average about fifteen days above the century mark. The increased humidity in the east, however, adds to that section of the state's summertime misery. Heat index values of 105 degrees or greater occur more than forty times per year in the far southeast and less than ten times per year in the far northwest. Years without triple-digit temperatures are rare, ranging from about one of every seven years in the eastern half of the state to somewhat rarer in the west.

The highest temperature ever recorded in the state was 120 degrees. This reading was first observed during the brutally hot summer of 1936: at Alva on July 18, at Altus on both July 19 and August 12, and at Poteau on August 10.

Temperatures of 32 degrees or less occur an average of sixty days per year in the southeast. This value increases to about 110 days per year where the panhandle joins the rest of the state, and to 140 days in the western panhandle. The lowest temperature on record is –31 degrees, set at Nowata on February 10, 2011.

The average length of the growing season or freeze-free period, is at a maximum of 225 to 230 days in the southern tier of counties and in the Arkansas River Valley downstream of Tulsa. The value generally decreases to about 195 days in the eastern panhandle, then more rapidly to 175 days in the western panhandle. The general northwest-to-southeast gradient is interrupted in the Ouachita Mountains, where growing seasons are three to four weeks shorter compared to surrounding areas. Along the Red River, the average date of the last freeze of spring ranges from about March 15 in the east to April 1 in the west. In northern Oklahoma, the last freeze of spring occurs, on average, from about April 8 near the Missouri border to April 15 in the eastern panhandle to the last week of April in the western panhandle. Freezing temperatures have occurred as late as April 20 along the southern border and in

Normal Annual Temperatures

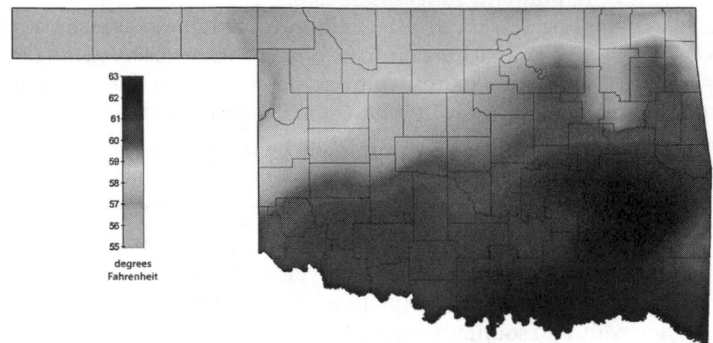

Calculated using normal data provided by NCDC. ©2011 Oklahoma Climatological Survey

east-central Oklahoma to about May 15 in northwest Oklahoma to the last days of May in the western panhandle.

The average date of the autumn's first freeze varies from about October 15 in the western panhandle, to about October 25 along the northern border and in northwestern Oklahoma, to about November 10 along the Red River and in the Arkansas River Valley downstream of Tulsa. Autumn freezes have occurred as early as about September 15 in the western third of the state to about October 15 in the southeast corner. Again, the Ouachita Mountains tend to differ from surrounding terrain by about two weeks during either season.

Frozen soil is not a major problem, nor much of a deterrent to seasonal activities. Its occurrence is rather infrequent, of very limited depth, and of brief duration.

Oklahoma's Weather Hazards

Thunderstorms and Tornadoes

On average, thunderstorms occur about fifty-five days per year in eastern Oklahoma, decreasing to about forty-five days per year in the southwest. The annual rate increases to near sixty days annually in the extreme western panhandle. Late spring and early summer are the peak seasons for thunderstorms. December and January, on average, feature the fewest thunderstorms.

Frequent cold fronts, a favorable jet stream, and dry line development make springtime the preferred season for violent thunderstorms, although they can occur at any time of year. Severe weather threats during spring include squall lines, mesoscale convective systems, heatbursts, and rotating supercell thunderstorms that can produce very large hail, damaging winds, and tornadoes. Autumn marks a secondary severe weather season, but the relative frequency of supercell thunderstorms is much lower than during spring. Individual thunderstorms are common during the summer, but tend to be less severe and shorter lived. These storms can produce locally heavy rain and hail.

Tornadoes are a particular hazard in Oklahoma. Since 1950, an average of fifty-five tornadoes have been observed annually within the state's borders. Tornadoes can occur at any time of year, but are most frequent during springtime. Three-fourths of Oklahoma's tornadoes have

Number of Tornadoes by County

Map of the number of tornadoes recorded by county using data from 1950 to 2011.

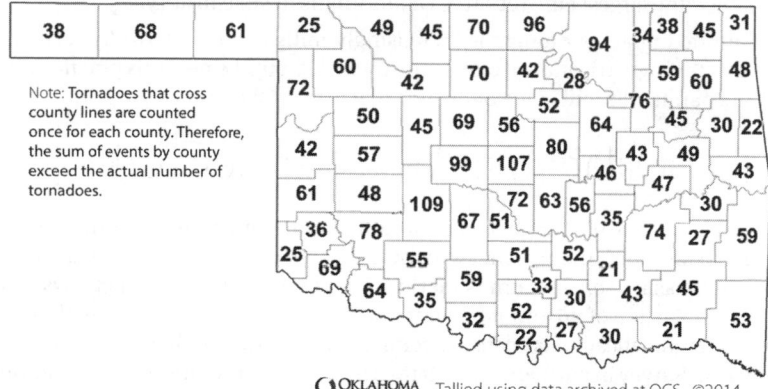

Note: Tornadoes that cross county lines are counted once for each county. Therefore, the sum of events by county exceed the actual number of tornadoes.

Ⓒ OKLAHOMA CLIMATOLOGICAL SURVEY   Tallied using data archived at OCS. ©2014

occurred during April, May, and June. May's average of twenty-one tornado observations per month is the greatest. The winter months each average less than one tornado per month.

Severe weather can occur at any time of day, but the maximum frequency for severe weather is from mid-afternoon to sunset. About 80 percent of tornadoes are observed between noon and midnight Central Standard Time, with the peak hours being between 4:00 and 8:00 PM.

Flooding

Floods of major rivers and tributaries may happen during any season, but they occur with greatest frequency during those spring and autumn months associated with greatest rainfall. Such floods cost many lives and property damage during the first fifty years of statehood, but flood prevention programs have reduced the frequency and severity of such events. Flash flooding of creeks and minor streams remains a serious threat, especially in urban and suburban areas, where development and removal of vegetation have increased runoff.

Drought

Drought is a recurring part of Oklahoma's climate cycle, as it is in all the Plains states. Almost all of Oklahoma's usable surface water comes from precipitation that falls within the state's borders. Therefore, drought in Oklahoma is tied almost entirely to local rainfall patterns (i.e., the influence of upstream events on drought is very small). Western Oklahoma is slightly more susceptible to drought because precipitation there tends to be more variable (percentage-wise) and marginal for dryland farm applications.

Drought episodes can last from a few months to several years. Those that last a few months can elevate wildfire danger and impact municipal water use. Seasonal droughts can occur at any time of the year, and those that coincide with crop production cycles can cause billions of dollars of damage to the farm economy. Multi-season and multi-year episodes can severely impact large reservoirs, streamflow, and groundwater.

Since modern climatological record-keeping began in the 1890s, the state has seen five major multi-year, regional drought events. These occurred in the late 1890s, from 1909 to 1918, 1930 to 1940, 1952 to 1956 and, to a lesser extent, 1962 to 1972. Each of these episodes contained at least one year of above-normal rainfall. The drought of the 1930s is associated with the Dust Bowl of the Great Plains, when socioeconomic conditions, agricultural practices and drought forced the largest emigration of Oklahomans in state history.

The agricultural impact of drought is increasingly mitigated on a farm-by-farm and year-by-year basis through irrigation of crops, mostly with groundwater. This practice dominates much of the panhandle and some of the rest of western Oklahoma.

Oklahoma's Weather Network

Oklahoma has acted to enhance its environmental monitoring through implementation of the Oklahoma Mesonet. The Mesonet is a world-class network of environmental monitoring stations that measure soil and atmospheric variables 24 hours a day, 365 days a year. The Mesonet is a collection of 116 towers, at least one in each county, equipped with sensors and configured to automatically relay data to a central collection point. Operated by the Oklahoma Climatological Survey in partnership with the University of Oklahoma and Oklahoma State University, the Mesonet monitors air and soil temperature, relative humidity, wind speed and direction, solar radiation, and precipitation at each of its sites. Many of the sites measure other information of agricultural or other scientific interest. Observations are made every five minutes and transmitted every five minutes. Reports are carried from the field sites to the central processing computer by a combination of radio and the dedicated high-speed telephone lines of the Oklahoma Law Enforcement Telecommunications System (OLETS).

The Mesonet is unique in its capability to measure a large variety of environmental conditions at so many sites across an area as large as Oklahoma. In addition, these conditions are relayed to a wide variety of customers very quickly after the observations are taken. Numerous agencies have fast and reliable access to Oklahoma Mesonet data, including the NWS Weather Forecast Offices in Oklahoma City, Tulsa, Amarillo, and Shreveport, the Arkansas-Red Basin River Forecast Center, the National Severe Storms Laboratory, and over 180 public safety offices across Oklahoma. These agencies use the data from the network to reduce loss of life and property damage in almost every community across the state.

The Oklahoma Climatological Survey has earned a world-class reputation for its operation of the Oklahoma Mesonet and its associated information infrastructure created and managed by scientists at the University of Oklahoma and at Oklahoma State University. The Oklahoma Mesonet has collected over 3 billion weather and soil observations—more than 99% of those possible—and produced millions of decision-making products for state and federal agencies, public safety officials, farmer and agricultural extension agents, university and K–12 students, scientific researchers, rural electric cooperatives, weather forecasters, and private citizens.

In January 2005, the Oklahoma Mesonet was awarded a Special Award from the American Meteorological Society "for serving Oklahoma and the meteorological community by providing high-quality data and information products used to protect lives, reduce costs, facilitate cutting-edge research, and educate the next generation."

A 2008 National Research Council report named the Oklahoma Mesonet as the "gold standard for statewide weather and climate networks."

Geology

Oklahoma is a region of complex geology where several major sedimentary basins are set amongst mountain ranges and uplifts. The state contains many classic areas where fundamental concepts of geology, petroleum exploration, and minerals production have been formulated during the years. Because of its geologic history, Oklahoma has abundant mineral resources that include petroleum (crude oil and natural gas), coal, nonfuel minerals (lead, zinc, gypsum, limestone, sand, and gravel), and water.

Major Geological Provinces

Geologic forces deep within the earth's crust hundreds of millions of years ago caused portions of Oklahoma to subside as major sedimentary basins, while adjacent areas were folded and thrust upward as major mountain uplifts. Most of the outcropping rocks in Oklahoma are of sedimentary origin, and they consist mainly of shale, sandstone, limestone, and gypsum. These sedimentary rocks typically are 2,000 to 10,000 feet thick in the northern shelf areas, and they increase sharply to 30,000 to 40,000 feet thick in the deep basins of the south. These sedimentary rocks contain most of the states' mineral resources, including petroleum, coal, water, and most of the nonfuel minerals. Sedimentary rocks rest upon a "basement" of igneous and metamorphic rocks that underlie all parts of the state.

Exposed in the southern Oklahoma mountain belts are a great variety of sedimentary and igneous rock units seen at few other places in the entire mid-continent region. Steeply dipping strata, such as those exposed along Interstate 35 through the Arbuckle Mountains, attest the strong geologic forces that folded and raised the mountain blocks. Outcropping rocks outside the mountain regions are essentially horizontal, with dips of less than one degree being most common. These strata typically form gently rolling hills and plains: thick shale units form broad, flat plains and valleys, whereas resistant layers of sandstone and limestone cap mesas, cuestas, and hills 100 to 500 feet high. Rocks and soils of western Oklahoma typically are red in color, due to iron oxides present in the bedrock, whereas rocks and soils elsewhere are shades of brown, gray, and black.

Major Geological Provinces

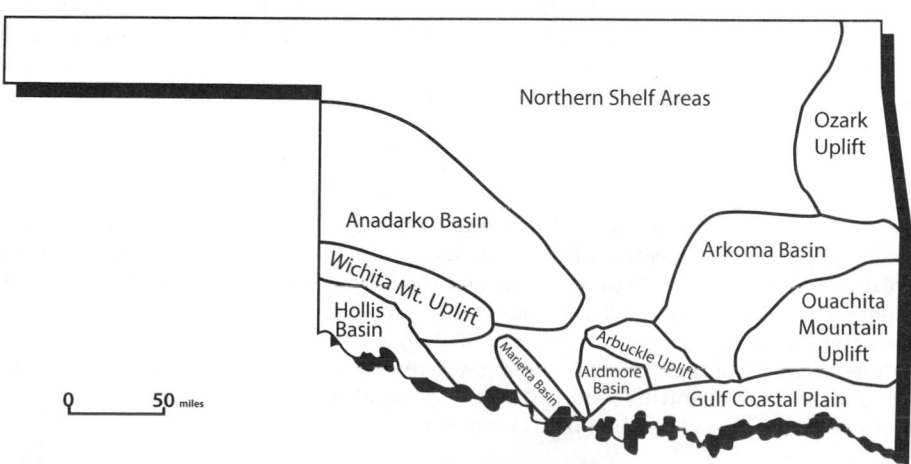

Physiographic Regions

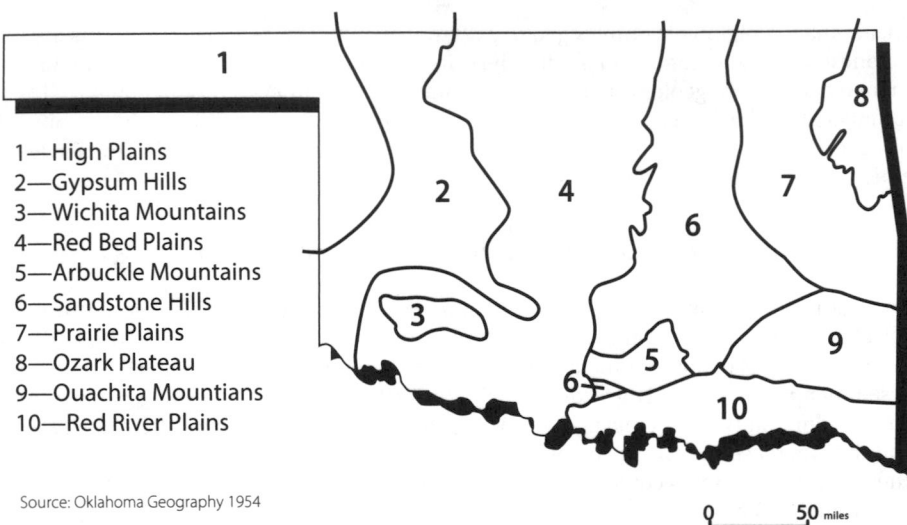

1—High Plains
2—Gypsum Hills
3—Wichita Mountains
4—Red Bed Plains
5—Arbuckle Mountains
6—Sandstone Hills
7—Prairie Plains
8—Ozark Plateau
9—Ouachita Mountians
10—Red River Plains

Source: Oklahoma Geography 1954

0 ——— 50 miles

In the Wichita Mountain Uplift, peaks of Cambrian granite and related igneous rocks tower 500 to 1,200 feet above surrounding plains. The province is composed mostly of granite, rhyolite, gabbro, and limestone. In the Hollis Basin, located in the extreme southwest corner of the state, thick formations of gypsum, shale, and sand are found. In the northeastern corner of the state, the Ozark Uplift is deeply dissected with Mississippian limestone and chert, shale, sandstone, and dolomite are also found in this area. The Arkoma Basin, in east central Oklahoma, is composed primarily of sandstone, shale, and limestone. The Ouachita Mountain Uplift consists of tightly folded sedimentary rock types, varying in age from Ordovician to Mississippian. The mountain ridges are folded Mississippian and Pennsylvanian sandstones that tower above valleys formed in shale.

The Gulf Coastal Plain is located in the southeast part of the state. Shale, limestone, sandstone, and large amounts of sand are present in this geological province. The Arbuckle Uplift is totally enclosed in Oklahoma. Thick limestone and dolomite units, varying in age from Cambrian to Mississippian, are found in addition to some sandstone and granite deposits. The Ardmore Basin is also located completely within Oklahoma's borders. It is composed mainly of Pennsylvanian sandstone and shale. The Marietta Basin consists mainly of outcrops of sandstones and shales of Pennsylvanian and Permian age.

Physiographic Regions

Oklahoma lies mostly in the Great Plains physiographic region and is characterized by low rolling plains that slope eastward. Although the state is often described as flat, local hilly areas rise a few hundred feet to more than 1,000 feet above the surrounding prairies. Three mountain ranges are present in the state: the Wichita Mountains in southwest Oklahoma, the Arbuckle Mountains in south central Oklahoma, and the Ouachita Mountains in the southeastern portion of the state. The highest vertical relief in Oklahoma occurs in the Ouachita Mountains and the southeast part of the prairie plains, with some peaks reaching more than 2,000 feet above their base elevations.

The major rivers of Oklahoma generally flow eastward. Listed from north to south these rivers are: the Arkansas, Cimarron, North Canadian, Canadian, Washita, and the Red. The Arkansas and its tributaries drain the northern two-thirds of the state, while the Red River and its tributaries drain the southern third.

Oklahoma can be divided into ten distinct regions, based on physical characteristics. Many of these areas are extensions of those found in surrounding states and extend to areas as far away as the Gulf of Mexico. The sharp contrasts between the regions give a broad overview of what to expect on a tour of the state.

The state's most level areas are those of the High, Red Bed, and Prairie Plains (regions 1, 4, and 7). Within these areas, the majority of Oklahoma's crops are produced and a great variation in population can be found. The Red River Plains (region 10) is located in the southern portion of the state and is endowed with fertile soil and low, rolling hills. Most of the rock in this region is composed of shale, sandstone, and limestone. A large portion of this area is located below 500 feet in elevation.

Interrupting the plains are the Sandstone and Gypsum Hill regions (2 and 6). The hills in these regions are aligned north to south. The Sandstone Hills resist general weathering because they are capped by resistant sandstone layers. The Gypsum Hills of western Oklahoma are known for the thick layers of white gypsum that cap mesas, buttes, and hilltops, and overlie layers of shale and sandstone that tend to erode easily.

The Arbuckle and Wichita Mountain regions (3 and 5) were formed through geologic uplift and folding. The Arbuckle Mountains contain limestone, sandstone, shale, and granite that have become important mineral sources to the mining industry. The Wichita Mountains, on the other hand, were formed from intrusive and extrusive igneous rocks that are very resistant to erosion. Granite and rhyolite remain where overlying rocks have been eroded.

The most pronounced of the mountain areas is the Ouachita Mountains (pronounced WA-she-taw) found in the southeastern section of the state (region 9). The rough terrain allows for farming only in the valleys, while some hillsides are grazed by cattle.

At one time the Ozark Plateau (region 8) was shaped like a large dome that rose high above the surrounding plains. It is now a hilly region with deeply dissected valleys as a result of the action of northeastern Oklahoma's numerous streams and rivers.

Generalized Topography

Oklahoma lies between the lower elevations of the Coastal Plain and the higher elevations of the Rocky Mountain foothills. The land surface of Oklahoma slopes gently from its northwest corner to the southeast with the steepest gradient of about twelve feet per mile in the Panhandle. Throughout the rest of the state, the slope averages about five feet per mile.

The contour lines shown in the diagram on previous page ("Physiographic Regions") connect points on the land surface having the same elevation. When contour lines are close together, they indicate that the slope of the land is steep.

Southeastern Oklahoma has many steep slopes and high mountains, while western Oklahoma has gentle slopes. In the extreme northwestern part of the state is Black Mesa, the highest point in Oklahoma, with an elevation of 4,973 feet above sea level. The lowest point, at 287 feet above sea level, is in the flood plain of the Little River near the state's southeastern corner. Oklahoma's best-known peak is Mount Scott in the Wichita Mountains.

Mineral Resources

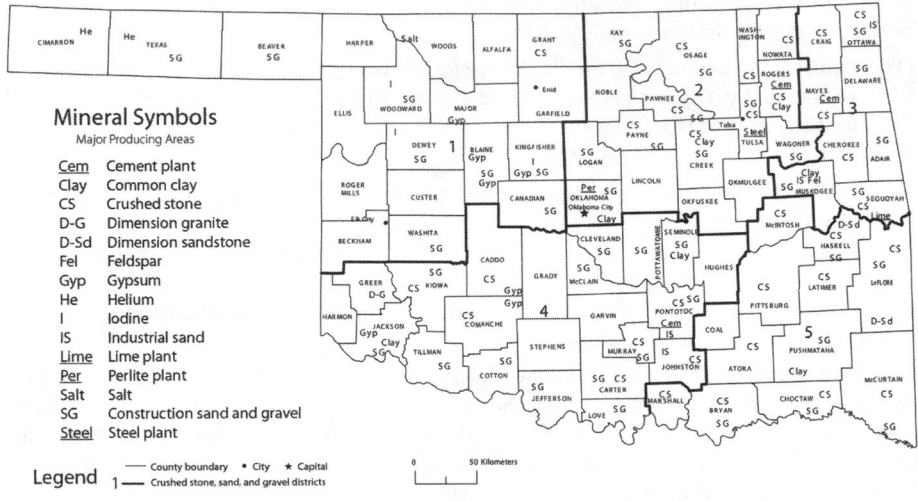

Mineral Symbols
Major Producing Areas

Cem   Cement plant
Clay   Common clay
CS   Crushed stone
D-G   Dimension granite
D-Sd   Dimension sandstone
Fel   Feldspar
Gyp   Gypsum
He   Helium
I   Iodine
IS   Industrial sand
Lime   Lime plant
Per   Perlite plant
Salt   Salt
SG   Construction sand and gravel
Steel Steel plant

Legend
------ County boundary   • City   ★ Capital
1 —— Crushed stone, sand, and gravel districts

0   50 Kilometers

Source: Oklahoma Geological Survey/U.S. Geological Survey, 2005

Minerals

According the United States Geological Survey 2009 Minerals Yearbook, in 2009 Oklahoma's nonfuel raw mineral production was valued at $667 million. This was a $153 million, or 18 percent decrease from the state's total nonfuel mineral value of $820 million in 2008, which then had increased by $86 million, or almost 12 percent from the total of $734 million in 2007. The state decreased to twenty-eighth from twenty-seventh rank among the fifty states in total nonfuel mineral production value, accounting for 1.1 percent of the U.S. total value. In 2009, crushed stone continued to be Oklahoma's leading nonfuel commodity, based upon value, accounting for 46 percent of the state's total nonfuel mineral production value, and increase from 42 percent in 2008. Crushed stone was followed by portland cement, construction sand and gravel, crude iodine, industrial sand and gravel, and Grade-A helium (descending

Nonfuel Mineral Production, 2009

Mineral	Quantity (in metric tons)	Value (in thousands)
Cement	W*	W*
Common Clay	572,000	$2,800
Gypsum	2,180,000	$15,900
Iodine	W*	W*
Sand & Gravel	13,010,000	$108,500
Stone	36,835,000	$312,330
Tripoli	W	W

* Data withheld to avoid disclosing company proprietary data.
Note: Total value presented in the table does not equal the total value of nonfuel mineral production in Oklahoma for 1999. The difference is in mineral values not released for public distribution.

order of value). Four of Oklahoma's leading industrial minerals: crushed stone, construction sand and gravel, industrial sand and gravel, and crude gypsum accounted for 65 percent of the state's total production value, essentially unchanged from 63 percent and 62 percent in 2008 and 2007, respectively.

According to the *Oklahoma Mining Commission Department of Mines 2013 Annual Report*, in 2013, Oklahoma's estimated value of non-coal raw mineral production was $755 million. The state ranked thirtieth in 2013 and thirty-second in 2012 among the fifty states in total non-fuel mineral production value, of which Oklahoma accounted for 0.94 percent of the U.S. total value. For 2013 the total mineral production for the state was 70,786,364 tons. Limestone production equaled 40,372,828 tons followed by: sand and gravel, 15,930,684 tons; gypsum, 5,354,300 tons; granite, 4,387,976 tons; coal, 1,167,208 tons; clay, 1,453,581 tons; select fill, 757,367 tons; shale, 434,382; dimensional stone, 420,859; chat, 301,240; salt, 133,120; tripoli, 84,052 tons; sandstone, 83,898 tons; topsoil, 4,133 tons; and caliche, 2,615 tons.

Oklahoma's enormous mineral reserve can be divided into three types of mineral products: mineral fuels, metals, and non-metals. Mineral fuels are materials that can be burned, such as petroleum (crude oil and natural gas), and coal. These account for more than 90 percent of Oklahoma's annual mineral output. Metals are substances that can be melted and molded into any shape desired and are usually hard and heat resistant. There presently are no metals mined in Oklahoma. Zinc and lead are the principal metals previously mined in Oklahoma, but copper, manganese, iron, and uranium also were produced. A non-metal (industrial mineral) is any rock, mineral or other select naturally occurring or synthetic material of economic value often used in combination with other materials, such as sand and stone used in concrete. The principal industrial minerals produced in Oklahoma include crushed stone, portland cement, construction sand and gravel, industrial sand and gravel, iodine, and gypsum. Other Oklahoma non-metals include tripoli, feldspar, helium, common clay, granite, salt, volcanic ash, and lime.

"River of Rocks" at Wichita Mountains Wildlife Refuge, near Lawton, Oklahoma.

Forests and Vegetation

Oklahoma's forests are vital to the economy and environmental quality of the state, providing a diverse scenic panorama, a wealth of intangible benefits, and a significant forest products industry. Forests protect our high quality waters, provide habitat for wildlife, supply opportunities for recreation, and enhance the environment.

Our forests have been shaped and altered by natural disturbances and human influences. Native Americans worked the forest for their own needs. They burned the forest floor to stimulate brushy growth favored by game species, cleared land for settlements, and used wood for their primary cooking fuel. The first European settlers found forests dominated by white and red oaks, shortleaf and loblolly pine, black walnut, maple, hickory, and pecan, elm, ash, cottonwood, baldcypress, and many other species.

> Nearly ten million acres—20 percent of the land—in Oklahoma is forest, with six million commercial-capable forest acres.

As logging dried up the forests of New England and the Great Lakes, the extensive pine and oak resources of the South beckoned. Although small "peckerwood" sawmills were scattered across southeastern Oklahoma by the late 1800s, intensive logging began in earnest around 1900. By 1930, much of Oklahoma's most valuable virgin pine timber had been removed to support the industrial growth of the upper midwest. Forests were cleared for cotton farming or livestock grazing. As the southern forests began to wane, loggers moved west, leaving behind an overcut forest plagued by wildfire.

Concerns about overcutting, wildfires, and lack of timbers to support local industry for the long term led citizen groups and private companies to support establishment of the Oklahoma Forestry Association and a State Forestry Service in 1925. Protection reduced wildfire damage and regeneration took hold. In western Oklahoma, President Franklin D. Roosevelt's Prairie States Forestry Project planted its first tree in a Greer County shelterbelt. The forest industry languished during the Great Depression, but the war brought renewed activity, relying on the growing "second forest." After World War II, social shifts in our population also affected the forests. The 1940s and 1950s saw urban dwellers leave inner cities in large numbers. Suburban developments cut into forest land and woodlots became more important as sources of recreation than income.

Oklahoma is often thought of as a state with only wide open prairies, wheat fields, and ranch land, but nearly ten million acres—20 percent of the land—is forest. More than six million forest acres are commercial-capable of growing wood as a crop. More than 90 percent of Oklahoma forests are owned by individuals, corporate owners, and the forest industry. Six percent is publicly owned.

Considerable value is also placed on forests in urban and community areas. Three-fourths of Oklahomans are now considered "urban" residents, which represents a significant change from the rural roots and image of the state. Forests are also highly valued outside traditional commercial areas, providing many environmental benefits.

Major forests are located in the Ouachita Mountains and the Ozark Plateau, in the eastern portion of the state, where rainfall is sufficient for tree growth. Also, the local topography in these areas is rough, which discourages the removal of forests for agricultural use. The Ozark Plateau is dominated by oak and hickory trees, while pine trees dominate the higher elevations of the Ouachita Mountains. There is, however, some mixing of these two types at

Natural Vegetation

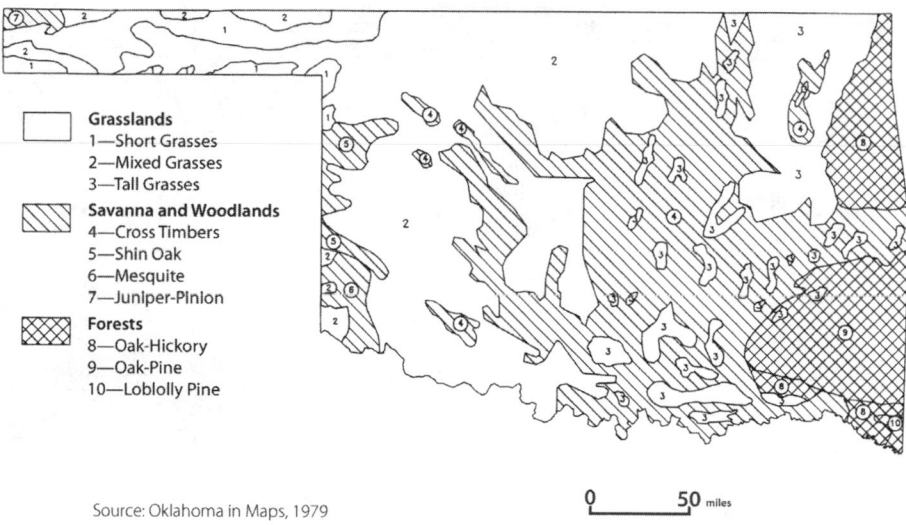

Grasslands
1—Short Grasses
2—Mixed Grasses
3—Tall Grasses

Savanna and Woodlands
4—Cross Timbers
5—Shin Oak
6—Mesquite
7—Juniper-Pinion

Forests
8—Oak-Hickory
9—Oak-Pine
10—Loblolly Pine

Source: Oklahoma in Maps, 1979

0   50 miles

all levels. Some sections of the Sandstone Hills, the Red River Plains, and the Prairie Plains are also covered by forests. The state has 144 native species of trees with common varieties including shortleaf and loblolly pine, sweetgum, pecan, several types of oak, cottonwood, and walnut.

Natural Vegetation

Oklahoma is situated in a transition zone between the humid eastern forests and the drier western grasslands. The state can be divided into three main types of vegetation: grassland, savannah, and woodlands, and forests. Grass areas are abundant within Oklahoma's boundaries and are used for grazing. Grasses in the western sections are primarily short and mixed. In the Panhandle, the soil is often parched and only the surface is moistened by rain. Tall grasses are found in the eastern section of the state. Savannah and woodland areas exist in all parts of the state with the exception of the rough terrain of the Ouachita Mountains in southeastern Oklahoma. The Cross Timbers of central Oklahoma is the largest woodland-savannah region and supports some the state's oldest known trees. Juniper-Pinyon is the least abundant vegetation type, found only in the state's far northwest corner.

Large expanses of forest are found primarily in eastern Oklahoma where rainfall is abundant. The Ouachita Mountains are home to the largest forested area in the state, and this is an extremely important region to the forest products, tree farming, and agritourism industries in Oklahoma.

Generalized Soils

Soil is a combination of loose rock material, organic matter, air, and water. Oklahoma has a great diversity of soils ranging from the rich limestone soils of the dark prairie lands to

Generalized Soils

Alfisols

Mollisols

Utilsols

Inceptisols

Vertisols

Entisols

Stony Rockland

Source: Oklahoma in Maps 1979

0 _____ 50 miles

the alluvial soils of river valleys, to thin sandy soils and poor red-clay soils. There are seven major soil groups in Oklahoma. The following is a breakdown of these groups:

Alfisols are found in central, south central, eastern, and western Oklahoma. They occur in climates that have a period when evapotranspiration (the rate at which water evaporates from the soil or is removed by plants) exceeds precipitation. Mollisols are commonly dark colored, base-rich soils of the grasslands that are found in central, western (including the central panhandle), eastern, and northeastern Oklahoma. They cover a larger area of Oklahoma than any other soil type.

Utisols occur only in eastern Oklahoma. They are usually found in warm and humid climates and are associated with a seasonal deficiency of rainfall. Low fertility and low base saturation in these soils are the major limitations to agricultural use. Inceptisols occupy a large portion of western Oklahoma and are found in climates where there is some leaching (filtering out) of soil nutrients. Vertisols occur mostly in southeastern Oklahoma and extend into Texas. They are clay soils that develop deep, wide cracks that allow the soil to be moistened from both above and below. Entisols occur mostly in floodplains and on steep slopes throughout the state. They show little or no evidence of active soil formation. Entisols found in western Oklahoma are shallow soils that show limited evidence of weathering processes. Stony Rockland areas, which are actually surface features and not a soil, are located in southwestern and south central Oklahoma and can be found in three small areas that boast a very rocky soil type.

The United States Congress created the Soil Conservation Service in 1935 to protect topsoil from becoming badly eroded by poor agricultural practices. Oklahomans were among the first to take advantage of the Soil Conservation Service, establishing the first soil conservation district in the United States.

Through the years, prior to statehood and even to the present, Oklahoma's most valuable resource has been its resourceful and imaginative people. For as many years, they have chosen numerous and varied official state symbols to recognize their special interests. Many of the state symbols come with stories as colorful and unusual as the symbols themselves. One of the more recently adopted state symbols was the selection of Port Silt Loam to represent the state soil for Oklahoma. This state soil was added to the list of state symbols by the state legislature in 1987.

Why have a state soil? The citizens of Oklahoma should have a keen awareness that soil is one of the most valuable resources. Food and much clothing and shelter come from plants growing in the soil. Individual and group action since statehood shows better care of this resource is important to the livelihood and well being of Oklahomans. More than 100 million tons of topsoil wash or blow away each year. Therefore, naming a state soil provides an educational purpose. It brings attention to the importance of soils and to the importance of conservation. Oklahoma has a variable climate and many kinds of geologic materials. These factors greatly influence the formation of different kinds of soil. More than 2,500 different kinds of soil are found in Oklahoma. Some soils are naturally fertile, and others are very limited in productivity. No one individual soil occurs throughout the state.

Port Silt Loam, the state soil, was selected because it occurs in more counties (thirty-three), and in about one million acres, more than any other particular soil. The Port soil is deep, well drained, and has a high productivity potential. It is suited for the production of alfalfa, cotton, wheat, sorghum, oats, and other sown crops. Port soil is usually dark brown to dark reddish brown, with the color derived from upland soil materials weathered from reddish sandstones, siltstones, and shales of the Permian Geologic Era. The natural soil supports a native, undisturbed vegetation of tall prairie grasses, with an overstory of pecan, walnut, bur oak, and cottonwood trees. This native condition offers a very desirable habitat for most of Oklahoma's wildlife species.

Soils are often named after an early pioneer, town, county, community, or stream in the vicinity where they are found. The name "Port" comes from a small community located in Washita County. The name "silt loam" is the texture of the topsoil. This texture consists mostly of silt-sized particles (.05 to .002mm) and when the moist soil is rubbed between the thumb and forefinger, it is loamy to the feel, thus the term "silt loam."

Mountains and Streams

Oklahoma Geological Survey

Mountains and streams have defined the landscape of Oklahoma in the geological past, and have helped create a beautiful landscape. Resistant rock masses have been folded, faulted, and thrust upward to form the mountains, while the streams have persisted in eroding less-resistant rock units and lowering the landscape to form the broad valleys, hills, and plains so typical of Oklahoma.

Mountains

Mountains are important not only because they expose much of the mineral wealth needed for the state's growth and industrial development, but, along with lakes and streams, they provide the unexpected beauty of Oklahoma's recreational areas. Although the three principal mountain systems—Wichitas, Arbuckles, and Ouachitas—occur in southern Oklahoma, other mountainous and hilly areas extend across many parts of the state.

Wichita Mountains in the southwest consist of a core of granite, rhyolite, and other igneous rocks emplaced during the Cambrian Period of geologic time, about 525 mya (million years ago). On the northeast they are flanked by thousands of feet of folded and steeply dipping marine limestones and other sedimentary rocks deposited during Late Cambrian and Ordovician time (515–425 mya). The relief between the hilltops and nearby lowlands generally ranges from 400 to 1,100 feet, and the highest elevation, about 2,475 feet above sea level, is on an unnamed peak four miles east, southeast of Cooperton. The best-known peak, Mount Scott, with a summit of 2,464 feet, can be reached by car or bus and commands the most spectacular view of the area. Important mineral resources produced here are granite, limestone, sand and gravel, and oil and gas. The mountains have been prospected, with limited success, for gold, silver, copper, lead, zinc, aluminum, and iron ores.

Arbuckle Mountains, an area of low to moderate hills in south-central Oklahoma, contain a core of Precambrian granite and gneiss (a metamorphic rock) formed about 1,300 mya. Most of the Arbuckles consist of 15,000 feet of folded and faulted limestones, dolomites, sandstones, and shales deposited in shallow seas from Late Cambrian through Pennsylvanian times (515–290 mya). Relief in the area ranges from 100 to 600 feet, with the highest elevation, 1,415 feet, in the West Timbered Hills, about seven miles west of Interstate 35. Although low, the relief is still impressive, as it is six times greater than any other topographic feature between Oklahoma City and Dallas, Texas. Two significant features in the mountains are the deep road cuts on I-35, and the "tombstone topography," which looks like rows of tombstones in a field, and is the result of differential weathering and erosion of alternating layers of hard and soft limestone. The Arbuckles contain the most diverse suite of mineral resources in Oklahoma. Limestone, dolomite, glass sand, granite, sand and gravel, shale, cement, iron ore, lead, zinc, tar sands, and oil and gas are all minerals which are being produced or have been produced here.

Ouachita Mountains (pronounced "Wa-she-tah"), in southeast Oklahoma, are made up of rocks deposited in a deep sea that covered the area from Late Cambrian through Early Pennsylvanian time (515–315 mya). The area was then folded and faulted in such a manner that resistant beds of sandstone, chert, and novaculite (a fine-grained silica rock, like flint) now form long, sinuous mountain ridges that tower 500–1,500 feet above adjacent valleys formed in easily eroded shales. The highest elevation is 2,666 feet on Rich Mountain. Major individual ridges within the Ouachitas are Winding Stair, Rich, Kiamichi, Blue, Jackfork,

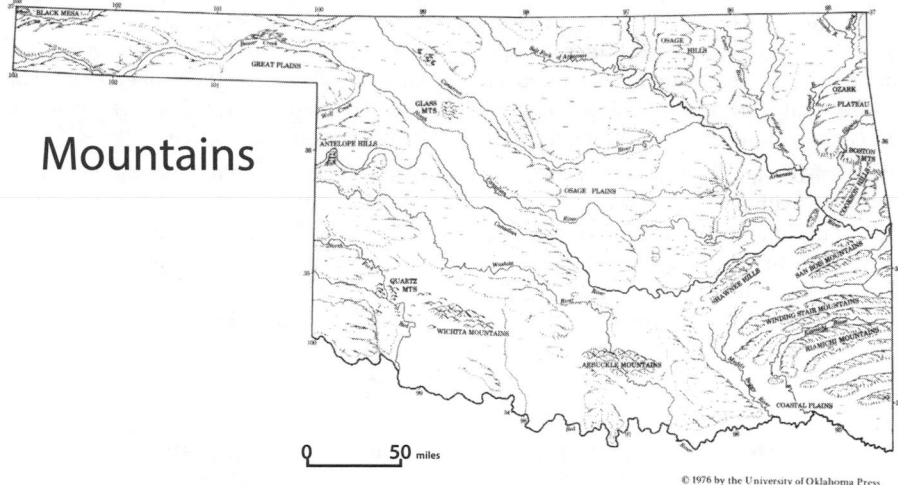

Mountains

0   50 miles

© 1976 by the University of Oklahoma Press

and Blackjack mountains. Mineral resources include limestone, quartzite, sand and gravel, asphaltite, lead, oil, and gas.

Mountains of the Arkansas River Valley are another group of high hills and mountains scattered in the Arkansas River Valley of east-central Oklahoma. They include Sans Bois, Cavanal, Sugar Loaf, Poteau, Beaver, Hi Early, and Rattlesnake mountains, among others. These mountains typically are broad featured, capped by thick and resistant sandstones that stand 300–2,000 feet above the wide, hilly plains formed on thick shale units. These sandstones and shales, deposited in the shallow seas and coastal areas covering eastern Oklahoma in Early and Middle Pennsylvanian times (330–310 mya), were broadly uplifted and folded during the Middle and Late Pennsylvanian uplift of the Ouachita Mountains. The largest mountain area is the Sans Bois Mountains, north of Wilburton and Red Oak. The highest summit, Sugar Loaf Mountain, is eight miles east of Poteau, and, at 2,568 feet, rises 2,000 feet above the surrounding plains. Principal mineral resources of the area are coal, oil and gas, clay, building stone, sand and gravel, and volcanic ash.

Ozark Plateau, or the Ozarks of northeast Oklahoma, is best described as a deeply dissected plateau. Bedrock units in the area are mostly flat-lying limestones and cherts deposited in shallow seas during the Mississippian Period (365–330 mya).

To the south and southwest, the Ozarks include outcrops of sandstones and shales deposited in shallow seas and coastal areas during Early Pennsylvanian time (330–315 mya). The Ozarks, including the Brushy or Boston mountains, were broadly uplifted during, and since, Pennsylvanian time causing streams to be incised into the bedrock. Relief in the Ozarks is 50 to 400 feet, typically, and the highest elevation, 1,745 feet, is on Workman Mountain, eight miles east, southeast of Stilwell. The beauty of the Ozarks and the abundant clear-water lakes have spawned many state parks. Important mineral resources being produced are limestone, shale, cement, tripoli, sand and gravel, oil, and gas. In the north is the world-famous Tri-State lead-zinc mining district (Miami-Picher area), which led the United States in zinc production almost every year from 1918–1945, and finally was closed in 1970.

Glass Mountains, in north-central Major County, about six miles west of Orienta, are an area of badlands topography, and are a prominent feature of the Blaine escarpment that extends southeast to northwest across northwest Oklahoma. Outcropping rocks are red-brown shales and siltstones, capped by several beds of resistant white gypsum; all were deposited during the Permian Period (about 270 mya). Much of the gypsum looks like glass fragments, and hence the name, "Glass Mountains." "Mountains" is a misnomer; they are actually prominent mesas, buttes, and escarpments. Flat-lying beds of caprock gypsum and underlying shales originally extended far to the north and east, but have been eroded back to the south and west to their present position. The local relief generally ranges from 150 to 200 feet, and the elevation at the top of the high buttes is about 1,585 feet.

Black Mesa, in the northwest corner of the Oklahoma Panhandle, is the highest point in the state, with an elevation of 4,973 feet. It is a plateau that rises about 600 feet above the adjacent Cimarron River and North Carrizo Creek. In Oklahoma, Black Mesa is 0.5 to one mile wide and three miles long, and is the erosional remnant of a finger-like basaltic lava flow extruded from a volcano in southeast Colorado. The lava flow formed during Tertiary time, about two to four mya, and occupied what was then a broad valley.

Streams

Oklahoma's stream systems, in terms of geologic time, are temporary as to location and flow rates. Eventually, streams will cut deeper, and their tributaries will erode nearby uplands, thereby shifting their positions. Major drainage systems in Oklahoma were initiated during the Pleistocene Epoch of geologic time (the last 1.65 million years or so), a time characterized by erosion in Oklahoma. Pleistocene terrace deposits, one hundred feet to more than 300 feet above modern flood plains, attests to the great erosion and down cutting performed by major rivers in this period.

Oklahoma's two major river basins are the Red River and Arkansas River basins. Flowing into Oklahoma from six neighboring states, all the surface water leaving the state flows into Arkansas via the Red, Arkansas, and Little rivers, and Lee Creek. The major rivers and their tributaries flow to the east and southeast across Oklahoma.

Red River and its tributaries drain about 23,000 square miles in the southern third of the state. The western most headwaters of Red River is a small tributary, Frio Draw, which begins about thirty miles south of Tucumcari, New Mexico. It flows across the Texas Panhandle through Palo Duro Canyon, and then marks Oklahoma's southern border (517 river miles) with Texas. From there it flows through Arkansas into Louisiana, where it joins the Atchafalaya River and enters Atchafalaya Bay and the Gulf of Mexico.

At the southwest corner of Oklahoma, the main stem is called Prairie Dog Town Fork Red River (PDTFRR); it is joined by Buck Creek two miles farther east, and from that point eastward, it is officially called Red River. Lake Texoma is the only reservoir on the main stem of Red River in Oklahoma; it holds the largest volume of water, 2.6 million acre feet, in the state, and has the second largest surface area of 88,000 acres. The tributaries to Red River have many other important lakes and reservoirs, such as Altus, Foss, Ellsworth, Waurika, Arbuckle, McGee Creek, Sardis, Hugo, Pine Creek, and Broken Bow.

Major Oklahoma tributaries to Red River include Salt Fork Red River, North Fork Red River, and Washita River, all of which contribute flow into Lake Texoma. Other tributaries are Muddy Boggy Creek, and Kiamichi and Little rivers, each having its own tributary system. There are also many other rivers and creeks that flow directly into Red River. At the southeast corner of the state, Red River has an elevation of 305 feet. The lowest elevation in the state, 287 feet, is twenty miles to the north where Little River enters Arkansas.

Arkansas River and its tributaries drain the northern two-thirds of Oklahoma, nearly 47,000 square miles. The source of the Arkansas River is near the town of Leadville, Colorado. The river flows eastward across southeast Colorado and western and central Kansas, turning south to enter Oklahoma at Kay County, north of Ponca City. It crosses northeast Oklahoma to leave the state at Fort Smith, Arkansas.

Much of the Arkansas River has a series of locks and dams, the McClellan-Kerr Navigation System, that link Oklahoma with barge traffic to the Mississippi River. Major lakes and reservoirs on the main stem of the Arkansas River include (from the southeast) Robert S. Kerr, Webbers Falls, Keystone, and Kaw. On the Canadian River, a major tributary to the Arkansas in eastern Oklahoma, Eufaula Lake has the largest surface area in the state, with 105,500 acres, and the second largest volume with 2.3 million acre-feet. Many tributaries to the Arkansas River have important lakes and reservoirs, such as Canton, Great Salt Plains, Hefner, Overholser, Thunderbird, Carl Blackwell, Hulah, Skiatook, Oologah, Fort Gibson, Hudson, Tenkiller Ferry, and Wister.

Major tributaries to the Arkansas River include the Canadian, North Canadian (named Beaver River in the Panhandle, above Wolf Creek), and Deep Fork rivers, all flowing into Eufaula Lake. Others are the Cimarron, Salt Fork, Caney, Verdigris, Neosho (Grand), and Illinois rivers, each having its own tributary system. Many other rivers and creeks flow directly into the Arkansas River. The lowest elevation, 385 feet, is where the river flows into Arkansas at Fort Smith.

Scenic Rivers of Oklahoma have such exceptional beauty and recreational value that six of them have been officially designated as "scenic rivers," and are protected by the state legislature. One scenic river is in the Red River System—the upper part of Mountain Fork, which flows into Broken Bow Lake in the Ouachita Mountains. The other five scenic rivers are in the Arkansas River System, in the Ozark Plateau, and include parts of the Illinois River and parts of Flint, Baron Fork, Lee, and Little Lee creeks.

Salt Plains and Saline Rivers are an unusual feature of the Oklahoma landscape. Natural dissolution of bedded salt (deposited during the Permian Period, about 270 mya) occurs at shallow depths in several parts of northwest and southwest Oklahoma. The resultant high-salinity brine seeps to the surface in some of the state's rivers. In the Arkansas River drainage, Great Salt Plains on Salt Fork covers about twenty-five square miles and is the largest salt flat. Others are Big Salt Plain and Little Salt Plain on Cimarron River, and Ferguson Salt Plain just north of Watonga in Blaine County. In the Red River drainage, the Caney, Kiser, and Robinson Salt plains are on Elm Fork in northern Harmon County, south of Erick. All of these Oklahoma salt plains discharge brines to the Arkansas and Red River systems, thus degrading the river waters and making them generally unsuitable for industrial, municipal, or irrigation uses in parts of western and central Oklahoma. The saline river waters are diluted

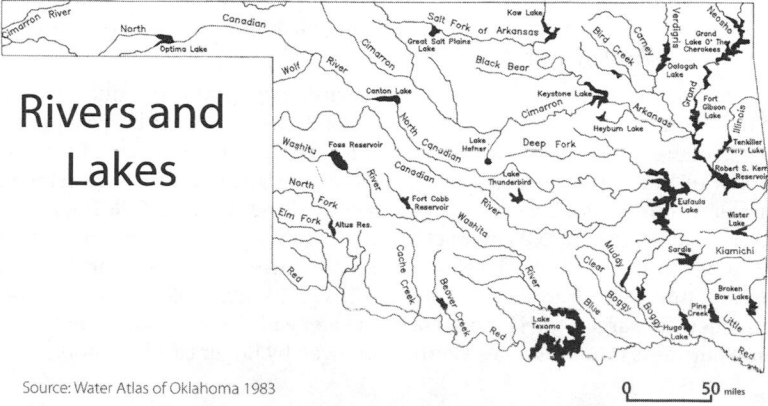

Groundwater

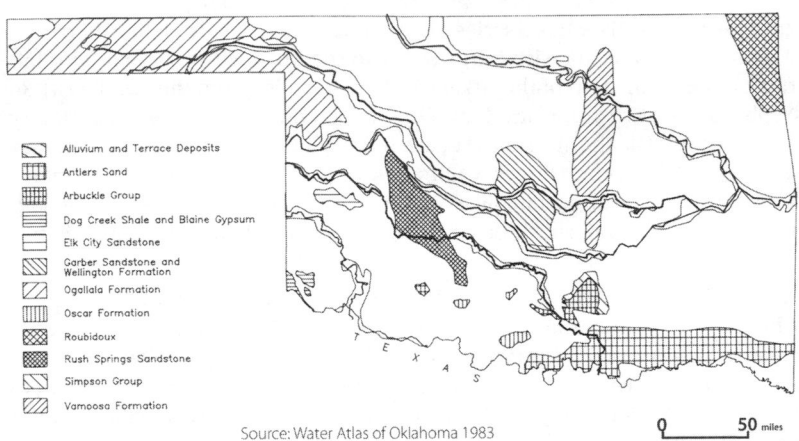

Alluvium and Terrace Deposits
Antlers Sand
Arbuckle Group
Dog Creek Shale and Blaine Gypsum
Elk City Sandstone
Garber Sandstone and Wellington Formation
Ogallala Formation
Oscar Formation
Roubidoux
Rush Springs Sandstone
Simpson Group
Vamoosa Formation

Source: Water Atlas of Oklahoma 1983

0   50 miles

by fresh-water inflow downstream from the salt plains, and thus the water is mostly usable by the time it reaches Keystone Lake and Lake Texhoma. Although the salt plains degrade the river waters, like most of nature's checks and balances they are a necessary part of the environment for the area's inhabitants, and they provide yet another aspect of the beautiful geological areas of the state of Oklahoma.

Water

Oklahoma contains thirty-four major reservoirs with a combined surface area of 543,450 acres and storing more than 13 million acre-feet of water. The state's largest lake in surface area is Eufaula (105,000 acres); Lake Texoma is second (88,000 acres). The state's largest lake in conservation storage is Texoma (2.6 million acre-feet of water); Eufaula is second (2.3 million ac-ft). Evaporation and percolation preclude immediate use of approximately 80 percent of Oklahoma's water. Average annual lake evaporation ranges from forty-eight inches in the extreme east to sixty-five inches in the southwest, numbers that far exceed the average yearly rainfall in those areas.

Groundwater is the prevalent source of water in the western half of the state, accounting for almost 90 percent of the total irrigation water use in Oklahoma. Underneath the state are twenty-three major groundwater basins containing 320 million acre-feet of water in storage, though only one-half of that amount may be recoverable.

According to the Oklahoma Water Resources Board, irrigation is the number one use of water in Oklahoma; water supply is a close second, followed distantly by livestock watering. The majority of the state's surface water (approximately 60 percent) is used for public water supply, followed by thermoelectric power generation and irrigation. The largest total amount of freshwater withdrawn for irrigation purposes was in Texas County, followed by Cimarron and Beaver counties, all in the Oklahoma Panhandle. The largest amount of water withdrawn for water-supply purposes is in Cleveland County, followed by Comanche and Oklahoma counties. Livestock withdrawals are largest in Texas County, followed by Cimarron and Alfalfa counties. The largest total amount of freshwater withdrawn for thermoelectric-power generation purposes is in Muskogee County, followed by Rogers and Seminole counties.

Wildlife

Oklahoma Department of Wildlife Conservation

The Oklahoma Department of Wildlife Conservation is the state agency responsible for managing fish and wildlife. The Wildlife Department receives no general state tax appropriations and is supported by hunting and fishing license fees and federal excise taxes on hunting and fishing equipment. The mission of the Oklahoma Department of Wildlife Conservation is to manage Oklahoma's wildlife resources and habitat to provide scientific, educational, aesthetic, economic, and recreational benefits for present and future generations of hunters, anglers, and others who appreciate wildlife.

In support of this statement, the agency is committed to: (1) conserving wildlife resources, habitat, and biodiversity through scientific research, propagation, and management; (2) balancing wildlife needs with those of people; supporting and promoting traditional uses of wildlife through regulated fishing, hunting, and trapping consistent with sound management principles; (3) informing and educating citizens so they will recognize the value of wildlife resources and support department regulations and programs; (4) protecting wildlife resources through increased awareness of and aggressive enforcement of wildlife laws and regulations; (5) identifying and acknowledging diverse public interests in wildlife resources and implementing responsible programs consistent with those interests; (6) promoting ethical private land and water practices; (7) maintaining and improving accessibility to wildlife on private and public waters and lands; (8) serving as advocate and legal representative for wildlife resources and habitat in environmental issues and actions that may impact these resources; (9) protecting unique, threatened and endangered species and preserving their habitats; (10) ensuring excellence in the pursuit of our mission through the hiring and continued training of qualified and experienced professionals; (11) and managing available funds efficiently and seeking innovative revenue sources for the accomplishment of this mission.

The department is organized into five major divisions: administration, fisheries, information and education, law enforcement and wildlife.

The Administration Division performs a great variety of tasks to support the agency's employees carrying out the department's mission. The division sections include accounting, licensing, information technology, human resources, communications, and property.

The department's Fisheries Division manages this important recreational resource, and meets the challenge by focusing on management, research, and production.

The Information and Education Division informs Oklahoma citizens about department programs, policies, and regulations.

The Law Enforcement Division enforces laws and regulations that protect Oklahoma's wildlife resources. Observance of wildlife laws protect the resource while providing opportunities for fair and equitable usage by the sporting public.

To manage the state's wildlife resources and their habitats the department's Wildlife Division provides hunting and other outdoor-recreational opportunities, through public lands acquisition and management, cooperative and technical assistance for private landowners, research and surveys, and education.

Oklahoma Wildlife Conservation Commission

The Wildlife Conservation Commission is the eight-member governing board of the Oklahoma Department of Wildlife Conservation. Commissioners serve eight-year terms and are appointed by the governor and confirmed by the Oklahoma Senate. The commission establishes state hunting and fishing regulations, sets policy for the Wildlife Department, and indirectly oversees all state fish and wildlife conservation activities. The commission also governs all department operations and financial transactions and meet the first Monday of each month to conduct business.

Department Funding

The department remains a non-appropriated, user-pay/user-benefit agency that is funded either directly or indirectly by hunting and fishing license sales. In fiscal year 2013 the department operated with an estimated $50.1 million in revenue. Specifically, major revenue sources are: annual license sales, $18.1 million; federal sportfish and wildlife restoration grant revenue, $15.5 million (grant income is based on a formula that includes a certified number of hunting and fishing licenses sold in the state); interest income, $6.3 million; other wildlife sales, $4.2 million; agriculture and oil leases, $2.5 million; and miscellaneous income including donations, $3.3 million.

Agency Expenditures

Annual expenditures in FY 2013 were approximately $46,910,673. Expenditures by area include $12.44 million for fisheries (26.52 percent of total budget); $13.6 million for wildlife (29.2 percent of total budget); $11.3 million for law enforcement (24.1 percent of total budget); $6.7 million for administration (14.3 percent of total budget); $2.6 million for information and education (5.7 percent of total budget); and, $128,201 for capital expenditures (0.27 percent of total budget).

Impact of Hunters and Anglers on Oklahoma's Economy and Environment

In FY 2013 Oklahoma's hunting and fishing license sales totaled $18,158,649. Hunting and fishing contribute to Oklahoma's economy generating jobs and tax revenues. Hunting and fishing also has an impact on the environment. In FY 2013-2014, Oklahoma hunters harvested a number of "big game" animals including 88,009 deer, thirteen Pronghorn Antelope, 113 elk; and twenty-eight black bears. The number of fished stocked in Oklahoma's public waters and private farm ponds numbered 11,285,397 in 2014. The total number of fish stocked in public waters in 2014 equaled 10,981,126. The most fish stocked in public waters was Walleye Bass numbering 6,661,976 and the fewest was the Redear Sunfish at twelve. The total number of fish stocked in private farm ponds in 2014 equaled 304,271, with the largest number being Bluegill at 165,505 and the lowest number being Channel Catfish at 37,751.

A Legacy of Conservation

The department was initially created as a one-man agency in 1909. The first hunting license was also created at a cost of $1.25 to fund the department, setting the precedent of a non-appropriated, user-pay/user-benefit agency. In 1956, state voters passed a constitutional amendment establishing the Oklahoma Department of Wildlife Conservation as the constitutional agency it is today. The amendment was enacted in 1957, and the first board of commissioners was created to oversee the department's operation.

Recent Accomplishments

2010

- Big game hunting season expanded when the holiday anterless deer season was extended to one 10–day season and antler point requirements on bull elk were reduced. Moreover, additional cow elk hunting days were added in portions of the state.
- Over 1,600 students participated in the "Archery in Schools" state shoot.
- Almost 4,000 Paddlefish were processed and studied at the state's Paddlefish Research and Processing Center. Prior to the center's opening, the Wildlife Department had only collected information from 240 fish since the late 1970s.
- The Oklahoma Department of Wildlife Conservation (ODWC) approved a memorandum of agreement with OG&E to offset impacts of a northwest Oklahoma wind farm on lesser prairie chickens. The agreement secures $4.9 million for projects such as conservation easements to protect undeveloped property, and management agreements to restore property with critical habitat for lesser prairie chickens.
- Oklahoma black bear archery season opened and closed in one day, when hunters reached the quota of twenty bears on October 1 in southeastern Oklahoma. A total of thirty-two black bears were harvested on October 1, which is thirteen more than were harvested in approximately one month's time in 2009.

2011

- The ODWC launched several research initiatives and joined with conservation groups to study possible causes of quail population decline in the state.
- The seventh-annual Oklahoma Wildlife Expo hosted record-breaking crowds of 59,000 visitors over the three-day event.
- ODWC acquired 8,000 new acres of public land in Love County to establish the Cross Timbers Wildlife Management Area.

2012

- The ODWC ramped up efforts to conserve the lesser prairie chicken in northwestern Oklahoma, working with other groups to keep the bird off the federal Endangered Species List. Efforts included a negotiated financial settlement with a wind energy company for habitat preservation and formulation of the Oklahoma Lesser Prairie Chicken Conservation Action Plan.
- ODWC renewed its commitment to continue working with the National Wild Turkey Federation on efforts to enhance turkey populations and generate interest among Oklahomans in the outdoors.
- A cooperative agreement with a timber company allowed ODWC to add 22,000 acres to the Honobia Creek Wildlife Management Area in southeastern Oklahoma.

Did you Know?

- Oklahoma ranks at the top of all states when it comes to diversity of plant and animal life.

- The Selman Bat Cave Wildlife Management Area in northwest Oklahoma is home to more that one million Mexican free-tailed bats. The Oklahoma Department of Wildlife Conservation offers guided evening tours on the area each summer.

- There are over 1.5 million acres of wildlife management areas in every corner of the state to explore.

- The four fish hatcheries run by the Oklahoma Department of Wildlife Conservation annually raise and stock about 12 million fish each year.

- One in three Oklahoma citizens hunt or fish and one in three Oklahoma citizens enjoy watching wildlife.

- Each year Oklahoma hunters donate about 16 tons of venison to the Hunters Against Hunger program. That is enough meat to provide nutritious meals for nearly 133,000 families across the state.

- The number of Oklahoma anglers in 2011 could fill the University of Oklahoma football stadium to capacity eight times! The number of Oklahoma hunters could fill the Oklahoma State University football stadium three and a half times.

- Opening day of deer season is the state's biggest single-day recreational attraction. It draws more participants than the busiest day of the Oklahoma State Fair or the Tulsa State Fair.

Medicine Creek at Fort Sill, circa 1860s. When Fort Sill was first staked out, Medicine Bluffs (in the background) was still used as a religious and ceremonial site by local Native American tribesmen. Later, Indians would refer to Fort Sill as "the Soldier House at Medicine Bluffs."

Astronomical Phenomena for Oklahoma, 2015 and 2016

Wayne Harris-Wyrick—Director, Kirkpatrick Planetarium

Eclipses

An eclipse occurs whenever the sun, Earth, and the Moon align in space. If the Moon is between the sun and Earth, a solar eclipse occurs. Whenever the Moon completely covers the sun as seen from some part of Earth, we experience a total solar eclipse. Total solar eclipses are rather common. One or two occur almost every year somewhere on our planet. They are quite rare, however, for any given location. A total solar eclipse is visible only over a rather narrow path on Earth's surface, although everyone for hundreds of miles either side of the path of totality experiences a partial eclipse. During a partial solar eclipse, the Moon only covers a piece of the sun's disk. They are more common from a given location, but much less spectacular. The central path of a total solar eclipse may miss Earth in such a way that some parts of our planet experience a partial solar eclipse even though no total eclipse is visible anywhere on the planet.

On some occasions, Earth experiences an annular solar eclipse. Since the Moon's distance from Earth varies slightly, it sometimes looks slightly smaller than the sun. The Moon is always nearly four hundred times smaller than the sun in actual size, but being four hundred times closer, it normally appears slightly larger. If a solar eclipse occurs when the Moon is farthest from Earth, it won't quite cover the sun. An "annulus", a ring of fire from the sun's edge, surrounds the Moon like a celestial donut in the sky. The rarest type of eclipse is a combination annual-total solar eclipse, known as a hybrid solar eclipse. During such an event, the Moon moves ever so slightly closer to Earth and what starts as an annular eclipse becomes a total eclipse during the event. Or it may begin as a total eclipse then become an annular eclipse as the Moon inches away from Earth. All four of these solar eclipse types occur over the two-year period, and one of those, a partial, will be visible from Oklahoma.

If Earth passes between the sun and Moon, our planet blocks the sunlight striking the Moon's surface, and we see a lunar eclipse. Because the sun is much larger then Earth, there exists a part of Earth's shadow where sunlight is only partially blocked. This is known as Earth's penumbra, and if the Moon is only eclipsed by Earth's penumbra, a penumbral eclipse, the slight darkening of the Moon during a penumbral eclipse may go completely unnoticed by the casual observer. The Moon may pass only partially into the deep part of Earth's shadow, the umbra, so that we experience a partial eclipse. Over the next two years, two total, one partial and two penumbral eclipses take place.

A lunar eclipse, whether penumbral, partial or total, is visible from most parts of Earth where it's night at the time of the eclipse. Five lunar eclipses occur over the two-year period, and all of those but the partial eclipse will be visible from Oklahoma. However, two of those will be the weak, penumbral type.

The Moon's color and brightness both change dramatically during an eclipse. The overall brightness decreases by a factor of several hundred or more. During a total lunar eclipse, the color changes can appear rather bizarre. The brilliant white Moon may become copper-colored or turn deep blood red. No wonder such sights frightened ancient civilizations.

A Solar eclipse can only occur at new Moon, when the Moon is directly between Earth and sun. A lunar eclipse can only occur at full Moon, when Earth is directly between the Moon and the sun. For most new and full Moon phases, the three objects, sun, Earth, and Moon, do not line up exactly and no eclipse occurs. This is due to the fact that the Moon's orbit is tilted compared the Earth's orbit around the sun.

Over the two-year spam 2015–16, four solar and four lunar eclipses occur. Unfortunately, none of the solar eclipses will be visible from Oklahoma. They happen on: March 20, 2015, a total eclipse visible from Iceland, Europe, northern Africa and Asia, but all but the North Atlantic region witnesses totality; partial solar eclipse on September 13, 2015, visible from southern Africa and India and Antarctica; A total on March 9, 2016, visible from eastern Asia, Australia, and the western Pacific Ocean; and an annular eclipse on September 1, 2016, visible from Africa and the Indian Ocean.

The four lunar eclipses include two total, but one, April 4, 2015, sets from use before it ends and the other, September 28, 2015, rises just after the eclipse begins. Two very weak penumbral eclipses occur on March 23, 2016, and September 16, 2016, and neither is visible from Oklahoma.

For more detailed information on eclipses, see NASA's eclipse page at eclipse.gsfc.nasa. gov/eclipse.html

Seasons

A common misconception holds that seasons come about because of the varying distance between Earth and the sun. Actually, Earth is closest to the sun in early January and at its most distant in early July. Seasons occur because our planet's north-south axis leans over a bit compared to our orbit around the sun. During summer, the North Pole slants toward the sun. We receive more direct sunlight, and because the sun passes higher overhead, we enjoy longer days. During winter, the North Pole tilts away from the sun. We receive less direct energy from the sun, and the shorter days mean colder temperatures (see the section Determining the Sun's Position and Number of Hours of Sunlight per Day). Technically, each season starts at a particular instant of time. The table below lists the beginning time of the seasons for 2015 and 2016.

Year	Spring	Summer	Fall	Winter
2015	Mar 20, 4:45 PM	Jun 21, 10:38 AM	Sep 23, 2:21 AM	Dec 21, 10:04 PM
2016	Mar 19, 10:30 PM	Jun 20, 4:34 PM	Sep 22, 8:21 AM	Dec 21, 4:44 AM

Moon Phases

The table below lists the phases of the Moon for 2015 and 2016. A full Moon rises more or less at sunset. A new Moon sits between Earth and the sun, and not visible. The quarter phases occur between the new and full phases. A "Blue Moon" refers to the second full Moon in the same calendar month, as occurs July, 2015. They happen, on average once every two and one-half years. Since February has only 28 or 29 days in it, and the full lunar cycle takes 29–1/2 days, February regularly contains only three of the four lunar phases. About every two or three decades, February's missed full Moon occurs on January 31, the second one in January, and the next full Moon also skips February, making another Blue Moon in March, a double Blue Moon year. The next double Blue Moon won't happen until 2018.

2015		2016	
New	Full	New	Full
	Jan 4 10:53 PM	Jan 10 01:30 AM	Jan 24 1:46 AM
Jan 20 7:14 AM	Feb 3 5:09 PM	Feb 8 2:39 PM	Feb 22 6:20 PM
Feb 18 5:47 PM	Mar 5 1:06 PM	Mar 9 1:54 AM	Mar 23 1:01 PM
Mar 20 4:36 AM	Apr 4 7:06 AM	Apr 7 12:24 PM	Apr 22 5:24 AM
Apr 18 1:57 PM	May 3 10:42 PM	May 6 8:30 PM	May 21 10:15 PM
May 17 11:13 PM	Jun 2 11:19 AM	Jun 5 4:00 AM	Jun 20 12:02 PM
Jun 16 9:05 AM	Jul 1 9:20 PM	Jul 4 12:01 PM	Jul 19 11:57 PM
Jul 15 8:24 PM	Jul 31 5:43 AM	Aug 2 7:45 PM	Aug 18 10:27 AM
Aug 14 09:54 AM	Aug 29 1:35 PM	Sep 1 10:03 AM	Sep 16 8:05 PM
Sep 13 1:41 AM	Sep 27 9:50 PM	Oct 1 1:12 AM	Oct 16 5:23 AM
Oct 12 5:06 PM	Oct 27 7:05 AM	Oct 30 6:38 PM	Nov 14 1:52 PM
Nov 11 11:47 AM	Nov 25 4:44 PM	Nov 29 12:18 PM	Dec 14 12:06 AM
Dec 11 4:29 AM	Dec 25 5:11 AM	Dec 29 6:53 AM	

Meteor Showers

On any dark, clear night away from artificial lights, you occasionally see a brief streak of light zip across the sky. We often call them "falling stars" or "shooting stars." They are actually meteors, tiny bits of space rock that enter our atmosphere at speeds up to 150,000 miles per hour. At such speeds they heat the surrounding air to incandescence from friction and pressure, creating the streak of light we see.

Several times a year we see greater numbers of meteors for a few nights. These events are called meteor showers. Meteor showers come from comets. Comets are huge, dirty snowballs that orbit our sun like the planets. When a comet enters the inner part of the solar system, the sun's heat will vaporize the outer layer of the comet's icy body, freeing the trapped dirt and rock. The debris remains in the comet's orbital path around the sun.

As it revolves around the sun, Earth may cross a comet's orbital path. Earth will encounter the comet's orbit on or near the same day each year. Our planet slams into the debris trail, and we see a meteor shower.

Several meteor showers occur throughout the year. Meteor showers are named for the constellation they appear to radiate from. The list below contains the most active meteor showers. A typical shower produces only one meteor every minute or two, so perhaps "meteor drizzle" is a better term.

The Leonid meteor shower occurs on November 17. Its parent comet, Tempel-Tuttle, orbits the sun every 33 years. The debris is heavily concentrated behind the comet, so every 33 years we see a spectacular Leonid meteor shower. The comet passed by in 1966. That year the Leonids set the record for meteor shower activity with as many as 140 visible per second for a brief period of time. The Leonids in 1998 peaked at around 1,000 per hour. In 1999 through 2002, Leonid meteor shower displayed dramatic activity, but has decreased steadily ever since.

While none of these showers were as active as the 1966 Leonids, they displayed numerous and bright fireballs. However on the last outbound leg, the comet and its debris trail passed very close to Jupiter. Jupiter's massive gravity altered the orbital path of the comet and its debris, possibly ending Leonid meteor storms forever. That may not be the end of meteor showers from Comet Tempel-Tuttle, though. In another one hundred years or so, the comet will again pass near Jupiter, bending its course back close to Earth's orbit. Since the meteor shower will appear to come out of a different constellation, it will have a new name.

Meteor Shower	Date	# per hour	Parent Comet
Quadrantids	January 3	50	2003 EH!
Lyrids	April 22	25	Thatcher
Eta Aquarids	May 6	20	Halley
Delta Aquarids	July 29	20	Unknown
Perseids	August 12	50	Swift-Tuttle
Orionids	October 21	25	Halley
Leonids	November 17	15	Tempel-Tuttle
Geminids	December 14	50	Phaethon
Ursids	December 22	20	Tuttle

Generally, the best viewing time for a meteor shower is from midnight to six a.m. The farther away from city lights, the more meteors you can see. A full or third quarter moon (see Moon Phases) will also hinder meteor observations. The date listed for each shower is the evening before the a.m. peak. For example, to see the Perseid shower, stay up past midnight on August 11 to the early morning hours of the 12.

Planet Visibility

The closer a planet orbits the sun, the faster it moves. Mercury and Venus orbit so rapidly, changes in their positions can be obvious from one night to the next. While Mars moves more slowly than either Mercury or Venus, an "optical illusion" occasionally makes Mars appear to really zip across the night sky. When Earth and Mars are on the same side of the sun, Earth's orbital motion makes Mars appear to move much faster than normal, sometimes even backward. This is much like passing a slower moving car on the highway. From your point of view, that slower car appears to be moving in reverse. The same apparent reverse motion also happens with all of the planets beyond Earth, but for Mars the effect is most obvious. While Mars, Jupiter, and Saturn never actually backtrack in their orbits around the sun, they do appear to back up once in a while, what astronomers call retrograde motion.

It's generally not difficult to distinguish planets from stars. You've never sung the song "Twinkle, Twinkle Little Planet" because planets don't twinkle, stars do. Also, the visible planets Mercury, Venus, Mars, Jupiter, and Saturn are brighter than most or all of the stars in the night sky. Bright non-twinkling "stars" are most likely planets.

Mercury

Never strays far from the sun as seen from Earth. As such, it can only be sighted in either the evening or morning twilight, almost never in a dark sky. Mercury begins 2015 in the evening twilight, close to Venus, the brightest regular object in the night other than the Moon. While

Venus remains there, Mercury rapidly plunges back towards the sun and by mid month and by the month's end, it's lost in the sun's glare. Over the rest of 2015, it shuttles between dawn (February, March, June, July, October) and dusk (April, May, August, September, December), hidden only in November. It hides too close to the sun for much of 2016, peeking out in the morning twilight in February, June, September, and October and in the evening twilight in April, August, and December.

Venus

Shines so brightly, surpassed only by the Moon in the night sky, it is nicknamed the Evening Star when seen after sunset and the Morning Star in the pre-dawn skies. Venus is the Evening Star from January through July, 2015, then passes between us and the sun in August to become the Morning Star from September until March 2016. Venus then spends 4 months passing on the far side of the sun to reappear in the evening from August through December 2016.

Mars

Begins 2015 low in the southwest through April, disappears behind the sun for three months, then reappears in the morning sky until April 2016. It then transitions back to the evening sky for the remainder of the year.

Jupiter

Our solar system's largest planet could swallow 1,400 Earths. Jupiter and the other outer planets move very slowly as they orbit the Sun, so slowly that these planets may spend an entire year, or even several, within the same constellation.

Jupiter begins 2015 in the evening sky on the Cancer-Leo border. It slowly moves into Leo where it remains until August, 2016. It's visible from midnight or earlier until August 2015, when it slips into the morning sky, remaining there until March 2016, when it slips back into the evening sky. In September 2016, Jupiter hides behind the sun to reappear in the morning sky for the rest of the year, in the constellation of Virgo.

Saturn

Moving even slower than Jupiter, it can stay in the same constellation for a year or more. Saturn begins 2015 in the morning sky, on the Libra-Scorpius border, moving into Scorpius. It moves into the evening sky in May as it also backtracks, or retrogrades, into Libra. By October, it's back in Scorpius, but then hides behind the sun during November, reappearing in the morning sky in December, where it remains until the middle of 2016, when it again moves into the evening sky, where it remains through 2016. By December 2015, Saturn slides out of Scorpius and into Ophiuchus, where it remains throughout 2016.

Uranus and Neptune

Both are so far from the sun they seem to barely creep along in the sky, moving very little over the course of two years. Uranus, just barely visible to the unaided human eye from a dark location, stays in Pisces all year. It begins 2015 in the evening sky, transitioning to the morning sky by May. By November it's back in the evening sky then repeats the entire cycle in 2016.

Neptune begins 2015 in the evening sky, but disappears quickly behind the sun to reappear in the morning sky until September, when it becomes an evening object again. It repeats the exact process in 2016 and remains in the constellation of Aquarius for the entire two-year period.

Pluto

In August, 2006, the International Astronomical Union, the governing body of astronomers world-wide, voted on a definition of the word "planet" that dropped Pluto from that classification. One astronomer described is as correcting a seventy-six year old mistake made when Pluto was discovered in 1930. The new definition of planet is: the object must be round, or nearly so, due to its gravity. It can't be a star—a round astronomical body that sustains nuclear reactions in its core—but it has to orbit one. It has to gravitationally dominate all other objects in its region of the solar system. That is, it has to be large enough that its gravity essentially sweeps up everything in its region of the solar system. This clause led to Pluto's demotion.

There are lots of things that share Pluto's region of the solar system. Pluto is less massive than the combined total mass of other objects in its orbital region. Pluto may not even be the largest object orbiting the sun in that part of the solar system, known as the Kuiper Belt. As the official definition of "planet" states, Pluto hasn't "gravitationally cleared the neighborhood around its orbit."

Pluto is now considered the prototype of a new class of solar system objects called "Dwarf Planets." Dwarf Planets meet all of the criteria of being a true planet except for that of gravitationally domination. There are 5 objects currently defined as Dwarf Planets in our solar system: Pluto, Makemake, Haumea, Eris (all in the Kuiper Belt) and Ceres, the largest member of the Asteroid Belt between Mars and Jupiter. Current astronomical discoveries include several other objects orbiting the sun that may eventually qualify as dwarf planets. Some astronomers believe there may be a hundred or more dwarf planets in our solar system. Dwarf Planets that orbit beyond Neptune have been grouped into a special classification: Plutoids to honor the former planet and its discoverer, Clyde Tombaugh.

Why Pluto Is Not A Planet: An Analogy

When Pluto was discovered in 1930 by Clyde Tombaugh, he was looking for a ninth planet. He discovered an object at the expected distance from the sun, moving at the right speed as it orbited the sun. Astronomers around the world declared it to be a planet. At first they thought it might even be about the size of Earth.

But all of that was before computers and modern instruments. The more astronomers studied Pluto, the more they realized that it wasn't really much like the other planets. It turned out to be very small: seven moons, including our own, are larger than Pluto. It had a weird orbit: long and skinny and tilted quite a bit compared to the other planets, both more like a comet than a planet. Its composition turned out to be more like a comet too: frozen methane, ammonia, carbon dioxide and water ice dominate its surface.

Think of it this way: suppose you have something that is hard, long, and skinny and round and if you sharpen one end of it, you find a dark material inside that can leave marks on paper. You decide to call it a pencil. You soon realize that pencils come in several variations: some are round, some are hexagonal; they come in different colors and sizes. Some even write in different colors.

Then one day you find something a bit different. It's round, has a thin paper covering over a thick center that's soft, but if you sharpen one end, you can draw on paper, so you call it a pencil. You call it a pencil because that's all you know that draws on paper. But later you find more of these, in all different colors and soon you have more of them than you do the other things you have been calling pencils. Eventually you realize that these are really different kinds of objects, so you no longer call them pencils, but instead call them crayons.

That's what happened to Pluto. Almost from its discovery, astronomers began to notice that it was really different from the other planets, more different than they were from each other.

In 2006, astronomers decided to reclassify Pluto, correcting a mistake they had made 76 years earlier. So the simple answer is that Pluto is no longer a planet because, really, it was never a planet. We just didn't know it at the time.

Conjunction

A conjunction occurs whenever two or more objects in our solar system appear close together in our sky. Many millions of miles separate the bodies in space, but from our viewpoint on Earth they seem to be very close. Two planets very rarely "line up," appearing as one bright object, but several conjunctions occur over the two-year period including some very close ones. While the table below lists times when two or more bodies within our solar system appear close together as seen from Earth, the planets move constantly, changing their relative positions nightly. On an even longer time frame, the stars themselves slowly move in their individual orbits around the Milky Way galaxy. Every night, every hour, every minute, presents an absolutely unique astronomical sight, never exactly the same as any other instant of time, ever.

On rare occasions, Mars passes close to the star Antares in Scorpius, the 11th brightest star visible from Oklahoma. The Greek god of war, what Romans call Mars and for whom the planet is named, is Ares. Mars and Antares both glow with a reddish-orang hue, and shine with similar intensity. The word "Antares" literally translates as "not Mars," in perhaps the oldest astronomical joke.

Objects	Date	Time	Comments
Mercury/Venus	Jan 11, 2015	Sunset	Evening Twilight
Venus/Mars	Feb 22, 2015	Sunset	Evening Twilight
Venus/Jupiter	Jul 1, 2015	Evening	
Mercury/Jupiter	Aug 7 2015	Sunset	Evening Twilight
Mars/Jupiter	Oct 18, 2015	5:00 AM	
Venus/Mars	Nov 3, 2015	4:00 AM	
Venus/Saturn	Jan 9, 2016	6:00 AM	
Mars/Antares	Apr 27, 2016	4:00 AM	Antares means "Not Mars"
Moon/Aldebaran	Jul 29, 2016	5:00 AM	
Moon/Jupiter	Aug 5, 2016	9:00 PM	
Venus/Jupiter	Aug 27, 2016	8:00 PM	Mercury nearby, below

The table above lists the good conjunctions to watch for in 2015–2016. For conjunctions to be listed, the two objects appear no more than two Moon diameters, one degree, apart. Only those conjunctions with the pair at least six degrees above the horizon, roughly the width of a fist held at arm's length, and the sun is at least six degrees below the horizon, are listed. "Time" indicates the best time to view the conjunction, not necessarily the closest approach of the two bodies. "AM" generally means looking in the morning before sunrise, and "PM" means after sunset in the evening. The closest spacing between the two objects may occur in daylight or when they are below the horizon. Conjunctions involving Neptune will require binoculars or a telescope due to its faintness. While Uranus is just within the visibility of the unaided human eye from a dark location, it is so faint you might need a pair of binoculars to see it.

Paper Strip Solar System Model

The planets of our solar system are so far apart in relationship to their sizes that no model can accurately recreate both the size of the planets and their spacing to the same scale. Either the spacing must be dramatically reduced relative to the scale of planetary diameters, or the planets themselves are too small to be seen without a microscope. Here is a model of the solar system that you can carry in your pocket. And although you won't be able to see the planets to the proper size scale, its size is personalized to you.

Materials: Cash Register paper roll, Pen, Scissors

Cut a strip of paper equal to your height (or your child's height), which is roughly the same as their fingertip-to-fingertip length of outstretched arms. This will represent your solar system, from the sun to the outermost parts. Label one end Sun and label the other end the Kuiper Belt. The Kuiper Belt is the outermost region of our solar system, the location of Pluto and the other Plutoids, and the source of large comets such as Halley's Comet.

Fold the strip in half so that the Sun and the Kuiper Belt ends touch, and crease it at the fold. Open it up and draw a line at the fold. Label that line Uranus.

Fold the Kuiper Belt end of the paper strip to Uranus and crease. Label that line Neptune.

Fold the Sun end of the paper strip to Uranus and crease. Label the line Saturn.

Fold the Sun to Saturn and crease. Label the line Jupiter.

Fold the Sun to Jupiter and crease. Label it Asteroid Belt (A.B. in illustration) or Ceres, the largest member of the asteroid belt. This is what you should have at this point:

The Paper Strip Model of the Solar System

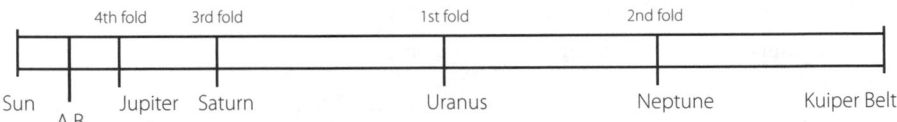

Now it gets crowded. Fold Sun to Asteroid Belt and crease. Draw line and label it Mars. Fold Sun to Mars and then fold new edge to Mars again, crease all, making 3 new crease lines. Unfold and draw lines at new creases. Label them (from Sun outward) Mercury, Venus, and Earth.

On this scale, the Sun is roughly the size of the pen tip used to write the names. It is the only object you could see on this scale without a powerful microscope.

Determining the Sun's Position and the Number of Hours of Sunlight Per Day

Because of Earth's daily rotation, the sun, moon, and the stars appear to move slowly across the sky. They "rise" in the east and "set" in the west. Of course they do not really move; we do. Earth rotates from west to east, so the sun, moon, planets, and the stars appear to move from east to west. Really, we are moving out from under them.

Over the course of a year, Earth orbits the sun, creating our seasons. This causes the sun's daily motion across the sky to vary at different times of the year. During summer, the sun passes nearly overhead. In winter, the sun arcs low across the sky in the south. The number of hours of daylight also varies with the seasons. Indeed this varying height of the sun, caused by Earth's tilt, and the subsequent varying number of daylight hours is the cause of our seasons. If Earth were not tilted, we would not have seasons and the amount of daylight would be constant.

The chart *Altitude and Azimuth of the Sun* (following page) gives the sun's location in the sky for any day and time, and can be used to calculate the number of daylight hours.

Altitude represents the height of the sun above the horizon, measured in degrees. The horizon is zero degrees. The point straight up at the center of the sky (the zenith) is altitude ninety degrees. Halfway up is forty-five degrees (see *How to Measure Distances and Time Using the Stars*). Azimuth represents the sun's compass direction, also measured in degrees. Due north is zero degrees, due east is ninety degrees, due south is 180 degrees, and due west is 270 degrees.

The graph shows the sun's altitude and azimuth throughout the day for the twenty-second of each month. Other days can be inferred easily from the chart. The sun's daily path is symmetrical in the morning and afternoon, so only half of the graph is shown.

At noon, the sun is due south (during daylight savings time, this occurs at 1:00; the sun does not care about saving daylight!). From the chart, the sun at noon would be zero degrees from south, or at azimuth 180. For morning hours, subtract the azimuth reading from 180; for afternoon hours add the reading to 180.

For example, on December 22, two hours before noon, the sun is at altitude twenty-six degrees, and is thirty degrees east of south or azimuth 150 (180 –30). At 2:00, the sun would be thirty degrees west of south, azimuth 210 degrees (180 +30).

On March 22 and September 22, the sun rises six hours before noon, and sets six hours after noon, so both of those days are exactly twelve hours long (those happen to be the vernal and autumnal equinoxes, the first day of spring and fall, respectively). On June 22, the summer solstice, the sun rises a bit over seven hours before noon, so that day is nearly fourteen and one-half hours long, the longest day of the year.

Light Pollution

Today, people who live in or near large cities have lost the beauty of the night sky. From within or near even small cities and towns, many stars are washed out by the increasing use of outdoor lighting at night. The graceful arch of the Milky Way across the night sky is visible only well away from urban lighting.

While there is a great need for nighttime lighting, there are adverse effects created by the many sources of outdoor light. Glare, light trespass, and light clutter contribute to inferior nighttime environment, reducing visibility and safety. Light, and the energy used to create it, are wasted if put where it is not needed, such as beaming upward into the night sky. It is simply wasted light, energy, and money.

Light that shines directly into a driver's eyes from a streetlight does not aid the driver in seeing at night. This glare actually deteriorates the driver's ability to see, and could lead to an accident. A security light that sprays bright light over a large area may make it impossible to see into the dark shadows, and may help create the very problem it was meant to solve. Good lighting, properly directed, provides safety, security, and reduces cost and energy waste.

Altitude (in degrees)

Altitude and Azimuth of the Sun
for the 22nd Day
of each Month
at 35° North Latitude

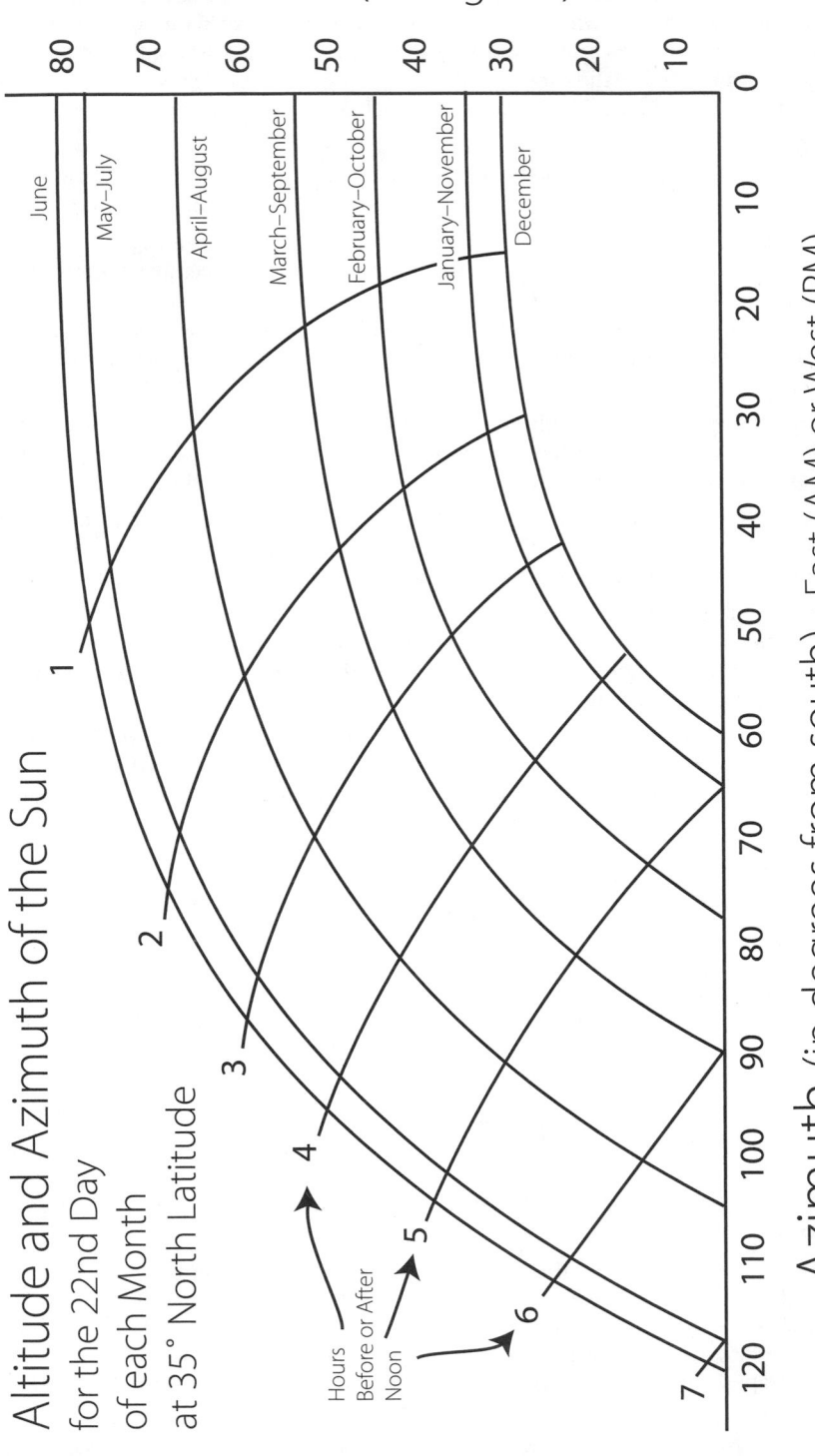

Azimuth (in degrees from south) • East (AM) or West (PM)

Astronomers suffer most severely from poorly designed and improperly aimed lighting. We have all seen billboards illuminated at night from upward-pointing lights. This lighting arrangement makes the beams of light visible for miles to drivers, calling attention to the billboard's message. While this may be a smart advertising ploy, it is terrible for astronomers trying to glean information from faint cosmic objects.

Many cities around major professional observatories have implemented outdoor lighting bans or strict lighting controls to aid astronomers. There are ways you can help in the fight against light pollution.

1. Use only as much light as you need, and put it where you want it. Excess light creates glare and dark shadows, both of which reduce safety and security. Use fixtures with recessed sockets, the type in which the lamp is not directly visible. This reduces glare and prevents stray light from getting up into the night sky.

2. Use the right kind of light. Incandescent light bulbs are not very cost effective. Vapor lights are generally cheaper. But not all vapor lights are equally good for astronomy. Mercury vapor lights shine with a bright blue-white light. High-pressure sodium vapor lights give off a yellowish glow. Both are commonly used in streetlights and home security lights.

Low-pressure sodium vapor lights are the best alternative for astronomy. They glow a deep yellow-orange color. That color makes objects look a bit odd, but this type of light has several advantages. They cost half as much as high-pressure sodium vapor lights and a third as much as mercury vapor lights to operate. Over the course of a year that savings could amount to millions of dollars for a typical city.

Since low-pressure sodium vapor lights emit a single color of light, it is very simple for astronomers to filter that light out. If all outdoor lighting consisted of low vapor sodium lights, astronomers would have no loss of ability to observe the heavens.

For more information about light pollution and proper lighting, visit the International Dark-Sky Association, www.darksky.org.

How To Find Directions

Directions are easily found at night, if the sky is clear and if you know the constellations. Look at the four seasonal star charts on previous pages. On all four charts the constellation Ursa Minor is in the north. We commonly call Ursa Minor the Little Dipper. The star that marks the end of the Little Dipper's handle is Polaris, the North Star. That star is almost directly over Earth's north pole. As our planet rotates, causing the stars to appear to rise, move, and set Polaris stays in the same spot, over Earth's north pole. Because of that special location, Polaris is the one star visible from the northern hemisphere that does not appear to move at all. It always marks the direction North.

In the daytime, we cannot use Polaris to determine North. But we can use the one star visible in the daytime, our sun. Our sun is always due south at solar noon. At that time, all shadows point due north. The problem is that solar noon does not occur when your clock says 12:00. Your location within your time zone affects exactly what the clock reads at solar noon. Because Earth orbits the sun in an ellipse, not a circle, the time from one solar noon to the next is not always exactly twenty-four hours.

To locate North, find a convenient pole (fence pole, flag pole, etc.) or push a straight stick upright in the ground. When clock time reaches 11:15 AM, start measuring the length of the pole or stick's shadow. The shadow gets shorter for the first few measurements, but eventually the shadow begins to lengthen. The shortest shadow occurs exactly at solar noon, and points due north.

To make such an activity more fun, try using people instead of sticks or poles. Go outside in the morning. While one student stands on a sidewalk or blacktop, have another trace out the location of the first student's feet. This is necessary so that the student can stand in the same place later. Trace out the standing student's shadow on the ground.

Come back to the same spot in the afternoon. Have the student place his feet in the exact same spot, as marked by the traced footprints. Once again trace the student's shadow. You now have a record of the different locations of the sun in the sky!

For young children, the concept of Earth's rotation is extremely difficult. After all, we do not feel any motion, although in Oklahoma we are moving at 850 miles per hour as Earth rotates. And we can easily see that the sun "moves" across the sky during the day and the Moon "moves" at night.

How to Measure Distances and Time Using the Stars

Distances in the sky are measured in degrees, just as the altitude and azimuth of the sun. Estimates of such distances can be made with your hand. Make a fist and stretch your arm out full length. The span across your knuckles from the first finger to the pinky equals ten degrees. Ten degrees is about equal to the span across the top of the Big Dipper's bowl. Stretch your fingers out wide and your hand spans about eighteen degrees, roughly two-thirds the width of the Big Dipper, or the distance diagonally across Orion (see star maps). The space between your knuckles is about three degrees, the length of Orion's belt. These measures can be used to estimate position in the sky. At 10:00 AM, December 22, the sun is twenty-six degrees above the horizon, or about 2.5 "fists" (see "Determining the Sun's Position"). The highest the sun gets in Oklahoma is eighty degrees, or eight "fists" high.

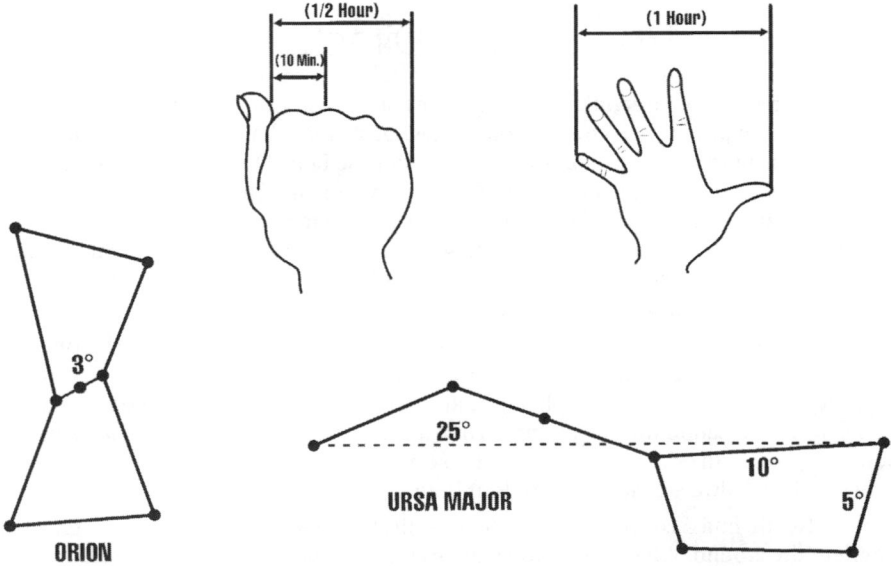

The diagram above indicates some distances using a few familiar constellations. Hand measurements let you quickly judge height or separation of objects in the sky. These hand measurements can be used to estimate the passage of time, too. Earth rotates once every day. In that twenty-four-hour period, Earth rotates through 360 degrees, or fifteen degrees per hour. By the time a star has moved the width of your outstretched hand, just over an hour has passed. Your closed fist measures about half an hour, and movement across your first two knuckles equals ten minutes. To measure the passage of time, note the location of some star, planet or the Moon near a tree, housetop, utility pole or other convenient marker, or find one near the eastern horizon. Periodically gauge its movement with your hand. Cowboys in the past measured time this same way when herding cattle at night.

Meteorites

Often while working in a field or yard, people stumble across an odd rock that just doesn't look or feel like other rocks in the area. These are often mistaken for a meteorite. Actual meteorite finds are quite rare, except in those areas near a known asteroid impact like the Barringer Crater near Flagstaff, Arizona.

Two common mistakes lead to most incorrect identifications of a terrestrial rock being a meteorite. Most people are not familiar with the variety of rocks that may be found in the area. Much of western Oklahoma is covered with red sandstone. Any other type of rock, especially dark-colored ones, may be mistaken for a meteorite by someone unaware that other types of rock might also exist in the area.

Often, rocks appear on the surface of a field where few if any other rocks are found, perhaps even in a small depression. Rocks buried underground can work their way up to the surface. You see a similar effect by opening a can of mixed nuts. The small peanuts are all at the bottom and the larger Brazil nuts and pecans lie on top. As the can of nuts is handled, the smaller peanuts fall through spaces between larger nuts, and the larger ones "float" to the top, even though they are much heavier than the smaller nuts. Large, dense rocks may work to the surface the same way.

Meteorites come in one of three types. Iron meteorites consist almost entirely of iron and nickel, and are thought to originate in the cores of large asteroids. Early in the life of our solar system, these large asteroids differentiated, that is iron, nickel, iridium, platinum, and other metals sunk to the center, just as in Earth, while the object remained in a liquefied state. The asteroids cooled and solidified with a metallic core and a rocky surface. Later, massive collisions with each other broke them apart, freeing the pure metallic parts, the source of iron meteorites. The outer, rocky material provides the source for stony meteorites, while the interface between the two regions is the source for stony-iron meteorites. All meteorites contain at least small amounts of nickel and iron, just as these metals can be found at the surface of Earth.

Most meteorites possess properties that distinguish them from terrestrial rocks. Meteorites tend to be far denser than ordinary rock; typically two to three times their density. All meteorites share at least some affinity for a magnet, and most are highly attracted to one. Meteorites never have a spongy or porous structure on the surface or in the interior.

As a meteorite flies through the atmosphere at tremendous speeds, it creates great friction with the air molecules around it. The heat generated by the friction heats the air to incandescence, the glowing trail behind a meteor in the night sky. The surface of the meteorite gets quite hot too, but the meteorite came from space where its temperature may have been below –2,000 F. for millions or billions of years. The flight of a few seconds through our atmosphere cannot warm the interior, and within a minute or two, the meteorite is freezing to the touch.

The heat of passage through the air creates a black "fusion crust" on the meteorite, although it will weather to a rusty brown color within a few months or years. The surface of the meteorite is often slightly melted by the heat of atmospheric entry, leaving small indentations resembling thumbprints, or flow lines where melted material flowed over the meteorite. The interiors of most meteorites shine like metallic silver. Meteorites are almost never round or rough, but have irregular shapes and a smooth surface.

In many locations around Oklahoma, iron smelting occurred in the past. It may have been a railroad foundry works, an old army base or blacksmith shop. Bits of old iron slag exist in many of these places, and are often mistaken for a meteorite. They generally will have little or no attraction for a magnet, but will show metallic luster on the inside.

If You Suspect You Have Found a Meteorite

Smithsonian Astrophysical Observatory suggests that you ask the following:

Yes or No   Is the object **solid**, not porous?

Yes or No   Is the object of **irregular** shape?

Yes or No   Is the object very **heavy** for its size?

Yes or No   Is the object **black** or **brown** on the outside?

Yes or No   Does the interior look **shiny** and **metallic**?

Yes or No   Is the object **different** from the country rocks?

If you answered, "Yes" to all these questions you almost certainly have a meteorite. If you answered "No" to most of the questions, it's probably not. With only one or two "No"s, it may still be a meteorite. Only sensitive chemical tests can answer the question for certain. Your local planetarium or university can usually recommend a testing facility. Inquiries may be made at the University of Oklahoma Department of Geology and Geophysics at 405/325-3253.

Does Life Exist Elsewhere in the Universe?

Life first appeared on Earth around 3.8 billion years ago; at least the oldest known fossils date from that time. Earth itself was formed 4.6 billion years ago, along with all the rest of the solar system. But for the first few hundred million years of its existence, Earth was a molten ball of magma. Almost as soon as Earth cooled to a reasonable temperature, the first simple, one-celled life forms came into existence. All other life on Earth evolved from those first living cells. Today, life exists everywhere on Earth where the temperature is below the boiling point of water, and even in some places where water is hotter than that. In every environment on Earth where water exists, life does, too.

Mars formed at the same time Earth did. Today, Mars is a frozen world, where temperatures rarely climb above the freezing point of water. It has one percent as much atmosphere as Earth, and no ozone layer to protect the surface from deadly cosmic rays and UV radiation.

Landers and rovers on the surface of Mars, in conjunction with orbiters taking high resolution images of the surface, have changed the standard scientific view of Mars. At one time Mars was very Earth-like. Geological evidence suggests that it had a thick atmosphere, rivers, lakes, and oceans. The surface water on Mars may have existed for geologically long periods of time. There are even caves on Mars and perhaps underground water exists in deep aquifers. In short, it was a perfect place for life to exist. And it reached those life-supporting conditions before Earth did. Did life form on Mars? No one knows yet, but if Earth is any example, it's certainly possible, if water existed for a long enough time.

In the young solar system, numerous asteroids constantly slammed into the various planets. That's what kept Earth and the other planets molten for so long after formation. Remnants of that early bombardment still exist today—asteroids that occasionally slam into our planet.

Oklahoma has only one known surface asteroid impact site, near Ponca City, although there are several other confirmed or suspected ones that are now buried.

Earth's gravity is strong enough that asteroid impacts don't knock debris into space. But Mars is a lot smaller, possessing only one-third the gravity of Earth. Asteroid impacts can and do knock pieces of Mars into space. And some of those have landed on Earth.

In 1996, a team of NASA scientists made a remarkable claim. A meteorite from Mars found in Antarctica contained the fossilized remains of Martian bacteria, or so the scientists claimed. The rock itself formed by geological processes that generally occur in a wet and warm climate, a perfect place to support life. Some sixteen million years ago, an asteroid slammed into Mars, knocking some of the Red Planet's rocks into space. One of those Martian rocks, containing the alleged fossils, landed in Antarctica. After years of analysis of the evidence, relatively few scientists now believe that the objects found are indeed fossilized bacteria, but the debate isn't over yet.

An important question remains: did life form on Mars before it did on Earth? Many biologists believe that is indeed feasible. And since Mars reached life-supporting conditions before Earth did, it is possible that an asteroid struck Mars 3.8 billion years ago and blasted a piece of rock containing live bacteria into space. That Martian rock eventually crashed to Earth. There is a real possibility that all life on Earth was seeded by life forms that first appeared on Mars.

One might wonder if it's possible that any living entity could survive years in space with no atmosphere, water or protection from cosmic rays and UV radiation. Experiments from our Apollo Moon program indicate that the answer may be yes.

Prior to the first manned landings on the Moon, NASA sent several Surveyor spacecraft that soft-landed on the lunar surface. These were NASA's way of testing lunar landing procedure, making sure we could safely land people there. Apollo 15 landed very near one of the Surveyor spacecraft and NASA directed the astronauts to retrieve the camera on board for return to Earth. When scientists studied the camera, they found to everyone's surprise, it contained dormant but living bacteria from Earth. The bacteria had survived for three years in condition almost identical to what a Martian meteorite would face in traveling from Mars to Earth.

Experiments have proven that bacteria buried inside a sufficiently large rock in space can survive by forming an endospore, a live but dormant state. Recent studies of that same Martian meteorite from Antarctica, known as ALH 84001, prove that conditions in the rock's interior would have gotten no hotter than 105 degrees, not hot enough to kill any hitchhiking bacteria. On Earth, biologists have found bacteria living inside rock two miles below Earth's surface. Would a wet Mars be any different?

Recently, scientists have found that a type of microbe called tardigrades, or water bears, can survive high doses of UV radiation and a strong vacuum, as in space. Tardigrades are commonly found in lichens or mosses, in soil, on mountaintops and in the sediment in the ocean. Their mossy homes can occasionally completely dry out yet some species can survive as long as a decade without moisture. Scientists put two different moss-dwelling species of tardigrades and their eggs on a European Space Agency's mission to the International Space Station. While orbiting Earth, the tardigrades were exposed to the vacuum of space for 10 days. Some were shielded from the sun's light; others were bathed in strong solar ultraviolet radiation. Both species of tardigrades survived exposure to space vacuum very well, although the samples exposed to both vacuum and solar radiation had significantly reduced survival rates.

The answer to the question of life on Mars, extant or extinct, probably won't be answered for at least another twenty or thirty years, when we land the first humans there. But there is no scientific reason to doubt the possibility that life did form on an ancient Mars. If so, there's a very real possibility that Martian microbes hitching a ride on a meteorite from the Red Planet seeded life on Earth.

Spacecraft sent to study Mars have found water—lots of it—enough to fill all of the Great Lakes several times over. The water currently exists in the form of ice, but the deeper layers may be liquid. We also know that in at least on some areas of Mars, sedimentary rocks formed in oceans, like much of the sandstone and limestone rocks in Oklahoma. There is an as yet unanswered question of whether those oceans lasted for a few thousand years or a few million years. Some evidence from recent studies of Mars indicates that liquid water existed at least for tens if not hundreds of thousands of years. If longer times frames are involved, life may have evolved there. On Earth, where water exists, so does life. Was Mars once inhabited, even if only by microbes, perhaps still inhabited? New missions to Mars will likely answer that question within a few decades.

Not all the data from satellites orbiting Mars is supportive of potential Martian life. The Martian geological crust is far more rigid than scientists had believed; the rocks making the crust of Mars can't flex much; the crust is frozen solid. That implies that any subsurface liquid water must be deeper below the surface and scarcer than previously assumed.

The Mars Science Laboratory, nicknamed Curiosity, landed in Gale Crater on Mars on August 6, 2012. This landing point was chosen because high-resolution images and other data from Mars-orbiting satellites indicated that it may once have contained water, and the floor of the crater indicated strong evidence of rocks that can only form in the presence of water. A major goal of the Curiosity Rover, to investigate the possible existence of organic chemistry or biological remains of past Martian life, is best served by NASA's Mars Mantra "Follow the Water." Where liquid water once existed, so the thinking goes, biology may have developed. As of this writing, Curiosity has discovered carbon-containing compounds, but no definitive signs of past biological activity on the Red Planet.

Mars isn't the only extraterrestrial location in our solar system that may harbor life. Jupiter's Moon Europa is, like Mars, a frozen world. Its surface is covered with a sheet of ice. But unlike Mars, Europa enjoys an extra source of heat beyond that coming from the sun. Jupiter, the largest planet with the strongest planetary gravitational field, possesses three other large moons: Io, Ganymede, and Callisto. Europa orbits Jupiter between Io and Ganymede, the largest moon of our solar system. Europa is squeezed and pulled between the gravity of Jupiter, Io, and Ganymede. This flexing heats the moon's core to temperatures high enough that the ice melts into a liquid ocean below the frozen surface.

At the bottom of Earth's oceans, where volcanic activity continually creates new ocean floor, energy from geothermal volcanic vents heats localized areas well above the near freezing temperatures of the typical sea bottom. At these locations, bizarre life forms flourish, life forms found nowhere else on our planet. Many biologists believe that all life on Earth may have come from single-celled microbes that first evolved at these mid-ocean rifts. Similar geological processes likely exist on Europa, and it's entirely within the realm of biological possibility that some form of life exists on the ocean floors of Europa.

Recently, the Cassini spacecraft orbiting Saturn discovered water geysers coming from the tiny moon Enceladus. It is so small that most astronomers assumed that it, like our much larger Moon, was geologically dead and frozen. But some force, perhaps tidal squeezing from Saturn and its rings, heats the interior, as with Europa. Continued studies have revealed that the plumes contain salt water and organic compounds like those found on comets and on the young Earth. Remember, on Earth, where there's liquid water, there's life. The possibility exists on Enceladus.

Saturn's largest moon, Titan, is intriguing from a biological perspective. The moon possess an atmosphere half again thicker than Earth's, and of a similar composition to what Earth had 3.8 billion years ago when life first began on our planet. But being farther from the sun, it is considerably colder. Water is so frozen that it is the geological equivalent of rock on Earth. But Titan does have a water analog, a solvent where biochemical reactions can occur: liquid methane and ethane. These "petrochemical" fluids form lakes and rivers. They generate a hydrologic cycle, including rain, evaporation, and clouds. The low temperatures imply that chemical reactions, including any biology, would proceed quite slowly by terrestrial standards, but could occur.

Potential homes for extraterrestrial life exist outside of our solar system as well. As of this writing, astronomers have discovered more than 1,800 confirmed or suspected exoplanets orbiting other stars, with numerous multi-planet systems. Another 2,000+ possible exoplanets await confirmation, with new discoveries announced regularly. Most of these extra-solar planets are the size of Jupiter or larger, and are not considered likely abodes of life. Smaller, Earth-like planets also exist out there. As of this writing, there are 21 known planets that are Earth-like or nearly so and orbit within their star's habitable zone, with another 90 awaiting confirmation. The smallest of these is still 1.4 times bigger than Earth. We've yet to find an exact Earth analog. Since so many of the known exoplanets are much larger, some may well have habitable moons, if they are at the right distance from their sun. Astronomers estimate that there are thirty habitable moons among the know exoplanets. Details on the known and suspected habitable planets can be found at phl.upr.edu/projects/habitable-exoplanets-catalog.

Life's requirements (as we currently understand them): temperatures capable of sustaining liquid water and a chemical environment complex enough to contain the necessary chemicals of life. Water is composed of two atoms of hydrogen and one atom of oxygen. Hydrogen is the most abundant element in the universe while oxygen is the third most common, and their combination, water, is the most common compound in the universe other than molecular hydrogen. The second most widespread element, helium, is a noble gas and is not involved in chemical reactions. In order, after oxygen, are carbon, neon (another noble gas), iron, and nitrogen. If these elements sound familiar they are among the basic building blocks of life on Earth, with the exception, of course, of the noble gases.

In at least one case, astronomers detected water vapor in the atmosphere of a large extra-solar planet. If the planet has water, any moons it has will also possess water. And our technology is improving all the time; soon we will be able to detect Earth-sized planets. Within a few years, we may find that we humans are merely one member of a vast cosmic civilization.

The Brightest Star

What is the brightest star we can see from Earth? Actually, astronomers have two different definitions of star brightness, or magnitude to use the technical term. So before you respond to that question let's define stellar magnitude.

"Absolute magnitude" refers to the actual energy output of the star, its luminosity. Generally speaking, hotter stars emit more energy than cooler stars and bigger stars emit more energy than smaller stars. That's not quite as straight forward as it seems: a large but cool star may or may not put out more light than a smaller but hotter star. The devil's in the details.

"Apparent magnitude" refers to the brightness of a star as seen in our sky, but that's actually affected by two parameters: the star's luminosity and its distance from us. Just as a distant street light appears fainter than a nearby one, a closer star will appear brighter in our sky than an identical one farther away. Absolute Magnitude is actually defined as the apparent magnitude at a fixed distance of ten parsecs, so distance is taken out of the absolute magnitude scale. A moderate star that is quite close may have a high apparent magnitude but a low absolute magnitude.

And to make matters even more confusing, the magnitude scale is backward. The modern stellar magnitude scale has its origins with the Greek astronomer Hipparchus in 129 B.C. when he produced one of the first known star charts. As a means of classifying stars, he divided them into brightness categories. The brightest stars, a few dozen in all, he described as "stars of the first magnitude." Somewhat less bright stars he declared were of the second magnitude, and so on. He divided all stars into one of six magnitude groups. So the brightest stars were Magnitude 1 and the faintest stars visible to the human eye were Magnitude 6. Thus, the bigger the number, the fainter the star.

In 1856, astronomers, after having developed instruments far more sensitive than their eyes, decided they needed to quantify this brightness scale more precisely. With their instruments, they determined that "stars of the First Magnitude" were, on average, a hundred times brighter than star of the sixth magnitude. A five-magnitude jump (6th magnitude to 1st magnitude) meant a change in brightness by a factor of one hundred. So they defined the magnitude scale in such a way that a change of one magnitude, from 1 to 2 or from 4 to 5 meant a change in brightness by a factor of 2.5 (technically, the 5th root of 100 or roughly 2.512). A difference in magnitude by one number between two stars means an increase of 2.512 times in brightness, with the smaller magnitude rating corresponding to the brighter star.

So what star seen in the skies over our planet has the lowest apparent magnitude number, the brightest as seen from Earth? Our sun, of course! It shines at apparent magnitude –26. But that's a trick question. What is the brightest nighttime star? It is likely that your answer when you first read the question at the beginning of this section is the same as it is now after the discussion of the astronomical magnitude scale. It is also likely that your answer is wrong. It is a common misconception that what we usually call the North Star is the brightest star in the sky. Actually, it's not even in the top ten. The North Star, whose proper name is Polaris, may be the best known star, so people often mistakenly believe it to be the brightest star. It's not. Polaris has an apparent magnitude of 2.02; it's not even a star "of the First Magnitude." It is actually the 48th brightest nighttime stars visible from Earth, the 33rd brightest as seen from Oklahoma.

The brightest star seen from Earth, the star with the lowest apparent magnitude, is Sirius at –1.44. It is one of a handful of stars so bright that the magnitude scale had to be extended into negative numbers. The scale factor is unchanged: a decrease in one magnitude, say, from 0 to –1, still means a brightness increase of 2.512. Sirius may be unfamiliar to you because it shines in the evening sky during our winter and spring months, when it is typically cold or cloudy, so it's not so well known to the casual sky observers of the northern hemisphere. If you lived in Australia, Sirius would be up during your summer and fall and therefore more familiar to you.

What star in the sky has the highest luminosity, that is to say, has the lowest absolute magnitude rating? It's difficult to say. We can directly measure the apparent magnitude of any star visible to us. But converting that to an absolute magnitude isn't always easy. Our ability to measure star distances may be no more accurate than 10%, even less so for very distant stars. Between stars, what astronomers call interstellar space, is not completely empty; there are tiny but varying amounts of dust and gas which can absorb and scatter starlight, making it tricky to measure exactly the amount of light coming from the star. And even with our best telescopes, we can only see a tiny fraction of the stars within our Milky Way galaxy, much less with stars in other galaxies.

One of the most luminous known stars is Eta Carina. Eta Carina isn't visible from Oklahoma; it's too far south to ever rise in our sky. This star is 100 to 150 times more massive than our sun. It ejected a shell of gas in 1843, one of several known explosions. That gas shell hides our direct view of the star but astronomers estimate its absolute magnitude at –12. By comparison, the absolute magnitude of Sirius is only +1.5. Our sun's absolute magnitude is +4.8, quite mediocre as stars go.

The Pistol Star, near the center of our Milky Way galaxy is another candidate for the brightest known star. Due to its distance and the dusty nature of its environs, the Pistol Star is harder to study, but it appears to be very close to Eta Carina in luminosity, probably a bit brighter.

A recent discovery shattered the record of those two stars. The Large Magellanic Cloud (LMC) is a small satellite galaxy of our Milky Way. The LMC is home to one of the most massive and prolific star forming regions ever seen, known as the Tarantula Nebula after its resemblance to that arachnid. Within the Tarantula Nebula sits the R136 cluster, forming stars at a furious rate. Its largest member, the star R136a1, currently holds the record of the most massive and luminous star ever found, with a current mass of about 265 solar masses and a birth weight of as much as 320 times that of the Sun (massive stars suffer from a rapid loss of material as a stellar wind). It shines with the incredible equivalent of 10,000,000 times the power of our sun. Prior to this discovery, astrophysicists believe that no star larger than 150 time the mass of the sun could survive with out tearing itself apart. Apparently astronomers still have a lot to learn about their main topic of study.

How Fast Are You Moving?

As you read this, you partake in several motions, even while sitting perfectly still. Earth rotates once a day and it orbits the sun once a year. In addition, our entire solar system orbits the center of the Milky Way Galaxy, which moves within our Local Cluster of Galaxies, which is itself moving. So how fast are you moving? What is your cosmic velocity?

Earth rotates once every 24 hours. Your rotational speed depends upon your latitude. At either pole, your rotational velocity is zero. Maximum velocity (just over 1,100 miles per hour) is achieved at Earth's equator. If you sat in one of the seats at the Kirkpatrick Planetarium in Science Museum Oklahoma, at north latitude 35.52344444 degrees, you'd travel due east at 840.6 miles per hour.

Earth orbits the sun once each year, from a distance of nearly ninety three million miles. We travel a distance of pi times twice the orbital radius, or 3.14159 times 2 times 92,955,629 miles or 584,057,451 miles each year. A year equals 8,766 hours. Crunch all the numbers and you'll discover that we travel at an average speed of 66,629 miles per hour orbiting our star.

Our solar system orbits the center of the Milky Way, as do all the stars in our galaxy. We are about 30,000 light years from the galactic center, and we take about 250,000,000 years to complete one orbit, one galactic year. When we were last at this location in our galactic orbit, dinosaurs were taking over our planet. Due to this orbital velocity, we travel at 495,000 miles per hour.

Our Milky Way is flying through space for a head-on collision with the Andromeda Galaxy. It's currently 2.2 million light years away, with one light year equal to 5,800,000,000,000 miles. We collide in about three billion years, which works out to 485,169,900 miles per hour. On top of that, the local Cluster of Galaxies (our Milky Way and the Andromeda galaxies are the largest members) is traveling towards the much larger Virgo Cluster of Galaxies at 53,654,400. Add all of these various motions together (some are opposite other motions) and the net speed of Earth through space is 20,937,683 miles per hour.

Remember that the next time you are pulled over for doing 50 in a 40 mph speed zone.

The Ultimate Fate of Oklahoma (and Earth)

At various times in its distant past, Oklahoma has been frozen, ocean front property, ocean bottom property, dinosaur playground and the land where the buffalo roam. At some time in its distant future, Oklahoma will become molten magma before turning into a frozen wasteland. These last two conditions will be shared with the entire planet Earth.

Earth, our sun, and all the other planets, dwarf planets, comets, asteroids, moons, and interplanetary dust formed four billion, six hundred million years ago from a cloud of interstellar gas—mostly hydrogen and helium with a smattering of oxygen, carbon, nitrogen, and other gasses—and dust—composed primarily of silicon, carbon, iron, and small amounts of other atoms. The moon came along shortly after that when a rogue planet the size of Mars collided with the young and still molten Earth. The debris from that collision cooled and eventually become our Moon.

The oldest evidence of life on Earth comes from a time 3.8 billion years ago. The Earth had barely cooled to the point that the surface was not constantly molten or covered by massive volcanoes, at least in a geological sense of time. Water became ubiquitous on the surface of our planet, a necessary ingredient for life. But periodically since then, Earth has experienced Ice Ages, where much of the planet's land masses were covered with glaciers. During a massive glaciation period lasting from roughly 750 million years ago to 580 millions ago, most of our planet, even a significant fraction of the surface of our oceans, froze in what geologists call Snowball Earth. Pockets of unfrozen ocean apparently remained, allowing a safe haven for life.

Around 544 million years ago, the ancient supercontinent Laurentia, which included what we today call North America and South America, began to separate. South America and North America were joined where what is now the Gulf of Mexico. The land that now makes up Oklahoma and Texas began to pull apart, creating what geologists call a rift valley. From 500 to 430 million years ago, as South America continued to move toward its current location, the rifting between Texas and Oklahoma ceased and this part of our country was covered in a vast shallow sea that waxed and waned. The vast amount of plant material that covered the floor of this shallow sea eventually became Oklahoma's oil, coal, and natural gas deposits. The sea became a haven for terrestrial life; the rift began slowly closing up. Starting around 280 million years ago, the land of southern Oklahoma lifted up, creating the Arbuckle and Wichita Mountains. Throughout this period, large reptiles and eventually dinosaurs roamed the land that would become Oklahoma.

Eventually the geology of North America settled down to what we have today. The central part of the country, including Oklahoma, became covered with short-and tall-grass prairies, home to incredible herds of buffalo, technically American Bison. The first Native Americans left important archeological evidence of the lifestyles of stone-age people in Oklahoma.

Our sun provides the life-giving warmth and light that makes all life possible by way of nuclear reactions deep in its core. Every tiny fraction of a second, four hydrogen atoms are converted into one helium atom in a round-about series of reactions that also releases energy as defined by Albert Einstein's famous equation $E=mc^2$. Our sun currently releases the equivalent of a million hydrogen bomb explosions every second from it 28–million-degree core.

Jump to the future, some two billion years from now. Our sun, which has been slowly growing larger and more luminous, has now increased so much in size and brightness, it has made the surface of Earth unlivable. The oceans have evaporated away and our once verdant planet can not support life of any kind. As the sun grows larger still, flares on its surface increase in strength and the flow of material away from the sun, the solar wind, has increased to gale strength. This would cause planet-wide aurora, except that the magnetic field of Earth died as the interior cooled below the melting point of iron, like what occurred on the much smaller Moon five billion years earlier. The increase in radiation we receive from the growing sun will eventually melt the surface rock of our planet.

As the sun continues to grow, it loses whole layers of itself out into space. This mass loss may ultimately save earth from total destruction by our parent star. As the sun's mass decreases, so does its gravitation pull on Earth and the other planets. Earth slowly pulls away, ultimately to where Mars is now. The expanding sun eventually engulfs Mercury and Venus, the two innermost planets. Whether or not Earths survives or is also swallowed and vaporized by in the sun's deep nuclear furnace, like Mercury and Venus, depends upon how fast the sun grows and how fast it loses mass. Astronomer's best current guess is that the sun wins out and Earth vanishes into the 100–million-degree core of the sun.

Mars, or perhaps the Moons of Jupiter, have become able to support life, so perhaps humanity moves there. But that would be only a short respite. Eventually the sun runs completely out of fuel, after shedding about half its mass creating a beautiful, ephemeral planetary nebula, visible across the neighboring regions of our Milky Way galaxy. Once the energy source is gone, the solar system freezes and the lights go out.

But a perhaps even more depressing fate awaits Earth in the far distant future, well beyond when the sun peters out. The latest cosmological observations indicate that not only is our universe expanding from the force of the Big Bang 14.7 billion years ago, the rate at which it is expanding is increasing. Some unknown force is pushing everything apart, a kind of universal antigravity. As the galaxies separate, this force, astronomers have dubbed it "Dark Energy" just to give it a name, becomes stronger.

We don't know the source of Dark Energy, but some scientists believe that it is a property of space itself. If that is so, it will grow exponentially stronger as space grows bigger. Eventually not only will galaxies be pushed apart, the stars within galaxies, four hundred billion or so in our Milky Way galaxy alone, will began to separate. Our galaxy will dissipate as the stars move away and our sky will go dark. Actually it will already *be* dark as the sun will have gone out a trillion years earlier. Soon the stars, planets, and any remaining life forms will be broken apart into individual atoms.

And the mysterious Dark Energy won't yet be finished. As space expands and the strength of the Dark Energy increases, it will eventually surpass the atomic and nuclear forces holding atoms together. The very structure of our universe will be ripped asunder and all that will eventually remain are those non-divisible entities in our universe: photons (particles of light), electrons, quarks, and gluons (the constituents that make up the atomic nucleus). And perhaps with such incredible forces acting on them, maybe even these "fundamental" particles will be torn apart and existence itself will cease altogether in our universe.

For now, just enjoy the wonderful scenery and great weather of our home state.

Astronomy Clubs, Planetariums, Observatories, and Astronomical Products

For those interested in further information on astronomical phenomena, the best sources are local astronomy clubs and planetariums. Astronomy clubs allow you to meet people who share a common interest. Clubs also provide opportunities to view astronomical objects through a telescope. Should buying a telescope be in your plans, clubs provide opportunities to "test drive" different telescopes before you buy one.

It's hard to beat the ability of a planetarium for teaching about the night sky. These domed theaters simulate the night sky beautifully, providing better views of the heavens than our light-polluted cities. Most offer a regular schedule of public performances, as well as school field trips with programs geared around public school curriculum. Some planetariums also include educational exhibits.

Oklahoma has few observatories, and most of those are privately owned. While membership in an astronomy club often provides access to a telescope, public-use observatories usually have larger instruments in a permanent, stable installation. They often have equipment for viewing celestial objects in a way astronomy clubs can't offer. Since universities or planetariums operate most public observatories, professional astronomers who offer greater insight or detailed explanations to questions often run the programs. Those listed below offer public viewing, but call ahead. The schedule may be limited or offered by reservation only.

Telescopes dealers not only maintain a selection of astronomical telescopes and binoculars, they often provide free handouts on various aspects of astronomy. If a telescope is in your future, it's worth sending for catalogues.

Astronomy Clubs

Astronomy Club of Tulsa
PO Box 470611, Tulsa, OK 74147
918/688–MARS
info@astrotulsa.com • www.astrotulsa.com

Leonardo's Star Quest Astronomy Club
200 E Maple Street, Enid, OK 73701
580/233-2787 • www.leonardos.org

Norman North High School Astronomy Club
1809 Stubbeman Drive, Norman, OK 73169 •
405/366-5954 • eileeng@norman.k12.ok.us

Odyssey Astronomy Club
Route 2 Box 154, Wanette, OK 74878
405/899-4016 • orion2c@aol.com

Telescope Dealers

Astronomics
680 SW 24 Ave, Norman, OK 73169
405-364-0858

Steve's Pro Shop
709-B S Air Depot Blvd, Midwest City, OK
73110 • 405-732-1350

Planetariums

Kirkpatrick Planetarium
2100 NE 52 St, Oklahoma City, OK 73111
405/602-3761

Oklahoma Baptist University
Shawnee, OK 74801 • 405/878-2028

Tulsa Air and Space Museum
3624 N 74 E Ave, Tulsa, OK 74115
918/834-9900

Observatories

University of Oklahoma
Physics and Astronomy Dept.
400 W Brooks, Norman, OK 73019
405-325-3961

RMMC Observatory
PO Box 470611, Tulsa, OK 74147
918-636-6682

Cheddar Ranch Observatory
PO Box 22804, Oklahoma City, OK 74123

During the late 1800s longhorn cattle were kept at Fort Sill to supply beef for the Indian Reservation.

GENERAL INDEX

SYMBOLS

A

J

K

T

OKLAHOMA BATTLEFIELDS & MILITARY FORTS